standard catalog of

WORLD PAPER MONEY

Volume Three – Modern Issues
1961-1996

Second Edition

Colin R. Bruce II
Senior Editor

George S. Čuhaj
Coordinating Editor

Neil Shafer
Technical Editor

Special Consultants

Milt Blackburn, Vladimir Duic, William G. Henderson, Arnoldo Efron
William McNatt, Tony Pisciotta, Jan Vandersande, Robert Wilhite,
Christof Zellweger

Man is not born to solve the problem of the universe, but to find out what he has to do; and to restrain himself within the limits of his comprehension. – *Goethe.*

Published in the United States by Krause Publications, Inc.
700 E. State Street, Iola, WI 54990
Telephone: 715-445-2214 • FAX: 715-445-4087

Copyright MCMXCVI by Krause Publications, Inc.

Library of Congress Catalog Card Number: 95-76858
International Standard Book Number: 0-87341-425-X

Printed in the United States of America

TABLE OF CONTENTS

INTRODUCTION

Welcome to this second edition of the Standard Catalog of World Paper Money, Modern Issues, 1961-1996. For the past several years the central bank and government notes of this modern era have been most avidly collected. With the addition of a dozen or so newly independent nations and many more stable countries changing designs and enhancing security devices, it was thought to better serve the collector, by the Krause Publications Numismatic Book division to divide the General Issues volume of the Standard Catalog of World Paper Money at the year 1961. In most cases a full issue is presented for continuity. We plan this volume 3 - Modern Issues to be an annual release, keeping pace with current developments in new issues, varieties, specimens and market valuations. Our Volume 2, General Issues prior to 1961, is being expanded to include many new photographs, signature charts, and other 'collector friendly' enhancements. Volume 1 of the World Paper Money Catalog contains Specialized Issues - those by banks, both commercial or private, but not of a national significance, issues of states or provinces. Future editions of those publications will be updated was demand makes it necessary.

Paper money collecting is undoubtedly nearly as old as paper money itself, but this segment of the numismatic hobby only began to reach a popularity approaching that of coin collecting since the latter half of the 1970s. While coins and paper money are alike in that both have served as legal obligations to facilitate commerce, long-time paper money enthusiasts know the similarity ends there.

Coins were historically guaranteed by the intrinsic value of their metallic content — at least until recent years when virtually all circulating coins have become little more than legal tender tokens, with very few containing precious metals except for many commemoratives never meant to circulate — while paper money possesses a value only when it is accepted for debts or converted into solid assets. With many note issues, this conversion privilege was limited and ultimately negated by the imposition of redemption cut-off dates.

Such conditions made the collecting of bank notes a risky business, particularly with notes possessing a face value of more than a nominal sum. This is why in most instances, except where issues were withdrawn shortly after release or became virtually worthless due to hyper-inflation, high denomination notes are extremely difficult to locate, especially in uncirculated or high grades of preservation.

In the not too distant past, security for bank notes was assured by good engraving, paper and inks. In the area covered by this book, you will see a gradual progression of security threads to the micro-printed filaments and segmented foil strips; from engraved underprints, to embedded cloth or nylon threads and now the addition of variable optical images; the inclusion of transparent register ornaments to aid in the detection of counterfeits for the sighted, and heightened design elements to aid the visually impaired. These, and many more developments create for you, the collector, varieties of older types, or new types for the collection.

Users familiar with the General Issues volumes of the past will notice the addition of a great many issues, signature and date varieties and specimen listings when these have become commercially available. While this book was being sent to press, even more new issues were making their appearances. Many dates and signatures are known to be scarcer or rarer than others, and the catalog now

reflects this specialization for its audience. Significant revision has taken place throughout the book, as usual, and each country has been brought up to date as available information allowed.

With this edition, and the soon to be released Volume 2, General Issues, extensive renumbering has been done to Austria, Belgium, Canada, Dominion Republic, Egypt, El Salvador, Ethiopia, France, Georgia and Great Britain. In all these cases, the old catalog number appears beneath the new number. This has been done to better organize the listings. Once the 8th Edition of General Issues is released wholesale renumbering should be curtailed.

"BNR", An Invitation

Users of this catalog may find a helpful adjunct in the *Bank Note Reporter*, the only monthly newspaper devoted exclusively to paper money of all kinds and from everyplace. Each issue presents up-to-date news, feature articles and informtion including World Paper Money Update, new discoveries, mystery notes, military notes and more. New issue listings in this paper are all keyed to the standard catalog numbering system.

All purchasers of this book are invited to subscribe to the *Bank Note Reporter*. Requests for more information and/or a free sample copy to U.S. addresses ($3.00 foreign) should be directed to the newspaper at 700 E. State St., Iola, WI 54990-0001. U.S.A.

ACKNOWLEDGMENTS

The contributions to this catalog have been many and varied, and to recognize them all would be a volume in itself. Accordingly, we wish to acknolwedge these invaluable collectors, scholars and dealers in the world paper money field, both past and present, for their specific contributions to this work through the submission of notes for illustration, improved descriptive information and valuations.

Jan Alexandersson
Milan Alusic
Donald Arnone
Jorge E. Arbelaez
David August
K. Austin
George Azuma
Cem Barlok
Richard Bates
Adriaan C.F. Beck
Milt Blackburn
Joseph E. Boling
Arthur John Boyko
Angus E. Bruce
Weldon D. Burson
Lance K. Campbell
Valikonagi Caddesi
Ramiro O. Casañas
George Conrad
Scott R. Cordry
Guido Crapanzano
Howard A. Daniel III
Paul Davis
Daniel Denis
Bob Diedrich
Richard G. Doty
Duane D. Douglas
Vladimir Duic
Arnoldo Efron
Wilhelm R. Eglseer
Joseph F. M. Eijsermans
Esko Ekman
Jean-Michel Engels
Paul Simon Essof
Edward Feltcorn
Güvendik Fisekciojlu

Jack G. Fisher
George A. Fisher, Jr.
Mark Fox
Ian Fraser
Gary Ganguillet
Brian G. Giese
Bernardo Gonzalez-White
Urs Graf
Mario Gutierrez Minera
John S. Haas
Ray Hackett
Edmond Hakimian
Brian Hannon
Flemming Lyngbeck Hansen
Sergio Heise-Fuenzalida
William G. Henderson
Melvin P. Hennisch
Dick Herman
Anton Holt
Armen Hovsepian
Nicolae Hridan
Sean Isaacs
Mikmail Istomin
Tomasz Jazwinski
Edouard Jean-Pierre
William M. Judd
Alex Kaglyan
Josef Klaus
Ladislav Klaus
John M. Kleeberg
Michael E. Knabe
Tristan Kolm
Lazare N. Kouame
Michael Kvasnica
Samuel Lachman
David Laties

Morris Lawing
Akos Ledai
Ricardo deLeon-Tallavas
Lee Shin Song
George Lill III
Raymond Lloyd
Claire Lobel
Dennis Luck
Alan Luedeking
Ma Tak Wo
Ranko Mandic
Ian Marshall
Arthur C. Matz
Leo May
Juozas Minikevicius
Lazar Mishev
Howard Mitchell
Michael Morris
Richard Murdoch
Collin Narbeth
Geoffrey P. Oldham
Andrew Oberbillig
Julian Papenfus
Frank Passic
Antonio E. Pedraza
William H. Pheatt
Albert Pick
Tony Pisciotta
Yahya J. Qureshi
Nazir Rahemtulla
Mircea Raicopol
Leo Reich
Jerome H. Remick
Rudolf Richter
Duane C. Riel
John Rishel

Thomas P. Rockwell
William H. Rosenblum
Arnaldo Russo
Alan Sadd
Karl Saethre
David M. Salem
Imre Scatmàri
Hartmut Schoenawa
Alan G. Sealey
Christian Selvais
Narenda S. Sengar
Joel Shafer
Ladislav Sin
Saran Singh
Arlie R. Slabaugh
Gary F. Snover
Jimmie C. Steelman
Mel Steinberg
Tim Steiner
Zeljko Stojanovic
Roger B. Stolberg
Steven Tan
David Tang
Guillermo Triana-Aguiar
Eduardo R. Trujillo
Anthony Tumonis
Gilbert Van Caelenberg
Jan W. Vandersande
Grobljar Vanjo
Igor V. Victorov-Orlov
Norbert Von Euw
A. Wang
Stewart Westdal
Christof Zellweger
Igor Zhuravliov

INSTITUTIONS

American Numismatic Association

American Numismatic Society

Bank of Slovenia

Central Bank of Dominican Republic
Central Bank of Iceland
International Bank Note Society
MTB Bank

National Bank of Poland

Newark Museum

Smithsonian Institution

PUBLICATIONS

Le Change Des Monnaies Étrangers
    by R.L. Martin. 12, rue Raymond-Poincaré, F55800 Revigny-Sur-Ornain, France.
        (Illustrated guide of new and current world bank notes.)

MRI Bankers' Guide To Foreign Currency
    by Arnoldo Efron, Monetary Research Institute, P.O. Box 3174, Houston, Texas, U.S.A., 77253-3174.
        (Quarterly illustrated guide of new and current world bank notes and travelers checks).

The Statesman's Year-Book, 1995-96.
132th Edition
    by Brian Hunter, editor, The Statesman's Year-Book Office, The Macmillan Press Ltd., 4-6 Crinan Street, London N1 9SQ , England.
        (Statistical and Historical Annual of the States of the World).

HOW TO USE THIS CATALOG

Catalog listings consist of all regular regional, provisional and military notes attaining wide circulation in their respective countries for the period covered. Cross-references are included for ease of identification and location. Where applicable, old catalog numbers appear in parentheses directly below the new number. Many listings have been regrouped by issue or inclusive date span rather than by denomination, and headings have been inserted. All this is to make the catalog as easy to use as possible for everyone.

The author, editors and publishers make no claim of absolute completeness, just as they acknowledge that some errors and pricing inequities will appear. Correspondence is invited with interested persons who have unlisted notes or who have date, signature or color information to enhance the presentation of existing listings in succeeding editions of this catalog.

Catalog Listings

Listings generally follow the following sequence:

Catalog number — the basic reference number at the beginning of each listing for each note. An 'S' is used as a prefix letter for listings in Volume 1, Specialized Issues. No prefix letter is used for listings in General Issues Volume 2 or 3.

Denomination — the value shown on the note, its nominal or face value.

Date — the actual issue date shown on the note. Where more than one date appears only the latest is used. Where the note has no date, the designation "ND" is used. When issue date is known even though the note has no date, the listing will show "ND" followed by a date in parentheses. Dates are always given in day-month-year order. Law or Decree dates are shown with an italic L or D before the date.

Color — included for all notes where known. The face color is given first, and if the back is different that comes later, after description of the face design.

Description — main design elements of the face side are described briefly immediately following color. The same is true for the back when information is known. Uniface notes are so designated. At times certain design elements consistent for a given series are shown just before the listing itself.

Printer — Abbreviations are used for larger or more prolific printers. See the list of printers' abbreviations on page 16. Smaller printers' names are shown in full. In the listings the word *imprint* refers to the logo of the printer's name usually appearing at the bottom margin.

Valuations — generally, modern issues are valued under the headings of Very Good, Very Fine, and Uncurculated. Listings which do not follow this pattern are clearly indicated.

Sample Listings

Following are three examples of catalog listings incorporating some of the features described in previous paragraphs:

Cat. #	Denomination	Date, description	VG	VF	Unc
10 (11)	5000 KORUN	1993. Black. blue-gray and violet in pink and lt. gray unpt. Pres. T. G. Masaryk at ro. Montage of Prague Gothic and Baroque buildings on back.	FV	FV	200.00

Explanation: catalog number is 10, changed from 11 in the last listing. Denomination is 5000 Korun, dated and issued in 1993. Face colors are black, blue-gray and violet on a pink and lt. gray unpt. The face design is a portrait of President T. G. Masaryk at right. The back colors are not listed as they are the same as the face. The back design is a montage of Prague's Gothic and Baroque buildings. As this is a recent issue, the only grade which commands a premium is that of uncirculated.

Cat. #	Denomination	Date, description	VG	VF	Unc
6	1 PULA	ND (1983). Dk. brown. Pres. O. Masire at l. Animals, plants and arms at ctr. on back.	FV	1.00	2.50

Explanation: catalog number is 6, denomination is 1 Pula and the date is not printed on the note, but it is known that is was released in 1983. The face color is dark brown and a portrait of President O. Masire is at the left. On the back are animals, plants and arms at the center.

Cat. #	Denomination	Date, description	VG	VF	Unc
M 45	10 NEW PENCE	ND (1972). Brown and green. Printer: DLR.	—	—	2.00

Explanation: This is a military use note catalogue number 45. Denomination is 10 New Pence, not dated on the note but known to have been released in 1972. The colors are brown and green. Printer is Thomas De La Rue (marked De La Rue on the note)

As a general rule, building, animals, etc. are not identified specifically unless such information helps to clarify the description. Portraits are identified whenever possible.

Renumbering

Very little renumbering has taken place for this edition. However, much hue and cry is raised about the havoc created when renumbering takes place. This is fully understood and appreciated by the catalogers, but we must all remember exactly what medium we are concerned with. Catalog numbers became very important as reference points very quickly, and everyone tags a number on a note and hopes it will never again have to be changed. That is the ideal to strive for, but it will probably take another generation of information and cataloging before numbers may reasonably be expected to remain constant. There is no other choice; as newer and better data is revealed, it is the duty of the cataloger to incorporate the necessary outline features to improve the accuracy of listings in volumes such as this. To do less would be an injustice to the hobby and all who care to improve it.

To ease the task of renumbering, in most cases previous catalog numbers are in parentheses immediately underneath the new numbers.

Dates and Date Listing Policy

The date listing in this catalog is intended to represent date information. We must all realize that paper money research is still in its relative infancy, and that a great many dates for a great many notes have never been set down. Moreover, even if they were, how could anyone know for certain at this time which of these are really rare and which are the more easily available? It will take many years, if ever, before such information is available, and even then its accuracy must be questioned. On the other hand, dates known to be scarce or rare are so indicated in this catalog.

In order to avoid any further difficulties, this is the date policy for catalog listings: in general, any note with up to three separate dates will have all of them shown in the listing. Notes with more than three issue dates will have an inclusive date span.

Examples:

242A 50 COLONES 15.7.1987; 26.4.1988

This shows all known dates for the note being listed.

242 100 COLONES 26.8.1969-26.4.1977.

The date span shows the earliest known date as 26.8.1969, and the latest 26.4.1977. Thus, ANY dates in between are automatically covered without their being listed.

Exceptions to this policy occur in certain series where collector interest requires the listing of all known dates, or where known dates include such a wide date span that to show inclusive dates would be misleading, or that pricing information is available for each date.

In later editions it is expected that more dates will be shown for some countries as signature or rarity information can be obtained to correlate with them.

As mentioned previously, Law or Decree dates will have *L* or *D* before the date.

Valuations

Valuations are given for most notes in three grades. The range of Very Good, Very Fine and Uncirculated is used for this modern book. While it is true that some notes have no premium value in Very Good, still it is felt this coverage provides the best uniformity of value data. Also, there are exceptional cases where headings are adjusted for either single notes or a series which really needs special treatment.

Valuations are determined generally from a concensus of individuals submitting prices for evaluation and averaging. Some notes have NO prices; this does not necessarily mean they are rare, but it does show that no pricing information was available. Some notes have a "Rare" designation, with no values. Such notes are generally not to be found on the market, and when they do appear their price is a matter between buyer and seller. No book can provide guidance in these instances except to indicate rarity.

All valuations are based on IBNS standards and American interests, and are stated in U.S. dollars. They serve only as aids in evaluating paper money since actual market conditions are constantly changing. Also, particularly choice examples of many issues listed in this book may bring higher premiums than those shown.

NOTE: Unless otherwise presented, values given are for types only, without regard for date and/or signature. In a number of instances, there are date or signature varieties worth a substantial premium over the listed value.

FV Instead of a Catalog Value

FV (face value): This designation has been used instead of a catalog value for currently circulating notes of most countries in less than new condition. FV may appear in one or both condition columns below Uncirculated, depending on the relative age and availability of the issue in question.

Values in Italics (Speculative)

In a few instances values are given in italics. This occurs when outside influences have made the collector market for the affected issue so unstable that any value shown is considered to be speculative.

Denominations

The denominations as indicated on many notes issued by a string of countries stretching from the eastern Orient, through western Asia and on across northern Africa often appear only in unfamiliar non-Western numeral styles. Within the listings which follow, however, denominations are always indicated in Western numerals.

A comprehensive chart keying Western numerals to their non-Western counterparts is included elsewhere in this introduction as an aid to the identification of note types. This compilation features not only the basic numeral systems such as Arabic, Japanese and Indian, but also the more restricted systems such as Burmese, Ethiopian, Siamese, Tibetan, Hebrew, Mongolian and Korean, plus other localized variations which have been applied to some paper money issues.

In consulting the numeral systems chart to determine the denomination of a note, one should remember that the actual numeral styles employed in any given area, or at a certain time, may vary significantly from these basic representations. Such variations can be deceptive to the untrained eye, just as variations from standard Western numeral styles can prove deceptive to individuals not acquainted with the particular style employed.

Letter Prefixes and Suffixes

A catalog number preceded by a capital "A" indicates the incorporation of an earlier listing as required by type or date; a capital letter following a catalog number shows the addition of a later issue. Both may also indicate newly discovered lower or higher denominations. Listings of notes for regional circulation are distinguished from regular national issues with the prefix "R" before the catalog number. Military issues use the prefix "M." Varieties are shown with small letters following a number, or by a listing of small letters with their respective entries.

Dating

Determining a note's date of issue is a basic consideration of attribution. As the reading of dates is subject not only to the vagaries of numeric styling, but to variations in dating roots caused by the observation of differing religious eras or regal periods from country to country, and in some instances even within a given country, making this determination can sometimes be quite difficult. Most countries outside the North Africa and Oriental spheres rely on Western date numerals and Christian era (AD) reckoning, although in a few instances note dating has been tied to the year of a reign or government.

Countries of the Arabic sphere generally date their issues to the Mohammedan era (AH) which commenced on July 16, 622 AD, when the prophet Mohammed fled from Mecca to Medina. As their calendar is reckoned by the lunar year of 354 days, which is about three percent (precisely 3.03 percent) shorter than the Christian year, a formula is required to convert the dating to its Western equivalent. To convert an AH date to the approximate AD date, subtract three percent of the AH date (round to the closest whole number) from the AH date, then add 621.

The Mohammedan calendar is not always based on the lunar year (AH), however, causing some confusion, particularly in Afghanistan and Iran (Persia) where a calendar based on the solar year (SH) was introduced around 1920. These dates can be converted to AD by simply adding 621. In 1976 the government of Iran implemented a new solar calendar based on the founding of the Iranian monarchy in 559 BC. The first year observed on the new calendar was 2535 (MS), which commenced on March 20, 1976.

Several different eras of reckoning, including Christian and Mohammedan (AH), have been used to date paper money of the Indian subcontinent. The two basic systems are the Vikrama Samvat era (VS), which dates from October 18, 58 BC, and the Saka era (SE), the origin of which is reckoned from March 3, 78 AD. Dating according to both eras appears on the notes of the various native states and countries of the area.

Thailand (Siam) has observed three different eras of dating. The most predominant is the Buddhist era (BE) which originated in 543 BC. Next is the Bangkok or Ratanakosind-sok era (RS) dating from 1781 AD (dates consist of only three numerals), followed by the Chula-Sakarat era (CS) which dates from 638 AD, with the latter also observed in Burma.

Other calendars include that of the Ethiopian era (EE) which commenced 7 years, 8 months after AD dating, and that of the Jewish people which commenced on October 7, 3761 BC. Korea claims a legendary dating from 2333 BC which is acknowledged on some issues of paper money.

The following table indicates the year dating for the various eras which correspond to 1990 by Christian calendar reckoning, but it must be remembered that there are overlaps between the eras in some instances:

Christian era (AD)	— 1990
Mohammedan era (AH)	— AH1411
Solar year (SH)	— SH1369
Monarchic Solar era (MS)	— MS2549
Vikrama Samvat era (VS)	— SE2047
Saka era (SE)	— Saka 1912
Buddhist era (BE)	— BE2533
Bangkok era (RS)	— RS209
Chula-Sakarat era (CS)	— CS1352
Ethiopian era (EE)	— EE1982
Jewish era	— 5750
Korean era	— 4323

Paper money of Oriental origin - principally Japan, Korea, China, Turkestan and Tibet - is generally dated to the year of the government, dynastic, regnal or cyclical eras, with the dates indicated in Oriental characters which usually read from right to left. In recent years, however, some dating has been according to the Christian calendar, and in Western numerals.

More detailed guides to the application of the less prevalent dating systems than those described, and others of strictly local nature, along with the numeral designations employed, are presented in conjunction with the appropriate listings.

Some notes carry dating according to both the locally observed and Christian eras. This is particularly true in the Arabic sphere, where the Mohammedan date may be indicated in Arabic numerals and the Christian date in Western numerals, or both dates may be represented in either Arabic or Western numerals.

In general the date actually carried on a given paper money issue is indicated. Notes issued by special Law or Decree will have L or D preceding the date. Dating listed which does not actually appear on a given note is generally bracketed by parentheses. Undated issues are indicated by the presence of the letters ND along with the year of issue in parentheses, if it is known.

Timing differentials between the 354 day Mohammedan and 365 day Christian years cause situations whereby paper money bearing dates for both eras exist bearing two year dates from one calendar in combination with a single date from the other.

China – Republic 9th year, 1st month, 15th day (15.1.1920), read r. to l.

Russia – 1 October 1920

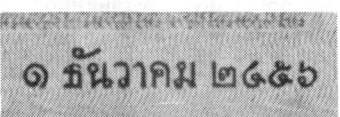

Thailand (Siam) – 1 December 2456

Korea – 4288 (1955)

Poland – 28 February 1919

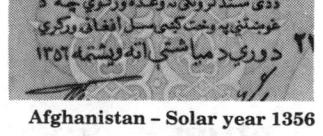

Afghanistan – Solar year 1356

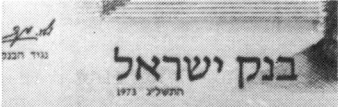

Israel – 1973, 5733

Indonesia – January 1950

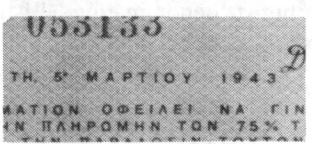

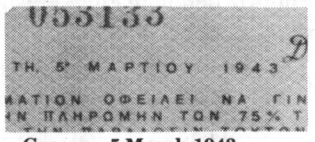

Egypt – 1967 December 2

Greece – 5 March 1943

English	January	February	March	April	May	June	July	August	September	October	November	December
Albanian	Kallnuer	Fruer	Mars	Prill	Maj	Qershuer	Korrik	Gusht	Shtatuer	Tetuer	Nanduer	Dhetuer
Czech	Leden	Unor	Brezen	Duben	Kveten	Cerven	Cervenec	Srpen	Zari	Rijen	listopad	Prosinec
Danish	Januar	Februari	Maart	April	Maj	Juni	Juli	August	September	Oktober	November	December
Dutch	Januari	Fevruari	Maart	April	Mei	Juni	Juli	Augustus	September	Oktober	November	December
Estonian	Jaanuar	Veebruar	Marts	Aprill	Mai	Juuni	Juuli	August	September	Oktoober	November	Detsember
French	Janvier	Fevrier	Mars	Avril	Mai	Juin	Jillet	Aout	Septembre	Octobre	Novembre	Decembre
Finnish	Tammikuu	Helmikuu	Maaliskuu	Huhtikuu	Toukokuu	Kesakuu	Heinakuu	Elokuu	Syyskuu	Lokakuu	Marraskuu	Joulukuu
German	Januar	Februar	Marz	April	Mai	juni	Juli	August	September	Oktober	Novembre	Dezember
Hungarian	Januar	Februar	Marcius	Aprilis	Majus	Junius	Julius	Augusztus	Szeptember	Oktober	November	December
Indonesian	Djanuari	Februari	Maret	April	Mai	Djuni	Djui	Augustus	September	Oktober	Nopember	Desember
Italian	Gennaio	Fabbraio	Marzo	Aprile	Maggio	Giugno	Luglio	Agosto	Settembre	Ottobre	Novembre	Dicembre
Lithuanian	Sausis	Vasaris	Kovas	Balandis	Geguzis	Birzelis	Liepos	Rugpiutis	Rugsejis	Spalis	Lapkritis	Gruodis
Norwegian	Januar	Februar	Mars	April	Mai	Juni	Juli	August	September	Oktober	November	Desember
Polish	Styczen	Luty	Marzec	Kwiecien	Maj	Cerwiec	Lipiec	Sierpien	Wrzesien	Pazdziernik	Listopad	Grudzien
Portuguese	Janerio	Fevereiro	Marco	Abril	Maio	Junho	Julho	Agosto	Setembro	Outubro	Novembro	Dezembro
Rombanian	Iannuario	Februarie	Martie	Aprilio	mai	Iunie	Iulie	August	Setembrie	Octombrie	Noiembrie	Decembrie
Croatian	Sijecanj	Veljaca	Ozujak	Travanj	Svibanj	Lipanj	Srpanj	Kolovoz	Rujan	Listopad	Studeni	Prosinac
Spanish	Enero	Febrero	Marzo	Abril	Mayo	Junio	Julio	Agosto	Septiembre	Octubre	Noviembre	Diciembre
Swedish	Januari	Februari	Mars	April	Maj	Juni	Juli	Augusti	September	Oktober	November	December
Turkish	Ocak	Subat	Mart Ayi	Nisan	Mayis Ayi	Haziran	Temmuz	Agusto	Eylul	Ekim	Kasim	Aralik
Arabic-New (condensed)	يناير	فبراير	مارس	ابريل	مايو	يونيو	يوليو	أغسطس	سبتمبر	أكتوبر	نوفمبر	ديسمبر
(extended)	يناير	فبراير	مارس	ابريل	مايو	يونيه	يوليه	اغسطس	سبتمبر	اكتوبر	نوفمبر	ديسمبر
Persian (Solar)	فروردين	اردیبهشت	خرداد	تیر	مرداد	شهریور	مهر	آبان	آذر	دی	بهمن	اسفند
(Lunar)	مُحَرَّم	صَفَر	رَبِيعُ الأَوَّل	رَبِيعُ الآخِر	جُمَادَى الأُولَى	جُمَادَى الآخِرَة	رَجَب	شَعْبَان	رَمَضَان	شَوَّال	ذُو القَعْدَة	ذُو الحِجَّة
Chinese	正月	二月	三月	四月	五月	六月	七月	八月	九月	十月	十一月	十二月
Japanese	月 一	月 二	月 三	月 四	月 五	月 六	月 七	月 八	月 九	月 十	月 一 十	月 二 十
Greek	Ιανοναριοδ	Φεβροναριοδ	Μαρτιοδ	Απιλιοδ	Μαιοδ	Ιουνιοδ	Ιουλιοδ	Αυγουατοδ	Εεπτεμβπιοδ	Οκτωβπιοδ	Νοεμπιοσ	Δεκεμβπιοδ
Russian	ЯНВАРЬ	ФЕВРАЛЬ	МАРТ	АПРЕЛЬ	МАИ	ИЮИЬ	ИЮЛЬ	АВГУСТ	СЕИТЯБРЬ	ОКТЯБРЬ	НОЯБРЬ	ДЕКАБРЬ
Serbian	Јануар	Фебруар	Марг	Април	Мај	Јун	Јул	Август	Септембар	Октобар	Новембар	Децембар
Yiddish	יאַנואַר	פֿעברואַר	מערץ	אַפּריל	מײַ	יוני	יולי	אויגוסט	סעפּטעמבער	אָקטיאַבער	נאָוועמבער	דעצעמבער
Hebrew (Israeli)	ינואר	פברואר	מרץ	אפריל	מאי	יוני	יולי	אוגוסט	ספטמבר	אוקטובר	נובמבר	דצמבר

Note: Word spellings and configurations as represented on actual notes may vary significantly from those shown on this chart.

Abbreviations

Certain abbreviations have been adopted for words occuring frequently in note descriptions. Following is a list of these:

#	—	number (catalog or serial)
bldg.	—	building
ctr.	—	center
dk.	—	dark
FV	—	face value
gen.	—	general
govt	—	government
Kg.	—	king
l.	—	left
lg.	—	large
lt.	—	light
m/c	—	multicolored
ND	—	no date
ovpt.	—	overprint
portr.	—	portrait
Qn.	—	queen
r.	—	right
sign.	—	signature or signatures
sm.	—	small
unpt.	—	underprint (background printing)
wmk.	—	watermark
w/	—	with
w/o	—	without

Housing and Caring for A Collection

The proper housing of a collection should be one of the first considerations of a beginning collector. Even the advanced collector needs to consider it from time to time. Only a person who has housed his notes in a manner giving pleasure to himself and others will keep alive the pleasure of collecting in the long run. The same applies to the way of housing as to the choce of the collecting specialty: it is chiefly a question of what most pleases the individual collector.

Sorting and proper arrangement of the ntes is most certainly a basic requirement. Storing the notes in envelopes and filing boxes should perhaps be considered only when building a new section of a collection, for accomodating varieties or for reasons of saving space when the collection begins to grow.

The grouping of notes on cardboard sheets and fixing them into position with photo corners is a mode of housing practiced for many years. The collector can arrange the notes to his own taste, letter and otherwise embellish them. Difficulties will arise in the accommodation of supplements and the exchanging of notes when acquiring pieces in better condition, since even slight differences in the formation will necessitate detaching and reaffixing the photo corners.

Most bank note collections are probably housed in some form of plastic-pocketed album which are today manufactured in many different sizes and styles to accommodate many types of world paper money.

Because the number of bank note collectors has grown continually during the past few years, some specialty manufacturers of postage stamp and coin albums have also developed new albums for paper money. The notes, housed in clear plastic pockets, individually or several in a pocket, can be viewed and exchanged without difficulty. These binders are not cheap, but the notes displayed in this manner should make the most lasting impression on the viewer. A large collection will hardly be accommodated in its entirety in this manner, thus many collectors limit themselves to partial areas or especially valuable notes which are displayed thus. CAUTION: certain types of plastic and all vinyl used for housing notes may cause brittleness in time and cause oiliness from fluids transferred from the vinyl to the notes.

The high demands which stamp collectors make in general on the quality of their objects cannot be transferred to paper money. A postage stamp is intended for use only once and is then embodied in a collection. or it may be purchased new as a mint specimen without the slightest trace of use. In paper money, it is difficult or impossible to acquire uncirculated specimens from a number of countries. Acquiring the circulating notes of such places in high grades is also not a simple matter. The collector must often content himself with notes showing more or less pronounced traces of use from circulation.

The fact that there is a classification and value difference between the notes with greater use or even damage is a matter of course. it is part of the opinion and personal taste of the individual collector to decide what he will consider worthy of collecting and what he will embody in his collection.

For the purposes of strengthening and backing torn paper money, under no circumstances should one use plain cellophane tape or a similar material. These tapes warp easily, with sealing marks forming at the edges, and the tape frequently discolors. Only with the greatest of difficulty (and often not at all) can these tape be removed, and the damage to the note or the printing is almost unavoidable. The best material for backing tears is the 3M Magic transparent tape, a self-adhesive tape especially recommended for the treatment and repair of documents.

There are collectors who, with great skill, remove unsightly spots, repair badly damaged notes, replace missing pieces and otherwise restore or clean a note. before venturing to take such work, one should first experiment with cheap duplicates and not endanger a collection piece by a daring attempt. Really difficult work of this nature should be left to the experienced restorer, provided the value of the note is a sensible ratio to the expenditure involved. On the same subject, there has recently arisen a school of thought which questions the wisdom and, indeed, the very morality of tampering with a piece of paper money to restore or improve its condition. Such a question must, in the final analysis, be left to the individual collector.

Unnatural Defects

Glue, tape or pencil marks may sometimes be successfully removed. While such removal will leave a cleaned surface, it will improve the overall appearance of the note without concealing any of its defects. Under such circumstances, the grade of that note may also be improved.

The words "pinholes", "staple holes", "trimmed", "writing on face", "tape marks" etc. should always be added to the description of a note. It is realized that certain countries routinely staple their notes together in groups before issue. In such cases, the description can include a comment such as "usual staple holes" or something similar. After all, not everyone knows that certain notes cannot be found otherwise.

The major point of this section is that one cannot lower the overall grade of a note with defects simply because of the defects. The price will reflect the lowered worth of a defective note, but the description must always include the specific defects.

The Term *Uncirculated*

The word *Uncirculated* is used in this grading guide only as a qualitive measurement of the appearance of a note. It has nothing at all to do with whether or not an issuer has actually released the note to circulation. Thus, the term About Uncirculated is justified and acceptable because so many notes that have never seen hand to hand use have been mishandled so that they are available at best in AU condition. Either a note is uncirculated in condition or it is not; there can be no degrees of uncirculated. Highlights or defects in color, centering and the like may be included in a description but the fact that a note is or is not in uncirculated condition should not be a disputable point.

GRADING GUIDE — Definitions of Terms

UNCIRCULATED: A perfectly preserved note, never mishandled by the issuing authority, a bank teller, the public or a collector.

Paper is clean and firm, without discoloration. Corners are sharp and square, witout any evidence of roudning. (Rounded corners are often a tell-tale sign of a cleaned or "doctored" note.)

An uncirculated note will have its original, natural sheen.

NOTE: Some note issuers are most often avaialble with slight eveidence of very light counting folds which do not "break" the paper. Also, French-printed notes usually have a slight ripple in the paper. Many collectors and dealers refer to such notes as AU-UNC.

ABOUT UNCIRCULATED: A virtually perfect note, with some minor handling. May show very slight evidence of bank counting folds at a corner or one light fold through the center, but not both. An AU note cannot be creased, a crease being a hard fold which has usually "broken" the surface of the note.

Paper is clean and bright with original sheen. Corners are not rounded.

NOTE: Europeans will refer to an About Uncirculated or AU note as "EF-Unc" or as just "EF". The Extremely Fine note described below will often be referred to as "GVF" or "Good Very Fine".

EXTREMELY FINE: A very attractive note, with light handling. May have a maximum of three light folds or one strong crease.

Paper is clean and bright with original sheen. Corners may show only the slightest evidence of rounding. There may also be the slightest sign of wear where a fold meets the edge.

VERY FINE: An attractive note, but with more evidence of handling and wear. May have scveral folds both vertically and horizontally.

Paper may have minimal dirt, or possible color smudging. Paper itself is still relatively crisp and not floppy.

There are no tears into the border area, although the edges do show slight wear. Corners also show wear but not full rounding.

FINE: A note which shows considerable circulation, with many folds, creases and wrinkling.

Paper is not excessively dirty but may have some softness.

Edges may show much handling, with minor tears in the border area. Tears may not extend into the design. There will be no center hole because of excessive folding.

Colors are clear but not very bright. A staple hole or two would not be considered unusual wear in a Fine note. Overall appearance is still on the desirable side.

VERY GOOD: A well used note, abused but still intact.

Corners may have much wear and rounding, tiny nicks, tears may extend into the design, some discoloration may be present, staining may have occurred, and a small hole may sometimes be seen at center from excessive folding.

Staple and pinholes are usually present, and the note itself is quite limp but NO pieces of the note can be missing. A note in VG condition may still have an overall not unattractive appearance.

GOOD: A well worn and heavily used note. Normal damage from prolonged circulation will include strong multiple folds and creases, stains, pinholes and/or staple holes, dirt, discoloration, edge tears, center hole, rounded corners and an overall unattractive appearance. No large pieces of the note may be missing. Graffiti is commonly seen on notes in G condition.

FAIR: A totally limp, dirty and very well used note. Larger pieces may be half torn off or missing besides the defects mentioned under the Good category. Tears will be larger, obscured portions of the note will be bigger.

POOR: A "rag" with severe damage because of wear, staining, pieces missing, graffiti, larger holes. May have tape holding pieces of the note together. Trimming may have taken place to remove rough edges. A Poor note is desirable only as a "filler" or when such a note is the only one known of that particular issue.

STANDARD INTERNATIONAL GRADING TERMINOLOGY AND ABBREVIATIONS

U.S. and ENGLISH SPEAKING LANDS	UNCIRCULATED	EXTREMELY FINE	VERY FINE	FINE	VERY GOOD	GOOD	POOR
Abbreviation	UNC	EF or XF	VF	FF	VG	G	PR
BRAZIL	(1) DW	(3) S	(5) MBC	(7) BC	(8)	(9) R	UTGeG
DENMARK	O	O1	1+	1	1÷	2	3
FINLAND	0	01	1+	1	1?	2	3
FRANCE	NEUF	SUP	TTB or TB	TB or TB	B	TBC	BC
GERMANY	KFR	II / VZGL	III / SS	IV / S	V / S.g.E.	VI / G.e.	G.e.s.
ITALY	FdS	SPL	BB	MB	B	M	—
JAPAN	未 使 用	極美品	美 品	並品	—	—	—
NETHERLANDS	FDC	Pr.	Z.F.	Fr.	Z.g.	G	—
NORWAY	0	01	1+	1	1÷	2	3
PORTUGAL	Novo	Soberbo	Muito bo	—	—	—	—
SPAIN	Lujo	SC, IC or EBC	MBC	BC	—	RC	MC
SWEDEN	0	01	1+	1	1?	2	—

BRAZIL

FE	— Flor de Estampa
S	— Soberba
MBC	— Muito Bem Conservada
BC	— Bem Conservada
R	— Regular
UTGeG	— Um Tanto Gasto e Gasto

DENMARK

O	— Uncirkuleret
01	— Meget Paent Eksemplar
1+	— Paent Eksemplar
1	— Acceptabelt Eksemplar
1	— Noget Slidt Eksemplar
2	— Darlight Eksemplar
3	— Meget Darlight Eskemplar

FINLAND

00	— Kiitolyonti
0	— Lyontiveres
01	— Erittain Hyva
1+	— Hyva
1?	— Keikko
3	— Huono

FRANCE

NEUF	— New
SUP	— Superbe
TTB	— Tres Tres Beau
TB	— Tres Beau
B	— Beau
TBC	— Tres Bien Conserve
BC	— Bien Conserve

GERMANY

VZGL	— Vorzüglich
SS	— Sehr schön
S	— Schön
S.g.E.	— Sehr gut erhalten
G.e.	— Gut erhalten
G.e.S.	— Gering erhalten
	Schlect

ITALY

Fds	— Fior di Stampa
SPL	— Splendid
BB	— Bellissimo
MB	— Molto Bello
B	— Bello
M	— Mediocre

JAPAN

未 使 用	— Mishiyo
極美品	— Goku Bihin
美 品	— Bihin
並品	— Futuhin

NETHERLANDS

Pr.	— Prachtig
Z.F.	— Zeer Fraai
Fr.	— Fraai
Z.g.	— Zeer Goed
G	— Good

NORWAY

0	— Usirkuleret eks
01	— Meget pent eks
1+	— Pent eks
1	— Fullgodt eks
1-	— Ikke Fullgodt eks
2	— Darlig eks

SPAIN

EBC	— Extraordinariamente Bien Conservada
SC	— Sin Circular
IC	— Incirculante
MBC	— Muy Bien Conservada
BC	— Bien Conservada
RC	— Regular Conservada
MC	— Mala Conservada

SWEDEN

0	— Ocirkulerat
01	— Mycket Vackert
1+	— Vackert
1	— Fullgott
1?	— Ej Fullgott
2	— Dalight

SPECIMEN NOTES

To familiarize private banks, central banks, law enforcement agencies and treasuries around the world with newly issued currency, many nations provide them with special "Specimen" examples of their notes. Specimens are actual bank notes, complete with dummy or all zero serial numbers and signatures and bearing the overprinted and/or perforated word "SPECIMEN" in the language of the country of origin itself or where the notes were printed.

Some countries have made specimen notes available for sale to collectors. These include Cuba, Czechoslovakia, Poland and Slovakia after World War II and a special set of four denominations of Jamaica notes bearing red matched star serial numbers. Also, in 1978, the Franklin Mint made available to collectors specimen notes from 15 nations, bearing matching serial numbers and a Maltese cross device used as a prefix. Several other countries have also participated in making specimen notes available to collectors at times.

Aside from these collectors issues, specimen notes may sometimes command higher prices than regular issue notes of the same type, even though there are far fewer collectors of specimens. In some cases, notably older issues in high denominations, specimens may be the only form of such notes available to collectors today. Specimen notes are not legal tender or redeemable, thus have no real "face value" which also is indicated on some examples.

The most unusual forms of specimens were produced by Waterlow and Sons. They printed special off colored notes for salesman's sample books adding the word SPECIMEN and their seal. These salesman's samples are not included in catalog listings. In most cases they are less valuable than true color specimens but may command a premium in more popularly collected countries.

Some examples of how the word "SPECIMEN" is represented in other languages or on notes of other countries follow:

AMOSTRA: Brazil
CAMPIONE: Italy
CONTOH: Malaysia
EKSEMPLAAR: South Africa
ESPÉCIME: Portugal and Colonies
ESPECIMEN: Various Spanish-speaking nations
GIAY MAU: Vietnam
MINTA: Hungary
MODELO: Brazil
MODEL: Albania
MUSTER: Austria, Germany
MUESTRA: Various Spanish-speaking nations
NUMUNEDIR GECMEZ: Turkey
ORNEKTIR GECMEZ: Turkey
ОБРАЗЕЦ or **ОБРАЗЕЦЪ:** Bulgaria, Russia, U.S.S.R.
PARAUGS: Latvia
PROFTRYK: Sweden
SPEZIMEN: Switzerland
UZORAK: Croatia
VZOREC: Slovenia
WZOR: Poland
ЗАГВАР: Mongolia

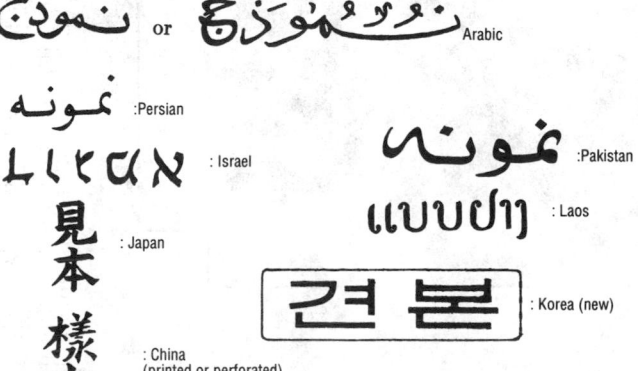

BANK NOTE PRINTERS

Printers' names, abbreviations or monograms will usually appear as part of the frame design or below it on face and/or back. In some instances the engraver's name may also appear in a similar location on a note, as well as part of the copyright notice. The following abbreviations identify printers for many of the notes listed in this volume:

ABNC	American Bank Note Company (USA)
BABNC	British American Bank Note Co., Ltd. (Canada)
BCdE	Banco Central de Ecuador
BDDK	Bundesdruckerei (Berlin)
BdM	Banco de Mexico
BEPP	Bureau of Engraving & Printing, Peking (China)
BF	Banque de France (France)
BWC	Bradbury, Wilkinson & Co. (England)
CABB	Compania Americana de Billetes de Banco (ABNC)
CBNC	Canadian Bank Note Company (Canada)
CdM-B	Casa da Moeda (Brazil)
CdM-A	Casa de Moneda (Argentina)
CdM-C	Casa de Moneda (Chile)
CMN	Casa de Moneda de la Nacion (Argentina)
CSABB	Compania Sud/Americana de Billetes de Banco (Argentina)
DBM-A	Deviet Banknot Matbassi, Ankara (Turkey)
DLR	Thomas De La Rue (England)
F-CO	Francios-Charles Oberthur
FNMT	Fabrica Nacional de Moneda y Timbre (Spain)
G&D	Giesecke & Devrient (Germany)
HdM-Z	Zaire
HKB	Hong Kong Banknote (Hong Kong)
H&S	Harrison & Sons Ltd. (England)
IBB	Imprenta de Billetes-Bogota (Colombia)
IBSFB	Imprenta de Billetes-Santa Fe de Bogota (Columbia)
IBNC	International Bank Note Company (US)
IPS-ROMA	Instituto Polygrafico Dello Statto (Italy)
JEZ	Johann Enschede en Zonen (Netherlands)
LN	Litografia Nacional (Colombia)
NBNC	National Bank Note Company (US)
OCV	Officina Carte-Valori (Italy)
ODBI	Officina Della Banca D'Italia (Italy)
OFZ	Orell Füssli Arts Grafiques, Zurich (Switzerland)
PPU	Indonesia
STC-P	Statni Tiskarna Cenin-Prague (Czech Rep)
TB	Tumba Bruk A.B. (Sweden)
TDLR	Thomas De La Rue (England)
USBNC	United States Banknote Corp. (USA)
W&S	Waterlow & Sons Ltd. (England)
ZZN-B	Zavod Zaizradu Novcanica-Belgrad (Yugoslavia)

**Application for Membership
in the
INTERNATIONAL BANK NOTE SOCIETY**

Name _____
  Last   First   Initial

Street _____

_____

City _____ Province or State _____

Country _____ Postal Code _____

Type of Membership:
  Individual: $17.50 per year_____
  Junior (Ages 11-17)
                $9.00 per year_____
  Family (Includes children under 18)
      $22.50 per year_____

Payment in US Dollars payable to IBNS.

Check _____ Money Order _____ Other _____

Do you wish your name and address to appear
in our Membership Directory?

    Yes _____   No _____

Collecting Interest _____

_____

_____

Mail to: Milan Alusic
            P.O. Box 1642
            Racine, Wisconsin
            U.S.A. 53401

International Bank Note Society

The International Bank Note Society was formed in 1961 to promote the collecting of world paper money.

More than 1,600 members in over 60 nations around the world draw on the services of the IBNS to advance their collecting.

The Society's benefits begin with the quarterly IBNS Journal, a magazine featuring learned writings on the notes of the world, their history, artistry and technical background.

Additionally, each member receives a directory which lists the membership by name as well as geographical location. Each member's collecting specialties are also given.

Other member benefits include a regular newsletter (3-4 times a year) plus twice-annual paper money auctions.

One of the greatest benefits of IBNS membership is the facility for correspondence with other members around the world, for purposes of exchanging notes, numismatic knowledge and assistance with research projects.

For persons with paper money they cannot identify, the Society offers an attribution service.

BANKNOTE MEASUREMENTS

When the size of a banknote is given to distinguish different printings of similar notes it is liested in millimeters width x height for both horizontal and vertical formats. In modern, accurately produced notes the dimensions of the paper are given.

**Dominican Republic #32A
157 x 67 mm**

Foreign Exchange Table

The latest foreign exchange fixed rates below apply to trade with banks in the country of origin. The left column shows the number of units per U.S. dollar at the official rate. The right column shows the number of units per dollar at the free market rate.

Country	Official #/$	Market #/$
Afghanistan (Afghani)	3,500	—
Albania (Lek)	100.	—
Algeria (Dinar)	43.	65.
Andorra uses French Franc and Spanish Peseta		
Angola (Novo Kwanza)	591,000	700,000
Anguilla uses E.C. Dollar	2.67	—
Antigua uses E.C. Dollar	2.67	—
Argentina (New Peso)	1.00	—
Armenia (Dram)	350.	404.
Aruba (Florin)	1.79	—
Australia (Dollar)	1.35	—
Austria (Schilling)	9.79	—
Azerbaijan (Manat)	N/A	4,376
Bahamas (Dollar)	1.00	—
Bahrain Is. (Dinar)	.3770	—
Bangladesh (Taka)	40.30	42.50
Barbados (Dollar)	1.98	2.05
Belarus (Ruble)	22,350	—
Belgium (Franc)	28.58	—
Belize (Dollar)	1.98	2.05
Benin uses CFA Franc West	496.	530.
Bermuda (Dollar)	1.00	—
Bhutan (Ngultrum)	31.30	33.
Bolivia (Boliviano)	4.64	—
Bosnia-Herzegovina, D.Mark		
Botswana (Pula)	2.77	—
Brazil (Real)	0.91	—
British Virgin Islands uses U.S. Dollar	1.00	—
Brunei/Ringgit	1.5125	—
Bulgaria (Lev)	53.75	—
Burkina Faso uses CFA Fr. West	496.	530.
Burundi (Franc)	270.	320.
Cambodia (Riel)	2,500	—
Cameroon uses CFA Franc Central	496.	530.
Canada (Dollar)	1.37	—
Cape Verde (Escudo)	84.40	92.
Central African Rep. (Franc)	496.	530.
CFA Franc Central	496.	530.
CFA Franc West	496.	530.
CFP Franc	98.82	—
Chad uses CFA Franc Central	496.	530.
Chile (Peso)	395.	—
China, P.R. (R. Yuan)	8.4241	9.00
Colombia (Peso)	865.	—
Comoros (Franc)	400.	—
Congo uses Franc CFA Central	496.	—
Cook Islands (Dollar)	1.67	—
Costa Rica (Colon)	167.	—
Croatia (Kuna)	5.73	—
Cuba (Peso)	.7575	140.
Cyprus (Pound)	.4717	—
Czech. (Koruna)	26.	—
Denmark (Krona)	5.459	—
Djibouti (Franc)	178.	—
Dominica uses E.C. Dollar	2.67	—
Dom. Rep. (Peso)	13.	—
East Caribbean (Dollar)	2.67	—
Ecuador (Sucre)	2,423	—
Egypt (Pound)	3.38	—
El Salvador (Colon)	8.75	—
England (Sterling Pound)	.6234	—
Equatorial Guinea uses CFA Fr Central	496.	530.
Eritrea, see Ethiopia		
Estonia (Kroon)	10.96	—
Ethiopia (Birr)	5.58	7.50
European Currency Unit	.7677	—
Falkland Is. (Pound)	.6234	—

Country	#/$	#/$
Faroe Islands (Krona)	6.10	—
Fiji Islands (Dollar)	1.448	—
Finland (Markka)	4.279	--
France (Franc)	4.854	—
French Polynesia uses Franc CFP	96.82	—
Gabon (Franc)	496.	530.
Gambia (Dalasi)	9.75	—
Georgia/Kupon	2,500,000	—
Germany (D. Mark)	1.39	—
Ghana (Cedi)	948.	—
Gibraltar (Pound)	.6234	—
Greece (Drachma)	226.	—
Greenland uses Denmark		
Grenada uses East Carib. Dollar	2.67	—
Guatemala (Quetzal)	5.60	—
Guernsey uses Sterling Pound	.6234	—
Guinea-Bissau (Peso)	12,300	—
Guinea Conakry (Fanc)	976.	—
Guyana (Dollar)	141.	—
Haiti (Gourde)	12.	15.
Honduras (Lempira)	8.60	—
Hong Kong (Dollar)	7.73	—
Hungary (Forint)	121.	—
Iceland (New Krona)	67.50	—
India (Rupee)	31.36	—
Indonesia (Rupiah)	2,231	—
Iran (Rial)	1,750	2,600
Iraq (Dinar)	.3125	450.
Ireland (Punt)	.6122	—
Isle of Man uses Sterling Pound	.6234	—
Israel (New Shekel)	2.958	—
Italy (Lira)	1,708	—
Ivory Coast uses CFA Franc West	496.	530.
Jamaica (Dollar)	33.25	34.
Japan (Yen)	83.30	—
Jersey Sterling Pound	.6234	—
Jordan (Dinar)	.6870	—
Kazakhstan/Tenga	61.	N/A
Kenya (Shilling)	55.90	56.50
Kiribati uses Australian Dollar		
Korea-PDR (Won)	2.15	N/A
Korea-Repub. (Won)	769.	—
Kuwait (Dinar)	.2926	—
Kyrgyzstan (Som)	10.90	—
Laos (Kip)	720.	—
Latvia (Lat)	.5200	—
Lebanon (Pound)	1,633	—
Lesotho (Maloti)	3.66	4.00
Liberia/Dollar "JJ"	1.00	40.
"Liberty"	—	20.
Libya (Dinar)	.3050	.833
Liechtenstein uses Swiss Franc		
Lithuania (Litas)	4.00	—
Luxembourg (Franc)	31.95	—
Macao (Pataca)	7.98	—
Macedonia (New Denar)	41.	—
Madagascar (Franc)	3,800	4,000
Maldives (Rufiya)	11.60	—
Malawi (Kwacha)	7.35	7.75
Malaysia (Ringgit)	2.465	—
Mali uses CFA West Franc	496.	530.
Malta (Lira)	.3481	—
Marshall Islands uses U.S. Dollar		
Mauritania (Ouguiya)	122.	130.
Mauritius (Rupee)	17.15	—
Mexico (New Peso)	6.295	—
Moldova (Leu)	4.430	—
Monaco uses French Franc		
Mongolia (Tugrik)	360.	—
Montenegro uses Yugo Super Dinar		
Montserrat uses E.C. Dollar	2.67	—
Morocco (Dirham)	8.95	—
Mozambique (Metical)	6,250	7,100
Myanmar (Burma) (Kyat)	5.81	120.
Nambia (Dollar)	3.66	4.00
Nauru uses Australian Dollar		
Nepal (Rupee)	49.25	—
Netherlands (Gulden)	1.5578	—

Country	#/$	#/$
Netherlands Antilles (Gulden)	1.79	—
New Caledonia uses CFP Franc		
New Zealand (Dollar)	1.4875	—
Nicaragua (Cordoba Oro)	6.75	—
Niger uses CFA Franc West	496.	530.
Nigeria (Naira)	22.	45.
Northern Ireland uses Sterling Pound	.6234	—
Norway (Krone)	6.23	—
Oman (Rial)	.3850	—
Pakistan (Rupee)	30.85	—
Palau uses U.S. Dollar		
Panama (Balboa) uses U.S. Dollar		
Papua-New Guinea (Kina)	0.94	—
Paraguay (Guarani)	1,765	—
Peru (Nuevo Sol)	2.250	—
Philippines (Piso)	26.10	—
Poland (Zloty)	2.3700	—
Portugal (Escudo)	146.80	—
Qatar (Riyal)	3.63	—
Romania (Leu)	1,680	—
Russia (Ruble)	4,896	—
Rwanda (Franc)	137.	N/A
St. Helena (Pound)	.6234	—
St. Kitts uses E.C. Dollar	2.67	—
St. Lucia uses E.C. Dollar	2.67	—
St. Vincent uses E.C. Dollar	2.67	—
San Marino uses Italian Lira		
Sao Tome e Principe (Dobra)	685.	—
Saudi Arabia (Riyal)	3.75	—
Scotland uses Sterling Pound	.6234	—
Senegal uses CFA Franc West	496.	530.
Seychelles (Rupee)	4.94	—
Sierra Leone (Leone)	580.	600.
Singapore (Dollar)	1.395	—
Slovakia (Koruna)	29.40	33.
Slovenia (Tolar)	121.	—
Solomon Is. (Dollar)	3.26	—
Somalia (Shillin)	2,620	4,600
Somaliland Somali Shillin		
South Africa (Rand)	3.6117	4.00
Spain (Peseta)	123.	—
Sri Lanka (Rupee)	48.90	—
Sudan (Dinar)	31.10	75.
Surinam (Gulden)	183.	—
Swaziland (Lilangeni)	3.66	4.00
Sweden (Krona)	7.301	—
Switzerland (Franc)	1.151	—
Syria (Pound)	45.	46.
Taiwan (NT Dollar)	25.35	—
Tajikistan uses Russian Ruble		
Tanzania (Shilling)	520.	550.
Thailand (Baht)	24.56	—
Togo uses CFA Franc West	496.	530.
Tonga (Pa'anga)	1.36	—
Transdniestra/new Coupon	N/A	230.
Trinidad & TobagoDollar	5.57	—
Tunisia (Dinar)	0.98	—
Turkey (Lira)	42,475	—
Turkmenistan (Manat)	60.	100.
Turks & Caicos uses U.S. Dollar		
Tuvalu uses Australian Dollar		
Uganda (Shilling)	925	—
Ukraine (Karbovanets)	N/A	153,081
United Arab Emirates (Dirham)	3.63	—
Uruguay (Peso Uruguayo)	6.02	—
Uzbekistan (Som)	N/A	26.09
Vanuatu (Vatu)	116.	—
Vatican City uses Italian Lira		
Venezuela (Bolivar)	169.78	190.
Vietnam (Dong)	11,200	—
Western Samoa (Tala)	2.52	—
Yemen (North)/Rial	12.	70.
Yemen South (Dinar)	.4609	2.70
Yugoslavia (Super Dinar)	1.552	—
Zaire (New Zaire)	1,445.	1,600.
Zambia (Kwacha)	695.	—
Zimbabwe (Dollar)	8.30	—

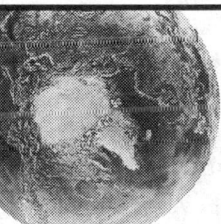

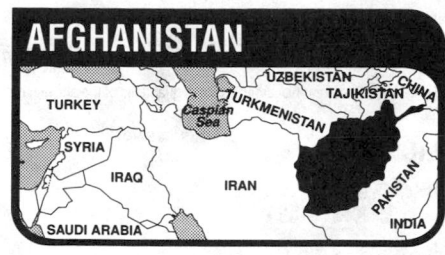

The Islamic Republic of Afghanistan, which occupies a mountainous region of Southwest Asia, has an area of 250,000 sq. mi. (647,497 sq. km.) and a population of 16.6 million. Presently about a fourth of the total population reside mostly in Pakistan in exile as refugees. Capital: Kabul. It is bordered by Iran, Pakistan, the USSR, and China's Sinkiang Province. Agriculture and herding are the principal industries; textile mills and cement factories are recent additions to the industrial sector. Cotton, wool, fruits, nuts, sheepskin coats and hand-woven carpets are exported but foreign trade has been interrupted since 1979.

Because of its strategic position astride the ancient land route to India, Afghanistan - formerly known as Aryana and Khorasan - was conquered by Darius I, Alexander the Great, various Scythian tribes, the Arabs, the Turks, Genghis Khan, Tamerlane, the Mughals, the Persians, and in more recent times by Great Britain.

It was a powerful empire under the Kushans, Hephthalites, Ghaznavids and Ghorids. The name Afghanistan, "Land of the Afghans," came into use in the eighteenth and nineteenth to describe the realm of the Afghan kings. Previously this mountainous region was the eastern most frontier of the Iranian world, with strong cultural influences from the Turks and Mongols to the north and India to the south.

The first Afghan king, Ahmad Shah Abdali, founder of the Durrani dynasty, established his rule at Qandahar in 1747. He conquered large territories in India and eastern Iran, which were lost by his grandson Zaman Shah. A new family, the Barakzays, drove the Durrani king out of Kabul, the capital, in 1819, but the Durranis were not eliminated completely until 1858. Further conflicts among the Barakzays prevented full unity until the reign of 'Abd al-Rahman in 1880. In 1929 the last Barakzay was Saqao, "Son of the Water-Carrier," who ruled as Habib Allah for less than a year before he was defeated by Muhammad Nadir Shah, a relative of the Barakzays. The last king, Muhammad Zahir, became a constitutional, though still autocratic, monarch in 1964. In 1973 a coup d'etat displaced him and created the Republic of Afghanistan. A subsequent military coup established the pro-Soviet Democratic Republic of Afghanistan in 1978. Mounting resistance in the countryside and violence within the government led to the Soviet invasion of late 1979 and the

RULERS
Muhammad Zahir Shah, SH1312-1352/1933-1973AD

MONETARY SYSTEM
1 Afghani = 100 Pul
1 Amani = 20 Afghani 1925-

REPLACEMENT NOTES:
#47-65: Very high series numbers.

KINGDOM

Bank of Afghanistan

1961 ISSUE
#37-42 Kg. Muhammad Zahir at l. and as wmk. Printer: TDLR. All notes 156 x 66mm.

Cat. #	Denomination	Date, description	VG	VF	Unc
37	10 AFGHANIS	SH1340 (1961). Brown on m/c unpt.	.50	1.00	5.00

| 38 | 20 AFGHANIS | SH1340 (1961). Blue on m/c unpt. | .50 | 1.00 | 6.00 |

Cat. #	Denomination	Date, description	VG	VF	Unc
39	50 AFGHANIS	SH1340 (1961). Green on m/c unpt.	1.00	3.00	11.00
40	100 AFGHANIS	SH1340 (1961). Red on m/c unpt.	5.00	10.00	22.50

41	500 AFGHANIS	SH1340 (1961); SH1342 (1963). Olive-brown on m/c unpt.			
		a. Prefix serial #.	25.00	45.00	85.00
		b. 8 digit serial #.	25.00	45.00	85.00
41A	500 AFGHANIS	SH1340 (1961). Orange on m/c unpt.	30.00	75.00	150.00

42	1000 AFGHANIS	SH1340 (1961); SH1342 (1963). Blue-gray on m/c unpt.			
		a. Prefix serial #.	45.00	85.00	225.00
		b. 8 digit serial #.	40.00	80.00	190.00

1967 ISSUE
#43-46 Kg. Muhammad Zahir at l. and as wmk. W/o imprint.

| 43 | 50 AFGHANIS | SH1346 (1967). Green on m/c unpt. | 1.25 | 2.50 | 7.50 |

44	100 AFGHANIS	SH1346 (1967). Lilac on m/c unpt.	2.00	4.00	12.00
45	500 AFGHANIS	SH1346 (1967). Blue on m/c unpt.	10.00	25.00	75.00
46	1000 AFGHANIS	SH1346 (1967). Brown on m/c unpt.	30.00	75.00	250.00

REPUBLIC

SH1352-1358/1973-1979 AD

1973–78 ISSUE

#47-53 Pres. Muhammad Daud at l. and as wmk.

Cat. #	Denomination	Date, description	VG	VF	Unc
47	10 AFGHANIS	SH1352 (1973); SH1354 (1975); SH1356 (1978). Green on m/c unpt.	.25	1.00	3.00

48	20 AFGHANIS	SH1352 (1973); SH1354 (1975); SH1356 (1978). Violet on m/c unpt.	.25	1.00	3.00

49	50 AFGHANIS	SH1352 (1973); SH1354 (1975); SH1356 (1977). Green on m/c unpt.	.25	1.00	3.00

50	100 AFGHANIS	SH1352 (1973); SH1354 (1975); SH1356 (1977). Brown-lilac on m/c unpt.	2.00	7.00	20.00

51	500 AFGHANIS	SH1352 (1973); SH1354 (1975). Blue and m/c.	1.00	4.00	12.50
52	500 AFGHANIS	SH1356 (1978). Brown on m/c unpt. Like #51.	4.00	15.00	50.00

53	1000 AFGHANIS	SH1352 (1973); SH1354 (1975); SH1356 (1977). Brown on m/c unpt.	2.00	8.00	25.00

NOTE: It is possible that all notes #47–53 dated SH1354 are replacements. Small quantities of the above have filtered into the market via Pakistan recently.

DEMOCRATIC REPUBLIC

SH1357-1370/1978-1992 AD

Da Afghanistan Bank

1978–79 ISSUE

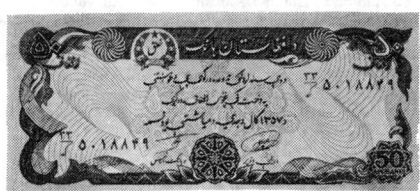

54	50 AFGHANIS	SH1357 (1978). Blue-green on m/c unpt. Arms w/star at top, and Arabic legend. Bldg. on back.	.30	1.50	8.50

#55-63 arms w/horseman and *DA AFGHANISTAN BANK* on face. Sign. varieties.

55	10 AFGHANIS	SH1358 (1979). Green and blue on m/c unpt. Mountain road scene on back.	.15	.25	.75

56	20 AFGHANIS	SH1358 (1979). Purple on m/c unpt. Bldg. and mountains on back. Sign. varieties.	.20	.40	1.25

Cat. #	Denomination	Date, description	VG	VF	Unc
57	50 AFGHANIS	SH1358– (1979). Greenish black with black text on m/c unpt. Similar to #54.			
		a. SH1358 (1979). 2 sign. varieties.	.10	.30	1.00
		b. SH1370 (1991).	.15	.20	2.00

Cat. #	Denomination	Date, description	VG	VF	Unc
62	5000 AFGHANIS	SH1372 (1993). Violet, dk. brown and black on m/c unpt. Mosque w/minaret at r. Mosque at ctr. on back. Wmk: Arms.	FV	FV	6.50

Cat. #	Denomination	Date, description	VG	VF	Unc
58	100 AFGHANIS	SH1358– (1979–). Deep red-violet on m/c unpt. Farmer worker in wheat field at r. Dam in mountains at ctr. on back.			
		a. SH1358 (1979). 2 sign. varieties.	.15	.40	1.25
		b. SH1369 (1990).	.35	1.00	3.50
		c. SH1370 (1991).	.35	1.00	3.50

Cat. #	Denomination	Date, description	VG	VF	Unc
59	500 AFGHANIS	SH1358 (1979). Violet and dk. blue on m/c unpt. Horsemen competing in Buzkashi at r. Fortress at Kabul on back.	.75	1.50	4.00
60	500 AFGHANIS	SH1358– (1979–). Like #59 but reddish brown, deep green and deep brown on m/c unpt. Back deep green on m/c unpt			
		a. SH1358 (1979).	FV	1.25	3.00
		b. SH1369 (1990).	.65	1.75	5.00
		c. SH1370 (1991).	.25	1.00	3.00

Cat. #	Denomination	Date, description	VG	VF	Unc
63	10,000 AFGHANIS	SH1372 (1993). Dk. blue, deep olive-green and black on m/c unpt. Gateway between minarets at r. Arched gateway at ctr. on back. Wmk: Arms.	FV	FV	12.50

Cat. #	Denomination	Date, description	VG	VF	Unc
61	1000 AFGHANIS	SH1358– (1979–). Dk. brown and deep red-violet on m/c unpt. Mosque at r. Shrine w/archways at l. ctr. on back.			
		a. SH1358 (1979).	1.25	4.00	10.00
		b. SH1370 (1991).	.25	1.00	3.00

ALBANIA

The Republic of Albania, a Balkan republic bounded by the rump Yugoslav state of Montenegro and Serbia, Macedonia, Greece and the Adriatic Sea, has an area of 11,100 sq. mi. (28,748 sq. km.) and a population of 3.3 million. Capital: Tirana. The country is predominantly agricultural, although recent progress has been made in the manufacturing and mining sectors. Petroleum, chrome, iron, copper, cotton textiles, tobacco and wood products are exported.

Since it had been part of the Greek and Roman Empires, little is known of the early history of Albania. After the disintegration of the Roman Empire, Albania was overrun by Goths, Byzantines, Venetians and Turks. Skanderbeg, the national hero, resisted the Turks and established an independent Albania in 1443, but in 1468 the country again fell to the Turks and remained part of the Ottoman Empire for more than 400 years.

Independence was re-established by revolt in 1912, and the present borders established in 1913 by a conference of European powers which, in 1914, placed Prince William of Wied on the throne; popular discontent forced his abdication within months. In 1920, following World War I occupancy by several nations, a republic was set up. Ahmet Zogu seized the presidency in 1925, and in 1928 proclaimed himself king with the title of Zog I. King Zog fled when Italy occupied Albania in 1939 and enthroned King Victor Emanuel of Italy. Upon the surrender of Italy to the Allies in 1943, German troops occupied the country. They withdrew in 1944, and communist partisans seized power, naming Gen. Enver Hoxha provisional president. In 1946, following a victory by the communist front in the 1945 elections, a new constitution modeled on that of the USSR was adopted. In accordance with the constitution of Dec. 28, 1976, the official name of Albania was changed from the People's Republic of Albania to the People's Socialist Republic of Albania. A general strike by trade unions in 1991 forced the communist government to resign. A new government was elected in Mar. 1992.

MONETARY SYSTEM
1 Lek = 100 Quintar 1948-

REPLACEMENT NOTES

#33-46: XA; YA; ZA prefix depending on denomination (1976-dated issue).

PEOPLE'S REPUBLIC
Banka E Shtetit Shqiptar

1964 ISSUE

#33-39 wmk: Curved *BSHSH* repeated.

Cat. #	Denomination	Date, description	VG	VF	Unc
33	1 LEK	1964. Green and deep blue on m/c unpt. Peasant couple at ctr.			
		a. Issued note.	.15	.50	1.50
		s. Specimen ovpt: *MODEL*.	—	—	3.00

34	3 LEKE	1964. Brown and lilac on m/c unpt. Woman w/basket of grapes at l.			
		a. Issued note.	.20	.65	2.25
		s. Specimen ovpt: *MODEL*.	—	—	4.00

35	5 LEKE	1964. Lilac and blue on m/c unpt. Truck and steam train. Ship at l. on back.			
		a. Issued note.	.25	.90	3.00
		s. Specimen ovpt: *MODEL*.	—	—	5.00

Cat. #	Denomination	Date, description	VG	VF	Unc
36	10 LEKE	1964. Dk. green on m/c unpt. Woman working w/cotton spinning frame.			
		a. Issued note.	.35	1.20	4.00
		s. Specimen ovpt: *MODEL*.	—	—	6.00

37	25 LEKE	1964. Blue-black on m/c unpt. Peasant woman w/sheaf at l., combine and truck at ctr.			
		a. Issued note.	.60	2.00	7.00
		s. Specimen ovpt: *MODEL*.	—	—	7.50

38	50 LEKE	1964. Red-brown. Marching soldiers at l., Skanderbeg at r.			
		a. Issued note.	1.00	3.50	12.00
		s. Specimen ovpt: *MODEL*.	—	—	8.50

Cat. #	Denomination	Date, description	VG	VF	Unc
39	100 LEKE	1964. Brown-lilac. Worker and boy at the coffer dam.			
		a. Issued note.	2.25	7.50	25.00
		s. Specimen ovpt: *MODEL*.	—	—	10.00

PEOPLE'S SOCIALIST REPUBLIC
Banka E Shtetit Shqiptar

1976 ISSUE

#40–46 wmk: Bank name around radiant star, repeated.

40	1 LEK	1976. Green and deep blue on m/c unpt. Like #33.			
		a. Issued note.	.10	.25	.75
		s1. Red ovpt: *SPECIMEN* w/all zeros serial #.	—	—	3.50
		s2. Red ovpt: *SPECIMEN* w/normal serial #.	—	—	.50
		s3. Lg. blue ovpt: *SPECIMEN* on face. Black ovpt: *E PRANUESHME* on back.	—	—	—
		s4. Lg. blue ovpt: *SPECIMEN* on face. Black bank 25th anniversary rectangular ovpt. on back.	—	—	—

41	3 LEKE	1976. Brown and lilac on m/c unpt. Like #34.			
		a. Issued note.	.10	.30	1.00
		s1. Red ovpt: *SPECIMEN* w/all zeros serial #.	—	—	4.00
		s2. Red ovpt: *SPECIMEN* w/normal serial #.	—	—	.75

42	5 LEKE	1976. Lilac and blue on m/c unpt. Like #35.			
		a. Issued note.	.10	.35	1.50
		s1. Red ovpt: *SPECIMEN* w/all zeros serial #.	—	—	4.50
		s2. Red ovpt: *SPECIMEN* w/normal serial #.	—	—	1.00
		s3. Lg. blue ovpt: *SPECIMEN* on face. Black ovpt: *E PRANUESHME* on back.	—	—	—
		s4. Lg. blue ovpt: *SPECIMEN* on face. Black bank 25th anniverary retangular ovpt. on back.	—	—	—

Cat. #	Denomination	Date, description	VG	VF	Unc
43	10 LEKE	1976. Dk. green on m/c unpt. Like #36.			
		a. Issued note.	.10	.40	2.00
		s1. Red ovpt: SPECIMEN w/all zeros serial #.	—	—	5.50
		s2. Red ovpt: SPECIMEN w/normal serial #.	—	—	1.25

44	25 LEKE	1976. Blue-black on m/c unpt. Like #37.			
		a. Issued note.	.15	.50	3.50
		s1. Red ovpt: *SPECIMEN* w/all zeros serial #.	—	—	6.50
		s2. Red ovpt: *SPECIMEN* w/normal serial #.	—	—	1.75

45	50 LEKE	1976. Red-brown on m/c unpt. Like #38.			
		a. Issued note.	.25	.75	8.50
		s1. Red ovpt: *SPECIMEN* w/all zeros serial #.	—	—	7.50
		s2. Red ovpt: *SPECIMEN* w/normal serial #.	—	—	2.50
		s3. Lg. blue ovpt: *SPECIMEN* on face. Black ovpt: *E PRANUESNHME* on back.	—	—	—
		s4. Lg. blue ovpt: *SPECIMEN* on face. Black bank 25th anniverary rectangular ovpt. on back.	—	—	—

46	100 LEKE	1976. Brown-lilac on m/c unpt.			
		a. Issued note.	.30	1.50	15.00
		s1. Red ovpt: *SPECIMEN* w/all zeros serial #.	—	—	8.50
		s2. Red ovpt: *SPECIMEN* w/normal serial #.	—	—	3.00

1991 ISSUE

#47-48 wmk: Bank name around radiant star, repeated.

Cat. #	Denomination	Date, description	VG	VF	Unc
47	**100 LEKE**	1991. Deep brown and deep purple on pale orange and m/c unpt. Steel workers at l., steel mill at r. Refinery at l. ctr., arms at upper r. on back.			
		a. Issued note.	FV	FV	5.00
		s. Specimen.	—	—	4.00

| 48 | **500 LEKE** | 1991. Purple, red and blue-green on lt. blue and lt. orange unpt. Peasant woman by sunflowers at l. ctr. Evergreen trees, mountains at l. ctr., arms at upper r. on back. | FV | 5.00 | 12.00 |

Lek Valute System

1 Lek Valute = 50 Lek

1992 ISSUE

#49-50 Steelworker at ctr., electrical transmission towers at l., arms at upper ctr., hydro-electric generator at r. on back. Wmk: *B.SH.SH.* **below star, repeated.**

| 49 | **10 LEK VALUTE** | ND (1992). Deep green and purple on m/c unpt. | 2.00 | 5.00 | 12.00 |

NOTE: Many examples of #49 have mismatched serial #s.

Cat. #	Denomination	Date, description	VG	VF	Unc
50	**50 LEK VALUTE**	ND (1992). Deep brown-violet and gray-green on m/c unpt. Like #49.			
		a. W/serial #.	5.00	15.00	40.00
		b. W/o serial #.	2.00	5.00	12.00
51	**Held in reserve.**				

REPUBLIC
Banka E Shqiperise

Lek System

1992 ISSUE

#52-54 wmk: Repeated ring of letters *B.SH.SH.*

| 52 | **200 LEKE** | 1992. Deep reddish-brown on brown and m/c unpt. I. Qemali at l. Citizens portrayed in double-headed eagle outline on back. | FV | FV | 4.00 |

| 53 | **500 LEKE** | 1992. Deep blue on blue and m/c unpt. N. Frasheri at l. Rural mountains at l., candle at ctr. on back. | FV | FV | 10.00 |

Cat. #	Denomination	Date, description	VG	VF	Unc
54	1000 LEKE	1992. Deep green and green on m/c unpt. Skanderbeg at l. Hillside fortress tower at l., crowned arms at ctr. on back.	FV	FV	18.00

1993–94 ISSUE

55	100 LEKE	1993–94. Purple on m/c unpt. L. Kombetar at l. Mountain peaks at l. ctr., falcon at ctr. on back.			
		a. 1993.	FV	FV	3.25
		b. 1994.	FV	FV	2.75
		s. Specimen.	—	—	2.50

#56-58 like #52-54 but w/vertical latent image at l. ctr.

56	200 LEKE	1994.			
		a. Issued note.	FV	FV	3.00
		s. Specimen.	—	—	4.00

Cat. #	Denomination	Date, description	VG	VF	Unc
57	500 LEKE	1994.			
		a. Issued note.	FV	FV	7.50
		s. Specimen.	—	—	7.00

58	1000 LEKE	1994.			
		a. Issued note.	FV	FV	15.00
		s. Specimen.	—	—	13.00

FOREIGN EXCHANGE CERTIFICATES
Banka E Shtetit Shqiptar

1965 ISSUE

#FX21-FX27 arms at r. Bank arms at ctr. on back.

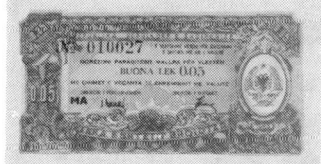

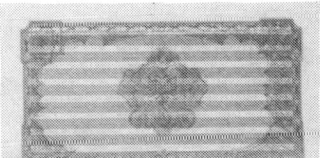

FX21	.05 LEK	1965. Deep blue-green on pink and pale yellow-orange unpt.	—	—	50.00
FX22	.10 LEK	1965. Deep olive-brown on pink and pale blue unpt.	—	—	50.00
FX23	1/2 LEK	1965. Deep purple on pink and lilac unpt.	—	—	50.00
FX24	1 LEK	1965. Blackish-green on pale yellow and pale yellow-orange unpt.	—	—	50.00
FX25	5 LEK	1965. Blue-black on pale yellow-green. unpt.	—	—	140.00
FX26	10 LEK	1965. Blue-green on pale yellow and pale grayish-green unpt.	—	—	140.00
FX27	50 LEK	1965. Deep red-brown on pink and pale yellow unpt.	—	—	140.00

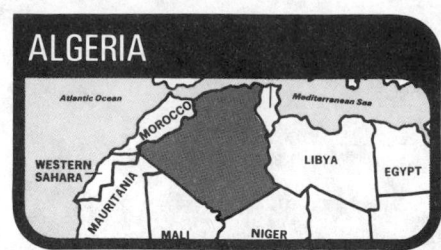

ALGERIA

The Democratic and Popular Republic of Algeria, a North African country fronting on the Mediterranean Sea between Tunisia and Morocco, has an area of 919,595 sq. mi. (2,381,741 sq. km.) and a population of 25.3 million. Capital: Algiers. Most of the country's working population is engaged in agriculture although a recent industrial diversification, financed by oil revenues, is making steady progress. Wines, fruits, iron and zinc ores, phosphates, tobacco products, liquified natural gas, and petroleum are exported.

Algiers, the capital and chief seaport of Algeria, was the site of Phoenician and Roman settlements before the present Moslem city was founded about 950. Nominally part of the sultanate of Tlemcen, Algiers had a large measure of independence under amirs of its own. In 1492 the Jews and Moors who had been expelled from Spain settled in Algiers and enjoyed an increasing influence until the imposition of Turkish control in 1518. For the following three centuries Algiers was the headquarters of the notorious Barbary pirates. The French took Algiers in 1830, and after a long and wearisome war completed the conquest of Algeria and annexed it to France, 1848. The inability to obtain equal rights with Frenchmen led to an organized revolt which began on Nov. 1, 1954 and lasted until a ceasefire was signed on July 1, 1962. Independence was proclaimed on July 5, 1962, following a self-determination referendum.

RULERS
French to 1962

MONETARY SYSTEM
1 Franc = 100 Centimes to 1960
1 Nouveau Franc = 100 Centimes, 1960–64
1 Dinar = 100 Centimes, 1964-

Banque de l'Algérie

1960 ISSUE

Nouveau (new) Franc System
1 "New" Franc = 100 "Old" Francs, 1960–64

Cat. #	Denomination	Date, description	VG	VF	Unc
47	5 NOUVEAUX FRANCS	31.7.1959; 18.12.1959. Green and m/c. Ram at bottom ctr., Bacchus at r.	10.00	60.00	150.00

			VG	VF	Unc
48	10 NOUVEAUX FRANCS	31.7.1959–2.6.1961. Isis at l.	15.00	85.00	210.00

			VG	VF	Unc
49	50 NOUVEAUX FRANCS	31.7.1959; 18.12.1959. Pythian Apollo at r.	35.00	125.00	325.00

Cat. #	Denomination	Date, description	VG	VF	Unc
50	100 NOUVEAUX FRANCS	1959–61. Seagulls w/city of Algiers in background.			
		a. 31.7.1959; 18.12.1959.	22.50	75.00	225.00
		b. 3.6.1960; 25.11.1960; 10.2.1961; 29.9.1961.	22.50	75.00	225.00

Banque Centrale d'Algérie
Dinar System
1964 ISSUE
#51-54 wmk: Emir Abd el-Kader.

			VG	VF	Unc
51	5 DINARS	1.1.1964. Violet and lilac. Vultures perched on rocks at l. ctr. Native objects on back. 2 styles of numerals in date and serial #.	3.00	20.00	65.00

			VG	VF	Unc
52	10 DINARS	1.1.1964. Lilac and m/c. Pair of storks and minaret. Native craft on back.	4.00	30.00	80.00
53	50 DINARS	1.1.1964. Lt. brown and m/c. 2 mountain sheep. Camel caravan on back.	12.50	35.00	90.00

Cat. #	Denomination	Date, description	VG	VF	Unc
54	100 DINARS	1.1.1964. M/c. Harbor scene. Modern bldg. complex at l. ctr. on back.	7.50	15.00	40.00

1970 ISSUE

#55–58 wmk: Emir Abd el-Kader.

Cat. #	Denomination	Date, description	VG	VF	Unc
55	5 DINARS	1.11.1970. Blue and m/c. Warrior w/shield and sword at ctr. r. Fox head on back. Sign. varieties.	.75	2.00	7.50

Cat. #	Denomination	Date, description	VG	VF	Unc
58	500 DINARS	1.11.1970. Purple. View of city. Ships on back.	6.00	20.00	75.00

1977; 1981 ISSUE

#59–60 wmk: Emir Abd el-Kader.

| 56 | 10 DINARS | 1.11.1970. Red-brown. Sheep at l., peacock at r. Man and ornate bldg. on back. Minor plate varieties in legend. | 2.00 | 6.00 | 15.00 |

| 59 | 50 DINARS | 1.11.1977. Dk. green on m/c unpt. Shepherd w/flock at lower l. ctr. Tractor on back. Sign. varieties. | 1.50 | 3.50 | 12.50 |

| 60 | 100 DINARS | 1.11.1981. Dk. blue and blue on lt. blue unpt. Village w/minarets at l. Man working w/plants at ctr. on back. | 3.00 | 8.00 | 15.00 |

1982–83 ISSUE

#60-65 wmk: Emir Abd el-Kader.

57	100 DINARS	1.11.1970. 2 men at l., wheat ears at r. Scenery w/antelope at r. on back.			
		a. Deep brown, brown-orange, blue-gray and pale yellow-orange.	4.00	12.00	27.50
		b. Brown, brown-orange, blue-gray and yellow-orange.	4.00	12.00	27.50

Cat. #	Denomination	Date, description	VG	VF	Unc
61	10 DINARS	2.12.1983. Black on brown and blue-green unpt. Diesel passenger train at ctr. Back blue, blue-green and brown; mountain village at ctr.	FV	1.00	3.00

| 62 | 20 DINARS | 2.1.1983. Red-brown on ochre unpt. Vase at l. ctr., handcrafts at r. Tower at ctr. on back. | FV | FV | 3.50 |
| 63 | Held in reserve. | | | | |

| 64 | 100 DINARS | 8.6.1982. Pale blue and gray. Similar to #60 but w/o bird at upper r. | FV | 10.00 | 25.00 |

| 65 | 200 DINARS | 23.3.1983. Brown, dk. green on m/c unpt. Monument at l. Canyon at ctr., amphora at r. on back. | FV | FV | 11.50 |

Banque de l'Algérie

1995 ISSUE

| 66 | 500 DINARS | | FV | FV | 20.00 |
| 67 | 1000 DINARS | 21.5.1992 (1995). Rose-orange. Animals at lower ctr., bull's head at r. | FV | FV | 35.00 |

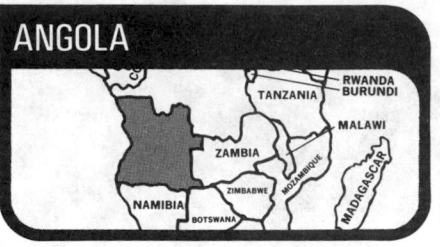

ANGOLA

The Peoples Republic of Angola, a country on the west coast of southern Africa bounded by Zaire, Zambia and Namibia (South-West Africa), has an area of 481,354 sq. mi. (1,246,700 sq. km.) and a population of 10.4 million, predominantly Bantu in origin. Capital: Luanda. Most of the people are engaged in subsistence agriculture. However, important oil and mineral deposits make Angola potentially one of the richest countries in Africa. Iron and diamonds are exported.

Angola was discovered by Portuguese navigator Diogo Cao in 1482. Portuguese settlers arrived in 1491, and established Angola as a major slaving center which sent about 3 million slaves to the New World.

A revolt against Portuguese rule, characterized by guerrilla warfare, began in 1961 and continued until 1974, when a new regime in Portugal offered independence. The independence movement was actively supported by three groups, the National Front, based in Zaire, the Soviet-backed Popular Movement, and the moderate National Union. Independence was proclaimed on Nov. 11, 1975.

RULERS

Portuguese to 1975

MONETARY SYSTEM

100 Centavos = 1 Escudo, 1954-77

1 Kwanza = 100 Lwei, 1977-95

1 Kwanza Reajustado = 1,0000 "old" Kwanzas, 1995–

REPLACEMENT NOTES

#118-125: ZA; ZB; ZC etc. prefix letters.

#126-131: AZ; BZ; CZ; DZ; EZ prefix letters.

PORTUGUESE INFLUENCE
Banco de Angola

1962 ISSUE

#92-96 portr. A. Tomas. at l. or r. Printer: TDLR.

Cat. #	Denomination	Date, description	VG	VF	Unc
92	20 ESCUDOS	10.6.1962. Black on m/c unpt. Dock at l. Gazelle running on back.	1.00	3.00	9.00

| 93 | 50 ESCUDOS | 10.6.1962. Lt. blue on m/c unpt. Airport at l. Animals at watering hole on back. | 1.50 | 4.50 | 15.00 |

Cat. #	Denomination	Date, description	VG	VF	Unc
94	100 ESCUDOS	10.6.1962. Lilac on m/c unpt. Salazar bridge at l. Elephants at watering hole on back.	2.00	10.00	45.00
95	500 ESCUDOS	10.6.1962. Red on m/c unpt. Port of Luanda at ctr. 2 rhinoceros on back.	6.00	25.00	150.00
96	1000 ESCUDOS	10.6.1962. Blue on m/c unpt. Dam at ctr. Herd on back.	8.00	35.00	225.00

1970 ISSUE

#97-98 portr. A. Tomas. at l. or r. Printer: TDLR.

97	500 ESCUDOS	10.6.1970. Red on m/c unpt. Like #95.	5.00	15.00	65.00
98	1000 ESCUDOS	10.6.1970. Blue on m/c unpt. Like #96.	7.50	30.00	110.00

1972 ISSUE

#99-103 M. Carmona at ctr. Printer: TDLR.

99	20 ESCUDOS	24.11.1972. Red, brown and m/c. Flowers on back.	.50	1.00	5.00

100	50 ESCUDOS	24.11.1972. Green, brown and m/c. Plants on back.	.35	.65	5.00

Cat. #	Denomination	Date, description	VG	VF	Unc
101	100 ESCUDOS	24.11.1972. Lt. and dk. brown and m/c. Tree and plants on back.	.50	1.00	5.50
102	500 ESCUDOS	24.11.1972. Blue and m/c. Rock hill w/huts on back.	1.50	4.50	12.50
103	1000 ESCUDOS	24.11.1972. Purple and m/c. Waterfalls on back.	2.00	7.00	25.00

1973 ISSUE

#104-108 Luiz de Camoes at r.

104	20 ESCUDOS	10.6.1973. Blue, purple and green. Cotton plant on back.	.50	2.00	7.50

105	50 ESCUDOS	10.6.1973. Blue and brown. Plant on back.	.35	.75	3.50

106	100 ESCUDOS	10.6.1973. Brown and maroon. Back green and maroon; tree at left.	.75	1.50	4.00

107	500 ESCUDOS	10.6.1973. Brown and purple. Rock hill on back.	1.50	3.50	9.50

108	1000 ESCUDOS	10.6.1973. Olive, blue and m/c. Waterfalls on back.	2.00	7.50	17.50

PEOPLES REPUBLIC
Banco Nacional de Angola
Kwanza System
1976 ISSUE

#109-113 Agostinho Neto at r. Arms at lower l. on back.

Cat. #	Denomination	Date, description	VG	VF	Unc
109	20 KWANZAS	11.11.1976. Brown, green and orange. Field soldiers on back.	1.00	2.50	5.00

110	50 KWANZAS	11.11.1976. Purple, brown and black. Field workers on back.	.75	1.50	4.00

111	100 KWANZAS	11.11.1976. Green. Cloth factory workers on back.	1.00	2.00	4.50

112	500 KWANZAS	11.11.1976. Blue. Cargo ships at dockside on back.	2.00	7.00	15.00

113	1000 KWANZAS	11.11.1976. Red. School class on back.	2.00	7.00	17.50

1979 ISSUE

#114-117 w/2 serial #. Sign. titles, date of independence added under Bank name on face. Arms at lower l. on back.

Cat. #	Denomination	Date, description	VG	VF	Unc
114	50 KWANZAS	14.8.1979. Purple, brown and black. Like #110.	.80	1.75	5.00

115	100 KWANZAS	14.8.1979. Green. Like #111.	.80	1.75	5.00
116	500 KWANZAS	14.8.1979. Blue. Like #112.	2.50	15.00	40.00

117	1000 KWANZAS	14.8.1979. Red. Like #113.	3.00	12.00	30.00

1984-87 ISSUE

#118-125 conjoined busts of Jose Eduardo Dos Santos and Antonio Agostinho Neto at r. Arms at lower l. on back. Wmk. (weak): bird. Sign. title varieties: 1984 issue sign. titles: *GOVERNADOR* and *VICE-GOVER-NADOR*; 1987 issue, both titles: *VICE-GOVERNADOR*.

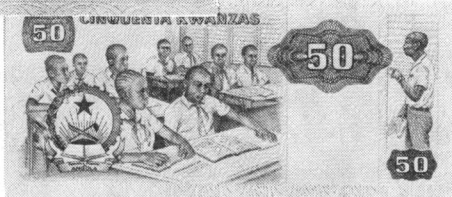

118	50 KWANZAS	7.1.1984. Deep brown and green on lt. green and tan unpt. Classroom and teacher on back.	.25	.75	2.50

NOTE: #118 dated 11.11.1987 may exist (see #122).

Cat. #	Denomination	Date, description	VG	VF	Unc
119	100 KWANZAS	7.1.1984; 11.11.1987. Deep blue, violet and brown on lt. blue and m/c unpt. Picking cotton on back.	1.50	3.50	7.50

NOTE: #119 dated 1987 was only issued w/ovpt. (see #125).

#120 and 121 wmk: Sculpture.

Cat. #	Denomination	Date, description	VG	VF	Unc
120	500 KWANZAS	1984; 1987. Black, red-brown and red on lilac and m/c unpt. Offshore oil platform at l., worker at r. on back.			
		a. Sign. titles: *GOVERNADOR* and *VICE–GOVERNADOR.* 7.1.1984.	3.00	10.00	25.00
		b. Sign. titles: *VICE–GOVERNADOR* and *VICE–GOVERNADOR.* 11.11.1987.	3.00	10.00	25.00

121	1000 KWANZAS	1984; 1987. Purple, blue-black and blue on lt. blue and m/c unpt. Soldiers embarking dockside and soldier on back.			
		a. Sign. titles: *GOVERNADOR* and *VICE–GOVERNADOR.* 7.1.1984.	3.00	8.50	30.00
		b. Sign. titles: *VICE–GOVERNADOR* and *VICE–GOVERNADOR.* 11.11.1987.	3.00	8.50	30.00

1991 PROVISIONAL ISSUE

122	50 NOVO KWANZA on 50 Kwanzas	ND (–old date 11.11.1987). Ovpt: *NOVO KWANZA* on unissued date of #118.		Reported, not confirmed.	

123	500 NOVO KWANZA on 500 Kwanzas	ND (–old date 11.11.1987). Ovpt: *NOVO KWANZA* in lt. green on #120.	7.50	30.00	—

Cat. #	Denomination	Date, description	VG	VF	Unc
124	1000 NOVO KWANZA on 1000 Kwanzas	ND (–old date 11.11.1987). Ovpt: *NOVO KWANZA* in red on #121.	5.00	17.50	50.00

125	5000 NOVO KWANZA on 100 Kwanzas	ND (–old date 11.11.1987). Ovpt: *NOVO KWANZA 5000* in brown on unissued date of #119.	25.00	75.00	—

1991 ISSUE

#126-134 portr. conjoined busts of J. E. Dos Santos and A. A. Neto at r. and as wmk. Arms at lower l. on back. Sign. titles: *GOVERNADOR* and *VICE-GOVERNADOR.*

126	100 KWANZAS	4.2.1991. Purple, green and brown. Rock formation at Pungo Andongo at l. ctr. Tribal mask at r. on back.	.25	1.00	2.50
127	500 KWANZAS	4.2.1991. Blue and violet. Back blue, violet, green and brown. Like #126. Specimen.	—	—	—

Cat. #	Denomination	Date, description	VG	VF	Unc
128	500 KWANZAS	4.2.1991. Purple and deep blue-green on m/c unpt. Serra da Leba at l. ctr; native pot at r. on back. 3 sign. varieties.	.60	2.50	5.00

| 129 | 1000 KWANZAS | 4.2.1991. Brown, orange, purple and red-violet on m/c unpt. Banco Nacional at l. ctr; native doll at r. on back. 2 sign. varieties. | .75 | 3.00 | 7.50 |

| 130 | 5000 KWANZAS | 4.2.1991. Dk. green, blue-green and dk. brown on m/c unpt. Waterfalls and stylized statue of "The Thinker" on back. 3 sign. varieties. | 1.00 | 4.00 | 10.00 |

| 131 | 10,000 KWANZAS | 4.2.1991. Red, olive-green and purple on m/c unpt. Palanca Negra, antelope herd and shell on back. | .50 | 2.00 | 5.00 |

| 132 | 50,000 KWANZAS | 4.2.1991. Bright green, yellow-green and dk. brown on m/c unpt. Like #130. | 1.00 | 4.00 | 10.00 |

| 133 | 100,000 KWANZAS | 4.2.1991 (1993). Orange and aqua on emerald green and m/c unpt. Like # 129 except for value. | 1.25 | 5.00 | 12.00 |

| 134 | 500,000 KWANZAS | 4.2.1991 (1994). Red, brown and violet on m/c unpt. Rhinoceros at l. on back. | .65 | 2.50 | 6.00 |

Currency Reform, 1995

1 Kwanza Reajustado = 1000 "Old" Kwanzas

1995 ISSUE

#135–137 portr. conjoined busts of J.E. Dos Santos and A.A. Neto at r. Arms at lower l., mask at upper r. on back. Wmk: Sculpture.

Cat. #	Denomination	Date, description	VG	VF	Unc
135	1000 KWANZAS REAJUSTADO	1.5.1995. Black and blue on m/c unpt. Palauca Negra Real, antelope at l. on back.	FV	FV	8.00
136	5000 KWANZAS REAJUSTADO	1.5.1995. Green and brown on m/c unpt. Banco Nacional at l. on back.	FV	FV	12.50
137	10,000 KWANZAS REAJUSTADO	1.5.1995. Red and purple on m/c unpt. Off shore oil platform at l. on back.	FV	FV	18.00

ARGENTINA

The Argentine Republic, located in southern South America, has an area of 1,068,301 sq. mi. (2,766,889 sq. km.) and a population of 32.4 million. Capital: Buenos Aires. Its varied topography ranges from the subtropical lowlands of the north to the towering Andean Mountains in the west and the windswept Patagonian steppe in the south. The rolling, fertile pampas of central Argentina are ideal for agriculture and grazing, and support most of the republic's population. Meat packing, flour milling, textiles, sugar refining and dairy products are the principal industries. Oil is found in Patagonia, but most of the mineral requirements must be imported.

Argentina was discovered in 1516 by the Spanish navigator Juan de Solis. A permanent Spanish colony was established at Buenos Aires in 1580, but the colony developed slowly. When Napoleon conquered Spain, the Argentines set up their own government in the name of the Spanish king on May 25, 1810. Independence was formally declared on July 9, 1816.

MONETARY SYSTEM

1 Peso (m/n) = 100 Centavos to 1970
1 New Peso (Ley 18.188) = 100 Old Pesos (m/n), 1970–83
1 Peso Argentino = 10,000 Pesos, (Ley 18.188) 1983–85
1 Austral = 1000 Pesos Argentinos, 1985–92
1 Austral = 100 Centavos, 1985–92
1 Peso = 10,000 Australes, 1992–

REPLACEMENT NOTES

#275-onward: "R" prefix before serial number.

Banco Central

NINTH ISSUE

W/o Ley

#275-277, 279-280 Gen. San Martin in uniform at r. Sign. varieties.

Cat. #	Denomination	Date, description	VG	VF	Unc
275	5 PESOS	ND (1960). Brown on yellow unpt. People gathering before bldg. on back. Printer: CMN.			
		a. Sign. titles: *SUBGERENTE GENERAL* and *VICE-PRESIDENTE*.	.20	.50	3.00
		b. Sign. titles: *GERENTE GENERAL* and *PRESIDENTE*.	.20	.60	2.50
		c. Sign. titles: *SUBGERENTE GENERAL* and *PRESIDENTE*.	.20	.60	3.00

Cat. #	Denomination	Date, description	VG	VF	Unc
276	50 PESOS	ND. Green on m/c unpt.	.20	.50	3.50

Cat. #	Denomination	Date, description	VG	VF	Unc
277	100 PESOS	ND. Brown on m/c unpt. 2 sign. varieties.	.20	.50	3.25

Cat. #	Denomination	Date, description	VG	VF	Unc
278	500 PESOS	ND (1964). Blue on m/c unpt. Older Gen. San Martin not in uniform at r. Grand Bourg House in France on back. 4 sign. varieties.			
		a. Sign. titles: *SUBGERENTE GENERAL* and *PRESIDENTE*.	.75	3.00	10.00
		b. Sign. titles: *GERENTE GENERAL* and *PRESIDENTE*.	.75	2.00	8.50

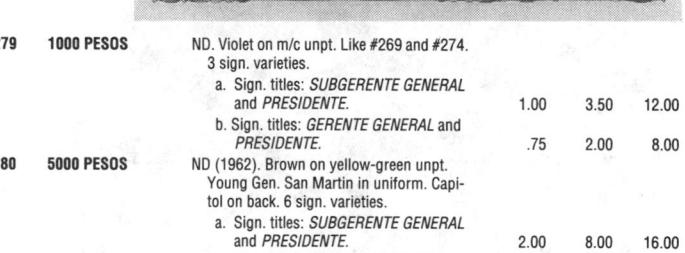

Cat. #	Denomination	Date, description	VG	VF	Unc
279	1000 PESOS	ND. Violet on m/c unpt. Like #269 and #274. 3 sign. varieties.			
		a. Sign. titles: *SUBGERENTE GENERAL* and *PRESIDENTE*.	1.00	3.50	12.00
		b. Sign. titles: *GERENTE GENERAL* and *PRESIDENTE*.	.75	2.00	8.00
280	5000 PESOS	ND (1962). Brown on yellow-green unpt. Young Gen. San Martin in uniform. Capitol on back. 6 sign. varieties.			
		a. Sign. titles: *SUBGERENTE GENERAL* and *PRESIDENTE*.	2.00	8.00	16.00
		b. Sign. titles: *GERENTE GENERAL* and *PRESIDENTE*.	2.00	8.00	16.00

Cat. #	Denomination	Date, description	VG	VF	Unc
281	10,000 PESOS	ND (1961). Red-brown on m/c unpt. Older Gen. San Martin not in uniform at r. Armies in the field on back. 5 sign. varieties.			
		a. Sign. titles: *SUBGERENTE GENERAL* and *PRESIDENTE.*	2.00	5.00	15.00
		b. Sign. titles: *GERENTE GENERAL* and *PRESIDENTE.*	3.00	8.00	22.50

Currency Reform

1 New Peso = 100 Old Pesos

PROVISIONAL ISSUE

Ley 18.188

282	1 PESO on 100 Pesos	ND (1970). New denomination ovpt. on #277.	.20	.50	1.75

283	5 PESOS on 500 Pesos	ND (1970). New denomination ovpt. on #278. 2 sign. varieties.	.25	1.00	4.00
284	10 PESOS on 1000 Pesos	ND (1970). New denomination ovpt. on #279.	.75	2.50	6.50

285	50 PESOS on 5000 Pesos	ND (1970). New denomination ovpt. on #280.	3.00	8.00	17.50

286	100 PESOS on 10,000 Pesos	ND (1970). New denomination ovpt. on #281. 2 sign. varieties.	6.00	12.50	45.00

REGULAR ISSUES

Ley 18.188

#287-289 Gen. Belgrano at r. Printer: CMN. Many sign. varieties. W/o colored threads in paper.

Cat. #	Denomination	Date, description	VG	VF	Unc
287	1 PESO	ND (1970–73). Orange on m/c unpt. Scene of Bariloche-Llao Llao on back. 5 sign. varieties.	.15	.25	1.25

288	5 PESOS	ND (1971–73). Blue on m/c unpt. Monument to the Flag at Rosario on back. 2 sign. varieties.	.15	.25	1.00

289	10 PESOS	ND (1970–73). Violet on m/c unpt. Waterfalls at Iguazu on back. 6 sign. varieties.	.15	.25	1.00

#290-292 Gen. San Martin at r. Colored threads in paper.

290	50 PESOS	ND (1972–73). Black and brown on m/c unpt. Hot springs at Jujuy on back. 3 sign. varieties.	.25	.75	2.00
291	100 PESOS	ND (1971–73). Red on m/c unpt. Coastline at Ushuaia on back. 4 sign. varieties.	.40	1.00	3.00
292	500 PESOS	ND (1972–73). Green on m/c unpt. Army monument at Mendoza on back. 2 sign. varieties.	1.00	3.00	8.00

Decreto - Ley No. 18.188/69

#293-295 Gen. Belgrano at r. Backs like #287–292. Sign. varieties. W/o colored threads in paper.

293	1 PESO	ND (1974). Orange on m/c unpt.	.15	.25	1.00

Cat. # 294	Denomination 5 PESOS	Date, description ND (1974–76). Blue on m/c unpt. 2 sign. varieties.	VG .15	VF .25	Unc .75

Cat. # 299	Denomination 1000 PESOS	Date, description ND (1973–76). Brown on m/c unpt. Plaza de Mayo in Buenos Aires on back. 3 sign. varieties.	VG 1.00	VF 3.00	Unc 10.00

W/o Decreto or Ley

295	10 PESOS	ND (1973–76). Violet on m/c unpt. 4 sign. varieties.	.15	.25	.75

#296-299 Gen. San Martin at r. Sign. varieties. Colored threads in paper.

300	10 PESOS	ND (1976). Violet on m/c unpt. Gen. Belgrano at r.	.10	.15	.50

#301-310 Gen. San Martin at r. Sign. varieties.

296	50 PESOS	ND (1974–76). Black and brown on m/c unpt. 3 sign. varieties.	.15	.25	1.50

301	50 PESOS	ND (1976–78). Black and brown on m/c unpt.			
		a. Colored threads in paper.	.10	.20	.75
		b. No colored threads in paper.	.10	.20	.75

297	100 PESOS	ND (1973–76). Red on m/c unpt. 3 sign. varieties.	.25	.50	1.50
298	500 PESOS	ND (1974–75). Green on m/c unpt. 2 sign. varieties.	1.00	3.00	7.00

302	100 PESOS	ND (1976–78). Red on m/c unpt.			
		a. Colored threads in paper. 2 sign. varieties.	.10	.20	.85
		b. No colored threads in paper. 2 sign. varieties.	.10	.20	.75

Cat. #	Denomination	Date, description	VG	VF	Unc
303	500 PESOS	ND (1977–82). Green on m/c unpt.			
		a. Wmk: Arms. Colored threads in paper.	.10	.20	1.00
		b. Wmk: Arms. No colored threads in paper. 4 sign. varieties.	.05	.10	.50
		c. Wmk: Multiple sunbursts. Colored threads. Back lithographed.	.05	.10	.40

304	1000 PESOS	ND (1976–82). Brown on m/c unpt.			
		a. Wmk: Arms. Colored threads in paper. 2 sign. varieties.	.10	.20	1.50
		b. Wmk: Arms. No colored threads in paper.	.10	.20	1.00
		c. Wmk: Multiple sunbursts. Back engraved.	.05	.10	.50
		d. Wmk: Multiple sunbursts. Back lithographed.	.05	.10	.50

#305-310 w/colored threads.

305	5000 PESOS	ND (1977–83). Blue and green on m/c unpt. Coastline of Mar del Plata on back.			
		a. Wmk: Arms. 2 sign. varieties.	.20	.50	3.50
		b. Wmk: Multiple sunbursts. 2 sign. varieties.	.10	.20	.75

306	10,000 PESOS	ND (1976–83). Orange on m/c unpt. National park on back.			
		a. Wmk: Arms. 3 sign. varieties.	.25	.75	3.00
		b. Wmk: Multiple sunbursts.	.20	.50	1.25

Cat. #	Denomination	Date, description	VG	VF	Unc
307	50,000 PESOS	ND (1979–83). Brown on m/c unpt. Banco Central on back. Wmk: Arms. 2 sign. varieties.	.30	1.00	2.00

308	100,000 PESOS	ND (1979–83). Gray on m/c unpt. Mint bldg. at l. ctr. on back.			
		a. Wmk: Arms.	.50	1.50	6.00
		b. Wmk: Multiple sunbursts. 2 sign. varieties.	.30	1.00	3.00

309	500,000 PESOS	ND (1980–83). Green and brown on m/c unpt. Founding of Buenos Aires on back. Wmk: Multiple sunbursts. 2 sign. varieties.	.30	1.00	4.50

Cat. #	Denomination	Date, description	VG	VF	Unc
310	1,000,000 PESOS	ND (1981). Pink and blue on m/c unpt. Independence Declaration w/*25 de Mayo* on back. Wmk: Multiple sunbursts. 3 sign. varieties.	1.00	3.00	17.50

Currency Reform

1 Peso Argentino = 10,000 Pesos, 1983-85

1983–85 ISSUE

#311-317 have face design w/San Martin at r. #311-315 have back designs like #287-291. #311-319 w/colored threads.

#311-316 wmk: Multiple sunbursts. Printer: CdM.

311	1 PESO ARGENTINO	ND (1983–84). Red-orange and purple on m/c unpt. 2 sign. varieties.	.05	.10	.35

312	5 PESOS ARGENTINOS	ND (1983–84). Brown-violet and black on m/c unpt. 2 sign. varieties.	.05	.15	.40

313	10 PESOS ARGENTINOS	ND (1983–84). Black and red-brown on green and m/c unpt. 2 sign. varieties.	.05	.15	.50
314	50 PESOS ARGENTINOS	ND (1983–85). Brown on m/c unpt. 2 sign. varieties.	.10	.20	.50
315	100 PESOS ARGENTINOS	ND (1983–85). Blue on m/c unpt. 2 sign. varieties.	.15	.40	1.25

316	500 PESOS ARGENTINOS	ND (1984). Violet on m/c unpt. Town meeting of May 22, 1810 on back.	.15	.40	1.75

Cat. #	Denomination	Date, description	VG	VF	Unc
317	1000 PESOS ARGENTINOS	ND. Blue-green and brown on m/c unpt. Military scene at "El Paso de Los Andes" on back.			
		a. Wmk: San Martin (1983). 2 sign. varieties.	.40	1.25	5.00
		b. Wmk: Multiple sunbursts (1984).	.25	.75	1.75
318	5000 PESOS ARGENTINOS	ND (1984–85). Red-brown on m/c unpt. J. B. Alberdi at r. Constitutional meeting of 1853 on back. Wmk: Young San Martin.	.35	1.00	3.00
319	10,000 PESOS ARGENTINOS	ND (1985). Blue-violet on m/c unpt. M. Belgrano at r. Creation of Argentine flag on back. Wmk: Young San Martin.	1.25	3.50	12.50

Currency Reform

1 Austral = 1000 Pesos Argentinos, 1985–92

1985 PROVISIONAL ISSUE

#320-322 ovpt. on Peso Argentino notes.

320	1 AUSTRAL	ND (1985). New denomination ovpt. in numeral and wording in box, green on face and blue on back. Ovpt. on #317b. Series D.	.15	.50	1.50

Cat. #	Denomination	Date, description	VG	VF	Unc
321	5 AUSTRALES	ND (1985). New denomination ovpt. as #320, purple on face and brown on back. Ovpt. on #318. Series B.	.35	1.00	3.00

322	10 AUSTRALES	ND (1985). New denomination ovpt. as #320. Ovpt. on #319.			
		a. Blue ovpt. on face and back. Wmk: San Martin. Series A.	1.50	4.00	8.00
		b. Like a., but wmk: Multiple sunbursts.	Reported, not confirmed.		
		c. Blue ovpt. on face, lt. olive-green ovpt. on back. Series B; C.	.75	1.75	4.00

1985–89 REGULAR ISSUE

#323-330 latent image "BCRA" on face. Liberty (Progreso) w/torch and shield seated at l. ctr. on back. Printer: CdM. Sign. varieties.

323	1 AUSTRAL	ND (1985). Blue-green and purple on m/c unpt. B. Rivadavia at ctr. Wmk: Multiple sunbursts.			
		a. Sign. titles: SUBGERENTE GENERAL and PRESIDENTE. Series A.	.10	.20	.50
		b. Sign. titles: GERENTE GENERAL and PRESIDENTE. Series B; C.	.10	.20	.50

324	5 AUSTRALES	ND (1986). Brown and deep olive-green on m/c unpt. J. J. de Urquiza at ctr. Wmk: Multiple sunbursts.			
		a. Sign. titles: SUBGERENTE GENERAL and PRESIDENTE. Series A.	.10	.25	.75
		b. Sign. titles: GERENTE GENERAL and PRESIDENTE. Series A.	.10	.20	.50

Cat. #	Denomination	Date, description	VG	VF	Unc
325	10 AUSTRALES	ND (1986). Dk. blue and purple on m/c unpt. S. Derqui at ctr. Wmk: Multiple sunbursts.			
		a. Coarse portrait in heavy horizontal wavy lines. Sign. titles: SUBGERENTE GENERAL and PRESIDENTE. Series A.	.10	.40	1.50
		b. Modified portrait in finer horizontal wavy lines. Sign. titles: GERENTE GENERAL and PRESIDENTE. Series A; B; C.	.10	.25	.75

326	50 AUSTRALES	ND (1986). Violet and deep brown on m/c unpt. B. Mitre at ctr. Wmk: Multiple sunbursts.			
		a. Sign. titles: SUBGERENTE GENERAL and PRESIDENTE. Series A.	.10	.50	2.00
		b. Sign titles: of GERENTE GENERAL and PRESIDENTE. Series A.	.10	.25	.75

327	100 AUSTRALES	ND (1985). Dk. red and purple on m/c unpt. D.F. Sarmiento at ctr. Wmk: Multiple sunbursts.			
		a. Sign. titles: SUBGERENTE GENERAL and PRESIDENTE. Series A.	.10	.50	2.00
		b. Sign. titles: GERENTE GENERAL and PRESIDENTE. Engraved back. Series A; B.	.10	.30	1.00
		c. Sign. titles like b., but back pink and lithographed; w/o purple and blue. Series C; D.	.10	.20	.50

Cat. #	Denomination	Date, description	VG	VF	Unc
328	500 AUSTRALES	ND (1988). Pale olive-green on m/c unpt. N. Avellaneda at ctr. Sign. titles: *GERENTE GENERAL* and *PRESIDENTE*.			
		a. Metallic green guilloche by *500*. Back olive-green, black and m/c. Wmk: Liberty. Series A. (1988).	.10	.50	2.00
		b. Dk. olive-green guilloche by *500*. Back pale olive-green and m/c; lithographed (w/o black). Wmk: Multiple sunbursts. Series A. (1990).	.10	.25	.75

Cat. #	Denomination	Date, description	VG	VF	Unc
329	1000 AUSTRALES	ND (1989). Violet-brown and purple on m/c unpt. J.A. Roca at ctr. Sign. titles: *GERENTE GENERAL* and *PRESIDENTE*.			
		a. Vertical green guilloche near *1000*. Wmk: Liberty. Series A.	.15	.75	2.50
		b. Vertical brown-violet guilloche near *1000*. Wmk: Multiple sunbursts. Series B.	.10	.45	1.50
		c. Like b. but sign. titles: *VICE PRESIDENTE* and *PRESIDENTE*. Series C.	.10	.45	1.50

Cat. #	Denomination	Date, description	VG	VF	Unc
330	5000 AUSTRALES	ND (1989). Dk. brown and red-brown on m/c unpt. M. Juarez at ctr.			
		a. Green shield design at upper ctr. r. Sign titles: *SUB-GERENTE GENERAL* and *PRESIDENTE*. Wmk: Liberty. Series A.	.50	2.50	6.50
		b. Green shield design at upper ctr. r. Sign titles: *GERENTE GENERAL* and *PRESIDENTE*. Wmk: Liberty. Series A.	.30	1.50	3.50
		c. Dk. brown shield design at upper ctr. r. Sign. titles: *SUB-GERENTE* and *PRESIDENTE*. Wmk: Liberty. Series B.	.25	1.00	3.00

Cat. #	Denomination	Date, description	VG	VF	Unc
		d. Dk. brown shield design. Sign. titles: *GERENTE* and *PRESIDENTE*. Wmk. Liberty. Series. B.	.25	1.00	3.00
		e. Dk. brown shield design. Sign. titles: *VICEPRESIDENTE* and *PRESIDENTE*. Lithographed back. Wmk: Multiple sunbursts. Series C.	.25	1.00	3.00

1989-91 PROVISIONAL ISSUE

#331-333 use modified face plates from earlier issue. Wmk: Multiple sunbursts. Series M. Printer: CdM.

			VG	VF	Unc
331	10,000 AUSTRALES	ND (1989). Black-blue, deep blue-green and brown on m/c unpt. Face similar to #306. Ovpt. value in olive-green in box at l. Word "PESOS" at ctr. blocked out. Denomination repeated in lines of text and ovpt. value at r. on back. Sign. titles: *GERENTE GENERAL* and *PRESIDENTE*.	2.00	7.50	20.00

			VG	VF	Unc
332	50,000 AUSTRALES	ND (1989). Deep olive-green and blue on m/c unpt. Face similar to #307. Ovpt. value in violet in box at l. Word "PESOS" at ctr. blocked out. Back similar to #331. Value in lt. brown at r. Sign. titles: *SUB-GERENTE GENERAL* and *PRESIDENTE*.	3.00	10.00	30.00
333	500,000 AUSTRALES	ND (1991). Black, purple and red on m/c unpt. Face similar to #309. Ovpt. value in box at l. Word "PESOS" at bottom r. blocked out. Back similar to #331. Value at r. Sign. titles: *VICEPRESIDENTE* and *PRESIDENTE*.	10.00	30.00	75.00

1989-91 REGULAR ISSUES

#334-338 Progreso on back. Wmk: Liberty head. Printer: CdM.

Cat. #	Denomination	Date, description	VG	VF	Unc
334	10,000 AUSTRALES	ND (1989). Black on deep blue, brown and m/c unpt. w/brown diamond design at upper ctr. r. C. Pellegrini at ctr.			
		a. Sign. titles: *GERENTE GENERAL* and *PRESIDENTE*. Series A; B.	.40	1.25	3.50
		b. Sign. titles: *VICEPRESIDENTE* and *PRESIDENTE*. Series C.	.50	1.50	4.50

| 335 | 50,000 AUSTRALES | ND (1989). Black on ochre, olive-green and m/c unpt. w/black flower design at upper ctr. r. L. Saenz Peña at ctr. Sign. titles: *GERENTE GENERAL* and *PRESIDENTE*. Series A; B. | 1.50 | 6.00 | 15.00 |

| 336 | 100,000 AUSTRALES | ND (1990–91). Dk. brown and reddish-brown on pale brown and m/c unpt. Coarsely engraved portr. of J. Evaristo Uriburu at ctr. Black sign. titles of *VICEPRESIDENTE* and *PRESIDENTE*. Series A; B. | 2.00 | 7.50 | 20.00 |

| 337 | 100,000 AUSTRALES | ND (1991). Dk. brown and reddish-brown on brown and m/c unpt. Finely engraved portr. of J. Evaristo Uriburu at ctr. Brown sign. titles. Series B. | 1.50 | 6.00 | 15.00 |

Cat. #	Denomination	Date, description	VG	VF	Unc
338	500,000 AUSTRALES	ND (1990). Black-violet, red and blue on m/c unpt. M. Quintana at ctr. Series A.	3.00	10.00	30.00

Currency Reform

1 Peso = 10,000 Australes, 1992–

1992 ISSUE

#339-341 wmk: Multiple sunbursts. Printer: CdM.

339	1 PESO	ND (1992–). Black and violet-brown on m/c unpt. C. Pelligrini at r. Back gray on m/c unpt; National Congress bldg. at l. ctr.			
		a. Sign. titles: *VICEPRESIDENTE* and *PRESIDENTE* (1992).	FV	FV	3.00
		b. Sign. titles: *PRESIDENTE B. C. R. A.* and *PRESIDENTE H. C. SENADORES* (1993).	FV	FV	2.75

340	2 PESOS	ND (1992–). Deep blue and red-violet on m/c unpt. B. Mitre at r. Back lt. blue on m/c unpt; Mitre Museum at l. ctr.			
		a. Sign. titles: *VICEPRESIDENTE* and *PRESIDENTE* (1992).	FV	FV	4.00
		b. Sign. titles: *PRESIDENTE B. C. R. A.* and *PRESIDENTE H. C. DIPUTADOS* (1993).	FV	FV	4.00

Cat. #	Denomination	Date, description	VG	VF	Unc
341	5 PESOS	ND (1992–). Deep olive-green and red-orange on m/c unpt. General J. de San Martin at r. Back lt. olive-gray on m/c unpt; monument to the Glory of Mendoza at l. ctr.			
		a. Sign. titles: *VICEPRESIDENTE* and *PRESIDENTE* (1992).	FV	FV	10.00
		b. Sign. titles: *PRESIDENTE B. C. R. A.* and *PRESIDENTE H. C. SENADORES* (1993).	FV	FV	9.00

Cat. #	Denomination	Date, description	VG	VF	Unc
344	50 PESOS	ND (1992–). Black and red on m/c unpt. D. Faustino Sarmiento at r. Government office w/monuments, palm trees in foreground at l. ctr. on back.			
		a. Sign. titles: *VICEPRESIDENTE* and *PRESIDENTE* (1992).	FV	FV	75.00
		b. Sign. titles: *PRESIDENTE B. C. R. A.* and *PRESIDENTE H. C. DIPUTADOS* (1993).	FV	FV	75.00

#342-343 wmk: Liberty head. Printer: CdM-Argentina.

342	10 PESOS	ND (1992–). Deep brown and dk. green on m/c unpt. M. Belgrano at r. Monument to the Flag – Rosario w/city in background at l. ctr. on back.			
		a. Sign. titles: *VICEPRESIDENTE* and *PRESIDENTE* (1992).	FV	FV	18.50
		b. Sign. titles: *PRESIDENTE B. C. R. A.* and *PRESIDENTE H. C. DIPUTADOS* (1993).	FV	FV	17.50

345	100 PESOS	ND (1992–). Violet, lilac, green and m/c. J.A. Roca at r. and as wmk. Back violet and m/c; "La Conquista del Desierto" scene.			
		a. Sign. titles: *VICEPRESIDENTE* and *PRESIDENTE* (1992).	FV	FV	140.00
		b. Sign. titles: *PRESIDENTE B. C. R. A.* and *PRESIDENTE H. C. SENADORES* (1993).	FV	FV	140.00

343	20 PESOS	ND (1992–). Carmine and deep blue on m/c unpt. J. Manuel de Rosas at r. Battle of the "Vuelta de Obligado" at l. ctr. on back.			
		a. Sign. titles: *VICEPRESIDENTE* and *PRESIDENTE* (1992).	FV	FV	32.50
		b. Sign. titles: *PRESIDENTE B. C. R. A.* and *PRESIDENTE H. C. SENADORES* (1993).	FV	FV	32.50

#344-345 portr. as wmk.

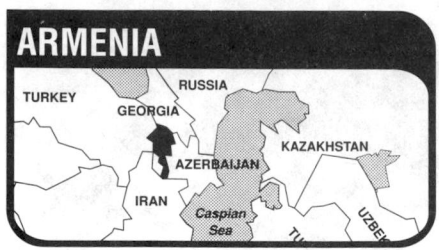

The Republic of Armenia (formerly Armenian S.S.R.) is bounded in the north by Georgia, to the east by Azerbaijan and to the south and west by Turkey and Iran. It has an area of 11,490 sq. mi. (29,800 sq. km) and a population of 3.3 million. Capital: Yerevan. Agriculture including cotton, vineyards and orchards, hydroelectricity, chemicals — primarily synthetic rubber and fertilizers, and vast mineral deposits of copper, zinc and aluminum and production of steel and paper are major industries.

The earliest history of Armenia records continuous struggles with expanding Babylonia and later Assyria. In the sixth century B.C. it was called Armina. Later under the Persian empire it enjoyed the position of a vassal state. Conquered by Macedonia, it later defeated the Seleucids and Greater Armenia was founded under the Artaxis dynasty. Christianity was established in 303 A.D. which led to religious wars with the Persians and Romans who divided it into two zones of influence. The Arabs succeeded the Persian Empire of the Sassanids which later allowed the Armenian princes to conclude a treaty in 653 A.D. In 862 A.D. Ashot V was recognized as the "prince of princes" and established a throne recognized by Baghdad and Constantinople in 886 A.D. The Seljuks overran the whole country and united with Kurdistan which eventually ran the new government. In 1240 A.D. onward the Mongols occupied almost all of western Asia until their downfall in 1375 A.D. when various Kurdish, Armenian and Turkoman independent principalities arose. After the defeat of the Persians in 1516 A.D. the Ottoman Turks gradually took control over a period of some 40 years, with Kurdish tribes settling within Armenian lands. In 1605 A.D. the Persians moved thousands of Armenians as far as India developing prosperous colonies. Persia and the Ottoman Turks were again at war, with the Ottomans once again prevailing. The Ottomans later gave absolute civil authority to a Christian bishop allowing them free enjoyment of their religion and traditions.

Russia occupied Armenia in 1801 until the Russo-Turkish war of 1878. British intervention excluded either side from remaining although the Armenians remained more loyal to the Ottoman Turks, but in 1894 the Ottoman Turks sent in an expeditionary force of Kurds fearing a revolutionary movement. Large massacres were followed by retaliations, then amnesty was proclaimed which led right into WW I and once again occupation by Russian forces in 1916. After the Russian revolution the Georgians, Armenians and Azerbaijanis formed the short lived Transcaucasian Federal Republic on Sept. 20, 1917 which broke up into three independent republics on May 26, 1918. Communism developed and in Sept. 1920 the Turks attacked the Armenian Republic; the Russians soon followed suit from Azerbaijan routing the Turks. On Nov. 29, 1920 Armenia was proclaimed a Soviet Socialist Republic. On March 12, 1922, Armenia, Georgia and Azerbaijan were combined to form the Transcaucasian Soviet Federated Socialist republic, which on Dec. 30, 1922, became a part of U.S.S.R. On Dec. 5, 1936, the Transcaucasian federation was dissolved and Armenia became a constituent republic of the U.S.S.R. A new constitution was adopted in April 1978. Elections took place on May 20, 1990. The Supreme Soviet adopted a declaration of sovereignty in Aug. 1991, voting to unite Armenia with Nagorno-Karabakh. This newly constituted "Republic of Armenia" became fully independent by popular vote in Sept. 1991. It became a member of the CIS in Dec.1991.

Fighting between Christians in Armenia and Muslim forces of Azerbaijan escalated in 1992 and continued through early 1994. Each country claimed the Nagorno-Karabakh, an Armenian ethnic enclave, in Azerbaijan. A temporary cease-fire was announced in May, 1994.

REPUBLIC

National Bank of the Republic of Armenia

1993–94 ISSUE

#33–38 wmk: Decorative design.

Cat. #	Denomination	Date, description	VG	VF	Unc
33	10 DRAM	1993. Dk. brown, lt. blue and pale orange on m/c unpt. Statue of David from Sasoun, and main railway station in Yerevan. Mt. Ararat on back.	FV	FV	.75

34	25 DRAM	1993. Brown, yellow and blue. Frieze w/lion from Erebuni Castle and cuneiform tablet. Ornament on back.	FV	FV	1.50

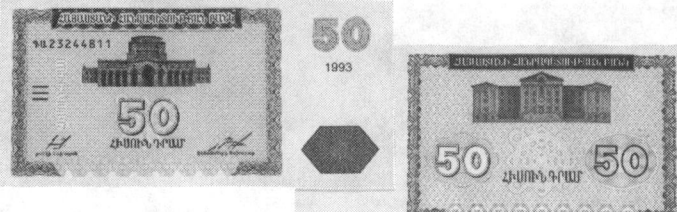

Cat. #	Denomination	Date, description	VG	VF	Unc
35	50 DRAMS	1993. Blue, red and violet. State Museum of History and National Gallery at upper l. ctr. Parliament bldg. at upper ctr. r. on back.	FV	FV	1.75

36	100 DRAM	1993. Violet, red and blue. Mt. Ararat at upper ctr. Zvarnots Temple at l. ctr. Opera and ballet theater in Yerevan on back.	FV	FV	2.50

37	200 DRAM	1993. Brown, green and red. St. Hegine Temple in Echmiadzin at upper ctr. Circular design on back.	FV	FV	4.00

38	500 DRAM	1993. Dk. green and red brown on m/c unpt. Tetradrachm of Kg. Tigran II the Great at l. ctr. and Mt. Ararat at upper ctr. Open book and quill pen on back.	FV	FV	6.00

39	1000 DRAM	1994. Dk. brown and brown on m/c unpt. Ancient statue at l. Ancient ruins on back. Wmk: Arms.	FV	FV	11.00

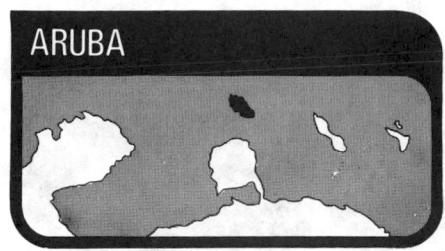

ARUBA

Aruba, formerly a part of the Netherlands Antilles, achieved on Jan. 1, 1986 a special status "status aparte" as the third state under the Dutch crown, together with the Netherlands and the remaining five islands of the Netherlands Antilles. On Dec. 15, 1954 the Netherlands Antilles were given complete domestic autonomy and granted equality within the Kingdom of the Netherlands. The "status aparte" is a step towards total independence of Aruba, scheduled for 1996. Aruba was the second-largest island of the Netherlands Antilles and is situated near the Venezuelan coast. The island has an area of 74 1/2 sq. mi. (193 sq. km.) and a population of 60,000. Capital: Oranjestad, named after the Dutch royal family. Chief industry is tourism. For earlier issues see Curaçao and the Netherlands Antilles. During Jan. 1986 the banknotes of the Netherlands Antilles were redeemed at a ratio of 1 to 1.

MONETARY SYSTEM

1 Florin = 100 Cents

Banco Central Di Aruba

#1-5 flag at l., coastal hotels at ctr. Arms of Aruba at ctr. on back. Printer: JEZ.

Cat. #	Denomination	Date, description	VG	VF	Unc
1	5 FLORIN	1.1.1986. Green.	FV	FV	6.50

2	10 FLORIN	1.1.1986. Green.	FV	FV	12.50

3	25 FLORIN	1.1.1986. Green.	FV	FV	28.50

4	50 FLORIN	1.1.1986. Green.	FV	FV	55.00

Cat. #	Denomination	Date, description	VG	VF	Unc
5	100 FLORIN	1.1.1986. Green.	FV	FV	110.00

Centrale Bank Van Aruba

#6-10 geometric forms with pre-Columbian Aruban art. Wmk: Stylized tree. Printer: JEZ.

6	5 FLORIN	1.1.1990. Purple and m/c. Tortuga Blanco (sea turtle) on back.	FV	FV	6.00

7	10 FLORIN	1.1.1990. Blue and m/c. Snail on back.	FV	FV	10.00

8	25 FLORIN	1.1.1990. Brown and m/c. Cascabel snake on back.	FV	FV	22.50

9	50 FLORIN	1.1.1990. Red-brown and m/c. Owl on back.	FV	FV	42.50

10	100 FLORIN	1.1.1990. Olive-green and m/c. Frog on back.	FV	FV	80.00
11	500 FLORIN	(1995).	FV	FV	325.00

COLLECTOR SERIES

Cat#	Date, denomination	Description	Issue Price	Mkt. Value
CS1	1990 (1995)	#6-10 w/matched serial # in special presenta-	—	200.00
	5-100 FLORIN	tion set.		

AUSTRALIA

The Commonwealth of Australia, the smallest continent and largest island in the world, is located south of Indonesia between the Indian and Pacific oceans. It has an area of 2,967,909 sq. mi. (7,686,849 sq. km.) and a population of 16.8 million. Capital: Canberra. Due to its early and sustained isolation, Australia is the habitat of such curious and unique fauna as the kangaroo, koala bear, platypus, wombat and barking lizard. The continent possesses extensive mineral deposits, the most important of which are gold, coal, silver, nickel, uranium, lead and zinc. Livestock raising, mining and manufacturing are the principal industries. Chief exports are wool, meat, wheat, iron ore, coal and nonferrous metals.

The first whites to see Australia probably were Portuguese and Spanish navigators of the late 16th century. In 1770, Captain James Cook explored the east coast and annexed it for Great Britain. The Colony of New South Wales was founded by Captain Arthur Phillip on Jan. 26, 1788, a date now celebrated as Australia Day. Dates of creation of six colonies that now comprise the states of the Australian Commonwealth are: New South Wales, 1823; Tasmania, 1825; Western Australia, 1838; South Australia, 1842; Victoria, 1851; Queensland, 1859. A constitution providing for federation of the colonies was approved by the British Parliament in 1900; the Commonwealth of Australia came into being in 1901. Australia passed the Statute of Westminster Adoption Act on Oct. 9, 1942, which officially established Australia's complete autonomy in external and internal affairs, thereby formalizing a situation that had existed for years. Australia is a member of the Commonwealth of Nations. The Queen of England is Chief of State.

Australia's currency system was changed from pounds - shillings - pence to a decimal system of dollars and cents on Feb.14, 1966.

RULERS
British

MONETARY SYSTEM
1 Shilling = 12 Pence
1 Pound = 20 Shillings to 1966
1 Dollar = 100 Cents, 1966-

REPLACEMENT NOTES:

#33, 34, 35: star after 5-digit serial number.
#37a, b, c; 38a, b, c; 39a, b; 40a, b, c; 41c: 3-letter prefix starting with Z, and an asterisk after the 5-digit serial number.

Commonwealth of Australia, Reserve Bank

1960–61 ISSUE

Pound System

#33-36 w/title: *GOVERNOR/RESERVE BANK OF AUSTRALIA* below lower l. sign.

Cat. #	Denomination	Date, description	VG	VF	Unc
33	10 SHILLINGS	ND (1961–65). Brown. M. Flinders at r. Parliament in Canberra on back. Sign. H. C. Coombs and R. Wilson.	1.25	3.50	25.00

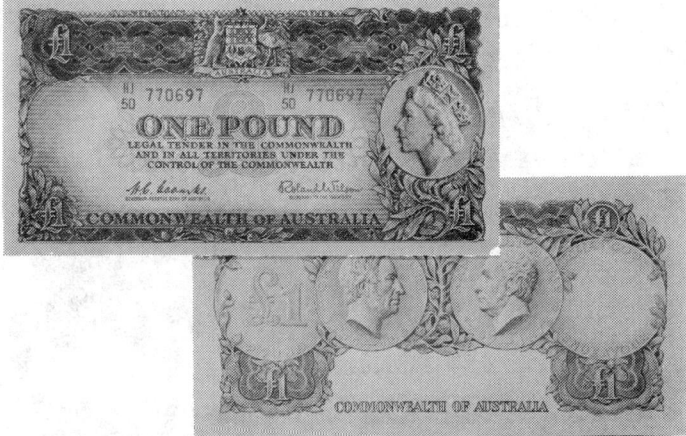

34	1 POUND	ND (1961–65). Green. Qn. Elizabeth II at r. Portr. C. Sturt and H. Hume on back. Sign. H. C. Coombs and R. Wilson.	1.50	5.00	30.00

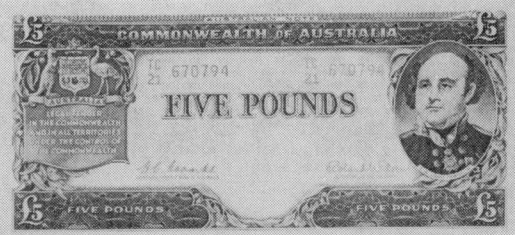

Cat. #	Denomination	Date, description	VG	VF	Unc
35	5 POUNDS	ND (1960–65). Blue. Sir J. Franklin at r. Cattle, sheep and agricultural products on back. Sign. H. C. Coombs and R. Wilson.	10.00	22.50	65.00

36	10 POUNDS	ND (1960–65). Red. Gov. Philip at l. Symbols of science and industry on back. Sign. H. C. Coombs and R. Wilson.	20.00	35.00	150.00

1966–67 ISSUE

Dollar System

#37-41 w/text: *COMMONWEALTH OF* in heading. Wmk: Capt. James Cook.

37	1 DOLLAR	ND (1966–72). Orange and brown. Arms at ctr., Qn. Elizabeth II at r. Stylized Aboriginal figures and animals on back.			
		a. Sign. H. C. Coombs and R. Wilson. (1966).	1.50	4.00	30.00
		b. Sign. H. C. Coombs and R. J. Randall. (1968).	4.00	17.50	180.00
		c. Sign. J. G. Phillips and R. J. Randall. (1969).	FV	3.00	20.00
		d. Sign. J. G. Phillips and F. H. Wheeler. (1972).	FV	2.00	12.50

38	2 DOLLARS	ND (1966–72). Green and yellow. J. MacArthur at r., sheep at ctr. Farrer at l., wheat at ctr. on back.			
		a. Sign. H. C. Coombs and R. Wilson. (1966).	FV	2.50	15.00
		b. Sign. H. C. Coombs and R. J. Randall. (1967).	3.00	8.50	50.00
		c. Sign. J. G. Phillips and R. J. Randall. (1968).	FV	2.50	12.50
		d. Sign. J. G. Phillips and F. H. Wheeler (1972).	FV	2.50	15.00
39	5 DOLLARS	ND (1967–72). Deep purple and m/c. Sir J. Banks at r., plants at ctr. C. Chisholm, ship, bldgs., and women on back.			
		a. Sign. H. C. Coombs and R. J. Randall. (1967).	FV	6.00	37.50
		b. Sign. J. G. Phillips and R. J. Randall. (1969).	FV	5.00	37.50
		c. Sign. J. G. Phillips and F. H. Wheeler. (1972).	FV	4.00	27.50

Cat. #	Denomination	Date, description	VG	VF	Unc
40	10 DOLLARS	ND (1966–72). Blue and orange. F. Greenway at r., village scene at ctr. H. Lawson and bldgs. on back.			
		a. Sign. H. C. Coombs and R. Wilson. (1966).	FV	9.00	25.00
		b. Sign. H. G. Coombs and R. J. Randall. (1967).	FV	20.00	120.00
		c. Sign. J. G. Phillips and R. J. Randall. (1968).	FV	9.00	25.00
		d. Sign. J. G. Phillips and F. H. Wheeler. (1972).	FV	10.00	30.00

			VG	VF	Unc
41	20 DOLLARS	ND (1966–72). Red and yellow. K. Smith at r. Hargrave at l., aeronautical devices on back.			
		a. Sign. H. C. Coombs and R. Wilson. (1966).	FV	17.50	35.00
		b. Sign. H. G. Coombs and R. J. Randall. (1968).	35.00	100.00	600.00
		c. Sign. J. G. Phillips and R. J. Randall. (1968).	FV	16.00	32.50
		d. Sign. J. G. Phillips and F. H. Whee-ler. (1972).	FV	16.00	32.50

Australia, Reserve Bank

1973; 1984 ISSUE

#42-48 w/o text: *COMMONWEALTH OF* in heading.

#42-46 like #37-41, wmk: Capt. James Cook.

			VG	VF	Unc
42	1 DOLLAR	ND (1974–83). Orange and brown.			
		a. Sign. J. G. Phillips and F. H. Wheeler. (1974).	1.00	2.50	12.00
		b. Sign. H. M. Knight and F. H. Wheeler. (1976).	1.00	1.75	8.00
		c. Sign. H. M. Knight and J. Stone. (1979).	1.00	1.50	3.50
		d. Sign. R. A. Johnston and J. Stone. (1983).	1.00	1.50	2.50

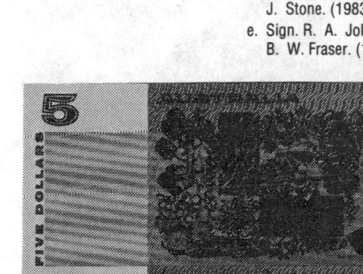

Cat. #	Denomination	Date, description	VG	VF	Unc
43	2 DOLLARS	ND (1974–85). Green and yellow.			
		a. Sign J. G. Phillips and F. H. Wheeler. (1974).	FV	3.00	17.50
		b. Sign. H. M. Knight and F. H. Wheeler. (1976). 2 serial # varieties.	FV	2.00	8.50
		c. Sign. H. M. Knight and J. Stone. (1979).	FV	2.00	5.00
		d. Sign. R. A. Johnston and J. Stone. (1983).	FV	2.00	4.00
		e. Sign. R. A. Johnston and B. W. Fraser. (1985).	FV	2.00	4.00

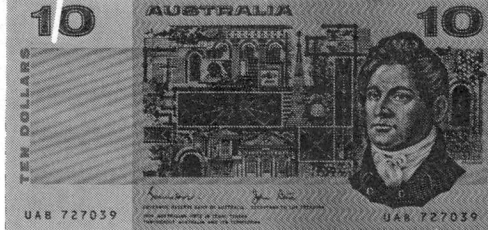

			VG	VF	Unc
44	5 DOLLARS	ND (1974–91). Deep purple and m/c.			
		a. Sign. J. G. Phillips and F. H. Wheeler. (1974).	FV	8.00	45.00
		b. Sign. H. M. Knight and F. H. Wheeler. (1976).	FV	4.50	15.00
		c. Sign. H. M. Knight and J. Stone. (1979). 2 serial # varieties.	FV	FV	9.00
		d. Sign. R. A. Johnston and J. Stone. (1983).	FV	FV	9.00
		e. Sign. R. A. Johnston and B. W. Fraser. (1985). 2 serial # varieties.	FV	FV	7.00
		f. Sign. B. W. Fraser and C. I. Higgins. (1990).	FV	FV	7.00
		g. Sign. B. W. Fraser and A. S. Cole. (1991).	FV	FV	7.00

Cat. #	Denomination	Date, description	VG	VF	Unc
45	10 DOLLARS	ND (1974–91). Blue and orange.			
		a. Sign. J. G. Phillips and F. H. Wheeler. (1974).	FV	14.00	100.00
		b. Sign. H. M. Knight and F. H. Wheeler. (1976).	FV	9.00	20.00
		c. Sign. H. M. Knight and J. Stone. (1979). 2 serial # varieties.	FV	FV	25.00
		d. Sign. R. A. Johnston and J. Stone. (1983).	FV	FV	22.50
		e. Sign. R. A. Johnston and B. W. Fraser. (1985).	FV	FV	13.50
		f. Sign. B. W. Fraser and C. I. Higgins. (1990).	FV	FV	13.50
		g. Sign. B. W. Fraser and A. S. Cole. (1991).	FV	FV	13.50

Cat. #	Denomination	Date, description	VG	VF	Unc
		a. Sign. J. G. Phillips and F. H. Wheeler. (1973).	FV	45.00	90.00
		b. Sign. H. M. Knight and F. H. Wheeler. (1975).	FV	45.00	100.00
		c. Sign. H. M. Knight and J. Stone. (1979).	FV	FV	70.00
		d. Sign. R. A. Johnston and J. Stone. (1983).	FV	FV	70.00
		e. Sign. R. A. Johnston and B. W. Fraser. (1985). 2 serial # varieties.	FV	FV	75.00
		f. Sign. M. J. Phillips and B. W. Fraser. (1989).	FV	FV	65.00
		g. Sign. B. W. Fraser and C. I. Higgins. (1989).	FV	FV	60.00
		h. Sign. B. W. Fraser and A. S. Cole. (1991).	FV	FV	60.00
		i. Sign. B.W. Fraser and A. S. Cole. (1994).	FV	FV	57.00

Cat. #	Denomination	Date, description	VG	VF	Unc
46	20 DOLLARS	ND (1974–). Red and yellow on m/c unpt.			
		a. Sign. J. G. Phillips and F. H. Wheeler. (1974).	FV	30.00	75.00
		b. Sign. H. M. Knight and F. H. Wheeler. (1975).	FV	18.00	40.00
		c. Sign. H. M. Knight and J. Stone. (1979). 2 serial # varieties.	FV	FV	35.00
		d. Sign. R. A. Johnston and J. Stone. (1983).	FV	FV	35.00
		e. Sign. R. A. Johnston and B. W. Fraser. (1985) 2 serial # varieties.	FV	FV	25.00
		f. Sign. M. J. Phillips and B. W. Fraser. (1989).	FV	FV	25.00
		g. Sign. B. W. Fraser and C. I. Higgins. (1989).	FV	FV	25.00
		h. Sign. B. W. Fraser and A. S. Cole. (1991).	FV	FV	25.00
		i. Sign. B.W. Fraser and E. A. Evans. (1994).	FV	FV	23.50

NOTE: See also "Collector Series" following note listings.

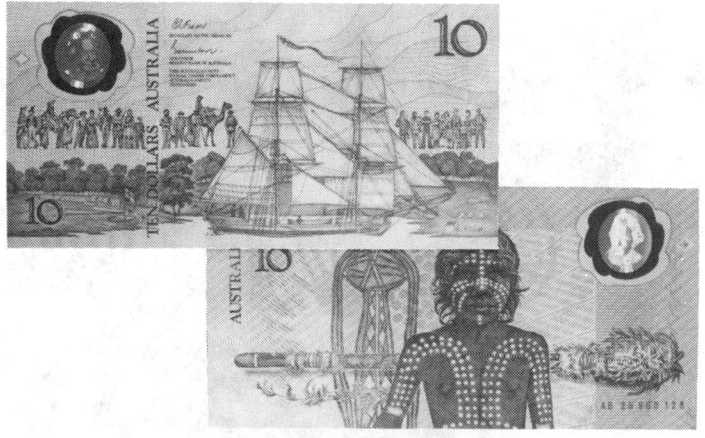

Cat. #	Denomination	Date, description	VG	VF	Unc
48	100 DOLLARS	ND (1984–). Blue and gray on m/c unpt. Sir Douglas Mawson at ctr. J. Tebbutt at I. ctr. on back.			
		a. Sign. R. A. Johnston and J. Stone. (1984).	FV	90.00	120.00
		b. Sign. R. A. Johnston and B. W. Fraser. (1985).	FV	FV	105.00
		c. Sign. B. W. Fraser and C. I. Higgins. (1990).	FV	FV	100.00
		d. Sign. B. W. Fraser and A. S. Cole. (1992).	FV	FV	100.00

NOTE: See also "Collector Series" following note listings.

1988 COMMEMORATIVE ISSUE

#49, Bicentennial of British Settlement–1988

Cat. #	Denomination	Date, description	VG	VF	Unc
47	50 DOLLARS	ND. (1973–). Yellow-brown and green on m/c unpt. Teaching implements at ctr., Sir W. Florey at r., I. Clunies-Ross at I., space research at ctr. on back.			

Cat. #	Denomination	Date, description	VG	VF	Unc
49	10 DOLLARS	1988; ND. Brown and green on m/c unpt. Capt. Cook OVD at upper I., colonists across background; Cook's ship supply at lower r. shoreline. Aboriginal youth, rock painting and ceremonial "Morning Star" pole at ctr. on back. Sign. R. A. Johnston and B. W. Fraser. Plastic.			
		a. 26.1.1988. Serial # prefix AA.	FV	FV	20.00
		b. ND. Serial # prefix AB.	FV	FV	14.00

NOTE: #49a was issued in a souvenir folder for U.S. $11.00, and also in sheets of 4, 12 and 24 subjects.

1992–95 ISSUES

#50-53 and 55 polymer plastic.

Cat. #	Denomination	Date, description	VG	VF	Unc
50	5 DOLLARS	1992; ND. Black, red and lilac on m/c unpt. Branch at l., Qn. Elizabeth II at ctr. r. Back black on lilac and m/c unpt., the old and the new Parliament House in Canberra at ctr. Sign. B. W. Fraser and A. S. Cole.			
		a. 7.7.1992.	FV	FV	10.00
		b. ND.	FV	FV	6.00

NOTE: #50a was issued in a souvenir folder containing a plastic and a paper note (#44g) for US $14.00. This issue marked the 25th anniversary of the $5 banknote.

Cat. #	Denomination	Date, description	VG	VF	Unc
51	10 DOLLARS	1993; ND. Purple on dk. blue and m/c unpt. Man on horseback at l., 'Banjo' Paterson at ctr., windmill OVD in transparent window at lower r. Dame M. Gilmore at ctr. r. on back. Sign. B. W. Fraser and E. A. Evans.			
		a. Red serial # 1993.	FV	FV	15.00
		b. Black serial # ND.	FV	FV	9.00

Cat. #	Denomination	Date, description	VG	VF	Unc
52	20 DOLLARS	1994; ND. Black and red on orange and pale green unpt. Biplane at l., Rev. J. Flynn at ctr. r., camel back at r. Sailing ship at l., M. Reiby at ctr. on back. Compass OVD in transparent window at lower r. Sign. B. W. Fraser.			
		a. Red serial #. 1994.	FV	FV	30.00
		b. Black serial #. ND.	FV	FV	23.50

Cat. #	Denomination	Date, description	VG	VF	Unc
53	50 DOLLARS	ND (1995). Yellow-brown and green on m/c unpt. D. Unaipon at l. ctr., Mission Church at Point McLeay at lower l., patent drawings at upper ctr. r., Southern Cross OVD at lower r. Portr. E. Cowan, foster mother w/children, at ctr., W. Australia's Parliament House at upper l., Cowan at lectern at r.			
		a. 1995.	FV	FV	52.50
		b. ND.	FV	FV	50.00
54	100 DOLLARS				Expected new issue.

55	5 DOLLARS	ND (1995). Like #50 but w/4 orientation bands in upper and lower margins. Red and orange circular unpt. on back. Sign. B. W. Fraser and E. A. Evans.	FV	FV	6.00

COLLECTOR SERIES

Cat#	Date, denomination	Description	Issue Price	Mkt. Value
CS1	1993. 20 DOLLARS	Ovpt. *NAAIC & BF* on #46h. Red serial # M000001-M000500	—	55.00
CS2	1993. 20 DOLLARS	As above, but higher serial #.	—	35.00

NOTE: 3000 notes were prepared for the International Coin and Banknote Fair held in Brisbane. A printing of 5000 is reported for the 80th anniversary of the first banknotes of the Commonwealth of Australia w/red serial # and beginning w/M000001.

Special printings:

#44f was issued in uncut vertical pairs and blocks of 4, 1000 half sheets (20 subjects) and 500 full sheets (40 subjects).

#44g was released in horizontal and vertical pairs at U.S. $24.00 and in blocks of 4 subjects at U.S. $45.00 at 3 different coin fairs in 1992 as the last paper 5 dollar note w/special serial prefix #*XXV-000001* thru *XXV-020000*. Only the note at l. was ovpt.: *25th ANNIVERSARY/1967–1992*.

#45g was issued in uncut form, vertical pairs, plain blocks of 4, and blocks of 4 w/ovpt: *NAAIC & BF* held in Sydney in 1991.

#46f was issued as uncut strips of 10 subjects (5 double rows), to a total of 36 strips.

#47f was issued in uncut blocks of 4, to a total of 72 blocks.

#47h was issued in 100 vertical pairs and 100 blocks of 4 w/gold serial #, also vertical pairs and blocks of 4 w/red serial #.

#47i was issued in uncut pairs and blocks of 4 to a total of 500 pairs and 250 blocks.

#48d includes 150 blocks of 4 and 300 pairs w/red serial # and 500 blocks of 4 and 700 pairs w/black serial #.

#51 includes 900 matched serial # sets of 2 $10 notes, paper and plastic in "prestigiously packaged" portfolio; a set of $10 notes in an "embossed collector folder," issue 9,000 sets; a set of $10 notes in a "presentation/collector" folder, larger quanities available.

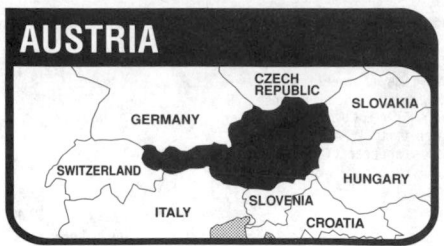

AUSTRIA

The Republic of Austria, a parliamentary democracy located in mountainous central Europe, has an area of 32,374 sq. mi. (83,849 sq. km.) and a population of 7.8 million. Capital: Vienna. Austria is primarily an industrial country. Machinery, iron and steel, textiles, yarns and timber are exported.

The territories later to be known as Austria were overrun in pre-Roman times by various tribes, including the Celts. Upon the fall of the Roman Empire, the country became a margravate of Charlemagne's Empire. Ottokar, King of Bohemia, gained possession in 1252, only to lose the territory to Rudolf of Habsburg in 1276. Thereafter, until World War I, the story of Austria was that of the ruling Habsburgs, German emperors from 1438-1806. From 1815-1867 it was a member of the "Deutsche Bund" (German Union).

During World War I, the Austro-Hungarian Empire was one of the Central Powers with Germany, Bulgaria and Turkey. At the end of the war, the Empire was dissolved and Austria established as an independent republic. In March 1938, Austria was incorporated into Hitler's short-lived German Third Reich. Allied forces of both East and West liberated Austria in April 1945, and subsequently divided it into four zones of military occupation. On May 15, 1955, the four powers formally recognized Austria as a "sovereign," independent democratic state.

MONETARY SYSTEM

1 Schilling = 100 Groschen, 1945–

NOTE: This section has been renumbered from the old 7th Edition of General Issues

---

REPUBLIC
Oesterreichische Nationalbank
Austrian National Bank

1956–65 ISSUE

Cat. #	Denomination	Date, description	VG	VF	Unc
136	20 SCHILLING	2.7.1956. Brown on red-brown and olive unpt. A. von Welsbach at r., arms at l. Church and mountains on back.	1.50	7.00	12.00

Cat. #	Denomination	Date, description	VG	VF	Unc
137 (140)	50 SCHILLING	2.7.1962. Purple on m/c unpt. R. Wettstein at r., arms at bottom ctr. Mauterndorf castle on back.	3.00	10.00	18.00

Cat. #	Denomination	Date, description	VG	VF	Unc
138 (137)	100 SCHILLING	1.7.1960. Dk. green on violet and m/c unpt. Violin and music at lower l., J. Strauss at r., arms at l. Schönbrunn Castle on back.	5.00	14.00	30.00

			VG	VF	Unc
139 (141)	500 SCHILLING	1.7.1965. Red-brown on m/c unpt. J. Ressel at r. Sailing ship at l., arms at lower r. on back.	FV	FV	85.00

			VG	VF	Unc
140 (138)	1000 SCHILLING	2.1.1961. Dk. blue on m/c unpt. V. Kaplan at r. Dam and Persenburg Castle, arms at r. on back. 148 x 75mm.	350.00	800.00	1200.
141 (139)	1000 SCHILLING	2.1.1961. Dk. blue on m/c unpt. Like #138 but w/blue lined unpt. up to margin. 158 x 85mm.	35.00	100.00	200.00

1967–70 ISSUE

			VG	VF	Unc
142	20 SCHILLING	2.7.1967. Brown on olive and lilac unpt. C. Ritter von Ghega at r., arms at lower ctr. Bridge and mountains on back.	FV	FV	4.00

Cat. #	Denomination	Date, description	VG	VF	Unc
143 (145)	50 SCHILLING	2.1.1970. Purple on m/c unpt. F. Raimund at r., arms at l. Theater in Vienna at l. ctr. on back.	FV	6.00	10.00

Cat. #	Denomination	Date, description	VG	VF	Unc
147 (143)	1000 SCHILLING	1.7.1966. Blue-violet on m/c unpt. B. von Suttner at r. ctr. Leopoldskron Castle and Hohensalzburg Fortress on back.	FV	110.00	140.00

1984–85 ISSUE

#148–153 Federal arms at upper l. Wmk: Federal arms and parallel vertical lines.

144 (147)	50 SCHILLING	(1983 - old date 2.1.1970). Like #145 but w/ ovpt: *2. AUFLAGE* (2nd issue) at lower l. ctr.	FV	6.00	10.00

148	20 SCHILLING	1.10.1986. Dk. brown and brown on m/c unpt. M. Daffinger at r. "Albertin" bldg. on back.	FV	FV	2.50

145 (144)	100 SCHILLING	2.1.1969. Dk. green on m/c unpt. A. Kauffman at r. Large house on back.	FV	FV	16.00

149	50 SCHILLING	2.1.1986. Purple and violet on m/c unpt. S. Freud at r. "Josephinum" bldg. in Vienna on back.	FV	FV	6.00

146	100 SCHILLING	2.1.1969. Like #144 but w/ovpt: *2 AUFLAGE* (2nd issue) at upper l.	FV	FV	16.00

Cat. #	Denomination	Date, description	VG	VF	Unc
150	100 SCHILLING	2.1.1984 (1985). Dk. green, gray and dk. brown on m/c unpt. E. Bohm v. Bawerk at r. Academy "Wissenschaften" at l. ctr. on back.	FV	FV	12.00

151	500 SCHILLING	1.7.1985 (1986). Dk. brown, deep violet and orange-brown on m/c unpt. O. Wagner at r. "Postsparkassengebäude" bldg. at ctr. on back.	FV	FV	65.00

152	1000 SCHILLING	3.1.1983. Dk. blue and purple on m/c unpt. E. Schrodinger at r. Vienna University at l. on back.	FV	FV	120.00

153	5000 SCHILLING	4.1.1988. Lt. brown and purple on m/c unpt. W.A. Mozart at r. Vienna's Opera House at ctr. on back.	FV	FV	550.00

AZERBAIJAN

The Republic of Azerbaijan (formerly Azerbaijan S.S.R.) includes the Nakhichevan Autonomous Republic and Nagorno-Karabakh Autonomous Region (which was abolished in 1991). Situated in the eastern area of Transcaucasia, it is bordered in the west by Armenia, in the north by Georgia and Dagestan, to the east by the Caspian Sea and to the south by Iran. It has an area of 33,430 sq. mi. (86,600 sq. km.) and a population of 7.1 million. Capital: Baku. The area is rich in mineral deposits of aluminum, copper, iron, lead, salt and zinc, with oil as its leading industry. Agriculture and livestock follow in importance.

In ancient times home of Scythian tribes and known under the Romans as *Albania* and to the Arabs as *Arran*, the country of Azerbaijan formed at the time of its invasion by Seljuk Turks a prosperous state under Persian suzerainty. From the 16th century the country was a theatre of fighting and political rivalry between Turkey, Persia and later Russia. Baku was first annexed to Russia by Czar Peter I in 1723 and remained under Russian rule for 12 years. After the Russian retreat the whole of Azerbaijan north of the Aras River became a khanate under Persian control until Czar Alexander I, after an eight-year war with Persia, annexed it in 1813 to the Russian empire.

Until the Russian Revolution of 1905 there was no political life in Azerbaijan. A Mussavat (Equality) party was formed in 1911 by Mohammed Emin Rasulzade, a former Social Democrat. After the Russian Revolution of March 1917, the party started a campaign for independence, but Baku, the capital, with its mixed population, constituted an alien enclave in the country. While a national Azerbaijani government was established at Gandzha (Elizavetpol), a Communist-controlled council assumed power at Baku with Stepan Shaumian, an Armenian, at its head. The Gandzha government joined first, on Sept. 20, 1917, a Transcaucasian federal republic, but on May 28, 1918, proclaimed the independence of Azerbaijan. On June 4, 1918, at Batum, a peace treaty was signed with Turkey and a Turko-Azerbaijani force started an offensive against Baku, but it was occupied on Aug. 17, 1918 by 1,400 British troops coming by sea from Anzali, Persia. On Sept. 14 the British evacuated Baku, returning to Anzali, and three days later the Azerbaijan government, headed by Fath Ali Khan Khoysky, established itself at Baku.

After the collapse of the Ottoman empire the British returned to Baku, at first ignoring the Azerbaijan government. A general election with universal suffrage for the Azerbaijan constituent assembly took place on Dec. 7, 1918 and out of 120 members there were 84 Mussavat supporters; Ali Marden Topchibashev was elected speaker, and Nasib Usubekov formed a new government. On Jan. 15, 1920, the Allied powers recognized Azerbaijan *de facto*, but on April 27 of the same year the Red army invaded the country, and a Soviet republic of Azerbaijan was proclaimed the next day. Later it became a member of the Transcaucasian Federation joining the U.S.S.R. on Dec. 30, 1922; it became a self-constituent republic in 1936.

The Azerbaijan Communist party held its first congress at Baku in Feb. 1920. From 1921 to 1925 its first secretary was a Russian, S.M. Kirov, who directed a mass deportation to Siberia of about 120,000 Azerbaijani "nationalist deviationists," among them the country's first two premiers.

In 1990 it adopted a declaration of republican sovereignty, and in Aug. 1991 declared itself formally independent; this action was approved by a vote of referendum in Jan. 1992. It announced its intention of joining the CIS in Dec. 1991, but a parliamentary resolution of Oct. 1992 declined to confirm its involvement. Communist President Mutaibov was relieved of his office in May, 1992. A National Council replaced Mutaibov and on June 7 elected Abulfez Elchibey in the first democratic election in the country's history. Surat Huseynov led a military coup against Elchibey and seized power on June 30, 1993. Huseynov became prime minister with former communist Geidar Aliyev, president.

Fighting commenced between Muslim forces of Azerbaijan and Christian forces of Armenia in 1992 and continued through early 1994. Each fraction claimed the Nagorno-Karabakh, an Armenian ethnic enclave, in Azerbaijan. A cease-fire was declared in May, 1994.

REPUBLIC
Azerbaycan Milli Banki
Manat System
1992 ISSUE

#11–13 Maiden Tower at ctr. Wmk: 3 flames.

Cat. #	Denomination	Date, description	VG	VF	Unc
11	1 MANAT	ND (1992). Deep olive-green on m/c unpt.	FV	FV	1.50
12	10 MANAT	ND (1992). Deep brown-violet on m/c unpt.	FV	FV	3.00

Cat. #	Denomination	Date, description	VG	VF	Unc
13	250 MANAT	ND (1992). Deep blue-gray on m/c unpt.	FV	FV	25.00

1993–94 ISSUE

#14-20 Ornate "value" backs. Wmk: 3 flames.

#14–18 different view Maiden Tower ruins at ctr.

Cat. #	Denomination	Date, description	VG	VF	Unc
14	1 MANAT	ND (1993). Deep blue and tan on dull orange and green unpt.	FV	FV	1.00
15	5 MANAT	ND (1993). Deep brown and pale purple on lilac and m/c unpt.	FV	FV	2.00
16	10 MANAT	ND (1993). Deep grayish blue-green on pale blue and m/c unpt.	FV	FV	2.50
17	50 MANAT	ND (1993). Brownish red and tan on ochre and m/c unpt.	FV	FV	3.00

Cat. #	Denomination	Date, description	VG	VF	Unc
18	100 MANAT	ND (1993). Red-violet and pale blue on m/c unpt.	FV	FV	4.00
19	500 MANAT	ND (1993). Deep brown on pale blue, pink and m/c unpt. N. Gencevi at r.	FV	FV	15.00
20	1000 MANAT	ND (1993). Dk. brown and blue on pink and m/c unpt. M.E. Resulzado at r.	FV	FV	25.00
21	10,000 MANAT	1994. Brown, maroon and violet on m/c unpt. Bldg. at ctr. r.	—	—	—

BAHAMAS

The Commonwealth of The Bahamas is an archipelago of about 3,000 islands, cays and rocks located in the Atlantic Ocean east of Florida and north of Cuba. The total land area of the 800-mile (1.287 km.) long chain of islands is 5,380 sq. mi. (13,935 sq. km.). They have a population of 255,000. Capital: Nassau. The Bahamas imports most of their food and manufactured products and exports cement, refined oil, pulpwood and lobsters. Tourism is the principal industry.

The Bahamas were discovered by Columbus in October, 1492, but Spain made no attempt to settle them. British influence began in 1626 when Charles I granted them to the lord proprietors of Carolina. They continued under British proprietors until 1717, when the civil and military governments were surrendered to the King and the islands designated a British Crown Colony. The Bahamas obtained complete internal self-government under the constitution of Jan. 7, 1964. Full independence was achieved on July 10, 1973. The Bahamas is a member of the Commonwealth of Nations. The Queen of England is Chief of State.

RULERS
British

MONETARY SYSTEM
1 Shilling = 12 pence
1 Pound = 20 Shillings to 1966
1 Dollar = 100 Cents 1966-

REPLACEMENT NOTES
#26-49, Z prefix letter.

Government

1953 ISSUE

#13-15 ship in circle frame at l., portr. Qn. Elizabeth II at r. Printer: TDLR.

Cat. #	Denomination	Date, description	VG	VF	Unc
13	4 SHILLINGS	ND (1953). Green.			
		a. Ctr. sign. H.R. Latreille, r.h. sign. Basil Burnside.	1.50	15.00	85.00
		b. Ctr. sign. W.H. Sweeting, r.h. sign. Basil Burnside.	1.00	10.00	65.00
		c. Ctr. sign. W.H. Sweeting, r.h. sign. Chas. P. Bethel.	1.00	12.50	75.00
		d. Ctr. sign. W.H. Sweeting, r.h. sign. George W.K. Roberts.	1.00	7.50	40.00

Cat. #	Denomination	Date, description	VG	VF	Unc
14	10 SHILLINGS	ND (1953). Red.			
		a. Ctr. sign. H. R. Latreille, r. h. sign. Basil Burnside.	4.00	25.00	165.00
		b. Ctr. sign. W. H. Sweeting, r. h. sign. Basil Burnside.	4.00	17.50	125.00
		c. Ctr. sign. W. H. Sweeting, r. h. sign. Chas. P. Bethel.	4.00	20.00	150.00
		d. Ctr. sign. W. H. Sweeting, r. h. sign. George W. K. Roberts.	2.00	12.50	90.00

Cat. #	Denomination	Date, description	VG	VF	Unc
15	1 POUND	ND (1953). Black.			
		a. Ctr. sign. H. R. Latreille, r. h. sign. Basil Burnside.	5.00	27.50	285.00
		b. Ctr. sign. W. H. Sweeting, r. h. sign. Basil Burnside.	5.00	22.50	235.00
		c. Ctr. sign. W. H. Sweeting, r. h. sign. Chas. P. Bethel.	5.00	28.50	265.00
		d. Ctr. sign. W. H. Sweeting, r. h. sign. George W. K. Roberts.	3.00	17.50	175.00

Cat. #	Denomination	Date, description	VG	VF	Unc
16	5 POUNDS	ND (1953). Blue.			
		a. Ctr. sign. W. H. Sweeting, r. h. sign. Basil Burnside.	35.00	275.00	1000.
		b. Ctr. sign. W. H. Sweeting, r. h. sign. Chas. P. Bethel.	40.00	350.00	1500.
		c. Ctr. sign. W. H. Sweeting, r. h. sign. George W. K. Roberts.	30.00	225.00	900.00

1965 Currency Note Act

#17-25 Qn. Elizabeth II at l. Sign. varieties. Wmk: Shellfish. Printer: TDLR.

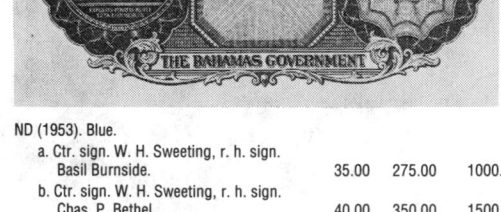

Cat. #	Denomination	Date, description	VG	VF	Unc
17	1/2 DOLLAR	*L.1965.* Purple on m/c unpt. Straw market on back.	FV	1.00	5.00

18	1 DOLLAR	*L.1965.* Green on m/c unpt. Sea garden on back.			
		a. 2 sign.	FV	2.50	20.00
		b. 3 sign.	FV	5.00	32.50

19	3 DOLLARS	*L.1965.* Red on m/c unpt. Paradise Beach on back.			
		a. Sign. Sands and Higgs.	3.50	7.00	17.50
		b. Sign. Francis and Higgs. Specimen.	—	—	200.00

20	5 DOLLARS	*L.1965.* Green on m/c unpt. Government House on back.	8.00	15.00	55.00
21	5 DOLLARS	*L.1965.* Orange on m/c unpt. Like #20.			
		a. 2 sign.	10.00	25.00	225.00
		b. 3 sign.	15.00	45.00	350.00

22	10 DOLLARS	*L.1965.* Dk. blue on m/c unpt. Flamingos on back.			
		a. 2 sign.	15.00	35.00	385.00
		b. 3 sign.	25.00	75.00	650.00
23	20 DOLLARS	*L.1965.* Dk. brown on m/c unpt. Surrey on back.	35.00	100.00	625.00
24	50 DOLLARS	*L.1965.* Brow on m/c unpt. Produce market on back.	75.00	200.00	950.00
25	100 DOLLARS	*L.1965.* Blue on m/c unpt. Deep sea fishing on back.	150.00	400.00	1500.

NOTE: #23-25 w/3 sign. exist in specimen form.

Bahamas Monetary Authority

1968 Monetary Authority Act

#26-33 Qn. Elizabeth II at l. Wmk: Shellfish. Printer: TDLR.

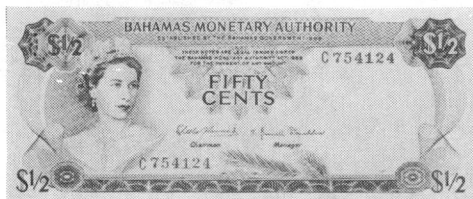

Cat. #	Denomination	Date, description	VG	VF	Unc
26	1/2 DOLLAR	*L.1968.* Purple on m/c unpt. Back similar to #17.	FV	1.00	3.00

27	1 DOLLAR	*L.1968.* Green on m/c unpt. Back similar to #18.	FV	2.50	12.50

28	3 DOLLARS	*L.1968.* Red on m/c unpt. Back similar to #19.	FV	3.50	12.50

29	5 DOLLARS	*L.1968.* Orange on m/c unpt. Back similar to #20.	7.00	20.00	135.00
30	10 DOLLARS	*L.1968.* Dk. blue on m/c unpt. Back similar to #22.	22.50	70.00	500.00

Cat. #	Denomination	Date, description	VG	VF	Unc
31	20 DOLLARS	*L.1968*. Dk. brown on m/c unpt. Back similar to #23.	37.50	175.00	850.00
32	50 DOLLARS	*L.1968*. Brown on m/c unpt. Back similar to #24.	100.00	350.00	1500.
33	100 DOLLARS	*L.1968*. Blue on m/c unpt. Back similar to #25.	185.00	400.00	2250.

Central Bank of the Bahamas

1974 Central Bank Act

#35-41 Qn. Elizabeth II. Wmk: Shellfish. Printer: TDLR.

Cat. #	Denomination	Date, description	VG	VF	Unc
35	1 DOLLAR	*L.1974*. Dk. blue-green on m/c unpt. Back similar to #18.			
		a. Sign. T. B. Donaldson.	1.25	2.00	8.50
		b. Sign. W. C. Allen.	1.50	7.50	22.50
36	*Deleted*				

Cat. #	Denomination	Date, description	VG	VF	Unc
37	5 DOLLARS	*L.1974*. Orange on m/c unpt. Back similar to #20.			
		a. Sign. T. B. Donaldson.	5.50	8.50	35.00
		b. Sign. W. C. Allen.	8.50	25.00	200.00

Cat. #	Denomination	Date, description	VG	VF	Unc
38	10 DOLLARS	*L.1974*. Dk. blue on m/c unpt. Back similar to #22.			
		a. Sign. T. B. Donaldson.	11.00	22.50	125.00
		b. Sign. W. C. Allen.	20.00	80.00	350.00

Cat. #	Denomination	Date, description	VG	VF	Unc
39	20 DOLLARS	*L.1974*. Dk. brown on m/c unpt. Back similar to #23.			
		a. Sign. T. B. Donaldson.	22.50	30.00	225.00
		b. Sign. W. C. Allen.	37.50	110.00	500.00
40	50 DOLLARS	*L.1974*. Brown on m/c unpt. Back similar to #24.			
		a. Sign. T. B. Donaldson.	55.00	125.00	525.00
		b. Sign. W. C. Allen.	65.00	200.00	900.00

Cat. #	Denomination	Date, description	VG	VF	Unc
41	100 DOLLARS	*L.1974*. Blue on m/c unpt. Back similar to #25.			
		a. Sign. T. B. Donaldson.	110.00	185.00	900.00
		b. Sign. W. C. Allen.	135.00	300.00	1500.

1974 Central Bank Act, 1984 Issue

#42-49 map at l. ctr., new portr. of Qn. Elizabeth II at r. ctr. Wmk: Sailing ship. Printer: TDLR.

Cat. #	Denomination	Date, description	VG	VF	Unc
42	1/2 DOLLAR	*L.1974* (1984). Green on m/c unpt. Baskets at l. Woman and market on back. Sign. W. C. Allen.	FV	FV	1.50

Cat. #	Denomination	Date, description	VG	VF	Unc
43	1 DOLLAR	*L.1974* (1984). Deep green on m/c unpt. Fish at l. Police band at ctr. on back.			
		a. Sign. W. C. Allen.	FV	FV	3.00
		b. Sign. F. H. Smith.	FV	FV	3.00

Cat. #	Denomination	Date, description	VG	VF	Unc
44	3 DOLLARS	*L.1974* (1984). Red-violet on m/c unpt. Beach at l. Sailboats on back. Sign. W. C. Allen.	FV	FV	5.00

Cat. #	Denomination	Date, description	VG	VF	Unc
45	5 DOLLARS	L.1974 (1984). Orange on m/c unpt. Statue at l. Native artwork on back.			
		a. Sign. W. C. Allen.	FV	6.00	18.50
		b. Sign. F. H. Smith. 2 horizontal serial #.	FV	FV	10.00

46	10 DOLLARS	L.1974 (1984). Pale blue on m/c unpt. 2 flamingos at l. Lighthouse and shoreline on back.			
		a. Sign. W. C. Allen.	FV	12.00	30.00
		b. Sign. F. H. Smith. 2 horizontal serial #.	FV	15.00	35.00

47	20 DOLLARS	L.1974 (1984). Red and black on m/c unpt. Horse and carriage at l. Nassau harbor on back.			
		a. Sign. W. C. Allen.	FV	25.00	75.00
		b. Sign. F. H. Smith. 2 horizontal serial #.	FV	22.50	55.00

48	50 DOLLARS	L.1974 (1984). Purple, orange and green on m/c unpt. Lighthouse at l. Bank on back.			
		a. Sign. W. C. Allen.	FV	65.00	185.00
		b. Sign. F. H. Smith. 2 horizontal serial #.	FV	75.00	275.00

Cat. #	Denomination	Date, description	VG	VF	Unc
49	100 DOLLARS	L.1974 (1984). Deep blue on m/c unpt. Sailboat at l. Blue marlin on back. Sign. W. C. Allen.	FV	125.00	275.00

1992 COMMEMORATIVE ISSUE

#50, Quincentennial of First Landfall by Christopher Columbus

50	1 DOLLAR	ND (1992). Dk. blue and deep violet on m/c unpt. Commercial seal at l., bust of C. Columbus r. w/compass face behind. Birds, lizard, islands outlined, ships across back with arms at lower r. Printer: CBNC.	FV	FV	2.75

1974 Central Bank Act; 1992 Issue

#51-56 printer: TDLR.

51	1 DOLLAR	L.1974 (1992). Deep green on m/c unpt. Like #43b but w/serial # vertical and horizontal.	FV	FV	2.50
52	5 DOLLARS	L.1974. Sir Cecil Wallace-Whitfield.			Expected new issue.
53	10 DOLLARS	L.1974 (1992). Pale blue on m/c unpt. Like #46b but w/serial # vertical and horizontal.	FV	FV	17.50
54	20 DOLLARS	L.1974 (1993). Black and red on m/c unpt. Sir M. B. Butler at r., horse drawn surrey at l. Aerial view of ships in Nassau's harbor at ctr., arms at r. on back. Wmk: Caravel.	FV	FV	30.00
55	50 DOLLARS	L.1974 (1992). Brown, blue-green and on m/c unpt. Like #48b but w/serial # vertical and horizontal.	FV	FV	80.00
56	100 DOLLARS	L.1974 (1992). Purple, deep blue and red-violet on m/c unpt. Like #49. Serial # vertical and horizontal. Sign. F. H. Smith.	FV	FV	150.00

COLLECTOR SERIES

Cat#	Date, denomination	Description	Issue Price	Mkt. Value
CS1	ND (1965) 1/2 - 100 DOLLARS	#17-25 ovpt: SPECIMEN.	—	1000.
CS2	ND (1968) 1/2 - 100 DOLLARS	#26-33 ovpt: SPECIMEN.	—	150.00

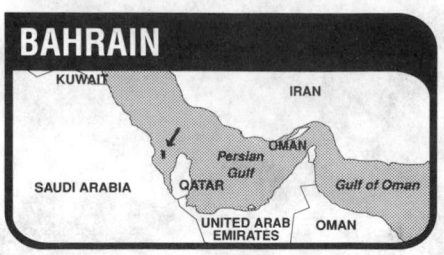

The State of Bahrain, a group of islands in the Persian Gulf off Saudi Arabia, has an area of 258 sq. mi. (622 sq. km.) and a population of 436,000. Capital: Manama. Prior to the depression of the 1930s, the economy was based on pearl fishing. Petroleum and aluminum industries and transit trade are the vital factors in the economy today.

The Portuguese occupied the islands in 1507 but were driven out in 1602 by Arab subjects of Persia. They in turn were ejected by Arabs of the Ataiba tribe from the Arabian mainland who have maintained possession up to the present time. The ruling sheikh of Bahrain entered into relations with Great Britain in 1805 and concluded a binding treaty of protection in 1861. In 1968 Great Britain decided to terminate treaty relations with the Persian Gulf sheikhdoms. Unable to agree on terms of union with the other sheikhdoms, Bahrain decided to seek independence as a separate entity and became fully independent on August 14, 1971.

RULERS
Isa Bin Sulman, 1961-

MONETARY SYSTEM
1 Dinar = 1000 Fils

Bahrain Currency Board
Authorization 6/1964

#1-6 sailboat at l., arms at r. Wmk: Falcon's head.

Cat. #	Denomination	Date, description	VG	VF	Unc
1	100 FILS	L.1964. Ochre on m/c unpt. Palm trees on back.	.25	1.00	5.50
2	1/4 DINAR	L.1964. Brown on m/c unpt. Oil derricks on back.	.50	1.50	7.00

3	1/2 DINAR	L.1964. Purple on m/c unpt. Ships on back.	1.00	2.00	10.00

4	1 DINAR	L.1964. Reddish-brown on m/c unpt. Minarets on back.	FV	4.00	15.00

Cat. #	Denomination	Date, description	VG	VF	Unc
5	5 DINARS	L.1964. Blue on m/c unpt. Sailboats on back.		FV	40.00	120.00

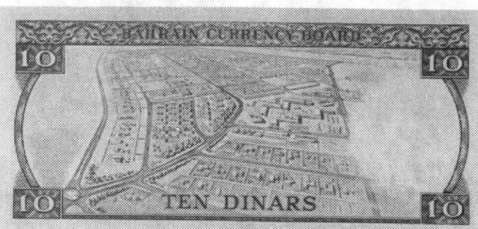

6	10 DINARS	L.1964. Green on m/c unpt. Aerial city view on back.		FV	35.00	95.00

Bahrain Monetary Agency
Authorization 23/1973

#7-11 map at l., sailboat at ctr., arms at r. Wmk: Falcon's head.

7	1/2 DINAR	L.1973. Brown on m/c unpt. Cow mask at lower l. Factory at l. on back.	FV	FV	4.00

8	1 DINAR	L.1973. Red on m/c unpt. Tower at l. Bldg. at l. on back.	FV	FV	7.00

8A	5 DINARS	L.1973. Blue on m/c unpt. Mosque at l. Pearl fishing scene on back.	FV	FV	30.00

Cat. #	Denomination	Date, description	VG	VF	Unc
9	10 DINARS	L.1973. Green on m/c unpt. Wind tower at l., dry dock on back.			
		a. 2 horizontal serial #.	FV	30.00	50.00
		b. Serial # vertical and horizontal.	FV	35.00	60.00

10	20 DINARS	L.1973. Reddish-brown on m/c unpt. Tower at l. Bldg. on back.	FV	85.00	160.00

11	20 DINARS	L.1973. Face like #10, but w/symbol changed at r. of map. Silvering added at lower l. denomination. Back has open frame and symbol around wmk. area. Also various color differences.			
		a. 2 horizontal serial #.	FV	FV	90.00
		b. Serial # vertical and horizontal.	FV	40.00	100.00

Authorization 23/1973 (1993 Issue)

#12-16 arms at ctr., outline map at l. Wmk: Antelope's head.

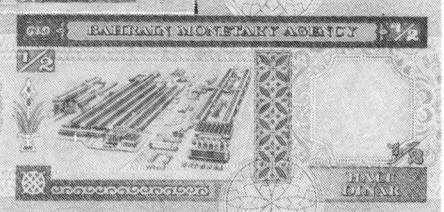

Cat. #	Denomination	Date, description	VG	VF	Unc
12	1/2 DINAR	L.1973 (1993). Deep brown, violet and brown-orange on m/c unpt. Man weaving at r. "Aluminum Bahrain" facility at l. ctr. on back.	FV	FV	3.50

13	1 DINAR	L.1973 (1993). Violet and red-orange on m/c unpt. Ancient seal at r. Modern office bldg. at l. ctr. on back.	FV	FV	6.00

14	5 DINARS	L.1973 (1993). Blue-black and deep blue-green on m/c unpt. Fortress at r. Bahrain International Airport at l. ctr. on back.	FV	FV	25.00

15	10 DINARS	L.1973 (1993). Deep olive-green and green on m/c unpt. Dhow at r. Aerial view of Kg. Fahad Causeway at l. ctr. on back.	FV	FV	45.00

Cat. #	Denomination	Date, description	VG	VF	Unc
16	20 DINARS	L.1973 (1993). Purple and violet m/c unpt. Government bldg. at r. Mosque at l. ctr. on back.	FV	FV	85.00

COLLECTOR SERIES

Cat. #	Date, denomination	Description	Issue Price	Mkt. Val.
CS1	ND (1978) 100 FILS - 20 DINARS	#1-6 and 10 w/ovpt: SPECIMEN and Maltese cross prefix serial #.	14.00	50.00

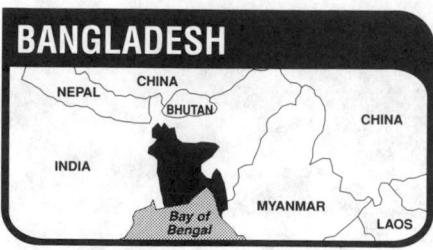

BANGLADESH

The Peoples Republic of Bangladesh (formerly East Pakistan), a parliamentary democracy located on the Bay of Bengal bordered by India and Burma, has an area of 55,598 sq. mi. (143,998 sq. km.) and a population of 122 million. Capital: Dacca. The economy is predominantly agricultural. Jute products and tea are exported.

British rule over the vast Indian sub-continent ended in 1947 when British India attained independence and was partitioned into the two successor states of India and Pakistan. Pakistan consisted of East and West Pakistan, two areas united by the Moslem religion but separated by culture and 1,000 miles of Indian territory. Restive under the de facto rule of the militant but fewer West Pakistanis, the East Pakistanis unsuccessfully demanded greater economic benefits and political reforms. The inability of the leaders of East and West Pakistan to resolve a political breakdown occasioned by the East Pakistan success in the general elections of 1970 precipitated massive civil disobedience in East Pakistan which West Pakistan sought to suppress militarily. East Pakistan seceded from Pakistan, March 26, 1971, and with the support of India declared an independent Peoples Republic of Bangladesh. Bangladesh is a member of the Commonwealth of Nations. The president is the Head of State and of Government.

MONETARY SYSTEM
1 Rupee = 100 Paise to 1972
1 Taka = 100 Poisha 1972-

REPLACEMENT NOTES
#12: Z prefix letter.

Peoples Republic of Bangladesh

1971 PROVISIONAL ISSUE

#1-3 w/BANGLADESH ovpt. in English or Bengali on Pakistan notes. The Bangladesh Bank never officially issued any Pakistan notes w/ovpt. These are considered locally issued by some authorities.

Cat. #	Denomination	Date, description	VG	VF	Unc
1	1 RUPEE	ND (1971). Blue. Purple BANGLADESH ovpt. on Pakistan #9.	20.00	35.00	75.00

1A	1 RUPEE	ND (1971). Blue. Purple Bengali ovpt. on Pakistan #9.	20.00	35.00	75.00

2	5 RUPEES	ND (1971). Brown-violet. Purple Bengali ovpt. on Pakistan #15.	15.00	30.00	70.00

Cat. #	Denomination	Date, description	VG	VF	Unc
3	10 RUPEES	ND (1971). Brown. Purple Bengali ovpt. on Pakistan #13.	15.00	30.00	70.00

1972–89 ISSUES

Cat. #	Denomination	Date, description	VG	VF	Unc
4	1 TAKA	ND (1972). Brown. Map of Bangladesh at l.	.10	.40	1.25

Cat. #	Denomination	Date, description	VG	VF	Unc
5	1 TAKA	ND (1973). Violet and ochre. Hand holding rice plants at l.			
		a. W/wmk.	.10	.40	1.25
		b. W/o wmk. (different sign.).	.10	.30	1.00

Cat. #	Denomination	Date, description	VG	VF	Unc
6	1 TAKA	ND (1974). Violet. Woman at l.	.10	.35	1.00

Cat. #	Denomination	Date, description	VG	VF	Unc
6A	1 TAKA	ND (1980). Violet and m/c. Deer on back.	FV	FV	.50
6B	1 TAKA	ND (1984). Violet and m/c. Similar to #6A but no printing on wmk. area at l. Also, different tiger wmk.	FV	FV	.50

Cat. #	Denomination	Date, description	VG	VF	Unc
6C (31)	2 TAKA	ND (1989). Black on green and orange unpt. Monument at r. Bird on back.	FV	FV	.75

Bangladesh Bank

1972 (ND) ISSUE

#7-9 map of Bangladesh at l., Mujibur Rahman at r.

Cat. #	Denomination	Date, description	VG	VF	Unc
7	5 TAKA	ND (1972). Purple on m/c unpt.	.50	1.50	7.50

Cat. #	Denomination	Date, description	VG	VF	Unc
8	10 TAKA	ND (1972). Blue on m/c unpt.	.75	2.00	8.00

Cat. #	Denomination	Date, description	VG	VF	Unc
9	100 TAKA	ND (1972). Green on m/c unpt.	1.50	5.00	17.50

1973 (ND) ISSUE

#10-12 Mujibur Rahman at l. Wmk: Tiger's head.

Cat. #	Denomination	Date, description	VG	VF	Unc
10	5 TAKA	ND (1973). Red. Lotus on back.	.25	1.00	4.00

Cat. #	Denomination	Date, description	VG	VF	Unc
11	10 TAKA	ND (1973). Green. River scene on back.			
		a. Serial # in Western numerals.	.50	2.50	10.00
		b. Serial # in Bengali numerals.	.50	1.75	7.00

Cat. #	Denomination	Date, description	VG	VF	Unc
12	100 TAKA	ND (1973). Brown. River scene on back.	.75	2.50	8.00

1974 (ND) ISSUE

#13-14 Mujibur Rahman at r. Wmk: Tiger's head.

13	5 TAKA	ND (1974). Red. Factory on back.	.25	.75	3.50

14	10 TAKA	ND (1974). Green. Rice harvesting on back.	.25	1.00	5.50

1976–77 (ND) ISSUE

#15-19 ornate bldg. at r. Wmk: Tiger's head.

15	5 TAKA	ND (1977). Lt. brown. Back like #13.	.15	.35	3.00

16	10 TAKA	ND (1977). Purple. Back like #14.	.25	.50	4.00

Cat. #	Denomination	Date, description	VG	VF	Unc
17	50 TAKA	ND (1976). Orange. Harvesting scene on back.	1.00	4.00	12.50

18	100 TAKA	ND (1976). Blue-violet on m/c unpt. Bldg. at l. Back like #12.	3.00	8.00	17.50

19	500 TAKA	ND (1977). Blue and lilac. Government bldg. on back.	20.00	50.00	110.00

NOTE: For similar 500 Taka but w/o printing on wmk. area, see #30.

1978–82 (ND) ISSUE

#20-24 wmk: Tiger's head.

20	5 TAKA	ND (1978). Lt brown on m/c unpt. Doorway at r. Back like #13.	.15	.25	1.00

Cat. #	Denomination	Date, description	VG	VF	Unc
21	10 TAKA	ND (1978). Purple. Mosque at r. Back like #14.	.20	.50	2.00

22	20 TAKA	ND (1980). Blue-green. Bldg. at r. Harvesting scene on back.	.50	1.50	3.50

23	50 TAKA	ND (1980). Orange on m/c unpt. Bldg. at r. Women harvesting on back.	.75	1.75	6.50

24	100 TAKA	ND (1982). Blue-violet, deep brown and m/c. Bldg. at r. Unpt. throughout wmk. area at l. Ruins of mosque at l. on back.	1.00	5.00	12.50

1982–88 (ND) ISSUE

#25-32 wmk: Different tiger's head. Sign. varieties.

Cat. #	Denomination	Date, description	VG	VF	Unc
25	5 TAKA	ND (1983). Similar to #20 but no printing on wmk. area at l. on face.			
		a. Black sign. Lg. serial #.	FV	FV	.50
		b. Black sign. Sm. serial #.	FV	FV	.50
		c. Brown sign. Sm. serial #.	FV	FV	.40

26	10 TAKA	ND (1982). Lilac on green and m/c unpt. Bldg. at r. Hydroelectric dam at ctr. on back. 2 sign. varieties.	FV	FV	1.50
27	20 TAKA	ND (1988). Design like #22 but no printing on wmk. area.			
		a. Black sign. Lg. serial #.	FV	FV	2.75
		b. Green sign. Sm. serial #.	FV	FV	2.25

28	50 TAKA	ND (1986). Black, red and deep green on m/c unpt. Monument at ctr. Modern bldg. at ctr. on back.	FV	FV	4.00

29	100 TAKA	ND (1984). Similar to #24 but no printing on wmk. area at l. on face.	FV	FV	8.50

Cat. #	Denomination	Date, description	VG	VF	Unc
30	500 TAKA	ND (1984). Gray, blue, violet and m/c. Similar to #19 but no printing on wmk. area at l. on face.	FV	FV	42.50

31 *Deleted. See #6c.*

1992–93 (ND) ISSUE

Cat. #	Denomination	Date, description	VG	VF	Unc
32	100 TAKA	ND (1992). Like #29 but w/circular toothed border added around wmk. area on face and back.	FV	FV	6.50
33	500 TAKA	ND (1993). Like #30, but w/segmented foil security thread.	FV	FV	27.50

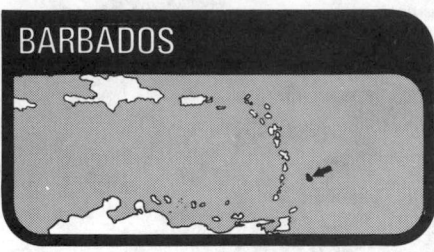

BARBADOS

Barbados, an independent state within the British Commonwealth, is located in the Windward Islands of the West Indies east of St. Vincent. The coral island has an area of 166 sq. mi. (431 sq. km) and a population of 258,600. Capital: Bridgetown. The economy is based on sugar and tourism. Sugar, petroleum products, molasses and rum are exported.

Barbados was named by the Portuguese who achieved the first landing on the island in 1563. British sailors landed at the site of present-day Holetown in 1624. Barbados was under uninterrupted British control from the time of the first British settlement in 1627 until it obtained independence on Nov. 30, 1966. It is a member of the Commonwealth of Nations. The Queen of England is Chief of State.

Barbados was included in the issues of the British Caribbean Territories - Eastern Group and later the East Caribbean Currency Authority until 1973.

RULERS
British to 1966

MONETARY SYSTEM
1 Dollar = 100 Cents, 1950-

Central Bank of Barbados

1973 (ND) ISSUE

#29-40 arms at l. ctr. Trafalgar Square in Bridgetown on back. Wmk: Map of Barbados. Printer: DLR.

Cat. #	Denomination	Date, description	VG	VF	Unc
29	1 DOLLAR	ND (1973). Red on m/c unpt. Portr. S. J. Prescod at r.	FV	.75	2.25

| 30 | 5 DOLLARS | ND (1973). Green on m/c unpt. Portr. S. J. Prescod at r. | FV | 4.00 | 12.00 |

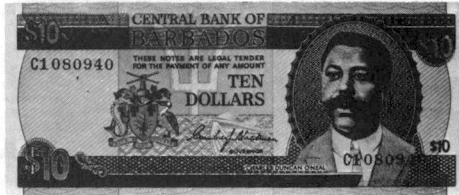

31	10 DOLLARS	ND (1973). Dk. brown on m/c unpt. Portr. C. D. O'Neal at r.			
		a. Sign. C. Blackman.	FV	7.00	13.50
		b. Sign K. King.	FV	6.00	9.00
32	20 DOLLARS	ND (1973). Purple on m/c unpt. Portr. S. J. Prescod at r.	FV	12.00	25.00

Cat. #	Denomination	Date, description	VG	VF	Unc
33	100 DOLLARS	ND (1973). Gray, blue on m/c unpt. Portr. Sir G. H. Adams at r. Treetops are grayish-blue on back. Serial # to E 3,200,000.	FV	70.00	125.00
34		*Deleted.* See #36.			

1975–80 (ND) ISSUE

35	2 DOLLARS	ND (1980). Blue on m/c unpt. Portr. J. R. Bovell at r.			
		a. Sign. C. Blackman.	FV	1.50	3.00
		b. Sign. K. King.	FV	FV	2.00

36 (34)	5 DOLLARS	ND (1975).Dk. green on m/c unpt. Portr. Sir F. Worrell at r.			
		a. Sign C. Blackman.	FV	3.50	7.50
		b. Sign. K. King.	FV	FV	6.50

1988–94 (ND) ISSUE

37	10 DOLLARS	ND (1994). Dk. brown and green on m/c unpt. Like #31 but seahorse in rectangle at l. on face, at r. on back.	FV	FV	12.50
38	20 DOLLARS	ND (1988). Purple on m/c unpt. Like #32, but bird emblem in rectangle at l. on face, at r. on back.			
		a. Sign. K. King.	FV	FV	22.50
		b. Sign. C. H. Springer.	FV	FV	17.50

Cat. #	Denomination	Date, description	VG	VF	Unc
39	50 DOLLARS	ND (1989). Orange, blue and gray on m/c unpt. Portr. Prime Minister E. W. Barrow at r.	FV	FV	50.00

40	100 DOLLARS	ND (1986). Brown, purple and gray-blue on m/c unpt. Like #33, but seahorse emblem in rectangle at l. on face, at r. on back. Treetops on back are green. Serial # above E 3,200,000.			
		a. Sign. C. Blackman.	FV	60.00	100.00
		b. Sign. K. King.	FV	FV	85.00

1995– (ND) ISSUE

#41– 44 like #35–38 but w/enhanced features such as "perfect register windows." Sign. C. M. Springer (?).

41	2 DOLLARS	ND (1996).			Expected new issue.
42	5 DOLLARS	ND (1995). Dk. green on m/c unpt.	FV	FV	5.00
43	10 DOLLARS	ND (1996).			Expected new issue.
44	20 DOLLARS	ND (1995). Red-violet and purple on m/c unpt. Like #38.	FV	FV	21.00

BELARUS

Belarus (Byelorussia, Belorussia, or White Russia — formerly the Belorussian S.S.R.) is situated along the Western Dvina and Dnieper, bounded in the west by Poland, to the north by Latvia and Lithuania, to the east by Russia and the south by the Ukraine. It has an area of 80,134 sq. mi. (207,600 sq. km.) and a population of 4.8 million. Capital: Minsk. Peat, salt, agriculture including flax, fodder and grasses for cattle breeding and dairy products, along with general manufacturing industries comprise the economy.

There never existed an independent state of Byelorussia. When Kiev was the center of Rus, there were a few feudal principalities in the Byelorussian lands, those of Polotsk, Smolensk and Turov being the most important. The principalities, protected by the Pripet marshes, escaped invasion when, in the first half of the 13th century, the Tatars destroyed the Kievan Rus, but soon they were all incorporated into the Grand Duchy of Lithuania. The Lithuanian conquerors were pagan and illiterate but politically wise. They respected the Christianity of the conquered and gradually Byelorussian became the official language of the grand duchy. When this greater Lithuania was absorbed by Poland in the 16th century, Polish replaced Byelorussian as the official language of the country. Until the partitions of Poland at the end of 18th century, the history of Byelorussia is identical with that of greater Lithuania.

When Russia incorporated the whole of Byelorussia into its territories in 1795, it claimed to be recovering old Russian lands and denied that the Byelorussians were a separate nation. The country was named Northwestern territory and in 1839 Byelorussian Roman Catholics of the Uniate rite were forced to accept Orthodoxy. A minority remained faithful to the Latin rite. The German occupation of western Byelorussia in 1915 created an opportunity for Byelorussian leaders to formulate in Dec. 1917 their desire for an independent Byelorussia. On Feb. 25, 1918, Minsk was occupied by the Germans, and in the Brest-Litovsk peace treaty of March 3 between the Central Powers and Soviet Russia the existence of Byelorussia was ignored. Nevertheless, on March 25, the National council headed by Lutskievich, Vatslav Lastovski and others proclaimed an independent republic. After the collapse of Germany the Soviet government repudiated the Brest treaties and on Jan. 1, 1919, proclaimed a Byelorussian S.S.R. The Red army occupied the lands evacuated by the Germans, and by February all Byelorussia was in Communist hands. The Polish army started an eastward offensive, however, and on Aug. 8 entered Minsk. In Dec. 1919 the Byelorussian National council gathered there but a split occurred in its ranks: Lastovski formed a pro-Soviet government, while Lutskievich formed an anti-Communist council. The Lastovski "government" soon took refuge in Lithuania, and later in Czechoslovakia. The peace treaty between Poland and the U.S.S.R. in March 1921 partitioned Byelorussia. In its eastern and larger part a Soviet republic was formed, which in 1922 became a founder member of the U.S.S.R. The eastern frontier was identical with the corresponding section of the Polish-Russian frontier before 1772. The first premier of the Byelorussian S.S.R., Dmitro Zhylunovich, persuaded Lastovski to return. Both perished in the purges of the 1930s. On Sept. 17, 1939, in accordance with the secret treaty partitioning Poland signed on Aug. 23 between Germany and the U.S.S.R., the Soviet army occupied eastern Poland, where a western Byelorussian people's assembly was elected on Oct. 22. The assembly "unanimously" demanded the incorporation of western Byelorussia into the U.S.S.R. On Nov. 2 the supreme soviet of the union proclaimed the unification of all Byelorussia. However, when the Moscow treaty of Aug. 16, 1945, fixed the Polish-Soviet frontier, it left Bialystok to Poland. From Jan. 1, 1955, the republic was divided into 7 *oblasti* or provinces; Minsk, Brest, Grodno, Molodechno, Mohylev (Mogilev), Homel (Gomel) and Vitebsk. On Aug. 25, 1991, following an unsuccessful coup, the Supreme Soviet adopted a declaration of independence, and the "Republic of Belarus" was proclaimed in Sept. Later in Dec. it became a founder member of the CIS.

MONETARY SYSTEM
1 Rubel = 100 Kapeek

КУПОН РЭСПУБЛІКА БЕЛАРУСБ

BELARUS REPUBLIC
КУПОН

Ruble Control Coupons

1991 FIRST ISSUE

#A1–A2 full sheet of 28 coupons of various denominations w/guilloche in unpt. in registry at ctr. Uniface.

Cat. #	Denomination	Date, description	VG	VF	Unc
A1	75 RUBLEI	ND (1991). Black text on blue and yellow unpt.			
		a. Issued full sheet.	—	2.00	4.00
		b. Remainder full sheet.	—	.75	1.50
		c. Coupon.	—	—	.05
A2	100 RUBLEI	ND (1991). Black text on pale red-orange and yellow unpt.			
		a. Issued full sheet.	—	2.00	4.00
		b. Remainder full sheet.	—	.75	1.50
		c. Coupon.	—	—	.05

1991 SECOND ISSUE

#A3–A8 w/o unpt. in registry at ctr. Uniface.

			VF	Unc
A3	20 RUBLEI	ND (1991). Black text on olive-green unpt. Sheet of 12 coupons of various denominations.		
		a. Issued full sheet.	2.00	4.00
		b. Remainder full sheet.	.75	1.50
		c. Coupon.	—	.10

#A4–A7 full sheet of 28 coupons of various denominations.

A4	50 RUBLEI	ND (1991). Black text on lt. blue unpt.

Cat. #	Denomination	Date, description	VG	VF	Unc
		a. Issued full sheet.	—	2.00	4.00
		b. Remainder full sheet.	—	.75	1.50
		c. Coupon.	—	—	.05
A5	75 RUBLEI	ND (1991). Dk. brown text on pale purple unpt.			
		a. Issued full sheet.	—	2.00	4.00
		b. Remainder full sheet.	—	.75	1.50
		c. Coupon.	—	—	.05
A6	200 RUBLEI	ND (1991). Black text on pink unpt.			
		a. Issued full sheet.	—	2.00	4.00
		b. Remainder full sheet.	—	.75	1.50
		c. Coupon.	—	—	.05

A7	300 RUBLEI	ND (1991). Black text on pale red-orange unpt.			
		a. Issued full sheet.	—	2.00	4.00
		b. Remainder full sheet.	—	.75	1.50
		c. Coupon.	—	—	.05

Cat. #	Denomination	Date, description	VG	VF	Unc
A8	500 RUBLE	ND (1991). Black text on pink, purple and yellow unpt.			
		a. Issued full sheet.	—	2.00	4.00
		b. Remainder full sheet.	—	.75	1.50
		c. Coupon.	—	—	.05

НАЦЫЯНАЛЬНАIА БАНКА БЕЛАРУСI

Belarus National Bank

РАЗЛIКОВЫ БIЛЕТ–Exchange Notes

1992–95 ISSUE

#1–10 "Pagonya," a defending warrior wielding sword on horseback at ctr. Wmk. paper.

1	50 KAPEEK	1992. Red and brown-orange on pink unpt. Squirrel at ctr. r. on back.	FV	FV	.25

2	1 RUBEL	1992. Yellow on green, purple and blue unpt. Rabbit at ctr. r. on back.	FV	FV	.30

3	3 RUBLI	1992. Green, red-orange and pale olive-green on m/c unpt. 2 beavers at ctr. r. on back.	FV	FV	.35

4	5 RUBLEI	1992. Deep blue on lt. blue, lilac, violet and m/c unpt. 2 wolves at ctr. r. on back.	FV	FV	.40

5	10 RUBLEI	1992. Deep green on lt. green, orange and m/c unpt. Lynx w/kitten at ctr. r. on back.	FV	FV	.50

Cat. #	Denomination	Date, description	VG	VF	Unc
6	25 RUBLEI	1992. Violet on red, green and m/c unpt. Moose at ctr. r. on back.	FV	FV	1.00

7	50 RUBLEI	1992. Deep purple on red and green unpt. Bear at ctr. r. on back.	FV	FV	.50

8	100 RUBLEI	1992. Brown, gray and tan on m/c unpt. Bison at ctr. r. on back.	FV	FV	1.50

9	200 RUBLEI	1992. Deep brown-violet, orange, green and ochre on m/c unpt. City view at ctr. r. on back.	FV	FV	1.50

10	500 RUBLEI	1992. Violet, tan, lt. blue and orange on m/c unpt. Victory Plaza in Minsk at ctr. r. on back.	FV	FV	1.75

11	1000 RUBLEI	1992 (1993). Blue, olive-green and pink. Back black, dk. blue and dk. green on m/c unpt.; Academy of Sciences bldg. at ctr. r. on back	FV	FV	1.35

12	5000 RUBLEI	1992 (1993). Red-violet and green on m/c unpt. Bldgs. in Minsk lower city at ctr. r. on back.	FV	FV	2.25
13 (14)	20,000 RUBLEI	1994. Dk. brown on m/c unpt. National Bank bldg. at l. ctr. on back.	FV	FV	5.00
14	50,000 RUBLEI	1995. City gate at l. on back.	FV	FV	12.00

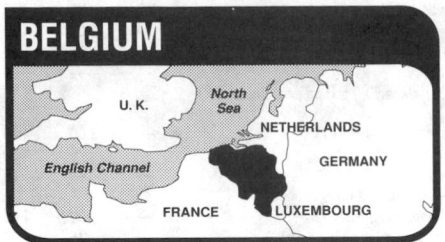

BELGIUM

The Kingdom of Belgium, a constitutional monarchy in northwest Europe, has an area of 11,779 sq. mi. (30,513 sq. km.) and a population of 10 million, chiefly Dutch-speaking Flemish and French-speaking Walloons. Capital: Brussels. Agriculture, dairy farming, and the processing of raw materials for re-export are the principal industries. Beurs voor Diamant in Antwerp is the world's largest diamond trading center. Iron and steel, machinery, motor vehicles, chemicals, textile yarns and fabrics comprise the principal exports.

The Celtic tribe called "Belgae," from which Belgium derived its name, was described by Caesar as the most courageous of all the tribes of Gaul. The Belgae eventually capitulated to Rome and the area remained for centuries as a part of the Roman Empire known as Belgica.

As Rome began its decline, Frankish tribes migrated westward and established the Merovingian, and subsequently, the Carolingian empires. At the death of Charlemagne, Europe was divided among his three sons Karl, Lothar and Ludwig. The eastern part of today's Belgium lay in the Duchy of Lower Lorraine while much of the western parts eventually became the County of Flanders. After further divisions, the area was absorbed into the Duchy of Burgundy from whence it passed into Hapsburg control when Marie of Burgundy married Maximilian of Austria. Phillip I (the Fair), son of Maximilian and Marie, then added Spain to the Hapsburg empire by marrying Johanna, daughter of Ferdinand and Isabella. Charles and Ferdinand, sons of Phillip and Johanna, began the separate Spanish and Austrian lines of the Hapsburg family. The Burgundian lands, along with the northern provinces which make up present day Netherlands, became the Spanish Netherlands. The northern provinces successfully rebelled and broke away from Hapsburg rule in the late 16th century and early 17th century. The southern provinces along with the Duchy of Luxembourg remained under the influence of Spain until the year 1700 when Charles II, last of the Spanish Hapsburg line, died without leaving an heir and the Spanish crown went to the Bourbon family of France. The Spanish Netherlands then reverted to the control of the Austrian line of Hapsburgs and became the Austrian Netherlands. The Austrian Netherlands along with the Bishopric of Liege fell to the French Republic in 1794.

At the Congress of Vienna in 1815 the area was united with the Netherlands but in 1830 independence was gained and the constitutional monarchy of Belgium was established. A large part of the Duchy of Luxembourg was incorporated into Belgium and the first king was Leopold I of Saxe-Coburg-Gotha. From 1920-1940 and since 1944 Eupen-Malmedy went from Germany to Belgium.

RULERS
Baudouin I, 1951-93
Albert II, 1993-

MONETARY SYSTEM
1 Franc = 100 Centimes
1 Belga = 5 Francs

REPLACEMENT NOTES
#60-69: Z1 Prefix.

KINGDOM
Banque Nationale de Belgique

1961–71 ISSUE

Cat. #	Denomination	Date, description	VG	VF	Unc
58	100 FRANCS	1.2.1962–30.4.1975. Lilac-brown on m/c unpt. Lombard at l. Allegorical figure on back. 4 sign. varieties.	FV	3.50	6.00

Cat. #	Denomination	Date, description	VG	VF	Unc
61	500 FRANCS	2.5.1961–28.4.1975. Blue-gray and m/c. B. Van Orley at ctr. Margaret of Austria on back. 4 sign. varieties.	FV	20.00	30.00

| 64 | 1000 FRANCS | 2.1.1961–11.12.1975. Brown and blue. Kremer (called Mercator) at l. Atlas holding globe on back. 4 sign. varieties. | FV | 37.50 | 55.00 |

| 65 | 5000 FRANCS | 6.1.1971–15.9.1977. Green. A. Vesalius at ctr. r. Statue and temple on back. 4 sign. varieties. | FV | 175.00 | 225.00 |

Royaume de Belgique - Koninkrijk Belgie

1964–66 Trésorerie - Thesaurie (Treasury Notes) Issue

| 67 | 20 FRANCS | 15.6.1964. Black on blue, orange and m/c unpt. Kg. Baudouin at l., arms at lower r. Atomic design at r. on back. 3 sign. varieties. | .25 | .50 | 2.00 |

| 69 | 50 FRANCS | 16.5.1966. Brown on m/c unpt. Arms at lower l. ctr., Kg. Baudouin, Qn. Fabiola at r. Parliament bldg. on back. 4 sign. varieties. | .25 | .75 | 2.50 |

Banque Nationale de Belgique

1978–82 ISSUES

#70-77 sign. varieties. Wmk: Kg. Baudonin.

Cat. #	Denomination	Date, description	VG	VF	Unc
70	100 FRANCS	ND (1978–81). Maroon, blue and olive-green on m/c unpt. H. Beyaert at ctr. r. Architectural view and plan at l. Geometric design on back. Sign. on back. 2 sign. varities.	FV	4.00	6.00

| 71 | 100 FRANCS | ND (1982–94). Like #70 but w/sign. on face and back. 7 sign. varieties. | FV | 4.00 | 5.00 |

| 72 | 500 FRANCS | ND (1980–81). Deep blue-violet and deep green on blue and m/c unpt. C. Meunier at l. ctr. Unpt. of 2 coal miners and mine conveyor tower at r. Five circular designs on back. Sign. on back. | FV | FV | 25.00 |

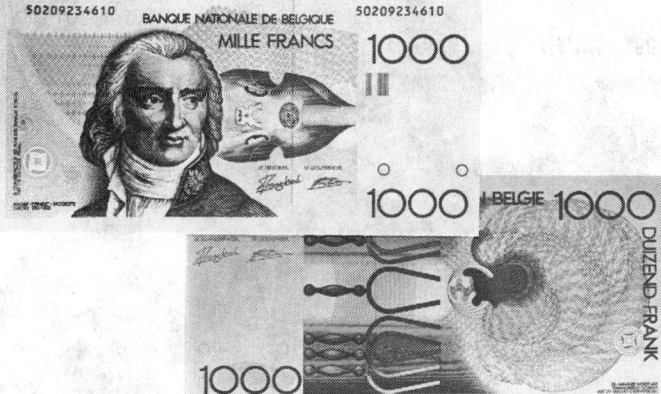

| 73 (72A) | 500 FRANCS | ND (1982–). Like #72 but w/sign. on face and back. 7 sign. varities. | FV | FV | 20.00 |

74 (73)	1000 FRANCS	ND (1981–). Brown and m/c. A. Gretry at l., viol in background. Tuning forks and sound wave designs on back. 7 sign. varities.			
		a. Name: *Andre Ernest Modeste Gretry. 1741–1813.*	FV	FV	40.00
		b. Error name: *Ernest Modeste. 1741–1813.*	FV	50.00	150.00
		c. Error name: *Andre Ernest Modeste, 1741–1813.*	FV	40.00	80.00

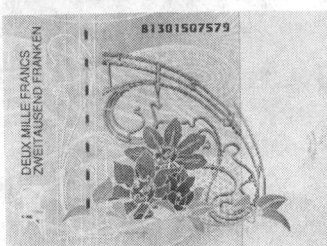

Cat. #	Denomination	Date, description	VG	VF	Unc
75 (76)	2000 FRANCS	ND (1994–). Purple and blue-green on m/c unpt. Baron V. Horton at l. and as wmk. Flora and *Art Nouveau* design at l. on back.	FV	FV	75.00
76 (74)	5000 FRANCS	ND (1982–). Green. G. Gezelle at l. ctr. Tree and stained glass window behind. Back green, red and brown; dragonfly and leaf. 5 sign. varieties.	FV	FV	200.00

77 (75)	10,000 FRANCS	ND (1992–). Grayish-purple on m/c unpt. Kg. Baudouin and Qn. Fabiola at l. aerial map as unpt. Flora and greenhouses at royal residence at Lacken at ctr.	FV	FV	350.00

1995 ISSUE

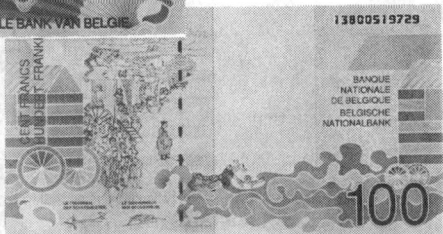

78	100 FRANCS	ND (1995–). Red-violet and black on m/c unpt. J. Ensor at l. and as wmk., masks at lower ctr. and at r. Beach scene at l. on back.	FV	FV	4.50
79	200 FRANCS	ND (1996).			Expected new issue

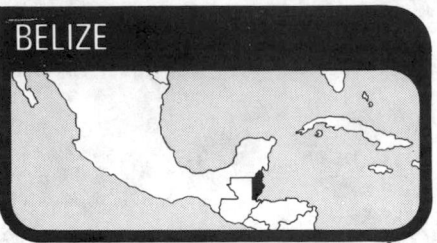

The British colony of Belize, formerly British Honduras, a self-governing dependency of the United Kingdom situated in Central America south of Mexico and east and north of Guatemala, has an area of 8,867 sq. mi. (22,965 sq. km.) and a population of 193,000. Capital: Belmopan. Sugar, citrus fruits, chicle and hard woods are exported.

The area, site of the ancient Mayan civilization, was sighted by Columbus in 1502, and settled by shipwrecked English seamen in 1638. British buccaneers settled the former capital of Belize in the 17th century. Britain claimed administrative right over the area after the emancipation of Central America from Spain, and declared it a colony subordinate to Jamaica in 1862. It established as the separate Crown Colony of British Honduras in 1884. The anti-British People's United Party, which attained power in 1954, won a constitution, effective in 1964 which established self-government under a British appointed governor. British Honduras became Belize on June 1, 1973, following the passage of a surprise bill by the Peoples United Party, but the constitutional relationship with Britain remained unchanged.

In Dec. 1975, the U.N. General Assembly adopted a resolution supporting the right of the people of Belize to self-determination, and asking Britain and Guatemala to renew their negotiations on the future of Belize. They obtained independence on Sept. 21, 1981.

Bank notes of the United States circulated freely in British Honduras until 1924.

RULERS
British

MONETARY SYSTEM
1 Dollar = 100 Cents

REPLACEMENT NOTES
#21-34 fraction, Z numerator with numeral as denominator. $1, Z/1, $5, Z/2, $10, Z/3, $20, Z/4, $100: Z/5.

#35-41, ZA or ZZ prefix.

BRITISH HONDURAS
Government of British Honduras

1952–53 ISSUE
#11-15 arms at l., portr. Qn. Elizabeth II at r.

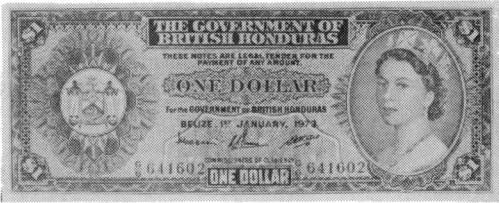

Cat. #	Denomination	Date, description	VG	VF	Unc
11	1 DOLLAR	1952–73. Green.			
		a. 1.2.1952–1.10.1958.	4.00	25.00	125.00
		b. 1.1.1961–1.5.1969.	2.00	10.00	50.00
		c. 1.1.1970–1.1.1973.	1.50	7.00	35.00

12	2 DOLLARS	1953–73. Purple.			
		a. 15.4.1953–1.10.1958.	7.50	40.00	350.00
		b. 1.10.1960–1.5.1965.	3.00	20.00	100.00
		c. 1.1.1971–1.1.1973.	2.00	15.00	55.00

Cat. #	Denomination	Date, description	VG	VF	Unc
13	5 DOLLARS	1953–73. Red.			
		a. 15.4.1953–1.1.1958.	10.00	50.00	325.00
		b. 1.3.1960–1.5.1969.	5.00	30.00	175.00
		c. 1.1.1970–1.1.1973.	4.50	20.00	100.00

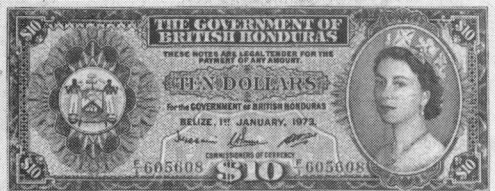

14	10 DOLLARS	1953–73. Black on m/c unpt.			
		a. 15.4.1953–1.10.1958.	15.00	100.00	600.00
		b. 1.5.1965–1.5.1969.	10.00	50.00	400.00
		c. 1.1.1971–1.1.1973.	7.50	35.00	300.00
15	20 DOLLARS	1952–73. Brown.			
		a. 1.12.1952–1.10.1958.	30.00	150.00	1000.
		b. 1.3.1960–1.5.1969.	20.00	120.00	700.00
		c. 1.1.1971–1.1.1973.	15.00	100.00	625.00

BELIZE
Government of Belize
1974–75 ISSUE

#16-20, arms at l., portr. Qn. Elizabeth II at r. Like #11–15.

16	1 DOLLAR	1.1.1974; 1.6.1975; 1.1.1976. Green.	.75	2.00	10.00
17	2 DOLLARS	1.1.1974; 1.6.1975; 1.1.1976. Violet and lilac.	2.00	5.00	22.50

18	5 DOLLARS	1.6.1975; 1.1.1976. Red.	3.00	8.50	40.00

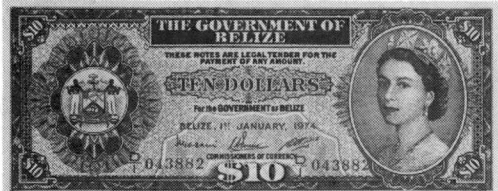

19	10 DOLLARS	1.1.1974; 1.6.1975; 1.1.1976. Black on m/c unpt.	6.00	20.00	100.00

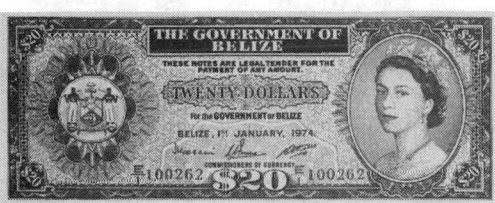

20	20 DOLLARS	1.1.1974; 1.6.1975; 1.1.1976. Brown.	12.00	37.50	225.00

Monetary Authority of Belize
Ordinance No. 9 of 1976

#21-25, linear border on arms in upper l. corner, Qn. Elizabeth II at ctr. r. 3/4 looking l., underwater scene w/reef and fish in ctr. background. House of Representatives in Belize on back. Wmk: Carved head of the "sleeping giant."

Cat. #	Denomination	Date, description	VG	VF	Unc
21	1 DOLLAR	1.6.1980. Green and m/c.	FV	1.00	5.00

22	5 DOLLARS	1.6.1980. Red and m/c.	FV	4.50	15.00

23	10 DOLLARS	1.6.1980. Violet and m/c.	FV	8.50	40.00

24	20 DOLLARS	1.6.1980. Brown and m/c.	FV	17.50	95.00

25	100 DOLLARS	1.6.1980. Blue and m/c.	FV	100.00	400.00

Central Bank of Belize
1983 ISSUE

#26-29 similar to #21–25. Wreath border on arms at upper l.

Cat. #	Denomination	Date, description	VG	VF	Unc
26	1 DOLLAR	1.7.1983. Green and m/c.	FV	1.50	7.50
27	Held in reserve				

| 28 | 10 DOLLARS | 1.7.1983. Gray and m/c. | FV | 7.00 | 35.00 |

| 29 | 20 DOLLARS | 1.7.1983. Brown on m/c unpt. | FV | 15.00 | 100.00 |

1983–87 ISSUE

#30-34, like #21–25. Lg. tree behind arms at upper l. Sign. varieties.

| 30 | 1 DOLLAR | 1.11.1983; 1.1.1986; 1.1.1987. Green and m/c. | FV | FV | 2.00 |

31	5 DOLLARS	1987; 1989.			
		a. 1.1.1987.	3.50	15.00	75.00
		b. 1.1.1989.	FV	3.00	12.00

32	10 DOLLARS	1987; 1989.			
		a. 1.1.1987.	FV	6.00	22.00
		b. 1.1.1989.	6.00	15.00	85.00

| 33 | 20 DOLLARS | 1.1.1986; 1.1.1987. | FV | 12.50 | 32.50 |

Cat. #	Denomination	Date, description	VG	VF	Unc
34	100 DOLLARS	1983; 1989.			
		a. 1.11.1983.	FV	85.00	250.00
		b. 1.1.1989.	FV	85.00	250.00

#35-41, older facing portr. of Qn. Elizabeth II at r. Wmk: Carved head of the "sleeping giant." Printer: TDLR.

| 35 | 1 DOLLAR | 1.5.1990. Green on lt. brown, blue and m/c unpt. Crustacean at l. Back green and red, marine life of Belize across ctr. | FV | FV | 1.50 |

| 36 | 2 DOLLARS | 1.5.1990; 1.6.1991. Purple on lt. green, blue and m/c unpt. Carved stone pillar at l. Mayan ruins of Belize on back. | FV | FV | 2.50 |

| 37 | 5 DOLLARS | 1.5.1990;1.6.1991. Red-orange, orange and violet on m/c unpt. Columbus medallion at l. St. George's Caye, coffin, outline map and bldg. on back. | FV | FV | 5.00 |

Cat. #	Denomination	Date, description	VG	VF	Unc
38	10 DOLLARS	1.5.1990; 1.6.1991. Black, olive-brown and deep blue-green on m/c unpt. Court House clock tower at l. Government House, Court House, and St. John's Cathedral on back.	FV	FV	8.50

| 39 | 20 DOLLARS | 1.5.1990. Dk. brown on m/c unpt. Jaguar at l. Fauna of Belize on back. | FV | FV | 16.00 |

| 40 | 50 DOLLARS | 1.5.1990; 1.6.1991. Purple, brown and red on m/c unpt. Boats at l. Bridges of Belize on back. | FV | FV | 40.00 |

| 41 | 100 DOLLARS | 1.5.1990; 1.6.1991. Blue-violet, orange and red on m/c unpt. Toucan at l. Birds of Belize on back. | FV | FV | 95.00 |

COLLECTOR SERIES

Cat#	Date, denomination	Desciption	Issue Price	Mkt. Val.
CS1	ND (1984) Collection	Stamped from paper bonded within gold foil. Denominations: $1 (1 pc.), $2 (2 pcs.), $5 (3 pcs.), $10 (4 pcs.), $20 (2 pcs.), $25 (6 pcs.), $50 (7 pcs.), $75 (5 pcs.), $100 (6 pcs.). Total 36 pcs. All have QE II and bldg. on face, different animals, ships, fish, birds etc. on backs.	—	500.00

NOTE: The Central Bank of Belize will exchange these notes for regular currency only in Belize (It is illegal to export the currency afterwards). Value is thus speculative.

The Parliamentary British Colony of Bermuda, situated in the western Atlantic Ocean 660 miles (1,062 km.) east of North Carolina, has an area of 20.6 sq. mi. (53 sq. km.) and a population of 60,470. Capital: Hamilton. Concentrated essences, beauty preparations, and cut flowers are exported. Most Bermudians derive their livelihood from tourism.

Bermuda was discovered by Juan de Bermudez, a Spanish navigator, in 1503. British influence dates from 1609 when a group of Virginia-bound British colonists under the command of Sir George Somers was shipwrecked on the islands for 10 months. The islands were settled in 1612 by 60 British colonists from the Virginia Colony and became a crown colony in 1684. Internal autonomy was obtained by the constitution of June 8, 1968.

In February, 1970, Bermuda converted from its former currency, the English pound, to a decimal currency, termed a dollar, which is equal to one U.S. dollar. On July 31, 1972, Bermuda severed its monetary link with the British pound sterling and pegged its dollar to be the same gold value as the U.S. dollar.

RULERS
British

MONETARY SYSTEM
1 Shilling = 12 Pence
1 Pound = 20 Shillings, to 1970
1 Dollar = 100 Cents, 1970-

REPLACEMENT NOTES
#23-40, Z/1 prefix.

Bermuda Government
Pound System
1952-66 ISSUE
#13-14, 16-17 portr. Qn. Elizabeth II. Printer: BWC.

Cat. #	Denomination	Date, description	VG	VF	Unc
13	5 SHILLINGS	1952; 1957. Brown on m/c unpt. Hamilton Harbor in frame at bottom ctr.			
		a. 20.10.1952.	3.00	10.00	65.00
		b. 1.5.1957.	2.00	7.50	45.00

Cat. #	Denomination	Date, description	VG	VF	Unc
14	10 SHILLINGS	1952–66. Red on m/c unpt. Gate's Fort in St. George in frame at bottom ctr.			
		a. 20.10.1952.	5.00	35.00	200.00
		b. 1.5.1957.	3.00	15.00	95.00
		c. 1.10.1966.	4.00	20.00	150.00

Cat. #	Denomination	Date, description	VG	VF	Unc
15	1 POUND	1952–66. Blue on m/c unpt. Bridge at l.			
		a. 20.10.1952.	7.50	30.00	250.00
		b. 1.5.1957. W/o security strip.	5.00	17.50	200.00
		c. 1.5.1957. W/security strip.	3.50	15.00	150.00
		d. 1.10.1966.	3.00	10.00	115.00
16	5 POUNDS	1952–66. Orange on m/c unpt. Ship entering Hamilton Harbor at l.			
		a. 20.10.1952.	25.00	100.00	550.00
		b. 1.5.1957. W/o security strip.	17.50	70.00	450.00
		c. 1.5.1957. W/security strip.	15.00	50.00	400.00
		d. 1.10.1966.	15.00	45.00	350.00

Cat. #	Denomination	Date, description	VG	VF	Unc
17	10 POUNDS	28.7.1964. Purple on m/c unpt. Bermuda arms at ctr. on back.	75.00	300.00	950.00

Dollar System
1970 ISSUE
#18-22 Qn. Elizabeth II at r. 3/4 looking l., arms at l. ctr. Wmk: Tuna fish.

Cat. #	Denomination	Date, description	VG	VF	Unc
18	1 DOLLAR	6.2.1970. Dk. blue on tan and aqua unpt. Sailboats on back.	FV	1.50	9.00

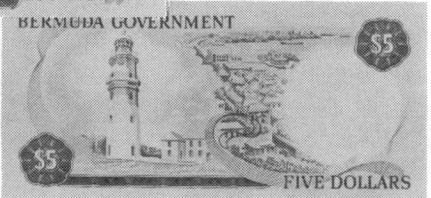

Cat. #	Denomination	Date, description	VG	VF	Unc
19	5 DOLLARS	6.2.1970. Red-violet on aqua and m/c unpt. Lighthouse at l., bldgs. at ctr. r. on back.	FV	6.00	17.50

Cat. #	Denomination	Date, description	VG	VF	Unc
20	10 DOLLARS	6.2.1970. Purple on brown and m/c unpt. Bird, seashell and beach on back.	FV	12.50	40.00
21	20 DOLLARS	6.2.1970. Green on m/c unpt. Sailboat and bridge on back.	FV	25.00	85.00
22	50 DOLLARS	6.2.1970. Brown on m/c unpt. Lighthouse and map on back.	FV	70.00	200.00

Bermuda Monetary Authority

1974–82 ISSUE

#23-28 Qn. Elizabeth II at r., 3/4 looking l. Wmk: Tuna fish. Like #18-22.

	Cat. #	Denomination	Date, description	VG	VF	Unc
26	20 DOLLARS		1974–86.			
		a.	1.4.1974.	25.00	45.00	185.00
		b.	1.3.1976.	FV	25.00	95.00
		c.	2.1. 1981; 1.5.1984.	FV	FV	37.50
		d.	Sign. title: *GENERAL MANAGER* at r. 1.1.1986.	FV	FV	37.50
27	50 DOLLARS		1974–82.			
		a.	1.5.1974.	60.00	150.00	600.00
		b.	1.4.1978; 2.1.1982.	FV	85.00	225.00

28	100 DOLLARS	1982–86. Orange and m/c. House of Assembly on back.			
		a. 2.1.1982.	FV	FV	185.00
		b. Sign. title: *GENERAL MANAGER* ovpt. at r. 14.11.1904.	FV	FV	175.00
		c. Sign title: *GENERAL MANAGER* at r. 1.1.1986.	FV	FV	165.00

1988–89 ISSUE

#29-34 older facing portr. of Qn. Elizabeth II at r. Back similar to #23-28 but w/stylistic changes; arms added at upper l. Sign. titles: *CHAIRMAN* and *DIRECTOR*. Wmk.: Tuna fish.

23	1 DOLLAR	1975–88.			
		a. Sign. titles: *CHAIRMAN* and *MANAGING DIRECTOR*. 1.7.1975; 1.12.1976.	FV	2.50	15.00
		b. 1.4.1978; 1.9.1979; 2.1.1982; 1.5.1984.	FV	1.50	7.50
		c. Sign. titles: *CHAIRMAN* and *GENERAL MANAGER*. 1.1.1986.	FV	1.50	7.00
		d. Sign. titles: *CHAIRMAN* and *DIRECTOR*. 1.1.1988.	FV	1.50	6.50

24	5 DOLLARS	1978–88.			
		a. Sign. titles: *CHAIRMAN* and *MANAGING DIRECTOR*. 1.4.1978.	FV	6.50	17.50
		b. 2.1.1981.	FV	6.00	15.00
		c. Sign. titles: *CHAIRMAN* and *GENERAL MANAGER*. 1.1.1986.	FV	6.00	15.00
		d. Sign. titles: *CHAIRMAN* and *DIRECTOR*. 1.1.1988.	FV	6.00	12.50
25	10 DOLLARS	1978; 1982.			
		a. 1.4.1978.	FV	17.50	75.00
		b. 2.1.1982.	FV	15.00	65.00

29	2 DOLLARS	1.10.1988; 1.8.1989. Blue-green on green and m/c unpt. Dockyards clock tower bldg. at l., map at ctr., arms at ctr. r. on back.	FV	FV	4.00

Cat. #	Denomination	Date, description	VG	VF	Unc
30	5 DOLLARS	20.2.1989. Red-violet, purple and m/c.			
		a. Sign. title: *DIRECTOR* on silver background at bottom ctr.	FV	7.00	20.00
		b. Sign. title: *DIRECTOR* w/o silver background.	FV	FV	10.00

| 31 | 10 DOLLARS | 20.2.1989. Purple, blue and ochre. | FV | FV | 20.00 |

| 32 | 20 DOLLARS | 20.2.1989. Green and red. | FV | FV | 32.50 |

| 33 | 50 DOLLARS | 20.2.1989. Brown and olive on m/c unpt. | FV | FV | 85.00 |

| 34 | 100 DOLLARS | 20.2.1989. Orange and brown on m/c unpt. | FV | FV | 145.00 |

1992–93 ISSUE

#35-40 issued under Bermuda Monetary Authority Act 1969. Authorization text in 3 lines at ctr. Wmk: Tuna fish.

#35-36 like #29-34.

| 35 | 5 DOLLARS | 12.11.1992; 25.3.1995. Like #30 but new 3-line text under value at ctr. | FV | FV | 8.50 |

| 36 | 10 DOLLARS | 4.1.1993. Like #31 but w/new text as #35. | FV | FV | 15.00 |

Cat. #	Denomination	Date, description	VG	VF	Unc
37	Held in reserve.				

| 38 | 50 DOLLARS | 12.10.1992; 25.3.1995. Dk. blue, brown and red on m/c unpt. Face similar to #33 but w/new text similar to #35. Scuba divers, shipwreck at l., island outline at upper r. above arms. | FV | FV | 75.00 |
| 39 | Held in reserve. | | | | |

1992 COMMEMORATIVE ISSUE

#40, Quincentenary of Christopher Columbus

| 40 | 50 DOLLARS | 12.10.1992. As #38 but w/commemorative details. Maltese cross as serial # prefix at upper l., c/c fractional prefix at r., and ovpt: *Christopher Columbus/Quincentenary/1492-1992* at l. | FV | FV | 100.00 |

1994 COMMEMORATIVE ISSUE

#41, 25th Anniversary Bermuda Monetary Authority

| 41 | 100 DOLLARS | 20.2.1994. Orange and brown on m/c unpt. Similar to #34 but new 3-line text under value. Ovpt: *25th Anniversary....* | FV | FV | 140.00 |

COLLECTOR SERIES

Cat#	Date, denomination,	Description	Issue Price	Mkt. Val.
CS1	1978–84 1-100 DOLLARS	#23-28 w/normal serial # but punched hole cancelled, ovpt: *SPECIMEN* (1985).	—	30.00
CS2	1981–82 1-100 DOLLARS	#23-28 w/all zero serial #, punched hole cancelled in all 4 corners, ovpt: *SPECIMEN* (1985).	—	30.00

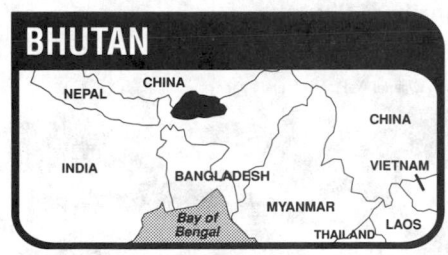

The Kingdom of Bhutan, a landlocked Himalayan country bordered by Tibet, India, and Sikkim, has an area of 18,147 sq. mi. (47,000 sq. km.) and a population of 600,000. Capital: Thimphu; Paro is the administrative capital. Virtually the entire population is engaged in agricultural and pastoral activities. Rice, wheat, barley, and yak butter are produced in sufficient quantity to make the country self-sufficient in food. The economy of Bhutan is primitive and many transactions are conducted on a barter basis.

Bhutan's early history is obscure, but is thought to have resembled that of rural medieval Europe. The country was conquered by Tibet, which still claims sovereignty over Bhutan, in the 9th century, and subjected to a dual temporal and spiritual rule until the mid-19th century, when the southern part of the country was occupied by the British and annexed to British India. Bhutan was established as a hereditary monarchy in 1907, and in 1910 agreed to British control of its external affairs. In 1949, India and Bhutan concluded a treaty whereby India assumed Britain's role in subsidizing Bhutan and conducting its foreign affairs.

RULERS

Jigme Singye Wangchuk, 1972-

MONETARY SYSTEM

1 Ngultrum (= 1 Rupee) = 100 Chetrums, 1974-

REPLACEMENT NOTES

#5-18, Z/1 prefix.

Royal Government of Bhutan

1974 ISSUE

#1-4 wmk: Ornate cruciform.

Cat. #	Denomination	Date, description	VG	VF	Unc
1	1 NGULTRUM	ND (1974). Blue on m/c unpt.	.20	.75	3.50

| 2 | 5 NGULTRUMS | ND (1974). Brown on m/c unpt. Jigme Singye Wangchuk at ctr. Simtokha Dzong palace on back. | 1.50 | 8.00 | 25.00 |

| 3 | 10 NGULTRUMS | ND (1974). Blue-violet on m/c unpt. Jigme Dorji Wangchuk at ctr. Paro Dzong palace on back. | 5.00 | 20.00 | 110.00 |

Cat. #	Denomination	Date, description	VG	VF	Unc
4	100 NGULTRUMS	ND (1978). Green and brown on m/c unpt. J. Singye Wangchuk at ctr., circle w/8 good luck symbols at r. Tashichho Dzong palace on back.	300.00	—	—

1981 ISSUE

#5-11 have serial # at upper l. and r.

| 5 | 1 NGULTRUM | ND (1981). Blue on m/c unpt. Royal emblem at ctr. Simtokha Dzong palace on back. | .10 | .20 | 1.25 |

| 6 | 2 NGULTRUM | ND (1981). Brown and green on m/c unpt. Similar to #5. | .15 | .50 | 2.50 |

| 7 | 5 NGULTRUM | ND (1981). Brown on m/c unpt. Birds l. and r., royal emblem at ctr. Paro Dzong palace on back. | .35 | 1.00 | 5.00 |

Royal Monetary Authority of Bhutan
1985–92 ISSUE
#12-18 similar to #5–11 but reduced size w/serial # at lower l. and upper r.

Cat. #	Denomination	Date, description	VG	VF	Unc
12	1 NGULTRUM	ND (1986). Blue on m/c unpt.	FV	FV	.75

Cat. #	Denomination	Date, description	VG	VF	Unc
8	10 NGULTRUM	ND (1981). Blue-violet on m/c unpt. J. Singye Wangchuk at r., royal emblem at l. Paro Dzong palace on back.	.65	2.00	10.00

13	2 NGULTRUM	ND (1986). Brown and green on m/c unpt.	FV	FV	1.50

9	20 NGULTRUM	ND (1981). Olive on m/c unpt. Jigme Dorji Wangchuk at r. Punakha Dzong palace on back.	1.20	3.50	17.50

14	5 NGULTRUM	ND (1985). Brown on m/c unpt.	FV	FV	3.00

10	50 NGULTRUM	ND (1981). Purple, violet and brown on m/c unpt. Like #9. Tongsa Dzong palace on back.	3.25	10.00	50.00

15	10 NGULTRUM	ND (1986; 1992). Blue-violet on m/c unpt.			
		a. Serial # w/fractional style prefix. (1986).	FV	FV	4.50
		b. Serial # w/2 lg. letters as prefix (printed in China). (1992).	FV	FV	3.00

11	100 NGULTRUM	ND (1981). Dk. green, olive-green and brown-violet on m/c unpt. Like #8; bird at ctr. Tashichho Dzong palace on back.	7.50	22.50	110.00

Cat. #	Denomination	Date, description	VG	VF	Unc
16	20 NGULTRUM	ND (1986; 1992). Olive on m/c unpt.			
		a. Serial # w/fractional style prefix. (1986).	FV	FV	6.00
		b. Serial # w/2 lg. letters as prefix (printed in China). (1992).	FV	FV	4.00

17	50 NGULTRUM	ND (1986; 1992). Purple, violet and brown on m/c unpt.			
		a. ND. Serial # w/fractional style prefix.	FV	3.00	15.00
		b. ND. Serial # w/2 large letters as prefix (printed in China). (1992).	FV	2.00	10.00

Cat. #	Denomination	Date, description	VG	VF	Unc
20	100 NGULTRUM	ND (1994). Green and brown on m/c unpt.	FV	FV	9.00

1994 COMMEMORATIVE ISSUE

#21, National Day

21	500 NGULTRUM	ND (1994). Orange on m/c unpt.	FV	FV	35.00

18	100 NGULTRUM	ND (1986; 1992). Green and brown on m/c unpt.			
		a. Serial # w/fractional style prefix. (1986).	FV	5.00	25.00
		b. Serial # w/2 lg. letters as prefix (printed in China). (1992).	FV	4.00	17.50

1994 ISSUE

#19 and 20 similar to #17 and 18 but with modified unpt. including floral diamond shaped registry design at upper ctr. Wmk: Wavy repeated text: *ROYAL MONETARY AUTHORITY*.

19	50 NGULTRUM	ND (1994). Purple, violet and brown on m/c unpt.	FV	FV	5.00

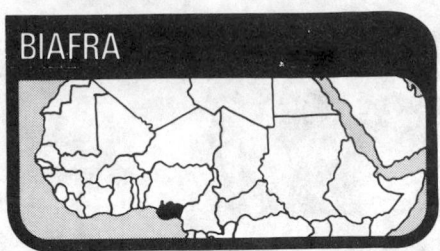

On May 27, 1967, Gen. Yakubu Gowon, head of the Federal Military Government of Nigeria, created three states from the Eastern Region of the country. Separation of the region, undertaken to achieve better regional and ethnic balance, caused Lt. Col. E. O. Ojukwu, Military Governor of the Eastern Region, to proclaim on May 30, 1967, the independence of the Eastern Region as the "Republic of Biafra." Fighting broke out between the Federal Military Government and the forces of Lt. Col. Ojukwu and continued until Biafra surrendered on Jan. 15, 1970. Biafra was then reintegrated into the republic as three states: East-Central, Rivers, and South-Eastern.

For additional history, see Nigeria.

MONETARY SYSTEM
1 Shilling = 12 Pence
1 Pound = 20 Shillings

Bank of Biafra
1967 ISSUE
#1-2 palm tree, lg. rising sun.

Cat. #	Denomination	Date, description	VG	VF	Unc
1	5 SHILLINGS	ND (1967). Blue on lilac unpt. Color varies from orange to yellow for rising sun. 4 girls at r. on back.			
		a. Serial #.	.75	3.00	10.00
		b. W/o serial #.	Reported, not confirmed.		

| 2 | 1 POUND | ND (1967). Blue and orange. Back brown; arms at r. | 1.50 | 10.00 | 80.00 |

1968 ISSUE
#3-7 palm tree and small rising sun at l. to ctr.

3	5 SHILLINGS	ND (1968–69). Blue on green and orange unpt. Back similar to #1.			
		a. Serial #.	1.00	3.00	12.50
		b. W/o serial #.	2.00	6.00	20.00

Cat. #	Denomination	Date, description	VG	VF	Unc
4	10 SHILLINGS	ND (1968–69). Green on blue and orange unpt. Bldgs. at r. on back.			
		a. Serial #.	1.00	3.00	10.00
		b. W/o serial #.	Reported, not confirmed.		

5	1 POUND	ND (1968–69). Dk. brown on green and brown unpt. Back similar to #2.			
		a. Serial #.	.10	.20	.50
		b. W/o serial #.	.50	2.00	9.50

6	5 POUNDS	ND (1968–69). Violet on m/c unpt. Arms at l., weaving at l. ctr. on back.			
		a. Serial #.	4.00	12.00	45.00
		b. W/o serial #.	2.00	6.00	25.00

7	10 POUNDS	ND (1968–69). Blue and brown on m/c unpt. Arms at l., carver at l. ctr. on back.			
		a. Serial #.	4.00	12.00	45.00
		b. W/o serial #.	2.50	7.50	30.00

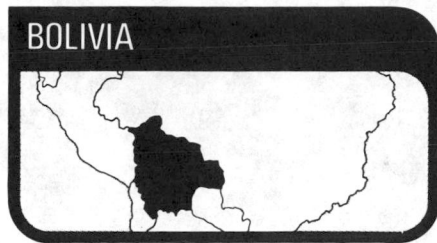

BOLIVIA

The Republic of Bolivia, a landlocked country in west central South America, has an area of 424,165 sq. mi. (1,098,581 sq. km.) and a population of 7.6 million. Capitals: La Paz (administrative); Sucre (constitutional). Mining is the principal industry and tin the most important metal. Minerals, petroleum, natural gas, cotton and coffee are exported.

The Incas, who ruled one of the world's greatest dynasties, incorporated the area that is now Bolivia into their empire about 1200AD. Their control was maintained until the Spaniards arrived in 1535 and reduced the predominantly Indian population to slavery. When Napoleon occupied Madrid in 1808 and placed his brother Joseph on the Spanish throne, a fervor of revolutionary activity quickened in Bolivia, culminating with the 1809 proclamation of independence. Sixteen years of struggle ensued before the republic, named for the famed liberator Simon Bolivar, was established on August 6, 1825. Since then, Bolivia has had more than 60 revolutions, 70 presidents and 11 constitutions.

MONETARY SYSTEM

1 Bolivar = 100 Centavos, 1945–62

1 Peso Boliviano = 100 Centavos, 1962–87

1 Boliviano = 100 Centavos, 1987–

REPLACEMENT NOTES

#162, 164, ZX, ZY or ZZ prefix letters and 6-digit serial number; #165–171, single ZX etc. and 8-digit serial #.

Series letters; #102–127, 26–letter alphabet used. # 128 and later, 24 letters used (no I; O).

Banco Central de Bolivia

Peso Boliviano System

1 Peso Boliviano = 1000 old Bolivianos

Ley de 13 de Julio de 1962

FIRST ISSUE

#152–157 old and new denomination on back at bottom. Arms at l. Sign. varieties. Printer: TDLR.

Cat. #	Denomination	Date, description	VG	VF	Unc
152	1 PESO BOLIVIANO	L.1962. Black on m/c unpt. Campesino at r. Agricultural scene at ctr. r. on back. Series A–E.	1.60	2.00	7.50

Cat. #	Denomination	Date, description	VG	VF	Unc
153	5 PESOS BOLIVIANOS	L.1962. Blue on m/c unpt. Villarroel at r. Petroleum refinery on back. Series A–C1.			
		a. Issued note.	.75	2.50	8.50
		b. Uncut sheet of 4 signed notes.	—	—	50.00

Cat. #	Denomination	Date, description	VG	VF	Unc
154	10 PESOS BOLIVIANOS	L.1962. Olive-green on m/c unpt. Busch at r. Mountain of Potosi on back.			
		a. Issued note.	.10	.40	.85
		b. Uncut sheet of 4 signed notes. Series U2.	—	—	25.00
		c. Uncut sheet of 4 specimen notes. Series U2.	—	—	20.00

155	20 PESOS BOLIVIANOS	L.1962. Purple on m/c unpt. Murillo at r. La Paz and mountain on back. Series A.	.75	4.00	25.00

156	50 PESOS BOLIVIANOS	L.1962. Orange on m/c unpt. Sucre at r. Puerta del Sol on back. Series A.	15.00	45.00	100.00

157	100 PESOS BOLIVIANOS	L.1962. Red on m/c unpt. Unpt. w/green at l., blue at r. Red serial #, and security thread at l. ctr. Bolivar at r. Back darker red, engraved; scene of the declaration of the Bolivian Republic. Series A.	12.00	40.00	80.00

SECOND ISSUE

#158–163 only new denomination on back. Sign. varieties. Printer: TDLR.

Cat. #	Denomination	Date, description	VG	VF	Unc
158	1 PESO BOLIVIANO	L.1962. Like #152. Series F–F1.	.30	1.00	5.00
159	Held in reserve.				
160	Held in reserve.				
161	20 PESOS BOLIVIANOS	L.1962. Like #155. Series B–H.	.30	1.00	7.50

162	50 PESOS BOLIVIANOS	L.1962. Like #156.			
		a. Issued note.	.10	.25	1.00
		b. Uncut sheet of 4 signed notes. Series V2.	—	—	40.00
		c. Uncut sheet of 4 notes w/sign. at top of notes. Series L2. (error.)	—	—	40.00
		d. Uncut sheet of 4 unsigned notes. Series AZ.	—	—	12.50

NOTE: Unsigned remainders appeared in vertical sheets of 4 subjects.

163	100 PESOS BOLIVIANOS	L.1962. Like #157. Unpt. w/green at l. and r. on face. Brighter red back, engraved. Lower # prefixes (from B to 10D).			
		a. Issued note.	.10	.25	.85
		b. Uncut sheet of 4 signed notes. Series X4; D5; U5.	—	—	40.00
		c. Uncut sheet of 4 unsigned notes. Series AZ.	—	—	12.50

Cat. #	Denomination	Date, description	VG	VF	Unc
164	100 PESOS BOLIVIANOS	L.1962 (1983). Design like #163.			
		a. Back dull red, lithographed w/poor detail. Black serial # and no security thread. Prefixes #10E–13D.	.25	.50	2.00
		b. Like #163 including engraved back, security thread and red serial #. Higher # prefixes (13E–19T) than for #164a.	.10	.25	1.00
		c. Unsigned remainder, prefix #12H.	—	—	15.00

NOTE: Unsigned remainders appeared in vertical sheets of 4 notes.

1981–84 Various Decrees

165	500 PESOS BOLIVIANOS	D. 1.6.1981. Deep blue, blue-green and black on m/c unpt. Arms at ctr., Avaroa at r. and as wmk. at l. Back blue on m/c unpt; view of Puerto de Antofagasta, ca.1879 at ctr. Series A; Z. Printer: ABNC.			
		a. Issued note.	.10	.25	1.00
		b. Error w/o series, decreto or sign. overprinting.	25.00	45.00	75.00
166	500 PESOS BOLIVIANOS	D. 1.6.1981. Like #165 but Series B; C; Z. Printer: TDLR.	.10	.25	1.25

167	1000 PESOS BOLIVIANOS	D. 25.6.1982. Black on m/c unpt. Arms at ctr., Juana Z. de Padilla at r. and as wmk. at l. House of Liberty on back. Sign. varieties. Printer: TDLR. Series A-Z9; ZY; ZZ (6 digits) A-L; (8 digits, each only to 49,999,999); Z (8 digits).	.10	.25	1.25

Cat. #	Denomination	Date, description	VG	VF	Unc
168	5000 PESOS BOLIVIANOS	D. 10.2.1984. Deep brown and m/c. Arms at ctr., Mariscal J. Ballivian y Segurola at r. and as wmk. at l. Stylized condor and leopard on back. Printer: BDDK. Series A.	.20	.40	1.50
169	10,000 PESOS BOLIVIANOS	D. 10.2.1984. Blackish-purple and purple w/ dk. green arms on m/c unpt. Arms at ctr., Marshall A. de Santa Cruz at r. and as wmk. at l. Back brown, bluish purple and green; Legislative palace at ctr. Printer: BDDK. Series A; Z.	.10	.30	1.00

Cat. #	Denomination	Date, description	VG	VF	Unc
170	50,000 PESOS BOLIVIANOS	D. 5.6.1984. Deep green on m/c unpt. Arms at l., Villaroel at r. Petroleum refinery on back. Printer: TDLR. Series A; B; Z.	.10	.25	.75

Cat. #	Denomination	Date, description	VG	VF	Unc
171	100,000 PESOS BOLIVIANOS	D. 5.6.1984. Brown-violet on m/c unpt. Arms at l., Campesino at r. Agricultural scene at ctr. r. on back. Printer: TDLR. Series A; B; Z.	.15	.30	1.00

1982–86 MONETARY EMERGENCY
Cheques de Gerencia (Official Checks)
Decreto 28.7.1982

#172–173 Dk. gray on lt. lilac and pale olive-green unpt. Central Bank seal in unpt. at ctr. Uniface. Unissued remainders.

Cat. #	Denomination	Date, description	VG	VF	Unc
172	5000 PESOS BOLIVIANOS	D.1982.			
		a. Stub w/text attached at r.	—	—	15.00
		b. W/o stub at r.	—	—	10.00

Cat. #	Denomination	Date, description	VG	VF	Unc
173	10,000 PESOS BOLIVIANOS	D.1982.			
		a. Stub w/text attached at r.	—	—	10.00
		b. W/o stub at r.	—	—	7.00

SANTA CRUZ BRANCH
1984 ISSUE

#176; 178 black, Mercury in green circular unpt. at ctr.

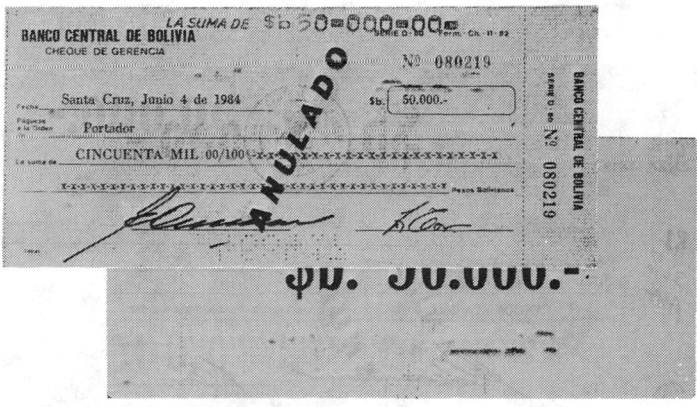

Cat. #	Denomination	Date, description	VG	VF	Unc
176	50,000 PESOS BOLIVIANOS	4.6.1984; 7.6.1984.			
		a. Issued note.	—	—	—
		b. Ovpt: *ANULADO* (cancelled) across face.	20.00	40.00	100.00
177	*Deleted.*				
178	1,000,000 PESOS BOLIVIANOS	4.6.1984; 7.6.1984.			
		a. Issued note.	—	—	—
		b. Ovpt: *ANULADO* across face.	30.00	60.00	120.00

LA PAZ BRANCH
1984 ISSUE

#180–182 like #176–178.

179	*Deleted.*				

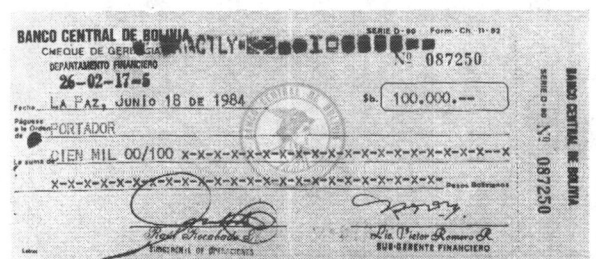

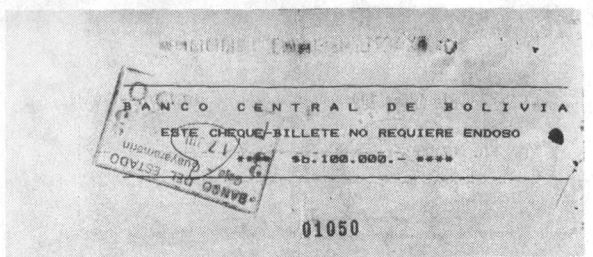

Cat. #	Denomination	Date, description	VG	VF	Unc
180	100,000 PESOS BOLIVIANOS	18.6.1984. Olive-green text on pale green unpt. Black text on back.			
		a. Issued note.	—	—	—
		b. Ovpt: *ANULADO* across face.	25.00	45.00	100.00
		c. Paid. Hole punched cancelled.	55.00	95.00	200.00

Cat. #	Denomination	Date, description	VG	VF	Unc
183	10,000 PESOS BOLIVIANOS	D.1984.	2.00	5.00	12.50

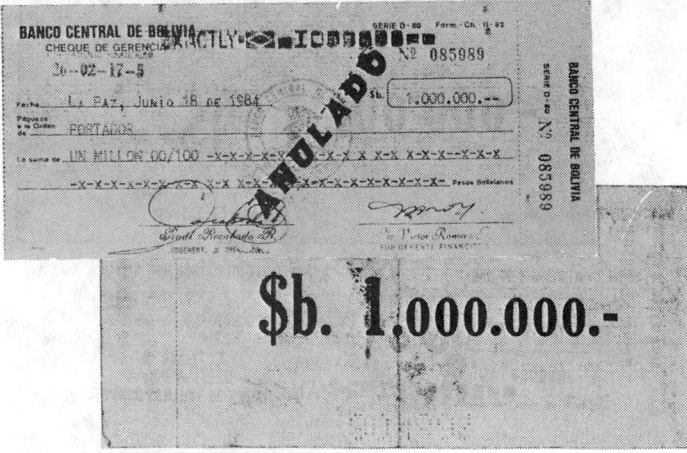

184	20,000 PESOS BOLIVIANOS	D.1984.	3.00	15.00	40.00

181	500,000 PESOS BOLIVIANOS	4.6.1984; 18.6.1984.			
		a. Issued note.	—	—	—
		b. Ovpt: *ANULADO* across face.	30.00	60.00	120.00
		c. Paid. Hole punched cancelled.	40.00	90.00	210.00

185	50,000 PESOS BOLIVIANOS	D.1984.	1.25	4.00	8.50

#186–187 like #183–185 but w/o 90-day use restriction text on back.

186	10,000 PESOS BOLIVIANOS	D.1984. Lt. blue on pink unpt. Series A.	.50	1.50	5.00

182	1,000,000 PESOS BOLIVIANOS	18.6.1984.			
		a. Issued note.	—	—	—
		b. Ovpt: *ANULADO* across face.	35.00	70.00	140.00
		c. Paid. Hole punched cancelled.	75.00	140.00	175.00

Decreto Supremo No. 20272, 5 June 1984

#183–185 brown on pink unpt. Mercury at upper l. Series A. Printer: JBNC. Usable for 90 days after date of issue (text in Spanish at lower r. on back).

NOTE: Unpt. of "B.C.B." and denom. boxes easily fade to lt. tan to pale yellow.

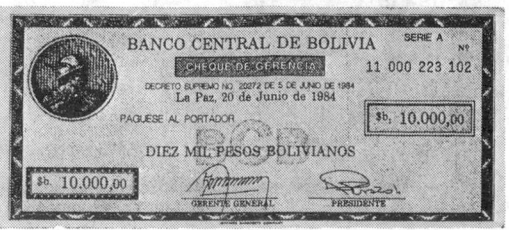

187	20,000 PESOS BOLIVIANOS	D.1984. Green on pink unpt. Series A.	1.00	2.50	7.50

#188 has 90-day use restriction clause similar to #183–185.

Cat. #	Denomination	Date, description	VG	VF	Unc
188	100,000 PESOS BOLIVIANOS	21.12.1984. Reddish-brown on lt. blue and lt. reddish-brown unpt. Series A. Imprint and wmk: CdMB.			
		a. Issued note.	.10	.50	1.75
		b. Error. Face only, back blank.	1.00	2.50	10.00

W/O BRANCH NAME

1984 ISSUE

189	500,000 PESOS BOLIVIANOS	D.1984. Deep green on green and peach unpt. No 90-day clause on back. Wmk: CdMB. W/o imprint.			
		a. Issued note.	.15	.60	3.00
		b. Error. Face only, back blank.	1.00	2.50	10.00

Decreto Supremo No. 20732, 8 March 1985

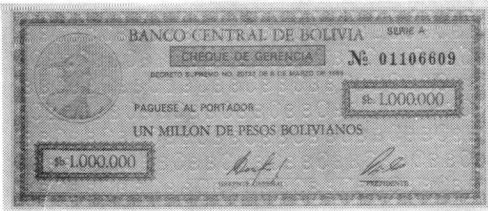

190	1 MILLION PESOS BOLIVIANOS	D.1985. Blue on yellow and pale blue unpt. Similar to previous issue. No 90-day restriction clause at lower r. on back. Series A. Wmk: CdMB. W/o imprint.	.25	1.00	4.50

#191–192 Series A. Printer: G&D.

Cat. #	Denomination	Date, description	VG	VF	Unc
191	5 MILLION PESOS BOLIVIANOS	D.1985. Brown-orange and red-brown on m/c unpt. Similar to previous issues but higher quality printing and appearance. M/c back; bank initials in ornate guilloche at ctr. No 90-day restriction clause.	2.00	6.50	12.50

192	10 MILLION PESOS BOLIVIANOS	D.1985. Rose and blue on tan unpt. Similar to #191.	3.00	10.00	22.50

#191A–192A similar to #191 and 192 but different style. Series B. Printer: CMB.

191A	5 MILLION PESOS BOLIVIANOS	D.1985. Similar to #191.	.85	2.50	5.50

192A	10 MILLION PESOS BOLIVIANOS	D.1985. Rose, violet and purple on m/c unpt. Similar to #192.	.75	3.25	6.50

#A193–194 printer: CdM-Argentina.

A193	1 MILLION PESOS BOLIVIANOS	D.1985. Blue and m/c. Lg. guilloche at l., Mercury head in unpt. at r. Series L.	.20	.75	3.00

Cat. #	Denomination	Date, description	VG	VF	Unc
193	5 MILLION PESOS BOLIVIANOS	*D.1985.* Brown w/reddish-brown text on m/c unpt. Similar to #A193. Series N.	.75	3.25	6.50

Cat. #	Denomination	Date, description	VG	VF	Unc
194	10 MILLION PESOS BOLIVIANOS	*D.1985.* Violet w/lilac text on m/c unpt. Similar to #A193. Series M.	3.00	6.00	15.00

Boliviano System

1 Centavo = 10,000 Pesos Bolivianos
1 Boliviano = 1,000,000 Pesos Bolivianos

1987 PROVISIONAL ISSUE

Cat. #	Denomination	Date, description	VG	VF	Unc
195	1 CENTAVO on 10,000 PB	ND (1987). Ovpt. at r. on back of #169.	.15	.35	1.25

Cat. #	Denomination	Date, description	VG	VF	Unc
196	5 CENTAVOS on 50,000 PB	ND (1987). Ovpt. at r. on back of #170.	.15	.35	1.25

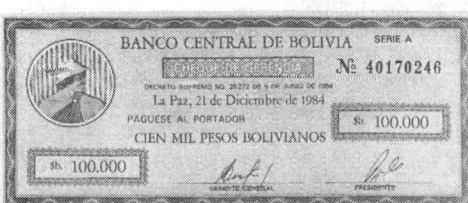

Cat. #	Denomination	Date, description	VG	VF	Unc
197	10 CENTAVOS on 100,000 PB	ND (1987). Ovpt. at r. on back of #188.	.15	.40	1.50

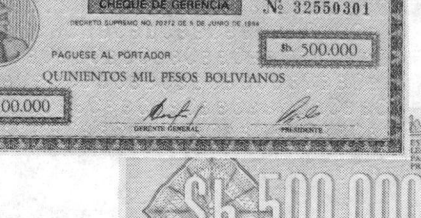

Cat. #	Denomination	Date, description	VG	VF	Unc
198	50 CENTAVOS on 500,000 PB	ND (1987). Ovpt. at r. on back of #189.	.15	.35	1.00

Cat. #	Denomination	Date, description	VG	VF	Unc
199	1 BOLIVIANO on 1,000,000 PB	ND (1987). Ovpt. at r. on back of #A193.	.25	.60	2.25

Cat. #	Denomination	Date, description	VG	VF	Unc
200	5 BOLIVIANOS on 5,000,000 PB	ND (1987). Ovpt. at l. or r. on back of #191A.	.50	2.50	5.00
		a. Issued note.	.50	2.50	5.00
		b. Error. Inverted overprint on left end.	2.00	5.50	15.00

Cat. #	Denomination	Date, description	VG	VF	Unc
201	10 BOLIVIANOS on 10,000,000 PB	ND (1987). Ovpt. at l. on back of #192A.	1.00	4.00	10.00

NOTE: During the preparation and overprinting of #195–201, a number of error notes were made. Examples: #195 with ovpt. at l. and r., #195 with 5 Centavos ovpt. at l. and 1 Centavo ovpt. at r., #196 with ovpt. at l. on face, ovpt. on #171 (wrong note), ovpt. on #188 (wrong note), and others. These errors were apparently made in quantities sufficient enough to have them available on the market from several sources. Prices vary from approximately $5 to $10 each.

1987; 1990 ISSUES
Ley 901 de 28-11-1986

#202–208 arms at lower l. or ctr. Issued under *L.28.11.1986*. Wmk: S. Bolivar. Printer: Oberthur
Series A. Sign. titles: *PRESIDENTE BCB* and *MINISTRO DE FINANZAS*. Serial # suffix *A*.
Series B. Sign. titles: *PRESIDENTE DEL B.C.B.* and *GERENTE GENERAL B.C.B.* Serial # suffix *B*.

202	2 BOLIVIANOS	*L.1986.* Black on m/c unpt. A. Vaca Diez at r. Trees and bldgs. at ctr. on back.			
		a. Series A (1987).	FV	FV	3.00
		b. Series B (1990).	FV	FV	4.00

203	5 BOLIVIANOS	*L.1986.* Olive-green on m/c unpt. Adela Zamudio at r. Religious shrine at l. ctr. on back.			
		a. Series A (1987).	FV	FV	5.00
		b. Series B (1990).	FV	FV	6.50

204	10 BOLIVIANOS	*L.1986.* Blue-black on m/c unpt. C. Guzman R. at r. Figures overlooking city view on back.			
		a. Series A (1987).	FV	FV	9.50
		b. Series B (1990).	FV	FV	12.50

Cat. #	Denomination	Date, description	VG	VF	Unc
205	20 BOLIVIANOS	*L.1986.* Orange and brown-orange on m/c unpt. P. Dalence at r. g. bldg. at ctr. on back.			
		a. Series A (1987).	FV	FV	20.00
		b. Series B (1990).	FV	FV	25.00
206	50 BOLIVIANOS	*L.1986* (1987). Purple on m/c unpt. M. Perez de Holguin at r. Tall bldg. at ctr. on back. Series A.	FV	FV	40.00

207	100 BOLIVIANOS	*L.1986* (1987). Red on m/c unpt. G. Rene Moreno at r. University bldg. at ctr. on back. Series A.	FV	FV	75.00

208	200 BOLIVIANOS	*L.1986* (1987). Brown on m/c unpt. F. Tamayo at r. Ancient statuary on back. Series A.	FV	FV	120.00

1993 ISSUE

#209–214 similar to #203-208 but many stylistic differences. Sign. titles: *PRESIDENTE BCB* and *GERENTE GENERAL BCB*. Serial # suffix *C*. Wmk: S. Bolivar. Printer: FNMT.

Cat. #	Denomination	Date, description	VG	VF	Unc
209	5 BOLIVIANOS	L.1986 (1993). Series C.	FV	FV	4.00

210	10 BOLIVIANOS	L.1986 (1993). Series C.	FV	FV	6.50

211	20 BOLIVIANOS	L.1986 (1993). Series C.	FV	FV	11.00

212	50 BOLIVIANOS	L.1986 (1993). Series C.	FV	FV	22.50

213	100 BOLIVIANOS	L.1986 (1993). Series C.	FV	FV	45.00

Cat. #	Denomination	Date, description	VG	VF	Unc
214	200 BOLIVIANOS	L.1986 (1993). Series C.	FV	FV	90.00

1995 FIRST ISSUE

#215 and 216 like #209 and 210 but w/4 control #. Wmk: S. Bolivar. Printer: TDLR.

215	5 BOLIVIANOS	L. 1986 (1995). Series C.	FV	FV	3.00

216	10 BOLIVIANOS	L. 1986 (1995). Series C.	FV	FV	5.50

1995 SECOND ISSUE

#217–220 like #209–212. Printer: TDLR.

Cat. #	Denomination	Date, description	VG	VF	Unc
217	**5 BOLIVIANOS**	L. 1986 (1995). Series D.	FV	FV	3.00

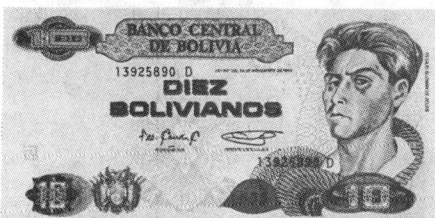

| 218 | **10 BOLIVIANOS** | L. 1986 (1995). Series D. | FV | FV | 5.50 |

| 219 | **20 BOLIVIANOS** | L. 1986 (1995). Series D. | FV | FV | 10.00 |

| 220 | **50 BOLIVIANOS** | L. 1986 (1995). Series D. | FV | FV | 20.00 |

The Republic of Bosnia-Herzegovina borders Croatia to the north and west, Serbia to the east and Montenegro in the southeast with only 12.4 miles of coastline. The total land area is 19,735 sq. mi. (51,129 sq. km.). They have a population of 4,366,000. Capital: Sarajevo. Electricity, mining and agriculture are leading industries.

Bosnia's first ruler of importance was the Ban Kulin, 1180–1204. Stephen Kotromanió was invested with Bosnia, held loyalty to Hungary and extended his rule to the principality of Hum or Zahumlje, the future Hercegovina. His daughter Elisabeth married Louis the Great and he died in the same year. His nephew Tvrtko succeeded and during the weakening of Serbian power he assumed the title "Stephen Tvrtko, in Christ God King of the Serbs and Bosnia and the Coastland." Later he assumed the title of "King of Dalmatia and Croatia," but died before he could consolidate power. Successors also asserted their right to the Serbian throne.

In 1459 the Turks invaded Serbia. Bosnia was invaded in 1463 and Hercegovina in 1483. During Turkish rule Islam was accepted rather than Catholicism. During the 16th and 17th centuries Bosnia was an important Turkish outpost in continuing warfare with the Hapsburgs and Venice. When Hungary was freed of the Turkish yoke, the Imperialists penetrated into Bosnia, and in 1697 Prince Eugene captured Sarajevo. Later, by the Treaty of Karlowitz in 1699, the northern boundary of Bosnia became the northernmost limit of the Turkish empire while the eastern area was ceded to Austria, but later restored to Turkey in 1739 lasting until 1878 following revolts of 1821, 1828, 1831 and 1862. On June 30, 1871 Serbia and Montenegro declared war on Turkey and were quickly defeated. The Turkish war with Russia led to the occupation by Austria-Hungary. Insurgents attempted armed resistance and Austria-Hungary invaded in mass, quelling the uprising in 1878. The Austrian occupation provided a period of prosperity while at the same time prevented relations with Serbia and Croatia. Strengthening political and religious movements from within forced the annexation by Austria on Oct. 7, 1908. Hungary's establishment of a dictatorship in Croatia following the victories of Serbian forces in the Balkan War roused the whole Yugoslav population of Austria-Hungary to feverish excitement. The Bosnian group, mainly students, devoted their efforts to revolutionary ideas. After Austria's Balkan front collapsed in Oct. 1918 the union with Yugoslavia developed and on Dec. 1, 1918 the former Kingdom of the Serbs, Croats and Slovenes was proclaimed (later to become the Kingdom of Yugoslavia on Oct. 3, 1929).

After the defeat of Germany in WW II during which Bosnia was under the control of Pavelic of Croatia, a new Socialist Republic was formed under Marshal Tito having six constituent republics all subservient, quite similar to the constitution of the U.S.S.R. Military and civil loyalty was with Tito. In Jan. 1990 the Yugoslav government announced a rewriting of the constitution, abolishing the Communist Party's monopoly of power. Opposition parties were legalized in July 1990. On Oct. 15, 1991 the National Assembly adopted a Memorandum on Sovereignty that envisaged Bosnian autonomy within a Yugoslav Federation. In March 1992 an agreement was reached under EC auspices by Moslems, Serbs and Croats to set up 3 autonomous ethnic communities under a central Bosnian authority. Independence was declared on April 5, 1992. The 2 Serbian members of government resigned and fighting broke out between all 3 ethnic communities. The United Nations is currently providing humanitarian aid while a recent peace treaty allowed NATO "Peace Keeping" forces be deployed in Dec. 1995 replacing the United Nations troops previously acting in a similar role.

NOTE: This section has been reorganized again, and referenced to the 1st Edition of Modern Issues.

1992 FIRST PROVISIONAL ISSUE

#1–2 violet handstamp NARODNA BANKA BOSNE I HERCEGOVINE, also in Cyrillic, around Yugoslav arms, on Yugoslav regular issues. Handstamp varieties exist.

Cat. #	Denomination	Date, description	Good	Fine	XF
1	**500 DINARA**	ND (1992). 31mm handstamp on Yugoslavia #107.			
		a. Handstamp w/o numeral.	10.00	22.00	55.00
		b. Handstamp w/numeral 1.	10.00	22.00	55.00

2	**1000 DINARA**	ND (1992). 48mm handstamp on Yugoslavia #108.			
		a. Handstamp w/o numeral.	16.00	35.00	90.00
		b. Handstamp w/numeral 1.	16.00	35.00	90.00
		c. Handstamp w/numeral 2.	16.00	35.00	90.00

3–4 held in reserve.

1992 SECOND PROVISIONAL ISSUE
Novcani Bon Series – Money Coupons

#5–9 issued in various Moslem cities. Dove of peace at upper l. ctr. Examples w/o indication of city of issue are remainders.

CITY CONTROL HANDSTAMPS AND OVPT.

a. BREZA	c. KRESEVO	e. VARES	g. ZENICA
b. FOJNICA	d. TESANJ	f. VISOKO	

Cat. #	Denomination	Date, description	Good	Fine	XF
5	*Deleted.*				

Cat. #	Denomination	Date, description	Good	Fine	XF
6	100 DINARA	1992. Deep pink on gray and yellow unpt.			
		a. Handstamped: *BREZA* on back.	3.00	9.00	25.00
		b. Circular red handstamp: *FOJNICA* on back.	2.50	7.50	22.50
		c. Rectangular purple handstamp on face, circular purple handstamp: *KRESEVO* on back.	6.50	20.00	60.00
		d. Handstamped: *TESANJ* on back.	6.50	20.00	60.00
		e. Handstamped: *VARES* on back.	2.50	7.50	22.50
		f. Handstamped: *VISOKO* on back (2 varieties).	2.00	6.00	18.00
		g. Circular red ovpt: *ZENICA, 11.5.1992.* on back r. W/printed sign. at either side.	1.00	3.00	9.00
		r. Remainder, w/o handstamp or ovpt.	.30	1.00	3.00

Cat. #	Denomination	Date, description	Good	Fine	XF
7	500 DINARA	1992. Pale greenish-gray on gray and yellow unpt.			
		a. Handstamped: *BREZA* on back.	2.50	8.00	24.00
		b. Circular red handstamp: *FOJNICA* on back.	2.50	7.50	22.50
		c. Handstamped: *KRESEVO* on back.	6.50	20.00	60.00
		d. Handstamped: *TESANJ* on back.	2.50	7.50	22.50
		e. Handstamped: *VARES* on back.	6.50	20.00	60.00
		f. Circular red handstamp: *VISOKO* on back.	4.50	14.00	42.00
		g. Circular red handstamp on back, details as #6g: *ZENICA* (small or large), *11.5.1992.*	1.00	3.00	9.00

Cat. #	Denomination	Date, description	Good	Fine	XF
8	1000 DINARA	1992. Blue on gray unpt.			
		a. Handstamped: *BREZA* on back.	5.00	16.00	48.00
		b. Handstamped: *FOJNICA* on back.	5.00	16.00	48.00
		c. Handstamped: *KRESEVO* on back.	8.00	25.00	75.00
		d. Handstamped: *TESANJ* on back.	6.50	20.00	60.00
		e. Handstamped: *VARES* on back.	6.50	20.00	60.00
		f. Handstamped: *VISOKO* on back (small or large).	2.00	6.00	18.00
		g. Handstamped: *ZENICA* on face, no date on stamping.	8.00	25.00	75.00
		h. Circular red ovpt. on back, details as 6g: *ZENICA, 11.5.1992.*	1.25	4.00	12.00

Cat. #	Denomination	Date, description	VG	VF	Unc
9	5000 DINARA	1992. Dull brown on gray and yellow unpt.			
		a. Handstamped: *BREZA* on back.	4.00	12.00	36.00
		b. Circular red handstamp: *FOJNICA* on back.	3.25	10.00	30.00
		c. Handstamped: *KRESEVO* on back.	6.50	20.00	60.00
		d. Handstamped: *TESANJ* on back.	10.00	30.00	—
		e. Handstamped: *VARES* on back.	3.25	10.00	30.00
		f. Handstamped: *VISOKO* on back (3 varieties).	2.00	6.00	18.00
		g. Handstamped: *ZENICA* on face, w/o date in stamping.	6.50	20.00	60.00
		h. Circular violet ovpt. on back, details as 6g: *ZENICA, 11.5.1992.*	1.00	3.00	9.00
		r. Remainder, w/o handstamp or ovpt.	5.00	16.00	48.00

MOSLEM REPUBLIC
РЕПУБЛИКА БОСНА И ХЕРЦЕГОВИНА
Republika Bosna I Hercegovina
НАРОДНА БАНКА БОСНЕ И ХЕРЦЕГОВИНЕ
Narodna Banka Bosne I Hercegovine
National Bank of Bosnia & Herzegovina

1992–93 ISSUES

#10–15 guilloche at l. ctr. 145x73mm. Wmk: Repeated diamonds. Printer: Cetis (Celje, Slovenia). #10–18 serial # varieties.

Cat. #	Denomination	Date, description	VG	VF	Unc
10	10 DINARA	1.7.1992. Purple on pink unpt. Mostar stone arch bridge at r. on back.			
		a. Issued note.	.10	.40	1.00
		s. Specimen.	—	—	30.00

Cat. #	Denomination	Date, description	VG	VF	Unc
11	25 DINARA	1.7.1992. Blue-black on lt. blue unpt. Crowned arms at ctr. r. on back.			
		a. Issued note.	.50	.50	1.25
		s. Specimen.	—	—	30.00

Cat. #	Denomination	Date, description	VG	VF	Unc
12	50 DINARA	1.7.1992. Blue-black on red-violet unpt. Mostar stone arch bridge at r. on back.			
		a. Issued note.	.20	.60	1.50
		s. Specimen.	—	—	30.00
12A	50 DINARA	ND (1993). Like #12 but reduced size.	—	—	—

Cat. #	Denomination	Date, description	VG	VF	Unc
13	100 DINARA	1.7.1992. Dull black on olive-green unpt. Crowned arms at ctr. r. on back.			
		a. Issued note.	.25	.75	1.75
		s. Specimen.	—	—	30.00

Cat. #	Denomination	Date, description	VG	VF	Unc
14	500 DINARA	1.7.1992. Dull violet-brown on pink and ochre unpt. Crowned arms at ctr. r. on back.			
		a. Issued note.	.50	1.50	3.50
		s. Specimen.	—	—	30.00

Cat. #	Denomination	Date, description	VG	VF	Unc
15	1000 DINARA	1.7.1992. Deep purple on lt. green and lilac unpt. Mostar stone arch bridge at r. on back.			
		a. Issued note.	.55	1.75	4.50
		s. Specimen.	—	—	30.00

#16 and 17 grayish-blue shield w/fleur-de-lis replaces crowned shield w/raised scimitar on back. Reduced size notes. Printed in Zenica.

Cat. #	Denomination	Date, description	VG	VF	Unc
16	5000 DINARA	25.1.1993. Pale olive-green on yellow-orange unpt.	1.00	3.00	7.50

Cat. #	Denomination	Date, description	VG	VF	Unc
17	10,000 DINARA	25.1.1993. Brown on pink unpt.	1.25	3.50	8.50
18	*Deleted*. See #29.				
19	*Deleted*. See #30.				
20	Held in reserve.				

National Bank (Moslem)

1992–93 BON ISSUE

#21–27 shield of arms at l. on back. Issued for Sarajevo area. Grayish-green or yellow unpt. on back.

Cat. #	Denomination	Date, description	VG	VF	Unc
21	10 DINARA	1.8.1992. Violet.			
		a. Issued note.	3.25	10.00	25.00
		s. Specimen.	—	—	30.00

Cat. #	Denomination	Date, description	VG	VF	Unc
22	20 DINARA	1.8.1992. Blue-violet.			
		a. Issued note.	3.25	10.00	25.00
		s. Specimen.	—	—	30.00

Cat. #	Denomination	Date, description		VG	VF	Unc
23	50 DINARA	1.8.1992. Pink.				
		a. Issued note.		3.25	10.00	25.00
		s. Specimen.		—	—	30.00

24	100 DINARA	1.8.1992. Green.				
		a. Issued note.		3.25	10.00	25.00
		s. Specimen.		—	—	30.00

25	500 DINARA	1.8.1992. Orange. Back red-orange on pale purple and grayish-green unpt.				
		a. Issued note.		3.25	10.00	25.00
		s. Specimen.		—	—	30.00

26	1000 DINARA	1.8.1992. Brown.				
		a. Issued note.		2.00	6.00	15.00
		s. Specimen.		—	—	30.00

27	5000 DINARA	1.8.1992. Violet.				
		a. Issued note.		2.25	7.00	18.00
		s. Specimen.		—	—	30.00

Cat. #	Denomination	Date, description		VG	VF	Unc
28	10,000 DINARA	6.4.1993. Lt. Blue.		2.25	7.00	18.00

29	50,000 DINARA	1.5.1993. Pink.		5.00	15.00	25.00

30	100,000 DINARA	1.8.1993. Green on m/c unpt. Back green on gray unpt.	1.65	5.00	12.00

31	100,000 DINARA	1.8.1993. Green. Back green on yellow unpt.	2.50	7.50	18.50

1993 EMERGENCY BON ISSUE

#33–35 not issued.

Cat. #	Denomination	Date, description	VG	VF	Unc
32 (30A)	100,000 DINARA	1993 (–old date 1.7.1992). Rectangular crenalated framed ovpt: *Novcani BON 100,000...* on face and back of 10 Dinara. #10.			
		a. Purple ovpt. 1.9.1993.	—	7.00	18.00
		b. Blue ovpt. and lt. blue sign. ovpt. 10.11.1993.	—	3.50	9.00
33	1 MILLION DINARA	10.11.1993 (old date–1.7.1992). Blue-violet ovpt on 25 Dinara, #11.	—	14.00	42.00

| 34 | 10 MILLION DINARA | 10.11.1993 (old date–1.7.1992). Blue-violet ovpt. on 50 Dinara, #12. | — | 12.00 | 36.00 |

| 35 | 100 MILLION DINARA | 10.11.1993 (old date–1.7.1992). Blue-violet on 100 Dinara, #12. | — | 12.00 | 36.00 |

1994 ISSUE

| 36 | 500 DINARA | 1.1.1994. Yellow unpt. | 1.65 | 5.00 | 15.00 |

| 37 (31) | 500,000 DINARA | 1.1.1994. Brown. Back: Brown on pale yellow-green unpt. | 2.50 | 7.50 | 18.50 |
| 38 (32) | 1 MILLION DINARA | 1.1.1994. Red. | 2.00 | 5.00 | 15.00 |

Currency Reform, 1994

1 'new' Dinar = 10,000 'old' Dinara

1994 ISSUE

#39-46 alternate with shield or Mostar stone bridge at ctr. r. on back.

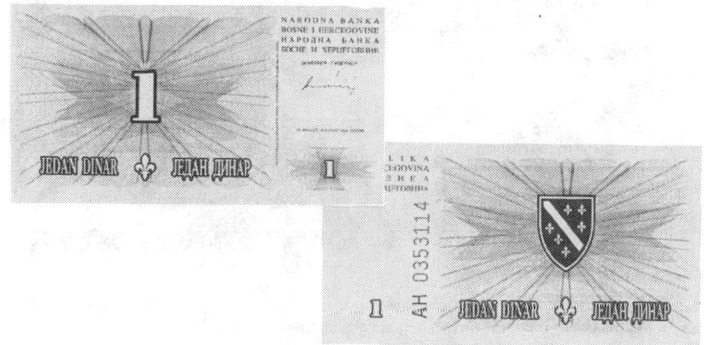

Cat. #	Denomination	Date, description	VG	VF	Unc
39 (33)	1 DINAR	15.8.1994. Purplish gray on red-violet and pale green unpt.			
		a. Issued note.	FV	FV	.35
		s. Specimen.	—	—	18.00

40 (34)	5 DINARA	15.8.1994. Purplish gray on lilac, red and orange unpt.			
		a. Issued note.	FV	FV	.50
		s. Specimen.	—	—	18.00

41 (35)	10 DINARA	15.8.1994. Purple on red, orange and red-violet unpt.			
		a. Issued note.	FV	FV	.65
		s. Specimen.	—	—	18.00

42 (36)	20 DINARA	15.8.1994. Brown on violet, red and yellow unpt.			
		a. Issued note.	FV	FV	1.00
		s. Specimen.	—	—	18.00

Cat. #	Denomination	Date, description	VG	VF	Unc
43 (37)	50 DINARA	15.8.1994. Purplish gray on red-violet and pale purple unpt.			
		a. Issued note.	FV	FV	1.25
		s. Specimen.	—	—	18.00

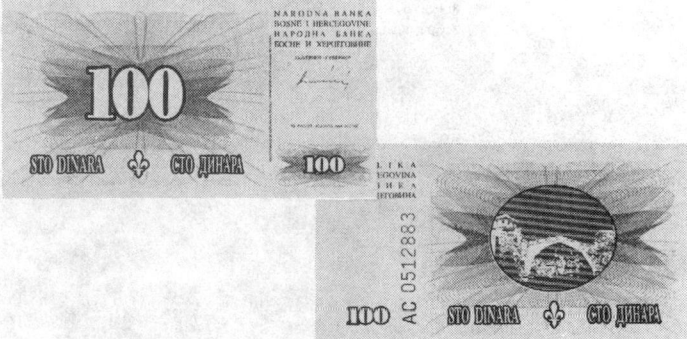

44 (38)	100 DINARA	15.8.1994. Dull black on aqua, yellow and olive-green unpt.			
		a. Issued note.	FV	FV	1.75
		s. Specimen.	—	—	18.00

45 (39)	500 DINARA	15.8.1994. Brown on pink, red and yellow-green unpt.			
		a. Issued note.	FV	FV	6.00
		s. Specimen.	—	—	18.00

46	1000 DINARA	15.8.1994. Blue-gray on gray-green, red-violet and lt. green unpt.			
		a. Issued note.	FV	FV	12.00
		s. Specimen.	—	—	18.00

SERBIAN REPUBLIC

НАРОДНА БАНКА СРПСЕ РЕПУБЛИКЕ БОСНЕ И ХЕРЦЕГОВИНЕ

Narodna Banka Srpske Republike Bosne I Hercegovine

National Bank of the Serbian Republic of Bosnia & Herzegovina

1992-93 BANJA LUKA ISSUE

#133–139 arms at l., numerals in heart-shaped design below guilloche at ctr. r. Curved artistic design at l. ctr., arms at r. on back.

#133–135 wmk: Portr. of a young girl.

Cat. #	Denomination	Date, description	VG	VF	Unc
133	10 DINARA	1992. Deep brown or orange and silver unpt. Back with ochre unpt.			
		a. Issued note.	.10	.35	1.00
		s. Specimen.	—	—	12.50

134	50 DINARA	1992. Deep olive-gray on ochre and m/c unpt.			
		a. Issued note.	.15	.40	1.25
		s. Specimen.	—	—	12.50

135	100 DINARA	1992. Dk. blue on lilac and silver unpt.			
		a. Issued note.	.35	1.00	3.00
		s. Specimen.	—	—	12.50

#136–140 wmk: Portr. of a young boy.

Cat. #	Denomination	Date, description	VG	VF	Unc
136	500 DINARA	1992. Dk. blue on pink and m/c unpt.			
		a. Issued note.	.65	2.00	6.00
		s. Specimen.	—	—	12.50

137	1000 DINARA	1992. Slate gray on pink and tan unpt. Back with orange unpt.			
		a. Issued note.	.40	1.20	3.50
		s. Specimen.	—	—	12.50
138	5000 DINARA	1992. Violet on lilac and lt. blue unpt.			
		a. Issued note.	.40	1.20	3.50
		s. Specimen.	—	—	12.50
139	10,000 DINARA	1992. Gray on tan and lt. blue unpt.			
		a. Issued note.	.40	1.20	3.50
		s. Specimen.	—	—	12.50
140	50,000 DINARA	1993. Brown on olive-green and m/c unpt.			
		a. Issued note.	.40	1.20	3.50
		s. Specimen.	—	—	12.50

NOTE: For similar notes to #136-140 but differing only in text at top, sign., and Knin as place of issue, see Croatia-Regional.

141	100,000 DINARA	1993. Purple on brown and m/c unpt. Wmk: Portr. of young woman w/headcovering.			
		a. Issued note.	.40	1.35	4.00
		s. Specimen.	—	—	15.00

#142-144 wmk: Portr. of a young girl.

142	1 MILLION DINARA	1993. Dp. purple on pink, yellow and m/c unpt.			
		a. Issued note.	.40	1.35	4.00
		s. Specimen.	—	—	15.00

Cat. #	Denomination	Date, description	VG	VF	Unc
143	5 MILLION DINARA	1993. Dk. brown on lt. blue and yellow-orange unpt.			
		a. Issued note.	.40	1.50	4.50
		s. Specimen.	—	—	15.00

144	10 MILLION DINARA	1993. Dk. blue-violet on olive-green and yellow-orange unpt.			
		a. Issued note.	.50	1.50	4.50
		s. Specimen.	—	—	15.00

NOTE: For similar notes to #141-144 but differing only in text at top, sign., and Knin as place of issue, see Croatia-Regional.

НАРОДНА БАНКА РЕПУБЛИКЕ СРПСКЕ
Narodna Banka Republike Srpske
National Bank of the Serbian Republic
1993 BANJA LUKA FIRST ISSUE

#145-148 wmk: Greek design repeated.

145	50 MILLION DINARA	1993. Dk. brown on pink and gray unpt.			
		a. Issued note.	.85	2.50	7.50
		s. Specimen.	—	—	15.00

146	100 MILLION DINARA	1993. Pale blue-gray on lt. blue and gray unpt.			
		a. Issued note.	.50	1.65	5.00
		s. Specimen.	—	—	15.00

147	1 MILLIARD DINARA	1993. Orange on pale blue and lt. orange unpt.			
		a. Issued note.	.65	2.00	6.00
		s. Specimen.	—	—	15.00

Cat. #	Denomination	Date, description	VG	VF	Unc
148	10 MILLIARD DINARA	1993. Black on pink and pale orange unpt.			
		a. Issued note.	1.00	3.00	9.00
		s. Specimen.	—	—	15.00

NOTE: For similar notes to #145–148 but differing only in text at top, sign., and Knin as place of issue, see Croatia – Regional.

Currency Reform, 1993

1 Dinar = 1,000,000 "old" Dinara

1993 BANJA LUKA SECOND ISSUE

#149–155 P. Kocic at l. Serbian arms at ctr. r. on back. Wmk: Greek design repeated.

Cat. #	Denomination	Date, description	VG	VF	Unc
149	5000 DINARA	1993. Red-violet and purple on pale blue-gray unpt.			
		a. Issued note.	.35	1.00	3.00
		s. Specimen.	—	—	15.00

Cat. #	Denomination	Date, description	VG	VF	Unc
150	50,000 DINARA	1993. Brown and dull red on ochre unpt.			
		a. Issued note.	.50	1.25	4.00
		s. Specimen.	—	—	15.00

Cat. #	Denomination	Date, description	VG	VF	Unc
151	100,000 DINARA	1993. Violet and blue-gray on pink unpt.			
		a. Issued note.	.40	1.35	4.00
		s. Specimen.	—	—	15.00

Cat. #	Denomination	Date, description	VG	VF	Unc
152	1 MILLION DINARA	1993. Black and blue-gray on pale purple unpt.			
		a. Issued note.	.65	2.00	6.00
		s. Specimen.	—	—	15.00

Cat. #	Denomination	Date, description	VG	VF	Unc
153	5 MILLION DINARA	1993. Orange and gray-blue on pale orange unpt.			
		a. Issued note.	.90	2.75	8.50
		s. Specimen.	—	—	15.00
154	100 MILLION DINARA	1993. Dull grayish-green and pale olive-brown on lt. blue unpt.			
		a. Issued note.	1.20	3.50	10.00
		s. Specimen.	—	—	15.00

Cat. #	Denomination	Date, description	VG	VF	Unc
155	500 MILLION DINARA	1993. Brown-violet and grayish green on pale olive-brown unpt.			
		a. Issued note.	1.20	3.50	10.00
		s. Specimen.	—	—	15.00

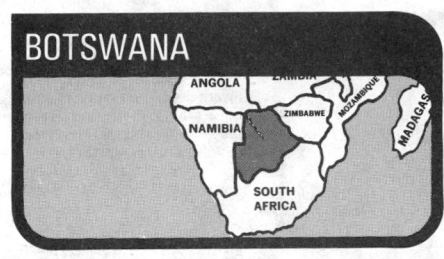

BOTSWANA

The Republic of Botswana (formerly Bechuanaland), located in south central Africa between Southwest Africa, (Namibia) and Zimbabwe has an area of 231,805 sq. mi (600,372 sq. km.) and a population of 1.35 million. Capital: Gaborone. Botswana is a member of a Customs Union with South Africa, Lesotho, and Swaziland. The economy is primarily pastoral with a rapidly developing mining industry, of which diamonds, copper and nickel are the chief elements. Meat products and diamonds comprise 85 percent of the exports.

Little is known of the origin of the peoples of Botswana. The early inhabitants, the Bushmen, did not develop a recorded history and are now dying out. The ancestors of the present Botswana probably arrived about 1600 AD in Bantu migrations from the north and east. Bechuanaland was first united early in the 19th century under Chief Khama III to more effectively resist incursions by the Boer trekkers from Transvaal and by the neighboring Matabeles. As the Boer threat intensified, appeals for protection were made to the British Government, which proclaimed the whole of Bechuanaland a British protectorate in 1885. In 1895, the southern part of the protectorate was annexed to Cape Province. The northern part, known as the Bechuanaland Protectorate, remained under British administration until it became the independent Republic of Botswana on Sept. 30, 1966. Botswana is a member of the Commonwealth of Nations. The president is Chief of State and Head of Government.

MONETARY SYSTEM

1 Pula (Rand) = 100 Thebe (Cents)

REPLACEMENT NOTES

#1–10, Z/1 prefix.

SIGNATURE VARIETIES

1	*Masire signature*	4	*P. S. Mmusi signature*
2	*Masire signature*	5	*P. S. Mmusi signature*
3	*P. S. Mmusi signature*	6	*signature*

Bank of Botswana

FIRST ISSUE

#1–5 Pres. Sir S. Khama at l., arms at upper r. Wmk: Rearing zebra. Printer: TDLR.

Cat. #	Denomination	Date, description	VG	VF	Unc
1	1 PULA	ND (1976). Brown and m/c. Milking cow on back.	.50	1.50	3.50

Cat. #	Denomination	Date, description	VG	VF	Unc
2	2 PULA	ND (1976). Blue and m/c. Various workers on back.	1.00	3.00	6.00

Cat. #	Denomination	Date, description	VG	VF	Unc
3	5 PULA	ND (1976). Purple and m/c. Gemsbok antelope on back.	2.50	7.00	20.00
4	10 PULA	ND (1976). Green and m/c. Lg. bldg. on back.			
		a. Sign. 1.	5.00	17.50	50.00
		b. Sign. 2.	10.00	60.00	150.00
5	20 PULA	ND (1979). Red and m/c. Mining conveyors on back.			
		a. Sign. 1.	15.00	75.00	175.00
		b. Sign. 2.	20.00	100.00	250.00

SECOND ISSUE

Cat. #	Denomination	Date, description	VG	VF	Unc
6	1 PULA	ND (1983). Dk. brown. Pres. O. Masire at l. Animals, plants and arms at ctr. on back.	.15	1.20	3.50

#7–10 Pres. O. Masire at l. Like #2–5. Wmk: Rearing zebra.

Cat. #	Denomination	Date, description	VG	VF	Unc
7	2 PULA	ND (1982). Blue and m/c.			
		a. Sign. 3.	FV	1.75	4.50
		b. Sign. 4.	FV	1.75	4.00
		c. Sign. 5.	FV	1.50	3.50
		d. Sign. 6.	FV	1.50	3.50

Cat. #	Denomination	Date, description	VG	VF	Unc
8	5 PULA	ND (1982). Deep violet and m/c.			
		a. Sign. 3.	FV	4.25	9.50
		b. Sign. 4.	FV	4.25	9.00
		c. Sign. 5.	FV	4.00	8.50

Cat. #	Denomination	Date, description	VG	VF	Unc
9	10 PULA	ND (1982). Green and m/c.			
		a. Sign. 3.	FV	7.00	17.50
		b. Sign. 4.	FV	7.00	16.00
		c. Sign. 5.	FV	7.00	15.00
		d. Sign. 6.	FV	7.00	13.00

Cat. #	Denomination	Date, description		VG	VF	Unc
10	20 PULA	ND (1982). Red and m/c.				
		a. Sign. 3.		FV	15.00	30.00
		b. Sign. 4.		FV	15.00	28.50
		c. Sign. 5.		FV	15.00	27.50
		d. Sign. 6.		FV	15.00	27.50

#11–15 Pres. O. Masire at l. Wmk: Rearing zebra. Metallic thread to r. of portr.

#11–13 printer: Harrison.

Cat. #	Denomination	Date, description	VG	VF	Unc
11	5 PULA	ND(1992). Similar to #8; sm. stylistic differences. Sign. 6.	FV	FV	6.00
12	10 PULA	ND(1992). Similar to #9; sm. stylistic differences. Sign. 6.	FV	FV	10.00
13	20 PULA	ND (1993). Similar to #10.	FV	FV	18.00

Cat. #	Denomination	Date, description	VG	VF	Unc
14	50 PULA	ND(1992). Brown and dk. green on m/c unpt. Pres. Masire at l., bird at ctr., arms at upper r. Man in canoe and bird w/fish on back. W/o imprint.	FV	FV	35.00
15	100 PULA	ND (1993). Purplish-blue, lt. brown and m/c. Pres. Masire at l., diamond and eagle at ctr. and r. Worker sorting rough diamonds on back.	FV	FV	60.00

COLLECTOR SERIES

Cat. #	Date, denomination	Description	Issue Price.	Mkt. Val.
CS1	ND (1979) 1–20 PULA	#1–5 ovpt: *SPECIMEN* and Maltese cross prefix serial #.	14.00	25.00
CS2	ND (1982) 1–20 PULA	#1–5 ovpt: *SPECIMEN* w/4 punched hole cancellation.	—	20.00
CS3	ND (1982) 1–20 PULA	#6–10 ovpt: *SPECIMEN* w/4 punched hole cancellation.	—	15.00

NOTE: #CS2 and CS3 were released in quantity by the Bank of Botswana.

BRAZIL

The Federative Republic of Brazil, which comprises half the continent of South America, is the only Latin American country deriving its culture and language from Portugal. It has an area of 3,286,470 sq. mi. (8,511,965 sq. km.) and a population of 146 million. Capital: Brasilia. The economy of Brazil is as varied and complex as any in the developing world. Agriculture is a mainstay of the economy, although but 4 percent of the area is under cultivation. Known mineral resources are almost unlimited in variety and size of reserves. A large, relatively sophisticated industry ranges from basic steel and chemical production to finished consumer goods. Coffee, cotton, iron ore and cocoa are the chief exports.

Brazil was discovered and claimed for Portugal by Admiral Pedro Alvares Cabral in 1500. Portugal established a settlement in 1532 and proclaimed the area a royal colony in 1549. During the Napoleonic Wars, Dom Joao VI established the seat of Portuguese government in Rio de Janeiro. When he returned to Portugal, his son Dom Pedro I declared Brazil's independence on Sept. 7, 1822, and became emperor of Brazil. The Empire of Brazil was maintained until 1889 when the federal republic was established. The Federative Republic was established in 1946 by terms of a constitution drawn up by a constituent assembly. Following a coup in 1964 the armed forces retained overall control under a dictatorship until a civilian government was restored on March 15, 1985. The current constitution was adopted in 1988.

MONETARY SYSTEM

1 Cruzeiro = 100 Centavos, 1942–67
1 Cruzeiro Novo = 1000 Old Cruzeiros, 1967–85
1 Cruzado = 1000 Cruzeiros Novos, 1986–89
1 Cruzado Novo = 1000 Cruzados, 1989–90
1 Cruzeiro = 1 Cruzado Novo, 1990–93
1 Cruzeiro Real (pl. Reais) = 1000 Cruzeiros, 93–

REPLACEMENT NOTES

#191–196, * after top row of numbers.

#197–211, sm. star instead of prefix letter.

#216-233, * prefix.

Tesouro Nacional, Valor Recebido

ESTAMPA 3

Cat. #	Denomination	Date, description	Series	VG	VF	Unc
166	5 CRUZEIROS	ND (1961–62). Dk. brown and brown. Raft w/sail at l., male Indian at r. Flower on back. Printer: CdM-B.				
		a. Sign. S. Paes de Almeida and C. Augusto Carrilho (1961).	1–75	.10	.30	1.00
		b. Sign. R. W. Moreira Salles and Fernandes Nunes (1961–62).	76–111	.10	.30	1.00

Tesouro Nacional, Valor Legal

ESTAMPA 1A

#167–173 dk. blue on m/c guilloches, 2 printed sign. Printer: ABNC.

Cat. #	Denomination	Date, description	Series	VG	VF	Unc
167	10 CRUZEIROS	ND (1961–63). Portr. G. Vargas at ctr. Back green; allegory of "Industry" at ctr.				
		a. Sign. C. Augusto Carrilho and C. Mariani (1961).	331–630	.15	.50	1.50
		b. Sign. R. Fernandes Nunes and M. Calmon du Pin (1963).	631–930	.15	.50	1.50
168	20 CRUZEIROS	ND (1961–63). Portr. D. da Fonseca at ctr. Back red; allegory of "the Republic" at ctr.				
		a. Sign. C. Augusto Carrilho and C. Mariani (1961).	461–960	.15	.50	2.00
		b. Sign. R. Fernandes Nunes and M. Calmon du Pin (1963).	961–1260	.15	.50	2.00

Cat. #	Denomination	Date, description	Series	VG	VF	Unc
169	50 CRUZEIROS	ND (1961). Portr. Princess Isabel at ctr. Back purple; allegory of "Law" at ctr. Sign. C. Augusto Carrilho and C. Mariani.	721–1220	.15	.65	3.50

Cat. #	Denomination	Date, description	Series	VG	VF	Unc
170	100 CRUZEIROS	ND (1961–64). Portr. D. Pedro at ctr. Back red-brown; allegory of "National Culture" at ctr.				
		a. Sign. C. Augusto Carrilho and C. Mariani (1961).	761–1160	.30	1.25	5.50
		b. Sign. R. Fernandes Nunes and O. Gouvea de Bulhoes (1964).	1161–1360	.30	1.00	5.00
		c. Sign. S. Augusto Ribeiro and O. Gouvea de Bulhoes (1964).	1361–1560	.30	1.50	6.00
171	200 CRUZEIROS	ND (1961–64). Portr. D. Pedro at ctr. Back olive-green; battle scene at ctr.				
		a. Sign. C. Augusto Carrilho and C. Mariani (1961).	671–1070	.50	1.50	7.50
		b. Sign. R. Fernandes Nunes and O. Gouvea de Bulhoes (1964).	1071–1370	.50	1.50	6.50
		c. Sign. S. Augusto Ribeiro and O. Gouvea de Bulhoes (1964).	1371–1570	.50	1.50	7.50

Cat. #	Denomination	Date, description	Series	VG	VF	Unc
172	500 CRUZEIROS	ND (1961–62). Portr. D. Joao VI at ctr. Back blue-black; allegory of "Maritime Industry" at ctr.				

Cat. #	Denomination	Date, description	Series	VG	VF	Unc
		a. Sign. C. Augusto Carrilho and C. Mariani (1961).	261–660	1.00	3.00	12.50
		b. Sign. R. Fernandes Nunes and W. Moreira Salles (1962).	661–1460	.75	2.50	12.00
173	1000 CRUZEIROS	ND (1961–63). Portr. P. Alvares Cabral at ctr. Back orange; scene of the "First Mass" at ctr.				
		a. Sign. C. Augusto Carrilho and C. Mariani (1961).	1331–1730	.75	3.00	27.50
		b. Sign. R. Fernandes Nunes and W. Moreira Salles (1962).	1731–3030	.75	3.00	18.50
		c. Sign. R. Fernandes Nunes and M. Calmon du Pin (1963).	3031–3830	1.00	4.00	15.00

Cat. #	Denomination	Date, description	Series	VG	VF	Unc
174	5000 CRUZEIROS	ND (1963–64). Blue-grayish. Portr. Tiradentes at r. Back red; Tiradentes in historical scene at ctr. Printer: ABNC.				
		a. Sign. R. Fernandes Nunes and M. Calmon du Pin (1963).	1–400	1.00	4.50	18.50
		b. Sign. R. Fernandes Nunes and O. Gouvea de Bulhoes (1964).	401–1400	1.00	4.00	16.00
		c. Sign. S. Augusto Ribeiro and O. Gouvea de Bulhoes (1964).	1401–1650	1.75	7.00	27.50
175		*Deleted.* See #182A.				

ESTAMPA 2A

#176–182 2 printed sign. Printer: TDLR.

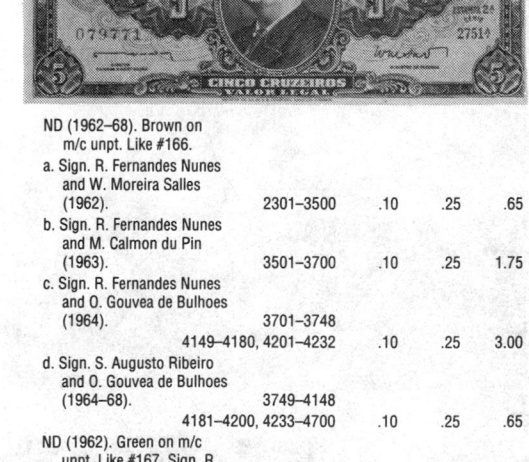

Cat. #	Denomination	Date, description	Series	VG	VF	Unc
176	5 CRUZEIROS	ND (1962–68). Brown on m/c unpt. Like #166.				
		a. Sign. R. Fernandes Nunes and W. Moreira Salles (1962).	2301–3500	.10	.25	.65
		b. Sign. R. Fernandes Nunes and M. Calmon du Pin (1963).	3501–3700	.10	.25	1.75
		c. Sign. R. Fernandes Nunes and O. Gouvea de Bulhoes (1964).	3701–3748			
			4149–4180, 4201–4232	.10	.25	3.00
		d. Sign. S. Augusto Ribeiro and O. Gouvea de Bulhoes (1964–68).	3749–4148			
			4181–4200, 4233–4700	.10	.25	.65
177	10 CRUZEIROS	ND (1962). Green on m/c unpt. Like #167. Sign. R. Fernandes Nunes and W. Moreira Salles.	2365–3055	.10	.25	.75

Cat. #	Denomination	Date, description	Series	VG	VF	Unc
178	20 CRUZEIROS	ND (1962). Red-brown. Like #168. Sign. R. Fernandes Nunes and W. Moreira Salles.	1576–2275	.15	.30	1.00
179	50 CRUZEIROS	ND (1963.) Purple on m/c unpt. Like #169. Sign. R. Fernandes Nunes and M. Calmon du Pin.	586–785	.25	1.00	4.00
180	100 CRUZEIROS	ND (1963). Red. Like #170. Sign. R. Fernandes Nunes and M. Calmon du Pin.	216–415	.35	1.50	6.00

Cat. #	Denomination	Date, description	Series	VG	VF	Unc
181	1000 CRUZEIROS	ND (1963). Orange on m/c unpt. Like #173. Sign. R. Fernandes Nunes and M. Calmon du Pin.	791–1590	.50	1.50	8.00
182	5000 CRUZEIROS	ND (1963–64). Red. Like #174. Sign. at l. w/Director Caixa de Amortizacao.				
	a.	Sign. R. Fernandes Nunes and M. Calmon du Pin (1963).	1–400	1.00	3.50	15.50
	b.	Sign. R. Fernandes Nunes and O. Gouvea de Bulhoes (1964).	401–1400	.85	3.00	15.00
	c.	Sign. S. Augusto Ribeiro and O. Gouvea de Bulhoes (1964).	1401–1700	1.50	5.00	25.00

Banco Central do Brazil

1965–66 ISSUE

A182	5000 CRUZEIROS	ND (1965). Red on m/c unpt. Like #174. Sign. D. Nogueira w/title: Presidente do Banco Central and O. Gouvea de Bulhoes.	1701–2200	1.00	3.50	16.50

182A	10,000 CRUZEIROS	ND (1966). Gray on m/c unpt. Portr. S. Dumont at r. Back blue; early airplane at r. Sign. D. Nogueira and O. Gouvea de Bulhoes. Printer: ABNC.				
	a.		1–493	4.00	16.00	40.00
	b.		561–590	20.00	80.00	200.00

Currency Reform, 1966

1 Cruzeiro Novo = 1000 "old" Cruzeiros

1966–67 PROVISIONAL ISSUE

#183–190 black circular ovpt: *BANCO CENTRAL* and new currency unit on Tesouro Nacional notes.

Cat. #	Denomination	Date, description	Series	VG	VF	Unc
183	1 CENTAVO on 10 Cruzeiros	ND (1966–67). Green on m/c unpt. Ovpt. on #177. Sign. D. Nogueira and O. Gouvea de Bulhoes.				
	a.	Error: *Minstro* below r. sign. (2 types of *1* in ovpt.) (1966).	3056–3151	.10	.20	.60
	b.	*Ministro* below r. sign. (1967).	3152–4055	.10	.20	.50
184	5 CENTAVOS on 50 Cruzeiros	ND (1966–67). Purple on m/c unpt. Ovpt. on #179. Sign. D. Nogueira and O. Gouvea de Bulhoes.				
	a.	Type of #183a.	786–1313	.10	.20	.60
	b.	Type of #183b.	1314–1885	.10	.20	.50

185	10 CENTAVOS on 100 Cruzeiros	ND (1966–67). Red on m/c unpt. Ovpt. on #180. Sign. D. Nogueira and O. Gouvea de Bulhoes.				
	a.	Type of #183a.	416–911	.10	.30	.85
	b.	Type of #183b.	912–1515	.10	.30	.85

186	50 CENTAVOS on 500 Cruzeiros	ND (1967). Blue on m/c unpt. Ovpt. on #172. Sign. D. Nogueira and O. Gouvea de Bulhoes.	1461–2360	.20	.50	2.00

187	1 CRUZEIRO N. on 1000 Cruzeiros	ND (1966–67). Blue on m/c unpt. Ovpt. on #173.				
	a.	Sign. S. Augusto Ribeiro and O. Gouvea de Bulhoes. (1966).	3831–3930	.25	.65	3.00
	b.	Sign. D. Nogueira and O. Gouvea de Bulhoes (1967).	3931–4830	.25	.60	2.50

Cat. #	Denomination	Date, description	Series	VG	VF	Unc
188	5 CRUZEIROS N. on 5000 Cruzeiros	ND (1966–67). Blue-green on m/c unpt. Ovpt. on #174.				
		a. Sign. S. Augusto Ribeiro and O. Gouvea de Bulhoes (1966–67).	1651–1700	1.00	4.50	15.00
		b. Sign. D. Nogueira and O. Gouvea de Bulhoes (1967).	1701–2900	.75	3.00	10.00

Cat. #	Denomination	Date, description	Series	VG	VF	Unc
189	10 CRUZEIROS N. on 10,000 Cruzeiros	ND (1966–67). Gray on m/c unpt. Bold or semi-bold ovpt. on #182A. Printer: ABNC.				
		a. Sign. D. Nogueira and O. Gouvea de Bulhoes (1966–67).	494–560 and 591–700	1.00	4.00	15.00
		b. Sign. R. Leme and A. Delfim Netto (1967).	701–1700	.75	3.00	10.00
		c. Sign. E. Galveas and A. Delfim Netto (1967).	1701–2700	.75	3.00	10.00
190	10 CRUZEIROS N. on 10,000 Cruzeiros	ND (1967). Brown, pink and m/c. Like #182A. Printer: TDLR.				
		a. Sign. R. Leme and A. Delfim Netto (1967).	1–1000	.75	3.00	10.00
		b. Sign. E. Galveas and A. Delfim Netto (1967).	1001–2100	.75	3.00	10.00

1970 ISSUES

#191–195 portr. as wmk. Sign. varieties.

#191–194, 195A printer: CdM-B.

Cat. #	Denomination	Date, description	Series	VG	VF	Unc
191 (191a)	1 CRUZEIRO	ND (1970–72). Dk. green. Bldg. at l. on back. W/medallic Liberty head at r. in brown. Serial # prefix A (1970–72).	1–3000	.20	.50	1.50
191A (191b)		ND (1972–81). Dk. green w/medallic Liberty head in green. Serial # prefix B (1972–81).	1–18094	.10	.25	.50

Cat. #	Denomination	Date, description	Series	VG	VF	Unc
192	5 CRUZEIROS	ND (1970). Blue on orange and green unpt. Portr. D. Pedro I at r. Back maroon; parade square.				
		a. Back darkly printed. Serial # prefix A (1970–71).	1–107	.10	.60	3.00
		b. Back lightly printed. Serial # prefix B (1973–79).	1–6841	.10	.25	.75

193	10 CRUZEIROS	ND (1970–80). Portr. D. Pedro II at r. Back green and brown; statue of the Prophet Daniel.				
		a. Brown, violet and green. Back darkly printed. Serial # prefix A (1970–78).	1–7745	.10	.50	2.50
		b. Brown and violet. Back lightly printed. Serial # prefix B (1979–80).	1–5131	.10	.25	1.00

194	50 CRUZEIROS	ND (1970–81). Black and violet on blue-black, lilac and m/c unpt. Portr. Mal. Deodora da Fonseca at r. Back brown, lilac and blue; coffee loading.	1–5233	.10	.25	.75

Cat. #	Denomination	Date, description	Series	VG	VF	Unc
195	100 CRUZEIROS	ND (1970–81). Carmine and violet. Portr. Marshal F. Peixoto at r. Back blue, brown and violet; National Congress. Printer: TDLR.	1–00500	1.00	3.00	25.00
195A	100 CRUZEIROS	ND. Like #195. Printer: CdM-B.	00501–12681	.25	.75	3.50

1972 COMMEMORATIVE ISSUE

#196, 150th Anniversary of Brazilian Independence

196	500 CRUZEIROS	1972 (1972/1822 dates in wmk.). Green, purple and m/c. Portraits of 5 men of differing racial groups. 5 different historical maps of Brazil on back. Printer: CdM-B. Sign. varieties.				
		a. A serial # (1972–79).	1–2636	1.00	5.00	15.00
		b. B serial # w/green lines and ornaments at l. (1979–80).	1–2763	.50	1.50	4.50

1978 ISSUE

#197–205 portr. as wmk. Sign. varieties. Printer: CdM-B.

#197–202 double portr. and vignettes.

197	1000 CRUZEIROS	ND (1978–80). Green and brown. B. do Rio Branco. *BANCO CENTRAL DO BRASIL* in 2 lines. Double view of machinery on back. Also, small plate modification on back.	1–3297	1.00	5.00	17.50

1981–85 ISSUE

Cat. #	Denomination	Date, description	VG	VF	Unc
198	100 CRUZEIROS	ND (1981). Red, purple and m/c. D. de Caxias. Back gray–blue and red; battle scene and sword.	.10	.15	.25

199	200 CRUZEIROS	ND (1981). Green, violet and m/c. Princess Isabel. Back brown and green; 2 women cooking outdoors.	.10	.15	.30

200	500 CRUZIEROS	ND (1981). Blue, brown and m/c. D. da Fonseca. Back pink, brown and purple; group of legislators.	.10	.20	.50

Cat. #	Denomination	Date, description	VG	VF	Unc
201	1000 CRUZEIROS	ND (1981). Brown, dk. olive and m/c. Similar to #197, but bank name in 1 line. Back tan and blue.	.10	.20	.50

| 202 | 5000 CRUZEIROS | ND (1981). Purple, brown and m/c. C. Branco. Back brown, purple and blue; antennas. | .10 | .30 | 1.00 |

| 203 | 10,000 CRUZEIROS | ND (1984). Brown on m/c unpt. Desk top at ctr., Rui Barbosa at r. Conference scene on back. | .20 | .60 | 3.00 |

204	50,000 CRUZEIROS	ND (1984). Violet on m/c unpt. Microscope at ctr., O. Cruz at r. Cruz Institute at ctr. on back.			
		a. Issued note.	.50	2.50	8.00
		x. Error, titles and sign. in reversed position so that *Presidente, Banco Central* is at l.	3.00	10.00	25.00

Cat. #	Denomination	Date, description	Series	VG	VF
205	100,000 CRUZEIROS	ND (1985). Black on blue, gold and m/c unpt. Electric power station at ctr., Pres. J. Kubitschek at r. Old and modern bldgs. at ctr. on back.	.50	2.50	7.50

Currency Reform
1 Cruzado = 1000 Cruzeiros

1986 PROVISIONAL ISSUE

#206–208 black circular ovpt: *Banco Central Do Brazil* and new currency unit on #203–205.

| 206 | 10 CRUZADOS on 10,000 Cruzeiros | ND (1986). Ovpt. on #203. | .10 | .20 | .60 |

| 207 | 50 CRUZADOS on 50,000 Cruzeiros | ND (1986). Ovpt. on #204. | .20 | .75 | 2.50 |

| 208 | 100 CRUZADOS on 100,000 Cruzeiros | ND (1986). Ovpt. on #205. | .20 | .75 | 3.00 |

1986 ISSUE

#209–211 printer: CdM-B.

Cat. #	Denomination	Date, description	Series	VG	VF
209	10 CRUZADOS	ND (1986). Similar to #203 except for denomination. 2 sign. varieties.	.10	.20	.50

210	50 CRUZADOS	ND (1986). Similar to #204 except for denomination.	.10	.25	.75

211	100 CRUZADOS	ND (1986). Similar to #205 except for denomination.	.10	.25	.75

1986 COMMEMORATIVE ISSUE

#212, Birth Centennial of H. Villa-Lobos

212	500 CRUZADOS	ND (1986). Blue-green on m/c unpt. H. Villa-Lobos at r. and as wmk. Villa-Lobos at l. ctr. on back. Printer: CdM-B. 4 sign. varieties.	.10	.20	.50

1988 ISSUE

#213–215 portr. as wmk. Printer: CdM-B.

Cat. #	Denomination	Date, description	Series	VG	VF
213	1000 CRUZADOS	ND (1988). Purple and brown-violet on m/c unpt. J. Machado at r. Street scene from old Rio de Janeiro on back.	.15	.75	2.50

214	5000 CRUZADOS	ND (1988). Blue and m/c. Portion of mural at ctr., C. Portinari at r. Examples of his artwork on back.	1.00	3.00	8.00

215	10,000 CRUZADOS	ND (1989). Red, brown and m/c. C. Chagas at r. Chagas w/lab instruments on back.	1.50	4.50	12.00

Currency Reform

1 Novo (new) Cruzado = 1000 old Cruzados

1989 PROVISIONAL ISSUE

#216–218 black triangular ovpt. of new currency unit on #213–215.

Cat. #	Denomination	Date, description	Series	VG	VF
216	1 CRUZADO N. on 1000 Cruzados	ND (1989). Ovpt. on #213.	.10	.20	.30

Cat. #	Denomination	Date, description		VG	VF	Unc
221	200 CRUZADOS NOVOS	ND (1989). Blue and black on m/c unpt. Political leaders at ctr., sculpture of the Republic at ctr. r., arms at r. Oil painting "Patria" by P. Bruno w/flag being embroidered by a family on back. Wmk: Liberty head. Printer: CdM-B.		FV	FV	3.50

1990 ISSUE

			VG	VF	Unc
222	500 CRUZADOS NOVOS	ND (1990). Green and purple on m/c unpt. Orchid at ctr., A. Ruschi at r. Back lt. orange, purple and blue; hummingbird, orchids and A. Ruschi at ctr.	FV	FV	7.50

			Series	VG	VF
217	5 CRUZADOS N. on 5000 Cruzados	ND (1989). Ovpt. on #214.	.15	.50	1.75

			Series	VG	VF
218	10 CRUZADOS N. on 10,000 Cruzados	ND (1989). Ovpt. on #215.	.15	.60	4.00

Currency Reform

1 Cruzeiro = 1 Cruzado Novo, 1990-93.

1991–92 PROVISIONAL ISSUE

#223–226 black rectangular ovpt. of new currency unit on #219–222.

1989 ISSUE

#219–220, 222 printer: CdM-B. Wmk: Liberty head.

			VG	VF	Unc
223	50 CRUZEIROS on 50 CRUZADOS N.	ND (1991). Ovpt. on #219.	.10	.20	.60

			Series	VG	VF
219	50 CRUZADOS N.	ND (1989). Brown and black on m/c unpt. C. Drummond de Andrade at r. Back black, red-brown and blue; de Andrade writing poetry.	.15	.50	2.50

			VG	VF	Unc
224	100 CRUZEIROS on 100 CRUZADOS N.	ND (1991). Ovpt. on #220.	.10	.30	1.00

			Series	VG	VF
220	100 CRUZADOS N.	ND (1989). Orange, purple and green on m/c unpt. C. Meireles at r. Back brown, black and m/c; child reading and people dancing.	.20	.65	3.00

			VG	VF	Unc
225	200 CRUZEIROS on 200 CRUZADOS N.	ND (1991). Ovpt. on #221.	FV	FV	1.00

1989 COMMEMORATIVE ISSUE

#221, Centenary of the Republic

			VG	VF	Unc
226	500 CRUZEIROS on 500 CRUZADOS N.	ND (1991). Ovpt. on #222.	FV	FV	1.50

Cat. #	Denomination	Date, description	VG	VF	Unc
227	5000 CRUZEIROS	ND (1992). Deep olive-green and deep brown on m/c unpt. Liberty head at r. and as wmk. Arms at l. on back. Printer: CdM–B. Provisional type.	FV	2.00	5.50

1991–93 ISSUE

#228–236 printer: CdM-B.

#228–231 similar to #220–223 but w/new currency unit and new sign. titles.

228	100 CRUZEIROS	ND (1992). Like #220.	.20	.40	.85

229	200 CRUZEIROS	ND (1992). Like #221.	FV	FV	1.00

230	500 CRUZEIROS	ND (1992). Like #222.	FV	FV	1.25

Cat. #	Denomination	Date, description	VG	VF	Unc
231	1000 CRUZEIROS	ND (1992). Dk. brown, brown, violet and black on m/c unpt. C. Rondon at r., native hut at ctr., map of Brazil in background. 2 Indian children and local food from Amazonia on back. Wmk: Liberty head.			
		a. Upper sign. title: *MINISTRA DA ECONOMIA,... .*	FV	FV	1.50
		b. Upper sign. title: *MINISTRO DA ECONOMIA,... .*	FV	FV	.75

232	5000 CRUZEIROS	ND (1992). Blue-black, black and deep brown on lt. blue and m/c unpt. C. Gomes at ctr. r., Brazilian youths at ctr. Statue of Gomes seated, grand piano at ctr. on back. Wmk: Liberty head.			
		a. Upper sign. title: *MINISTRO DA ECONOMIA,... .*	FV	FV	2.00
		b. Upper sign. title: *MINISTRO DA FAZENDA,... .*	FV	FV	1.00

233	10,000 CRUZEIROS	ND (1992). Black and brown-violet on m/c unpt. V. Brazil at r. and as wmk. Extracting poison at ctr. One snake swallowing another at ctr. on back.	FV	FV	1.00

Cat. #	Denomination	Date, description	VG	VF	Unc
234	50,000 CRUZEIROS	ND (1991). Dk. brown and red-orange on m/c unpt. C. Cascudo at ctr. r. and as wmk. 2 men on raft at l. ctr. background. Folklore dancers at l. ctr. on back.			
		a. Upper sign. title: *MINISTRO DA ECONOMIA,... .*	FV	FV	1.50
		b. Upper sign. title: *MINISTRO DA FAZENDA,... .*	FV	FV	1.50

#235–236 wmk: Sculptured head of *"Brasillia."*

235	100,000 CRUZEIROS	ND (1992). Hummingbird feeding nestlings at ctr., butterfly at r. Butterfly at l., Ignacu cataract at ctr. on back.	FV	FV	4.50
		a. Upper sign. title: *MINISTRO DA ECONOMIA,... .*	FV	FV	4.50
		b. Upper sign. title: *MINISTRO DA FAZENDA,... .*	FV	FV	4.50

236	500,000 CRUZEIROS	ND (1993). Red-violet, brown and deep purple on m/c unpt. M. de Andrade at r., native indian art in unpt. Bldg., de Andrade teaching children at ctr. on back.	FV	FV	20.00

Currency Reform, 1993

1 Cruzeiro Real = 1000 Cruzeiros

1993 PROVISIONAL ISSUE

#237-239 black circular ovpt. of new value on #234b–236b.

Cat. #	Denomination	Date, description	VG	VF	Unc
237	50 CRUZEIROS REAIS on 50,000 Cruzeiros	ND (1993). Ovpt. on #234b.	FV	FV	1.00

238	100 CRUZEIROS REAIS on 100,000 Cruzeiros	ND (1993). Ovpt. on #235b.	FV	FV	2.00

239	500 CRUZEIROS REAIS on 500,000 Cruzeiros	ND (1993). Ovpt. on #236b.	FV	FV	6.50

1993–94 ISSUE

#240–242 wmk: Sculptured head of *"Brasillia."* Printer: CdM-B.

240	1000 CRUZEIROS REAIS	ND (1993). Black, dk. blue and brown on m/c unpt. A. Teixeira at ctr. r. "Parque" school at l. ctr. Children and workers on back.	FV	FV	2.50

241	5000 CRUZEIROS REAIS	ND (1993). Black, red-brown and dk. olive-green on m/c unpt. Gaucho at ctr. r., ruins of São Miguel das Missões at l. ctr. Back vertical; gaucho, horseback, roping steer at ctr.	FV	FV	9.00

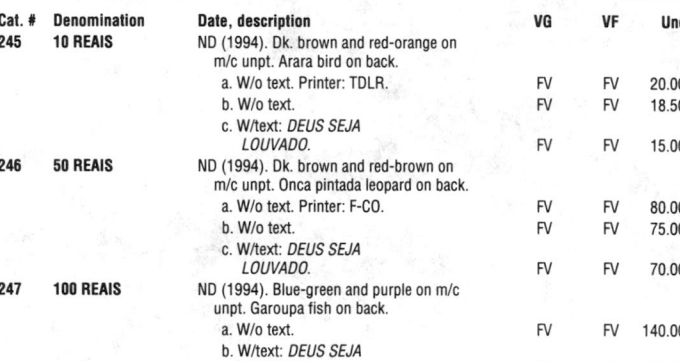

Cat. #	Denomination	Date, description	VG	VF	Unc
242	50,000 CRUZEIROS REAIS	ND (1994). Deep purple and brown-violet on m/c unpt. Native dancer and Baiana at l. and ctr. r. Back vertical; Baiana Acarajé preparing food at ctr.	FV	FV	50.00

Currency Reform, April 1994

1 Real = 1 U.S.A. Dollar

#243-247 Sculpture of the Republic at ctr. r. and as wmk. Printer: CdM-B or w/additional imprint of secondary printer. 4 sign. varieties.

243	1 REAL	ND (1994). Black and green on m/c unpt. Hummingbirds on back.			
		a. W/o text.	FV	FV	3.00
		b. W/text: *DEUS SEJA LOUVADO.*	FV	FV	2.25

244	5 REAIS	ND (1994). Purple and blue on m/c unpt. Crane on back.			
		a. W/o text. Printer: G&D.	FV	FV	11.00
		b. W/o text.	FV	FV	10.00
		c. W/text: *DEUS SEJA LOUVADO.*	FV	FV	8.50

Cat. #	Denomination	Date, description	VG	VF	Unc
245	10 REAIS	ND (1994). Dk. brown and red-orange on m/c unpt. Arara bird on back.			
		a. W/o text. Printer: TDLR.	FV	FV	20.00
		b. W/o text.	FV	FV	18.50
		c. W/text: *DEUS SEJA LOUVADO.*	FV	FV	15.00
246	50 REAIS	ND (1994). Dk. brown and red-brown on m/c unpt. Onca pintada leopard on back.			
		a. W/o text. Printer: F-CO.	FV	FV	80.00
		b. W/o text.	FV	FV	75.00
		c. W/text: *DEUS SEJA LOUVADO.*	FV	FV	70.00
247	100 REAIS	ND (1994). Blue-green and purple on m/c unpt. Garoupa fish on back.			
		a. W/o text.	FV	FV	140.00
		b. W/text: *DEUS SEJA LOUVADO.*	FV	FV	125.00

Listings For:

BRITISH EAST CARIBBEAN TERRITORIES, see East Caribbean States

BRITISH HONDURAS, see Belize

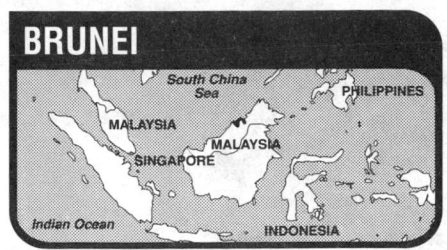

BRUNEI

Negara Brunei Darussalam (The State of Brunei), a British protected state on the northwest coast of the island of Borneo, has an area of 2,226 sq. mi. (5,765 sq. km.) and a population of 256,500. Capital: Bandar Seri Begawan. Crude oil and rubber are exported.

Magellan was the first European to visit Brunei in 1521. It was a powerful state, ruling over Northern Borneo and adjacent islands from the 16th to the 19th century. Brunei became a British protectorate in 1888 and a British dependency in 1905. The Constitution of 1959 restored control over internal affairs to the sultan, while delegating responsibility for defense and foreign affairs to Britain.

The island of Labuan (formerly Sultana), located 6 miles off the northwest coast of Borneo, has an area of 35 sq. mi. (90.6 sq. km.) and a population of 10,000. It is now part of Sabah (British North Borneo), and consequently of Malaysia. The East India Co. sought to make Labuan a trading station in 1775, but the island reverted to a pirate refuge. In 1846 it was ceded by the sultan of Brunei to Britain. Labuan was a crown colony from 1848 to 1890, when its administration was handed over to British North Borneo, which ruled it until 1905, when it became part of the Straits Settlements. Labuan became a part of Sabah in 1946.

RULERS
Sultan Sir Omar Ali Saifuddin III, 1950–67
Sultan Hassanal Bolkiah I, 1967–

MONETARY SYSTEM
1 Dollar = 100 Sen to 1967
1 Ringgit (Dollar) = 100 Sen, 1967–

Kerajaan Brunei–Government of Brunei

1967 ISSUE

#1–5 Sultan Omar Ali Saifuddin III w/military cap at r. and as wmk. Mosque on back.

Cat. #	Denomination	Date, description	VG	VF	Unc
1	1 RINGGIT	1967. Dk. blue on m/c unpt. Back gray, lavender and pink.	FV	5.50	22.50

2	5 RINGGIT	1967. Dk. green on m/c unpt. Back green and pink.	FV	7.50	30.00
3	10 RINGGIT	1967. Red on m/c unpt. Back red.	FV	10.00	35.00
4	50 RINGGIT	1967. Dk. brown on m/c unpt. Back olive.	FV	60.00	150.00

5	100 RINGGIT	1967. Blue on m/c unpt. Back purple.	FV	100.00	225.00

1972-79 ISSUE

#6–10 Sultan Hassanal Bolkiah I in military uniform at r. and as wmk. Mosque on back.

Cat. #	Denomination	Date, description	VG	VF	Unc
6	1 RINGGIT	1972–88. Blue on m/c unpt.			
		a.1972; 1976; 1978.	FV	1.25	4.00
		b.1980; 1982.	FV	1.00	3.50
		c.1983–1988.	FV	.85	3.00

7	5 RINGGIT	1979–86. Green on m/c unpt.			
		a. 1979; 1981.	FV	4.50	12.00
		b. 1983; 1984; 1986.	FV	4.00	10.00
8	10 RINGGIT	1976–86. Red on m/c unpt.			
		a. 1976; 1981.	FV	8.50	20.00
		b. 1983; 1986.	FV	7.50	18.50

9	50 RINGGIT	1973–86. Dk. brown on m/c unpt.			
		a.1973.	FV	40.00	100.00
		b.1977; 1982.	FV	37.50	80.00
		c.1986.	FV	FV	60.00

10	100 RINGGIT	1972–88. Blue on m/c unpt.			
		a.1972; 1976.	FV	85.00	175.00
		b.1978; 1980.	FV	80.00	140.00
		c.1982; 1983; 1988.	FV	75.00	130.00

#11–12 Sultan Bolkiah I in royal uniform at r.

11	500 RINGGIT	1979; 1987. Orange on m/c unpt. Mosque at ctr. on back.	FV	400.00	600.00

Cat. #	Denomination	Date, description	VG	VF	Unc
12	1000 RINGGIT	1979; 1987. Gray, brown and greenish-blue. Brunei Museum on back.	FV	800.00	1150.

Negara Brunei Darussalam

1989 ISSUE

#13–20 Sultan Bolkiah at r. and as wmk.

| 13 | 1 RINGGIT | 1989–91; 1994. Purple on m/c unpt. Aerial view on back. | FV | FV | 1.50 |

| 14 | 5 RINGGIT | 1989–91; 1993. Blue-gray and deep green on m/c unpt. Houses and boats on back. | FV | FV | 5.50 |

| 15 | 10 RINGGIT | 1989–92. Purple and red-orange on m/c unpt. Houses and mosque on back. | FV | FV | 10.00 |

Cat. #	Denomination	Date, description	VG	VF	Unc
16	50 RINGGIT	1989–91. Brown, olive-green, and orange on m/c unpt. People in power launch on back.	FV	FV	47.50

| 17 | 100 RINGGIT | 1989–91; 94. Blue and violet on m/c unpt. River scene on back. | FV | FV | 90.00 |

18	500 RINGGIT	1989–92. Red-orange, purple, olive and black on m/c unpt. Woman in boat on back.	FV	FV	400.00
19	1000 RINGGIT	1989–91. Red-violet, purple, olive and blue-green on m/c unpt. Waterfront village on back.	FV	FV	750.00
20	10,000 RINGGIT	1989. Green and yellow on m/c unpt. Aerial view of harbor on back.	FV	FV	7250.

1992 COMMEMORATIVE ISSUE

#21, 25th Anniversary of Accession

Cat. #	Denomination	Date, description	VG	VF	Unc
21	25 RINGGIT	1992. Brown, lilac, green and m/c. Royal procession at ctr., Sultan at r. and as wmk. at l. Crown at l., coronation at ctr. on back. Dates *1967* and *1992* with text at top.	FV	FV	35.00

The Republic of Bulgaria (formerly the Peoples Republic of Bulgaria), a Balkan country on the Black Sea in southeastern Europe, has an area of 44,365 sq. mi. (110,912 sq. km.) and a population of 8.47 million. Capital: Sofia. Agriculture remains a key component of the economy but industrialization, particularly heavy industry, has been emphasized since the late 1940's. Machinery, tobacco and cigarettes, wines and spirits, clothing and metals are the chief exports.

The area now occupied by Bulgaria was conquered by the Bulgars, an Asiatic tribe, in the 7th century. Bulgarian kingdoms continued to exist on the Bulgarian peninsula until it came under Turkish rule in 1395. In 1878, after nearly 500 years of Turkish rule, Bulgaria was made a principality under Turkish suzerainty. Union seven years later with Eastern Rumelia created a Balkan state with borders approximating those of present-day Bulgaria. A Bulgarian kingdom fully independent of Turkey was proclaimed Sept. 22, 1908. That monarchy was abolished by plebiscite in 1946 and Bulgaria became a People's Republic on the Soviet pattern. Following demonstrations and a general strike the communist government resigned in Nov. 1990. A new government was elected in Oct. 1991.

MONETARY SYSTEM

1 Lev ЛЕВ = 100 Stotinki СТОТИНКИ

TITLES

Bulgarian People's Republic = НАРОДНА РЕПУБЛИКА БЪЛГАРИЯ

Bulgarian National Bank = БЪЛГАРСКАТА НАРОДНА БАНКА

State banknote = ЦАРСТВО БЪЛГАРА

PEOPLES REPUBLIC
БЪЛГАРСКАТА НАРОДНА БАНКА
Bulgarian National Bank

1962 ISSUE

#88–92 arms at l.

Cat. #	Denomination	Date, description	VG	VF	Unc
88	1 LEV	1962. Brown-lilac. Tower on back.	.10	.25	2.50

89	2 LEVA	1962. Green. Woman picking grapes in vineyard on back.	.20	.40	3.50
90	5 LEVA	1962. Red-brown. Coastline village.	.25	.50	5.50
91	10 LEVA	1962. Blue. Factory. Dimitrov on back.	.35	.70	8.00
92	20 LEVA	1962. Brown-lilac. Factory. Dimitrov on back.	.50	1.00	15.00

1974 ISSUE

#93–97 modified arms w/dates *681–1944* at l.

#93–95 wmk: Decorative design.

93	1 LEV	1974. Brown. Like #88.	.10	.20	1.00

Cat. #	Denomination	Date, description	VG	VF	Unc
94	2 LEVA	1974. Green. Like #89.	.10	.25	1.25

| 95 | 5 LEVA | 1974. Red-brown. Like #90. | .15 | .30 | 1.50 |

#96 and 97 wmk: Hands holding hammer and sickle.

| 96 | 10 LEVA | 1974. Blue. Like #91. | .25 | .50 | 2.50 |

| 97 | 20 LEVA | 1974. Brown-lilac. Like #92. | .50 | 1.00 | 6.00 |

1989-90 ISSUES

Cat. #	Denomination	Date, description	VG	VF	Unc
98	50 LEVA	1990. Brown and dk. blue on m/c unpt. Arms at l. ctr. Back brown and dk. green; castle ruins at ctr. r. on back. Wmk: Hands holding hammer and sickle.	1.00	10.00	50.00

NOTE: #98 was withdrawn from circulation shortly after its release.

| 99 | 100 LEVA | 1989. Purple on lilac unpt. Arms at l. ctr. Horseman w/2 dogs at ctr. r. on back. Wmk: Rampant lion. (Not issued). | — | — | 250.00 |

NOTE: #99 carries the name of the Bulgarian Peoples Republic, probably the reason it was not released. An estimated 500-600 pieces were "liberated" from the recycling process.

REPUBLIC
БЪЛГАРСКАТА НАРОДНА БАНКА
Bulgarian National Bank
1991–94 ISSUE

#100–105 wmk: Rampant lion.

| 100 | 20 LEVA | ND(1992). Blue-black and blue-green on m/c unpt. Dutchess Sevastokratoritza Desislava on l. ctr. Boyana Church at r. on back. | FV | FV | 2.50 |

| 101 | 50 LEVA | 1992. Purple and violet on m/c unpt. Khristo G. Danov at l. Platen printing press at r. on back. | FV | FV | 3.50 |

| 102 | 100 LEVA | 1991. Dk. brown and maroon on m/c. unpt. Zhary Zograf (artist) at l. ctr. Wheel of life at r. on back. Cream paper. | FV | FV | 5.50 |

Cat. #	Denomination	Date, description	VG	VF	Unc
103	200 LEVA	1992. Deep violet and brown-orange on m/c. unpt. Ivan Vazov at l. village in unpt. Lyre w/laurel wreath at r. on back.	FV	FV	9.00

| 104 | 500 LEVA | 1993. Dk. green and black on m/c unpt. D. Hristor at l. and as wmk. Opera house in Varna at ctr. r., sea gulls at lower r. on back. | FV | FV | 20.00 |

| 105 | 1000 LEVA | 1994. Dk. green and olive-brown on m/c unpt. V. Levski at l. and as wmk., Liberty w/flag, sword and lion at upper ctr. r. Monument and writings of Levski at ctr. r. on back. | FV | FV | 35.00 |

106	2000 LEVA	1994. Black and dk. blue on m/c unpt. N. Ficev at l. and as wmk., bldg. outlines at ctr., wide hologram foil strip at l. Steeple, bldg. plans at ctr. r. on back.	FV	FV	65.00
107	5000 LEVA	Expected new issue.			
108	10,000 LEVA	Expected new issue.			

Listings For:

BURMA, see Myanmar

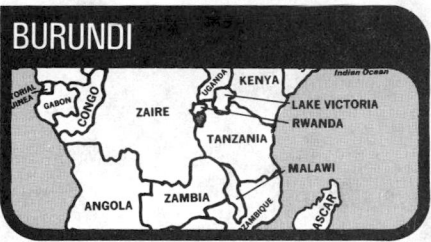

BURUNDI

The Republic of Burundi, a landlocked country in central Africa, was a kingdom with a feudalistic society, caste system and Mwami (king) for more than 400 years before independence. It has an area of 10,759 sq. mi. (27,834 sq. km.) and a population of 5.3 million. Capital: Bujumbura. Plagued by poor soil, irregular rainfall and a single-crop economy - coffee - Burundi is barely able to feed itself. Coffee, tea and cotton are exported.

Although the area was visited by European explorers and missionaries in the latter half of the 19th century, it wasn't until the 1890s that it, together with Rwanda, fell under European domination as part of German East Africa. Following World War I, the territory was mandated to Belgium by the League of Nations and administered with the Belgian Congo. After World War II it became a U.N. Trust Territory. Limited self-government was established by U.N.-supervised elections in 1961. Burundi gained independence as a kingdom under Mwami Mwambutsa IV on July 1, 1962. The republic was established by military coup in 1966.

RULERS
Mwambutsa IV, 1962–1966
Ntare V, 1966

MONETARY SYSTEM
1 Franc (Amafranga) = 100 Centimes

REPLACEMENT NOTES
#20-34, ZZ prefix.

Banque d'Emission du Rwanda et du Burundi

1964 PROVISIONAL ISSUE

#1–7 lg. *BURUNDI* ovpt. on face.

Cat. #	Denomination	Date, description	VG	VF	Unc
1	5 FRANCS	ND (1964 - old dates 15.5.1961; 15.4.1963). Lt. brown. Black ovpt. on Rwanda-Burundi #1.	25.00	60.00	150.00

| 2 | 10 FRANCS | ND (1964 - old date 5.10.1960). Gray. Red ovpt. on Rwanda-Burundi #2. | 15.00 | 45.00 | 125.00 |

| 3 | 20 FRANCS | ND (1964 - old date 5.10.1960). Green. Black ovpt. on Rwanda-Burundi #3. | 20.00 | 50.00 | 150.00 |

| 4 | 50 FRANCS | ND (1964 - old date 1.10.1960). Red. Black ovpt. on Rwanda-Burundi #4. | 35.00 | 75.00 | 275.00 |

Cat. #	Denomination	Date, description	VG	VF	Unc
5	100 FRANCS	ND (1964 - old dates 1.10.1960; 31.7.1962). Blue. Red ovpt. on Rwanda-Burundi #5.	15.00	45.00	150.00
6	500 FRANCS	ND (1964 - old date 15.5.1961). Lilac brown. Black ovpt. on Rwanda-Burundi #6.	175.00	550.00	—

Cat. #	Denomination	Date, description	VG	VF	Unc
7	1000 FRANCS	ND (1964 - old date 31.7.1962). Green. Black ovpt. on Rwanda-Burundi #7.	125.00	375.00	900.00

Banque du Royaume du Burundi

1964 ISSUE

#8–14 arms at ctr. on back.

8	5 FRANCS	1.10.1964; 1.12.1964; 1.5.1965. Lt. brown on gray-green unpt. 2 young men picking coffee beans at l.	2.00	6.00	25.00

9	10 FRANCS	20.11.1964; 25.2.1965; 20.3.1965; 31.12.1965. Dk. brown on lilac-brown unpt. Cattle at ctr.	3.50	9.00	30.00

10	20 FRANCS	20.11.1964; 25.2.1965; 20.3.1965. Blue-green. Dancer at ctr.	10.00	30.00	100.00

11	50 FRANCS	1964–66. Red-orange. View of Bujumbura.			
		a. Sign. titles: *LE VICE PRESIDENT* and *LE PRESIDENT.* 1.10.1964–31.12.1965.	18.00	75.00	165.00

Cat. #	Denomination	Date, description	VG	VF	Unc
		b. Sign. titles: *L'ADMINISTRATEUR* and *LE PRESIDENT.* 1.7.1966.	—	—	—

NOTE: #11b was prepared but apparently not released w/o ovpt. See #16b.

12	100 FRANCS	1964–66. Bluish-purple. Prince Rwagasore at ctr.			
		a. Sign. titles: *LE VICE PRESIDENT* and *LE PRESIDENT.* 1.10.1964; 1.12.1964; 1.5.1965.	6.00	20.00	140.00
		b. Sign. titles: *L'ADMINISTRATEUR* and *LE PRESIDENT.* 1.7.1966.	7.00	25.00	160.00

13	500 FRANCS	5.12.1964; 1.8.1966. Brown on yellow unpt. Bank at r.	45.00	175.00	—

14	1000 FRANCS	1.2.1965. Green on m/c unpt. Kg. Mwami Mwambutsa IV at r.	110.00	360.00	—

Banque de la République du Burundi

1966 PROVISIONAL ISSUE

#15-19 black ovpt: *DE LA REPUBLIQUE* and *YA REPUBLIKA* on face only of Banque du Royaume notes.

15	20 FRANCS	ND (1966 - old date 20.3.1965). Ovpt. on #10.	15.00	35.00	120.00
16	50 FRANCS	ND (1966 - old dates 1.5.1965; 31.12.1965; 1.7.1966).			
		a. Ovpt. on #11a.	17.50	45.00	150.00
		b. Ovpt. on #11b.	35.00	85.00	260.00

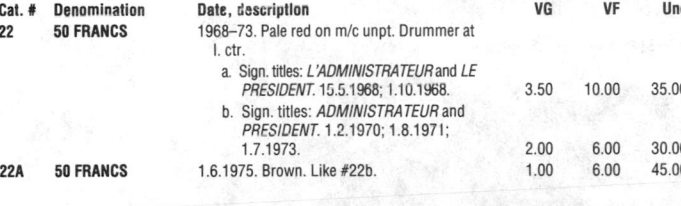

Cat. #	Denomination	Date, description	VG	VF	Unc
17	100 FRANCS	ND (1966).			
		a. Ovpt. on #12a. (- old date 1.5.1965).	15.00	45.00	150.00
		b. Ovpt. on #12b. (- old date 1.7.1966).	15.00	45.00	150.00

NOTE: Ovpt. on #17 has letters either 3.2 or 2.6mm high.

| 18 | 500 FRANCS | ND (1966 - old dates 5.12.1964; 1.8.1966). Ovpt. on #13. | 90.00 | 250.00 | — |

| 19 | 1000 FRANCS | ND (1966 - old date 1.2.1965). Ovpt. on #14. | 175.00 | 450.00 | — |

1968–75 ISSUES

Sign. varieties.

20	10 FRANCS	1968; 1970. Red on green and blue unpt. "Place De La Revolution" monument at r. Sign. titles: *L'ADMINISTRATEUR* and *LE PRESIDENT*.			
		a. 1.11.1968.	1.25	3.00	10.00
		b. 1.4.1970.	.15	.50	2.00

21	20 FRANCS	1968–73. Blue on green and violet unpt. Dancer at ctr. Text on back.			
		a. Sign. titles: *LE PRESIDENT* and *LE VICE-PRESIDENT*. 1.11.1968.	3.00	10.00	32.50
		b. Sign. titles: *LE PRESIDENT* and *L'ADMINISTRATEUR*. 1.4.1970; 1.11.1971; 1.7.1973.	1.75	5.00	15.00

Cat. #	Denomination	Date, description	VG	VF	Unc
22	50 FRANCS	1968–73. Pale red on m/c unpt. Drummer at l. ctr.			
		a. Sign. titles: *L'ADMINISTRATEUR* and *LE PRESIDENT*. 15.5.1968; 1.10.1968.	3.50	10.00	35.00
		b. Sign. titles: *ADMINISTRATEUR* and *PRESIDENT*. 1.2.1970; 1.8.1971; 1.7.1973.	2.00	6.00	30.00
22A	50 FRANCS	1.6.1975. Brown. Like #22b.	1.00	6.00	45.00

23	100 FRANCS	1968–75. Brown on pale orange, lilac and blue unpt. Prince Rwagasore at r.			
		a. Sign. titles: *LE VICE-PRESIDENT* and *LE PRESIDENT*. 15.5.1968; 1.10.1968.	5.00	15.00	75.00
		b. Sign. titles: *ADMINISTRATEUR* and *LE PRESIDENT*. 1.2.1970; 1.8.1971; 1.7.1973; 1.6. 1975.	4.00	9.00	45.00

24	500 FRANCS	1968–75. Brown. Bank at r.			
		a. Sign. titles: *LE PRESIDENT* and *LE VICE–PRESIDENT*. 1.8.1968.	50.00	130.00	265.00
		b. Sign. titles: *LE PRESIDENT* and *L'ADMINISTRATEUR*. 1.4.1970; 1.8.1971.	60.00	150.00	285.00
		c. Sign. titles: *LE PRESIDENT* and *LE VICE–PRESIDENT*. 1.7.1973; 1.6.1975.	50.00	130.00	265.00

25	1000 FRANCS	1968–75. Blue and m/c. Bird and flowers. Back blue and lt. brown; cattle at ctr.			
		a. Sign. titles: *L'ADMINISTRATEUR* and *LE PRESIDENT*. 1.4.1968; 1.5.1971; 1.2.1973.	45.00	150.00	375.00
		b. Sign. title: *LE VICE–PRESIDENT*. 1.6.1975; 1.9.1976.	45.00	150.00	375.00

Cat. #	Denomination	Date, description	VG	VF	Unc
26	5000 FRANCS	1968; 1971; 1973. Blue. Pres. Micombero in military uniform at r. Loading at dockside on back.			
		a. Sign. titles: *LE VICE-PRESIDENT* and *LE PRESIDENT.* 1.4.1968; 1.7.1973.	115.00	300.00	800.00
		b. Sign. title: *L'ADMINISTRATEUR.* 1.5.1971.	125.00	325.00	875.00

1975–78 ISSUE

#27–31 face like #20-26. Arms at ctr. on back.

Cat. #	Denomination	Date, description	VG	VF	Unc
27	20 FRANCS	1977–91. Red on m/c unpt. Face design like #21. Sign. titles: *LE GOUVERNEUR* and *L'ADMINISTRATEUR.*			
		a. 1.7.1977; 1.6.1979; 1.12.1981.	FV	.50	2.00
		b. 1.12.1983; 1.12.1986; 1.5.1988; 1.10.1989; 1.10.1991.	FV	FV	1.00
28	50 FRANCS	1.7.1977–1.5.1993. Brown on m/c unpt. Face like #22.			
		a. 1.7.1977; 1.8.1979.	.15	.75	2.50
		b. 1.12.1981; 1.12.1983.	FV	.50	2.00
		c. 1.5.1988; 1.10.1989; 1.10.1991; 1.5.1993.	FV	.35	1.00
29	100 FRANCS	1977–93. Purple. Face design like #23. Sign. titles: *L'ADMINISTRATEUR* and *LE GOUVERNEUR.*			

Cat. #	Denomination	Date, description	VG	VF	Unc
		a. 1.7.1977; 1.5.1979.	FV	1.00	3.50
		b. 1.1.1981; 1.7.1982; 1.1.1984; 1.11.1986.	FV	.85	2.75
		c. 1.5.1988; 1.7.1990.	FV	.65	1.75

Cat. #	Denomination	Date, description	VG	VF	Unc
30	500 FRANCS	1977–88. Dk. blue on m/c unpt. Face design like #24. Numeral and date style varieties. Sign. titles: *LE GOUVERNEUR* and *LE VICE-GOUVERNEUR.*			
		a 1.7.1977; 1.9.1981.	FV	6.00	22.50
		b. 1.7.1985; 1.9.1986; 1.5.1988.	FV	5.00	15.00

Cat. #	Denomination	Date, description	VG	VF	Unc
31	1000 FRANCS	1977–89. Dk. green on m/c unpt. Like #25.			
		a. Sign. titles: *LE VICE-GOUVERNEUR* and *LE GOUVERNEUR.* 1.7.1977; 1.1.1978; 1.5.1979; 1.1.1980.	FV	15.00	30.00
		b. 1.1.1981; 1.5.1982; 1.1.1984; 1.12.1986.	FV	10.00	27.50
		c. Sign. titles: *L'ADMINISTRATEUR* and *LE VICE-GOUVERNEUR.* 1.6.1987.	FV	7.50	25.00
		d. Sign. titles: *LE VICE-GOUVERNEUR* and *LE GOUVERNEUR.* 1.5.1988; 1.10.1989.	FV	FV	20.00
32	5000 FRANCS	1978-91. Purple on m/c unpt. Bldg. at r., arms at ctr. Dock scene on back.			
		a. 1.7.1978; 1.10.1981.	30.00	60.00	175.00
		b. 1.9.1986.	FV	28.00	85.00
		c. 1.10.1989; 1.10.1991.	FV	FV	70.00
		d. Sign titles: *LE 1ST VICE-GOUV-ERNEUR* and *LE GOUVERNEUR.* 25.5.1995.	FV	FV	62.50

1979–81 ISSUES

Cat. #	Denomination	Date, description	VG	VF	Unc
33	10 FRANCS	1.6.1981; 1.12.1983; 1.12.1986; 1.5.1988; 1.10.1989; 1.10.1991. Blue-green on tan unpt. Map of Burundi w/arms superimposed at ctr. Text on back. Sign. titles: *LE GOUVERNEUR* and *L'ADMINISTRATEUR.*	FV	.30	.75

Cat. #	Denomination	Date, description	VG	VF	Unc
34	500 FRANCS	1.6.1979; 1.1.1980. Tan, blue, violet and green. Back purple, brown and orange. Similar to #30. Sign titles: *LE GOU-VERNEUR* and *LE VICE-GOUVERNEUR*.	5.00	12.50	40.00

1993–95 ISSUE

| 35 | 100 FRANCS | 1.151993. Dull purple on m/c unpt. Similar to #29. Arms at lower l., brick home construction at ctr. on back. Sign. titles: *LE 2ème VICE-GOUVERNEUR* and *LE GOU-VERNEUR*. | FV | FV | 3.00 |

| 36 | 1000 FRANCS | 19.5.1994. Greenish-black and brown-violet on m/c unpt. Steers at l., arms at lower ctr. Monument at ctr. on back. Sign. titles: *LE GOUVERNEUR* and *LE 1ER VICE-GOU-VERNEUR*. Wmk: Pres. Micombero. | FV | 7.50 | 15.00 |

| 37 | 5000 FRANCS | 25.5.1995. Dk. brown and grayish-purple on m/c unpt. Arms at upper ctr., bldg. at lower r. Ship dockside on back. Sign. titles: *LE GOUVERNEUR* and *LE 1ER VICE-GOUVERNEUR*. | FV | FV | 60.00 |

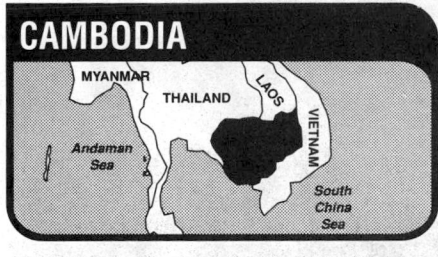

CAMBODIA

Cambodia, formerly known as Democratic Kampuchea and the Khmer Republic, a land of paddy fields and forest-clad hills located on the Indo-Chinese peninsula fronting on the Gulf of Thailand, has an area of 69,898 sq. mi. (181,035 sq. km.) and a population of 12 million. Capital: Phnom Penh. Agriculture is the basis of the economy, with rice the chief crop. Native industries include cattle breeding, weaving and rice milling. Rubber, cattle, corn, and timber are exported.

The region was the nucleus of the Khmer empire which flourished from the 5th to the 12th century and attained an excellence in art and architecture still evident in the magnificent ruins at Angkor. The Khmer empire once ruled over much of Southeast Asia, but began to decline in the 13th century as the Thai and Vietnamese invaded the region and attached its territories. At the request of the Cambodian king, a French protectorate attached to Cochin-China was established over the country in 1863, saving it from dissolution, and in 1885, Cambodia was included in the French Union of Indo-China. France established a constitutional monarchy for Cambodia within the French Union in 1949. The 1954 Geneva Convention resulted in full independence for the Kingdom of Cambodia. King Sihanouk abdicated to his father and won the office of Prime Minister.

Prince Sihanouk was toppled by a bloodless coup led by Lon Nol in March of 1970. Sihanouk moved to Peking to head a government-in-exile. On Oct. 9, 1970, Cambodia became the Khmer Republic, and Lon Nol its President. The government of Lon Nol was in turn toppled, April 17, 1975, by the Khmer Rouge insurgents who took control of the government and renamed the country Democratic Kampuchea.

The Khmer Rouge completely eliminated the economy and created a state without money, exchange or barter. Everyone worked for the state and was taken care of by the state. The Vietnamese supported People's Republic of Kampuchea was installed in accordance with the constitution of January 5, 1976. The name of the country was changed from Democratic Cambodia to Democratic Kampuchea, afterwards reverting to Cambodia.

In the early 1990's the UN attempted to supervise a ceasefire and in 1992 Norodom Sihanouk returned as Chief of State.

RULERS

Norodom Sihanouk, (as Chief of State) 1960–1970
Lon Nol, 1970–1975
Pol Pot, 1975–1979
Heng Samrin, 1979–92
Norodom Sihanouk (as Chief of State), 1992-

MONETARY SYSTEM

1 Riel = 100 Sen to 1975
1 New Riel = 10 Kak = 100 Su, 1975–

REPLACEMENT NOTES

10c, 11, 13, 15, 16, use 3 special Cambodian prefix characters (equivalent to Z90).

	SIGNATURE VARIETIES			
	GOVERNOR [ចៅហ្វាយិណាល]	CHIEF INSPECTOR [អគ្គនិរ័យ]	ADVISOR [ឲ្យប្រឹក្សាមួយទាន់]	DATE
3				1956
4				Late 1961
5				Mid 1962
6				1963
7				1965
8				1968
9				1968
10				1969
11				1970
12				1972
13				1972
14				1974
15				March, 1975 (Printed 1974)

Signature varieties reprinted from *Spink's Numismatic Circular*, March 1979.

CAMBODIA
Banque Nationale du Cambodge

Cat. #	Denomination	Date, description	VG	VF	Unc
4	1 RIEL	ND (1956–72). Grayish green on m/c unpt. Boats dockside in port of Phnom-Penh. Temple on back			
		a. Sign. 1.	1.00	3.00	15.00
		b. Sign. 2; 6; 7; 8; 10; 100.	.15	.25	1.25
		c. Sign. 12.	.10	.15	.25

			VG	VF	Unc
5	20 RIELS	ND (1957–72). Brown. Combine harvester at r. Pagoda on back.			
		a. Sign. 3; 6; 7; 8; 10.	.25	1.00	5.00
		b. Sign. 12.	.15	.25	1.25
6		*Deleted.* See #3A.			

			VG	VF	Unc
7	50 RIELS	ND (1956–72). Blue and orange. Fishermen fishing from boats w/lg. nets in Lake Tonle Sap at l. and r. Back blue and brown; Angkor Wat.			
		a. Western numeral in plate block designator. Sign. 3.	.25	.75	2.00
		b. Cambodian numeral in plate block designator. 5-digit serial #. Sign. 7; 10; 12.	.25	.75	3.00
		c. Cambodian serial # 6-digits. Sign. 12.	.10	.20	.35

Cat. #	Denomination	Date, description	VG	VF	Unc
8	100 RIELS	ND (1957). Brown and green on m/c unpt. Statue of Lokecvara at l. Long boat on back.			
		a. Imprint: *Giesecke & Devrient Munchen, AG.* Sign. 3; 7; 8; 11.	.50	1.50	8.00
		b. Imprint: *Giesecke & Devrient Mun-chen.* Sign. 12; 13.	.10	.20	.65

			VG	VF	Unc
9	500 RIELS	ND (1958). Green and brown on m/c unpt. Sculpture of 2 women dancers (Tevodas) at l. 2 persons in ceremonial costume on back. Printer: G&D.			
		a. Sign. 3, 6.	5.00	20.00	75.00
		b. Sign. 9.	.25	.75	3.50

1961-62 ISSUE

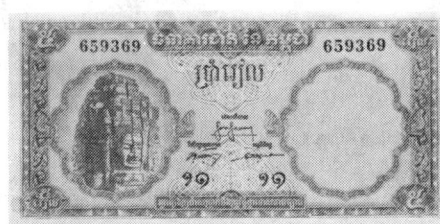

			VG	VF	Unc
10	5 RIELS	ND (1961). Red on m/c unpt. Bayon stone 4 faces of Avalokitesvara at l. Pagoda on back.			
		a. Sign. 4.	1.00	4.00	40.00
		b. Sign. 6; 7; 8; 11.	.20	.50	2.00
		c. Sign. 12.	.10	.25	65

			VG	VF	Unc
11	10 RIELS	ND (1962). Brown on m/c unpt. Temple of Bantael Srei. Bldg. at l. on back. Sign. 5; 6; 7; 8; 11; 12.	.20	.40	1.00
12	100 RIELS	ND (1962). Blue-black, dk. green and dk. brown on m/c unpt. Sun rising behind Temple of Preah Vihear at l. Back blue, green and brown, w/distant view of road to a city on mountaintop. Wmk: Statue head. Printer: G&D.			
		a. Sign. 6.	1.00	3.00	20.00
		b. Sign. 13. (Not issued).	.10	.20	.60

KHMER REPUBLIC
1970 ISSUE

Cat. #	Denomination	Date, description	VG	VF	Unc
13	100 RIELS	ND (1970). Blue on m/c unpt. 2 oxen at r. 3 ceremonial women on back.			
		a. ABNC imprint on lower margins, face and back. Sign. 3.	3.00	20.00	75.00
		b. W/o imprint on either side. Sign. 12.	.15	.25	.65

Cat. #	Denomination	Date, description	VG	VF	Unc
16	500 RIELS	ND (1973). Green on m/c unpt. Girl w/vessel on head at l. Rice paddy scene on back.			
		a. Sign. 13; 14.	.15	.25	1.00
		b. Sign. 15.	.10	.20	.60

14	500 RIELS	ND (1970). M/c. Farmer plowing w/2 oxen. Pagoda at r., doorway at l. on back. French printing.			
		a. Sign. 3.	1.00	7.50	30.00
		b. Sign. 5; 7.	.50	6.00	20.00
		c. Sign. 9.	.50	4.00	15.00
		d. Sign. 12.	.15	.50	4.00
		x. Lithograph counterfeit; wmk. barely visible. Sign. 3; 5; 7; 9.	.50	2.00	10.00

17	1000 RIELS	ND. Green on m/c unpt. School children. Large sculptured head on back. Sign. 13. Printer: BWC. (Not issued).	.10	.20	.60

KAMPUCHEA
Bank of Kampuchea

#18–24 prepared by the Khmer Rouge (Communist insurgents) but not issued. New regime under Pol Pot instituted an "agrarian moneyless society." All notes dated 1975.

1973 ISSUE

18	0.1 RIEL (1 Kak)	1975. Purple, green, and orange on m/c unpt. Mortar crew. at l. Threshing rice on back.	.20	.50	3.00

15	100 RIELS	ND. Purple on m/c unpt. Carpet weaving. Angkor Wat on back. (Not issued).			
		a. Sign. 13.	.10	.20	.50
		b. Sign. 14.	1.00	2.50	8.00

19	0.5 RIEL (5 Kak)	1975. Red on lt. green and m/c unpt. Troops marching at l. ctr. Ancient sculpture at l., machine and worker at r. on back.	.20	.50	3.00

#20–24 wmk: Angkor Wat.

State Bank of Democratic Kampuchea

1979 ISSUE

#25–32 issued 20.3.1980 by the Vietnamese-backed regime of Heng Samrin which overthrew Pol Pot in 1979.

Cat. #	Denomination	Date, description	VG	VF	Unc
20	1 RIEL	1975. Red-violet and red on m/c unpt. Farm workers. at l. ctr. Woman operating machine on back.	.20	.50	2.00

Cat. #	Denomination	Date, description	VG	VF	Unc
25	0.1 RIEL (1 Kak)	1979. Green on blue unpt. Arms at ctr. Water buffalos on back.	.10	.15	.25

| 21 | 5 RIELS | 1975. Deep green on m/c unpt. Ancient temples of Angkor Wat. at ctr. r. Landscaping crew on back. | .20 | .40 | 1.50 |

| 26 | 0.2 RIEL (2 Kak) | 1979. Dk. green on tan unpt. Arms at ctr. Rice workers on back. | .10 | .20 | .50 |

| 27 | 0.5 RIEL (5 Kak) | 1979. Red-orange on yellow unpt. Arms at l., train at r. Men fishing from boats w/nets on back. | .10 | .20 | .50 |

| 22 | 10 RIELS | 1975. Brown and red on m/c unpt. Machine gun crew. at ctr. r. Harvesting rice on back. | .25 | .75 | 4.00 |

28	1 RIEL	1979. Brown on yellow and m/c unpt. Arms at ctr. Women harvesting rice on back.			
		a. Issued note.	.10	.20	.50
		s. Specimen.	—	—	35.00

| 23 | 50 RIELS | 1975. Purple on m/c unpt. Planting rice at l., ancient sculpture at r. Woman's militia at ctr. r. on back. | 1.00 | 4.00 | 20.00 |

| 29 | 5 RIELS | 1979. Dk. brown on lt. green and m/c unpt. 4 people at l., arms at r. Independence monument on back. | .10 | .30 | 1.00 |

| 24 | 100 RIELS | 1975. Deep green on m/c unpt. Factory workers at l. ctr. Back black; harvesting rice. | 2.00 | 6.00 | 30.00 |

Cat. #	Denomination	Date, description	VG	VF	Unc
30	10 RIELS	1979. Gray and blue on m/c unpt. Arms at l., harvesting fruit trees at r. School on back.	.20	.50	2.00

Cat. #	Denomination	Date, description	VG	VF	Unc
31	20 RIELS	1979. Violet on pink and m/c unpt. Arms at l. Water buffalos hauling logs on back. Wmk: Arms.			
		a. Issued note.	.10	.35	1.50
		x. Lithograph counterfeit.	—	—	2.00

Cat. #	Denomination	Date, description	VG	VF	Unc
32	50 RIELS	1979. Red on green and m/c unpt. Arms at l., Bayon stone head at ctr. Angkor Wat on back. Wmk: Arms.	.10	.25	.75

1987 ISSUE

Cat. #	Denomination	Date, description	VG	VF	Unc
33	5 RIELS	1987. Like #29 but red and brown on lt. yellow and lt. green unpt. Back red on pale yellow unpt.	.10	.35	1.25
34	10 RIELS	1987. Like #30 but green on lt. blue and m/c unpt. Back deep green and lilac on lt. blue unpt.	.10	35	1.50

CAMBODIA

National Bank Of Cambodia–State Bank

1990–92 ISSUE

Cat. #	Denomination	Date, description	VG	VF	Unc
35	50 RIELS	1992. Dull brown on m/c. Arms at ctr., male portrait at r. Ships dockside on back. Wmk: Floral design. Printer: NBC.	FV	FV	.50
36	100 RIELS	1990. Dk. green and brown on lt. blue and lilac unpt. Independence monument at l. ctr., Achar Mean at r. Rubber trees on back. Wmk: Crowned monogram C-C. Issuer: State Bank.	FV	FV	1.00

Cat. #	Denomination	Date, description	VG	VF	Unc
37	200 RIELS	1992. Deep olive-green and brown on m/c unpt. Floodgates at r. Sculpture in Angkor Wat at ctr. on back. Wmk: Floral design. Printer: NBC.	FV	FV	1.50

Cat. #	Denomination	Date, description	VG	VF	Unc
38	500 RIELS	1991. Red, purple and brown-violet on m/c unpt. Arms above Angkor Wat at ctr. Animal statue at l., cultivating with tractors at ctr. on back. Wmk: Sculptured heads.	FV	FV	3.00

Cat. #	Denomination	Date, description	VG	VF	Unc
39	1000 RIELS	1992. Dk. green, brown and black on m/c unpt. Temple ruins in Angkor Wat. Fisherman fishing in boats w/lg. nets in Lake Tonle Sap on back. Wmk: Chinze.	—	—	1.25

Cat. #	Denomination	Date, description	VG	VF	Unc
40	2000 RIELS	1992. Black on dp. blue and violet-brown and m/c unpt. Prince N. Sihanouk at l., and as wmk., Temple portral at r.	—	—	3.25

NOTE: #39 and 40 were not released into circulation.

1995 ISSUE

#41–47 printer: F-CO.

#41 and 42 wmk: Cube design.

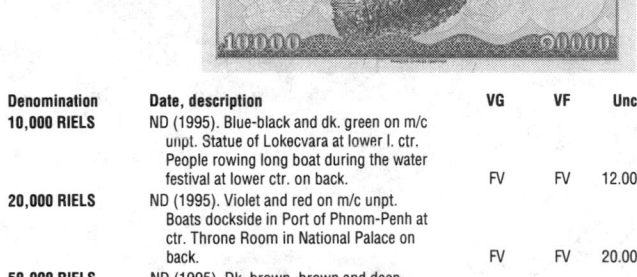

Cat. #	Denomination	Date, description	VG	VF	Unc
44	10,000 RIELS	ND (1995). Blue-black and dk. green on m/c unpt. Statue of Lokecvara at lower l. ctr. People rowing long boat during the water festival at lower ctr. on back.	FV	FV	12.00
45	20,000 RIELS	ND (1995). Violet and red on m/c unpt. Boats dockside in Port of Phnom-Penh at ctr. Throne Room in National Palace on back.	FV	FV	20.00
46	50,000 RIELS	ND (1995). Dk. brown, brown and deep olive-green on m/c unpt. Preah Vihear Temple at ctr. Road to Preah Vihear Temple on back.	FV	FV	50.00
47	100,000 RIELS	ND (1995). Green, blue-green and black on m/c unpt. Kg. and Qn. receiving homage of the people on back.	FV	FV	95.00

| 41 | 1000 RIELS | ND. (1995). Blue-green on m/c unpt. Bayon stone 4 faces of Avalokitesvara at l. Back green on m/c unpt.; Prasat Chan Chaya at r. | FV | FV | 2.00 |

REGIONAL

Khmer Rouge Influence

#R1-R4 w/sign. of Pres. Khieu Samphan. No details about the notes are available.

R1	5 RIELS		—	—	—
R2	10 RIELS		—	—	—
R3	50 RIELS		—	—	—
R4	100 RIELS	Workers in field.	—	—	—

| 42 | 2000 RIELS | ND (1995). Reddish brown on m/c unpt. Fishermen fishing from boats w/nets in Lake Tonle Sap at l. and r. Temple ruins at Angkor Wat on back. | FV | FV | 3.50 |

#43–46 Kg. Sihanouk at r. and as wmk.

| 43 | 5000 RIELS | ND (1995). Deep purple and blue-black w/black text on m/c unpt. Temple of Banteai Srei at lower l. ctr. New market in Phnom-Penh on back. | FV | FV | 6.50 |

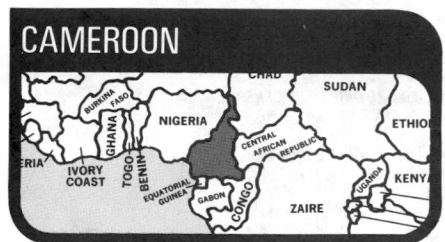

CAMEROON

The United Republic of Cameroon, located in west-central Africa on the Gulf of Guinea, has an area of 185,568 sq. mi. (475,442 sq. km.) and a population of 12.2 million. Capital: Yaounde. About 90 per cent of the labor force is employed on the land; cash crops account for 80 per cent of the country's export revenue. Cocoa, coffee, aluminum, cotton, rubber and timber are exported.

European contact with what is now the United Republic of Cameroon began in the 16th century with the voyage of Portuguese navigator Fernando Po. The following three centuries saw continuous activity by Spanish, Dutch and British traders and missionaries. The land was spared colonial rule until 1884, when treaties with tribal chiefs brought German domination. In 1919, the League of Nations divided the Cameroons between Great Britain and France, with the larger eastern area going to France. The French and British mandates were converted into United Nations trusteeships in 1946. French Cameroon became the independent Cameroon Republic on Jan. 1, 1960. The federation of East (French) and West (British) Cameroon was established in 1961 when the southern part of British Cameroon voted for reunification with the Cameroon Republic, and the northern part for union with Nigeria.

See also Central African States, French Equatorial Africa and Equatorial African States.

MONETARY SYSTEM
1 Franc = 100 Centimes

SIGNATURE VARIETIES
Refer to introduction to Central African States.

RÉPUBLIQUE DU CAMEROUN
Banque Centrale

#1–2A denominations in French only, or French and English.

Cat. #	Denomination	Date, description	Good	Fine	XF
1	1000 FRANCS	ND (1961). M/c. Man w/basket harvesting cocoa. Sign. 1A.	150.00	450.00	1000.
2	5000 FRANCS	ND (1961). M/c. Pres. A. Ahidjo at r. Sign. 1A.	75.00	200.00	750.00

| 2A | 5000 FRANCS | ND. Like #2 but denomination also in English words at lower l. ctr. Sign. 1A. | 150.00 | 400.00 | 1000. |

RÉPUBLIQUE FÉDÉRALE DU CAMEROUN
Banque Centrale

#3–7 denominations in French and English.

Cat. #	Denomination	Date, description	VG	VF	Unc
3	100 FRANCS	ND (1962). M/c. Pres. of the Republic at l. Ships on back. Sign. 1A.	5.00	20.00	60.00

| 4 | 500 FRANCS | ND (1962). M/c. Man w/2 oxen. Man w/bananas, road w/ truck, 2 ships on back. Sign. 1A. | 12.00 | 40.00 | 125.00 |

NOTE: Engraved and litho varieties exist for #4.

5	1000 FRANCS	ND (1962). M/c. Like #1 but *REPUBLIQUE FEDERALE . . .* on back. Sign. 1A.	15.00	60.00	175.00
6	5000 FRANCS	ND (1962). M/c. Like #2A but *REPUBLIQUE FEDERALE . . .* on back. Sign. 1A.	50.00	150.00	425.00
7	10,000 FRANCS	ND (1972). M/c. Pres. A. Ahidjo at l., fruit at ctr., wood carving at r. Statue at l. and r., tractor plowing at ctr. on back. Sign. 2.	35.00	75.00	160.00

RÉPUBLIQUE UNIE DU CAMEROUN
Banque des Etats de l'Afrique Centrale

Cat. #	Denomination	Date, description	VG	VF	Unc
8	500 FRANCS	ND (1974; 1984); 1978–83. Red-brown and m/c. Woman wearing hat at l., aerial view of modern bldgs. at ctr. Mask at l., students and chemical testing at ctr., statue at r. on back.			
		a. Sign. titles: *LE DIRECTEUR GENERAL and UN CENSEUR*. Engraved. (Wmk: Antelope in half profile. Sign. 3. ND (1974).	10.00	50.00	125.00
		b. Like a. Sign. 5.	FV	4.00	10.00
		c. Sign. titles: *LE GOUVERNEUR and UN CENSEUR*. Wmk: Antelope in profile. Sign. 10. 1.4.1978.	FV	3.50	9.00
		d. Sign. 12. 1.6.1981; 1.1.1982; 1.1.1983.	FV	3.00	7.50

Cat. #	Denomination	Date, description	VG	VF	Unc
9	1000 FRANCS	ND (1974); 1978–82. Blue and m/c. Hut at ctr., girl w/plaits at r. Mask at l., trains, planes and bridge at ctr., statue at r. on back.			
		a. Sign. titles: *LE DIRECTEUR GENERAL and UN CENSEUR*. Engraved. Wmk: Antelope in half profile. Sign. 5. ND (1974).	FV	8.00	20.00
		b. Sign. titles like a. Lithographed. Wmk. like c. Sign. 8. ND (1978).	20.00	50.00	125.00
		c. Sign. titles: *LE GOUVERNEUR and UN CENSEUR*. Lithographed. Wmk: Antelope in profile. Sign.10. 1.4.1978; 1.7.1980.	FV	7.50	17.00
		d. Sign. 12. 1.6.1981; 1.1.1982; 1.1.1983.	FV	7.50	15.00

Cat. #	Denomination	Date, description	VG	VF	Unc
10	5000 FRANCS	ND (1974).Brown and m/c.. Pres. A. Ahidjo at l., railway loading equipment at r. Mask at l., industrial college at ctr., statue at r. on back.			
		a. Sign. titles: *LE DIRECTEUR GENERAL and UN CENSEUR*. Engraved. Sign. 3. ND (1974).	50.00	150.00	325.00
		b. Like a. Sign. 5.	30.00	60.00	175.00
		c. Sign. titles: *LE GOUVERNEUR and UN CENSEUR*. Sign. 11; 12.	FV	30.00	60.00

Cat. #	Denomination	Date, description	VG	VF	Unc
11	10,000 FRANCS	ND (1974; 1978; 1981). M/c. Pres. A. Ahidjo at l. Similar to #7 except for new bank name on back.			
		a. Sign. titles: *LE DIRECTEUR GENERAL and UN CENSEUR*. Sign. 5. ND (1974).	FV	60.00	125.00
		b. Sign. titles: *LE GOUVERNEUR and UN CENSEUR*. Sign. 11; 12. ND (1978; 1981).	FV	55.00	100.00
12	5000 FRANCS	ND (1981). Brown and m/c. Mask at l., woman carrying bundle of fronds at r. Plowing and mine ore conveyor on back. Sign. 12.	FV	21.50	40.00

Cat. #	Denomination	Date, description	VG	VF	Unc
13	10,000 FRANCS	ND (1981). Brown, green and m/c. Stylized antelope heads at l., woman at r. Loading of fruit onto truck at l. on back. Sign. 12.	FV	FV	75.00

RÉPUBLIQUE DU CAMEROON
Banque des Etats de l'Afrique Centrale

Cat. #	Denomination	Date, description	VG	VF	Unc
14	1000 FRANCS	1.6.1984. Blue and m/c. Like #9 except for new country name. Sign. 12	FV	7.00	15.00
15	5000 FRANCS	ND (1984; 1990). Brown and m/c. Like #12 except for new country name. Sign. 12; 13.	FV	12.50	25.00
16	10,000 FRANCS	ND (1984; 1990). Brown, green and m/c. Like #13 except for new country name. Sign. 12; 13.	FV	25.00	50.00

1985 ISSUE

#17–19 wmk: Carving (as on notes).

Cat. #	Denomination	Date, description	VG	VF	Unc
17	500 FRANCS	1985–. Brown on m/c unpt. Carving and jug at ctr. Man carving mask at l. ctr. on back.			
		a. Sign. 12. 1.1.1985–1.1.1988.	FV	3.00	5.00
		b. Sign. 13. 1.1.1990.	FV	FV	3.50

Cat. #	Denomination	Date, description	VG	VF	Unc
18	1000 FRANCS	1.1.1985. Dk. blue on m/c unpt. Carving at l., small figurines at ctr., man at r. Incomplete map of Chad at top. Elephant at l., carving at r.on back.	FV	10.00	17.50

19	1000 FRANCS	1986–. Like #18 but w/completed outline map of Chad at top ctr.			
		a. Sign. 12. 1.1.1986–1.1.1989.	FV	6.00	10.00
		b. Sign. 13. 1.1.1990.	FV	7.00	11.00
		c. Sign. 15.1.1.1992.	FV	2.75	5.00

CANADA

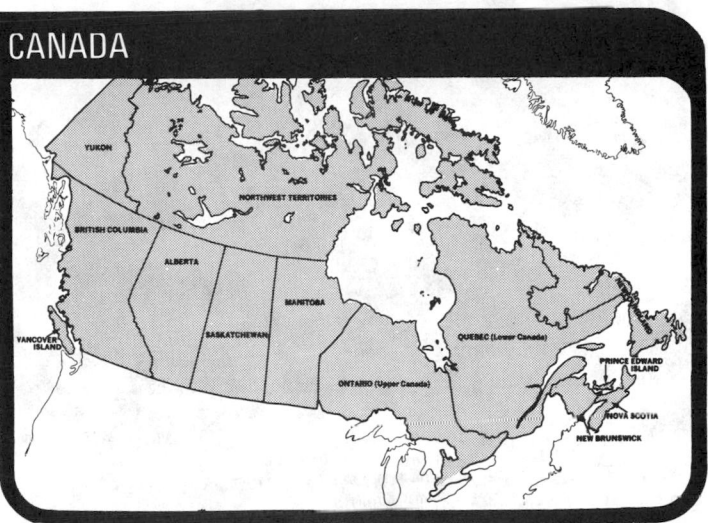

Jacques Cartier, a French explorer, took possession of Canada for France in 1534, and for more than a century the history of Canada was that of a French colony. Samuel de Champlain helped to establish the first permanent colony in North America, in 1604 at Port Royal, Acadia — now Annapolis Royal, Nova Scotia. Four years later he founded the settlement of Quebec.

The British settled along the coast to the south while the French, motivated by a grand design, pushed into the interior. France's plan for a great American empire was to occupy the Mississippi heartland of the country, and from there to press in upon the narrow strip of English coastal settlements from the rear. Inevitably, armed conflict erupted between the French and the British; consequently, Britain acquired Hudson Bay, Newfoundland and Nova Scotia from the French in 1713. British control of the rest of New France was secured in 1763, largely because of James Wolfe's great victory over Montcalm near Quebec in 1759.

During the American Revolution, Canada became a refuge for great numbers of American loyalists, most of whom settled in Ontario, thereby creating an English majority west of the Ottawa River. This ethnic imbalance contravened the effectiveness of the prevailing French type of government, and in 1791 the Constitutional act was passed by the British parliament, dividing Canada at the Ottawa River into two parts, each with its own government: Upper Canada, chiefly English and consisting of the southern section of what is now Ontario; and Lower Canada, chiefly French and consisting principally of the southern section of Quebec. Subsequent revolt by dissidents in both sections caused the British government to pass the Union act, July 23, 1840, which united Lower and Upper Canada (as Canada East and Canada West) to form the Province of Canada, with one council and one assembly in which the two sections had equal numbers.

The union of the two provinces did not encourage political stability; the equal strength of the French and British made the task of government all but impossible. A further change was made with the passage of the British North American act, which took effect on July 1, 1867, and established Canada as the first federal union in the British Empire. Four provinces entered the union at first: Upper Canada as Ontario, Lower Canada as Quebec, Nova Scotia and New Brunswick. The Hudson's Bay Company's territories were acquired in 1869 out of which were formed the provinces of Manitoba, Saskatchewan and Alberta. British Columbia joined in 1871 and Prince Edward Island in 1873. Canada took over the Arctic Archipelago in 1895. In 1949 Newfoundland came into the confederation. Canada is a member of the Commonwealth of Nations. The Queen of England is Chief of State.

> **NOTE:** This section has been renumbered from the old 7th Edition of General Issues

RULERS
British

MONETARY SYSTEM
1 Dollar = 100 Cents

REPLACEMENT NOTES

#66–70A and 74b, asterisk in front of fractional prefix letters. #76, 78-81, triple letter prefix ending in X (AAX, BAX, etc.). Exceptions: #82, no asterisk but serial number starts with 510 or 516; #83, serial number starts with 31 (instead of 30). #84-90, as #76 and 78-81.

Banque Du Canada/Bank of Canada

NOTE: Dates reflect those as seen on the various issues. They remain constant even though signatures may change several times.

1954 "Devil's Head" ISSUE

#66–83 Qn. Elizabeth II at r.

"Devil's face"   Retouched

Cat #	Denomination	Date, description	VG	VF	Unc
66	1 DOLLAR	1954. Black on green unpt. "Devil's face" in hairdo of Qn. Back green; Western prairie scene. Printer: CBNC.			
		a. Sign. Coyne-Towers.	2.50	5.50	30.00
		b. Sign. Beattie-Coyne.	2.00	5.00	25.00
67	2 DOLLARS	1954. Black on red-brown unpt. "Devil's face" in hairdo of Qn. Back red-brown; Quebec scenery. Printer: BABNC.			
		a. Sign. Coyne-Towers.	5.00	12.50	55.00
		b. Sign. Beattie-Coyne.	5.00	10.00	45.00
68	5 DOLLARS	1954. Black on blue unpt. "Devil's face" in Qn's. hairdo. Back blue; river in the North Country. Printer: BABNC.			
		a. Sign. Coyne-Towers.	8.50	17.50	75.00
		b. Sign. Beattie-Coyne.	7.50	15.00	65.00
69	10 DOLLARS	1954. Black on purple unpt. "Devil's face" in Qn's. hairdo. Back purple; Rocky Mountain scene. Printer: BABNC.			
		a. Sign. Coyne-Towers.	15.00	25.00	95.00
		b. Sign. Beattie-Coyne.	12.00	20.00	80.00
70	20 DOLLARS	1954. Black on olive green unpt. "Devil's face" in Qn's. hairdo. Back olive-green; Laurentian Hills in winter. Printer: CBNC.			
		a. Sign. Coyne-Towers.	22.50	45.00	165.00
		b. Sign. Beattie-Coyne.	22.50	40.00	135.00
71	50 DOLLARS	1954. Black on orange unpt. "Devil's face" in Qn's. hairdo. Back orange: Atlantic coastline. Printer: CBNC.			
		a. Sign. Coyne-Towers.	55.00	90.00	225.00
		b. Sign. Beattie-Coyne.	55.00	85.00	200.00
72	100 DOLLARS	1954. Black on brown unpt. "Devil's face" in Qn's. hairdo. Back brown; mountain lake. Printer: CBNC.			
		a. Sign. Coyne-Towers.	100.00	145.00	285.00
		b. Sign. Beattie-Coyne.	100.00	150.00	300.00
73	1000 DOLLARS	1954. Black on rose unpt. "Devil's face" in Qn's. hairdo. Back rose; Central Canadian landscape. Sign: Coyne-Towers.	1000.	1200.	1650.

1954 "Modified Hairstyle" ISSUES

Cat #	Denomination	Date, description	VG	VF	Unc
74 (66A)	1 DOLLAR	1954. Like #66 but Qn.'s hair in modified style. Printer: CBNC.			
		a. Sign. Beattie-Coyne.	1.25	3.00	12.50
		b. Sign. Beattie-Rasminsky.	1.00	1.50	7.50
75 (66B)	1 DOLLAR	1954. Like #74. Printer: BABNC.			
		a. Sign. Beattie-Coyne.	1.00	2.00	12.50
		b. Sign. Beattie-Rasminsky.	1.00	1.50	5.00
		c. Sign. Bouey-Rasminsky.	1.00	1.50	5.00
		d. Sign. Lawson-Bouey.	1.00	1.50	5.50

Cat. #	Denomination	Date, description	VG	VF	Unc
77 (68A)	5 DOLLARS	1954. Like #68 but Qn's. hair in modified style. Printer: CBNC.			
		a. Sign. Beattie-Coyne.	7.50	15.00	45.00
		b. Sign. Beattie-Rasminsky.	5.00	7.50	27.50
		c. Sign. Bouey-Rasminsky.	5.00	7.50	27.50
78 (68B)	5 DOLLARS	1954. Like #77. Sign. Beattie-Coyne. Printer: BABNC.	7.50	15.00	45.00

Cat. #	Denomination	Date, description	VG	VF	Unc
79 (69A)	10 DOLLARS	1954. Like #69 but Qn's. hair in modified style. Printer: BABNC.			
		a. Sign. Beattie-Coyne.	10.00	12.50	65.00
		b. Sign. Beattie-Rasminsky.	10.00	12.50	40.00

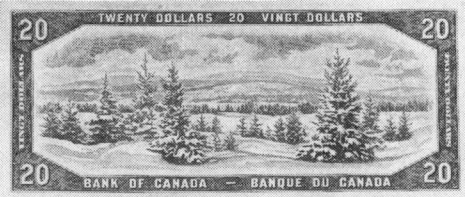

Cat. #	Denomination	Date, description	VG	VF	Unc
80 (70A)	20 DOLLARS	1954. Like #70 but Qn's. hair in modified style.			
		a. Sign. Beattie-Coyne.	22.50	27.50	100.00
		b. Sign. Beattie-Rasminsky.	20.00	25.00	75.00

Cat. #	Denomination	Date, description	VG	VF	Unc
76 (67A)	2 DOLLARS	1954. Like #67 but Qn's. hair in modified style. Printer: BABNC.			
		a. Sign. Beattie-Coyne.	2.00	5.50	25.00
		b. Sign. Beattie-Rasminsky.	2.00	3.50	10.00
		c. Sign. Bouey-Rasminsky.	2.00	3.50	11.00
		d. Sign. Lawson-Bouey.	2.00	3.00	9.50

Cat. # 81 (71A)	Denomination 50 DOLLARS	Date, description 1954. Like #71 but Qn's. hair in modified style. Printer: CBNC.	VG	VF	Unc
		a. Sign. Beattie-Coyne.	50.00	65.00	165.00
		b. Sign. Beattie-Rasminsky.	50.00	65.00	150.00
		c. Sign. Lawson-Bouey.	50.00	85.00	275.00

82 (72A)	100 DOLLARS	1954. Like #72 but Qn's. hair in modified style. Printer: CBNC.			
		a. Sign. Beattie-Coyne.	100.00	135.00	250.00
		b. Sign. Beattie-Rasminsky.	100.00	125.00	235.00
		c. Sign. Lawson-Bouey.	100.00	135.00	250.00
83 (73A)	1000 DOLLARS	1954. Like #73 but Qn's. hair in modified style.			
		a. Sign. Beattie-Coyne.	1000.	1200.	1750.
		b. Sign. Beattie-Rasminsky.	950.00	1100.	1750.
		c. Sign. Bouey-Rasminsky.	950.00	1100.	1500.
		d. Sign. Lawson-Bouey.	900.00	1050.	1350.
		e. Sign. Thiessen-Crow.	950.00	1100.	1500.

1967 COMMEMORATIVE ISSUE

#74, Centennial of Canadian Confederation

Dates: *1867–1967* replace regular serial #.

Regular serial #.

Cat # 84 (74)	Denomination 1 DOLLAR	Date, description 1967. Black on green unpt. Qn. Elizabeth II at r. First Parliament on green back.	VG	VF	Unc
		a. *1867–1967* replacing serial #.	1.00	1.50	3.50
		b. Serial #.	1.00	1.50	4.50

1969–75 ISSUE

85 (78)	1 DOLLAR	1973. Black, lt. green on m/c unpt. Qn. Eliza- beth II at r. Parliament across the Ottawa river on back.			
		a. Sign. Lawson-Bouey.	FV	1.00	3.50
		b. Sign. Crow-Bouey.	FV	1.00	2.50

NOTE: Two formats of uncut 40-note sheets of #85b were sold to collectors in 1988 (BABN) and again in 1989 (CBNC). BABN format: 5x8 notes regular prefix BFD, BFK, BFL replacement prefix BAX. CBNC format: 4x10 notes: regular prefix ECP, ECR, ECV, ECW, replacement prefix EAX.

86 (79)	2 DOLLARS	1974. Red-brown on m/c unpt. Qn. Elizabeth II at r. Inuits preparing for whaling on back.			
		a. Sign. Lawson-Bouey.	FV	2.00	6.50
		b. Sign. Crow-Bouey.	FV	2.00	6.00

87 (77)	5 DOLLARS	1972. Blue on m/c unpt. Sir Wilfred Laurier at r. Serial # on face. Salmon fishing along Pacific coast on back.			
		a. Sign. Bouey-Rasminsky.	FV	6.00	25.00
		b. Sign. Lawson-Bouey.	FV	6.00	22.50

Cat #	Denomination	Date, description	VG	VF	Unc
88	10 DOLLARS	1971. Purple on m/c unpt. Sir John A. Mac-			
(76)		Donald at r. Oil refinery on back.			
		a. Sign. Beattie-Rasminsky.	FV	12.00	40.00
		b. Sign. Bouey-Rasminsky.	FV	12.00	45.00
		c. Sign. Lawson-Bouey.	FV	FV	25.00
		d. Sign. Crow-Bouey.	FV	FV	22.50
		e. Sign. Thiessen-Crow.	FV	FV	20.00

Cat #	Denomination	Date, description	VG	VF	Unc
89	20 DOLLARS	1969. Green on m/c unpt. Arms at l. Qn. Eliz-			
(75)		abeth II at r. Serial # on face. Lake, Rocky			
		Mountains on back.			
		a. Sign. Beattie-Rasminsky.	FV	22.50	50.00
		b. Sign. Lawson-Bouey.	FV	22.50	50.00

Cat #	Denomination	Date, description	VG	VF	Unc
90	50 DOLLARS	1975. Red on m/c unpt. W.L. MacKenzie			
(80)		King at r. Mounted Police in formation on			
		back.			
		a. Sign. Lawson-Bouey.	FV	55.00	100.00
		b. Sign. Crow-Bouey.	FV	50.00	95.00

Cat #	Denomination	Date, description	VG	VF	Unc
91	100 DOLLARS	1975. Brown on m/c unpt. Sir Robert Bor-			
(81)		den at r. 3 ships dockside on back.			
		a. Sign. Lawson-Bouey.	FV	105.00	160.00
		b. Sign. Crow-Bouey.	FV	100.00	150.00

1979 ISSUE

Cat #	Denomination	Date, description	VG	VF	Unc
92	5 DOLLARS	1979. Blue on m/c unpt. Similar to #87, but			
(83)		different guilloches on face. Serial # on			
		back.			
		a. Sign. Lawson-Bouey.	FV	FV	15.00
		b. Sign. Crow-Bouey.	FV	FV	22.50

Cat #	Denomination	Date, description	VG	VF	Unc
93	20 DOLLARS	1979. Deep olive-green on m/c unpt. Similar			
(82)		to #89, but different guilloches on face.			
		Serial # on back.			
		a. Sign. Lawson-Bouey.	FV	FV	60.00
		b. Sign. Crow-Bouey.	FV	FV	45.00
		c. Sign. Thiessen-Crow.	FV	FV	25.00

1986–91 ISSUE

Cat #	Denomination	Date, description	VG	VF	Unc
94	2 DOLLARS	1986. Brown on m/c unpt. Qn. Elizabeth II,			
(84)		Parliament Bldg. at r. Robins on back.			
		a. Sign. Crow-Bouey.	FV	FV	4.00
		b. Sign. Thiessen-Crow.	FV	FV	3.00
		c. Sign. Bonnin-Thiessen.	FV	FV	2.50

NOTE: Two formats of uncut 40-note sheets of #86b were sold to collectors in 1995-96. BABN format: 5x8 notes. CBNC format: 4x10 notes.

Cat #	Denomination	Date, description	VG	VF	Unc
99 (89)	100 DOLLARS	1988. Dk. brown on m/c unpt. Sir R. Bordon, Parliament bldg. at r., green optical device w/denomination at upper l. Canada goose on back. Sign. Thiessen-Crow.	FV	FV	90.00

Cat #	Denomination	Date, description	VG	VF	Unc
95 (85)	5 DOLLARS	1986. Blue-gray on m/c unpt. Sir Wilfred Laurler, bldgs. at r. Kingfisher on back.			
		a. Sign. Crow-Bouey.	FV	FV	7.00
		b. Sign. Thiessen-Crow.	FV	FV	5.50

	1000 DOLLARS	1988. Pink on m/c unpt. Face similar to 2 dollars, #94 w/optical device w/denomi- nations at upper l. 2 pine grosbeaks on branch at r. on back. Sign. Thiessen- Crow.	VG	VF	Unc
100 (90)	1000 DOLLARS		FV	FV	875.00

			VG	VF	Unc
96 (86)	10 DOLLARS	1989. Purple on m/c unpt. Sir John A. Mac- donald at l. ctr. w/bldgs. Osprey on back. Sign. Thiessen-Crow.	FV	FV	11.00
97 (87)	20 DOLLARS	1991. Dccp olive-green and ollve-green on m/c unpt. Green foil optical device w/denom. at upper l. Qn. Elizabeth II, Parli- ement library at r. Loon on back. Sign. Thiessen-Crow.	FV	FV	20.00

NOTE: The letter "I" in prefix also appears as "I".

			VG	VF	Unc
98 (88)	50 DOLLARS	1988. Red on m/c unpt. W. L. MacKenzie King, Parliament bldg. at r., gold optical device w/denomination at upper l. Snowy owl on back. Sign. Thiessen-Crow.	FV	FV	47.00

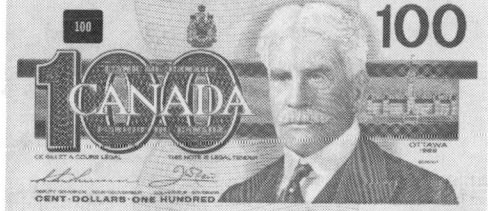

The Republic of Cape Verde, Africa's smallest republic, is located in the Atlantic Ocean, about 370 miles (595 km.) west of Dakar, Senegal, off the coast of Africa. The 14–island republic has an area of 1,557 sq. mi. (4,033 sq. km.) and a population of 380,000. Capital: Praia. The refueling of ships and aircraft is the chief economic function of the country. Fishing is important and agriculture is widely practiced, but the Cape Verdes are not self-sufficient in food. Fish products, salt, bananas, coffee, peanuts and shellfish are exported.

The date of discovery of the islands is uncertain. Possibly they were visited by Venetian Captain Alvise Cadamosto in 1456. Portuguese navigator Diogo Gomes claimed them for Portugal in May of 1460. Settlement began two years later. The early importance and wealth of the islands, which caused them to be attacked by Sir Francis Drake and the Dutch, resulted from the monopoly of the Guinea slave trade granted the inhabitants in 1466. Poverty and famine occasioned by frequent periods of severe drought have marked the history of the country since abolition of the slave trade in 1876.

After 500 years of Portuguese rule, the Cape Verdes became independent on July 5, 1975. At the first general election, all seats of the new national assembly were won by the Party for the Independence of Guinea–Bissau and Cape Verde (PAIGC). The PAIGC plans to link the two former colonies into one state.

RULERS
Portuguese to 1975

MONETARY SYSTEM
1 Mil Reis = 1000 Reis
1 Escudo = 100 Centavos

PORTUGUESE INFLUENCE
Banco Nacional Ultramarino
1958 ISSUE
Decreto Lei 39221

#47–50 portr. S. Pinto at r., bank seal at l., arms at lower ctr. Sign titles: *O-ADMINISTRADOR* and *O VICE-GOVERNADOR*. Printer: BWC.

Cat. #	Denomination	Date, description	VG	VF	Unc
47	20 ESCUDOS	16.6.1958. Green on m/c unpt.	1.50	5.00	25.00
48	50 ESCUDOS	16.6.1958. Blue on m/c unpt.	5.00	25.00	125.00

| 49 | 100 ESUCUDOS | 16.6.1958. Red on m/c unpt. | 3.00 | 10.00 | 25.00 |
| 50 | 500 ESCUDOS | 16.6.1958. Brown-violet on m/c unpt. | 20.00 | 40.00 | 135.00 |

1971–72 ISSUE

Decreto Lei 39221 and 44891.

| 51 | *Deleted.* See #53A. |

#52 and #53A like #47 and 48 but w/security thread. Sign. titles: *ADMINISTRADOR* and *VICE-GOVERNADOR*.

Cat. #	Denomination	Date, description	VG	VF	Unc
52	20 ESCUDOS	4.4.1972. Green on m/c unpt. 2 sign. varieties.	1.50	5.00	15.00

| 53 | 50 ESCUDOS | 4.4.1972. Blue on m/c unpt. | 2.00 | 10.00 | 30.00 |

| 53A | 500 ESCUDOS | 16.6.1971; 29.6.1971. Olive-green on m/c unpt. Infante D. Henrique at r. | 15.00 | 50.00 | 150.00 |

REPUBLIC
Banco De Cabo Verde
1977 ISSUE

#54-56 A. Cabral w/native hat at r. and as wmk. w/security thread. Printer: BWC.

| 54 | 100 ESCUDOS | 20.1.1977. Red and m/c. Bow and musical instruments at l. Mountain on back. | FV | 2.50 | 5.00 |

| 55 | 500 ESCUDOS | 20.1.1977. Blue and m/c. Shark at l. Harbor at Praia on back. | FV | 7.00 | 15.00 |

Cat. #	Denomination	Date, description	VG	VF	Unc
56	1000 ESCUDOS	20.1.1977. Brown and m/c. Electrical appliance at l. Workers at quarry on back.	FV	15.00	35.00

1989 ISSUE

#57–61 A. Cabral at r. and as wmk. Serial # black at l., red at r. Printer: TDLR.

57	100 ESCUDOS	20.1.1989. Red and brown on m/c unpt. Festival on back.	FV	FV	4.50

58	200 ESCUDOS	20.1.1989. Green and black on m/c unpt. Modern airport collage vertically on back.	FV	FV	8.00
59	500 ESCUDOS	20.1.1989. Blue on m/c unpt. Shipyard on back.	FV	FV	15.00
60	1000 ESCUDOS	20.1.1989. Brown and red-brown on m/c unpt. Insects on back.	FV	FV	30.00
61	2500 ESCUDOS	20.1.1989. Violet on m/c unpt. Palace of National Assembly on back.	FV	FV	75.00

1992 ISSUE

#63-64 wmk: A. Cabral. Printer: TDLR.

Cat. #	Denomination	Date, description	VG	VF	Unc
63	200 ESCUDOS	8.8.1992. Black and blue-green on m/c unpt. Sailing ship *Ernestina* at r. Back like #58.	FV	FV	7.00

64	500 ESCUDOS	23.4.1992. Purple, blue and dk. brown on m/c unpt. Dr. B. Lopes da Silva at r. Back like #59.	FV	FV	14.00

65	1000 ESCUDOS	5.6.1992. Dk. brown, red-orange and purple on m/c unpt. Bird at ctr. r. Grasshopper on back.	FV	FV	30.00

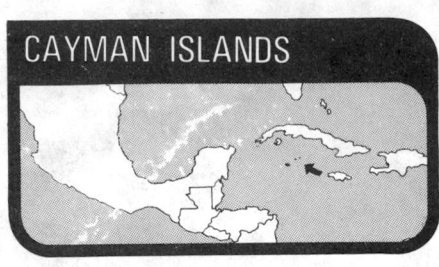

The Cayman Islands, a British dependency situated about 180 miles (290 km.) northwest of Jamaica, consists of three islands: Grand Cayman, Little Cayman and Cayman Brac. The islands have an area of 102 sq. mi. (259 sq. km.) and a population of 26,950. Capital: Georgetown. Seafaring, commerce, banking and tourism are the principal industries. Rope, turtle shells and shark skins are exported.

The islands were discovered by Columbus in 1503, and were named by him, Tortugas (Spanish for "turtles") because of the great number of turtles in the nearby waters. The Cayman Islands were colonized from Jamaica by the British and remained dependencies of Jamaica until 1959, when they became a unit territory within the West Indies Federation. They became a separate colony when the Federation was dissolved in 1962.

RULERS
British

MONETARY SYSTEM
1 Dollar = 100 Cents

REPLACEMENT NOTES
#1–15, Z/1 prefix.

Cayman Islands Currency Board

1971 Currency Law

#1–4 arms at upper ctr., Qn. Elizabeth II at r. Wmk: Tortoise. Printer: TDLR.

Cat. #	Denomination	Date, description	VG	VF	Unc
1	1 DOLLAR	L.1971 (1972). Blue on m/c unpt. Fish, coral at ctr. on back.	1.50	2.00	5.00

2	5 DOLLARS	L.1971 (1972). Green on m/c unpt. Sailboat at ctr. on back.	8.00	10.00	17.50

3	10 DOLLARS	L.1971 (1972). Red on m/c unpt. Beach scene at ctr. on back.	14.00	18.00	45.00

Cat. #	Denomination	Date, description	VG	VF	Unc
4	25 DOLLARS	L.1971 (1972). Brown on m/c unpt. Compass and map at ctr. on back.	35.00	45.00	100.00

1974 Currency Law

#5–11 arms at upper ctr., Qn. Elizabeth II at r. Wmk: Tortoise. Printer: TDLR.

5	1 DOLLAR	L.1974 (1985). Like #1.			
		a. Sign. as #1 illustration.	FV	1.75	4.50
		b. Sign. Jefferson.	FV	1.50	2.50

6	5 DOLLARS	L.1974. Like #2.	FV	7.00	10.00

7	10 DOLLARS	L.1974. Like #3.	FV	13.00	20.00

8	25 DOLLARS	L.1974. Like #4.	FV	32.50	45.00

9	40 DOLLARS	L.1974. (1981). Purple and m/c. Pirates Week Festival (crowd on beach) at ctr. on back.	FV	55.00	85.00

Cat. #	Denomination	Date, description	VG	VF	Unc
10	50 DOLLARS	L.1974. (1987). Blue on m/c unpt. Govt. house at ctr. on back.	FV	70.00	90.00

Cat. #	Denomination	Date, description	VG	VF	Unc
15	100 DOLLARS	1991. Orange and dk. brown on m/c unpt. Harbor view at ctr. on back.	FV	FV	160.00

COLLECTOR SERIES

Cat. #	Date, denomination	Description	Issue Price	Mkt. Val.
CS1	L.1974 1–100 DOLLARS	#5–11 ovpt: SPECIMEN.	—	110.00

NOTE: Estimated availability of #CS1 is 300 sets.

CS2	1991 5–100 DOLLARS	#12–15 ovpt: SPECIMEN.	61.35	80.00

11	100 DOLLARS	L.1974. (1982). Deep orange and m/c. Sea-coast view of George Town at ctr. on back.	FV	1.35	175.00

1991 ISSUE

#12–15 arms at upper ctr., Qn. Elizabeth II at r. Red coral at l. on back. Wmk: Tortoise. Printer: TDLR.

12	5 DOLLARS	1991. Dark green and olive-brown on m/c unpt. Sailboat in harbor waters at ctr. on back.	FV	FV	9.00

13	10 DOLLARS	1991. Red and purple on m/c unpt. Open chest, palm tree along coastline at ctr. on back.	FV	FV	17.50

14	25 DOLLARS	1991. Dk. brown and brown on m/c unpt. Island outlines and compass at ctr. on back.	FV	FV	40.00

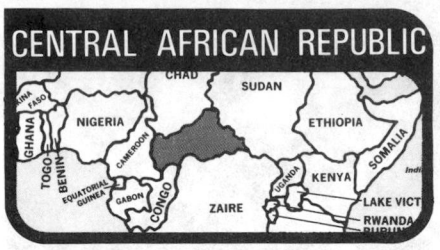

CENTRAL AFRICAN REPUBLIC

The Central African Republic, a landlocked country in Central Africa, bounded by Chad on the north, Cameroon on the west, Congo (Brazzaville) and Zaire on the south, and The Sudan on the east, has an area of 240,535 sq. mi. (622,984 sq. km.) and a population of 3.13 million. Capital: Bangui. Deposits of uranium, iron ore, manganese and copper remain to be developed. Diamonds, cotton, timber and coffee are exported.

The area that is now the Central African Republic was constituted as the French territory of Ubangi-Shari in 1894. It was united with Chad in 1905 and joined with Middle Congo and Gabon in 1910, becoming one of the four territories of French Equatorial Africa. Upon dissolution of the federation on Dec. 1, 1958, the constituent territories became full autonomous members of the French Community. Ubangi-Shari proclaimed its complete independence as the Central African Republic on Aug. 13, 1960.

On Jan. 1, 1966, Col. Jean-Bedel Bokassa, Chief of Staff of the Armed Forces, overthrew the government of President David Dacko and assumed power as president of the republic. President Bokassa abolished the constitution of 1959 and dissolved the National Assembly. In 1972 the Congress of the sole political party appointed Bokassa president for life. The republic became a constitutional monarchy on Dec. 4, 1976; President Bokassa was named Emperor Bokassa I. Bokassa was ousted as Central African emperor in a bloodless takeover of the government led by former president David Dacko on Sept. 20, 1979, and the African nation proclaimed once again a republic.

See also French Equatorial Africa and Equatorial African States. It is a member of the "Union Monetaire des Etats de l'Afrique Centrale."

NOTE: For later issues see Central African States.

RULERS
Emperor Bokassa I, 1976–79

MONETARY SYSTEM
1 Franc = 100 Centimes

SIGNATURE VARIETIES
Refer to introduction to Central African States.

RÉPUBLIQUE CENTRAFRICAINE
Banque des Etats de L'Afrique Centrale

#1–4 Pres. Bokassa at r. in military uniform w/ or w/o cap. Wmk: Antelope's head.

Cat. #	Denomination	Date, description	VG	VF	Unc
1	500 FRANCS	ND (1974). Lilac-brown and m/c. Landscape at ctr. Mask at l., students and chemical testing at ctr., statue at r. on back. Sign. 6.	5.00	20.00	60.00

Cat. #	Denomination	Date, description	VG	VF	Unc
2	1000 FRANCS	ND (1974). Blue and m/c. Rhinoceros at l., water buffalo at ctr. Mask at l., trains, planes and bridge at ctr., statue at r. on back. Sign. 6.	8.00	30.00	80.00

3	5000 FRANCS	ND (1974). Brown and m/c. Field workers hoeing at l., combine at ctr. Mask at l., bldgs. at ctr., statue at r. on back.			
		a. Sign. 4.	35.00	95.00	250.00
		b. Sign. 6.	32.50	85.00	200.00

| 4 | 10,000 FRANCS | ND (1976). M/c. Sword hilts at l. and ctr. Mask at l., tractor cultivating at ctr., statue at r. on back. Sign. 6. | 75.00 | 175.00 | 450.00 |

EMPIRE CENTRAFRICAIN
Banque des Etats de L'Afrique Centrale

#5–8 Emp. Bokassa I at r. Wmk: Antelope's head.

| 5 | 500 FRANCS | 1.4.1978. Similar to #1. Specimen. | — | — | 1500. |
| 6 | 1000 FRANCS | 1.4.1978. Similar to #2. Sign. 9. | 75.00 | 185.00 | 450.00 |

| 7 | 5000 FRANCS | ND (1979). Similar to #3. Sign. 9. | 75.00 | 185.00 | 450.00 |

Cat. #	Denomination	Date, description	VG	VF	Unc
8	10,000 FRANCS	ND (1978). Similar to #4. Sign. 6.	65.00	150.00	300.00

RÉPUBLIQUE CENTRAFRICAINE
Banque des Etats de l'Afrique Centrale

#9–10 wmk: Antelope's head.

| 9 | 500 FRANCS | 1.1.1980; 1.7.1980; 1.6.1981. Red and m/c. Woman weaving basket at r. Back like #1. Lithographed. Sign. 9. | FV | 3.00 | 6.00 |

| 10 | 1000 FRANCS | 1.1.1980; 1.7.1980; 1.6.1981; 1.1.1982; 1.6.1984. Blue and m/c. Butterfly at l., waterfalls at ctr., water buffalo at r. Back like #2. Lithographed. Sign. 9. | FV | 7.50 | 15.00 |

Cat. #	Denomination	Date, description	VG	VF	Unc
11	5000 FRANCS	1.1.1980. Brown and m/c. Girl at l., village scene at ctr. Carving at l., airplane, train crossing bridge and tractor hauling logs at ctr., man smoking a pipe at r. Similar to Equatorial African States #6. Sign. 9.		FV 35.00	70.00

NOTE: For notes with similar back designs see Cameroon Republic, Chad, Congo (Brazzaville) and Gabon.

| 12 | 5000 FRANCS | ND (1984). Brown and m/c. Mask at l., woman w/bundle of fronds at r. Plowing and mine ore conveyor on back. Sign. 9, 14. | FV | 22.50 | 35.00 |

| 13 | 10,000 FRANCS | ND (1983). Brown, green and m/c. Stylized antelope heads at l., woman at r. Loading fruit onto truck at l. on back. Sign. 9. | FV | 40.00 | 65.00 |

1985 ISSUE

#14–16 wmk: Carving (as printed on notes). Sign. 9.

Cat. #	Denomination	Date, description	VG	VF	Unc
14	500 FRANCS	1.1.1985; 1.1.1986; 1.1.1987; 1.1.1989. Brown on orange and m/c unpt. Carving and jug at ctr. Man carving mask at l. ctr. on back.	FV	3.00	6.00

15	1000 FRANCS	1.1.1985. Deep blue on m/c unpt. Carving at l., map at ctr., Gen. Kolingba at r. Incomplete map of Chad at top ctr. Elephant at l., animals at ctr., carving at r. on back.	FV	8.00	15.00
16	1000 FRANCS	1.1.1986-1.1.1990. Like #15 but completed outline map of Chad at top ctr.	FV	4.00	10.00

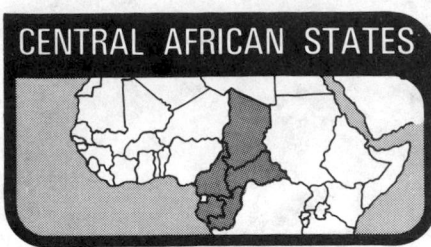

CENTRAL AFRICAN STATES

The Bank of the Central African States (BEAC) is a regional central bank for the monetary and customs union formed by Cameroon, Central African Republic, Chad, Congo (Brazzaville), Gabon, and (since 1985) Equatorial Guinea. It succeeded the Equatorial African States Bank in 1972–73 when the latter was reorganized and renamed to provide greater African control over its operations. The seat of the BEAC was transferred from Paris to Yaounde in 1977 and an African governor assumed responsibility for direction of the bank in 1978. The BEAC is a member of the franc zone with its currency denominated in CFA francs and pegged to the French franc at a rate of 50–1.

BEAC notes carry country names on the face and the central bank name on the back. The 1974–84 series had common back designs but were face-different. A new series begun in 1983–85 uses common designs also on the face except for some 1000 franc notes. The notes carry the signatures of *LE GOUVERNEUR (LE DIRECTEUR GENERAL* prior to 1-4-78) and *UN CENSEUR* (since 1972). Cameroon, Gabon, and France each appoint one censeur and one alternate. Cameroon and Congo notes carry the Cameroon censeur signature. Central African Republic, Equatorial Guinea, and Gabon notes carry the Gabon censeur signature. Chad notes have been divided between the two.

Prior to 1978, all BEAC notes were printed by the Bank of France. Since 1978, the 500 and 1000 franc notes have been printed by the private French firm Oberthur. The Bank of France notes are engraved and usually undated. The Oberthur notes are lithographed and most carry dates.

See the individual member countries for specific note listings. Also see Equatorial African States and French Equatorial Africa.

Banque des Etats de l'Afrique Centrale

CONTROL LETTER or SYMBOL CODE		
Country	Until 1993	1993 onward
Cameroun	*	E
Central African Republic	B	F
Chad	A	P
Congo	C	C
Equatorial Guinea		N
Gabon	D	L

SIGNATURE COMBINATIONS				
1.	Panouillot Le Directeur-General		Gautier Le President	1955–72
1A.	Panouillot Le Directeur-General		Duouedi Un Censeur	1961–72
2.	Panouillot Le Directeur-General		Koulla Un Censeur	1972–73
3.	Joudiou Le Directeur-General		Koulla Un Censeur	1974
4.	Joudiou Le Directeur-General		Renombo Un Censeur	1974
5.	Joudiou Le Directeur-General		Ntang Un Censeur	1974–77
6.	Joudiou Le Directeur-General		Ntoutoume Un Censeur	1974–78
7.	Joudiou Le Directeur-General		Beke Bihege Un Censeur	1977
8.	Joudiou Le Directeur-General		Kamgueu Un Censeur	1978
9.	Oye Mba Le Gouverneur		Ntoutoume Un Censeur	1978–90
10.	Oye Mba Le Gouverneur		Kamgueu Un Censeur	1978–86
11.	Oye Mba Le Gouverneur		Kamgueu Un Censeur	1978–80
12.	Oye Mba Le Gouverneur		Tchepannou Un Censeur	1981–89

13.	Oye Mba		Dang		1990	
	Le Gouverneur		Un Censeur			
14.	Mamalepot		Ntoutoume		1991	
	Le Gouverneur		Un Censeur			
15.	Mamalepot		Mebara		1991–93	
	Le Gouverneur		Un Censeur			
16.	Mamalepot		Ognagma		1994	
17.	Mamalepot				1994–	

CODE LETTERS

Code letters appear at lower left and upper right. Dates appear as first two digits of serial number.

C – Congo (c)
E – Cameroon (e)
F – Central African Republic (f)
L – Gabon (l)
N – Equatorial Guinea (n)
P – Chad (p)

#1-3 map of Central African States at lower l. ctr.

Cat. #	Denomination	Date, description	VG	VF	Unc
3	2000 FRANCS	(19)93–. Dk. brown and green w/black text on m/c unpt. Woman's head at r, and as wmk. surrounded by tropical fruit. Exchange of passengers and produce w/ship at l. ctr. on back.			
		c. Sign. 15. (19)93. Sign. 16. (19)94.	FV	FV	13.50
		c. Sign. 15. (19)93.	FV	FV	13.50
		f. Sign. 15. (19)94.	FV	FV	13.50
		l. Sign. 15. (19)93.	FV	FV	13.50
		n. Sign. 15. (19)93.	FV	FV	13.50
		p. Sign. 15. (19)93.	FV	FV	13.50

Cat. #	Denomination	Date, description	VG	VF	Unc
1	500 FRANCS	(19)93–. Dk. brown and gray on m/c unpt. Shepherd at r. and as wmk., zebus at ctr. Baobab, antelopes and Kota mask on back.			
		c. Sign. 15. (19)93. Sign. 16. (19)94.	FV	FV	4.00
		e. Sign. 15. (19)93. Sign. 17. (19)94.	FV	FV	4.00
		f. Sign. 15. (19)93.	FV	FV	4.00
		l. Sign. 15. (19)93; Sign. 16. (19)94.	FV	FV	4.00
		n. Sign. 15. (19)93.	FV	FV	4.00
		p. Sign. 15. (19)93; Sign. 16. (19)94.	FV	FV	4.00

Cat. #	Denomination	Date, description	VG	VF	Unc
4	5000 FRANCS	(19)94–. Dk. brown, brown and blue w/violet text on m/c unpt. Laborer wearing hard hat at ctr.r., riggers w/well drill at r. Woman w/head basket at lower l., fisherman along shoreline at ctr. on back.			
		c. Sign. 16. (19)94.	FV	FV	25.00
		e. Sign. 17. (19)94.	FV	FV	25.00
		f. Sign. 16. (19)94.	FV	FV	25.00
		l. Sign. 15. (19)93.	FV	FV	25.00
		n. Sign. 16. (19)94.	FV	FV	25.00
		p. Sign. 16. (19)94.	FV	FV	25.00

Cat. #	Denomination	Date, description	VG	VF	Unc
5	10,000 FRANCS	(19)94–. Dk. brown and blue w/blue-black text on m/c unpt. Modern bldg. at ctr., young woman at r. Fisherman, boats and villagers along shoreline at l. ctr. on back.			
		c. Sign. 16. (19)94.	FV	FV	45.00
		e. Sign. 15. (19)93.	FV	FV	45.00
		f. Sign. 16. (19)94.	FV	FV	45.00
		l. Sign. 15. (19)93.	FV	FV	45.00
		n. Sign. 16. (19)94.	FV	FV	45.00
		p. Sign. 16. (19)94.	FV	FV	45.00

Cat. #	Denomination	Date, description	VG	VF	Unc
2	1000 FRANCS	(19)93–. Dk. brown and red w/black text on m/c unpt. Young man at r. and as wmk., harvesting coffee beans at ctr. Forest harvesting, Okoume raft and Bakele wood mask on back.			
		c. Sign. 15. (19)93. Sign. 16. (19)94.	FV	FV	7.00
		e. Sign. 15. (19)93. Sign. 17. (19)94.	FV	FV	7.00
		f. Sign. 15. (19)93. Sign. 16. (19)94.	FV	FV	7.00
		l. Sign. 15. (19)93.	FV	FV	7.00
		n. Sign. 15. (19)93.	FV	FV	7.00
		p. Sign. 15. (19)93.	FV	FV	7.00

Listings For:

CEYLON, see Sri Lanka

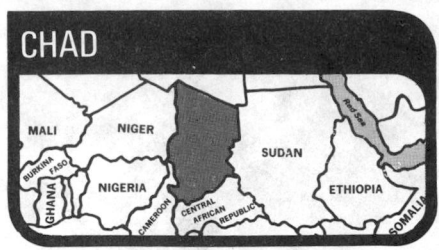

The Republic of Chad, a land-locked country of central Africa, is the largest country of former French Equatorial Africa. It has an area of 495,755 sq. mi. (1,284,000 sq. km.) and a population of 5.96 million. Capital. N'Djaména. An expanding livestock industry produces camels, cattle and sheep. Cotton (the chief product), ivory and palm oil are important exports.

Although supposedly known to Ptolemy, the Chad area was first visited by white men in 1823. Exaggerated estimates of its economic importance led to a race for its possession (1890–93) which resulted in territory being divided by treaty between Great Britain, France and Germany. As a consequence of World War I, the German area was mandated to France in 1919. Chad was absorbed into the colony of French Equatorial Africa, as a part of Ubangi-Shari, in 1910 and became a separate colony in 1920. Upon dissolution of French Equatorial Africa in 1959, the component states became autonomous members of the French Union. Chad became an independent republic on Aug. 11, 1960.

CEYLON, see Shri Lanka MONETARY SYSTEM
 1 Franc = 100 Centimes
SIGNATURE VARIETIES
Refer to introduction to Central African States.

NOTE: For later issues see Central African States

RÉPUBLIQUE DU TCHAD
Banque Centrale

Cat. #	Denomination	Date, description	VG	VF	Unc
1	10,000 FRANCS	ND (1971). M/c. Pres. Tombalbaye at l., cattle watering at ctr. Mask at l., tractor plowing at ctr., statue at r. on back. Sign. 1.	125.00	350.00	850.00

Banque des Etats de l'Afrique Central

Cat. #	Denomination	Date, description	VG	VF	Unc
2	500 FRANCS	ND (1974); 1978. Brown and m/c. Woman at l., birds at ctr. and at r. Mask at l., students and chemical testing at ctr., statue at r. on back.			
		a. Sign. titles: and wmk. like #3a. Sign. 6. (1974).	FV	6.00	17.50
		b. Sign. titles, wmk. and date like #3c. Sign. 10. 1.4.1978.	20.00	75.00	150.00

Cat. #	Denomination	Date, description	VG	VF	Unc
3	1000 FRANCS	ND; 1.4.1978. Blue and m/c. Woman at r. Mask at l., trains, planes and bridge at ctr., statue at r. on back.			
		a. Sign. titles: *LE DIRECTEUR GENERAL* and *UN CENSEUR*. Engraved. Wmk: Antelope in half profile. Sign. 5; 7. (1974).	6.00	15.00	45.00
		b. Sign. titles: *LE DIRECTEUR GENERAL* and *UN CENSEUR*. Lithographed. Wmk: Antelope in profile. Sign. 8. (1978).	5.00	10.00	30.00
		c. Sign. titles: *LE GOUVERNEUR* and *UN CENSEUR*. Sign. 10. 1.4.1978.	4.50	8.50	18.50
4	5000 FRANCS	ND (1974). Brown-orange and m/c. Pres. Tombalbaye at l. Mask at l., industrial college at ctr., statue at r. on back. Sign. 4.	100.00	250.00	625.00
5	5000 FRANCS	ND. Brown and m/c. Woman at l. Like #4 on back.			
		a. Sign. 6. (1976).	22.50	45.00	115.00
		b. Sign. 9. (1978).	21.50	35.00	75.00

1980 ISSUE

Cat. #	Denomination	Date, description	VG	VF	Unc
6	500 FRANCS	1.6.1980; 1.6.1984. Red and m/c. Woman weaving basket at r. Sign. 10	FV	3.00	9.00

Cat. #	Denomination	Date, description	VG	VF	Unc
7	1000 FRANCS	1.6.1980; 1.6.1984. Blue and m/c. Water buffalo at r. Back like #3. Sign. 9; 10.	FV	5.00	15.00

Cat. #	Denomination	Date, description	VG	VF	Unc
8	5000 FRANCS	1.1.1980. Brown and m/c. Girl at l., village scene at ctr. Back w/carving, airplane, train, tractor and man smoking pipe. Similar to Central African Republic #11 and others. Sign. 9.	FV	30.00	70.00

1984–85 ISSUE

Cat. #	Denomination	Date, description	VG	VF	Unc
9	500 FRANCS	1985–92. Brown on m/c unpt. Carved statue and jug at ctr. Man carving mask at l. ctr. on back. Wmk: Carving.			
		a. Sign. 10. 1.1.1985; 1.1.1986.	FV	3.00	8.50
		b. Sign. 12. 1.1.1987.	FV	3.00	8.00
		c. Sign. 13. 1.1.1990.	FV	3.00	7.50
		d. Sign. 15. 1.1.1991; 1.1.1992.	FV	2.50	7.00

Cat. #	Denomination	Date, description	VG	VF	Unc
11	5000 FRANCS	ND (1984–91). Brown and m/c. Mask l., woman w/bundle of fronds at r. Plowing and mine ore conveyor on back. Sign. 9; 15.	FV	25.00	40.00
12	10,000 FRANCS	ND (1984–91). Brown, green and m/c. Stylized antelope heads at l., woman at r. Loading fruit onto truck at l. on back. Sign. 9; 15.	FV	FV	70.00

NOTE: For notes with similar back designs see Cameroon Republic, Central African Republic, Congo (Brazzaville) and Gabon.

Cat. #	Denomination	Date, description	VG	VF	Unc
10	1000 FRANCS	1.1.1985. Blue and m/c. Animal carving at lower l., map at ctr., starburst at lower r. Incomplete outline map of Chad at top ctr. Elephant at l., statue at r. on back. Wmk: Animal carving. Sign. 9.	15.00	30.00	75.00

NOTE: #10 was withdrawn shortly after issue because of the error (incompleteness) at top of the map.

Cat. #	Denomination	Date, description	VG	VF	Unc
10A	1000 FRANCS	1985–91. Like #10 but completed outline map of Chad at top ctr.			
		a. Sign. 9. 1.1.1985; 1.1.1988; 1.1.1989; 1.1.1990.	FV	7.50	12.50
		b. Sign. 15. 1.1.1991.	FV	6.00	11.00

The Republic of Chile, a ribbonlike country on the Pacific coast of southern South America, has an area of 292,258 sq. mi. (756,945 sq. km.) and a population of 13.3 million. Capital: Santiago. Historically, the economic base of Chile has been the rich mineral deposits of its northern provinces. Copper, of which Chile has 25 percent of the free world's reserves, has accounted for more than 75 per cent of Chile's export earnings in recent years. Other important exports are iron ore, iodine, fruit and nitrate of soda.

Diego de Almargo was the first Spaniard to attempt to wrest Chile from the Incas and Araucanian tribes, 1536. He failed, and was followed by Pedro de Valdivia, a favorite of Pizarro, who founded Santiago in 1541. When the Napoleonic Wars involved Spain, leaving the constituent parts of the Spanish Empire to their own devices, Chilean patriots formed a national government and proclaimed the country's independence, Sept. 18, 1810. Independence, however, was not secured until Feb. 12, 1818, after a bitter struggle led by Bernardo O'Higgins and San Martin.

MONETARY SYSTEM

1 Escudo = 100 Centesimos, 1960–75

1 Peso = 100 Escudos, 1975–

Banco Central de Chile

Monetary Reform

1000 Pesos = 1 Escudo (= 100 Centesimos)

1960 PROVISIONAL ISSUE

#124–133 Escudo denominations in red as part of new plates (not ovpt., except #124). on back. Sign. varieties. Printer: CdM- Chile.

Cat. #	Denomination	Date, description	VG	VF	Unc
124	1/2 CENTESIMO on 5 Pesos	ND (1960-61). Blue. Ovpt. on #119.	—	—	—

Cat. #	Denomination	Date, description	VG	VF	Unc
125	1 CENTESIMO on 10 Pesos	ND (1960-61). Red-brown ovpt. on #120.	.50	1.00	6.00

126	5 CENTESIMOS on 50 Pesos	ND (1960-61). Green ovpt. on #121. Wmk: L, V or X below portr.			
		a. Imprint 25mm wide on bottom.	.50	2.00	5.00
		b. Imprint 22mm wide on bottom.	.10	.20	.50

Cat. #	Denomination	Date, description	VG	VF	Unc
127	10 CENTESIMOS on 100 Pesos	ND (1960-61). Red ovpt. on #122. Wmk: C, L, V or X below portr.	.10	.25	.75

128	50 CENTESIMOS on 500 Pesos	ND (1960-61). Blue ovpt. on #115.	.50	2.50	10.00

129	1 ESCUDO on 1000 Pesos	ND (1960-61). Brown ovpt. on #116.	.50	1.50	7.50

130	5 ESCUDOS on 5000 Pesos	ND (1960-61). Brown-violet ovpt. on #117.	1.00	3.00	15.00

131	10 ESCUDOS on 10,000 Pesos	ND (1960-61). Purple on lt. blue unpt.ovpt. on #118. Dual wmk: Head at l., words DIEZ MIL at r.	2.00	10.00	35.00
132	10 ESCUDOS on 10,000 Pesos	ND (1960-61). Red-brown. Similar to #131 but w/o wmk. at r.	2.50	15.00	45.00
133	50 ESCUDOS on 50,000 Pesos	ND (1960-61). Blue-green and brown on m/c unpt. ovpt. on #123.	4.50	17.50	60.00

REGULAR ISSUES
FIRST ISSUE

#134–140 sign. varieties. Wmk: D. Diego Portales P. Printer: CdM-Chile.

Cat. #	Denomination	Date, description	VG	VF	Unc
134	1/2 ESCUDO	ND (1962). Blue. B. O'Higgins at ctr. Explorer on horseback at l. ctr. on back.			
		a. Lt. blue and peach unpt. Red serial #.	.15	.50	1.50
		b. Lt. brown unpt. Black serial #.	.10	.25	1.00

135	1 ESCUDO	ND Brown-violet w/lilac guilloche on tan unpt. Prat at ctr. Red-brown arms w/ founding of Santiago on back. Engraved. Serial # black (3mm) or brown (4mm).			
		a. Wmk: 1000 at r.	.50	2.00	7.50
		b. Wmk: 500 at r.	.50	1.50	4.00
		c. W/o wmk. at r. Arms in red-brown on back.	.20	.50	1.00
		d. W/o wmk. at r. Arms in olive on back.	.10	.20	.75

136	1 ESCUDO	ND. Dull violet on tan unpt. Like #135 but arms on back in lt. olive. Lithographed.	.10	.30	1.00

Cat. #	Denomination	Date, description	VG	VF	Unc
137	5 ESCUDOS	ND. Brown. Bulnes at ctr. Yellow-orange arms at l. Battle of Rancagua at ctr. on back.	.75	2.00	5.00
138	5 ESCUDOS	ND. Red. Like #137. Red-brown arms at l. on back.	.10	.25	1.00

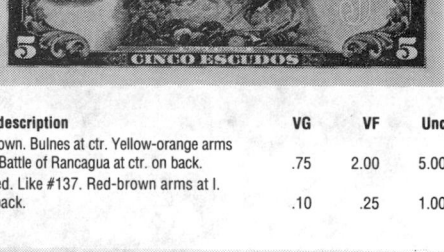

139	10 ESCUDOS	ND. Lilac. M. Balmaceda at ctr. Dk. or lt. brown seal on back. Soldiers meeting at ctr. on back.	.25	.75	4.00

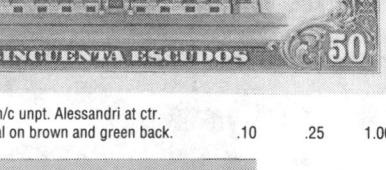

140	50 ESCUDOS	ND. Green on m/c unpt. Alessandri at ctr. Banco Central on brown and green back.	.10	.25	1.00

141	100 ESCUDOS	ND. Blue and brown on tan unpt. Rengifo at r. Sailing ships at ctr. on back.	.25	.75	3.00

SECOND ISSUE

#142–148 sign. varieties. Wmk: D. Diego Portales P. Printer: CdM-Chile.

Cat. #	Denomination	Date, description	VG	VF	Unc
142	10 ESCUDOS	ND (1970). Red-brown, blue and green. M. Balmaceda at r.			
		a. Brown lower margin on back. Engraved.	.20	.50	2.00
		b. Green lower margin on back. Lithographed.	.20	.50	2.00
143	10 ESCUDOS	ND (1973). Brown. Like #142 but lithographed.	.10	.25	.75

Cat. #	Denomination	Date, description	VG	VF	Unc
147	5000 ESCUDOS	ND (1974). Dk. green and brown on m/c unpt. Carrera at l. Carrera House at ctr. r. on back.			
		a. Back w/deep green vignette. Lithographed.	.50	1.50	5.00
		b. Back w/dk. olive-green vignette. Partially engraved.	.30	.75	3.00

148	10,000 ESCUDOS	ND (1974). Red-brown on m/c unpt. B. O'Higgins at l. Blue serial #. Battle of Rancagua on back.	.50	2.00	6.00

144	500 ESCUDOS	ND (1972). Red-brown and m/c. Steel worker at l. Strip mining at ctr. r. on back (mining). W/o 3–line text: *NO DEBEMOS CONSENTIRE…*at bottom.	65.00	200.00	—
145	500 ESCUDOS	ND. Like #144 but w/3–line text: *NO DEBEMOS CONSENTIRE…*on back at bottom.	.15	.50	2.50

Monetary Reform

1 Peso = 100 Escudos

#149–151 wmk: D. Diego Portales P.

146	1000 ESCUDOS	ND (1973). Purple and m/c. Carrera at l. Back like #147.	.15.	.50	3.00

149	5 PESOS	1975–76. Green on olive unpt. Carrera at r. and as wmk. Back similar to #147.	.40	1.00	3.00

Cat. #	Denomination	Date, description	VG	VF	Unc
150	10 PESOS	1975–76. Red. B. O'Higgins at r. and as wmk. Back similar to #148.			
		a. *B. O'HIGGINS* under portr. 1975.	.40	1.00	3.00
		b. *LIBERTADOR B. O'HIGGINS* under portr. 1975; 1976.	.25	.75	2.00

151	50 PESOS	1975–81. Aqua, purple and green. Prat at r. Sailing ships at ctr. on back. Wmk: Men in uniform.			
		a. 1975–78.	FV	.50	2.00
		b. 1980; 1981.	FV	.25	1.00

#152–156 printer: CdM-Chile.

#152 and 153 wmk: D. Diego Portales P.

152	100 PESOS	1976–84. Purple and m/c unpt. Portales at r. 1837 meeting at ctr. on back.			
		a. Normal serial #. 1976.	FV	1.00	3.00
		b. Electronic sorting serial #. 1976–84.	FV	FV	2.50

153	500 PESOS	1977–. Dk. brown w/black text on m/c unpt. Valdivia at r. wmk. Founding of Santiago at ctr. on back.			
		a. 1977; 1978.	FV	1.50	6.00
		b. 1980–82; 1985–90; 1992; 1994.	FV	FV	3.00

Cat. #	Denomination	Date, description	VG	VF	Unc
154	1000 PESOS	1978–. Dk. blue-green and dk. olive-brown, green and m/c. I. Carrera Pinto at r. and as wmk., military arms at ctr. Monument to Chilean heroes on back.			
		a. Sign. titles: *PRESIDENTE* and *GERENTE GENERAL*. 1978–80.	FV	2.00	8.00
		b. 1982; 1985–87.	FV	FV	5.50
		c. 1988–93.	FV	FV	5.00
		d. Sign. titles: *PRESIDENTE* and *GERENTE GENERAL INTERINO*. 1990–91.	FV	FV	4.50
		e. Sign. titles like a. 1992–94.	FV	FV	4.00

155	5000 PESOS	1981–. Brown and red-violet on m/c unpt. Allegorical woman w/musical instrument, seated male at ctr. Statue of woman w/children at l. ctr., G. Mistral at r. on back. Wmk: G. Mistral.			
		a. Sign. titles: *PRESIDENTE* and *GERENTE GENERAL*. 1981. Plain security thread.	FV	FV	35.00
		b. 1986–90.	FV	FV	23.00
		c. Sign. titles: *PRESIDENTE* and *GERENTE GENERAL INTERINO*. 1991.	FV	FV	25.00
		d. Sign. titles: *PRESIDENTE* and *GERENTE GENERAL*. 1992–93.	FV	FV	21.00
		e. As d but w/segmented foil security thread. 1994; 1995.	FV	FV	20.00

156	10,000 PESOS	1989–. Dk. blue and dk. olive-green on m/c unpt. Capt. A. Prat C. at r. and as wmk. Statue of Liberty at l., Hacienda San Agustin de Punual Cuna at l. ctr. on back.			
		a. Plain security thread. 1989–93.	FV	FV	42.50
		b. Segmented foil security thread. 1994.	FV	FV	40.00

CHINA

The People's Republic of China, located in eastern Asia, has an area of 3,696,100 sq. mi. (9,572,900 sq. km.), including Manchuria and Tibet, and a population of 1.14 billion. Capital: Beijing (Peking). The economy is based on agriculture, mining and manufacturing. Textiles, clothing, metal ores, tea and rice are exported.

In the fall of 1911, the middle business class of China and Chinese students educated in Western universities started a general uprising against the Manchu dynasty which forced the abdication on Feb. 12, 1912, of the boy emperor Hsuan T'ung (Pu-yi), thus bringing to an end the Manchu dynasty that had ruled China since 1644. Five days later, China formally became a republic with physician and revolutionist Sun Yat-sen as first provisional president.

Dr. Sun and his supporters founded a new party called the Kuomintang, and planned a Chinese republic based upon the Three Principles of Nationalism, Democracy and People's Livelihood. They failed, however, to win control of all China, and Dr. Sun resigned the presidency in favor of Yuan Shih Kai, the most powerful of the Chinese generals. Yuan ignored the constitution of the republic and tried to make himself emperor.

After the death of Yuan in 1917, Sun Yat-sen and the Kuomintang established a republic in Canton. It also failed to achieve the unification of China, and in 1923 Dr. Sun entered into an agreement with the Soviet Union known as the Canton-Moscow Entente. The Kuomintang agreed to admit Chinese communists to the party. The Soviet Union agreed to furnish military advisers to train the army of the Canton Republic. Dr. Sun died in 1925 and was succeeded by one of his supporters, General Chiang Kai-shek.

Chiang Kai-shek launched a vigorous campaign to educate the Chinese and modernize their industries and agriculture. Under his command, the armies of the Kuomintang captured Nanking (1927) and Peking (1928). In 1928, Chiang was made president of the Chinese Republic. His government was recognized by most of the great powers, but he soon began to exercise dictatorial powers. Prodded by the conservative members of the Kuomintang, he initiated a break between the members and the Chinese Communists which, once again, prevented the unification of China.

Persuaded that China would fare better under the leadership of its businessmen in alliance with the capitalist countries than under the guidance of the Chinese Communists and in alliance with the Soviet Union, Chiang expelled all Communists from the Kuomintang, sent the Russian advisers home, and hired German generals to train his army.

The Communists responded by setting up a government and raising an army that during the period of 1930-34 acquired control over large parts of Kiangsi, Fukien, Hunan, Hupeh and other provinces. These early Communist centers issued currency in the form of copper and silver coins and many varieties of notes printed on paper and cloth. A lack of minting facilities limited the issue of coins. Low mintage and the demonetization of silver in China in 1935 have elevated the surviving coinage specimens to the status of highly valued numismatic rarities. The issues of notes, the majority of which bore revolutionary slogans and often cartoon-like vignetts have also suffered a high attrition rate and certain issues command appreciable premiums in today's market.

When his army was sufficiently trained and equipped, Chiang Kai-shek led several military expeditions against the Communist Chinese which, while unable to subdue them, dislodged them south of the Yangtze, forcing them to undertake in 1935 a celebrated "Long March" of 6,000 miles (9,654 km.) from Hunan northwest to a refuge in Shensi province just south of Inner Mongolia from which Chiang was unable to displace them.

The Japanese menace had now assumed warlike proportions. Chiang rejected a Japanese offer of cooperation against the Communists, but agreed to suppress the movement himself. His generals, however, persuaded him to negotiate a truce with the Communists to permit united action against the greater menace of Japanese aggression. Under the terms of the truce, Communists were again admitted to the Kuomintang. They, in turn, promised to dissolve the Soviet Republic of China and to cease issuing their own currency.

The war with Japan all but extinguished the appeal of the Kuomintang, appreciably increased the power of the Communists, and divided China into three parts. The east coast and its principal cities - Peking, Tientsin, Nanking, Shanghai and Canton - were in Japanese-controlled, puppet-ruled states. The Communists controlled the countryside in the north where they were the de facto rulers of 100 million peasants. Chiang and the Kuomintang were driven toward the west, from where they returned with their prestige seriously damaged by their wartime performance.

At the end of World War II, the United States tried to bring the Chinese factions together in a coalition government. American mediation failed, and within weeks the civil war resumed.

By the fall of 1947, most of northeast China was under Communist control. During the following year, the war turned wholly in favor of the Communists. The Kuomintang armies in the northeast surrendered, two provincial capitals in the north were captured, a large Kuomintang army in the Huai river basin surrendered. Four Communist armies converged upon the demoralized Kuomintang forces. The Communists crossed the Yangtse in April 1949. Nanking, the Nationalist capital, fell. The civil war on the mainland was virtually over.

Chiang Kai-shek relinquished the presidency to Li Tsung-jen, his deputy, and after moving to Canton, to Chungking and Chengtu, retreated from the mainland to Taiwan (Formosa) where he resumed the presidency.

The Communist Peoples Republic of China was proclaimed on September 2, 1949. Thereafter relations between the Peoples Republic and the Soviet Union steadily deteriorated. China emerged as independent center of Communist power in 1958.

During and following World War II, the Chinese Communists again established banks at the various Communist centers to issue local currency. Prominent among Communist regional banks were the Bank of Central China, Bank of Peihai, and Bank of Shansi, Chahar and Hopeh.

The complexity of regional banks with their widely varying exchange rates were replaced in December 1948 by the Peoples Bank of China. Beneficial effects of the centralization were not immediately apparent. The pace of inflation was unslowed and regional note-issuing agencies continued to operate in remote areas for more than a year. Upon the defeat of the Kuomintang and the establishment of the Peoples Republic of China, the Communist government issued a new form of currency, the "Peoples Currency," as a replacement for all other notes in an effort to inject a stabilizing influence into the disorganized economy. Peoples Currency, Foreign Exchange Certificates and certain local or emergency issues are the only forms of paper money permitted to circulate by the Communist government.

PEOPLE'S REPUBLIC OF CHINA

MONETARY SYSTEM
1 Yuan = 10 Jiao
1 Jiao = 10 Fen

MONETARY UNITS	
Yuan	圓 or 圜
Pan Yuan	圓半
5 Jiao	角伍
1 Jiao	角壹
1 Fen	分壹

NUMERICAL CHARACTERS

No.	CONVENTIONAL			FORMAL		
1	一	正	元	壹	弌	
2	二			弍	貳	
3	三			弎	叁	
4	四			肆		
5	五			伍		
6	六			陸		
7	七			柒		
8	八			捌		
9	九			玖		
10	十			拾	什	
20	十二	廿		拾貳	念	
25	五十二	五廿		伍拾貳		
30	十三	卅		拾叁		
100	百一			佰壹		
1,000	千一			仟壹		
10,000	萬一			萬壹		
100,000	萬十	億一		萬拾	億壹	
1,000,000	萬百一			萬佰壹		

Peoples Bank of China

行銀民人國中
Chung Kuo Jen Min Yin Hang
中國人民銀行
Zhong Guo Ren Min Yin Hang

1960 ISSUE

#873–879 arms at r. on back.

Cat. #	Denomination	Date, description	VG	VF	Unc
873	1 JIAO	1960. Red-brown. Workers at ctr. (S/M #C284–1).	1.00	3.00	6.00

Cat. #	Denomination	Date, description	VG	VF	Unc
874	1 YUAN	1960. Red-brown and red-violet on m/c unpt. Woman driving tractor at ctr. (S/M #C284–).	.10	.30	1.25

Cat. #	Denomination	Date, description	VG	VF	Unc
875	2 YUAN	1960. Black and green on m/c unpt. Machinist working at lathe at ctr.			
		a. Wmk: Lg. star and 4 small stars. (S/M #C284–10a).	.15	.50	2.00
		b. Wmk: Lt. stars and dark spades. (S/M #C284–106).	.10	.35	1.00

Cat. #	Denomination	Date, description	VG	VF	Unc
876	5 YUAN	1960. Brown and black on m/c unpt. Foundry worker at ctr. Wmk: Lg. star and 4 small stars. (S/M #C284–11).	.25	1.00	4.00

1962;1965 ISSUE

#877-879 arms at r. on back.

Cat. #	Denomination	Date, description	VG	VF	Unc
877	1 JIAO	1962. Brown on m/c unpt. Workers at l.			
		a. Back brown on green and lt. orange unpt. (S/M #C284–30a).	.75	1.50	5.00
		b. Back brown on lilac and lt. orange unpt. Blue serial #. (S/M #C284–30b).	.05	.10	.25
		c. Like #877b but only partially engraved. Red serial #. (S/M #C284–30c).	.05	.15	.50
		d. Lithograph. (S/M #C284–30d).	.05	.10	.20

Cat. #	Denomination	Date, description	VG	VF	Unc
878	2 JIAO	1962. Green. Bridge at l.			
		a. Engraved face. (S/M #C284–31a).	.25	1.00	3.00
		b. Lithographed face. (S/M #C284–31b).	.05	.15	.40

Cat. #	Denomination	Date, description	VG	VF	Unc
879	10 YUAN	1965. Black on m/c unpt. Group of people at ctr. Wmk: Great Hall w/rays. (S/M #C284–40).	1.50	2.25	.500

1972 ISSUE

Cat. #	Denomination	Date, description	VG	VF	Unc
880	5 JIAO	1972. Purple and m/c. Women working in factory. Arms at r. on back. (S/M #C284–41).			
		a. Engraved bank title and denomination. Wmk: Lg. star and 4 small stars.	.20	.50	1.00
		b. Lithographed face. W/o wmk.	—	.20	.50

1980 ISSUE

#881–883 arms at ctr. on back.

Cat. #	Denomination	Date, description	VG	VF	Unc
885	2 YUAN	1980. Dk. olive-green on m/c unpt. 2 youths at r. Rocky shoreline on back. (S/M #C284–46).	FV	FV	1.25

Cat. #	Denomination	Date, description	VG	VF	Unc
881	1 JIAO	1980. Dk. brown on m/c unpt. 2 men at l. (S/M #C284–42).	FV	FV	.20

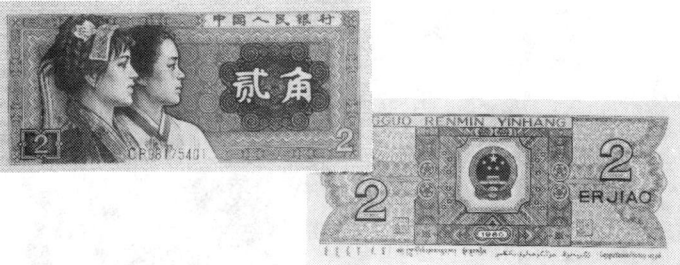

882	2 JIAO	1980. Grayish olive-green on m/c unpt. 2 youths at l. (S/M #C284–43).	FV	FV	.35

886	5 YUAN	1980. Dk. brown on m/c unpt. Old man and young woman at r. Yangtze Gorges on back. Wmk: Ancient Pu coin. (S/M #C284–47).	FV	FV	3.00

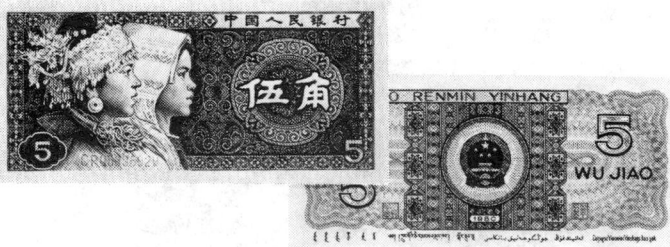

883	5 JIAO	1980. Purple on red-violet and lt. blue unpt. 2 children at l. Back brown-violet on m/c unpt. (S/M #C284–44).	FV	FV	.50

#884–889 arms at upper l., stylized birds in unpt. at ctr., dot patterns for poor of sight at lower l. or r.

887	10 YUAN	1980; 1990 Black on blue and m/c unpt. Old and young man at r. Mountains on back. Wmk: Young man.			
		a. 1980.	FV	FV	7.50
		b. 1990.	FV	FV	5.00

884	1 YUAN	1980; 1990. Brown-violet on m/c unpt. 2 youths at r. Great Wall at ctr. on back.			
		a. Blue ser. #. 1980. (S/M #C284–45a).	FV	FV	.65
		b. Black ser. #. 1990. (S/M #C284–45b).	FV	FV	.50

Cat. #	Denomination	Date, description	VG	VF	Unc
888	50 YUAN	1980; 1990. Black on lt. green and m/c unpt. Intellectual, student girl and industrial male worker at ctr. Waterfalls on back. Wmk: Industrial male worker.			
		a. 1980. (S/M #C284–49a).	FV	10.00	16.50
		b. Security thread at r. 1990. (S/M #C284–49b).	FV	FV	15.00

Cat. #	Denomination	Date, description	VG	VF	Unc
889	100 YUAN	1980; 1990. Black on m/c unpt. 4 great leaders at ctr. Mountains on back.			
		a. 1980. (S/M #C284–50a).	FV	FV	30.00
		b. Security thread at r. 1990. (S/M #C284–50b).	FV	FV	27.50

NOTE: #890 used in inter-bank transfers only.

FOREIGN EXCHANGE CERTIFICATES
Bank of China

中國銀行
Chung Kuo Yin Hang

1979 ISSUE

Cat. #	Denomination	Date, description	VG	VF	Unc
FX1	10 FEN	1979. Brown on m/c unpt. Waterfalls at ctr. (S/M #C294–301).			
		a. Wmk: Lg. star and 4 small stars.	FV	.25	1.00
		b. Wmk: Star and torch.	FV	FV	.50

Cat. #	Denomination	Date, description	VG	VF	Unc
FX2	50 FEN	1979. Purple on m/c unpt. Temple of Heaven at l. ctr. (S/M #C294–302).	FV	FV	1.00

Cat. #	Denomination	Date, description	VG	VF	Unc
FX3	1 YUAN	1979. Deep green on m/c unpt. Pleasure boats in lake w/mountains behind at ctr. (S/M #C294–303).	FV	FV	1.75

Cat. #	Denomination	Date, description	VG	VF	Unc
FX4	5 YUAN	1979. Deep brown on m/c unpt. Mountain scenery at ctr. (S/M #C294–304).	FV	FV	4.50

Cat. #	Denomination	Date, description	VG	VF	Unc
FX5	10 YUAN	1979. Deep blue on m/c/ unpt. Yangtze Gorges at ctr. (S/M #C294–305).	FV	FV	7.50

Cat. #	Denomination	Date, description	VG	VF	Unc
FX6	50 YUAN	1979. Purple and red on m/c unpt. Mountain lake at ctr. (S/M #C294–306).	FV	FV	22.50

Cat. #	Denomination	Date, description	VG	VF	Unc
FX7	100 YUAN	1979. Black and blue on m/c unpt. Great Wall at ctr. (S/M #C294–307).	FV	FV	35.00

1988 ISSUE

Cat. #	Denomination	Date, description	VG	VF	Unc
FX8	50 YUAN	1988. Black, orange-brown and green on m/c unpt. Shoreline rock formations at ctr. (S/M #C294–308).	FV	FV	15.00
FX9	100 YUAN	1988. Olive-green on m/c unpt. Great Wall at ctr. (S/M #C294–309).	FV	FV	30.00

NOTE: #FX1–FX9 were discontinued in 1995, they are redeemable at the Bank of China.

MILITARY
Military Payment Certificates

軍用代金券

Chün Yung Tai Chin Ch'üan

1965 ISSUE

M41	1 FEN	1965. Greenish brown. Airplane at l. ctr. (S/M #C250.5–11).	5.00	15.00	27.50

M42	5 FEN	1965. Red. Airplane at ctr. (S/M #C250.5–12).	7.00	20.00	35.00

M43	1 CHIAO	1965. Purple. Steam passenger train at ctr. r. (S/M #C250.5–13).	8.50	25.00	45.00
M44	Held in Reserve.				

M45	1 YUAN	1965. Green. Truck convoy at l. (S/M #C250.5–15).	12.00	35.00	65.00
M46	5 YUAN	1965. Truck convoy at l. (S/M #C250.5 –17).	—	—	—

REPUBLIC OF CHINA (TAIWAN)

The Republic of China, comprising Taiwan (an island located 90 miles (145 km.) off the southeastern coast of mainland China), the offshore islands of Quemoy and Matsu and nearby islets of the Pescadores chain, has an area of 14,000 sq. mi. (35,981 sq. km.) and a population of 20.2 million. Capital: Taipei. During the past decade, manufacturing has replaced agriculture in importance. Fruits, vegetables, plywood, textile yarns and fabrics and clothing are exported.

Chinese migration to Taiwan began as early as the sixth century. The Dutch established a base on the island in 1624 and held it until 1661, when they were driven out by supporters of the Ming dynasty who used it as a base for their unsuccessful attempt to displace the ruling Manchu dynasty of mainland China. After being occupied by Manchu forces in 1683, Taiwan remained under the suzerainty of China until its cession to Japan in 1895. It was returned to China following World War II. On December 8, 1949, Taiwan became the last remnant of Sun Yatsen's Republic of China when Chiang Kai-shek moved his army and government from mainland China to the island following his defeat by the Communist forces of Mao Tse-tung.

MONETARY SYSTEM
1 Chiao = 10 Fen (Cents)
1 Yuan (Dollar) = 10 Chiao

PORTRAIT ABBREVIATIONS

SYS = Sun Yat-sen, 1867–1925
President of Canton Government, 1917–25

CKS = Chaing Kai-shek 1886–1975
President in Nanking, 1927–31
Head of Foromosa Government, Taiwan, 1949–1975

NOTE: Because of the frequency of the above appearing in the following listings their initials are used only in reference to their portraits.

NOTE: S/M # in reference to *CHINESE BANKNOTES* by Ward D. Smith and Brian Matravers.

CHINESE ADMINISTRATION
Bank of Taiwan

臺灣銀行

T'ai Wan Yin Hang

PRINTERS 1946–

CPF: 廠製印央中
(Central Printing Factory)

CPFT: 廠北台廠製印央中
(Central Printing Factory, Taipei)

FPFT: 廠刷印一第
(First Printing Factory)

PFBT: 所刷印行銀灣臺
(Printing Factory of Taiwan Bank)

CIRCULATING BANK CASHIER'S CHECKS

1960 ISSUE

#969–984 horizontal format.

Cat. #	Denomination	Date, description	VG	VF	Unc
969	10 YUAN	1960. Blue on m/c unpt. SYS at l., bridge at r. (S/M #T73–50).	.20	.50	2.00

970	10 YUAN	1960. Red on yellow and lt. green unpt. Like #969 but w/o printer. (S/M #T73–51).	.35	1.25	6.00

1961 ISSUE

Cat. #	Denomination	Date, description	VG	VF	Unc
971	1 YUAN	1961. Dk. blue-green and purple. SYS at l., steep coastline at r. Printer: PFBT.			
		a. Engraved. *(S/M #T73–60).*	.20	.75	3.50
		b. Lithographed. (1972). *(S/M #T73–60).*	.10	1.50	2.50

#972–975 SYS at l. Printer: CPF.

Cat. #	Denomination	Date, description	VG	VF	Unc
972	5 YUAN	1961. Red on m/c unpt. House w/tower at r. *(S/M #T73–61).*	.20	.75	3.00
973	5 YUAN	1961. Brown on m/c unpt. Similar to #972. *(S/M #T73–62).*	.25	1.00	5.50
974	50 YUAN	1961. Violet on m/c unpt. *(S/M #T73–63).*	.60	2.50	9.00
975	100 YUAN	1961. Green on m/c unpt. SYS at l. *(S/M #T73–64).*	.75	3.00	10.00

1964 ISSUE

#976–977 SYS at l. Printer: CPF.

976	50 YUAN	1964. Violet on m/c unpt. Similar to #974. *(S/M #T73–70).*	.50	2.00	6.00

977	100 YUAN	1964. Green on m/c unpt. Similar to #975. *(S/M #T73–71).*	.60	3.00	9.00

Republic of China/Taiwan Bank

行銀灣臺　國民華中
Chung Hua Min Kuo/T'ai Wan Yin Hang

1969 ISSUE

#978 and 979 SYS at l. Printer: CPF.

Cat. #	Denomination	Date, description	VG	VF	Unc
978	5 YUAN	1969. Blue. *(S/M #T73–72).*	.15	.35	1.50

979	10 YUAN	1969. Red. Similar to #978. *(S/M #T73–73).*			
		a. W/o plate letter.	.20	.50	2.00
		b. Plate letter *A* at lower r. on face.	.15	.35	1.50

1970 ISSUE

#980–983 SYS at l. Printer: CPF.

980	50 YUAN	1970. Violet. *(S/M #T73–75).*	FV	2.25	4.00

981	100 YUAN	1970. Green. *(S/M #T73–).*	FV	4.50	8.50

1972 ISSUE

Cat. #	Denomination	Date, description	VG	VF	Unc
982	50 YUAN	1972. Violet, purple and lt. blue. Chungshan bldg. on back. Wide margin w/guilloche at r. (S/M #T73–76).	FV	2.00	4.50

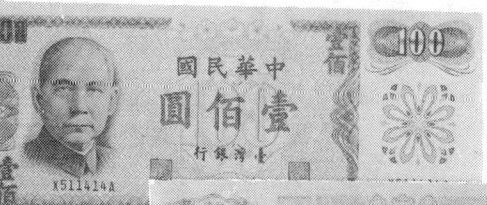

| 983 | 100 YUAN | 1972. Dk. green, lt. green and orange. Palace on back. (S/M #T73–77). | FV | 4.00 | 7.00 |

1976 ISSUE

#984–986 SYS at l. Printer: CPF.

| 984 | 10 YUAN | 1976. Red and m/c. Bank on back. (S/M #T73–78). | FV | .50 | 1.50 |
| 985 | 500 YUAN | 1976. Olive, purple and m/c. CKS at l. Chungshan bldg. on back. W/o wmk. at r. (S/M #T73–79). | FV | 20.00 | 35.00 |

| 986 | 1000 YUAN | 1976. Blue-black, olive-brown and violet on m/c. unpt. CKS at l. Presidential Office bldg. on back. W/o wmk. at r. (S/M #T73–80). | FV | 40.00 | 65.00 |

1981 ISSUE

#987 and 988 SYS at l. Printer: CPF.

Cat. #	Denomination	Date, description	VG	VF	Unc
987	500 YUAN	1981. Brown, red-brown and m/c. Similar to #985 but wmk. of CKS at r. (S/M #T73–81).	FV	FV	30.00

| 988 | 1000 YUAN | 1981. Blue-black and m/c. Similar to #986 but wmk: CKS at r. (S/M #T73–82). | FV | FV | 55.00 |

1987 ISSUE

| 989 | 100 YUAN | 1987 (1988). Red, red-brown and brown-violet on m/c unpt. SYS at l. and as wmk. Chungshan bldg. on back. (S/M #T73–83). | FV | FV | 6.00 |

OFF-SHORE ISLAND CURRENCY

KINMEN (Quemoy) ISSUES

限金門通用

Hsien Chin Men T'ung Yung

Notes of the Bank of Taiwan and later notes of the Republic of China/Bank of Taiwan w/ovpt: 金門

#R1001–R1009 vertical format w/SYS at upper ctr.

#R1001

Cat. #	Denomination	Date, description	VG	VF	Unc
R1001	1 YUAN	1949 (1963). Green. Printer: CPF. *(S/M #T74–1).*	.25	1.25	5.50
R1006	10 YUAN	1950 (1963). Blue. Printer: CPF. *(S/M #T74–20).*	.50	1.50	7.50

Cat. #	Denomination	Date, description	VG	VF	Unc
R1012A	10 YUAN	1976. Ovpt. on #984. *(S/M #T74–).*	.20	.50	3.00
R1012B	100 YUAN	1981. Ovpt. on #988. *(S/M #T74–).*	5.00	7.00	20.00
R1012C	1000 YUAN	1981. Ovpt. on #988. *(S/M #T74–).*	40.00	50.00	85.00

MATSU ISSUES

限馬祖地區通用

Hsien Ma Tsu Ti Ch'u T'ung Yung

Notes of the Bank of Taiwan and later notes of the Republic of China/Bank of Taiwan w/ovpt: 馬祖

			VG	VF	Unc
R1017	10 YUAN	1950 (1964). Blue. Printer: CPF. *(S/M #T75–2).*	1.00	2.50	12.50

#R1007

R1007	50 YUAN	1951 (1967). Green. Printer: FPFT. *(S/M #T74–30).*	3.00	10.00	55.00
R1009	5 YUAN	1966. Violet-brown. Printer: CPF. *(S/M #T74–50).*	.60	3.00	12.00

R1018	50 YUAN	1951 (1967). Green. Printer: FPFT. *(S/M #T75–10).*	3.50	7.50	27.50

R1010	10 YUAN	1969 (1975). Red ovpt. on #979a. *(S/M #T74–60).*	.25	1.00	5.00

R1021	5 YUAN	1955 (1959). Dk. green. Printer: PFBT. *(S/M #T75–30).*	.35	2.00	10.00

R1011	50 YUAN	1969 (1970). Dk. blue. SYS at r. *(S/M #T74–61).*	.50	2.00	10.00

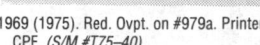

R1012	100 YUAN	1972 (1975). Green ovpt. on #983. *(S/M #T74–70).*	1.00	4.00	20.00

R1022	10 YUAN	1969 (1975). Red. Ovpt. on #979a. Printer: CPF. *(S/M #T75–40).*	.35	1.00	5.00

Cat. #	Denomination	Date, description	VG	VF	Unc
R1023	50 YUAN	1969 (1970). Violet on m/c unpt. Printer: CPF. (S/M #T75–45).	1.00	4.00	20.00
R1024	100 YUAN	1972 (1975). Green ovpt. on #983. Printer: CPF. (S/M #T75–50).	3.00	10.00	35.00

Cat. #	Denomination	Date, description	VG	VF	Unc
R1025	10 YUAN	1976. Ovpt. on #984. (S/M #T75–55).	.25	1.00	4.00
R1026	500 YUAN	1981. Ovpt. on #987. (S/M #T75–60).	FV	20.00	45.00
R1027	1000 YUAN	1981. Ovpt. on #988. (S/M #T75–61).	FV	35.00	85.00

COLOMBIA

The Republic of Colombia, located in the northwestern corner of South America, has an area of 439,737 sq. mi. (1,138,914 sq. km.) and a population of 33.4 million. Capital: Bogota. The economy is primarily agricultural with a mild, rich coffee the chief crop. Colombia has the world's largest platinum deposits and important reserves of coal, iron ore, petroleum and limestone; precious metals and emeralds are also mined. Coffee, crude oil, bananas, sugar, coal and flowers are exported.

The northern coast of present Colombia was one of the first parts of the American continent to be visited by Spanish navigators, and the site, at Darien in Panama, of the first permanent European settlement on the American mainland in 1510. New Granada, as Colombia was known until 1861, stemmed from the settlement of Santa Maria in 1525. New Granada was established as a Spanish Colony in 1549. Independence was declared in 1813, and secured in 1824. In 1819, Simon Bolivar united Colombia, Venezuela, Panama and Ecuador as the Republic of Greater Colombia. Venezuela withdrew from the Republic in 1829; Ecuador in 1830; and Panama in 1903.

MONETARY SYSTEM

1 Peso = 100 Centavos

Replacement Notes:

Earlier issues, small R just below and between signatures. Larger R used later. Some TDLR printings have R preceding serial number. Later Colombian-printed notes use circled asterisk usually close to sign. or a star at r. of upper serial #. Known replacements: #404, 406, 407, 409, 413–15, 417–18, 420–22, 425–428, 430, 432, 433.

Banco de la República

PESOS ORO System

Gold Certificates

1941 ISSUE

Cat. #	Denomination	Date, Description	VG	VF	Unc
389	10 PESOS	1941–63. Portr. Nariño at r. w/o title: *CAJERO* and sign. on back.			
		a. Series N in red. 20.7.1941; 20.7.1943.	1.00	6.00	20.00
		b. Seriens N in violet. 20.7.1944; 1.1.1945; 7.8.1947.	.50	4.00	15.00
		d. Series N. 12.10.1949.	.25	2.00	10.00
		e. Series EE. 1.1.1950.	.25	2.00	10.00
		f. Series EE. 2.1.1963.	.20	1.50	5.00

1943 ISSUE

Cat. #	Denomination	Date, Description	VG	VF	Unc
395	20 PESOS	1943–63. Purple and m/c. Caldas at l., S. Bolívar at r. Liberty at ctr. on back. Printer: ABNC.			
		a. Series U in red. 20.7.1943.	12.50	50.00	
		b. Series U in purple. 20.7.1944; 1.1.1945.	10.00	40.00	
		c. Series U. 7.8.1947.	1.00	4.00	
		d. Series DD. 1.1.1950; 1.1.1951.	1.00	3.00	
		e. Series DD. 2.1.1963.	.50	2.00	

1953 ISSUE

Cat. #	Denomination	Date, Description	VG	VF	Unc
400	10 PESOS	1953–61. Blue on m/c unpt. Portr. Nariño at l., palm trees at r. Bank w/Mercury alongside at Cali on back. Series N.			
		a. 1.1.1953.	.25	2.00	8.00
		b. 1.1.1958; 1.1.1960.	.25	1.25	6.00
		c. 2.1.1961.	.25	1.00	5.00

401	20 PESOS	1953–65. Red-brown on m/c unpt. Portr. Caldas and allegory at l. Liberty in frame at r. Newer bank at Barranquilla on back. Series O.			
		a. 1.1.1953.	.25	3.00	10.00
		b. 1.1.1960.	.25	3.00	10.00
		c. 2.1.1961; 2.1.1965.	.20	1.00	5.00

1958 ISSUE

#402–403 printer: ABNC.

402	50 PESOS	1958–67. Lt. brown on m/c unpt. Sucre at l. Back olive-green; Liberty at ctr. Series Z.			
		a. 20.7.1958; 7.8.1960.	.50	3.50	10.00
		b. 1.1.1964; 12.10.1967.	.25	2.50	9.00

403	100 PESOS	1958–67. Gray on m/c unpt. Santander at r. Back green; like #402. Series Y.			
		a. 7.8.1958.	.50	3.00	10.00
		b. 1.1.1960; 1.1.1964; 20.7.1965; 20.7.1967.	.50	3.00	10.00

1959-60 ISSUE

Cat. #	Denomination	Date, Description	VG	VF	Unc
404	1 PESO	1959–77, Blue on m/c unpt. S. Bolivar at l., Santander at r. Liberty head and condor w/waterfall and mountain at ctr. on back.			
		a. Security thread. 12.10.1959.	.10	1.00	4.00
		b. Security thread. 2.1.1961; 7.8.1962; 2.1.1963; 12.10.1963; 2.1.1964; 12.10.1964.	.10	.50	2.00
		c. W/o security thread. 20.7.1966; 20.7.1967; 1.2.1968; 2.1.1969.	.10	.25	1.00
		d. W/o security thread. 1.5.1970; 12.10.1970; 7.8.1971; 20.7.1972; 7.8.1973; 7.8.1974.	.10	.25	1.00
		e. As d. 1.1.1977.	.50	1.50	10.00
405	5 PESOS	20.7.1960. Green on m/c unpt. Portr. Cordoba and seated allegory at l. New bank bldg. at Bogota on back. Series M. Printer: TDLR.	.25	1.50	5.00

1961-64 ISSUE

406	5 PESOS	1961–81. Deep greenish-black and deep brown on m/c unpt. Condor at l., Cordoba at r. Fortress at Cartagena at ctr. on back.			
		a. Security thread. 2.1.1961; 1.5.1963; 2.1.1964.	1.00	4.00	15.00
		b. Security thread. 11.11.1965; 20.7.1966; 12.10.1967; 20.7.1968.	.25	1.50	4.00
		c. Security thread. 20.7.1971.	.20	.60	2.00
		d. W/o security thread. 1.1.1973; 20.7.1974; 20.7.1975; 20.7.1976; 20.7.1977.	.10	.30	1.00
		e. W/o security thread. 1.10.1978; 1.4.1979; 1.1.1980; 1.1.1981.	.10	.25	1.00

Cat. #	Denomination	Date, Description	VG	VF	Unc
407	10 PESOS	1963–80. Lilac and slate blue on green and m/c unpt. Nariño at l., condor at r. Back red-brown and slate blue; archeological site w/monoliths.			
		a. Security thread. 20.7.1963; 20.7.1964.	1.00	5.00	20.00
		b. Security thread. 20.7.1965; 20.7.1967; 2.1.1969.	.25	.75	4.00
		c. Security thread. 12.10.1970.	.25	.75	4.00
		d. W/o security thread. 1.1.1973; 20.7.1974; 1.1.1975; 20.7.1976; 1.1.1978.	.20	.40	1.00
		e. W/o security thread. 7.8.1979; 7.8.1980.	.10	.30	1.00
		f. Like e., but *SERIE AZ* at l. ctr. and upper r. on face. 7.8.1980.	.10	.30	1.00

Cat. #	Denomination	Date, Description	VG	VF	Unc
408	500 PESOS	20.7.1964. Olive-green on m/c unpt. Portr. Bolívar at r. Back has no open space under Liberty head. Series AA. Printer: ABNC.	5.00	17.50	55.00

1966–68 ISSUE

Cat. #	Denomination	Date, Description	VG	VF	Unc
409	20 PESOS	1966–83. Brown, gray and green on m/c unpt. Caldas w/globe at r. Back brown and green on m/c unpt.; artifacts from the Gold Museum.			
		a. Security thread. 12.10.1966; 2.1.1969.	.30	1.00	4.00
		b. W/o security thread. 1.5.1972; 1.5.1973; 20.7.1974; 20.7.1975; 20.7.1977.	.20	.40	1.00
		c. W/o security thread. 1.4.1979; 1.1.1981; 1.1.1982; 1.1.1983.	.10	.30	1.00

Cat. #	Denomination	Date, Description	VG	VF	Unc
410	100 PESOS	1968–71. Blue on m/c unpt. Santander at r. Capital at Bogota on back. Series Y.			
		a. 1.1.1968; 2.1.1969.	.50	2.50	10.00
		b. 1.5.1970; 20.7.1971.	.50	1.50	5.00

Cat. #	Denomination	Date, Description	VG	VF	Unc
411	500 PESOS	1968–71. Green on m/c unpt. S. Bolivar at r. Subterranean caves on back. Series A. Printer: ABNC.			
		a. 1.1.1968.	4.00	10.00	25.00
		b. 12.10.1971.	3.50	7.00	17.50

1969 ISSUE

Cat. #	Denomination	Date, Description	VG	VF	Unc
412	50 PESOS	1969–70. Brown-violet on m/c unpt. Blue design w/o border at l., Torres at r. Arms and flowers on back. Printer: TDLR.			
		a. 2.1.1969.	.25	1.00	5.00
		b. 12.10.1970.	.25	.75	3.00

1972–73 ISSUE

Cat. #	Denomination	Date, Description	VG	VF	Unc
413	2 PESOS	1972–77. Purple on m/c unpt. P. Salavari-etta at l. Back brown; "El Dorado" replica from the Gold Museum.			
		a. Lg. size serial #, and # at r. near upper border. 1.1.1972; 20.7.1972; 1.1.1973.	.10	.15	.50
		b. Sm. size serial #, and # at r. far from upper border. 20.7.1976; 1.1.1977; 20.7.1977.	.10	.15	.50

Cat. #	Denomination	Date, Description	VG	VF	Unc
414	50 PESOS	20.7.1973; 20.7.1974. Similar to #412 but curved dk. border added at l. and r., also at r. on back. Printer: TDLR.	.30	.60	3.00

Cat. #	Denomination	Date, Description	VG	VF	Unc
415	100 PESOS	20.7.1973; 20.7.1974. Similar to #410 but curved dk. border added at l. and r., also at r. on back. Series Y.	.50	1.00	7.00

Cat. #	Denomination	Date, Description	VG	VF	Unc
416	500 PESOS	7.8.1973. Red on m/c unpt. Like #411. Series A. Printer: ABNC.	2.00	5.00	20.00

1974 ISSUE

Cat. #	Denomination	Date, Description	VG	VF	Unc
417	200 PESOS	20.7.1974; 7.8.1975. Green on m/c unpt. Bolivar at ctr. r., church at r. *BOGOTA COLOMBIA* at lower l. ctr. Man picking coffee beans on back. Printer: TDLR.	.50	1.75	6.00

1977–79 ISSUE

Cat. #	Denomination	Date, Description	VG	VF	Unc
418	100 PESOS	1977–80. Violet on m/c unpt. Santander at r. ctr. Capitol at Bogota on back. Printer: TDLR.			
		a. 1.1.1977.	.25	.75	3.00
		b. Serial # prefix A-C. 1.1.1980.	.15	.60	2.50

NOTE: Numerals at upper ctr. and upper r. are darker on 1980 dated notes, also the word *CIEN*.

Cat. #	Denomination	Date, Description	VG	VF	Unc
419	500 PESOS	1977–79. Olive and m/c. Santander at l. Back gray; subterranean cave and Liberty head. Printer: ABNC.			
		a. 20.7.1977.	FV	2.00	10.00
		b. 1.4.1979.	FV	1.50	8.00

Cat. #	Denomination	Date, Description	VG	VF	Unc
420	200 PESOS	20.7.1978; 1.1.1979; 1.1.1980. Like #417 but only *COLOMBIA* at lower l. ctr.	FV	.75	3.00

Cat. #	Denomination	Date, Description	VG	VF	Unc
421	1000 PESOS	1.4.1979. Black and m/c. J. Antonio Galan at r. Nariño Palace on back. Printer: ABNC.	FV	2.50	15.00

1980–84 ISSUES

Cat. #	Denomination	Date, Description	VG	VF	Unc
422	50 PESOS	1980–85. Like #414 but *COLOMBIA* added near border at upper l. ctr. Imprint of TDLR removed from back.			
		a. 1.1.1980; 7.8.1981.	FV	.75	1.50
		b. 1.1.1983.	FV	.20	1.00
422A	50 PESOS	1984–86. Like #422, but w/o wmk. Printer: IBB.			
		a. 12.10.1984; 1.1.1985.	FV	.20	1.00
		b. 1.1.1986.	FV	FV	.75

423	500 PESOS	1981–86. Brown, dk. green and red-brown on m/c unpt. Santander at l., Bogota Mint on back; screw coinage press at lower r. Wmk: Santander. Printer: TDLR.			
		a. 20.7.1981.	FV	1.25	5.00
		b. 20.7.1984; 20.7.1985.	FV	1.00	4.00
		c. 12.10.1985; 20.7.1986.	FV	FV	3.00

424	1000 PESOS	1982–87. Blue and m/c. S. Bolívar at l. Scene honoring 1819 battle heroes on back. Printer: TDLR.			
		a. 1.1.1982.	FV	2.50	8.00
		b. 7.8.1984.	FV	2.00	6.00
		c. 1.1.1986; 1.1.1987.	FV	FV	4.50

1983 ISSUE

425	100 PESOS	1983–91. Violet, brown, orange and dk. red on m/c unpt. Nariño at l. and as wmk. Villa on back; flat bed printing press at lower r.			
		a. Printer: IBB. 1.1.1983; 12.10.1984.	FV	FV	1.50
		b. 12.10.1985; 1.1.1986; 12.10.1986; 1.1.1987.	FV	FV	1.00
		c. 12.10.1988; 7.8.1989; 1.1.1990; 1.1.1991.	FV	FV	1.00
		d. Printer: IBSFB. 7.8. 1991.	FV	FV	1.00
426	200 PESOS	1.1.1982. Like #420 but printer: IBB.	FV	FV	2.50

Cat. #	Denomination	Date, Description	VG	VF	Unc
426A	200 PESOS	1.4.1983. Green on m/c unpt. Church and Father Mutis at l. and as wmk. Cloister in Bogota on back. Printer: TDLR.	FV	1.50	6.00
426B	200 PESOS	1983–92. Like #426A.			
		a. Printer: IBB. 1.4.1983.	FV	.75	4.00
		b. 20.7.1984; 1.11.1984; 1.4.1985	FV	FV	2.00
		c. 1.11.1985; 1.4.1987.	FV	FV	2.00
		d. Larger stylized and bold serial #. 1.4.1987; 1.4.1988; 1.11.1988; 1.4.1989; 1.11.1989; 1.4.1991.	FV	FV	2.00
		e. Printer: IBSFB. 10.8.1992.	FV	FV	1.25

427	2000 PESOS	1983–86. Dk. brown on m/c unpt. S. Bolivar at l. and as wmk. Scene at Paso dei Paramo de Pisba at ctr. r. on back. Printer: TDLR.			
		a. 24.7.1983.	FV	2.50	10.00
		b. 24.7.1984.	FV	2.00	9.00
		c. 17.12.1985; 17.12.1986.	FV	FV	7.00
428	Held in reserve.				

1986–87 ISSUE

429	500 PESOS	1986–94. Like #423.			
		a. Printer: IBB. 20.7.1986; 12.10.1987; 20.7.1989; 12.10.1990.	FV	FV	2.50
		b. Printer: IBSFB. 2.3.1992.	FV	FV	2.50
		c. 4.1.1993; 1994.	FV	FV	2.00
430	1000 PESOS	1987–94. Like #424.			
		a. Printer: IBB. 1.1.1987; 1.1.1990; 1.1.1991.	FV	FV	3.50
		b. Printer: IBSFB. 31.1.1992; 1.4.1992; 4.1.1993; 3.1.1994; 1.11.1994.	FV	FV	3.00
431	2000 PESOS	1986–92. Like #427.			
		a. Printer: IBB. 17.12.1986; 17.12.1988; 17.12.1990.	FV	FV	5.00
		b. Printer: IBSFB. 1.4.1992; 2.3.1992; 3.8.1992; 1.7.1993; 1.7.1994.	FV	FV	5.00

1986 COMMEMORATIVE ISSUE

#432, Centennial of the Constitution

Cat. #	Denomination	Date, Description	VG	VF	Unc
432	5000 PESOS	5.8.1986. Deep violet and red-violet on m/c unpt. R. Nuñez at l. and as wmk. Statue at ctr. r. on back. Printer: BDDK.	FV	FV	15.00

1987–90 ISSUES

433	5000 PESOS	5.8.1987; 5.8.1988. Similar to #432 but printer: IPS-Roma.	FV	FV	12.50
434	5000 PESOS	1990-93 Like #432.			
		a. Printer: IBB. 1.1.1990.	FV	FV	12.50
		b. Printer: IBSFB. 31.1.1992; 4.1.1993; 3.1.1994; 4.7.1994; 2.1.1995.	FV	FV	12.50

1992 COMMEMORATIVE ISSUE

#435 Quincentennial of Columbus' Voyage, 12.10.1492

| 435 | 10,000 PESOS | 1992. Deep brown and black on m/c unpt. Early sailing ships at ctr., youthful woman "Majer Embera" at ctr. r. and as wmk, native gold statue at r. Native birds around antique world map at l. ctr., Santa Maria sailing ship at lower r. on back. Printer: BdM. | FV | FV | 30.00 |

Peso System
1993–95 ISSUES

#436–440 portr. as wmk.
#436–438 printer: IBSFB.

| 436 | 2000 PESOS | 1.11.1994. Like #431 but EL deleted from title, ORO deleted from value. | FV | FV | 4.00 |
| 437 | 5000 PESOS | 3.1.1994; 2.1.1995. Like #432–434 but EL deleted from the title, ORO deleted from value. | FV | FV | 9.00 |

NOTE: Large quantities of #437 were stolen in 1994.

438	5000 PESOS	1.3.1995. Dk. brown, brown and deep blue-green on m/c unpt. Trees at l. and ctr. J. Asuncion Silva and bug at r. Woman, trees and monument at ctr. on back.	FV	FV	9.00
439	5000 PESOS	1.7.1995. Like #439. Printer: TDLR.	FV	FV	9.0
440 (436)	10,000 PESOS	1993–94. Like #435, but EL deleted from title, ORO deleted from value, diff. sign. and titles. Printer: IBSFB.	FV	FV	22.50

NOTE: Large quantities of #440 were stolen in 1994.

| 441 | 20,000 PESOS | Expected new issue. | | | |

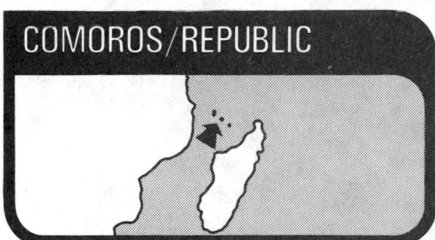

COMOROS/REPUBLIC

The Federal Islamic Republic of the Comoros, a volcanic archipelago located in the Mozambique Channel of the Indian Ocean 300 miles (483 km.) northwest of Madagascar, has an area of 838 sq. mi. (1,797 sq. km.) and a population of 570,000. Capital: Moroni. The economy of the islands is based on agriculture. There are practically no mineral resources. Vanilla, essence for perfumes, copra and sisal are exported.

Ancient Phoenician traders were probably the first visitors to the Comoro Islands, but the first detailed knowledge of the area was gathered by Arab sailors. Arab dominion and culture were firmly established when the Portuguese, Dutch and French arrived in the 16th century. In 1843 a Malagasy ruler ceded the island of Mayotte to France; the other three principal islands of the archipelago - Anjouan, Moheli and Grand Comore - came under French protection in 1886. The islands were joined administratively with Madagascar in 1912. The Comoros became partially autonomous, with the status of a French overseas territory, in 1946, and achieved complete internal autonomy in 1961. On Dec. 31, 1975, after 133 years of French association, the Comoro Islands became the independent Republic of the Comoros.

Mayotte retained the option of determining its future ties and in 1976 voted to remain French. Its present status is that of a French Territorial Collectivity. French currency also circulates there.

RULERS
French to 1975

MONETARY SYSTEM
1 Franc = 100 Centimes

Banque de Madagascar et des Comores
1960 PROVISIONAL ISSUE

#2-6 additional red ovpt: COMORES.

Cat. #	Denomination	Date, description	VG	VF	Unc
2	50 FRANCS	ND (1960–63). Brown and m/c. Ovpt. on Madagascar #45.			
		a. Sign. titles: LE CONTROLEUR GAL. and LE DIRECTEUR GAL. ND (1960).	5.00	20.00	60.00
		b. Sign. titles: LE DIRECTEUR GAL. ADJOINT and LE PRESIDENT DIRECTEUR GAL. ND (1963). 2 sign. varieties.	1.00	4.00	15.00

3	100 FRANCS	ND (1960–63). M/c. Ovpt. on Madagascar #46.			
		a. Sign. titles: LE CONTROLEUR GAL. and LE DIRECTEUR GAL. ND (1960).	6.00	25.00	75.00
		b. Sign. titles: LE DIRECTEUR GAL. ADJOINT and LE PRESIDENT DIRECTEUR GAL. ND (1963).	1.00	3.50	10.00

#4–6 dated through 1952 have titles "a," dated 1955 and ND have titles "b."

Cat. #	Denomination	Date, description	VG	VF	Unc
4	500 FRANCS	ND (1960–63). M/c. Ovpt. on Madagascar #47.			
		a. Sign. titles: *LE CONTROLEUR GAL.* and *LE DIRECTEUR GAL.;* –old date 30.6.1950; 9.10.1952 (1960).	30.00	100.00	250.00
		b. Sign. titles: *LE DIRECTEUR GAL. ADJOINT* and *LE PRESIDENT DIRECTEUR GAL.* ND (1963).	15.00	55.00	165.00
5	1000 FRANCS	ND (1960–63). M/c. Ovpt. on Madagascar #48.			
		a. Sign. titles: *LE CONTROLEUR GAL.* and *LE DIRECTEUR GAL.;* –old date 1950–52; 9.10.1952 (1960).	45.00	125.00	325.00
		b. Sign. titles: *LE DIRECTEUR GAL. ADJOINT* and *LE PRESIDENT DIRECTEUR GAL.* ND (1963).	25.00	75.00	225.00

Cat. #	Denomination	Date, description	VG	VF	Unc
6	5000 FRANCS	ND (1960–63). M/c. Ovpt. on Madagascar #49.			
		a. Sign. titles: *LE CONTROLEUR GAL.* and *LE DIRECTEUR GAL.;* –old date 30.6.1950 (1960).	200.00	450.00	750.00
		b. Sign. titles: *LE DIRECTEUR GAL. ADJOINT* and *LE PRESIDENT DIRECTEUR GAL.* ND (1963).	150.00	350.00	600.00

Institut d'Émission des Comores

#7–9 wmk: Crescent on Maltese cross.

			VG	VF	Unc
7	500 FRANCS	ND (1976). Blue-gray, brown and red on m/c unpt. Bldg. at ctr., young woman wearing a hood at r. 2 women at l., boat at r. on back. 2 sign. varities.	FV	3.00	7.50

Cat. #	Denomination	Date, description	VG	VF	Unc
8	1000 FRANCS	ND (1976). Blue-gray, brown and red on m/c unpt. Woman at r., palm trees at waters edge in background. Women on back.	FV	6.00	15.00
9	5000 FRANCS	ND (1976). Green on m/c unpt. Man and woman at ctr., boats and bldg. in l. background. Man at ctr. on back.	FV	35.00	75.00

Banque Centrale des Comores

#10-12 similar to #7-9 but w/new bank name. Wmk: Maltese cross w/crescent.

			VG	VF	Unc
10	500 FRANCS	ND (1986–). Similar to #7.			
		a. Engraved. Sign. titles: *LE DIRECTEUR GÉNÉRAL* and *LE PRÉSIDENT DU CONSEIL D'ADMINISTRATION* (1986).	FV	2.25	5.50
		b. Offset. Sign. titles: *LE GOUVERNEUR* and *PRÉSIDENT DU...*(1994).	FV	FV	4.50

			VG	VF	Unc
11	1000 FRANCS	ND (1984–). Similar to #8.			
		a. Engraved. Sign. titles as #10a (1984).	FV	4.00	10.00
		b. Offset. Sign. titles as #10b (1994).	FV	3.25	8.00

Cat. #	Denomination	Date, description	VG	VF	Unc
12	5000 FRANCS	ND (1984–). Similar to #9. Engraved. Sign. titles as #10a.	FV	16.50	40.00

The Republic of the Congo (formerly the Peoples Republic of the Congo), located on the equator in west-central Africa, has an area of 132,047 sq. mi. (342,000 sq. km.) and a population of 2.26 million. Capital: Brazzaville. Agriculture forestry, mining, and food processing are the principal industries. Timber, industrial diamonds, potash, peanuts, and cocoa beans are exported.

The Portuguese were the first Europeans to explore the Congo (Brazzaville) area, 14th century. They conducted a slave trade with the tribal kingdoms of Teke, Loango, and Kongo without attempting developmental colonization. French influence was established in 1883 when the King of Teke signed a treaty with Savorgnan de Brazza, thereby placing his kingdom under the protection of France. While a French protectorate, the area was known as Middle Congo. In 1910 Middle Congo became a part of French Equatorial Africa, which also included Gabon, Ubangi-Shari (now the Central African Republic), and Chad. Following World War II, during which it was an important center of Free French activities, the Middle Congo was given a large measure of internal autonomy, and its inhabitants were made French citizens. Upon approval of the constitution of the Fifth French Republic, 1958, it became a member of the new French Community. On Aug. 15, 1960, Middle Congo became the independent Republic of the Congo-Brazzaville. In Jan. 1970 the country's name was changed to Peoples Republic of the Congo. A new constitution which asserts the government's advocacy of socialism was adopted in 1973.

In June and July of 1992, a new 125-member National Assembly was elected. Later that year a new president, Pascal Lissouba, was elected. In November, President Lissouba dismissed the previous government and dissolved the National Assembly. A new 23-member government, including members of the opposition, was formed in December 1992 and the name was changed to Republique du Congo.

RULERS
French to 1960

MONETARY SYSTEM
1 Franc = 100 Centimes

SIGNATURE LISTINGS

NOTE: For later issues and signature chart see Central African States.

Banque Centrale, République Populaire du Congo

Cat. #	Denomination	Date, description	VG	VF	Unc
1	10,000 FRANCS	ND (1971). M/c. Young Congolese woman at l., people marching w/sign at ctr. Statue at l. and r., tractor plowing at ctr. on back. Sign. 1.	125.00	350.00	900.00

Banque des Etats de l'Afrique Centrale, République Populaire du Congo/Congo Peoples Republic

1974 ISSUE

Cat. #	Denomination	Date, description	VG	VF	Unc
2	500 FRANCS	ND (1974)–1983. Lilac-brown and m/c. Woman at l., river scene at ctr. Mask at l., students and chemical testing at ctr., statue at r. on back.			
		a. Sign. titles: *LE DIRECTEUR GENERAL* and *UN CENSEUR*. Engraved. Sign. 5. ND (1974).	2.50	6.00	15.00
		b. Sign. titles: *LE GOUVERNEUR* and *UN CENSEUR*. Lithographed. Sign. 10. 1.4.1978.	5.00	17.50	35.00
		c. Titles as b. Sign. 10; 1.7.1980.	2.00	5.00	12.50
		d. Titles as b. Sign. 12; 1.6.1981; 1.1.1982; 1.1.1983; 1.6.1984.	1.50	4.00	7.50

Cat. #	Denomination	Date, description	VG	VF	Unc
3	1000 FRANCS	ND (1974)–1984. Blue and m/c. Industrial plant at ctr., man at r. Mask at l., trains, planes and bridge at ctr., statue at r. on back.			
		a. Sign. titles: *LE DIRECTEUR GENERAL* and *UN CENSEUR*. Engraved. . Wmk: Antelope head in half profile. Sign. 3. ND (1974).	10.00	25.00	65.00
		b. Like a. Sign. 5.	5.00	10.00	25.00
		c. Sign. titles: *LE DIRECTEUR GENERAL* and *UN CENSEUR*. Lithographed. . Wmk: Antelope head in profile. Sign. 8. ND (1978).	4.50	9.00	17.50
		d. Sign. titles: *LE GOUVERNEUR* and *UN CENSEUR*. Lithographed. Wmk. like b. Sign. 10. 1.4.1978.	5.00	10.00	22.50
		e. Titles as c. Sign. 12. 1.6.1981; 1.1.1982; 1.1.1983; 1.6.1984.	3.50	7.00	15.00

Cat. #	Denomination	Date, description	VG	VF	Unc
4	5000 FRANCS	ND (1974; 1978). Brown. Woman at l. Mask at l., bldgs. at ctr., statue at r. on back.			
		a. Sign. titles: *LE DIRECTEUR GENERAL* and *UN CENSEUR*. Sign. 3. ND (1974).	35.00	85.00	175.00
		b. Like a. Sign. 5.	20.00	45.00	90.00
		c. Sign. titles: *LE GOUVERNEUR* and *UN CENSEUR*. Sign. 11; 12. ND (1978).	25.00	32.50	50.00
5	10,000 FRANCS	ND (1974-81). M/c. Like #1 except for new bank name on back.			
		a. Sign. titles: *LE DIRECTEUR GENERAL* and *UN CENSEUR*. Sign. 5; 7. ND (1974; 1977).	45.00	65.00	110.00
		b. Sign. titles: *LE GOUVERNEUR* and *UN CENSEUR*. Sign. 11; 12. ND (1978; 1981).	25.00	45.00	80.00

1983–84 ISSUE

Cat. #	Denomination	Date, description	VG	VF	Unc
6	5000 FRANCS	ND (1984; 1991). Brown and m/c. Mask at l., woman w/bundle of fronds at r. Plowing and mine ore conveyor on back. Sign. 12; 15.	FV	12.50	35.00
7	10,000 FRANCS	ND (1983). Brown, green and m/c. Stylized antelope heads at l., woman at r. Loading fruit onto truck at l. on back. Sign. 12.	FV	25.00	65.00

1985–87 ISSUE

#8–10 sign. titles: *LE GOUVERNEUR* and *UN CENSEUR*.

Cat. #	Denomination	Date, description	VG	VF	Unc
8	500 FRANCS	1985–. Brown on m/c unpt. Statue at l. ctr. and as wmk., jug at ctr. Man carving mask at l. ctr. on back.			
		a. Sign. 12. 1.1.1985; 1.1.1987; 1.1.1988; 1.1.1989.	FV	1.75	7.50
		b. Sign. 13. 1.1 1990.	FV	1.25	5.00
		c. Sign. 15. 1.1.1991.	FV	1.25	5.00

Cat. #	Denomination	Date, description	VG	VF	Unc
9	1000 FRANCS	1.1.1985. Blue and m/c. Animal carving at lower l., map of 6 member states at ctr. Unfinished map of Chad at upper ctr. Elephant at l., animals at ctr., carving at r. on back. Wmk: Animal carving. Sign. 12.	FV	5.00	15.00

Cat. #	Denomination	Date, description	VG	VF	Unc
10	1000 FRANCS	1987–. Like #9 but completed map of Chad at top on face.			
		a. Sign. 12. 1.1.1987; 1.1.1988.	FV	4.00	13.50
		b. Sign. 13. 1.1.1990.	FV	3.00	11.00
		c. Sign. 15. 1.1.1991.	FV	2.50	10.00

NOTE: For issues w/similar back designs see Cameroon Republic, Central African Republic, Chad and Gabon.

République du Congo/Congo Republic
Banque des Etats de l'Afrique Centrale

Cat. #	Denomination	Date, description	VG	VF	Unc
11	5000 FRANCS	ND (1992). Black text and brown on pale yellow and m/c unpt. African mask at l. and as wmk., woman carrying bundle of cane at r. African string instrument at far l., farm tractor plowing at l. ctr., mineshaft cable ore bucket lift at r. on back. Sign. 15.	FV	12.50	27.50

| 12 | 10,000 FRANCS | ND (1992). Greenish-black text, brown on pale green and m/c unpt. Artistic antelope masks at l., woman's head at r. and as wmk. Loading produce truck w/bananas at l. on back. Sign. 15. | FV | 25.00 | 50.00 |

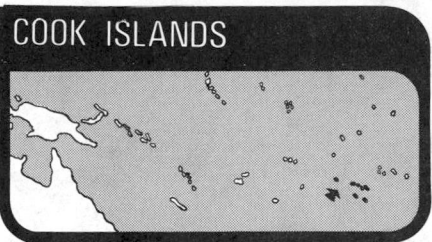

COOK ISLANDS

Cook Islands, a political dependency of New Zealand consisting of 15 islands located in the South Pacific Ocean about 2,000 miles (3,218 km.) northeast of New Zealand, has an area of 93 sq. mi. (234 sq. km.) and a population of 16,900. Capital: Avarua. The United States claims the islands of Danger, Manahiki, Penrhyn and Rakahanga atolls. Citrus and canned fruits and juices, copra, clothing, jewelry and mother-of-pearl shell are exported.

The islands were first sighted by Spanish navigator Alvaro de Mendada in 1595. Portuguese navigator Pedro Fernandes de Quieros landed on Rakahanga in 1606. English navigator Capt. James Cook sailed to the islands on three occasions: 1773, 1774 and 1777. He named them Hervey Islands, in honor of Augustus John Hervey, a lord of the Admiralty. The islands were declared a British protectorate in 1888, and were annexed to New Zealand in 1901. They were granted internal self-government in 1965. New Zealand provides an annual subsidy and retains responsibility for defense and foreign affairs.

As a territory of New Zealand, the Cook Islands are considered to be within the Commonwealth of Nations.

NOTE: In June 1995 the Government of the Cook Islands began redeeming all 10, 20 and 50 dollar notes in exchange for New Zealand currency while all coinage and their 3 dollar notes will remain in circulation.

RULERS
New Zealand, 1901–

MONETARY SYSTEM
1 Dollar = 100 Cents, 1967–

Government of the Cook Islands

1987 ISSUE

#3–5 Ina and the shark at l.

Cat. #	Denomination	Date, description	VG	VF	Unc
3	3 DOLLARS	ND (1987). Deep green, blue-black and black on m/c. Fishing canoe and statue of the god Te-Rongo on back.	FV	2.50	5.00

| 4 | 10 DOLLARS | ND (1987). Violet-brown, blue-black and black on m/c unpt. Pantheon of gods on back. | FV | 7.50 | 10.00 |

Cat. #	Denomination	Date, description	VG	VF	Unc
5	20 DOLLARS	ND (1987). Purple, blue-black and black on m/c unpt. Conch shell, turtle shell and drum on back.			
		a. Sign.T. Davis.	FV	16.50	25.00
		b. Sign. M. J. Fleming.	FV	15.00	19.00

COMMEMORATIVE ISSUE

#6, 6th Festival of Pacific Arts, Rarotonga, Oct. 16-27, 1992

Cat. #	Denomination	Date, description	VG	VF	Unc
6	3 DOLLARS	Oct.1992. Black commemorative text ovpt. at l. on back of #3.	FV	2.50	5.00

1992 ISSUE

#7-10 Worshippers at church w/cemetery at ctr. Wmk: Sea turtle

Cat. #	Denomination	Date, description	VG	VF	Unc
7	3 DOLLARS	ND (1992). Lilac and green on m/c unpt. Back purple, orange and m/c. AITUTAKI at upper ctr., local drummers at l., dancers at ctr., fish at r.	FV	FV	4.00

Cat. #	Denomination	Date, description	VG	VF	Unc
8	10 DOLLARS	ND (1992). Green and olive on m/c unpt. RAROTONGA above hillside gathering on back.	FV	FV	9.00

Cat. #	Denomination	Date, description	VG	VF	Unc
9	20 DOLLARS	ND (1992). Brown-orange and olive on m/c unpt. NGAPUTORU & MANGAIA above 2 islanders w/canoe at ctr. on back.	FV	FV	17.50

Cat. #	Denomination	Date, description	VG	VF	Unc
10	50 DOLLARS	ND (1992). Blue and green on m/c unpt. NORTHERN GROUP above 3 islanders in canoe at l. 2 women seated weaving at ctr. on back.	FV	FV	42.50

COLLECTOR SERIES

Cat. #	Date, denomination	Description	Issue Price	Mkt. Val.
CS1	ND (1987). 3–20 DOLLARS	#3–5 w/matched serial # in collector pack.	55.00	60.00

COSTA RICA

The Republic of Costa Rica, located in southern Central America between Nicaragua and Panama, has an area of 19,575 sq. mi. (50,700 sq. km.) and a population of 3.03 million. Capital: San Jose. Agriculture predominates; coffee, bananas, beef and sugar contribute heavily to the country's export earnings.

Costa Rica was discovered by Christopher Columbus in 1502, during his last voyage to the new world, and was a colony of Spain from 1522 until independence in 1821. Columbus named the territory Nueva Cartago; the name Costa Rica wasn't generally employed until 1540. Bartholomew Columbus attempted to found the first settlement but was driven off by Indian attacks and the country wasn't pacified until 1530. Costa Rica was absorbed for two years (1821–23) into the Mexican Empire of Agustin de Iturbide. From 1823 to 1848 it was a constituent state of the Central American Republic (q.v.). It was established as a republic in 1848. Today, Costa Rica remains a model of orderly democracy in Latin America.

MONETARY SYSTEM

1 Colon = 100 Centavos, 1896–

Banco Central de Costa Rica

PROVISIONAL ISSUE

#214 ovpt: *BANCO CENTRAL DE COSTA RICA/SERIE PROVISIONAL* on Banco Nacional notes.

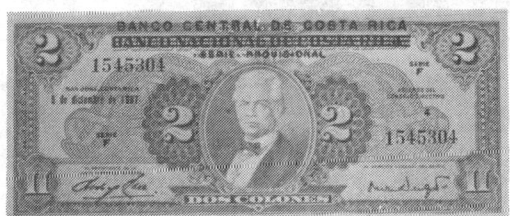

Cat. #	Denomination	Date, description	VG	VF	Unc
214	2 COLONES	5.12.1967. Black ovpt. on #203. Series F.	.35	1.50	6.50

REGULAR ISSUES

SERIES A

#221–224 printer: W&S.

221	10 COLONES	1951–62. Blue on m/c unpt. Portr. A. Echeverria at ctr. Back blue; ox-cart at ctr.			
		a. W/POR added to l. of sign. title at l. 8.11.1951; 29.10.1952.	3.00	8.00	50.00
		b. W/o sign. title changes. 7.9.1955–27.6.1962.	2.00	6.00	40.00
		c. W/POR added to both sign. titles. 28.11.1951	3.00	8.00	50.00

Cat. #	Denomination	Date, description	VG	VF	Unc
222	20 COLONES	1952–64. Red on m/c unpt. Portr. C. Picado at ctr. Back red, university bldg. at ctr.			
		a. Date at l. ctr., w/o sign. title changes. 11.6.1952; 10.12.1952; 11.8.1954; 14.10.1955; 13.2.1957.	3.00	15.00	75.00
		b. Sign. title: *SUB-GERENTE* ovpt. at r. 20.4.1955.	2.25	11.00	65.00
		c. Date at lower l. 7.11.1957–9.9.1964.	2.00	10.00	60.00
		d. *POR* added at l. of sign. title at l. 25.3.1953; 25.2.1954.	3.00	15.00	75.00

223	50 COLONES	31.1.1957–27.11.1963. Olive on m/c unpt. Portr. R.F. Guardia at ctr. Back olive; National Library at ctr.	5.00	25.00	100.00

224	100 COLONES	1955–60. Black on m/c unpt. Portr. J.R. Mora at ctr. Back black; statue of J. Santamaria at ctr.			
		a. W/o sign. title changes: 19.10.1955; 6.10.1959; 25.11.1959; 29.4.1960.	7.50	27.50	125.00
		b. Sign. title: *SUB-GERENTE* ovpt. at r. 27.3.1957.	7.50	27.50	125.00

#225–226 printer: ABNC.

Cat. #	Denomination	Date, description	VG	VF	Unc
225	500 COLONES	2.4.1973; 4.5.1974; 4.5.1976; 26.4.1977. Purple on m/c unpt. Portr. M.M. Gutierrez at r. Back purple; National Theater at ctr.	45.00	160.00	350.00

226	1000 COLONES	26.3.1958; 2.4.1973; 18.10.1973; 12.6.1974. Red on m/c unpt. Portr. J. Pena at l. Back red; Central and National Bank at ctr.	80.00	225.00	450.00

SERIES B

227	5 COLONES	20.5.1959–3.11.1962. Green on m/c unpt. Portr. B. Carrillo at ctr. Back green; coffee worker at ctr. Printer: W&S.	1.00	4.00	15.00

#228–232 printer: TDLR.

228	10 COLONES	19.9.1962–9.10.1967. Blue on m/c unpt. Portr. Echeverria at ctr. Back blue; ox-cart at ctr.	1.50	5.00	25.00

229	20 COLONES	11.11.1964–30.6.1970. Brown on m/c unpt. Portr. Picado at ctr. Back brown; university bldg. at ctr.	2.00	7.50	37.50

Cat. #	Denomination	Date, description	VG	VF	Unc
230	50 COLONES	4.6.1965–30.6.1970. Greenish-brown on m/c unpt. Portr. Guardia at ctr. Back greenish-brown; National Library at ctr.	3.00	12.50	55.00

231	100 COLONES	1961–66. Black on m/c unpt. Portr. Mora at ctr. Statue of J. Santamaria at ctr. on back.			
		a. Brown unpt. 18.12.1961-3.12.1964.	4.00	20.00	90.00
		b. Olive unpt. and w/security thread. 9.6.1965; 27.4.1966.	3.50	17.50	85.00

232	500 COLONES	1980–85. Purple on m/c unpt. M.M. Gutierrez at r. National Theatre on back.			
		a. Red serial #. 18.12.1980; 12.3.1981.	FV	12.50	25.00
		b. Black serial #. 17.9.1981; 18.5.1982; 20.3.1985.	FV	FV	15.00

233	1000 COLONES	9.6.1975–7.4.1983; 20.3.1985. Red on m/c unpt. T. Soley Guell at l. National Insurance Institute on back. Printer: ABNC.	FV	FV	35.00

SERIES C

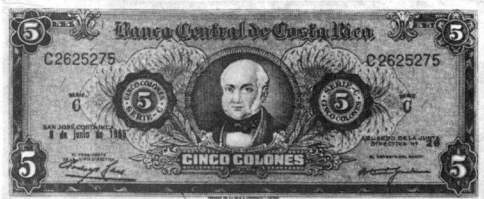

234	5 COLONES	3.10.1963–29.5.1967. Green on m/c unpt. Portr. Carrillo at ctr. Back green; coffee worker at ctr. Printer: TDLR.	.75	2.50	12.50

Cat. #	Denomination	Date, description	VG	VF	Unc
235	10 COLONES	1969–70; ND. Blue on m/c unpt. Portr. R. Facio Brenes at r. Back blue; Banco Central bldg. at ctr. Printer: ABNC.			
		a. 4.3.1969; 17.6.1969; 30.6.1970.	.75	2.50	12.50
		b. W/o date or sign.	—	—	—

NOTE: It is reported that 10,000 pieces of #235b mistakenly reached circulation.

236	20 COLONES	1972–83. Dk. brown on m/c unpt. C.G. Viquez at l., bldgs. and trees at r. Allegorical scene on back.			
		a. BARBA … etc. text under bldgs. at ctr. Sign. titles: *EL PRESIDENTE DE LA JUNTA DIRECTIVA* and *EL GERENTE DEL BANCO.* Date at upper r., w/ security strip. 10.7.1972; 6.9.1972.	.75	2.50	7.50
		b. Text and sign. as a., date position at upper ctr., w/security strip. 13.11.1972–26.4.1977.	.75	2.00	5.00
		c. Lt. brown. Sign. titles: *PRESIDENTE EJECUTIVO* and *GERENTE.* W/o security thread. *BARVA…* etc. text under bldgs. at ctr. Date at upper ctr. r. or upper ctr. 1.6.1978–7.4.1983.	FV	.50	1.50
236A	20 COLONES	28.6.1983. Design like #236d, but Series Z. Printed on Tyvek (plastic).	1.00	3.00	7.00

237	50 COLONES	10.9.1973–26.4.1977. Olive on m/c unpt. Meeting scene at l., M.M. de Peralta y Alfaro at r. *Casa Amarilla* (Yellow House) on back.	1.00	4.00	15.00

Cat. #	Denomination	Date, description	VG	VF	Unc
238	100 COLONES	29.8.1966–27.8.1968. Black on m/c unpt. Portr. Mora at ctr., w/o *C* in corners or at r. Back black; w/statue of J. Santamaria at ctr. Printer: TDLR.	5.00	15.00	65.00

238A	500 COLONES	21.1.1987; 21.8.1987; 14.6.1989. Brown-orange and olive-brown on m/c unpt. Similar to #232, but clear wmk. area at l. Printer: TDLR.	FV	FV	12.50

238B	1000 COLONES	19.11.1986; 17.6.1987; 6.1.1988; 17.1.1989. Red on m/c unpt. Similar to #233. Printer: ABNC.	FV	FV	20.00

238C	1000 COLONES	1990–. Red on m/c unpt. Similar to #233 and #238B. Printer: USBN.			
		a. 24.4.1990; 3.10.1990; 23.10.1991.	FV	FV	17.50
		b. 2.2.1994; 15.6.1994.	FV	FV	12.50

SERIES D

Cat. #	Denomination	Date, description	VG	VF	Unc
239	5 COLONES	1968–92. Deep green and lilac on m/c unpt. R.Y. Castro at l., flowers at r. Back green and m/c; National Theater scene. Printer: TDLR.			
		a. Date at ctr. w/wmk. and security thread. Error name *T. VILLA* on back. 20.8.1968; 11.12.1968.	1.00	2.50	7.50
		b. Date at ctr. r. w/wmk. and security thread. Error name *T. VILLA* on back. 1.4.1969; 30.6.1970; 8.5.1972.	.50	1.50	4.00
		c. Date at ctr. r. w/wmk. and security thread. Corrected name *J. VILLA* on back. 4.5.1973–4.5.1976.	.25	.50	2.50
		d. W/o wmk. or security thread. Changed sign. titles. 28.6.1977–15.1.1992.	.10	.20	.75
		e. Like d. but w/error date: 7.4.1933 (instead of 1983).	1.00	2.00	5.00

240	10 COLONES	1972–87. Blue on m/c unpt. University bldg. at l., R. Facio Brenes at r. Central Bank on back. W/o imprint.			
		a. Security thread. 6.9.1972–26.4.1977.	.25	.75	3.00
		b. W/o security thread. 26.4.1977–18.2.1987.	FV	FV	.75

1978 COMMEMORATIVE ISSUE

#241, Centennial of Bank of Costa Rica 1877–1977

241	50 COLONES	1978-86. Olive-green and m/c. Obverse of 1866 50 Centimos coin at l., G. Ortuno y Ors at r. Bank, reverse of 50 Centimos coin and commemorative text: *1877–CENTENARIO…* on back. Printer: TDLR.			
		a. 30.10.1978; 30.4.1979; 18.3.1980; 2.4.1981.	1.00	3.50	7.50
		b. 18.5.1982; 22.11.1984; 20.3.1985; 2.4.1986.	.75	1.50	4.50

REGULAR ISSUE

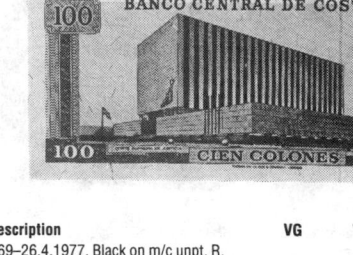

Cat. #	Denomination	Date, description	VG	VF	Unc
242	100 COLONES	26.8.1969–26.4.1977. Black on m/c unpt. R. Jimenez O. at l., cows and mountains at ctr. Supreme Court at ctr., figures at r. on back. Printer: TDLR.	2.00	5.00	27.50

SERIES E

#242A–243 sign. titles: *PRESIDENTE EJECUTIVO* and *GERENTE*.

242A (A243)	50 COLONES	15.7.1987; 26.4.1988. Olive green on m/c unpt. Similar to #241 but text: *ANTIGUO EDIFICIO…* on back. Printer: CdM Brazil.	FV	FV	2.25

242B	50 COLONES	19.6.1991; 28.8.1991; 29.7.1992; 2.6.1993. Similar to #242A. Printer: TDLR.	FV	FV	1.50

243	100 COLONES	26.4.1977–9.11.1988. M/c. R. Jimenez O. at l. Similar to #242. Printer: TDLR.	FV	FV	2.75

SERIES Z

NOTE: For 20 Colones 1983 printed on Tyvek plastic, see #236A.

1971 COMMEMORATIVE ISSUE

#244–249 circular ovpt: *150 AÑOS DE INDEPENDENCIA 1821–1971.*

Cat. #	Denomination	Date, description	VG	VF	Unc
244	5 COLONES	24.5.1971. Ovpt. on #239b. Series D.	1.00	5.00	12.50

245	10 COLONES	24.5.1971. Ovpt. on #235. Series C.	3.00	15.00	35.00
246	50 COLONES	24.5.1971. Ovpt. on #230. Series B.	15.00	45.00	110.00

247	100 COLONES	24.5.1971; 13.12.1971. Ovpt. on #242. Series D.	20.00	65.00	175.00

248	500 COLONES	24.5.1971. Ovpt. on #225. Series A.	145.00	325.00	—
249	1000 COLONES	24.5.1971. Ovpt. on #226. Series A.	175.00	400.00	—

#250 circular ovpt: *XXV ANIVERSARIO BANCO CENTRAL DE COSTA RICA / 1950 / 1975.*

250	5 COLONES	20.3.1975. Ovpt. on #239. Series D.	1.00	3.50	8.50

#251–253 Held in reserve.

REGULAR ISSUES

SERIES F (and later issues)

Cat. #	Denomination	Date, description	VG	VF	Unc
254	100 COLONES	30.11.1988; 4.10.1989; 5.10.1990 Black on m/c unpt. Similar to #242 and 243. Printer: ABNC.	FV	FV	4.00

SERIES G

255	100 COLONES	17.9.1992. Like #254 but printer: CdM.	FV	FV	3.50

SERIES H

256	100 COLONES	28.9.1993. Like #254. Printer: ABNC.	FV	FV	2.75

SERIES A

257	5000 COLONES	28.8.1991; 11.3.1992; 29.7.1992. Dk. blue and dk. brown on m/c unpt. Local sculpture at l. ctr. Bird, leopard, local carving, foliage and sphere on back. Printer: TDLR.	FV	FV	65.00

Croatia (Hrvatska), formerly a federal republic of the Socialist Federal Republic of Yugoslavia, has an area of 21,829 sq. mi. (56,538 sq. km.) and a population of about 5 million. Capital: Zagreb.

The country was attached to the Kingdom of Hungary until Dec. 1, 1918, when it joined with Serbia, Slovenia, Bosnia-Herzegovina, Macedonia and Montenegro to form the Kingdom of the Serbs, Croats and Slovenes, which changed its name to the Kingdom of Yugoslavia on Oct. 3, 1929. On April 6, 1941, Hitler, angered by the coup d'etat that overthrew the pro-Nazi regime of regent Prince Paul, sent the Nazi armies crashing across the Yugoslav borders from Germany, Hungary, Romania and Bulgaria. Within a week the army of the Balkan Kingdom was broken. Yugoslavia was dismembered to reward Hitler's Balkan allies. Croatia, reconstituted as a nominal kingdom, was given to the administration of an Italian princeling, who wisely decided to remain in Italy.

Croatia proclaimed its independence from Yugoslavia on Oct. 8, 1991. Serbian forces had developed a military stronghold in the area around Knin, located in southern Croatia. In August 1995 Croat forces overran this political-military enclave.

MONETARY SYSTEM
1 Dinar = 100 Para, 1945–1994
1 Kuna = 100 Lipa, 1994–

REPUBLIKA HRVATSKA – REPUBLIC OF CROATIA

1991–93 ISSUE

#16–27 R. Boskovic at ctr., geometric calculations at upper r. (Printed in Sweden).
#16–22 vertical back with Zagreb cathedral and artistic rendition of city buildings behind.

Cat. #	Denomination	Date, description	VG	VF	Unc
16	1 DINAR	8.10.1991. Dull orange-brown on m/c unpt. 4.5mm serial #. Wmk: Lozenges.			
		a. Issued note.	FV	FV	.15
		s. Specimen.	—	—	20.00

17	5 DINARA	8.10.1991. Pale violet on m/c unpt. 4mm serial #. Wmk: Lozenges.			
		a. Issued note.	FV	FV	.30
		s. Specimen.	—	—	20.00

18	10 DINARA	8.10.1991. Pale red-brown on m/c unpt. 4.5mm serial #. Wmk: Lozenges.			
		a. Issued note.	FV	FV	.50
		s. Specimen.	—	—	20.00

Cat. #	Denomination	Date, description	VG	VF	Unc
19	25 DINARA	8.10.1991. Dull violet on m/c unpt. Buff paper w/2.8mm serial #. Wmk: 5's in crossed wavy lines.	FV	FV	.75
		a. Issued note.	FV	FV	.75
		b. Inverted wmk.	6.50	16.00	32.50
		s. Specimen.	—	—	30.00

NOTE: The wmk. paper actually used in the production for #19 was originally prepared for printing Sweden 5 Kronor, #14.

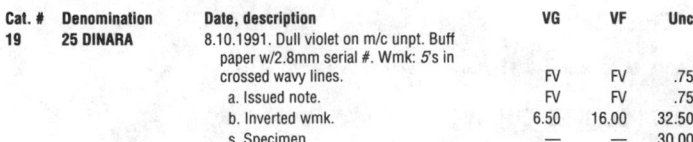

20	100 DINARA	8.10.1991. Pale green on m/c unpt. W/o wmk.			
		a. Issued note.	FV	FV	3.25
		s. Specimen.	—	—	40.00

#21–26 wmk: Baptismal font.

21	500 DINARA	8.10.1991. Lilac on m/c unpt.			
		a. Issued note.	FV	FV	4.50
		s. Specimen.	—	—	30.00

22	1000 DINARA	8.10.1991. Pale blue-violet on m/c unpt.			
		a. Issued note.	FV	FV	8.50
		s. Specimen.	—	—	30.00

#23-26 statue of woman seated at ctr. on back.

23	2000 DINARA	15.1.1992. Deep brown on m/c unpt.			
		a. Issued note.	FV	FV	10.00
		s. Specimen.	—	—	30.00

Cat. #	Denomination	Date, description	VG	VF	Unc
24	5000 DINARA	15.1.1992. Dark gray on m/c unpt.			
		a. Issued note.	FV	FV	12.00
		s. Specimen.	—	—	30.00

25	10,000 DINARA	15.1.1992. Olive-green on m/c unpt.			
		a. Issued note.	FV	FV	10.00
		s. Specimen.	—	—	30.00

26	50,000 DINARA	30.5.1993. Deep red on m/c unpt.			
		a. Issued note.	FV	FV	25.00
		s. Specimen.	—	—	30.00
27	100,000 DINARA	30.5.1993. Dk. blue-green on m/c unpt.			
		a. Issued note.	FV	FV	50.00
		s. Specimen.	—	—	30.00

Currency Reform, 1994

1 Kuna = 1,000 Dinara

#28–35 shield at upper l. ctr. Printer: G & D.

28	5 KUNA	31.10.1993 (1994). Dk. green and green on m/c unpt. F. K. Frankopan and P. Zrinski at r. and as wmk. Fortress in Varazdin at l. ctr. on back.			
		a. Issued note.	FV	FV	3.00
		b. Error w/o date or sign.	12.00	30.00	60.00
		s. Specimen.	—	—	30.00

29	10 KUNA	31.10.1993 (1994). Purple and violet on m/c unpt. J. Dobrila at r. and as wmk. Pula arena at l. ctr. on back.			
		a. Issued note.	FV	FV	5.50
		s. Specimen.	—	—	30.00

Cat. #	Denomination	Date, description	VG	VF	Unc
30	20 KUNA	31.10.1993 (1994). Brown, red and violet on m/c unpt. J. Jelacic at r. and as wmk. Pottery dove and castle of Count Fltz in Vukovar at l. ctr. on back.			
		a. Issued note.	FV	FV	10.00
		s. Specimen.	—	—	30.00
31	50 KUNA	31.10.1993 (1994). Dk. blue and blue-green on m/c unpt. I. G. Dubrovnik at r. and as wmk. Aerial view of old Dubrovnik at l. ctr. on back.			
		a. Issued note.	FV	FV	20.00
		s. Specimen.	—	—	30.00

32	100 KUNA	31.10.1993 (1994). Red-brown and brown-orange on m/c unpt. I. Mazuranic at r. and as wmk. Plan of and church of St. Vitus in Rijeka at l. ctr. on back.			
		a. Issued note.	FV	FV	35.00
		b. Error w/o serial #.	13.50	32.50	65.00
		s. Specimen.	—	—	30.00

Cat. #	Denomination	Date, description	VG	VF	Unc
33	200 KUNA	31.10.1993 (1994). Dk. brown and brown on m/c unpt. S. Radic at r. and as wmk. Town command in Osijek at l. ctr. on back.			
		a. Issued note.	FV	FV	60.00
		s. Specimen.	—	—	30.00
34	500 KUNA	31.10.1993 (1994). Dk. brown and olive-brown on m/c unpt. M. Marulic at r. and as wmk. Palace of Diocletian in Spit at l. ctr. on back.			
		a. Issued note.	FV	FV	130.00
		s. Specimen.	—	—	30.00
35	1,000 KUNA	31.10.1993 (1994). Dk. brown and purple on m/c unpt. A. Starcevic at r. and as wmk. Equestrian statue of Kg. Tomislav at l. ctr., Zagreb Cathedral at ctr. r. on back.			
		a. Issued note.	FV	FV	240.00
		s. Specimen.	—	—	30.00

1995 ISSUE

36	10 KUNA	15.1.1995. Black and brown on m/c unpt. Like #29. Printer: G&D.			
		a. Issued note.	FV	FV	5.50
		s. Specimen.	—	—	30.00

REGIONAL
РЕПУБЛИКА СРПСКА КРАЈИНА
Republika Srpska Krajina

KNIN ISSUE

REPLACEMENT NOTES
#R1–R34, ZA prefix letters.

#R1–R6 arms at l., numerals in heartshaped design below guilloche at r. ctr. Curved artistic design at l. ctr., arms at r. on back. Headings in Serbo-Croatian and Cyrillic.

#R1–R3 wmk: Portr. of a young girl. .

R1	10 DINARA	1992. Deep brown on orange and silver unpt. Back with ochre unpt.			
		a. Issued note.	.40	1.00	2.50
		b. Specimen.	—	—	13.50

Cat. #	Denomination	Date, description	VG	VF	Unc
R2	50 DINARA	1992. Gray on tan and yellow unpt.			
		a. Issued note.	.50	1.25	3.00
		s. Specimen.	—	—	13.50

R3	100 DINARA	1992. Blue-gray on lilac and silver unpt.			
		a. Issued note.	.40	1.00	4.00
		s. Specimen.	—	—	13.50

#R4–R5 wmk: Young boy.

R4	500 DINARA	1992. Blue-gray on pink and m/c unpt.			
		a. Issued note.	2.75	7.00	22.00
		s. Specimen.	—	—	13.50

R5	1000 DINARA	1992. Deep gray on pink and tan unpt.			
		a. Issued note.	1.65	5.00	15.00
		s. Specimen.	—	—	13.50
R6	5000 DINARA	1992. Violet on lt. blue, pink and lilac unpt.			
		a. Issued note.	1.00	2.00	5.00
		s. Specimen.	—	—	13.50

НАРОДНА БАНКА РЕПУБЛИКЕ СРПСКЕ КРАЈИНЕ
Narodna Banka Republike Srpske Krajine
National Bank of the Serbian Republic – Krajina

1992–93 ISSUE

#R7–R16 like #R1–R6.

#R7–R8 wmk: Portr. of young boy.

Cat. #	Denomination	Date, description	VG	VF	Unc
R7	10,000 DINARA	1992. Deep gray-green on lt. blue and tan unpt.			
		a. Issued note.	.50	1.00	3.00
		s. Specimen.	—	—	13.50

R8	50,000 DINARA	1992. Brown on pale orange and pale olive-green unpt.			
		a. Issued note.	1.00	1.75	4.50
		s. Specimen.	—	—	13.50

R9	100,000 DINARA	1993. Dull purple and brown on m/c unpt. Wmk: Young woman.			
		a. Issued note.	1.50	2.50	6.00
		s. Specimen.	—	—	13.50

#R10–R12 wmk: Portr. of young girl.

R10	1 MILLION DINARA	1993. Deep purple on m/c unpt.			
		a. Issued note.	5.00	10.00	20.00
		s. Specimen.	—	—	13.50

Cat. #	Denomination	Date, description	VG	VF	Unc
R11	5 MILLION DINARA	1993. Dk. brown on orange and blue-gray unpt.			
		a. Issued note.	1.00	2.50	7.50
		s. Specimen.	—	—	13.50

R12	10 MILLION DINARA	1993. Deep blue on pale olive-green and m/c unpt.			
		a. Issued note.	2.00	4.00	10.00
		s. Specimen.	—	—	13.50

#R13–R19 wmk: Greek design repeated.

R13	20 MILLION DINARA	1993. Olive-gray on orange and tan unpt.			
		a. Issued note.	2.00	4.00	10.00
		s. Specimen.	—	—	13.50

R14	50 MILLION DINARA	1993. Brown-violet on pink and lt. gray unpt.			
		a. Issued note.	2.00	4.00	10.00
		s. Specimen.	—	—	13.50

R15	100 MILLION DINARA	1993. Blue-black on lt. blue and gray unpt.			
		a. Issued note.	2.00	4.00	10.00
		s. Specimen.	—	—	13.50

Cat. #	Denomination	Date, description	VG	VF	Unc
R16	500 MILLION DINARA	1993. Orange on lilac and yellow unpt.			
		a. Issued note.	2.00	4.00	10.00
		s. Specimen.	—	—	13.50

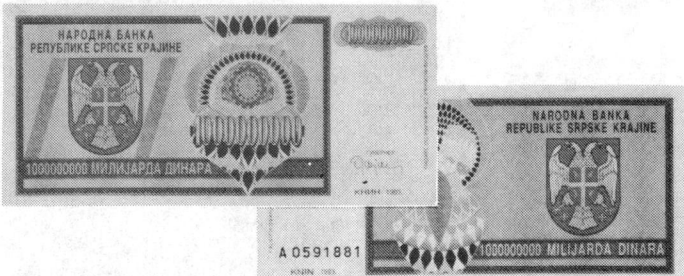

R17	1 MILLIARD DINARA	1993. Dull brownish orange on pale blue and lt. orange unpt.			
		a. Issued note.	2.00	4.00	10.00
		s. Specimen.	—	—	13.50

R18	5 MILLIARD DINARA	1993. Purple on lilac and gray unpt.			
		a. Issued note.	2.00	4.00	10.00
		s. Specimen.	—	—	13.50

R19	10 MILLIARD DINARA	1993. Black on orange and pink unpt.			
		a. Issued note.	2.00	4.00	10.00
		s. Specimen.	—	—	13.50

NOTE: For notes identical in color and design to #R1–R19 but differing only in text at top, sign. and place of issue Banja Luka, see Bosnia & Herzegovina #33–47.

Currency Reform, 1993
1 Dinar = 1,000,000 "old" Dinara

1993 ISSUE
#R20-R27 Knin fortress on hill at l. ctr. Serbian arms at ctr. r. on back. Wmk: Greek design repeated.

R20	5000 DINARA	1993. Red-violet and violet on blue-gray unpt.			
		a. Issued note.	.50	1.25	4.00
		s. Specimen.	—	—	13.50

Cat. #	Denomination	Date, description	VG	VF	Unc
R21	50,000 DINARA	1993. Brown, red and red-orange on ochre unpt.			
		a. Issued note.	.75	1.75	5.50
		s. Specimen.	—	—	13.50

R22	100,000 DINARA	1993. Violet and blue-gray on pink unpt.			
		a. Issued note.	.75	1.75	5.50
		s. Specimen.	—	—	13.50

R23	500,000 DINARA	1993. Brown and gray-green on pale green unpt.			
		a. Issued note.	1.00	2.00	6.00
		s. Specimen.	—	—	13.50

R24	5 MILLION DINARA	1993. Orange and gray-green on pale orange unpt.			
		a. Issued note.	1.00	2.00	6.00
		s. Specimen.	—	—	13.50

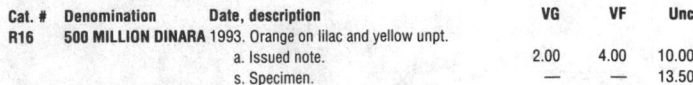

Cat. #	Denomination	Date, description	VG	VF	Unc
R25	100 MILLION DINARA	1993. Olive-brown and gray-green on lt. blue unpt.			
		a. Issued note.	1.25	2.50	7.50
		s. Specimen.	—	—	13.50

R26	500 MILLION DINARA	1993. Chocolate brown and gray-green on pale olive-green unpt.			
		a. Issued note.	.50	1.00	4.00
		s. Specimen.	—	—	13.50

R27	5 MD DINARA	1993. Brown-orange and aqua on gray unpt.			
		a. Issued note.	1.25	2.50	7.50
		s. Specimen.	—	—	13.50

R28	10 MD DINARA	1993. Purple and red on aqua unpt.			
		a. Issued note.	1.25	2.50	7.50
		s. Specimen.	—	—	13.50
R29	50 MD DINARA	1993. Brown and olive-green on reddish brown unpt.			
		a. Issued note.	1.25	2.50	7.50
		s. Specimen.	—	—	13.50

Currency Reform, 1994

1 "new" Dinar = 10,000 "old" Dinara

1994 ISSUE

#R30–R34 like #R2–R29.

R30	1,000 DINARA	1994. Dk. brown and slate-gray on yellow-orange unpt.			
		a. Issued note.	.50	1.00	2.50
		s. Specimen.	—	—	13.50

Cat. #	Denomination	Date, description	VG	VF	Unc
R31	10,000 DINARA	1994. Red-brown and dull purple on ochre unpt.			
		a. Issued note.	.50	1.00	2.50
		s. Specimen.	—	—	13.50

R32	500,000 DINARA	1994 Dk. brown and blue-gray on grayish green unpt.			
		a. Issued note.	.75	1.50	3.00
		s. Specimen.	—	—	13.50

R33	1 MILLION DINARA	1994. Purple and aqua on lilac unpt.			
		a. Issued note.	1.00	2.00	4.50
		s. Specimen.	—	—	13.50

R34	10 MILLION DINARA	1994. Gray and red-brown on pink unpt.			
		a. Issued note.	1.50	3.00	8.00
		s. Specimen.	—	—	13.50

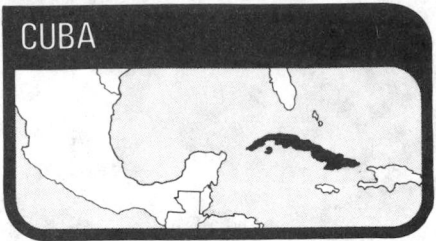

The Republic of Cuba, situated at the northern edge of the Caribbean Sea about 90 miles (145 km.) south of Florida, has an area of 44,218 sq. mi. (114,524 sq. km.) and a population of 10.7 million. Capital: Havana. The Cuban economy is based on the cultivation and refining of sugar, which provides 80 percent of export earnings.

Discovered by Columbus in 1492 and settled by Diego Velasquez in the early 1500s, Cuba remained a Spanish possession until 1898, except for a brief British occupancy in 1762–63. Cuban attempts to gain freedom were crushed, even while Spain was granting independence to its other American possessions. Ten years of warfare, 1868–78, between Spanish troops and Cuban rebels exacted guarantees of right which were never implemented. The final revolt, begun in 1895, evoked American sympathy, and with the aid of U.S. troops independence was proclaimed on May 20, 1902. Fulgencio Batista seized the government in 1952 and established a dictatorship. Opposition to Batista, led by Fidel Castro, drove him into exile on Jan. 1, 1959. A communist-type, 25 member collective leadership headed by Castro was inaugurated in March 1962.

MONETARY SYSTEMS

1 Peso = 100 Centavos
1 Peso Convertibles = 1 U.S.A. Dollar, 1995–

REPLACEMENT NOTES

#108-112: an EX, DX, CX, BX, AX series #, by denomination.

Banco Nacional de Cuba / National Bank of Cuba

1961 ISSUE

#94–99 denomination at l. and r. Sign. titles: *PRESIDENTE DEL BANCO* at l., *MINISTRO DE HACIENDA* at r. Printer: STC-P.

Cat. #	Denomination	Date, description	VG	VF	Unc
94	1 PESO	1961–65. Olive green on ochre unpt. Portr. J. Martí at ctr. F. Castro w/rebel soldiers entering Havana in 1959 on back.			
		a. 1961.	1.75	3.00	17.50
		b. 1964.	1.25	2.25	8.50
		c. 1965.	FV	2.00	7.00

95	5 PESOS	1961–65. Dull deep green on pink unpt. Portr. A. Maceo at ctr. Invasion of 1958 on back.			
		a. 1961.	FV	5.00	40.00
		b. 1964.	FV	5.00	22.50
		c. 1965.	FV	5.00	20.00

Cat. #	Denomination	Date, description	VG	VF	Unc
96	10 PESOS	1961–65. Brown on tan and yellow unpt. Portr. M. Gomez at ctr. Castro addressing crowd in 1960 on back.			
		a. 1961.	FV	12.00	50.00
		b. 1964.	FV	10.00	37.50
		c. 1965.	FV	10.00	32.50

97	20 PESOS	1961–65. Blue on pink unpt. Portr. C. Cienfuegos at ctr. Soldiers on the beach in 1956 on back.			
		a. 1961.	FV	22.50	90.00
		b. 1964.	FV	20.00	65.00
		c. 1965.	FV	20.00	60.00
		x. U.S.A.counterfeit. Series F69; F70.			
		1961.	3.50	15.00	75.00

NOTE: Each member of the "Bay of Pigs" invasion force was reportedly issued one hundred each of #97x.

98	50 PESOS	1961. Purple on green unpt. Portr. C. Garcia Iniguez at ctr. Nationalization of international industries on back.	30.00	75.00	200.00

Cat. #	Denomination	Date, description	VG	VF	Unc
99	100 PESOS	1961. Lt. red on orange unpt. Portr. C. M. de Cespedes at ctr. Attack on Moncada in 1953 on back.	55.00	125.00	350.00

1966 ISSUE

#100–101 denomination at l. and r. Sign. titles: *PRESIDENTE DEL BANCO* at l. and r. Printer: STC-P (w/o imprint).

Cat. #	Denomination	Date, description	VG	VF	Unc
100	1 PESO	1966. Like #94.	FV	1.25	10.00
101	10 PESOS	1966. Like #96.	FV	8.50	35.00

1967; 1971 ISSUE

#102–105 Denomination at l. Sign. title: *PRESIDENTE DEL BANCO* at r. Printer: STC-P (w/o imprint).

Cat. #	Denomination	Date, description	VG	VF	Unc
102	1 PESO	1967–88. Like #94.			
		a. 1967–70; 1972.	FV	1.00	5.00
		b. 1978–86.	FV	FV	4.00
		c. 1986.	FV	1.50	8.00
		d. 1988.	FV	FV	2.00

Cat. #	Denomination	Date, description	VG	VF	Unc
103	5 PESOS	1967–90. Like #95.			
		a. 1967–68.	FV	4.00	20.00
		b. 1970; 1972.	FV	FV	15.00
		c. 1984–87.	FV	FV	10.00
		d. 1988; 1990.	FV	FV	6.00

Cat. #	Denomination	Date, description	VG	VF	Unc
104	10 PESOS	1967–89. Like #96.			
		a. 1967–71.	FV	8.00	35.00
		b. 1978.	FV	FV	25.00
		c. 1983–84; 1986–87.	FV	FV	18.00
		d. 1988–89.	FV	FV	11.00

Cat. #	Denomination	Date, description	VG	VF	Unc
105	20 PESOS	1971–90. Like #97.			
		a. 1971.	FV	16.00	50.00
		b. 1978.	FV	FV	40.00
		c. 1983.	FV	FV	35.00
		d. 1987–90.	FV	FV	20.00

1975 COMMEMORATIVE ISSUE

#106, 15th Anniversary Nationalization of Banking

Cat. #	Denomination	Date, description	VG	VF	Unc
106	1 PESO	1975. Olive on violet unpt. Portr. J. Martí at l., arms at r. Ship at dockside on back.	2.50	8.00	25.00

1983 ISSUE

Cat. #	Denomination	Date, description	VG	VF	Unc
107	3 PESOS	1983–89. Red on m/c unpt. Portr. E. "Che" Guevara at ctr. Back red on orange unpt.; "Che" cutting sugar cane at ctr.			
		a. 1983–86.	FV	3.00	12.00
		b. 1988–89.	FV	FV	4.00

1990–91 ISSUE

Cat. #	Denomination	Date, description	VG	VF	Unc
108	5 PESOS	1991. Deep green and deep blue on m/c unpt. A. Maceo at r. Secret meeting of the rebel military in the woods at l. ctr. on back. Wmk: J. Marti.	.25	1.00	2.50

Cat. #	Denomination	Date, description	VG	VF	Unc
109	10 PESOS	1991. Deep brown and deep olive-green on m/c unpt. M. Gomez at r. "Guerra de todo el Pueblo" at l. ctr. on back. Wmk: J. Marti.	.50	2.00	5.00

Cat. #	Denomination	Date, description	VG	VF	Unc
110	20 PESOS	1991. Deep blue and purple on m/c unpt. Agricultural scenes at l. ctr. on back. Wmk: National heroine.	1.00	4.00	10.00
111	50 PESOS	1990. Deep violet and dk. green on m/c unpt. Arms at ctr. C. Garcia Iniguez at r. Center of Genetic Engineering and Biotechnology at l. ctr. on back. Wmk: Woman's head.	1.25	5.00	15.00

1995 ISSUE

#112 and 113 arms at upper ctr. r.

Cat. #	Denomination	Date, description	VG	VF	Unc
112	1 PESO	1995. Dull olive-green on lt. blue and m/c unpt. J. Marti at l., arms at upper ctr. r. F. Castro w/rebel soldiers entering Havana in 1959 on back.	FV	FV	.75

Cat. #	Denomination	Date, description	VG	VF	Unc
113	3 PESOS	1995. E. "Che" Guevara at rl. "Che" cutting sugar cane on back.	FV	FV	1.50

NOTE ON VALUATIONS: Values for #94–113 are given for issued notes. See "COLLECTOR SERIES" after "FOREIGN EXCHANGE CERTIFICATES" for Specimen note listings and market values.

FOREIGN EXCHANGE CERTIFICATES

The Banco Nacional de Cuba issues four types of certificates in series A, B, C and D. The C and D series require issue dates, sign. at redemption, etc. resembling traveler's checks.

A SERIES

#FX1–FX5 red-violet. Arms at l. Various fortresses depicted on back.

	Denomination	Date, description	VG	VF	Unc
FX1	1 PESO	ND(1985–). Orange and olive green unpt. Castillo San Salvador de la Punta on back.	FV	1.50	3.50

	Denomination	Date, description	VG	VF	Unc
FX2	3 PESOS	ND(1985–). Orange and pink unpt. Castillo San Pedro de la Roca on back.	FV	3.00	7.00
FX3	5 PESOS	ND(1985–). Orange and blue-green unpt. Castillo de Los Tres Reyes on back.	FV	5.00	10.00
FX4	10 PESOS	ND(1985–). Orange and brown unpt. Castillo Nuestra Señora de Los Angeles de Jagua on back.	FV	10.00	18.00

	Denomination	Date, description	VG	VF	Unc
FX5	20 PESOS	ND (1985–). Orange and blue unpt. Castillo de la Real Fuerza on back.	FV	20.00	40.00

B SERIES

#FX6–FX10 dk. green. Arms at l. Various fortresses depicted on back.

Cat. #	Denomination	Date, description	VG	VF	Unc
FX6	1 PESO	ND (1985–). Lt. green and olive-brown unpt. Back like #FX1.	FV	1.00	2.50

Cat. #	Denomination	Date, description	VG	VF	Unc
FX7	5 PESOS	ND (1985–). Lt. green and blue-green unpt. Back like #FX3.	FV	5.00	20.00
FX8	10 PESOS	ND (1985–). Lt. green and brown unpt. Back like #FX4.	FV	10.00	30.00
FX9	20 PESOS	ND (1985–). Lt. green and blue unpt. Back like #FX5.	FV	20.00	40.00

Cat. #	Denomination	Date, description	VG	VF	Unc
FX10	50 PESOS	ND (1985–). Lt. green and dull violet unpt. Castillo de la Chorrera on back.	FV	50.00	100.00

C SERIES

#FX11–18 pale blue. Arms at l.

Cat. #	Denomination	Date, description	VG	VF	Unc
FX11	1 PESO	ND. Lt. blue and lt. red-brown unpt.	FV	1.50	3.50

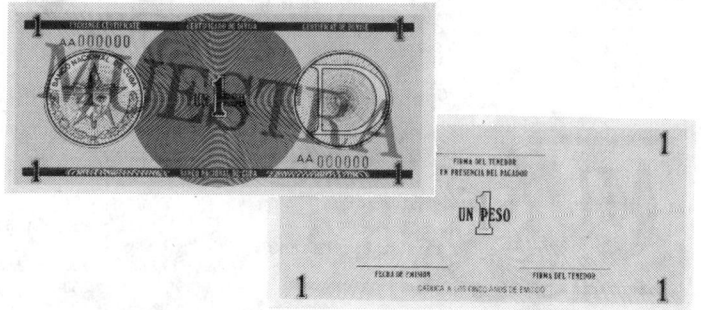

Cat. #	Denomination	Date, description	VG	VF	Unc
FX12	3 PESOS	ND. Lt. blue and violet unpt.	FV	3.00	7.00
FX13	5 PESOS	ND. Lt. blue and lt. olive unpt.	FV	5.00	10.00
FX14	10 PESOS	ND. Lt. blue and lilac unpt.	FV	10.00	18.00
FX15	20 PESOS	ND. Lt. blue and tan unpt.	FV	20.00	32.00
FX16	50 PESO	ND. Lt. blue and rose unpt.	FV	50.00	75.00
FX17	100 PESOS	ND. Lt. blue and ochre unpt.	FV	100.00	150.00
FX18	500 PESOS	ND. Lt. blue and tan unpt.	FV	450.00	675.00

D SERIES

FX19–23 pale red-brown. Arms at l.

Cat. #	Denomination	Date, description	VG	VF	Unc
FX19	1 PESO	ND. Lt. orange and orange-brown unpt.	FV	1.50	3.50
FX20	3 PESOS	ND. Lt. orange and pale blue unpt.	FV	3.00	7.00
FX21	5 PESOS	ND. Lt. orange and lt. green unpt.	FV	5.00	10.00
FX22	10 PESOS	ND. Lt. orange and lilac unpt.	FV	10.00	18.00
FX23	20 PESOS	ND. Lt. orange and ochre unpt.	FV	20.00	32.00

Pesos Convertibles System

1 Peso Convertibles = 1 U.S.A. Dollar

1994 ISSUE

#FX–FX30 arms on back.

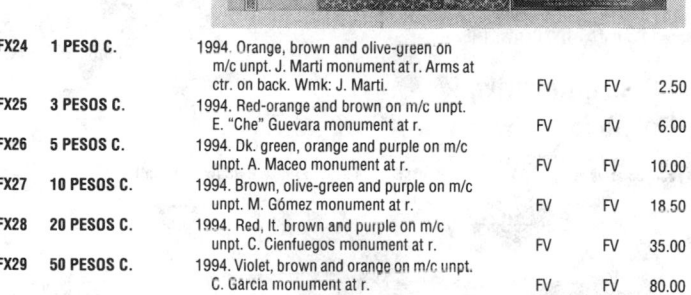

Cat. #	Denomination	Date, description	VG	VF	Unc
FX24	1 PESO C.	1994. Orange, brown and olive-green on m/c unpt. J. Marti monument at r. Arms at ctr. on back. Wmk: J. Marti.	FV	FV	2.50
FX25	3 PESOS C.	1994. Red-orange and brown on m/c unpt. E. "Che" Guevara monument at r.	FV	FV	6.00
FX26	5 PESOS C.	1994. Dk. green, orange and purple on m/c unpt. A. Maceo monument at r.	FV	FV	10.00
FX27	10 PESOS C.	1994. Brown, olive-green and purple on m/c unpt. M. Gómez monument at r.	FV	FV	18.50
FX28	20 PESOS C.	1994. Red, lt. brown and purple on m/c unpt. C. Cienfuegos monument at r.	FV	FV	35.00
FX29	50 PESOS C.	1994. Violet, brown and orange on m/c unpt. C. García monument at r.	FV	FV	80.00
FX30	100 PESOS C.	1994. Red, brown-orange and purple on m/c C. Manuel de Céspedes monument at r.	FV	FV	150.00

COLLECTOR SERIES

The Banco Nacional de Cuba has been selling specimen notes of the 1961–1989 issues. Specimen notes dated 1961–66 have normal block # and serial # while notes from 1967 to date all have normal block # and all zero serial #.

Cat. #	Date, denomination	Description	Issue Price	Mkt. Val.
CS1	1961 1–100 PESOS	Ovpt: SPECIMEN on #94a-97a, 98, 99.	—	125.00
CS2	1964 1–20 PESOS	Ovpt: SPECIMEN on #94b-97b.	—	16.50
CS3	1965 1–20 PESOS	Ovpt: SPECIMAN on #94c-97c.	—	14.00
CS4	1966 1, 10 PESOS	Ovpt: SPECIMEN on #100, 101.	—	7.00
CS5	1967 1–10 PESOS	Ovpt: SPECIMEN on #102a-104a.	—	10.00
CS6	1968 1–10 PESOS	Ovpt: SPECIMEN on #102a-104a.	—	10.00
CS7	1969 1, 10 PESOS	Ovpt: SPECIMEN on #102a, 104a.	—	7.00
CS8	1970 1–10 PESOS	Ovpt: SPECIMEN on #102a, 103b, 104a.	—	7.00
CS9	1971 10, 20 PESOS	Ovpt: SPECIMEN on #104a, 105a.	—	8.00
CS10	1972 1, 5 PESOS	Ovpt: SPECIMEN on #102a, 103b.	—	7.00
CS11	1975 1 PESO	Ovpt: SPECIMEN on #106.	—	8.00
CS12	1978 1, 10, 20 PESOS	Ovpt: SPECIMEN on #102b, 104b, 105b.	—	11.00
CS13	1979 1 PESO	Ovpt: SPECIMEN on #102b.	—	3.00
CS14	1980 1 PESO	Ovpt: SPECIMEN on #102b.	—	3.00
CS15	1981 1 PESO	Ovpt: SPECIMEN on #102b.	—	3.00
CS16	1982 1 PESO	Ovpt: MUESTRA on #102b.	—	3.00
CS17	1983 3, 10, 20 PESOS	Ovpt: MUESTRA on #104c, 105c, 107a.	—	12.00
CS18	1984 3, 5, 10 PESOS	Ovpt: MUESTRA on #103c, 104c, 107a.	—	12.00
CS19	1985 1, 3, 5 PESOS	Ovpt: MUESTRA on #102b, 103c, 107a.	—	12.00
CS20	1986 1-10 PESOS	Ovpt: MUESTRA on #102b, 103c, 104c, 107a.	—	12.50
CS21	1987 5, 10, 20 PESOS	Ovpt: MUESTRA on #103c-105c.	—	12.00
CS22	1988 1-20 PESOS	Ovpt: MUESTRA on #102c, 103d-105d, 107b.	—	12.50
CS23	1989 3, 20 PESOS	Ovpt: MUESTRA on #105d, 107b.	—	7.00
CS24	1990 5, 20, 50 PESOS	Ovpt: MUESTRA on #103d, 105d, 111	—	10.00
CS25	1991 5, 10, 20 PESOS	Ovpt: SPECIMEN on #108-110.	—	10.00
CS26	1995 1, 3 PESOS	Ovpt: MUESTRA on #112 and 113.	—	5.00

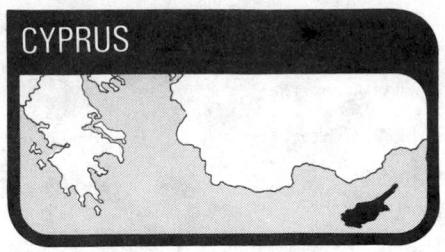

CYPRUS

The Republic of Cyprus, a member of the British Commonwealth, lies in the eastern Mediterranean Sea 44 miles (71 km.) south of Turkey and 60 miles (97 km.) west of Syria. It is the third largest island in the Mediterranean Sea, having an area of 3,572 sq. mi. (9,251 sq. km.) and a population of 710,200. Capital: Nicosia. Agriculture and mining are the chief industries. Asbestos, copper, citrus fruit, iron pyrites and potatoes are exported.

The importance of Cyprus dates from the Bronze Age when it was desired as a principal souce of copper (from which the island derived its name) and as a strategic trading center. Its role as an international marketplace made it a prime disseminator of the then prevalent cultures, a role that still influences the civilization of Western man. Because of its fortuitous position and influential role, Cyprus was conquered by a succession of empires; the Assyrian, Egyptian, Persian, Macedonian, Ptolemaic, Roman and Byzantine. It was taken from Isaac Comnenus by Richard the Lion-Hearted in 1191, sold to the Knights Templars, conquered by Venice and Turkey, and made a crown colony of Britain in 1925. Finally on Aug. 16, 1960, it became an independent republic.

In 1964, the ethnic Turks, who favor partition of Cyprus into separate Greek and Turkish states, withdrew from active participation in the government. Turkish forces invaded Cyprus in 1974 and gained control of 40 percent of the island. In 1975, Turkish Cypriots proclaimed their own state in northern Cyprus.

Cyprus is a member of the British Commonwealth of Nations. The president is Chief of State and Head of Government.

MONETARY SYSTEM

1 Shilling = 9 Piastres
1 Pound = 20 Shillings to 1963
1 Shilling = 50 Mils
1 Pound = 1000 Mils, 1963-83
1 Pound = 100 Cents, 1983–

Kibris Cumhuriyeti
Republic of Cyprus

#30–33 arms at r., map at lower r. Wmk: Eagle's head. Printer: BWC (w/o imprint).

Cat. #	Denomination	Date, description	VG	VF	Unc
30	250 MILS	1.12.1961. Blue on m/c unpt. Fruit at l. Mine on back.	2.00	6.00	22.50
31	500 MILS	1.12.1961. Green on m/c unpt. Mountain road lined w/trees on back.	5.00	15.00	45.00

Cat. #	Denomination	Date, description	VG	VF	Unc
32	1 POUND	1.12.1961. Brown on m/c unpt. Viaduct and pillars on back.	5.00	12.50	35.00
33	5 POUNDS	1.12.1961. Dk. green on m/c unpt. Embroidery and floral design on back.	12.00	30.00	85.00

Kibris Merkez Bankasi
Central Bank of Cyprus

1964–66 ISSUE

#34–37 like #30-33. Various date and sign. varieties.

Cat. #	Denomination	Date, description	VG	VF	Unc
34	250 MILS	1964–82. Like #30.			
		a. 1.12.1964–1.12.1969; 1.9.1971.	.50	2.00	7.00
		b. 1.3.1971; 1.6.1972; 1.5.1973; 1.6.1974.	.40	1.50	3.50
		c. 1.7.1975–1.6.1982.	.30	1.00	2.50

Cat. #	Denomination	Date, description	VG	VF	Unc
35	500 MILS	1964–79. Like #31.			
		a. 1.12.1964–1.6.1972.	1.25	2.50	9.50
		b. 1.5.1973; 1.6.1974; 1.7.1975; 1.8.1976.	.75	2.00	5.00
		c. 1.6.1979; 1.9.1979.	.50	1.50	4.00

Cat. #	Denomination	Date, description	VG	VF	Unc
36	1 POUND	1966–78. Like #32.			
		a. 1.8.1966–1.6.1972.	1.50	3.50	12.50
		b. 1.11.1972; 1.5.1973; 1.6.1974; 1.8.1976.	1.00	3.00	8.50
		c. 1.7.1975; 1.5.1978.	.75	2.50	6.50

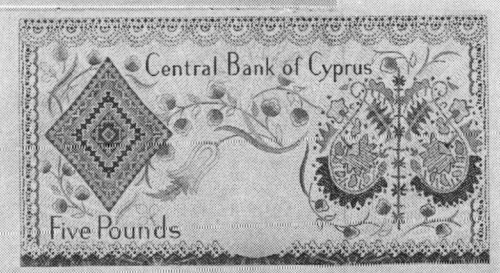

Cat. #	Denomination	Date, description	VG	VF	Unc
37	5 POUNDS	1966–76. Blue on m/c unpt. Like #33.			
		a. 1.8.1966; 1.9.1967; 1.12.1969.	4.00	15.00	45.00
		b. 1.6.1972; 1.11.1972; 1.7.1975.	FV	10.00	30.00
		c. 1.5.1973; 1.6.1974; 1.8.1976.	FV	7.00	25.00

1977–82 ISSUE

#38–41 wmk: Moufflon (ram's head).

38	500 MILS	1.6.1982. Brown and m/c. Woman seated at r., arms at top l. ctr. Dam on back.	FV	FV	4.50

39	1 POUND	1.6.1979. Brown and m/c. Nymph at r., arms at top l. ctr. Abbey on back.	FV	2.00	8.00

Cat. #	Denomination	Date, description	VG	VF	Unc
40	5 POUNDS	1.6.1979. Purple and m/c. Limestone head from Hellenistic period at l., arms at upper ctr. r. Theater at Salamis (Roman period) on back.	FV	10.00	30.00

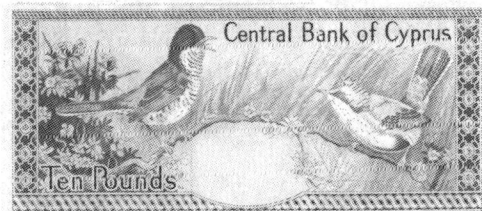

41	10 POUNDS	1977–85. Dk. green and blue-black on m/c unpt. Archaic bust at l., arms at r. 2 birds on back.			
		a. 1.4.1977; 1.5.1978; 1.6.1979.	FV	20.00	50.00
		b. 1.7.1980; 1.10.1981; 1.6.1982; 1.6.1985.	FV	18.00	45.00

Pound/Cent System 1983-

1982–87 ISSUE

#42–44 wmk: Moufflon (ram's head).

42	50 CENTS	1.10.1983; 1.12.1984. Brown and m/c. Similar to #38.	FV	FV	3.50

43	1 POUND	1.2.1982; 1.11.1982; 1.3.1984; 1.11.1985. Dk. brown and m/c. Like #39 but bank name in outlined (white) letters by dk. unpt.	FV	FV	7.00

Cat. #	Denomination	Date, description	VG	VF	Unc
44	10 POUNDS	1.4.1987; 1.10.1988. Dk. green and blue-black on m/c unpt. Similar to #41 but w/date above at l. of modified arms on r.	FV	FV	40.00

1987–92 ENHANCED ISSUE

#45-49 w/micro-printing. Wmk: Moufflon (ram's) head.

Cat. #	Denomination	Date, description	VG	VF	Unc
45	50 CENTS	1.4.1987; 1.10.1988; 1.11.1989. Like #42 but w/bank name in micro-printing alternately in Greek and Turkish just below upper frame.	FV	FV	2.00

Cat. #	Denomination	Date, description	VG	VF	Unc
46	1 POUND	1987-. Like #43 but w/bank name in unbroken line of microprinting with Greek at left and Turkish at right just below upper frame.			
		a. W/o lt. beige unpt. color on back. Micro-print line under dark bar at top.1.4.1987; 1.10.1988; 1.11.1989.	FV	FV	6.00
		b. Lt. beige color added to ctr. unpt. on back for security. 1.11.1989; 1.2.1992.	FV	FV	5.00
		c. Dot added near upper l. corner. 1.3.1993.	FV	FV	5.00

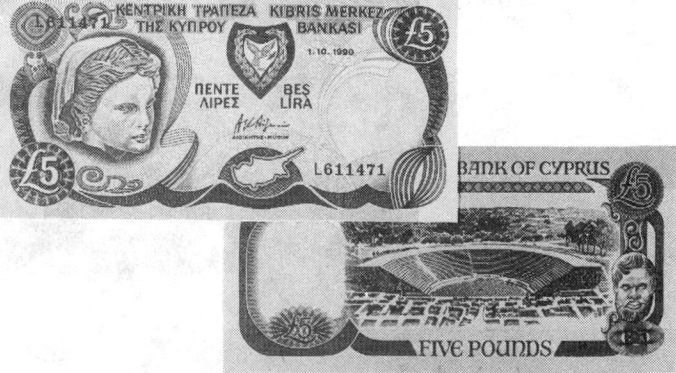

Cat. #	Denomination	Date, description	VG	VF	Unc
47	5 POUNDS	1.10.1990. Like #40 but line of micro-printing added.	FV	FV	22.50

Cat. #	Denomination	Date, description	VG	VF	Unc
48	10 POUNDS	1.1.1989; 1.10.1990; 1.2.1992. Dk. green and blue-black on m/c unpt. Similar to #44 but w/enhanced security features.	FV	FV	35.00

Cat. #	Denomination	Date, description	VG	VF	Unc
49	20 POUNDS	1.2.1992. Deep blue on m/c unpt. Bust of Aphrodite at l., arms at upper ctr., ancient bird (pottery art) at r. Ancient merchant boat of Kyrenia at ctr., ancient pottery jugs at lower r. on back. Printer: TDLR.			
		a. YIRMI LIRA (error).	FV	FV	70.00
		b. YIRMI LIRA.	FV	FV	70.00

1996 ISSUE

Cat. #	Denomination	Date, description	VG	VF	Unc
50	20 POUNDS	(1996).			Expected new issue.

CZECHOSLOVAKIA

The Republic of Czechoslovakia, located in central Europe, had an area of 49,365 sq. mi. (127,859 sq. km.) and a population of 15.7 million. Capital: Prague. Machinery was the chief export of the highly industrialized economy.

Czechoslovakia proclaimed itself a republic on Oct. 28, 1918. with T. G Masaryk as president. Hitler provoked Czechoslovakia's German minority in the Sudentenland to agitate for autonomy. At Munich in Sept. of 1938, France and Britain, forced the cession of the Sudentenland to Germany. In March 1939, Germany invaded Czechoslovakia and established the Protectorate of Bohemia and Moravia. Slovakia, a province in southeastern Czechoslovakia, was constituted as a republic under Nazi influence. After the World War II defeat of the Axis powers re-established the physical integrity and independence of Czechoslovakia, while bringing it within the Russian sphere of influence. On Feb. 23-25, 1948, the Communists seized control of the government in a coup d'etat, and adopted a constitution making the country a "people's republic." A new constitution adopted June 11, 1960, converted the country into a "socialist republic" which lasted until 1989. On Nov. 11, 1989, public demonstrations against the communist government began and in Dec. of that same year, communism was overthrown and the Czech and Slovak Federal Republic was formed. On January 1, 1993 this was split to form the Czech Republic and the Republic of Slovakia.

MONETARY SYSTEM
1 Koruna = 100 Haleru

SPECIMEN NOTES

Large quantities of specimens were formerly made available to collectors. Most notes issued after 1945 are distinguished by a perforation consisting of a few small holes or letter *S*. Since the difference in price between original and specimen notes is frequently very great, both types of notes are valued. The earlier issues were recalled from circulation and then perforated: *SPECIMEN* or *NEPLATNE* for collectors. Caution should be exercised while examining notes as we have been notified of examples of perforated specimen notes having the holes filled back in.

> **NOTE:** This section has been renumbered since the 7th Edition of General Issues.

SOCIALIST REPUBLIC
Ceskoslovanska Socialisticka Republika
1961 ISSUE

#81–82 wmk: Star in circle, repeated.

Cat. #	Denomination	Date, description	VG	VF	Unc
81	3 KORUN	1961. Blue-black on blue-green unpt. Similar to #79.			
		a. Issued note.	.20	.50	2.50
		s. Perforated w/3 holes or *SPECIMEN*.	—	.50	2.00

82	5 KORUN	1961. Dull black on pale green unpt. Similar to #80.			
		a. Issued note.	.20	.50	2.50
		s. Perforated w/3 holes or *SPECIMEN*.	—	.50	2.00

Státní Banky Ceskoslovenské
(Czechoslovak State Bank)
1960–64 ISSUE

#88–98 printer: STC-Prague.

Cat. #	Denomination	Date, description	VG	VF	Unc
88	10 KORUN	1960. Brown on m/c unpt. 2 girls w/flowers at r. Orava Dam on back.	.10	.50	4.00

90 (89)	25 KORUN	1961. Blue. Socialist arms at l. ctr. J. Zizka at r. Tabor town square on back.			
		a. Issued note.	1.00	2.50	10.00
		s. Perforated: *SPECIMEN*.	—	—	5.00

90 (91)	50 KORUN	1964. Red-brown. Russian soldier and partisan at r. Refinery on back.	1.00	2.50	7.00

91 (90)	100 KORUN	1961. Deep green on m/c unpt. Factory at lower l., farm couple at r. Charles Bridge and Prague castle on back.			
		a. Wmk: Star within linden leaf, repeated. Series prefix: B, C, D, P, R, T, Z and X01–X24.	1.00	4.50	12.50
		b. Reissue wmk: Multiple stars and linden leaves. Series prefix: X25–. (1990–92).	1.00	2.00	8.00

NOTE: #91b w/added 'C-100' adhesive stamp, see Czech Republic. With *SLOVENSKA REPUBLIKA* adhesive stamp, see Slovakia.

1970 ISSUE

Cat. #	Denomination	Date, description	VG	VF	Unc
92	20 KORUN	1970. Blue on lt. blue and m/c unpt. Arms at ctr., J. Zizka at r. Medieval procession on back.	1.00	2.00	5.00

1973 ISSUE

Cat. #	Denomination	Date, description	VG	VF	Unc
93	500 KORUN	1973. Deep brown-violet and m/c. Soldiers at r. Medieval shield al lower ctr., mountain fortress ruins at Devon at r. on back.	8.00	15.00	50.00

NOTE: #93 w/additional 'D-500' adhesive stamp, see Czech Republic. With *SLOVENSKA REPUBLIKA* adhesive stamp, see Slovakia.

1985–89 ISSUE

Cat. #	Denomination	Date, description	VG	VF	Unc
94 (95)	10 KORUN	1986. Deep br View of orava bird at lower l. w/trees and mountains on back.	.25	1.00	2.25

Cat. #	Denomination	Date, description	VG	VF	Unc
95 (96)	20 KORUN	1988. Blue and m/c. J. Komensky at r., alphabet at l. Tree of life growing from bank at ctr., man and woman at l. on back.	.30	1.25	3.50

NOTE: #96 w/additional *SLOVENSKA REPUBLIKA* adhesive stamp, see Slovakia.

Cat. #	Denomination	Date, description	VG	VF	Unc
96 (97)	50 KORUN	1987. Brown-violet and blue on red and orange unpt. L. Stur at r. Bratislava castle on back.	.50	2.00	7.50

NOTE: #97 w/additional *SLOVENSKA REPUBLIKA* adhesive stamp, see Slovakia.

Cat. #	Denomination	Date, description	VG	VF	Unc
97 (98)	100 KORUN	1989. Dk. green on green and red unpt. K. Gottwald at r. Prague castle on back.	2.00	5.00	15.00

NOTE: #97 was withdrawn shortly after issue, apparently because of objections to the portrayal of Czech Communist Party chief secretary Klement Gottwald. In circulation from 1.10.1989 to 31.12.1990.

Cat. #	Denomination	Date, description	VG	VF	Unc
98 (94)	1000 KORUN	1985. Blue black, blue and purple on m/c unpt. B. Smetana at r. Vysehrad Castle at l. on back.	15.00	30.00	85.00

NOTE: #98 w/additional 'M-1000' adhesive stamp or printed, see Czech Republic. With *SLOVENSKA REPUBLIKA* adhesive stamp, see Slovakia.

FOREIGN EXCHANGE CERTIFICATES
Odberní Poukaz

These certificates were issued by the government-owned company "Tuzex." Foreign visitors could exchange their hard currency for regular Korun or the Tuzex vouchers. Ther vouchers were accepted at special stores where imported or exported goods could be bought.

The usual black market rate for Tuzex vouchers was 5 to 7 regular Korun for 1 Tuzex Koruna.

#FX1–FX8 white outer edge, *TUZEX* once in text. Dates of issue up to Dec. 1988. Several text varieties exist. Listings are for types only. Printer: STC–P.

 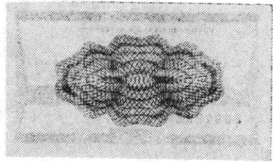

Cat. #	Denomination	Date, description	VG	VF	Unc
FX1	0.50 KORUNA	ND. Violet and green.	.50	1.00	2.50
FX2	1 KORUNA	ND. Green on ochre unpt.	.50	1.00	2.50

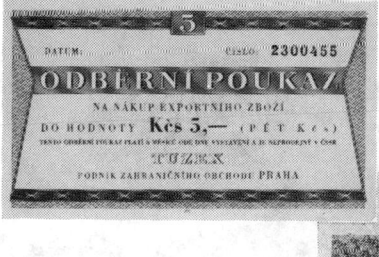

FX3	5 KORUN	ND. Violet on blue and ochre unpt.	1.00	2.00	5.00
FX4	10 KORUN	ND. Dk. green on green unpt.	2.00	4.50	10.00
FX5	20 KORUN	ND. Brown on orange and green unpt.	4.00	8.50	20.00
FX6	50 KORUN	ND. Brown on pink and orange unpt.	8.00	17.50	40.00
FX7	100 KORUN	ND. Violet on green and violet unpt.	10.00	25.00	60.00
FX8	500 KORUN	ND. Gray on brown unpt.	20.00	45.00	100.00

1989 ISSUE

#FX9–16 lg. globe w/*TUZEX* at l. and r. Colors as previous issue, but outer edge w/design. Printer: STC–P.

FX9	0.50 KORUNA	1989; 1990. Violet edge.	.30	.75	2.00
FX10	1 KORUNA	1989; 1990. Yellow-brown edge.	.30	.75	2.00
FX11	5 KORUN	1989; 1990. Blue and ochre edge.	.60	1.50	4.50
FX12	10 KORUN	1989; 1990. Lt. and dk. green edge.	1.50	4.00	9.00
FX13	20 KORUN	1989; 1990. Yellow-brown and green edge.	3.00	8.00	18.00
FX14	50 KORUN	1989; 1990. Pink and orange edge.	6.00	15.00	35.00
FX15	100 KORUN	1989; 1990. Violet and green edge.	8.00	20.00	50.00
FX16	500 KORUN	1989; 1990. Brown edge.	17.50	40.00	85.00

NOTE: #FX4–FX8 and FX12–FX16 were redeemable 1 year from issue date.

The Czech Republic, formerly united with Slovakia in the Czech & Slovak Federal Republic, is bordered in the west by Germany, to the north by Poland, to the east by Slovakia and to the south by Austria. It consists of 3 major regions: Bohemia, Moravia and Silesia. It has an area of 20,431 sq. mi. (78,864 sq. km.) and a population cf 10.3 million. Capital: Prague (Praha). Agriculture and livestock are chief occupations while coal deposits are the main mineral resources.

The Czech lands in the western part were united with the Slovaks to form the Czechoslovak Republic, on Oct. 28, 1918 upon the dissolution of Austria-Hungarian Empire. This territory was broken up for the benefit of Germany, Poland and Hungary by the Munich agreement signed by the United Kingdom, France, Germany and Italy on Sept. 29, 1938. In March 1939 the German influenced Slovak government proclaimed Slovakia independent. Germany incorporated the Czech lands into the Third Reich as the "Protectorate of Bohemia and Moravia." A government-in-exile was set up in London in July 1940. The Soviets and USA forces liberated the area by May 1945. Communist influence increased steadily while pressure for liberalization culminated in the overthrow of the Stalinist leader Antonín Novotny and his associates in 1968. The Communist Party then introduced far reaching reforms which received warnings from Moscow, followed by occupation of Warsaw Pact forces resulting in stationing of Soviet forces. Mass demonstrations for reform began in Nov. 1989 and the Federal Assembly abolished the Communist Party's sole right to govern. New governments followed on Dec. 3. and Dec. 10. The Movement for Democratic Slovakia was apparent in the June 1992 elections with the Slovak National Council adopting a declaration of sovereignty, later a constitution for an independent Slovakia, with the Federal Assembly voting for the dissolvement of the Czech and Slovak Federal Republic. This came into effect on Dec. 31, 1992 and both new republics came into being on Jan. 1, 1993.

MONETARY SYSTEM

1 Czechoslovak Koruna (Kcs) = 1 Czech Koruna (Kc)
1 Koruna = 100 Haleru

REPUBLIC

Ceská Národní Banka
Czech National Bank

1993 PROVISIONAL ISSUE

#1–3 were released 8.2.1993 having adhesive revalidation stamps affixed (later a printed *1000* was also circulated.) Valid until 31.8.1993 but could be exchanged in deposits until 31.5.1994. Old Czechoslovak notes of 100 Korun and higher denominations became worthless on 7.2.1993. Smaller denominations remained in circulation until 30.11.1993.

Cat. #	Denomination	Date, description	VG	VF	Unc
1	100 KORUN	ND (1993–old date 1961). Dk. green "C-100" adhesive stamp affixed to Czechoslovakia #90A.	3.00	7.00	15.00

| 2 | 500 KORUN | ND (1993–old date 1973). Dk. green "D-500" adhesive stamp affixed to Czechoslovakia #93. | 15.00 | 30.00 | 65.00 |

Cat. #	Denomination	Date, description	VG	VF	Unc
3	1000 KORUN	ND (1993–old date 1985). Deep green "M-1000" revalidation stamp on Czechoslovakia #94.			
		a. Adhesive stamp affixed.	25.00	60.00	150.00
		b. Stamp image printed on note.	30.00	65.00	200.00

NOTE: #1-3 were in circulation from Feb. 8 to Aug. 31, 1993.

1993 ISSUE

#4–9 new arms at ctr. r. on back.

#4–5 printer: TDLR.

4	50 KORUN	1993. Violet and black on pink and gray unpt. St. A. Ceska at r. and w/crown as wmk. Lg. A at l. within gothic window frame at l. ctr. on back.	FV	FV	5.50

5	100 KORUN	1993. Blue-green, green and blue-black on lilac and m/c unpt. Kg. Karel IV at r. and as wmk. Lg. seal of Charles University at l. ctr. on back.	FV	FV	8.50

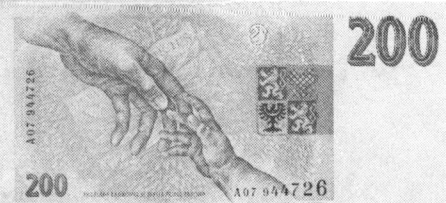

6	200 KORUN	1993. Deep brown on lt. orange and lt. green unpt. J. A. Komensky at r. and as wmk. Hands outreached at l. ctr. on back. Printer: STC-P.			
		a. Security filament w/200 KCS.	FV	FV	12.50
		b. Security filament w/200 KC.	FV	FV	12.50
		c. Security filament from Ziare note.	—	—	80.00

Cat. #	Denomination	Date, description	VG	VF	Unc
7	500 KORUN	1993. Dk. brown, brown & brown-violet on pink and tan unpt. Rose in unpt. al upper ctr., Mrs. B. Nemcová at r. and as wmk. Laureate young woman's head at l. ctr. on back. Printer: TDLR.	FV	FV	24.00

#8–9 printer: STC-P.

8	1000 KORUN	1993. Purple and lilac on m/. unpt. F. Palacky at r. and as wmk. Eagle and Kromeriz Castle on back.	FV	FV	45.00

9	5000 KORUN	1993. Black, blue-gray and violet on pink and lt. gray unpt. Pres. T.G. Masaryk at r. Montage of Prague Gothic and Baroque buildings on back.	FV	FV	200.00

1994-95 ISSUE

Cat. #	Denomination	Date, description	VG	VF	Unc
10	20 KORUN	1994. Blue-black and gray on lt. blue unpt, Kg. P. Otakar I. and as wmk. Crown with seal above at ctr., stylized crown lower l. on back. Printer: STC-P.	FV	FV	2.00

11	50 KORUN	1994. Like #5 but w/o gray in unpt. Stylized heart lower l. on back.	FV	FV	5.00
12	100 KORUN	1995. Like #6.			Expected new issue.
13	500 KORUN	1995. Like #8.			Expected new issue.

DENMARK

The Kingdom of Denmark, a constitutional monarchy located at the mouth of the Baltic Sea, has an area of 16,633 sq. mi. (43,069 sq. km.) and a population of 5.16 million. Capital: Copenhagen. Most of the country is arable. Agriculture, which employs the majority of the people, is conducted by small farmers served by cooperatives. The largest industries are food processing, iron and metal, and fishing. Machinery, meats (chiefly bacon), dairy products and chemicals are exported.

Denmark, a great power during the Viking period of the 9th–11th centuries, conducted raids on western Europe and England, and in the 11th century united England, Denmark and Norway under the rule of King Canute. Despite a struggle between the crown and the nobility (13th–14th centuries) which forced the King to grant a written constitution, Queen Margaret (1353–1412) succeeded in uniting Denmark, Norway, Sweden, Finland and Greenland under the Danish crown, placing all of Scandinavia under the rule of Denmark. An unwise alliance with Napoleon contributed to the dismembering of the empire and fostered a liberal movement which succeeded in making Denmark a constitutional monarchy in 1849.

RULERS

Frederik IX, 1947–1972
Margrethc II, 1972–

MONETARY SYSTEM

1 Krone = 100 Øre 1874–

REPLACEMENT NOTES

#42–47, suffix OJ (for whole sheets) or OK (for single notes).

#42–45 although dated (19)50, they were issued from 1952 onwards.

Danmarks Nationalbank

DATING

For #42–47, 5 and 10 Kroner w/date of the ordinance of 7.4.1936; the year dates are incorporated in the left-hand serial number (the 2 middle figures). Example: H 6 63 7 E = (19)63. The other denominations have this characteristic but also continue with year dates in the conventional manner

1952–63 ISSUE

Law of 7.4.1936

#42–47 first sign. changes. Second sign. Riim, 1952–67 for #42a, 42b, 43, 44, 45a, 45b, 46a, 46b, 47; Valeur from 1970– for #44, 45b, 46b.

Cat. #	Denomination	Date, description	VG	VF	Unc
42	5 KRONER	(19)50–60. Blue-green. Portr. Thorvaldsen at l., 3 Graces at r. Kalundborg city view on back. Wmk: 5 repeated.			
		a. 5 in the wmk. 10.55mm high. w/o dot after 7 in law date. (19)52. Series A0; A1; A2.	2.75	13.50	45.00
		b. As a but w/dot after 7 in law date. (19)52.	1.85	9.00	30.00
		c. 5 in the wmk. 13mm high. (19)55–60.	1.50	7.50	25.00
		r. Replacement note. (19)50 (sic).	1.50	7.50	25.00

Cat. #	Denomination	Date, description	VG	VF	Unc
43	10 KRONER	(19)50–52. Black and olive-brown. Portr. Andersen at l., birds in nest at r. Green landscape on back. Wmk: *5* repeated.			
		a. Issued note. (19)51–52.	4.00	20.00	65.00
		r. Replacement note. (19)50 (sic).	5.00	25.00	85.00

44	10 KRONER	(19)50–74. Black and brown. Portr. Andersen at l. Black landscape on back.			
		a. Top and bottom line in frame commences w/10.	7.50	37.50	125.00
		b. As a but w/10's in wmk. 14mm high. (19)54–57.	5.50	27.50	90.00
		c. 1957–74. Top and bottom line in frame commences with *TI*. (19)57-59.	2.00	9.00	30.00
		d. As c. (19)60–69.	2.00	6.00	20.00
		e. As c. (19)70–74	FV	2.75	5.50
		r. Replacement note. (19)50 (sic).	2.50	4.50	10.00

45	50 KRONER	(19)50–70. Blue on green unpt. Portr. O. Romer at l., tower at r. Rock formation on blue back.			
		a. Hand-made paper. Wmk: Crowns and *50*. (19)56–61.	15.00	35.00	150.00
		b. Wmk: Rhombuses and *50*. (19)62–70.	10.00	15.00	35.00
		r. Replacement note. (19)50 (sic).	12.50	22.50	75.00

46	100 KRONER	(19)61–70. Red on red-brown unpt. Portr. H. C. Orsted at l., compass at r. Kronborg city view.			
		a. Hand-made paper. Wmk: Close wavy lines. (19)61.	30.00	50.00	125.00
		b. Wmk: *100*. (19)61–70.	22.50	35.00	60.00
47	500 KRONER	(19)63–67. Green. Portr. C. D. F. Reventlow at l., farmer plowing at r. Roskilde city view on back.			
			100.00	150.00	250.00

1972–79 ISSUE

#48–52 portr. at r. of all notes painted by Danish artist Jens Juel (1745–1802). Issued under L.1936. The year of issue is shown by the 2 middle numerals within the series code at lower l. or r. Sign. varieties. Wmk: Head of J. Juel and value repeated vertically.

Cat. #	Denomination	Date, description	VG	VF	Unc
48	10 KRONER	(19)72–78. Black on olive and m/c unpt. Portr. S. Kirchhoff at r. Duck at l. on back.	FV	2.50	5.00

49	20 KRONER	(19)79–88. Dk. blue on brown and m/c unpt. Portr. Tutein at r. 2 birds on back.	FV	FV	8.00

50	50 KRONER	(19)72–90. Blue. Portr. Ryberg at r. Fish at l. on back.	FV	FV	15.00

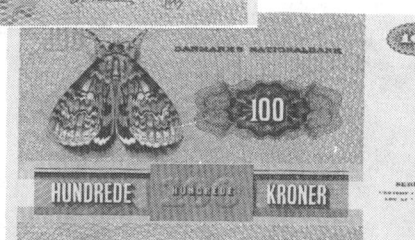

51	100 KRONER	(19)72–91. Red and m/c. J. Juel's self-portrait at r. Butterfly at l. on back.	FV	FV	28.50

Cat. #	Denomination	Date, description	VG	VF	Unc
52	500 KRONER	(19)72–88. Black on green and m/c unpt. "Unknown lady of Qualen" at r. Reptile on back.	FV	FV	120.00

53	1000 KRONER	(19)72–86. Black on gray and m/c unpt. Portr. T. Heiberg at r. Long eared squirel on back.	FV	FV	235.00

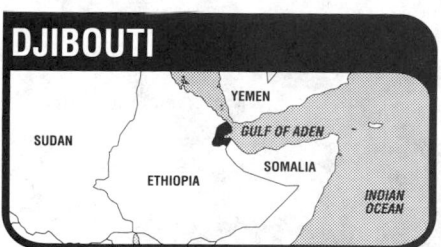

The Republic of Djibouti (formerly French Somaliland and the French Overseas Territory of Afars and Issas), located in northeast Africa at the Bab el Mandeb Strait connecting the Suez Canal and the Red Sea with the Gulf of Aden and the Indian Ocean, has an area of 8,494 sq. mi. (22,000 sq. km.) and a population of 542,000. Capital: Djibouti. The tiny nation has less than one sq. mi. of arable land, and no natural resources except salt, sand and camels. The commercial activities of the trans-shipment port of Djibouti and the Addis Ababa-Djibouti railroad are the basis of the economy. Salt, fish and hides are exported.

French interest in former French Somaliland began in 1839 with concessions obtained by a French naval lieutenant from the provincial sultans. French Somaliland was made a protectorate in 1884 and its boundaries were delimited by the Franco-British and Ethiopian accords of 1887 and 1897. It became a colony in 1896 and a territory within the French Union in 1946. In 1958, it voted to join the new French Community as an overseas territory, and reaffirmed that choice by a referendum in March 1967. Its name was changed from French Somaliland to the French Territory of Afars and Issas on July 5, 1967.

The French Tricolor, which had flown over the strategically important territory for 115 years, was lowered for the last time on June 27, 1977, when French Afars and Issas became Africa's 49th independent state, under the name of the Republic of Djibouti.

Djibouti, a seaport and capital city of the Republic of Djibouti (and formerly of French Somaliland and French Afars and Issas) is located on the east coast of Africa and the southernmost entrance to the Red Sea. The capital was moved from Obok to Djibouti in 1892 and established as the transshipment point for Ethiopia's foreign trade via the Franco-Ethiopian railway linking Djibouti and Addis Ababa.

RULERS

French to 1977

MONETARY SYSTEM

1 Franc = 100 Centimes

FRENCH AFARS and ISSAS

Trésor Public, Territoire Français des Afars et des Issas

1969 (ND) ISSUE

Cat. #	Denomination	Date, description	VG	VF	Unc
30	5000 FRANCS	ND (1969). M/c. Aerial view of Dijouti harbor at ctr.	55.00	175.00	350.00

1973–74 (ND) ISSUE

31	500 FRANCS	ND (1973). M/c. Ships at l. ctr.	8.50	20.00	80.00

Cat. #	Denomination	Date, description	VG	VF	Unc
32	1000 FRANCS	ND (1974). M/c. Woman holding jug at l. ctr. on face and back.	15.00	50.00	200.00

1975 (ND) ISSUE

Cat. #	Denomination	Date, description	VG	VF	Unc
33	500 FRANCS	ND (1975). M/c. Man at l., rocks in sea and storks at r. Stern of ship at r. on back.	5.00	15.00	60.00

34	1000 FRANCS	ND (1975). M/c. Woman at l., people by trains at ctr. Camels and driver on back.	8.00	17.50	85.00

35	5000 FRANCS	ND (1975). M/c. Man at r., forest scene at ctr.	35.00	65.00	165.00

REPUBLIC OF DJIBOUTI
Banque Nationale

1979; 1984 (ND) ISSUE

Cat. #	Denomination	Date, description	VG	VF	Unc
36	500 FRANCS	ND (1979; 1988). Like #33.			
		a. Blue unpt. W/o sign. (1979).	FV	5.00	10.00
		b. Pale blue unpt. Sign title: *LE GOUVERNEUR* added. (1988).	FV	4.50	8.50

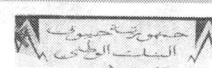

(1979)

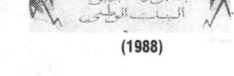

(1988)

37	1000 FRANCS	ND (1979; 1988). Like #34.			
		a. W/o sign. (1979).	FV	10.00	21.50
		b. Sign. title: *LE GOUVERNEUR* added above *MILLE*. Shorter Arabic text at top on back. (1988).	FV	8.00	18.50
		c. W/segmented foil security thread (ca.1991).	FV	7.50	16.50
		d. Litho.	FV	FV	14.00

38	5000 FRANCS	ND (1979). Like #35.			
		a. W/o security thread.	FV	35.00	65.00
		b. W/segmented foil security thread.	FV	25.00	55.00

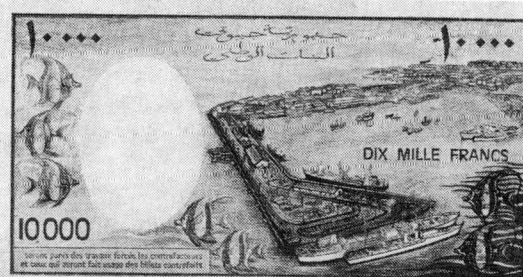

Cat. #	Denomination	Date, description	VG	VF	Unc
39	10,000 FRANCS	ND (1984). Brown and red on yellow and green. Woman holding baby at l., goats in tree at r. Fish and harbor scene on back.	FV	FV	110.00
		a. W/o security thread.	FV	50.00	120.00
		b. W/segmented foil security thread.	FV	FV	100.00

The Dominican Republic, which occupies the eastern two-thirds of the island of Hispaniola, has an area of 18,816 sq. mi. (48,734 sq. km.) and a population of 7.3 million. Capital: Santo Domingo. The agricultural economy produces sugar, coffee, tobacco and cocoa.

Columbus discovered Hispaniola in 1492, and named it *La Isla Espanola* — "the Spanish Island." Santo Domingo, the oldest white settlement in the Western Hemisphere, was the base from which Spain conducted its exploration of the New World. Later, French buccaneers settled the western third of Hispaniola, which in 1697 was ceded to France by Spain, and in 1804 became the Republic of Haiti —"mountainous country." At this time, the Spanish called their part of Hispaniola Santo Domingo, and the French called their part Saint-Domingue. In 1822, the Haitians conquered the entire island and held it until 1844, when Juan Pablo Duarte, the national hero of the Dominican Republic, drove them out of eastern Hispaniola and established an independent Dominican Republic. The republic returned voluntarily to Spanish dominion — after being rejected by France, Britain and the United States — from 1861 to 1865, when independence was restored.

NOTE: This section has been renumbered from the old 7th Edition of General Issues

MONETARY SYSTEM
1 Peso = 100 Centavos

REPLACEMENT NOTES
#117–124: Z prefix and suffix (TDLR printings).

Banco Central de la República Dominicana
1961 (ND) ISSUES

Cat. #	Denomination	Date, description	VG	VF	Unc
85 (35)	10 CENTAVOS	ND (1961). Blue and black. Banco de Reservas in round frame at ctr. Back blue. Printer: ABNC.	1.00	3.50	12.50

| 86 (35A) | 10 CENTAVOS | ND (1961). Black on lt. blue-green safety paper. Banco de Reservas in oval frame at ctr. Back green. Local printer. | 2.00 | 6.00 | 20.00 |

| 87 (36) | 25 CENTAVOS | ND (1961). Red and black. Entrance to the Banco Central in rectangular frame at ctr. Back red. Printer: ABNC. | 1.00 | 4.00 | 15.00 |

Cat. #	Denomination	Date, description	VG	VF	Unc
88 (37)	25 CENTAVOS	ND (1961). Black. Entrance to the Banco Central in oval frame at ctr. Back green. Local printer.			
		a. Pink safety paper.	1.75	5.00	20.00
		b. Plain cream paper.	2.50	7.50	22.50

Cat. #	Denomination	Date, description	VG	VF	Unc
89 (38)	50 CENTAVOS	ND (1961). Purple and black. Palacio Nacional in circular frame at ctr. Back purple. Printer: ABNC.	1.75	4.50	17.50

Cat. #	Denomination	Date, description	VG	VF	Unc
90 (38A)	50 CENTAVOS	ND (1961). Black on yellow safety paper. Palacio Nacional in oval frame at ctr. Back green. Local printer.	5.50	25.00	60.00

1962 (ND) ISSUE

#91–98 w/text over seal: *SANTO DOMINGO/DISTRITO NACIONAL/REPUBLICA DOMINICANA.* Printer: ABNC.

Cat. #	Denomination	Date, description	VG	VF	Unc
91 (39)	1 PESO	ND (1962–63). Red. Portr. Duarte at ctr.	4.00	16.00	48.00

Cat. #	Denomination	Date, description	VG	VF	Unc
92 (40)	5 PESOS	ND (1962). Red. Portr. Sanchez at ctr.	6.00	24.00	72.00

Cat. #	Denomination	Date, description	VG	VF	Unc
93 (41)	10 PESOS	ND (1962). Red. Portr. Mella at ctr.	12.50	50.00	150.00

Cat. #	Denomination	Date, description	VG	VF	Unc
94 (42)	20 PESOS	ND (1962). Red. "Puerta del Conde" at ctr.	25.00	100.00	300.00
95 (43)	50 PESOS	ND (1962). Red. Tomb of Columbus at ctr.	50.00	150.00	450.00

Cat. #	Denomination	Date, description	VG	VF	Unc
96 (44)	100 PESOS	ND (1962). Red. Woman w/coffee pot and cup at ctr.	75.00	175.00	525.00
97 (44A)	500 PESOS	ND (1962). "Obelisco de Ciudad Trujillo" at ctr.	—	—	—
98 (44B)	1000 PESOS	ND (1962). Minor Basilica of Santa Maria at ctr.	—	Unique	—

1964 (ND) ISSUE

#99–106 Liberty head and arms on back. Sign. varieties. Printer: TDLR.

Cat. #	Denomination	Date, description	VG	VF	Unc
99 (45)	1 PESO	ND (1964–73). Portr. black on lt. green and pinkish tan unpt. Duarte at ctr. w/eyes looking l., white bow tie. Back black.	.50	2.50	10.00

Cat. #	Denomination	Date, description	VG	VF	Unc
100 (46)	5 PESOS	ND (1964–74). Brown on lt. green and lilac unpt. Portr. Sanchez at ctr.	3.00	10.00	30.00

| 101 (47) | 10 PESOS | ND (1964–74). Green on lt. green and lt. lilac unpt. Portr. Mella at ctr. | 5.00 | 16.00 | 48.00 |

| 102 (48) | 20 PESOS | ND (1964–74). Brown on lt. green and blue unpt. National shrine at ctr. | 8.00 | 30.00 | 75.00 |

| 103 (49) | 50 PESOS | ND (1964–74). Purple. Ox cart at ctr. | 20.00 | 65.00 | 130.00 |

| 104 (50) | 100 PESOS | ND (1964–74). Orange. Banco Central at ctr. | 40.00 | 125.00 | 250.00 |

Cat. #	Denomination	Date, description	VG	VF	Unc
105 (51)	500 PESOS	ND (1964–74). Blue. Columbus' tomb and cathedral at ctr.	100.00	400.00	750.00

| 106 (52) | 1000 PESOS | ND (1964–74). Red. National Palace at ctr. | 200.00 | 750.00 | 1500. |

1973 (ND) ISSUE

| 107 (45A) | 1 PESO | ND (1973–74). Like #99 but Duarte w/eyes looking front, black bow tie. | .50 | 2.00 | 8.50 |

1975 ISSUE

#108–115 dates in upper margin on back.

108 (45B)	1 PESO	1975–78. Like #107.	.25	1.50	4.50
109 (46A)	5 PESOS	1975–76. Like #100.	.50	5.00	15.00
110 (47A)	10 PESOS	1975–76. Like #101.	1.50	9.00	27.00
111 (48A)	20 PESOS	1975–76. Like #102.	2.50	15.00	45.00
112 (49A)	50 PESOS	1975–76. Like #103.	5.50	33.50	100.00
113 (50A)	100 PESOS	1975–76. Like #104.	10.00	60.00	180.00
114 (51A)	500 PESOS	1975. Like #105.	50.00	250.00	750.00
115 (52A)	1000 PESOS	1975–76. Like #106.	95.00	500.00	1500.

1977-80 ISSUES

#116–124 dates in upper margin on back.

Cat. #	Denomination	Date, description	VG	VF	Unc
116 (53)	1 PESO	1978–79. Black and m/c. Duarte at r. Sugar factory on back. Printer: ABNC.	.20	1.00	3.50

#117–124 printer: TDLR.

Cat. #	Denomination	Date, description	VG	VF	Unc
117 (53A)	1 PESO	1980–82. Like #116. Dates very lightly printed.	.75	1.00	3.00

Cat. #	Denomination	Date, description	VG	VF	Unc
118 (54)	5 PESOS	1978–88. Deep brown, red brown, red on m/c unpt. Sanchez at r., arms at ctr. Hydroelectric dam on back.			
		a. 1978.	.50	2.50	7.50
		b. 1980–82.	FV	2.00	6.00
		c. 1984; 1985; 1987; 1988.	FV	1.50	4.50

Cat. #	Denomination	Date, description	VG	VF	Unc
119 (55)	10 PESOS	1978–88. Deep green and black on m/c unpt. Mella at r., Liberty head at ctr. Quarry mining scene on back.			
		a. 1978.	1.00	4.00	12.50
		b. 1980–82.	FV	3.00	9.00
		c. 1985; 1987; 1988.	FV	2.50	7.50

Cat. #	Denomination	Date, description	VG	VF	Unc
120 (56)	20 PESOS	1978–88. Deep brown and brown on m/c unpt. National shrine at ctr. Puerta del Conde on back.			
		a. 1978.	2.00	7.00	21.00
		b. 1980–82.	FV	5.50	17.50
		c. 1985; 1987; 1988.	FV	5.00	15.00

Cat. #	Denomination	Date, description	VG	VF	Unc
121 (57)	50 PESOS	1978; 1980. Purple on m/c unpt. Basilica at ctr. First cathedral in America on back.	5.00	22.50	45.00

Cat. #	Denomination	Date, description	VG	VF	Unc
122 (58)	100 PESOS	1977–87. Orange and violet on m/c unpt. Entrance to 16th century mint at ctr. Banco Central on back.			
		a. Wmk: Indian head. 1977; 1978; 1980; 1981.	10.00	42.50	125.00
		b. Wmk: Duarte. 1984; 1987.	FV	50.00	150.00

Cat. #	Denomination	Date, description	VG	VF	Unc
123 (59)	500 PESOS	1978; 1980. Deep blue-green, black and brown on m/c unpt. National Theater at ctr. Fort San Felipe on back.	50.00	200.00	400.00

Cat. #	Denomination	Date, description	VG	VF	Unc
124 (60)	1000 PESOS	1978–87. Red, purple and violet on m/c unpt. National Palace at ctr. Columbus' fortress on back.			
		a. Wmk: Indian head. 1978; 1980.	100.00	275.00	550.00
		b. Wmk: Duarte. 1984; 1987.	90.00	225.00	450.00

1982 COMMEMORATIVE ISSUE

#125, 35th Anniversary Banco Central, 1947-1982

125 (74)	100 PESOS	1982 (– old date 1978). Special commemorative text ovpt. in black below bank on back of #122. Specimen.	—	—	150.00

1984 ISSUE

126 (61)	1 PESO	1984; 1987; 1988. Black, brown and m/c. New portrait of Duarte at r., otherwise like #117.	FV	FV	.85

1988 ISSUE

#127–130 printer: USBNC.

127 (67)	50 PESOS	1988. Purple on m/c unpt. Similar to #121.	FV	FV	12.00
128 (68)	100 PESOS	1988. Orange and violet on m/c unpt. Similar to #122.	FV	FV	18.50
129 (69)	500 PESOS	1988. Deep blue-green, black and brown on m/c unpt. Similar to #123.	FV	FV	75.00
130 (72)	1000 PESOS	1988; 1990. Red, purple and violet on m/c unpt. Similar to #124.	FV	FV	135.00

1990 ISSUE

#131-134 w/silver leaf-like underlays at l. and r. on face. Printer: H&S.

131 (62)	5 PESOS	1990. Deep brown, red-brown, red on m/c unpt. Similar to #118.	FV	FV	1.75
132 (63)	10 PESOS	1990. Deep green and black on m/c unpt. Similar to #119.	FV	FV	2.75
133 (64)	20 PESOS	1990. Deep brown and brown on m/c unpt. Similar to #120	FV	FV	5.00
134 (70)	500 PESOS	1990. Deep blue-green, black and brown on m/c unpt. Similar to #123.	FV	FV	7.00

1991; 1992 ISSUE

#135-138 printer: TDLR.

135 (66)	50 PESOS	1991. Purple on m/c unpt. Similar to #127.	FV	FV	11.00

Cat. #	Denomination	Date, description	VG	VF	Unc
1356 (68)	100 PESOS	1991. Orange and violet on m/c unpt. Similar to #128.	FV	FV	17.50
137 (71)	500 PESOS	1991; 1994. Deep blue-green, black and brown on m/c unpt. Similar to #134.	FV	FV	65.00
138 (73)	1000 PESOS	1992; 1994. Red, purple and violet on m/c unpt. Similar to #130.	FV	FV	125.00

1993 ISSUE

143	5 PESOS	1993. Deep brown, red-brown, red on m/c unpt. Similar to #131. Printer: USBNC.	FV	FV	1.50

#144 and 145 printer: FNMT.

144	100 PESOS	1993. Orange and violet on m/c unpt. Similar to #136.	FV	FV	15.00
145	1000 PESOS	1993. Red, purple and violet on m/c unpt. Similar to #138.	FV	FV	120.00

1994 ISSUE

146	5 PESOS	1994. Deep brown, red-brown, red on m/c unpt. Similar to #143. Printer: TDLR.	FV	FV	1.25

1995 ISSUE

#147 and 148 similar to #146 and #132 but w/brighter colored arms. Printer: F-CO.

147	5 PESOS	1995.	FV	FV	1.35
148	10 PESOS	1995.	FV	FV	2.50

1992 COMMEMORATIVE ISSUE

#139–142, Quincentennial of First Landfall by Christopher Columbus, 1992.

139 (75)	20 PESOS	1992. Similar to #133 but w/brown commemorative text: *1492-1992 V Centenario…* at l. over seal. Printer: BABNC.	FV	FV	4.00

140 (76)	500 PESOS	1992. Brown and blue-black on m/c unpt. Sailing ships at ctr., C. Columbus at ctr. r. and as wmk. Columbus Lighthouse, placement of Cross of Christianity and map outline on back. Printer: CBNC.	FV	FV	65.00

Cat. #	Denomination	Date, description	VG	VF	Unc
141 (77)	500 PESOS	1992. Black commemorative text ovpt. at r. on #123.	FV	FV	65.00

| 142 (78) | 1000 PESOS | 1992. Black commemorative text ovpt. at r. on #124. | FV | FV | 125.00 |

COLLECTOR SERIES

Cat. #	Date, denomination	Description	Issue Price	Mkt. Val.
CS1	ND (ca.1974). 1–1000 PESOS	#99–106. Ovpt.: *MUESTRA* twice on face.	—	200.00
CS2	ND (ca. 1974). 1–1000 PESOS	#99–106. Ovpt.: *MUESTRA* on face and back.	40.00	125.00
CS3	1978. 1–1000 PESOS	#116, 118–124. Ovpt.: *MUESTRA/SIN VALOR* on face, *ESPECIMEN* on back.	40.00	100.00
CS4	1978. 1–1000 PESOS	#116, 118, 1240. Ovpt.: *SPECIMEN* and Maltese cross prefix serial #. #58 is dated 1977.	14.00	60.00

EAST AFRICA

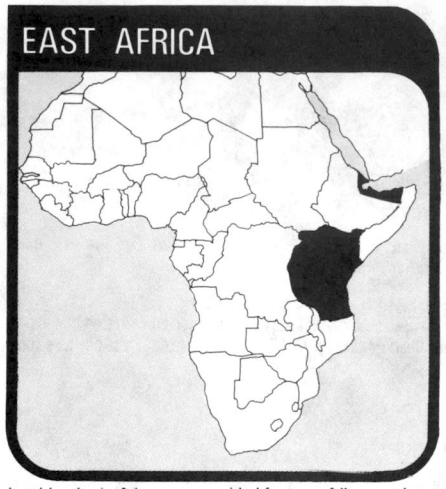

East Africa was an administrative grouping of five separate British territories: Kenya, Tanganyika (now part of Tanzania), the Sultanate of Zanzibar and Pemba (now part of Tanzania), Uganda and British Somaliland (now part of Somalia). See individual entries for specific statistics and history.

The common interest of Kenya, Tanzania and Uganda invited cooperation in economic matters and consideration of political union. The territorial governors, organized as the East Africa High Commission, met periodically to administer such common activities as taxation, industrial development and education. The authority of the Commission did not infringe upon the constitution and internal autonomy of the individual colonies. A common coinage and banknotes, which were also legal tender in Aden, was provided for use of the member colonies by the East Africa Currency Board.

Also see British Somaliland, Zanzibar, Kenya, Uganda and Tanzania.

RULERS

British

MONETARY SYSTEM

1 Shilling = 100 Cents, 1921–

East African Currency Board, Nairobi

W/O OFFICE OF ISSUE

#37–44 portr. Qn. Elizabeth II at l. wmk. area bottom ctr. Printer: TDLR.

#37–40 w/4 sign. at r.

Cat. #	Denomination	Date, description	VG	VF	Unc
37	5 SHILLINGS	ND (1958–60). Brown.	2.50	10.50	185.00
38	10 SHILLINGS	ND (1958–60). Green.	2.50	12.50	150.00
39	20 SHILLINGS	ND (1958–60). Blue.	3.00	15.00	165.00

| 40 | 100 SHILLINGS | ND (1958–60). Red. | 20.00 | 100.00 | 650.00 |

#41–44 w/3 sign. at l. and 4 at r.

41	5 SHILLINGS	Brown. Like #37.			
		a. ND (1961). Top l. sign: E.B. David.	2.50	12.50	150.00
		b. ND (1962–63). Top l. sign: A.L. Adu.	2.00	10.00	100.00

42	10 SHILLINGS	Green. Like #38.			
		a. ND (1961). Top l. sign: E.B. David.	3.50	13.50	175.00
		b. ND (1962–63). Top l. sign: A.L. Adu.	3.00	10.00	125.00

Cat. #	Denomination	Date, description	VG	VF	Unc
43	20 SHILLINGS	Blue. Like #39.			
		a. ND (1961). Top l. sign: E.B. David.	6.50	35.00	350.00
		b. ND (1962–63). Top l. sign: A.L. Adu.	5.00	22.50	225.00

44	100 SHILLINGS	Red. Like #40			
		a. ND (1961). Top l. sign: E.B. David.	15.00	90.00	700.00
		b. ND (1962–63). Top l. sign: A.L. Adu.	8.50	47.50	475.00

#45–48 wmk. area at l., sailboat at l. ctr.

45	5 SHILLINGS	ND (1964). Brown and m/c.	1.50	7.50	50.00

47	20 SHILLINGS	ND (1964). Blue and m/c.	5.00	25.00	200.00

48	100 SHILLINGS	ND (1964). Red and m/c.	7.50	35.00	160.00

Cat. #	Denomination	Date, description	VG	VF	Unc
46	10 SHILLINGS	ND (1964). Green and m/c.	2.00	10.00	65.00

EAST CARIBBEAN STATES

The East Caribbean States, formerly the British Caribbean Territories (Eastern Group), a currency board formed in 1950, comprised the British West Indies territories of Trinidad and Tobago; Barbados; the Leeward Islands of Anguilla, Saba, St. Christopher, Nevis and Antigua; the Windward Islands of St. Lucia, Dominica, St. Vincent and Grenada; British Guiana and the British Virgin Islands.

As time progressed, the members of this Eastern Group varied which is reflected on the backs of #13–16. The first issue includes Barbados but not Grenada, while the second issue includes both Barbados and Grenada and the third issue retains Grenada while Barbados is removed.

RULERS
British

MONETARY SYSTEM
1 Dollar = 100 Cents

REPLACEMENT NOTES

#13–16 Var. II onward: Z1 prefix (may continue to Z2).

#17–onward: Z prefix.

British Caribbean Territories, Eastern Group

1953–64 ISSUE

#7–12 map at l., portr. Qn. Elizabeth II at r. Printer: BWC.

Cat. #	Denomination	Date, description	VG	VF	Unc
7	1 DOLLAR	1953–64. Red.			
		a. Wmk: sailing ship. 5.1.1953.	6.00	35.00	150.00
		b. Wmk: Qn. Elizabeth II. 1.3.1954–2.1.1957.	3.00	15.00	75.00
		c. 2.1.1958–2.1.1964.	1.50	12.00	60.00
8	2 DOLLARS	1953–64. Blue.			
		a. Wmk: Like #7a: 5.1.1953.	20.00	175.00	425.00
		b. Wmk: Like #7b: 1.3.1954–1.7.1960.	7.50	35.00	300.00
		c. 2.1.1961–2.1.1964.	3.00	15.00	250.00

Cat. #	Denomination	Date, description	VG	VF	Unc
9	5 DOLLARS	1953–64. Green.			
		a. Wmk: Like #7a: 5.1.1953.	22.50	185.00	450.00
		b. Wmk: Like #7b: 3.1.1955–2.1.1959.	10.00	35.00	375.00
		c. 2.1.1961–2.1.1964.	7.50	25.00	350.00

Cat. #	Denomination	Date, description	VG	VF	Unc
10	10 DOLLARS	1953–64. Brown.			
		a. Wmk: Like #7a: 5.1.1953.	37.50	300.00	1500.
		b. Wmk: Like #7b: 3.1.1955–2.1.1959.	20.00	125.00	950.00
		c. 2.1.1961; 2.1.1962; 2.1.1964.	15.00	85.00	450.00

Cat. #	Denomination	Date, description	VG	VF	Unc
11	20 DOLLARS	1953–64. Purple.			
		a. Wmk: Like #7a: 5.1.1953.	50.00	400.00	2000.
		b. Wmk: Like #7b: 2.1.1957–2.1.1964.	25.00	75.00	1000.
12	100 DOLLARS	1953–63. Black.			
		a. Wmk: Like #7a: 5.1.1953.	375.00	1250.	—
		b. Wmk: Like #7b: 1.3.1954; 2.1.1957; 2.1.1963.	225.00	750.00	—

East Caribbean Currency Authority

SIGNATURE VARIETIES			
1	Chairman / Director Director Director	6	Chairman / Director Director Director
2	Chairman / Director Director Director	7	Chairman / Director Director Director
3	Chairman / Director Director Director	8	Chairman / Director Director Director
4	Chairman / Director Director Director	9	Chairman / Director Director Director
5	Chairman / Director Director Director	10	Chairman / Director Director Director

ISLAND PARTICIPATION

| Variety I | Variety II | Variety III |

VARIETY I: Listing of islands on back includes Barbados but not Grenada.

VARIETY II: Listing includes Barbados and Grenada.

VARIETY III: Listing retains Grenada while Barbados is deleted.

1965 (ND) ISSUE

#13–16 map at l., Qn. Elizabeth II at r. Coastline w/rocks and trees at l. on back. Sign. varieties. Wmk: QE II. Printer: TDLR.

Beginning in 1983, #13–16 were ovpt. with circled letters at l. indicating their particular areas of issue within the Eastern Group. Letters and their respective areas are as follows:

A, Antigua	L, St. Lucia
D, Dominica	M, Montserrat
G, Grenada	U, Anguilla
K, St. Kitts	V, St. Vincentl.

Cat. #	Denomination	Date, description	VG	VF	Unc
14	5 DOLLARS	ND (1965). Green. Flying fish at ctr.			
		Variety I. Sign. 1; 2.			
		a. Sign. 1.	6.00	25.00	125.00
		b. Sign. 2.	5.50	20.00	125.00
		Variety II. Sign. 3–7.			
		c. Sign. 3.	Reported, not confirmed.		
		d. Sign. 4.	4.00	10.00	85.00
		e. Sign. 5; 6.	3.50	7.50	45.00
		f. Sign. 7.	4.00	10.00	65.00
		Variety III. Sign. 8–10.			
		g. Sign. 8.	2.00	5.00	20.00
		h. Sign. 9; 10.	FV	3.00	12.00
		i. Ovpt: *A* in circle.	FV	2.50	10.00
		j. Ovpt: *D* in circle.	FV	2.50	15.00
		k. Ovpt: *G* in circle.	FV	2.50	11.00
		l. Ovpt: *K* in circle.	FV	2.50	12.50
		m. Ovpt: *L* in circle.	FV	2.50	75.00
		n. Ovpt: *M* in circle.	FV	2.50	11.00
		o. Ovpt: *U* in circle.	FV	2.50	11.00
		p. Ovpt: *V* in circle.	FV	2.50	11.00

Cat. #	Denomination	Date, description	VG	VF	Unc
13	1 DOLLAR	ND (1965). Red. Fish at ctr.			
		a. Variety I. Sign. 1; 2.	1.00	5.00	27.50
		Variety II. Sign. 3–7.			
		b. Sign. 3.	.75	3.00	12.50
		c. Sign. 4.	1.00	5.00	55.00
		d. Sign. 5; 6; 7.	.50	2.00	9.50
		Variety III. Sign. 8–10.			
		e. Sign. 8.	.45	1.50	5.00
		f. Sign. 9; 10. Darker red on back as previous varieties, to Series B77.	FV	.65	4.00
		g. Sign. 10. Brighter red on back. Series B83–B91.	FV	.65	3.50
		h. Ovpt: *A* in circle.	FV	.50	4.00
		i. Ovpt: *D* in circle.	FV	.50	5.00
		j. Ovpt: *G* in circle.	FV	.50	5.00
		k. Ovpt: *K* in circle.	FV	.50	4.00
		l. Ovpt: *L* in circle.	FV	.50	6.00
		m. Ovpt: *M* in circle.	FV	.50	4.00
		n. Ovpt: *V* in circle.	FV	.50	4.00

Cat. #	Denomination	Date, description	VG	VF	Unc
15	20 DOLLARS	ND (1965). Purple. Turtles at ctr.			
		Variety I. Sign. 1; 2.			
		a. Sign. 1.	15.00	65.00	500.00
		b. Sign. 2.	20.00	75.00	600.00
		Variety II. Sign. 3–7.			
		c. Sign. 3.	Reported, not confirmed.		
		d. Sign. 4.	12.50	50.00	300.00
		e. Sign. 5; 6; 7.	10.00	40.00	250.00
		Variety III. Sign. 8–10.			
		f. Sign. 8	10.00	12.50	30.00
		g. Sign. 9, 10.	FV	10.00	25.00
		h. Ovpt: *A* in circle.	FV	10.00	22.50
		i. Ovpt: *D* in circle.	FV	10.00	27.50
		j. Ovpt: *G* in circle.	FV	10.00	25.00
		k. Ovpt: *K* in circle.	FV	15.00	100.00
		l. Ovpt: *L* in circle.	FV	10.00	22.50
		m. Ovpt: *M* in circle.	FV	10.00	25.00
		n. Ovpt: *U* in circle.	FV	10.00	22.50
		o. Ovpt: *V* in circle.	FV	10.00	22.50

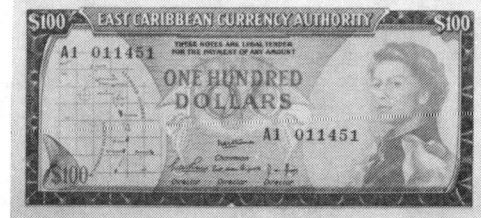

Cat. #	Denomination	Date, description	VG	VF	Unc
16	100 DOLLARS	ND (1965). Black. Sea horses at ctr.			
		Variety I. Sign. 1; 2.			
		a. Sign. 1.	150.00	400.00	1250.
		b. Sign. 2.		Reported, not confirmed.	
		Variety II. Sign. 3–7.			
		c. Sign. 5.	100.00	325.00	1000.
		d. Sign. 3; 4; 6; 7.		Reported, not confirmed.	
		Variety III. Sign. 8–10.			
		e. Sign. 8.		Reported, not confirmed.	
		f. Sign. 9; 10.	FV	60.00	175.00
		g. Ovpt: A in circle.	FV	60.00	250.00
		h. Ovpt: D in circle.	50.00	125.00	450.00
		i. Ovpt: G in circle.	FV	85.00	275.00
		j. Ovpt: K in circle.	FV	95.00	350.00
		k. Ovpt: L in circle.	FV	60.00	200.00
		l. Ovpt: M in circle.	FV	50.00	185.00
		m. Ovpt: V in circle.	FV	55.00	195.00

Eastern Caribbean Central Bank

SIGNATURE VARIETIES			
1	 Governor	3	
2	K. Dwight Venner Governor	4	

1985–87 (ND) ISSUE

#17–25 have windsurfer at l., Qn. Elizabeth II at r. ctr., map at r. on face. Wmk: QEII. Printer: TDLR.

Notes w/suffix letter of serial # indicating particular areas of issue (as with ovpt. letters on previous issue).

#17–20 do not have name Anguilla at island near top of map at r. Palm tree, swordfish at r. ctr., shoreline in background on back. No $10 without Anguilla was issued. Sign. 1.

Cat. #	Denomination	Date, description	VG	VF	Unc
17	1 DOLLAR	ND (1985–88). Red on m/c unpt.			
		a. Suffix letter A.	FV	1.00	3.00
		b. Suffix letter D.	FV	1.00	3.00
		c. Suffix letter G.	FV	1.00	3.00
		d. Suffix letter K.	FV	1.00	3.00
		e. Suffix letter L.	FV	1.00	3.00
		f. Suffix letter M.	FV	1.00	3.00
		g. Suffix letter V.	FV	1.00	3.00
		h. Ovpt: U in circle on suffix letter V issue (1988).	FV	1.00	3.00

Cat. #	Denomination	Date, description	VG	VF	Unc
18	5 DOLLARS	ND (1986–88). Deep green on m/c unpt.			
		a. Suffix letter A.	FV	FV	6.00
		b. Suffix letter D.	FV	FV	6.00
		c. Suffix letter G.	FV	FV	6.00
		d. Suffix letter K.	FV	FV	5.00
		e. Suffix letter L.	FV	FV	6.00
		f. Suffix letter M.	FV	FV	5.00
		g. Suffix letter V.	FV	FV	5.00
		h. Ovpt: U in circle on suffix letter V issue (1988).	FV	FV	6.00

Cat. #	Denomination	Date, description	VG	VF	Unc
19	20 DOLLARS	ND (1987–88). Purple and brown on m/c unpt.			
		a. Suffix letter A.	FV	FV	20.00
		b. Suffix letter D.	FV	FV	22.00
		c. Suffix letter G.	FV	10.00	25.00
		d. Suffix letter K.	FV	FV	22.00
		e. Suffix letter L.	FV	FV	20.00
		f. Suffix letter M.	FV	12.50	30.00
		g. Suffix letter V.	FV	FV	20.00
		h. Ovpt. U in circle.	FV	FV	30.00

Cat. #	Denomination	Date, description	VG	VF	Unc
20	100 DOLLARS	ND (1986–88). Black and orange on m/c unpt.			
		a. Suffix letter A.	FV	FV	95.00
		b. Suffix letter D.	FV	50.00	125.00
		c. Suffix letter G.	FV	50.00	110.00
		d. Suffix letter K.	FV	FV	95.00
		e. Suffix letter L.	FV	FV	95.00
		f. Suffix letter M.	FV	FV	95.00
		g. Suffix letter V.	FV	FV	95.00
		h. Ovpt: U in circle on suffix letter V issue (1988).	FV	FV	100.00

1985-89 (ND) ISSUE

#21–25 with ANGUILLA island named near top of map at r.

#21, 22, 24 and 25 harbor at St. Lucia on back.

Cat. #	Denomination	Date, description	VG	VF	Unc
21	1 DOLLAR	ND (1988–89). Like #17 but Anguilla named. Sign. 1.			
		a. Suffix letter D.	FV	1.00	4.00
		b. Suffix letter K.	FV	1.00	4.00
		c. Suffix letter L.	FV	1.00	4.00
		d. Suffix letter U.	FV	1.00	4.00

#22–25 have 2 sign. varieties.

Cat. #	Denomination	Date, description	VG	VF	Unc
22	5 DOLLARS	ND (1988–93). Like #18 but Anguilla named.			
		a. Suffix letter A. Sign. 1.	FV	FV	5.00
		b. Like a. Sign. 2.	FV	FV	5.00
		c. Suffix letter D. Sign. 1.	FV	FV	5.00
		g. Suffix letter K. Sign 1.	FV	FV	5.00
		h. Like g. Sign. 2.	FV	FV	5.00
		i. Suffix letter L. Sign. 1.	FV	FV	5.00
		j. Like i. Sign. 2.	FV	FV	5.00

Cat. #	Denomination	Date, description	VG	VF	Unc
		m. Suffix letter *U*. Sign. 1.	FV	FV	7.00
		p. Suffix letter *V*. Sign. 2.	FV	FV	5.00

23   10 DOLLARS ND (1985–93). Blue on m/c unpt. Harbor at Grenada, sailboats at l. and ctr. on back.

		VG	VF	Unc
a. Suffix letter *A*. Sign. 1.		FV	FV	9.00
b. Like a. Sign. 2		FV	FV	10.00
c. Suffix letter *D*. Sign. 1.		FV	FV	9.00
d. Like c. Sign. 2.		FV	FV	10.00
e. Suffix letter *G*. Sign. 1.		FV	FV	9.00
g. Suffix letter *K*. Sign. 1.		FV	FV	9.00
h. Like g. Sign. 2.		FV	FV	10.00
i. Suffix letter *L*. Sign. 1.		FV	FV	9.00
j Like i. Sign. 2.		FV	FV	9.00
k. Suffix letter *M*. Sign. 1.		FV	FV	10.00
m. Suffix letter *U*. Sign. 1.		FV	FV	9.00
o. Suffix letter *V*. Sign. 1.		FV	FV	9.00
p. Like o. Sign. 2.		FV	FV	9.00

24   20 DOLLARS ND (1988–93). Like #19 but Anguilla named.

		VG	VF	Unc
a. Suffix letter *A*. Sign. 1.		FV	FV	18.00
b. Like a. Sign. 2.		FV	FV	18.00
c. Suffix letter *D*. Sign. 1.		FV	FV	20.00
d. Like c. Sign. 2.		FV	FV	18.00
e. Suffix letter *G*. Sign. 1.		FV	FV	22.50
g. Suffix letter *K*. Sign. 1.		FV	FV	20.00
h. Like g. Sign. 2.		FV	FV	18.00
i. Suffix letter *L*. Sign. 1.		FV	FV	20.00
j. Like i. Sign. 2.		FV	FV	18.00
k. Suffix letter *M*. Sign. 1.		FV	FV	18.00
l. Like k. Sign. 2.		FV	FV	18.00
m. Suffix letter *U*. Sign. 1.		FV	FV	20.00
o. Suffix letter *V*. Sign. 1.		FV	FV	20.00

25   100 DOLLARS ND (1988–93). Like #20 but Anguilla named.

		VG	VF	Unc
a. Suffix letter *A*. Sign. 1.		FV	FV	95.00
b. Like a. Sign. 2.		FV	FV	95.00
c. Suffix letter *D*. Sign. 1.		FV	FV	95.00
d. Like c. Sign. 2.		FV	FV	95.00
e. Suffix letter *G*. Sign. 1.		FV	FV	100.00
g. Suffix letter *K*. Sign. 1.		FV	FV	100.00
h. Like g. Sign. 2.		FV	FV	100.00
i. Suffix letter *L*. Sign. 1.		FV	FV	95.00
j. Like i. Sign. 2.		FV	FV	95.00
k. Suffix letter *M*. Sign. 1.		FV	FV	100.00
l. Like k. Sign. 2.		FV	FV	95.00
m. Suffix letter *U*. Sign. 1.		VF	FV	100.00
o. Suffix letter *V*. Sign. 1.		FV	FV	95.00

1993 (ND) ISSUE

#26-30 Qn. Elizabeth II at ctr. r. and as wmk., turtle at ctr. Island map at ctr. on back. Sign. 2. Printer: TDLR.

Cat. #	Denomination	Date, description	VG	VF	Unc
26	5 DOLLARS	ND (1993). Dk. green and black on m/c unpt. Admiral's House in Antigua and Barbuda at l., Trafalgar Falls in Dominica at r. on back.	FV	FV	6.50

| 27 | 10 DOLLARS | ND (1993). Blue and black on m/c unpt. Admiralty Bay in St. Vincent & the Grenadines at l., Sailing ship *Warspite* at r. ctr. on back. | FV | FV | 11.50 |

| 28 | 20 DOLLARS | ND (1993). Brown-violet and blue on m/c unpt. Govt. House in Montserrat at l., nutmeg in Grenada at r. on back. | FV | FV | 20.00 |

Cat. #	Denomination	Date, description	VG	VF	Unc
29	50 DOLLARS	ND (1993). Purple and olive-green on m/c unpt. Brimstone Hill in St. Kitts at l., Les Pitons mountains in St. Lucia at r. on back.	FV	FV	45.00

| 30 | 100 DOLLARS | ND (1993). Dk. brown, dk. green and m/c. Sir Arthur Lewis at l., E.C.C.B. Central Bank bldg. at r. on back. | FV | FV | 85.00 |

1995 (ND) SERIES

| 31 | 5 DOLLARS | ND (1995). Dk. green and black on m/c unpt. Like #26 but w/redesigned corner 5's. | FV | FV | 5.50 |

NOTE: It is expected that most, if not all, suffix letter varieties will be issued for #26-30.

COLLECTOR SERIES

The following 2 sets are made of paper-thin gold and silver foil.

Cat. #	Date, denomination	Description	Issue Price	Mkt. Val.
CS1	ND (1983). 30 DOLLARS	12 different showing various flowers and animals. Notes titled *ANTIGUA & BARBUDA*.	—	300.00
CS2	ND (1988). 100 DOLLARS	30 different showing various pirate ships.	—	500.00

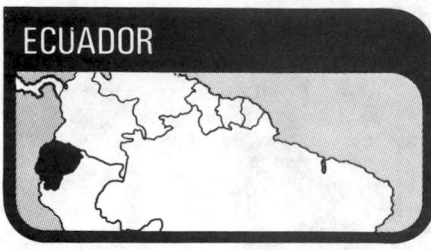

ECUADOR

The Republic of Ecuador, located astride the equator on the Pacific coast of South America, has an area of 109,484 sq. mi. (283,561 sq. km.) and a population of 9.65 million. Capital: Quito. Agriculture is the mainstay of the economy but there are appreciable deposits of minerals and petroleum. It is the world's largest exporter of bananas and balsa wood. Coffee, cacao and shrimp are also valuable exports.

Ecuador was first sighted, 1526, by Bartolome Ruiz. Conquest was undertaken by Sebastian de Benalcazar who founded Quito in 1534. Ecuador was part of the province, later Vice-royalty, of Peru until 1739 when it became part of the Vice-royalty of New Granada. After two failed attempts to attain independence in 1810 and 1812, it successfully declared its independence in October 1820, and won final victory over Spanish forces May 24, 1822. Incorporated into the Gran Colombia confederacy, it loosened its ties in 1830 and regained full independence in 1835.

MONETARY SYSTEM

1 Peso = 100 Centavos
1 Sucre = 10 Decimos = 100 Centavos
1 Condor = 25 Sucres

Banco Central del Ecuador

1944 SECOND ISSUE

#96–97 w/text: *CAPITAL AUTORIZADO 20,000,000 SUCRES.* 3 sign.; various sign. title ovpts. Printer: ABNC.

Cat. #	Denomination	Date, description	VG	VF	Unc
96	500 SUCRES	12.5.1944–17.11.1966. Mercury seated at ctr. Back deep orange.	150.00	250.00	550.00

| 97 | 1000 SUCRES | 12.5.1944–6.4.1967. Woman reclining w/globe and telephone at ctr. Back gray. | — | — | — |

1950–71 ISSUES

Various dates found w/ or w/o dot after *1* in year.

#100–107 black on m/c unpt. Several date varieties, sign. title ovpts. and serial # styles. Arms on back 31mm. wide, w/o flagpole stems below. Printer: ABNC.

100	5 SUCRES	1956–73. Portr. Sucre at ctr. Back red-violet.			
		a. 19.6.1956–24.9.1957.	.50	2.50	10.00
		b. 1.1.1966.	.25	.50	3.50
		c. 27.2.1970– 3.9.1973.	.15	.25	2.00

Cat. #	Denomination	Date, description	VG	VF	Unc
101	10 SUCRES	1950–74. Portr. S. de Benalcazar at ctr. Back blue.			
		a. Plain background. 14.1.1950–28.11.1955.	1.50	5.00	20.00
		b. Ornate background, different background guilloches. 15.6.1956–27.4.1966.	.50	2.00	8.50
		c. 24.5.1968–2.1.1974.	.25	1.00	4.00

Cat. #	Denomination	Date, description	VG	VF	Unc
105	100 SUCRES	1956–80. Like #A105 but w/diff. guilloches.			
		a. 19.6.1956; 19.7.1957; 7.11.1957; 6.6.1958; 8.4.1959.	4.00	20.00	60.00
		b. 1.1.1966–7.7.1970.	2.00	4.00	15.00
		c. 1.2.1980.	1.00	2.00	5.00
106	500 SUCRES	ND (ca.1971). Similar to #96, but w/diff. guilloches and other changes. Back brown. (Not issued). Archive example.	—	—	—

102	20 SUCRES	28.2.1950–28.7.1960. Church facade at ctr. Back brown.	1.00	4.50	20.00

103	20 SUCRES	1962–73. Like #102 but different guilloche and darker unpt.			
		a. 12.12.1962-27.4.1966.	1.00	3.00	10.00
		b. 17.11.1966-3.9.1973.	.50	1.50	5.50

107	1000 SUCRES	17.11.1966–20.9.1973. Banco Central bldg. at ctr. Back olive-gray.	20.00	50.00	160.00

1975–80 ISSUE

#108–112 face like #100-105. Arms on back 29mm. Wide, new rendition w/flagpole stems below. Printer: ABNC.

104	50 SUCRES	1968–71. Like #99. Back green.			
		a. 24.5.1968; 5.11.1969.	1.50	3.50	15.00
		b. 20.5.1971.	1.00	2.50	8.00
A105	100 SUCRES	7.11.1952. Portr. S. Bolivar at ctr. Back purple.	8.00	35.00	60.00

108	5 SUCRES	1975–83. Like #100.			
		a. 14.3.1975; 29.4.1977.	.15	.40	1.00
		b. 20.8.1982; 20.4.1983.	FV	FV	.50

Cat. #	Denomination	Date, description	VG	VF	Unc
109	10 SUCRES	14.3.1975; 10.8.1976; 29.4.1977; 24.5.1978. Like #101.	.10	.30	2.00

110	20 SUCRES	10.8.1976. Like #103.	.50	1.00	3.50

111	50 SUCRES	10.8.1976. Like #104.	1.00	2.50	5.00

112	100 SUCRES	24.5.1980. Like #105.	FV	FV	3.00

1957–76 ISSUE

#113–118 black on m/c unpt. Similar to #108-112. Several sign. title ovpt. varieties. Printer: TDLR.
#113–117 security thread used intermittently through 1969.

Cat. #	Denomination	Date, description	VG	VF	Unc
113	5 SUCRES	1958–88. Similar to #108.			
		a. 2.1.1958–7.11.1962.	.60	2.00	7.50
		b. 23.5.1963-27.2.1970.	.25	.50	3.00
		c. 25.7.1979-24.5.1980.	FV	FV	1.00
		d. 22.11.1988.	FV	FV	.50

114	10 SUCRES	1968–83. Similar to #109.			
		a. 24.5.1968; 20.5.1971.	.25	.50	3.00
		b. 24.5.1980; 30.9.1982; 20.4.1983.	FV	FV	.50

115	20 SUCRES	1961–83. Similar to #110.			
		a. 7.6.1961; 27.2.1962; 6.7.1962.	1.00	3.50	12.50
		b. 1.5.1978; 24.5.1980; 20.4.1983.	FV	FV	.75

116	50 SUCRES	1957–82. Similar to #111.			
		a. 2.4.1957; 7.7.1959; 7.4.1960; 7.11.1962; 29.10.1963; 29.1.1965; 6.8.1965.	1.00	5.00	15.00
		b. 1.1.1966; 27.4.1966; 17.11.1966; 4.10.1967; 30.5.1969; 17.7.1974.	.50	2.00	6.00
		c. 24.5.1980; 20.8.1982.	FV	FV	1.50

117	100 SUCRES	6.7.1962; 23.7.1964; 6.8.1965. Similar to #112 but crude portr. w/lt. clouds behind.	4.00	15.00	50.00

Cat. #	Denomination	Date, description	VG	VF	Unc
118	100 SUCRES	1965–80. Like #117 but better portr. w/dk. clouds behind.			
		a. 6.8.1965; 20.5.1971; 17.7.1974.	2.00	4.00	15.00
		b. 10.8.1976; 10.8.1977; 24.5.1980.	FV	1.50	4.00

Cat. #	Denomination	Date, description	VG	VF	Unc
119	500 SUCRES	1976–82. Black, purple and dk. olive-green on m/c unpt. Dr. E. de Santa Cruz y Espejo at l. Back blue and m/c; arms at ctr. Printer: TDLR.			
		a. 24.5.1976; 10.8.1977; 9.10.1978; 25.1.1979.	1.00	7.50	25.00
		b. 20.7.1982.	FV	4.00	10.00

Cat. #	Denomination	Date, description	VG	VF	Unc
120	1000 SUCRES	1976–82. Dk. green and red-brown on m/c unpt. Ruminahui at r. Back dk. green and m/c; arms at ctr. and as wmk.			
		a. 24.5.1976-25.7.1979.	1.00	9.00	25.00
		b. 20.7.1982.	FV	4.00	12.00

1984–88 ISSUES

#121–125 w/o text: *SOCIEDAD ANONIMA* below bank title. Sign. varieties. W/o imprint.

Cat. #	Denomination	Date, description	VG	VF	Unc
121	10 SUCRES	29.4.1986; 22.11.1988. Like #114.	FV	FV	.50

Cat. #	Denomination	Date, description	VG	VF	Unc
121A	20 SUCRES	29.4.1986; 22.11.1988. Like #115.	FV	FV	.60

Cat. #	Denomination	Date, description	VG	VF	Unc
122	50 SUCRES	5.9.1984; 29.4.1986; 22.11.1988. Like #116.	FV	FV	.75

Cat. #	Denomination	Date, description	VG	VF	Unc
123	100 SUCRES	29.4.1986; 20.4.1990. Like #118.	FV	FV	.85

Cat. #	Denomination	Date, description	VG	VF	Unc
123A	100 SUCRES	1988–. Like #112. Serial # style varieties.			
		a. Blue serial #. 8.6.1988; 21.6.1991.	FV	FV	1.00
		b. 21.2.1992; 9.3.1992; 4.12.1992; 20.8.1993.	FV	FV	.50
		c. Black serial #. 21.2.1994.	FV	FV	.25

#124–125 wmk: Arms. W/o imprint.

124	500 SUCRES	5.9.1984. Like #119.	FV	FV	2.00

124A	500 SUCRES	8.6.1988. Similar to #124 but many minor plate differences.	FV	FV	1.25

125	1000 SUCRES	1984–. Like #120 but w/o *EL* in bank title. Serial # style varieties.			
		a. 5.9.1984; 29.9.1986.	FV	FV	3.00
		b. 8.6.1988.	FV	FV	1.50

NOTE: Later dates of 100–1000 Sucres were made by different printers (w/o imprint) and vary slightly.

#126–128 printer: BCdE.

Cat. #	Denomination	Date, description	VG	VF	Unc
126	5000 SUCRES	1987–92. Purple on m/c unpt. Juan Montalvo at l., arms at ctr. r. 2 birds and sea tortoise on back.			
		a. 1.12.1987.	FV	FV	8.00
		b. 21.6.1991; 17.3.1992; 22.6.1992.	FV	FV	6.50

NOTE: Designed in Mexico and printed in England.

1993–96 ISSUE

127	5000 SUCRES	20.8.1993; 31.1.1995. Like #126 but w/repositioned sign. and both serial # horizontal.	FV	FV	5.00

128 (127)	10,000 SUCRES	30.7.1988; 21.2.1994; 6.2.1995. Dk.brown and reddish-brown on m/c unpt. Vicente Rocafuerte at l. and as wmk. Arms upper l. ctr., Independence monument in Quito at ctr. r. on back.	FV	FV	9.00

129	20,000 SUCRES	31.1.1995. Brown, black and deep blue on m/c unpt. Dr. G. Garcia Moreno at r. and as wmk. Arms at ctr. on back.	FV	FV	17.50
130	50,000 SUCRES	Expected new issue.			
131	100,000 SUCRES	Expected new issue.			

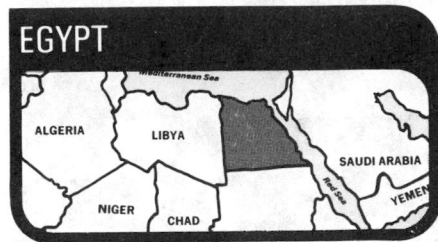

EGYPT

The Arab Republic of Egypt, located on the northeastern corner of Africa, has an area of 386,650 sq. mi. (1,000,000 sq. km.) and a population of 56 million. Capital: Cairo. Although Egypt is an almost rainless expanse of desert, its economy is predominantly agricultural. Cotton, rice and petroleum are exported.

Egyptian history dates back to about 4000 B.C. when the empire was established by uniting the upper and lower kingdoms. Following its 'Golden Age' (16th to 13th centuries B.C.), Egypt was conquered by Persia (525 B.C.) and Alexander the Great (332 B.C.) The Ptolemies ruled until the suicide of Cleopatra (30 B.C.) when Egypt became a Roman colony. Arab caliphs ruled Egypt from 641 to 1517, when the Turks took it for their Ottoman Empire. Turkish rule, interrupted by the occupation of Napoleon (1798–1801), became increasingly casual, permitting Great Britain to inject its influence by purchasing shares in the Suez Canal. British troops occupied Egypt in 1882, becoming the de facto rulers. On Dec. 14, 1914, Egypt was made a protectorate of Britain. British occupation ended on Feb. 28, 1922, when Egypt became a sovereign, independent kingdom. The monarchy was abolished and a republic proclaimed on June 18, 1952.

On Feb. 1, 1958, Egypt and Syria formed the United Arab Republic. Yemen joined on March 8 in an association known as the United Arab States. Syria withdrew from the United Arab Republic on Sept. 29, 1961, and on Dec. 26 Egypt dissolved its ties with Yemen in the United Arab States. On Sept. 2, 1971, Egypt shed the name United Arab Republic in favor of the Arab Republic of Egypt.

MONETARY SYSTEM
1 Piastre (Guerche) = 10 Milliemes
1 Pound (Junayh) = 100 Piastres, 1916–

REPLACEMENT NOTES
Starting in 1969, 2 types exist. Earlier system uses a single Arabic letter as series prefix instead of normal number/letter prefix. Known notes: #38–. Later system has the equivalent of English "200" or "300" in front of a single Arabic series letter. Known notes: #46–.

Central Bank of Egypt

1961–64 ISSUE
#31–37 sign. and date varieties.

Cat. #	Denomination	Date, description	VG	VF	Unc
31	25 PIASTRES	1.11.1961–18.8.1966. Blue. U. A. R. arms at r.	.50	1.50	6.00

Cat. #	Denomination	Date, description	VG	VF	Unc
32	50 PIASTRES	1.11.1961–14.8.1966. Black. U. A. R. arms at r., also in wmk.	1.00	5.00	15.00

Cat. #	Denomination	Date, description	VG	VF	Unc
33	1 POUND	1.11.1961–23.2.1967. Blue-green and lilac. Tutankhamen's mask at r. Back green.	1.00	2.50	7.00

Cat. #	Denomination	Date, description	VG	VF	Unc
34	5 POUNDS	1.11.1961–12.11.1961. Green and brown. Circular guilloche at l., Tutankhamen's mask at r. Wmk: Flower.	7.50	25.00	95.00

35	5 POUNDS	13.11.1961–16.6.1964. Green and brown. Similar to #34, but circular area at l. is blank. Guilloche at bottom ctr. on face and back. Wmk: U. A. R. arms.	3.00	10.00	25.00
36	5 POUNDS	17.6.1964–13.2.1965. Lilac and brown. Like #35.	2.50	7.50	22.50

Cat. #	Denomination	Date, description	VG	VF	Unc
37	10 POUNDS	1.11.1961–13.2.1965. Dk. green and dk. brown on m/c unpt. Tutankhamen's mask at r. Wmk: U. A. R. arms.	5.00	12.00	30.00

1967–69 ISSUE

Cat. #	Denomination	Date, description	VG	VF	Unc
38	25 PIASTRES	6.2.1967–4.1.1975. Blue, green and brown on m/c unpt. Sphinx w/statue at l. ctr. U. A. R. arms at ctr. on back. Wmk: Egyptian scribe.	.25	1.00	4.50

| 39 | 50 PIASTRES | 2.12.1967–28.1.1978. Red-brown and brown. Al Azhar Mosque at r., University of Cairo at l. ctr. Ramses II on back. Wmk: Egyptian scribe. | .50 | 1.00 | 3.50 |

Cat. #	Denomination	Date, description	VG	VF	Unc
40	1 POUND	12.5.1967–19.4.1978. Brown and m/c. Mosque of Sultan Quayet Bey. Ancient statues on back. Wmk: Egyptian scribe.	1.00	2.00	4.00

| 41 | 5 POUNDS | 1.1.1969–78. Blue, gray and green. Mosque of Ahmad ibn Tulun at Cairo at ctr. Ruins at l., frieze at ctr. r. on back. Wmk: Egyptian scribe. | 2.00 | 5.00 | 18.50 |

| 42 | 10 POUNDS | 1.9.1969–78. Red-brown and brown. Sultan Hassan Mosque at Cairo at l. ctr. Pharaoh and pyramids on back. Wmk: Egyptian scribe. | 4.00 | 7.50 | 22.50 |

1976 ISSUE

| 43 | 25 PIASTRES | 12.4.1976–28.8.1978. Blue, green and grayish brown on blue and orange unpt. Face and wmk. like #38. A. R. E. arms on back. | .25 | .50 | 2.50 |

Cat. #	Denomination	Date, description	VG	VF	Unc
44	20 POUNDS	5.7.1976; 1978. Green. Mosque of Moham-med Ali at l., Arabic legends at r. Ancient war chariot and frieze on back. Wmk: Egyptian scribe.	8.50	15.00	35.00

1978–79 ISSUE

#45–57 no longer have conventional reading dates with Arabic day, month and year. In place of this are six Arabic numerals, the first and last making up the year of issue; next 2 digits represent the day and following 2 digits represent the month; i.e. 822119 = 22.11.(19)89. Another example including raised diamonds (= zeroes) 804107 = 4.10.(19)87. Wmk: Tutankhamen's mask.

45	25 PIASTRES	2.1.–14.3.(19)79. Black on gray, pale blue and m/c unpt. Al-Sayida Aisha Mosque at ctr. Stylized A.R.E. arms, cotton, wheat and corn plants on back.	.25	.50	2.50

46	1 POUND	29.5.(19)78–. Brown, purple and deep olive-green on m/c unpt. Mosque of Sultan Quayet Bey at ctr. Ancient statues on back.			
		a. Back deep brown. Solid security thread. 29.5.(19)78–10.4.(19)87.	FV	FV	1.50
		b. Back pale brown. Solid security thread. 19.11.(19)86–24.6.(19)87.	FV	FV	1.50
		c. Back pale brown. Segmented security thread with bank name repeated. 13.8.(19)89–17.1.(19)93.	FV	FV	1.50

Cat. #	Denomination	Date, description	VG	VF	Unc
47	10 POUNDS	24.6.(19)78–. Brown and brown-violet. Mosque of Ar-Rifai at ctr. Pharaoh on back.	FV	FV	12.00

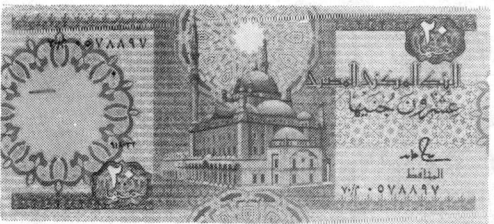

48	20 POUNDS	6.9.(19)78–. Black, gray-violet and deep green on m/c unpt. Mohammed Ali Mosque at ctr. Ancient sculptures from Chapel of Sesostris I and ancient war chariot on back.			
		a. Date below wmk. Solid security thread. 6.9.(19)78–22.4.(19)82.	FV	FV	20.00
		b. Date at lower r. of wmk. Solid security thread. 9.12.(19)86; 4.10.(19)87.	FV	FV	18.50
		c. Segmented security thread w/bank name repeated. (19)88–18.3.(19)92.	FV	FV	17.50

49	100 POUNDS	(19)78; (19)92. Blue and m/c. Mosque of Al Sayida Zaynab at ctr. Pharaoh's mask above frieze at ctr. on vertical back.			
		a. Series 1–6.(19)78.	FV	60.00	120.00
		b. (19)92.	FV	FV	70.00

1980–81 ISSUE

Cat. #	Denomination	Date, description	VG	VF	Unc
50	25 PIASTRES	17.1.(19)80–84. Dk. green on dk. green and m/c unpt. Like #45.	FV	.25	1.25

Cat. #	Denomination	Date, description	VG	VF	Unc
53	25 PIASTRES	4.4.(19)85–. Purple on pale blue, lilac and m/c unpt. Face and wmk. like #45 and #50. Standard A.R.E. arms at l. ctr. on back.			
		a. Solid security thread. 4.4.(19)85–30.1.(19)89.	FV	FV	.85
		b. Segmented security thread w/bank name repeated. 17.12.(19)90–8.10.(19)91.	FV	FV	.75

54	50 PIASTRES	(19)85–. Black on pale orange, pink and m/c unpt. Mosque at r. Back like #51.			
		a. No text line at lower l. on face. Solid security thead. 2.7.(19)85–.	FV	.35	2.00
		b. Text line added at lower l. on face. 10.2.(19)87–.	FV	FV	1.25
		c. Segmented security thread w/bank name repeated. 19.8.(19)91–.	FV	FV	1.00

51	50 PIASTRES	1.1.(19)81–83. Green, brown and m/c. Al Ahzar Mosque at ctr. Sculptured wall design at l., Ramses II at ctr., ancient seal at r. on back.	FV	.50	1.50

1989–94 ISSUE

55	5 POUNDS	2.4.(19)89–. Black and blue-black on m/c unpt. Like #52 but m/c scrollwork added in unpt. and into wmk. area. Ancient design over wmk. area at r. on back.			
		a. Solid security thread. 2.4.(19)89–5.7.(19)90.	FV	FV	650
		b. Segmented security thread w/bank name repeated. 3.4.(19)91; 4.4.(19)91.	FV	FV	5.50

52	5 POUNDS	(19)81–89. Black and blue-black on m/c unpt. Ibn Toulon Mosque at ctr. Design symbolizing bounty of the Nile River on back.			
		a. 1.2.(19)81.	FV	3.00	10.00
		b. (19)82–89.	FV	2.50	8.50

1985 ISSUE

Cat. #	Denomination	Date, description	VG	VF	Unc
56	50 POUNDS	9.2.(19)93–. Brown, violet and m/c. Mosque at r. Isis above ancient boat, ruins at l. ctr. on back.	FV	FV	30.00

Cat. #	Denomination	Date, description	VG	VF	Unc
57	100 POUNDS	14.9.(19)94. Dk. brown and brown-violet on m/c unpt. Mosque at lower l. ctr. Sphinx at ctr. on back.	FV	FV	55.00

Arab Republic of Egypt

1971–91 CURRENCY NOTE ISSUES

Face: *ARAB REPUBLIC OF EGYPT* in Arabic.

Back: *ARAB REPUBLIC OF EGYPT* in English. Various sign. Imprint: Survey Authority or Postal Printing House.

Cat. #	Denomination	Date, description	VG	VF	Unc
80	5 PIASTRES	ND. Lilac. Qn. Nefertiti at r. Wmk: *U A R.*			
		a. Sign. Baghdady w/titles: *VICE-PRESIDENT AND MINISTER OF TREASURY.* Series 15; 16.	1.25	5.00	20.00
		b. Sign. Baissouni w/titles: *MINISTER OF TREASURY AND PLANNING.* Series 16-18.	.25	1.00	5.00
		c. Sign. Daif w/titles: *MINISTER OF TREASURY.* Color lilac to blue. Wmk: 3mm tall. Series 18-22.	.20	.75	4.00
		d. Sign. and titles as c. Wmk: 5mm tall. Series 22-26.	.20	.75	4.00
		e. Sign. Hegazy w/titles as d. Series 26-33.	.20	.75	4.00
80A	5 PIASTRES	ND. Face like #80. Back w/sign. Kaissouni title: *MINISTER OF TREASURY* (error). Series 16.	15.00	40.00	100.00
81	10 PIASTRES	ND. Black. Group of militants w/flag having only 2 stars.			
		a. Sign. Baghdady w/titles: *VICE-PRESIDENT AND MINISTER OF TREASURY.* Series 16.	1.50	6.00	22.00
		b. Sign. Kaissouni w/titles: *MINISTER OF TREASURY AND PLANNING.*	.40	1.50	6.00
		c. Sign. Kaissouni w/titles: *MINISTER OF TREASURY.* Series 16.	.05	.25	1.00
		d. Sign. Daif w/title as c. Series 18-24.	.25	1.00	5.00
		e. Sign. Hegazy w/title as c. Series 24-29.	.25	1.00	5.00

Cat. #	Denomination	Date, description	VG	VF	Unc
82	5 PIASTRES	ND. Lilac. Similar to #80. Imprint: Survey of Egypt.			
		a. Sign. Hegazy w/title: *MINISTER OF TREASURY.* Wmk: *U A R.* Series 33; 34.	1.00	3.50	15.00
		b. Sign. Hegazy w/title: *MINISTER OF TREASURY.* Wmk: *A R E.* Series 34-36.	.75	3.00	12.00
		c. Sign. Ibrahim w/title: *MINISTER OF FINANCE.* Wmk: *A R E.* Series 36; 37.	.35	1.50	6.00
		d. Sign. El Nashar w/title as c. Series 37.	.60	2.50	10.00
		e. Sign. Ismail. w/title as c. Series 37-40.	.20	.75	3.00
		f. Sign. M. S. Hamed. Series 40-42.	.25	1.00	4.00
		g. Sign. Loutfy. Series 42-47.	.20	.75	3.00
		h. Sign. Meguid. Series 47-50.	.15	.60	2.50
		i. Sign. Hamed. Series. 50.	2.00	6.00	20.00
		j. Like c. Imprint. Postal Printing House. Sign. Hamed. Series 50-72.	.10	.35	1.50
		k. Sign. El Razaz. Series 72.	.25	1.00	5.00
83	10 PIASTRES	ND. Black. Similar to #81. Imprint: Survey Authority.			
		a. Sign. Hegazy w/title: *MINISTER OF TREASURY.* Wmk: U A R. Series 29; 30.	2.00	8.00	35.00
		b. Sign. Hegazy w/title: *MINISTER OF TREASURY.* Wmk: A R E. Series 30; 31.	1.00	4.00	15.00
		c. Sign. Ibrahim w/title: *MINISTER OF FINANCE.* Wmk: A R A. Series 31; 32.	.45	1.75	7.00
		d. Sign. El Nashar w/titles as c. Series 32-33.	1.00	4.00	15.00
		e. Sign. Ismail w/titles as c. Series 33-35.	.25	1.00	4.00
		f. Sign. M. S. Hamed w/titles as c. Series 35-38.	.45	1.75	7.00
		g. Sign. Loutfy w/titles as c. Series 38-43.	.25	1.00	4.00
		h. Sign. Meguid w/titles as c. Series 43-46.	.20	.75	3.00
		i. Sign. Hamed w/titles as c. Series 46.	3.00	10.00	30.00
84	10 PIASTRES	ND. Black. Similar to #83 but new flag w/eagle instead of 2 starf. Sign. title: *MINISTER OF FINANCE.*			
		a. Sign. Hamed. Series 46-49.	.15	.50	2.00
		b. Sign. El Razaz. Series 69-75.	.20	.75	3.00

NOTE: Transitional series numbers from one signature to the next are generally much scarcer and command a premium. As of July, 1991 all Egyptian currency notes have been denomatized and withdrawn from circulation.

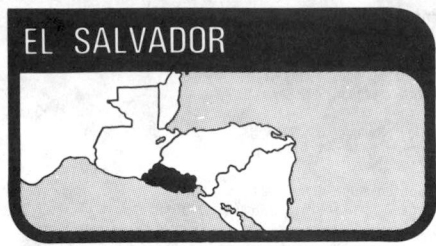

EL SALVADOR

The Republic of El Salvador, a Central American country bordered by Guatemala, Honduras and the Pacific Ocean, has an area of 8,260 sq. mi. (21,041 sq. km.) and a population of 5.05 million. Capital: San Salvador. This most intensely cultivated country of Latin America produces coffee (the major crop), cotton, sugar and balsam for export. Gold, silver and other metals are largely unexploited.

The first Spanish attempt to subjugate the area was undertaken in 1523 by Pedro de Alvarado, Cortes' lieutenant. He was forced to retreat by superior Indian forces, but returned in 1525 and succeeded in bringing the region under control of the captain generalcy of Guatemala, where it remained until 1821. In 1821, El Salvador and the other Central American provinces declared their independence from Spain. In 1823, the Federal Republic of Central America was formed by the five Central American States. When this federation was dissolved in 1829, El Salvador became an independent republic.

MONETARY SYSTEM
1 Colon = 100 Centavos 1919–

NOTE: This section has been reorgainzed by date issues from printing firms. The catalog numbers have been changed and are referenced to the old 7th Edition of General Issues.

Banco Central de Reserva de El Salvador

SUPERINTENDENCIA DE BANCOSE Y OTRAS INSTITUCIONES FINANCIERAS

Juan S. Quinteros	1962–1975	Marco T. Guandique	1977–Feb. 1981
Jose A. Mendoza	1968–1975	Rafael T. Carbonell	1981
Jorge A. Dowson	1975–1977	Raul Nolasco	1981–

1962–63 ISSUES

#100–138 backs w/Columbus at ctr., I. and later as wmk. also. Various date and sign. ovpts. on back w/different shields and seals.

#100–122, 133, and 138 black on m/c unpt.

#100–104 printer: TDLR.

Cat. #	Denomination	Date, description	VG	VF	Unc
100 (84)	1 COLON	12.3.1963; 25.1.1966; 23.8.1966. Central Bank at ctr. Back orange	1.00	2.50	10.00

Cat. #	Denomination	Date, description	VG	VF	Unc
101 (90)	2 COLONES	15.2.1962; 9.6.1964. Coffee bush at I. Back red-brown.	2.00	6.00	30.00

Cat. #	Denomination	Date, description	VG	VF	Unc
102 (94)	5 COLONES	15.2.1962; 12.3.1963. Woman w/basket of fruit on her head. Back green.	2.50	7.50	30.00

			VG	VF	Unc
103 (101A)	10 COLONES	15.2.1962; 9.6.1964; 27.12.1966. M. J. Arce at ctr., serial # at lower I. and upper r. Back brown.	3.00	10.00	40.00

			VG	VF	Unc
104 (105)	25 COLONES	12.3.1963; 27.12.1966. Reservoir at ctr. Back dk. blue.	6.50	20.00	70.00

1964–65 ISSUES

#105–107 printer: ABNC.

			VG	VF	Unc
105 (83A)	1 COLON	8.9.1964. Farmer plowing at ctr., SAN SALVADOR at upper I. Black serial # and series letters. Back orange.	2.00	8.00	22.50
106 (95)	5 COLONES	8.9.1964. Delgado addressing crowd at ctr., SAN SALVADOR at upper I. Black serial # at lower I. and upper r. Back green.	2.50	7.50	30.00

Cat. #	Denomination	Date, description	VG	VF	Unc
107 (110)	100 COLONES	12.1.1965. Brown and green unpt. Independence monument at ctr. but *SAN SALVA-DOR* at upper l. Serial # at lower l. and upper r. Back olive-green.	20.00	65.00	200.00

1967 COMMEMORATIVE ISSUE

#108–109 printer: TDLR.

Cat. #	Denomination	Date, description	VG	VF	Unc
108 (85)	1 COLON	20.6.1967. *UN COLON* at ctr. Jose Cañas, *SAN SALVADOR* and date at r. Back orange.	1.00	2.00	9.00

Cat. #	Denomination	Date, description	VG	VF	Unc
109 (96)	5 COLONES	20.6.1967. Pink and green unpt. Scene of 31.12.1823 at ctr.	2.00	5.00	20.00

NOTE: #108 and 109 are reportedly a commemorative for the bicentennial of the birth of Jose Cañas.

1968–70 ISSUE

#110–114 printer: USBNC.

Cat. #	Denomination	Date, description	VG	VF	Unc
110 (86)	1 COLON	1968; 1970. *1 COLON* at ctr., Jose Cañas at r. Back orange.			
		a. Sign. title: *CAJERO* at r. 13.8.1968.	.75	1.50	6.00
		b. Sign. title: *GERENTE* at r. 12.5.1970.	.75	1.50	6.00

Cat. #	Denomination	Date, description	VG	VF	Unc
111 (97)	5 COLONES	1968–70. Delgado addressing crowd at ctr., *5 COLONES* at r. Back dk. green; Columbus at l. and as wmk.			
		a. Sign. title: *CAJERO* at r. 13.8.1968; 4.2.1969.	1.25	3.50	12.50
		b. Sign. title: *GERENTE* at r. 12.5.1970.	1.25	3.50	12.50

Cat. #	Denomination	Date, description	VG	VF	Unc
112 (102)	10 COLONES	13.8.1968. *10 COLONES* at ctr., M. J. Arce at r. Back black. Wmk: Columbus.	3.00	8.00	30.00
113 (106)	25 COLONES	12.5.1970. Reservoir at r. Back dk. blue. Wmk: Columbus.	7.00	17.50	50.00

Cat. #	Denomination	Date, description	VG	VF	Unc
114 (111)	100 COLONES	12.5.1970. Brown and green unpt. Independence monument at ctr. Back olive-green.	17.50	45.00	145.00

1971–72 ISSUE

#115–119 printer: TDLR.

Cat. #	Denomination	Date, description	VG	VF	Unc
115 (87)	1 COLON	31.8.1971; 24.10.1972. *SAN SALVADOR* and date at l., *UN COLON* at ctr., Jose Cañas at r. Back red.	.50	1.00	2.50

Cat. #	Denomination	Date, description	VG	VF	Unc
116 (91)	2 COLONES	24.10.1972; 15.10.1974. Colonial church of Panchimalco at ctr., *DOS COLONES* at r., w/o wmk. Back red-brown.	.50	1.00	2.25

Cat. #	Denomination	Date, description	VG	VF	Unc
117 (98)	5 COLONES	31.8.1971–24.6.1976. Face like #97 but w/o *5 COLONES* at l., Delgado addressing crowd at ctr. Wmk: Columbus. Back green; Columbus at l. ctr. and as wmk.	FV	1.50	5.00

Cat. #	Denomination	Date, description	VG	VF	Unc
118 (103)	10 COLONES	13.8.1971–23.12.1976. *DIEZ COLONES* at ctr., M. J. Arce at r. Back black. Wmk: Columbus.	2.50	4.50	15.00

Cat. #	Denomination	Date, description	VG	VF	Unc
119 (107)	25 COLONES	31.8.1971. Reservoir at ctr. Similar to #106 but different design on face and back. Wmk: Columbus.	7.00	12.50	35.00

1974 ISSUE

#120–122 printer: TDLR.

120 (87A)	1 COLON	15.10.1974. Hydroelectric dam at ctr., w/o *UN COLON* at l. Back red, like #115.	.30	.75	2.25

121 (108)	25 COLONES	15.10.1974; 24.6.1976; 23.12.1976. Acajutla port scene. Back blue. Wmk: Columbus.	FV	8.00	22.50

122 (112)	100 COLONES	1974–79. Indian pyramid at Tazumal at ctr. Back olive. Wmk: Columbus.			
		a. Regular serial #. 15.10.1974–11.5.1978.	FV	20.00	80.00
		b. Electronic sorting serial #. 3.5.1979.	FV	FV	65.00

1976 ISSUE

#123–124 printer: TDLR.

123 (87B)	1 COLON	28.10.1976. Similar to #120 but *UN COLON* at l. Back like #125. W/o wmk.	.50	1.50	4.50

Cat. #	Denomination	Date, description	VG	VF	Unc
124 (91A)	2 COLONES	24.6.1976. Like #116, w/*DOS COLONES* at l. and r., but m/c unpt. in margins, w/o wmk. Denomination added to face at l. Arms at r. on back.	FV	FV	2.00

1977–79 ISSUE

Cat. #	Denomination	Date, description	VG	VF	Unc
125 (87C)	1 COLON	1977–82. Like #123 but m/c unpt. on margins Arms at r. on back. Printer: TDLR.			
		a. Regular style serial #. 7.7.1977; 11.5.1978.	FV	FV	1.75
		b. Electronic sorting serial #. 3.5.1979; 19.6.1980.	FV	FV	1.50
		c. W/o sign. title: *GERENTE* at r. 3.6.1982.	FV	FV	1.00

Cat. #	Denomination	Date, description	VG	VF	Unc
126 (98A)	5 COLONES	6.10.1977. Like #117, but *5 COLONES* at l. and r., m/c unpt. in margins, w/o wmk.	FV	FV	3.00

NOTE: For similar 5 Colones dated 19.6.1980 see #137.

Cat. #	Denomination	Date, description	VG	VF	Unc
127 (103A)	10 COLONES	1977–. *DIEZ COLONES* at ctr., M. J. Arce at ctr. r. Back black. Wmk: Columbus. Printer: ABNC.			
		a. Sign. title: *GERENTE* at r. 7.7.1977.	FV	4.00	7.00
		b. W/o sign. title: *GERENTE* at r. 25.8.1983; 17.3.1988.	FV	FV	4.00

Cat. #	Denomination	Date, description	VG	VF	Unc
128 (103B)	10 COLONES	13.10.1977. Like #127 but blue arms added to face and back. W/o wmk. Printer: ABNC.	2.50	4.00	9.50

Cat. #	Denomination	Date, description	VG	VF	Unc
129 (103C)	10 COLONES	1978–80. Black on m/c unpt. M.J. Arce at r., m/c unpt in margins. Back black. Wmk: Columbus. Printer: TDLR.			
		a. Regular serial #. 11.5.1978.	FV	2.50	6.00
		b. Electronic sorting serial #. 3.5.1979; 21.7.1980.	FV	2.00	5.00

Cat. #	Denomination	Date, description	VG	VF	Unc
130 (108A)	25 COLONES	1978–80. Like #121 but m/c unpt. in margins on face.			
		a. Regular serial #. 11.5.1978.	FV	6.00	20.00
		b. Electronic sorting serial #. 3.5.1979; 19.6.1980.	FV	5.00	12.00

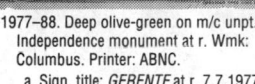

Cat. #	Denomination	Date, description	VG	VF	Unc
131 (115)	50 COLONES	1979; 1980. Purple and m/c. Lg. bldg. and statue at l., Capt. Gen. G. Barrios at r. Ships at l. on back. Wmk: Columbus. Printer: TDLR.			
		a. 3.5.1979.	FV	8.00	20.00
		b. 19.6.1980.	FV	7.50	17.50

Cat. #	Denomination	Date, description	VG	VF	Unc
132 (113)	100 COLONES	1977–88. Deep olive-green on m/c unpt. Independence monument at r. Wmk: Columbus. Printer: ABNC.			
		a. Sign. title: *GERENTE* at r. 7.7.1977.	FV	FV	55.00
		b. W/o sign. title: *GERENTE* at r. 29.9.1983.	FV	FV	37.50
		c. Like b. 17.3.1988.	FV	FV	30.00

Cat. #	Denomination	Date, description	VG	VF	Unc
133 (116)	100 COLONES	17.7.1980. Like #122 but w/flag below date at l. Printer: TDLR.	FV	FV	40.00

1983 ISSUE

134 (98Bb)	5 COLONES	25.8.1983; 17.3.1988. Delgade addressing crowd at ctr. W/o sign. title: *GERENTE* at r. Back green.	FV	FV	1.50
135 (108B)	25 COLONES	29.9.1983. Black on m/c unpt. Bridge and reservoir at ctr. W/o sign. title: *GERENTE* at r. Wmk: Columbus. Printer: ABNC.	FV	FV	8.00

1990–93 ISSUE

136 (98C)	5 COLONES	16.5.1990. Similar to #126 but w/o sign. title: *GERENTE* at r., w/electronic sorting serial #. Back olive-green and dk. gray. Printer: TDLR.	FV	FV	1.50
137 (98B)	5 COLONES	19.6.1980 (1992). Similar to #109 but w/sign. title: *GERENTE* at r. Printer: ABNC.	FV	FV	2.50
138 (117)	100 COLONES	12.3.1993. Black on pink, blue and pale green unpt. Like #133 but w/arms at upper l., flag at lower r. Printer: TDLR.	FV	FV	27.50

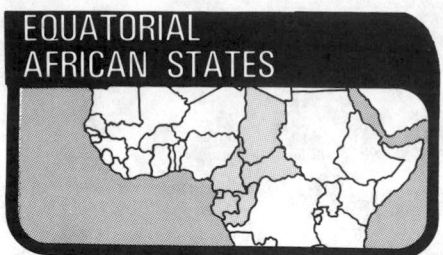

EQUATORIAL AFRICAN STATES

Equatorial African States (Central African States), a monetary union comprising the former French possessions and now independent states of the Republic of Congo (Brazzaville), Gabon, Central African Republic, Chad and Cameroon, issues a common currency for the member states from a common central bank. The monetary unit, the African Financial Community Franc, is tied to and supported by the French franc.

In 1960, an abortive attempt was made to form a union of the newly independent republics of Chad, Congo, Central Africa and Gabon. The proposal was discarded when Chad refused to become a constituent member. The four countries then linked into an Equatorial Customs Unit, to which Cameroon became an associate member in 1961. A more extensive cooperation of the five republics, identified as the Central African Customs and Economic Union, was entered into force at the beginning of 1966.

In 1974 the Central Bank of the Equatorial African States, which had issued coins and paper currency in its own name and with the names of the constituent member nations, changed its name to the Bank of the Central African States.

MONETARY SYSTEM

1 Franc (C.F.A.) = 100 Centimes

CONTROL LETTER or SYMBOL CODE		
Country	**Until 1993**	**1993 onward**
Cameroun	*	E
Central African Republic	B	F
Chad	A	P
Congo	C	C
Equatorial Guinea		N
Gabon	D	L

NOTE: Issues for the individual states are identified by a single code letter or symbol following the control #.

Banque Centrale des Etats de l'Afrique Equatoriale et du Cameroun

1961 (ND) ISSUES

Cat. #	Denomination	Date, description	VG	VF	Unc
1	100 FRANCS	ND (1961–62). Blue and m/c. Woman w/jug at l., Gov. Felix Eboue at ctr., people in canoe at r. Cargo ships at ctr., man at r. on back.			
		a. Code letter *A*.	15.00	60.00	200.00
		b. Code letter *B*.	15.00	65.00	225.00
		c. Code letter *C*.	15.00	60.00	200.00
		d. Code letter *D*.	15.00	60.00	200.00
		e. * for Cameroun.	50.00	150.00	350.00
		f. W/o code letter.	12.50	45.00	150.00
2	100 FRANCS	ND (1961–62). M/c. Like #1 but denomination also in English. W/* for Cameroun.	40.00	120.00	300.00

Banque Centrale des Etats de l'Afrique Equatoriale

1963 (ND) ISSUES

Cat. #	Denomination	Date, description	VG	VF	Unc
3	100 FRANCS	ND (1963). Brown and m/c. Musical instrument at l., hut at l. ctr., man at r. Elephant at l., tools at r. on back.			
		a. Code letter *A*.	8.00	25.00	60.00
		b. Code letter *B*.	8.00	25.00	60.00
		c. Code letter *C*.	8.00	25.00	60.00
		d. Code letter *D*.	8.00	25.00	60.00

Cat. #	Denomination	Date, description	VG	VF	Unc
7	10,000 FRANCS	ND (1968). M/c. Pres. Bokassa at r., highrise bldg. in background. Arms of Central African Republic at lower l. on back.			
		a. Code letter *A*.	200.00	425.00	900.00
		b. Code letter *B*.	200.00	425.00	900.00
		c. Code letter *C*.	200.00	425.00	900.00
		d. Code letter *D*.	200.00	425.00	900.00

Cat. #	Denomination	Date, description	VG	VF	Unc
4	500 FRANCS	ND (1963). Green and m/c. Girl wearing bandana at r., track mounted crane w/ore bucket in background. Radar unit at l., man on camel at r. on back.			
		a. Engraved. Code letter *A*.	15.00	70.00	250.00
		b. As a. Code letter *B*.	15.00	70.00	250.00
		c. As a. Code letter *C*.	18.00	85.00	300.00
		d. As a. Code letter *D*.	15.00	70.00	250.00
		e. Lithographed. Code letter *A*.	10.00	55.00	185.00
		f. As e. Code letter *B*.	10.00	55.00	185.00
		g. As e. Code letter *C*.	12.00	60.00	200.00
		h. As e. Code letter *D*.	10.00	55.00	185.00

Cat. #	Denomination	Date, description	VG	VF	Unc
5	1000 FRANCS	ND (1963). M/c. People gathering cotton. Young men logging on back.			
		a. Engraved. Code letter *A*.	15.00	70.00	250.00
		b. As a. Code letter *B*.	15.00	70.00	250.00
		c. As a. Code letter *C*.	18.00	90.00	300.00
		d. As a. Code letter *D*.	15.00	75.00	250.00
		e. Lithographed. Code letter *A*.	12.00	60.00	210.00
		f. As e. Code letter *B*.	12.00	60.00	210.00
		g. As e. Code letter *C*.	15.00	80.00	275.00
		h. As e. Code letter *D*.	12.00	60.00	210.00

Cat. #	Denomination	Date, description	VG	VF	Unc
6	5000 FRANCS	ND (1963). M/c. Girl at l., village scene at ctr. Carving at l., airplane, train crossing bridge and tractor hauling logs at ctr., man smoking a pipe at r. on back.			
		a. Code letter *A*.	125.00	300.00	650.00
		b. Code letter *B*.	125.00	300.00	650.00
		c. Code letter *C*.	125.00	300.00	650.00
		d. Code letter *D*.	125.00	300.00	650.00
		s. Specimen.	—	—	450.00

The Republic of Equatorial Guinea (formerly Spanish Guinea) consists of Rio Muni, located on the coast of west-central Africa between Cameroon and Gabon, and the off-shore islands of Fernando Po, Annobon, Corisco, Elobey Grande and Elobey Chico. The equatorial country has an area of 10,831 sq. mi. (28,051 sq. km.) and a population of 417,000. Capital: Malabo. The economy is based on agriculture and for-estry. Cacao, wood and coffee are exported.

Fernando Po was discovered between 1474 and 1496 by Portuguese navigators charting a route to the spice islands of the Far East. Portugal retained control of it and the adjacent islands until 1778 when they, together with trading rights to the African coast between the Ogooue and Niger rivers, were ceded to Spain. Fernando Po was administered, with Spanish consent, by the British from 1827 to 1844 when it was reclaimed by Spain. Mainland Rio Muni was granted to Spain by the Berlin Conference of 1885. The name of the colony was changed from Spanish Guinea to Equatorial Guinea in Dec. of 1963. Independence was attained on Oct. 12, 1968.

MONETARY SYSTEM

1 Peseta Guineana = 100 Centimos to 1975
1 Ekuele = 100 Centimos, 1975–80
1 Epkwele (pl. Bipkwele) = 100 Centimos, 1980–85
1 Franc (C.F.A.) = 100 Centimes, 1985–
1 Franco (C.F.A.) = 4 Bipkwele

REPLACEMENT NOTES

#4–8A, Z/1 prefix.

REPUBLIC
Banco Central
Peseta System

1969 ISSUE

#1–3 printer: FNMT.

Cat. #	Denomination	Date, description	VG	VF	Unc
1	100 PESETAS GUINEANAS	12.10.1969. Red-brown on lt. tan unpt. Banana tree at l. Shoreline and man w/boat on back. Wmk: Woman's head.	1.00	3.00	9.00

Cat. #	Denomination	Date, description	VG	VF	Unc
2	500 PESETAS GUINEANAS	12.10.1969. Green. Derrick loading logs at l., shoreline at ctr. Woman w/bundle on head at r. on back. Wmk: Man's head.	2.00	6.00	18.00

3	1000 PESETAS GUINEANAS	12.10.1969. Blue. Pres. M. Nguema Biyogo at ctr. Tree at l., arms at ctr. on back. Wmk: King and queen.	2.75	6.50	20.00

Banco Popular

Ekuele System

1975 FIRST DATED ISSUE

#4–8 w/Pres. M.N. Biyogo at r. and as wmk. Name under portrait: *MACIAS NGUEMA BIYOGO.* Printer: TDLR.

4	25 EKUELE	7.7.1975. Purple on lt. orange and green unpt. Trees at ctr. Arms at l., bridge at ctr. on back. Name underneath: *PUENTE MACIAS NGUEMA BIYOGO.*	.65	1.60	3.75

5	50 EKUELE	7.7.1975. Brown on green and pink unpt. Plants at ctr. Arms at l., logging at ctr. on back.	.65	1.60	4.00

#6–8 arms at ctr.

Cat. #	Denomination	Date, description	VG	VF	Unc
6	100 EKUELE	7.7.1975. Green on pink and m/c unpt. Bridge and boats on back.	.65	1.60	4 50

7	500 EKUELE	7.7.1975. Blue on m/c unpt. National Palace on back.	1.25	4.00	12.50

8	1000 EKUELE	7.7.1975. Red on m/c unpt. Bank on back.	2.00	4.00	10.00

1975 SECOND DATED ISSUE

#4A–8A like #4-8 but name under portrait: *MASIE NGUEMA BIYOGO NEGUE NDONG*. Different sign. also.

4A	25 EKUELE	7.7.1975. Like #4 except for name change on both sides.	1.00	2.00	6.00
5A	50 EKUELE	7.7.1975. Like #5 except for name change.	1.00	2.50	6.00

Cat. #	Denomination	Date, description	VG	VF	Unc
6A	100 EKUELE	7.7.1975. Like #6 except for name change on both sides.	1.00	2.50	6.00
7A	500 EKUELE	7.7.1975. Like #7 except for name change.	1.50	4.00	10.00
8A	1000 EKUELE	7.7.1975. Like #8 except for name change.	1.50	3.50	8.50

Banco de Guinea Ecuatorial

Bipkwele System

1979 ISSUE

#9–12 wmk: T.E. Nkogo. Printer: FNMT.

9	100 BIPKWELE	3.8.1979. Dk. olive-green and m/c. Arms at ctr., T.E. Nkogo at r. Boats along pier of Puerto de Bata on back.	1.75	4.00	10.00

10	500 BIPKWELE	3.8.1979. Black on green and pink unpt. Arms at ctr., R. Uganda at r. Back brown and black; sailboat, shoreline and trees.	3.00	8.00	20.00

11	1000 BIPKWELE	3.8.1979. Brown, black and m/c. Arms at ctr., R. Bioko at r. Back maroon and brown; men cutting food plants.	5.00	12.50	35.00

Cat. #	Denomination	Date, description	VG	VF	Unc
12	5000 BIPKWELE	3.8.1979. Blue-gray on m/c unpt. Arms at ctr., E.N. Okenve at r. Back blue-gray and blue; logging scene at ctr.	3.00	7.50	22.50

1980 PROVISIONAL ISSUE

| 13 | 1000 BIPKWELE | 21.10.1980. Black ovpt. of new denomination and date on #1. (Not issued). | — | 3.50 | 17.50 |

| 14 | 5000 BIPKWELE | 21.10.1980. Similar red ovpt. on #2. (Not issued). | — | 6.00 | 22.50 |

NOTE: #13 and 14 were prepared for issue but not released to circulation. Shortly afterwards, Equatorial Guinea began the use of CFA franc currency. #3 was not ovpt. because it carries the portrait of former Pres. Biyogo.

Banque des Etats de l'Afrique Centrale

Franco/Franc System

1985 ISSUE

#15–17 wmk: Carving (as printed on notes). Sign. 9 (from list at Central African States).

Cat. #	Denomination	Date, description	VG	VF	Unc
15	500 FRANCOS	1.1.1985. Brown on m/c unpt. Carving and jug at ctr. Man carving mask at l. ctr. on back.	FV	3.00	6.00

| 16 | 1000 FRANCOS | 1.1.1985. Blue and m/c. Animal carving at lower l., map at ctr., starburst at lower r. Incomplete map of Chad at upper ctr. Elephant at l., statue at r. on back. | FV | 6.00 | 10.00 |

| 17 | 5000 FRANCOS | 1.1.1985; 1.1.1986. Brown, yellow and m/c. Carved mask at l., woman carrying bundle at r. Farmer plowing w/tractor at l., ore lift at r. on back. | FV | 20.00 | 35.00 |

1995 ISSUE

| 18 | 2000 FRANCS | (1995). | — | — | 11.00 |

ESTONIA

The Republic of Estonia (formerly the Estonian Soviet Socialist Republic of the U.S.S.R.) is the northernmost of the three Baltic states in eastern Europe. It has an area of 17,413 sq. mi. (45,100 sq. km.) and a population of 1.6 million. Capital: Tallinn. Agriculture and dairy farming are the principal industries. Butter, eggs, bacon, timber and petroleum are exported.

This small and ancient Baltic state has enjoyed but two decades of independence since the 13th century. After having been conquered by the Danes, the Livonian Knights, the Teutonic Knights of Germany (who reduced the people to serfdom), the Swedes, the Poles and Russia, Estonia declared itself an independent republic on Nov. 15, 1917, but was not freed until Feb. 1919. The peace treaty was signed Feb. 2, 1920. Shortly after the start of World War II, it was again occupied by Russia and incorporated as the 16th state of the U.S.S.R. Germany occupied the tiny state from 1941 to 1944, after which it was retaken by Russia. Some of the nations of the world, including the United States and Great Britain, did not recognize Estonia's incorporation as an S.S.R. into the Soviet Union.

On August 20, 1991, the Parliament of the Estonian S.S.R. voted to reassert the republic's independence.

MONETARY SYSTEM
1 Kroon = 100 Senti, 1928–1941

The U.S.S.R. ruble circulated from 1944 until 1991.

REPLACEMENT NOTES

#69-70, asterisk in front of serial #. #71-75, ZZ prefix.

Eesti Pank — Bank of Estonia

1991–92 ISSUE

#69–70 wmk: Parliament bldg. in Tallinn. Paper w/vertical security thread.

Cat. #	Denomination	Date, description	VG	VF	Unc
69	1 KROON	1992. Brownish black on yellow-orange and dull violet-brown unpt. K. Raud at l. Toompea Castle w/Tall Hermann (national landmarks) on back.	FV	FV	.50

Cat. #	Denomination	Date, description	VG	VF	Unc
70	2 KROONI	1992. Black on lt. blue-violet and grayish-green unpt. K.E. von Baer at l. Tartu University bldg. at ctr. on back.	FV	FV	.75

#71–75 Bank arms at upper r. Wmk: Three lions. Paper w/vertical security thread.

Cat. #	Denomination	Date, description	VG	VF	Unc
71	5 KROONI	1991 (1993). Black and tan on m/c unpt. P. Keres at ctr., chessboard and arms at upper r. Teutonic Fortress along Narva River, church on back.	FV	FV	1.50

| 72 | 10 KROONI | 1991 (1993). Purple and red-violet on m/c unpt. J. Hurt at l. ctr. Tamme-lauri oak tree at Urvaste at r. on back. | FV | FV | 2.50 |

| 73 | 25 KROONI | 1991 (1993). Deep olive-green on m/c unpt. A. Hansen-Tammsaare at l. ctr., wilderness in background at r. Early rural log construction farm; view of Vargamäe on back. | FV | FV | 6.00 |

| 74 | 100 KROONI | 1991 (1993). Black and deep blue on lt. blue and m/c unpt. L. Koidula at l. ctr., cuckoo bird at lower r. Waves breaking against rocky cliffs of Northcoast at ctr. to r. on back. | FV | FV | 22.50 |

Cat. #	Denomination	Date, description	VG	VF	Unc
75	500 KROONI	1991 (1993). Blue-black and purple on m/c unpt. C. R. Jakobson at l. ctr., harvest between 2 farmers with Sakala above at r. Barn swallow in flight over rural pond at r. on back.	FV	FV	80.00

1995–96 ISSUE

76	5 KROONI				Expected new issue.
77	10 KROONI				Expected new issue.

78	50 KROONI	1994. Green and black on m/c unpt. R. Tobias at l. ctr., gates at lower ctr. r. Opera House in Tallinn at ctr. r. on back.	FV	FV	11.00
79	100 KROONI	1994. Black and dk. blue on m/c unpt. Like #74 but w/gray seal at upper l.	FV	FV	20.00
80	500 KROONI	1994. Like #75.	FV	FV	75.00

ETHIOPIA

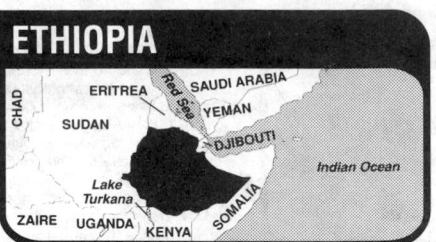

The Peoples Democratic Republic of Ethiopia, faces on the Red Sea in east-central Africa. The country has an area of 424,214 sq. mi. (1.099,900 sq. km.) and a population of 55 million people who are divided among 40 tribes and speak 270 languages and dialects. Capital: Addis Ababa. The economy is predominantly agricultural and pastoral. Gold and platinum are mined and petroleum fields are being developed. Coffee, oil-seeds, hides and cereals are exported.

Legend claims that Menelik I, the son born to Solomon, King of Israel, by the Queen of Sheba, settled in Axum in Northern Ethiopia to establish the dynasty which then reigned – with only brief interruptions – until 1974. Modern Ethiopian history began with the reign of Emperor Menelik II (1889–1913) under whose guidance the country emerged from medieval isolation. Ethiopia was invaded by Mussolini in 1935, and together with Italian Somaliland and Eritrea became part of Italian East Africa until liberated by British and Ethiopian troops in 1941. Haile Selassie I, 225th consecutive Solomonic ruler, was deposed by a military committee on Sept. 12, 1974. In July 1976, Ethiopia's military provisional government referred to the country as Socialist Ethiopia.

Eritrea, a former Ethiopian province fronting on the Red Sea, was an Italian colony from 1890 until its incorporation into Italian East Africa in 1936. It was under British military administration from 1941 to Sept. 15, 1952, when the United Nations designated it an autonomous unit within the federation of Ethiopia and Eritrea. On Nov. 14, 1962, it was fully integrated with Ethiopia. On May 24, 1993, Eritrea became an independent nation.

RULERS
Haile Selassie I, 1930–1936, 1941–1974

MONETARY SYSTEM
1 Birr (Dollar) = 100 Canteems (Cents), 1941–

REPLACEMENT NOTES
#30–39, ZZ prefix.

KINGDOM
State Bank of Ethiopia

Dollar System

1961 (ND) ISSUE
#18–24 Haile Selassie at r. Arms at ctr. on back. Printer: BWC.

Cat. #	Denomination	Date, description	VG	VF	Unc
18	1 DOLLAR	ND (1961). Green on lilac and lt. orange unpt. Coffee bushes at l.	3.00	15.00	45.00

19	5 DOLLARS	ND (1961). Orange on green and m/c unpt. University (old palace) at l.	7.50	35.00	125.00
20	10 DOLLARS	ND (1961). Red on m/c unpt. Harbor at Massawa at l.	20.00	65.00	250.00

Cat. #	Denomination	Date, description	VG	VF	Unc
21	20 DOLLARS	ND (1961). Brown on m/c unpt. Ancient stone monument (Axum) at l.	30.00	125.00	385.00
22	50 DOLLARS	ND (1961). Blue on m/c unpt. Bridge over Blue Nile at l.	90.00	250.00	700.00
23	100 DOLLARS	ND (1961). Purple on m/c unpt. Trinity Church at Addis Ababa at l.			
		a. Sign. title: *GOVERNOR*.	100.00	250.00	700.00
		b. Sign. title: *ACTING GOVERNOR*.	70.00	200.00	550.00
24	500 DOLLARS	ND (1961). Dk. green on m/c unpt. Castle at Gondar at l.	250.00	600.00	1500.

National Bank of Ethiopia

1966 ISSUE

#25–29 Emperor Haile Selassie at r. Arms at ctr. on back. Printer: TDLR.

25	1 DOLLAR	ND (1966). Green on m/c unpt. Aerial view of Massawa harbor, city at l.	2.00	6.00	20.00

26	5 DOLLARS	ND (1966). Brown on m/c unpt. Bole-Airport Addis Ababa at l. Back orange.	5.00	20.00	85.00

27	10 DOLLARS	ND (1966). Dk. red on m/c unpt. National Bank at Addis Ababa at l.	3.00	10.00	40.00

28	50 DOLLARS	ND (1966). Blue on m/c unpt. Koka High Dam at l.	20.00	75.00	275.00

Cat. #	Denomination	Date, description	VG	VF	Unc
29	100 DOLLARS	ND (1966). Purple on green and m/c unpt. Bet Giorgis in Lalibela (rock church) at l.	15.00	55.00	175.00

REPUBLIC

Birr System

Law EE 1969 (1976 AD)

ARMS VARIETIES

Type A   Type B   Type C   Type D

SIGNATURE VARIETIES			
1 T. Deguefe, 1974–76 CHAIRMAN OF THE BOARD		**3** B. Tamirat, 1987–91 ADMINISTRATOR	
2 T. G. Kidan, 1978–87 ADMINISTRATOR		**4** L. Berhann, 1991– GOVERNOR	

1976 (ND) ISSUE

#30–34 have map at l., lion head in unpt. at l. ctr.

30	1 BIRR	L.EE1969 (1976). Black on green on lt. brown and green unpt. Young man at ctr. r., longhorns at r. Back black on m/c unpt; birds and Tisisat waterfalls of Blue Nile on back.			
		a. Sign. 1.	.50	2.00	5.00
		b. Sign. 2.	.25	1.50	2.50

31	5 BIRR	L.EE1969 (1976). Black and brown-orange on m/c unpt. Man picking coffee beans at ctr. r., plant at r. Kudu, leopard and Semien Mountains on back.			
		a. Sign. 1.	1.00	4.00	8.00
		b. Sign. 2.	1.25	3.50	7.00

Cat. #	Denomination	Date, description	VG	VF	Unc
32	10 BIRR	*L.EE1969* (1976). Brown, violet and red on m/c unpt. Woman weaving basket at ctr. r., basket w/lid at r. Plowing w/tractor on back.			
		a. Sign. 1.	3.00	8.00	15.00
		b. Sign. 2.	2.50	5.00	10.00

33	50 BIRR	*L.EE1969* (1976). Blue-black and dk. brown on lilac and m/c unpt. Science students at ctr. r., musical instrument at r. Fasilides Castle on back.			
		a. Sign. 1.	12.50	22.50	50.00
		b. Sign. 2.	11.50	20.00	40.00

34	100 BIRR	*L.EE1969* (1976). Purple, violet and dk. brown on m/c unpt. Warrior standing at ctr. r., flowers at r. Young man w/microscope on back.			
		a. Sign. 1.	25.00	45.00	75.00
		b. Sign. 2.	20.00	35.00	65.00

1987 (ND) ISSUE

#36–40 similar to #30–34 but w/ornate tan design at l. and r. edges on back. Sign. 3.

36 (30A)	1 BIRR	*L.EE1969* (1987). Like #30.	.20	1.00	1.75
37 (31c)	5 BIRR	*L.EE1969* (1987). Like #31.	.85	2.50	5.00
38 (32c)	10 BIRR	*L.EE1969* (1987). Like #32.	1.50	3.50	7.50
39 (33c)	50 BIRR	*L.EE1969* (1987). Like #33.	10.00	17.50	35.00
40 (35)	100 BIRR	*L.EE1969* (1976). Like #34 but w/flowers and dark shield at r.	20.00	32.50	55.00

1991 ISSUE

#41–45 like #36–40 but w/new arms Type B, C or D at r. on back.

Cat. #	Denomination	Date, description	VG	VF	Unc
41 (36)	1 BIRR	*L.EE1969* (1991). Like #36. Arms Type D.			
		a. Sign. 3 w/title in Amharic script.	FV	FV	1.50
		b. Sign. 4 w/title: *GOVERNOR* and also in Amharic script.	FV	FV	1.25
42 (37)	5 BIRR	*L.EE1969* (1991). Like #37. Arms Type B.			
		a. Sign 3 w/title in Amharic script. Arms Type B.	FV	FV	4.50
		b. Sign. 4 w/title *GOVERNOR* and also in Amheric script. Arms Type C.	FV	FV	4.00

43 (38)	10 BIRR	*L.EE1969* (1991). Like #38. Arms Type D.			
		a. Sign. 3 w/title in Amharic script.	FV	FV	7.50
		b. Sign. 4 w/title: *GOVERNOR* and also in Amharic script. Sign. 4	FV	FV	6.00

44 (39)	50 BIRR	*L.EE1969* (1991). Like #33.			
		a. Sign. 3 w/title in Amharic script. Arms Type B.	FV	FV	40.00
		b. Sign. 4 w/title: *GOVERNOR* and also in Amharic script. Arms Type C.	FV	FV	35.00
		c. As b. Arms Type D.	FV	FV	30.00

45 (40)	100 BIRR	*L.EE1969* (1991). Like #34 and #35. Arms Type D.			
		a. Sign. 3 w/title in Amharic script.	FV	FV	50.00
		b. Sign. 4 w/title: *GOVERNOR* and also in Amharic script.	FV	FV	45.00

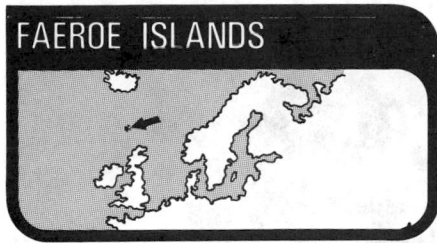

FAEROE ISLANDS

The Faeroe Islands, a self-governing community within the kingdom of Denmark, are situated in the North Atlantic between Iceland and the Shetland Islands. The 17 inhabited islets and reefs have an area of 540 sq. mi. (1,399 sq. km.) and a population of 48,000. Capital: Thorshavn. The principal industries are fishing and grazing. Fish and fish products are exported.

While it is thought that Irish hermits lived on the islands in the 7th and 8th centuries, the present inhabitants are descended from the 6th century Norse settlers. The Faeroe Islands became a Norwegian fief in 1035 and became Danish in 1380 when Norway and Denmark were united. They have ever since remained in Danish possession and were granted self-government (except for an appointed governor-general) with their own legislature, executive and flag in 1948.

The islands were occupied by British troops during World War II, after the German occupation of Denmark.

RULERS
Danish

MONETARY SYSTEM
1 Króne = 100 Øre

NOTE: This section has been reorgainzed by date issues from printing firms. The catalog numbers have been changed and are referenced to the old 7th Edition of General Issues.

REPLACEMENT NOTES

#16–23: suffix OJ or OK on series number.

Føroyar

Law of 12.4.1949

1951–54 ISSUE

Cat. #	Denomination	Date, description	VG	VF	Unc
13	5 KRÓNER	*L.1949* (1951–60). Black on green unpt. Coin w/ram at l. Fishermen w/boat on green back.			
		a. Sign. C. A. Vagn-Hansen and Kr. Djurhuus.	5.00	30.00	100.00
		b. Sign. N. Elkaer-Hansen and Kr. Djurhuus.	5.00	30.00	100.00

14	10 KRÓNER	*L.1949* (1954). Black on orange unpt. Shield w/ram at l. Rural scene on orange back.			
		a. Sign. C. A. Vagn-Hansen and Kr. Djurhuus. Wmk: *10. 10.5mm.*	3.00	5.00	25.00
		b. Sign. M. Wahl and P. M. Dam. Wmk: *10.* 13mm.	2.50	4.00	12.50
		c. Sign. M. Wahl and A. P. Dam.	2.00	3.50	8.00

Cat. #	Denomination	Date, description	VG	VF	Unc
15	100 KRÓNER	*L.1949* (1952–63). Blue-green. Porpoises on back. Irregular margins at l. and r. (straight margins are trimmed).			
		a. Sign. C. A. Vagn-Hansen and Kr. Djurhuus.	25.00	65.00	200.00
		b. Sign. N. Elkaer-Hansen and Kr. Djurhuus.	25.00	65.00	200.00
		c. Sign. M. Wahl and P. M. Dam.	25.00	65.00	200.00

1964–74 ISSUE

#16–23 have coded year dates in the l. series # (the 2 middle digits). Wmk: Anchor chain.

16 (18)	10 KRÓNER	*L.1949* (19)74. Green. Like #14. Sign. of L. Groth and A. P. Dam.	FV	FV	5.00
		e. Sign. B. Klinte and J. Sundstein. (19)90.	FV	FV	27.50
17	50 KRÓNER	*L.1949* (19)67. Black on lt. blue and blue-green unpt. N. Pall at l. Back blue on green unpt. Drawing of homes and church across ctr. Sign. M. Wahl and P. M. Dam.	11.50	17.50	27.50

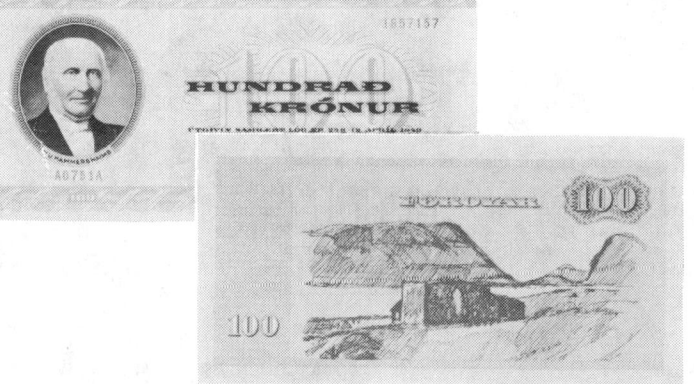

Cat. #	Denomination	Date, description	VG	VF	Unc
18 (16)	100 KRÓNER	L.1949 (19)64; 69; 72; 75. Black on pink and gold unpt. V. U. Hammershaimb at l. Back blue on tan unpt. Drawing of house and mountains on back.			
		a. Sign. M. Wahl and H. Djurhuus (19)64.	20.00	32.50	60.00
		b. Sign. M. Wahl and Kr. Djurhuus (19)69; 72.	20.00	32.50	60.00
		c. Sign. L. Groth and A. P. Dam. (19)75.	20.00	30.00	50.00

1976–86 ISSUE

Cat. #	Denomination	Date, description	VG	VF	Unc
19 (23)	20 KRONOR	L.1949 (19)86; 88. Deep purple on pink and aqua unpt. Man w/ice tool at r. Back red and black; drawing of animals at ctr.			
		a. Sign. N. Bentsen and A. P. Dam. (19)86.	FV	FV	5.50
		b. Sign. B. Klinte and A. P. Dam. (19)88.	FV	FV	5.50

Cat. #	Denomination	Date, description	VG	VF	Unc
20 (20)	50 KRÓNER	L.1949 (19)78; 87. Black on lt. blue and gray unpt. Similar to #17 but reduced size. 140 x 72mm. Back black on gray unpt. Wmk: Chain links.			
		a. Sign. L. Groth and A. P. Dam. (19)78.	FV	FV	15.00
		b. Sign. N. Bentsen and A. P. Dam. (19)87.	FV	FV	14.00

Cat. #	Denomination	Date, description	VG	VF	Unc
21 (19)	100 KRÓNER	L.1949 (19)78; 83; 87; 88; 90. Black on tan unpt. Similar to #16 but reduced size. Back black and green on ochre unpt. Wmk: Chain links.			
		a. Sign. L. Groth and A. P. Dam (19)78.	FV	FV	35.00
		b. Sign. N. Bentsen and P. Ellefsen. (19)83.	FV	FV	32.50
		c. Sign. N. Bentsen and A. P. Dam. (19)87.	FV	FV	30.00
		d. Sign. B. Klinte and A. P. Dam. (19)88.	FV	FV	28.50

Cat. #	Denomination	Date, description	VG	VF	Unc
22 (21)	500 KRÓNER	L.1949 (19)78–. Black on green and dull purple unpt. Fisherman at r. Fishermen in boat at sea on back. Sign. L. Groth and A. P. Dam.	FV	FV	135.00

Cat. #	Denomination	Date, description	VG	VF	Unc
23 (22)	1000 KRÓNER	L.1949 (19)78; 83; 87; 89. Blue-green, black and green. H. O. Djurhuus at l. Street scene on back.			
		a. Sign. L. Groth and A. P. Dam. (19)78.	FV	FV	250.00
		b. Sign. N. Bentsen and P. Ellefsen. (19)83.	FV	FV	225.00
		c. Sign. N. Bentsen and A. P. Dam. (19)87.	FV	FV	210.00
		d. Sign. B. Klinte and A. P. Dam. (19)89.	FV	FV	200.00

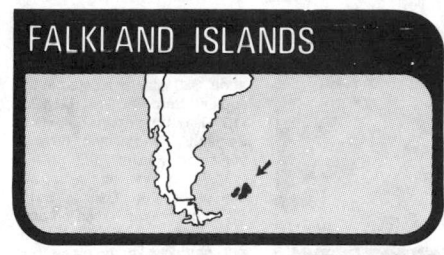

FALKLAND ISLANDS

The Colony of the Falkland Islands and Dependencies, a British colony located in the South Atlantic about 500 miles northeast of Cape Horn, has an area of 4,700 sq. mi. (12,173 sq. km.) and a population of 2,100. East Falkland, West Falkland, South Georgia, and South Sandwich are the largest of the 200 islands. Capital: Stanley. Sheep grazing is the main industry. Wool, whale oil, and seal oil are exported.

The Falklands were discovered by British navigator John Davis (Davys) in 1592, and named by Capt. John Strong — for Viscount Falkland, treasurer of the British navy — in 1690. French navigator Louis De Bougainville established the first settlement, at Port Louis, in 1764. The following year Capt. John Byron claimed the islands for Britain and left a small party at Saunders Island. Spain later forced the French and British to abandon their settlements but did not implement its claim to the islands. In 1829 the Republic of Buenos Aires, which claimed to have inherited the Spanish rights, sent Louis Vernet to develop a colony on the islands. In 1831 he seized three American sailing vessels, whereupon the men of the corvette, *U.S.S. Lexington*, destroyed his settlement and proclaimed the Falklands to be "free of all governance." Britain, which had never renounced its claim, then re-established its settlement in 1833.

RULERS
British

MONETARY SYSTEM
1 Shilling = 12 Pence
1 Pound = 20 Shillings to 1966
1 Pound = 100 Pence, 1966–

The Government of the Falkland Islands

Pound/Shilling System

1960–67 ISSUE

#7–11 portr. Qn. Elizabeth II at r. Printer: TDLR.

Cat. #	Denomination	Date, description	VG	VF	Unc
7	10 SHILLINGS	10.4.1960. Brown on gray unpt.	5.00	20.00	90.00

Cat. #	Denomination	Date, description	VG	VF	Unc
8	1 POUND	1967–82. Blue on gray-green and lilac unpt.			
		a. 2.1.1967.	2.00	5.00	27.50
		b. 20.2.1974.	1.75	3.50	20.00
		c. 1.12.1977.	2.50	10.00	40.00
		d. 1.1.1982.	2.00	6.00	28.50
		e. 15.6.1982.	1.75	3.00	20.00

Cat. #	Denomination	Date, description	VG	VF	Unc
9	5 POUNDS	1960; 1975. Red on green unpt.			
		a. Sign: L. Gleadell: 10.4.1960.	9.00	20.00	95.00
		b. Sign: H. T. Rowlands: 30.1.1975.	7.50	15.00	75.00

Pound/Pence System

1969–84 ISSUE

Cat. #	Denomination	Date, description	VG	VF	Unc
10	50 PENCE	1969; 1974. Brown on gray unpt.			
		a. Sign: L. Gleadell. 25.9.1969.	1.50	3.50	18.00
		b. Sign: H.T. Rowlands. 20.2.1974.	1.25	3.00	15.00

Cat. #	Denomination	Date, description	VG	VF	Unc
11	10 POUNDS	1975–82. Green on lt. orange and yellow-green unpt. Sign. H. T. Rowlands.			
		a. 5.6.1975.	17.50	25.00	100.00
		b. 1.1.1982.	18.50	30.00	150.00
		c. 15.6.1982.	16.50	20.00	90.00

Cat. #	Denomination	Date, description	VG	VF	Unc
12	1 POUND	1.10.1984. Blue on brown and yellow unpt. Qn. Elizabeth II at r., penguins and shield at l., seals at r. Governor's home and church on back.	FV	2.50	15.00

1983 COMMEMORATIVE ISSUE

#13, 150th Anniversary of English rule 1833–1983

Cat. #	Denomination	Date, description	VG	VF	Unc
13	5 POUNDS	14.6.1983. Red on m/c unpt. Like #12. Commemorative legend at lower ctr.	FV	FV	15.00

1984–90 ISSUE

#14–16 Qn. Elizabeth II at r.

14	10 POUNDS	1.9.1986. Gray-green on m/c unpt. Like #12.	FV	FV	27.00

15	20 POUNDS	1.10.1984. Brown on m/c unpt. Like #12.	FV	FV	50.00

16	50 POUNDS	1.7.1990. Blue on m/c unpt. Like #12.	FV	FV	115.00

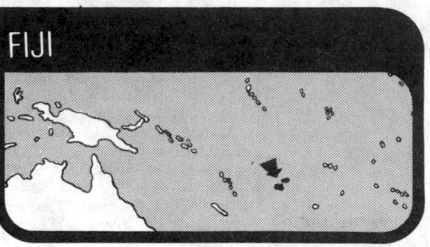

FIJI

The Dominion of Fiji, an independent member of the British Commonwealth, consists of about 320 islands located in the southwestern Pacific 1,100 miles (1,770 km.) north of New Zealand. The islands have a combined area of 7,056 sq. mi. (18,274 sq. km.) and a population of 747,000. Capital: Suva. Fiji's economy is based on agriculture and mining. Sugar, coconut products, manganese and gold are exported.

The Fiji Islands were discovered by Dutch navigator Abel Tasman in 1643 and visited by British naval captain James Cook in 1774. The first complete survey of the island was conducted by the United States in 1840. Settlement by missionaries from Tonga and traders attracted by the sandalwood trade began in 1835. Following a lengthy period of intertribal warfare, the islands were unconditionally and voluntarily ceded to Great Britain in 1874 by King Thakombau. Fiji became a sovereign and independent nation on Oct. 10, 1970, the 96th anniversary of the cession of the islands to Queen Victoria. It is a member of the Commonwealth of Nations. The Queen of England is Chief of State.

RULERS
British

MONETARY SYSTEM
1 Shilling = 12 Pence
1 Pound = 20 Shillings to 1969
1 Dollar = 100 Cents, 1969–

REPLACEMENT NOTES
#37–72: Z/1 prefix.

Government of Fiji
Pound/Shilling System
1953–57 ISSUE

#30–36 arms at upper ctr., portr. Qn. Elizabeth II at r. Printer: BWC.

Cat. #	Denomination	Date, description	VG	VF	Unc
30	5 SHILLINGS	1957–65. Green and blue on lilac and green unpt.			
		a. 1.6.1957; 28.4.1961; 1.12.1962.	2.00	7.50	65.00
		b. 1.9.1964; 1.12.1964; 1.10.1965.	1.50	6.00	50.00

31	10 SHILLINGS	1957–65. Brown on lilac and green unpt.			
		a. 1.6.1957; 28.4.1961; 1.12.1962.	3.00	22.50	235.00
		b. 1.9.1964; 1.10.1965.	2.50	15.00	185.00

Cat. #	Denomination	Date, description	VG	VF	Unc
32	1 POUND	1954–67. Green on yellow and blue unpt.			
		a. 1.7.1954; 1.6.1957; 1.9.1959.	8.00	25.00	170.00
		b. 1.12.1961–1.1.1967.	3.00	20.00	150.00
33	5 POUNDS	1954–67. Purple on lt. orange and green unpt.			
		a. 1.7.1954; 1.9.1959; 1.10.1960.	40.00	225.00	1000.
		b. 1.12.1962; 20.1.1964; 1.12.1964; 1.1.1967.	30.00	200.00	750.00

Cat. #	Denomination	Date, description	VG	VF	Unc
34	10 POUNDS	1954–64. Blue.			
		a. 1.7.1954.	75.00	375.00	1500.
		b. 1.9.1959; 1.10.1960; 20.1.1964; 11.6.1964.	50.00	285.00	700.00
35	20 POUNDS	1.1.1953. Black and violet. *GOVERNMENT OF FIJI* at ctr. on back.	350.00	1500.	3750.
36	20 POUNDS	1.1.1953; 1.7.1954; 1.11.1958. Red. *GOVERNMENT OF FIJI* at top on back.	350.00	1750.	4500.

Dollar System

1968 (ND) ISSUE

#37–42 Qn. Elizabeth at r. Arms and heading: *GOVERNMENT OF FIJI* at top ctr. 2 sign. Ritchie and Barnes. Wmk: Head of Fijian. Printer: TDLR.

Cat. #	Denomination	Date, description	VG	VF	Unc
37	50 CENTS	ND (1968). Green on m/c unpt. Thatched house and palms on back.	1.00	2.50	15.00

Cat. #	Denomination	Date, description	VG	VF	Unc
38	1 DOLLAR	ND (1968). Brown on lilac and lt. green unpt. Scene of Yanuca in the Mamanuca Group of Islands, South Yasewas on back.	1.00	5.00	20.00

#39–42 w/o pictorial designs on back.

Cat. #	Denomination	Date, description	VG	VF	Unc
39	2 DOLLARS	ND (1968). Green on yellow and lt. blue unpt.	3.00	10.00	55.00
40	5 DOLLARS	ND (1968). Orange on lilac and gray unpt.	7.00	25.00	185.00
41	10 DOLLARS	ND (1968). Purple on lt. orange and lilac unpt.	15.00	40.00	265.00
42	20 DOLLARS	ND (1968). Blue on lt. green and orange unpt.	27.50	85.00	500.00

1971 (ND) ISSUE

#43–48 like #37-42. Only 1 sign.

Cat. #	Denomination	Date, description	VG	VF	Unc
43	50 CENTS	ND (1971). Green on m/c unpt. Like #37.			
		a. Sign. Wesley Barrett.	1.00	2.50	12.00
		b. Sign. C.A. Stinson.	1.00	2.00	10.00
44	1 DOLLAR	ND (1971). Brown on lilac and lt. green unpt. Like #38.			
		a. Sign. Wesley Barrett.	1.50	3.50	32.50
		b. Sign. C.A. Stinson.	1.50	5.00	45.00
45	2 DOLLARS	ND (1971). Green on yellow and lt. blue unpt. Like #39.			
		a. Sign. Wesley Barrett.	2.50	7.50	85.00
		b. Sign. C.A. Stinson.	Reported, not confirmed.		

Cat. #	Denomination	Date, description	VG	VF	Unc
46	5 DOLLARS	ND (1971). Like #40.			
		a. Sign. Wesley Barrett.	5.00	20.00	165.00
		b. Sign. C.A. Stinson.	5.00	25.00	250.00
47	10 DOLLARS	ND (1971). Like #41.			
		a. Sign. Wesley Barrett.	12.00	37.50	250.00
		b. Sign. C.A. Stinson.	12.50	45.00	350.00
48	20 DOLLARS	ND (1971). Like #42.			
		a. Sign. Wesley Barrett.	25.00	65.00	400.00
		b. Sign. C.A. Stinson.	25.00	75.00	450.00

Central Monetary Authority of Fiji

1974 (ND) ISSUE

#48–53 like #37-42. New heading: *FIJI* at top, and issuing authority name across lower ctr. 2 sign. Printer: TDLR.

Cat. #	Denomination	Date, description	VG	VF	Unc
48A	50 CENTS	ND (1974). Like #37. Sign. D.J. Barnes and R.J.A. Earland. (Not issued.)	—	—	—
49	1 DOLLAR	ND (1974). Like #38.			
		a. Sign. D.J. Barnes and R.J. Earland.	1.00	2.00	9.00
		b. Sign. D.J. Barnes and H.J. Tomkins.	1.00	2.00	9.00

Cat. #	Denomination	Date, description	VG	VF	Unc
50	2 DOLLARS	ND (1974). Like #39.			
		a. Sign. D.J. Barnes and I.A. Craik.	3.00	12.00	75.00
		b. Sign. D.J. Barnes and R.J. Earland.	1.50	3.00	22.50
		c. Sign. D.J. Barnes and H.J. Tomkins.	1.50	3.00	25.00
51	5 DOLLARS	ND (1974). Like #40.			
		a. Sign. D.J. Barnes and I.A. Craik.	7.50	25.00	185.00
		b. Sign. D.J. Barnes and R.J. Earland.	3.50	10.00	65.00
		c. Sign. D.J. Barnes and H.J. Tomkins.	3.50	8.50	57.50
52	10 DOLLARS	ND (1974). Like #41.			
		a. Sign. D.J. Barnes and I.A. Craik.	17.50	50.00	375.00
		b. Sign. D.J. Barnes and R.J. Earland.	8.50	17.50	135.00
		c. Sign. D.J. Barnes and H.J. Tomkins.	7.50	15.00	100.00
53	20 DOLLARS	ND (1974). Like #42.			
		a. Sign. D.J. Barnes and I.A. Craik.	30.00	75.00	525.00
		b. Sign. D.J. Barnes and R.J. Earland.	15.00	30.00	150.00
		c. Sign. D.J. Barnes and H.J. Tomkins.	15.00	55.00	200.00

1980 (ND) ISSUE

#54–58 Qn. Elizabeth II at r. ctr., arms at ctr., artifact at r. Sign. D.J. Barnes and H.J. Tomkins. Printer: TDLR.

Cat. #	Denomination	Date, description	VG	VF	Unc
54	1 DOLLAR	ND (1980). Brown on m/c unpt. Open air fruit market on back.	FV	1.00	7.50

| 55 | 2 DOLLARS | ND (1980). Green on m/c unpt. Harvesting sugar cane on back. | FV | 2.50 | 17.50 |

| 56 | 5 DOLLARS | ND (1980). Orange on m/c unpt. Circle of fishermen w/net on back. | FV | 7.00 | 37.50 |

| 57 | 10 DOLLARS | ND (1980). Purple on m/c unptl. Men doing a dance on back. | FV | 15.00 | 90.00 |

| 58 | 20 DOLLARS | ND (1980). Blue on m/c unpt. Native hut on back. | FV | 35.00 | 200.00 |

1983 ISSUE

#59–60 like #54-58. Backs retouched and lithographed. Sign. D.J. Barnes and S. Siwatibaku.

Cat. #	Denomination	Date, description	VG	VF	Unc
59	1 DOLLAR	ND (1983). Black on m/c unpt. Like #54.	FV	FV	5.50

| 60 | 2 DOLLARS | ND (1983). Green on m/c unpt. Like #55. | FV | FV | 12.50 |

| 61 | 5 DOLLARS | ND (1986). Orange on m/c unpt. Like #56. | FV | FV | 15.00 |

| 62 | 10 DOLLARS | ND (1986). Purple on m/c unpt. Like #57. | FV | FV | 27.50 |

| 63 | 20 DOLLARS | ND (1986). Blue on m/c unpt. Like #58. | FV | FV | 60.00 |

Reserve Bank Of Fiji

1987-91 (ND) ISSUE

#64–68 modified portr. of Qn. Elizabeth II at r., and new banking authority. Similar to #59-63. Sign. S. Siwatibau.

#64, 65, 68 printer: BWC.

Cat. #	Denomination	Date, description	VG	VF	Unc
64	1 DOLLAR	ND (1987). Similar to #59.	FV	FV	2.50
65	2 DOLLARS	ND (1988). Similar to #60.	FV	FV	4.50
66	5 DOLLARS	ND. (ca.1991). Similar to #61. Printer: TDLR.	FV	FV	12.00
67	10 DOLLARS	ND (1989). Similar to #62. Printer: TDLR.	FV	FV	20.00
68	20 DOLLARS	ND (1988). Similar to #63.	FV	FV	35.00

1992–95 ISSUE

#69-73 similar to #64-68. Vertical serial # at l., heavy segmented security thread, slightly redesigned portr. Sign. Kubuabola. Printer: TDLR.

Cat. #	Denomination	Date, description	VG	VF	Unc
69	1 DOLLAR	ND (1993). Similar to #64. W/o segmented security thread.	FV	FV	2.00
70	2 DOLLARS	ND (1995). Similar to #65.	FV	FV	4.00
71 (70)	5 DOLLARS	ND (1992). Similar to #66.	FV	FV	7.50
72 (71)	10 DOLLARS	ND (1992). Similar to #67.	FV	FV	12.50
73 (72)	20 DOLLARS	ND (1992). Similar to #68.	FV	FV	25.00

1995–96 ISSUE

#74–78 mature bust of Qn. Elizabeth II.

Cat. #	Denomination	Date, description	VG	VF	Unc
74	2 DOLLARS	ND.			Expected new issue.
76	5 DOLLARS	ND (1995). Brown on m/c unpt. Nadi International Airport.	FV	FV	6.50
76	10 DOLLARS	ND.			Expected new issue.
77	20 DOLLARS	ND.			Expected new issue.
78	50 DOLLARS	ND (1996).	FV	FV	55.00

The Republic of Finland, the second most northerly state of the European continent, has an area of 130,120 sq. mi. (337,009 sq. km.) and a population of 5 million. Capital: Helsinki. Lumbering, shipbuilding, metal and woodworking are the leading industries. Paper, timber, woodpulp, plywood and metal products are exported.

The Finns, who probably originated in the Volga region of Russia, took Finland from the Lapps late in the 7th century. They were conquered in the 12th century by Eric IX of Sweden, and brought into contact with Western Christendom. In 1809, Sweden was conquered by Alexander I of Russia, and the peace terms gave Finland to Russia which became a grand duchy within the Russian Empire until Dec. 6, 1917, when, shortly after the Bolshevik revolution, it declared its independence. After a brief but bitter civil war between the Russian sympathizers and Finnish nationalists in which the Whites (nationalists) were victorious, a new constitution was adopted, and on Dec. 6, 1917 Finland was established as a republic. In 1939 Soviet troops invaded Finland over disputed territorial concessions which were later granted in the peace treaty of 1940. When the Germans invaded Russia, Finland also became involved and in the Armistice of 1944 lost the Petsamo area also to the Soviets.

MONETARY SYSTEM
1 Markka = 100 Penniä 1860-1963
1 New Markka = 100 Old Markkaa 1963–

REPLACEMENT NOTES
#91-111, asterisk after serial number.
#112-115, 117, #9 as 2nd and 3rd digits in serial #.

Suomen Pankki - Finlands Bank

1963 DATED ISSUES

#98–102 w/o *Litt.* designation.

Cat. #	Denomination	Date, description	VG	VF	Unc
98	1 MARKKA	1963. Lilac-brown on olive unpt. Wheat ears.	FV	.50	2.00

99	5 MARKKAA	1963. Blue. Conifer branch.	FV	1.50	5.00

#106A–107 *Litt. B.*

Cat. #	Denomination	Date, description	VG	VF	Unc
100	10 MARKKAA	1963. Dk. green. Paaslkivi at l.	FV	8.00	20.00

Cat. #	Denomination	Date, description	VG	VF	Unc
106A	5 MARKKAA	1963. Blue. Like #99.	FV	FV	2.00
107	50 MARKKAA	1963. Brown. Like #101 and #105.	FV	FV	20.00

1975–77 ISSUE

101	50 MARKKAA	1963. Brown. K. J. Stahlberg at l.	FV	20.00	40.00

108 (110)	50 MARKKAA	1977. Brown and m/c. K.J. Stahlberg at l. and as wmk.	FV	FV	18.00

102	100 MARKKAA	1963. Violet. J. V. Snellman at l.	FV	FV	50.00

#103–106 *Litt. A.*

103	5 MARKKAA	1963. Blue. Similar to #99, but border and date designs are more detailed.	FV	FV	3.00
104	10 MARKKAA	1963. Dk. green. Like #100.	FV	3.00	5.00

109	100 MARKKAA	1976. Violet. J.V. Snellman at l. and as wmk.	FV	FV	33.00

105	50 MARKKAA	1963. Brown. Like #101.	FV	15.00	30.00

106	100 MARKKAA	1963. Violet. Like #102.	FV	FV	35.00

110 (108)	500 MARKKAA	1975. Blue and violet. Urho Kekkonen at l. and as wmk. Arms and 9 small shields on back.	FV	FV	150.00

1980 ISSUES

Cat. #	Denomination	Date, description	VG	VF	Unc
111	10 MARKKAA	1980. Green on brown and orange unpt. Like #100 except for color and addition of 4 raised discs at r. ctr. for denomination identification by the blind. Back green and purple. Wmk: Paasikivi.	FV	FV	5.00

| 112 | 10 MARKKAA | 1980. Similar to #111 but date under portr., and 5 small circles at bottom. *Litt. A.* | FV | FV | 5.00 |

1986 ISSUE

#113–117 wmk as portr. Circles above lower r. serial #.

| 113 | 10 MARKKAA | 1986. Deep blue on blue and green unpt. P. Nurmi at l. and as wmk. Helsinki Olympic Stadium on back. | FV | FV | 4.50 |

| 114 | 50 MARKKAA | 1986. Black on red-brown and m/c unpt. A. Aalto at l. and as wmk. 4 raised circles at lower r. for the blind. Finlandia Hall on back. | FV | FV | 18.50 |

Cat. #	Denomination	Date, description	VG	VF	Unc
115	100 MARKKAA	1986. Black on green and m/c unpt. J. Sibelius at l. and as wmk. 3 raised circles at lower r. for the blind. Swans on back.	FV	FV	35.00

| 116 | 500 MARKKAA | 1986. Black on red, brown and yellow unpt. E. Lonnrot at l. and as wmk. Punkaharjuesker on back. | FV | FV | 140.00 |

| 117 | 1000 MARKKAA | 1986. Blue and purple on m/c unpt. D'Anders Chydenium at l. and as wmk. King's gate, sea fortress of Suomenlinna in Hel-sinki harbor, seagulls on back. | FV | FV | 275.00 |

1991-93 ISSUE

#118–122 wmk as portr.

| 118 | 20 MARKKAA | 1993. Black on blue and gold unpt. V. Linna at l. and as wmk. Optical variable device at upper r. Lg. bldgs. at l. and r. on back. | FV | FV | 6.50 |

#119-122 like #114–117 but w/*Litt. A* above denomination added to lower l. and variable optical device (VOD) added at upper r. to higher denominations. Circles above bank name.

| 119 | 50 MARKKAA | 1986 (1991). Like #114. | FV | FV | 16.00 |
| 120 | 100 MARKKAA | 1986 (1991). Like #115. | FV | FV | 30.00 |

| 121 | 500 MARKKAA | 1986 (1991). Like #116. | FV | FV | 120.00 |

| 122 | 1000 MARKKAA | 1986 (1991). Like #117. | FV | FV | 235.00 |

FRANCE

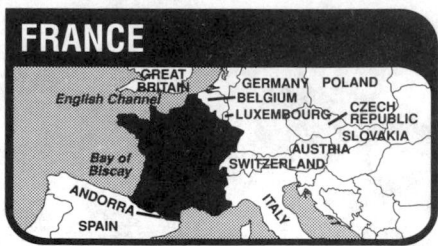

The French Republic, largest of the West European nations, has an area of 220,668 sq. mi. (547,026 sq. km.) and a population of 57.5 million. Capital: Paris. Agriculture, mining and manufacturing are the most important elements of France's diversified economy. Textiles and clothing, iron and steel products, machinery and transportation equipment, agricultural products and wine are exported.

France, the Gaul of ancient times, emerged from the Renaissance as a modern centralized national state which reached its zenith during the reign of Louis XIV (1643–1715) when it became an absolute monarchy and the foremost power in Europe. Although his reign marks the golden age of French culture, the domestic abuses and extravagance of Louis XIV plunged France into a series of costly wars. This, along with a system of special privileges granted the nobility and other favored groups, weakened the monarchy, brought France to bankruptcy - and laid the way for the French Revolution of 1789–94 that shook Europe and affected the whole world.

The monarchy was abolished and the First Republic formed in 1793. The new government fell in 1799 to a coup led by Napoleon Bonaparte who, after declaring himself First Consul for life, had himself proclaimed emperor of France and king of Italy. Napoleon's military victories made him master of much of Europe, but his disastrous Russian campaign of 1812 initiated a series of defeats that led to his abdication in 1814 and exile to the island of Elba. The monarchy was briefly restored under Louis XVIII. Napoleon returned to France in March 1815, but his efforts to regain power were totally crushed at the Battle of Waterloo. He was exiled to the island of St. Helena where he died in 1821.

The monarchy under Louis XVIII was again restored in 1815, but the ultrareactionary regime of Charles X (1824–30) was overthrown by a liberal revolution and Louis Philippe of Orleans replaced him as monarch. The monarchy was ousted by the Revolution of 1848 and the Second Republic proclaimed. Louis Napoleon Bonaparte (nephew of Napoleon I) was elected president of the Second Republic. He was proclaimed emperor in 1852. As Napoleon III, he gave France two decades of prosperity under a stable, autocratic regime, but led it to defeat in the Franco-Prussian War of 1870, after which the Third Republic was established.

The Third Republic endured until 1940 and ended by the capitulation of France to the swiftly maneuvering German forces. Marshal Henri Petain formed a puppet government that sued for peace and ruled unoccupied France from Vichy. Meanwhile, General Charles de Gaulle escaped to London where he formed a wartime government in exile and the Free French army. De Gaulle's provisional exile government was officially recognized by the Allies after the liberation of Paris in 1944, and De Gaulle, who had been serving as head of the provisional government, was formally elected to that position. In October 1945, the people overwhelmingly rejected a return to the prewar government, thus paving the way for the formation of the Fourth Republic.

De Gaulle was unanimously elected president of the Fourth Republic, but resigned in January 1946 when leftists withdrew their support. In actual operation, the Fourth Republic was remarkably like the Third, with the National Assembly the focus of power. The later years of the Fourth Republic were marked by a burst of industrial expansion unmatched in modern French history. The growth rate, however, was marred by a nagging inflationary trend that weakened the franc and undermined the competitive posture of France's export trade. This and the Algerian conflict led to the recall of De Gaulle to power, the adoption of a new constitution vesting strong powers in the executive, and establishment in 1958 of the current Fifth Republic.

MONETARY SYSTEM
1 Franc = 100 Centimes, 1794–

Banque de France

Nouveaux Franc (NF) System

1959 ISSUE

| 73 | 5 NF | 5.3.1959–5.11.1965. Blue, orange and m/c. Bldg. at l. Village at l. Pantheon in Paris on back. | 1.50 | 9.00 | 30.00 |

Cat. #	Denomination	Date, description	VG	VF	Unc
74	10 NF	5.3.1959–4.1.1963. M/c. Skyline across, Richelieu at r. Similar scene on back, Richelieu at l.	2.50	10.00	35.00
75	50 NF	5.3.1959–5.4.1962. M/c. Henry IV at ctr., castly and bridge in background. Similar scene on back.	12.50	37.50	125.00
76	100 NF	5.3.1959–6.5.1964. M/c. Arch at l. Bonaparte at r. Capital bldg. at r. Bonaparte at l. on back.	20.00	33.50	110.00

77	500 NF	1959–66. M/c. Moliere at ctr.			
		a. Sign. G. Gouin d'Ambrieres, R. Tondu and P. Gargam. 2.7.1959–8.1.1965.	FV	200.00	300.00
		b. Sign. H. Morant, R. Tondu and P. Gargam. 6.1.1966–1.9.1966.	200.00	250.00	350.00

Franc System
1962–66 ISSUE

78	5 FRANCS	1966–70. Brown, purple and m/c. L. Pasteur at l., bldg. at r. Laboratory implements, Pasteur at r. on back.			
		a. Sign. R. Tondu, P. Gargam and H. Morant. 5.5.1966–4.11.1966.	1.00	3.00	20.00
		b. Sign. R. Tondu, H. Morant and G. Bouchet. 5.5.1967–8.1.1970.	1.00	3.50	22.50

79	10 FRANCS	1963–73. Red and m/c. Bldg. at ctr., Voltaire at r. Similar scene w/Voltaire at l. on back.			
		a. Sign. G. Gouin d'Ambrieres, P. Gargam and R. Tondu. 4.1.1963–2.12.1965.	FV	3.00	17.50
		b. Sign. H. Morant, P. Gargam and R. Tondu. 6.1.1966–6.4.1967.	FV	3.00	15.00
		c. Sign. G. Bouchet, H. Morant and R. Tondu. 6.7.1967–4.2.1971.	FV	3.00	15.50
		d. Sign. G. Bouchet, H. Morant and P. Vergnes. 3.6.1971–6.12.1973.	FV	3.00	12.50

Cat. #	Denomination	Date, description	VG	VF	Unc
80	50 FRANCS	1962–76. M/c. Bldgs. w/courtyard at ctr., Racine at r. Racine at l., bldgs. across on back.			
		a. Sign. G. Gouin d'Ambrieres, R. Tondu and P. Gargam. 7.6.1962–4.3.1965.	FV	15.00	45.00
		b. Sign. H. Morant, R. Tondu and P. Gargam. 2.2.1967.	20.00	30.00	50.00
		c. Sign. G. Bouchet, R. Tondu and H. Morant. 7.12.1967–5.11.1970.	FV	15.00	35.00
		d. Sign. G. Bouchet, P. Vergnes and H. Morant. 3.6.1971–3.10.1974.	FV	15.00	35.00
		e. Sign. G. Bouchet, Tronche and H. Morant. 6.2.1975–2.10.1975.	FV	15.00	35.00
		f. Sign. P.A. Strohl, G. Bouchet and J.J. Tronche. 2.1.1976–3.6.1976.	FV	15.00	35.00

81	100 FRANCS	1964–79. M/c. P. Corneille at ctr. surrounded by arches.			
		a. Sign. R. Tondu, G. Gouin d'Ambrieres and P. Gargam. 2.4.1964–2.12.1965.	FV	25.00	75.00
		b. Sign. R. Tondu, H. Morant and P. Gargam. 3.2.1966–6.4.1967.	FV	25.00	50.00
		c. Sign. R. Tondu, G. Bouchet and H. Morant. 5.10.1967–1.4.1971.	FV	25.00	40.00
		d. Sign. P. Vergnes, G. Bouchet and H. Morant. 1.7.1971–3.10.1974.	FV	25.00	37.50
		e. Sign. J. Tronche, G. Bouchet and H. Morant. 6.2.1975–6.11.1975.	FV	25.00	37.50
		f. Sign. P. A. Strohl, G. Bouchet and J. Tronche. 2.1.1976–1.2.1979.	FV	25.00	37.50

1968–81 ISSUE
#82–88 wmk. as portr.

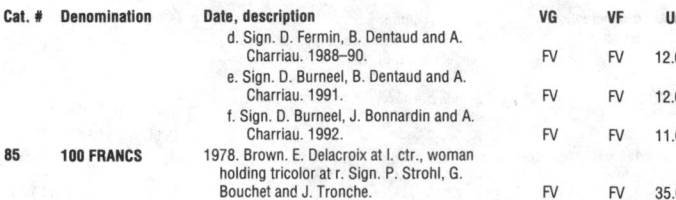

Cat. #	Denomination	Date, description	VG	VF	Unc
		d. Sign. D. Fermin, B. Dentaud and A. Charriau. 1988–90.	FV	FV	12.00
		e. Sign. D. Burneel, B. Dentaud and A. Charriau. 1991.	FV	FV	12.00
		f. Sign. D. Burneel, J. Bonnardin and A. Charriau. 1992.	FV	FV	11.00
85	100 FRANCS	1978. Brown. E. Delacroix at l. ctr., woman holding tricolor at r. Sign. P. Strohl, G. Bouchet and J. Tronche.	FV	FV	35.00

Cat. #	Denomination	Date, description	VG	VF	Unc
82 (83)	10 FRANCS	1972–79. Red, brown and olive. H. Berlioz conducting at r. Berlioz at l., musical instrument at r. on back.			
		a. Sign. H. Morant, G. Bouchet and P. Vergnes. 23.11.1972–3.11.1974.	FV	2.50	4.50
		b. Sign. H. Morant, G. Bouchet and J. Tronche. 6.2.1975–4.12.1975.	FV	2.50	3.50
		c. Sign. P. Strohl, G. Bouchet and Tronche. 2.1.1976–31.1.1979.	FV	2.25	3.00

Cat. #	Denomination	Date, description	VG	VF	Unc
83 (87)	20 FRANCS	1980–. Dull violet, brown and m/c. C. Debussy at r., sea scene in background (La Mer). Similar but w/lake scene on back.			
		a. Sign. P. A. Strohl, J. Tronche and B. Dentaud. 1980–86.	FV	FV	5.50
		b. Sign. P. A. Strohl, D. Ferman and B. Dentaud. 1987.	FV	FV	5.00
		c. W/security thread. Sign. D. Ferman, B. Dentaud and A. Charriau. 1990.	FV	FV	5.00
		d. Sign. D. Burneel, B. Dentaud and A. Charriau. 1991.	FV	FV	5.00
		e. Sign. D. Burneel, J. Bonnardin and A. Charriau. 1992; 1993.	FV	FV	4.50
		f. Sign. D. Burneel, J. Bonnardin and C. Vigier. 1994.	FV	FV	4.50

Cat. #	Denomination	Date, description	VG	VF	Unc
86	100 FRANCS	1978–. Brown. Like #85 but retouched 100 CENT FRANCS w/heavier diagonal lines at upper l.			
		a. Sign. P. Strohl, G. Bouchet and J. Tronche. 1978–79.	FV	FV	25.00
		b. Sign. P. Strohl, J. Tronche and B. Dentaud. 1979–86.	FV	FV	25.00
		c. Sign. P.A. Strohl, Ferman and B. Dentaud. 1987.	FV	FV	22.00
		d. Sign. D. Ferman, B. Dentaud and Charriau. 1988–90.	FV	FV	22.00
		e. Sign. D. Burneel, , B. Dentaud and A. Charriau. 1991.	FV	FV	22.00
		f. Sign. D. Burneel, J. Bonnardin and A. Charriau. 1992; 1993.	FV	FV	22.00
		g. Sign. D. Burneel, J. Bonnardin and C. Vigier. 1994..	FV	FV	22.00

Cat. #	Denomination	Date, description	VG	VF	Unc
84	50 FRANCS	1976–92. Deep blue-black on m/c unpt. M. Quentin de la Tour at r. ctr. Similar scene reversed on back.			
		a. Sign. P. Strohl, G. Bouchet and J. Tronche. 1976–79.	FV	FV	15.00
		b. Sign. P. Strohl, J. Tronche and B. Dentaud. 1979–86.	FV	FV	13.00
		c. Sign. P. Strohl, Ferman and B. Dentaud. 1987.	FV	FV	12.00

Cat. #	Denomination	Date, description	VG	VF	Unc
87 (88)	200 FRANCS	1981–. Blue-green, yellow and m/c. Figure w/staff at l., Baron de Montesquieu at r. Similar but w/town view on back.			
		a. Sign. P. A. Strohl, J. Tronche and B. Dentaud. 1981–86.	FV	FV	55.00
		b. Sign. P. A. Strohl, D. Ferman and B. Dentaud. 1987.	FV	FV	45.00
		c. Sign. D. Fermin, B. Dentaud and A. Charriau. 1988–90.	FV	FV	45.00

Cat. #	Denomination	Date, description	VG	VF	Unc
		d. Sign. D. Burneel, B. Dentaud and A. Charriau. 1991.	FV	FV	45.00
		e. Sign. D. Burneel, J. Bonnardin and A. Charriau. 1992; 1993.	FV	FV	42.00
		f. Sign. D. Burneel, J. Bonnardin and C. Vigier. 1994.	FV	FV	42.00

Cat. #	Denomination	Date, description	VG	VF	Unc
		a. Sign. D. Burneel, J. Bonnardin and A. Charriau.	FV	FV	11.00
		b. Sign. D. Burneel, J. Bonnardin and C. Vigier. 1994.	FV	FV	11.00
90	100 FRANCS	(1997).			Expected new issue.
91	200 FRANCS	(1996).			Expected new issue.

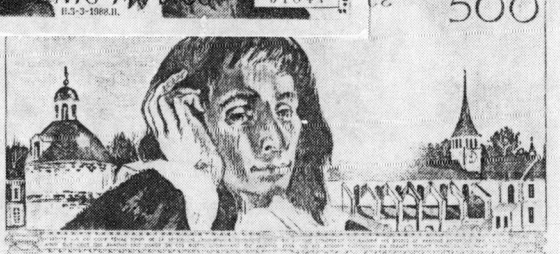

88 (82) **500 FRANCS** 1968–. Yellow-brown and dk. brown. Tower of St. Jacques Church in Paris at l., B. Pascal at ctr., B. Pascal at l., abbey of Port Royal on back.

			VG	VF	Unc
		a. Sign. G. Bouchet, R. Tondu and H. Morant. 4.1.1968–8.1.1970.	FV	115.00	150.00
		b. Sign. G. Bouchet, P. Vergnes and H. Morant. 5.8.1971–5.9.1974.	FV	110.00	150.00
		c. Sign. G. Bouchet, J. Tronche and H. Morant. 5.12.1974–6.11.1975.	FV	FV	130.00
		d. Sign. P. A. Strohl, G. Bouchet and J. Tronche. 1.4.1976–7.6.1979.	FV	FV	125.00
		e. Sign. P. A. Strohl, J. Tronche and B. Dentaud. 7.6.1979–6.2.1986.	FV	FV	125.00
		f. Sign. P. A. Strohl, Ferman and B. Dentaud. 8.1.1987; 22.1.1987; 5.11.1987.	FV	FV	125.00
		g. Sign. of D. Ferman, R. Dentaud and A. Charriau. 3.3.1988; 2.2.1989.	FV	FV	120.00
		h. Sign. D. Burneel, B. Dentaud and A. Charrlau. 1991.	FV	FV	120.00
		i. Sign. D. Burneel, J. Bonnardin and A. Charrlau. 1992; 1993.	FV	FV	120.00
		j. Sign. D. Burneel, J. Bonnardin and C. Vigier. 1994.	FV	FV	120.00

92 500 FRANCS 1994 (1995). Dk. green and black on m/c unpt. M. and P. Curie at ctr. r. Segmented foil strip at l. Laboratory utencils at l. ctr. on back. Wmk: M. Curie. Sign. as #89b.   FV   FV   720.00

1993–97 ISSUE

89 50 FRANCS 1992 (1993). Purple and dk. blue on blue, green and m/c unpt. Drawing of small child at l. Old airplane at upper border, topographical map of Africa at ctr., A. de Saint-Exupéry at r. and as wmk. Biplane on back. Many technical anti-counterfeiting techniques used.

Listings For:

FRENCH AFARS and ISSAS, see Djibouti

FRENCH ANTILLES

Three French overseas departments, Guiana, Guadeloupe and Martinique which issued a common currency from 1961–1975. Since 1975 Bank of France notes have circulated.

RULERS
French

MONETARY SYSTEM
1 Nouveau Franc = 100 "old" Francs
1 Franc = 100 Centimes

Institut d'Emission des Départements d'Outre-Mer

Nouveaux Franc System

1961 PROVISIONAL ISSUE

#1–3 ovpt: *GUADELOUPE, GUYANE, MARTINIQUE.*

Cat. #	Denomination	Date, description	VG	VF	Unc
1	1 NF on 100 Francs	ND (1961). M/c. La Bourdonnais at l. Woman at r. on back.	10.00	40.00	165.00
2	10 NF on 1000 Francs	ND (1961). M/c. Fishermen from the Antilles.	35.00	175.00	525.00

3	50 NF on 5000 Francs	ND (1961). M/c. Woman w/fruit bowl.	125.00	450.00	1300.

SECOND 1961 PROVISIONAL ISSUE

#4, ovpt: *DÉPARTEMENT DE LA GUADELOUPE — DÉPARTEMENT DE LA GUYANE — DÉPARTEMENT DE LA MARTINIQUE.*

Cat. #	Denomination	Date, description	VG	VF	Unc
4	5 NF on 500 Francs	ND (1961). Brown and m/c. Sailboat at l., 2 native women at r. Men w/carts containing plants and wood on back.	35.00	125.00	425.00

Institut d'Emission des Départements d'Outre-Mer
République Francaise

#5–10 ovpt: *DÉPARTEMENT DE LA GUADELOUPE — DÉPARTEMENT DE LA GUYANE — DÉPARTEMENT DE LA MARTINIQUE.*

1963 ISSUE

5	10 NOUVEAUX FRANCS	ND (1963). Brown, green and m/c. Girl at r., coastal scenery in background. People cutting sugar cane on back.	3.00	12.50	80.00

6	50 NOUVEAUX FRANCS	ND (1963). Green and m/c. Banana harvest. Shoreline w/houses at l., man and woman at r. on back.	12.50	45.00	125.00

Franc System

1964 ISSUE

#7–10 w/2 sign. varieties.

7	5 FRANCS	ND (1964). Like #4, but smaller size.	7.50	20.00	120.00

8	10 FRANCS	ND (1964). Like #5.	3.00	12.50	55.00
9	50 FRANCS	ND (1964). Like #6.	7.50	22.00	95.00

10	100 FRANCS	ND (1964). Brown and m/c. Gen. Schoelcher at ctr. r. Schoelcher at l. ctr., various arms and galleon around on back.	25.00	50.00	200.00

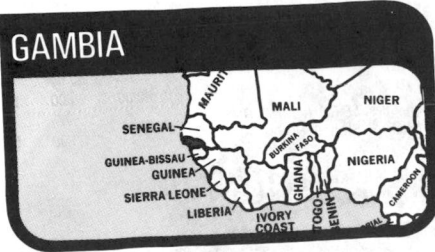

GAMBIA

The Republic of The Gambia, an independent member of the British Commonwealth, occupies a strip of land 7 miles (11 km.) to 20 miles (32 km.) wide and 200 miles (322 km.) long encompassing both sides of West Africa's Gambia River, and completely surrounded by Senegal. The republic, one of Africa's smallest countries, has an area of 4,361 sq. mi. (11,295 sq. km.) and a population of 840,000. Capital: Banjul. Agriculture and tourism are the principal industries. Peanuts constitute 95 per cent of export earnings.

The Gambia was once part of the great empires of Ghana and Songhay. When Portuguese gold seekers and slave traders visited The Gambia in the 15th century, it was part of the Kingdom of Mali. In 1588 the territory became, through purchase, the first British colony in Africa. English slavers established Fort James, the first settlement, on a small island a dozen miles up the Gambia River in 1664. After alternate periods of union with Sierra Leone and existence as a separate colony, The Gambia became a British colony in 1888. On Feb. 18, 1965, The Gambia achieved independence as a constitutional monarchy within the Commonwealth of Nations, with the Queen of England as Chief of State. It became a republic on April 24, 1970, remaining a member of the Commonwealth, but with the president as Chief of State and Head of Government.

RULERS
British to 1970

MONETARY SYSTEM
1 Shilling = 12 Pence
1 Pound = 20 Shillings to 1970
1 Dalasi = 100 Bututs 1970–

REPLACEMENT NOTES
#13–16, Z prefix.

SIGNATURE VARIETIES

1	CHAIRMAN / DIRECTOR	7	
2	GENERAL MANAGER / GOVERNOR	8	
3	GENERAL MANAGER / ACTING GOVERNOR	9	
4	GENERAL MANAGER / GOVERNOR	10	
5		11	
6		12	

The Gambia Currency Board

Pound Sterling System
#1–3 sailboat at l. Wmk: Crocodile's head. Sign. 1.

			VG	VF	Unc
	9 but w/outline map of Chad pleted.		FV	FV	10.00
	9. 1.1.1986; 1.1.1987; 1.1.1990.		FV	FV	10.00
	14. 1.1.1991.				

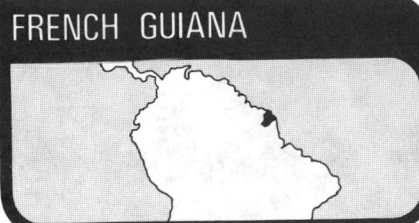

FRENCH GUIANA

The French Overseas Department of French Guiana, located on the northeast coast of South America, bordered by Surinam and Brazil, has an area of 32,252 sq. mi. (91,000 sq. km.) and a population of 114,800. Capital: Cayenne. Placer gold mining and shrimp processing are the chief industries. Shrimp, lumber, gold, cocoa and bananas are exported.

The coast of Guiana was sighted by Columbus in 1498 and explored by Amerigo Vespucci in 1499. The French established the first successful trading stations and settlements, and placed the area under direct control of the French Crown in 1674. Portuguese and British forces occupied French Guiana for five years during the Napoleonic Wars. Devil's Island, the notorious penal colony in French Guiana where Capt. Alfred Dreyfus was imprisoned, was established in 1852 — and finally closed in 1947. When France adopted a new constitution in 1946, French Guiana voted to remain within the French Union as an overseas department.

RULERS
French

MONETARY SYSTEM
1 Franc = 100 Centimes
1 Nouveaux Franc = 100 "old" Francs

Caisse Centrale de la France d'Outre-Mer

Nouveaux Franc System

1961 (ND) ISSUE
#29–34 ovpt. GUYANE and nouveaux franc denominations.

Cat. #	Denomination	Date, description	VG	VF	Unc
29	1 NF on 100 Francs	ND (1961). Ovpt. on #23. M/c. B. d'Esnambuc at l., sailing ship at r.	15.00	45.00	175.00

30	5 NF on 500 Francs	ND (1961). Ovpt. on #24. M/c. La Bourdeonnais at l., women at r.	50.00	150.00	475.00
31	10 NF on 100 Francs	ND (1961). Ovpt. on #27. M/c. Fishermen.	125.00	350.00	875.00

32	10 NF on 1000 Francs	ND. Ovpt. on #25. M/c. 2 women at r.	110.00	300.00	650.00
33	50 NF on 5000 Francs	ND. Ovpt. on #28. Woman w/fruit bowl.	375.00	800.00	1500.

NOTE: For later issues see French Antilles.

Listings For:

FRENCH GUINEA, see Guinea

FRENCH PACIFIC TERRITORIES

The French Pacific Territories include French Polynesia, New Caledonia and formerly the New Hebrides Condominium. For earlier issues also refer to French Oceania and Tahiti.

Institut d'Emission d'Outre-Mer

1985–96 ISSUE

Cat. #	Denomination	Date, description	VG	VF	Unc
1	500 FRANCS	ND (1992). M/c. Sailboat at ctr., fisherman at r., Man at l., objects at r. on back.	FV	FV	12.50

NOTE: For #1 w/ovpt: NOUMEA on back see New Caledonia #45.

2	1000 FRANCS	ND (1996). M/c. Hut in palm trees at l., girl at r.	FV	FV	22.50
3	5000 FRANCS	ND (1996). M/c. Bouganville at l., sailing ships at ctr.	FV	FV	90.00

4	10,000 FRANCS	ND (1985). M/c. Tahitian girl w/ headdress at l., touristic bungalows at ctr. Fish at ctr., Melanesian girl wearing flower at r. on back. Wmk: 2 ethnic heads.	FV	FV	175.00

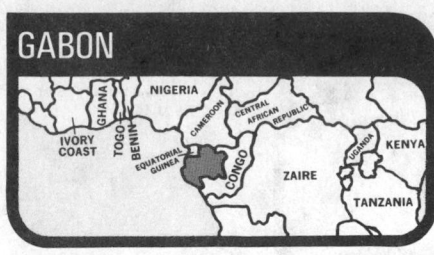

GABON

The Gabonese Republic, a member of the French Community, straddles the equator on the west coast of Africa. The hot and humid rain forest country has an area of 103,347 sq. mi. (267,667 sq. km.) and a population of 1.1 million, almost all of Bantu origin. Capital: Libreville. Extravagantly rich in resources, Gabon exports crude oil, manganese ore, gold and timbers.

Gabon was first visited by Portuguese navigator Diego Cam in the 15th century. Dutch, French and British traders, lured by the rich stands of hard woods and oil palms, quickly followed. The French founded their first settlement on the left bank of the Gabon River in 1839 and established their presence by signing treaties with the tribal chiefs. After gradually extending their influence into the interior during the last half of the 19th century, France occupied Gabon in 1885 and, in 1910, organized it as one of the four territories of French Equatorial Africa. It became an autonomous republic within the French Union in 1946, and on Aug. 17, 1960, became a completely independent republic within the new French Community.

NOTE: For related currency see the Equatorial African States.

RULERS
French to 1960

MONETARY SYSTEM
1 Franc = 100 Centimes

SIGNATURE VARIETIES
Refer to introduction to Central African States.

Banque Centrale

1971 ISSUE

Cat. #	Denomination	Date, description	VG	VF	Unc
1	10,000 FRANCS	ND (1971). M/c. Mask at r., Pres. O. Bongo at r., mine elevator at ctr. Statue at l. and r., tractor plowing at ctr. on back. Sign. 1.	30.00	85.00	225.00

Banque des Etats de l'Afrique Centrale

1974 ISSUE

Cat. #	Denomination	Date, description	VG	VF	Unc
2	500 FRANCS	ND (1974); 1978. Lilac-brown and m/c. Woman wearing kerchief at l., logging at ctr. Mask at l., students and chemical testing at ctr., statue at r. on back.			
		a. Engraved. Sign. 6. ND (1974).	2.50	5.00	10.00
		b. Lithographed. Sign. 9. 1.4.1978.	2.00	4.00	7.00

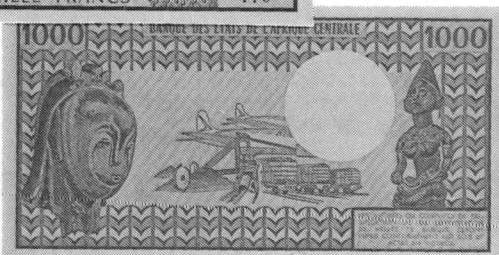

3	1000 FRANCS	ND (1974; 1978); 1978–84. Red, blue and m/c. Ship and oil refinery at ctr., Pres. O. Bongo at r. Mask at l., trains, planes and bridge at ctr., statue at r. on back.			
		a. Sign. titles: LE DIRECTEUR GENERAL and UN CENSEUR. Engraved. Wmk: Antelope head in half profile. Sign. 4. ND (1974).	45.00	125.00	195.00
		b. Like a. Sign. 6.	FV	8.00	20.00
		c. Sign. titles: LE DIRECTEUR GENERAL and UN CENSEUR. Lithographed. Wmk: Antelope head in profile. Sign. 6. ND (1978).	FV	8.00	18.00
		d. Sign titles: LE GOUVERNEUR and UN CENSEUR. Lithographed. Wmk. like b. Sign. 9. 1.4.1978; 1.1.1983; 1.6.1984.	FV	7.50	15.00

| 4 | 5000 FRANCS | ND (1974; 1978). Brown. Oil refinery at l., open pit mining and Pres. O. Bongo at r. Mask at l., bldgs. at ctr., statue at r. on back. | | | |

Cat. #	Denomination	Date, description	VG	VF	Unc
		a. Sign. titles: LE DIRECTEUR GENERAL and UN CENSEUR. Sign. 4. ND (1974).	35.00	85.00	
		b. Like a. Sign. 6.	20.00	40.00	
		c. Sign. titles: LE GOUVERNEUR and UN CENSEUR. Sign. 9. ND (1978).	FV	25.00	

5	10,000 FRANCS	ND (1974; 1978). M/c. Similar to #1 except for new bank name on back.			
		a. Sign. titles: LE DIRECTEUR GENERAL and UN CENSEUR. Sign. 6. ND (1974).	40.00	65.00	110.00
		b. Sign. titles: LE GOUVERNEUR and UN CENSEUR. Sign. 9. ND (1978).	40.00	50.00	80.00

1983–84 ISSUE

| 6 | 5000 FRANCS | ND (1984–). Brown and m/c. Mask at l., woman w/fronds at r. Plowing and mine ore conveyor on back. Sign. 9; 14. | FV | FV | 30.00 |

Cat. #					
7					

1985 ISSUE

#8–10 Wmk: carving

8	500 FRANCS	1.1.1985. Brown on orange and m/c unpt. Carving and jug at ctr. Man carving mask at l. ctr. on back.			FV
9	1000 FRANCS	1.1.1985. Deep blue on m/c unpt. Carving at l., map at ctr., Pres. O. Bongo at r. Incomplete outline map of Chad at top ctr. Elephant at l., animals at ctr., man carving at r. on back.	FV	FV	

FRENCH GUIANA

The French Overseas Department of French Guiana, located on the northeast coast of South America, bordered by Surinam and Brazil, has an area of 32,252 sq. mi. (91,000 sq. km.) and a population of 114,800. Capital: Cayenne. Placer gold mining and shrimp processing are the chief industries. Shrimp, lumber, gold, cocoa and bananas are exported.

The coast of Guiana was sighted by Columbus in 1498 and explored by Amerigo Vespucci in 1499. The French established the first successful trading stations and settlements, and placed the area under direct control of the French Crown in 1674. Portuguese and British forces occupied French Guiana for five years during the Napoleonic Wars. Devil's Island, the notorious penal colony in French Guiana where Capt. Alfred Dreyfus was imprisoned, was established in 1852 — and finally closed in 1947. When France adopted a new constitution in 1946, French Guiana voted to remain within the French Union as an overseas department.

RULERS
French

MONETARY SYSTEM
1 Franc = 100 Centimes
1 Nouveaux Franc = 100 "old" Francs

Caisse Centrale de la France d'Outre-Mer

Nouveaux Franc System

1961 (ND) ISSUE

#29–34 ovpt: *GUYANE* and nouveaux franc denominations.

Cat. #	Denomination	Date, description	VG	VF	Unc
29	1 NF on 100 Francs	ND (1961). Ovpt. on #23. M/c. B. d'Esnambuc at l., sailing ship at r.	15.00	45.00	175.00

30	5 NF on 500 Francs	ND (1961). Ovpt. on #24. M/c. La Bourdeonnais at l., women at r.	50.00	150.00	475.00
31	10 NF on 100 Francs	ND (1961). Ovpt. on #27. M/c. Fishermen.	125.00	350.00	875.00

32	10 NF on 1000 Francs	ND. Ovpt. on #25. M/c. 2 women at r.	110.00	300.00	650.00
33	50 NF on 5000 Francs	ND. Ovpt. on #28. Woman w/fruit bowl.	375.00	800.00	1500.

NOTE: For later issues see French Antilles.

Listings For:

FRENCH GUINEA, see Guinea

FRENCH PACIFIC TERRITORIES

The French Pacific Territories include French Polynesia, New Caledonia and formerly the New Hebrides Condominium. For earlier issues also refer to French Oceania and Tahiti.

Institut d'Emission d'Outre-Mer

1985–96 ISSUE

Cat. #	Denomination	Date, description	VG	VF	Unc
1	500 FRANCS	ND (1992). M/c. Sailboat at ctr., fisherman at r., Man at l., objects at r. on back.	FV	FV	12.50

NOTE: For #1 w/ovpt: *NOUMEA* on back see New Caledonia #45.

2	1000 FRANCS	ND (1996). M/c. Hut in palm trees at l., girl at r.	FV	FV	22.50
3	5000 FRANCS	ND (1996). M/c. Bouganville at l., sailing ships at ctr.	FV	FV	90.00

4	10,000 FRANCS	ND (1985). M/c. Tahitian girl w/ headdress at l., touristic bungalows at ctr. Fish at ctr., Melanesian girl wearing flower at r. on back. Wmk: 2 ethnic heads.	FV	FV	175.00

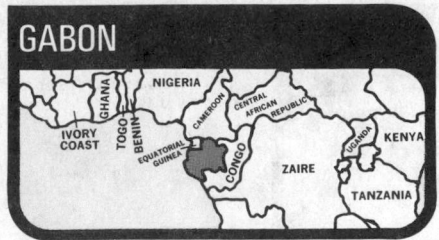

GABON

The Gabonese Republic, a member of the French Community, straddles the equator on the west coast of Africa. The hot and humid rain forest country has an area of 103,347 sq. mi. (267,667 sq. km.) and a population of 1.1 million, almost all of Bantu origin. Capital: Libreville. Extravagantly rich in resources, Gabon exports crude oil, manganese ore, gold and timbers.

Gabon was first visited by Portuguese navigator Diego Cam in the 15th century. Dutch, French and British traders, lured by the rich stands of hard woods and oil palms, quickly followed. The French founded their first settlement on the left bank of the Gabon River in 1839 and established their presence by signing treaties with the tribal chiefs. After gradually extending their influence into the interior during the last half of the 19th century, France occupied Gabon in 1885 and, in 1910, organized it as one of the four territories of French Equatorial Africa. It became an autonomous republic within the French Union in 1946, and on Aug. 17, 1960, became a completely independent republic within the new French Community.

NOTE: For related currency see the Equatorial African States.

RULERS
French to 1960

MONETARY SYSTEM
1 Franc = 100 Centimes

SIGNATURE VARIETIES
Refer to introduction to Central African States.

Banque Centrale

1971 ISSUE

Cat. #	Denomination		VG	VF	Unc
1	10,000 FRANCS	ND (1971). M/c. Mask at l., Pres. O. Bongo at r., mine elevator at ctr. Statue at l. and r., tractor plowing at ctr. on back. Sign. 1.	30.00	85.00	225.00

Banque des Etats de l'Afrique Centrale

1974 ISSUE

Cat. #	Denomination	Date, description	VG	VF	Unc
2	500 FRANCS	ND (1974); 1978. Lilac-brown and m/c. Woman wearing kerchief at l., logging at ctr. Mask at l., students and chemical testing at ctr., statue at r. on back.			
		a. Engraved. Sign. 6. ND (1974).	2.50	5.00	10.00
		b. Lithographed. Sign. 9. 1.4.1978.	2.00	4.00	7.00

3	1000 FRANCS	ND (1974; 1978); 1978–84. Red, blue and m/c. Ship and oil refinery at ctr., Pres. O. Bongo at r. Mask at l., trains, planes and bridge at ctr., statue at r. on back.			
		a. Sign. titles: *LE DIRECTEUR GENERAL* and *UN CENSEUR.* Engraved. Wmk: Antelope head in half profile. Sign. 4. ND (1974).	45.00	125.00	195.00
		b. Like a. Sign. 6.	FV	8.00	20.00
		c. Sign. titles: *LE DIRECTEUR GENERAL* and *UN CENSEUR.* Lithographed. Wmk: Antelope head in profile. Sign. 6. ND (1978).	FV	8.00	18.00
		d. Sign titles: *LE GOUVERNEUR* and *UN CENSEUR.* Lithographed. Wmk. like b. Sign. 9. 1.4.1978; 1.1.1983; 1.6.1984.	FV	7.50	15.00

4	5000 FRANCS	ND (1974; 1978). Brown. Oil refinery at l., open pit mining and Pres. O. Bongo at r. Mask at l., bldgs. at ctr., statue at r. on back.			

Cat. #	Denomination	Date, description	VG	VF	Unc
		a. Sign. titles: *LE DIRECTEUR GENERAL* and *UN CENSEUR*. Sign. 4. ND (1974).	35.00	85.00	175.00
		b. Like a. Sign. 6.	20.00	40.00	90.00
		c. Sign. titles: *LE GOUVERNEUR* and *UN CENSEUR*. Sign. 9. ND (1978).	FV	25.00	55.00

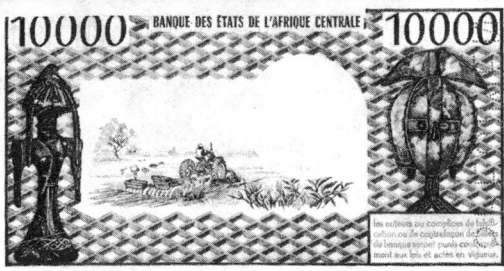

5	10,000 FRANCS	ND (1974; 1978). M/c. Similar to #1 except for new bank name on back.			
		a. Sign. titles: *LE DIRECTEUR GENERAL* and *UN CENSEUR*. Sign. 6. ND (1974).	40.00	65.00	110.00
		b. Sign. titles: *LE GOUVERNEUR* and *UN CENSEUR*. Sign. 9. ND (1978).	40.00	50.00	80.00

1983–84 ISSUE

6	5000 FRANCS	ND (1984–). Brown and m/c. Mask at l., woman w/fronds at r. Plowing and mine ore conveyor on back. Sign. 9; 14.	FV	FV	30.00

Cat. #	Denomination	Date, description	VG	VF	Unc
7	10,000 FRANCS	ND (1983–91). Brown, green and m/c. Stylized antelope heads at l., woman at r. Loading fruit onto truck at l. on back. Sign. 9; 14.	FV	FV	55.00

1985 ISSUE

#8–10 Wmk: carving (same as printed on notes).

8	500 FRANCS	1.1.1985. Brown on orange and m/c unpt. Carving and jug at ctr. Man carving mask at l. ctr. on back.	FV	FV	5.00

9	1000 FRANCS	1.1.1985. Deep blue on m/c unpt. Carving at l., map at ctr., Pres. O. Bongo at r. Incomplete outline map of Chad at top ctr. Elephant at l., animals at ctr., man carving at r. on back.	FV	FV	15.00

Cat. #	Denomination	Date, description	VG	VF	Unc
10	1000 FRANCS	1986–91. Like #9 but w/outline map of Chad at top completed.			
		a. Sign. 9. 1.1.1986; 1.1.1987; 1.1.1990.	FV	FV	10.00
		b. Sign. 14. 1.1.1991.	FV	FV	10.00

GAMBIA

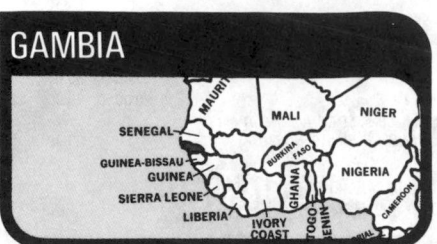

The Republic of The Gambia, an independent member of the British Commonwealth, occupies a strip of land 7 miles (11 km.) to 20 miles (32 km.) wide and 200 miles (322 km.) long encompassing both sides of West Africa's Gambia River, and completely surrounded by Senegal. The republic, one of Africa's smallest countries, has an area of 4,361 sq. mi. (11,295 sq. km.) and a population of 840,000. Capital: Banjul. Agriculture and tourism are the principal industries. Peanuts constitute 95 per cent of export earnings.

The Gambia was once part of the great empires of Ghana and Songhay. When Portuguese gold seekers and slave traders visited The Gambia in the 15th century, it was part of the Kingdom of Mali. In 1588 the territory became, through purchase, the first British colony in Africa. English slavers established Fort James, the first settlement, on a small island a dozen miles up the Gambia River in 1664. After alternate periods of union with Sierra Leone and existence as a separate colony, The Gambia became a British colony in 1888. On Feb. 18, 1965, The Gambia achieved independence as a constitutional monarchy within the Commonwealth of Nations, with the Queen of England as Chief of State. It became a republic on April 24, 1970, remaining a member of the Commonwealth, but with the president as Chief of State and Head of Government.

RULERS
British to 1970

MONETARY SYSTEM
1 Shilling = 12 Pence
1 Pound = 20 Shillings to 1970
1 Dalasi = 100 Bututs 1970–

REPLACEMENT NOTES
#13-16, Z prefix.

SIGNATURE VARIETIES					
1	J.B. Loynes (CHAIRMAN)	(DIRECTOR)	7		D.Macklan
2	(GENERAL MANAGER)	(GOVERNOR)	8	A.H.Humphreys	D.Macklan
3		S.S. Sisay	9	Edward Fishingham (GENERAL MANAGER)	(ACTING GOVERNOR)
4	m.ooronqai	S.S. Sisay	10	Edward Fishingham (GENERAL MANAGER)	(GOVERNOR)
5	A.K.N.Ahmed	S.S. Sisay	11		
6		S.S. Sisay	12		

The Gambia Currency Board

Pound Sterling System
#1–3 sailboat at l. Wmk: Crocodile's head. Sign. 1.

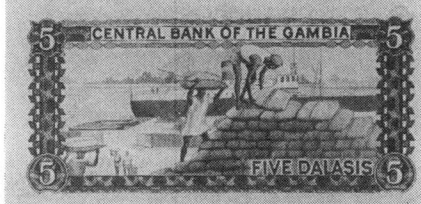

Cat. #	Denomination	Date, description	VG	VF	Unc
1	10 SHILLINGS	ND (1965–70). Green and brown on m/c unpt. Workers in field on back.	3.00	9.00	28.50

Cat. #	Denomination	Date, description	VG	VF	Unc
5	5 DALASIS	ND (1972–86). Red on m/c unpt. Back like #2.			
		a. Sign. 2.	12.50	30.00	70.00
		b. Sign. 4.	2.00	6.00	15.00
		c. Sign. 6.	1.50	4.00	7.50
		d. Sign. 7.	FV	2.00	5.00

| 2 | 1 POUND | ND (1965–70). Red and brown on m/c unpt. Loading sacks at dockside on back. | 5.00 | 15.00 | 50.00 |

6	10 DALASIS	ND (1972–86). Green on m/c unpt. Fishermen in boat w/net on back.			
		a. Sign. 3.	3.00	12.00	30.00
		b. Sign. 4.	Reported, not confirmed.		
		c. Sign. 6.	2.25	4.50	10.00
		d. Sign. 7.	1.35	3.50	7.50

| 3 | 5 POUNDS | ND (1965–70). Blue and green on m/c unpt. Back blue; man and woman operating agricultural machine at ctr. r. | 15.00 | 35.00 | 80.00 |

Central Bank of The Gambia

Dalasi System

ND 1971-72 ISSUE

#4–8 sailboat at l., Pres. D. Kairaba Jawara at r. Sign. varieties. Wmk: Crocodile's head.

7	25 DALASIS	ND (1972–83). Blue on m/c unpt. Back similar to #3 but design is at l. ctr.			
		a. Sign. 2.	35.00	80.00	190.00
		b. Sign. 6.	17.50	40.00	90.00

1978 COMMEMORATIVE ISSUE

#8, Opening of Central Bank on 18.2.1978

4	1 DALASI	ND (1971–87). Purple on m/c unpt. Back like #1.			
		a. Sign. 2.	3.00	10.00	25.00
		b. Sign. 3.	1.25	4.00	10.00
		c. Sign. 4.	1.00	3.00	7.00
		d. Sign. 5.	.50	2.00	5.00
		e. Sign. 6.	.25	.75	2.50
		f. Sign. 7.	.25	.75	2.50
		g. Sign. 8.	.50	2.00	4.50

Cat. #	Denomination	Date, description	VG	VF	Unc
8	1 DALASI	ND (1978). Purple on m/c unpt. Central bank bldg. on back; commemorative legend beneath. Sign. 5.	4.00	10.00	25.00

1987 ISSUE

#9–11 w/line of micro printing under *PROMISE TO PAY…* . Wmk: Crocodile's head.

9	5 DALASIS	ND (1987–90). Like #5 but back red and orange.			
		a. Sign. 8.	.75	2.00	5.00
		b. Sign. 10.	.65	1.50	5.00

10	10 DALASIS	ND (1987–90). Like #6 but back green and lt. olive.			
		a. Sign. title: *GOVERNOR* at r. Sign. 8.	1.50	4.00	10.00
		b. Sign. title: *ACTING GOVERNOR* at r. Sign. 9.	1.25	3.00	7.50

11	25 DALASIS	ND (1987–90). Like #7 but back blue, black and aqua.			
		a. Sign. title: *GOVERNOR* at r. Sign. 8.	4.00	10.00	25.00
		b. Sign. title: *ACTING GOVERNOR* at r. Sign. 9.	3.00	8.00	20.00
		c. Sign. 10.	2.75	6.00	15.00

1989–91 ISSUE

#12–15 Pres. Jawara at r. Micro printing of bank name above and below title. Wmk: Crocodile's head.

Cat. #	Denomination	Date, description	VG	VF	Unc
12	5 DALASIS	ND (1991–). Red and orange on m/c unpt. Giant kingfisher at ctr. Herding cattle on back.			
		a. Sign. 10.	FV	FV	2.50
		b. Sign. 11.	FV	FV	2.00

13	10 DALASIS	ND (1991–). Dk. green and olive on m/c unpt. Sacred ibis at ctr. Lg. dish antenna, communications station at l. ctr. on back.			
		a. Sign. 10.	FV	FV	4.50
		b. Sign. 11.	FV	FV	4.50

14	25 DALASIS	ND (1991–). Dk. blue on green and lavender unpt. Carmine bee eater at ctr. Govt. house at l. ctr. on back. Sign. 10.	FV	FV	9.00

15	50 DALASIS	ND (1989–). Purple on m/c unpt. Crested birds at ctr. Stones in a circle on back. Sign. 10.	FV	FV	17.00

GEORGIA

Georgia (formerly the Georgian Social Democratic Republic under the U.S.S.R.), is bounded by the Black Sea to the west and by Turkey, Armenia and Azerbaijan. It occupies the western part of Transcaucasia covering an area of 26,900 sq. mi. (69,700 sq. km.) Capital: Tbilisi. Hydro-electricity, minerals, forestry and agriculture are the chief industries.

The Georgian dynasty first emerged after the Macedonian victory over the Achaemenid Persian empire in the 4th century B.C. Roman "friendship" was imposed in 65 B.C. after Pompey's victory over Mithradates. The Georgians embraced Christianity in the 4th century A.D. During the next three centuries Georgia was involved in the ongoing conflicts between the Byzantine and Persian empires. The latter developed control until Georgia regained its independence in 450-503 A.D. but then it reverted to a Persian province in 533 A.D., Then restored as a kingdom by the Byzantines in 562 A.D. It was established as an Arab emirate in the 8th century. The Seljuk Turks invaded but the crusades thwarted their interests. Over the following centuries Turkish and Persian rivalries along with civil strife divided the area under the two influences.

Czarist Russian interests increased and a treaty of alliance was signed on July 24, 1773 whereby Russia guaranteed Georgian independence and it acknowledged Russian suzerainty. Persia invaded again in 1795 leaving Tiflis in ruins. Russia slowly took over annexing piece by piece and soon developed total domination. After the Russian Revolution the Georgians, Armenians and Azerbaijanis formed the short-lived Transcaucasian Federal Republic on Sept. 20, 1917 which broke up into three independent republics on May 26, 1918. A Germano-Georgian treaty was signed on May 28, 1918, followed by a Turko-Georgian peace treaty on June 4. The end of WW I and the collapse of the central powers allowed free elections.

On May 20, 1920, Soviet Russia concluded a peace treaty, recognizing its independence, but later invaded on Feb. 11, 1921 and a soviet republic was proclaimed. On March 12, 1922 Stalin included Georgia in a newly formed Transcaucasian Soviet Federated Socialist Republic. On Dec. 5, 1936 the T.S.F.S.R. was dissolved and Georgia became a direct member of the U.S.S.R. The collapse of the U.S.S.R. allowed full transition to independence and on April 9, 1991 a unanimous vote declared the republic an independent state based on its original treaty of independence of May 1918.

NOTE: This section has been renumbered from the old 7th Edition of General Issues

REPUBLIC

Georgian National Bank

FIRST 1993 *KUPONI* ISSUE

#23–32, view of Tbilisi at ctr. r. w/equestrian statue of Kg. V. Gorgosal in foreground, Mt. Tatzminda in background. Cave dwellings at l. ctr. on back. Fractional serial # prefix w/*1* as denominator. Wmk: Hexagonal design repeated.

#23–28 w/o ornate triangular design at l. and r. of lg. value in box at l. ctr. on face, or at sides of value at r. on back.

Cat. #	Denomination	Date, description	VG	VF	Unc
23	1 (LARIS)	ND (1993).		Reported, not confirmed.	
24	3 (LARIS)	ND (1993).		Reported, not confirmed.	

Cat. #	Denomination	Date, description	VG	VF	Unc
25	5 (LARIS)	ND (1993). Dull brown on lilac unpt. W/rosettes at sides of value on face and back.	.05	.20	1.00

26	10 (LARIS)	ND (1993). Yellow-brown on lilac unpt.	.10	.30	1.50

27	50 (LARIS)	ND (1993). Lt. blue on lilac unpt.	.20	.50	2.50
28	100 (LARIS)	ND (1993). Greenish gray and lt. brown on lilac unpt.	.30	.75	4.00

Cat. #	Denomination	Date, description	VG	VF	Unc
29	500 (LARIS)	ND (1993). Purple on lilac unpt.	.35	.90	4.50

30	1000 (LARIS)	ND (1993). Blue-gray and brown on lilac unpt.	.60	1.50	8.00

31	5000 (LARIS)	ND (1993). Green and brown on lilac unpt. Back green on pale brown-orange.	.50	1.25	6.00
32	10,000 (LARIS)	ND (1993). Violet on lilac and brown unpt.	1.25	3.00	15.00

SECOND 1993 ISSUE

#33–38 like #25–28 but w/ornate triangular design at l. and r. of lg. value in box at l. ctr. on face, and at sides of value at r. on back. Fractional serial # prefix w/*2* as denominator. Wmk: Hexagonal design repeated.

Cat. #	Denomination	Date, description	VG	VF	Unc
33	1 (LARIS)	ND (1993). Red-orange and lt. brown on lilac unpt. Like #25.	—	.05	.25

34	3 (LARIS)	ND (1993). Purple and lt. brown on lilac unpt. Like #25.	.05	.10	.50

35	5 (LARIS)	ND (1993). Like #25.	.05	.10	.60

36	10 (LARIS)	ND (1993). Like #26.	.05	.15	.75

Cat. #	Denomination	Date, description	VG	VF	Unc
37	50 (LARIS)	ND (1993). Like #27.	.10	.20	1.00

| 38 | 100 (LARIS) | ND (1993). Like #28. | .20 | .50 | 2.50 |

THIRD 1993 ISSUE

#39–42 similar to first and second 1993 issue but fractional serial # prefix w/*3* as denominator.

| 39 (43) | 10,000 (LARIS) | 1993. Violet on lilac and brown unpt. | .30 | .75 | 3.50 |

| 40 (44) | 25,000 (LARIS) | 1993. Orange and dull brown on lilac unpt. | .40 | 1.00 | 4.50 |

| 41 (45) | 50,000 (LARIS) | 1993. Pale red-brown and tan on lilac unpt. Back dull red-brown on pale brown-orange unpt. | .40 | 1.00 | 4.50 |

Cat. #	Denomination	Date, description	VG	VF	Unc
42 (46)	100,000 (LARIS)	1993. Olive-green and brown on lilac unpt. Back pale olive-green on dull brown-orange unpt.	.40	1.00	5.00

FOURTH 1993 ISSUE

#43–46 griffin at l. and r. of ornate round design at ctr. on face. 2 bunches of grapes w/vine above and below value on back. Wmk. Isometric rectangular design.

43 (39)	250 (LARIS)	1993. Dk.-blue on green, lilac and lt. blue unpt.	FV	FV	.75
		a. W/security thread.	.05	.15	.75
		b. W/o security thread.	—	—	—

| 44 (40) | 2000 (LARIS) | 1993. Green and blue on gold and green unpt. | .20 | .50 | 2.50 |

| 45 (41) | 3000 (LARIS) | 1993. Brown and yellow on lt. brown unpt. | .20 | .45 | 2.25 |

46 (42)	20,000 (LARIS)	1993–. Purple on lt. red and blue unpt.			
		a. Lg. wmk. 1993.	.20	.50	2.50
		b. Sm. wmk. 1994.	.20	.50	2.50

1994 ISSUE

#47–52 similar to #43–46. Wmk. Geometric rectangular pattern repeated.

Cat. #	Denomination	Date, description	VG	VF	Unc
47	30,000 (LARIS)	1994. Dull red-brown on pale orange and lt. gray unpt.	.20	.55	2.75

48	50,000 (LARIS)	1994. Dk. olive-green and dull black on pale olive-green and tan unpt.	.25	.70	3.50

48A	100,000 (LARIS)	1994. Dk. gray on lt. blue and lt. gray unpt.			
		a. Lg. wmk.	.35	.90	4.50
		b. Sm. wmk.	.35	.90	4.50

49	150,000 (LARIS)	1994. Dk. blue-green on pale blue, lt. gray and lilac unpt.	.35	.90	4.50

50	250,000 (LARIS)	1994. Brown-orange on pale orange and lt. green unpt.	.40	1.00	5.00

51	500,000 (LARIS)	1994. Deep violet on pale purple and pink unpt.	.40	1.00	5.50

52	1 MILLION (LARIS)	1994. Red on pink and pale yellow-brown unpt.	.90	2.25	11.00

Currency Reform, 1995

1 "New" Lari = 1,000,000 "Old" Laris

1995 ISSUE

#53–59 arms at l. to ctr.

Cat. #	Denomination	Date, description	VG	VF	Unc
53	1 LARI	1995. Deep purple on m/c unpt. N. Pirosmani between branches at ctr. View of Tbilisi, painting of deer at ctr. r. on back.	FV	FV	3.50

54	2 LARI	1995 Deep olive-green on m/c unpt. Bars of music at l., Z. Paliashvili at ctr. r. Opera House in Tbilisi at ctr. r. on back.	FV	FV	6.00

55	5 LARI	1995. Brown on m/c unpt. I. Javakhishvili at ctr., map above ornate lion statue at l. ctr., Tbilisi State University above open book at r.	FV	FV	12.50

56	10 LARI	1995. Blue-black on m/c unpt. Flowers at l., A. Tsereteli and swallow at ctr. r. Woman seated on stump while spinning yarn with a crop spindle between ornamental brances at ctr. r. on back. Wmk: Arms repeated vertically.	FV	FV	12.50

#57–59 wmk: Griffon.

Cat. #	Denomination	Date, description	VG	VF	Unc
57	20 LARI	1995. Dk. brown on m/c unpt. Open book and newspaper at upper l., I. Chavchavadze at ctr. Statue of Kg. V. Gorgosal between views of Tbilisi at ctr. r. on back.	FV	FV	35.00

58	50 LARI	1995. Dk. brown and deep blue-green on m/c unpt. Griffon at l., Princess Tamara at ctr. r. Mythical figure at ctr. r. on back.	FV	FV	65.00

59	100 LARI	1995. Dk. brown, purple and black on m/c unpt. Carved bust of S. Rustaveli at ctr. r., Frieze at upper ctr. r. on back.	FV	FV	125.00

GERMANY-FEDERAL REP.

The Federal Republic of Germany (formerly West Germany), located in north-central Europe, since 1990 with the unification of East Germany, has an area of 137.82 sq. mi. (356,854 sq. km.) and a population of 79.75 million. Capital: Bonn. The economy centers about one of the world's foremost industrial establishments. Machinery, motor vehicles, iron, steel, yarns and fabrics are exported.

During the post-Normandy phase of World War II, Allied troops occupied the western German provinces of Schleswig-Holstein, Hamburg, Lower Saxony, Bremen, North Rhine-Westphalia, Hesse, Rhineland-Palatinate, Baden-Wurttemberg, Bavaria and Saarland. The conquered provinces were divided into American, British and French occupation zones. Five eastern German provinces were occupied and administered by the forces of the Soviet Union.

The western occupation forces restored the civil status of their zones on Sept. 21, 1949, and resumed diplomatic relations with the provinces on July 2, 1951. On May 5, 1955, nine of the ten western provinces, organized as the Federal Republic of Germany, became fully independent. The tenth province, Saarland, was restored to the republic on Jan. 1, 1957.

The post-WW II division of Germany ended on Oct. 3, 1990, when the German Democratic Republic (East Germany) ceased to exist and its five constituent provinces were formally admitted to the Federal Republic of Germany. An election Dec. 2, 1990, chose representatives to the united federal parliament (Bundestag), which then conducted its opening session in Berlin in the old Reichstag building. Although Berlin technically is the capital of the reunited Germany, the actual seat of government remains for the time being in Bonn.

MONETARY SYSTEM
1 Deutsche Mark (DM) = 100 Pfennig

REPLACEMENT NOTES

#18–43: single Y or Z, or double letter prefix starting with Y or Z.

Deutsche Bundesbank

#18–43 portr. as wmk.

1960 ISSUE

Cat. #	Denomination	Date, description	VG	VF	Unc
18	5 DEUTSCHE MARK	2.1.1960. Green on m/c unpt. Young Venetian woman by A. Durer at r. Sprig on back.	FV	5.00	13.00

#19–21 and 23 w/ or w/o ultraviolet senstive features.

19	10 DEUTSCHE MARK	2.1.1960. Blue on m/c unpt. Young man at r. Sailing ship *Gorch Fock* on back.	FV	20.00	45.00
20	20 DEUTSCHE MARK	2.1.1960. Black and green on m/c unpt. E. Tucher by A. Durer ar r. Violin, bow and clarinet on back.	FV	35.00	80.00

21	50 DEUTSCHE MARK	2.1.1960. Brown and olive-green on m/c unpt. Chamberlain H. Urmiller at r. Turreted bldg. Holsten-Tor (in Lübeck) on back.	FV	45.00	95.00
22	100 DEUTSCHE MARK	2.1.1960. Blue on m/c unpt. Master Seb. Munster at r. Eagle on back.	FV	80.00	175.00

Cat. #	Denomination	Date, description	VG	VF	Unc
23	500 DEUTSCHE MARK	2.1.1960. Brown-lilac on m/c unpt. Male portrait by Hans Maler zu Schwaz. Castle Elta on back.	FV	FV	650.00

Cat. #	Denomination	Date, description	VG	VF	Unc
29	100 DEUTSCHE MARK	2.1.1970. Blue. Like #22.	FV	FV	130.00
30	500 DEUTSCHE MARK	2.1.1970. Brown-lilac. Similar to #23.	FV	FV	500.00

1977 ISSUE

#31–36 like #25–30 but different date and sign.

31	10 DEUTSCHE MARK	1.6.1977. Blue. Like #26.	FV	FV	12.00

24	1000 DEUTSCHE MARK	2.1.1960. Dk. brown on m/c unpt. Astronomer Schoner (by Lucas Cranach the Elder) at r. and as wmk. Cathedral of Limburg on the Lahn on back.	FV	FV	1150.

1970 ISSUE

#25–30 like #18–24 but different sign. and legal penalty.

25	5 DEUTSCHE MARK	2.1.1970. Green. Like #18.	FV	10.00	25.00

#26–29 letters of serial # either 2.8 or 3.3 mm.

26	10 DEUTSCHE MARK	2.1.1970. Blue. Like #19.	FV	FV	32.50

32	20 DEUTSCHE MARK	1.6.1977. Green. Like #27.	FV	FV	30.00
33	50 DEUTSCHE MARK	1.6.1977. Brown and green. Like #28.	FV	FV	50.00
34	100 DEUTSCHE MARK	1.6.1977. Blue. Like #29.	FV	FV	90.00
35	500 DEUTSCHE MARK	1.6.1977. Like #30.	FV	FV	425.00
36	1000 DEUTSCHE MARK	1.6.1977. Brown. Like #24, but different sign. and legal penalty.	FV	FV	800.00

1980 ISSUE

#38–41 like #25–30 but different date, w/or w/o copyright notice at lower l. margin on back.

37	5 DEUTSCHE MARK	2.1.1980. Like #25 but w/© DEUTSCHE BUNDESBANK 1963 on back.	FV	FV	5.00

27	20 DEUTSCHE MARK	2.1.1970. Green. Like #20.	FV	FV	50.00
28	50 DEUTSCHE MARK	2.1.1970. Brown and green. Like #21.	FV	FV	80.00

Cat. #	Denomination	Date, description	VG	VF	Unc
38	10 DEUTSCHE MARK	2.1.1980. Like #26.			
		a. W/o copyright notice.	FV	FV	17.50
		b. W/© *DEUTSCHE BUNDESBANK 1963* on back.	FV	FV	11.00
39	20 DEUTSCHE MARK	2.1.1980. Like #27.			
		a. W/o copyright notice.	FV	FV	60.00
		b. W/© *DEUTSCHE BUNDESBANK 1961* on back.	FV	FV	20.00
40	50 DEUTSCHE MARK	2.1.1980. Like #28.			
		a. W/o copyright notice.	FV	FV	62.50
		b. W/© *DEUTSCHE BUNDESBANK 1962* on back.	FV	FV	45.00

Cat. #	Denomination	Date, description	VG	VF	Unc
41	100 DEUTSCHE MARK	2.1.1980. Like #29.			
		a. W/o copyright notice.	FV	FV	95.00
		b. W/© *DEUTSCHE BUNDESBANK 1962* on back.	FV	FV	90.00
42	500 DEUTSCHE MARK	2.1.1980. Like #30.	FV	FV	400.00
43	1000 DEUTSCHE MARK	2.1.1980. Like #36.	FV	FV	800.00

1989–91 ISSUE

#44–51 portr. as wmk.

Cat. #	Denomination	Date, description	VG	VF	Unc
44	5 DEUTSCHE MARK	1.8.1991. Green and olive-green on m/c unpt. B. von Arnim at r. Bank seal and Brandenburg Gate at l. ctr. on back.	FV	FV	5.00

Cat. #	Denomination	Date, description	VG	VF	Unc
45	10 DEUTSCHE MARK	2.1.1989; 1.8.1991; 1.10.1993. Bluish purple and blue. C.F. Gauss at r. Sextant on back.	FV	FV	10.00

Cat. #	Denomination	Date, description	VG	VF	Unc
46	20 DEUTSCHE MARK	1.8.1991; 1.10.1993. Green, black and red-violet on m/c unpt. A. von Druste-Hülshoff at r. Quill pen and tree at l. ctr., open book at lower r. on back.	FV	FV	18.50

Cat. #	Denomination	Date, description	VG	VF	Unc
47	50 DEUTSCHE MARK	2.1.1989; 1.8.1991; 1.10.1993. Dark brown on m/c unpt. B. Neuman at r. Architectural drawings on back.	FV	FV	45.00

Cat. #	Denomination	Date, description	VG	VF	Unc
48	100 DEUTSCHE MARK	2.1.1989; 1.8.1991; 1.10.1993. Blue and m/c. C. Schumann at r. Building, grand piano on back. Multiple tuning forks in wmk. area.	FV	FV	85.00

Cat. #	Denomination	Date, description	VG	VF	Unc
49	200 DEUTSCHE MARK	2.1.1989. Red-orange and m/c. P. Ehrlich at r. Microscope on back.	FV	FV	160.00

| 50 | 500 DEUTSCHE MARK | 1.8.1991; 1.10.1993. Reddish purple and m/c. Maria S. Merian at r. Dandelion w/ butterfly and caterpillar on back. | FV | FV | 400.00 |

| 51 | 1000 DEUTSCHE MARK | 1.8.1991; 1.10.1993. Deep violet brown and blue-green on m/c unpt. City drawing at ctr., Wilhelm and Jacob Grimm at ctr. r. Bank seal at l., book frontipice of "Deutches Wörterbuch" over entry for freedom. Child collecting falling stars in wmk. area at ctr. on back. | FV | FV | 775.00 |

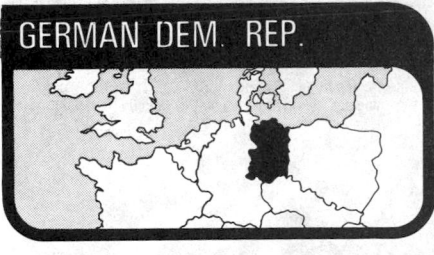

The German Democratic Republic (East Germany), located on the great north European plain ceased to exist in 1990.

During the closing days of World War II in Europe, Soviet troops advancing into Germany from the east occupied the German provinces of Mecklenburg, Brandenburg, Saxony-Anhalt, Saxony and Thuringia. These five provinces comprised the occupation zone administered by the Soviet Union after the cessation of hostilities. The other three zones were administered by the U.S., Great Britain and France. Under the Potsdam agreement, questions affecting Germany as a whole were to be settled by the commanders in chief of the occupation zones acting jointly and by unanimous decision. When Soviet intransigence rendered the quadripartite commission inoperable, the three western zones were united to form the Federal Republic of Germany, May 23, 1949. Thereupon the Soviet Union dissolved its occupation zone and established it as the Democratic Republic of Germany, Oct. 7, 1949. East and West Germany became reunited as one country on July 1, 1990.

MONETARY SYSTEM

1 Mark = 100 Pfennig

REPLACEMENT NOTES

#22–33, YA-YZ, XA-XZ and ZA–ZZ.

Deutsche Notenbank

1964 ISSUE

#22 and 25 arms at l. on back.

Cat. #	Denomination	Date, description	VG	VF	Unc
22	5 MARK	1964. Brown on m/c unpt. A. von Humboldt at r. Humboldt University at l. ctr. on back.	1.25	3.00	8.00

#23, 24 and 26 arms at upper r. ctr.

| 23 | 10 MARK | 1964. Green on m/c unpt. F. von Schiller at r. Zeiss Factory at l. ctr. on back. | 3.00 | 6.00 | 15.00 |

#24-26 portr. as wmk.

Cat. #	Denomination	Date, description	VG	VF	Unc
24	20 MARK	1964. Red-brown on m/c unpt. J.W. von Goethe at r. National Theater in Weimar at l. ctr. on back.	2.00	8.50	18.00
25	50 MARK	1964. Blue-green on m/c unpt. F. Engels at r. Wheat threshing at l. ctr. on back.	5.00	10.00	40.00

| 26 | 100 MARK | 1964. Blue on m/c unpt. K. Marx at r. Brandenburg Gate at l. ctr. on back. | 4.00 | 12.00 | 50.00 |

Staatsbank der DDR

1971; 1975 ISSUE

#27–31 arms at upper l. on face. Arms at l. on back. Portr. as wmk.

27	5 MARK	1975. Purple on m/c unpt. T. Muntzer at r. Harvesting on back.			
		a. 6 digit lg. serial #.	.50	1.00	3.50
		b. 6 digit sm. serial #.	.25	.75	3.00

28	10 MARK	1971. Brown on m/c unpt. C. Zetkin at r. Woman at radio station on back.			
		a. 6 digit lg. serial #.	.50	2.00	6.00
		b. 7 digit sm. serial #.	.40	1.50	4.50

29	20 MARKS	1975. Green on m/c unpt. Goethe at r. Children leaving school on back.			
		a. 6 digit lg. serial #.	.85	2.50	10.00
		b. 7 digit sm. serial #.	1.00	3.50	8.50

30	50 MARK	1971. Red on m/c unpt. F. Engels at r. Oil refinery on back.			
		a. 7 digit lg. serial #.	2.00	7.00	15.00
		b. 7 digit sm. serial #.	1.50	6.00	12.50

Cat. #	Denomination	Date, description	VG	VF	Unc
31	100 MARK	1975. Blue on m/c unpt. K. Marx at r. Street scene in East Berlin on back.			
		a. 7 digit lg. serial #.	4.00	10.00	20.00
		b. 7 digit sm. serial #.	3.00	7.50	18.50

| 32 | 200 MARK | 1985. Dk. olive-green and dk. brown on m/c unpt. Family at r. Teacher dancing w/children in front of modern school bldg. at ctr. on back. Wmk: Dove. (Not issued.) | — | — | 80.00 |

| 33 | 500 MARK | 1985. Dk. brown on m/c unpt. Arms at r. and as wmk. Govt. bldg. Staatsrat (in Berlin) at ctr. on back. (Not issued.) | — | — | 80.00 |

FOREIGN EXCHANGE CERTIFICATES
Forum–Aussenhandelsgesellschaft M.B.H.

Certificates issued by state–owned export–import company These were in the form of checks for specified amounts for purchase of goods.

1 Mark = 1 DM (West German Mark)

| FX1 | 50 PFENNIG | 1979. Violet and orange. | 1.00 | 2.00 | 4.00 |

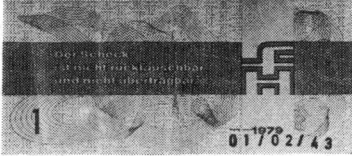

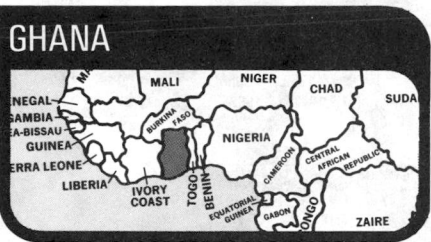

GHANA

The Republic of Ghana, a member of the British Commonwealth situated on the West Coast of Africa between the Ivory Coast and Togo, has an area of 92,098 sq. mi. (238,537 sq. km.) and a population of 14.8 million, almost entirely African. Capital: Accra. Cocoa (the major crop), coconuts, palm kernels and coffee are exported. Mining, second in importance to agriculture, is concentrated on gold, manganese and industrial diamonds.

Ghana was first visited by Portuguese traders in 1470, and through the 17th century was used by various European powers — England, Denmark, Holland, Germany — as a center for their slave trade. Britain achieved control of the Gold Coast in 1821, and established the colony of Gold Coast in 1874. In 1901, Britain annexed the neighboring Ashanti Kingdom; the same year a northern region known as the Northern Territories became a British protectorate. Part of the former German colony of Togoland was mandated to Britain by the League of Nations and administered as part of the Gold Coast. The state of Ghana, comprising the Gold Coast and British Togoland, obtained independence on March 6, 1957, becoming the first black African colony to do so. On July 1, 1960, Ghana adopted a republican constitution, changing from a ministerial to a presidential form of government. The government was overthrown, the constitution suspended and the National Assembly dissolved by the Ghanaian Army and police on Feb. 24, 1966. The government was returned to civilian authority in Oct. 1969, but was again seized by military officers in a bloodless coup on Jan. 13, 1972. Ghana remains a member of the Commonwealth of Nations, with executive authority vested in the Supreme Military Council.

Ghana's monetary denomination of "cedi" is derived from the word "sedie" meaning cowrie, a shell money commonly employed by coastal tribes.

MONETARY SYSTEM
1 Shilling = 12 Pence
1 Pound = 20 Shillings to 1965
1 Cedi = 100 Pesewas, 1965–

REPLACEMENT NOTES
#10–16: Z/99 prefix. #17–22: dated 1979-80: ZZ prefix; 1982 date: XX prefix. #23–28: Z/1 prefix.

Bank of Ghana

Pound System

#1–3 various date and sign. varieties. Wmk: *GHANA* in star.

Cat. #	Denomination	Date, description	VG	VF	Unc
FX2	1 MARK	1979. Brown and rose.	1.00	2.00	4.00
FX3	5 MARK	1979. Green and rose.	1.50	3.00	6.00
FX4	10 MARK	1979. Blue and lt. green.	2.00	4.50	10.00
FX5	50 MARK	1979. Red and orange.	3.00	7.00	15.00
FX6	100 MARK	1979. Olive and yellow.	4.00	10.00	30.00
FX7	500 MARK	1979. Gray-brown, violet and light blue.	8.00	20.00	80.00

Cat. #	Denomination	Date, description	VG	VF	Unc
1	10 SHILLINGS	1958–63. Green and brown. Bank in Accra at ctr. r. Star on back.			
		a. 2 sign. Printer: TDLR. 1.7.1958.	2.00	5.00	15.00
		b. W/o imprint. 1.7.1961; 1.7.1962.	1.00	3.00	10.00
		c. 1 sign. 1.7.1963.	.75	2.50	8.00

Cat. #	Denomination	Date, description	VG	VF	Unc
2	1 POUND	1958–62. Red-brown and blue. Bank in Accra at ctr. Coconuts in 2 piles on back.			
		a. Printer: TDLR. 1.7.1958; 1.4.1959.	1.00	3.00	10.00
		b. W/o imprint. 1.7.1961; 1.7.1962.	1.00	2.50	8.50

3	5 POUNDS	1.7.1958–1.7.1962. Purple and orange. Bank in Accra at ctr. Ships and logs on back.	5.00	15.00	35.00

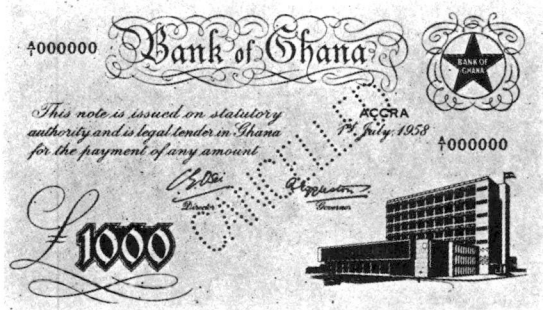

4	1000 POUNDS	1.7.1958. Black-brown. Bank in Accra at lower r.	—	100.00	300.00

NOTE: #4 was used in interbank transactions.

Cedi System

1965 ISSUE

#5–9 portr. Kwame Nkrumah and as wmk.

5	1 CEDI	ND (1965). Blue on m/c unpt. K. Nkrumah at r. Bank on back.	.50	2.00	4.00
6	5 CEDIS	ND (1965). Dk. brown on m/c unpt. K. Nkrumah at r. Parliament House on back.	1.00	3.00	7.50

7	10 CEDIS	ND (1965). Green on m/c unpt. K. Nkrumah at l. Freedom and Justice shrine on back.	2.00	5.00	15.00

Cat. #	Denomination	Date, description	VG	VF	Unc
8	50 CEDIS	ND (1965). Red on m/c unpt. K. Nkrumah at l. Island and palm trees on back.	6.00	12.50	35.00

9	100 CEDIS	ND (1965). Purple on m/c unpt. K. Nkrumah at r. Hospital on back.	10.00	25.00	60.00

9A	1000 CEDIS	ND(1965). Black. Lg. star at upper l. Central Bank in Accra at r. on back.	—	—	—

1967 ISSUE

Various date and sign. varieties.

#10–16 wmk: Arms.

10	1 CEDI	23.2.1967–1.10.1973. Blue on m/c unpt. Cocoa beans at r. Shield and implements on back.	.25	1.00	3.50

Cat. #	Denomination	Date, description	VG	VF	Unc
11	5 CEDIS	23.2.1967; 8.1.1969. Dk. brown on m/c unpt. Wood carving of a bird at r. Animal carvings on back.	2.00	8.00	30.00

Cat. #	Denomination	Date, description	VG	VF	Unc
12	10 CEDIS	23.2.1967; 8.1.1969; 1.10.1970. Red on m/c unpt. Art products at r. Small statuettes on back.	1.00	5.00	17.50

1972–73 ISSUE

			VG	VF	Unc
13	1 CEDI	1973–78. Blue-black on deep green, deep purple and m/c unpt. Young boy w/slingshot at r. Man cutting fruit from a tree on back.			
		a. 2.1.1973.	.20	.50	1.50
		b. 2.1.1975; 2.1.1976; 2.1.1978.	.10	.20	.50

NOTE: Date 2.1.1976 has 2 minor varieties in length of *"2nd"* as part of date.

Cat. #	Denomination	Date, description	VG	VF	Unc
14	2 CEDIS	1972–78. Green on m/c unpt. Young man w/hoe at r. Workers in field on back.			
		a. 21.6.1972. Sign. 1. Serial # prefix A.	.25	.60	2.00
		b. 21.6.1972. Sign. 2. Serial # prefix B.	.25	.60	2.00
		c. 2.1.1977; 2.1.1978.	.10	.25	.65

			VG	VF	Unc
15	5 CEDIS	1973–78. Brown on m/c unpt. Woman wearing lg. hat at r. Huts on back.			
		a. 2.1.1973; 2.1.1975.	.25	.60	2.00
		b. 2.1.1977; 4.7.1977; 2.1.1978.	.20	.50	1.00

			VG	VF	Unc
16	10 CEDIS	1973–78. Red on m/c unpt. Elderly man smoking a pipe at r. Dam on back.			
		a. 2.1.1973. Sign. 1. Serial # prefix A/1.	.35	1.25	4.50
		b. 2.1.1973. Sign. 2. Serial # prefix B/1.	.35	1.25	4.50
		c. 2.1.1975.	.35	1.25	4.50
		d. 2.1.1976; 2.1.1977; 2.1.1978.	.10	.20	.40

1979 ISSUE

#17–21, 2 serial # varieties.

#17–22 wmk: Arms.

			VG	VF	Unc
17	1 CEDI	7.2.1979; 6.3.1982. Green and m/c. Young man at r. Man weaving on back.	.10	.20	1.00

Cat. #	Denomination	Date, description	VG	VF	Unc
18	2 CEDIS	7.2.1979; 2.1.1980; 6.3.1982. Blue and m/c. School girl at r. Workers w/plants in field on back.	.10	.25	.75

| 19 | 5 CEDIS | 7.2.1979; 2.1.1980; 6.3.1982. Red and m/c. Elderly man at r. Men cutting log on back. | .15 | .35 | 1.25 |

| 20 | 10 CEDIS | 7.2.1979–6.3.1982. Purple and m/c. Young woman at r. Fishermen w/long net on back. | .25 | 1.50 | 4.00 |

Cat. #	Denomination	Date, description	VG	VF	Unc
21	20 CEDIS	7.2.1979; 2.7.1980; 6.3.1982. Green and m/c. Miner at r. Man weaving on back.	.35	1.00	3.00

| 22 | 50 CEDIS | 7.2.1979; 2.7.1980. Brown and m/c. Old man at r. Men cutting coconuts on back. | .20 | .60 | 1.75 |

NOTE: Date 2.1.1980 is reported for #22, not confirmed.

1983–91 ISSUE

| 23 | 10 CEDIS | 15.5.1984. Purple and m/c. W. Larbi, F. Otoo, E. Nukpor at l. People going to rural bank on back. | FV | .25 | .75 |

#24–28 wmk: Eagle's head above star.

| 24 | 20 CEDIS | 15.5.1984; 15.7.1986. Shades of green and aqua. Qn. Mother Yaa Asantewa at l. Workers and flag procession on back. | FV | .50 | 1.75 |

Cat. #	Denomination	Date, description	VG	VF	Unc
28	500 CEDIS	1986–. Purple and blue-green on m/c unpt. Arms at r. Trees, fruit and miner at ctr. on back.			
		a. Sign. J. S. Addo. 31.12.1986.	FV	2.00	7.00
		b. Sign. G. K. Agama. 20.4.1989; 19.7.1990; 19.9.1991; 14.10.1992; 10.8.1993; 10.6.1994.	FV	FV	3.75

#29–31 arms at lower l. and as wmk. Sign. G. K. Agama.

Cat. #	Denomination	Date, description	VG	VF	Unc
25	50 CEDIS	1.4.1983; 15.5.1984; 15.7.1986. Brown, violet and m/c. Boy w/hat at l. ctr. Drying grain at ctr. on back.	FV	.60	2.00

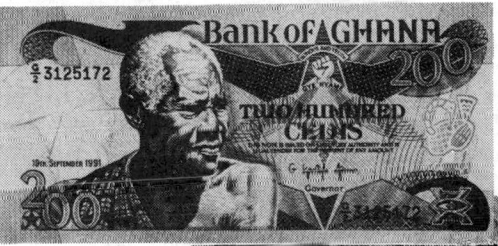

Cat. #	Denomination	Date, description	VG	VF	Unc
26	100 CEDIS	1983–. Purple, blue and m/c. Woman at l. ctr. Loading produce onto truck at ctr. on back.			
		a. Sign. J. S. Addo. 1.4.1983; 15.5.1984; 15.7.1986.	FV	.75	3.50
		b. Sign. G. K. Agama. 19.7.1990; 19.9.1991.	FV	FV	2.50

Cat. #	Denomination	Date, description	VG	VF	Unc
29	1000 CEDIS	1991–. Dk. brown, dk. blue and dk. green on m/c unpt. Jewels at r. Harvesting fruit at ctr. on back.			
		a. 22.2.1991.	FV	2.00	7.00
		b. Segmented foil security thread. 22.7.1993; 10.6.1994.	FV	FV	4.50

Cat. #	Denomination	Date, description	VG	VF	Unc
27	200 CEDIS	1983–. Lt. brown, orange and m/c. Old man at l. ctr. Children in classroom at ctr. on back.			
		a. Sign. J. S. Addo. 1.4.1983; 15.5.1984; 15.7.1986.	FV	1.25	4.00
		b. Sign. G. K. Agama. 20.4.1989; 19.7.1990; 19.9.1991; 14.10.1992; 10.8.1993.	FV	FV	2.50

Cat. #	Denomination	Date, description	VG	VF	Unc
30	2000 CEDIS	16.6.1994. Red-brown, violet and black on m/c unpt. Suspension bridge at r. Fisherman loading nets into boat at l. ctr. on back.	FV	FV	9.00

Cat. #	Denomination	Date, description	VG	VF	Unc
31	5000 CEDIS	29.6.1994. Lg. stars in unpt. at ctr., supported shield of arms at upper r. Red-brown and green on m/c unpt. Map at l., freighter in harbor, log flow in foreground on back.	FV	FV	22.00

COLLECTOR SERIES

Cat. #	Date, denomination	Description	Issue Price	Mkt. Val.
CS1	1977 1–10 CEDIS	#13–16 w/ovpt: *SPECIMEN* and Maltese cross prefix serial #.	14.00	25.00

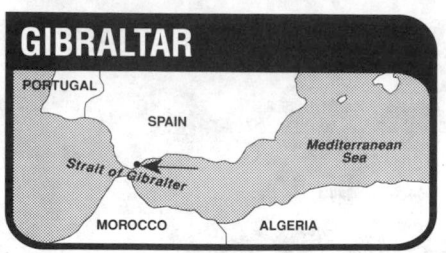

GIBRALTAR

PORTUGAL

SPAIN

Mediterranean Sea

Strait of Gibraltar

MOROCCO ALGERIA

The British Colony of Gibraltar, located at the southernmost point of the Iberian Peninsula, has an area of 2.25 sq. mi. (5.8 sq. km.) and a population of 29,048 Capital (and only town): Gibraltar. Aside from its strategic importance as guardian of the western entrance to the Mediterranean Sea, Gibraltar is also a free port, British naval base, and coaling station.

Gibraltar, rooted in Greek mythology as one of the Pillars of Hercules, has long been a coveted stronghold. Moslems took it from Spain and fortified it in 711. Spain retook it in 1309, lost it again to the Moors in 1333, and retook it in 1462. After Barbarossa sacked Gibraltar in 1540, Spain strengthened its defenses and held it until the War of the Spanish Succession when it was captured by a combined British and Dutch force, 1704. Britain held it against the Franco-Spanish attacks of 1704–05 and through the historic "Great Siege" of 1779–83. Recently Spain has attempted to discourage British occupancy by harassment and economic devices. In 1967, Gibraltar's inhabitants voted 12,138 to 44 to remain under British rule.

RULERS
British

MONETARY SYSTEM
1 Shilling = 12 Pence
1 Pound = 20 Shillings to 1971
1 Pound = 100 New Pence, 1971–

Government of Gibraltar

1958 ISSUE

#17–19 printer: TDLR.

Cat. #	Denomination	Date, description	VG	VF	Unc
17	10 SHILLINGS	3.10.1958; 1.5.1965. Blue on yellow-brown unpt. Rock of Gibraltar at l.	2.50	15.00	95.00

			VG	VF	Unc
18	1 POUND	1958–75. Green on yellow-brown unpt. Rock of Gibraltar at bottom ctr.			
		a. Sign. title: *FINANCIAL SECRETARY.* 3.10.1958; 1.5.1965.	2.50	8.50	37.50
		b. Sign. title: *FINANCIAL AND DEVELOPMENT SECRETARY.* 20.11.1971.	2.00	5.00	17.00
		c. 20.11.1975.	3.00	15.00	85.00

			VG	VF	Unc
19	5 POUNDS	1958–75. Brown. Rock of Gibraltar at bottom ctr.			
		a. Sign. title: *FINANCIAL SECRETARY.* 3.10.1958; 1.5.1965.	12.50	35.00	165.00
		b. Sign. title: *FINANCIAL AND DEVELOPMENT SECRETARY.* 1.5.1965; 20.11.1971; 20.11.1975.	10.00	27.50	125.00

1975 DATED ISSUE

#20–24 Qn. Elizabeth II at ctr. and as wmk. Sign. varieties. Printer: TDLR.

Cat. #	Denomination	Date, description	VG	VF	Unc
20	1 POUND	1975–. Brown and red on m/c unpt. Bldg. w/flag on back. 3 sign. varieties.			
		a. 20.11.1975 (1978).	FV	FV	6.00
		b. 15.9.1979.	FV	FV	5.50
		c. 21.10.1986; 4.8.1988.	FV	FV	4.50

			VG	VF	Unc
21	5 POUNDS	1975; 1988. Green on m/c unpt. Back like #20. 2 sign. varieties.			
		a. 20.11.1975.	FV	FV	20.00
		b. 4.8.1988.	FV	FV	13.50
22	10 POUNDS	20.11.1975 (1977). Blue on m/c unpt. Lg. bldg. on back.	FV	FV	22.50

			VG	VF	Unc
23	20 POUNDS	1975–. Lt. brown on m/c unpt. Back similar to #22. 3 sign. varieties.			
		a. 20.11.1975 (1978).	FV	50.00	195.00
		b. 15.9.1979.	FV	40.00	140.00
		c. 1.7.1986.	FV	FV	60.00

1986 ISSUE

Cat. #	Denomination	Date, description	VG	VF	Unc
24	50 POUNDS	27.11.1986. Purple and m/c. Rock of Gibraltar on back.	FV	FV	120.00

COLLECTOR SERIES

Cat. #	Date, denomination	Description	Issue Price	Mkt. Val.
CS1	1975 1–20 POUNDS.	#20–23 w/ovpt: *SPECIMEN* and Maltese cross prefix serial #.	14.00	35.00

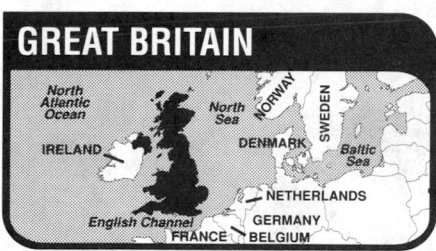

GREAT BRITAIN

The United Kingdom of Great Britain and Northern Ireland, located off the northwest coast of the European continent, has an area of 94,227 sq. mi. (244,046 sq. km.) and a population of 56.6 million. Capital: London. The economy is based on industrial activity and trading. Machinery, motor vehicles, chemicals, and textile yarns and fabrics are exported.

After the departure of the Romans, who brought Britain into an active relationship with Europe, Britain fell prey to invaders from Scandinavia and the Low Countries who drove the original Britons into Scotland and Wales, and established a profusion of kingdoms that finally united in the 11th century under the Danish King Canute. Norman rule, following the conquest of 1066, stimulated the development of those institutions which have since distinguished British life. Henry VIII (1509–47) turned Britain from continental adventuring and faced it to the sea — a decision that made Britain a world power during the reign of Elizabeth I (1558–1603). Strengthened by the Industrial Revolution and the defeat of Napoleon, 19th century Britain turned to the remote parts of the world and established a colonial empire of such extent and prosperity that the world has never seen its like. World Wars I and II sealed the fate of the Empire and relegated Britain to a lesser role in world affairs by draining her resources and inaugurating a worldwide movement toward national self-determination in her former colonies.

By the mid-20th century, most of the territories formerly comprising the British Empire had gained Independence, and the empire had evolved into the Commonwealth of Nations, an association of equal and autonomous states which enjoy special trade interests. The Commonwealth is presently (1983) composed of 49 member nations, including the United Kingdom. All recognize the British monarch as head of the Commonwealth. Fourteen continue to recognize the British monarch as Chief of State. They are: United Kingdom, Australia, New Zealand, Bahamas, Barbados, Canada, Fiji, Jamaica, Mauritius, Papua New Guinea, Solomon Islands, St. Lucia, Kiribati and Tuvalu.

RULERS
Elizabeth II, 1952–

MONETARY SYSTEM
1 Shilling = 12 Pence
1 Pound = 20 Shillings to 1971
1 Pound = 100 New Pence, 1971–

REPLACEMENT NOTES
#130–133, letter M as one of the letters in series prefix. #134–137, Page sign. only, M## or ##M series prefix.

NOTE: This section has been renumbered from the old 7th Edition of General Issues.

Bank of England

Founded in 1694, the Bank of England is the greatest banking institution formed. Although torn by crisis in its infancy, today it enjoys the public's confidence in the expression "As safe as the Bank of England".

The earliest recorded notes were all handwritten promissory notes and certificates of deposit of 1694. The first partially printed notes were introduced ca. 1696 with handwritten amounts. By 1745 all notes were printed with partial denominations of round figures in denominations of 20 Pounds through 1000 Pounds, allowing handwritten denominations of shillings to be added on.

In 1759 the word *POUNDS was also printed on the notes.*

From 1752 the Chief Cashier's handwritten name as payee is usually found and from 1782 it was used exclusively. From 1798 until 1855 it was actually printed on the notes. In 1855 notes were produced made simply payable to *bearer. Notes were issued in denominations of 1 Pound through 1000 Pounds.*

For specialized listings of early Bank of England notes refer to *English Paper Money*, by Vincent Duggleby.

1957 ISSUE

Cat. #	Denomination	Date, description	VG	VF	Unc
371 (128)	5 POUNDS	ND (1957–61). Blue and m/c. Helmeted Britannia hd. at l., St. George and dragon at lower ctr., denomination £5 in blue print on back. Sign. L.K. O'Brien.	10.00	20.00	45.00
372 (129)	5 POUNDS	ND (1961–63). Blue and m/c. Like #371 but denomination £5 recessed in white on back.	10.00	20.00	45.00

1960–64 ISSUE

#130–138 Qn. Elizabeth II at r.

Cat. #	Denomination	Date, description	VG	VF	Unc
373 (130)	**10 SHILLINGS**	ND (1960–70). Brown on m/c unpt.			
		a. Sign. L. K. O'Brien. (1960–61).	2.00	4.00	12.00
		b. Sign. J. Q. Hollom. (1962–66).	1.50	3.00	10.00
		c. Sign. J. S. Fforde. (1966–70).	1.50	2.50	7.00

Cat. #	Denomination	Date, description	VG	VF	Unc
374 (131)	**1 POUND**	ND (1960–77). Deep green on m/c unpt.			
		a. Sign. L. K. O'Brien. (1960–61).	2.00	3.00	10.00
		b. Sign. J. Q. Hollom. (1962–66).	2.00	3.00	8.00
		c. Sign. J. S. Fforde. (1966–70).	2.00	3.00	7.00
		d. Sign. J. B. Page. (1970–77).	2.00	3.00	6.00

Cat. #	Denomination	Date, description	VG	VF	Unc
375 (132)	**5 POUNDS**	ND (1963–72). Deep blue on m/c unpt.			
		a. Sign. J. Q. Hollom. (1962–66).	9.00	17.50	32.50
		b. Sign. J. S. Fforde. (1966–70).	9.00	15.00	30.00
		c. Sign. J. B. Page. (1970–71).	9.00	15.00	30.00

Cat. #	Denomination	Date, description	VG	VF	Unc
376 (133)	**10 POUNDS**	ND (1964). Deep brown on m/c unpt.			
		a. Sign. J. Q. Hollom. (1964–66).	18.00	25.00	45.00
		b. Sign. J. S. Fforde. (1966–70).	18.00	22.50	40.00
		c. Sign. J. B. Page. (1970–77).	18.00	22.50	40.00

1971–82 ISSUE

Cat. #	Denomination	Date, description	VG	VF	Unc
377 (134)	**1 POUND**	ND (1978–82). Deep green on m/c unpt. Back guilloches gray at lower l. and r. corners. Sir I. Newton at ctr. r. on back and in wmk.			
		a. Green sign. J. B. Page. (1978–82).	2.00	3.00	6.00
		b. Back guilloches lt. green at lower l. and r. Black sign. D. H. F. Somerset. (1982–84).	2.00	3.00	5.00

#135–138 Qn. Elizabeth II in robes on r.

Cat. #	Denomination	Date, description	VG	VF	Unc
378 (135)	5 POUNDS	ND (1971–90). Blue-black on m/c unpt. Duke of Wellington on back and in wmk.			
		a. Blue-gray sign. J. B. Page. (1971–72).	FV	FV	27.50
		b. Black sign. J. B. Page. Litho back w/ small *L* at lower l. (1973–82).	FV	FV	22.50
		c. Black sign. D. H. F. Somerset. (1982–88). Thin security thread.	FV	FV	20.00
		d. Sign. D. H. F. Somerset. Thick security thread.	FV	FV	25.00
		e. Sign. G. M. Gill (1988–91).	FV	FV	18.50

Cat. #	Denomination	Date, description	VG	VF	Unc
381 (138)	50 POUNDS	ND (1981–93). Olive-green and brown on m/c unpt. . Wmk: Qn. Elizabeth II at l., w/o imprint. View and plan of St. Paul's Cathedral at l., Sir C. Wren at ctr. r. on back.			
		a. Black sign. D. H .F. Somerset (1981–88).	FV	FV	175.00
		b. Modified background and guilloche colors. Segmented foil on security thread on surface. Sign. G. M. Gill (1988–91).	FV	FV	135.00
		c. Sign. G. E. A. Kentfield (1991–93).	FV	FV	185.00

1990–92 ISSUE
#139-141 Qn. Elizabeth II at r. and as wmk.

Cat. #	Denomination	Date, description	VG	VF	Unc
379 (136)	10 POUNDS	ND (1975–91). Deep brown on m/c unpt. F. Nightingale on back and as wmk.			
		a. Brown sign. J. B. Page. (1978–82).	FV	20.00	40.00
		b. Black sign. D. H. F. Somerset (1982–88).	FV	FV	35.00
		c. Black sign. D. H. F. Somerset.W/segmented security thread. (1982–88).	FV	FV	35.00
		d. Sign. G. M. Gill (1988–91).	FV	FV	32.50
		e. Sign. G. E. A. Kentfield (1991).	FV	FV	45.00

Cat. #	Denomination	Date, description	VG	VF	Unc
382 (139)	5 POUNDS	©1990 (1990–93). Dk. brown and deep blue-green on m/c unpt. Britannia seated at upper l.; Rocket locomotive at l.; G. Stephenson at r. on back.			
		a. Lt. blue-gray sign. of G. M. Gill (1990–91).	FV	FV	15.00
		b. Blue-black sign. of G. M. Gill, darker brownish-black portr. of Q.E. II (1991).	FV	FV	15.00
		c. Like b. Sign. G. E. A. Kentfield (1991).	FV	FV	15.00

Cat. #	Denomination	Date, description	VG	VF	Unc
380 (137)	20 POUNDS	ND (1970–91). Purple on m/c unpt. Shakespeare statue on back. Wmk: Qn. Elizabeth.			
		a. Wmk: Qn. Sign. J. S. Fforde. (1970).	35.00	60.00	150.00
		b. Wmk: Qn. Sign. J. B. Page. (1970–82).	35.00	50.00	90.00
		c. Wmk: Qn. Sign. D. H. F. Somerset. (1982–84).	FV	FV	85.00
		d. Wmk: Shakespeare. Modified background colors. Segmented security thread. Sign. D. H. F. Somerset. (1984–88).	FV	FV	75.00
		e. Sign. G. M. Gill (1988–91).	FV	FV	70.00

Cat. #	Denomination	Date, description	VG	VF	Unc
383 (140)	10 POUNDS	©1992 (1992–93). Black, brown and red on m/c unpt. Arms at l. Cricket match at l., Charles Dickens at r. on back. Sign. G. E. A. Kentfield (1992).	FV	FV	25.00

Cat. #	Denomination	Date, description	VG	VF	Unc
387 (144)	20 POUNDS	©1993 (1993–). Like #384 but w/dk. value symbol at upper l. corner and substitution of value symbol for crown at upper r. corner on face. Additional value symbol at top r. on back.	FV	FV	37.50

Cat. #	Denomination	Date, description	VG	VF	Unc
384 (141)	20 POUNDS	©1991 (1991–93). Black, teal-violet and purple on m/c unpt. Britannia arms at l. Broken vertical foil strip and purple optical device at l. ctr. M. Faraday w/students at l., portr. at r. on back. Serial # olive-green to maroon at upper l. and dk. blue at r.			
		a. Sign. G. M. Gill (1990–91).	FV	FV	55.00
		b. Sign. G. E. A. Kentfield (1991).	FV	FV	60.00

1993 MODIFIED ISSUE

#142–145 Qn. Elizabeth II at r. and as wmk. Sign. G. E. A. Kentfield.

Cat. #	Denomination	Date, description	VG	VF	Unc
385 (142)	5 POUNDS	©1990 (1993–). Like #382 but w/dk. value symbol at upper l. corner, also darker shading on back.	FV	FV	12.00

| 388 (145) | 50 POUNDS | ©1994 (1994–). Brownish-black, red and violet on m/c unpt. Allegory in oval in unpt. at l. Bank gatekeeper at lower l., his house at l. and Sir J. Houblon at r. on back. | FV | FV | 100.00 |

MILITARY
British Armed Forces, Special Vouchers

SIXTH SERIES (1972)

#M44–M46 printer: DLR.

Cat. #	Denomination	Date, description	VG	VF	Unc
386 (143)	10 POUNDS	©1993 (1993–). Like #383 but w/enhanced symbols for value and substitution of value £10 for crown at upper r. on face. Additional value symbol at top r. on back.	FV	FV	20.00
M44	5 NEW PENCE	ND (1972). Brown and green.	—	—	2.00

Cat. #	Denomination	Date, description	VG	VF	Unc
M45	10 NEW PENCE	ND (1972). Violet and green.	—	—	3.00

M46	50 NEW PENCE	ND (1972). Green.	—	—	4.00

#M47–M49 printer: BWC.

M47	5 NEW PENCE	ND (1972). Like #M44.	—	—	1.50
M48	10 NEW PENCE	ND (1972). Like #M45.	—	—	2.00
M49	50 NEW PENCE	ND (1972). Like #M46.	—	—	3.00

COLLECTOR SERIES

Cat. #	Date, denomination	Description	Issue Price	Mkt. Val.
CS1	1995 5 POUNDS	Uncut sheet of 3 notes #385 in folder. Serial #AB16–AB18. Last web printing.	68.00	70.00
CS2	1995 5 POUNDS	Uncut sheet 3 notes #385 in folder. Serial #AC01–AC03. First sheet printing.	68.00	70.00

NOTE: Issued to commemorate the 200th Anniversary of the first 5 Pound note.

GREECE

The Hellenic Republic of Greece is situated in southeastern Europe on the southern tip of the Balkan Peninsula. The republic includes many islands, the most important of which are Crete and the Ionian Islands. Greece (including islands) has an area of 51,146 sq. mi. (131,944 sq. km.) and a population of 10 million. Capital: Athens. Greece is still largely agricultural. Tobacco, cotton, fruit and wool are exported.

Greece, the Mother of Western civilization, attained the peak of its culture in the 5th century BC, when it contributed more to government, drama, art and architecture than any other people to this time. Greece fell under Roman domination in the 2nd and 1st centruries BC, becoming part of the Byzantine Empire until Constantinople fell to the Crusaders in 1202. With the fall of Constantinople to the Turks in 1453, Greece became part of the Ottoman Empire. Independence from Turkey was won with the revolution of 1821–27. In 1833, Greece was established as a monarchy, with sovereignty guaranteed by Britain, France and Russia. After a lengthy power struggle between the monarchist forces and democratic factions, Greece was proclaimed a republic in 1925. The monarchy was restored in 1935 and reconfirmed by a plebiscite in 1946. The Italians invaded Greece via Albania on Oct. 28,1940 but were driven back well within the Albanian border. Germany began its invasion in April 1941 and quickly overran the entire country, driving off a British Expeditionary force by the end of April. King George II and his new government went into exile. The German - Italian occupation of Greece lasted until Oct. 1944. On April 21, 1967, a military junta took control of the government and suspended the constitution. King Constantine II made an unsuccessful attempt against the junta in the fall of 1968 and consequently fled to Italy. The monarchy was formally abolished by plebiscite, Dec. 8, 1974, and Greece established as the "Hellenic Republic," the third republic in Greek history.

The island of Crete (Kreti), located 60 miles southeast of the Peloponnesus, was the center of a brilliant civilization that flourished before the advent of Greek culture. After being conquered by the Romans, Byzantines, Moslems and Venetians, Crete became part of the Turkish Empire in 1669. As a consequence of the Greek Revolution of the 1820s, it was ceded to Egypt. Egypt returned the island to the Turks in 1840, and they ceded it to Greece in 1913, after the Second Balkan War.

The Ionian Islands, situated in the Ionian Sea to the west of Greece, is the collective name for the islands of Corfu, Cephalonia, Zante, Santa Maura, Ithaca, Cthera and Paxo, with their minor dependencies. Before Britain acquired the islands, 1809–1814, they were at various times subject to the authority of Venice, France, Russia and Turkey. They remained under British control until their cession to Greece on March 29, 1864.

RULERS

Paul I, 1947–1964
Constantine II, 1964–1973

MONETARY SYSTEM

1 Drachma = 100 Lepta, 1831–

REPLACEMENT NOTES

#195–: OOA prefix.

GREEK ALPHABET

A	α	Alpha	(ā)	I	ι	Iota	(ē)	P	ρ	Rho	(r)
B	β	Beta	(b)	K	κ	Kappa	(k)	Σ	σ	Sigma	(s)6
Γ	γ	Gamma	(g)	Λ	λ	Lambda	(l)	T	τ	Tau	(t)
Δ	δ	Delta	(d)	M	μ	Mu	(m)	Y	υ	Upsilon	(oo)
E	ε	Epsilon	(e)	N	ν	Nu	(n)	Φ	φ	Phi	(f)
Z	ζ	Zeta	(z)	Ξ	ξ	Xi	(ks)	X	χ	Chi	(H)
H	η	Eta	(ā)	O	o	Omicron	(o)	Ψ	ψ	Psi	(ps)
Θ	θ	Theta	(th)	Π	π	Pi	(p)	Ω	ω	Omega	(ō)

KINGDOM

ΤΡΑΠΕΖΑ ΤΗΣ ΕΛΛΑΔΟΣ

Bank of Greece

1964–70 ISSUE

REPUBLIC

ΤΡΑΠΕΖΑ ΤΗΣ ΕΛΛΑΔΟΣ

Bank of Greece

REPUBLIC

ΤΡΑΠΕΖΑ ΤΗΣ ΕΛΛΑΔΟΣ

Bank of Greece

1978 ISSUE

#199 and 200 wmk: Man's head from Delphi.

Cat. #	Denomination	Date, description	VG	VF	Unc
195	50 DRACHMAI	1.10.1964. Blue on m/c unpt. Arethusa at l., galley at bottom r. Shipyard on back.	.45	.85	2.00

Cat. #	Denomination	Date, description	VG	VF	Unc
199	50 DRACHMAI	8.12.1978. Blue on m/c unpt. Poseidon at l. Sailing ship at ctr., man and woman at r. on back.	FV	FV	1.00

196	100 DRACHMAI	1966–67. Red-brown on m/c unpt. Demokritos at l., bldg. and atomic symbol at r. University at ctr. on back.			
		a. Sign. Zolotas as Bank President. 1.7.1966.	8.00	20.00	65.00
		b. Sign. Galanis as Bank President. 1.10.1967.	.90	1.50	4.00

200	100 DRACHMAI	8.12.1978. Brown and violet on m/c unpt. Athena at l. Back maroon, green and orange; A. Korans at l., church at bottom r.	FV	FV	1.75

197	500 DRACHMAI	1.11.1968. Olive on m/c unpt. Relief of Elusis at ctr. Relief of animals at bottom l., fruit at bottom ctr. on back.	FV	FV	9.00

1983–87 ISSUE

#201–203 wmk: Man's head from Delphi.

198	1000 DRACHMAI	1.11.1970. Brown on m/c unpt. Zeus at l., stadium at bottom ctr. Back brown and green; woman at l. and view of city.			
		a. Wmk: Head of Aphrodite of Knidus in 3/4 profile (1970).	FV	20.00	50.00
		b. Wmk: Head of Ephebus of Anticythera in profile (1972).	FV	FV	15.00

201	500 DRACHMAI	1.2.1983. Deep green on m/c unpt. I. Capodistrias at l. ctr., his birthplace at lower r. Fortress overlooking Corfu on back.	FV	FV	4.50

Cat. #	Denomination	Date, description	VG	VF	Unc
202	1000 DRACHMAI	1.7.1987. Brown on m/c unpt. Ancient coin at lower ctr., Apollo at ctr. r. Discus thrower and Hera Temple ruins on back.	FV	FV	8.00

			VG	VF	Unc
203	5000 DRACHMAI	23.3.1984. Deep blue on m/c unpt. T. Kolokotronis at l. Landscape and view of town of Karytaina at ctr. r. on back.	FV	FV	35.00

1995 ISSUE

#204 and 204 wmk: Man's head from Delphi.

204	200 DRACHMAI	1995.			Expected new issue.

205 (204)	10,000 DRACHMAI	16.1.1995. Deep purple and purple on m/c unpt. Dr. G. Papanikolaou at l. ctr., microscope at lower ctr. r. Medical care frieze at bottom ctr., statue of Asklápios at ctr. r.	FV	FV	65.00

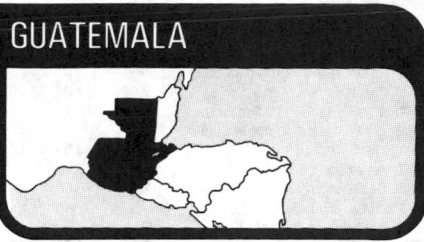

GUATEMALA

The Republic of Guatemala, the northernmost of the five Central American republics, has an area of 42,042 sq. mi. (108,889 sq. km.) and a population of 9.4 million. Capital: Guatemala City. The economy of Guatemala is heavily dependent on resources which are being developed. Coffee, cotton and bananas are exported.

Guatemala, once the site of the ancient Mayan civilization, was conquered by Pedro de Alvarado, the lieutenant of Cortes who undertook the conquest from Mexico. Skilled in strategy and cruelty, he progressed rapidly along the Pacific coastal lowlands to the highland plain of Quezaltenango where the decisive battle for Guatemala was fought. After routing the Mayan forces, he established the first capital of Guatemala in 1524.

Guatemala of the colonial period included all of Central America but Panama. Guatemala declared its independence of Spain in 1821 and was absorbed into the short-lived Mexican empire of Augustin Iturbide, 1822–23. From 1823 to 1839 Guatemala was a constituent state of the Central American Republic. Upon dissolution of the federation, Guatemala became an independent republic.

MONETARY SYSTEM
1 Quetzal = 100 Centavos, 1924–

Banco de Guatemala

1957-63 ISSUE

#91A–109 sign. title: *JEFE DE...* at r.

#91A–95A printer: ABNC.

Cat. #	Denomination	Date, description	VG	VF	Unc
91A	1/2 QUETZAL	22.1.1958. Brown. Hermitage of Cerro del Carmen at l. 2 Guatemalans on back.	2.00	7.50	40.00
92A	1 QUETZAL	16.1.1957; 22.1.1958. Green. Palace of the Captains General at l. Lake Atitlan on back.	2.00	6.00	32.50

93A	5 QUETZALES	22.1.1958. Purple vase (Vasija de Vaxactum) at l. Mayan-Spanish battle on back.	8.00	25.00	90.00
94A	10 QUETZALES	12.1.1962; 9.1.1963; 8.1.1964. Red. Stone-carving (Ara de Tikal) at l. Founding of old Guatemala on back.	10.00	40.00	125.00

95A	20 QUETZALES	9.1.1963; 8.1.1964; 15.1.1965. Blue. R. Landivar at l. Meeting of Independence on back.	17.50	70.00	225.00

1959-60 ISSUE

#A97A–102A sign. varieties. Printer: W&S.

Cat. #	Denomination	Date, description	VG	VF	Unc
A97A	1/2 QUETZAL	18.2.1959. Like #97. Lighter brown shadings around value guilloche at l. Printed area 2mm. smaller than #97A. 6-digit serial #.	2.00	7.00	40.00
97A	1/2 QUETZAL	18.2.1959; 13.1.1960; 18.1.1961. Similar to #A97A but darker brown shadings around value guilloche at l. 7-digit serial #.	.75	2.50	20.00
A98A	1 QUETZAL	18.2.1959. Green palace. Like #98. Dull green back. 6-digit serial #.	2.00	6.00	35.00
98A	1 QUETZAL	18.2.1959–8.1.1964. Black and green. Like #A98A, but black palace. Back bright green. 7-digit serial #.	1.00	3.50	17.50

Cat. #	Denomination	Date, description	VG	VF	Unc
99A	5 QUETZALES	18.2.1959. Like #99. Vase in purple.	8.00	25.00	90.00
99B	5 QUETZALES	18.2.1959–8.1.1964. Similar to #99A but redesigned guilloche. Vase in brown.	5.00	20.00	75.00

Cat. #	Denomination	Date, description	VG	VF	Unc
100A	10 QUETZALES	18.2.1959. Like #100. Stone in red.	15.00	40.00	135.00
100B	10 QUETZALES	18.2.1959; 13.1.1960; 18.1.1961. Similar to #100A but redesigned guilloche. Stone in brown.	12.50	30.00	100.00

Cat. #	Denomination	Date, description	VG	VF	Unc
101A	20 QUETZALES	13.1.1960–15.1.1965. Similar to #101, but portr. at r.	20.00	65.00	165.00
101B	100 QUETZALES	18.2.1959. Like #102, w/portr. at ctr.	115.00	250.00	500.00

Cat. #	Denomination	Date, description	VG	VF	Unc
102A	100 QUETZALES	13.1.1960–15.1.1965. Portr. at r.	115.00	250.00	450.00

1964-67 ISSUE

#103–109 sign. varieties. Printer: TDLR.

Cat. #	Denomination	Date, description	VG	VF	Unc
103	1/2 QUETZAL	8.1.1964–5.1.1972. Like #97A.	1.00	2.00	10.00

Cat. #	Denomination	Date, description	VG	VF	Unc
104	1 QUETZAL	8.1.1964–5.1.1972. Like #98A.	1.00	2.00	13.50

#105–109, 2 wmk. varieties.

Cat. #	Denomination	Date, description	VG	VF	Unc
105	5 QUETZALES	8.1.1964–6.1.1971. Like #99B.	3.00	7.50	25.00

Cat. #	Denomination	Date, description	VG	VF	Unc
106	10 QUETZALES	15.1.1965–7.1.1970. Similar to #100B.	8.00	25.00	85.00
107	20 QUETZALES	15.1.1965–6.1.1971. Like #101A.	17.50	45.00	165.00

Cat. #	Denomination	Date, description	VG	VF	Unc
108	50 QUETZALES	13.1.1967–5.1.1973. Orange and blue. Gen. J. Maria Orellana at r. Back orange; bank at ctr.	60.00	120.00	275.00
109	100 QUETZALES	21.1.1966–7.1.1970. Dk. blue and brown. Face like #102A. City and mountain on back.	75.00	140.00	300.00

1969-74 ISSUE

#110–116 various date and sign. varieties. Printer: TDLR.

Cat. #	Denomination	Date, description	VG	VF	Unc
110	1/2 QUETZAL	1972–83. Brown and m/c. Tecun Uman (National Hero) at r. Tikal Temple on back.			
		a. W/o security (flourescent) imprint. 5.1.1972; 5.1.1973.	.25	1.00	4.50
		b. Security (flourescent) imprint on back. 2.1.1974–20.4.1977.	.25	.60	2.50
		c. 4.1.1978–6.1.1983. Date at r.	FV	.50	2.50

Cat. #	Denomination	Date, description	VG	VF	Unc
111	1 QUETZAL	1972–83. Green and m/c. Gen. J. Maria Orellana at r. Banco de Guatemala on back.			
		a. Security (flourescent) imprint on face. Date at lower r. 5.1.1972; 5.1.1973.	.30	.25	5.50
		b. Security imprint as a. on face and back. 2.1.1974–2.1.1976.	.25	1.00	4.50
		c. Date at r. 5.1.1977–30.12.1983.	FV	.50	2.50

#112–116 wmk: Tecun Uman.

Cat. #	Denomination	Date, description	VG	VF	Unc
112	5 QUETZALES	1969–83. Purple and m/c. Gen. (later Pres.) J. Rufino Barrios at r. Classroom scene on back.			
		a. 3.1.1969–5.1.1973.	1.25	3.75	15.00
		b. 2.1.1974–20.4.1977	FV	2.50	10.00
		c. Date at r. 4.1.1978–6.1.1983.	FV	2.00	8.00

Cat. #	Denomination	Date, description	VG	VF	Unc
116	100 QUETZALES	1975–82. Brown and m/c. F. Marroquin at r. University of San Carlos de Borromeo on back.			
		a. 5.1.1972.	25.00	37.50	125.00
		b. 3.1.1975; 7.1.1976.	20.00	32.50	110.00
		c. 6.1.1982; 6.1.1983.	FV	30.00	100.00

1983 ISSUE

#117–123 design characteristics similar to previous issue. Wmk: Tecun Uman. Printer: G&D.

113	10 QUETZALES	1971–79; 1983. Red and m/c. Gen. M. Garcia Granados at r. National Assembly session of 1872 on back.			
		a. 6.1.1971; 5.1.1972.	2.25	5.00	28.50
		b. 3.1.1975; 7.1.1976; 5.1.1977; 20.4.1977.	2.00	4.50	18.50
		c. 3.1.1979–6.1.1983.	FV	3.75	15.00

117	1/2 QUETZAL	6.1.1983–4.1.1989. Brown and m/c. Tecun Uman at r. Tikal Temple on back. Similar to #110.	FV	.25	1.25
118	1 QUETZAL	30.12.1983–4.1.1989. Blue-green and m/c. Gen. J. Orellana at r. Banco de Guatemala bldg. on back. Similar to #111.	FV	.40	1.50
119	5 QUETZALES	6.1.1983–6.1.1988. Purple and m/c. J. Rufino Barrios at r. Similar to #112. Classroom scene on back.	FV	1.75	7.00

114	20 QUETZALES	1972–74; 1983; 1988. Blue and m/c. Dr. M. Galvez at r. Granting of Independence to Central America on back.			
		a. 5.1.1972; 5,1,1973; 2.1.1974.	4.00	7.50	30.00
		b. 6.1.1983.	3.50	6.00	25.00
		c. 6.1.1988.	FV	5.00	20.00

120	10 QUETZALES	30.12.1983–6.1.1988. Red-violet, red-brown and m/c. Gen. M. Garcia Granados at r. Similar to #113. National Assembly session of 1872 on back.	FV	3.50	10.00
121	20 QUETZALES	6.1.1983–7.1.1987. Blue and m/c. Dr. M. Galvez at r. Similar to #114.	FV	3.00	16.50

115	50 QUETZALES	1974; 1981–83. Orange and m/c. Carlos O. Zachrisson at r. Crop workers on back.			
		a. 2.1.1974.	10.00	18.50	75.00
		b. 7.1.1981; 6.1.1982; 6.1.1983.	9.00	15.00	60.00

122	50 QUETZALES	30.12.1983–7.1.1987. Orange, yellow-orange and m/c. Carlos O. Zachrisson at r. Similar to #115. Crop workers on back.	FV	16.50	32.50

Cat. #	Denomination	Date, description	VG	VF	Unc
123	100 QUETZALES	30.12.1983–7.1.1987. Brown and m/c. F. Marroquin at r. Similar to #116.	FV	25.00	55.00

1989-90 ISSUE
#124–126 printer: CBN.

124	1/2 QUETZAL	4.1.1989; 14.2.1992; 27.10.1993. Similar to #117.	FV	FV	.85

125	1 QUETZAL	3.1.1990; 6.3.1991; 14.2.1992. Similar to #118.	FV,	FV	1.00

126	5 QUETZALES	3.1.1990; 6.3.1991; 22.1.1992. Similar to #119.	FV	FV	3.00

#127–130 design characteristics similar to #120-123. Vertical serial # at l. Printer: TDLR.

Cat. #	Denomination	Date, description	VG	VF	Unc
127	10 QUETZALES	4.1.1989; 3.1.1990. Brown-violet, red and m/c. Similar to #120.	FV	FV	5.00

128	20 QUETZALES	4.1.1989; 3.1.1990; 22.1.1992. Blue-black, purple and blue on m/c unpt. Similar to #121.	FV	FV	9.50

129	50 QUETZALES	4.1.1989; 3.1.1990; 1994. Orange, green and m/c. Similar to #122.	FV	FV	20.00

130	100 QUETZALES	4.1.1989; 3.1.1990; 22.1.1992. Brown, red-brown and m/c. Similar to #123. Back lilac and m/c.	FV	FV	35.00

1992 ISSUE
#131-134 similar to #117-120 but more colorful backs. Printer: Oberthur.

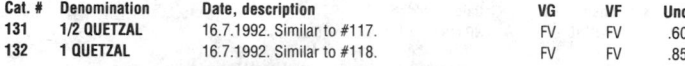

Cat. #	Denomination	Date, description	VG	VF	Unc
131	1/2 QUETZAL	16.7.1992. Similar to #117.	FV	FV	.60
132	1 QUETZAL	16.7.1992. Similar to #118.	FV	FV	.85

| 133 | 5 QUETZALES | 16.7.1992. Similar to #119. | FV | FV | 3.00 |
| 134 | 10 QUETZALES | 16.7.1992. Similar to #120. | FV | FV | 4.00 |

#135-137 similar to #121-122 but more colorful backs. Printer: BABN.

| 135 | 20 QUETZALES | 12.8.1992. Similar to #121. | FV | FV | 8.00 |
| 136 | 50 QUETZALES | 12.8.1992. Similar to #122. | FV | FV | 18.00 |

| 137 | 100 QUETZALES | 27.5.1992. Similar to #123. Date at lower l., gold colored device at r. Back lt. brown and m/c. | FV | FV | 32.50 |

1993 ISSUE

| 138 | 5 QUETZALES | 27.10.1993. Similar to #133. Printer: CBNC. | FV | FV | 3.00 |

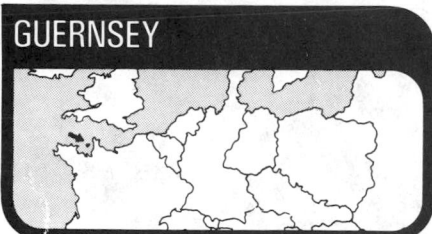

GUERNSEY

The Bailiwick of Guernsey, a British crown dependency located in the English Channel 30 miles (48 km.) west of Normandy, France, has an area of 30 sq. mi. (78 sq. km.), including the Isles of Alderney, Jethou, Herm, Brechou and Sark, and a population of 53,794. Capital: St. Peter Port. Agriculture and cattle breeding are the main occupations.

Militant monks from the Duchy of Normandy established the first permanent settlements on Guernsey prior to the Norman invasion of England, but the prevalence of prehistoric monuments suggests an earlier occupancy. The island, the only part of the Duchy of Normandy belonging to the British crown, has been a possession of Britain since the Norman Conquest of 1066. During the Anglo-French Wars, the harbors of Guernsey were employed in the building and outfitting of ships for the English privateers preying on French shipping. Guernsey is administered by its own laws and customs. Acts passed by the British Parliament are not applicable to Guernsey unless the island is specifically mentioned. During World War II, German troops occupied the island from June 30, 1940 to June 6, 1944.

RULERS
British

MONETARY SYSTEM
1 Penny = 8 Doubles
1 Shilling = 12 Pence
5 Shillings = 6 Francs
1 Pound = 20 Shillings to 1971
1 Pound = 100 New Pence 1971–

REPLACEMENT NOTES
#48–55, Z prefix.

States of Guernsey
1945; 1956 ISSUE
#42–44 printer: PBC.

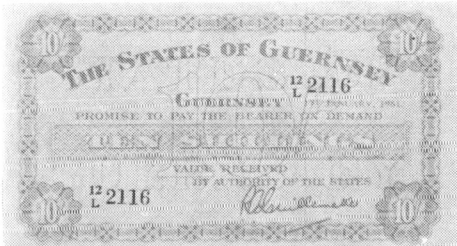

Cat. #	Denomination	Date, description	VG	VF	Unc
42	10 SHILLINGS	1945–66. Lilac on lt. green unpt. Back purple.			
		a. 1.8.1945–1.9.1957.	12.50	40.00	180.00
		b. 1.7.1958–1.3.1965.	5.00	15.00	80.00
		c. 1.7.1966.	3.00	10.00	40.00

43	1 POUND	1945–66. Purple on green unpt. Harbor entrance across ctr. Back green.			
		a. 1.8.1945–1.3.1957.	7.50	30.00	180.00
		b. 1.9.1957–1.3.1962 1.6.1963; 1.3.1965.	5.00	20.00	100.00
		c. 1.7.1966.	3.50	15.00	65.00

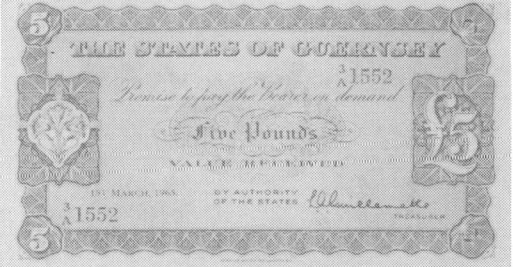

Cat. #	Denomination	Date, description	VG	VF	Unc
44	5 POUNDS	1.12.1956; 1.3.1965; 1.7.1966. Green and blue. Flowers at l.	35.00	100.00	525.00

1969; 1975 ISSUE

#45–47 printer: BWC.

45	1 POUND	ND (1969–75). Olive on pink and yellow unpt. Arms at ctr. Castle Cornet on back.			
		a. Sign. Guillemette.	2.00	5.00	25.00
		b. Sign. Hodder.	2.00	4.50	20.00
		c. Sign. Bull.	2.00	4.50	15.00

46	5 POUNDS	ND (1969–75). Purple on lt. brown unpt. Arms at r. City view and harbor wall on back.			
		a. Sign. Guillemette.	9.00	20.00	85.00
		b. Sign. Hodder.	9.00	15.00	50.00
		c. Sign. Bull.	9.00	17.50	57.50

47	10 POUNDS	ND (1975–80). Blue, green and m/c. Britannia w/lion and shield at l. Sir Isaac Brock and Battle of Queenston Hgts. on blue back. Sign. Hodder.	20.00	45.00	165.00

1980 ISSUE

#48–51 states seal at lower l. on face and as wmk. Printer: DLR.

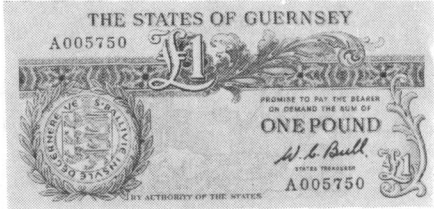

Cat. #	Denomination	Date, description	VG	VF	Unc
48	1 POUND	ND (1980). Dk. green and black on m/c unpt. Market square scene of 1822 at lower ctr. in unpt. D. De Lisle Brock and Royal Court of St. Peter Port on back. 135 x 67mm.			
		a. Black sign. W. C. Bull.	FV	FV	6.00
		b. Sign. M. J. Brown.	FV	FV	5.00

49	5 POUNDS	ND (1980). Purple, dk. brown and olive-brown on m/c unpt. Fort Grey at lower ctr. in unpt. T. De La Rue and Fountain St. at ctr., workers at envelope making machine at lower r. on back. Black sign. W. C. Bull. 146 x 78mm.	FV	FV	18.50

50	10 POUNDS	ND (1980). Purple, blue and blue-black on m/c unpt. Castle Cornet at lower ctr. Maj. Gen. Sir Isaac Brock and battle of Queenston Hgts. on back. 151 x 85mm.			
		a. Black sign. W. C. Bull.	FV	FV	32.50
		b. Sign. M. J. Brown.	FV	FV	30.00

Cat. #	Denomination	Date, description	VG	VF	Unc
51	20 POUNDS	ND (1980). Red, red-violet, brown and orange on m/c unpt. 1815 scene of Saumarez Park at lower ctr. in unpt. Adm. Lord de Saumarez and ships on back. 161 x 90mm.			
		a. Black sign. W. C. Bull.	FV	FV	60.00
		b. Sign. M. J. Brown.	FV	FV	55.00

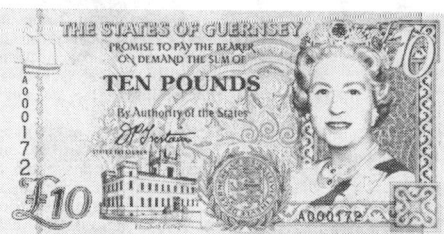

1991 ISSUE

#52–55 similar to #48-51 but reduced size. Wmk: Seal. Printer: DLR.

52	1 POUND	ND (ca.1991–). Similar to #48. 128 x 65mm.			
		a. Green sign. M. J. Brown.	FV	FV	3.75
		b. Sign. D. P. Trestain.	FV	FV	3.25

Cat. #	Denomination	Date, description	VG	VF	Unc
57	10 POUNDS	ND (1995). Violet, blue and dk. blue on m/c unpt. Elizabeth College at lower l. Saumarez Park above Le Niaux Watermill and Le Trepid Dolmen at l. ctr. on back.	FV	FV	25.00
58	20 POUNDS	ND (1996).	FV	FV	45.00

53	5 POUNDS	ND (1990–). Similar to #49. 136 x 70mm.			
		a. Brown sign. M. J. Brown.	FV	FV	13.50
		b. Sign. D. P. Trestain.	FV	FV	12.50
54	10 POUNDS	ND (ca.1991–). Similar to #50. 142 x 75mm.	FV	FV	22.50
		a. Blue sign. M. J. Brown.	FV	FV	27.00
		b. Sign. D. P. Trestain.	FV	FV	25.00

59 (56)	50 POUNDS	ND (1994). Dk. brown, dk. green and blue-black on m/c unpt. Royal Court House at lower l. Stone carving, letter of Marque at lower l., St. Andrew's Church at ctr. r. on back.	FV	FV	110.00

55	20 POUNDS	ND (ca.1991–). Similar to #51. 149 x 80mm.			
		a. Red-orange sign. M. J. Brown.	FV	FV	50.00
		b. Sign. D. P. Trestain.	FV	FV	47.50

1994–96 ISSUE

#56–59 Qn. Elizabeth II at r. and as wmk. States' seal at lower ctr. R. Sign. D. P. Trestain. Printer: TDLR.

56	5 POUNDS	ND (1996).	FV	FV	12.50

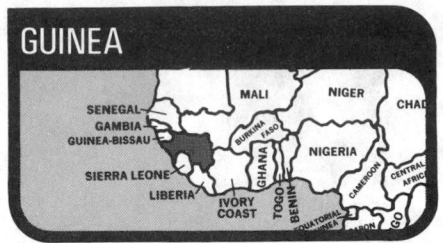

GUINEA

The Republic of Guinea (formerly French Guinea), situated on the Atlantic coast of Africa between Sierra Leone and Guinea-Bissau, has an area of 94,964 sq. mi. (245,957 sq. km.) and a population of 6.1 million. Capital: Conakry. Although Guinea contains one-third of the world's reserves of bauxite and significant deposits of iron ore, gold and diamonds, the economy is still dependent on agriculture. Aluminum, bananas, copra and coffee are exported.

The coast of Guinea was known to Portuguese navigators of the 15th century but was seldom visited by European traders of the 16th-18th centuries because of its dangerous coastal waters. French penetration of the area began in the mid-19th century with the entering into of protectorate treaties with several of the coastal chiefs. After a long struggle with Guinea's native leader Samory Toure, France secured the area and until 1890 administered it as a part of Senegal. In 1895 the colony (Guinee Francaise) became an autonomous part of the federation of French West Africa. The inhabitants were extended French citizenship in 1946 when the colony became an overseas territory of the French Union. Guinea became an independent republic on Oct. 2, 1958, when it declined to enter the new French Community.

MONETARY SYSTEM

1 Franc = 100 Centimes to 1971
1 Syli = 10 Francs, 1971–80
Franc System 1985–

REPLACEMENT NOTES

#12–15, ZZ prefix.

Banque Centrale de la République de Guinée

Franc System

1960 ISSUE

#12–15 Pres. Sekou Toure at l. Wmk: Dove.

Cat. #	Denomination	Date, description	VG	VF	Unc
12	50 FRANCS	1.3.1960. Brown and m/c. Heavy machinery on back.	.65	2.00	6.00

Cat. #	Denomination	Date, description	VG	VF	Unc
13	100 FRANCS	1.3.1960. Brown-violet and m/c. Pineapple field workers on back.	1.25	4.00	12.00
14	500 FRANCS	1.3.1960. Blue and m/c. Men pulling long boats ashore on back.	3.00	10.00	50.00

Cat. #	Denomination	Date, description	VG	VF	Unc
15	1000 FRANCS	1.3.1960. Green and m/c. Banana harvesting on back.	1.75	5.00	35.00

Syli System

1971 ISSUE

Law of 1.3.1960

#16–19 wmk: Dove.

16	10 SYLIS	1971. Brown and m/c. Patrice Lumumba at r. People w/bananas on back.	.20	.60	1.75

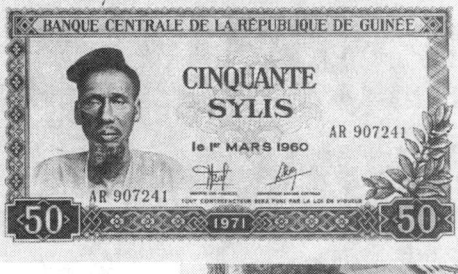

17	25 SYLIS	1971. Dk. brown and m/c. Man smoking a pipe at r. Man and cows on back.	.30	.85	2.50

18	50 SYLIS	1971. Green and m/c. Bearded man at l. Landscape w/large dam and reservoir on back.	1.00	3.00	9.00

Cat. #	Denomination	Date, description	VG	VF	Unc
19	100 SYLIS	1971. Purple and m/c. A.S. Toure at l. Steam shovel and 2 dump trucks on back.	.75	2.25	6.50

1980–81 ISSUE

Law of 1.3.1960

#20–27 wmk: Multiple stars and design.

Cat. #	Denomination	Date, description	VG	VF	Unc
20	1 SYLI	1981. Olive on green unpt. Mafori Bangoura at r.			
		a. Issued note.	.05	.15	.50
		s. Specimen.	—	—	3.50

21	2 SYLIS	1981. Black and brown on orange unpt. Green guilloche at ctr. Kg. Mohammed V of Morocco at l.			
		a. Issued note.	.10	.25	.75
		s. Specimen.	—	—	3.50

22	5 SYLIS	1980. Blue on pink unpt. Kwame Nkrumah at r. Back like #16.			
		a. Issued note.	.20	.65	1.75
		s. Specimen.	—	—	5.00

23	10 SYLIS	1980. Red-violet and red-orange on m/c unpt. Like #16.			
		a. Issued note.	.25	.75	2.25
		s. Specimen.	—	—	6.50

24	25 SYLIS	1980. Dk. green and m/c. Like #17. Back green and m/c.			
		a. Issued note.	.40	1.20	3.50
		s. Specimen.	—	—	7.50

Cat. #	Denomination	Date, description	VG	VF	Unc
25	50 SYLIS	1980. Dk. red, brown and m/c. Like #18.			
		a. Issued note.	.65	2.00	6.00
		s. Specimen.	—	—	8.50
26	100 SYLIS	1980. Blue and m/c. Like #19.			
		a. Issued note.	1.75	6.00	14.00
		s. Specimen.	—	—	10.00

| 27 | 500 SYLIS | 1980. Dk. brown and m/c. J. Broz Tito at l. Modern bldg. on back. | .85 | 2.50 | 10.00 |

NOTE: #27 is purported to commemorate Marshal Tito's visit to Guinea.

Franc System

1985 ISSUE

Law of 1.3.1960

#28–33 arms at ctr.

28	25 FRANCS	1985. Blue and m/c. Young boy at l. Girl by huts at ctr. r. on back.			
		a. Issued note.	.25	.75	2.25
		s. Specimen.	—	—	2.50

Cat. #	Denomination	Date, description	VG	VF	Unc
29	50 FRANCS	1985. Dk. red and m/c. Bearded man at l. Plowing w/water buffalo at ctr. on back.			
		a. Issued note.	FV	.75	.75
		s. Specimen.	—	—	3.50
30	100 FRANCS	1985. Purple and m/c. Young woman at l. Harvesting bananas at ctr. on back.			
		a. Issued note.	FV	.50	1.50
		s. Specimen.	—	—	4.50

31	500 FRANCS	1985. Green and m/c. Woman at l. Minehead at ctr. on back.			
		a. Issued note.	FV	1.25	3.50
		s. Specimen.	—	—	5.50

32	1000 FRANCS	1985. Blue, brown and m/c. Girl at l. Shovel loading ore into open end dump trucks at ctr., mask at r. on back.			
		a. Issued note.	FV	1.85	5.50
		s. Specimen.	—	—	7.50
33	5000 FRANCS	1985. Blue, brown and m/c. Woman at l. Dam at ctr., mask at r. on back.			
		a. Issued note.	FV	6.00	18.00
		s. Specimen.	—	—	9.00

GUINEA-BISSAU

The Republic of Guinea-Bissau, a former Portuguese overseas province on the west coast of Africa between Senegal and Guinea, has an area of 13,948 sq. mi. (36,125 sq. km.) and a population of 929,000. Capital: Bissau. The country has undeveloped deposits of oil and bauxite. Peanuts, oil-palm kernels and hides are exported.

The African Party for the Independence of Guinea-Bissau was founded in 1956, and several years later began a guerrilla warfare that grew in effectiveness until 1974, when the rebels controlled most of the colony. Portugal's costly overseas wars in her African territories resulted in a military coup in Portugal in April 1974, that appreciably brightened the prospects for freedom for Guinea-Bissau. In August 1974, the Lisbon government signed an agreement granting independence to Portuguese Guinea effective Sept. 10, 1974. The new republic took the name of Guinea-Bissau.

RULERS
Portuguese until 1974

MONETARY SYSTEM
1 Peso = 100 Centavos, 1975–

REPLACEMENT NOTES
#6-9, Z prefix. #10-15, AZ, BZ, CZ, DZ, ZA or ZZ prefix, depending on denomination.

Banco Nacional da Guiné-Bissau
1975 ISSUE
#1–4 wmk: A. Cabral.

Cat. #	Denomination	Date, description	VG	VF	Unc
1	50 PESOS	24.9.1975. Blue. P. Nalsna at l. Field workers at ctr., woman at r. on back.	1.00	2.50	6.50

2	100 PESOS	24.9.1975. Brown. D. Ramos at l. Objects and woman on back.	1.00	2.50	7.50

Cat. #	Denomination	Date, description	VG	VF	Unc
3	500 PESOS	24.9.1975. Green and brown. Pres A. Cabral at I. Carving and 2 youths on back.	7.50	15.00	37.50
4	*Deleted.* See #8.				

1978–83 ISSUES

#5–9 arms at lower r. on face. Wmk: A. Cabral.

Cat. #	Denomination	Date, description	VG	VF	Unc
5	50 PESOS	28.2.1983. Orange on m/c unpt. Artifact at I. ctr., P. Nalsna at r. Local scene on back. Printer: BWC.	FV	1.00	2.50

Cat. #	Denomination	Date, description	VG	VF	Unc
6	100 PESOS	28.2.1983. Red on m/c unpt. Carving at I., D. Ramos at r. Bldg. on back. W/o imprint.	FV	1.25	3.50

Cat. #	Denomination	Date, description	VG	VF	Unc
7	500 PESOS	28.2.1983. Deep blue on m/c unpt. Carving at I., F. Mendes at r. Slave trade scene on back. W/o imprint.	FV	2.00	5.00

Cat. #	Denomination	Date, description	VG	VF	Unc
8	1000 PESOS	24.9.1978. Green on brown and m/c unpt. Weaver and loom at lower I. ctr., Pres. A. Cabral at r. Allegory w/title: *Apoteose ao Triunfo* on back. Printer: BWC.			
		a. Sign. titles: *COMISSARIO PRINCIPAL, COMISSARIO DE ESTADO DES FINANCAS* and *GOVERNADOR.*	5.00	12.50	50.00
		b. Sign. titles: *PRIMEIRO MINISTRO, MINISTRO DE ECONOMIA E FINANCAS* and *GOVERNADOR.*	FV	2.00	5.00

Cat. #	Denomination	Date, description	VG	VF	Unc
9	5000 PESOS	12.9.1984. Brown-orange and m/c. Map at ctr., Pres. A. Cabral at r. Harvesting grain at ctr. on back. W/o imprint.	FV	3.00	9.00

1990 ISSUE

#10–15 sign. titles: *MINISTRO-GOVERNADOR* and *VICE-GOVERNADOR.* Printer: TDLR.
#10–12 wmk: *BCG.*

Cat. #	Denomination	Date, description	VG	VF	Unc
10	50 PESOS	1.3.1990. Red on m/c unpt. Similar to #5 but reduced size w/o wmk. area.	FV	FV	1.00

Cat. #	Denomination	Date, description	VG	VF	Unc
11	100 PESOS	1.3.1990. Olive-gray on m/c unpt. Similar to #6 but reduced size w/o wmk. area.	FV	FV	.75

Cat. #	Denomination	Date, description	VG	VF	Unc
12	500 PESOS	1.3.1990. Deep blue on m/c unpt. Similar to #7 but reduced size w/o wmk. area.	FV	FV	2.00

#13–15 wmk: Portr. A. Cabral.

13	1000 PESOS	1.3.1990. Dk. brown, brown-violet and orange on m/c unpt. Similar to #8.	FV	FV	2.50

14	5000 PESOS	1990–. Purple, violet and brown on m/c unpt. Similar to #9.			
		a. Sign. titles: *MINISTRO-GOVERNA-DOR* and *VICE-GOVERNADOR* 1.3.1990.	FV	FV	4.25
		b. Sign. titles: *GOVERNADOR* and *VICE-GOVERNADOR*. 1.3.1993.	FV	FV	3.75

15	10,000 PESOS	1990–. Green, olive-brown and blue on m/c unpt. Statue at lower l. ctr., outline map at ctr., A. Cabral at r. Local people fishing w/nets in river at ctr. on back.			
		a. Sign titles: *MINISTRO-GOVERNADOR* and *VICE-GOVERNADOR*. 1.3.1990.	FV	FV	8.00
		b. Sign. titles: *GOVERNADOR* and *VICE-GOVERNADOR*. 1.3.1993.	FV	FV	7.00

GUYANA

The Cooperative Republic of Guyana, an independent member of the British Commonwealth situated on the northeast coast of South America, has an area of 83,000 sq. mi. (214,969 sq. km.) and a population of 779,000. Capital: Georgetown. The economy is basically agrarian. Sugar, rice and bauxite are exported.

The original area of Guyana, which included present-day Surinam, French Guiana, and parts of Brazil and Venezuela, was sighted by Columbus in 1498. The first European settlement was made late in the 16th century by the Dutch. For the next 150 years, possession alternated between the Dutch and the British, with a short interval of French control. The British exercised de facto control after 1796, although the area, which included the Dutch colonies of Essequebo, Demerary and Berbice, wasn't ceded to them by the Dutch until 1814. From 1803 to 1831, Essequebo and Demerary were administered separately from Berbice. The three colonies were united in the British Crown Colony of British Guiana in 1831. British Guiana won internal self-government in 1952 and full independence, under the traditional name of Guyana, on May 26, 1966.

Notes of the British Caribbean Currency Board circulated from 1950–1965.

RULERS
British to 1966

MONETARY SYSTEM
1 Dollar = 4 Shillings 2 Pence, 1837–1965
1 Dollar = 100 Cents, 1966–

SIGNATURE VARIETIES					
1	GOVERNOR	MINISTER OF FINANCE	6	GOVERNOR	VICE PRESIDENT ECONOMIC PLANNING AND FINANCE
2			7	GOVERNOR	MINISTER OF FINANCE
3			8		
4			9		
5			10		

Bank of Guyana

1966 ISSUE

#21–29 wmk: Macaw's (parrot) head. Printer: TDLR.

#21–27 Kaieteur Falls at r.

Cat. #	Denomination	Date, description	VG	VF	Unc
21	1 DOLLAR	ND (1966–). Red on m/c unpt. Black bush polder at l., rice harvesting at r. on back.			
		a. Sign. 1; 2; 5.	.25	1.00	4.00
		b. Sign. 3; 4.	1.00	2.50	8.00
		c. Sign. 6. (1983).	.10	.40	1.50

Cat. #	Denomination	Date, description	VG	VF	Unc
		d. Serial # prefix B/1 or higher. Sign. 7. (1989).	FV	.20	.75
		e. Sign. 8. (1992).	FV	FV	.50

22	5 DOLLARS	ND (1966–). Dk. green on m/c unpt. Cane sugar harvesting at l., conveyor at r. on back.			
		a. Sign. 1; 2; 5.	.50	2.00	5.00
		b. Sign. 6. (1983).	.15	.65	2.50
		c. Serial # prefix A/27 or higher. Sign. 7.	FV	FV	.75

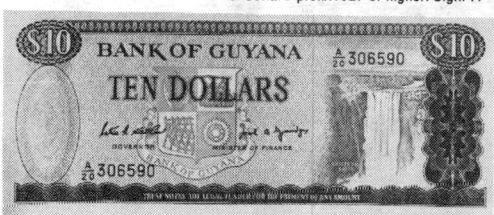

23	10 DOLLARS	ND (1966–). Dk. brown on m/c unpt. Bauxite mining at l., aluminum plant at r. on back.			
		a. Sign. 1; 5.	.75	3.00	12.50
		b. Sign. 6. (1983).	.30	1.25	5.00
		c. Serial # prefix A/16 or higher. Sign. 7. (1989).	FV	FV	1.00

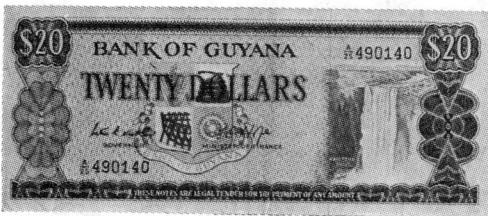

24	20 DOLLARS	ND (1966–88). Purple on m/c unpt. Ship-building at l., ferry vessel at r. on back.			
		a. Sign. 1; 5.	FV	4.00	15.00
		b. Sign. 6. (1983).	FV	2.50	10.00
		c. Serial # prefix A/42 or higher. Sign. 7.	FV	FV	7.00

25	Held in reserve.				
26	Held in reserve.				

1989–92 ISSUE

27	20 DOLLARS	ND (1989). Brown on m/c unpt. Similar to #24, but design element added at l. and r. Sign. 7.	FV	FV	2.00

Cat. #	Denomination	Date, description	VG	VF	Unc
28	100 DOLLARS	ND (1989). Blue o m/c unpt. Arms at ctr., map at r. Cathedral at ctr. on back. Sign. 7.	FV	FV	6.00

29	500 DOLLARS	ND (ca. 1992). Lilac brown and purple on m/c unpt. Map of Guyana at r. Public bldgs. in Georgetown on back. Sign 8.	FV	FV	10.00
30	1000 DOLLARS	ND.			Expected new issue.

HAITI

The Republic of Haiti, which occupies the western one third of the island of Hispañola in the Caribbean Sea between Puerto Rico and Cuba, has an area of 10,714 sq. mi. (27,750 sq. km.) and a population of 6.2 million. Capital: Port-au-Prince. The economy is based on agriculture, light manufacturing and tourism which is becoming increasingly important. Coffee, bauxite, sugar, essential oils and handicrafts are exported.

Columbus discovered Hispañola in 1492. Spain colonized the island, making Santo Domingo the base for exploration of the Western Hemisphere. Later French buccaneers settled the western third of Hispañola which was ceded to France by Spain in 1697. Slaves brought over from Africa to work the coffee and sugar cane plantations made it one of the richest colonies of the French Empire. The Republic of Haiti was established in 1804 by the slave revolt of the 1790's, making it the oldest black republic in the world and the second oldest republic (after the United States) in the Western Hemisphere.

MONETARY SYSTEM
5 Gourdes = 1 U.S. Dollar, 1919–89

REPLACEMENT NOTES
#239 and later notes printed by TDLR, ZZ prefix.

Banque Nationale de la République d'Haiti

SIXTH ISSUE (ca.1951–64)

Convention du 12 Avril 1919

#178-184 arms at ctr. on back. First sign. title: *Le President*. Printer: ABNC.

Cat. #	Denomination	Date, description	VG	VF	Unc
178	1 GOURDE	*L.1919.* Dk. brown on lt. blue and m/c. unpt. Citadel rampart at ctr. Prefix letters AS-BM. 5 sign. varieties.	.75	2.00	10.00
179	2 GOURDES	*L.1919.* Blue and m/c. Lt. green in unpt. Like #178. Prefix letters Z-AF. 6 sign. varieties.	1.00	3.00	15.00
180	5 GOURDES	*L.1919.* Orange on green unpt. Woman harvesting coffee beans at l. Prefix letters G-M. 3 sign. varieties.	1.50	4.50	12.50

Cat. #	Denomination	Date, description	VG	VF	Unc
181	10 GOURDES	*L.1919.* Green on m/c unpt. Coffee plant at ctr. Prefix letters B-D. 2 sign. varieties.	3.00	10.00	30.00
183	50 GOURDES	*L.1919.* Olive-green on m/c unpt. Cotton bolls at ctr. Specimen.	—	—	160.00

Cat. #	Denomination	Date, description	VG	VF	Unc
184	100 GOURDES	*L.1919.* Purple on m/c unpt. Field workers at l. Back purple. Prefix letter A.	20.00	50.00	200.00

SEVENTH ISSUE (ca.1964)

Convention du 12 Avril 1919

#185–189 like #178–180 but new guilloche patterns, w/o green in unpt. Arms at ctr. on back. Printer: ABNC.

Cat. #	Denomination	Date, description	VG	VF	Unc
185	1 GOURDE	*L.1919.* Dk. blue on lt. blue and m/c unpt. Like #178. Prefix letters BK-BT.	.50	1.50	7.00

| 186 | 2 GOURDES | *L.1919.* Blue on lt. blue and m/c unpt. Like #179. Prefix letters AF-AJ. | .75 | 2.50 | 12.00 |

| 187 | 5 GOURDES | *L.1919.* Orange on lt. pale blue and m/c unpt. Like #180. Prefix letter N. | .50 | 1.00 | 5.00 |

NOTE: It is reported that the entire shipment of #187 was stolen and never officially released.

| 188 | 50 GOURDES | *L.1919.* Olive-green on blue and magenta unpt. Similar to #183. (Not issued). Archive example. | — | — | — |
| 189 | 100 GOURDES | *L.1919.* Purple on m/c unpt. Similar to #184. (Not issued). Archive example. | — | — | — |

EIGHTH ISSUE (ca.1967)

Convention du 12 Avril 1919

#190-195 arms at ctr. on back. Printer: TDLR.

#190-193 second sign. title: *LE DIRECTEUR.*

Cat. #	Denomination	Date, description	VG	VF	Unc
190	1 GOURDE	*L.1919.* Brown on m/c unpt. Similar to #185. Prefix letters DA-DL.	.30	1.00	6.50

| 191 | 2 GOURDES | *L.1919.* Grayish-blue on m/c unpt. Similar to #186. Prefix letters DA-DF. | .50 | 1.50 | 7.50 |

Cat. #	Denomination	Date, description	VG	VF	Unc
192	5 GOURDES	L.1919. Similar to #187. Prefix letters DA-DK.	1.00	4.00	12.00

| 193 | 10 GOURDES | L.1919, Similar to #181. Prefix letters DA. | 3.00 | 8.00 | 30.00 |

| 194 | 50 GOURDES | L.1919. Similar to #183. Prefix letters DA. Second sign. title: *UN DIRECTEUR*. | 10.00 | 17.50 | 75.00 |

| 195 | 100 GOURDES | L.1919. Similar to #205. Prefix letters DA. | 20.00 | 35.00 | 150.00 |

NINTH ISSUE

Convention du 12 Avril 1919

#196-198 Pres. Dr. F. Duvalier at ctr. or l. Arms at ctr. on back. Printer: TDLR.

| 196 | 1 GOURDE | L.1919. Dk. brown on m/c unpt. Prefix letters DK-DT. | .25 | .60 | 3.50 |

Cat. #	Denomination	Date, description	VG	VF	Unc
197	2 GOURDES	L.1919. Grayish-blue on m/c unpt. Like #196. Prefix letters DG-DJ.	.50	1.25	4.50

| 198 | 5 GOURDES | L.1919. Orange on m/c unpt. Portr. Pres. Duvalier at l. Prefix letters DJ-DK. | 1.00 | 2.50 | 7.50 |
| 199 | Held in reserve. | | | | |

TENTH ISSUE

Convention du 12 Avril 1919

#200-203 arms at ctr. on back. Printer: ABNC.

| 200 | 1 GOURDE | l.1919. Dk. brown on m/c unpt. Portr. Pres. F. Duvalier at ctr. Prefix letters A-Z; AA-CR. 3 sign. varieties. | .25 | .60 | 2.00 |

#201-207 w/4 lines of text on back (like previous issues).

| 201 | 2 GOURDES | L.1919. Blue on m/c unpt. Like #200. First issued w/o prefix, then letters A-Q. | .50 | 1.25 | 3.50 |

| 202 | 5 GOURDES | L.1919. Orange on m/c unpt. Portr. Pres. F. Duvalier at l. First issued w/o prefix, then letters A-Z; AA-AP. 3 sign. varieties. | 1.00 | 2.00 | 4.50 |
| 203 | 10 GOURDES | L.1919. Dk. green on m/c unpt. Portr. Pres. F. Duvalier at ctr. First issued w/o prefix, then letter A. | 2.50 | 5.00 | 12.50 |

| 204 | 50 GOURDES | L.1919. Dk. gray on m/c unpt. Portr. Pres. L. F. Salomon Jeune at ctr. First issued w/o prefix, then letters A-C. 2 sign. varieties. | 10.00 | 17.50 | 30.00 |

Cat. #	Denomination	Date, description	VG	VF	Unc
205	100 GOURDES	*L.1919.* Purple on m/c unpt. Portr. H. Christophe (Pres., later Kg.) at l. W/o prefix letter. 2 sign. varieties.	20.00	40.00	70.00

| 206 | 250 GOURDES | *L.1919.* Dk. yellow-green on m/c unpt. J. J. Dessalines at r. W/o prefix letter. | 55.00 | 110.00 | 200.00 |

207	500 GOURDES	*L.1919.* Red on m/c unpt. Similar to #203. W/o prefix letter.	82.50	165.00	300.00
208	Held in reserve.				
209	Held in reserve.				

ELEVENTH ISSUE (ca.1973)

Lois des 21 Mai 1935 et 15 Mai 1953 et au Décret du 22 Novembre 1973 (issued 1979)

#210–214 arms at ctr. on back. Printer: ABNC.

| 210 | 1 GOURDE | *L.1973, etc.* Like #200. Prefix letters A-Z; AA-AC. | .30 | .60 | 2.00 |

#211-214 w/3 lines of text on back.

| 211 | 2 GOURDES | *L.1973, etc.* Like #201. Prefix letters A-J. | .60 | 1.25 | 3.00 |
| 212 | 5 GOURDES | *L.1973, etc.* Like #202. Prefix letters A-AA. | 1.00 | 2.00 | 4.00 |

| 213 | 50 GOURDES | *L.1973, etc.* Like #204. Prefix letter A. | 10.00 | 17.50 | 27.50 |
| 214 | 100 GOURDES | *L.1973, etc.* Like #205. W/o prefix letter. 2 serial # varieties. | 20.00 | 35.00 | 70.00 |

#215–217 held in reserve.

TWELFTH ISSUE

Lois des 21 Mai 1935 et 15 Mai 1953 et au Décret du 22 Novembre 1973

Cat. #	Denomination	Date, description	VG	VF	Unc
218	25 GOURDES	*L.1973, etc.* Dk. blue, and brown-violet on m/c unpt. Pres. Jean-Claude Duvalier at l., antenna at r. Prefix letters DA-DD. National Palace on back. Printer: TDLR.	3.00	7.50	15.00

#219–229 held in reserve.

Banque de la République d'Haiti

1980–82 ISSUE

Loi du 17 Aout 1979

#230-232, 235–238 sign. titles: *LE GOUVERNEUR, LE GOUVERNEUR ADJOINT* and *LE DIRECTEUR*. Arms at ctr. on back. Printer: ABNC.

230	1 GOURDE	*L.1979.* Like #210. W/ or w/o prefix letter.			
		a. Printed on paper w/planchettes. Smaller size numerals in serial #.	FV	.20	.75
		b. Printed on Tyvek. Larger size numerals in serial #.	FV	.50	1.50

231	2 GOURDES	*L.1979.* W/o or w/ prefix letter.			
		a. Printed on paper w/planchettes. Smaller size numerals in serial #.	FV	.50	1.50
		b. Printed on Tyvek. Larger size numerals in serial #.	FV	.75	2.00
232	5 GOURDES	*L.1979.* Like #212. Prefix letters A-T.	FV	1.00	3.00

#233 and 234 held in reserve.

235	50 GOURDES	*L.1979.* Like #213.			
		a. Printed on dull white paper w/planchettes. W/o prefix letter or letter A; B; G.	FV	12.00	25.00
		b. Printed on Tyvek. Prefix letter C. Wmk: American bald eagle symbol of ABNC.	FV	12.00	27.50
		c. Printed on Tyvek but w/o wmk. Prefix letter D; F.	FV	12.00	25.00

236	100 GOURDES	*L.1979.* Like #205.			
		a. Printed on paper w/planchettes. Prefix letters A; B.	FV	16.00	40.00
		b. Printed on Tyvek. Prefix letter C; D.	FV	16.00	40.00
237	250 GOURDES	*L.1979.* Similar to #206. Printed on Tyvek.	FV	45.00	100.00
238	500 GOURDES	*L.1979.* Similar to #207. Printed on Tyvek.	FV	90.00	200.00

1984–85 ISSUE

#239-240 arms at ctr. on back. Printer: TDLR.

Cat. #	Denomination	Date, description	VG	VF	Unc
239	1 GOURDE	L.1979 (1984). Brown. Like #196. Double prefix letters. Sign. titles like #230.	FV	.20	.60

240	2 GOURDES	L.1979 (1985). Similar to #191.			
		a. Sign. titles like #239.	FV	.50	1.50
		b. Sign. titles like #241.	FV	.35	1.25

#241-243 sign. title at r: LE DIRECTEUR GENERAL. Arms at ctr. on back.

241	5 GOURDES	L.1979 (1985). Orange on m/c unpt. Portr. Pres. Jean-Claude Duvalier at l. Arms at ctr. on back. Printer: G&D.	FV	1.00	4.00

242	10 GOURDES	L.1979 (1984). Similar to #203, but portr. Jean-Claude Duvalier at ctr. Printer: ABNC.	FV	2.00	6.00

Cat. #	Denomination	Date, description	VG	VF	Unc
243	25 GOURDES	L.1979 (1985). Blue-violet on pink and m/c unpt. Like #241. Printer: G&D.	FV	4.50	15.00
244	*Deleted.* See #240.				

1986–88 ISSUE

#245–252 sign. title at r: *LE DIRECTEUR GENERAL.* Arms at ctr. on back.

245	1 GOURDE	1987. Dk. brown and brown-black on m/c unpt. Toussaint L'Ouverture at ctr. Printer: G&D.	FV	FV	.50

246	5 GOURDES	1987. Orange and brown on m/c unpt. Statue of Combat de Vertiéres at upper ctr. Wmk: Palm tree. Printer: G&D.	FV	FV	2.50

Cat. #	Denomination	Date, description	VG	VF	Unc
247	10 GOURDES	1988. Green, red and blue on m/c unpt. Catherine Flon Arcahaie seated sewing the first flag of the Republic at r. Back green. Printer: ABNC.	FV	FV	4.50

248	25 GOURDES	1988. Purple and dk. blue on m/c unpt. Palace of Justice at ctr. Wmk: Palm tree. Printer: G&D.	FV	FV	9.00

249	50 GOURDES	1986. Green and m/c. Design and sign. titles like #235. Printer: ABNC.	FV	FV	30.00
250	100 GOURDES	1986. Similar to #236 but printer: TDLR.	FV	FV	45.00
251	250 GOURDES	1988. Tan on m/c unpt. Similar to #237. Printer: ABNC.	FV	FV	80.00
252	500 GOURDES	1988. Red. Pres. A. Pétion at r. Printer: ABNC.	FV	FV	150.00

1989–91 ISSUE

#253–255 arms at ctr. on back. Printer: USBC.

253	1 GOURDE	1989. Dk. brown and brown-black on m/c unpt. Toussaint L'Ouverture w/short hair at ctr.	FV	FV	.60

Cat. #	Denomination	Date, description	VG	VF	Unc
254	2 GOURDES	1990. Blue-black on m/c unpt. Citadel rampart. Shortened legal clause w/o reference to United States on face and back.	FV	2.00	10.00

255	5 GOURDES	1989. Orange and brown on m/c unpt. Like #246. Wmk: Palm tree.	FV	FV	1.75

#256–258 legal clause on face and back w/o reference to the United States. Arms at ctr. on back. Wmk: Palm tree. Printer: G&D.

256	10 GOURDES	1991. Green, red and blue on m/c unpt. Similar to #247.	FV	FV	4.00

257	50 GOURDES	1991. Dk. olive-green and black-green on m/c unpt. Portr. Pres. L. F. Salomon Jeune at ctr.	FV	FV	10.00

Cat. #	Denomination	Date, description	VG	VF	Unc
258	100 GOURDES	1991. Purple on m/c unpt. Portr. H. Christophe at l.	FV	FV	20.00

1992 ISSUE

#259–261 w/o laws. Shortened clause on face and back: *CE BILLET EST EMIS CONFORMEMENT…* Arms at ctr. on back. Printer: TDLR.

259	1 GOURDE	1992. Like #245.	FV	FV	.35

260	2 GOURDES	1992. Like #254.	FV	FV	.75

261	5 GOURDES	1992. Like #246.	FV	FV	1.50

HONDURAS

The Republic of Honduras, situated in Central America between Nicaragua and Guatemala, has an area of 43,277 sq. mi. (112,088 sq. km.) and a population of 5.1 million. Capital: Tegucigalpa. Agriculture, mining (gold and silver), and logging are the chief industries. Bananas, timber and coffee are exported.

Honduras, a site of the ancient Mayan Empire, was claimed for Spain by Columbus in 1502, during his last voyage to the Americas. The first settlement was made by Cristobal de Olid under orders of Hernan Cortes, then in Mexico. The area, regarded as one of the most promising sources of gold and silver in the new world, was a part of the Captaincy General of Guatemala throughout the colonial period. After declaring its independence from Spain, in 1821, Honduras fell briefly to the Mexican empire of Agustin de Iturbide, and then joined the Central American Federation (1823–39). Upon dissolution of the federation, Honduras became an independent republic.

MONETARY SYSTEM
1 Lempira = 100 Centavos, 1926–

Banco Central de Honduras

Established 1950 by merger of Banco Atlantida and Banco de Honduras.

1951 ISSUE

Cat. #	Denomination	Date, description	VG	VF	Unc
49	100 LEMPIRAS	1951–72. Yellow on m/c unpt. Valle at l., arms at r. Village and bridge on back.			
		a. W/o security thread, lilac-pink unpt. Printer: W&S. 16.3.1951; 8.3.1957.	85.00	225.00	—
		b. W/o security thread, w/fibers at r. ctr., lt. green and lt. orange unpt. Printer: W&S. 10.12.1969.	65.00	150.00	—
		c. W/security thread, yellow unpt. 13.10.1972.	55.00	125.00	225.00

1953–61 ISSUE

50	1 LEMPIRA	10.2.1961; 30.7.1965. Red on m/c unpt. Lempira at l., modified design of #45 w/black serial #. Dios del Maiz/Idolo Maya and Mayan artifacts on back. 2 sign. varieties. Printer: TDLR.	1.00	4.00	15.00

51	5 LEMPIRAS	1953–67. Gray on m/c unpt. Morazan at l., arms at r. Serial # at upper l. and upper r. Battle of Trinidad on back. Printer: ABNC.			
		a. Date horizontal. 17.3.1953; 7.1.1966.	4.00	20.00	75.00
		b. Date vertical. 15.4.1966; 29.9.1967.	3.50	17.50	60.00

Cat. #	Denomination	Date, description	VG	VF	Unc
52	10 LEMPIRAS	1954–70. Brown on m/c unpt. Cabanas at l., arms at r. Old bank on back. Date and sign. style varieties. Printer: TDLR.			
		a. R. sign. title: *MINISTRO DE HACIENDA...* 19.11.1954.	15.00	60.00	125.00
		b. R. sign. title: *MINISTRO DE ECONOMIA...* 19.2.1960–15.1.1970.	10.00	25.00	75.00

53	20 LEMPIRAS	4.6.1954; 8.5.1959–18.2.1972. Green. D. Herrera at l., arms at r. Waterfalls on back. Printer: TDLR.	15.00	37.50	125.00

54	50 LEMPIRAS	20.1.1956. Deep blue on m/c unpt. Dr. J. Trinidad Reyes at l., arms at r. University of Honduras on back. Printer: TDLR.	35.00	100.00	350.00

1968–70 ISSUE

55	1 LEMPIRA	1968–72. Red on green and pink unpt. Lempira at l., design different from #50 and 45. *Ruinas de Copan Juego de Pelota* on back. Printer: TDLR.			
		a. R. sign. title: *MINISTRO DE ECONOMIA...* 25.10.1968.	.80	2.50	8.00
		b. R. sign. title: *MINISTRO DE HACIENDA...* 21.1.1972.	.75	1.00	3.50

56	5 LEMPIRAS	1968–74. Gray on m/c unpt. Like #51. Serial # at lower l. and upper r. Printer: ABNC.			
		a. Date horizontal. 29.11.1968; 11.4.1969.	3.00	15.00	55.00
		b. Date vertical. 11.4.1969–24.8.1974.	2.50	8.00	30.00

57	10 LEMPIRAS	18.12.1970–13.11.1975. Brown on m/c unpt. Cabanas at l., arms at r. Ruins and new bank on back. Printer: ABNC.	3.50	10.00	35.00

1973–74 ISSUE

Cat. #	Denomination	Date, description	VG	VF	Unc
58	1 LEMPIRA	11.3.1974. Red on green and lilac unpt. Lempira w/o feather at l., arms at r. Different view of Ruinas de Copan on back. Printer: TDLR.	.50	.70	1.50

59	5 LEMPIRAS	1974–78. Gray on m/c unpt. Morazan at l., arms at r. Battle of Trinidad at l. on back. Printer: ABNC.			
		a. Date vertical. 24.10.1974.	2.50	7.50	27.50
		b. Date horizontal. 12.12.1975–13.2.1978.	2.00	4.00	18.00

60	20 LEMPIRAS	2.3.1973–18.8.1978. Green on m/c unpt. D. Herrera at l., arms at r. Presidential residence on back. Date placement varieties. Printer: TDLR.	8.50	25.00	75.00

1976 COMMEMORATIVE ISSUE

#61, Centennial of the Marco Aurelio Soto Government

Cat. #	Denomination	Date, description	VG	VF	Unc
61	2 LEMPIRAS	23.9.1976. Purple on m/c unpt. Arms at l., M. Aurelio Soto at r. Island and Port of Amapala on back. Printer: TDLR.	FV	.60	2.00

1975–78 REGULAR ISSUE

Cat. #	Denomination	Date, description	VG	VF	Unc
62	1 LEMPIRA	30.6.1978. Red. Like #58 but Indian symbols added below bank name on back. Printer: TDLR.	FV	.35	1.50

63	5 LEMPIRAS	1978–. Black, dk. blue, and deep green on m/c unpt. Arms at l., Morazan at r. Battle of Trinidad Nov. 11, 1827 on back. Printer: TDLR.			
		a. 4.10.1978; 8.5.1980.	FV	1.25	3.50
		b. 8.12.1985; 30.3.1989.	FV	1.00	2.50
		c. Serial # at upper l. in ascending size. 14.1.1993.	FV	FV	1.75

64	10 LEMPIRAS	1976–89. Brown on m/c unpt. Cabanas at l. Scene of City University on back. Printer: ABNC.			
		a. 18.3.1976; 13.2.1978.	FV	2.50	6.50
		b. 8.9.1983; 24.9.1987; 22.6.1989.	FV	2.00	5.50
65	20 LEMPIRAS	1978–93. Deep green on m/c unpt. D. de Herrera at r. Port of Cortes on back. Date placement varieties. Printer: ABNC.			
		a. 2.11.1978.	FV	5.00	10.00
		b. Vertical date at r. 23.6.1982; 5.1.1984; 9.4.1987.	FV	4.00	8.50
		c. Horizontal date at upper l. 5.10.1989; 24.1.1991; 9.5.1991; 29.8.1991.	FV	3.50	7.00
		d. 10.12.1992; 1.7.1993.	FV	FV	5.50

66	50 LEMPIRAS	29.1.1976–1.7.1993. Deep blue on m/c unpt. J. Manuel Galvez D. at l. National Development Bank on back. Wmk: Tree. Printer: ABNC.			
		a. Vertcal date at r. 29.1.1976; 10.9.1979.	FV	12.50	20.00
		b. 3.7.1986; 10.11.1989.	FV	8.00	16.50
		c. Horizontal date at upper l. 13.12.1990; 29.8.1991.	FV	7.00	13.50
		d. 1.7.1993; 18.3.1993.	FV	FV	9.00

67	100 LEMPIRAS	16.1.1975; 29.1.1976; 18.3.1976; 10.9.1979. Brown-orange on m/c unpt. Valle at l. Signatepeque school of forestry on back. Printer: TDLR.	FV	20.00	45.00

1980–81 ISSUE

Cat. #	Denomination	Date, description	VG	VF	Unc
68	1 LEMPIRA	1980; 1984; 1989. Red on m/c unpt. Arms at l., Lempira at r. Ruins of Copan on back. Printer: TDLR.			
		a. W/o security thread. 29.5.1980; 16.10.1984.	FV	.30	1.00
		b. W/security thread. 30.3.1989	FV	FV	./5

69	100 LEMPIRAS	1981–93. Brown-orange, dk. olive-green, and dp. purple on m/c unpt. Valle at r. and as wmk. Different view of forestry school on back. Printer: TDLR.			
		a. Regular serial #. 8.1.1981; 23.6.1982; 8.9.1983.	FV	15.00	28.50
		b. 3.7.1986; 10.12.1987; 21.12.1989.	FV	12.50	25.00
		c. 13.12.1989; 9.15.1991; 10.12.1992; 14.1.1993; 18.3.1993.	FV	FV	22.50

1989 ISSUE

#70 enhanced unpt. in wmk. area on back. 14.1.1993.

70	10 LEMPIRAS	21.9.1989. Dk. brown and red on m/c unpt. Arms at l. Cabanas at r. City University on back. Printer: TDLR.	FV	1.50	3.75

1992–93 ISSUE

Cat. #	Denomination	Date, description	VG	VF	Unc
71	1 LEMPIRA	10.9.1992. Dk. red on m/c unpt. Similar to #47a but back in paler colors. Printer: CBNC.	FV	FV	.65

#72–74 printer: TDLR.

Cat. #	Denomination	Date, description	VG	VF	Unc
72	2 LEMPIRA	14.1.1993. Like #61 but w/lt. blue unpt. at l. Serial # at upper l. in ascending size.	FV	FV	1.00

Cat. #	Denomination	Date, description	VG	VF	Unc
73 (72)	20 LEMPIRAS	14.1.1993 (1994); 25.2.1993 (1995). Deep green and dk. brown on m/c unpt. D. de Herrera at r. and as wmk. Back vertical, Presidential House at ctr. Wmk: tree.	FV	FV	5.00

Cat. #	Denomination	Date, description	VG	VF	Unc
74 (73)	50 LEMPIRAS	14.1.1993 (1994); 25.2.1993 (1995). Blue-black and dk. brown on m/c unpt. J. M. Galvez D. at r. and as wmk. Back vertical, Central Bank Annex at ctr.	FV	FV	11.00
75 (74)	100 LEMPIRAS	14.1.1993. Like #69 but w/engraved date.Serial # at upper l. in ascending size. Enhanced unpt. in wmk. area on back.	FV	FV	20.00
76 (75)	500 LEMPIRAS	(1996).			Expected new issue

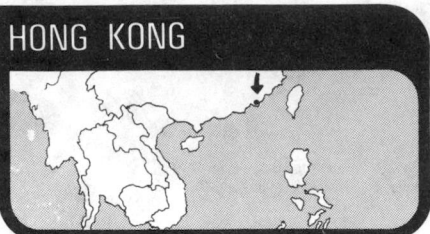

HONG KONG

Hong Kong, a British colony situated at the mouth of the Canton or Pearl River 90 miles (145 km.) southeast of Canton, has an area of 409 sq. mi. (1,045 sq. km.) and a population of 5.6 million. Capital: Victoria. The free port of Hong Kong, the commercial center of the Far East, is a transshipment point for goods destined for China and the countries of the Western Pacific. Light manufacturing and tourism are important components of the economy.

Long a haven for fishermen-pirates and opium smugglers, the island of Hong Kong was ceded to Britain at the conclusion of the first Opium War (1839–1842). At the time, the acquisition of "a barren rock" was ridiculed by both London and English merchants operating in the Far East. The Kowloon Peninsula and Stonecutter's Island were ceded in 1860 and the so-called New Territories, comprising most of the mainland of the colony, were leased to Britain for 99 years in 1898. They will return to mainland China's rule on Dec. 20, 1999.

When the Japanese opened hostilities in World War II, on Dec. 7, 1941, they immediately attacked Hong Kong which fell, after some bitter fighting, on Christmas day. The colony was liberated by British troops on Aug. 30, 1945, when it was found that the population was no more than 600,000, of whom 80 percent were suffering from malnutrition. Hong Kong's economic life was dead. A brief period of military administration was followed by the formal re-establishment of civil government in May 1946. Hong Kong made a dramatic recovery and at the close of 1947 the population had reached 1,800,000. With the disintegration of the Nationalist Chinese forces and the establishment of the Central Peoples government, from 1948 to April 1950, an unprecedented influx of refugees took place, raising the population to about 2,360,000.

RULERS
British

MONETARY SYSTEM
1 Dollar = 100 Cents

REPLACEMENT NOTES
#191–197, ZZ prefix. #278–283, Z prefix.

NOTE ON VALUATIONS: Most valuations are for issued notes. At times specimen or proof notes have valuations, but these are only cases where a regularly issued example is not known to exist.

Chartered Bank

行銀打渣[1]
Cha Ta Yin Hang
香港渣打銀行
Hong Kong Cha Ta Yin Hang

Later became the Standard Chartered Bank.

1961–67 (ND) ISSUES
#68–72 wmk: Helmeted warrior's head. Printer: TDLR.

Cat. #	Denomination	Date, description	VG	VF	Unc
68	5 DOLLARS	1961–62; ND. Black and green on m/c unpt. Arms at lower l. Chinese junk and sampan at ctr. on back.			
		a. 1.7.1961.	12.00	37.50	100.00
		b. 3.3.1962.	15.00	50.00	150.00
		c. ND (1962–70).	4.00	17.50	60.00

Cat. #	Denomination	Date, description	VG	VF	Unc
69	5 DOLLARS	ND (1967). Black and yellow-brown on m/c unpt. Like #68.	3.50	15.00	50.00
70	10 DOLLARS	1961–62; ND. Black and red-violet on red unpt. Arms at l. Chartered Bank bldg. at ctr. on back.			
		a. 1.7.1961; 3.3.1962.	16.50	42.50	100.00
		b. ND (1962–70).	2.50	11.00	40.00

Cat. #	Denomination	Date, description	VG	VF	Unc
71	100 DOLLARS	ND; 1961. Dk. green and brown on m/c unpt. Arms at ctr. Harbor view on back.			
		a. 1.7.1961.	60.00	150.00	900.00
		b. ND (1961–70).	32.00	80.00	450.00

72	500 DOLLARS	1961–77. Black and dk. brown on m/c unpt. Male portr. at l., boat, harbor view at ctr. on back.			
		a. Sign. titles: *ACCOUNTANT* and *MANAGER*. 1.7.1961.	160.00	400.00	1500.
		b. Sign. titles as a. ND (1962–?).	FV	120.00	400.00
		c. Sign. titles: *ACCOUNTANT* and *CHIEF MANAGER IN HONG KONG*. ND (?–1975).	FV	120.00	400.00
		d. Sign. titles as c. 11.1.1977.	FV	100.00	350.00

1970–77 ISSUE

#73–76 bank bldg. at l., bank crest at ctr. Wmk: Helmeted warrior's head. Printer: TDLR.

73	5 DOLLARS	ND (1970-75); 1975. Dk. brown on m/c unpt. City Hall at ctr. r. on back.			
		a. Sign. title: *MANAGER* at r. ND (1970–75).	.85	1.75	6.50
		b. Sign. title: *CHIEF MANAGER IN HONG KONG* at r. 1.6.1975.	1.25	2.50	10.00

Cat. #	Denomination	Date, description	VG	VF	Unc
74	10 DOLLARS	ND; 1975; 1977. Dk. green on m/c unpt. Ocean terminal at ctr. r.			
		a. Sign. titles: *ACCOUNTANT* and *MANAGER*. ND (1970–75).	FV	3.00	10.00
		b. Sign. titles: *ACCOUNTANT* and *CHIEF MANAGER IN HONG KONG*. ND; 1.6.1975.	FV	4.00	15.00
		c. Sign. titles as b. 1.1.1977.	FV	2.50	7.00

75	50 DOLLARS	ND (1970–75). Blue on m/c unpt. City Hall at ctr. r. on back	FV	20.00	100.00
76	100 DOLLARS	ND; 1977. Red on m/c unpt.			
		a. ND (1970–75).	FV	25.00	90.00
		b. 1.1.1977.	FV	20.00	70.00

1979-80 ISSUE

#77–81 bank bldg. at l., arms at ctr. on back. Wmk: Helmeted warrior's head. Printer: TDLR (w/o imprint).

77	10 DOLLARS	1.1.1980; 1.1.1981. Green. Stylistic carp at r.	FV	FV	4.00
78	50 DOLLARS	1.1.1979; 1.1.1981; 1.1.1982. Blue on m/c unpt. Chinze at r.			
		a. 1.1.1979.	FV	FV	20.00
		b. 1.1.1981; 1.1.1982.	FV	FV	16.50

79	100 DOLLARS	1.1.1979; 1.1.1980; 1.1.1982. Red on m/c unpt. Mythical horse *Qilin* at r.			
		a. 1.1.1979.	FV	FV	35.00
		b. 1.1.1980.	FV	FV	30.00
		c. 1.1.1982.	FV	FV	25.00

Cat. #	Denomination	Date, description	VG	VF	Unc
80	500 DOLLARS	1979; 1982. Brown on m/c unpt. Mythical phoenix at r.			
		a. 1.1.1979.	FV	FV	150.00
		b. 1.1.1982.	FV	FV	120.00

Cat. #	Denomination	Date, description	VG	VF	Unc
81	1000 DOLLARS	1979; 1982. Yellow-orange on m/c unpt. Dragon at r.			
		a. 1.1.1979.	FV	FV	275.00
		b. 1.1.1982.	FV	FV	225.00

Hong Kong and Shanghai Banking Corporation

行銀理滙海上港香

Hsiang K'ang Shang Hai Hui Li Yin Hang

1949–68 ISSUE

#181–184 wmk: Helmeted warrior's head and denomination.

Cat. #	Denomination	Date, description	VG	VF	Unc
181	5 DOLLARS	1959–75. Brown. Similar to #173 and 180 but smaller size. New bank bldg. at ctr. on back.			
		a. Sign. titles: *CHIEF ACCOUNTANT* and *CHIEF MANAGER.* 2.5.1959–29.6.1960.	1.75	5.00	14.00
		b. 1.5.1963.	5.50	14.00	140.00
		c. 1.5.1964–27.3.1969.	1.50	4.00	10.00
		d. Sign. titles: *CHIEF ACCOUNTANT* and *GENERAL MANAGER.* 1.4.1970–18.3.1971.	.60	1.35	6.00
		e. 13.3.1972; 31.10.1972.	.50	1.25	3.50
		f. Sm. serial #. 31.10.1973; 31.3.1975.	FV	1.00	2.00
181A	10 DOLLARS	1949–59. Dk. green on m/c unpt. Like #178 but w/HONG KONG at date divided.			
		a. 1.7.1949; 31.12.1953.	5.00	12.50	70.00
		b. 1.7.1954–14.1.1958.	3.50	8.50	55.00
		c. 26.3.1958.	7.00	17.50	90.00
		d. 14.9.1958; 24.9.1958.	3.50	8.50	52.50
		e. 4.2.1959.	5.00	12.50	70.00

Cat. #	Denomination	Date, description	VG	VF	Unc
182	10 DOLLARS	1959–83. Dk. green on m/c unpt. Woman w/sheaf of grain at upper l., arms below. Back similar to #184.			
		a. Sign. titles: *CHIEF ACCOUNTANT* and *CHIEF MANAGER.* 21.5.1959 – 1.9.1962.	FV	2.75	14.00
		b. 1.5.1963; 1.9.1963.	1.85	5.50	35.00
		c. 1.5.1964; 1.9.1964.	FV	2.75	14.00
		d. 1.10.1964.	4.00	10.00	100.00
		e. 1.2.1965; 1.8.1966; 31.7.1967.	FV	2.50	12.50
		f. 20.3.1968; 23.11.1968; 27.3.1969; 18.3.1971.	FV	2.00	7.00
		g. Sign. titles: *CHIEF ACCOUNTANT* and *GENERAL MANAGER.* 1.4.1970–31.3.1977.	FV	1.75	6.00
		h. Sign. titles: *CHIEF ACCOUNTANT* and *EXECUTIVE DIRECTOR.* 31.3.1978; 31.3.1979.	FV	FV	5.00
		i. Sign. titles: *CHIEF ACCOUNTANT* and *GENERAL MANAGER.* 31.3.1980; 31.3.1981.	FV	FV	3.50
		j. Sign. titles: *MANAGER* and *GENERAL MANAGER.* 31.3.1982; 31.3.1983.	FV	FV	3.00

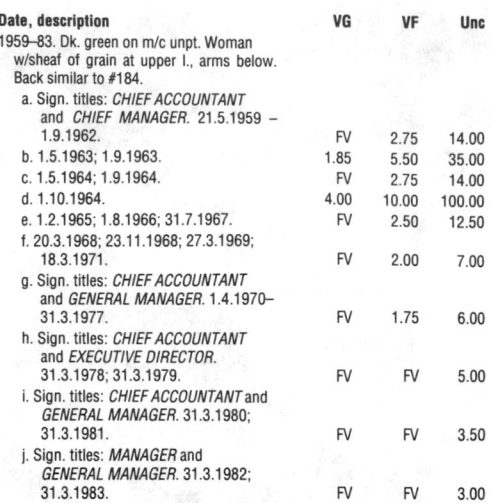

Cat. #	Denomination	Date, description	VG	VF	Unc
183	100 DOLLARS	1959–72. Red on m/c unpt. Woman seated at l. w/open book, arms at upper ctr.			
		a. Sign. titles: *CHIEF ACCOUNTANT* and *GENERAL MANAGER.* 12.8.1959–1.10.1964.	18.00	40.00	125.00
		b. 1.2.1965–27.3.1969.	14.00	30.00	90.00
		c. Sign. titles: *CHIEF ACCOUNTANT* and *GENERAL MANAGER.* 1.4.1970; 18.3.1971; 13.3.1972.	14.00	30.00	90.00

Cat. #	Denomination	Date, description	VG	VF	Unc
184	50 DOLLARS	1968–83. Dk. blue on m/c unpt. Arms at r. New bank bldg. at l. ctr. on back.			
		a. Sign. titles: *CHIEF ACCOUNTANT* and *CHIEF MANAGER.* 31.5.1968; 27.3.1969.	FV	10.00	37.50
		b. Sign. titles: *CHIEF ACCOUNTANT* and *GENERAL MANAGER.* 31.10.1973; 31.3.1975; 31.3.1978.	FV	8.50	32.50
		c. Sign. titles as b. 31.3.1977.	FV	14.00	62.50
		d. Sign. titles: *CHIEF ACCOUNTANT* and *EXECUTIVE DIRECTOR.* 31.3.1979.	FV	14.00	70.00
		e. Sign. titles: *CHIEF ACCOUNTANT* and *GENERAL MANAGER.* 31.3.1980.	FV	FV	25.00
		f. 31.3.1981.	FV	FV	22.50
		g. Sign. titles: *MANAGER* and *GENERAL MANAGER.* 31.3.1982; 31.3.1983.	FV	FV	20.00
185	*Deleted.*				

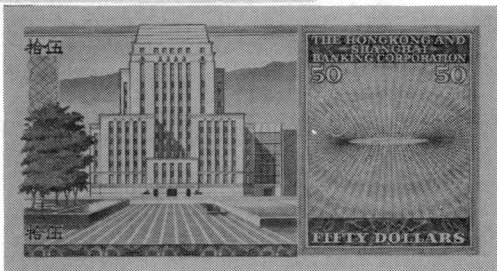

1972–78 ISSUES

#186–190 wmk: Lion's head. Printer: BWC.

Cat. #	Denomination	Date, description	VG	VF	Unc
186	100 DOLLARS	1972–76. Red on m/c unpt. Arms at l. Facing lions at lower l. and r.; bank bldg. at ctr., dragon in medallion at r.			
		a. W/4 lg. serial # on back. 13.3.1972; 31.10.1972.	FV	20.00	80.00
		b. Smaller electronic sorting serial # on face. W/o serial # on back. 31.10.1972.	FV	22.50	100.00
		c. 31.10.1973.	FV	18.50	65.00
		d. 31.3.1975; 31.3.1976.	FV	17.50	40.00

187	100 DOLLARS	1977–83. Red on lighter m/c unpt. Similar to #186.			
		a. Sign. titles: *CHIEF ACCOUNTANT* and *EXECUTIVE DIRECTOR.* 31.3.1977; 31.3.1978.	FV	14.00	35.00
		b. Sign. titles as a. 31.3.1979; 31.3.1980; 31.3.1981.	FV	FV	32.50
		c. Sign. titles: *MANAGER* and *GENERAL MANAGER.* 31.3.1982; 31.3.1983.	FV	FV	30.00

188	500 DOLLARS	31.10.1973; 31.3.1975; 31.3.1976. Brown on m/c unpt. Arms at l. Bank bldg. at l., lion's head at r. on back.	FV	FV	150.00
189	500 DOLLARS	1978–83. Brown and black on m/c unpt. Similar to #188 but w/modified frame designs.			
		a. 31.3.1978; 31.3.1980; 31.3.1981.	FV	FV	120.00
		b. 31.3.1982; 31.3.1983.	FV	FV	110.00

Cat. #	Denomination	Date, description	VG	VF	Unc
190	1000 DOLLARS	1977–83. Gold and black on m/c unpt. Arms at r. Lion at l., bank bldg. at ctr. r. on back.			
		a. 31.3.1977.	FV	FV	200.00
		b. 31.3.1979; 31.3.1980; 31.3.1981; 31.3.1983.	FV	FV	185.00

1985–87 ISSUE

#191–196 arms at l. Facing lions at lower l. and r. w/new bank bldg. at ctr. on back. Sign. varieties. Wmk: Lion's head. Printer: TDLR.

191	10 DOLLARS	1985–92. Deep green on m/c unpt. Sampan and ship at r. on back.			
		a. Sign. title: *GENERAL MANAGER.* 1.1.1985; 1.1.1986; 1.1.1987.	FV	FV	4.50
		b. Sign. title: *EXECUTIVE DIRECTOR.* 1.1.1988.	FV	FV	4.00
		c. Sign. title: *GENERAL MANAGER.* 1.1.1989; 1.1.1990; 1.1.1992.	FV	FV	3.50

192	20 DOLLARS	1986–89. Deep gray-green and brown on m/c unpt. Clock tower, ferry in harbor view at r. on back.			
		a. Sign. title: *GENERAL MANAGER.* 1.1.1986; 1.1.1987.	FV	FV	8.50
		b. Sign. title: *EXECUTIVE DIRECTOR.* 1.1.1988.	FV	FV	7.50
		c. Sign. title: *GENERAL MANAGER.* 1.1.1989.	FV	FV	6.50
193	50 DOLLARS	1985–92. Violet on m/c unpt. Men in boats at r. on back.			
		a. Sign. title: *GENERAL MANAGER.* 1.1.1985; 1.1.1986; 1.1.1987.	FV	FV	17.50
		b. Sign. title: *EXECUTIVE DIRECTOR.* 1.1.1988.	FV	FV	15.00

Cat. #	Denomination	Date, description	VG	VF	Unc
		c. Sign. title: *GENERAL MANAGER.* 1.1.1989; 1.1.1991; 1.1.1992.	FV	FV	12.50
194	100 DOLLARS	1985–88. Red on m/c unpt. Tiger Balm Garden pagoda at r.			
		a. Sign. title: *GENERAL MANAGER.* 1.1.1985; 1.1.1986; 1.1.1987.	FV	FV	27.50
		b. Sign. title: *EXECUTIVE DIRECTOR.* 1.1.1988.	FV	FV	25.00

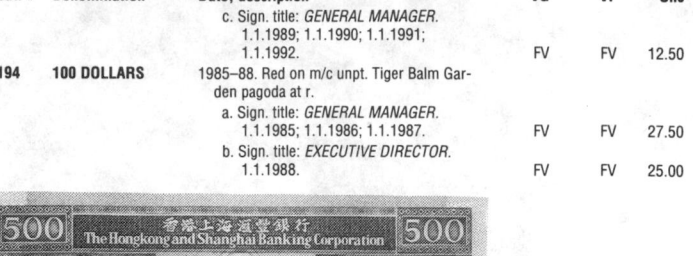

195	500 DOLLARS	1987–92. Brown on m/c unpt. Old tower at r. on back.			
		a. Sign. title: *GENERAL MANAGER.* 1.1.1987.	FV	FV	100.00
		b. Sign. title: *EXECUTIVE DIRECTOR.* 1.1.1988.	FV	FV	95.00
		c. Sign. title: *GENERAL MANAGER.* 1.1.1989; 1.1.1990; 1.1.1991; 1.1.1992.	FV	FV	90.00
196	1000 DOLLARS	1.1.1985; 1.1.1986; 1.1.1987. Red, brown and orange on m/c unpt. Old Supreme Court bldg. at r. on back.	FV	FV	175.00

1988–90 ISSUE

197	20 DOLLARS	1.1.1990; 1.1.1991; 1.1.1992. Like #192 but gray on orange, pink and m/c unpt. Sign. title: *GENERAL MANAGER.*	FV	FV	6.00
198	100 DOLLARS	1.1.1989; 1.1.1990; 1.1.1991; 1.1.1992. Similar to #194 Sign. title: *GENERAL MANAGER.* Back red and black on m/c unpt.	FV	FV	22.50
199	1000 DOLLARS	1988–1991. Similar to #196. Back orange, brown and olive-brown on m/c unpt.			
		a. Sign. title: *EXECUTIVE DIRECTOR.* 1.1.1988.	FV	FV	175.00
		b. Sign title: *GENERAL MANAGER.* 1.1.1989; 1.1.1990; 1.1.1991.	FV	FV	170.00

1993 ISSUE

#200–205 lion's head at l. and as wmk., city view in unpt. at ctr. New bank bldg. at ctr. between facing lions on back. Sign. title: *EXECUTIVE DIRECTOR.* Printer: TDLR.

200	10 DOLLARS				Expected new issue.

Cat. #	Denomination	Date, description	VG	VF	Unc
201	20 DOLLARS	1.1.1993; 1.1.1994. Gray on m/c unpt.	FV	FV	5.00

202	50 DOLLARS	1.1.1993; 1.1.1994. Purple and violet on m/c unpt.	FV	FV	11.00

203	100 DOLLARS	1.1.1993; 1.1.1994. Red, orange and black on m/c unpt. Ten Thousand Buddha Pagoda at Shatin at r. on back.	FV	FV	20.00
204	500 DOLLARS	1.1.1993; 1.1.1994. Brown and red-orange on m/c unpt. Government house at upper r. on back.	FV	FV	85.00
205	1000 DOLLARS	1.1.1993; 1.1.1994. Orange, red-brown and olive-green on pink and m/c unpt. Legislative Council bldg. at r. on back.	FV	FV	165.00

Mercantile Bank Limited

行銀利有港香

Hsiang K'ang Yu Li Yin Hang

In 1978 this bank was absorbed by the Hong Kong & Shanghai Banking Corp. and its note issuing right ended.

1964 ISSUE

244–245 wmk: Dragon. Printer: TDLR.

244	100 DOLLARS	1964–73. Red-brown on m/c unpt. Aerial view of coastline. Woman standing w/pennant and shield at ctr. on back.			
		a. 28.7.1964.	35.00	85.00	500.00
		b. 5.10.1965; 27.7.1968.	15.00	37.50	325.00
		c. 16.4.1970; 1.11.1973.	FV	32.50	275.00

1974 ISSUE

Cat. #	Denomination	Date, description	VG	VF	Unc
245	100 DOLLARS	4.11.1974. Red, purple and brown on m/c unpt. Woman standing w/pennant and shield at l. Back red on m/c unpt.; city view at ctr.	FV	16.50	40.00

Standard Chartered Bank

香港渣打銀行

Hong Kong Cha Ta Yin Hang

1985; 1988 ISSUE

#278 –283 bank bldg. at l., bank arms at ctr. on back. Sign. titles: *FINANCIAL CONTROLLER* and *AREA GENERAL MANAGER*. Wmk: Helmeted warrior's head.

Cat. #	Denomination	Date, description	VG	VF	Unc
278	10 DOLLARS	1.1.1985. Dk. green on yellow-green unpt. Similar to #77.	FV	FV	3.50

279	20 DOLLARS	1.1.1985; 1.1.1992. Dk. gray, orange and brown on m/c unpt. Turtle at r.	FV	FV	6.00

280	50 DOLLARS	1.1.1985–1.1.1992. Purple, violet and dk. gray on m/c unpt. Similar to #78.	FV	FV	13.50

Cat. #	Denomination	Date, description	VG	VF	Unc
281	100 DOLLARS	1.1.1985–1.1.1992. Red on m/c unpt. Similar to #79.	FV	FV	22.50
282	500 DOLLARS	1.1.1988–1.1.1992. Maroon, gray and green on m/c unpt. Similar to #80.	FV	FV	90.00

283	1000 DOLLARS	1.1.1985–. Yellow-orange on m/c unpt. Similar to #81.	FV	FV	185.00

1993 ISSUE

#284–289 Bauhinia flower blossom replaces bank arms at ctr. on back. Sign. titles: *CHIEF FINANCIAL OFFICER* and *AREA GENERAL MANAGER*. Wmk: *SCB* above helmeted warrior's head.

284	10 DOLLARS	1.1.1993; 1.1.1994. Dk. green on yellow-green unpt. Face like #278.	FV	FV	2.75
285	20 DOLLARS	1.1.1993; 1.1.1994. Dk. gray, orange and brown on m/c unpt. Face like #279.	FV	FV	5.00
286	50 DOLLARS	1.1.1993; 1.1.1994. Purple, violet and dk. gray on m/c unpt. Face like #280.	FV	FV	12.00

Cat. #	Denomination	Date, description	VG	VF	Unc
287	100 DOLLARS	1.1.1993; 1.1.1994. Red and purple on m/c unpt. Face like #281.	FV	FV	20.00
288	500 DOLLARS	1.1.1993; 1.1.1994. Brown and blue-green on m/c unpt.	FV	FV	85.00
289	1000 DOLLARS	1.1.1993; 1.1.1994.	FV	FV	175.00

Government of Hongkong

府政港香

Hsiang K'ang Cheng Fu

FINANCIAL SECRETARY: SIGNATURE VARIETIES

1	J.J. Cowperthwaite, 1961–71	4	Sir Piers Jacobs, 1986–92
2	C. P. Haddon-Cave, 1971–81	5	Sir Hamish Macleod, 1992–
3	Sir J. H. Bremridge, 1981–86	6	

1952; 1961 (ND) ISSUE

#325–328 Qn. Elizabeth II at r.

#325–327 uniface.

#325

#326

325	1 CENT	ND (1961–). Brown on lt. blue unpt.			
		a. Sign. 1.	—	.05	.20
		b. Sign. 2.	—	.10	.65
		c. Sign. 3.	.10	.65	3.00
		d. Sign. 4.	—	.05	.20
		d. Sign. 5.	—	FV	.10

NOTE: #325 ceased to be legal tender on 30.9.1995, and was redeemable until 31.12.1995.

326	5 CENTS	ND (1961–65). Green on lilac unpt.	.20	.50	2.50

327	10 CENTS	ND (1961–65). Red on grayish unpt.	.15	.35	1.50

Cat. #	Denomination	Date, description	VG	VF	Unc
328	1 DOLLAR	1952–59. Dk. green on m/c unpt. Printer: BWC.			
		a. 1.7.1952; 1.7.1954; 1.7.1955.	.75	3.00	15.00
		b. 1.6.1956–1.7.1959.	.35	2.00	8.00

P.R.C. BRANCH BANK

Bank of China

中國銀行

Chung Kuo Yin Hang

1994 ISSUE

#329–333 Bank of China Tower at l. Wmk: Stone lion statue. Printer: TDLR (HK) Ltd. (W/o imprint).

329	20 DOLLARS	1.5.1994. Blue-black, blue and violet on m/c unpt. Narcissus flowers at lower ctr. r. Aerial view of Wanchai and Central Hong Kong at ctr. r. on back.	FV	FV	4.50

330	50 DOLLARS	1.5.1994. Purple and blue on violet and m/c unpt. Chrysanthemum flowers at lower ctr. r. Aerial view of cross-harbor tunnel at ctr. r. on back.	FV	FV	10.00

Cat. #	Denomination	Date, description	VG	VF	Unc
331	100 DOLLARS	1.5.1994. Red-violet, orange and red on m/c unpt. Lotus flowers at lower ctr. r. Aerial view of Tsimshatsui, Kowloon Peninsula at ctr. r. on back.	FV	FV	18.00

| 332 | 500 DOLLARS | 1.5.1994; 1.1.1995.Dk. brown and blue on m/c unpt. Peony flowers at lower ctr. r. Hong Kong Container Terminal in Kwai Chung at ctr. r. on back. | FV | FV | 80.00 |

| 333 | 1000 DOLLARS | 1.5.1994; 1.1.1995. Reddish-brown, orange and pale olive green on m/c unpt. Bauhinia flowers at lower ctr. r. Aerial view overlooking the Central district at ctr. r. on back. | FV | FV | 155.00 |

HUNGARY

The Hungarian Republic, located in central Europe, has an area of 35,919 sq. mi. (93,030 sq. km.) and a population of 10.6 million. Capital: Budapest. The economy is based on agriculture, bauxite and a rapidly expanding industrial sector. Machinery, chemicals, iron and steel, and fruits and vegetables are exported.

The ancient kingdom of Hungary, founded by the Magyars in the 9th century, achieved its greatest extension in the mid-14th century when its dominions touched the Baltic, Black and Mediterranean Seas. After suffering repeated Turkish invasions, Hungary accepted Habsburg rule to escape Turkish occupation, regaining independence in 1867 with the Emperor of Austria as king of a dual Austro-Hungarian Empire. Sharing the defeat of the Central Powers in World War I, Hungary lost the greater part of its territory and population and underwent a period of drastic political revision. The short-lived republic of 1918 was followed by a chaotic interval of communist rule, 1919, and the restoration of the monarchy in 1920 with Admiral Horthy as regent of a kingdom without a king. Although a German ally in World War II, Hungary was occupied by German troops who imposed a pro-Nazi dictatorship, 1944. Soviet armies drove out the Germans in 1945 and assisted the communist minority in seizing power. A revised constitution published on Aug. 20, 1949, had established Hungary as a "People's Republic" of the Soviet type, but it is once again a republic as of Oct. 23, 1989.

MONETARY SYSTEM

1 Forint = 100 Fillér 1946–

DENOMINATIONS

Egy = 1	Ötven = 50
Két = 2	Száz = 100
Öt = 5	Ezer = 1000
Tiz = 10	Millió = Million
Húsz = 20	Milliárd = 1,000 Million
Huszonöt = 25	

These words used separately or in combination give denomination.

Magyar Nemzeti Bank —Hungarian National Bank

1957-83 ISSUE

#168—173 arms of 3-bar shield w/star and wreath.

Cat. #	Denomination	Date, description	VG	VF	Unc
168	10 FORINT	1957-75. Deep olive-green and blue-black on m/c unpt. Value at l., portr. S. Petófi at r. Trees and river at ctr. on back.			
		a. 23.5.1957.	.75	3.00	7.50
		b. 24.8.1960.	.50	2.00	7.00
		c. 12.10.1962.	.50	1.50	5.00
		d. 30.6.1969.	.25	1.00	3.00
		e. 28.10.1975.	.10	.35	2.00

169	20 FORINT	1957–80. Deep blue on m/c unpt. Value at l., portr. G. Dózsa at r. Nude male with hammer and wheat at ctr. on back.			
		a. 23.5.1957.	.75	3.00	10.00
		b. 24.8.1960.	2.00	5.00	25.00
		c. 12.10.1962.	.75	2.00	7.50
		d. 3.9.1965.	.50	1.00	6.00
		e. 30.6.1969.	.20	.65	5.00
		f. 28.10.1975. Serial # varieties.	.50	1.00	4.50
		g. 30.9.1980.	.25	.50	2.00

Cat. #	Denomination	Date, description	VG	VF	Unc
173	1000 FORINT	1983. Deep green on m/c unpt. Portr. Bela Bartok at r. Back green on m/c unpt. Mother nursing baby at ctr.			
		a. 25.3.1983.	FV	FV	30.00
		b. 10.11.1983.	FV	FV	25.00

1990-92 ISSUE

#174–177 St. Stephan's Crown over Hungarian Arms replaces 3-bar shield.

Cat. #	Denomination	Date, description	VG	VF	Unc
170	50 FORINT	1965–89. Deep brown and brown on m/c unpt. Value at l., portr. Prince F. Rakoczi at r. Battle scene at ctr. on back.			
		a. 3.9.1965.	1.50	3.00	6.00
		b. 30.6.1969.	1.50	2.50	5.00
		c. 28.10.1975. Serial # varieties.	1.50	2.50	5.00
		d. 30.9.1980.	FV	FV	3.00
		e. 10.11.1983.	FV	FV	2.75
		f. 4.11.1986.	FV	FV	2.50
		g. 10.1.1989.	FV	FV	1.50

Cat. #	Denomination	Date, description	VG	VF	Unc
174	100 FORINT	15.1.1992. Like #171 but w/new arms.	FV	FV	2.50

Cat. #	Denomination	Date, description	VG	VF	Unc
171	100 FORINT	1957–89. Violet and deep brown on m/c unpt. Value at l., port. L. Kossath at r. Horse drawn wagon at ctr. on back.			
		a. 23.5.1957.	4.00	8.00	25.00
		b. 24.8.1960.	4.00	8.00	25.00
		c. 12.10.1962.	2.00	4.00	12.00
		d. 24.10.1968.	FV	3.00	10.00
		e. 28.10.1975. Serial # varieties.	FV	2.00	8.50
		f. 30.9.1980.	FV	FV	6.50
		g. 30.10.1984.	FV	FV	5.50
		h. 10.1.1989.	FV	FV	2.25

Cat. #	Denomination	Date, description	VG	VF	Unc
175	500 FORINT	31.7.1990. Like #172 but w/new arms.	FV	FV	10.00
176	1000 FORINT	1992; 1993. Like #173 but w/new arms.			
		a. 30.10.1992.	FV	FV	18.50
		b. 16.12.1993.	FV	FV	15.00

Cat. #	Denomination	Date, description	VG	VF	Unc
172	500 FORINT	1969–80. Purple on m/c unpt. Portr. E. Ady at r. Aerial view of Budapest and Danube river on back. Sign. varieties.			
		a. 30.6.1969.	FV	10.00	45.00
		b. 28.10.1975. Serial # varieties.	FV	FV	25.00
		c. 30.9.1980.	FV	FV	20.00

Cat. #	Denomination	Date, description	VG	VF	Unc
177	5000 FORINT	1990–93. Deep brown and brown on orange and m/c unpt. Portr. I. Széchenyi at r. Academy of Science at ctr. on back.			
		a. 31.7.1990.	FV	FV	80.00
		b. 30.10.1992.	FV	FV	75.00
		c. 16.12.1993.	FV	FV	70.00

1996 ISSUE

Cat. #	Denomination	Date, description			
178	100 FORINT	1996. L. Kossuth.			Expected new issue.
179	200 FORINT	1996. R. Károly.			Expected new issue.
180	500 FORINT	1996. F. Rákóczi II.			Expected new issue.
181	1000 FORINT	1996. Kg. Mátyas.			Expected new issue.
182	2000 FORINT	1996. B. Gábor.			Expected new issue.
183	5000 FORINT	1996. Count I. Széchenyi.			Expected new issue.
184	10,000 FORINT	1996. St. Stephan.			Expected new issue.

ICELAND

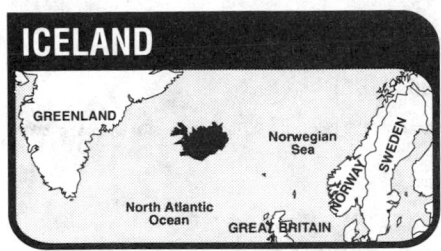

The Republic of Iceland, an island of recent volcanic origin in the North Atlantic east of Greenland and immediately south of the Arctic Circle, has an area of 39,768 sq. mi. (103,000 sq. km.) and a population of 262,193. Capital: Reykjavík. Fishing is the chief industry and accounts for more than 70 percent of the exports.

Iceland was settled by Norwegians in the 9th century and established as an independent republic in 930. The Icelandic assembly called the "Althing," also established in 930, is the oldest parliament in the world. Iceland came under Norwegian sovereignty in 1262, and passed to Denmark when Norway and Denmark were united under the Danish crown in 1384. In 1918, it was established as a virtually independent kingdom in union with Denmark. On June 17, 1944, while Denmark was still under occupation by troops of the Third Reich, Iceland was established by plebiscite as an independent republic.

MONETARY SYSTEM

1 Krona = 100 Aurar, 1874–

SIGNATURE VARIETIES

31	V. Thor – J. G. Mariasson, 1961–1964	43	J. Nordal – G. Hjartarson, 1974–84
32	J. Nordal – V. Thor, 1961–64	44	G. Hjartarson – T. Arnason, 1984
33	J. G. Mariasson – J. Nordal, 1961–67	45	T. Arnason – J. Nordal, 1984–93
34	J. Nordal – J. G. Mariasson, 1961–67	46	T. Arnason – D. Olafsson, 1984–93
35	S. Klemenzson – J. G. Mariasson, 1966–67	47	J. Nordal – T. Arnason, 1984–93
36	J. Nordal – S. Klemenzson, 1966–67	48	G. Hallgrimsson – T. Arnason, 1986–90
37	J. Nordal – D. Olafsson, 1967–86	49	J. Nordal – G. Hallgrimsson, 1986–90
38	D. Olafsson – J. Nordal, 1967–86	50	B. I. Gunnarsson – T. Arnason, 1991–93
39	S. Klemenzson – D. Olafsson, 1967–71	51	J. Nordal – B. I. Gunnarsson, 1991–93
40	S. Frimannsson – D. Olafsson, 1971–73	52	J. Sigurthsson – B. I. Gunnarsson, 1994
41	J. Nordal – S. Frimannsson, 1971–73	53	B. I. Gunnarsson – J. Sigurthsson, 1994
42	G. Hjartarson – D. Olafsson, 1974–84	54	E. Gudnason – S. Hermansson, 1994–
		55	S. Hermansson – E. Gudnason, 1994–

Sedlabanki Íslands
Central Bank of Iceland

Law of 29.3.1961

#42–47 sign. varieties. Printer: BWC (w/o imprint).

Cat. #	Denomination	Date, description	VG	VF	Unc
42	10 KRÓNUR	*L.1961.* Brown-violet on green and orange unpt. J. Eiriksson at I. Ship in harbor lower ctr. Dock scene on back. 2 sign. varieties.			
		a. Issued note.	1.00	2.00	4.00
		s. Specimen.	—	—	75.00

#43–47 wmk: Male portr.

43	25 KRÓNUR	*L.1961.* Purple on m/c unpt. M. Stephensen-Logmadur at I. Fjord at ctr. Fishing boats near large rock formation on back.			
		a. Issued note.	1.00	2.00	5.00
		s. Specimen.	—	—	85.00

44	100 KRÓNUR	*L.1961.* Dk. blue-green on m/c unpt. T. Gunnarsson at I. Sheepherders, horseback, sheep w/mountains in background on back. 12 sign. varieties.			
		a. Issued note.	.30	1.00	2.50
		s. Specimen.	—	—	100.00

Cat. #	Denomination	Date, description	VG	VF	Unc
45	500 KRÓNUR	L.1961. Green on lilac and m/c unpt. H. Haf-stein at l. Sailors on back. 7 sign. varieties.			
		a. Issued note.	1.00	2.00	6.00
		s. Specimen.	—	—	125.00

46	1000 KRÓNUR	L.1961. Blue on m/c unpt. J. Sigurdsson at r., building at lower ctr. Rock formations on back. 11 sign. varieties.			
		a. Issued note.	2.50	4.00	7.00
		s. Specimen.	—	—	150.00

47	5000 KRÓNUR	L.1961. Brown on m/c unpt. Similar to #41. E. Benediktsson at l., dam at lower ctr. Man overlooking waterfalls on back. 8 sign. varieties.			
		a. Issued note.	5.00	12.00	25.00
		s. Specimen.	—	—	175.00

Currency Reform, 1981

100 old Kronur = 1 new Krona

Law 29 March 1961 (1981–86 ISSUE)

#48-52 Printer: BWC (w/o imprint), then later by TDLR (w/o imprint). These made after takeover of BWC by TDLR.

#48–53 sign. varieties. Wmk: J. Sigurdsson.

Cat. #	Denomination	Date, description	VG	VF	Unc
48	10 KRÓNUR	L.1961 (1981). Blue on m/c unpt. A. Jónsson at r. Old Icelandic household scene on back. 4 sign. varieties.			
		a. Issued note.	FV	FV	1.00
		s. Specimen.	—	—	65.00

49	50 KRÓNUR	L.1961 (1981). Brown on m/c unpt. Bishop Guobrandur Þorlaksson at l. 2 printers on back. 4 sign. varieties.			
		a. Issued note.	FV	FV	2.00
		s. Specimen.	—	—	80.00

50	100 KRÓNUR	L.1961 (1981). Dk. green and m/c. Prof. Á. Magnússon at r. Monk w/illuminated manuscript on back. 11 sign. varieties.			
		a. Issued note.	FV	FV	4.00
		s. Specimen.	—	—	100.00

Cat. #	Denomination	Date, description	VG	VF	Unc
51	500 KRÓNUR	L.1961 (1981). Red on m/c unpt. J. Sigurdsson at l. ctr. Sigurdsson working at his desk on back. 8 sign. varieties.			
		a. Issued note.	FV	FV	15.00
		s. Specimen.	—	—	125.00

52	1000 KRÓNUR	L.1961 (1984). Purple on m/c unpt. Bishop B. Sveinsson w/book at r. Church at ctr. on back. 8 sign. varieties.			
		a. Issued note.	FV	FV	25.00
		s. Specimen.	—	—	150.00

53	5000 KRÓNUR	L.1961 (1986). Blue on m/c unpt. R. Jónsdóttir at ctr. Bishop G. Þorláksson w/ two previous wives at r. Jónsdóttir and two girls examining embroidery on back. 3 sign. varieties.			
		a. Issued note.	FV	FV	125.00
		s. Specimen.	—	—	200.00

Law 5 Mai 1986 (1994– ISSUE)

#54–56 like #50–52 but w/new sign. and law date.

Cat. #	Denomination	Date, description	VG	VF	Unc
54	100 KRÓNUR	L.1986 (1994). 2 sign. varieties.	FV	FV	3.00
55	500 KRÓNUR	L.1986 (1994). 3 sign. varieties.	FV	FV	13.50

56	1000 KRÓNUR	L.1986 (1994).	FV	FV	22.50

57	2000 KRÓNUR	L.1986 (1995). Brown and blue-violet on m/c unpt. Painting "Inside, outside" at ctr., J. S. Kjarval at r. Painting "Yearning for Flight" (Leda and the Swan) and "Woman with Flower" on back.	FV.	FV	45.00
58	5000 KRÓNUR	L.1986 (1994). Like #53.		Expected new issue.	

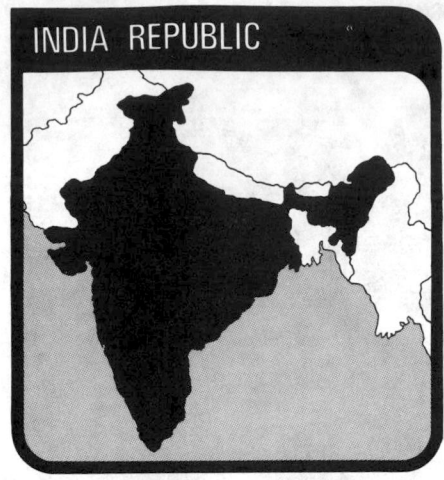

INDIA REPUBLIC

The Republic of India, a subcontinent jutting southward from the mainland of Asia, has an area of 1,266,595 sq. mi. (3,287,590 sq. km.) and a population of 833.4 million, second only to that of the Peoples Republic of China. Capital: New Delhi. India's economy is based on agriculture and industrial activity. Engineering goods, cotton apparel and fabrics, handicrafts, tea, iron and steel are exported.

The people of India have had a continuous civilization since about 2500 BC, when an urban culture based on commerce and trade, and to a lesser extent, agriculture, was developed by the inhabitants of the Indus River Valley. The origins of this civilization are uncertain, but it declined about 1500 B.C., when the region was conquered by the Aryans. Over the following 2,000 years, the Aryans developed a Brahmanic civilization and introduced the caste system. Several successive empires flourished in India over the following centuries, notably those of the Mauryans, Guptas and Mughals. In the 7th and 8th centuries AD, the Arabs expanded into western India, bringing with them the Islamic faith. A Muslim dynasty (the Mughal Empire) controlled virtually the entire subcontinent during the period preceding the arrival of the Europeans; an Indo-Islamic style of art and architecture evolved, of which the Taj Mahal is a splendid example.

The Portuguese were the first to arrive, off Calicut in May 1498. It wasn't until 1612, after Portuguese and Spanish power began to wane, that the English East India Company established its initial settlement at Surat. By the end of the century, English traders were firmly established in Bombay, Madras and Calcutta, as well as in some parts of the interior, and Britain was implementing a policy to create the civil and military institutions that would insure British dominion over the country. By 1757, following the successful conclusion of a war of colonial rivalry with France, the British were firmly established in India as not only traders, but as conquerors. During the next 60 years, the English East India Company acquired dominion over most of India by bribery and force, and ruled directly, or through puppet princelings.

The Indian Mutiny (also called Sepoy Mutiny) of 1857–59, begun by Indian troops in the service of the British East India Company, revealed the intensity of the growing resentment against British domination. The widespread rebellion against British rule was unsuccessful, but resulted in the transfer of government from the company to the British crown, and was a source of inspiration to later Indian nationalists. Agitation for representation in the government continued.

Following World War I, in which India sent six million troops to fight at the side of the Allies, Indian nationalism intensified under the banner of the Indian National Congress and the leadership of Mohandas Karamchand Gandhi, who called the non-violent revolt against British authority. The Government of India Act of 1935 proposed a federal status linking the British India provinces with the many princely states; in addition, provincial legislatures were to be created. The federal status was never implemented, but the legislatures were created after the election of 1937, with the National Congress winning majorities in most of the provinces.

When Britain declared war on Germany in Sept., 1939, the viceroy declared India also to be at war with a common enemy. The Congress, however, demanded independence as a condition for cooperation. Britain refused. But as the Japanese advanced into Asia, Britain offered to transfer to Indians power over all but military affairs during the war, and set forth a plan for postwar independence. Congress was willing to accept the wartime transfer of power, but both Congress and the Muslim League rejected Britain's plan for independence; Congress because it did not sufficiently safeguard Indian unity, the Muslims (who wanted a separate Muslim state) because of fears of what would happen to Muslims within a united India.

Early in 1947, Prime Minister Clement Attlee announced that Britain would leave India "by a date not later than June 1948," even though the Hindus and Muslims could not agree among themselves on a plan for self-government. The National Congress, aware that the Muslim League would revolt rather than accept an all-India government, reluctantly agreed to the formation of a separate Muslim state. The Muslim-populated provinces of the northwest frontier, Sindh and West Punjab in the west, and East Bengal in the east were separated from India to form the Muslim state of Pakistan, which became independent on August 14, 1947. India became independent on the following day. Initially, Pakistan consisted of East and West Pakistan, two areas separated by 1,000 miles of Indian territory. East Pakistan seceded from Pakistan on March 26, 1971, and with the support of India established itself as the independent Peoples Republic of Bangladesh.

The Republic of India is a member of the Commonwealth of Nations. The president is the Chief of State. The prime minister is the Head of Government.

MONETARY SYSTEM

1 Rupee = 100 Naye Paise, 1957–1964
1 Rupee = 100 Paise, 1964–

STAPLE HOLES AND CONDITION

Perfect uncirculated notes are rarely encountered without having at least two tiny holes made by staples, stick pins or stitching having been done during age old accounting practices before and after a note is released to circulation.

SIGNATURE VARIETIES

Governors, Reserve Bank of India (all except 1 Rupee notes)

1	C. D. Deshmukh February 1943–June 1949	10	K. R Puri August 1975–May 1977
2	B. Rama Rau July 1949–January 1957	11	M. Narasimham May 1977–November 1977
3	K.G. Ambegaokar January 1957–February 1957	12	I. G. Patel December 1977–1981
4	H.V.R. Iengar March 1957–February 1962	13	Manmohan Singh, 1981–1983
5	P.C. Bhattacharyya March 1962–June 1967	14	R. N. Malhotra 1983–1984
6	L.K. Jha July 1967–May 1970	15	Abhitam Ghosh 1984 (in office 20 days)
7	B.N. Adarkar May 1970–June 1970	16	S. Venkitaramanan
8	S. Jagannathan	17	C. R. (?)
9	N. C. Sen Gupta May 1975–August 1975		

Reserve Bank of India

FIRST SERIES

#27–47 Asoka column at r. Lg. letters in unpt. beneath serial #. Wmk: Asoka column.

पांच रूपया
Error singular Hindi = RUPAYA

पांच रूपये
Corrected plural Hindi = RUPAYE

VARIETIES: #27–28, 33, 38, 42, 46, 48 and 50 have large headings in Hindi expressing value incorrectly in the singular form Rupaya.

Cat. #	Denomination	Date, description	VG	VF	Unc
29	2 RUPEES	ND. Red-brown on violet and green unpt. Tiger head at l. on back. Value in English and corrected Hindi on both sides. Third value text line on back 24mm long. Tiger's head to l.			
		a. Sign. 2.	.75	3.00	12.00
		b. Sign. 4.	.50	2.00	10.00

30	2 RUPEES	ND. Red-brown on green unpt. Face like #29. Tiger head at l. looking to r., w/13 value text lines at ctr. on back. Sign. 5.	.50	2.50	10.00

31	2 RUPEES	ND. Olive on tan unpt. Like #30. Sign. 5.	.50	2.00	6.00

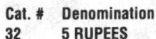

Cat. #	Denomination	Date, description	VG	VF	Unc
32	5 RUPEES	ND. Green on brown unpt. English value only on face, serial # at ctr. *Rs. 5* and antelope on back. Sign B. Rama Rau.	1.00	4.00	15.00

Cat. #	Denomination	Date, description	VG	VF	Unc
36	5 RUPEES	Like #35 but sign. title: *GOVERNOR* centered. 13 value text lines on back.			
		a. Letter A. Sign. 5.	1.50	4.00	12.50
		b. Letter B. Sign. 5.	1.50	4.00	12.50

33	5 RUPEES	ND. Like #32 but value in English and error Hindi on face, serial # at r. 8 value lines on back, fourth line 21mm long. Sign. B. Rama Rau.	.75	2.00	9.00

39	10 RUPEES	ND. Violet on m/c unpt. English and correct Hindi value. Dhow at ctr. on back. Third value text line on back 29mm long.			
		a. W/o letter. Sign. 2.	1.50	4.00	12.50
		b. W/o letter. Sign. 4.	.75	3.00	9.00
		c. Letter A. Sign. 4.	.75	3.00	9.00

NOTE: For similar note but in red, see #R3 (Persian Gulf listings); in blue, see #R5 (Haj Pilgrim listings).

34	5 RUPEES	ND. Fourth value text line on back 26mm long. Sign. 2.	.75	3.00	9.00

40	10 RUPEES	ND. Like #39 but sign. title: *GOVERNOR* centered. 13 value text lines on back.			
		a. Letter A. Sign. 5.	1.50	4.00	12.50
		b. Letter B. Sign. 5.	1.50	4.00	12.50

35	5 RUPEES	ND. Green on brown unpt. Value in English and correct Hinki. *Rs. S* and antelope on back. but redesigned panels at l. and r.			
		a. W/o letter. Sign. 4.	.75	2.00	9.00
		b. Letter A. Sign. 4.	.50	2.00	6.00

NOTE: For similar note but in orange, see #R2 (Persian Gulf listings).

Cat. #	Denomination	Date, description	VG	VF	Unc
43	100 RUPEES	ND. Purplish-blue on m/c unpt. Value in English and correct Hindi. Bank emblem at l. on back. Third value text line 40mm long.			
		a. W/o letter, thin paper. Sign. 2.	15.00	40.00	85.00
		b. W/o letter, thin paper. Sign. 4.	15.00	40.00	85.00
		c. Letter A, thick paper. Sign. 4.	15.00	40.00	85.00

NOTE: For similar note but in green, see #R4 (Persian Gulf listings); in red, see #R6 (Haj Pilgrim listings).

44	100 RUPEES	ND. Violet and m/c. Heading in rectangle at top, serial # at upper l. and lower r. Sign. title: *GOVERNOR* at ctr. r. Dam at ctr. w/ 13 value text lines at l. on back. Sign. 4.	12.50	25.00	65.00
45	100 RUPEES	ND. Like #44 but sign. title: *GOVERNOR* is centered. Sign. 5.	12.50	25.00	65.00
47	1000 RUPEES	ND. Brown on green and blue unpt. Value in English and correct Hindi. Tanjore Temple at ctr. 13 value lines on back. BOMBAY. Sign. 5.	50.00	110.00	—

48	5000 RUPEES	ND. Green, violet and brown. Asoka column at l. Value in English and in error Hindi on face and back. Gateway of India on back. Sign. 2.			
		a. BOMBAY.	—	Rare	—
		b. CALCUTTA.	—	Rare	—
		c. DELHI.	—	Rare	—

Cat. #	Denomination	Date, description	VG	VF	Unc
49	5000 RUPEES	ND. Green, violet and brown. Osoka column at l. Value in English and correct Hindi. Gateway of India on back. BOMBAY. Sign. 4.	—	Rare	—

50	10,000 RUPEES	ND. Blue, violet and brown. Asoka column at ctr. Value in English and in error Hindi on face and back.			
		a. BOMBAY. Sign. 2.	—	Rare	—
		b. CALCUTTA. Sign. 2.	—	Rare	—
		c. MADRAS. Sign. 4.	—	Rare	—
50A	10,000 RUPEES	ND. Like #50 but Hindi corrected. BOMBAY. Sign. 4.	—	Rare	—

SECOND SERIES

Most notes reduced size. Large letters found in unpt. beneath serial #.
#51–65 Asoka column at r.

پیے
Urdu Incorrect (actually Persian)

پیے
Corrected to Urdu

VARIETIES: #51–52, 54–55, 57–59, 62–63, 67–70 have bottom value line on back in Urdu expressed incorrectly ending in Persian (Farsi) at l.

51	2 RUPEES	ND. Brown and m/c. Numeral *2* at ctr. 7mm high. Tiger at ctr. on back.			
		a. Sign. title: *GOVERNOR* centered at bottom. Sign. 5.	.70	2.00	6.00
		b. Sign. title: *GOVERNOR* at ctr. r. Sign. 6.	.50	1.00	4.00

52	2 RUPEES	ND. Deep pink and m/c. Numeral *2* at ctr. 15mm high. Tiger at ctr. on back. Sign. 8.	.50	1.00	4.00
53	2 RUPEES	ND. Like #52 but corrected Urdu at bottom l. on back. English text at l. on face.			
		a. W/o letter. Sign. 8.	.30	.85	3.00
		b. W/o letter. Sign. 10.	.30	.85	3.00
		c. Letter A. Sign. 10.	.30	.85	3.00
		d. Letter A. Sign. 11.	.30	.85	3.00
		e. Letter A. Sign.12.	.25	.75	2.00
		f. Letter B. Sign. 12.	.20	.75	2.00
		g. Letter C. Sign. 12.	.20	.75	2.00

Cat. #	Denomination	Date, description	VG	VF	Unc
53A	2 RUPEES	ND. Similar to #53 but English text at r. on face.			
		a. W/o letter. Sign. 13.	.30	1.00	3.00
		b. Letter A. Sign. 14.	.30	1.00	3.00
		c. Letter B. Sign. 14.	.30	1.00	3.00
			.30	1.00	3.00
			.15	.50	1.50

Cat. #	Denomination	Date, description	VG	VF	Unc
54	5 RUPEES	ND. Green and m/c. Numeral *5* at ctr. 11mm high. Antelope at ctr. on back.			
		a. Sign. title: *GOVERNOR* centered at bottom. Sign. 5.	.40	1.25	4.00
		b. Sign. title: *GOVERNOR* at ctr. r. Sign. 6.	.25	.75	3.00

Cat. #	Denomination	Date, description	VG	VF	Unc
55	5 RUPEES	ND. Dk. green on m/c unpt. Numeral *5* at ctr. 17mm high. Antelope at ctr. on back. Sign. 8.	.40	1.00	3.00
56	5 RUPEES	ND. Like #55 but corrected Urdu at bottom l. on back.			
		a. W/o letter. Sign. 8.	.40	1.00	3.00
		b. Letter A. Sign. 8.	.40	1.00	3.00
		c. Letter A. Sign. 10.	.40	1.00	3.00
		d. Letter A. Sign. 11.	.40	1.00	3.00

Cat. #	Denomination	Date, description	VG	VF	Unc
57	10 RUPEES	ND. Purple and m/c. Numeral *10* at ctr. 30mm broad. Dhow at ctr. on back.			
		a. Sign. title: *GOVERNOR* centered at bottom. Sign. 5.	1.00	2.50	7.50
		b. Sign. title: *GOVERNOR* at ctr. r. Sign. 6.	1.00	2.50	7.50

Cat. #	Denomination	Date, description	VG	VF	Unc
58	10 RUPEES	ND. Brown and m/c. Numeral *10* at ctr. 18mm broad. Heading in English and Hindi on back. Sign. 6.	2.00	7.50	20.00

Cat. #	Denomination	Date, description	VG	VF	Unc
59	10 RUPEES	ND. Dk. brown on m/c unpt. Like #58. Heading only in Hindi on back.			
		a. W/o letter. Sign. 8.	.75	2.00	7.00
		b. Letter A. Sign. 8.	.75	2.00	7.00
60	10 RUPEES	ND. Like #59 but corrected Urdu at bottom l. on back.			
		a. Letter A. Sign. S8.	.75	2.00	7.50
		b. Letter B. Sign. 8.	.75	2.00	7.50
		c. Letter B. Sign. 10.	.75	2.00	7.50
		d. Letter B. Sign. 11.	.75	2.00	7.50
		e. Letter C. Sign. 11.	.75	2.00	7.50
		f. Letter C. Sign. 12.	.75	1.50	6.00
		g. Letter D. Sign. 12.	.75	1.50	6.00
		h. Letter D. Sign.13.	.50	1.00	4.00
		i. Letter E. Sign. 14.	.50	1.00	4.00
		j. Letter F. Sign. 14.	.50	1.00	4.00
		k. Letter G. Sign. 14.	.50	1.00	4.00
		l. W/o letter. Sign. 14.	.50	1.00	4.00
		m. Sign. 15.	.60	1.50	10.00

Cat. #	Denomination	Date, description	VG	VF	Unc
60A	10 RUPEES	ND. Similar to #60 but w/Hindi title above *RESERVE BANK OF INDIA* and Hindi text at l. of *10* and *I PROMISE...* at r. Sanskrit title added under Asoka column at r. Sign. 16.	FV	FV	2.00

Incorrect Kashmiri
(actually Persian)   Corrected Kashmiri

Cat. #	Denomination	Date, description	VG	VF	Unc
61	20 RUPEES	ND. Orange and m/c. Parliament House at ctr. on back. Sign. 8.			
		a. Dk. colors under sign., error in Kashmiri in fifth line on back.	2.00	6.00	17.50
		b. Lt. colors under sign., error in Kashmiri in fifth line on back.	1.50	5.00	12.00
		c. Lt. colors under sign., corrected Kashmiri line on back.	1.50	5.00	12.00

Cat. #	Denomination	Date, description	VG	VF	Unc
62	100 RUPEES	ND. Blue and m/c. Numeral *100* at ctr. 43mm broad. Dam at ctr. w/only English heading on back.			
		a. Sign. 5.	6.00	15.00	45.00
		b. Sign. 6.	6.00	15.00	45.00
63	100 RUPEES	ND. Blue and m/c. Numeral *100* at ctr. 28mm broad. Dam at ctr. w/only Hindi heading on back. Sign. 8.	6.00	14.00	35.00

Cat. #	Denomination	Date, description	VG	VF	Unc
64	100 RUPEES	ND. Like #63 but corrected Urdu value line on back.			
		a. W/o letter. Sign. 8.	5.00	14.00	35.00
		b. W/o letter. Sign. 10.	5.00	14.00	35.00
		c. W/o letter. Sign. 11.	5.00	14.00	35.00
		d. Letter A. Sign. 12.	5.00	12.00	30.00

Cat. #	Denomination	Date, description	VG	VF	Unc
65	1000 RUPEES	ND. Brown on m/c unpt. Text in English and Hindi on face. Temple at ctr. on back. BOMBAY.			
		a. Sign. 9.	30.00	50.00	100.00
		b. Sign. 10.	30.00	50.00	100.00

Government of India

1969 COMMEMORATIVE ISSUE

#66, Centennial of Birth of Gandhi

Cat. #	Denomination	Date, description	VG	VF	Unc
66	1 RUPEE	ND (1969–70). Violet and m/c. Coin w/Gandhi and *1869–1948* at r. Reverse of Gandhi coin on back at l. Sign. 12.	.25	.75	2.00

Reserve Bank of India

1969 Commemorative Issue

#67–70, Centennial of Birth of Ghandi

Cat. #	Denomination	Date, description	VG	VF	Unc
67	2 RUPEES	ND (1969–70). Red-violet and m/c. Face like #52. Gandhi seated at ctr. on back.			
		a. Sign. 6.	.50	3.00	6.00
		b. Sign. 7.	.75	4.00	7.50

Cat. #	Denomination	Date, description	VG	VF	Unc
68	5 RUPEES	ND (1969–70). Dk. green on m/c unpt. Face like #55. Back like #67.			
		a. Sign. 6.	.50	3.00	6.00
		b. Sign. 7.	.75	4.00	7.50

Cat. #	Denomination	Date, description	VG	VF	Unc
69	10 RUPEES	ND (1969–70). Brown and m/c. Face like #59. Back like #68.			
		a. Sign. 6.	.50	2.00	6.00
		b. Sign. 7.	.60	2.50	7.50

Cat. #	Denomination	Date, description	VG	VF	Unc
70	100 RUPEES	ND (1969–70). Blue and m/c. Face like #63. Back like #68.			
		a. Sign. 6.	5.50	22.00	65.00
		b. Sign. 7.	5.50	22.00	65.00

Government of India

SIGNATURE VARIETIES			
Various Secretaries, (1 Rupee notes only)			
33	H. M. Patel, 1951–1957	35	L. K. Jha, 1957–1963
34	A. K. Roy, 1957	36	S. Boothalingam, 1964–1966

NOTE: The sign. H. M. Patel is often misread as "Mehta." There was never any such individual serving as Secretary. Do not confuse H. M. Patel with I. G. Patel who served later.

37	S. Jagannathan, 1967–1968	43	Pratap Kishen Kaul, 1983–1985
38	I. G. Patel, 1968–1972	44	S. Venkitaramanan, 1985–88
39	M. G. Kaul, 1973–1976	45	Gopi Arora, 1989
40	Manomohan Singh, 1976–1980	46	Bimal Jalan, 1990
41	R. N. Malhotra, 1980–1981	47	Montek Singh Ahluwalia, 1991–
42	M. Narasimham, 1981–85	48	

1957; 63 ISSUE

#75–78A wmk: Asoka column.

Cat. #	Denomination	Date, description	VG	VF	Unc
75	1 RUPEE	1957. Violet and m/c. Redesigned coin w/Asoka column at r. Coin dated 1957 and *100 Naye Paise* in Hindi, 7 value lines on back.			
		a. W/o letter. Sign. 33 w/sign. title: *SECRETARY* ... (1956).	Reported, not confirmed.		
		b. Letter A. Sign. 33 w/sign. title: *SECRETARY*	.30	1.00	3.00
		c. Letter A. Sign. 33 w/sign. title: *PRINCIPAL SECRETARY*...	.30	1.00	3.00
		d. Letter B. Sign. 34 w/sign. title: *SECRETARY* ...	.30	1.00	3.00
		e. Letter B. Sign. 35.	.25	.75	2.00

Cat. #	Denomination	Date, description	VG	VF	Unc
		f. Letter C. Sign. 35.	.25	.75	2.00
		g. Letter D. Sign. 35.	.25	.75	2.00

			VG	VF	Unc
76	1 RUPEE	1963–65. Violet on m/c unpt. Redesigned note. Coin w/various dates and *1 Rupee* in Hindi, 13 value lines on back.			
		a. Letter A. Sign. 35. 1963.	.25	.75	2.00
		b. Letter B. Sign. 36. 1964.	.25	1.00	3.00
		c. Letter B. Sign. 36. 1965.	.25	.75	2.00

			VG	VF	Unc
77	1 RUPEE	1966–80. Violet on m/c unpt. Redesigned note, serial # at l. Coin w/various dates on back.			
		a. W/o letter. Sign. 37. 1966.	.25	.75	2.00
		b. Letter A. Sign. 37. 1967.	.25	.75	2.00
		c. Letter B. Sign. 37. 1968.	.25	.75	2.00
		d. Letter B. Sign. 38 w/sign. title: *SPECIAL SECRETARY* ... . 1968.	.20	.50	1.50
		e. Letter B. Sign. 38 w/sign. title: *SPECIAL SECRETARY* ... . 1969.	.20	.50	1.50
		f. Letter C. Sign. 38 w/title: *SPECIAL SECRETARY* ...1969.	.20	.50	1.50
		g. Letter C. Sign. 38. 1970.	.20	.50	1.50
		h. Letter C. Sign. 38. 1971.	.20	.50	1.50
		i. Letter D. Sign. 38. 1971.	.20	.50	1.50
		j. Letter D. Sign. 38. 1972.	.20	.50	1.50
		k. Letter E. Sign. 38. 1972.	.20	.50	1.50
		l. Letter F. Sign. 39. 1973.	.20	.50	1.50
		m. Letter F. Sign. 39. 1973.	.20	.50	1.50
		n. Letter F. Sign. 39. 1974.	.20	.50	1.50
		o. Letter G. Sign. 39. 1974.	.20	.50	1.50
		p. Letter G. Sign. 39. 1975.	.20	.50	1.50
		q. Letter H. Sign. 39. 1975.	.20	.50	1.50
		r. Letter H. Sign. 39. 1976.	.20	.50	1.50
		s. Letter I. Sign. 39. 1976.	.20	.50	1.50
		t. W/o letter. Sm. serial #. Sign. 40. 1976.	.20	.40	1.00
		u. Sm. serial #. Sign. 40. 1977.	.20	.40	1.00
		v. Letter A. Sign. 40. 1978.	.20	.40	1.00
		w. Letter A. Sign. 40. 1979.	.20	.40	1.00
		x. Letter A. Sign. 40. 1980.	.20	.40	1.00
		y. Letter A. Sign. 41. 1980.	.20	.40	1.00
		z. Letter B. Sign. 41. 1980.	.20	.40	1.00

			VG	VF	Unc
78	1 RUPEE	1981–82. Purple and violet on lt. blue, brown and m/c unpt. Coin w/Asoka column at upper r. Offshore oil drilling platform and reverse of coin w/date on back.			
		a. Sign. 41. 1981.	FV	FV	.50
		b. Sign. 42. 1981.	FV	FV	.50
		c. Sign. 42. 1982.	FV	FV	.50

Cat. #	Denomination	Date, description	VG	VF	Unc
78A	1 RUPEE	1983–. Similar to #78 but w/new coin design.			
		a. Sign. 43 w/title: *SECRETARY* .... 1983–85.	FV	FV	.40
		b. Sign. 44 w/title: *FINANCE SECRETARY* .... 1985–86.	FV	FV	.40
		c. Letter A. Sign. 44. 1986–88.	FV	FV	.40
		d. Letter B. Sign. 45. 1989.	FV	.15	.50
		e. Letter B. Sign. 46. 1990.	FV	FV	.30
		f. Letter B. Sign. 47 w/title: *SECRETARY* .... 1991.	FV	FV	.30
		g. Letter B. Sign. 47. 1992.	FV	FV	.30
		h. Letter B. Sign. 47 w/title: *FINANCE SECRETARY*. 1993.	FV	FV	.30
		i. Letter B. Sign. 47. 1994.	FV	FV	.30

Reserve Bank of India

THIRD SERIES

Lg. letters in unpt. beneath serial #.

#79–88 Asoka column at r. and as wmk.

Cat. #	Denomination	Date, description	VG	VF	Unc
79	2 RUPEES	ND. Orange on m/c unpt. Space craft at ctr. on back.			
		a. Sign. 10.	FV	.25	1.00
		b. Sign. 11.	FV	.25	1.00
		c. W/o letter. Sign. 12.	FV	.25	1.00
		d. Letter A. Sign. 12.	FV	.25	1.00
		e. W/o letter. Sign. 13.	FV	.25	1.00
		f. Letter A. Sign. 13.	FV	.25	1.00
		g. W/o letter. Sign. 14.	FV	.25	1.00
		h. Letter A. Sign. 14.	FV	.15	.75
		i. Letter B. Sign. 14.	FV	.15	.75
		j. Letter A. Sign. 15.	.40	1.50	7.50

Cat. #	Denomination	Date, description	VG	VF	Unc
80	5 RUPEES	ND. Gray-green on m/c unpt. Farmer plowing w/tractor at ctr. on back.			
		a. W/o letter. Sign. 8.	FV	.50	1.25
		b. W/o letter A. Sign. 10.	FV	.50	1.25
		c. Letter A. Sign. 10.	FV	.50	1.25
		d. Letter A. Sign. 11.	FV	.50	1.25
		e. Letter A. Sign. 12.	FV	.50	1.25
		f. Letter B. Sign. 12.	FV	.50	1.25
		g. Letter C. Sign. 12.	FV	.50	1.25
		h. Letter D. Sign. 13.	FV	.50	1.25
		i. W/o letter. New seal in Hindi and English. Sign. 14.	FV	.50	1.25
		j. Letter A. New seal. Sign. 14.	FV	.50	1.25
		k. Letter E. Sign. 14.	FV	.50	1.25
		l. Letter F. Sign. 14.	FV	.50	1.5
		m. Letter G. Sign. 14.	FV	.50	1.5
		n. Letter D. Sign. 15.	.50	2.00	10.00
		o. W/o letter. Sign. 16.	FV	.40	1.00
		p. Letter B. Sign. 16.	VG	.40	1.00
		q. Letter B. Sign. 17.	FV	FV	.85

Cat. #	Denomination	Date, description	VG	VF	Unc
81	10 RUPEES	ND. Lilac and brown on m/c unpt. Tree w/ peacocks at ctr. on back.			
		a. W/o letter. Sign. 8.	FV	.85	3.00
		b. W/o letter. Sign. 10.	FV	.85	3.00
		c. W/o letter. Sign. 11.	FV	.85	3.00
		d. Letter A. Sign. 12.	FV	.85	3.00
		e. W/o letter. Sign.12.	FV	.85	3.00
		f. W/o letter. Sign. 13.	FV	.85	3.00
		g. Letter A. Sign. 13.	FV	.85	3.00
		h. Sign. 14.	FV	.75	2.00
		i. Letter B. Sign. 14.	FV	.75	2.00
		j. Letter C. Sign. 14.	FV	.75	2.00
		k. Sign. 15.	.75	3.00	12.50

Cat. #	Denomination	Date, description	VG	VF	Unc
82	20 RUPEES	ND. Red and purple on m/c unpt. Back orange on m/c unpt. Buddhist Wheel of Life at lower ctr. on back.			
		a. Sign. 8.	FV	1.25	4.00
		b. Sign. 10.	FV	1.25	4.00
		c. Sign. 11.	FV	1.25	4.00
		d. W/o letter. Sign. 12	FV	1.25	4.00
		e. Letter A. Sign. 12.	FV	1.25	4.00
		f. Letter A. Sign. 13.	FV	1.25	4.00
		g. Letter A. Sign. 14.	FV	1.25	4.00
		h. Letter B. Sign. 14.	FV	1.25	4.00
		i. Sign. 15.	1.00	3.50	10.00
		j. Sign. 17.	FV	1.00	2.00

Cat. #	Denomination	Date, description	VG	VF	Unc
83	50 RUPEES	ND. Black and purple on lilac and m/c unpt. Parliament House at ctr. on back.			
		a. W/o flag at top of flagpole on back. Sign. 8.	FV	3.00	8.00
		b. W/o flag at top of flagpole on back. Sign. 10.	FV	3.00	8.00
		c. Flag at top of flagpole. Sign.12..	FV	3.00	8.00

Cat. #	Denomination	Date, description	VG	VF	Unc
84	50 RUPEES	ND. Black and purple on orange, lilac and m/c unpt. Similar to #83.			
		a. Sign.12.	FV	2.25	7.00
		b. Sign. 13.	FV	2.25	7.00
		c. Sign. 14.	FV	2.25	6.00
		d. Letter A. Sign. 14.	FV	2.25	6.00
		e. Letter B. Sign. 14.	FV	2.25	6.00
		f. Sign. 15.	2.00	8.00	20.00
		g. Sign. 16.	FV	2.00	6.00
		h. Sign. 17.	FV	1.75	3.50

Cat. #	Denomination	Date, description	VG	VF	Unc
86	100 RUPEES	ND. Black, deep red and purple on m/c unpt. (pink at ctr.). Like #85A. Deep red sign.			
		a. Sign. 12.	FV	3.50	15.00
		b. Sign. 13.	FV	3.50	15.00
		c. Sign. 14.	FV	3.50	7.50
		d. Sign. 16.	FV	3.50	6.50
		e. Sign. 17.	FV	3.50	8.00

87	500 RUPEES	ND (1987). Brown, deep blue-green and deep blue on m/c unpt. M. K. Gandhi at ctr. r. Electronic sorting marks at lower l. Gandhi leading followers across back. Wmk: Asoka column.			
		a. Sign. 14.	FV	20.00	35.00
		b. Sign. 16.	FV	18.50	32.50

85	100 RUPEES	ND. Black, brown-violet and dk. green on blue-violet on brown and m/c unpt. (tan at ctr.). Dam, agricultural work at ctr. on back. Denomination above bar at lower r. Black sign.			
		a. Sign. 8.	FV	5.00	20.00
		b. Sign. 10.	FV	4.00	17.50
		c. Sign. 11.	FV	4.00	17.50
		d. Sign. 12.	FV	4.00	17.50
		e. Sign. 14.	FV	3.50	15.00
		f. Sign. 15.	4.00	10.00	25.00

1992 ISSUE

85A	100 RUPEES	ND. Like #85 but w/o bar under denomination at lower r. Sign. 14.	FV	3.50	10.00

88	10 RUPEES	ND (1992).Dull brown-violet on orange and m/c unpt. Rural temple at l. ctr. on back.			
		a. Sign. 16.	FV	.50	1.75
		b. Sign. 17.	FV	.50	1.50

PERSIAN GULF

Intended for circulation in area of Oman, Bahrain, Qatar and Trucial States during 1950s and early 1960s. Z prefix in serial #. Known as "Gulf Rupees."

Reserve Bank of India

(ND) ISSUE

Cat. #	Denomination	Date, description	VG	VF	Unc
R2	5 RUPEES	ND. Like #35a but orange. Sign. 4.	5.00	15.00	60.00

R3	10 RUPEES	ND. Like #39c but red. Sign. 4.	7.00	20.00	90.00

R4	100 RUPEES	ND. Like #43b but green. Sign. 4.	40.00	150.00	450.00

HAJ PILGRIM

Reserve Bank of India

(ND) ISSUE

#R5-R6, for use by Moslem pilgrims in Mecca, Saudi Arabia. Letters HA near serial #, and *HAJ* l. and r. of bank title at top.

Cat. #	Denomination	Date, description	VG	VF	Unc
R5	10 RUPEES	ND. Like #39c but blue. Sign. 4.	25.00	75.00	350.00
R6	100 RUPEES	ND. Like #43b but red. Sign. 4.	85.00	250.00	650.00

INDONESIA

The Republic of Indonesia, the world's largest archipelago, extends for more than 3,000 miles (4,827 km.) along the equator from the mainland of southeast Asia to Australia. The more than 13,500 islands comprising the archipelago have a combined area of 735,268 sq. mi. (2,042,005 sq. km.) and a population of 187.7 million, including East Timor. Capital: Jakarta. Petroleum, timber, rubber and coffee are exported.

Had Columbus succeeded in reaching the fabled Spice Islands, he would have found advanced civilizations a millennium old, and temples still ranked among the finest examples of ancient art. During the opening centuries of the Christian era, the islands were influenced by Hindu priests and traders who spread their culture and religion. Moslem invasions began in the 13th century, fragmenting the island kingdoms into small states which were unable to resist Western colonial infiltration. Portuguese traders established posts in the 16th century, but they were soon outnumbered by the Dutch who arrived in 1602 and gradually asserted control over the islands comprising present-day Indonesia, Dutch dominance, interrupted by British incursions during the Napoleonic Wars, established the Netherlands East Indies as one of the richest colonial possessions in the world.

The Indonesian independence movement, which began between the two world wars, was encouraged by the Japanese during their 3-year occupation during World War II. Indonesia proclaimed its independence on Aug. 17, 1945, three days after the surrender of Japan, and established it on Dec. 28, 1949, after four years of Dutch military efforts to reassert control. West Irian, formerly Netherlands New Guinea, came under the administration of Indonesia on May 1, 1963.

MONETARY SYSTEM

1 Rupiah = 100 Sen, 1945–

Republik Indonesia

1961 ISSUE

Cat. #	Denomination	Date, description	VG	VF	Unc
78	1 RUPIAH	1961. Dk. green. Rice field workers at l. Farm produce on back.	.10	.25	.75

79	2 1/2 RUPIAH	1961. Black, dk. blue and brown on blue-green unpt. Corn field work at l.	.10	.20	.50

BORNEO ISSUE

#79A–79B Sukarno at l, Javanese dancer at r. on back.

79A	1 RUPIAH	1961. Green on orange unpt.	1.00	2.00	6.00

79B	2 1/2 RUPIAH	1961. Blue on gray-brown unpt.	1.00	2.00	6.00

1964 ISSUE

#80–81 Sukarno at l.

Cat. #	Denomination	Date, description	VG	VF	Unc
80	1 RUPIAH	1964. Red and brown.			
		a. Imprint: *Pertjetakan Kebajoran* at bottom ctr. on face.	.75	2.00	5.00
		b. W/o imprint.	.25	.50	2.00

81	2 1/2 RUPIAH	1964. Blue and brown.			
		a. Imprint like #80a.	1.00	2.50	6.00
		b. W/o imprint.	1.00	2.50	6.00

Bank Indonesia

1963 ISSUE

89	10 RUPIAH	1963. Blue and brown. Wood carver at l. Huts, shrine at ctr., mythical figure at r. on back.	.10	.25	1.00

1964 ISSUE

90	1 SEN	1964. Green-blue. Man w/straw hat at r.	—	—	.10

Cat. #	Denomination	Date, description	VG	VF	Unc
91	5 SEN	1964. Lilac-brown. Girl in uniform at r.	—	—	.10
92	10 SEN	1964. Dk. green. Like #91.	—	—	.10

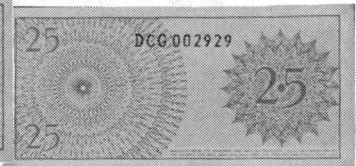

93	25 SEN	1964. Red. Man in uniform at r.	—	—	.10

94	50 SEN	1964. Purple. Like #93.	—	.10	.30

#95–96, 98 and 101 have printed Indonesian arms in wmk. area at r.

95	25 RUPIAH	1964. Green. Woman weaver at l.	.15	.50	1.50

96	50 RUPIAH	1964. Dk. brown and green. Woman spinner at l.	.15	.50	1.50

97	100 RUPIAH	1964. Brown and red. Worker on rubber plantation at l.			
		a. Printer's name: *P.T. Pertjetakan Kebajoran Imp.* 16mm. long at r. on back.	1.00	2.50	5.00
		b. Printer's name: *PN Pertjetakan Kebajoran Imp.* 22mm. long at r. on back.	.25	.75	3.00

Cat. #	Denomination	Date, description	VG	VF	Unc
98	100 RUPIAH	1964. Blue and brown. Worker on rubber plantation at l.	.50	1.00	3.00
99	10,000 RUPIAH	1964. Red and dk. brown. 2 men pulling rope at l. Wmk: Water buffalo.	1.00	4.00	20.00
100	10,000 RUPIAH	1964. Green. Like #99.	.50	1.00	4.00

101	10,000 RUPIAH	1964. Green. Like #100, but w/wmk. arms.			
		a. Wmk. at ctr.	.35	2.00	6.00
		b. Wmk. at l. and r.	.25	1.00	4.00

1968 ISSUE

#102–112 Gen. Sudirman at l.
#102–103 wmk: Arms at ctr.

102	1 RUPIAH	1968. Red. Woman shelling coconut at l. on back.	.10	.25	1.50

103	2 1/2 RUPIAH	1968. Dk. blue. Arms at r. Woman holding rice stalks at l. on back.	.10	.25	1.50

#104–110 wmk: Arms at r.

Cat. #	Denomination	Date, description	VG	VF	Unc
104	5 RUPIAH	1968. Dull violet on m/c unpt. Dam construction scene on back.	.10	.25	2.00

105	10 RUPIAH	1968. Lt. brown. Oil refinery on back.	.25	.50	2.00

106	25 RUPIAH	1968. Green and brown. Bridge over Musi River at ctr. r. on back.	.25	.75	3.00

107	50 RUPIAH	1968. Violet and dk. blue. Airplanes on back.	.35	1.00	6.00

108	100 RUPIAH	1968. Deep red on m/c unpt. Rail coalyard on back.	.50	1.50	4.00

Cat. #	Denomination	Date, description	VG	VF	Unc
109	500 RUPIAH	1968. Dk. green. Yarn spinning on back.	.50	1.75	7.50

110	1000 RUPIAH	1968. Orange and dk. brown. Petro–chemical plant on back.	.50	1.50	6.00

NOTE: Deceptive forgeries of #110 are very common.

111	5000 RUPIAH	1968. Blue-green. Industrial plant on back.	4.00	12.50	50.00
112	10,000 RUPIAH	1968. Red brown and violet. Industrial scene on back.	10.00	25.00	60.00

1975 ISSUE

112A	500 RUPIAH	ND. Prince Diponegoro at l. Terraced fields on back. (Not issued.)	—	—	—

113	1000 RUPIAH	1975. Blue-green. Prince Diponegoro at l. Farm scene on back. Wmk: Man's head.	.50	1.50	5.00

Cat. #	Denomination	Date, description	VG	VF	Unc
113A	5000 RUPIAH	ND. Brown. Prince Diponegoro at r. Back like #114. (Not issued.)	—	—	—

114	5000 RUPIAH	1975. Brown and m/c. Fisherman w/net at r. 3 men sailing ships on back. Wmk: Tjut Njak Din's head.	1.65	5.00	20.00

114A	10,000 RUPIAH	ND. Green and red. Like #113A. Peasants at ctr. on back. (Not issued.)	—	—	—

Cat. #	Denomination	Date, description	VG	VF	Unc
115	10,000 RUPIAH	1975. Brown and m/c. Stone relief at Borobudur Temple. Large mask from Bali at l. on back. Wmk: Gen. Soedirman.	3.50	10.00	50.00

1977 ISSUE

116	100 RUPIAH	1977. Red and m/c. Rhinoceros at l. Rhinoceros in jungle scene at ctr. r. on back. Wmk: Arms.	.05	.20	1.25

117	500 RUPIAH	1977. Green and m/c. Woman w/2 orchids at l. Bank of Indonesia at ctr. on back and as wmk.	.25	.75	3.00

1979 ISSUE

118	10,000 RUPIAH	1979. M/c. Musicians playing the "Gamelan" at ctr. Prambanan Temple on back. Wmk: Dr. Soetomo.	3.00	9.00	22.50

1980 ISSUE

Cat. #	Denomination	Date, description	VG	VF	Unc
119	1000 RUPIAH	1980. Blue and m/c. Dr. Soetomo at ctr. r. Mountain scene in Sianok Valley on back. Wmk: Sultan Hasanudin.	.15	.50	2.00

120	5000 RUPIAH	1980. Brown and m/c. Diamond cutter at ctr. Back brown, green and m/c. 3 Torajan houses from Celebes at ctr. Wmk: D. Sartika.	2.00	6.00	17.50

1982 ISSUE

121	500 RUPIAH	1982. Dk. green and m/c. Man standing by Amorphophallus Titanum flower at l. Bank of Indonesia on back. Wmk: Gen. A. Yani.	.35	1.00	2.25

1984–88 ISSUE

122	100 RUPIAH	1984. Red on m/c unpt. Goura Victoria at l. Asahan Dam on back. Wmk: Arms.			
		a. Engraved.	FV	FV	.75
		b. Litho.	FV	FV	.50

1992 ISSUE

#127–132 arms at upper r. area. Printer: PPU.

Cat. #	Denomination	Date, description	VG	VF	Unc
123	500 RUPIAH	1988. Brown and dk. green on m/c unpt. Stag at l. Branch Bank of Indonesia at Cirebon at r. on back. Wmk: Gen. A. Yani.	FV	FV	1.50

Cat. #	Denomination	Date, description	VG	VF	Unc
127	100 RUPIAH	1992. Red on orange and m/c unpt. Sailboat "Pinici" at l. Volcano "Anak Krakatau" at r. on back. Wmk: K. H. Dewantara.	FV	FV	.75

| 124 | 1000 RUPIAH | 1987. Blue-black on m/c unpt. Arms at l.; Raja Sisingamangaraja XII at ctr. Yogyakarta Palace at ctr. on back. Wmk: Sultan Hasanuddin. | FV | FV | 2.00 |

| 128 | 500 RUPIAH | 1992. Dk. gray and deep brown on green and m/c unpt. Orangutan resting on limb at l. Native huts at E. Kalimanan at r. on back. Wmk: H. O. S. Tjokroaminoto. | FV | FV | 1.25 |

| 125 | 5000 RUPIAH | 1986. Dk. brown on m/c unpt. Teuku Umar at ctr. Minaret of Kudus mosque at r. on back. Wmk: C. M. Tijahahu. | FV | FV | 10.00 |

| 129 | 1000 RUPIAH | 1992. Deep blue on lt. blue and m/c unpt. Aerial view of Lake Toba at l. ctr. Native huts, stone monument at Nias Island at ctr. on back. Wmk: Tjut Njak Meutia. | FV | FV | 2.00 |

| 126 | 10,000 RUPIAH | 1985. Purple and m/c. R. A. Kartini at l. Temple at ctr. Female graduate at ctr. r. on back. Wmk: Dr. T. Mangoenkoesoemo. | FV | FV | 20.00 |

Cat. #	Denomination	Date, description	VG	VF	Unc
130	5000 RUPIAH	1992. Black, brown and dk. brown on m/c unpt. Musical instrument, tapestry at ctr. Volcano w/3-color "Kelimutu" Lake at ctr. on back. Wmk: Tjut Njak Din.	FV	FV	5.50
131	10,000 RUPIAH	1992. Rose and purple on m/c unpt. Sri Sultan Hamengku Buwono IX at l., girl scouts at ctr. r. Borobudur Temple on hillside on back. Wmk: W. R. Soepratman.	FV	FV	12.50

| 132 | 20,000 RUPIAH | 1992. Black, dark grayish-green and red on m/c unpt. Red Cendrawasih bird at ctr. Cloves flower at ctr., map of Indonesian Archipeligo at r. Wmk: K. H. Dewantara. | FV | FV | 25.00 |

COMMEMORATIVE 1993 ISSUE

#133 and 133A, 25 Years of Economic Development

| 133 | 50,000 RUPIAH | 1993. Greenish-blue, tan and gray. Pres. Soeharto at l. ctr., surrounded by various scenes of development. Anti-counterfeiting design at r. Jet plane over Soekarno-Hatta International Airport at ctr. on back. Wmk: W. R. Soepratman. | FV | FV | 65.00 |

| 133A | 50,000 RUPIAH | 1993. Design like #133, but pale gray plastic. Soeharto in optical variable device at r. | — | — | 95.00 |

NOTE: #133A issued in commemorative folder.

REGIONAL

Irian Barat — West Irian

1963 PROVISIONAL ISSUE

#R1 and R2 Pres. Sukarno at l. w/ovpt: *IRIAN BARAT* on Rebublik Indonesia issue.

| R1 | 1 RUPIAH | ND (1963 – old date 1961). Orange. | 2.50 | 7.50 | 20.00 |

| R2 | 2 1/2 RUPIAH | ND (1963 – old date 1961). Violet. | 3.50 | 8.50 | 25.00 |

#R3-R5 Pres. Sukarno at l., ovpt: *IRIAN BARAT* on Bank Indonesia issue.

Cat. #	Denomination	Date, description	VG	VF	Unc
R3	5 RUPIAH	ND (1963 – old date 1960). Gray-olive.	4.00	15.00	40.00
R4	10 RUPIAH	ND (1963 – old date 1960). Red.	6.00	17.50	35.00
R5	100 RUPIAH	ND (1963 – old date 1960). Green.	10.00	25.00	60.00

Riau

1963 PROVISIONAL ISSUE

#R96 and R7 Pres. Sukarno at l. w/ovpt: *RIAU* on Republik Indonesia issue.

| R6 (R9) | 1 RUPIAH | ND (1963 – old date 1961). Orange. | 4.00 | 15.00 | 40.00 |

| R7 (R10) | 2 1/2 RUPIAH | ND (1963 – old date 1961). Blue. | 6.00 | 20.00 | 50.00 |

#R8–R10 Pres. Sukarno at l., ovpt: *RIAU* on Bank Indonesia issue.

| R8 (R6) | 5 RUPIAH | ND (1963 – old date 1960). Violet. Ovpt. on #82a, w/prefix X in serial #. | 4.00 | 15.00 | 40.00 |

NOTE: Counterfeits on #82a but w/o prefix X on serial # exist.

| R9 (R7) | 10 RUPIAH | ND (1963 – old date 1960). Red. | 4.00 | 10.00 | 30.00 |
| R10 (R8) | 100 RUPIAH | ND (1963 – old date 1960). Green. | 20.00 | 45.00 | 100.00 |

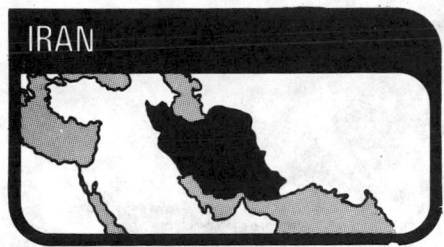

IRAN

The Islamic Republic of Iran, located between the Caspian Sea and the Persian Gulf in southwestern Asia, has an area of 636,296 sq. mi. (1,648,000 sq. km.) and a population of 51 million. Capital: Tehran. Although predominantly an agricultural state, Iran depends heavily on oil for foreign exchange. Crude oil, carpets and agricultural products are exported.

Iran (historically known as Persia) is one of the world's most ancient and resilient nations. Strategically astride the lower land gate to Asia, it has been conqueror and conquered, sovereign nation and vassal state, ever emerging from its periods of glory or travail with its culture and political individuality intact. Iran (Persia) was a powerful empire under Cyrus the Great (600–529 B.C.), its borders extending from the Indus to the Nile. It has also been conquered by the predatory empires of antique and recent times - Assyrian, Medean, Macedonia, Seljuq, Turk, Mongol - and more recently been coveted by Russia, Germany and Great Britain. Revolts against the absolute power of the Shahs resulted in the establishment of a constitutional monarchy in 1906. In 1931 the Kingdom of Persia became known as the Kingdom of Iran. In 1979, the monarchy was toppled and an Islamic Republic proclaimed.

RULERS

Pahlavi Dynasty

Mohammad Reza Pahlavi, SH1320–58/1941–79AD

PRESIDENTS

Islamic Republic of Iran

Abolhassan Bani Sadr, SH1358–60 (AD1979–Jun 81)

Mohammad Ali Rajai, SH1360 (AD–1981 Jun-Oct)

Hojjatoleslam Ali Khamene'i, SH1360–(AD1981–)

MONETARY SYSTEM

1 Shahi = 5 Dinars

1 Rial (100 Dinars) = 20 Shahis

1 Toman = 10 Rials SH1310– (1932–)

REPLACEMENT NOTES

#100-108 (and ovpt. notes of #110-126), 01, 02, 03 or 99/9, 98/9, 97/9. #132 and later, 99/99, 98/99, 97/99, etc.

SIGNATURE/TITLE VARIETIES		
Kingdom: Mohammad Reza Pahlavi		
	GENERAL DIRECTOR	**MINISTER OF FINANCE**
7	Ebrahim Kashani	Abdolbagi Shoaii
8	Dr. Ali Asghar Pourhomayoun	Abdul Hossein Behnia
9	Mehdi Samii	Abdul Hossein Behnia
10	Mehdi Samii	Amir Abbas Hoveyda
11	Mehdi Samii	Dr. Jamshid Amouzegar
12	Khodadad Farmanfarmaian	Dr. Jamshid Amouzegar
13	Abdol Ali Jahanshahi	Dr. Jamshid Amouzegar
14	Mohammad Yeganeh	Dr. Jamshid Amouzegar

	GENERAL DIRECTOR		**MINISTER OF ECONOMIC AND FINANCIAL AFFAIR**
15	Mohammad Yeganeh		Hushang Ansary
16	Hassan Ali Mehran		Hushang Ansary
17	Hassan Ali Mehran		Mohammad Yeganeh

NOTE: Some signers used more than one signature (Jamshid Amouzegar), some held more than one term of office (Mehdi Samii) and others held the office of both General Director and Minister of Finance (Mohammad Yeganeh) at different times.

Shah Mohammad Reza Pahlavi, SH1323–58/1944–79 AD

Type V. Imperial Iranian Army (IIA). Uniform. Full face. SH1337–40.

Type VI. Imperial Iranian Air Force (IIAF) Uniform. Three quarter face. SH1341–44.

Type VII. Imperial Iranian Army (IIA) Uniform. Full face. SH1347–48.

Type VIII. Commander in Chief of Iran's Armed Forces. Three quarter face. Large portrait. MS2535 to SH1358.

Type IX. Shah Pahlavi in CinC Uniform and his father Shah Reza in Imperial Iranian Army (IIA) Uniform. MS2535.

Bank Markazi Iran

FIRST ISSUE

#71–72 fifth portr. of Shah Pahlavi in army uniform at r. Wmk: Young Shah Pahlavi. Yellow security thread runs vertically. Sign. 7. Printer: Harrison (w/o imprint).

Cat. #	Denomination	Date, description	VG	VF	Unc
71	10 RIALS	SH1340 (1961). Blue, green and orange. Geometric design at ctr. Amir Kabir dam near Karaj on back.	.50	1.00	2.75

Cat. #	Denomination	Date, description	VG	VF	Unc
72	20 RIALS	SH1340 (1961). Dk. brown, lt. brown and orange. Geometric design at ctr. Statue of Shah and Ramsar Hotel on back.	.60	1.50	3.50

#73–75 sixth portr. of Shah Pahlavi in air force uniform. Wmk: Young Shah Pahlavi. Yellow security thread runs vertically. Sign. 8. Printer: Harrison (w/o imprint).

Cat. #	Denomination	Date, description	VG	VF	Unc
73	50 RIALS	SH1341 (1962). Green, orange and blue. Shah Pahlavi at r. Koohrang dam and tunnel on back.			
		a. Sm. date 2.5mm high.	1.00	2.00	5.00
		b. Lg. date 4.0mm high.	1.00	2.00	5.00

Cat. #	Denomination	Date, description	VG	VF	Unc
78	20 RIALS	ND (1965). Dk. brown, pink and green. Ornate design at ctr. Oriental hunters on horseback on back.			
		a. Sign. 9.	.35	.85	2.25
		b. Sign. 10.	.50	1.50	4.00
79	50 RIALS	ND (1965). Dk. green, orange and blue. Ornate design at ctr. Koohrang dam and tunnel on back.			
		a. Sign. 9.	1.75	5.00	15.00
		b. Sign. 10.	1.75	5.00	15.00
80	200 RIALS	ND (1965). Dk. blue, orange and lavender. M/c ornate design at ctr. Railroad bridge on back. Sign. 9.	2.00	8.00	25.00
81	500 RIALS	ND (1965). Black, pink and purple. Shah at ctr. Winged horses on back. Sign. 9.	6.00	20.00	70.00
82	1000 RIALS	ND (1965). Brown, red and blue. Shah at ctr. Tomb of Hafez at Shiraz on back. Sign. 9.	10.00	35.00	115.00
83	100 RIALS	ND (1965). Maroon and olive-green. M/c ornate design. Oil refinery at Abadan on back. Sign. 10.	1.50	4.50	12.50

Cat. #	Denomination	Date, description	VG	VF	Unc
74	500 RIALS	SH1341 (1962). Black, pink and purple. Shah Pahlavi at ctr. Winged horses on back.	7.50	20.00	70.00

THIRD ISSUE

#84–87 seventh portr. of Shah Pahlavi in army uniform at r. Wmk: Young Shah Pahlavi. Yellow security thread runs vertically. Sign. 11 or 12. Printer: Harrison (w/o imprint).

#84–89 are called "Dark Panel" notes. The bank name is located on a contrasting dk. ornamental panel at the top ctr.

			VG	VF	Unc
84	20 RIALS	ND (1969). Dk. brown, pink and green. Ornate design at ctr. Oriental hunters on horseback on back.	.35	.85	2.25
85	50 RIALS	ND (1969–71). Green, orange and blue. Ornate design at ctr. Koohrang dam and tunnel on back.			
		a. Sign. 11.	.35	.85	2.25
		b. Sign. 12.	.75	1.50	4.00
86	100 RIALS	ND (1969–71). Maroon and lt. green. Ornate design at ctr. Oil refinery at Abadan on back.			
		a. Sign. 11.	1.00	2.00	5.00
		b. Sign. 12.	1.00	2.00	5.00
87	200 RIALS	ND (1969–71). Dk. blue, orange and purple. M/c ornate design. Railroad bridge on back.			
		a. Sign. 11.	3.00	8.00	20.00
		b. Sign. 12.	4.00	11.00	25.00

Cat. #	Denomination	Date, description	VG	VF	Unc
75	1000 RIALS	SH1341 (1962). Brown, red and blue. Shah Pahlavi at ctr. Tomb of Hafez in Shiraz on back.	12.00	45.00	145.00

SECOND ISSUE

#76–82 sixth portr. of Shah Pahlavi in armed forces uniform at r. Wmk: Young Shah Pahlavi. Yellow security thread runs vertically. Printer: Harrison (w/o imprint).

			VG	VF	Unc
76	100 RIALS	SH1342 (1963). Maroon and lt. green. Ornate design at ctr. Oil refinery at Abadan on back. Sign. 9.	1.00	3.00	8.00
77	50 RIALS	SH1343 (1964). Dk. green, orange and blue. Ornate design at ctr. Koohrang dam and tunnel on back. Sign. 9.	1.00	3.50	9.00

#88- 89A seventh portr. of Shah Pahlavi in army uniform at ctr. Sign. 11.

			VG	VF	Unc
88	500 RIALS	ND (1969). Black, pink and purple. Ornate frame at ctr. Winged horses on back.	4.00	12.00	40.00

Cat. #	Denomination	Date, description	VG	VF	Unc
89	1000 RIALS	ND (1969). Brown, red and blue. Ornate frame at ctr. Tomb of Hafez at Shiraz on back.	6.00	18.00	60.00
89A	5000 RIALS	ND (1969). Purple. Ornate frame at ctr. Golestan Palace in Tehran on back. Printed in Pakistan.	90.00	450.00	1000.

FOURTH ISSUE

#90–92 seventh portr. of Shah Pahlavi in army uniform at r. Wmk: Young Shah Pahlavi. Yellow security thread runs vertically. Printer: Harrison w/o imprint).

#90–96 are called "Light Panel" notes. The bank name is located on a contrasting lt. ornamental background panel at the top ctr.

| 90 | 50 RIALS | ND (1971). Dk. green, orange and blue. Ornamental design at ctr. Koohrang dam and tunnel on back. Sign. 13. | 1.00 | 2.75 | 7.00 |

91	100 RIALS	ND (1971–73). Maroon and lt. green. Ornate design at ctr. Oil refinery at Abadan on back.			
		a. Sign. 11.	1.00	2.50	6.00
		b. Sign. 12.	1.00	4.00	9.00
		c. Sign. 13.	1.00	2.50	6.00

92	200 RIALS	ND (1971–73). Blue, orange and purple. Ornate design at ctr. Railroad bridge on back.			
		a. Sign. 11.	2.00	8.00	20.00
		b. Sign. 12.	3.00	10.00	30.00
		c. Sign. 13.	1.50	4.00	10.00

#93-96 seventh portr. of Shah Pahlavi in army uniform at ctr. Wmk: Young Shah Pahlavi.

Cat. #	Denomination	Date, description	VG	VF	Unc
93	500 RIALS	ND (1971–73). Black, pink and purple. Ornate frame at ctr. Winged horses on back.			
		a. Sign. 11.	3.00	10.00	30.00
		b. Sign. 12.	6.00	15.00	60.00
		c. Sign. 13.	5.00	15.00	40.00

94	1000 RIALS	ND (1971–73). Brown, red and blue. Ornate design at ctr. Tomb of Hafez at Shiraz on back.			
		a. Sign. 11.	7.50	20.00	70.00
		b. Sign. 12.	6.50	17.50	65.00
		c. Sign. 13.	5.00	15.00	40.00

95	5000 RIALS	ND (1971–72). Purple and red. Ornate frame at ctr. Golestan Palace in Tehran on back.			
		a. Sign. 12.	20.00	60.00	200.00
		b. Sign. 13.	15.00	50.00	150.00

Cat. #	Denomination	Date, description	VG	VF	Unc
96	10,000 RIALS	ND (1972–73). Dk. green and brown. Ornate frame at ctr. National Council of Ministries in Tehran on back.			
		a. Sign. 11.	75.00	150.00	400.00
		b. Sign. 13.	60.00	125.00	350.00

FIFTH ISSUE - Commemorative

2,500th Anniversary of the Persian Empire

#97–98 lg. eighth portr. of Shah Pahlavi in the "Commander in Chief" of Iranian armed forces uniform at r. Wmk: Young Shah Pahlavi. Yellow security thread runs vertically. Sign. 11 or 12. Printer: TDLR.

97	50 RIALS	SH1350 (1971). Green, blue and brown. M/c. Floral design. Shah Pahlavi giving land deeds to villager on back.			
		a. Sign. 11.	1.00	2.50	6.00
		b. Sign. 13.	1.00	2.50	6.00

98	100 RIALS	SH1350 (1971). Dk. red, purple and orange. M/c geometric and floral design. 3 vignettes labeled: *HEALTH, AGRICULTURE* and *EDUCATION* on back.	.50	1.50	4.50
99		*Deleted.* See #101a.			

SIXTH ISSUE

#100–107 lg. eighth portr. of Shah Pahlavi at r. Wmk: Young Shah Pahlavi. Yellow security thread runs vertically. Printer: TDLR.

Cat. #	Denomination	Date, description	VG	VF	Unc
100	20 RIALS	ND (1974–79). Brown, orange and pink. Persian carpet design, shepherd and ram. Amir Kabir Dam near Karaj on back.			
		a. Sign. 16.	.50	1.00	2.50
		b. Sign. 17.	.50	1.00	3.00
		c. Sign. 18.	.50	1.00	2.50

101	50 RIALS	ND (1974–79). Green, brown and blue. Persian carpet design. Tomb of Cyrus the Great at Persepolis on back.			
		a. Yellow security thread. Sign. 14.	.50	1.00	2.50
		b. Yellow security thread. 15.	.20	.50	1.25
		c. Yellow security thread. Sign. 16.	.50	1.00	2.50
		d. Black security thread. Sign: 17.	.50	1.00	3.00
		e. Black security thread. Sign. 18.	.50	1.00	3.00

102	100 RIALS	ND (1974–79). Maroon, purple and orange. Persian carpet design. Marmar Palace on back.			
		a. Yellow security thread. Sign. 15.	1.00	2.50	6.50
		b. Yellow security thread. Sign. 16.	.50	1.25	3.00
		c. Black security thread. Sign. 17.	.50	1.25	3.00
		d. Black security thread. Sign. 18.	.50	1.25	3.00

Cat. #	Denomination	Date, description	VG	VF	Unc
103	200 RIALS	ND (1974–79). Blue and green. Persian carpet design. Shahyad Square in Tehran on back.			
		a. 6 point star in design on back. Yellow security thread. Monument name as Maidane Shahyad at lower l. on back. Sign. 15.	2.50	6.00	15.00
		b. 12 point star in design on back. Yellow security thread. Monument name as Maidane Shahyad. Sign. 16.	1.00	4.00	9.00

		c. 12 point star in design on back. Yellow security thread. Monument name changed to Shahyad Aryamer. Sign. 16.	1.00	3.50	8.00
		d. 12 point star in design on back. Black security thread and Shahyad Aryamer monument. Sign. 17.	1.00	4.00	9.00
		e. 12 point star in design on back. Black security thread and Shahyad Aryamer monument. Sign. 18.	1.00	2.00	5.00

Cat. #	Denomination	Date, description	VG	VF	Unc
106	5000 RIALS	ND (1974–79). Purple, pink and green. Persian carpet design. Golestan Palace in Tehran on back.			
		a. Yellow security thread. Sign.15.	12.00	45.00	145.00
		b. Yellow security thread. Sign.16.	8.50	22.00	55.00
		c. Black security thread. Sign. 17.	7.50	20.00	75.00
		d. Black security thread. Sign. 18.	7.50	20.00	75.00

104	500 RIALS	ND (1974–79). Black, green and orange. Persian carpet design. Winged horses on back.			
		a. 6 point star in design below Shah Pahlavi. Yellow security thread. Sign. 15.	1.50	4.00	15.00
		b. 6 point star in design below Shah Pahlavi. Yellow security thread. Sign. 16.	1.00	3.00	10.00
		c. Diamond design below Shah Pahlavi. Black security thread. Sign. 17.	1.00	3.50	10.00
		d. Diamond design below Shah Pahlavi. Black security thread. Sign. 18.	1.00	3.00	10.00

107	10,000 RIALS	ND (1974–79). Green and brown. Persian carpet design. National Council of Ministries in Tehran on back.			
		a. Yellow security thread. Sign. 15.	30.00	90.00	300.00
		b. Yellow security thread. Sign. 16.	7.50	20.00	75.00
		c. Black security thread. Sign. 17.	20.00	60.00	200.00
		d. Black security thread. Sign. 18.	12.50	40.00	100.00

COMMEMORATIVE ISSUE

50th Anniversary of the founding of the Pahlavi Dynasty

#108, ninth portr. of Shah Pahlavi w/Shah Reza at r. Wmk: Young Shah Pahlavi. Yellow security thread runs vertically. Sign. 16. Printer: TDLR.

105	1000 RIALS	ND (1974–79). Brown, green and yellow. Persian carpet design. Tomb of Hafez in Shiraz on back.			
		a. Yellow security thread. Sign.15.	4.00	11.00	30.00
		b. Yellow security thread. Sign. 16.	1.00	3.00	10.00
		c. Black security thread. Sign. 17.	1.00	3.00	9.00
		d. Black security thread. Sign. 18.	1.50	4.00	13.50

Cat.#	Denomination	Date, description	VG	VF	Unc
108	100 RIALS	ND (1976). Maroon, orange and green. Persian carpet design w/old Bank Melli at bottom ctr. 50th anniversary design in purple and lavender consisting of 50 suns surrounding Pahlavi Crown on back.	.50	1.50	4.50

ISLAMIC REPUBLIC

REVOLUTIONARY OVERPRINTS

After the Islamic Revolution of 1978–79, the Iranian government used numerous overprints on existing stocks of unissued paper money to obliterate Shah Pahlavi's portrait. There were numerous unauthorized and illegal crude stampings and hand obliterations used by zealous citizens which circulated freely, but only three major types of official overprints were used by the government.

PROVISIONAL ISSUES

All provisional government ovpt. were placed on existing notes of Shah Pahlavi already printed. Overprinting was an interim action meant to discredit and disgrace the deposed Shah as well as to publicize and give credence to the new Islamic Republic. The overprints themselves gave way to more appropriate seals and emblems, changes of watermarks and finally to a complete redesigning of all denominations of notes.

In all cases the Shah's portr. was covered by an arabesque design. Eight different styles and varieties of this ovpt. were used. Watermark ovpt., when used, are either the former Iranian national emblem of Lion and Sun or the calligraphic Persian text of *JUMHURI-YE-ISLAMI-YE-IRAN* (Islamic Republic of Iran) taken from the obverse of the country's new emblem. All ovpt. colors are very dark and require careful scrutiny to distinguish colors other than black.

Three major types of official ovpt. were used by the government.

Measurements of ovpt. in mm.

At times there are variances in size of the ovpt. on the Shah's portr. The place to measure for the correct mm. size is across the widest part of the top of the ovpt., approximately a position from "ear to ear".

Type I ovpt: Arabesque design over portr. Wmk. area w/o ovpt.

109 *Deleted.*

Cat.#	Denom.	Date, description	VG	VF	Unc
110	20 RIALS	ND. Black 27mm ovpt. on #100a.	.75	2.50	7.50
111	50 RIALS	ND. Ovpt. on #101b.			
		a. Black 27mm ovpt.	.75	2.00	5.00
		b. Green 27mm ovpt.	1.00	2.50	7.00
112	100 RIALS	ND. Ovpt. on #102c.			
		a. Black 27mm ovpt.	1.00	3.00	10.00
		b. Maroon 27mm ovpt.	2.50	10.00	25.00

Cat.#	Denom.	Date, description	VG	VF	Unc
113	200 RIALS	ND. Ovpt. on #103.			
		a. Black 28mm. ovpt. on #103a.	2.50	10.00	30.00
		b. Black 28mm. ovpt. on #103b.	2.50	10.00	30.00
		c. Black 28mm. ovpt on #103d.	1.50	8.00	20.00
		d. Black 32mm. ovpt. on #103d.	2.50	10.00	30.00
114	500 RIALS	ND. Ovpt. on #104.	8.50	17.50	35.00
		a. Black 28mm. ovpt. on #104b.	4.00	12.00	40.00
		b. Black 28mm. ovpt. on #104d.	4.00	11.00	35.00
115	1000 RIALS	ND. Ovpt. on #105.			
		a. Black 32mm ovpt. on #105b.	4.00	12.00	45.00
		b. Black 32mm. ovpt. on #105d.	7.00	20.00	65.00
		c. Brown 32mm. ovpt. on #105d.	7.00	20.00	65.00
116	5000 RIALS	ND. Ovpt. on #106.			.00
		a. Black 32mm. ovpt. on #106b.	17.50	60.00	175.00
		b. Black 32mm. ovpt. on #106c.	17.50	60.00	175.00
		c. Black 32mm. ovpt. on #106d.	15.00	50.00	160.00

Type II ovpt: Arabesque design over portr. and lion and sun national emblem over wmk. area.

Cat.#	Denomination	Date, description	VG	VF	Unc
117	50 RIALS	ND. Ovpt. on #101.			
		a. Black 27mm ovpt. on #101b.	1.50	5.00	15.00
		b. Black 27mm ovpt. on #101c.	2.50	7.00	20.00
118	100 RIALS	ND. Ovpt. on #102.			
		a. Black 28mm ovpt. on #102c.	2.00	5.00	15.00
		b. Black 33mm ovpt. on #102d.	.35	1.00	3.00
119	200 RIALS	ND. Ovpt. on #103.			
		a. Black 28mm ovpt. on #103d.	4.00	12.00	35.00
		b. Black 33mm ovpt. on #103d.	5.00	15.00	40.00
120	500 RIALS	ND. Ovpt. on #104.			
		a. Black 28mm ovpt. on #104d.	7.00	20.00	65.00
		b. Black 22mm ovpt. on #104d.	7.00	20.00	70.00
121	1000 RIALS	ND. Ovpt. on #105.			
		a. Black 32mm ovpt. on #105b.	5.00	15.00	50.00
		b. Black 32mm ovpt. on #105d.	4.00	12.50	45.00
122	5000 RIALS	ND. Ovpt. on #106.			
		a. Black 32mm ovpt. on #106b.	25.00	70.00	200.00
		b. Black 32mm ovpt. on #106d.	25.00	70.00	200.00

Type III ovpt: Arabesque design over portr. and the calligraphic Persian text *JUMHURI-YE ISLAMI-YE-IRAN* (Islamic Republic of Iran) over wmk. area.

Cat.#	Denom.	Date, description	VG	VF	Unc
123	50 RIALS	ND. Black arabesque ovpt. over portr. on #101.			
		a. 28mm ovpt., dk. green script on #101b.	2.00	6.00	20.00
		b. 33mm ovpt., black script on #101d.	.35	1.00	3.00
124	500 RIALS	ND. Black arabesque and script ovpt. on #104.			
		a. 28mm ovpt. on #104b.	3.00	10.00	35.00
		b. 33mm ovpt. on #104d.	2.50	7.50	22.50
125	1000 RIALS	ND. Ovpt. on #105.			
		a. Black 32mm ovpt., black script on #105b.	5.00	15.00	50.00
		b. Black 32mm ovpt., black script on #105d.	4.50	14.00	45.00
		c. Brown 32mm ovpt., violet script on #105b.	7.50	20.00	75.00

Cat.#	Denom.	Date, description	VG	VF	Unc
126	5000 RIALS	ND. Ovpt. on #106.			
		a. Purple 32mm. ovpt., purple script on #106b.	20.00	60.00	200.00
		b. Black 32mm. ovpt., purple script on #106d.	20.00	60.00	200.00

NOTE: Some notes w/Shah portr. are found w/unofficial ovpts., i.e. large purple or black stamped *X* on portr. and wmk. area.

1980 EMERGENCY CIRCULATING CHECK ISSUE

Cat.#	Denomination	Date, description	VG	VF	Unc
126A	10,000 RIALS	ND (1980). Dk. blue w/black text on green unpt. Drawings of modern bldgs. at l. and ctr. Wmk: Bank name repeated. Uniface.	20.00	55.00	120.00

Notes of the Islamic Republic of Iran

18	Yousef Khoshkish (on ovpt.)		Mohammad Yeganeh (on ovpt.)
19	Mohammad Ali Mowlavi		Ali Ardalan
20	Ali Reza Nobari		Abol Hassan Bani-Sadr
21	Dr. Mohsen Nourbakhsh		Hossein Nemazi
22	Dr. Mohsen Nourbakhsh		Iravani
23	Ghasemi		Iravani
24	Ghasemi		Dr. Mohsen Nourbakhsh
25	Mohammad Hossein Adeli		Dr. Mohsen Nourbakhsh

1981 (ND) FIRST ISSUE

#127–131 calligraphic Persian (Farsi) text from republic seal at l., Iman Reza mosque at r. W/o wmk. Yellow security thread w/*BANK MARKAZI IRAN* in black runs through vertically. Sign.19. Printer: TDLR (w/o imprint).

#127 and #130 have calligraphic seal printed in the same color as the note (blue and lavender, respectively) and with no variation. #128, 129 and 131 had the calligraphic seal applied locally after notes were printed. Numerous color varieties, misplacement or total omission can be seen on face or back, or both.

127	200 RIALS	ND (1981). Blue and green. Tomb of Ibn-E-Sina in Hamadan at l. on back.			
		a. Ovpt. lion and sun on face.	.75	2.00	5.50
		b. Ovpt. dk. brown seal.			

Cat.#	Denomination	Date, description	VG	VF	Unc
128	500 RIALS	ND (1981). Brown, orange and green. Winged horses on back.	.30	1.50	4.50

129	1000 RIALS	ND (1981). Rust, brown and green. Tomb of Hafez in Shiraz on back.	2.00	6.00	15.00

130	5000 RIALS	ND (1981). Lavender and green. Oil refinery at Tehran on back.			
		a. Security thread.	4.00	15.00	50.00
		b. W/o security thread.	10.00	35.00	100.00

Cat.#	Denomination	Date, description	VG	VF	Unc
131	10,000 RIALS	ND (1981). Green and brown. National Council of Ministries in Tehran on back.			
		a. Dk. brown circular seal on wmk.	8.00	25.00	80.00
		b. No dk. brown seal, exposing lion and sun ovpt.	10.00	35.00	100.00
		c. No lion and sun ovpt.	10.00	35.00	100.00

NOTE: #131 first ovpt. w/circular gray-yellow lion and sun on both sides, then additional ovpt. regular black calligraphic seal on top of first ovpt. Notes w/o black seal, or misplaced seal, are errors.

1981 (ND) SECOND ISSUE

#132–134 Islamic motifs. Wmk.: Islamic Republic seal. White security thread w/*BANK MARKAZI IRAN* in black Persian script runs vertically. Sign. 20 unless 21 noted. Printer: TDLR (w/o imprint).

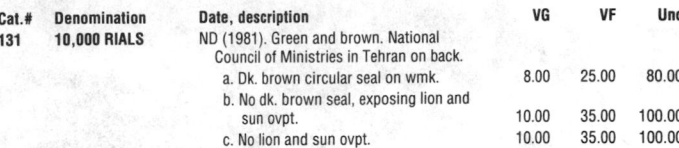

132	100 RIALS	ND (1981). Maroon and brown. Imam Reza shrine at Mashad at r. Madressa Chahr-Bagh in Isfahan on back.	.50	1.00	3.50

133	5000 RIALS	ND (1981). Violet, red-orange and brown on m/c unpt. Mullahs leading marchers carrying posters of Ayatollah Khomeini at ctr. Hazrat Masoumeh shrine at l. ctr. on back.	5.00	12.00	30.00

Cat.#	Denomination	Date, description	VG	VF	Unc
134	10,000 RIALS	ND (1981). Deep blue-green on yellow and m/c unpt. Face like #133. Imam Reza shrine in Mashad at ctr. on back. Wmk: Arms.			
		a. Sign. 20. Wmk: Republic seal.	6.00	15.00	50.00
		b. Sign. 21. Wmk: Arms.	6.00	15.00	50.00

1982; 1983 (ND) ISSUE

#135–139 Islamic motifs. Wmk: Upraised broadsword in 2 curved arcs (arms) at l. White security thread w/black *BANK MARKAZI IRAN* in Persian letters repeatedly runs vertically. Printer: TDLR.

135	100 RIALS	ND (1982). Maroon and brown. Imam Reza shrine. at r. Madressa Chahr-Bagh on back. Like #132.	.40	1.00	2.00

136	200 RIALS	ND (1982). Grayish blue and m/c. Mosque. Farmers and tractor on back.			
		a. Sign. 21.	.30	.75	2.25
		b. Sign. 23.	FV	FV	2.00

137	500 RIALS	ND (1982). Gray and olive. Feyzieh Madressa seminary at lower l., lg. prayer gathering at ctr. Tehran University on back.			
		a. Sign. 21. Wmk: Arms.	FV	FV	7.50
		b. Sign. 22.	FV	5.00	25.00
		c. Sign. 23.	FV	FV	7.00
		d. Sign. 23. Wmk: Mohd. H. Fahmideh (youth).	FV	FV	3.75
		e. Sign. 24.	FV	FV	3.50
		f. Sign. 25.	FV	FV	3.50

Wmk:

Cat.#	Denomination	Date, description	VG	VF	Unc
138	1000 RIALS	ND (1982; 1986). Lt. green, red-brown and brown. Feyzieh Madressa seminary at ctr. Mosque of Omar (Dome of the Rock) in Jerusalem on back.			
		a. Sign. 21. Additional short line of text under bldg. on back. Wmk: Arms.	FV	FV	12.50
		b. Sign. like a. No line of text under bldg. on back.	FV	FV	30.00
		c. Sign. 22.	FV	FV	15.00
		d. Sign. 23.	FV	FV	10.00
		e. Sign. 23. Wmk: Mohd. H. Fahmideh (youth).	FV	FV	7.00
		f. Sign. 24.	FV	FV	6.00
		g. Sign. 25.	FV	FV	5.00

| 139 | 5000 RIALS | ND (1983). Red and m/c. Similar to #133; reduced crowd. Radiant sun removed from upper l. on face. 2 small placards of Khomeini added to crowd. | FV | FV | 24.00 |

NOTE: #139 exists w/2diff. sign. 21 style of Nemazi.

Central Bank of the Islamic Republic of Iran
1985–86 (ND) ISSUE

140	100 RIALS	ND (1985). Purple and m/c. Ayatollah Moddaress at r. Parliament at l. on back. Wmk.: Arms. Printer: TDLR.			
		a. Sign. 21.	FV	FV	3.00
		b. Sign. 22.	FV	FV	2.50
		c. Sign. 23.	FV	FV	2.25
		d. Sign. 23. Wmk: Mohd. M. Fahmideh (youth).	FV	FV	2.00
		e. Sign. 24.	FV	FV	2.00
		f. Sign. 25.	FV	FV	1.75

Cat.#	Denomination	Date, description	VG	VF	Unc
141 (144)	2000 RIALS	ND(1986). Violet, dk. brown and m/c. Revolutionists before mosque at ctr. r. Kaabain Mecca on back.			
		a. Sign. 21. Wmk: Arms.	FV	FV	7.50
		b. Sign. 22.	FV	FV	7.50
		c. Sign. 23.	FV	FV	10.00
		d. Sign. 23. Wmk: Mohd. H. Fahmideh (youth).	FV	FV	7.50
		e. Sign. 24.	FV	FV	7.50
		f. Sign. 25.	FV	FV	7.50

1992–93 (ND) ISSUE
#143–146 Khomeini at r. Sign. 25.

142	500 RIALS				Expected new issue.

| 143 | 1000 RIALS | ND(1992). Brown and deep olive-green on m/c unpt. Mosque of Omar (Dome of the Rock) in Jerusalem at ctr. on back. Wmk: Youthful revolutionary male portrait. | FV | FV | 4.00 |
| 144 | 2000 RIALS | | | | Expected new issue. |

#145-146 wmk: Khomeini.

| 145 | 5000 RIALS | ND(1993). Dk. brown and olive-green on m/c unpt. Flowers and birds at ctr. r. on back. | FV | FV | 14.50 |

| 146 | 10,000 RIALS | ND(1992). Deep blue-green, blue and olive-green on m/c unpt. Mount Damavand at ctr. r. on back. | FV | FV | 25.00 |
| 147 | 50,000 RIALS | | | | Expected new issue. |

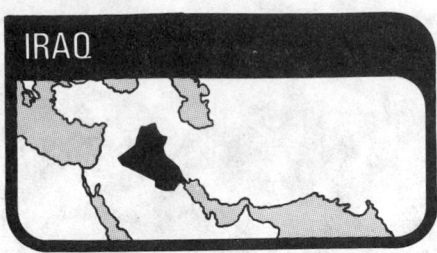

The Republic of Iraq, historically known as Mesopotamia, is located in the Near East and is bordered by Kuwait, Iran, Turkey, Syria, Jordan and Saudi Arabia. It has an area of 167,925 sq. mi. (434,924 sq. km.) and a population of 17.6 million. Capital: Baghdad. The economy of Iraq is based on agriculture and petroleum. Crude oil accounts for 94 percent of the exports before the war with Iran began in 1980.

Iraq was the site of a number of flourishing civilizations of antiquity — Sumerian, Assyrian, Babylonian, Parthian, Persian — and of the Biblical cities of Ur, Nineveh and Babylon. Desired because of its favored location which embraced the fertile alluvial plains of the Tigris and Euphrates Rivers, Mesopotamia — "land between the rivers" — was conquered by Cyrus the Great of Persia, Alexander of Macedonia and by Arabs who made the legendary city of Baghdad the capital of the ruling caliphate. Suleiman the Great conquered Mesopotamia for Turkey in 1534, and it formed part of the Ottoman Empire until 1623, and from 1638 to 1917. Great Britain, given a League of Nations mandate over the territory in 1920, recognized Iraq as a kingdom in 1922. Iraq became an independent constitutional monarchy presided over by the Hashemite family, direct descendants of the prophet Mohammed, in 1932. In 1958, the army-led revolution of July 14 overthrew the monarchy and proclaimed a republic.

MONETARY SYSTEM
- 1 Dirham = 50 Fils
- 1 Riyal = 200 Fils
- 1 Dinar (Pound) = 1000 Fils

REPUBLIC
Central Bank of Iraq
1958 ISSUE

#51–55 Republic arms w/1958 at r. and as wmk. Sign. varieties.

Cat. #	Denomination	Date, description	VG	VF	Unc
51	1/4 DINAR	1958. Green on m/c unpt unpt. Palm tree at ctr. on back.	1.00	5.00	15.00
52	1/2 DINAR	1958. Brown on m/c unpt.	2.00	8.00	30.00

53	1 DINAR	1958. Blue on m/c unpt. Ornate rectangular piece w/strings on back.	1.50	6.50	20.00

Cat. #	Denomination	Date, description	VG	VF	Unc
54	5 DINARS	1958. Lt. purple on m/c unpt.	2.50	12.50	35.00

55	10 DINARS	1958. Dk. blue on m/c unpt.	6.00	30.00	90.00

ND 1971 ISSUE

#56–60 wmk: Falcon's head. Sign. varieties.

56	1/4 DINAR	ND (1971). Green and brown on m/c unpt. Harbor at ctr. Back like #51. *1/4 Dinar* at l. on back.	1.00	4.00	12.50

Cat. #	Denomination	Date, description	VG	VF	Unc
57	1/2 DINAR	ND (1971). Brown on m/c unpt. Oil refinery. Walled fort and minaret at ctr., *1/2 Dinar* at l. on back.	2.00	7.50	20.00

58	1 DINAR	ND (1971). Blue and brown on m/c unpt. Factory at ctr. Doorway at ctr., *1 Dinar* at l. on back.	2.00	5.00	15.00

59	5 DINARS	ND (1971). Lilac on brown and m/c unpt. Parliament bldg. across face. 2 ancient figures at ctr., *5 Dinars* at l. on back.	9.00	45.00	135.00

60	10 DINARS	ND (1971). Purple, blue and brown on m/c unpt. Coffer dam at ctr. Ancient carvings of winged creatures at ctr., *10 Dinars* at l. on back.	7.00	35.00	100.00

ND 1973; 1978–80 ISSUE

#61–66 wmk: Falcon's head. Sign. varieties.

Cat. #	Denomination	Date, description	VG	VF	Unc
61	1/4 DINAR	ND (1973). Green and black on m/c unpt. Similar to #56. *Quarter Dinar* at bottom r. on back.	1.00	5.00	15.00

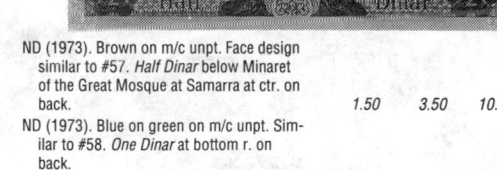

62	1/2 DINAR	ND (1973). Brown on m/c unpt. Face design similar to #57. *Half Dinar* below Minaret of the Great Mosque at Samarra at ctr. on back.	1.50	3.50	10.00
63	1 DINAR	ND (1973). Blue on green on m/c unpt. Similar to #58. *One Dinar* at bottom r. on back.			
		a. W/o line of Arabic inscription below factory.	1.00	5.00	15.00
		b. 1 line of Arabic inscription below factory.	1.00	4.50	20.00

64	5 DINARS	ND (1973). Lilac on m/c unpt. Similar to #59. *Five Dinars* at bottom on back.	1.25	6.00	18.00

Cat. #	Denomination	Date, description	VG	VF	Unc
65	10 DINARS	ND (1973). Purple on m/c unpt. Coffer dam at r. Back similar to #60, but *Ten Dinars* at bottom.	1.00	5.00	15.00

Cat. #	Denomination	Date, description	VG	VF	Unc
66	25 DINARS	1978–AH1398; 1980–AH1400. Green and brown on m/c unpt. 3 Arabian horses at ctr., date below sign. at lower r. Abbaside Palace on back. 182 x 88mm.	.75	4.00	12.50

1979–86 ISSUE

#67–72 wmk: Arabian horse's head. Sign. varieties.

| 67 | 1/4 DINAR | 1979/AH1399. Green and m/c. Palm trees at ctr. Bldg. on back. | .20 | 1.00 | 4.00 |

Cat. #	Denomination	Date, description	VG	VF	Unc
68	1/2 DINAR	1980/AH1400; 1985/AH1405. Brown and m/c. Astrolabe at r. Minaret of Samarra on back.	.15	.75	2.00

| 69 | 1 DINAR | 1979/AH1399; 1980/AH1400; 1984/AH1404; 1984 AH1405. Olive-green and deep blue on m/c unpt. Coin design at ctr. Musanteriah School in Baghdad on back. | .30 | 1.50 | 4.50 |

| 70 | 5 DINARS | 1980/AH1400; 1981/AH1401; 1982/AH1402. Brown-violet on deep blue and m/c unpt. Waterfalls at ctr. Walled city on back. | .45 | 2.25 | 7.00 |

Cat. #	Denomination	Date, description	VG	VF	Unc
71	10 DINARS	1980/AH1400; 1981/AH1401; 1982/AH1402. Purple and m/c. A. Abulhasan ibn al Hisham at r. Tower on back.	.20	2.00	6.00

Cat. #	Denomination	Date, description	VG	VF	Unc
75	50 DINARS	1991/AH1411. Brown and blue-green on m/c unpt. S. Hussein at r. Minaret of the Great Mosque at Samarra at ctr. r. on back.	FV	FV	7.50

| 72 | 25 DINARS | 1982/AH1402. Green and brown. Similar to #66 but date below horses. Reduced size, 175 x 80mm. | .60 | 3.00 | 9.00 |

| 76 | 100 DINARS | 1991/AH1411. Dk. blue-green on lilac and m/c unpt. S. Hussein at r. Crossed swords below Iraqi flag at ctr. on back. | FV | FV | 4.00 |

| 73 | 25 DINARS | 1986. Brown and black on green, blue and m/c unpt. Medieval horsemen charging at ctr., S. Hussein at r. City gate at l., monument at ctr. on back. Wmk.: Hussein. | .60 | 3.00 | 9.00 |

NOTE: In a sudden economic move during summer of 1993, it was announced that all previous 25 Dinar notes issued before #74 had become worthless.

1991 EMERGENCY GULF WAR ISSUE

#74-76 local printing.

| 74 | 25 DINARS | 1991/AH1411. Similar to #72 but green and gray on lt. green unpt. Litho. | FV | FV | 5.00 |

1992–93 EMERGENCY ISSUE

#77-79 dull lithograph printing.

| 77 | 1/4 DINAR | 1993/AH1413. Like #67. | FV | FV | .75 |
| 78 | 1/2 DINAR | 1993/AH1413. Like #68. | FV | FV | 1.00 |

Cat. #	Denomination	Date, description	VG	VF	Unc
79	1 DINAR	1992/AH1412. Green and blue-black on m/c unpt. Like #69.	FV	FV	1.25

#80–85 S. Hussein at r.

#80-81 printed in China.

80	5 DINARS	1992/AH1412. Red-brown on pale orange, lilac and m/c unpt. Temple at l. ctr. Monument at ctr., ancient stone carvings at l. on back. Shade varieties.			
		a. W/border around embossed text at ctr.	FV	FV	3.50
		b. W/o border around embossed text at ctr.	FV	FV	3.50

81	10 DINARS	1992/AH1412. Violet, blue-green and m/c. Winged lion sculpture at l. on back.	FV	FV	5.50
82	Held in reserve.				

1994–95 ISSUE

Cat. #	Denomination	Date, description	VG	VF	Unc
83	50 DINARS	1994/AH1414. Brown and pale green on m/c unpt. Ancient statuette, monument at l. ctr. Modern Saddam bridge at ctr. on back.	FV	FV	4.00

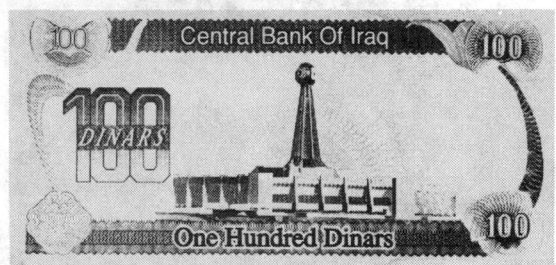

| 84 | 100 DINARS | 1994/AH1414. Blue-black on lt. blue and pale ochre unpt. Walled compound at ctr. Modern bldg. at ctr. on back. Printed wmk: Falcon's head. | FV | FV | 4.00 |

NOTE: Shade varieties exist.

| 85 | 250 DINARS | 1995/AH1415. Purple on m/c unpt. Hydroelectric dam at l. ctr., Archaic frieze across back. | FV | FV | 5.00 |

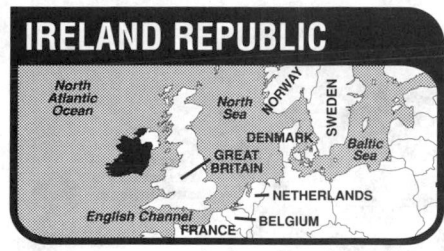

IRELAND REPUBLIC

The Republic of Ireland which occupies five-sixths of the island of Ireland located in the Atlantic Ocean west of Great Britain, has an area of 27,136 sq. mi. (70,283 sq. km.) and a population of 3.5 million. Capital: Dublin. Agriculture and dairy farming are the principal industries. Meat, livestock, dairy products and textiles are exported.

The Irish Free State was established as a dominion on Dec. 6, 1921. Ireland withdrew from the Commonwealth and proclaimed itself a republic on April 18, 1949. The government, however, does not use the term "Republic of Ireland," which tacitly acknowledges the partitioning of the island into Ireland and Northern Ireland, but refers to the country simply as "Ireland".

MONETARY SYSTEM
1 Shilling = 12 Pence
1 Pound = 20 Shillings to 1971
1 Pound = 100 New Pence 1971–

REPLACEMENT NOTES

#63–67, earlier dates use different letter than normal run of series letters. Later dates use different letter but have "OO" in front of the letter.

#70–74 use a triple letter (3 of the same) to indicate replacement.

Central Bank of Ireland
1961-63 ISSUE

#63–65 portr. Lady Hazel Lavery at l., denomination at bottom ctr.

Cat. #	Denomination	Date, description	VG	VF	Unc
63	10 SHILLINGS	3.1.1962–6.6.1968. Orange. Sign. M. O. Muimhneachain and T. K. Whitaker.	1.00	5.00	15.00

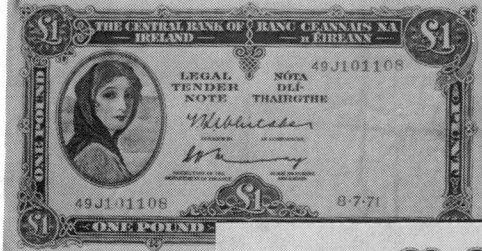

Cat. #	Denomination	Date, description	VG	VF	Unc
64	1 POUND	1962–76. Green.			
		a. Sign. M. O. Muimhneachain and T. K. Whitaker. 16.3.1962–8.10.1968.	2.50	6.00	20.00
		b. Sign. T. K. Whitaker and C. H. Murray. 1.3.1969–17.9.1970.	2.00	5.00	17.50
		c. Sign. like b, but metallic security thread at l. of ctr. 8.7.1971–21.4.1975.	2.00	4.00	12.50
		d. Sign. C. H. Murray and M. O. Murchu. 30.9.1976.	2.00	3.00	10.00

Cat. #	Denomination	Date, description	VG	VF	Unc
65	5 POUNDS	1961–75. Brown.			
		a. Sign. M. O. Muimhneachain and T. K. Whitaker. 15.8.1961–12.8.1968.	12.50	25.00	85.00
		b. Sign. T. K. Whitaker and C. H. Murray. 12.5.1969; 27.2.1970.	10.00	20.00	70.00
		c. Sign. like b, but metallic security thread at l. of ctr. 18.1.1971–5.9.1975.	9.00	12.50	50.00

#66–69 Lady Hazel Lavery in Irish national costume w/chin resting on her hand and leaning on an Irish harp.

Cat. #	Denomination	Date, description	VG	VF	Unc
66	10 POUNDS	1962–76. Blue.			
		a. Sign. M. O. Muimhneachain and T. K. Whitaker. 2.5.1962–16.7.1968.	20.00	45.00	120.00
		b. Sign. T. K. Whitaker and C. H. Murray. 5.5.1969; 9.3.1970.	18.00	35.00	95.00
		c. Sign. like b, but metallic security thread at l. of ctr. 19.5.1971–10.2.1975.	16.00	25.00	70.00
		d. Sign. C. H. Murray and M. O. Murchu. 2.12.1976.	15.00	22.50	65.00
67	20 POUNDS	1961–76. Red.			
		a. Sign. M. O. Muimhneachain and T. K. Whitaker. 1.6.1961–15.6.1965.	37.50	85.00	250.00
		b. Sign. T. K. Whitaker and C. H. Murray. 3.3.1969–6.1.1975.	35.00	60.00	185.00
		c. Sign. C. H. Murray and M. O. Murchu. 24.3.1976.	32.00	50.00	150.00
68	50 POUNDS	1962–77. Purple.			
		a. Sign. M. O. Muimhneachain and T. K. Whitaker. 1.2.1962–6.9.1968.	95.00	150.00	325.00
		b. Sign. T. K. Whitaker and C. H. Murray. 4.11.1970–16.4.1975.	85.00	125.00	250.00
		c. Sign. C. H. Murray and M. O. Murchu. 4.4.1977.	80.00	100.00	200.00

Cat. #	Denomination	Date, description	VG	VF	Unc
69	100 POUNDS	1963–77. Green.			
		a. Sign. M. O. Muimhneachain and T. K. Whitaker. 16.1.1963–9.9.1968.	175.00	275.00	525.00
		b. Sign. T. K. Whitaker and C. H. Murray. 26.10.1970; 4.5.1972; 26.2.1973.	150.00	225.00	425.00
		c. Sign. C. H. Murray and M. O. Murchu. 4.4.1977.	160.00	200.00	375.00

1976-82 ISSUE

Cat. #	Denom.	Date, description	VG	VF	Unc
70	1 POUND	1977–89. Dk. olive-green and green on m/c unpt. Qn. Medb at r. Old writing on back. Wmk: Lady Lavery.			
		a. Sign. C. H. Murray and M. O. Murchu. 10.6.1977–29.11.1977.	2.00	3.00	8.50
		b. Sign. C. H. Murray and T. O'Cofaigh. 30.8.1978–30.10.1981.	FV	2.50	7.50
		c. Sign. T. O'Cofaigh and M. F. Doyle. 30.6.1982–22.4.1987.	FV	2.00	6.50
		d. Sign. M. F. Doyle and S. P. Cromien. 23.3.1988–17.7.1989.	FV	2.00	6.50

Cat. #	Denom.	Date, description	VG	VF	Unc
71	5 POUNDS	1976–93. Brown and red. J. S. Eriugena at r. Old writing on back.			
		a. Sign. T. K. Whitaker and C. H. Murray. 26.2.1976.	FV	FV	25.00
		b. Sign. C. H. Murray and M. O. Murchu. 18.5.1976–17.10.1977.	FV	FV	25.00
		c. Sign. C. H. Murray and T. O'Cofaigh. 25.4.1979–13.10.1981.	FV	FV	22.50
		d. Sign. T. O'Cofaigh and M. F. Doyle. 1982; 7.10. 1983–22.4.1987.	FV	FV	17.50
		e. Sign. M. F. Doyle and S. P. Cromien. 12.8.1988–7.5.1993.	FV	FV	15.00

Cat. #	Denomination	Date, description	VG	VF	Unc
72	10 POUNDS	1978–92. Violet and purple. J. Swift at r. Old street map on back.			
		a. Sign. C. H. Murray and T. O'Cofaigh. 1.6.1978–20.10.1981.	FV	FV	40.00
		b. Sign. T. O'Cofaigh and M. F. Doyle. 1982; 25.2.1983–4.4.1986.	FV	FV	35.00
		c. Sign. M. F. Doyle and S. P. Cromien. 1.2.1988–14.4.1992.	FV	FV	32.50

Cat. #	Denom.	Date, description	VG	VF	Unc
73	20 POUNDS	1980–92. Blue and m/c. W. B. Yeats at r., Abbey Theatre symbol at ctr. Map on back.			
		a. Sign. C. H. Murray and T. O'Cofaigh. 7.1.1980–28.10.1981.	FV	FV	75.00
		b. Sign. T. O'Cofaigh and M. F. Doyle. 11.7.1983–28.8.1986.	FV	FV	65.00
		c. Sign. M. F. Doyle and S. P. Cromien. 5.7.1988–21.1.1992.	FV	FV	60.00

Cat. #	Denom.	Date, description	VG	VF	Unc
74	50 POUNDS	1982; 1991. Red and brown. Carolan playing harp in front of group. Musical instruments on back.			
		a. Sign. T. O'Cofaigh and M. F. Doyle. 1.11.1982.	FV	FV	150.00
		b. Sign. M. F. Doyle and S. P. Cromien. 5.11.1991.	FV	FV	120.00

1992-95 ISSUE

#75-77 wmk: Lady Lavery and value. Sign. M.F. Doyle and S.P. Cromien or as noted.

Cat. #	Denomination	Date, description	VG	VF	Unc
75	5 POUNDS	1994–. Dk. brown, reddish brown, and grayish purple on m/c unpt. Mater Misericordiae Hospital at bottom l. ctr., C. McAuley at r. School children at ctr. on back.			
		a. Sign. M. F. Doyle and S. P. Cromien. 15.3.1994.	FV	FV	12.50
		b. Sign. O'Connell and Mullarkey. 27.4.1994.	FV	FV	11.50

76	10 POUNDS	14.7.1993–. Dk. green, brown, blue and m/c. Aerial iew of Dublin at ctr., J. Joyce at r. Sculpted head representing Liffey River at l., map in unpt. on back.	FV	FV	23.50

77	20 POUNDS	21.9.1992–. Violet, brown and dk. grayish blue on m/c unpt. Derryname Abbey at l. ctr., D. O'Connell at r. Writings and bldg. on back.	FV	FV	45.00
78	50 POUNDS	(1995). Blue on m/c unpt. D. Hyde.	FV	FV	110.00

NORTHERN IRELAND

From 1800 to 1921 Ireland was an integral part of the United Kingdom. The Anglo-Irish treaty of 1921 established the Irish Free State of 26 counties within the Commonwealth of Nations and recognized the partition of Ireland. The six predominantly Protestant counties of northeast Ulster chose to remain a part of the United Kingdom with a limited self-government.

Up to 1928 the notes of the private or commerical banks were circulating in the whole of Ireland. After the establishment of the Irish Free State, the private or commercial notes were valid only in Northern Ireland.

For notes of the Irish Republic see Ireland/Republic.

RULERS
British

MONETARY SYSTEM
1 Shilling = 12 Pence
1 Pound = 20 Shillings to 1971
1 Pound = 100 New Pence 1971–

REPLACEMENT NOTES
#61–63: Z prefix. #245–249: ZY or ZZ prefix letters.

Allied Irish Banks Ltd.

Formerly Provincial Bank of Ireland Ltd., later became First Trust Bank.

1982 ISSUE

#1–5 designs similar to Provincial Bank of Ireland Ltd. (#247–251) except for bank title and sign. Printer: TDLR.

Cat. #	Denomination	Date, description	VG	VF	Unc
1	1 POUND	1.1.1982; 1.7.1983; 1.12.1984. Green on m/c unpt. Young girl at r. Sailing ship *Girona* at ctr. on back.	FV	2.75	10.00

2	5 POUNDS	1.1.1982. Blue and purple on m/c unpt. Young woman at r. Dunluce Castle at ctr. on back.	FV	12.50	22.50

Cat. #	Denomination	Date, description	VG	VF	Unc
3	10 POUNDS	1.1.1982; 1.12.1984. Brown and gray-green on m/c unpt. Young man at r. Wreck of the *Girona* at ctr. on back.	FV	22.50	40.00
4	20 POUNDS	1.1.1982. Purple and green. Elderly woman at r. Chimney at Lacada Pt. at ctr. on back.	FV	42.50	75.00
5	100 POUNDS	1.1.1982. Black, olive and green. Elderly man at r. The *Armada* at ctr. on back.	FV	185.00	300.00

Allied Irish Banks Public Limited Company

Formerly Allied Irish Banks Ltd., later became First Trust Bank.

1987–88 ISSUE

#6–9 like #2–5 except for bank title and sign. Printer: TDLR.

			VG	VF	Unc
6	5 POUNDS	1.1.1987; 1.1.1990. Similar to #2.	FV	FV	16.50
7	10 POUNDS	1.3.1988; 1.1.1990; 18.5.1993. Similar to #3.	FV	FV	30.00
8	20 POUNDS	1.4.1987. Similar to #4.	FV	FV	57.50

			VG	VF	Unc
9	100 POUNDS	1.12.1988. Similar to #5.	FV	FV	250.00

Bank of Ireland

BELFAST BRANCH

1967 (ND) ISSUE

#56–64 Mercury at l., woman w/harp at r. Airplane, bank bldg. and boat on back.

Cat. #	Denomination	Date, description	VG	VF	Unc
56	1 POUND	ND (1967). Green-lilac. 151 x 72mm. Sign. W. E. Guthrie w/title: *Agent*.	2.00	5.00	20.00
57	5 POUNDS	ND (1967–68). Brown-violet.			
		a. Sign. W. E. Guthrie w/title: *Agent*. (1967).	9.00	17.50	65.00
		b. Sign. H. H. M. Chestnutt w/title: *Agent*. (1968).	8.00	15.00	55.00
58	10 POUNDS	ND (1967). Brown and yellow. Sign. W. E. Guthrie w/title: *Agent*.	18.00	35.00	120.00
59	*Deleted.*				
60	*Deleted.*				

1971; 1972 (ND) ISSUES

Cat. #	Denomination	Date, description	VG	VF	Unc
61	1 POUND	ND (1972–77). Black on lt. green and lilac unpt. Like #56, but smaller size. 134 x 66mm.			
		a. W/o £ signs in corners. Sign. H. H. M. Chestnutt title: *MANAGER* (1972).	FV	3.00	18.50
		b. Corners as a. Sign. A. S. J. O'Neill w/ title: *MANAGER* (1977).	FV	FV	12.00
62 (63)	5 POUNDS	ND (1971–77). Blue on lt. green and lilac unpt. 146 x 78mm.			
		a. W/o £ signs in corners. Sign. of H. H. M. Chestnutt w/title: *Manager (1971)*.	FV	13.50	37.50
		b. Corners as a. Sign. of A. S. J. O'Neill w/title: *Manager* (1977).	FV	12.50	27.50
63 (65)	10 POUNDS	ND (1971–77). Brown on lt. green and lt. orange unpt.			
		a. Sign. of H. H. M. Chestnutt w/title: *Manager* (1971).	FV	22.50	55.00
		b. Sign. of A. S. J. O'Neill w/title: *Manager* (1977).	FV	18.50	45.00
64 (68)	100 POUNDS	ND (1974–78). Red on m/c unpt.			
		a. Sign. of H. H. M. Chestnutt w/title: *Manager* (1974).	FV	FV	375.00
		b. Sign. of A. S. J. O'Neill w/title: *Manager* (1978).	FV	FV	300.00

1980'S ISSUES

Cat. #	Denomination	Date, description	VG	VF	Unc
65 (62)	1 POUND	ND. Like #61 but w/*STERLING* added.	FV	FV	4.50
66 (64)	5 POUNDS	ND. £ signs added in corners.			
		a. Sign. A. S. J. O'Neill.	FV	11.00	25.00
		b. Sign. D. F. Harrison.	FV	10.00	22.50
67	20 POUNDS	ND (1984). Dk. green on m/c unpt. Sign. A. S. J. O'Neill.	FV	18.50	60.00
68 (69)	100 POUNDS	ND. Similar to #64 but w/£ sign at upper r. and lower l. corners on face and back. *Sterling* added at lower ctr. on face.			
		a. Sign. A. S. J. O'Neill.	FV	FV	285.00
		b. Sign. D. F. Harrison.	FV	FV	210.00

1983 COMMEMORATIVE ISSUE

#66, Bank of Ireland Bicentenary, 1783–1983

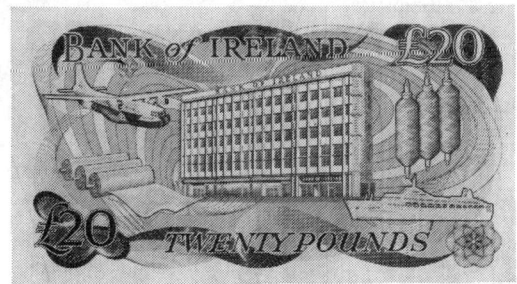

Cat. #	Denomination	Date, description	VG	VF	Unc
69 (66)	20 POUNDS	1983. Dk. green on m/c unpt. Like #67 but commemorative text below bank title.	55.00	125.00	325.00

1990–92 ISSUE

#70–73 bank seal (Hibernia seated) at l. Queen's University in Belfast on back. Sign. D. F. Harrison. Wmk: Medusa head.

70	5 POUNDS	28.8.1990. Blue and purple on m/c unpt.	FV	FV	13.50
71	10 POUNDS	14.5.1991. Purple and maroon on m/c unpt.	FV	FV	23.50
72	20 POUNDS	9.5.1991. Green and brown on m/c unpt.	FV	FV	45.00
73	100 POUNDS	28.8.1992. Red on m/c unpt.	FV	FV	200.00

NOTE: Specimens and 3-subject sheets were sold to collectors. Low numbers were also available in special folders.

First Trust Bank

Formerly Allied Irish Banks PLC, which acquired the Trustee Savings Bank. Member AIB Group Northern Ireland PLC.

1994 ISSUE

#132-135 five shields at bottom ctr. Printer: TDLR. Sign. title: GROUP MANAGING DIRECTOR. Wmk: Young woman.

132	10 POUNDS	10.1.1994. Dk. brown and violet. Face similar to #3. Sailing ship Girona at ctr. on back.	FV	FV	23.50

Cat. #	Denomination	Date, description	VG	VF	Unc
133	20 POUNDS	10.1.1994. Violet, dk. brown and red-brown on m/c unpt. Face similar to #4. Chimney at Lacada Pt. at ctr. on back.	FV	FV	45.00

134	50 POUNDS	10.1.1994. Black, dk. olive-green and blue on m/c unpt. Face similar to #5. Cherubs holding armada medallion at ctr. on back.	FV	FV	110.00

135	100 POUNDS	10.1.1994. Black and olive-brown on m/c unpt. Elderly couple at r. The Armada at ctr. on back.	FV	FV	200.00

Northern Bank Ltd.

1929–30 ISSUE

#178-186 sailing ship, plow and man at grindstone at upper ctr.

178	1 POUND	1929–68. Black. Blue guilloche.			
		a. Red serial #. 6.5.1929; 1.7.1929; 1.8.1929.	10.00	25.00	85.00
		b. Black prefix letters and serial #. 1.1.1940.	6.00	12.50	35.00
		c. 1.10.1968.	3.00	9.00	35.00

Cat. #	Denomination	Date, description	VG	VF	Unc
181	10 POUNDS	1930–68. Black on red unpt.			
		a. Red serial #. 1.1.1930–1.1.1940.	40.00	80.00	225.00
		b. Black serial #. 1.8.1940; 1.9.1940.	30.00	70.00	200.00
		c. Red serial #. 1.1.1942–1.11.1943.	25.00	50.00	150.00
		d. Imprint on back below central design. 1.10.1968.	FV	25.00	70.00

1968 ISSUE

Cat. #	Denomination	Date, description	VG	VF	Unc
184	5 POUNDS	1.10.1968. Black on green unpt.	10.00	17.50	40.00
185	50 POUNDS	1.10.1968. Black on dk. blue unpt. *NBLD* monogram on back.	85.00	150.00	300.00
186	100 POUNDS	1.10.1968. Black on dk. blue unpt. *NBLD* monogram on back.	175.00	300.00	500.00

1970 ISSUE

#187–192 cows at l., ship yard at bottom ctr., loom at r. Sign. varieties.

Cat. #	Denomination	Date, description	VG	VF	Unc
187	1 POUND	1.7.1970; 1.10.1971; 1.8.1978; 1.7.1979. Green on pink unpt. Printer: BWC.	FV	2.50	10.00
188	5 POUNDS	1.7.1970–1.4.1982. Lt. blue.	FV	11.00	27.50
189	10 POUNDS	1.7.1970; 1.10.1971; 1.1.1975; 15.6.1988. Brown.	FV	20.00	45.00
190	20 POUNDS	1.7.1970; 15.6.1988. Purple.	FV	37.50	85.00
191	50 POUNDS	1.7.1970. Orange.	FV	87.50	200.00
192	100 POUNDS	1.7.1970; 1.10.1971; 1.1.1975. Red.	FV	175.00	350.00

1988-90 ISSUE

#193–197 dish antenna at l., stylized *N* at ctr. and computero r. n back. Printer: TDLR.

Cat. #	Denomination	Date, description	VG	VF	Unc
193	5 POUNDS	24.8.1988; 24.8.1989; 24.8.1990. Blue and m/c. Station above trolley car at ctr., W. A. Traill at r.	FV	FV	15.00

Cat. #	Denomination	Date, description	VG	VF	Unc
194	10 POUNDS	24.8.1988; 14.5.1991. Red and brown on m/c unpt. Early automobile above bicyclist at ctr., J. B. Dunlop at r.	FV	FV	27.50

Cat. #	Denomination	Date, description	VG	VF	Unc
195	20 POUNDS	24.8.1988; 24.8.1989; 9.5.1991; 30.3.1992. Purple brown, red and m/c. Airplane at ctr., H. G. Ferguson at r., tractor at bottom r.	FV	FV	45.00

Cat. #	Denomination	Date, description	VG	VF	Unc
196	50 POUNDS	1.11.1990. Bluish-green, black and m/c. Tea dryer, centrifugal machine at ctr, Sir S. Davidson at r.	FV	FV	125.00

Cat. #	Denomination	Date, description	VG	VF	Unc
197	100 POUNDS	1.11.1990. Lilac, black, blue and m/c. Airplanes and ejection seat at ctr., Sir J. Martin at r.	FV	FV	225.00

Provincial Bank of Ireland Ltd.

See also Ireland-Republic and Northern - Allied Irish Banks Ltd

BELFAST BRANCH

1965 ISSUE

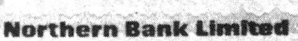

Cat. #	Denomination	Date, description	VG	VF	Unc
243	1 POUND	1.12.1965. Green. Woman at ctr. Printer: TDLR.	4.00	10.00	30.00
242	5 POUNDS	5.10.1954–5.7.1961. Brown. Woman at ctr. Printer: W&S.	12.50	25.00	65.00
244	5 POUNDS	6.12.1965. Similar to #243 but printer: TDLR.	11.00	22.50	50.00

1968 ISSUE

Cat. #	Denomination	Date, description	VG	VF	Unc
245	1 POUND	1.1.1968–1.1.1972. Green. Like #241. 150 x 71mm.	2.00	5.00	20.00
246	6 POUNDS	5.1.1968; 5.1.1970; 5.1.1972. Brown. Like #243. 139 x 84mm.	10.00	15.00	45.00

1977-81 ISSUE

#247–251, designs similar to Allied Irish Banks Ltd. issues except for bank title and sign. Printer: TDLR.

Cat. #	Denomination	Date, description	VG	VF	Unc
247	1 POUND	1977; 1979. Green on m/c unpt. Young girl at r. Sailing ship *Girona* at ctr. on back.			
		a. Sign. J. G. McClay. 1.1.1977.	2.00	4.00	15.00
		b. Sign. F. H. Hollway. 1.1.1979.	FV	3.00	12.50

248	5 POUNDS	1977; 1979. Blue and purple on m/c unpt. Young woman at r. Dunluce Castle at ctr. on back.			
		a. Sign. J. G. McClay. 1.1.1977.	8.50	12.00	32.50
		b. Sign. F. H. Hollway. 1.1.1979.	FV	10.00	27.50
249	10 POUNDS	1977; 1979. Brown and gray-green on m/c unpt. Young man at r. Wreck of the *Girona* at ctr. on back.			
		a. Sign. J. G. McClay. 1.1.1977.	17.50	22.50	57.50
		b. Sign. F. H. Hollway. 1.1.1979.	FV	20.00	50.00

Cat. #	Denomination	Date, description	VG	VF	Unc
250	20 POUNDS	1.3.1981. Purple and green. Elderly woman at r. Chimney at Lacada Pt. at ctr. on back.	FV	45.00	90.00
251	100 POUNDS	1.3.1981. Black, olive and green. Elderly man at r. The *Armada* at ctr. on back.	FV	175.00	350.00

Ulster Bank Ltd.

BELFAST BRANCH

1966-70 ISSUE

#321–324 view of Belfast at lower l. and r., port w/bridge at lower ctr. below sign., date to r. Arms at ctr. on back. Sign. Jno. J. A. Leitch. Printer: BWC.

321	1 POUND	4.10.1966. Dk. blue on m/c unpt. 151 x 72 mm.	2.50	5.50	17.50
322	5 POUNDS	4.10.1966. Brown on m/c unpt. 140 x 85 mm.	10.00	20.00	55.00
323	10 POUNDS	4.10.1966. Green on m/c unpt. 151 x 93 mm.	20.00	40.00	100.00
324	20 POUNDS	1.7.1970. Lilac on m/c unpt. 161 x 90 mm. Specimen.	—	—	—

1971-82 ISSUE

#325–330 similar to #321–324 but date at l., sign. at ctr. r. Printer: BWC.

325	1 POUND	1971–76. 135 x 67 mm.			
		a. Sign. H. E. O'B. Traill. 15.2.1971.	2.25	5.00	12.50
		b. Sign. R. W. Hamilton. 1.3.1973; 1.3.1976.	2.00	3.50	8.50
326	5 POUNDS	1971–83. 146 x 78 mm.			
		a. Sign. H. E. O'B. Traill. 15.2.1971.	9.00	20.00	50.00
		b. Sign R. W. Hamilton. 1.3.1973; 1.3.1976.	8.50	13.50	30.00
		c. Sign. V. Chambers. 1.10.1982; 1.10.1983.1.3.1976.	FV	10.00	25.00

327	10 POUNDS	1971–88. 151 x 86 mm.			
		a. Sign. H. E. O'B. Traill. 15.2.1971.	18.50	35.00	85.00
		b. Sign. R. W. Hamilton. 1.3.1973; 1.3.1976.	17.50	25.00	65.00
		c. Sign. V. Chambers. 2.1.1980; 1.10.1982; 1.10.1983; 1.2.1988.	FV	22.50	50.00
328	20 POUNDS	1.10.1982; 1.10.1983. Sign. V. Chambers.	FV	47.50	85.00
329	50 POUNDS	1.10.1982. Brown on m/c unpt. Sign. V. Chambers.	FV	90.00	150.00
330	100 POUNDS	1.3.1973. Red on m/c unpt. Sign. R. W. Hamilton.	FV	FV	350.00

1989-90 ISSUE

#331–334 similar to previous issue but smaller size notes. Sign. J. Wead. Printer: TDLR.

Cat. #	Denomination	Date, description	VG	VF	Unc
331	5 POUNDS	1.12.1989. Similar to #326.	FV	FV	13.50

332	10 POUNDS	1.12.1990. Similar to #327. Printer: TDLR.	FV	FV	25.00
333	20 POUNDS	1.11.1990. Similar to #32.	FV	FV	47.50
334	100 POUNDS	1.12.1990. Similar to #330.	FV	FV	225.00

NOTE: The Bank of Ireland sold to collectors matched serial # sets off £5-10-20 notes as well as 100 sets of replacement serial II, Z prefix.

COLLECTOR SERIES

Cat. #	Date, denomination	Description	Issue Price	Mkt. Val.
CS1	ND (1978) 1, 5, 10, 100 POUNDS	#61b, #63b, #65b, and #68b ovpt: SPECIMEN and Maltese cross prefix serial #.	7.00	50.00

| CS2 | 1978 1, 5, 10 POUNDS | #247a–249a dated 1.1.1977. Ovpt: SPECIMEN and Maltese cross prefix serial #. | 7.00 | 30.00 |

NOTE: Sheets of 3 specimen notes of Bank of Ireland 1989-90 issue were sold to collectors.

ISLE OF MAN

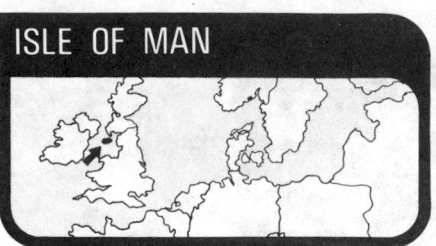

The Isle of Man, a dependency of the British Crown located in the Irish Sea equidistant from Ireland, Scotland and England, has an area of 227 sq. mi. (588 sq. km.) and a population of 61,000. Capital: Douglas. Agriculture, dairy farming, fishing and tourism are the chief industries.

The prevalence of prehistoric artifacts and monuments on the island give evidence that its mild, almost sub-tropical climate was enjoyed by mankind before the dawn of history. Vikings came to the Isle of Man during the 9th century and remained until ejected by Scotland in 1266. The island came under the protection of the British Crown in 1288, and in 1406 was granted, in perpetuity, to the Earls of Derby, from whom it was inherited, 1736, by the Duke of Atholl. Rights and title were purchased from the Duke of Atholl in 1765 by the British Crown; the remaining privileges of the Atholl family were transferred to the crown in 1829. The Isle of Man is ruled by its own legislative council and the House of Keys, one of the oldest legislative assembiles in the world. Acts of Parliament passed in London do not affect the island unless it is specifically mentioned.

RULERS
British

MONETARY SYSTEM
1 Pound = 20 Shillings to 1971
1 Pound = 100 New Pence, 1971–

Lloyds Bank Ltd.

Cat. #	Denomination	Date, description	Good	Fine	XF
13	1 POUND	21.1.1955–14.3.1961. Black on green unpt. Bank arms at upper ctr.			
		a. Issue note.	75.00	150.00	300.00
		b. Unsigned remainder. ND.	—	—	40.00

Westminster Bank Ltd.

#23A various date and sign. varieties.

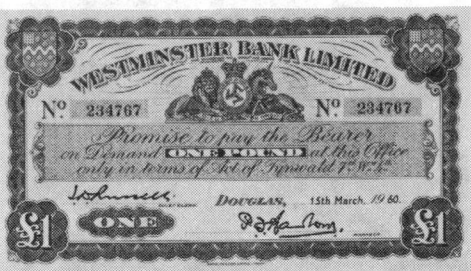

23A	1 POUND	1955–61. Black on lt. yellow unpt. Crowned Triskele arms supported by lion and unicorn at upper ctr. W/text: INCORPORATED IN ENGLAND added below bank name. Printer: W&S.			
		a. 23.11.1955.	125.00	250.00	500.00
		b. 4.4.1956–10.3.1961.	35.00	70.00	140.00

Government

SIGNATURE VARIETIES			
1	Garvey	5	Dawson
2	Stallard	6	Cashen
3	Paul (26mm)		
4	Paul (20mm)		

1961 (ND) ISSUE

#24–27 Triskele arms at lower ctr., young portr. of Qn. Elizabeth II at r. Printer: BWC.

Cat. #	Denomination	Date, description	VG	VF	Unc
24	10 SHILLINGS	ND (1961). Red on m/c unpt. Old sailing boat on back.			
		a. Sign. 1.	1.50	5.00	30.00
		b. Sign. 2.	1.50	5.00	27.50
		s. Sign. 1. Specimen.	—	—	45.00

25	1 POUND	ND (1961). Purple on m/c unpt. Tynwald Hill on back.			
		a. Sign. 1.	2.50	8.00	45.00
		b. Sign. 2.	2.00	7.00	37.50
		s. Sign. 1. Specimen.	—	—	55.00

26	5 POUNDS	ND (1961). Green and blue. Castle Rushen on back.			
		a. Sign. 1.	22.50	100.00	400.00
		b. Sign. 2.	20.00	85.00	350.00
		s. Sign. 1. Specimen w/normal serial # blocked out.	—	—	125.00

1969 (ND) ISSUE

Cat. #	Denomination	Date, description	VG	VF	Unc
27	50 NEW PENCE	ND (1969). Blue on m/c unpt. Back like #24. 139 x 66mm. Sign. 2.	1.00	3.00	15.00

1972 (ND) ISSUE

#28–31 Triskele arms at ctr., mature portr. Qn. Elizabeth II at r. Sign. title: *LIEUTENANT GOVERNOR*. Printer: BWC.

28	50 NEW PENCE	ND (1972). Blue on m/c unpt. Back like #24. 126 x 62 mm.			
		a. Sign. 2.	1.00	5.00	30.00
		b. Sign. 3.	1.00	2.50	18.00
		c. Sign. 4.	1.00	2.00	12.00

29	1 POUND	ND (1972). Purple on m/c unpt. Back similar to #25.			
		a. Sign. 2.	4.00	15.00	65.00
		b. Sign. 3.	2.00	10.00	75.00
		c. Sign. 4.	1.50	3.00	18.50

30	5 POUNDS	ND (1972). Blue and lilac-brown. Back similar to #26.			
		a. Sign. 2.	15.00	35.00	200.00
		b. Sign. 3.	8.00	15.00	85.00

Cat. #	Denomination	Date, description	VG	VF	Unc
31	10 POUNDS	ND (1972). Brown and green. Peel Castle ca.1830 on back. Sign. 3.			
		a. Sign. 2.	150.00	350.00	1000.
		b. Sign. 3.	50.00	150.00	400.00
		s. Sign. 2. Specimen.	—	—	165.00

1979 COMMEMORATIVE ISSUE

#32, Millennium Year 1979

32	20 POUNDS	1979. Red-orange, orange and dk. brown on m/c unpt. Triskele at ctr., Qn. Elizabeth II at r. Island outline at upper r. Commemorative text at lower r. of triskele. Laxey wheel ca. 1854, crowd of people and hills in background on back. Printer: BWC.	50.00	100.00	350.00

1979; 1983 (ND) ISSUES

#33–37 new sign. title: *TREASURER OF THE ISLE OF MAN.* Wmk: Triskele arms. Printer: BWC.

33	50 PENCE	ND. Like #28. Sign. 5.	FV	FV	4.00
34	1 POUND	ND. Like #29. Sign. 5.	FV	FV	7.00
35	5 POUNDS	ND. Like #30.			
		a. Sign. 5. Series C.	FV	15.00	65.00
		b. Sign. 5. Series D, guilloche variety.	FV	12.00	40.00
36	10 POUNDS	ND. Like #31.	FV	22.50	40.00
37	20 POUNDS	ND (1979). Like #32 but w/o commemorative text.	FV	38.50	85.00
38	50 POUNDS	ND (1983). Lt. blue and green. Qn. Elizabeth II at r. Douglas Bay on back.	FV	90.00	150.00

39	1 POUND	ND (1983). Green on m/c unpt. Like #25 but printed on Bradvek, a special plastic.	FV	2.50	8.50

1983 (ND) REDUCED SIZE ISSUE

#40–44 smaller format. QE II at r. Wmk: Triskele. Printer: TDLR.

Cat. #	Denomination	Date, description	VG	VF	Unc
40	1 POUND	ND. Purple and m/c. Back like #25.			
		a. Sign. 5.	FV	FV	6.00
		b. Sign. 6.	FV	FV	4.50

41	5 POUNDS	ND. Greenish blue, lilac brown and m/c. Back like #30.			
		a. Sign. 5.	FV	FV	20.00
		b. Sign. 6.	FV	FV	17.50

42	10 POUNDS	ND. Brown, green and m/c. Back brown, orange and m/c. Like #31. Sign. 6.			
		a. Sign. 5.	FV	\multicolumn{2}{}{Reported, not confirmed.}	
		b. Sign. 6.	FV	FV	22.50

43	20 POUNDS	ND. Brown, red-orange and m/c. Back like #32.			
		a. Sign. 5.	FV	FV	100.00
		b. Sign. 6.	FV	FV	67.50
44	50 POUNDS	ND.			Expected new issue.

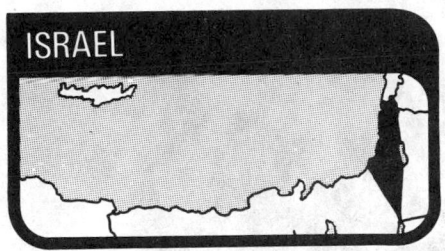

ISRAEL

The State of Israel, at the eastern end of the Mediterranean Sea, bounded by Lebanon on the north, Syria on the northeast, Jordan on the east, and Egypt on the southwest, has an area of 7,847 sq. mi. (23,309 sq. km.) and a population of 4.5 million. Capital: Jerusalem. Diamonds, chemicals, citrus, textiles, and minerals are exported.

Palestine, which corresponds to Canaan of the Bible, was settled by the Philistines about the 12th century B.C. and shortly thereafter was invaded by the Jews who established the kingdoms of Israel and Judah. Because of its position as part of the land bridge connecting Asia and Africa, Palestine was invaded and conquered by nearly all of the historic empires of ancient Europe and Asia. In the 16th century it became a Turkish satrap. After falling to the British in World War I, it, together with Transjordan, was mandated to Great Britain by the League of Nations, 1922.

For more than half a century prior to the termination of the British mandate over Palestine, 1948, Zionist leaders had sought to create a Jewish homeland for Jews dispersed throughout the world. For almost as long, Jews fleeing persecution had immigrated to Palestine. The Nazi persecutions of the 1930s and 1940s increased the Jewish movement to Palestine and generated international support for the creation of a Jewish state, first promulgated by the Balfour Declaration of 1917 which asserted British support for the endeavor. The dream of a Jewish homeland was realized on May 14, 1948 when Palestine was proclaimed the State of Israel.

MONETARY SYSTEM

1 Lira = 100 Agorot, 1960–80
1 Sheqel = 10 "old" Lirot, 1980–85
1 New Sheqel = 1000 "old" Sheqalim, 1985–

Bank of Israel

Lira System

1958-60/5718-20 ISSUE

#29, 30 printer: JEZ (w/o imprint).

Cat. #	Denomination	Date, description	VG	VF	Unc
29	1/2 LIRA	1958/5718. Green. Woman soldier w/basket full of oranges at l. and as wmk. Tombs of the Sanhedrin on back.	.50	1.25	5.00

30	1 LIRA	1958/5718. Blue. Fisherman w/net and anchor at l. and as wmk. Wreath on back.			
		a. Paper w/security thread at l. Black serial #.	.25	.75	3.00
		b. Red serial #	.25	.75	3.00
		c. Paper w/security thread and morse tape, brown serial #.	.15	.50	2.00

#31, 32 printer: TDLR (w/o imprint).

Cat. #	Denomination	Date, description	VG	VF	Unc
31	5 LIROT	1958/5718. Brown. Worker w/hammer in front of factory at l. and as wmk. Seal of Shema on back.	.40	1.25	5.00

32	10 LIROT	1958/5718. Lilac and violet. Scientist w/microscope and test tube at l. and as wmk. Dead Sea scroll and vases on back.			
		a. Paper w/security thread. Black serial #.	.35	1.00	4.00
		b. Paper w/security thread and morse tape. Red serial #.	.35	1.00	4.00
		c. Paper w/security thread and morse tape. Blue serial #.	.35	1.00	4.00
		d. Paper w/security thread and morse tape. Brown serial #.	.35	1.00	4.00

33	50 LIROT	1960/5720. Brown and m/c. Boy and girl at l. and as wmk. Mosaic of menorah on back. Printer: JEZ (w/o imprint).			
		a. Paper w/security thread. Black serial #.	1.00	3.00	12.50
		b. Paper w/security thread. Red serial #.	1.00	3.00	12.50
		c. Paper w/security thread and morse tape. Blue serial #.	.85	2.50	10.00
		d. Paper w/security thread and morse tape. Green serial #.	.85	2.50	10.00
		e. Paper w/security thread and morse tape. Brown serial #.	.60	1.75	7.00

1968/5728 ISSUE

#34–37 printer: JEZ (w/o imprint).

Cat. #	Denomination	Date, description	VG	VF	Unc
34	5 LIROT	1968/5728. Gray-green and blue on m/c unpt. A. Einstein at r. and as wmk. Bldg. on back.			
		a. Black serial #.	.40	1.25	5.00
		b. Red serial #.	.40	1.25	5.00

Cat. #	Denomination	Date, description	VG	VF	Unc
37	100 LIROT	1968/5728. Blue and green on m/c unpt. Dr. T. Herzl at r. and as wmk. Menorah and surrounding objects on back.			
		a. Wmk: Profile. Black serial # 3.5mm.	2.00	5.00	12.50
		b. Wmk: 3/4 profile r. Red serial #.	2.00	5.00	12.50
		c. Wmk: Profile. Red serial #.	Reported, not confirmed		
		d. Wmk: Profile. Black serial # 2.8mm. W/o series letter.	1.00	4.00	9.00
		e. Wmk: Profile. Brown serial #.	1.00	3.00	8.00

1973-75/5733-35 ISSUE

All the following notes except #41 and 45 have marks for the blind on the face. #38–46 have barely discernible bar code strips at lower l. and upper r. on back. All have portr. as wmk. Various gates in Jerusalem are shown on the backs.

#38–51 printer: JEZ (w/o imprint).

Cat. #	Denomination	Date, description	VG	VF	Unc
35	10 LIROT	1968/5728. Brown, violet and m/c. C. Nachman Bialik at r. and as wmk. House on back.			
		a. Black serial #.	.25	.75	3.00
		b. Green serial #.	.25	.75	3.00
		c. Blue serial #.	.25	.75	3.00

Cat. #	Denomination	Date, description	VG	VF	Unc
38	5 LIROT	1973/5733. Lt. and dk. brown. H. Szold at r. Lion's Gate on back.	.15	.50	2.00

Cat. #	Denomination	Date, description	VG	VF	Unc
36	50 LIROT	1968/5728. Lt. brown and green on m/c unpt. Pres. C. Weizmann at r. and as wmk. Knesset bldg. on back.			
		a. Black serial #.	1.00	3.00	6.50
		b. Blue serial #.	1.00	2.50	5.50

Cat. #	Denomination	Date, description	VG	VF	Unc
39	10 LIROT	1973/5733. Purple on lilac unpt. Sir M. Montefiore at r. Jaffa Gate on back.	.15	.50	2.00

| 40 | 50 LIROT | 1973/5733. Green on olive unpt.. C. Weizmann at r. Sichem Gate on back. | .35 | 1.00 | 4.00 |

| 41 | 100 LIROT | 1973/5733. Blue on blue and brown unpt. Dr. T. Herzl at r. Zion Gate on back. | .35 | 1.00 | 4.00 |

| 42 | 500 LIROT | 1975/5735. Black on tan and brown unpt. D. Ben-Gurion at r. Golden Gate on back. | 1.65 | 5.00 | 20.00 |

Sheqel System
1978–84/5738–44 ISSUE

Cat. #	Denomination	Date, description	VG	VF	Unc
43	1 SHEQEL	1978/5738 (1980). Purple. Like #39.	.15	.40	1.50

| 44 | 5 SHEQALIM | 1978/5738 (1980). Green. Like #40. | .40 | 1.25 | 5.00 |

| 45 | 10 SHEQALIM | 1978/5738 (1980). Blue. Like #41. | .25 | .75 | 3.00 |

46	50 SHEQALIM	1978/5738 (1980). Black on tan and brown unpt. Like #42.			
		a. W/o small bars below serial # or barely discernible bar code strips on back.	.15	.50	2.00
		b. W/o small bars below serial #, but w/ bar code strips on back.	.50	1.50	6.00
		c. 2 green bars below serial # on back.	3.00	15.00	75.00
		d. 4 black bars below serial # on back.	3.00	15.00	75.00
		e. 12-subject sheet.	—	—	15.00

Cat. #	Denomination	Date, description	VG	VF	Unc
47	100 SHEQALIM	1979/5739. Red-brown. Ze'ev Jabotinsky at r. Herod's Gate on back.			
		a. W/o bars below serial # on back.	.15	.50	2.00

| | | b. 2 bars below serial # on back. | 2.00 | 10.00 | 50.00 |

NOTE: Colored bars on #46–47 were used to identify various surfaced coated papers, used experimentally.

| 48 | 500 SHEQALIM | 1982/5742. Red and m/c. Farm workers at ctr., Baron E. de Rothschild at r. Vine leaves on back. | .50 | 1.50 | 6.00 |

Cat. #	Denomination	Date, description	VG	VF	Unc
49	1000 SHEQALIM	1983/5743. Green and m/c. Rabbi M. B. Maimon-Maimonides at r. View of Tiberias at l. on back.			
		a. Error in first letter *he* of second word at r. in vertical text (right to left), partly completed letter resembling *7*.	.85	2.50	10.00
		b. Corrected letter resembling *17*.	.65	2.00	8.00

| 50 | 5000 SHEQALIM | 1984/5744. Blue and m/c. City view at ctr., L. Eshkol at r. Water pipe and modern design on back. | .65 | 2.00 | 8.00 |

| 51 | 10,000 SHEQALIM | 1984/5744. Brown, black, orange and dk. green on m/c unpt. Stylized tree at ctr., G. Meir at r. and as wmk. Gathering in front of Moscow synagogue on back. | 1.65 | 5.00 | 20.00 |

New Sheqel System

1 New Shekel = 1000 Sheqalim

SIGNATURE VARIETIES			
5	Mandelbaum, 1986	7	Lorincz and Bruno, 1987–91
6	Shapira and Mandelbaum, 1985	8	Lorincz and Frankel, 1992

1985-92/5745–52 ISSUE

#51A–53 use design concepts like previous issue. #51A–56 have marks for the blind. All have portr. as wmk. Printer: JEZ (w/o imprint).

Cat. #	Denomination	Date, description	VG	VF	Unc
51A	1 NEW SHEKEL	1986/5746. Like #49 except for denomination. Sign. 5.	FV	.35	2.00

Cat. #	Denomination	Date, description	VG	VF	Unc
52	5 NEW SHEQALIM	1985/5745; 1987/5747. Like #50 except for denomination.			
		a. Sign. 6. 1985/5745.	FV	FV	10.00
		b. Sign. 7. 1987/5747.	FV	FV	8.00

53	10 NEW SHEQALIM	1985/5745; 1987/5747; 1992/5752. Like #51 except for denomination.			
		a. Sign. 6. 1985/5745.	FV	FV	20.00
		b. Sign. 7. 1987/5747.	FV	FV	12.50
		c. Sign. 8. 1992/5752.	FV	FV	10.00

Cat. #	Denomination	Date, description	VG	VF	Unc
54	20 NEW SHEQALIM	1987/5747; 1993/5753. Dk. gray and m/c. M. Sharett standing holding flag at ctr., his bust at r. and as wmk. Herzlya High School at ctr. on back.			
		a. W/o sm. double circle w/dot in wmk. area face and back. Sign. 7. 1987/5747.	FV	FV	25.00
		b. W/sm. double circle w/dot in wmk. area face and back. Sign. 7. 1987/5747.	FV	FV	20.00
		c. Sign. 8. 1993/5753.	FV	FV	16.50

55	50 NEW SHEQALIM	1985/5745–1992/5752. Purple and m/c. S.J. Agnon at r. and as wmk. Various bldgs. and book titles on back.			
		a. Sign. 6. 1985/5745.	FV	FV	40.00
		b. Sign. 7. Slight color variations. 1988/5748.	FV	FV	35.00
		c. Sign 8. 1992/5752.	FV	FV	30.00

56	100 NEW SHEQALIM	1986/5746; 1989/5749; 1995/5755. Brown and m/c. Y. Ben-Zvi at r. and as wmk. Stylized village and carob tree on back.			
		a. Sign. 5. Plain security thread and plain white paper. 1986/5746.	FV	FV	75.00
		b. Sign. 6. W/security thread inscribed: *Bank Israel*, paper w/colored threads. 1989/5749.	FV	FV	60.00
		c. Sign. 8. 1995/5755.	FV	FV	57.50

57	200 NEW SHEQALIM	1991/5751. Deep red, purple and blue-green on m/c unpt. Z. Shazar at r. and as wmk. School girl writing at ctr. on back. Sign. 8.	FV	FV	110.00

ITALY

The Italian Republic, a 700-mile-long peninsula extending into the heart of the Mediterranean Sea, has an area of 116,304 sq. mi. (301,255 sq. km.) and a population of 57.4 million. Capital: Rome. The economy centers about agriculture, manufacturing, forestry and fishing. Machinery, textiles, clothing and motor vehicles are exported.

From the fall of Rome until modern times, "Italy" was little more than a geographical expression. Although nominally included in the Empire of Charlemagne and the Holy Roman Empire, it was in reality divided into a number of independent states and kingdoms presided over by wealthy families, soldiers of fortune or hereditary rulers. The 19th century unification movement fostered by Mazzini, Garibaldi and Cavor attained fruition in 1860–1870 with the creation of the Kingdom of Italy and the installation of Victor Emanuele, King of Italy. Benito Mussolini came to power during the post-World War I period of economic and political unrest, installed a Fascist dictatorship with a figurehead king as titular Head of State, and allied with Germany for the pursuit of World War II. Following the defeat of the Axis powers, the Italian monarchy was dissolved by plebiscite, and the Italian Republic proclaimed.

MONETARY SYSTEM
 1 Lira = 100 Centesimi

SEALS

Type C
Facing head of Medusa

Type D
Winged lion of St. Mark of Venice above 3 shields

Banca d'Italia — Bank of Italy

DECREES

There are many different dates found on the following notes of the Banca d'Italia. These include *ART. DELLA LEGGE* (law date) and the more important *DECRETO MINISTERIALE* –(D.M. date). The earliest *D.M.* date is usually found on the back of the note while later *D.M.* dates are found grouped together. The actual latest date (of issue) is referred to in the following listings.

Decreto Ministeriale 10.2 and 9.2.1948, also 1959 and 1961

Cat. #	Denomination	Date, description	VG	VF	Unc
39	1000 LIRE	1948–61. Purple and brown. Portr. "Italia" at l. and as wmk. Back blue on gray unpt. Seal: Type C.			
		a. Sign. Einaudi and Urbini. 10.2.1948.	2.00	10.00	140.00
		b. Sign. Menichella and Urbini. 11.2.1949.	2.00	10.00	140.00
		c. Blue-gray. Sign. Menichella and Boggione. 15.9.1959.	3.00	20.00	200.00
		d. Color like c. Sign. Carli and Ripa. 25.9.1961.	2.00	10.00	140.00

Repubblica Italiana

			VG	VF	Unc
64	500 LIRE	1966–75. Dk. gray on m/c unpt. Eagle w/snake at l., Arethusa at r. 3 sign. varieties.			
		a. 20.6.1966; 20.10.1967; 23.2.1970.	1.00	2.00	10.00
		b. 23.4.1975.	10.00	30.00	240.00

Decreto Ministeriale 14.2.1974

Cat. #	Denomination	Date, description	VG	VF	Unc
64A	500 LIRE	14.2.1974; 2.4.1979. Green-blue. Mercury at r. 3 sign. varieties.	.50	1.00	2.00

Decreto Ministeriale 6.8.1976

| 64B | 500 LIRE | 20.12.1976. Like #64A. | .50 | 1.50 | 3.50 |

Banca d'Italia — Bank of Italy

Decreto Ministeriale 12.4.1962

			VG	VF	Unc
70	10,000 LIRE	1962–73. Brown, purple, orange and red-brown w/dk. brown text on m/c unpt. Michaelangelo at r. Bldg. w/courtyard on back.			
		a. Sign. Carli and Ripa. 3.7.1962; 14.1.1964; 27.7.1964.	FV	10.00	30.00
		b. Sign. Carli and Febbraio. 20.5.1966.	FV	10.00	30.00
		c. Sign. Carli and Pacini. 4.1.1968.	FV	10.00	35.00
		d. Sign. Carli and Lombardo. 8.6.1970.	FV	10.00	30.00
		e. Sign. Carli and Barbarito. 15.2.1973; 27.11.1973.	FV	FV	30.00

Decreto Ministeriale 28.6.1962

			VG	VF	Unc
71	1000 LIRE	1962–68. Blue on red and brown unpt. G. Verdi at r.			
		a. Sign. Carli and Ripa. 14.7.1962; 14.1.1964.	FV	1.50	25.00
		b. Sign. Carli and Ripa. 5.7.1963; 25.7.1964.	FV	4.00	65.00
		c. Sign. Carli and Febbraio. 10.8.1965; 20.5.1966.	FV	1.50	30.00
		d. Sign. Carli and Pacini. 4.1.1968.	FV	4.00	80.00

Decreto Ministeriale 20.8.1964

Cat. #	Denomination	Date, description	VG	VF	Unc
72	5000 LIRE	1964–70. Green on pink unpt. Columbus at r. Ship on back.			
		a. Sign. Carli and Ripa. 3.9.1964.	4.00	10.00	140.00
		b. Sign. Carli and Pacini. 4.1.1968.	4.00	10.00	140.00
		c. Sign. Carli and Lombardo. 20.1.1970.	4.00	10.00	140.00

Decreto Ministeriale 27.6.1967

Cat. #	Denomination	Date, description	VG	VF	Unc
73	50,000 LIRE	1967–74. Brownish-black, dk. brown and reddish brown w/black text on m/c unpt. Leonardo da Vinci at r. Bldgs. on back. Wmk: bust of Madonna.			
		a. Sign. Carli and Febbraio. 4.12.1967.	FV	80.00	350.00
		b. Sign. Carli and Lombardo. 19.7.1970.	FV	50.00	280.00
		c. Sign. Carli and Barbarito. 16.5.1972; 4.2.1974.	FV	50.00	280.00

Cat. #	Denomination	Date, description	VG	VF	Unc
74	100,000 LIRE	1967–74. Brownish-black, brown and deep olive-green on m/c unpt. A. Manzoni at r. Mountains on back. Wmk: Archaic female bust.			
		a. Sign. Carli and Febbraio. 3.7.1967.	FV	100.00	400.00
		b. Sign. Carli and Lombardo. 19.7.1970.	FV	90.00	300.00
		c. Sign. Carli and Barbarito. 6.2.1974.	FV	90.00	300.00

Decreto Ministeriale 26.2.1969

Cat. #	Denomination	Date, description	VG	VF	Unc
75	1000 LIRE	1969–81. Blue and lilac. Harp at l. ctr., G. Verdi at r. Paper w/security thread. La Scala opera house on back.			
		a. Sign. Carli and Lombardo. 25.3.1969; 11.3.1971.	FV	1.00	4.00
		b. Sign. Carli and Barbarito. 15.2.1973.	FV	1.25	7.00
		c. Sign. Carli and Barbarito. 5.8.1975.	FV	1.00	4.00
		d. Sign. Baffi and Stevani. 10.1.1977; 10.5.1979.	FV	1.00	7.00
		e. Sign. Ciampi and Stevani. 20.2.1980; 6.9.1980; 30.5.1981.	FV	1.00	4.00

Decreto Ministeriale 15.5.1971

Cat. #	Denomination	Date, description	VG	VF	Unc
76	5000 LIRE	1971–77. Olive. Mythical seahorse at ctr., Columbus at r. 3 sailing ships of Columbus on back.			
		a. Sign. Carli and Lombardo. 20.5.1971.	FV	4.00	20.00
		b. Sign. Carli and Barbarito. 11.4.1973.	FV	5.00	30.00
		c. Sign. Baffi and Stevani. 10.11.1977.	FV	5.00	30.00

Decreto Ministeriale 10.9.1973

Cat. #	Denomination	Date, description	VG	VF	Unc
77	2000 LIRE	1973; 1976; 1983. Brown and green. Galileo at ctr. Zodiac signs on back.			
		a. Sign. Carli and Barbarito. 8.10.1973.	FV	2.50	15.00
		b. Sign. Baffi and Stevani. 22.10.1976.	FV	2.00	10.00
		c. Sign. Ciampi and Stevani. 24.10.1983.	FV	FV	4.00

Decreto Ministeriale 20.12.1974

78	20,000 LIRE	21.2.1975. Brownish-black and dk. brown on red-brown and pale olive-green unpt. Titian at ctr. Painting at l. ctr. on back. Wmk: Woman's head. Sign. Carli and Barbarito.	FV	30.00	90.00

Decreto Ministeriale 2.3.1979

79	5000 LIRE	1979–83. Brown and green. Man at l. Bldg. and statuary on back.			
		a. Sign. Baffi and Stevani. 9.3.1979.	FV	5.50	10.00
		b. Sign. Ciampi and Stevani. 1.7.1980; 3.11.1982; 19.10.1983.	FV	5.00	10.00

Decreto Ministeriale 25.8.1976

80	10,000 LIRE	1976–84. Black and m/c. Man at l. Column at r. on back.			
		a. Sign. Baffi and Stevani. 30.10.1976; 29.12.1978.	FV	11.00	18.50
		b. Sign. Ciampi and Stevani. 6.9.1980; 3.11.1982; 8.3.1984.	FV	10.00	16.50

Decreto Ministeriale 20.6.1977

Cat. #	Denomination	Date, description	VG	VF	Unc
81	50,000 LIRE	1977–82. Blue, red and green. Young women and lion of St. Mark at l. Modern design of arches on back.			
		a. Sign. Baffi and Stevani. 20.6.1977; 12.6.1978; 23.10.1978.	FV	30.00	40.00
		b. Sign. Ciampi and Stevani. 11.4.1980.	FV	30.00	40.00
		c. Sign. Ciampi and Stevani. 2.11.1982.	FV	35.00	100.00

Decreto Ministeriale 16.6.1978

82	100,000 LIRE	D.1978. Red-violet and black on m/c unpt. Woman's bust at l. and as wmk. Modern bldg. design at r. on back			
		a. Sign. Ciampi and Stevani. 20.6.1978.	FV	65.00	100.00
		b. Sign. Ciampi and Stevani. 1.7.1980–10.5.1982.	FV	65.00	135.00

Decreto Ministeriale 6.1.1982

83	1000 LIRE	D.1982. Dk. green, tan and m/c. Marco Polo at r. and as wmk. Bldg. on vertical back. Printer: ODBI.			
		a. Sign. Ciampi and Stevani. 6.1.1982.	FV	FV	2.00
		b. Sign. Ciampi and Speziali. 6.1.1982.	FV	FV	2.00

Decreto Ministeriale 1.9.1983

Cat. #	Denomination	Date, description	VG	VF	Unc
84	100,000 LIRE	D.1983. Dk. brown and brown on green and olive-green unpt. Couple at ctr., Caravaggio at r. and as wmk. Fruit basket at l., castle at upper ctr. on back.			
		a. Sign. Ciampi and Stevani. 1.9.1983.	FV	FV	125.00
		b. Sign. Ciampi and Speziali. 1.9.1983.	FV	FV	110.00

Decreto Ministeriale 4.1.1985

85	5,000 LIRE	ND (1985). Olive green and m/c unpt. Coliseum at ctr., V. Bellini at r. and as wmk. Scene from opera "Norma" on back.			
		a. Sign. Ciampi and Stevani. 4.1.1985.	FV	FV	7.50
		b. Sign. Ciampi and Speziali. 4.1.1985.	FV	FV	7.50

Decreto Ministeriale 3.9.1984

86	10,000 LIRE	D.1984. Dk. blue on m/c unpt. Lab instrument at ctr. A. Volta at r. and as wmk. Mausoleum on back.			
		a. Sign. Ciampi and Stevani. 3.9.1984.	FV	FV	14.00
		b. Sign. Ciampi and Speziali. 3.9.1984.	FV	FV	14.00

Decreto Ministeriale 6.2.1984

Cat. #	Denomination	Date, description	VG	VF	Unc
87	50,000 LIRE	D.1984. Red-violet and m/c. Figurine at ctr., G.L. Bernini at r. and as wmk. Equestrian statue on back.			
		a. Sign. Ciampi and Stevani. 5.12.1984; 28.10.1985; 1.12.1986.	FV	FV	55.00
		b. Sign. Ciampi and Speziali. 25.1.1990.	FV	FV	50.00

Decreto Ministeriale 3.10.1990

88	1000 LIRE	D.1990. Red-violet and m/c. M. Montessori at r. and as wmk. Teacher and student on back. Sign. Ciampi and Speziali.	FV	FV	1.75

89	2000 LIRE	D.1990. Dk. brown on m/c unpt. Arms at l. ctr.; G. Marconi at r. and as wmk. Ship, radio tower and early radio set on back. Sign. Ciampi and Speziali.	FV	FV	3.00

Decreto Ministeriale 27.5.1992

90	50,000 LIRE	D.1992. Violet and dull green on m/c unpt. Similar to #87. Sign. Ciampi and Speziali.	FV	FV	50.00

Decreto Ministeriale 6.5.1994

Cat. #	Denomination	Date, description	VG	VF	Unc
91	100,00 LIRE	D.1994. Dk. brown, reddish brown and pale green on m/c unpt. Similar to #84.			
		a. Sign. Fazio and Speciali. 6.5.1994.	FV	FV	90.00
		b. Sign. Fazio and Amici. 6.5.1994.	FV	FV	87.50

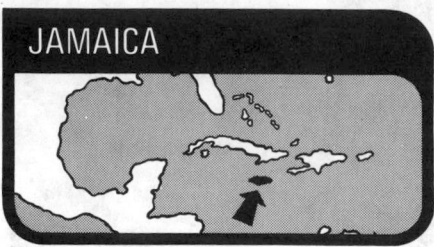

Jamaica, a member of the British Commonwealth situated in the Caribbean Sea 90 miles south of Cuba, has an area of 4,232 sq. mi. (10,991 sq. km.) and a population of 2.4 million. Capital: Kingston. The economy is founded chiefly on mining, tourism and agriculture. Alumina, bauxite, sugar, rum and molasses are exported.

Jamaica was discovered by Columbus on May 3, 1494, and settled by Spain in 1509. The island was captured in 1655 by a British naval force under the command of Admiral William Penn, and ceded to Britain by the Treaty of Madrid, 1670. For more than 150 years, the Jamaican economy of sugar, slaves and piracy was one of the most prosperous in the new world. Dissension between the property-oriented island legislature and the home government prompted parliament to establish a crown colony government for Jamaica in 1866. From 1958 to 1961 Jamaica was a member of the West Indies Federation, withdrawing when Jamaican voters rejected the association. The colony attained independence on Aug. 6, 1962. Jamaica is a member of the Commonwealth of Nations. The Queen of England is Chief of State.

A decimal standard currency system was adopted on Sept. 8, 1969.

RULERS
  British

MONETARY SYSTEM
  1 Shilling = 12 Pence
  1 Pound = 20 Shillings to 1969
  1 Dollar = 100 Cents, 1969–

Replacement Notes:

#53–74, ZY or ZZ prefix letters.

Bank of Jamaica

SIGNATURE VARIETIES			
1	Stanley W. Payton, 1960–64	7	Horace G. Barber, 1983–86
2	Richard T. P. Hall, **Acting Governor** – 1964–66	8	Headley A. Brown, 1986–89
3	Richard T. P. Hall **Governor** – 1966–67	9	Dr. Owen C. Jefferson, **Acting Governor** – 1989–90
4	G. Arthur Brown, 1967–77	10	G. A. Brown, 1990–93
5	Herbert Samuel Walker, 1977–81	11	R. Rainsford, 1993
6	Dr. Owen C. Jefferson, **Acting Governor** – 1981–83	12	J. Bussieres, 1994–

Pound System

FIRST ISSUE

Law 1960

#49–51/Qn. Elizabeth II at l. Latin motto below arms. Sign. 1. Printer: TDLR.

Cat. #	Denomination	Date, description	VG	VF	Unc
49	5 SHILLINGS	L.1960. Red on m/c unpt. River rapids on back.	3.00	12.50	40.00
50	10 SHILLINGS	L.1960. Purple on m/c unpt. Men w/bananas on back.	5.00	17.50	140.00

SECOND ISSUE

Cat. #	Denomination	Date, description	VG	VF	Unc
51	1 POUND	L.1960. Green on m/c unpt. Harvesting on back.	5.90	20.00	150.00

#49A–51A like previous issue, but English motto below arms. Printer: TDLR.

49A	5 SHILLINGS	L.1960. Red on m/c unpt,			
		a. Sign. 1. 2 serial # varieties.	2.00	7.00	45.00
		b. Sign. 2.	2.50	8.00	55.00
		c. Sign. 4.	1.50	5.00	40.00
50A	10 SHILLINGS	L.1960. Purple on m/c unpt.			
		a. Sign. 1. 2 serial # varieties.	3.00	7.50	55.00
		b. Sign. 2.	3.00	8.50	70.00
		c. Sign. 3.	3.50	12.50	85.00
		d. Sign. 4.	2.00	6.00	60.00
51A	1 POUND	L.1960. Green on m/c unpt.			
		a. Sign. 1. 2 serial # varieties, Gothic and Roman.	5.00	17.50	130.00
		b. Sign. 2..	5.00	17.50	140.00
		c. Sign. 3.	7.50	25.00	150.00
		d. Sign. 4.	4.00	15.00	125.00
52	5 POUNDS	L.1960. Blue on m/c unpt. Storage plant at ctr., woman w/fruit basket at r. on back.			
		a. Sign. 1. 2 serial # varieties, Gothic and Roman.	30.00	125.00	350.00
		b. Sign. 3.	27.50	110.00	325.00
		c. Sign. 4.	25.00	100.00	300.00

Dollar System

FIRST ISSUE

Law 1960

#53–55 wmk: Pineapple. Sign. 4. Printer: TDLR.

53	50 CENTS	L.1960 (1970). Red and m/c. M. Garvey at l. National shrine on back.	.50	1.00	4.50

54	1 DOLLAR	L.1960 (1970). Purple and m/c. Sir Alexander Bustamante at l. Tropical harbor on back.	.50	1.50	5.50

Cat. #	Denomination	Date, description	VG	VF	Unc
55	2 DOLLARS	L.1960 (1970). Dk. green and m/c. P. Dogle at l., bird at ctr. Group of people on back.	.85	2.50	10.00

NOTE: For #54 and 55 w/red serial # see #CS1–CS3.

56 (57)	5 DOLLARS	L.1960 (1970). Dk. brown, green and blue-gray on m/c unpt. N. Manley at l. Old Parliament on back.	2.50	7.50	22.50

57 (58)	10 DOLLARS	L.1960 (1970). Blue-black and black on m/c unpt. G. William Gordon at l. Bauxite industry on back.	5.00	15.00	50.00

1973 FAO COMMEMORATIVE ISSUE
#58, 25th Anniversary Declaration of Human Rights 1948–73

Cat. #	Denomination	Date, description	VG	VF	Unc
58 (56)	2 DOLLARS	1973. Like #55 but *Universal Declaration/of Human Rights/1948 - 10 December - 1973. Toward Food Education/Employment for All/Articles 23-26* added on back. Serial # double prefix FA-O...	1.00	3.25	13.50

1970 SECOND ISSUE

#59–63 new guilloches in corners and some larger denomination numerals on face and back.

Cat. #	Denomination	Date, description	VG	VF	Unc
59	1 DOLLAR	*L.1960*. Like #54 but w/corner design modifications.			
		a. Sign. 4.	.35	1.50	6.00
		b. Sign. 5.	.25	1.00	3.00
60	2 DOLLARS	*L.1960*. Like #55 but w/corner design modifications.			
		a. Sign. 4.	.50	2.00	8.50
		b. Sign. 5.	.50	2.00	5.50

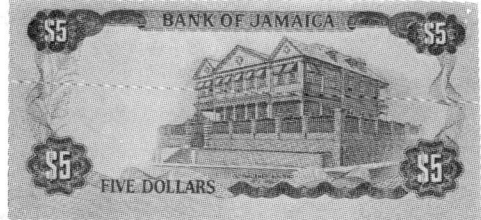

Cat. #	Denomination	Date, description	VG	VF	Unc
61	5 DOLLARS	*L.1960*. Like #57 but w/corner design modifications.			
		a. Sign. 4.	1.25	5.00	17.50
		b. Sign. 5.	.85	3.50	12.00
62	10 DOLLARS	*L.1960*. Like #58 but w/corner design modifications. Sign. 4.	3.00	12.50	40.00

Cat. #	Denomination	Date, description	VG	VF	Unc
63	20 DOLLARS	*L.1960* (1977). Maroon and m/c. N. Nethersole at l., flag at ctr. Bank of Jamaica on back. Sign. 4.	4.00	15.00	65.00

1978–84 ISSUE

Bank of Jamaica Act

#64–68 wmk: Pineapple. Printer: TDLR.

Cat. #	Denomination	Date, description	VG	VF	Unc
64	1 DOLLAR	ND (1982–86). Like #59.			
		a. Sign. 6.	.15	.50	2.50
		b. Sign. 7.	.10	.35	1.50
65	2 DOLLARS	ND (1982–86). Like #60.			
		a. Sign. 6.	.20	.65	5.00
		b. Sign. 7.	.10	.30	4.00
66	5 DOLLARS	ND (1984). Similar to #61. Sign.7.	.15	.60	6.00

Cat. #	Denomination	Date, description	VG	VF	Unc
67	10 DOLLARS	1978–81. Bluish purple on m/c unpt. Like #62.			
		a. Sign. 5. 1.10.1978; 1.10.1979.	.50	1.50	17.50
		b. Sign. 9. 1.12.1981.	.40	1.00	7.50

Cat. #	Denomination	Date, description	VG	VF	Unc
68	20 DOLLARS	1978–83. Red and m/c. Like #63.			
		a. Sign. 5. 1.10.1978; 1.10.1979; 1.10.1981.	1.00	2.50	25.00
		b. Sign. 6. 1.12.1981.	.85	2.00	20.00
		c. Sign. 7. 1.12.1983.	.75	1.25	12.50

1985 REDUCED SIZE ISSUE

#68A–76 note size: 144 x 68mm. Wmk: Pineapple. Printer: TDLR.

Cat. #	Denomination	Date, description	VG	VF	Unc
68A	1 DOLLAR	1985–90. Similar to #64; lower corner guilloches modified.			
		a. Sign. 7. 1.1.1985.	FV	FV	1.50
		b. Sign. 8. 1.3.1986; 1.2.1987; 1.9.1987.	FV	FV	1.00
		c. Sign. 9. 1.7.1989.	FV	FV	1.00
		d. Sign. 10. 1.1.1990.	FV	FV	.75

69	2 DOLLARS	1985–. Dk. green and violet on m/c unpt. Similar to #65 but lithographed. Horizontal sorting bar at r.			
		a. Sign. 7. 1.1.1985.	FV	FV	2.50
		b. Sign. 8. 1.3.1986; 1.2.1987; 1.9.1987.	FV	FV	2.00
		c. Sign. 9. 1.7.1989.	FV	FV	1.75
		d. Sign. 10. 1.1.1990; 29.5.1992.	FV	FV	1.00
		e. Sign. 11. 1.2.1993.	FV	FV	.50

#70-76 arms at bottom ctr.

70	5 DOLLARS	1985–. Similar to #66 but w/2 horizontal blue-green sorting bars at l. and r.			
		a. Sign. 7. 1.1.1985.	FV	FV	4.00
		b. Sign. 8. 1.9.1987.	FV	FV	3.00
		c. Sign. 9. 1.5.1989.	FV	FV	2.00
		d. Sign. 10. 1.7.1991; 1.8.1992.	FV	FV	.85

71	10 DOLLARS	1985–. Similar to #67 but 3 horizontal sorting bars at l. and r.			
		a. Sign. 7. 1.1.1985.	FV	FV	6.00
		b. Sign. 8. 1.9.1987.	FV	FV	5.00
		c. Sign. 9. 1.8.1989.	FV	FV	4.00
		d. Sign. 10. 1.5.1991; 1.8.1992.	FV	FV	1.50

Cat. #	Denomination	Date, description	VG	VF	Unc
72	20 DOLLARS	1985–. Red-orange, violet and black on m/c unpt. Similar to #68 but circular electronic sorting mark at l.			
		a. Sign. 7. 1.1.1985.	FV	FV	8.00
		b. Sign. 8. 1.3.1986; 1.2.1987; 1.9.1987.	FV	FV	6.00
		c. Sign. 9. 1.9.1989.	FV	FV	4.00
		d. Sign. 10.	FV	FV	2.00

1986–94 ISSUE

73	50 DOLLARS	1.8.1988. Brown, purple, red-violet on m/c unpt. S. Sharpe at l. Doctor's Cave Beach on back. Sign. 8.	FV	FV	3.50

74	100 DOLLARS	1.12.1986; 1.9.1987. Black and purple on m/c unpt. Sir D. Sangster at l. Dunn's River Falls at r. on back. Sign. 8.	FV	5.00	12.00

Cat. #	Denomination	Date, description	VG	VF	Unc
75	100 DOLLARS	1.7.1991; 1.6.1992; 1.2.1993; 1.3.1994. Like #74 but w/lilac unpt. and 2 circles at r., w/vertical orange bar. More silver waves added to both $100 on back. Sign. 10.	FV	FV	6.50

76	500 DOLLARS	1.5.1994. Purple, violet and brown on m/c unpt. Nanny of the Maroons at l. Map of islands above Fort Royal at ctr. r. on back. Sign. 12.	FV	FV	25.00
77	1000 DOLLARS				Expected new issue.

COLLECTOR SERIES

Cat. #	Date, denomination	Description	Issue Price	Mkt. Val.
CS1	1976 1-10 DOLLARS	#54–57 w/matching red star prefix serial # and SERIES 1976. (5000 sets issued).	30.00	20.00
CS2	1977 1–10 DOLLARS	#54–57 w/matching red star prefix serial # and SERIES 1977. (7500 sets issued).	29.50	15.00

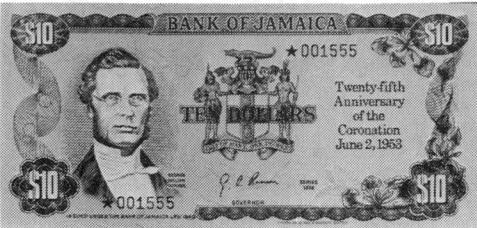

CS3	1978 1–10 DOLLARS	#54–57 in double set. One is like #CS1–2 w/ SERIES 1978 and the other w/additional ovpt: Twenty-fifth Anniversary of the Coronation June 2, 1953 and SERIES 1978 at r. All w/ matching red star prefix serial #. (6250 sets issued).	61.00	30.00

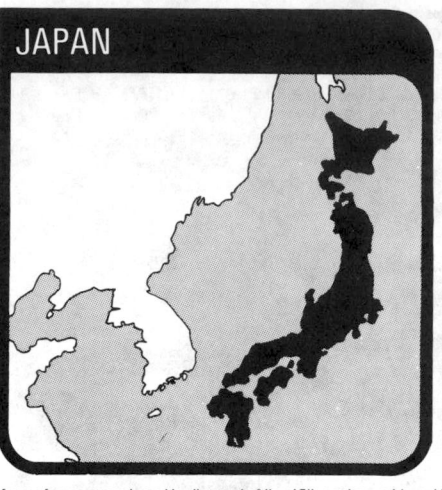

JAPAN

Japan, a constitutional monarchy situated off the east coast of Asia, has an area of 145,856 sq. mi. (377,644 sq. km.) and a population of 123.2 million. Capital: Tokyo. Japan, one of the three major industrial nations of the free world, exports machinery, motor vehicles, textiles and chemicals.

Japan, founded (so legend holds) in 660 BC by a direct descendant of the Sun Goddess, was first brought into contact with the west by a storm-blown Portuguese ship in 1542. European traders and missionaries proceeded to enlarge the contact until the Shogunate, sensing a military threat in the foreign presence, expelled all foreigners and severed relations with the outside world in the 17th century. After contact was reestablished by Commodore Perry of the U.S. Navy in 1854, Japan rapidly industrialized, abolished the Shogunate and established a parliamentary form of government, and by the end of the 19th century achieved the status of a modern economic and military power. A series of wars with China and Russia, and participation with the Allies in World War I, enlarged Japan territorially but brought its interests into conflict with the Far Eastern interests of the United States and Britain, causing it to align with the Axis powers for the pursuit of World War II. After its defeat in World War II, Japan renounced military aggression as a political instrument, established democratic self-government, and quickly reasserted its position as an economic world power.

See also Burma, China (Japanese military issues, Central Reserve Bank, Federal Reserve Bank, Hua Hsing Commercial Bank, Mengchiang Bank, Chanan Bank and Chi Tung Bank and Manchukuo), Hong Kong, Indochina, Malaya, Netherlands East Indies, Oceania, the Philippines, Korea and Taiwan.

RULERS		REIGN NAME	YEAR
Hirohito, 1926–89		Showa	1–64
Akihito, 1989–		Heisei	1–

MONETARY SYSTEM
1 Yen = 100 Sen
MONETARY UNITS

厘 Rin; 錢 Sen; 圓 or 圓 or ¥ or 円 Yen

NOTE: This section has been partially renumbered and is referenced to the old 7th Edition of General Issues

Nippon Ginko Ken 日本銀行券
Nip-pon Gin-ko Ken

Bank of Japan—Notes
1950–58 ISSUE
#90–99 w/ single or double letter serial # prefix. Issuer's name reads l. to r.

Cat. #	Denomination	Date, description	VG	VF	Unc
90	100 YEN	ND (1953). Brown-violet on green unpt. Portr. l. Taisuke at r. 12 varieties exist. Diet Bldg. at r. on back.			
		a. Single letter serial # prefix.	6.00	20.00	65.00
		b. Double letter serial # prefix. Lt. brown paper.	1.50	5.00	15.00
		c. As b, but white paper.	FV	1.50	2.50

Cat. #	Denomination	Date, description	VG	VF	Unc
91	500 YEN	ND (1951). Blue. Portr. I. Tomomi at r. Back gray and pale green; Mt. Fuji at r.			
		a. Single letter serial # prefix.	8.00	25.00	80.00
		b. Double letter serial # prefix. Cream paper	5.50	7.00	30.00
		c. As b, but white paper.	FV	5.50	11.50

92 (93)	1000 YEN	ND (1950). Black on green unpt. Portr. Shotoku-Taishi at r. Back brown and blue; Yumedono Pavilion at l.			
		a. Single letter serial # prefix.	12.00	40.00	125.00
		b. Double letter serial # prefix.	FV	15.00	45.00

93 (95)	5000 YEN	ND (1957). Green and m/c. Portr. Shotoku-Taishi at ctr. and as wmk. Back green; Bank of Japan at ctr.			
		a. Single letter serial # prefix.	FV	65.00	115.00
		b. Double letter serial # prefix.	FV	FV	70.00

94 (96)	10,000 YEN	ND (1958). Dk. brown and dk. green. Portr. Shotohu-Taishi at l. and r. in unpt. within ornate frame. Wmk: Yumedono Pavilion.			
		a. Single letter serial # prefix.	FV	125.00	200.00
		b. Double letter serial # prefix.	FV	FV	130.00

1963–69 ISSUE

Cat. #	Denomination	Date, description	VG	VF	Unc
95 (92)	500 YEN	ND (1969). Blue. Portr. I. Tomomi at r. Back steel blue; Mt. Fuji at l. ctr.			
		a. Single letter serial # prefix	FV	7.50	20.00
		b. Double letter serial # prefix.	FV	5.50	7.50

96 (94)	1000 YEN	ND (1963). Dk. green on m/c unpt. I. Hirobumi at r. and as wmk. Back brown; Bank of Japan at ctr.			
		a. Single letter serial # prefix. Black serial #.	FV	15.00	65.00
		b. As a but w/double letter serial # prefix.	FV	FV	15.00
		c. Single letter serial # prefix. Blue serial #.	FV	12.00	37.50
		d. As c but w/double letter serial # prefix.	FV	FV	13.00

1984 ISSUE

#97–99 wmk. same as portr.

97	1000 YEN	ND (1984–93). Blue and m/c. N. Soseki at r. Crane at l. and r. on back.			
		a. Single letter serial # prefix. Black serial #	FV	12.00	25.00
		b. As a but w/double letter serial # prefix.	FV	FV	13.50
		c. Single letter serial # prefix. Blue serial #.	FV	FV	20.00
		d. As c but w/double letter serial # prefix.	FV	FV	15.00

Cat. #	Denomination	Date, description	VG	VF	Unc
98	5000 YEN	ND (1984–). Violet and m/c. N. Inazo at r. Lake and Mt. Fuji at ctr. on back.			
		a. Single letter serial # prefix. Black serial #.	FV	50.00	75.00
		b. As a but w/double letter serial # prefix.	FV	FV	70.00

99	10,000 YEN	ND (1984–93). Lt. brown and m/c. F. Yuki-chi at r. Pheasant at l. and r. on back.			
		a. Single letter serial # prefix.	FV	110.00	140.00
		b. As a but w/double letter serial # prefix.	FV	FV	130.00

1993 ISSUE

#100–102 microprinting added. Wmk: Same as portr.

100	1000 YEN	ND (1993). Blue and m/c. Like #97			
		a. Single letter serial # prefix. Brown serial # (1993).	FV	FV	15.00
		b. As a but w/double letter serial # prefix.	FV	FV	12.50
101	5000 YEN	ND (1993). Violet and m/c. Like #98.			
		a. Single letter serial # prefix letter. Brown serial # (1993).	FV	FV	65.00
		b. As a but w/double letter serial # prefix.	FV	FV	60.00
102	10,000 YEN	ND (1993). Lt. brown and m/c. Like #99.			
		a. Single letter serial # prefix. Brown serial # (1993).	FV	FV	125.00
		b. As a but w/double letter serial # prefix.	FV	FV	120.00

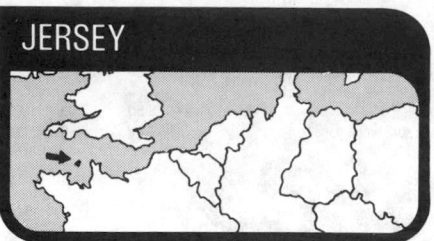

JERSEY

The Bailiwick of Jersey, a British Crown dependency located in the English Channel 12 miles (19 km.) west of Normandy, France, has an area of 45 sq. mi. (117 sq. km.) and a population of 72,691. Capital: St. Helier. The economy is based on agriculture and cattle breeding — the importation of cattle is prohibited to protect the purity of the island's world-famous strain of milk cows.

Jersey was occupied by Neanderthal man 100,000 years B.C., and by Iberians of 2000 B.C. who left their chamber tombs in the island's granite cliffs. Roman legions almost certainly visited the island although they left no evidence of settlement. The country folk of Jersey still speak an archaic form of Norman-French, lingering evidence of the Norman annexation of the island in 933 B.C. Jersey was annexed to England in 1206, 140 years after the Norman Conquest. The dependency is administered by its own laws and customs; laws enacted by the British Parliament do not apply to Jersey unless it is specifically mentioned. During World War II, German troops occupied the island from July 1, 1940 until June 6, 1944.

RULERS
British

MONETARY SYSTEM
1 Shilling = 12 Pence
1 Pound = 20 Shillings, 1877–1971
1 Pound = 100 New Pence, 1971–

REPLACEMENT NOTES
#8–10: w/Clennett sign., Z prefix. #11–19 and presumably to #23: ZB, CZ prefix letters.

States of Jersey, Treasury

SIGNATURE VARIETIES			
1	F.N. Padgham, 1963–72	4	Baird, 1993-
2	J. Clennett, 1972–83	5	
3	Leslie May, 1983–93	6	

1963 (ND) ISSUE

#7–10 Qn. Elizabeth II at r. looking l., wearing cape. Printer: TDLR.

Cat. #	Denomination	Date, description	VG	VF	Unc
7	10 SHILLINGS	ND (1963). Brown on m/c unpt. St. Ouen's Manor on back.	1.00	2.00	7.50

Cat. #	Denomination	Date, description	VG	VF	Unc
8	1 POUND	ND (1963). Green. Mont Orgueil Castle on back. 2 sign. varieties.			
		a. Sign. 1.	2.00	7.50	35.00
		b. Sign. 2.	2.00	4.50	20.00
		c. W/o sign.	15.00	30.00	75.00
		s. Specimen.	—	—	8.00
9	5 POUNDS	ND (1963). Dk. red. St. Aubin's Fort on back.			
		a. Sign. 1.	10.00	25.00	125.00
		b. Sign. 2.	8.50	12.00	30.00
		s. Specimen.	—	—	12.00

Cat. #	Denomination	Date, description	VG	VF	Unc
10	10 POUNDS	ND (1972). Purple and m/c. Back similar to #7.			
		a. Sign. 2.	18.00	25.00	55.00
		s. Specimen.	—	—	15.00

1976 (ND) ISSUE

#11–14 Qn. Elizabeth at ctr. r. looking l., wearing a tiara. #11–13 sign. varieties. Printer: TDLR.

Cat. #	Denomination	Date, description	VG	VF	Unc
11	1 POUND	ND (1976–88). Blue. Battle of Jersey scene on back.			
		a. Sign. 2.	FV	2.00	6.00
		b. Sign. 3.	FV	1.75	5.00
		s. Specimen.	—	—	5.00

Cat. #	Denomination	Date, description	VG	VF	Unc
12	5 POUNDS	ND (1976–88). Brown. Sailing ships, Elizabeth Castle on back.			
		a. Sign. 2.	FV	10.00	22.50
		b. Sign. 3.	FV	9.00	20.00
		s. Specimen.	—	—	10.00

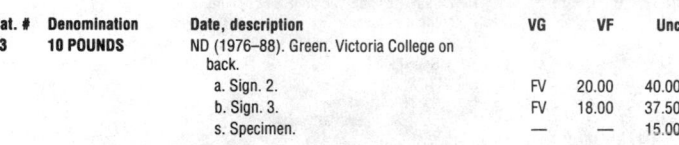

Cat. #	Denomination	Date, description	VG	VF	Unc
13	10 POUNDS	ND (1976–88). Green. Victoria College on back.			
		a. Sign. 2.	FV	20.00	40.00
		b. Sign. 3.	FV	18.00	37.50
		s. Specimen.	—	—	15.00

Cat. #	Denomination	Date, description	VG	VF	Unc
14	20 POUNDS	ND (1976–88). Red-brown. Sailing ship, Gorey Castle on back.			
		a. Sign. 2.	FV	42.50	90.00
		b. Sign. 3.	FV	35.00	85.00
		s. Specimen.	—	—	24.00

1989 (ND) ISSUE

#15–19 birds at l. corner, arms at ctr., Qn. Elizabeth II at r. facing, wearing cape. Wmk: Cow's head.

Cat. #	Denomination	Date, description	VG	VF	Unc
15	1 POUND	ND (1989). Dk. green and violet on m/c unpt. Church at l. ctr. on back.			
		a. Sign. 3.	FV	FV	4.00
		s. Specimen.	—	—	4.00

Cat. #	Denomination	Date, description	VG	VF	Unc
16	5 POUNDS	ND (1989). Rose on m/c unpt. La Corbiere lighthouse on back.			
		a. Sign. 3.	FV	FV	16.00
		s. Specimen.	—	—	8.00

17	10 POUNDS	ND (1989). Orange-brown on m/c unpt. Battle of Jersey on back.			
		a. Sign. 3.	FV	FV	35.00
		s. Specimen.	—	—	15.00

18	20 POUNDS	ND (1989). Blue on m/c unpt. St. Ouen's Manor on back.			
		a. Sign. 3.	FV	FV	67.50
		s. Specimen.	—	—	25.00

Cat. #	Denomination	Date, description	VG	VF	Unc
19	50 POUNDS	ND (1989). Dk. gray on m/c unpt. Government House on back.			
		a. Sign. 3.	FV	FV	135.00
		s. Specimen.	—	—	50.00

1993 (ND) ISSUE

#20-24 like #15-19 but w/solid color denomination at upper r. Wmk: Cow's head.

20	1 POUND	ND (1993). Like #15.			
		a. Sign. 4.	FV	FV	3.75
		s. Specimen.	—	—	4.00

21 (20)	5 POUNDS	ND (1993). Like #16.			
		a. Sign. 4.	FV	FV	12.50
		s. Specimen.	—	—	8.00

22 (21)	10 POUNDS	ND (1993). Like #17.			
		a. Sign. 4.	FV	FV	23.50
		s. Specimen.	—	—	15.00

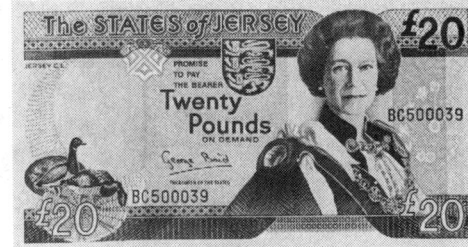

23 (22)	20 POUNDS	ND (1993). Like #18.			
		a. Sign. 4.	FV	FV	45.00
		s. Specimen.	—	—	25.00
24 (23)	50 POUNDS	ND (1993). Like #19.			
		a. Sign. 4.	FV	FV	110.00
		s. Specimen.			

1995 COMMEMORATIVE ISSUE

#25, 50th Anniversary Liberation of Jersey

Cat. #	Denomination	Date, description	VG	VF	Unc
25	1 POUND	9.5.1995. Face like #15 w/text: 50th Anniversary...at l. in wmk. area. Face and back of German Occupation 1 Pound #6 on back. Wmk: Cow's head. Sign. 4. Printer: TDLR.	FV	FV	3.50

COLLECTOR SERIES

Cat. #	Date, denomination	Description	Issue Price	Mkt. Val.
CS1	ND(1978) 1–20 POUNDS	#11a–14a w/ovpt: *SPECIMEN* and Maltese cross prefix serial #.	14.00	30.00

JORDAN

The Hashemite Kingdom of Jordan, a constitutional monarchy in southwest Asia, has an area of 37,738 sq. mi. (97,740 sq. km.) and a population of 3 million. Capital: Amman. Agriculture and tourism comprise Jordan's economic base. Chief exports are phosphates, tomatoes and oranges.

Jordan is the Edom and Moab of the time of Moses. It became part of the Roman province of Arabia in 106 AD, was conquered by the Arabs in 633–36, and was part of the Ottoman Empire from the 16th century until World War I. At that time, the regions presently known as Jordan and Israel were mandated to Great Britain by the League of Nations as Transjordan and Palestine. In 1922 Transjordan was established as the semi-autonomous Emirate of Transjordan, ruled by the Hashemite Prince Abdullah but still nominally a part of the British mandate. The mandate over Transjordan was terminated in 1946, the country becoming the independent Hashemite Kingdom of Transjordan. The kingdom was renamed the Hashemite Kingdom of The Jordan in 1950.

RULERS
Hussein I, 1952–

MONETARY SYSTEM
1 Dirham = 100 Fils
1 Dinar = 10 Dirhams, until 1993
1 Dinar = 10 Piastres, 1993–

REPLACEMENT NOTES
#9-27, jj prefix (YY).

SIGNATURE VARIETIES			
10		16	
11		17	
12		18	
13		19	
14		20	
15		21	

Central Bank of Jordan
1959 FIRST ISSUE

Law 1959

#9–12 Kg. Hussein at l. Wmk: Kg. Hussein wearing turban.

Cat. #	Denomination	Date, description	VG	VF	Unc
9	500 FILS	L.1959. Brown on m/c unpt. Forum Jerash on back. W/FIVE HUNDRED FILS at bottom margin on back. Sign. 10–12.	3.50	15.00	42.50

10	1 DINAR	L.1959. Green on m/c unpt. al-Aqsa Mosque "Dome of the Rock" at ctr. w/columns at r. on back. Sign. 10–12.	3.00	10.00	40.00

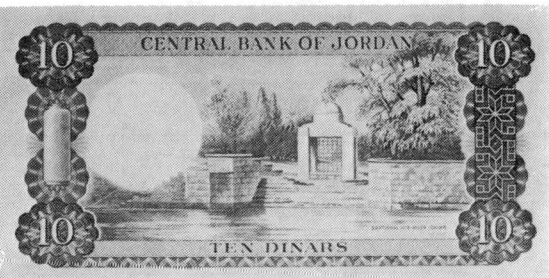

Cat. #	Denomination	Date, description	VG	VF	Unc
11	5 DINARS	L.1959. Red-brown on m/c unpt. El Hazne, Treasury of Pharaoh at Petra at ctr. r. on back. Sign. 10–12.	10.00	25.00	90.00
12	10 DINARS	L.1959. Blue-gray on m/c unpt. Baptismal site on River Jordan on back. Sign. 10; 11.	25.00	65.00	190.00

1959 SECOND ISSUE

#13–16 Kg. Hussein I at l., w/o law date 1959. Wmk: Kh. Hussein wearing turban.

13	1/2 DINAR	ND. Like #9, but w/HALF DINAR at bottom margin on back. Sign. 12–15.	1.00	3.00	13.50
14	1 DINAR	ND. Like #10. Sign. 12–15.	1.75	5.00	21.00
15	5 DINARS	ND. Like #11. Sign. 12–15.	2.25	9.00	37.50

16	10 DINARS	ND. Like #12. Sign. 12–15.	4.00	16.50	65.00

1975; 1977 ISSUE

#17–21 Kg. Hussein at l. Wmk: Kg. Hussein wearing turban.

Cat. #	Denomination	Date, description	VG	VF	Unc
17	1/2 DINAR	ND (1975–92). Brown on m/c unpt. Jerash at r. on back. Sign. 15–18.	FV	.60	3.00

18	1 DINAR	ND (1975–92). Dk. green on m/c unpt. al-Aqsa Mosque "Dome of the Rock" behind columns at r. on back. Sign. 15–18.			
		a. Sign. 15.	FV	FV	10.00
		b. Sign. 16	FV	FV	8.50
		c. Sign. 17.	FV	FV	7.50
		d. Sign. 18.	FV	FV	6.50
		e. Sign. 19.	FV	FV	4.50

19	5 DINARS	ND (1975–92). Red on m/c unpt. El Hazne, Treasury of the Pharaoh at Petra at r. on back.			
		a. Sign. 15.	FV	FV	30.00
		b. Sign. 16	FV	FV	27.50
		c. Sign. 17.	FV	FV	25.00
		d. Sign. 18.	FV	FV	22.50
		e. Sign. 19.	FV	FV	20.00

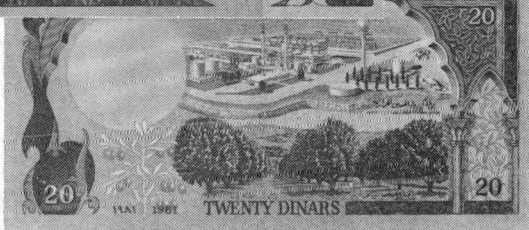

1992 ISSUE

#23–27 Kg. Hussein wearing headdress at ctr. r. and as wmk. Sign. 19.

Cat. #	Denomination	Date, description	VG	VF	Unc
20	10 DINARS	ND (1975–92). Blue on m/c unpt. Cultural palace above and amphitheater at ctr. r. on back. Sign. 15–18.			
		a. Sign. 15.	FV	FV	85.00
		b. Sign. 16.	FV	FV	65.00
		c. Sign. 17.	FV	FV	50.00
		d. Sign. 18.	FV	FV	45.00
		e. Sign. 19.	FV	FV	35.00

Cat. #	Denomination	Date, description	VG	VF	Unc
23	1/2 DINAR	AH 1412/1992. Lilac-brown and dk. brown on m/c unpt. Qusayr Amra fortress at r. on back.	FV	FV	2.50

| 21 | 20 DINARS | 1977; 1981; 1985; 1987; 1988. Deep brown on m/c unpt. Electric power station of Zerga on back. Sign. 16–18. | FV | FV | 57.50 |

| 24 | 1 DINAR | AH 1412/1992. Green on olive and m/c unpt. Ruins of Jerash at ctr. r. on back. | FV | FV | 4.50 |

1991 ISSUE

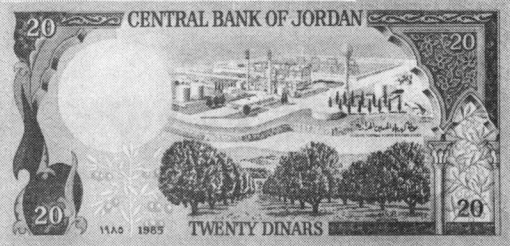

| 25 | 5 DINARS | AH 1412/1992. Red, violet-brown on m/c unpt. Treasury at Petra on back. | FV | FV | 15.00 |

| 22 | 20 DINARS | 1977 (1991); 1982 (1991); 1985 (1992). Like #21 but blue on m/c unpt. (Sign. 16; 15; 17, respectively.) | FV | FV | 65.00 |

Cat. #	Denomination	Date, description	VG	VF	Unc
26	10 DINARS	AH1412/1992. Blue, gray-violet, green on m/c unpt. al-Rabadh Castle on back.	FV	FV	27.50

27	20 DINARS	AH 1412/1992. Dk. brown, green and red-brown on m/c unpt. Dome of the Rock at l. ctr. on back.	FV	FV	50.00

1995–96 ISSUE

#27–32 w/title: *THE HASHEMITE KINGDOM KINGDOM OF JORDAN* on back.

28	1/2 DINAR	(1996).		Expected new issue.	
29	1 DINAR	AH 1415/1995. Like #24.	FV	FV	4.00
30	5 DINARS	(1996).		Expected new issue.	
31	10 DINARS	(1996).		Expected new issue.	
32	20 DINARS	(1996). Like #27.		Expected new issue.	

Listings For:

KAMPUCHEA, see Cambodia

KATANGA

Katanga, the southern province of Zaire (formerly Belgian Congo) extends northeast to Lake Tanganyika, east and south to Zambia, and west to Angola. It was inhabited by Luba and Bantu peoples, and was one of Africa's richest mining areas.

In 1960, Katanga, under the leadership of provincial president Moise Tshombe and supported by foreign mining interests, seceded from newly independent Republic of the Congo. A period of political confusion and bloody fighting involving Congolese, Belgian and United Nations forces ensued. At the end of the rebellion in 1962, Katanga was reintegrated into the republic, and was known as Shaba region.

For additional history, see Zaire.

MONETARY SYSTEM
1 Franc = 100 Centimes

GOVERNMENT

PROVISIONAL ISSUE

#1–4 w/red ovpt: *GOUVERNEMENT KATANGA* on face and back of Banque D'Emission du Rwanda et du Burundi notes.

Cat. #	Denomination	Date, description	Good	Fine	VF
1	5 FRANCS	ND (– old date 15.5.1961). Ovpt. on Rwanda & Burundi #1.	—	—	—
2	10 FRANCS	ND (– old date 15.9.1960; 5.10.1960). Ovpt. on Rwanda & Burundi #2.	—	—	—

3	20 FRANCS	ND (– old date 5.9.1960; 5.10.1960). Ovpt. on Rwanda & Burundi #3.	—	—	—

4	50 FRANCS	ND (– old date 1.10.1960). Ovpt. on Rwanda & Burundi #4.	—	—	—

Banque Nationale du Katanga

1960 ISSUE

#5–10 Moise Tshombe at r. Various dates.

Cat. #	Denomination	Date, description	VG	VF	Unc
5	10 FRANCS	1.12.1960; 15.12.1960. Lilac and yellow.			
		a. Issued note.	10.00	30.00	75.00
		b. Remainder, no serial #.	—	—	40.00

Cat. #	Denomination	Date, description	VG	VF	Unc
11	10 FRANCS	ND. Green, brown and red. Moise Tshombe at l., flag at r. Foundry on back. Printer: W&S. (Not issued).	—	—	500.00

1962 ISSUE
#12–14 wheel of masks and spears on back. Wmk: elephant. Various dates.

12	100 FRANCS	18.5.1962; 15.8.1962; 15.9.1962; 14.1.1963. Dk. green and brown on m/c unpt. Woman carrying ears of corn at r.	15.00	30.00	75.00
13	500 FRANCS	17.4.1962. Purple and m/c. Man w/fire at r.	100.00	200.00	375.00

6	20 FRANCS	21.11.1960. Blue-green.			
		a. Issued note.	12.00	35.00	85.00
		b. Remainder, no serial #.	—	—	40.00
7	50 FRANCS	10.11.1960. Brown and salmon.			
		a. Issued note.	13.50	40.00	100.00
		b. Remainder, no serial #.	—	—	60.00

14	1000 FRANCS	26.2.1962. Dk. blue, red and brown on m/c unpt. Woman carrying child on back and picking cotton at r.	50.00	100.00	250.00

8	100 FRANCS	31.10.1960. Brown, green and yellow.			
		a. Issued note.	20.00	60.00	150.00
		b. Remainder, no serial #.	—	—	75.00
9	500 FRANCS	31.10.1960. Green, violet and olive.			
		a. Issued note.	60.00	175.00	350.00
		b. Remainder, no serial #.	—	—	100.00
10	1000 FRANCS	31.10.1960. Blue and brown.			
		a. Issued note.	100.00	200.00	375.00
		b. Remainder, no serial #.	—	—	150.00

1960 (ND) ISSUE

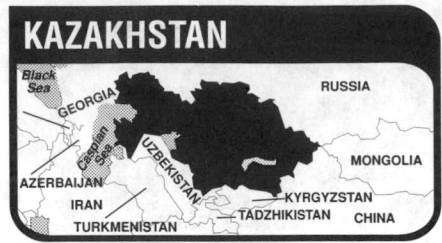

KAZAKHSTAN

The Republic of Kazakhstan (formerly Kazakhstan S.S.R.) is bordered to the west by the Caspian Sea and Russia, to the north by Russia, in the east by the Peoples Republic of China and in the south by Uzbekistan and Kirghizia and has an area of 1,049,155 sq. mi. (2,717,300 sq. km.) and a population of 16.7 million. Capital: Alma-Ata (formerly Verny). Rich in mineral resources including coal, tungsten, copper, lead, zinc and manganese with huge oil and natural gas reserves; while agriculture is important, as it was at once, 20 percent of the total acreage of the combined U.S.S.R. Non-ferrous metallurgy, heavy engineering and chemical industries are leaders in its economy.

The Kazakhs are a branch of the Turkic peoples which led the nomadic life of herdsman until WW I. In the 13th century they come under Genghis Khan's eldest son Juji and later became a part of the Golden Horde, a western Mongol empire. Around the beginning of the 16th century they were divided into 3 confederacies, known as *zhuz* or hordes, in the steppes of Turkistan. At the end of the 17th century an incursion by the Kalmucks, a remnant of the Oirat Mongol confederacy, resulted in heavy losses on both sides which facilitated Russian penetration. Resistance to Russian settlements varied throughout the 1800's, but by 1900 over 100 million acres was declared Czarist state property and used for a planned peasant colonization. After a revolution in 1905 Kazakh deputies were elected. In 1916 the tsarist government ordered mobilization of all males, between 19 and 43, for auxilary service. The Kazakhs rose in defiance which led the governor general of Turkistan to send troops against the rebels. Shortly after the Russian revolution Kazakh Nationalists asked for full autonomy. The Communist *coup d'état* of Nov. 1917 led to civil war. In 1919–20 the Red army defeated the "White" Russian forces and occupied Kazakhstan and fought against the Nationalist government formed on Nov. 17, 1917 by Ali Khan Bukey Khan. The Kazakh Autonomous Soviet Socialist Republic was proclaimed on Aug. 26, 1920 within the R.S.F.S.R. Russian and Ukrainian colonization continued while 2 purges in 1927 and 1935 quelled any Kazakh feelings of priority in the matters of their country. On Dec. 5, 1936 Kazakhstan qualified for full status as an S.S.R. and held its first congress in 1937. Independence was declared on Dec. 16, 1991 and Kazakhstan joined the C.I.S.

MONETARY SYSTEM

1 Tenge =100 Tyin = 500 Rubles (Russian), 1993 –

КАЗАКСТАН ҮЛТТЫҚ БАНКІ

Kazakstan National Bank

1993 ISSUE

#1-6 ornate denomination in circle at r. Circular arms at l. on back. Serial # at l. or lower l. for each. Wmk. paper.

Tenge System

Cat. #	Denomination	Date, description	VG	VF	Unc
1	1 TYIN	1993. Violet and blue-violet on m/c unpt.	FV	FV	.15
2	2 TYIN	1993. Blue-violet on lt. blue and m/c unpt.	FV	FV	.25
3	5 TYIN	1993. Violet on lt. blue and m/c unpt.	FV	FV	.35

Cat. #	Denomination	Date, description	VG	VF	Unc
4	10 TYIN	1993. Deep red on pink and m/c unpt.	FV	FV	.50

| 5 | 20 TYIN | 1993. Black and blue-gray on m/c unpt. | FV | FV | .65 |

| 6 | 50 TYIN | 1993. Dk. brown and black on m/c unpt. | FV | FV | .75 |

#7–15 arms at upper ctr. r. on back.
#7–9 wmk: symetrical design repeated

| 7 | 1 TENGE | 1993. Blue-black on m/c unpt. al-Farabi at ctr. r. Back lt. blue on m/c unpt; architectural drawings of mosque at l. ctr., arms at upper r. | FV | FV | .45 |

| 8 | 3 TENGE | 1993. Dk. green on m/c unpt. Suinbai at ctr. r. Mountains, forest, and river at l. ctr. on back. | FV | FV | .85 |

Cat. #	Denomination	Date, description	VG	VF	Unc
9	5 TENGE	1993. Dk. brown-violet on m/c unpt. Kurmangazy at ctr. r. Cemetary at l. ctr. on back.	FV	FV	1.25

Cat. #	Denomination	Date, description	VG	VF	Unc
13	100 TENGE	1993. Purple and kd. blue on m/c unpt. Abylai Khan at ctr. r. and as wmk. Domed bldg. at l. ctr. on back.	FV	FV	5.50

#14–16 al-Farabi at r. and as wmk.

14	200 TENGE	1993. Red and brown on m/c unpt. Domes of bldg. at l. on back.	FV	FV	10.00
15	500 TENGE	1994. Blue-black and violet on m/c unpt. Ancient bldg. on back.	FV	FV	22.50
16	1000 TENGE	1994. Deep green, red and orange on m/c unpt. Ancient bldg. on back.	FV	FV	40.00

10	10 TENGE	1993. Dk. green on m/c unpt. Shoqan Valikhanov at ctr. r. and as wmk. Mountains, forest, and lake at l. ctr. on back.	FV	FV	2.00

11	20 TENGE	1993. Brown on m/c unpt. A. Kunanbrev at ctr. r. and as wmk. Equestrian hunter at l. ctr. on back.	FV	FV	2.50

12	50 TENGE	1993. Red-brown and deep violet on m/c unpt. Abilkhair Khan at ctr. r. and as wmk. Native artwork at l. ctr. on back.	FV	FV	3.50

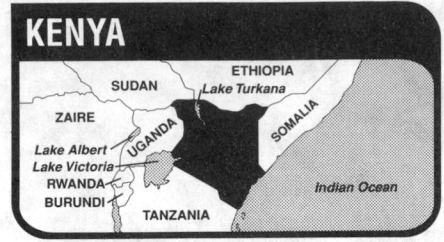

KENYA

SUDAN
ETHIOPIA
Lake Turkana
ZAIRE
SOMALIA
UGANDA
Lake Albert
Lake Victoria
RWANDA
BURUNDI
TANZANIA
Indian Ocean

The Republic of Kenya, located on the east coast of Central Africa, has an area of 224,961 sq. mi. (582,646 sq. km.) and a population of 25.9 million. Capital: Nairobi. The predominantly agricultural country exports coffee, tea and petroleum products.

The Arabs came to the coast of Kenya in the 8th century and established posts to conduct an ivory and slave trade. The Portuguese, the inveterate wanderers of the Age of Exploration, followed in the 16th century. After a lengthy and bitter struggle with the sultans of Zanzibar who controlled much of the southeastern coast of Africa, the Portuguese were driven away (late 17th century) and for many years Kenya was simply a port of call on the route to India. German and British interests in the 19th century produced agreements defining their respective spheres of influence. The British sphere was administrated by the Imperial East Africa Co. until 1895, when the British government purchased the company's rights in the East Africa Protectorate which in 1920, was designated as Kenya Colony and protectorate — the latter being a 10-mile wide coastal strip together with Mombasa, Lamu and other small islands nominally retained by the Sultan of Zanzibar. Kenya achieved self-government in June of 1963 as a consequence of the 1952–60 Mau Mau terrorist campaign to secure land reforms and political rights for Africans. Independence was attained on Dec. 12, 1963. Kenya became a republic in 1964. It is a member of the Commonwealth of Nations. The president is Chief of State and Head of Government.

Notes of the East African Currency Board were in use during the first years.

RULERS
British to 1964

MONETARY SYSTEM
1 Shilling (shilingi) = 100 Cents

REPLACEMENT NOTES
#24-30, ZZ prefix.

REPUBLIC
Central Bank of Kenya
1966 ISSUE
#1–5 M. Jomo Kenyatta at l. Values also in Arabic numerals and letters. Various dates. Wmk: Lion's head.

Cat. #	Denomination	Date, description	VG	VF	Unc
1	5 SHILLINGS	1966–68. Brown on m/c unpt. Woman picking coffee beans at r. on back.			
		a. 1.7.1966.	2.00	7.00	35.00
		b. 1.7.1967; 1.7.1968.	2.50	8.00	37.50

2	10 SHILLINGS	1966–68. Green on m/c unpt. Tea pickers in field on back.			
		a. 1.7.1966.	3.00	10.00	60.00
		b. 1.7.1967; 1.7.1968.	4.00	12.50	65.00

Cat. #	Denomination	Date, description	VG	VF	Unc
3	20 SHILLINGS	1966–68. Blue on m/c unpt. Plants and train w/sisal on back.			
		a. 1.7.1966.	6.00	30.00	125.00
		b. 1.7.1967; 1.7.1968.	6.00	30.00	125.00

4	50 SHILLINGS	1966–68. Dk. brown on m/c unpt. Cotton picking below Mt. Kenya on back.			
		a. 1.7.1966.	90.00	250.00	550.00
		b. 1.7.1967; 1.7.1968.	95.00	275.00	600.00

5	100 SHILLINGS	1966; 1968. Purple on m/c unpt. Workers at pineapple plantation on back.			
		a. 1.7.1966.	25.00	70.00	350.00
		b. 1.7.1968.	25.00	75.00	400.00

1969 ISSUE
#6–10 M. Jomo Kenyatta at l., values w/o Arabic numerals and letters. Different text at lower ctr. Sign. varieties. Wmk: Lion's head.

6	5 SHILLINGS	1.7.1969–1.7.1973. Brown. Similar to #1.	1.00	3.50	12.50
7	10 SHILLINGS	1.7.1969–1.7.1974. Green. Similar to #2.	2.00	5.00	25.00
8	20 SHILLINGS	1.7.1969–1.7.1973. Blue. Similar to #3.	3.00	10.00	75.00

Cat. #	Denomination	Date, description	VG	VF	Unc
9	50 SHILLINGS	1.7.1969; 1.7.1971. Dk. brown. Similar to #4.	90.00	250.00	600.00
10	100 SHILLINGS	1.7.1969–1.7.1973. Purple. Similar to #5.	10.00	45.00	150.00

1974 ISSUE

#11–14 M. Jomo Kenyatta at l., values indistinct or barely visible at bottom l. corners. Various date and sign. varieties. Wmk: Lion's head.

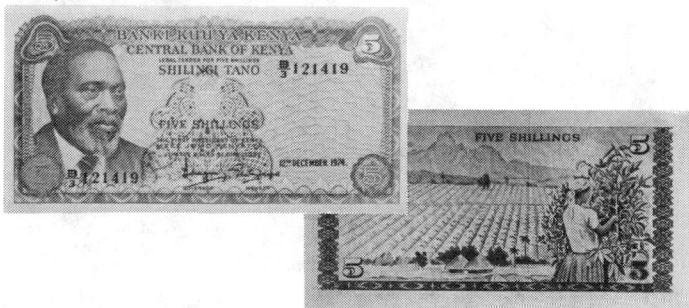

11	5 SHILLINGS	12.12.1974; 1.1.1975; 1.7.1976; 1.7.1977. Brown-orange on m/c unpt. Woman picking coffee beans on back.	.50	1.75	5.00

12	10 SHILLINGS	1.1.1975; 1.7.1976; 1.7.1977. Dk. green and dk. brown on m/c unpt. Cattle on back.	1.00	3.00	9.00

13	20 SHILLINGS	12.12.1974; 1.1.1975; 1.7.1976; 1.7.1977. Blue-black and blue on m/c unpt. Lions on back.	2.00	6.00	22.50

14	100 SHILLINGS	12.12.1974; 1.1.1975; 1.7.1976; 1.7.1977. Violet, dk. brown and dk. blue on m/c unpt. Kenyatta statue and tower on back. 153 x 79mm.	7.50	25.00	60.00

1978 ISSUE

#15–18 M. Jomo Kenyatta at l., w/English value in 3rd line only on face. Wmk: Lion's head.

Cat. #	Denomination	Date, description	VG	VF	Unc
15	5 SHILLINGS	1.7.1978. Brown-orange on m/c unpt.. Similar to #11. W/English value on face in third line only.	.50	1.25	3.00
16	10 SHILLINGS	1.7.1978. Dk. green and dk. brown on m/c unpt. Similar to #12.	1.00	2.00	5.00
17	20 SHILLINGS	1.7.1978. Blue-black and blue on m/c unpt. Similar to #13.	1.50	3.50	8.00
18	100 SHILLINGS	1.7.1978. Violet, dk. brown and dk. blue on m/c unpt. Similar to #14 but w/different colors in guilloches. 157 x 81mm.	3.50	10.00	20.00

NOTE: #15-18 were withdrawn soon after Kenyatta's death. A shortage of currency resulted in a limited reissue during Dec. 1993 – Jan. 1994 of mostly circulated notes.

1980–81 ISSUE

#19–23 arms at ctr., Pres. Daniel T.A. Moi at r. Wmk: Lion's head.

19	5 SHILLINGS	1.1.1981; 1.1.1982; 1.7.1984. Brown and m/c. 3 rams w/giraffes and mountain in background on back.	FV	.75	3.00

20	10 SHILLINGS	1.1.1981–1.7.1988. Green and m/c. 2 cows at l., 2 schoolchildren drinking milk at ctr. on back.	FV	.50	3.00

Cat. #	Denomination	Date, description	VG	VF	Unc
21	20 SHILLINGS	1.1.1981–1.7.1987. Blue and m/c. 4 women reading newspaper at ctr. on back.	FV	1.50	5.50

Cat. #	Denomination	Date, description	VG	VF	Unc
25	20 SHILLINGS	1988–92. Dk. blue, violet and dk. green on m/c unpt. Moi International Sports Complex on back.			
		a. 12.12.1988.	1.35	4.00	12.50
		b. 1.7.1989; 1.7.1990.	.50	1.60	4.00
		c. 1.7.1991; 2.1.1992.	FV	1.00	3.00

NOTE: #25 dated 12.12.1988 is believed to be a commemorative for the 25th anniversary of independence.

22	50 SHILLINGS	1.6.1980; 1.7.1985; 14.9.1986; 1.7.1987; 1.7.1988. Dk. red and m/c. Back olive; jet aircraft flying over Jomo Kenyatta airport.	FV	2.50	7.00

23	100 SHILLINGS	1.6.1980–1.7.1988. Purple and m/c. Kenyatta statue, tower and mountains on back.	2.50	5.00	12.50

26	50 SHILLINGS	10.10.1990; 1.7.1992. Red-brown on m/c unpt. Back green; modern bldgs. at l.	1.25	2.50	7.50

1986–90 ISSUES

#24–30 arms at l. ctr., Pres. D. T. A. Moi at r. Wmk: Lion's head.

24	10 SHILLINGS	1989–. Dk. green, dk. blue and brown on m/c unpt. University at l. ctr. on back.			
		a. 14.10.1989; 1.7.1990.	.25	.75	2.00
		b. 1.7.1991; 2.1.1992.	FV	.50	1.50
		c. 1.7.1993; 1.1.1994.	FV	FV	1.25

27	100 SHILLINGS	1989–. Purple, dk. green and red on m/c unpt. Monument to 25th anniversary of independence w/Mt. Kenya on back.			
		a. 14.10.1989; 1.7.1991.	2.75	3.00	8.00
		b. 2.1.1992.	FV	3.00	7.50
		c. 1.7.1992; 1.1.1994.	FV	3.00	7.50

Cat. #	Denomination	Date, description	VG	VF	Unc
28	200 SHILLINGS	14.9.1986; 1.7.1987; 1.7.1988. Brown on m/c unpt. Triangle in lower l. border. No silvering on value at upper r. Fountain at ctr. on back.	FV	FV	20.00

Cat. #	Denomination	Date, description	VG	VF	Unc
31	20 SHILLINGS	14.9.1993; 1.1.1994. Similar to #25 but w/roses added to l. border, vertical red serial #, engraved date and m/c symmetrical design below upper border. Male runner and other artistic enhancements on back.	FV	FV	2.25

			VG	VF	Unc
29	200 SHILLINGS	1989–. Similar to #28 but rose replaces colored triangle to r. of *200* at lower l. Additional silver diamond design under *200* at upper r. Vertical serial # at l.			
		a. 1.7.1989; 1.7.1990.	FV	FV	11.00
		b. 2.1.1992.	FV	FV	11.00
		c. 1.7.1992; 14.9.1993; 1.1.1994.	FV	FV	11.00

			VG	VF	Unc
32	1000 SHILLINGS	12.12.1994. Brown and violet on m/c unpt. Pres. D. T. A. Moi at l. ctr., arms at upper r. Water buffalo, elephants and bird on back. Wmk: Lion's head.	FV	FV	40.00

			VG	VF	Unc
30	500 SHILLINGS	1988–. Black, deep green and red on m/c unpt. Roses at l. Modern bldg., Mt. Kenya on back.			
		a. 14.10.1988.	FV	16.50	50.00
		b. 1.7.1990–1.1.1995.	FV	FV	27.50

1993–94 ISSUE

Listings For:

KHMER REPUBLIC, see Cambodia

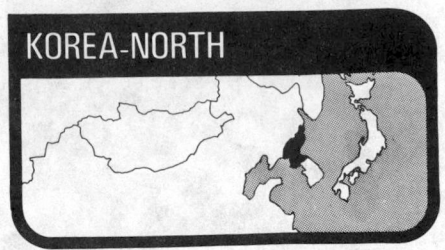

KOREA-NORTH

The Democratic Peoples Republic of Korea, situated in northeastern Asia on the northern half of the Korean peninsula between the Peoples Republic of China and the Republic of Korea, has an area of 46,540 sq. mi. (120,538 sq. km.) and a population of 22.4 million. Capital: Pyongyang. The economy is based on heavy industry and agriculture. Metals, minerals and farm produce are exported.

Japan replaced China as the predominant foreign influence in Korea in 1895 and annexed the peninsular country in 1910. Defeat in World War II brought an end to Japanese rule. U.S. troops entered Korea from the south and Soviet forces entered from the north. The Cairo conference (1943) had established that Korea should be "free and independent." The Potsdam conference (1945) set the 38th parallel as the line dividing the occupation forces of the United States and Russia. When Russia refused to permit a U.N. commission designated to supervise reunification elections to enter North Korea, an election was held in South Korea which established the Republic of Korea on Aug. 15, 1948. North Korea held an unsupervised election on Aug. 25, 1948, and on the following day proclaimed the establishment of the Democratic Peoples Republic of Korea.

MONETARY SYSTEM
1 Won = 100 Chon

DEMOCRATIC PEOPLES REPUBLIC

Korean Central Bank

1959 ISSUE

Cat. #	Denomination	Date, description	VG	VF	Unc
12	50 CHON	1959. Blue. Arms at upper l.	.15	.50	2.00

13	1 WON	1959. Red-brown. Fishing boat at ctr.	.15	.50	2.00

14	5 WON	1959. Green and m/c. Lg. bldg. at ctr.	.15	.40	2.00

Cat. #	Denomination	Date, description	VG	VF	Unc
15	10 WON	1959. Red and m/c. Pagoda at ctr. r. Woman picking fruit on back.	.20	.50	2.00

16	50 WON	1959. Purple and m/c. Bridge and city at ctr. Woman w/wheat on back.	.20	.50	2.00

17	100 WON	1959. Green and m/c. Train w/fuel at loading area at ctr. River w/cliffs on back.	.25	.75	3.00

1978 ISSUE

#18–22, arms.

18	1 WON	1978. Green and m/c. 2 adults and 2 children at ctr. Back purple and m/c. Soldier at l., woman w/flowers at ctr., woman at r.			
		a. Red and black serial #. No seal on back.	.20	.60	2.50
		b. Black serial #. Green seal at l. on back.	.25	.75	3.00
		c. Red serial #. Red seal at l. on back.	.20	.60	2.50
		d. Red serial #. Lg. numeral 1 in red guilloche on back.	.20	.60	2.50
		e. Black serial #. Lg. number 1 in blue guilloche on back.	.35	1.00	4.00

Cat. #	Denomination	Date, description	VG	VF	Unc
21	50 WON	1978. Olive and m/c. Soldier w/man holding torch, woman w/wheat, man w/book at ctr. Lake scene on back.			
		a. Red and black serial #. No seal on back.	.50	1.50	6.00
		b. Black serial #. Green seal at lower r. on back.	.35	1.10	4.50
		c. Red serial #. Red seal at lower r. on back.	.35	1.10	4.50
		d. Red serial #. Lg. numeral 50 in red guilloche on back.	.50	1.50	6.00
		e. Black serial #. Lg. numeral 50 in blue guilloche on back.	.50	1.50	6.00

Cat. #	Denomination	Date, description	VG	VF	Unc
19	5 WON	1978. Blue-gray and m/c. Worker w/book and gear, and woman w/wheat at ctr. Mt Gumgang on back.			
		a. Red and black serial #. No seal on back.	.25	.75	3.00
		b. Black serial #. Green seal at l. on back.	.25	.85	3.50
		c. Red serial #. Red seal at l. on back.	.25	.85	3.50
		d. Red serial #. Lg. numeral 5 in red guilloche on back.	.25	.85	3.50
		e. Black serial #. Lg. numeral 5 in blue guilloche on back.	.25	.85	3.50

			VG	VF	Unc
22	100 WON	1978. Purple and m/c. Kim Il Sung at ctr. r. House w/trees on back. Red and black serial #. No seal on back.	.75	2.50	10.00

NOTE: Circulation of above varieties #18–21: a., for general circulation; b., for Socialist visitors; c., for non-Socialist visitors; d. replaced a., and e., not known.

1988 ISSUE

#23–26 have arms at upper l. on face; red serial #. 'Value' backs.

Cat. #	Denomination	Date, description	VG	VF	Unc
23	1 CHON	1988. Blue on purple unpt.	.10	.20	.40
24	5 CHON	1988. Blue on pink unpt.	.15	.25	.50
25	10 CHON	1988. Blue and black on green-yellow unpt.	.20	.40	.75
26	50 CHON	1988. Blue on yellow unpt.	.25	.50	1.00

Cat. #	Denomination	Date, description	VG	VF	Unc
20	10 WON	1978. Brown and m/c. Winged equestrian statue 'Chonllima' at ctr. Waterfront factory on back.			
		a. Red and black serial #. No seal on back.	.40	1.25	5.00
		b. Black serial #. Green seal at upper r. on back.	.30	1.00	4.00
		c. Red serial #. Red seal at upper r. on back.	.30	1.00	4.00
		d. Red serial #. Lg. numeral 10 in red guilloche on back.	.30	1.00	4.00
		e. Black serial #. Lg. numeral 10 in blue guilloche on back.	.30	1.00	4.00

#27–30, dk. green on blue and pink unpt. w/winged equestrian statue. "Chonllima" at ctr., arms at upper r. Red serial #.

			VG	VF	Unc
27	1 WON	1988.	.30	.75	2.50

			VG	VF	Unc
28	5 WON	1988.	.40	1.50	7.50
29	10 WON	1988.	.75	3.00	12.50
30	50 WON	1988.	1.50	8.00	40.00

1988 SOCIALIST VISITOR ISSUE

#31–38, arms at upper r. Denomination on back. Black serial #.

			VG	VF	Unc
31	1 CHON	1988. Red-brown on pink and blue unpt.	FV	FV	1.25

Cat. #	Denomination	Date, description	VG	VF	Unc
32	5 CHON	1988. Purple on pink and blue unpt.	FV	FV	1.75
33	10 CHON	1988. Olive-green on pink and blue unpt.	FV	FV	2.50
34	50 CHON	1988. Brown-violet on pink and blue unpt.	FV	FV	3.00

#35–38 red on blue and ochre unpt. Temple at ctr., olive sprig on globe on r. Olive sprig on globe on back.

35	1 WON	1988.		FV	FV	3.50
36	5 WON	1988.		FV	FV	12.50
37	10 WON	1988.		FV	FV	25.00
38	50 WON	1988.		FV	FV	100.00

1992 ISSUE

#39–42 arms at upper l. Wmk: Winged Equestrian statue "Chonllima".

39	1 WON	1992. Grayish olive-green and olive-brown on m/c unpt. Young woman w/flower basket at ctr. r. Mt. Gumgang on back.	FV	FV	1.50

40	5 WON	1992. Blue-black and deep purple on m/c unpt. Students at ctr. r. w/modern bldg. and factory in background. Palace on back.	FV	FV	4.00

41	10 WON	1992. Deep brown and red-brown on m/c unpt. Factory worker, winged equestrian statue "Chonllima" at ctr., factories in background at r. Flood gates on back.	FV	FV	7.50

Cat. #	Denomination	Date, description	VG	VF	Unc
42	50 WON	1992. Deep brown and deep olive-brown on m/c unpt. Monument to 5 year plan at l. and as wmk., young professionals at ctr. r., arms at upper r. Landscape of pine trees and mountains on back.	FV	FV	35.00

Cat. #	Denomination	Date, description	Good	Fine	XF
43	100 WON	1992. Deep brown and brown-violet on m/c unpt. Arms at lower l. ctr., Kim Il Sung at r. Rural home at ctr. on back. Wmk: Arched gateway.	FV	FV	65.00

COLLECTOR SERIES

Cat. #	Date, denomination,	Description	Issue Price	Mkt. Val.
CS1	1978 1-100 WON.	Red ovpt. Korean characters for specimen on #18a–22a (w/all zero serial #).	—	30.00

| CS2 | 1992 1-100 WON. | Red, rectangular ovpt. Korean characters for specimen on #39–43. (39, 42 and 43 all zero serial #, 40–41 w/normal serial #). | — | 50.00 |

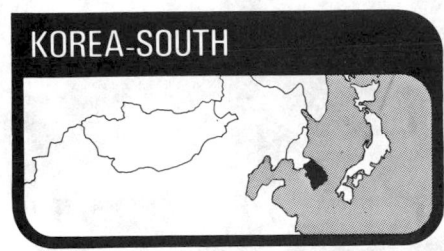

KOREA-SOUTH

The Republic of Korea, situated in northeastern Asia on the southern half of the Korean peninsula between North Korea and the Korean Strait, has an area of 38,025 sq. mi. (98,484 sq. km.) and a population of 43.27 million. Capital: Seoul. The economy is based on agriculture and textiles. Clothing, plywood and textile products are exported.

Japan replaced China as the predominant foreign influence in Korea in 1895 and annexed the peninsular country in 1910. Defeat in World War II brought an end to Japanese rule. U.S. troops entered Korea from the south and Soviet forces entered from the north. The Cairo Conference (1943) had established that Korea should be "free and independent." The Potsdam Conference (1954) set the 38th parallel as the line dividing the occupation forces of the United States and Russia. When Russia refused to permit a U.N. commission designated to supervise reunification elections to enter North Korea, an election was held in South Korea on May 10, 1948. By its determination, the Republic of Korea was inaugurated on Aug. 15, 1948.

MONETARY SYSTEM

1 Won (Hwan) = 100 Chon
1 new Won = 10 old Hwan, 1962–

DATING

The modern notes of Korea are dated according to the founding of the first Korean dynasty, that of the house of Tangun, in 2333 BC.

REPLACEMENT NOTES

#3: H prefix. #13–15: D prefix and no suffix letter. #30-32, 34, 36–37, sm. crosslet design in front of serial #. #35, 38, 38A, 39, 43-49: notes w/first digit 9 in serial number.

Bank of Korea

Hwan System

1960–61 ISSUE

				VG	VF	Unc
25	1000 HWAN	4293 (1960); 4294 (1961); 1962. Black on olive unpt. Kg. Sejong the Great at r. Back blue-green and lt. brown; flaming torch at ctr.		1.50	7.50	45.00

| 26 | 500 HWAN | 4294 (1961). Blue-green on m/c unpt. Kg. Sejong the Great at r. Back green; bldg. at r. 8-character imprint. | | 10.00 | 60.00 | 300.00 |

Cat. #	Denomination	Date, description	VG	VF	Unc
27	100 HWAN	1962. Green on orange and m/c unpt. Woman reading to child at r. Archway at l., date at bottom r. margin on back.	12.50	50.00	250.00

Currency Reform

1 new Won = 10 old Hwan

1962 ISSUE

28	10 JEON	1962. Deep blue on pale blue and pink unpt.	.05	.10	.50

29	50 JEON	1962. Black on pale green and ochre unpt.	.05	.10	.50

30	1 WON	ND (1962). Violet on brown unpt.	.05	.10	1.00

31	5 WON	ND (1962). Black on gray-green unpt.	.10	.25	1.50

32	10 WON	ND (1962). Brown on green unpt.	.35	1.00	6.00

Cat. #	Denomination	Date, description	VG	VF	Unc
33	10 WON	1962–65; ND. Brown on lilac and green unpt. Tower at l. Medieval tortoise warship at ctr. on back.			
		a. Date at lower r. on back.	1.65	5.50	47.50
		b. W/o date at lower r. on back.	.15	.75	2.25

34	50 WON	ND (1962). Red-brown on blue and lilac unpt. Rock in the sea at l. Torch at ctr. on back.	2.00	7.00	45.00

35	100 WON	1962–65. Green on olive unpt. Archway at l. Unpt: *100 Won* at ctr. Pagoda and date on back.	1.00	6.00	48.50

36	100 WON	ND (1962). Green on blue and gold unpt. Archway similar to #35 at l. Unpt. 5-petaled blossom at ctr. Back like #34.	2.00	10.00	55.00
37	500 WON	ND (1962). Blue on lilac and green unpt. Pagoda portal at l. Back like #34.	4.00	17.50	85.00

38	100 WON	ND (1965). Dk. green. Bank name and denomination in red. Kg. Sejong the Great at r. Bldg. on back.	.65	1.75	7.50

Cat. #	Denomination	Date, description	VG	VF	Unc
38A	100 WON	ND (1965). Dk. blue-green. Bank name and denomination in maroon. Like #38.	.75	2.25	10.00

39	500 WON	ND (1966). Gray on m/c unpt. City gate at l. Medieval tortoise warships on back.	.75	1.50	6.00

40	50 WON	ND (1969). Black on green and brown unpt. Pavilion at l. Back blue; torch at ctr.	.25	1.00	4.00

41	5000 WON	ND (1972). Brown on green and m/c unpt. Yi I at r. Lg. bldg. on back.	7.50	12.50	40.00

Cat. #	Denomination	Date, description	VG	VF	Unc
42	10,000 WON	ND (1973). Dk. brown and m/c. Kg. Sejong the Great at l. ctr. Bldgs. and pavilion on back.	15.00	25.00	60.00

Cat. #	Denomination	Date, description	VG	VF	Unc
47	1000 WON	ND (1983). Purple on m/c unpt. Yi Hwang at r. One raised colored dot for blind at lower l. Bldgs. in courtyard on back.	FV	FV	4.00

| 43 | 500 WON | ND (1973). Blue and m/c. Adm. Yi Sun-shin at l., medieval tortoise warship at ctr. Bldg. w/steps on back. | FV | 1.00 | 3.00 |

| 48 | 5000 WON | ND (1983). Brown on m/c unpt. Yi I at r. Two raised colored dots for blind at lower l. Sm. bldg. w/steps on back. | FV | FV | 13.00 |

| 44 | 1000 WON | ND (1975). Purple and m/c. Yi Hwang at r. Do-San Academy in black on back. | FV | 2.00 | 6.00 |
| 45 | 5000 WON | ND (1977). Brown on m/c unpt. Yi I at r. Sm. bldg. w/steps on back. | FV | 8.50 | 20.00 |

| 49 | 10,000 WON | ND (1983). Dk. green on m/c unpt. Monument at l; Kg. Sejong at r. Three raised colored dots for blind at lower l. Pavilion at ctr. on back. | FV | FV | 24.00 |

AUXILIARY MILITARY PAYMENT CERTIFICATE COUPONS

Issued to Korean troops in Vietnam to facilitate their use of United States MPC. These coupons could not be used as currency by themselves.

SERIES I

#M1–M8 were issued on Dec. 29, 1969, and were valid only until June or Oct. 7, 1970. Anchor on glove crest. Validation stamp on back. Uniface.

| 46 | 10,000 WON | ND (1979). Black, dk. green and m/c. Monument at l., Kg. Sejong at r. Pavilion at ctr. on back. | FV | 20.00 | 40.00 |

1983 ISSUE

Cat. #	Denomination	Date, description	VG	VF	Unc
M1	5 CENTS	ND (1969). Maroon, red-brown and yellow ctr. Flowering branch at l., lg. *5* at r.	90.00	225.00	—
M2	10 CENTS	ND (1969). Dk. blue w/lt. blue-green ctr. Flowers at l., lg. *10* at. r.	90.00	225.00	—
M3	25 CENTS	ND (1969). Brown and yellow ctr. Flower at l., lg. *25* at r.	—	—	—
M4	50 CENTS	ND (1969). Green and yellow ctr. Flower at l., lg. *50* at r.	—	—	—
M5	1 DOLLAR	ND (1969). Brown and yellow ctr. Korean flag at l., lg. *1* at r.	—	—	—
M6	5 DOLLARS	ND (1969). Blue and turquoise ctr. Flowers at l., lg. *5* at r.	—	—	—
M7	10 DOLLARS	ND (1969). Brown and yellow ctr. Flowers at l.	—	—	—
M8	20 DOLLARS	ND (1969). Green and yellow ctr. Flowers at l.	—	—	—

SERIES II

#M9–M16 were issued June (or Oct.) 1970. Anchor aymbol ctr., 702 at l., lg. denomination numerals r. Fact and back similar.

M9	5 CENTS	ND (1970). Maroon and violet on ochre unpt. Space capsule at l.	20.00	65.00	200.00

M10	10 CENTS	ND (1970). Red and yellow on green paper. Flowers at l. Back red.	30.00	90.00	275.00

M11	25 CENTS	ND (1970). Green and blue. Crown at l.	90.00	225.00	—

M12	50 CENTS	ND (1970). Blue and green. Pottery w/legs at l.	90.00	225.00	—
M13	1 DOLLAR	ND (1970). Maroon and red on lt. green paper. Torch at l.	—	—	—
M14	5 DOLLARS	ND (1970). Red, ochre and yellow on lt. blue paper. Holed coin at l.	—	—	—
M15	10 DOLLARS	ND (1970). Blue on yellow paper. Pagoda at l.	—	—	—
M16	20 DOLLARS	ND (1970). Green on pink paper. Vignette at l.	—	—	—

SERIES III

#M17–M24, military symbol in circle at ctr. on face.

Cat. #	Denomination	Date, description	VG	VF	Unc
M17	5 CENTS	ND. Brown and maroon on yellow paper. "5" at l., clam shell and pearl at ctr. Kettle on back.	20.00	65.00	200.00
M18	10 CENTS	ND. Blue w/green tint. "10" at l., snail at ctr. Candle holder on back.	30.00	75.00	275.00

M19	25 CENTS	ND. Red. lilac and ochre. "25" at l., crest seal on turtle at r. Back pink; archway at r.	90.00	225.00	—
M20	50 CENTS	ND. Green and blue. "50" at l., tiger at ctr. Balancing rock on back.	90.00	225.00	—

M21	1 DOLLAR	ND. Brown and maroon. Flowers at l. Shrine on back.			

 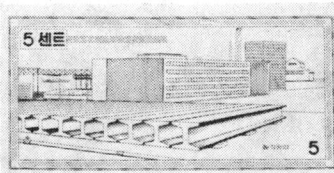

M22	5 DOLLARS	ND. Blue and lt. blue on yellow paper. Bush at l., crest seal on rayed cloud at r. Tower at ctr. on back.	—	—	—
M23	10 DOLLARS	ND. Yellow and maroon. Pagoda on face. Turtle boat on back.			
M24	20 DOLLARS	ND. 2 dragons at ctr. Korean house on back.			

SERIES IV

#M25–M32, Korean warrior at ctr. on face.

M25	5 CENTS	ND. Pink, deep green and lt. blue. Beams and steel mill at ctr. on back.	20.00	40.00	185.00

M26	10 CENTS	ND. Deep green on yellow-green. Modern city complex on back. Thick or thin paper.	20.00	40.00	185.00
M27	25 CENTS	ND. Yellow and maroon. 2 bridges on back.	60.00	200.00	—
M28	50 CENTS	ND. Blue-green and maroon. Back blue-green and red; dam.	90.00	225.00	—

Cat. #	Denomination	Date, description	VG	VF	Unc
M29	1 DOLLAR	ND. Green on lt. green unpt. Oil refinery on back.	35.00	100.00	250.00

| M30 | 5 DOLLARS | ND. Brown on gold unpt. Back red-orange; natural gas tank. | 350.00 | 700.00 | — |

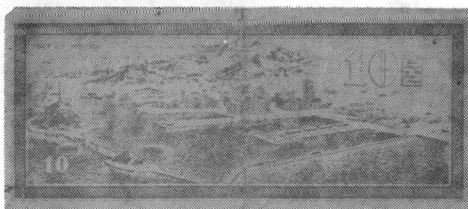

| M31 | 10 DOLLARS | ND. Pink and green. Back pink and blue; loading area at docks. | 60.00 | 200.00 | — |
| M32 | 20 DOLLARS | ND. Blue and purple. Back green; 4-lane superhighway. | — | — | — |

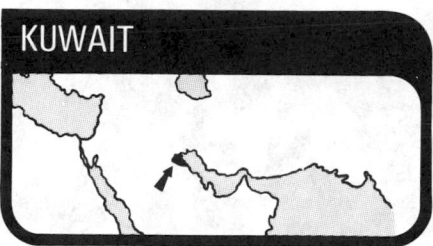

KUWAIT

The State of Kuwait, a constitutional monarchy located on the Arabian Peninsula at the north-western corner of the Persian Gulf, has an area of 6,880 sq. mi. (17,818 sq. km.) and a population of 2.1 million. Capital: Kuwait. Petroleum, the basis of the economy, provides 95 per cent of the exports.

The modern history of Kuwait began with the founding of the men who wandered northward from the region of the Qatar Peninsula of eastern Arabia. Fearing that the Turks would take over the sheikhdom, Shaikh Mubarak entered into an agreement with Great Britain, 1899, placing Kuwait under the protection of Britain and empowering Britain to conduct its foreign affairs. Britain terminated the protectorate on June 19, 1961, giving Kuwait its independence (by a simple exchange of notes) but agreeing to furnish military aid on request.

The Kuwait dinar, one of the world's strongest currencies, is backed 100 percent by gold and foreign exchange holdings.

On Aug. 2, 1990 Iraqi forces invaded and rapidly overran Kuwaiti forces. Annexation by Iraq was declared on Aug. 8. The Kuwaiti government established itself in exile in Saudi Arabia. The United Nations forces attacked on Feb. 24, 1991 and Kuwait City was liberated on Feb. 26. Iraq quickly withdrew remaining forces.

RULERS

British to 1961
Abdullah, 1961–1965
Sabah Ibn Salim Al Sabah, 1965–1977
Jabir Ibn Ahmad Al Sabah, 1977–

MONETARY SYSTEM

1 Dinar = 1000 Fils

SIGNATURE VARIETIES			
1	Amir H. Sheik Jaber Al-Ahmad		
	BANK GOVERNOR	FINANCE MINISTER	
2	Hamza Abbas	Abdul Rehman Al Atiquei	6 Salem Abdul Aziz Al Sabah / Jassem Mohammad Al Kharafi
3	Hamza Abbas	Abdul Latif Al Hamad	7 Salem Abul Aziz Al Sabah
4	Abdul Wahab Al Tammar	Ali Khalifa Al Sabah	8
5	Abdul Wahab Al Tammar	Jassem Mohammad Al Kharafi	9

Kuwait Currency Board

Law of 1960

#1–5 Amir Shaikh Abdullah at r. and as wmk. All have sign. #1.

Cat. #	Denomination	Date, description	VG	VF	Unc
1	1/4 DINAR	L.1960. Brown on m/c unpt. Aerial view, Port of Kuwait at ctr. on back.	4.00	15.00	35.00

Central Bank of Kuwait

Law of 1968

#6–10 Amir Shaikh Sabah at r. All have sign. #2.

Cat. #	Denomination	Date, description	VG	VF	Unc
2	1/2 DINAR	L.1960. Purple on m/c unpt. School at ctr. on back.	4.50	17.50	50.00

Cat. #	Denomination	Date, description	VG	VF	Unc
6	1/4 DINAR	L.1968. Brown on m/c unpt. Back like #1.	1.00	3.00	12.00

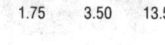

3	1 DINAR	L.1960. Red-brown on m/c unpt. Cement plant at ctr. on back.	7.50	20.00	110.00

7	1/2 DINAR	L.1968. Purple on m/c unpt. Back like #2.	1.75	3.50	13.50

4	5 DINARS	L.1960. Blue on m/c unpt. Street scene on back.	50.00	150.00	400.00

8	1 DINAR	L.1968. Red-brown on m/c unpt. Oil refinery on back.	3.50	6.00	30.00

5	10 DINARS	L.1960. Green on m/c unpt. Dhow on back.	60.00	200.00	450.00

Cat. #	Denomination	Date, description	VG	VF	Unc
9	5 DINARS	*L.1968.* Blue on m/c unpt. View of Kuwait on back.	12.50	30.00	80.00

| 10 | 10 DINARS | *L.1968.* Green on m/c unpt. Back similar to #5. | 20.00 | 50.00 | 120.00 |

#11–16 arms at r. Black serial #. #11–15 wmk.: Dhow.

11	1/4 DINAR	*L.1968* (1980–91). Brown and purple on m/c unpt. Oil rig at l. Oil refinery on back.			
		a. Sign. 2; 4.	.50	1.00	3.00
		b. Sign. 6.	.40	.75	2.50

NOTE: Contraband stolen by invading Iraqi forces included prefix denominators #54–68.

12	1/2 DINAR	*L.1968* (1980). Purple on m/c unpt. Tower at l. Harbor scene on back.			
		a. Sign. 2–4.	.60	1.25	6.00
		b. Sign. 6.	.50	1.00	5.00

NOTE: Contraband stolen by invading Iraqi forces include prefix denominators #30–37.

13	1 DINAR	*L.1968* (1980–91). Brown-violet, purple and black on m/c unpt. Modern bldg. at l. Old fortress on back.			
		a. Overall ornate unpt. Sign. 2; 4.	1.00	2.50	12.50
		b. Plain colored unpt. at top and bottom. Sign. 6.	.75	2.00	7.50

NOTE: Contraband stolen by invading Iraqi forces include prefix denominators #47–53.

Cat. #	Denomination	Date, description	VG	VF	Unc
14	5 DINARS	*L.1968* (1980–91). Deep blue and black on m/c unpt. Minaret at l. Lg. bldg. on back.			
		a. Overall ornate unpt. Sign. 2; 4.	3.00	8.00	30.00
		b. Plain colored unpt. at top and bottom. Sign. 6.	2.50	7.00	17.50

NOTE: Contraband stolen by invading Iraqi forces include prefix denominators #18–20.

| 15 | 10 DINARS | *L.1968* (1980–91). Green on m/c unpt. Falcon at l. Sailing boat on back. Sign. 2–4. | 4.00 | 10.00 | 40.00 |

NOTE: Contraband stolen by invading Iraqi forces include prefix denominators #70–87.

| 16 | 20 DINARS | *L.1968* (1986–91). Brown and olive-green on m/c unpt. Bldg. at l. Central Bank at l. ctr. on back. Wmk: Eagle's head. Sign. 5; 6. | 12.50 | 35.00 | 125.00 |

NOTE: Contraband stolen by invading Iraqi forces include prefix denominators #9–13.

1992 POST LIBERATION ISSUE

After the 1991 Gulf War, Kuwait declared all previous note issues worthless.

#17–22 like previous issue. Red serial # at top r. Sign. 7.

Cat. #	Denomination	Date, description	VG	VF	Unc
17	1/4 DINAR	L.1968 (1992). Violet and black on silver and m/c unpt. Like #11.	FV	1.00	2.75

| 18 | 1/2 DINAR | L.1968 (1992). Deep blue, blue-green and deep violet on silver and m/c unpt. Like #12. | FV | 2.00 | 5.00 |

| 19 | 1 DINAR | L.1968 (1992). Deep olive-green, green and deep blue on silver and m/c unpt. Like #13. | FV | FV | 7.50 |

| 20 | 5 DINARS | L.1968 (1992). Olive-brown, pink, green and m/c. Like #14. | FV | FV | 35.00 |

Cat. #	Denomination	Date, description	VG	VF	Unc
21	10 DINARS	L.1968 (1992). Orange-red, brown-olive and m/c. Like #15.	FV	FV	65.00
22	20 DINARS	L.1968 (1992). Violet-brown and m/c. Like #16.	FV	FV	120.00

1994 ISSUE

#23–28 outline of falcon's head above arms at l., segmented silver vertical thread at ctr. r. Wmk: Falcon's head. Sign. 8.

| 23 | 1/4 DINAR | L.1968 (1994). Brown, grayish purple and red-orange on m/c unpt. Ship at bottom ctr. r. Girls playing game on back. | FV | FV | 3.50 |

| 24 | 1/2 DINAR | L.1968 (1994). Brown and dk. grayish green on m/c unpt. Souk shops at lower r. Boys playing game on back. | FV | FV | 5.00 |

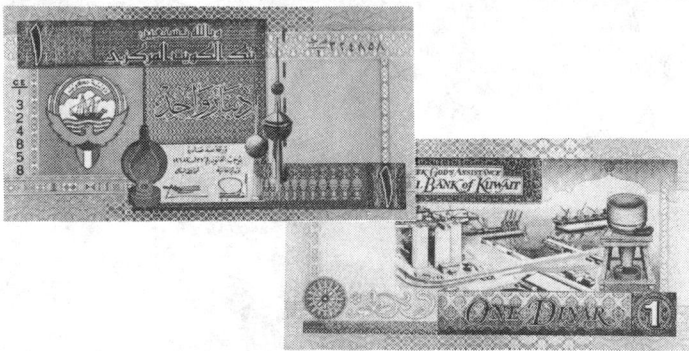

| 25 | 1 DINAR | L.1968 (1994). Deep brown, purple and dk. gray on m/c unpt. Pinnacles at ctr. r. Aerial view of harbor docks on back. | FV | FV | 9.00 |

#26–28 silver foiling of falcon's head at l. ctr.

KYRGYZSTAN

The Republic of Kyrgyzstan, (formerly Kirghiz S.S.R., a Union Republic of the U.S.S.R.), independent state since Aug. 31, 1991, member of the UN and of the C.I.S. It was the last state of the Union Republics to declare its sovereignty. Capital: Bishkek (formerly Frunze).

Originally part of the Autonomous Turkestan S.S.R. founded on May 1, 1918, the Kyrgyz ethnic area was established on October 14, 1924 as the Kara-Kirghiz Autonomous Region within the R.S.F.S.R. Then on May 25, 1925 the name Kara (black) was dropped. It became an A.S.S.R. on Feb. 1, 1926 and a Union Republic of the U.S.S.R. in 1936. On Dec. 12, 1990, the name was then changed to the Republic of Kyrgyzstan.

MONETARY SYSTEM
1 COM = 100 ТЫЙЫН
1 SOM = 100 Tyiyn

КЫРГЫЗ РЕСПУБЛИКАСЫ

Kyrgyz Republic

1993 ISSUE

#1–3 bald eagle at ctr. Ornate design at ctr. on back. Wmk: Eagle in repeating pattern.

Cat. #	Denomination	Date, description	VG	VF	Unc

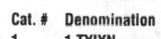

| 1 | 1 TYIYN | ND (1993). Dk. brown on pink and brown- | | | |
| | | orange unpt. | FV | FV | .20 |

| 2 | 10 TYIYN | ND (1993). Brown on pale green and brown-orange unpt. | FV | FV | 1.00 |

| 3 | 50 TYIYN | ND (1993). Gray on blue and brown-orange unpt. | FV | FV | 1.75 |

КЫРГЫЗСТАН БАНКЫ

Kyrgyzstan Bank

1993 ISSUE

#4–6 Equestrian statue of Manas the Noble at r. Manas' mausoleum at l. on back. Wmk: Eagle in repeating pattern.

Kuwait (left column)

Cat. #	Denomination	Date, description	VG	VF	Unc
26	5 DINARS	L.1968 (1994). Grayish green and red-violet on m/c unpt. Pinnacle at r. Oil refinery at ctr. on back.	FV	FV	35.00
27	10 DINARS	L.1968 (1994). Purple, violet and dk. brown on m/c unpt. Mosque at lower r. Pearl fisherman at l. ctr., dhow at r. on back.	FV	FV	60.00

NOTE: #23–27 were reported as withdrawn in early 1995 due to the word *Allah* being present.

| 28 | 20 DINARS | L.1968 (1994). Dk. olive-green, orange and olive-brown on m/c unpt. Fortress at lower r. Central bank at bottom l. ctr., old fortress gate, pinnacle at r. on back. | FV | FV | 110.00 |

COLLECTOR SERIES

Cat. #	Date, denomination	Description	Issue Price	Mkt. Val.
CS1	26.2.1993 1 DINAR	Orange-red, violet-blue and blue. Plastic w/silver seal on window. Issued in special folder for "Second Anniversary of Liberation of Kuwait." Text on back includes: *"THIS IS NOT LEGAL TENDER."*	—	12.50

Cat. #	Denomination	Date, description	VG	VF	Unc
4	1 SOM	ND (1993). Red on m/c unpt.	FV	FV	1.50

| 5 | 5 SOM | ND (1993). Deep grayish-green on m/c unpt. | FV | FV | 7.50 |

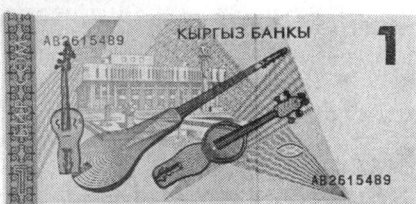

| 6 | 20 SOM | ND (1993). Purple on m/c unpt. | FV | FV | 25.00 |

1994 ISSUE

Cat. #	Denomination	Date, description	VG	VF	Unc
8	5 SOM	ND (1994). Blue and yellow on m/c unpt. B. Beishenalieva at r. Classical bldg. on back.	FV	FV	3.00

9	10 SOM	ND (1994). Green and brown on m/c unpt. Kassim at r. Mountains on back.	FV	FV	5.50
10	20 SOM	ND (1994). Red-orange on m/c unpt. T. Moldo at r.	FV	FV	8.50
11	50 SOM	ND (1994). Reddish-brown on m/c unpt. K. Datka at r. Mausoleum and minaret on back.	FV	FV	16.00
12	100 SOM	ND (1995).	FV	FV	22.50

| 7 | 1 SOM | ND (1994). Yellow-brown A. Maldubayer at r. String musical instruments, modern bldg. on back. | FV | FV | 1.25 |

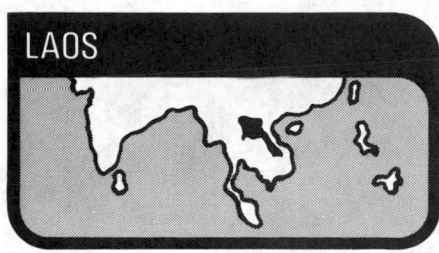

LAOS

The Lao People's Democratic Republic, located on the Indo-Chinese Peninsula between the Socialist Republic of Vietnam and the Kingdom of Thailand, has an area of 91,429 sq. mi. (236,800 sq. km.) and a population of 4.2 million. Captial: Vientiane. Agriculture employs 95 percent of the people. Tin, lumber and coffee are exported.

The first United Kingdom of Laos was established in the mid-14th century by King Fa Ngum who ruled an area including present Laos, northeastern Thailand, and the southern part of China's Yunnan province from his capital at Luang Prabang. Thailand and Vietnam obtained control over much of the present Lao territory in the 18th century and remained dominant until France established a protectorate over the area in 1893 and incorporated it into the Union of Indo-China. The Independence of Laos was proclaimed in March of 1945, during the last days of the Japanese occupation of World War II. France reoccupied Laos in 1946, and established it as a constitutional monarchy within the French Union in 1949. In 1953, war erupted between the government and the Pathet Lao, a Communist movement supported by the Vietnamese Communist forces. Peace was declared in 1954 with Laos becoming fully independent in 1955 and the Pathet Lao being permitted to occupy two northern provinces. Civil war broke out again in 1960 with the United States supporting the government of the Kingdom of Laos and the North Vietnamese helping the Communist Pathet Lao, and continued, with intervals of truce and political compromise, until the formation of the Lao People's Democratic Republic on Dec. 2, 1975.

RULERS

Savang Vatthana, 1959–1975

MONETARY SYSTEM

1 Kip = 100 At, 1955–78
100 "Old" Kip = 1 "New" Kip, 1979–

REPLACEMENT NOTES

#7, 11–14, 16, 17, 19: S9 (Z9 in English) as series number.

#25-29, ZA; ZB; ZC prefix. #30-32, ZM; ZK; ZL prefix.

KINGDOM
Banque Nationale du Laos

SIGNATURE VARIETIES		
	LE GOUVERNEUR ຜູ້ອຳນວຍການ	UN CENSEUR ຜູ້ກວດການຜູ້ນຶ່ງ
1	*Rhay Panya*	*le louidos*
2	*Rhay Panya*	*Rewly*
3	*Odry Panya*	*Seven*
4	*mony huanamy*	*Seven*
5	*mony huanamy*	*Mph*
6	*mony huanamy*	*Eg*

1962–63 REGULAR ISSUE

Cat. #	Denomination	Date, description	VG	VF	Unc
8	1 KIP	ND (1962). Brown on pink and blue unpt. Stylized figure at l. Arms on back. Sign. 3; 4.	.10	.20	.75

Cat. #	Denomination	Date, description	VG	VF	Unc
9	5 KIP	ND (1962). Green on m/c unpt. S. Vong at r. Temple at l., man on elephant at ctr. on back.			
		a. Sign. 2.	4.50	17.50	42.50
		b. Sign. 5.	.15	.35	1.35

10	10 KIP	ND (1962). Blue on yellow and green unpt. Woman at l. (like back of Fr. Indochina #102). Stylized sunburst on back (like face of #102).			
		a. Sign. 1.	12.50	50.00	—
		b. Sign. 5.	.15	.35	1.50

#11–14 Kg. Savang Vatthana at l.

11	20 KIP	ND (1963). Brown on tan and blue unpt. Bldg. at ctr. Pagoda at ctr. r. on back.			
		a. Sign 5.	.15	.35	1.50
		b. Sign 6.	.10	.30	1.25

Cat. #	Denomination	Date, description	VG	VF	Unc
15	10 KIP	ND (1974). Blue on m/c unpt. Kg. Savang Vatthana at ctr. r. Back blue and brown; ox cart. Sign. 6. Specimen.	—	100.00	350.00

#16–19 Kg. Savang Vatthana at l. Sign. 6.

Cat. #	Denomination	Date, description	VG	VF	Unc
12	50 KIP	ND (1963). Purple on brown and blue unpt. Pagoda at ctr. Back purple; bldg. at r. Sign. 5; 6.	.10	.25	1.00

13	200 KIP	ND (1963). Blue on green and gold unpt. Temple of That Luang at ctr. Waterfalls on back.			
		a. Sign. 4.	.40	1.25	5.00
		b. Sign. 6.	.20	.50	2.00

16	100 KIP	ND (1974). Brown on blue, green and pink unpt. Pagoda at ctr. Ox cart on back.	.15	.35	1.50

14	1000 KIP	ND (1963). Brown on blue and gold unpt. Temple at ctr. 3 long canoes on back.			
		a. Sign. 5.	.40	1.00	5.00
		b. Sign. 6.	.25	.75	3.00

17	500 KIP	ND (1974). Red on m/c unpt. Pagoda at ctr. Dam on back.	.20	.40	1.75

1974–75 ISSUE

Cat. #	Denomination	Date, description	VG	VF	Unc
18	1000 KIP	ND. Black on m/c unpt. Elephant on back. Specimen only.	—	Rare	—

| 19 | 5000 KIP | ND (1975). Blue-gray on m/c unpt. Pagoda at ctr. Musicians w/instruments on back. | .75 | 2.50 | 10.00 |

STATE OF LAOS
Pathet Lao Government

#A20-24 printed in Peoples Republic of China and circulated in areas under control of Pathet Lao insurgents. Later these same notes became the accepted legal tender for the entire country.

Cat. #	Denomination	Date, description	VG	VF	Unc
A20	1 KIP	ND. Green on yellow and blue unpt. Threshing grain at ctr. Medical clinic scene on back. (Not issued).	—	—	50.00

20	10 KIP	ND. Lilac and red on m/c unpt. Medical examination scene. Fighters in the brush on back.			
		a. Wmk: Temples.	.10	.25	.75
		b. Wmk: 5-pointed stars.	.05	.15	.50

Cat. #	Denomination	Date, description	VG	VF	Unc
21	20 KIP	ND. Brown on green unpt. Rice distribution. Forge workers on back.			
		a. Wmk: Temples.	.10	.25	1.00
		b. Wmk: 5-pointed stars.	.10	.25	1.00

22	50 KIP	ND. Purple on m/c unpt. Factory workers. Plowing ox on back.			
		a. Wmk: Temples.	.05	.35	1.50
		b. Wmk: 5-pointed stars.	.10	.25	1.25

| 23 | 100 KIP | ND. Blue on m/c unpt. Long boats on lake. Scene in textile store on back. Wmk: Temples. | .10 | .25 | 1.50 |

Cat. #	Denomination	Date, description	VG	VF	Unc
23A	200 KIP	ND. Green on m/c unpt. Road and trail convoys. Factory scene on back. Wmk: Temples.			
		a. Issued note.	.15	.40	1.75
		x. Lithograph counterfeit (1974) on plain paper, w/o serial #. Ho Chi Minh at r. on back.	12.00	40.00	100.00

Cat. #	Denomination	Date, description	VG	VF	Unc
24	500 KIP	ND. Brown on m/c unpt. Armed field workers in farm scene. Soldiers shooting down planes on back. Wmk: Temples.	.15	.35	1.50

PEOPLES DEMOCRATIC REPUBLIC

Currency Reform
1 new Kip = 100 old Kip

1972 PROVISIONAL ISSUE

Cat. #	Denomination	Date, description	VG	VF	Unc
24A	50 KIP on 500 Kip	ND. New legends and denomination ovpt. on #24. (Not issued).	15.00	35.00	150.00

1979-92 ISSUE

Cat. #	Denomination	Date, description	VG	VF	Unc
25	1 KIP	ND (1979). Blue-gray. Militia unit at l., arms at r. Schoolroom scene on back.	.05	.10	.20

Cat. #	Denomination	Date, description	VG	VF	Unc
26	5 KIP	ND (1979). Green. Shoppers at a store, arms at r. Logging elephants on back.	.05	.15	.40

Cat. #	Denomination	Date, description	VG	VF	Unc
27	10 KIP	ND (1979). Brown on green and yellow unpt. Lumber mill at l., arms at r. Medical scenes on back.	.10	.20	.50

Cat. #	Denomination	Date, description	VG	VF	Unc
28	20 KIP	ND (1979). Brown on green and pink unpt. Arms at l., tank w/troop column at ctr. Back brown and maroon; textile mill at ctr.	.10	.20	.50

Cat. #	Denomination	Date, description	VG	VF	Unc
29	50 KIP	ND (1979). Brownish red on green unpt. Rice planting at l. ctr., arms at r. Back red and brown; hydroelectric dam.	.15	.35	1.00

Cat. #	Denomination	Date, description	VG	VF	Unc
30	100 KIP	ND. Deep blue-green and deep blue on yellow and pink unpt. Grain harvesting at l., arms at r. Bridge, storage tanks, and soldier on back.	FV	FV	1.00

Cat. #	Denomination	Date, description	VG	VF	Unc
31	500 KIP	1988. Brown and deep blue on m/c unpt. Modern irrigation systems at ctr. below arms. Harvesting fruit at ctr. on back.	FV	FV	3.75

| 32 | 1000 KIP | 1992. Blue-black and green on m/c unpt. 3 women at l., temple at ctr. r., arms at r. Cattle at ctr. on back. | FV | FV | 4.00 |

LATVIA

The Republic of Latvia, the central Baltic state in east Europe, has an area of 24,595 sq. mi. (43,601 sq. km.) and a population of *2.6 million. Capital: Riga. Livestock raising and manufacturing are the chief industries. Butter, bacon, fertilizers and telephone equipment are exported.

The Latvians, of Aryan descent, were nomadic tribesmen who settled along the Baltic prior to the 13th century. Lacking a central government, they were easily conquered by the German Teutonic knights, Russia, Sweden and Poland. Following the third partition of Poland by Austria, Prussia and Russia in 1795, Latvia came under Russian domination and did not experience autonomy until the Russian Revolution of 1917 provided an opportunity for freedom. The Latvian republic was established on Nov. 18, 1918. It was occupied by Soviet troops in 1939 and annexed to the Soviet Union in 1940. Following the German occupation of 1941–44, it was retaken by Russia and reestablished as a member S.S. Republic of the Soviet Union. Western countries, including the United States, did not recognize Latvia's incorporation into the Soviet Union.

Latvia declared Its independence from the former U.S.S.R. on Aug. 22, 1991.

MONETARY SYSTEM
1 Rublis = 1 Russian Ruble, 1992
1 Lat = 200 Rublu, 1993
1 Lat = 100 Santimu

REPUBLIC

1992 ISSUE

#35–40 wmk: Symmetrical design.

Cat. #	Denomination	Date, description	VG	VF	Unc
35	1 RUBLIS	1992. Violet on yellow and ochre unpt. Back violet-brown on lt. green and yellow unpt.	—	.10	.25

| 36 | 2 RUBLI | 1992. Purple on brown-orange and yellow unpt. | — | .10 | .25 |

| 37 | 5 RUBLI | 1992. Deep blue on lt. blue and lt. yellow-orange unpt. Back blue-black on blue and lt. blue unpt. | — | .15 | .50 |

Cat. #	Denomination	Date, description	VG	VF	Unc
38	10 RUBLU	1992. Purple on red-orange and pale orange unpt.	.10	.25	.75

Cat. #	Denomination	Date, description	VG	VF	Unc
39	20 RUBLU	1992. Violet on lilac and pink unpt.	.15	.60	1.75

| 40 | 50 RUBLU | 1992. Gray-green on lt. blue and pink unpt. | .20 | .85 | 2.75 |

| 41 | 200 RUBLU | 1992. Greenish black on yellow and blue-green unpt. Back greenish-black on lt. blue and pink unpt. | .50 | 2.00 | 5.00 |

| 42 | 500 RUBLU | 1992. Violet-brown on gray and dull orange unpt. | 1.35 | 4.00 | 10.00 |

Currency Reform, 1993
1 Lat = 200 Rublu

#43–48 Lielvarde belt vertically at r. Metalized belt at l., arms at lower r. on back. Wmk: Young woman in national costume.

Cat. #	Denomination	Date, description	VG	VF	Unc
43	5 LATI	1992 (1993). Varied shades of green on tan and pale green unpt. Oak tree at ctr. r. Local art at ctr. on back.	FV	FV	13.50

| 44 | 10 LATU | 1992 (1993). Violet and purple on m/c unpt. Landscape of Daugava River at ctr. National bow broach at ctr. on back. | FV | FV | 25.00 |

| 45 | 20 LATU | 1992 (1993). Brown and dk. brown on m/c unpt. Rural house at r. National ornamented woven linen at l. ctr. on back. | FV | FV | 47.50 |

| 46 | 50 LATU | 1992 (1994). Deep blue on m/c unpt. Sailing ship at r. Two crossed kegs and a cross on back. | FV | FV | 115.00 |

| 47 | 100 LATU | 1992 (1994). Red and dk. brown on m/c unpt. K. Barons at r. Ornaments of the woven national belt on back. | FV | FV | 220.00 |
| 48 | 500 LATU | 1992. Purple on m/c unpt. Young woman in national costume at r. Small ornamental brass crowns on back. (Not released). | — | — | — |

LEBANON

The Republic of Lebanon, situated on the eastern shore of the Mediterranean Sea between Syria and Israel, has an area of 4,015 sq. mi. (10,400 sq. km.) and a population of 2.8 million. Capital: Beirut. The economy is based on agriculture, trade and tourism. Fruit, other foodstuffs and textiles are exported.

Almost at the beginning of recorded history, Lebanon appeared as the well-wooded hinterland of the Phoenicians who exploited its famous forests of cedar. The mountains were a Christian refuge and a Crusader stronghold. Lebanon, the history of which is essentially the same as that of Syria, came under control of the Ottoman Turks early in the 16th century. Following the collapse of the Ottoman Empire after World War I, Lebanon, along with Syria, became a French mandate. The French drew a border around the predominantly Christian Lebanon Sanjak or administrative subdivision and on Sept. 1, 1920 proclaimed the area the State of Grand Lebanon (Etat du Grand Liban) a republic under French control. France announced the independence of Lebanon on Nov. 26, 1941, but the last British and French troops did not leave until the end of August 1946.

MONETARY SYSTEM

1 Livre (Pound) = 100 Piastres

Banque de Syrie et du Liban

1952; 1956 ISSUE

#55–60 all dated 1 January. Sign. varieties. Printer: TDLR.

Cat. #	Denomination	Date, description	VG	VF	Unc
55	1 LIVRE	1.1.1952–64. Brown and m/c. Boats at dockside (Saida) at I. Columns of Baalbek on back. W/ or w/o security strip.	.50	3.00	15.00

Cat. #	Denomination	Date, description	VG	VF	Unc
56	5 LIVRES	1.1.1952–64. Blue and m/c. Courtyard of the Palais de Beit-Eddine. Snowy mountains w/trees on back. W/ or w/o security strip.	2.00	10.00	75.00

Cat. #	Denomination	Date, description	VG	VF	Unc
57	10 LIVRES	1.1.1956; 1.1.1961; 1.1.1963. Green and m/c. Ruins of pillared temple. Shoreline w/city on hills on back.	5.00	15.00	100.00

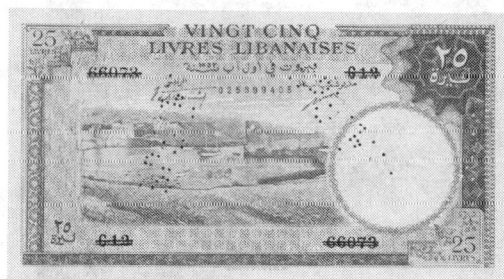

			VG	VF	Unc
58	25 LIVRES	1.1.1952; 1.1.1953. Blue-gray on m/c unpt. Harbor town. Stone arch bridge at ctr. r. on back. Wmk: Lion's head.	10.00	50.00	235.00

			VG	VF	Unc
59	50 LIVRES	1.1.1952; 1.1.1953; 1.1.1964. Deep brown on m/c unpt. Coast landscape. Lg. rock formations in water on back. Wmk: Lion's head.	20.00	65.00	325.00

			VG	VF	Unc
60	100 LIVRES	1.1.1952; 1.1.1953; 1.1.1958; 1.1.1963. Blue. View of Beyrouth. Cedar tree at ctr. on back and as wmk.	10.00	30.00	90.00

Banque du Liban

1964; 1978 ISSUE

#61–69 printer: TDLR.

Cat. #	Denomination	Date, description	VG	VF	Unc
61	1 LIVRE	1964–80. Brown on blue unpt. Columns of Baalbek. Cavern on back. Wmk: 2 eagles.			
		a. 1964; 1968.	.85	2.50	10.00
		b. 1971; 1972; 1974.	.65	2.00	6.50
		c. 1978; 1980.	.50	1.50	5.00

Cat. #	Denomination	Date, description	VG	VF	Unc
64	25 LIVRES	1964–83. Brown on gold unpt. Citadel on the sea (Saida). Ruin on rocks on back. Wmk: Lion's head.			
		a. 1964; 1967; 1968.	4.00	12.50	35.00
		b. 1972; 1973; 1974; 1978.	2.50	8.50	27.50
		c. 1983.	.15	.30	1.00

Cat. #	Denomination	Date, description	VG	VF	Unc
62	5 LIVRES	1964–88. Green on blue and lt. yellow unpt. Bldgs. Footbridge on back. Wmk: Ancient galley.			
		a. 1964.	1.65	5.00	15.00
		b. 1967; 1968.	1.00	3.00	11.50
		c. 1972; 1974; 1978.	.85	2.50	8.50
		d. 1986; 1988.	.10	.15	.35

Cat. #	Denomination	Date, description	VG	VF	Unc
65	50 LIVRES	1964–88. Dk. gray, purple and dk. olive-green on m/c unpt. Ruins of Temple of Bacchus on face. Bldg. on back. Wmk: Cedar tree.			
		a. 1964; 1967; 1968.	4.50	15.00	45.00
		b. 1972; 1973; 1974; 1978.	3.50	10.00	30.00
		c. Guilloche added above temple ruins w/10-petaled rosette at l. in unpt. 1983; 1985.	.25	.30	1.50
		d. W/o control # above ruins on face. 1988.	FV	FV	1.00

Cat. #	Denomination	Date, description	VG	VF	Unc
63	10 LIVRES	1964–86. Purple on m/c unpt. Ruins of Anjar. Lg. rocks in water on back. Wmk: Man's head.			
		a. 1964.	2.00	6.00	18.50
		b. 1967; 1968.	1.65	5.00	15.00
		c. 1971; 1973; 1974; 1978.	.90	2.75	9.50
		d. 1986.	.10	.20	.50

Cat. #	Denomination	Date, description	VG	VF	Unc
66	100 LIVRES	1964–88. Blue-black on lt. pink and l. blue unpt. Palais Beit-Eddine w/inner court-yard. Snowy trees in mountains on back. Wmk: Bearded male elder.			
		a. 1964; 1967; 1968.	5.50	13.50	40.00
		b. 1973; 1974; 1977; 1978.	4.00	8.50	25.00
		c. Guilloche added under bank name on back. 1983; 1985.	.15	.60	2.50
		d. Guilloche added under title on face. 1988.	.10	.30	1.00

Cat. #	Denomination	Date, description	VG	VF	Unc
67	250 LIVRES	1978–88. Deep gray-green and blue-black on m/c unpt. Ruins on face and back. Wmk: Ancient circular sculpture w/ head at ctr. from the Grand Temple Podium			
		a. 1978.	3.00	16.50	50.00
		b. 1983. Control # at top ctr.	1.50	7.50	40.00
		c. 1985–87.	.20	1.00	5.00
		d. W/o control # above sign. at archway on face. 1988.	.15	.50	2.25

1988; 1993 ISSUE

Law of 19883

68	500 LIVRES	1988. Brown and olive-green on m/c unpt. City scene at ctr. Ruins at l. ctr. on back. Wmk: Lion's head.	.50	.85	1.75

69	1000 LIVRES	1988; 1990; 1991. Dk. blue, blue-black and green on m/c unpt. Map at r. Ruins at ctr., modern bldg. at ctr. on back. Wmk: Cedar tree.	.85	1.50	3.00

Cat. #	Denomination	Date, description	VG	VF	Unc
70	10,000 LIVRES	1993. Violet, olive-brown and purple on m/c unpt. Ancient ruins at ctr. City ruins w/5 archaic statues on back. Wmk: Ancient circular sculpture w/head at ctr. from of the Grand Temple Podium.	FV	FV	14.00

1994 ISSUE

#71–74 ornate block designs and as unpt. Arabic serial # and matching bar code, #. Wmk: Cedar tree. Printer: BABN.

71	5000 LIVRES	1994. Red and purple on pink and m/c unpt. Geometric designs on back.	FV	FV	9.00

72	20,000 LIVRES	1994. Red-brown and orange on yellow and m/c unpt. Geometric designs w/lg. LIBAN at lower l. ctr. on back.	FV	FV	25.00

Cat. #	Denomination	Date, description	VG	VF	Unc
73	50,000 LIVRES	1994. Blue-black and brown-violet on m/c unpt. Cedar tree at upper l., artistic boats at lower l. ctr. Lg. diamond w/BDL at l. ctr., cedar tree at lower l. on back.	FV	FV	62.50

| 74 | 100,000 LIVRES | 1994. Dk. blue-green and dk. green on m/c unpt. Cedar tree at lower r. Artistic bunch of grapes and grain stalks at l. ctr. on back. | FV | FV | 120.00 |

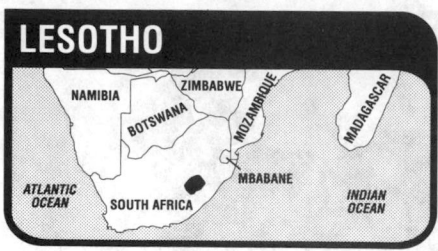

LESOTHO

The Kingdom of Lesotho, a constitutional monarchy located within the east-central part of the Republic of Africa, has an area of 11,716 sq. mi. (30,355 sq. km.) and a population of 1.7 million. Capital: Maseru. The economy is based on subsistence agriculture and livestock raising. Wool, mohair, and cattle are exported. Lesotho (formerly Basutoland) was sparsely populated until the end of the 16th century. Between the 16th and 19th centuries an influx of refugees from tribal wars led to the development of a distinct Basotho group. During the reign of tribal chief Moshesh I (1823–70), a series of wars with the Orange Free State resulted in the loss of large areas of territory to South Africa. Moshesh appealed to the British for help, and Basutoland was constituted a native state under British protection. In 1871 it was annexed to Cape Colony, but was restored to direct control by the Crown in 1884. From 1884 to 1959 legislative and executive authority was vested in a British High Commissioner. The constitution of 1959 recognized the expressed wish of the people for independence, which was attained on Oct. 4, 1966. Lesotho is a member of the Commonwealth of Nations. The king of Lesotho is Chief of State.

MONETARY SYSTEM
1 Maloti = 100 Licente

RULERS
King Motlotlehi Moshoeshoe II, 1966–

DATING
Partial date given in the 2 numbers of the serial # prefix for #1–8.

Lesotho Monetary Authority

1979 ISSUE

#1–3A arms at ctr., military bust of Kg. Moshoeshoe II at r. Wmk: Basotho hat.

Cat. #	Denomination	Date, description	VG	VF	Unc
1	2 MALOTI	(19)79. Dk. brown on m/c unpt. Bldg. and Lesotho flag at l. on back.			
		a. Blue and brown unpt. at r. of Kg.	1.00	2.00	6.00
		b. Brown unpt. at r. of Kg.	Reported, not confirmed.		

| 2 | 5 MALOTI | (19)79. Deep blue on m/c unpt. Craftsmen weaving at l. ctr. on back. | 2.00 | 5.00 | 15.00 |

Cat. #	Denomination	Date, description	VG	VF	Unc
3	10 MALOTI	(19)79. Red and purple on m/c unpt. Basotho horseman in maize field at ctr. on back.	5.00	12.00	45.00

Cat. #	Denomination	Date, description	VG	VF	Unc
6	10 MALOTI	(19)81. Like #3.			
		a. Sign. 1 (19)81.	FV	4.50	15.00
		b. Sign. 2 (19)81 (issued 1984).	FV	4.25	13.50

| 3A | 20 MALOTI | (19)79. Herdsmen w/cattle at l. ctr. on back. Specimen. | — | — | — |

Central Bank of Lesotho

SIGNATURE VARIETIES

| 1 | *[signature]* | 3 | |
| 2 | *[signature]* | 4 | |

1981; 1984 ISSUE

#4–8 arms at ctr., military bust of Kg. Moshoeshoe II at r. Partial year date given as the denominator of the serial # prefix. Wmk: Basotho hat.

7	20 MALOTI	(19)81; 84. Dk. green and olive-green on m/c unpt. Mosotho herdsboy w/cattle at l. ctr on back.			
		a. Sign. 1 (19)81.	FV	10.00	35.00
		b. Sign. 2 (19)84.	FV	8.50	25.00

4	2 MALOTI	(19)81; 84. Like #1.			
		a. Sign. 1 (19)81.	FV	1.25	4.00
		b. Sign. 2 (19)84.	FV	1.00	3.50

8	50 MALOTI	(19)81. Purple and deep blue on m/c unpt. "Qiloane" mountain at l. on back.			
		a. Sign. 1.	FV	25.00	65.00

1989; 1992 ISSUE

#9–13 arms at ctr., civilian bust of Kg. Moshoeshoe II in new portr. at r. Designs similar to #4–8 but w/Kg. also as wmk. Sign. 3.

5	5 MALOTI	(19)81. Face like #2. Waterfalls at ctr. on back.			
		a. Sign. 1.	FV	2.50	8.00

Cat. #	Denomination	Date, description	VG	VF	Unc
9	2 MALOTI	1989. Similar to #4.	FV	FV	2.00

10	5 MALOTI	1989. Similar to #5.	FV	FV	4.00

11	10 MALOTI	1989; 1990. Similar to #6.	FV	FV	7.50

12	20 MALOTI	1989; 1990. Dk. green and blue-black on m/c unpt. Similar to #7.	FV	FV	13.50
13	50 MALOTI	1989. Similar to #8.	FV	FV	45.00
14	50 MALOTI	1992. Violet and green on m/c unpt. Seated Kg. Moshoeshoe I at r. "Qiloane" mountain on back.	FV	FV	35.00

1994 ISSUE

#15–18 seated Kg. Moshoeshoe I at l., arms at ctr. and as wmk. Sign. 4.

15	20 MALOTI	1994. Deep green and blue-green on m/c unpt. Mosotho herdsboy w/cattle near huts at ctr. r. on back.	FV	FV	11.50
16	50 MALOTI	1994. Violet and green on m/c unpt. Herdsman horseback w/packmule at ctr., "Qiloane" mountain at r. on back.	FV	FV	25.00
17 (15)	100 MALOTI	1994.	FV	FV	42.50
18 (16)	200 MALOTI	1994.	FV	FV	80.00

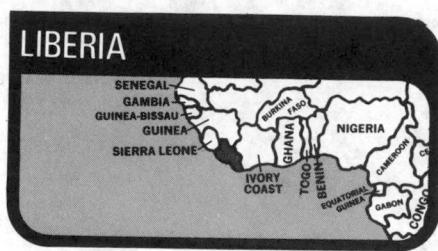

LIBERIA

The Republic of Liberia, located on the southern side of the west African bulge between Sierra Leone and the Ivory Coast, has an area of 38,250 sq. mi. (111,369 sq. km.) and a population of 2.5 million. Capital: Monrovia. The major industries are agriculture, mining and lumbering. Iron ore, diamonds, rubber, coffee and cocoa are exported.

The Liberian coast was explored and chartered by Portuguese navigator Pedro de Cintra in 1461. For the following three centuries Portuguese traders visited the area regularly to trade for gold, slaves and pepper. The modern country of Liberia, Africa's first republic, was settled in 1822 by the American Colonization Society as a homeland for American freed slaves, with the U.S. government furnishing funds and assisting in negotiations for procurement of land from the native chiefs. The various settlements united in 1839 to form the Commonwealth of Liberia, and in 1847 established the country as a republic with a constitution modeled after that of the United States.

Notes were issued until 1880; thereafter the introduction of dollar notes of the United States took place. U.S. money was declared legal tender in Liberia in 1943, replacing British West African currencies. Not until 1989 was a distinctive Liberian currency again issued.

MONETARY SYSTEM
1 Dollar = 100 Cents

REPLACEMENT NOTES

#19, 20: ZZ prefix.

National Bank of Liberia

#19–20 printer: TDLR.

Cat#	Denomination	Date, description	VG	VF	Unc
19	5 DOLLARS	12.4.1989. Black and deep green on m/c unpt. J. J. Roberts at ctr., tapping trees at r. Back deep green on m/c unpt.; National Bank bldg. at ctr.	FV	FV	6.50

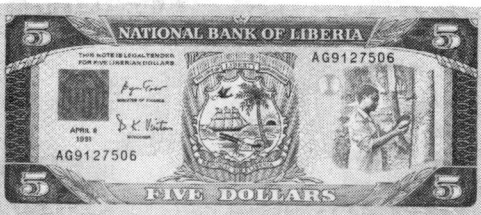

20	5 DOLLARS	6.4.1991. Similar to #19 but w/arms at ctr.	FV	FV	3.25

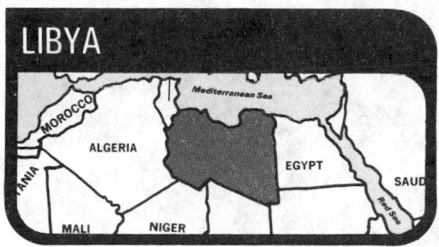

The Socialist People's Libyan Arab Jamahiriya, located on the north central coast of Africa between Tunisia and Egypt, has an area of 679,359 sq. mi. (1,759,540 sq. km.) and a population of 4 million. Capital: Tripoli. Crude oil, which accounts for 90 per cent of the export earnings, is the mainstay of the economy.

Libya has been subjected to foreign rule throughout most of its history, various parts of it having been ruled by the Phoenicians, Carthaginians, Vandals, Byzantines, Greeks, Romans, Egyptians, and in the following centuries the Arab's language, culture and religion were adopted by the indigenous population. Libya was conquered by the Ottoman Turks in 1553, and remained under Turkish domination, becoming a Turkish vilayet in 1835, until it was conquered by Italy and made into a colony in 1911. The name "Libya", the ancient Greek name for North Africa exclusive of Egypt, was given to the colony by Italy in 1934. Libya came under Allied administration after the fall of Tripoli on Jan. 23, 1943 and was divided into zones of British and French control. On Dec. 24, 1951, in accordance with a United Nations resolution, Libya proclaimed its independence as a constitutional monarchy, thereby becoming the first country to achieve independence through the United Nations. The monarchy was overthrown by a coup d'etat on Sept. 1, 1969, and Libya was established as a republic.

RULERS
Idris I, 1951–1969

MONETARY SYSTEM
1 Piastre = 10 Milliemes
1 Pound = 100 Piastres – 1000 Milliemes, 1951–1971
1 Dinar = 1000 Dirhams, 1971–

Bank of Libya
Law of 5.2.1963
FIRST ISSUE
#23–27 crowded arms at l. Wmk: Arms.

Cat. #	Denomination	Date, description	VG	VF	Unc
23	1/4 POUND	L.1963/AH1382. Red on m/c unpt.	3.50	15.00	60.00
24	1/2 POUND	L.1963/AH1382. Purple on m/c unpt.	5.00	25.00	90.00
25	1 POUND	L.1963/AH1382. Blue on m/c unpt.	8.00	35.00	140.00

| 26 | 5 POUNDS | L.1963/AH1382. Green on m/c unpt. | 15.00 | 85.00 | — |

Cat. #	Denomination	Date, description	VG	VF	Unc
27	10 POUNDS	L.1963/AH1382. Brown on m/c unpt.	20.00	120.00	—

SECOND ISSUE
#28–32 crowned arms at l. Reduced size notes. Wmk: Arms.

28	1/4 POUND	L.1963/AH1382. Red on m/c unpt.	4.00	17.50	75.00
29	1/2 POUND	L.1963/AH1832. Purple on m/c unpt.	5.00	27.50	100.00
30	1 POUND	L.1963/AH1382. Blue on m/c unpt.	7.00	35.00	120.00

| 31 | 5 POUNDS | L.1963/AH1382. Green on m/c unpt. | 15.00 | 65.00 | 225.00 |
| 32 | 10 POUNDS | L.1963/AH1382. Brown on m/c unpt. | 25.00 | 100.00 | 350.00 |

SOCIALIST PEOPLES REPUBLIC
Central Bank of Libya

SIGNATURE VARIETIES			
1	المحافظ	3	
2		4	

1971 ISSUE
#33–37 w/ or w/o Arabic inscription at lower r. on face. Sign. 1.

Cat. #	Denomination	Date, description	VG	VF	Unc
33	1/4 DINAR	ND. Orange-brown on m/c unpt. Heraldic eagle at l. Doorway on back.			
		a. W/o inscription (1971).	5.00	20.00	85.00
		b. W/ inscription (1972).	1.00	3.50	28.50

Cat. #	Denomination	Date, description	VG	VF	Unc
37	10 DINARS	ND. Blue-gray on m/c unpt. Omar El Mukhtar at l. 3 horsemen at ctr. on back.			
		a. W/o inscription (1971).	35.00	100.00	300.00
		b. W/ inscription (1972).	8.50	28.50	65.00

38–42 *Deleted*. See #33b–37b.

1980-81 ISSUE

34	1/2 DINAR	ND. Purple on m/c unpt. Heraldic eagle at l. Oil refinery on back.			
		a. W/o inscription (1971).	7.50	35.00	125.00
		b. W/inscription (1972).	2.00	10.00	25.00

35	1 DINAR	ND. Blue on m/c unpt. Gate and minaret at l. Hilltop fort on back.			
		a. W/o inscription (1971).	10.00	40.00	150.00
		b. W/ inscription (1972).	3.00	7.50	30.00

42A	1/4 DINAR	ND (1981). Green on m/c unpt. Ruins at l. Fortress and palms on back. 2 sign. varieties.			
		a. Sign. 1.	.45	1.75	5.50
		b. Sign. 2.	.40	1.50	4.50

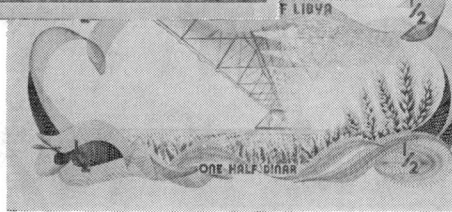

36	5 DINARS	ND. Olive on m/c unpt. Arms at l. Fortress on back.			
		a. W/o inscription (1971).	20.00	65.00	200.00
		b. W/ inscription (1972).	8.00	27.50	60.00

43	1/2 DINAR	ND (1981). Green on m/c unpt. Petroleum refinery at l. Irrigation system above wheat field on back.			
		a. Sign. 1.	.75	3.00	9.00
		b. Sign. 2.	.50	2.25	7.00

Cat. #	Denomination	Date, description	VG	VF	Unc
44	1 DINAR	ND (1981). Green on m/c unpt. Mosque at l. Interior of mosque on back. Sign. 1.	2.00	4.00	10.00

45	5 DINARS	ND (1980). Green on m/c unpt. Camels at l. Crowd around monument on back. 2 sign. varieties.			
		a. Sign. 1.	2.50	10.00	30.00
		b. Sign. 2.	2.25	9.00	27.00

46	10 DINARS	ND (1980). Green on m/c unpt. Omar El Mukhtar at l. Lg. crowd below hilltop fortress at ctr. on back.			
		a. Sign. 1.	5.50	22.00	65.00
		b. Sign. 2.	5.00	20.00	60.00

1984 ISSUE

#47–51 designs generally similar to previous issue. Sign. 2.

Cat. #	Denomination	Date, description	VG	VF	Unc
47	1/4 DINAR	ND (1984). Green and brown on m/c unpt. Similar to #42A.	FV	1.50	4.50

48	1/2 DINAR	ND (1984). Green and purple on m/c unpt. Similar to #43.	FV	6.50	20.00

49	1 DINAR	ND (1984). Green and dk. blue on m/c unpt. Similar to #44.	FV	6.50	20.00

50	5 DINARS	ND (1984). Dk. green and lt. green on m/c unpt. Similar to #45.	FV	8.00	25.00

Cat. #	Denomination	Date, description	VG	VF	Unc
51	10 DINARS	ND (1984). Dk. green on m/c unpt. Similar to #46.	FV	14.00	42.00

1988–90 ISSUE

#52–58 wmk: Heraldic falcon.

Cat. #	Denomination	Date, description	VG	VF	Unc
54 (56)	1 DINAR	ND (1988). Blue and m/c. Kadaffy at l. ctr. Temple at lower ctr. on back.			
		a. Sign. 3.	FV	FV	8.00
		b. Sign. 4.	FV	FV	12.00

52	1/4 DINAR	ND (ca.1990). Dk. green, blue and m/c. Ruins at ctr. Back brown; English text at top. Design features similar to #47. Sign. 3. Wmk: Heraldic Falcon.	FV	FV	4.00

55 (58)	5 DINARS	ND (ca.1991). Gray and violet on m/c unpt. Camel at ctr. Back similar to #50 but w/English text. Sign. 3.	FV	FV	30.00

53 (54)	1/2 DINAR	ND (ca.1990). Dk. purple, blue and m/c. Oil refinery at l. ctr. Back purple; English text at top. Design features similar to #48.			
		a. Sign. 3.	FV	FV	5.00
		b. Sign. 4.	FV	FV	4.00

56 (59)	10 DINARS	ND (1989). Green on m/c unpt. Omar el Mukhtar at l. Arabic text; lg. crowd before hilltop fortress at ctr., octagonal frame w/o unpt. at upper r. on back. Sign. 3.	FV	FV	45.00

1991–93 ISSUE

Cat. #	Denomination	Date, description	VG	VF	Unc
57 (53)	1/4 DINAR	ND (ca.1991). Like #52, but w/all Arabic text on back. More pink in unpt. on face.			
		a. Sign. 3.	FV	FV	3.00
		b. Sign. 4.	FV	FV	2.75
58 (55)	1/2 DINAR	ND (ca. 1991). Like #54, but w/all Arabic text on back. More pinkish unpt. at upper corners. Sign. 3.	FV	FV	3.50
59 (57)	1 DINAR	ND (1993). Like #56 but w/modified green and pink unpt.	FV	FV	6.50
60 (58)	5 DINARS	ND (ca. 1991). Gray and violet on m/c unpt. Like #58 but w/all Arabic text on back.			
		a. Sign. 3.	FV	FV	27.50
		b. Sign. 4.	FV	FV	22.50
61 (59)	10 DINARS	ND (1991). Green on m/c unpt. Like #59 but w/unpt. in octagonal frame at upper r. on back. Sign. 4.	FV	FV	40.00

The Republic of Lithuania (formally the Lithuanian Soviet Federated Socialist Republic), southernmost of the Baltic states in east Europe, has an area of 26,173 sq. mi. (65,201 sq. km.) and a population of 3.72 million. Capital: Vilnius. The economy is based on livestock raising and manufacturing. Hogs, cattle, hides and electric motors are exported.

Lithuania emerged as a grand duchy joined to Poland through the Lublin Union in 1569. In the 15th century it was a major power of central Europe, stretching from the Baltic to the Black Sea. Following the third partition of Poland by Austria, Prussia and Russia, 1795, Lithuania came under Russian domination and did not regain its independence until shortly before the end of World War I when it declared itself a sovereign republic. The republic was occupied by Soviet troops in June of 1940 and annexed to the U.S.S.R. Following the German occupation of 1940-44, it was retaken by Russia and reestablished as a member republic of the Soviet Union. Western countries, including the United States, did not recognize Lithuania's incorporation into the Soviet Union.

Lithuania declared its independence March 11, 1990, and it was recognized by the United States on Sept. 2, 1991, followed by the Soviet government in Moscow on Sept. 6. They were seated in the UN General Assembly on Sept. 17, 1991.

MONETARY SYSTEM
1 Litas = 100 Centu

Lietuvos Ukio Bankas
Talonas System
1991 ISSUE

#29–31 plants on face, arms at ctr. in gray on back. W/ and w/o counterfeiting clause at bottom.

Cat#	Denomination	Date, description	VG	VF	Unc
29	0.10 TALONAS	1991. Brown on green and yellow unpt.			
		a. W/o 3 lines of black text at ctr.	.05	.10	.25
		b. W/3 lines of black text at ctr.	.05	.10	.25

30	0.20 TALONAS	1991. Lilac on green and yellow unpt. W/3 lines of black text at ctr.	.05	.10	.25

31	0.50 TALONAS	1991. Blue-green on green and yellow unpt.			
		a. W/o 3 lines of black text at ctr.	.05	.10	.25
		b. W/3 lines of black text at ctr.	.05	.10	.25
		c. As b. but first word of text VALSTYBI-NIS (error).	2.00	5.00	10.00

#32–38 value w/plants at ctr., arms in gray at r. Animals or birds on back. Wmk: Lg. squarish diamond w/symbol of the republic throughout paper. W/ and w/o counterfeiting clause at bottom on face.

Cat#	Denomination	Date, description	VG	VF	Unc
32	1 (TALONAS)	1991. Brown on yellow-gold unpt. Numeral w/cranberry branch at ctr. 2 lizards on back.			
		a. W/o text.	.05	.10	.25
		b. W/ text.	.05	.10	.25

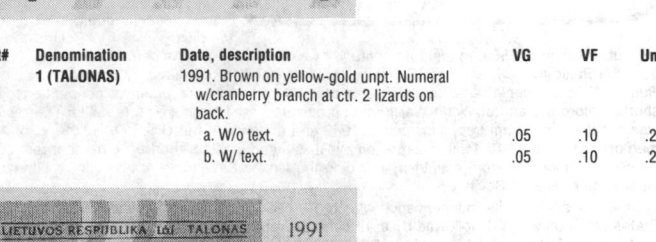

Cat#	Denomination	Date, description	VG	VF	Unc
36	25 (TALONU)	1991. Purplish gray on blue and orange unpt. Numerals w/pine tree branch at ctr. Lynx on back.			
		a. W/o text.	2.00	5.00	10.00
		b. W/ text.	.40	1.00	3.00

33	3 (TALONU)	1991. Dk. green and gray on blue-green, ochre and brown unpt. Numeral w/juniper branch at ctr. 2 birds (pewits) on back.			
		a. W/o text.	.10	.25	.75
		b. W/ text.	.10	.25	.75

37	50 (TALONU)	1991. Green and orange on orange unpt. Numerals w/seashore plant at ctr. Elk on back.			
		a. W/o text.	1.50	4.00	8.00
		b. W/ text.	.50	1.35	4.00

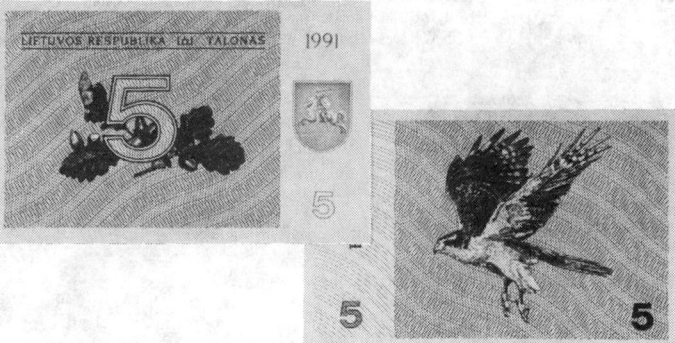

34	5 (TALONU)	1991. Dk. purple and gray on blue-green, green and gray unpt. Numeral w/oak tree branch at ctr. Hawk at ctr. on back.			
		a. W/o text.	.40	1.00	3.00
		b. W/ text.	.50	.75	1.00

38	100 (TALONU)	1991. Green and brown on brown unpt. Numerals and dandelions at ctr. European bison on back.			
		a. W/o text.	2.00	5.00	10.00
		b. W/ text.	1.00	2.50	7.50

1992 ISSUE

#39–44 value on plant at ctr., shield of arms at r. on face. Wmk. as #32–38. Smaller size than #32–38.

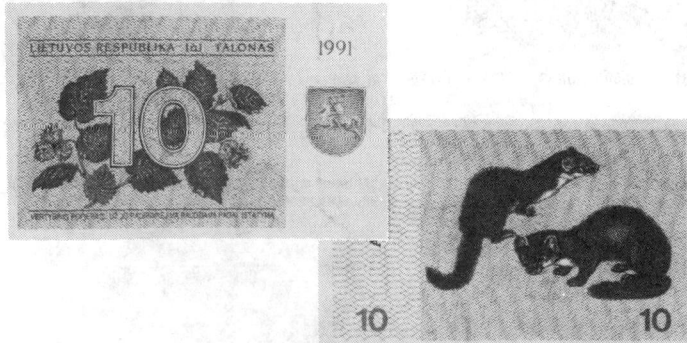

35	10 (TALONU)	1991. Brown on pinkish unpt. Numerals w/walnut tree branch at ctr. 2 martens on back.			
		a. W/o text.	.50	1.35	4.00
		b. W/ text.	.50	1.00	2.00

39	1 (TALONAS)	1992. Brown on orange and ochre unpt., dk. brown shield. 2 birds on back.	.05	.10	.20

Cat#	Denomination	Date, description	VG	VF	Unc
40	10 (TALONU)	1992. Brown on tan and ochre unpt., gray shield. Nest w/birds on back.	.10	.25	.75

| 41 | 50 (TALONU) | 1992. Dk. grayish green on lt. green and gray unpt., dk. gray-green shield. 2 birds on back. | .15 | .35 | 1.00 |

| 42 | 100 (TALONU) | 1992. Grayish purple on blue and red-orange unpt., gray shield. 2 martens on back. | .25 | .65 | 2.00 |

| 43 | 200 (TALONU) | 1992. Dk. brown on red and brown unpt., gray shield. 2 deer on back. | .40 | 1.00 | 3.00 |

| 44 | 500 (TALONU) | 1992. Brown-violet on blue unpt., brown shield. Bear on back. | 2.00 | 6.00 | 10.00 |

1993 ISSUE

#45–46 arms in brown at l., value w/branches at ctr. Animals on back. Wmk: Pattern repeated, circle w/design inside.

| 45 | 200 TALONU | 1993. Brown and red on blue unpt. 2 deer on back. | .65 | 1.65 | 5.00 |

Cat#	Denomination	Date, description	VG	VF	Unc
46	500 TALONU	1993. Brown on blue and brown unpt. 2 wolves on back.	.30	.75	2.25

NOTE: #46 was withdrawn after 6 weeks.

Litu System, 1993–

#47–50 arms "Vytis" at upper r. on back. Printer: USBNC (w/o imprint).

47	10 LITU	1991 (1993). Brownish black and dk. brown on tan unpt. Aviators S. Darius and S. Girénas at ctr. Monoplane "Lituanica" at upper ctr. on back.			
		a. *GIRFNAS* name w/o accent on E (error).	.60	2.00	6.00
		b. *GIRÉNAS* name w/accent on E.	.50	1.65	5.00

| 48 | 20 LITU | 1991 (1993). Dk. brown and green on violet and tan unpt. Bishop Maironis at r., Liberty at l. Museum of History in Kaunas at ctr. on back. | .85 | 3.00 | 10.00 |

| 49 | 50 LITU | 1991 (1993). Yellowish black and brown on ochre and tan unpt. J. Basanavicius at r. Cathedral at Vilnius at l. on back. | 2.00 | 7.00 | 20.00 |

Cat#	Denomination	Date, description	VG	VF	Unc
50	100 LITU	1991 (1993). Deep green, blue and brown on m/c unpt. Arms "Vytis" at ctr., S. Daukantas at r. Aerial view of University of Vilnius at l. ctr. on back.	3.00	10.00	30.00
51	500 LITU	1991. Arms "Vytis" at ctr. V. Kuoirka at r. Liberty bell on back. (Not issued).	—	—	—
52	1000 LITU	1991. Arms "Vytis" at ctr. M. Ciurliouis at r. 2 people on back. (Not issued).	—	—	—

1993–94 Dated Notes

#53–58 wmk: arms "Vytis." Shield w/"Vytis" at ctr. r. on back. Printer: TDLR (w/o imprint).

Cat#	Denomination	Date, description	VG	VF	Unc
56	10 LITU	1993. Dk. blue, dk. green, and brown-violet on m/c unpt. Similar to #47 but pilots at r.	FV	FV	5.00

53	1 LITAS	1994. Black and dk. brown on orange and m/c unpt. J. Zemaite at r.	FV	FV	1.00
57	20 LITU	1993. Dk. brown-violet and dk. green on m/c unpt. Similar to #48.	FV	FV	9.00

54	2 LITAI	1993. Black and dk. green on pale green and m/c unpt. Samogitian Bishop Valancius at r. Trakai castle at l. on back.	FV	FV	1.75
58	50 LITU	1993. Dk. brown, red-brown and blue-black on m/c unpt. Similar to #49.	FV	FV	17.50

55	5 LITAI	1993. Purple, violet and dk. blue-green on m/c unpt. J. Jablonskis at ctr. r. Mother and daughter at spinning wheel at l. on back.	FV	FV	2.75

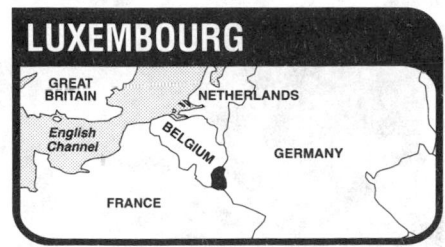

LUXEMBOURG

The Grand Duchy of Luxembourg is located in western Europe between Belgium, Germany and France, has an area of 998 sq. mi. (2,586 sq. km.) and a population of 390,000. Capital: Luxembourg. The economy is based on steel - Luxembourg's per capita production of 16 tons is the highest in the world.

Founded about 963, Luxembourg was a prominent country of the Holy Roman Empire; one of its sovereigns became Holy Roman Emperor as Henry VII, 1308. After being made a duchy by Emperor Charles IV, 1534, Luxembourg passed under the domination of Burgundy, Spain, Austria and France in 1443–1815. It regained autonomy under the Treaty of Vienna, 1815, as a grand duchy in union with the Netherlands, though ostensibly a member of the German Confederation. When Belgium seceded from the Kingdom of the Netherlands, 1830, Luxembourg was forced to cede its greater western section to Belgium. The tiny duchy left the German Confederation in 1867 when the Treaty of London recognized it as an independent state and guaranteed its perpetual neutrality. Luxembourg was occupied by Germany and liberated by American troops in both World Wars.

RULERS

Charlotte, 1919–64

Jean, 1964–

MONETARY SYSTEM

1 Franc = 100 Centimes

Die Internationale Bank in Luxemburg

International Bank in Luxembourg

Cat. #	Denomination	Date, description	VG	VF	Unc
14	100 FRANCS	1.5.1968. Green-blue and blue on m/c unpt. Tower at l., Grand Duke Jean at r. Steelworks and dam on back. Wmk: BIL.	2.00	4.00	15.00

14A	100 FRANCS	8.3.1981. Brown and purple on m/c unpt. Bridge to Luxembourg City at l., Grand Duke Jean at r., Henry in background. Two stylized female figures swirling around wmk. area on back. Wmk: BIL.	FV	3.50	4.50

1961–63 ISSUE

Cat. #	Denomination	Date, description	VG	VF	Unc
51	50 FRANCS	6.2.1961. Brown on m/c unpt. Grand Duchess Charlotte at r. Landscape w/combine harvester on back.	2.00	4.00	10.00
52	100 FRANCS	18.9.1963. Red-brown on m/c unpt. Grand Duchess Charlotte at r. Hydroelectric dam on back.	5.00	10.00	30.00

1966–70 ISSUE

#53–57, Grand Duke Jean at l. ctr. #53, 55–59 wmk: Grand Duke Jean.

53	10 FRANCS	20.3.1967. Green on m/c unpt. Grand Duchess Charlotte Bridge in city on back.	.50	1.25	3.50

54	20 FRANCS	7.3.1966. Blue on m/c unpt. Moselle River w/dam and lock on back.	FV	1.75	4.50

Cat. #	Denomination	Date, description	VG	VF	Unc
55	100 FRANCS	15.7.1970. Red on m/c unpt. View of Adolphe Bridge on back.	FV	4.00	8.50

1972; 1980 ISSUE

56	50 FRANCS	25.8.1972. Dk. brown on m/c unpt. Guilloche unpt at l. Factory on back.			
		a. Sign. title: *LE MINISTRE DES FINANCES.*	FV	FV	8.50
		b. Sign. title: *LE MINISTRE D'ETAT.*	FV	FV	7.00

57	100 FRANCS	14.8.1980. Red on m/c unpt. Grand Duke Jean at ctr. r., bldg. at l. Back gold and red; city of Luxembourg scene. Sign. varieties.	FV	FV	6.50

Institut Monetaire Luxembourgeois

SIGNATURE VARIETIES		
MINISTRE DU TRESOR		
1	J. Poos	2	J. Santer

#68–60, Grand Duke Jean at ctr. r. and as wmk.

58	100 FRANCS	ND (1986). Red on m/c unpt. Like #57 but w/new issuer's name.			
		a. W/o © symbol. Sign. 1. Series A-K.	FV	FV	6.50
		b. W/© symbol. Sign. 2. Series L-.	FV	FV	4.50

Cat. #	Denomination	Date, description	VG	VF	Unc
59	1000 FRANCS	ND (1985). Brown on m/c unpt. Castle of Vianden at l., Grand Duke Jean at ctr. Bldg. sketches at r. ctr. on back.	FV	FV	45.00

60	5000 FRANCS	ND (1993). Green, orange and olive-green on brown and m/c unpt. Chateau de Clevaux at l. 17th century map, European Center at Luxembourg-Kirchberg at ctr. r. on back.	FV	FV	200.00

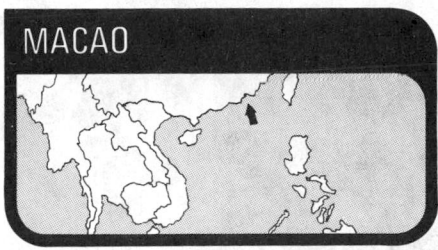

MACAO

The Province of Macao, a Portuguese overseas province located in the South China Sea 35 miles southwest of Hong Kong, consists of the peninsula of Macao and the islands of Taipa and Coloane. It has an area of 6 sq. mi. (16. sq. km.) and a population of 433,000. Capital: Macao. Macao's economy is based on light industry, commerce, tourism, fishing and gold trading - Macao is one of the few entirely free markets for gold in the world. Cement, textiles, firecrackers, vegetable oils and metal products are exported.

Established by the Portuguese in 1557, Macao is the oldest European settlement in the Far East. The Chinese, while agreeing to Portuguese settlement, did not recognize Portuguese sovereign rights and the Portuguese remained largely under control of the Chinese until 1849, when the Portuguese abolished the Chinese custom house and declared the independence of the port. The Manchu government formally recognized the Portuguese right to "perpetual occupation" of Macao in 1887, but its boundaries are still not delimited. In Mar. 1940 the Japanese army demanded recognition of the nearby "puppet" government at Changshan. in Sept. 1943 they demanded installation of their "advisors" in lieu of a military occupation.

Macao is scheduled to become a special administrative area under The Peoples Republic of China in 1999.

RULERS
Portuguese

MONETARY SYSTEM
1 Pataca = 100 Avos

PORTUGUESE INFLUENCE

Banco Nacional Ultramarino 大西洋國海外滙理銀行
Ta Hsi Yang Kuo Hai Wai Hui Li Yin Hang

1963–73 ISSUE

#49 and 50 O. Bispo D. Belchior Carneiro at r. Printer: BWC.

Cat. #	Denomination	Date, description	VG	VF	Unc
49	10 PATACAS	8.4.1963. Deep blue on m/c unpt. Portr. Bishop D. Belchlor Carneiro at r. Sign. varieties.	1.50	3.00	11.00
50	500 PATACAS	8.4.1963. Green on m/c unpt.	75.00	150.00	240.00

51	100 PATACAS	1.8.1966. Brown on m/c unpt. Portr. M. de Arriaga Brum da Silveira a t r. Flag atop archway at ctr. on back. Printer: TDLR.	20.00	30.00	60.00

Cat. #	Denomination	Date, description	VG	VF	Unc
52	5 PATACAS	21.3.1968. Brown on m/c unpt. Portr. Bishop D. Belchlor Carneiro at r. Sign. varieties.	1.00	2.50	8.50

53	100 PATACAS	13.12.1973. Blue on m/c unpt. Ruin of S. Paulo Cathedral at r. and as wmk. Sailing ship at l. on back. Sign. titles: *GOVERNADOR* and *ADMINISTRADOR* above signs.	15.00	25.00	50.00

1976–79 ISSUE

#54–57 w/text: *CONSELHO DE GESTAO* at ctr.

54	5 PATACAS	18.11.1976. Brown on m/c unpt. Portr. Bishop D. Belchlor Carneiro at r. Sign. varieties.	.75	1.25	5.00
55	10 PATACAS	7.12.1977. Blue on m/c unpt. Portr. Bishop D. Belchlor Carneiro at r.	1 50	2.50	7.50

56	50 PATACAS	1.9.1976. Greenish-gray on m/c unpt. Portr. L. de Camoes at r.	7.00	12.50	35.00

Cat. #	Denomination	Date, description	VG	VF	Unc
57	100 PATACAS	8.6.1979. Blue on m/c unpt. Like #53. Sign. title: *PRESIDENTE* at l. sign.	12.50	20.00	45.00
57A	500 PATACAS	24.4.1979. Green on m/c unpt. Like #50.	75.00	140.00	225.00

1981; 1988 ISSUE

#58–62 19th century harbor scene on back.

58	5 PATACAS	8.8.1981. Green and m/c. Temple at r.			
		a. W/sign. title: *PRESIDENTE* at l.	FV	FV	3.50
		b. W/o sign. title: *PRESIDENTE* at l. 2 sign. varieties.	FV	FV	3.00

59	10 PATACAS	8.8.1981; 12.5.1984. Brown and m/c. Light-house w/flag at r.			
		a. W/sign. title: *PRESIDENTE* at l.	FV	FV	6.00
		b. W/sign. title: *VICE-PRESIDENTE* at l.	FV	FV	5.50
		c. W/o sign. title at l. 2 sign. varieties.	FV	FV	4.50
		d. 3 decrees at upper l. 12.5.1984.	FV	FV	4.00

Cat. #	Denomination	Date, description	VG	VF	Unc
60	50 PATACAS	8.8.1981. Purple on m/c unpt. Portr. L. de Camoes at r.	FV	FV	16.50

61	100 PATACAS	1981; 1984. Blue, purple and m/c. Portr. C. Pessanha at r.			
		a. W/sign. title: *PRESIDENTE* at l. 8.8.1981.	FV	FV	30.00
		b. W/o sign. title: *PRESIDENTE* at l. 12.5.1984.	FV	FV	25.00

62	500 PATACAS	8.8.1981; 12.5.1984. Olive and m/c. Portr. V. de Morais at r. Peninsula on back.	FV	FV	100.00
63	1000 PATACAS	8.8.1988. Brown and yellow-orange on m/c unpt. Stylized dragon at r. Modern view of bridge to Macao on back.	FV	FV	185.00

1988 COMMEMORATIVE ISSUE

#64, 35th Anniversary Grand Prix

64	10 PATACAS	11.26–27.1988 (–old date 1984). Black ovpt. at l. on face, at ctr. on back of #59a.	—	—	10.00

1990–92 ISSUE

#65–69, bridge and city view on back. Wmk: Junk.

Cat. #	Denomination	Date, description	VG	VF	Unc
65	10 PATACAS	8.7.1991. Brown, olive and m/c. Bldg. at r.	FV	FV	3.00
66	50 PATACAS	13.7.1992. Olive-brown and m/c. Holiday marcher w/dragon costume at ctr. r., man at r.	FV	FV	12.50

67	100 PATACAS	13.7.1992. Black and m/c. Early painting of settlement at ctr., junk at r.	FV	FV	22.50
68	500 PATACAS	3.9.1990. Olive and m/c. Bldg. at r.	FV	FV	90.00
69	1000 PATACAS	8.7.1991. Orange and m/c. Dragon at r.	FV	FV	175.00

Banco da China

Chung Kuo Yin Hang

1995 ISSUE

#70–74 Bank of China-Macao bldg. at l., lotus blossom at lower ctr. on back. Wmk: Lotus blossom(s).

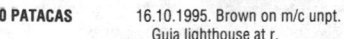

| 70 | 10 PATACAS | 16.10.1995. Brown on m/c unpt. Farel de Guia lighthouse at r. | FV | FV | 3.00 |

Cat. #	Denomination	Date, description	VG	VF	Unc
71	50 PATACAS	16.10.1995. Dk. Brown and brown on m/c unpt. University of Macao at r.	FV	FV	12.50

| 72 | 100 PATACAS | 16.10.1995. Brown and purple on m/c unpt. New terminal of Port Exterior at r. | FV | FV | 22.50 |

| 73 | 500 PATACAS | 16.10.1995. Black and greenish-black on m/c unpt. Ponte de Amizade bridge at r. | FV | FV | 90.00 |

| 74 | 1000 PATACAS | 16.10.1995. Brown, orange and red on m/c unpt. Aerial view of Praia Oeste. | FV | FV | 175.00 |

MACEDONIA

The Republic of Macedonia is land-locked, and is bordered in the north by Yugoslavia, to the east by Bulgaria, in the south by Greece and to the west by Albania. It has an area of 9,923 sq. mi. (25,713 sq. km.) and a population at the 1991 census was 2,038,847, of which the predominating ethnic groups were Macedonians. The capital is Skopje.

The Slavs, settled in Macedonia since the 6th century, who had been Christianized by Byzantium, were conquered by the non-Slav Bulgars in the 7th century and in the 9th century formed a Macedo-Bulgarian empire, the western part of which survived until Byzantine conquest in 1014. In the 14th century it fell to Serbia, and in 1355 to the Ottomans. After the Balkan Wars of 1912–13 Turkey was ousted, and Serbia received the greater part of the territory, the balance going to Bulgaria and Greece. In 1918, Yugoslav Macedonia was incorporated into Serbia as 'South Serbia,' becoming a republic in the S.F.R. of Yugoslavia. Claims to the historical Macedonian territory have long been a source of contention between Bulgaria and Greece.

On Nov. 20, 1991 parliament promulgated a new constitution, and declared its independence on Nov. 20, 1992, but failed to secure EC and US recognition owing to Greek objections to its use of the name "Macedonia." In December of 1992, the UN Security Council authorized the expedition of a small peacekeeping force to prevent hostilities spreading to Macedonia.

There is a 120-member single-chamber National Assembly.

MONETARY SYSTEM
1 Dena = 100 Deni

НАРОДНА БАНКА НА МАКЕДОНИЈА
(National Bank of Macedonia)

1992 ISSUE
#1–6 farmers harvesting at I. Ilenden monument in Krushevo at I. on back. Wmk. paper.

Cat. #	Denomination	Date, description	VG	VF	Unc
1	10 (DENAR)	1992. Blue-black on lilac unpt.	.05	.10	.25

Cat. #	Denomination	Date, description	VG	VF	Unc
2	25 (DENAR)	1992. Red on lilac unpt.	.10	.20	.35

Cat. #	Denomination	Date, description	VG	VF	Unc
3	50 (DENAR)	1992. Brown on ochre unpt.	.10	.25	.75

| 4 | 100 (DENAR) | 1992. Blue-black on lt. blue unpt. | .15 | .35 | 1.00 |

| 5 | 500 (DENAR) | 1992. Bright green on ochre unpt. | .40 | 1.65 | 5.00 |

| 6 | 1000 (DENAR) | 1992. Dull blue-violet on pink unpt. | .50 | 2.00 | 8.00 |

Cat. #	Denomination	Date, description	VG	VF	Unc
7	5000 (DENAR)	1992. Deep brown and dull red on m/c unpt. Woman at desk top computer at ctr. Ilenden monument at l. on back. Wmk. paper.	2.00	4.00	10.00

			VG	VF	Unc
8	10,000 (DENAR)	1992. Blue-black on pink and gray unpt. Bldgs. at ctr r. Musicians at l. of Ilenden monument at ctr. r. on back. Wmk. paper.	3.00	6.00	15.00

НАРОДНА БАНКА РЕПУБЛИКА МАКЕДОНИЈА
National Bank of the Republic of Macedonia

Currency Reform
1 "New" Denar = 100 "Old' Denari

1993 ISSUE

#9–12 wmk: Ilenden monument at Krushero.

			VG	VF	Unc
9	10 DENARI	1993. Lt. blue on m/c unpt. Ilenden monument at l. Houses on mountainside in Krushevo on back.	FV	FV	1.50

Cat. #	Denomination	Date, description	VG	VF	Unc
10	20 DENARI	1993. Wine-red on m/c unpt. Turkish bath in Skopje at l. Tower in Skopje vertically on back.	FV	FV	2.75

			VG	VF	Unc
11	50 DENARI	1993. Lt. red on m/c unpt. Church of St. Pantaleimon at l. Bldg. of National Bank in Skopje on back.	FV	FV	6.00

			VG	VF	Unc
12	100 DENARI	1993. Brown on m/c unpt. St. Sophia church in Ohrid at l. National Museum in Ohrid on back.	FV	FV	10.00

			VG	VF	Unc
13	500 DENARI	1993. Greenish gray on m/c unpt. Orthodox church at l. and as wmk. City Wall across upper back.	FV	FV	35.00

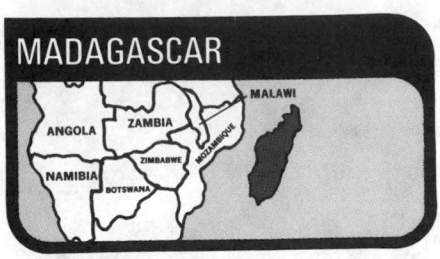

The Democratic Republic of Madagascar, an independent member of the French Community located in the Indian Ocean 250 miles (402 km.) off the southeast coast of Africa, has an area of 226,658 sq. mi. (587,041 sq. km.) and a population of 12.4 million. Capital: Antananarivo. The economy is primarily agricultural; large bauxite deposits are presently being developed. Coffee, vanilla, graphite and rice are exported.

Diago Diaz, a Portuguese navigator, sighted the island of Madagascar on Aug. 10, 1500, when his ship became separated from an India-bound fleet. Attempts at settlement by the British during the reign of Charles I and by the French during the 17th and 18th centuries were of no avail, and the island became a refuge and supply base for Indian Ocean pirates. Despite considerable influence on the island, the British accepted the imposition of a French protectorate in 1886 in return for French recognition of Britain's sphere of influence in Zanzibar. Madagascar was made a French colony in 1896 after absolute control had been established by military force. Britain occupied the island after the fall of France in 1942, to prevent its seizure by the Japanese, and gave it to the Free French in 1943. On Oct. 14, 1958, following a decade of intermittent but bitter warfare, Madagascar, as the Malagasy Republic, became an autonomous state within the French Community. On June 27, 1960, it became a sovereign independent nation, though remaining nominally within the French Community. The Malagasy Republic was renamed the Democratic Republic of Madagascar in 1976.

MONETARY SYSTEM

1 CFA Franc = 2 French Francs, 1948–59
1 CFA Franc = 0.02 French Franc, 1959–61
5 Malagasy Francs (F. M. G.) = 1 Ariary, 1961-

REPLACEMENT NOTES

#62-70, Z one or two numbers. #71–, ZZ prefix.

MALAGASY

Institut d'Emission Malgache

1961 (ND) PROVISIONAL ISSUE

#51–55 new bank name and new Ariary denominations ovpt. on previous issue of Banque de Madagascar et des Comores.

Cat. #	Denomination	Date, description	VG	VF	Unc
51	50 FRANCS= 10 Ariary	ND (1961). M/c. Woman w/hat at r. Man on back. Ovpt. on #45.			
		a. Sign. title: *LE CONTROLEUR GENERAL*.	3.00	12.50	50.00
		b. Sign. title: *LE DIRECTEUR GENERAL ADJOINT*.	3.00	15.00	60.00

Cat. #	Denomination	Date, description	VG	VF	Unc
52	100 FRANCS= 20 Ariary	ND (1961). M/c. Woman at r., palace of the Qn. of Tananariva in background. Woman, boats and animals on back. Ovpt. on #46b.	4.00	20.00	65.00

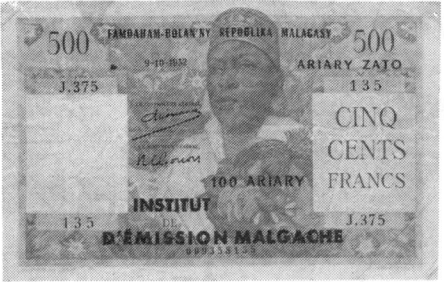

Cat. #	Denomination	Date, description	VG	VF	Unc
53	500 FRANCS= 100 Ariary	ND (1961). M/c. Man w/fruit at ctr. Ovpt. on #47.	15.00	65.00	200.00

Cat. #	Denomination	Date, description	VG	VF	Unc
54	1000 FRANCS= 200 Ariary	ND (1961 –old date 9.10.1952). M/c. Man and woman at l. ctr. Ox cart on back. Ovpt. on #48.	20.00	125.00	325.00
55	5000 FRANCS= 1000 Ariary	ND (1961). M/c. Gallieni at upper l., woman at r. Woman and baby on back. Ovpt. on #49.	50.00	275.00	650.00

NOTE: #53–55 some notes also have old dates of intended or original issue (1952–55).

1963 (ND) REGULAR ISSUE

Cat. #	Denomination	Date, description	VG	VF	Unc
56	1000 FRANCS= 200 Ariary	ND (1963). M/c. People in canoes at l., president at ctr. Wmk: Woman's head.			
		a. W/o sign. and title.	50.00	375.00	600.00
		b. W/sign. and title.	40.00	250.00	550.00

1966 (ND) ISSUE

#57–60 wmk: Woman's head.

Cat. #	Denomination	Date, description	VG	VF	Unc
57	100 FRANCS= 20 Ariary	ND (1966). M/c. 3 women spinning. Trees on back. 2 sign. varieties.	2.50	10.00	30.00

Cat. #	Denomination	Date, description	VG	VF	Unc
58	500 FRANCS= 100 Ariary	ND (1966). M/c. Woman at l., landscape in background. River scene on back. 2 sign varieties.	5.00	35.00	165.00

Cat. #	Denomination	Date, description	VG	VF	Unc
59	1000 FRANCS= 200 Ariary	ND (1966). M/c. Woman and man at l. Similar to #48 and #54 but size 150 x 80mm.	7.50	40.00	175.00

Cat. #	Denomination	Date, description	VG	VF	Unc
60	5000 FRANCS= 1000 Ariary	ND (1966). M/c. President at l., workers in rice field at r. Women and boy on back.	12.50	45.00	200.00

1969 ISSUE

61	50 FRANCS= 10 Ariary	ND (1969). M/c. Like #45 and #51. Different sign. title.	2.25	7.50	25.00

MADAGASCAR DEMOCRATIC REPUBLIC
Banque Centrale de la République Malgache
1974 (ND) ISSUE

Cat. #	Denomination	Date, description	VG	VF	Unc
62	50 FRANCS= 10 Ariary	ND (1974–75). Violet and m/c. Young man at r. Fruit market on back.	1.50	4.00	10.00
63	100 FRANCS= 20 Ariary	ND. Brown and m/c. Old man at r. Rice planting on back.	1.50	4.00	12.00

#64–66 wmk: Zebu's head.

64	500 FRANCS= 100 Ariary	ND. Green and m/c. Butterfly at l., young woman at r. Dancers on back.	2.50	6.00	20.00
65	1000 FRANCS= 200 Ariary	ND. Blue and m/c. Lemurs at l., man in straw hat at r. Trees and designs on back.	3.50	8.00	37.50

66	5000 FRANCS= 1000 Ariary	ND. Red, violet and m/c. Oxen at l., young woman at r. Back violet and orange; tropical plants and African carving at ctr.	15.00	30.00	70.00

Banky Foiben'i Madagasikara
1983 (ND) ISSUE

#67–70 wmk: Zebu's head. Sign. varieties.

67	500 FRANCS= 100 Ariary	ND (1983–87). Brown, gray and m/c. Boy w/fish in net at ctr. Aerial view of port at r. on back.	FV	1.50	5.00

Cat. #	Denomination	Date, description	VG	VF	Unc
71	500 FRANCS= 100 Ariary	ND (1988–93). Similar to #67, but modified unpt.	FV	1.50	4.00

Cat. #	Denomination	Date, description	VG	VF	Unc
68	1000 FRANCS= 200 Ariary	ND (1983–87). Violet and m/c. Man w/hat playing flute at ctr. Fruits and vegetables at r. on back.	FV	2.00	7.50

| 72 | 1000 FRANCS= 200 Ariary | ND (1988–93). Similar to #68, but modified unpt. | FV | 2.50 | 7.50 |

| 69 | 5000 FRANCS= 1000 Ariary | ND (1983–87). Blue and m/c. Woman and child at ctr. School, book and monument at r. on back. | FV | 9.00 | 32.50 |

| 73 | 5000 FRANCS= 1000 Ariary | ND (1988–). Similar to #69, but modified unpt. | FV | 7.00 | 20.00 |

| 70 | 10,000 FRANCS= 2000 Ariary | ND (1983–87). Green on m/c unpt. Young girl w/sheaf at ctr. Harvesting rice at r. on back. | FV | 20.00 | 65.00 |

1988 (ND) ISSUE

#71–76 vertical serial # at r. Sign. varieties. Wmk: Zebu's head.

| 74 | 10,000 FRANCS= 2000 Ariary | ND (1988–). Similar to #70, but modified unpt. | FV | 10.00 | 30.00 |

1993–95 (ND) ISSUE

#75–78 wmk: Zebu's head.

Cat. #	Denomination	Date, description	VG	VF	Unc
75 (77)	500 FRANCS= 100 Ariary	ND (1994). Dk. brown and dk. green on m/c unpt. Girl at r., village in unpt. at upper ctr. Herdsmen w/Zebus, village in background at l. ctr. on back.	FV	FV	2.00

76 (78)	1000 FRANCS= 200 Ariary	ND (1994). Dk. brown and dk. blue on m/c unpt. Young man at r., boats in background. Young woman w/basket of shellfish, fisherman working w/net at l. ctr. on back.	FV	FV	3.00
77 (75)	2500 FRANCS= 500 Ariary	ND (1993). Red, green, blue and black on m/c unpt. Older woman at ctr. Heron, tortoise, monkey, butterfly in foliage on back.	FV	FV	6.50
78	5000 FRANCS= 1000 Ariary	ND (1995). Dk. brown and violet on lilac and m/c unpt. Young make head at r., ox cart, cane cutters at ctr. Animals, birds and seashells on back.	FV	FV	5.00
79	10,000 FRANCS= 2000 Ariary	ND (1995). Dk. brown on tan and m/c unpt. Old man at r., statuette, local artifacts at ctr. e artisans at work on back.	FV	FV	8.50

| 80 (76) | 25,000 FRANCS= 5000 Ariary | ND (1993) Olive-green and green on m/c unpt. Old man at ctr., island outline at l. Scene of traditional bullfighting at r. on back. | FV | FV | 20.00 |

MALAWI

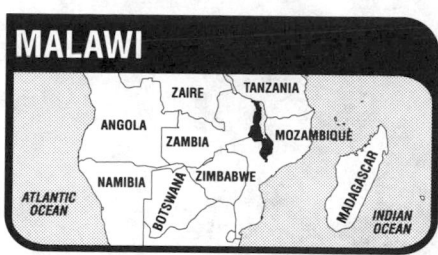

The Republic of Malawi (formerly Nyasaland), located in southeastern Africa to the west of Lake Malawi (Nyasa), has an area of 45,747 sq. mi. (118,484 sq. km.) and a population of 8.6 million. Capital: Lilongwe. The economy is predominantly agricultural. Tobacco, tea, peanuts and cotton are exported.

Although the Portuguese, heirs to the restless spirit of Prince Henry, were the first Europeans to reach the Malawi area, the first meaningful contact was made by missionary-explorer Dr. David Livingstone who arrived at Lake Malawi on Sept. 16, 1859, and remained to make extensive explorations in the 1860s. Subsequent clashes between settlements of Scottish missionaries and Arab slave traders, and the procurement of development rights by Cecil Rhodes, 1884, stimulated British interest and brought about the establishment of the Nyasaland protectorate in 1891. In 1953, Nyasaland reluctantly joined the Federation of Rhodesia and Nyasaland and, after prolonged protest, was granted self-government within the federation. Nyasaland became the independent nation of Malawi on July 6, 1964, and became a republic two years later. Malawi is a member of the Commonwealth of Nations. The president is the Chief of State and Head of Government.

Also see Rhodesia, Rhodesia and Nyasaland.

RULERS

British to 1964

MONETARY SYSTEM

1 Pound = 20 Shillings to 1971
1 Kwacha = 100 Tambala 1971–

REPLACEMENT NOTES

#13–17, ZZ prefix. #18-22, V/1, W/1, X/1, Y/1, Z/1 prefix by denomination.

#23-27, ZZ prefix.

Reserve Bank of Malawi

1964 Reserve Bank Act

Pound System

1964 FIRST ISSUE

#1–4 portr. Dr. H. K. Banda at l., sunrise, fishermen in boat on Lake Malawi at ctr. Sign. title: *GOVERNOR* only. Wmk: Rooster.

Cat. #	Denomination	Date, description	VG	VF	Unc
1	5 SHILLINGS	L.1964. Blue-gray. Arms w/bird on back.	4.00	14.00	65.00
2	10 SHILLINGS	L.1964. Brown. Workers in tobacco field on back.	7.50	55.00	225.00

| 3 | 1 POUND | L.1964. Green. Workers picking cotton on back. | 7.50 | 62.50 | 250.00 |

Cat. #	Denomination	Date, description	VG	VF	Unc
4	5 POUNDS	*L.1964.* Blue and brown. Tea pickers below Mt. Mulanje on back.	20.00	100.00	600.00

1964 SECOND ISSUE

#1A–3A portr. Dr. H. K. Banda at l., fishermen at ctr. Sign. titles: *GOVERNOR* and *GENERAL MANAGER*.

Cat. #	Denomination	Date, description	VG	VF	Unc
1A	5 SHILLINGS	*L.1964.* Like #1.	2.50	10.00	42.50

| 2A | 10 SHILLINGS | *L.1964.* Like #2. | 3.50 | 14.50 | 57.50 |
| 3A | 1 POUND | *L.1964.* Like #3. | 5.50 | 22.50 | 90.00 |

Kwacha System

1964 Reserve Bank Act

1971 ISSUE

5	50 TAMBALA	*L.1964* (1971). Blue-gray. Face Like #1A. Roadway border checkpoint on back.	5.50	22.50	90.00
6	1 KWACHA	*L.1964* (1971). Brown. Like #2A.	12.00	48.50	185.00
7	2 KWACHA	*L.1964* (1971). Green. Like #3A.	14.00	55.00	225.00

Cat. #	Denomination	Date, description	VG	VF	Unc
8	10 KWACHA	*L.1964* (1971). Blue and brown. Like #4 but 2 signs.	22.00	87.50	350.00

1973-74 ISSUE

#9–12 portr. Dr. H. K. Banda as Prime Minister at r. W/ or w/o dates. Wmk: Rooster.

9	50 TAMBALA	*L.1964* (ND); 1974–75. Gray-green. Sugar cane harvesting on back.			
		a. ND (1973).	3.75	15.00	90.00
		b. 30.6.1974.	1.50	6.50	37.50
		c. 31.1.1975.	.85	3.50	20.00
10	1 KWACHA	*L.1964* (ND); 1974–75. Brown. Plantation worker, hill in background on back.			
		a. ND (1973).	4.00	16.50	100.00
		b. 30.6.1974.	3.00	12.00	60.00
		c. 31.1.1975.	1.25	5.00	30.00
11	5 KWACHA	*L.1964* (ND); 1974–75. Red. Worker w/basket at ctr., *K5* at upper l. on back.			
		a. ND (1973).	11.00	45.00	275.00
		b. 30.6.1974.	8.50	35.00	210.00
		c. 31.1.1975.	6.50	26.50	160.00
12	10 KWACHA	*L.1964* (ND); 1974–75. Blue. Plantation workers, w/mountains in background on back.			
		a. ND (1973).	12.50	50.00	300.00
		b. 30.6.1974.	13.50	53.50	325.00
		c. 31.1.1975.	7.50	30.00	185.00

1976; 1983 ISSUE

#13–17 portr. Dr. H. K. Banda as President at r. Wmk: Rooster. Sign. varieties.

Cat. #	Denomination	Date, description	VG	VF	Unc
13	50 TAMBALA	1976–84. Gray-blue. Cotton harvest on back.			
		a. 31.1.1976; 1.7.1978.	.75	3.00	15.00
		b. 1.5.1982.	.50	2.00	10.00
		c. 1.1.1983.	.75	3.00	15.00
		d. 1.11.1984.	1.00	4.50	22.50

Cat. #	Denomination	Date, description	VG	VF	Unc
14	1 KWACHA	1976–84. Violet-brown on m/c unpt. Workers harvesting, mountains in background on back.			
		a. 31.1.1976; 1.7.1978; 30.6.1979.	.75	3.00	15.00
		b. 1.1.1981; 1.5.1982; 1.1.1983; 1.4.1984	.50	2.00	10.00
		c. 1.11.1984.	.60	1.75	9.00

Cat. #	Denomination	Date, description	VG	VF	Unc
15	5 KWACHA	1976–84. Red. Field workers, *K5* at upper r. on back.			
		a. 31.1.1976; 1.7.1978; 30.6.1979.	2.75	11.00	55.00
		b. 1.1.1981–1.1.1983.	1.75	7.00	35.00
		c. 1.11.1984.	2.00	8.00	40.00

Cat. #	Denomination	Date, description	VG	VF	Unc
16	10 KWACHA	1976–84. Deep blue and brown on m/c unpt. Capital bldg. at Lilongwe on back.			
		a. 31.1.1976; 1.7.1978; 30.6.1979.	5.00	20.00	100.00
		b. 1.1.1981; 1.1.1983.	3.75	15.00	75.00
		c. 1.11.1984; 1.8.1985.	5.00	20.00	100.00

Cat. #	Denomination	Date, description	VG	VF	Unc
17	20 KWACHA	1983; 1984. Green, brown-violet and m/c. Back green and m/c. Bank at ctr.			
		a. 1.7.1983.	3.75	15.00	75.00
		b. 1.11.1984.	8.75	35.00	175.00

1986 ISSUE

#18–22 Pres. Banda at r. Wmk: Rooster.

Cat. #	Denomination	Date, description	VG	VF	Unc
18	50 TAMBALA	1.3.1986. Dk. brown on m/c unpt. Picking corn on back.	.15	.75	4.00

Cat. #	Denomination	Date, description	VG	VF	Unc
19	1 KWACHA	1986; 1988. Brown-violet on m/c unpt. Cultivating tobacco on back.			
		a. 1.3.1986.	.45	1.75	7.00
		b. 1.4.1988.	.15	.75	4.00

Cat. # 20	Denomination 5 KWACHA	Date, description 1986; 1988. Red-orange on m/c unpt. University of Malawi on back.	VG	VF	Unc
		a. 1.3.1986.	1.85	7.50	30.00
		b. 1.4.1988.	.90	3.75	15.00

Cat. # 21	Denomination 10 KWACHA	Date, description 1986; 1988. Blue-black on m/c unpt. Lilongwe, capital city, on back.	VG	VF	Unc
		a. 1.3.1986.	3.00	12.50	50.00
		b. 1.4.1988.	2.00	8.50	35.00

22	20 KWACHA	1986; 1988. Deep green on m/c unpt. Kamuzu International Airport on back.			
		a. 1.3.1986.	6.00	25.00	100.00
		b. 1.4.1988.	3.00	13.00	52.00

1990–94 ISSUES

Act 1989

#23–28 palm tree, man in dugout canoe, and rayed silver circle at ctr., portr. Dr. H. K. Banda as President at r. Ascending vertical serial # at l. Wmk: Rooster.

Cat. # 23	Denomination 1 KWACHA	Date, description 1990; 1992. Brown-violet on m/c unpt. Back like #19.	VG	VF	Unc
		a. 1.12.1990.	FV	FV	2.50
		b. 1.5.1992.	FV	FV	1.75

24	5 KWACHA	1990; 1994. Red-orange and olive-green on m/c unpt. University of Malawi at l. ctr. on back.			
		a. 1.12.1990.	FV	FV	7.00
		b. 1.1.1994.	FV	FV	3.50

25	10 KWACHA	1990–94. Blue-gray, blue-violet and dk. brown on m/c unpt. Lilongwe City municipal bldg. at l. ctr. on back.			
		a. 1.12.1990.	FV	FV	12.50
		b. 1.9.1992.	FV	FV	8.50
		c. Smaller sign. as b. 1.1.1994.	FV	FV	5.00
26	20 KWACHA	1.9.1990. Green, orange and blue on m/c unpt. Kamuzu International Airport at l. ctr. on back.	FV	FV	10.00
27	20 KWACHA	1.7.1993. Like #26 but w/larger airplane on back.	FV	FV	5.50

Cat. #	Denomination	Date, description	VG	VF	Unc
28	50 KWACHA	1990; 1994. Pale purple, violet and blue on m/c unpt.			
		a. 1.6.1990.	FV	11.00	45.00
		b. 1.1.1994.	—	—	22.50

MALAYA & BRITISH BORNEO

Malaya and British Borneo, a Currency Commission named the Board of Commissioners of Currency, Malaya and British North Borneo, was initiated on Jan. 1, 1952, for the purpose of providing a common currency for use in Johore, Kelantan, Kedah, Perlis, Trengganu, Negri Sembilan, Pahang, Perak, Salangor, Penang, Malacca, Singapore, North Borneo, Sarawak and Brunei. For later issues see Brunei, Malaysia and Singapore.

RULERS
British

MONETARY SYSTEM
1 Dollar = 100 Cents

Board of Commissioners of Currency

#8–9 arms of 5 states on back. Wmk: Tiger's head.

Cat. #	Denomination	Date, description	VG	VF	Unc
8	1 DOLLAR	1.3.1959. Blue on m/c unpt. Sailing boat at l. Men w/boat on back.			
		a. Printer: W&S.	3.75	15.00	60.00
		b. Printer: TDLR.	1.75	7.00	28.00

29	100 KWACHA	1993; 1994. Blue-violet, purple, violet and bright green on m/c unpt. Trucks hauling grain to storage facility at ctr. on back.			
		a. 1.4.1993.	FV	15.00	60.00
		b. 1.1.1994.	FV	FV	18.50
30	200 KWACHA	1.6.1995. Brown-violet, olive-green and silver on m/c unpt. Pres. Muluzi at r., sunrise, fisherman in boat on Lake Malawi at ctr., bird at upper l. Elephants on back.	FV	FV	35.00

Cat. #	Denomination	Date, description	VG	VF	Unc
9	10 DOLLARS	1.3.1961. Red and dk. brown on m/c unpt. Farmer plowing w/ox at r. Printer: TDLR.			
		a. Sm. serial #. Series A.	16.50	50.00	150.00
		b. Lg. serial #. Series A.	17.50	52.50	160.00
		c. Lg. serial #. Series B.	18.50	55.00	165.00

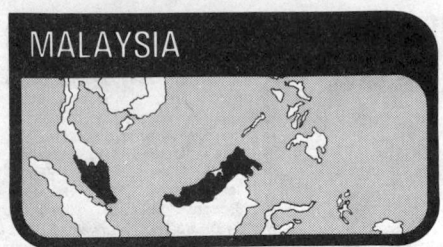

Malaysia, an independent federation of southeast Asia consisting of 11 states of West Malaysia on the Malay Peninsula and two states of East Malaysia on the island of Borneo, has an area of 127,316 sq. mi. (329,747 sq. km.) and a population of 18.6 million. Capital: Kuala Lumpur. The federation came into being on Sept. 16, 1963. Rubber, timber, tin, iron ore and bauxite are exported.

The constituent states of Malaysia are Johore, Kedah, Kelantan, Malacca, Negri Sembilan, Pahang, Penang, Perak, Perlis, Selangor and Trengganu of West Malaysia; and Sabah and Sarawak of East Malaysia. Singapore joined the federation in 1963, but broke away on Aug. 9, 1965, to become an independent republic. Malaysia is a member of the Commonwealth of Nations. The "Paramount Ruler" is Chief of State. The prime minister is Head of Government.

MONETARY SYSTEM

1 Ringgit (Dollar) = 100 Sen

REPLACEMENT NOTES

#1 3-5, 7-11, 13, Z/# prefix. #15b–17b, X/# prefix. #19–24, 27-34, a BA, WA, UZ or ZZ prefix by denomination.

Bank Negara Malaysia

All notes w/Yang Di-Pertuan Agong, Tunku Abdul Rahman, first Head of State of Malaysia (died 1960).

1967 ISSUE

#1–6 old spelling of *DI-PERLAKUKAN*. Arms on back. Wmk: Tiger's head. Sign. of Ismail Md. Ali w/title: *GABENOR*.

#1–2 printer: BWC.

Cat. #	Denomination	Date, description	VG	VF	Unc
1	1 RINGGIT	ND (1967–72). Blue on m/c unpt.			
		a. Solid security thread.	FV	1.00	5.00
		b. Segmented foil security thread.	FV	1.25	5.50

2	5 RINGGIT	ND (1967–72). Green on m/c unpt.			
		a. Solid security thread.	FV	5.00	25.00
		b. Segmented foil security thread.	FV	5.50	27.50

#3–5 printer: TDLR.

3	10 RINGGIT	ND (1967–72). Red-orange on m/c unpt. (SA-PULOH).			
		a. Solid security thread.	FV	5.50	20.00
		b. Segmented foil security thread.	FV	6.00	22.50
4	50 RINGGIT	ND (1967–72). Blue on m/c unpt. (LIMA PULOH).			
		a. Solid security thread.	FV	25.50	60.00
		b. Segmented foil security thread.	FV	25.00	62.50

Cat. #	Denomination	Date, description	VG	VF	Unc
5	100 RINGGIT	ND (1967–72). Violet on m/c unpt. (SA-RATUS).			
		a. Solid security thread.	FV	50.00	150.00
		b. Segmented foil security thread.	FV	FV	140.00
6	1000 RINGGIT	ND (1967–72). Brown-violet on m/c unpt. (SA-RIBU). Printer: BWC.	FV	500.00	850.00

1972 ISSUE

#7–12 new spelling *DIPERLAKUKAN*. Arms on back. Wmk: Tiger's head. Sign. of of Ismail Md. Ali w/title: *GABENUR*.

#7–8 printer: BWC.

7	1 RINGGIT	ND (1972–76). Blue on m/c unpt.	FV	1.00	3.50

8	5 RINGGIT	ND (1976). Green on m/c unpt.	FV	3.00	7.50

#9 and 10 printer: TDLR.

9	10 RINGGIT	ND (1972–76). Red-orange and brown on m/c unpt. (SEPULUH). Printer: TDLR.			
		a. Solid security thread.	FV	5.00	12.50
		b. Segmented foil security thread.	FV	5.00	13.50

Cat. #	Denomination	Date, description	VG	VF	Unc
10	50 RINGGIT	ND (1972–76). Blue on m/c unpt. *(LIMA PULUH)*.			
		a. Solid security thread.	FV	22.50	50.00
		b. Segmented foil security thread.	FV	22.50	52.50

#11 and 12 printer: BWC.

| 11 | 100 RINGGIT | ND (1972–76). Violet on m/c unpt. *(SERATUS)*. | FV | 50.00 | 100.00 |
| 12 | 1000 RINGGIT | ND (1972–76). Brown-violet on m/c unpt. *(SERIBU)*. | FV | FV | 650.00 |

1976; 1981 ISSUE

#13–18 arms on back. Wmk: Tiger's head.

#13–16 different guilloche w/latent image numeral at lower l.

#13–15 printer: BWC.

13	1 RINGGIT	ND (1976–83). Blue on m/c unpt. Like #7.			
		a. Sign. Ismail Md. Ali. (1976).	FV	.75	2.00
		b. Sign. Abdul Aziz Taha. (1981).	FV	.70	1.50
14	5 RINGGIT	ND (1976–83). Green on m/c unpt. Like #8.			
		a. Sign. Ismail Md. Ali. (1976).	FV	3.00	6.00
		b. Sign. Abdul Aziz Taha. (1981).	FV	2.50	5.00
15	10 RINGGIT	ND (1976–81). Red-orange and brown on m/c unpt. Like #9. Sign. Ismail Md. Ali. (1976).	FV	6.00	9.00
15A	10 RINGGIT	ND (1981–83). Like #15 but printer: TDLR. Sign. Abdul Aziz Taha.	FV	5.00	8.00

16	50 RINGGIT	ND (1976–83). Blue on m/c unpt. Like #10. Printer: BWC.			
		a. Sign. Ismail Md. Ali. (1976).	FV	30.00	40.00
		b. Sign. Abdul Aziz Taha. (1981).	FV	30.00	40.00
17	100 RINGGIT	ND (1976–83). Purple on m/c unpt. Like #11. Printer: TDLR.			
		a. Sign. Ismail Md. Ali. (1976).	FV	50.00	70.00
		b. Sign. Abdul Aziz Taha. (1981).	FV	FV	65.00
18	1000 RINGGIT	ND (1976–81). Purple and green on m/c unpt. Like #12. Sign. Ismail Md. Ali. Printer: BWC.	FV	FV	550.00

1981-83 ISSUES

#19–26 new design w/marks for the blind. Sign. of Abdul Aziz Taha. Wmk: Portr. of T.A. Rahman.

Cat. #	Denomination	Date, description	VG	VF	Unc
19	1 RINGGIT	ND (1982–84). Blue and brown on pink and m/c unpt. National Monument Kuala Lumpurate at ctr. on back. Printer: BWC.	FV	.50	1.25

#19A–21 printer: TDLR.

| 19A | 1 RINGGIT | ND (1981–83). Like #19. | FV | .50 | 1.00 |

| 20 | 5 RINGGIT | ND (1983–84). Dk. green and blue on m/c unpt. King's Palace at Kuala Lumpur on back. | FV | 2.50 | 4.00 |

| 21 | 10 RINGGIT | ND (1983–84). Red and brown on m/c unpt. Railway station at Kuala Lumpur on back. | FV | 4.50 | 7.50 |

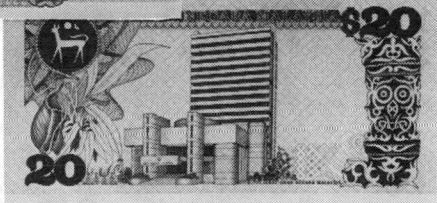

Cat. #	Denomination	Date, description	VG	VF	Unc
22	20 RINGGIT	ND (1982–84). Deep. brown and dk. blue on m/c unpt. Bank Negara Malaysia bldg. in Kuala Lumpur on back. Printer: BWC.	FV	9.00	15.00

| 23 | 50 RINGGIT | ND (1983–84). Black and blue-gray on m/c unpt. National Museum at Kuala Lumpur on back. Printer: TDLR. | FV | 22.50 | 32.00 |

| 24 | 100 RINGGIT | ND (1983–84). Red-brown and violet on m/c unpt. National Mosque in Kuala Lumpur on back. Printer: TDLR. | FV | 45.00 | 65.00 |

| 25 | 500 RINGGIT | ND (1982–84). Dk. red and purple on m/c unpt. High Court bldg. in Kuala Lumpur on back. Printer: BWC. | FV | 225.00 | 300.00 |

Cat. #	Denomination	Date, description	VG	VF	Unc
26	1000 RINGGIT	ND (1983–84). Gray-green on m/c unpt. Parliament bldg. in Kuala Lumpur on back. Printer: TDLR.	FV	425.00	550.00

1986-95 ISSUES

#27–34 similar to #19–26 but no mark for the blind, white space for wmk. (both sides), and vertical serial #. Sign. Datuk Jaafar Hussein. Wmk: Portr. T.A. Rahman.

#27-31 printer: TDLR.

27	1 RINGGIT	ND (1986; 1989). Blue on m/c unpt.			
		a. Usual security thread (1986).	FV	FV	1.00
		b. Segmented foil security thread (1989).	FV	FV	.85

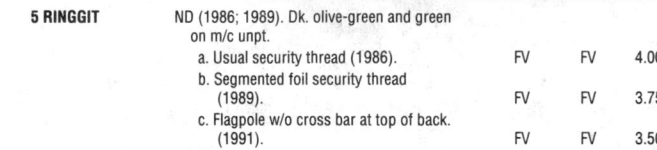

28	5 RINGGIT	ND (1986; 1989). Dk. olive-green and green on m/c unpt.			
		a. Usual security thread (1986).	FV	FV	4.00
		b. Segmented foil security thread (1989).	FV	FV	3.75
		c. Flagpole w/o cross bar at top of back. (1991).	FV	FV	3.50

| 29 | 10 RINGGIT | ND (1989). Brown, red-orange and violet on m/c unpt. Segmented foil security thread (1989). | FV | FV | 7.50 |

Cat. #	Denomination	Date, description	VG	VF	Unc

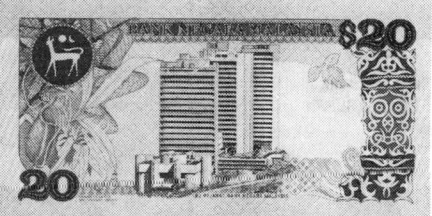

| 30 | 20 RINGGIT | ND (1989). Deep. brown, olive and m/c. | FV | FV | 12.50 |

| 31 | 50 RINGGIT | ND (1989). Blue and m/c. Segmented silver foil over security thread. | FV | FV | 27.50 |
| 31A | 50 RINGGIT | ND (1991–92). Like #31, but printer: BABN. | FV | FV | 25.00 |

| 32 | 100 RINGGIT | ND (1989). Purple and m/c. Segmented silver foil over security thread. Printer: TDLR. | FV | FV | 55.00 |
| 32A | 100 RINGGIT | ND (1991–93). Like #32, but printer: USBNC. | FV | FV | 50.00 |

#33–34 printer: TDLR.

| 33 | 500 RINGGIT | ND (1989). Red, brown and yellow. Segmented foil security thread. | FV | FV | 225.00 |
| 34 | 1000 RINGGIT | ND (1989). Blue, green and purple. Segmented foil security thread. | FV | FV | 450.00 |

1995 ISSUE

#35–38 sign. Ahmed Mohd. Don. Wmk. portr. T.A. Rahman.

Cat. #	Denomination	Date, description	VG	VF	Unc
35	5 RINGGIT	ND (1995). Like #28 but printer: TDLR.	FV	FV	3.50

36	10 RINGGIT	ND (1995). Like #29 but printer: F-CO.	FV	FV	6.50
37 (29A)	10 RINGGIT	ND (1995). Dk. brown, red-orange and violet on m/c unpt. Like #29 but printer: BABN.	FV	FV	10.00
38	10 RINGGIT	ND (1995). Like #29 but printer: G&D.	FV	FV	6.50

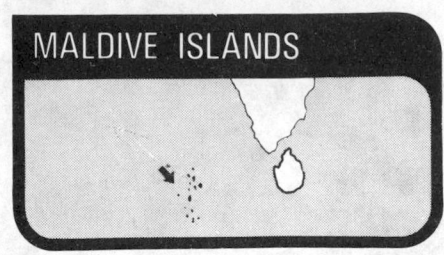

The Republic of Maldives, an archipelago of 2,000 coral islets in the northern Indian Ocean 417 miles (671 km.) southwest of Ceylon, has an area of 115 sq. mi. (298 sq. km.) and a population of 213,200. Capital: Malé. Fishing employs 95 percent of the work force. Dried fish, copra and coir yarn are exported.

The Maldive Islands were visited by Arab traders and converted to Islam in 1153. After being harassed in the 16th and 17th centuries by Mopla pirates of the Malabar coast and Portuguese raiders, the Maldivians voluntarily placed themselves under the suzerainty of Ceylon. In 1887, the islands became an internally self-governing British protectorate and a nominal dependency of Ceylon. Traditionally a sultanate, the Maldives became a republic in 1953 but restored the sultanate in 1954. The Sultanate of the Maldive Islands attained complete internal and external autonomy on July 26, 1965, and on Nov. 11, 1968 again became a republic.

RULERS

British to 1965

MONETARY SYSTEM

1 Rupee = 100 Lari

Maldivian State, Government Treasurer

#2–7 palm tree and dhow at l., dhow at r.

Cat. #	Denomination	Date, description	VG	VF	Unc
2	1 RUPEE	1947; 1960. Blue and green on m/c unpt. Bldgs. on back.			
		a. 14.11.1947/AH1367.	2.00	6.00	15.00
		b. 4.6.1960/AH1379.	.50	1.00	2.50

3	2 RUPEES	1947; 1960. Brown and blue on m/c unpt. Pavilion on back.			
		a. 14.11.1947/AH1367.	2.50	7.50	17.50
		b. 4.6.1960/AH1379.	.75	1.50	3.00
4	5 RUPEES	1947; 1960. Violet and orange on m/c unpt. Bldg. on back.			
		a. 14.11.1947/AH1367.	2.00	6.00	15.00
		b. 4.6.1960/AH1379.	1.00	2.50	6.00

Cat. #	Denomination	Date, description	VG	VF	Unc
5	10 RUPEES	1947; 1960. Brown on m/c unpt. Bldg. on back.			
		a. 14.11.1947/AH1367.	2.50	5.00	15.00
		b. 4.6.1960/AH1379.	5.00	15.00	40.00

6	50 RUPEES	1951-80. Blue on m/c unpt. Waterfront bldg. on back.			
		a. 1951/AH1371.	30.00	75.00	200.00
		b. 4.6.1960/AH1379.	5.50	15.00	30.00
		c. Litho. 1.8.1980/AH17.7.1400.	6.00	17.50	35.00

7	100 RUPEES	1951; 1960. Green on m/c unpt. Back brown, violet and m/c; park and bldg.			
		a. 1951/AH1371.	35.00	95.00	300.00
		b. 4.6.1960/AH1379.	7.50	20.00	45.00

Maldives Monetary Authority

1983 ISSUE

#9–14 dhow at r. Wmk: Arms. Printer: BWC.

Cat. #	Denomination	Date, description	VG	VF	Unc
9	2 RUFIYAA	7.10.1983/AH1404. Black on olive-brown and m/c unpt. Shoreline village on back.	FV	FV	1.50

10	5 RUFIYAA	7.10.1983/AH1404. Deep purple on green and m/c unpt. Fishing boats at ctr. on back.	FV	FV	2.25

11	10 RUFIYAA	7.10.1983/AH1404. Brown on m/c unpt. Villagers working at ctr. on back.	FV	FV	3.50

12	20 RUFIYAA	7.10.1983/AH1404. Red-violet on m/c unpt. Fishing boats at dockside in Malé Harbour on back.			
		a. 7.10.1983/AH1404.	FV	FV	6.50
		b. 1987/AH1408.	FV	FV	5.50

13	50 RUFIYAA	1983; 1987. Blue on m/c unpt. Village market in Malé at ctr. on back.			
		a. Imprint at bottom ctr. on back. 7.10.1983/AH1404.	FV	FV	13.50
		b. W/o imprint. 1987/AH1408.	FV	FV	11.50

Cat. #	Denomination	Date, description	VG	VF	Unc
14	100 RUFIYAA	1983; 1987. Green on m/c unpt. Tomb of Medhuziyaarath at ctr. on back.			
		a. Imprint at bottom ctr. on back. 7.10.1983/AH1404.	FV	FV	25.00
		b. W/o imprint. 1987/AH1408.	FV	FV	22.00

1990 ISSUE

#15-21 like #9–14. Printer: TDLR.

15	2 RUFIYAA	1990/AH1411. Like #9, but darker dhow and trees, also slightly diff. unpt. colors.	FV	FV	1.00
16	5 RUFIYAA	1990/AH1411. Like #10, but brown unpt. at ctr., also darker boats on back.	FV	FV	2.00
17-20	**Held in reserve.**				
21	500 RUFIYAA	1990/AH1411. Orange and green on m/c unpt. Grand Friday Mosque and Islamic Ctr. on back.	FV	FV	80.00

The Republic of Mali, formerly the French Sudan, a landlocked country in the interior of West Africa southwest of Algeria, has an area of 478,764 sq. mi. (1,240,000 sq. km.) and a population of 9.36 million. Capital: Bamako. Livestock, fish, cotton and peanuts are exported.

Malians are descendants of the ancient Malinke Kingdom of Mali that controlled the middle Niger from the 11th to the 17th centuries. The French penetrated the Sudan (now Mali) about 1880, and established their rule in 1898 after subduing fierce native resistance. In 1904 the area became the colony of Upper Senegal-Niger (changed to French Sudan in 1920), and became part of the French Union in 1946. In 1958 French Sudan became the Sudanese Republic with complete internal autonomy. Senegal joined with the Sudanese Republic in 1959 to form the Mali Federation which, in 1960, became a fully independent member of the French Community. Upon Senegal's subsequent withdrawal from the Federation, the Sudanese, on Sept. 22, 1960, proclaimed their nation the fully independent Republic of Mali and severed all ties with France.

Mali seceded from the African Financial Community in 1962, then rejoined in 1984. Issues specially marked with letter *D* for Mali were made by the Banque des Etats de l'Afrique de l'Ouest.

See also French West Africa, and West African States.

MONETARY SYSTEM

1 Franc = 100 Centimes

Banque de la République du Mali

1960 ISSUE

#1–5 Modibo Keita at l.

Cat. #	Denomination	Date, description	VG	VF	Unc
1	50 FRANCS	22.9.1960. Purple on m/c unpt. Village on back.	5.00	25.00	110.00

| 2 | 100 FRANCS | 22.9.1960. Brown on yellow unpt. Cattle on back. | 5.00 | 28.00 | 135.00 |
| 3 | 500 FRANCS | 22.9.1960. Red on lt. blue and orange unpt. Woman and tent on back. | 55.00 | 175.00 | 425.00 |

Cat. #	Denomination	Date, description	VG	VF	Unc
4	1000 FRANCS	22.9.1960. Blue on lt. green and orange unpt. Farmers w/oxen at lower r. Back blue; man and huts.	20.00	85.00	275.00
5	5000 FRANCS	22.9.1960. Green on m/c unpt. 2 farmers plowing w/oxen at r. Market scene and bldg. on back.	120.00	300.00	650.00

1970 ISSUE

#6–10 Modibo Keita at r. Printer: TDLR.

| 6 | 50 FRANCS | 22.9.1960 (1970). Purple on blue and lt. green unpt. Dam at lower l. Back purple; woman and village. | 17.50 | 50.00 | 185.00 |

| 7 | 100 FRANCS | 22.9.1960 (1970). Brown on green and lilac unpt. Tractors at lower l. Back brown; old man at r., canoes at ctr., city view behind. | 12.50 | 35.00 | 150.00 |
| 8 | 500 FRANCS | 22.9.1960 (1970). Green on yellow, blue and red unpt. Bldg. at lower l. Longhorn cattle on back. | 30.00 | 100.00 | 350.00 |

| 9 | 1000 FRANCS | 22.9.1960 (1970). Blue on lilac and brown unpt. Bank at lower l. Back blue; people and Djenne mosque. | 25.00 | 135.00 | 300.00 |
| 10 | 5000 FRANCS | 22.9.1960 (1970). Dk. red on green unpt. Farmers at ctr. Market scene and bldgs. on back. | 65.00 | 250.00 | 525.00 |

Banque Centrale du Mali

Cat. #	Denomination	Date, description	VG	VF	Unc
11	100 FRANCS	ND (1971–73). M/c. Woman at l., hotel at r. Woman at l., boats docking at ctr. on back.	6.00	20.00	60.00

#12–15 sign. varieties.

Cat. #	Denomination	Date, description	VG	VF	Unc
14	5000 FRANCS	ND (1971–73). M/c. Cattle at lower l., man w/turban at r. Woman and flowers at l., woman w/machinery at r. on back.	10.00	25.00	50.00

			VG	VF	Unc
12	500 FRANCS	ND (1971–73). M/c. Soldier at l., tractors at r. Men and camels on back. 4 sign. varieties.	1.50	4.00	10.00

15	10,000 FRANCS	ND (1971–73). M/c. Man w/fez at l., factory at lower r. Weaver at l., young woman w/coin headband at r. on back.	16.50	40.00	70.00

13	1000 FRANCS	ND (1971–73). M/c. Bldg. at l., older man at r. Carvings at l., mountain village at ctr. on back. 6 sign. varieties.	2.50	6.00	15.00

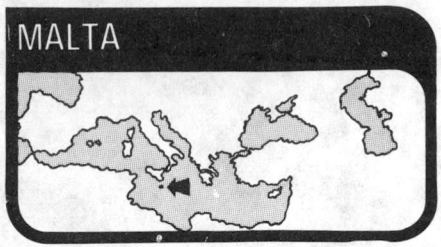

The Republic of Malta, an independent parliamentary democracy within the British Commonwealth, is situated in the Mediterranean Sea between Sicily and North Africa. With the islands of Gozo and Comino, Malta has an area of 122 sq. mi. (316 sq. km.) and a population of 359,900. Capital: Valletta. Malta has no proven mineral resources, an agriculture insufficient to its needs and a small but expanding, manufacturing facility. Clothing, textile yarns and fabrics, and knitted wear are exported.

For more than 3,500 years Malta was ruled, in succession, by Phoenicians, Carthaginians, Romans, Arabs, Normans, the Knights of Malta, France and Britain. Napoleon seized Malta by treachery in 1798. The French were ousted by a Maltese insurrection assisted by Britain, and in 1814 Malta, of its own free will, became part of the British Empire. Malta obtained full independence in Sept., 1964; electing to remain within the Commonwealth with the British monarch as the nominal head of state.

Malta became a republic on Dec. 13, 1974, but remained a member of the Commonwealth of Nations. The president is Chief of State. The prime minister is the Head of Government.

RULERS

British to 1974

MONETARY SYSTEM

1 Shilling = 12 Pence

1 Pound = 20 Shillings to 1971

1 Cent = 10 Mils

1 Lira (Pound) = 100 Cents, 1971–

REPLACEMENT NOTES

#31-33, X/1, Y/1 or Z/1 prefix by denomination.

#34-36, X/2, Y/2, or Z/2 prefix by denomination.

#37-40 and #41-44, W/2, X/2, Y/2, or Z/2 prefix by denomination.

Government of Matta

1949 Ordinance; 1963 (ND) ISSUE

#25–27 Qn. Elizabeth II at r. Printer: BWC.

Cat. #	Denomination	Date, description	VG	VF	Unc
25	10 SHILLINGS	L.1949 (1963). Green, blue and m/c. Cross at ctr. Mgarr Harbour, Gozo on back.	4.00	10.00	70.00

Cat. #	Denomination	Date, description	VG	VF	Unc
26	1 POUND	L.1949 (1963). Brown. Violet and m/c. Cross at ctr. Industrial Estate, Marsa on back.	5.00	20.00	75.00

Cat. #	Denomination	Date, description	VG	VF	Unc
27	5 POUNDS	L.1949 (1961). Blue and m/c. Cross at ctr. Grand Harbour on back.			
		a. Sign. D. A. Shepherd (1961).	30.00	150.00	500.00
		b. Sign. R. Soler (1963).	30.00	150.00	500.00

Central Bank of Malta

1967 Central Bank Act; 1968–69 (ND) ISSUE

#28–30 designs similar to #25–27. Printer: BWC.

28	10 SHILLINGS	L.1967 (1968). Red and m/c. Similar to #25.	3.50	10.00	37.50

29	1 POUND	L.1967 (1969). Olive and m/c. Similar to #26.	3.00	12.50	65.00

Cat. #	Denomination	Date, description	VG	VF	Unc
30	5 POUNDS	*L.1967* (1968). Brown, violet and m/c. Similar to #27.	10.00	35.00	150.00

Bank Centrali ta'Malta / Central Bank of Malta

1967 Central Bank Act; 1973 (ND) ISSUE

#31–33 arms at r., map at ctr. Printer: TDLR.

31	1 LIRA	*L.1967* (1973). Green and m/c. War Memorial at l. Prehistoric Temple in Tarxien at l., old capital city of Medina at ctr. on back.			
		a. Sign J. Sammut and A. Camilleri.	FV	4.00	17.50
		b. Sign. H. de Gabriele and J. Laspina.	FV	4.00	17.50
		c. Sign. H. de Gabriele and A. Camilleri.	FV	4.00	17.50
		d. Sign. J. Laspina and J. Sammut.	FV	4.00	17.50
		e. Sign. A. Camilleri and J. Laspina.	FV	4.00	17.50
		f. Sign. J. Sammut and H. de Gabriele.	FV	4.00	17.50

32	5 LIRI	*L.1967* (1973). Blue and m/c. Neptune at l. Yacht marina and boats on back.			
		a. Sign. H. de Gabriele and J. Laspina.	FV	15.00	55.00
		b. Sign. H. de Gabriele and A. Camilleri.	FV	15.00	55.00
		c. Sign. J. Laspina and J. Sammut.	FV	15.00	55.00
		d. Sign. A. Camilleri and J. Laspina.	FV	15.00	55.00
		e. Sign. J. Sammut and H. de Gabriele.	FV	15.00	55.00
		f. Sign J. Sammut and A. Camilleri.	FV	15.00	55.00

Cat. #	Denomination	Date, description	VG	VF	Unc
33	10 LIRI	*L.1967* (1973). Brown and m/c. Like #32. View of Grand Harbour and boats on back.			
		a. Sign. of H. de Gabriele and A. Camilleri.	FV	30.00	100.00
		b. Sign. of J. Laspina and J. Sammut.	FV	35.00	150.00
		c. Sign of A. Camilleri and J. Laspina.	FV	35.00	150.00
		d. Sign. of J. Sammut and H. de Gabriele.	FV	35.00	150.00
		e. Sign. of L. Spiteri w/title: *DEPUTAT GOVERNATUR.*	FV	35.00	100.00

1979 (ND) ISSUE

Central Bank Act, 1967

#34–36 map at upper l. Wmk: Allegorical head of Malta. Printer: TDLR.

34	1 LIRA	*L.1967* (1979). Brown and m/c. Watch tower "Gardjola" at ctr. New University on back.			
		a. W/o dot.	FV	3.50	10.00
		b. W/1 dot added for poor of sight at upper r.	FV	3.00	8.50

35	5 LIRI	*L.1967* (1979). Violet and m/c. Statue of "Culture" at ctr. Marsa Industrial Estate on back.			
		a. W/o 2 dots.	FV	14.00	40.00
		b. W/2 dots added for poor of sight at upper r.	FV	13.00	35.00

Cat. #	Denomination	Date, description	VG	VF	Unc
40	20 LIRA	L.1967 (1986). Brown on m/c unpt. 4 brown horizontal accounting bars at lower r. Statue and govt. bldg. at ctr. on back.	FV	FV	120.00

1989 (ND) ISSUE

#41–44 doves at l., Malta w/musical instrument at ctr. r. Wmk: Turreted head of Malta. Printer: TDLR.

Cat. #	Denomination	Date, description	VG	VF	Unc
36	10 LIRI	L.1967 (1979). Gray, pink and m/c. Statue of "Justice" at ctr. Part of Malta Drydocks on back.			
		a. W/o 3 dots.	FV	28.00	55.00
		b. W/3 dots added for poor of sight at upper r.	FV	28.00	60.00

1986 (ND) ISSUE

#37–40 sailing craft and map of Malta at ctr., A. Barbara at r.

41	2 LIRI	L.1967 (1989). Violet on m/c unpt. Bldgs. in Malta and Gozo on back.	FV	FV	13.50
42	5 LIRI	L.1967 (1989). Blue on m/c unpt. Historical tower on back.	FV	FV	26.50
43	10 LIRI	L.1967 (1989). Green on m/c unpt. Wounded people being brought into National Assembly on back.	FV	FV	50.00
44	20 LIRA	L.1967 (1989). Brown on m/c unpt. Prime Minister Dr. G. B. Olivier on back.	FV	FV	95.00

1994 (ND) ISSUE

45	2 LIRI	L.1967 (1994).	FV	FV	12.00
46	5 LIRI	L.1967 (1994).	FV	FV	23.50
47	10 LIRI	L.1967 (1994).	FV	FV	45.00
48	20 LIRA	L.1967 (1994).	FV	FV	87.50

#45–48 like 41-44 but w/enhanced colors and segmented foil security threads.

COLLECTOR SERIES

CSI	ND (1979) 1–10 LIRI	#34–36 w/ovpt: SPECIMEN and Maltese cross prefix serial #.		14.00	25.00

37	2 LIRI	L.1967 (1986). Red-orange on m/c unpt. Dockside crane at l., aerial harbor view at r. on back.	FV	FV	15.00

38	5 LIRI	L.1967 (1986). Gray-green and blue; 2 black horizontal accounting bars at lower r. Sailboats in harbor and repairing of fishing nets on back.	FV	FV	27.50

39	10 LIRI	L.1967. (1986). Olive and dk. green on m/c unpt. 3 dk. green horizontal accounting bars at lower r. Shipbuilding on back.	FV	FV	60.00

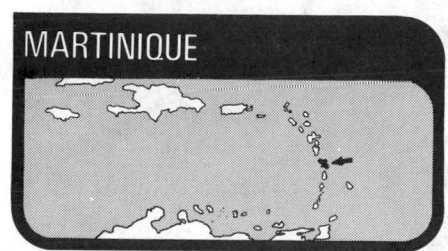

The French Overseas Department of Martinique, located in the Lesser Antilles of the West Indies between Dominica and Saint Lucia, has an area of 425 sq. mi. (1,101 sq. km.) and a population of 329,000. Capital: Fort-de-France. Agriculture and tourism are the major sources of income. Bananas, sugar and rum are exported.

Christopher Columbus discovered Martinique, probably on June 15, 1502. France took possession on June 25, 1635, and has maintained possession since that time except for three short periods of British occupation during the Napoleonic Wars. A French department since 1946, Martinique voted a reaffirmation of that status in 1958, remaining within the new French Community. Martinique was the birthplace of Napoleon's Empress Josephine, and the site of the eruption of Mt. Pelee in 1902 that claimed 40,000 lives.

RULERS
French

MONETARY SYSTEM
1 Franc = 100 Centimes

Caisse Centrale de la France d'Outre-Mer

Nouveaux Francs System

1961 (ND) PROVISIONAL ISSUE

#37–39B ovpt: *MARTINIQUE* and new denominations on previous "old" Franc issues.

Cat. #	Denomination	Date, description	VG	VF	Unc
37	1 NF on 100 Francs	ND (1961). M/c. La Bourdonnais at l., native coupe at r.	9.00	65.00	225.00

| 38 | 5 NF on 500 Francs | ND (1961). M/c. 2 women at r., sailboat at l. Farmers w/ox carts on back. | 20.00 | 160.00 | 375.00 |

Cat. #	Denomination	Date, description	VG	VF	Unc
39	10 NF on 1000 Francs	ND (1961). M/c. Fisherman. Woman w/box of produce on her head at l. ctr. on back.	35.00	185.00	575.00
40 (39A)	50 NF on 5000 Francs	ND (1961). M/c. Woman holding fruit bowl at ctr. Harvesting scene on back.	150.00	650.00	—
41 (39B)	50 NF on 5000 Francs	ND (1961). M/c. Gen. Schoelcher. Specimens.	—	—	—

NOTE: For later issues see French Antilles.

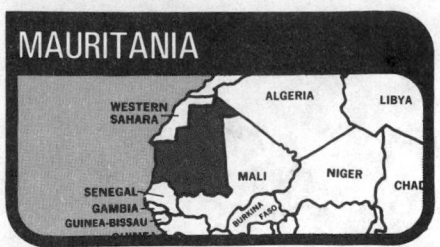

The Islamic Republic of Mauritania, located in northwest Africa bounded by Spanish Sahara, Mali, Algeria, Senegal and the Atlantic Ocean, has an area of 397,955 sq. mi. (1,030,700 sq. km.) and a population of 2.11 million. Capital: Nouakchott. The economy centers about herding, agriculture, fishing and mining. Iron ore, copper concentrates and fish products are exported.

The indigenous Negroid inhabitants were driven out of Mauritania by Berber invaders of the Islamic faith in the 11th century. The Berbers in turn were conquered by Arab invaders, the Beni Hassan, in the 16th century. Arab traders carried on a gainful trade in gum arabic, gold and slaves with Portuguese, Dutch, English and French traders until late in the 19th century when France took control of the area, and in 1920 made it a part of French West Africa. Mauritania became a part of the French Union in 1946 and was made an autonomous republic within the new French Community in 1958, when the Islamic Republic of Mauritania was proclaimed. The republic became independent on November 28, 1960, and withdrew from the French Community in 1966.

On June 28, 1973, in a move designed to emphasize its non-alignment with France, Mauritania converted its currency from the old French-supported CFA franc unit to a new unit called the Ouguiya.

MONETARY SYSTEM
1 Ouguiya = 5 Khoum
100 Ouguiya = 500 CFA Francs, 1973–

NOTE: Issues specially marked with letter *E* for Mauritania were made by the Banque Centrale des Etats de l'Afrique de l'Ouest. These issues were used before Mauritania seceded from the French Community of the West African States in 1973. For listing see West African States.

Banque Centrale de Mauritanie

1973 ISSUE

Cat. #	Denomination	Date, description	VG	VF	Unc
1	100 OUGUIYA	20.6.1973. Blue. Mauritanian girl at ctr. Men loading boat on back.			
		a. Issued note.	10.00	20.00	60.00
		s. Specimen.	—	—	17.50

2	200 OUGUIYA	20.6.1973. Brown. Bedouin woman at l., tents in background. Camels and huts on back.			
		a. Issued note.	11.00	22.00	65.00
		s. Specimen.	—	—	15.00

Cat. #	Denomination	Date, description	VG	VF	Unc
3	1000 OUGUIYA	20.6.1973. Green. Woman weaving on loom at l., metal worker at r. ctr. Local musicians and scenes on back.			
		a. Issued note.	15.00	35.00	100.00
		s. Specimen.	—	—	25.00

1974–79 ISSUE

#4–7 wmk: Old man w/beard. Sign. varieties.

4	100 OUGUIYA	1974–89. Purple, violet and brown on m/c unpt. Musical instruments at l., cow and tower at r. on back.			
		a. 28.11.1974.	4.00	10.00	25.00
		b. 28.11.1983.	7.50	15.00	35.00
		c. 28.11.1985.	2.00	7.50	13.50
		d. 28.11.1989.	FV	3.25	10.00
		e. 28.11.1992.	FV	3.00	9.00
		f. 28.11.1993.	FV	FV	9.00

5	200 OUGUIYA	1974–89. Brown, dk. olive-green and brown-orange on m/c unpt. Bowl, dugout canoe and palm tree on back.			
		a. 28.11.1974.	6.00	15.00	30.00
		b. 28.11.1985.	4.00	10.00	22.50
		c. 28.11.1989.	FV	6.00	18.00
		d. 28.11.1992.	FV	5.00	15.00
		e. 28.11.1993.	FV	FV	12.50

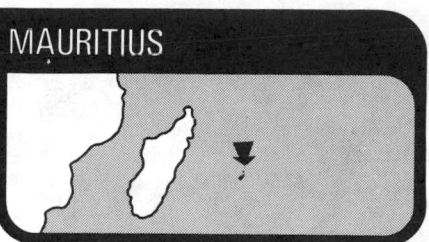

The island of Mauritius, a member nation of the British Commonwealth located in the Indian Ocean 500 miles (805 km.) east of Madagascar, has an area of 790 sq. mi. (2,045 sq. km.) and a population of 1.01 million. Capital: Port Louis. Sugar provides 90 percent of the export revenue.

Cartographic evidence indicates that Arabs and Malays arrived at Mauritius during the Middle Ages. Domingo Fernandez, a Portuguese navigator, visited the island in the early 16th century, but Portugal made no attempt at settlement. The Dutch took possession, and named the island, in 1598. Their colony failed to prosper and was abandoned in 1710. France claimed Mauritius in 1715 and developed a strong and prosperous colony that endured until the island was captured by the British, 1810, during the Napoleonic Wars. British possession was confirmed by the Treaty of Paris, 1814. Mauritius became independent on March 12, 1968. It is a member of the Commonwealth of Nations. The Queen of England is Chief of State.

RULERS

British

MONETARY SYSTEM

1 Rupee = 100 Cents, 1848–

REPLACEMENT NOTES

#30–33, Z/# prefix.

Bank of Mauritius

1967 ISSUE

Cat. #	Denomination	Date, description	VG	VF	Unc
6	500 OUGUIYA	1979–1985. Green, brown and dk. green on m/c unpt. Back brown, green and black; field workers at l., factory at r.			
		a. 28.11.1979.	18.00	40.00	100.00
		b. 28.11.1983.	16.00	35.00	90.00
		c. 28.11.1985.	8.50	15.00	40.00
		d. 28.11.1989.	FV	12.00	36.00
		e. 28.11.1991.	FV	10.00	30.00
		f. 28.11.1992.	FV	8.00	24.00
		g. 28.11.1993.	FV	FV	24.00

SIGNATURE VARIETIES

1	GOVERNOR OF THE BANK / MANAGING DIRECTOR	4	GOVERNOR OF THE BANK / MANAGING DIRECTOR
2		5	
3		6	

#30–33 Qn. Elizabeth II at r. Wmk: Dodo bird. Printer: TDLR.

Cat. #	Denomination	Date, description	VG	VF	Unc
7	1000 OUGUIYA	1974–1991. Blue, violet and blue-black on m/c unpt. Bowl of fish, camel, hut and tower on back.			
		a. 28.11.1974.	18.00	40.00	100.00
		b. 28.11.1985.	10.00	22.50	60.00
		c. 28.11.1989.	FV	20.00	45.00
		d. 28.10.1991.	FV	15.00	40.00
		e. 28.11.1992.	FV	12.00	40.00
		f. 28.11.1993.	FV	12.00	35.00

Cat. #	Denomination	Date, description	VG	VF	Unc
30	5 RUPEES	ND (1967). Blue on m/c unpt. Sailboat on back.			
		a. Sign. 1.	.75	1.75	7.00
		b. Sign. 3.	1.00	3.00	22.50
		c. Sign. 4.	.50	1.25	4.00

Cat. #	Denomination	Date, description	VG	VF	Unc
31	10 RUPEES	ND (1967). Red on m/c unpt. Government bldg. on back.			
		a. Sign. 1.	.85	2.00	11.50
		b. Sign. 2.	1.00	3.00	15.00
		c. Sign. 4.	.75	1.25	6.50
32	25 RUPEES	ND (1967). Green on m/c unpt. Ox-cart on back.			
		a. Sign. 1.	2.50	4.50	25.00
		b. Sign. 4.	2.00	3.50	22.50

Cat. #	Denomination	Date, description	VG	VF	Unc
35	10 RUPEES	ND (1985). Green on m/c unpt. Arms at lower l. ctr., bldg. w/flag at ctr. r. Bridge on back.			
		a. Dk. green printing.	FV	FV	3.00
		b. Lt. green printing.	FV	FV	1.75

			VG	VF	Unc
36	20 RUPEES	ND. Bluish purple, blue-green, blue and orange on m/c unpt. Lady Jugnauth at l., arms at ctr. bldg. w/flag at lower r. Satellite dishes at ctr. on back.	FV	FV	3.00

#37–41 arms at lower l. to lower ctr., bldg. w/flag at r. Wmk: Dodo bird. Printer: BWC.

			VG	VF	Unc
33	50 RUPEES	ND (1967). Purple on m/c unpt. Ships docked at Port Louis harbor on back.			
		a. Sign. 1.	5.00	12.00	55.00
		b. Sign. 2.	7.50	20.00	85.00
		c. Sign. 4.	4.00	10.00	40.00

1985 ISSUE

#34–36 outline of Mauritius map on back. Wmk: Dodo bird. Printer: TDLR.

			VG	VF	Unc
37	50 RUPEES	ND (1986). Dk. blue on m/c unpt. 2 deer and butterfly on back.	FV	FV	7.50

			VG	VF	Unc
34	5 RUPEES	ND (1985). Brown on m/c unpt. Arms at lower l. ctr., bldg. w/flag at r. Bank on back.	FV	FV	1.00

			VG	VF	Unc
38	100 RUPEES	ND (1986). Red on m/c unpt. Landscape on back.	FV	FV	8.00

Cat. #	Denomination	Date, description	VG	VF	Unc
39	200 RUPEES	ND (1985). Blue on m/c unpt. Sir Seewoodsagur Ramgoolam at l. Lg. home (Le Réduit) on back. Printer: TDLR.	FV	FV	22.50

| 40 | 500 RUPEES | ND (1988). Brown and orange on m/c unpt Bldg. w/flag at ctr., arms below, Sir A. Jugnauth (Prime Minister) at r. Sugar cane field workers loading wagon w/mountains in background on back. | FV | FV | 55.00 |

| 41 | 1000 RUPEES | ND (1991). Blue and purple on m/c unpt. Sir V. Ringadoo at l., palm trees and bldg. w/flag at ctr. Port Louis harbor on back. | FV | FV | 100.00 |

COLLECTOR SERIES

Cat. #	Date, denomination	Description	Issue Price	Mkt. Val.
CS1	ND (1978) 5–50 RUPEES	#30–33 w/ovpt.: *SPECIMEN* and Maltese cross prefix serial #.	14.00	25.00

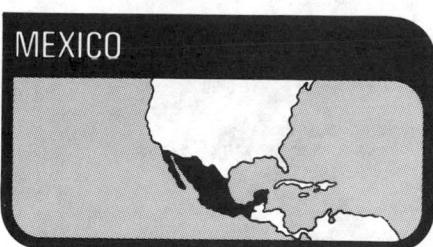

MEXICO

The United Mexican States located immediately south of the United States has an area of 761,604 sq. mi. (1,978,750 sq. km.) and a population of 84.4 million. Capital: Mexico City. The economy is based on agriculture, manufacturing and mining. Cotton, sugar, coffee and shrimp are exported.

Mexico was the site of highly advanced Indian civilizations 1,500 years before conquistador Hernando Cortes conquered the wealthy Aztec empire of Montezuma. 1519–1521, and founded a Spanish colony which lasted for nearly 300 years. During the Spanish period, Mexico, then called New Spain, stretched from Guatemala to the present states of Wyoming and California, its present northern boundary having been established by the secession of Texas (1836) and the 1846–1848 war with the United States.

Independence from Spain was declared by Father Miguel Hidalgo on Sept. 16, 1810, (Mexican Independence Day) and was achieved by General Augustin de Iturbide in 1821. Iturbide became emperor in 1822 but was deposed when a republic was established a year later. For more than half a century following the birth of the republic, the political scene of Mexico was characterized by turmoil which saw two emperors (including the unfortunate Maximilian), several dictators and an average of one new government every nine months passing swiftly from obscurity to oblivion. The land, social, economic and labor reforms promulgated by the Reform Constitution of 1917 established the basis for a sustained economic development and participative democracy that have made Mexico one of the most politically stable countries of modern Latin America.

MONETARY SYSTEM
1 Peso = 100 Centavos
1 Nuevo Peso = 1000 old Pesos, 1992–

NOTE: The monument referred to is of the Angel of Independence and National Heroes located in México City.

Banco de México, S.A.

1948–61 ISSUES

#712 sign. varieties. Printer: ABNC.

Cat. #	Denomination	Date, description	Series	VG	VF	Unc
712	1 PESO	1957–70. Black on m/c unpt. Aztec calendar stone at ctr. Text: *MEXICO D.F.* added above date at l. Back red; Independence Monument at ctr.				
		a. 19.6.1957.	FW-GF	.10	.50	3.00
		b. 24.7.1957.	GH-GR	.10	.40	2.50
		c. 4.12.1957.	GS-HB	.10	.30	2.00
		d. 1. 20.8.1958.	HC-HL	.10	.30	2.00
		e. 2. 18.3.1959.	HS-IB	.10	.25	1.75
		f. 20.5.1959.	IQ-IZ	.10	.25	1.75
		g. 25.1.1961.	JO-KC	.10	.25	1.50
		h. 8.11.1961.	LC-LD	.10	.25	1.50
		i. 9.6.1965.	BCO-BCX	.10	.20	1.00
		j. 10.5.1967.	BCY-BEB	.10	.25	1.00
		k. 27.8.1969.	BGA-BGJ	.10	.25	1.00
		l. 22.7.1970.	BIG-BIP	.10	.20	.75

714A	5 PESOS	1957–70. Black on m/c unpt. Portr. Faure at ctr. Text: *MEXICO D.F.* before date. Back gray; Independence Monument at ctr.				
		a. 19.6.1957.	FW, FX	.40	1.50	6.00
		b. 24.7.1957.	GQ, GR	.40	1.50	6.00
		c. 20.8.1958.	HC-HJ	.25	1.00	4.00
		d. 18.3.1959.	HS-HV	.25	1.00	4.00
		e. 20.5.1959.	IQ-IT	.25	1.00	4.00
		f. 25.1.1961.	JO-JV	.15	.75	3.00
		g. 8.11.1961.	LC-MP	.15	.75	3.00

Cat. #	Denomination	Date, description	Series	VG	VF	Unc
		h. 24.4.1963.	AIE-AJJ	.15	.50	2.00
		i. 19.11.1969.	BGK-BGT	.15	.50	2.00
		j. 22.7.1970.	BIG-BII	.15	.50	2.00

Cat. #	Denomination	Date, description	Series	VG	VF	Unc
716	10 PESOS	1954–67. Black on m/c unpt. Portr. E. Ruiz de Valezquez at r. Text: *MEXICO D.F.* above series letters. Back brown; road to Guanajuato at ctr.				
		a. 10.2.1954.	DW, DX	.50	1.00	7.00
		b. 8.9.1954.	EI-EN	.25	1.00	4.00
		c. 19.6.1957.	FW, FX	.60	2.50	8.00
		d. 24.7.1957.	GQ	.60	2.50	8.00
		e. 20.8.1958.	HC-HF	.25	1.00	4.00
		f. 18.3.1959.	HS-HU	.25	1.00	4.00
		g. 20.5.1959.	IQ-IS	.25	1.00	4.00
		h. 25.1.1961.	JO-JT	.25	1.00	4.00
		i. 8.11.1961.	LC-LV	.25	1.00	4.00
		j. 24.4.1963.	AIE-AIT	.25	1.00	4.00
		k. 17.2.1965.	BAQ-BAX	.25	1.00	4.00
		l. 10.5.1967.	BCY-BDA	.25	1.00	3.00
717C	20 PESOS	1950–70. Black on m/c unpt. Portr. J. Ortiz de Dominguez at l. W/o *No* above serial #. Back olive-green; Federal Palace courtyard at ctr.				
		a. 27.12.1950. Black series letters.	CS-CT	1.10	2.00	9.00
		b. 19.1.1953.	DK	1.10	2.00	9.00
		c. 10.2.1954. Red series letters.	DW	1.10	2.00	8.50
		d. 11.1.1956.	FK	1.10	2.00	8.50
		e. 19.6.1957.	FW	1.10	2.00	8.00
		f. 20.8.1958.	HC, HD	1.10	2.00	8.00
		g. 18.3.1959.	HS, HT	1.10	1.75	7.00
		h. 20.5.1959.	IQ, IR	1.10	1.75	7.00
		i. 25.1.1961.	JO, JP	.75	1.50	6.00
		j. 8.11.1961.	LC-LG	.75	1.50	6.00
		k. 24.4.1963.	AIE-AIH	.50	1.25	5.00
		l. 17.2.1965.	BAQ-BAV	.50	1.25	5.00
		m. 10.5.1967.	BCY-BDB	.50	1.25	5.00
		n. 27.8.1969.	BGA-BGB	.50	1.25	5.00
		o. 18.3.1970.	BID-BIF	.50	1.25	5.00
		p. 22.7.1970.	BIG-BIK	.50	1.25	5.00
718A	50 PESOS	1948–72. Deep blue on m/c unpt. Portr. I. de Allende at l. Middle sign. title: *INTERVENTOR DE LA COM. NAC. BANCARIA.* Engraved dates. Back blue; Independence Monument.				
		a. 22.12.1948. Black series letters.	BA-BD	3.00	6.00	15.00
		b. 23.11.1949.	BU-BX	3.00	6.00	15.00
		c. 26.7.1950.	BY-CF	3.00	5.00	12.50
		d. 27.12.1950.	CS-DH	3.00	5.00	12.50
		e. 19.1.1953.	DK-DV	3.00	4.00	11.00
		f. 10.2.1954.	DW-EE	2.00	4.00	10.00
		g. 8.9.1954.	EF-FF	2.00	4.00	10.00
		h. 11.1.1956.	FK-FV	2.00	4.00	10.00
		i. 19.6.1957.	FW-GP	2.00	4.00	10.00
		j. 20.8.1958.	HC-HR	2.00	4.00	10.00
		k. 18.3.1959. Red series letters.	HS-IP	2.00	4.00	10.00
		l. 20.5.1959.	IQ-JN	2.00	4.00	10.00
		m. 25.1.1961.	JO-LB	1.50	3.00	8.00
		n. 8.11.1961.	LC-ZZ, AAA-AID	1.50	3.00	8.00
		o. 24.4.1963.	AIF-BAM	1.50	3.00	8.00
		p. 17.2.1965.	BAQ-BCD	1.00	2.50	5.50
		q. 10.5.1967.	BCY-BEN	1.00	2.50	5.00
		r. 19.11.1969.	BGK-BIC	1.00	2.50	4.50
		s. 22.7.1970.	BIG-BKN	1.00	2.50	4.50
		t. 27.6.1972.	BLI-BMG	1.00	2.50	4.50
		u. 29.12.1972.	BNB-BRB	1.00	2.00	5.00
719A	100 PESOS	1950–61. Brown on m/c unpt. Portr. M. Hidalgo at l. Middle sign. title: *INTERVENTOR DE LA COM. NAC. BANCARIA.* Engraved dates. Back olive-green; coin w/national seal at ctr.				
		a. 27.12.1950. Black series letters.	CS-CZ	6.00	10.00	25.00
		b. 19.1.1953.	DK-DP	3.50	7.00	15.00
		c. 8.9.1954.	EI-ET	3.50	7.00	15.00

Cat. #	Denomination	Date, description	Series	VG	VF	Unc
		d. 11.1.1956.	FK-FV	3.50	7.00	15.00
		e. 19.6.1957.	FW-GH	3.50	7.00	12.00
		f. 20.8.1958.	HC-HQ	3.50	7.00	12.00
		g. 18.3.1959.	HS-IH	3.50	7.00	12.00
		h. 20.5.1959.	IQ-JF	3.50	7.00	12.00
		i. 25.1.1961.	JO-KL	3.50	7.00	12.00

Cat. #	Denomination	Date, description	Series	VG	VF	Unc
719B	100 PESOS	1961–73. Brown on m/c unpt. Like #719 but series letters below serial #.				
		a. 8.11.1961. Red series letters.	LE-ZZ, AAA-AEG	2.00	5.00	10.00
		b. 24.4.1963.	AIK-AUS	2.00	5.00	10.00
		c. 17.2.1965.	BAQ-BCD	2.00	5.00	10.00
		d. 10.5.1967.	BCY-BFZ	2.00	5.00	10.00
		e. 22.7.1970.	BIO-BJX	1.00	3.00	7.50
		f. 24.3.1971.	BLH	1.00	3.00	7.50
		g. 27.6.1972.	BLI-BNF	2.00	5.00	10.00
		h. 29.12.1972.	BNG-BUX	1.00	2.00	7.50
		i. 18.7.1973.	BUY-BXU	1.00	2.00	7.50

Cat. #	Denomination	Date, description	Series	VG	VF	Unc
720B	500 PESOS	1948–78. Black on m/c unpt. Portr. J. M. Morelos y Pavon at r. W/o *No.* above serial #. Middle sign. title: *INTERVENTOR DE LA COM. NAC. BANCARIO.* Back green; Palace of Mining at ctr.				
		a. 22.12.1948.	BA	15.00	40.00	150.00
		b. 27.12.1950.	CS, CT	15.00	40.00	150.00
		c. 3.12.1951.	DI, DJ	15.00	40.00	150.00
		d. 19.1.1953.	DK-DN	12.00	25.00	60.00
		e. 31.8.1955.	FH-FJ	12.00	20.00	50.00
		f. 11.1.1956.	FK, FL	12.00	20.00	50.00
		g. 19.6.1957.	FW, FY, GA, GB	12.00	20.00	50.00
		h. 20.8.1958.	HC-HH	10.00	20.00	40.00
		i. 18.3.1959.	HS-HX	10.00	20.00	40.00
		j. 20.5.1959.	IM-IV	10.00	20.00	40.00
		k. 25.1.1961.	JO-JT	10.00	20.00	40.00
		l. 8.11.1961.	LC-MS	10.00	20.00	40.00
		m. 17.2.1965.	BAQ-BCN	6.00	12.00	25.00
		n. 24.3.1971.	BKD-BKT	2.50	5.00	12.50
		o. 27.6.1972.	BLI-BL	2.50	5.00	12.50
		p. 29.12.1972.	BNG-BNP	2.50	5.00	12.50
		q. 18.7.1973.	BUJ-BWB	1.75	5.00	12.50
		r. 2.8.1974.	BXV-BZI	1.75	3.50	8.00
		s. 18.2.1977.	BZJ-CCK	1.00	3.50	7.50
		t. 18.1.1978.	CCL-CDY	1.00	3.50	7.50

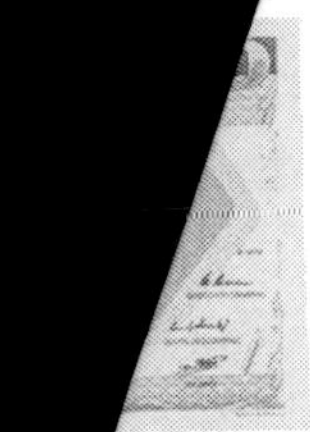

...n		VG	VF	Unc
	...e and brown-orange on m/c ...45 but design continued over ... W/o wmk.			
	...NTANA vertically at lower l. ...1985; 24.2.1987.	1.75	2.50	5.00
	... SANTANA. 28.3.1989.	1.75	2.50	3.00

	10,...SOS	19.7.1985; 24.2.1987. Like #742.	2.00	5.00	12.00
	10,...ESOS	1987-91. Deep blue-black on brown and blue-green unpt. Similar to #747 but wmk. area filled in.			
		a. W/*SANTANA* at lower l. under refinery design. 24.2.1987.	3.50	5.00	8.00
		b. W/o *SANTANA* 1.2.1988	3.50	4.50	7.00
		c. 28.3.1989; 16.5.1991	3.50	4.50	4.0

749	20,000 PESOS	19.7.1985; 24.2.1987; 27.8.1987. Deep blue on blue and m/c unpt. Fortress above coastal cliffs at ctr. Don A. Quintana Roo at r. and as wmk. Artwork on back.	6.00	9.00	20.00

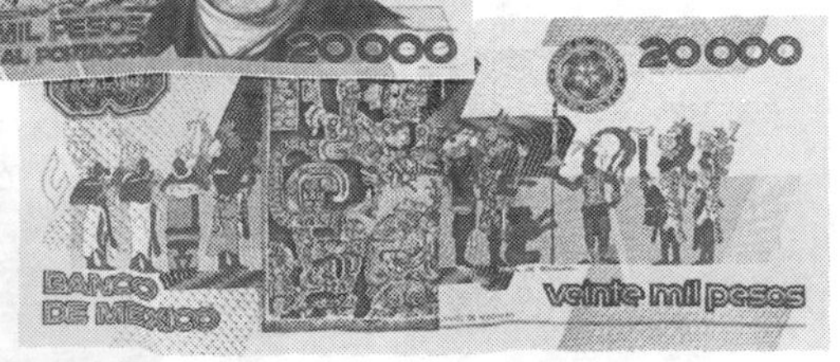

750	20,000 PESOS	1.2.1988; 28.3.1989. Blue-black on blue and pink unpt. Similar to #749 but design continued over wmk. area.	FV	5.00	8.60

751	50,000 PESOS	1986-90. Purple and m/c. Cuauhtémoc at r. and as wmk. Aztec and Spaniard fighting at l. ctr. on back.			
		a. 12.5.1986; 24.2.1987; 27.8.1987.	FV	15.00	30.00
		b. 28.3.1989; 10.1.1990; 20.12.1990.	FV	12.50	25.00

752	100,000 PESOS	1988-1991. Black and maroon on m/c unpt. P. F. Calles at l. and as wmk. Banco de Mexico at ctr. Deer, cactus, lake and mountain on back.			
		a. 4.1.1988.	FV	25.00	55.00
		b. 20.12.1990; 2.9.1991.	FV	20.00	45.00

Currency Reform

1 Nuevo Peso = 1000 "old" Pesos

1992 ISSUE

#753-756 similar to #748-752. 3 sign.; sign. varieties. Printer: BdM.

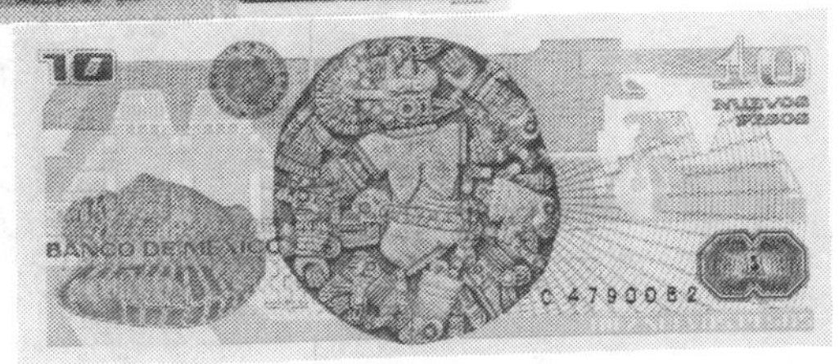

753	10 NUEVOS PESOS	31.7.1992. Similar to #748.			
		a. Series A.	FV	FV	5.00
		b. Series B–.	FV	FV	4.00

Cat. #	Denomination	Date, description	Series	VG	VF	Unc
721B	1000 PESOS	1948–77. Black on m/c unpt. Cuauhtemoc at r. Middle sign. title: *INTERVENTOR DE LA COM. NAC. BANCARIO.* Back brown; Chichen Itzá pyramid at ctr.				
		a. 22.12.1948.	BA	25.00	45.00	150.00
		b. 23.11.1949.	BU	25.00	45.00	150.00
		c. 27.12.1950.	CS	25.00	45.00	125.00
		d. 3.12.1951.	DI, DJ	25.00	45.00	125.00
		e. 19.1.1953.	DK, DL	25.00	45.00	125.00
		f. 31.8.1955.	FG, FH	20.00	40.00	75.00
		g. 11.1.1956.	FK, FL	20.00	40.00	75.00
		h. 19.6.1957.	FN-FW	20.00	35.00	60.00
		i. 20.8.1958.	HC-HE	20.00	35.00	60.00
		j. 18.3.1959.	HS-HU	18.00	30.00	50.00
		k. 20.5.1959.	IQ-IS	18.00	30.00	50.00
		l. 25.1.1961.	JO-JQ	18.00	30.00	45.00
		m. 8.11.1961.	LC-LV	18.00	30.00	45.00
		n. 17.2.1965.	BAQ-BCN	7.00	15.00	30.00
		o. 24.3.1971.	BKO-BKT	2.00	4.00	10.00
		p. 27.6.1972.	BLI-BLM	2.00	4.50	12.00
		q. 29.12.1972.	BNG-BNK	8.00	20.00	30.00
		r. 18.7.1973.	BUY-BWB	2.00	4.50	12.00
		s. 2.8.1974.	BXV-BYY	2.00	4.50	12.00
		t. 18.2.1977.	BZL-CBQ	2.00	4.00	10.00

1969–80 ISSUES

#723–730 3 sign. w/varieties. Bank title w/*S.A.* Printer: BdM-Bank of Mexico.

Cat. #	Denomination	Date, description	VG	VF	Unc
723	5 PESOS	1969–72. Black on m/c unpt. J. Ortiz de Dominguez at r. Yucca plant, aqueduct, village of Queretaro and national arms on back.			
		a. 3.12.1969.	.15	.25	2.00
		b. 27.10.1971.	.15	.25	1.00
		c. 27.6.1972.	.15	.25	.75

724	10 PESOS	1969–77. Dk. green and m/c. Bell at l., M. Hidalgo y Castilla at r. National arms and Dolores Cathedral on back.			
		a. 16.9.1969.	.25	.50	4.00
		b. 3.12.1969.	.15	.25	1.50
		c. 22.7.1970.	.15	.25	1.00
		d. 3.2.1971.	.15	.25	1.00
		e. 29.12.1972.	.15	.25	1.00
		f. 18.7.1973.	.10	.20	.50
		g. 16.10.1974.	.10	.20	.50
		h. 15.5.1976.	.10	.20	.50
		i. 18.2.1977.	.10	.20	.50

Cat. #	Denomination	Date, description	VG	VF	Unc
725	20 PESOS	1972–77. Red and black on m/c unpt. J. Morelos y Pavon at r. w/bldg. in background. Pyramid of Quetzalcoatl on back.			
		a. 29.12.1972.	.25	.50	2.00
		b. 18.7.1973.	.10	.20	.50
		c. 8.7.1976.	.10	.20	.50
		d. 8.7.1977.	.10	.20	.50

726	50 PESOS	1973; 1976. Blue on m/c unpt. Government palace at l., B. Juárez at r. Red and black series letters and serial #. Temple and Aztec god on back.			
		a. 18.7.1973.	.30	1.00	4.00
		b. 8.7.1976.	.30	1.00	2.00
726A	50 PESOS	1978; 1979. Blue on m/c unpt. Like #726 but only red series letters and a black serial #.			
		a. 5.7.1978.	.30	1.00	2.00
		b. 17.5.1979.	.20	.40	1.00

727	100 PESOS	30.5.1974. Purple on m/c unpt. V. Carranza at l., "La Trinchera" painting at ctr. Red and black series letters and serial #. Stone figure on back.	.30	1.00	3.00
727A	100 PESOS	1978; 1979. Purple on m/c unpt. Like #727 but only red series letters and a black serial #.			
		a. 5.7.1978.	.20	.60	2.00
		b. 17.5.1979.	.20	.40	1.00

Cat. #	Denomination	Date, description	VG	VF	Unc
728	500 PESOS	29.6.1979. Black on dk. olive-green and m/c unpt. F. I. Madero at l. and as wmk. Aztec calendar stone on back.	1.00	3.00	9.00

729	1000 PESOS	1978–79. Brown on m/c unpt. J. de Asbaje at r. and as wmk. Santo Domingo plaza at l. ctr. on back.			
		a. 5.7.1978.	2.00	4.50	15.00
		b. 17.5.1979.	1.00	4.00	10.00
		c. 29.6.1979.	1.00	3.00	9.00

| 730 | 5000 PESOS | 25.3.1980. Red and m/c unpt. on blue paper. Cadets at l. ctr., one of them as wmk. Chapultepec castle on back. | 4.00 | 10.00 | 35.00 |
| 730A (722A) | 10,000 PESOS | 18.1.1978. Purple on m/c unpt. Portr. M. Romero at l. Back green; National palace at ctr. Printer: ABNC. Series CCL-CFH. | 5.00 | 20.00 | 60.00 |

1981 ISSUE

#731-736 w/4 sign. and varieties. Bank title w/*S.A.* Printer: BdM.

| 731 | 50 PESOS | 27.1.1981. Blue on m/c unpt. Similar to #726A but 4 sign. | .10 | .20 | .50 |

Cat. #	Denomination	Date, description	VG	VF	Unc
732	100 PESOS	1981–82. Purple on m/c unpt. Similar to #727A but 4 sign.			
		a. 27.1.1981.	.10	.20	.50
		b. 3.9.1981.	.10	.20	.50
		c. 25.3.1982.	.10	.20	.50

733	500 PESOS	1981–82. Green on m/c unpt. Similar to #728 but 4 sign. and narrower serial #.			
		a. 27.1.1981.	.25	1.00	4.50
		b. 25.3.1982.	.25	1.00	4.00

734	1000 PESOS	1981–82. Dk. brown and brown on m/c unpt. Similar to #729 but 4 sign. and narrower serial #.			
		a. Engraved bldgs. on back. 27.1.1981.	2.00	4.00	8.00
		b. 3.9.1981.	2.00	4.00	8.00
		c. 25.3.1982.	2.00	4.00	8.00
735	5000 PESOS	1981–82. Red and black on m/c unpt., lt. blue paper. Similar to #730 but 4 sign. and narrower serial #.			
		a. 27.1.1981.	5.00	10.00	25.00
		b. 25.3.1982.	5.00	10.00	25.00

736	10,000 PESOS	1981–82. Blue-black, brown and deep blue-green on grayish green and m/c unpt. Gen. Lazaro Cardenas at r. and as wmk. Back dk. green, red and blue; Coyolxauhqui stone carving at ctr.			
		a. 8.12.1981.	3.00	12.00	40.00
		b. 25.3.1982.	3.00	10.00	30.00
		c. 30.9.1982.	3.00	10.00	30.00

1983-84 ISSUE

#737-742 w/4 sign. *S.A.* removed from bank title, Printer: BdM.

Cat. #	Denomination	Date, description	VG	VF	Unc
737	500 PESOS	1983–84. Similar to #733 but silk threads and w/o wmk. Design continued over wmk. area on both sides.			
		a. 14.3.1983.	.20	.50	2.50
		b. 7.8.1984.	.20	.50	2.50
738	1000 PESOS	13.5.1983; 7.8.1984. Like #734 but *S.A.* removed from title.	1.00	2.50	6.00

| 739 | 1000 PESOS | 30.10.1984. Similar to #734 but rayed quill pen printed over wmk. area at l. | .35 | .85 | 2.50 |

740	2000 PESOS	1983–84. Black, dk. green, brown and m/c. J. Sierra at l. ctr., University bldg. at r. 19th century courtyard on back.			
		a. 26.7.1983.	1.00	3.00	10.00
		b. 7.8.1984.	.75	1.25	4.00
		c. 30.10.1984.	.75	1.25	4.00

Cat. #					
741					
742					

1985-88 ISSUE

#743-752 w/3 sign. *S.A.* r...

| 746 | | | | | |

743	1000 PESOS	19.7.1985. Like #739.			
744	2000 PESOS	1985-89. Like #740.			
		a. W/*SANTANA* at lower l. 19.7.1985; 24.2.1987.	.75	1.25	3.00
		b. W/o *SANTANA*. 28.3.1989.	.75	1.25	1.50

| 747 | | | | | |
| 748 | | | | | |

| 745 | 5000 PESOS | 19.7.1985. Red and m/c unpt. Blue tint paper. Like #741. | 1.75 | 2.25 | 8.00 |

Cat. #	Denomination	Date, description	VG	VF	Unc
754	20 NUEVOS PESOS	31.7.1992. Similar to #750.			
		a. Series A.	FV	FV	10.00
		b. Series B–.	FV	FV	9.00

755	50 NUEVOS PESOS	31.7.1992. Similar to #751.			
		a. Series A.	FV	FV	22.50
		b. Series B–.	FV	FV	20.00

756	100 NUEVOS PESOS	31.7.1992. Similar to #752.			
		a. Series A.	FV	FV	45.00
		b. Series B–.	FV	FV	40.00

1994 ISSUE

#757–762 printer: BdM.

757	10 NUEVOS PESOS	10.12.1992 (1994). Blue-green on m/c unpt. E. Zapata at r., hands holding ears of corn at ctr. Machinery at lower l., statue of Zapata horseback by peasant at ctr. r., bldg. in background.	FV	FV	3.50

Cat. #	Denomination	Date, description	VG	VF	Unc
758	20 NUEVOS PESOS	10.12.1992 (1994). Purple, blue and violet on m/c unpt. B. Juárez at r., heraldic eagle at ctr. Monument, statues "Hemicicio a Juárez" on back.	FV	FV	6.50

759	50 NUEVOS PESOS	10.12.1992 (1994). Violet and red on m/c unpt. J. M. Morelos at r., crossed cannons below his flag at ctr. Butterflies at l., boat fishermen at ctr. on back.	FV	FV	15.00

760	100 NUEVOS PESOS	10.12.1992 (1994). Red and brown on m/c unpt. Nezahualcóyoti at r., and as wmk., Aztec figure at ctr. Xochipilli on back.	FV	FV	25.00

Cat. #	Denomination	Date, description	VG	VF	Unc
761	200 NUEVOS PESOS	10.12.1992 (1994). Dk. brown and olive-brown on m/c unpt. J. de Asbaje at r., and as wmk., open book and quill pen at ctr. Temple de San Jerónimo on back.	FV	FV	45.00

| 762 | 500 NUEVOS PESOS | 10.12.1992 (1994). Red-brown and dk. brown on m/c unpt. I. Zaragoza at ctr. r., and as wmk., Battle of Puebla at l. ctr. Cathedral at Puebla at ctr. on back. | FV | FV | 110.00 |

1996 ISSUE

#763–768 similar to #757–762 except *NUEVOS* and *PAGARA A LA VISTA AL PORTADOR* are omitted. Sign. are rearranged. Printer: BdM.

| 763 | 10 PESOS | 6.5.1994 (1996). Blue-green on m/c unpt. Similar to #757. | FV | FV | 3.50 |

764	20 PESOS	6.5.1994 (1996). Purple, violet and blue on m/c unpt. Similar to #758.	FV	FV	6.50
765	50 PESOS	6.5.1994 (1996). Violet and red on m/c unpt. Similar to #759.	FV	FV	15.00
766	100 PESOS	6.5.1994 (1996). Red and brown on m/c unpt. Similar to #760.	FV	FV	28.50
767	200 PESOS	6.5.1994 (1996). Dk. brown and olive-brown on m/c unpt. Similar to #761.	FV	FV	50.00
768	500 PESOS	6.5.1994 (1996). Red-brown and dk. brown on m/c unpt. Similar to #762.	FV	FV	120.00

COLLECTOR SERIES

Matched serial # sets of ABNC 1-100 Pesos and BdM 5-1000 Pesos series A were released at the International Coin Convention in México City. Unc. set $30.00.

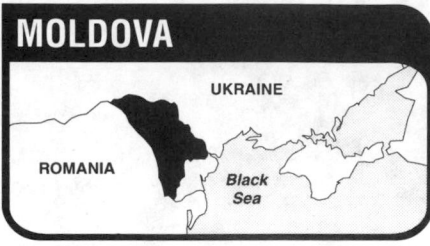

MOLDOVA

The Republic of Moldova (formerly the Moldavian S.S.R.) is bordered in the east and south by the Ukraine and on the west by Romania. It has an area of 13,000 sq. mi. (33,700 sq. km.) and a population of 4.4 million. (This includes the area and people of Transdniestria, an area in dispute.) Fish, agricultural products including canned goods, steel, concrete and dairy products are leading industries.

The Moldavian A.S.S.R. was created on Oct. 12, 1924, as part of the Ukrainian S.S.R., a Soviet protest against the recovery of Bessarabia by Romania. In 1940 Romania yielded to a Soviet ultimatum and ceded Bessarabia to the U.S.S.R. and the Soviet government formed a Moldavian S.S.R. comprised of the major part of Bessarabia. In June 1941, the Romanians allied with Germany reincorporated the whole of Bessarabia into Romania. Soviet armies reconquered it late in 1944 restoring the Moldavian S.S.R. A new constitution was adopted in April 1978. A declaration of republican sovereignty was adopted in June 1990 and the area was renamed Moldova, an independent republic, declared in Aug. 1991. In Dec. 1991 Moldova became a member of the Commonwealth of Independent States. Separatists and government forces clashed in 1992. A joint declaration by Russian and Moldavian presidents on July 3, 1992 envisaged a demarcation line held by neutral forces and withdrawal of the Russian army from Transdniestria, which had developed into a self-styled republic.

MONETARY SYSTEM

1 Leu = 1000 Cupon = 100 Rubles (Russian), 1993–

REPUBLIC

Ruble Control Coupons

Cat. #	Denomination	Date, description	VG	VF	Unc
A11	20 RUBLE	1992.			
		a. Full sheet.	—	.50	1.00
		b. Coupon.	—	—	.10

Banca Nationala a Moldovei

1992-93 "CUPON" ISSUE

#1–4 arms at l. Castle at r. on back. Wmk: Wavy lines.

| 1 | 50 CUPON | 1992. Gray-green on gray unpt. | .10 | .40 | 1.65 |

| 2 | 200 CUPON | 1992. Blue-black on gray unpt. Back purple on lilac unpt. | .20 | .65 | 2.50 |

| 3 | 1000 CUPON | 1993. Brown on pale blue-green and ochre unpt. Bank monogram at upper l. | .25 | .75 | 3.00 |

Cat. #	Denomination	Date, description	VG	VF	Unc
4	5000 CUPON	1993. Pale brown-violet, orange and pale olive-green unpt. Bank monogram at upper l. Back pale brown-violet on pale brown-orange unpt.	.45	1.35	5.50

Currency Reform

1 Leu = 1000 Cupon, 1993–

1992 DATED ISSUE

#5–7 Kg. Stefan at l., arms at upper ctr. r. Cetatea Soroca Castle at ctr. r. on back.

| 5 | 1 LEU | 1992 (1993). Brown and dk. olive-green on ochre unpt. | FV | .45 | 1.75 |

| 6 | 5 LEI | 1992 (1993). Purple on lt. blue and ochre unpt. | FV | 1.00 | 4.00 |

| 7 | 10 LEI | 1992 (1993). Red brown and olive-green on pale orange unpt. | FV | 1.75 | 7.00 |

1992; 1994 DATED ISSUE

#18–16 Kg. Stefan at l. and as wmk., arms at upper ctr. r.

#18–14 bank monogram at upper r.

Cat. #	Denomination	Date, description	VG	VF	Unc
8 (10)	1 LEU	1994; 1995. Brown on ochre and pale yellow-green on m/c unpt. Monastary at Capriana at ctr. r on back. Monastary at Hërbovet at ctr. r. on back.	FV	FV	1.50

| 9 (11) | 5 LEI | 1994; 1995. Grayish blue-green on lilac and pale aqua. Basillica of St. Dumitrudln Orhei at ctr. r. on back. | FV | FV | 2.75 |

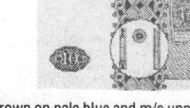

| 10 (12) | 10 LEI | 1994. Red-brown on pale blue and m/c unpt. Monastary at Hîrjauca at ctr. r. on back. | FV | FV | 5.00 |

13 (8)	20 LEI	1992 (1993); 1994; 1995. Blue-green on lt. green, aqua and ochre. Back dk. green and blue-green on lt. green unpt.	FV	2.75	9.00
14 (9)	50 LEI	1992 (1993); 1994. Red violet on lilac and m/c unpt. Monastary at Hîrbovet at ctr. r. on back.	FV	FV	17.50
15	100 LEI	(1996).	FV	FV	32.50
16	200 LEI	1992 (1996).	FV	FV	60.00

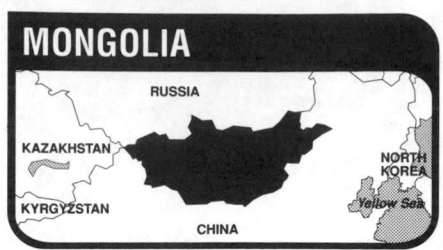

MONGOLIA

RUSSIA
KAZAKHSTAN
KYRGYZSTAN
CHINA
NORTH KOREA
Yellow Sea

The State of Mongolia (formerly the Mongolian Peoples Republic), a landlocked country in central Asia between the Soviet Union and the Peoples Republic of China, has an area of 604,247 sq. mi. (1,565,000 sq. km.) and a population of 2.26 million. Capital: Ulan Bator. Animal herds and flocks are the chief economic asset. Wool, cattle, butter, meat and hides are exported.

Mongolia (often referred to as Outer Mongolia), one of the world's oldest countries, attained its greatest power in the 13th century when Genghis Khan and his successors conquered all of China and extended their influence westward as far as Hungary and Poland. The empire dissolved in later centuries and in 1691 was brought under suzerainty of the Manchus, who had conquered China in 1644. After the Chinese republican movement led by Sun Yat-sen overthrew the Manchus and set up the Chinese Republic in 1911, Mongolia, with the support of Russia, proclaimed its independence from China, and on March 13, 1921 a Provisional Peoples Government was established. Later, on Nov. 26, 1924, the government proclaimed the Mongolian Peoples Republic. Opposition to the communist party developed in late 1989 and after demonstrations and hunger strikes the Politburo resigned on Mar. 12, 1990 and the new State of Mongolia was organized.

MONETARY SYSTEM
1 Tugrik (Tukhrik) = 100 Mongo

REPLACEMENT NOTES

#35-41; 3A, 3B, or ЯА prefix.

#42-48; ЯА, ЯВ prefix.

УЛСЫН БАНК – State Bank

1966 ISSUE

#35-41 Socialist arms at upper l.

Cat. #	Denomination	Date, description	VG	VF	Unc
35	1 TUGRIK	1966. Brown. No portr.	.20	.50	1.00

#36-41 portr. Sukhe-Bataar at r.

Cat. #	Denomination	Date, description	VG	VF	Unc
36	3 TUGRIK	1966. Green.	.25	.60	1.25
37	5 TUGRIK	1966. Blue.	.25	.60	1.25
38	10 TUGRIK	1966. Red-brown.	.25	.75	1.50
39	25 TUGRIK	1966. Brown-violet.	.50	1.00	2.50
40	50 TUGRIK	1966. Green. Govt. bldg. and Ulan-Bataar on back.	1.00	2.50	5.00

41	100 TUGRIK	1966. Brown. Back like #40	2.00	4.00	7.50

1981-83 ISSUE

#42-45 and 47-48 like #36-41.

Cat. #	Denomination	Date, description	VG	VF	Unc
42	1 TUGRIK	1983. Brown.	FV	FV	.65

43	3 TUGRIK	1983. Green.	FV	FV	.85

44	5 TUGRIK	1981. Blue-green on blue-gray & pale green unpt.	FV	FV	1.00

45	10 TUGRIK	1981. Red-brown on pale orange & blue-green unpt.	FV	FV	1.75

46	20 TUGRIK	1981. Yellow-green. Sukhe-Bataar at ctr. Power station at Ulan-Bataar at ctr. on back.	FV	FV	2.00

Cat. #	Denomination	Date, description	VG	VF	Unc
47	50 TUGRIK	1981. Dk. green.	FV	FV	4.00

| 48 | 100 TUGRIK | 1981. Dk. brown on ochre & blue-green unpt. | FV | FV | 8.00 |

STATE

МОНГОЛ ЪАНК – Mongol Bank

1993 (ND) ISSUE

#49–51 "Soemba" arms at upper ctr.

	#49		#50			#51

49	10 MONGO	ND (1993). Red-violet on pale red orange. 2 archers at lower ctr. on face and back.	FV	FV	.50
50	20 MONGO	ND (1993). Brown on ochre and yellow-brown unpt. 2 atheletes at lower ctr. on face and back.	FV	FV	.50
51	50 MONGO	ND (1993). Greenish-black on blue and pale green unpt. 2 horseman at lower ctr. on face and back.	FV	FV	.50

#52–60 wmk: Genghis Khan.

Cat. #	Denomination	Date, description	VG	VF	Unc
52	1 TUGRIK	ND (1993). Dull olive-green and brown-orange on ochre unpt. Chinze at l. "Soemba" arms at ctr. r. on back.	FV	FV	.85

#53–57 youthful portr. Suhe-Bator at l., "Soemba" arms at ctr. Horses grazing in mountainous landscape at ctr. r. on back.

53	5 TUGRIK	ND (1993). Red-orange, ochre and brown on m/c unpt.	FV	FV	1.00

54	10 TUGRIK	ND (1993). Green, blue and lt. green on m/c unpt.	FV	FV	1.00

55	20 TUGRIK	ND (1993). Violet, orange and red on m/c unpt.	FV	FV	1.25

56	50 TUGRIK	ND (1993). Dk. brown on m/c unpt.	FV	FV	1.25

Cat. #	Denomination	Date, description	VG	VF	Unc
57	100 TUGRIK	ND (1993). Purple, red-brown and dk. blue on m/c unpt.	FV	FV	1.75

#58–59 Genghis Khan at l., "Soemba" arms at ctr. Ox drawn yurte, village at ctr. r. on back.

58	500 TUGRIK	ND (1993). Dk. green, brown and yellow-green on m/c unpt.	FV	FV	4.50

59	1000 TUGRIK	ND (1993). Blue-gray, brown and blue on m/c unpt.	FV	FV	8.50
60	5000 TUGRIK	ND.		Expected new issue.	

MOROCCO

The Kingdom of Morocco situated on the northwest corner of Africa south of Spain, has an area of 172,413 sq. mi. (712,550 sq. km.) and a population of 25.7 million. Capital: Rabat. The economy is essentially agricultural. Phosphates, fresh and preserved vegetables, canned fish, and raw material are exported.

Morocco's strategic position at the gateway to western Europe has been the principal determinant of its violent, frequently unfortunate history. Time and again the fertile plain between the rugged Atlas Mountains and the sea has echoed the battle's trumpet as Phoenicians, Romans, Vandals, Visigoths, Byzantine Greeks and Islamic Arabs successively conquered and occupied the land. Modern Morocco is a remnant of an early empire formed by the Arabs at the close of the 7th century which encompassed all of northwest Africa and most of the Iberian Peninsula. During the 17th and 18th centuries, while under the control of native dynasties, it was the headquarters of the famous Sale pirates. Morocco's strategic position involved it in the competition of 19th century European powers for political influence in Africa, and resulted in the division of Morocco into French and Spanish spheres of interest which were established as protectorates in 1912. Morocco became independent on March 2, 1956, after France agreed to end its protectorate. Spain signed similar agreements on April 7 of the same year.

RULERS

Muhammad V, AH1346–80/1927–61AD
Hassan II, AH1380– /1961– AD

MONETARY SYSTEM

1 Franc = 100 Centimes
1 Dirham = 100 Francs, 1921–1974
1 Dirham = 100 Santimat, 1974–

Banque du Maroc

Established June 30, 1959

1960 (ND); 1965 ISSUE

#53–55 wmk: Lion's head.

Cat. #	Denomination	Date, description	VG	VF	Unc
53	5 DIRHAMS	ND; 1965–69. M/c. Kg. Muhammad V wearing a fez at r. Harvesting on back. 6 sign. varieties.			
		a. ND(1960).	2.50	8.00	32.50
		b. 1965/AH1384; 1966/AH1386; 1968/AH1387; 1969/AH1389.	1.50	6.00	27.50

Cat. #	Denomination	Date, description	VG	VF	Unc
54	10 DIRHAMS	ND; 1965–69. M/c. Kg. Muhammad V wearing a fez at l. Orange picking on back. 5 sign. varieties.			
		a. ND.	3.00	10.00	45.00
		b. 1965/AH1384; 1968/AH1387; 1969/AH1389.	2.00	6.50	30.00

| 55 | 50 DIRHAMS | 1965/AH1385; 1966/AH1386; 1968/AH1387; 1969/AH1389. M/c. Kg. Hassan II at r. Miners at work on back. 4 sign. varieties. | 15.00 | 50.00 | 200.00 |

1970 ISSUE

#56–59 Kg. Hassan II at l. and as wmk. Printer: TDLR.

| 56 | 5 DIRHAMS | 1970/AH1390. Purple. Castle at ctr. Industrial processing on back. | FV | 1.50 | 5.00 |

| 57 | 10 DIRHAMS | 1970/AH1390; 1985/AH1405. Brown. Villa at ctr. Processing oranges on back. | FV | 2.00 | 5.50 |

Cat. #	Denomination	Date, description	VG	VF	Unc
58	50 DIRHAMS	1970/AH1390; 1985/AH1405. Green. City at ctr. Dam on back.	FV	12.00	20.00

| 59 | 100 DIRHAMS | 1970/AH1390; 1985/AH1405. Brown, blue and m/c. Bldg. at ctr. Oil refinery on back. | FV | 20.00 | 30.00 |

Bank Al-Maghrib

1987 ISSUE

#60–62 Kg. Hassan II facing at r. and as wmk. Sign. varieties.

| 60 | 10 DIRHAMS | 1987/AH1407. Red-brown, red and m/c. Musical instrument and pillar at l. ctr. on back. | FV | FV | 6.50 |

| 61 | 50 DIRHAMS | 1987/AH1407. Green and m/c. Mounted militia charging, flowers at ctr. on back. | FV | 10.00 | 20.00 |
| 62 | 100 DIRHAMS | 1987/AH1407. Brown and m/c. Demonstration on back. | FV | FV | 27.50 |

1991 ISSUE

#63–66 older bust of Kg. Hassan II at r. facing half l. Wmk: Kg. facing.

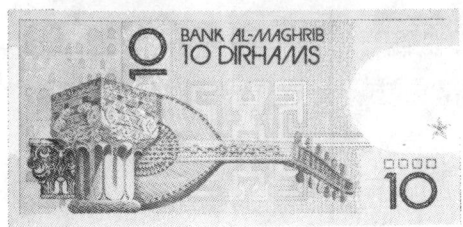

Cat. #	Denomination	Date, description	VG	VF	Unc
63	10 DIRHAMS	1987/AH407 (ca.1991). Brown-violet and purple on m/c unpt. Back like #60, but diff. colors of unpt.	FV	FV	3.50
64	50 DIRHAMS	1987/AH1407 (ca.1991). Green and m/c. Back like #61.	FV	FV	13.50
65	100 DIRHAMS	1987/AH1407 (ca.1991). Brown, blue and m/c. Back like #62.	FV	FV	26.00

66	200 DIRHAMS	1987/AH1407 (ca.1991). Blue-violet, blue and m/c. Mausoleum of Kg. Muhammad V at ctr. Sailboat, shell and coral on back.	FV	FV	50.00

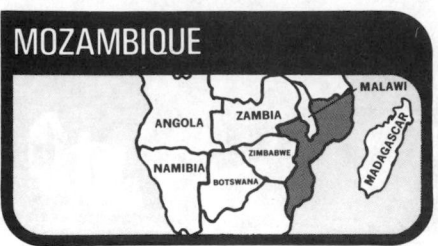

MOZAMBIQUE

The People's Republic of Mozambique, a former overseas province of Portugal stretching for 1,430 miles (2,301 km.) along the southeast coast of Africa, has an area of 309,494 sq. mi. (783,030 sq. km.) and a population of 16.1 million, 99 percent of whom are native Africans of the Bantu tribes. Capital: Maputo. Agriculture is the chief industry. Cashew nuts, cotton, sugar, copra and tea are exported.

Vasco da Gama explored all the coast of Mozambique in 1498 and found Arab trading posts already along the coast. Portuguese settlement dates from the establishment of the trading post of Mozambique in 1505. Within five years Portugal absorbed all the former Arab sultanates along the east African coast. The area was organized as a colony in 1907 and became an overseas province in 1952. In Sept. of 1974, after more than a decade of guerrilla warfare with the forces of the Mozambique Liberation Front, Portugal agreed to the independence of Mozambique, effective June 25, 1975.

RULERS
Portuguese to 1975

MONETARY SYSTEM
1 Escudo = 100 Centavos, 1907–1975
1 Metica = 100 Centimos, 1975–

REPLACEMENT NOTES
#116, 117, 119: Z prefix.
#125-133, ZA, ZB, ZC prefix.
#134-137, AW, BW, CY, DZ prefix by denomination.

PORTUGUESE INFLUENCE
Banco Nacional Ultramarino
Escudo System
1961–67 ISSUE
#109–110 printer: BWC.

Cat. #	Denomination	Date, description	VG	VF	Unc
109	100 ESCUDOS	27.3.1961. Green on m/c unpt. Portr. A. de Ornelas at r. Bank (steamship) seal at l. on back.			
		a. Wmk: Arms.	1.50	3.50	8.00
		b. W/o wmk.	1.00	3.00	7.00

110	500 ESCUDOS	22.3.1967. Brown-violet on m/c unpt. Portr. C. Xavier at r.	8.00	20.00	45.00

1970 ISSUE
Sign. varieties.

Cat. #	Denomination	Date, description	VG	VF	Unc
111	50 ESCUDOS	27.10.1970. Black on m/c unpt. J. de Aze-vedo Coutinho at l. ctr. Back green; bank (steamship) seal at l. Wmk: Arms.	.75	3.00	6.00

FIRST 1972 ISSUE

| 112 | 1000 ESCUDOS | 16.5.1972. Black-blue on m/c unpt. Afonso V at r. Allegorical woman w/ships at l. on back, bank (steamship) seal at upper ctr. 3 sign. varieties. | 5.00 | 20.00 | 75.00 |

NOTE: #112 has 2 1/2mm. serial # w/o prefix or 3mm. serial # and 3-letter prefix.

SECOND 1972 ISSUE

| 113 | 100 ESCUDOS | 23.5.1972. Blue on m/c unpt. G. Coutinho and S. Cabral at l. ctr. Surveyor at ctr. on back. Wmk: Coutinho. | 1.00 | 3.00 | 8.50 |

| 114 | 500 ESCUDOS | 23.5.1972. Violet on m/c unpt. G. Coutinho at l. ctr. and as wmk. Cabral and airplane on back. | 4.00 | 10.00 | 35.00 |

Cat. #	Denomination	Date, description	VG	VF	Unc
115	1000 ESCUDOS	23.5.1972. Green on m/c unpt. Likc #114. 2 men in cockpit of airplane on back.	10.00	20.00	60.00

PEOPLES REPUBLIC

Banco de Moçambique

1976 PROVISIONAL ISSUE

#116–119 black ovpt. of new bank name.

| 116 | 50 ESCUDOS | ND (1976 - old date 27.10.1970). Ovpt. on #111. | .10 | .20 | .50 |

| 117 | 100 ESCUDOS | ND (1976 - old date 27.3.1961). Ovpt. on #109. | .10 | .20 | .50 |

| 118 | 500 ESCUDOS | ND (1976 - old date 22.3.1967). Ovpt. on #110. | .10 | .30 | .75 |

Cat. #	Denomination	Date, description	VG	VF	Unc
119	1000 ESCUDOS	ND (1976 - old date 23.5.1972). Ovpt. on #115.	.15	.40	1.00

Metica System

1976 ISSUE

#120–124 Pres. S. Machel at l. ctr. Printer: TDLR.

120	5 METICAS	25.6.1976. Brown and m/c. Kudo on back. Specimens only.	—	—	—
121	10 METICAS	25.6.1976. Blue on m/c. Lions on back. Specimens only.	—	—	—
122	20 METICAS	25.6.1976. Red and m/c. Giraffes on back. Specimens only.	—	—	—
123	50 METICAS	25.6.1976. Purple and m/c. Cape buffalo on back. Specimens only.	—	—	—

| 124 | 100 METICAS | 25.6.1976. Green and m/c. Elephants on back. Specimens only. | — | — | — |

NOTE: #120–124 appear to be unadopted designs.

República Popular De Moçambique

1980 ISSUE

#125–128 arms at ctr.

| 125 | 50 METICAIS | 16.6.1980. Dk. brown and brown on m/c unpt. Soldiers at l., flag ceremony at r. Soldiers in training on back. | .15 | .40 | 1.25 |

Cat. #	Denomination	Date, description	VG	VF	Unc
126	100 METICAIS	16.6.1980. Green on m/c unpt. Soldiers at flagpole at l., E. Mondlane at r. Public ceremony on back.	.20	.50	1.50

| 127 | 500 METICAIS | 16.6.1980. Blue on m/c unpt. Government assembly at l., chanting crowd at r. Chemists and school scene on back. | .40 | 1.00 | 3.50 |

| 128 | 1000 METICAIS | 16.6.1980. Red on m/c unpt. Pres. S. Machel w/3 young boys at r., revolutionary monument at l. Mining and harvesting scenes on back. | .75 | 2.00 | 5.00 |

1983–88 ISSUE

#129–132 modified arms at ctr. Smaller size serial #.

| 129 | 50 METICAIS | 16.6.1983; 16.6.1986. Similar to #125 except for arms. | .10 | .35 | 1.00 |

Cat. #	Denomination	Date, description	VG	VF	Unc
130	100 METICAIS	16.6.1983; 16.6.1986; 16.6.1989. Similar to #126 except for arms.	.10	.35	1.00

| 131 | 500 METICAIS | 16.6.1983; 16.6.1989. Similar to #127 except for arms. | .25 | 1.00 | 2.50 |

| 132 | 1000 METICAIS | 16.6.1983; 16.6.1986; 16.6.1989. Similar to #128 except for arms. | .60 | 1.75 | 4.00 |

| 133 | 5000 METACAIS | 3.2.1988; 3.2.1989. Purple, brown and violet on m/c unpt. Carved statues at l., painting at r. Dancers and musicians on back. Wmk: Pres. Machel. | .60 | 1.75 | 4.00 |

1991–93 ISSUE

#134–137 arms at upper ctr. r. printed on silver or gold underlay. Bank seal at lower l. on back. Wmk: J. Chissano. Printer: TDLR.

Cat. #	Denomination	Date, description	VG	VF	Unc
134	500 METICAIS	16.6.1991. Brown and grayish blue on m/c unpt. Native statue of couple in grief at l. ctr., native art at r. Back blue; dancing warriors at ctr.	FV	.35	1.50

| 135 | 1000 METICAIS | 16.6.1991. Brown and red on m/c unpt. E. Mondlane at l. ctr., military flag raising ceremony at r. Back red; monument at l. ctr. | FV | .50 | 2.25 |

| 136 | 5000 METICAIS | 16.6.1991. Purple, red and orange-brown on m/c unpt. S. Machel at l. ctr., monument to the Socialist vanguard at r. Foundry workers at ctr. on back. | FV | 1.00 | 4.00 |

Cat. #	Denomination	Date, description	VG	VF	Unc
137	10,000 METICAIS	16.6.1991. Blue-green, brown and orange on m/c unpt. J. Chissano at l. ctr., high tension electrical towers at r. w/farm tractor in field and high-rise city view in background at r. Plowing with oxen at ctr on back.	FV	1.50	6.50

#138 and 139 Bank of Mozambique bldg. at l. ctr. arms at upper r. Cabora Bassa hydroeletric dam on back.

Cat. #	Denomination	Date, description	VG	VF	Unc
138	50,000 METICAIS	16.6.1993 (1994). Red-brown and brown on m/c unpt.	FV	6.50	15.00
139	100,000 METICAIS	16.6.1993 (1994). Red and black on m/c unpt.	FV	12.50	28.50

Listings For:

MUSCAT and OMAN, see Oman

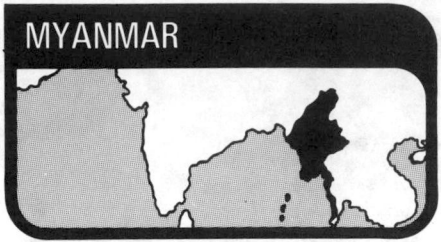

MYANMAR

The Socialist Republic of the Union of Myanmar (Burma), a country of Southeast Asia fronting on the Bay of Bengal and the Andaman Sea, has an area of 261,789 sq. mi. (676,552 sq. km.) and a population of 41.5 million. Capital: Rangoon. Burma is an agricultural country heavily dependent on its leading product (rice) which occupied two-thirds of the cultivated area and accounts for 40 per cent of the value of exports. Petroleum, lead, tin, silver, zinc, nickel, cobalt and precious stones are exported.

The first European to reach Burma, about 1435, was Nicolo Di Conti, a merchant of Venice. During the beginning of the reign of Bodawpaya (1782-1819AD) the kingdom comprised most of the same area as it does today including Arakan which was taken over in 1784-85. The British East India Company, while unsuccessful in its 1612 effort to establish posts along the Bay of Bengal, was enabled by the Anglo-Burmese Wars of 1824-86 to expand to the whole of Burma and to secure its annexation to British India. In 1937, Burma was separated from India, becoming a separate British colony with limited self-government. The Japanese occupied Burma in 1942, and in late 1943 Burma became an "independent and sovereign state" under Dr. Ba Maw who was appointed the Adipadi (head of state). Burma became an independent nation outside the British Commonwealth on Jan. 4, 1948, the constitution of 1948 providing for a parliamentary democracy and the nationalization of certain industries. However, political and economic problems persisted, and on March 2, 1962, Gen. Ne Win took over the government, suspended the constitution, installed himself as chief of state, and pursued a socialistic program with nationalization of nearly all industry and trade. On Jan. 4, 1974, a new constitution adopted by referendum established Burma as a "socialist republic" under one-party rule. The country name was changed to Union of Myanmar in 1989.

MONETARY SYSTEM
1 Kyat = 100 Pya, 1952–

REPLACEMENT NOTES
#52–55, special Burmese characters.

Peoples Bank of Burma

#52–55 portr. Gen. Aung San at ctr. Wmk. pattern throughout paper. Printed in East Berlin.

Cat. #	Denomination	Date, description	VG	VF	Unc
52	1 KYAT	ND (1965). Violet and blue. Back violet; fisherman at ctr. Serial # varieties.	.15	.30	1.00

Cat. #	Denomination	Date, description	VG	VF	Unc
53	5 KYATS	ND (1965). Green and lt. blue. Back green; man w/ox at ctr. r.	.15	.40	1.50

Cat. #	Denomination	Date, description	VG	VF	Unc
54	10 KYATS	ND (1965). Red-brown and violet. Back red-brown, woman picking cotton at r.	.20	.50	2.00

Cat. #	Denomination	Date, description	VG	VF	Unc
58	10 KYATS	ND (1973). Red, violet and m/c. Native ornaments on back.	.15	.40	1.00

| 55 | 20 KYATS | ND (1965). Brown and tan. Back brown; farmer on tractor at ctr. r. | .40 | 1.00 | 3.00 |

Union of Burma Bank

1972–79 ISSUE

#56–61 various military portrs. of Gen. Aung San at l. and as wmk.

| 56 | 1 KYAT | ND (1972). Green and blue on m/c unpt. Ornate native wheel assembly on back. | .10 | .15 | .40 |

| 59 | 25 KYATS | ND (1972). Brown and tan on m/c unpt. Mythical winged creature at ctr. on back. | .25 | .60 | 1.50 |

| 57 | 5 KYATS | ND (1973). Blue and purple on m/c unpt. Palm tree on back. | .15 | .35 | .75 |

| 60 | 50 KYATS | ND (1979). Brown and violet on m/c unpt. Mythical dancer on back. | 2.00 | 5.00 | 17.50 |

Cat. #	Denomination	Date, description	VG	VF	Unc
61	100 KYATS	ND (1976). Blue and green on m/c unpt. Native wheel and musical string instrument at l. ctr. on back.	1.50	4.00	15.00

1985–94 ISSUE

#62–66 smaller notes. Various portr. Gen. Aung San. as wmk.

Cat. #	Denomination	Date, description	VG	VF	Unc
65	75 KYATS	ND (1985). Brown and m/c. Gen. Aung San at l. ctr. Dancer at l. on back.	FV	1.00	2.50

			VG	VF	Unc
62	15 KYATS	ND (1986). Blue-gray and green on m/c unpt. Gen. Aung San at l. ctr. Mythical dancer at l. on back.	FV	.65	1.75

| 66 | 90 KYATS | ND (1987). Brown and green on m/c unpt. Seya San at r. Farmer plowing w/oxen and rice planting on back. | FV | FV | 5.50 |

| 63 | 35 KYATS | ND (1986). Brown-violet and purple on m/c unpt. Gen. Aung San in military hat at l. ctr. Mythical dancer at l. on back. | FV | 1.00 | 3.00 |

Central Bank Of Myanmar

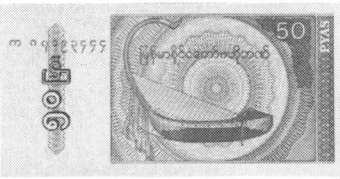

| 66A | 50 PYA | ND (1994). Dull purple and dull brown on gray and tan unpt. Musical string instrument at ctr. Wmk: OM. | FV | FV | .20 |

| 64 | 45 KYATS | ND (1987). Blue-gray and blue on m/c unpt. Po Hla Gyi at r. Two workers w/rope and bucket, oil field on back. | FV | FV | 4.00 |

| 67 | 1 KYAT | ND (1990). Pale brown, orange and m/c. Gen. Aung San at l. and as wmk. Dragon carving at l. on back. | FV | FV | .35 |

#68 and 69 Held in reserve.

Cat. #	Denomination	Date, description	VG	VF	Unc
70	20 KYATS	ND (1994). Deep olive-green, brown, and blue-green on m/c unpt. Chinze at l. Fountain of elephants in park at ctr. r. on back. Wmk: Chinze over value.	FV	FV	1.25

71	50 KYATS	ND (1994). Red-brown, tan, and dk. brown on m/c unpt. Chinze at r. and as wmk. Coppersmith at l. ctr. on back.	FV	FV	2.25

72	100 KYATS	ND (1994). Blue-violet, blue-green and dk. brown on m/c unpt. Chinze at l. Workers restoring temple and grounds at ctr. r. on back. Wmk: Chinze over value.	FV	FV	4.50

Cat. #	Denomination	Date, description	VG	VF	Unc
73	200 KYATS	ND (ca.1991). Dk. blue and green on m/c unpt. Chinze at r., his head as wmk. Elephant pulling log at ctr. r. on back.	FV	FV	10.00

74	500 KYATS	ND (1994). Purple, brown-violet and brown-orange on m/c unpt. Chinze at l. Workers restoring medieval statue, craftsman and water hauler at ctr. r. on back. Wmk: Chinze over value.	FV	FV	13.50

FOREIGN EXCHANGE CERTIFICATES

Central Bank

#FX1-FX3 statue at r.

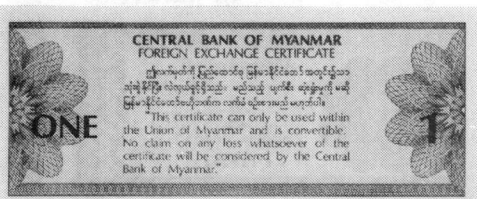

FX1	1 DOLLAR (USA)	ND (1993). Blue, brown, yellow and green.	FV	FV	3.00

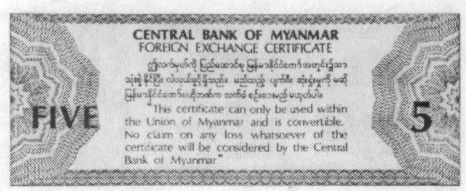

Cat. #	Denomination	Date, description	VG	VF	Unc
FX2	5 DOLLARS (USA)	ND (1993). Maroon, yellow and blue.	FV	FV	13.50

FX3	10 DOLLARS (USA)	ND (1993). Blue, green and gray.	FV	FV	25.00

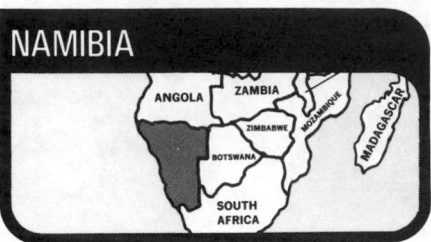

NAMIBIA

The Republic of Namibia (formerly the international territory of Namibia), once the German colonial territory of German South West Africa and later South West Africa, is situated on the Atlantic coast of southern Africa, bounded on the north by Angola, on the east by Botswana, and on the south by South Africa. It has an area of 318,261 sq. mi. (824, 290 sq. km.) and a population of 1.4 million. Capital: Windhoek. Diamonds, copper, lead, zinc and cattle are exported.

South Africa undertook the administration of South West Africa under the terms of a League of Nations mandate on Dec. 17, 1920. When the League of Nations was dissolved in 1946, its supervisory authority for South West Africa was inherited by the United Nations. In 1946 the UN denied South Africa's request to annex South West Africa. South Africa responded by refusing to place the territory under a UN trusteeship. In 1950 the International Court of Justice ruled that South Africa could not unilaterally modify the international status of South West Africa. A 1966 UN resolution declaring the mandate terminated was rejected by South Africa, and the status of the area remained in dispute. In June 1968 the UN General Assembly voted to rename the territory Namibia. In 1971 the International Court of Justice ruled that South Africa's presence in Namibia was illegal. In Dec. 1973 the UN appointed a UN Commissioner, and a multi-racial Advisory Council was also appointed. An interim government was formed in 1977 and independence was to be declared by Dec. 31, 1978. This resolution was rejected by major UN powers. In April 1978 South Africa accepted a plan for UN-supervised elections which led to political abstention by the South West Africa People's Organization (SWAPO) party. The result was the dissolution of the Minister's Council and National Assembly in Jan. 1983. A Multi-Party Conference (MPC) was formed in May 1984 which held talks with SWAPO. The MPC petitioned South Africa for Namibian self-government and on June 17, 1984 the Transitional Government of National Unity was installed. Negotiations were held in 1988 between Angola, Cuba and South Africa reaching a peaceful settlement on Aug. 5, 1988. By April 1, 1989, Cuban troops were to withdraw from Angola and South African troops from Namibia. The Transitional Government resigned on Feb. 28, 1988 for the upcoming elections of the constituent assembly in Nov. 1989. Independence was finally achieved on March 21, 1990.

MONETARY SYSTEM
1 Namibia Dollar = 1 South African Rand

NOTE: For notes of the 3 commercial banks that circulated until 1963 see South West Africa listings in Vol. I.

Bank of Namibia

#1–3 Capt. H. Wittbooi at l. ctr. Printer: TB.

Cat#	Date, denomination	Description	VG	VF	Unc
1	10 NAMIBIA DOLLARS	ND (1993). Blue-black on m/c unpt. Arms at upper l. Springbok at r. on back.	FV	FV	6.50
1A	20 NAMIBIA DOLLARS			Expected new issue.	

Cat#	Date, denomination	Description	VG	VF	Unc
2	50 NAMIBIA DOLLARS	ND (1993). Blue-green and dk. brown on m/c unpt. Arms at upper ctr. Antelope at r. on back.	FV	FV	25.00

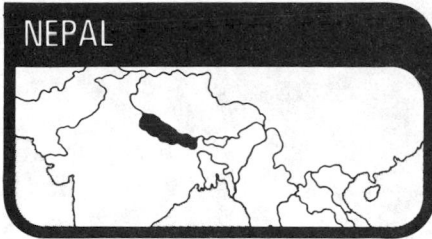

3	100 NAMIBIA DOLLARS	ND (1993). Red, brown and red-brown on m/c unpt. Arms at upper ctr. r. Oryx at r. on back.	FV	FV	45.00
4	200 NAMIBIA DOLLARS			Expected new issue.	

COLLECTOR SERIES

Cat#	Date, denomination	Description	Issue Price	Mkt. Val.
CS1	ND (1993) 10-100 Dollars	#1-3 w/matched serial # mounted in a special plexiglass frame.	150.00	150.00

NOTE: #CS1 was initially designated for distribution among foreign dignitaries.

NEPAL

The Kingdom of Nepal, the world's only Hindu kingdom, is a landlocked country located in central Asia along the southern slopes of the Himalayan Mountains. It has an area of 56,136 sq. mi. (140,797 sq. km.) and a population of 19.4 million. Capital: Kathmandu. Nepal has substantial deposits of coal, copper, iron and cobalt but they are largely unexploited. Agriculture is the principal economic activity. Livestock, rice, timber and jute are exported.

Prithvi Narayan Shah, ruler of the principality of Gurkha, formed Nepal from a number of independent mountain states in the latter half of the 18th century. After his death a period of political instability ensued which lasted until the 1840s when the Rana family reduced the monarch to a figurehead and established itself as hereditary Prime Ministers. A popular revolution (1950–51) toppled the Rana family and reconstituted the power in the throne. In 1959 King Mahendra declared Nepal a constitutional monarchy. A new constitution promulgated in 1962 instituted a system of panchayat (village council) democracy from the village to the national levels.

RULERS
Mahendra Vira Vikrama Shahi Deva, 1955–1972
Birendra Bir Bikram Shahi Deva, 1972–

MONETARY SYSTEM
1 Rupee = 100 Paisa

SIGNATURE VARIETIES			
1	Janaph Raja	7	Prhadimhalal Rajbhandari
2	Bharana Raja	8	Yadavnath Panta
3	Narendra Raja	9	Kirisherkher Sharma
4	Himalaya Shamsher	10	Kalyan Bikram Adhikari
5	Laxminath Gautam	11	Ganesh Raj Thapa
6	Besh Bahadur Thapa	12	

State Bank of Nepal

1956 (ND) ISSUE

Cat. #	Denomination	Date, description	VG	VF	Unc
12	1 RUPEE	ND (1956). Coin at l., temple at ctr. Sign. 8.	.50	1.50	3.50

Cat. #	Denomination	Date, description	VG	VF	Unc
13	5 RUPEES	ND (1956). Portr. Stupa at ctr. Himalayas on back. Sign. 5; 6; 7; 8.	.50	1.65	5.00

14	10 RUPEES	ND (1956). Temple at ctr. Arms at ctr. on back.. Sign. 5; 6; 7; 8.	.90	2.75	8.00

15	100 RUPEES	ND (1956). Temple at Lalitpor at ctr. Rhinoceros on back. Sign. 5; 6; 7.	3.00	10.00	35.00

1972 (ND) ISSUE

#16–21 Kg. Mahendra Vira Vikrama wearing military uniform w/white cap at l. Sign. 8. Wmk: Crown.

16	1 RUPEE	ND (1972). Brown and blue. Back brown and purple; 4-chair rotary device and arms.	.20	.65	1.75

17	5 RUPEES	ND (1972). Green and lilac. Back green and blue. Terraces w/Himalayas in background.	.30	.85	2.50

Cat. #	Denomination	Date, description	VG	VF	Unc
18	10 RUPEES	ND (1972). Tan on dull olive-green and lt. blue unpt. Back green and brown; Royal Palace at Kathmandu.	.40	1.25	3.50
19	100 RUPEES	ND (1972). Green and lilac. Temple at r. Back green; Royal Palace at Bhaktapur.	3.00	7.00	27.00
20	500 RUPEES	ND (1972). Brown and violet. 2 tigers on back.	13.50	35.00	110.00

21	1000 RUPEES	ND (1972). Blue and m/c. Great Stupa at Bodhnath. Houses and mountains on back.	26.50	70.00	200.00

1974 (ND) ISSUE

#22–28 Kg. Birendra Bir Bikram in military uniform w/dk. cap at l. Wmk: Crown.

22	1 RUPEE	ND (1974). Blue, purple and gold. Temple at ctr. Back blue and brown; 2 musk deer at ctr. r. Sign. 9; 10; 11.	.05	.20	.80

23	5 RUPEES	ND (1974). Red, brown and green. Temple at ctr. Back red and brown; 2 yaks. Sign. 9; 10; 11.	.15	.40	1.60

Cat. #	Denomination	Date, description	VG	VF	Unc
28A	1 RUPEE	ND. Blue on m/c unpt. Back similar to #22. Sign. 12.	FV	FV	.40
29	2 RUPEES	ND (1981). Green, blue and lilac. Temple at ctr. Back m/c; leopard at ctr.			
		a. Line from king's lower lip extending downward. Sign. 10.	FV	FV	.75
		b. No line from king's lower lip. Sign. 10; 11.	FV	FV	.50

Cat. #	Denomination	Date, description	VG	VF	Unc
24	10 RUPEES	ND (1974). M/c. Mythological figures at ctr. Back brown and green; 2 antelopes at ctr. Sign. 9; 10; 11.	.30	.85	2.75

30	5 RUPEES	ND (1987). Brown on red and m/c unpt. Temple at ctr. Back similar to #23. Sign. 11.	FV	FV	1.25

25	50 RUPEES	ND (1974). Purple and green. Bldg. at ctr. Back blue and brown; mountain goat standing l. at ctr. Sign. 9.	1.50	3.50	10.00
31	10 RUPEES	ND (1985). Dk. brown, orange, lilac and m/c. Religious figure at ctr. Animals at ctr. on back. Sign. 11.	FV	FV	1.75

26	100 RUPEES	ND (1974). Green and purple. Mountains at ctr. Back green; rhinoceros walking l., "eye" at upper l. corner. Sign. 9.	3.00	7.00	20.00
27	500 RUPEES	ND (1974). Brown. Temple at ctr. Back brown and gold; 2 tigers. Sign. 9.	12.50	30.00	100.00
28	1000 RUPEES	ND (1974). Blue and m/c. Temple and Great Stupa at Bodhnath at ctr. Elephant on back.	25.00	55.00	225.00
32	20 RUPEES	ND (1982–87). Orange on m/c unpt. Temple at ctr. Back orange and m/c; deer at ctr. Sign. 9; 10.	FV	FV	4.00

1981–87 (ND) ISSUE

#28A–36 Kg. Birendra Bir Bikram wearing plumed crown at l. Wmk: Crown.

32A	20 RUPEES	ND (1988). Orange on m/c unpt. Like #32, but m/c border. M/c borders on back. Sign. 11.	FV	FV	1.75

Cat. #	Denomination	Date, description	VG	VF	Unc
33	50 RUPEES	ND (1983–). Blue on m/c unpt. Palace at ctr. Mountain goat at ctr. on back.			
		a. Sign. 10 w/title at r. (1983).	FV	FV	5.00
		b. Sign. 11 w/title at ctr. (1988).	FV	FV	3.75

34	100 RUPEES	ND (1981). Green on pale purple and tan unpt. Temple at r. Back green; rhinoceros walking l. Similar to #26, but w/o "eye" at upper l. Sign. 10; 11.			
		a. Line from king's lower lip extending downward.	FV	FV	10.00
		b. No line from king's lower lip.	FV	FV	8.00
35	500 RUPEES	ND (1981). Brown and blue-violet on m/c unpt. Temple at ctr. Back brown and gold; 2 tigers. Sign. 10; 11.			
		a. Regular security thread.	FV	FV	25.00
		b. Segmented foil security thread.	FV	FV	20.00

36	1000 RUPEES	ND (1981). Blue and brown on m/c unpt. Stupa and temple on face, elephant at ctr. on back. Sign. 10; 11.			
		a. Regular security thread.	FV	FV	50.00
		b. Segmented foil security thread.	FV	FV	40.00

NETHERLANDS

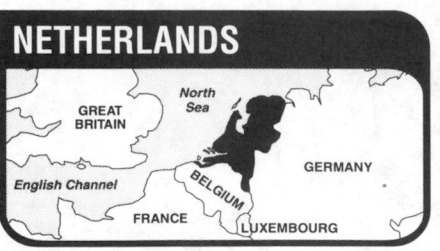

The Kingdom of the Netherlands, a country of western Europe fronting on the North Sea and bordered by Belgium and Germany, has an area of 15,770 sq. mi. (40,844 sq. km.) and a population of 15.1 million. Capital: Amsterdam, but the seat of government is at The Hague. The economy is based on dairy farming and a variety of industrial activities. Chemicals, yarns and fabrics, and meat products are exported.

After being a part of Charlemagne's empire in the 8th and 9th centuries, the Netherlands came under control of Burgundy and the Austrian Hapsburgs, and finally was subjected to Spanish dominion in the 16th century. Led by William of Orange, the Dutch revolted against Spain in 1568. The seven northern provinces formed the Union of Utrecht and declared their independence, in 1581, becoming the Republic of the United Netherlands. In the following century, the "Golden Age" of Dutch history, the Netherlands became a great sea and colonial power, a patron of the arts and a refuge for the persecuted. In 1814, all the provinces of Holland and Belgium were merged into the Kingdom of the United Netherlands under William I. The Belgians withdrew in 1830 to form their own kingdom, the last substantial change in the configuration of European Netherlands.

RULERS
Juliana I, 1948–81
Beatrix, 1981–

MONETARY SYSTEM
1 Gulden = 100 Cents
1 Rijksdaalder = 2 1/2 Gulden

De Nederlandsche Bank

#86–102 printer: JEZ.

1953–56 ISSUE

Cat. #	Denomination	Date, description	VG	VF	Unc
85	10 GULDEN	23.3.1953. Blue, brown and green. H. de Groot. at r.	FV	6.50	17.50

| 86 | 20 GULDEN | 8.11.1955. Green and lilac. Boerhaave at r. Serpent at l. on back. | 5.00 | 17.50 | 60.00 |
| 87 | 25 GULDEN | 10.4.1955. Red, orange and brown. C. Huygens at r. | FV | 15.00 | 35.00 |

Cat. #	Denomination	Date, description	VG	VF	Unc
88	100 GULDEN	2.2.1953. Dk. brown. Erasmus at r. Back red-brown; stylized bird at l.	FV	60.00	100.00

			VG	VF	Unc
89	1000 GULDEN	15.7.1956. Brown and green. Rembrandt at r. Hand w/brush and palette on back.	FV	600.00	750.00

1966–72 ISSUE

			VG	VF	Unc
90	5 GULDEN	26.4.1966. Green. Vondel at r. Modern bldg. design on back. Wmk: Inkwell, quill pen and scroll.			
		a. Serial # at upper l. and lower r. Gray paper w/clear wmk.	FV	FV	10.00
		b. Serial # at upper l. and lower r. White paper w/vague wmk. Series XA/XM.	FV	FV	12.50
		c. Serial # at upper l. and ctr. r. in smaller type. (Experimental issue only; circulated in the province of Utrecht.) Series 6AA.	30.00	60.00	150.00

			VG	VF	Unc
91	10 GULDEN	25.4.1968. Dk. blue on violet and m/c unpt. Stylized self-portrait of F. Hals at r. Wmk: Cornucopia.			
		a. O in "bullseye" at upper l. on back.	FV	6.00	12.00
		b. Plain "bullseye" at upper l. on back.	FV	FV	10.00

Cat. #	Denomination	Date, description	VG	VF	Unc
92	25 GULDEN	10.2.1971. Red. J. Pietersz Sweelinck at r. Wmk: Rectangular wave design.	FV	FV	22.50

			VG	VF	Unc
93	100 GULDEN	14.5.1970. Dk. brown. Adm. M. Adriaensz de Ruyter at r.	FV	FV	90.00
94	1000 GULDEN	30.3.1972. Black on dk. blue-green unpt. B. d' Espinoza at r. Wmk: Pyramid.	FV	FV	700.00

1973–85 ISSUE

			VG	VF	Unc
95	5 GULDEN	28.3.1973. Dk. green on green and m/c unpt. J. Vondel at r. Wmk. like #90.	FV	FV	7.50

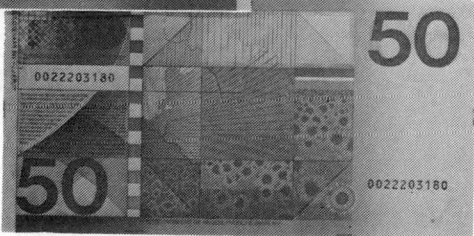

Cat. #	Denomination	Date, description	VG	VF	Unc
96	50 GULDEN	4.1.1982. Orange on m/c unpt. Sunflower w/bee at lower ctr. Vertical format. Map and flowers on back. Wmk: Bee.	FV	FV	40.00

Cat. #	Denomination	Date, description	VG	VF	Unc
97	100 GULDEN	28.7.1977 (1981). Dk. brown on m/c unpt. Water- snipe bird at r. Head of great snipe bird on back and as wmk.	FV	FV	80.00

Cat. #	Denomination	Date, description	VG	VF	Unc
98	250 GULDEN	25.7.1985 (1986). Violet on m/c unpt. Lighthouse. Vertical format. Lighthouse and map on back. Wmk: Rabbit and *VHP*.	FV	FV	185.00

1989– ISSUE

99	10 GULDEN				Expected new issue.

100	25 GULDEN	5.4.1989. Red on m/c unpt. Value and geometric designs on face and back. Wmk: Robin.	FV	FV	20.00
101	Held in reserve.				

Cat. #	Denomination	Date, description	VG	VF	Unc
102	100 GULDEN	9.1.1992 (7.9.1993). Dk. and lt. brown, gray and gold on m/c unpt. Value and geometric designs on face and back. Wmk: Little owl.	FV	FV	77.50
103	Held in reserve.				
104	1000 GULDEN				Expected new issue.

NETHERLANDS ANTILLES

The Netherlands Antilles, part of the Netherlands realm, comprise two groups of islands in the West Indies: Bonaire and Curacao near the Venezuelan coast; and St. Eustatius, Saba and the southern part of St. Martin (St. Maarten) southeast of Puerto Rico. The island group has an area of 385 sq. mi. (961 sq. km.) and a population of 191,000. Capital: Willemstad. Chief industries are the refining of crude oil, and tourism. Petroleum products and phosphates are exported.

On Dec. 15, 1954, the Netherlands Antilles were given complete domestic autonomy and granted equality within the Kingdom with Surinam and the Netherlands.

The island of Aruba gained independence in 1986.

RULERS
Dutch

MONETARY SYSTEM
1 Gulden = 100 Cents

Bank van de Nederlandse Antillen

1962 ISSUE

#1–7 woman seated w/scroll and flag in oval at l. Printer: JEZ.

Cat. #	Denomination	Date, description	VG	VF	Unc
1	5 GULDEN	2.1.1962. Blue. View of Curacao at ctr.	4.00	10.00	40.00
2	10 GULDEN	2.1.1962. Green. Highrise bldg. (Aruba) at ctr.	7.50	18.00	75.00
3	25 GULDEN	2.1.1962. Black-gray. View of Bonaire at ctr.	20.00	40.00	115.00

4	50 GULDEN	2.1.1962. Brown. City by the seaside (St. Maarten) at ctr.	35.00	85.00	225.00
5	100 GULDEN	2.1.1962. Violet. Monument (St. Eustatius) at ctr.	70.00	125.00	300.00
6	250 GULDEN	2.1.1962. Olive. Boats on the beach (Saba) at ctr.	175.00	350.00	600.00

| 7 | 500 GULDEN | 2.1.1962. Red. Oil refinery (Curacao) at ctr. | 350.00 | 425.00 | 700.00 |

1967 ISSUE

#8–13 monument *Steunend op eigen Kracht* ... at l. Printer: JEZ.

8	5 GULDEN	1967; 1972. Dk. blue and green. View of Curacao at ctr.			
		a. 28.8.1967.	3.50	6.00	20.00
		b. 1.6.1972.	3.50	5.00	15.00

Cat. #	Denomination	Date, description	VG	VF	Unc
9	10 GULDEN	1967; 1972. Green. View of Aruba at ctr.			
		a. 28.8.1967.	7.00	10.00	30.00
		b. 1.6.1972.	6.50	6.50	25.00
10	25 GULDEN	1967; 1972. Black-gray. View of Bonaire at ctr.			
		a. 28.8.1967.	14.00	27.50	75.00
		b. 1.6.1972.	13.00	20.00	50.00
11	50 GULDEN	1967; 1972. Brown. Beach (St. Maarten) at ctr.			
		a. 28.8.1967.	28.00	65.00	150.00
		b. 1.6.1972.	26.00	45.00	95.00

12	100 GULDEN	1967; 1972. Violet. Boats and fishermen on the beach (St. Eustatius) at ctr.			
		a. 28.8.1967.	75.00	100.00	250.00
		b. 1.6.1972.	70.00	85.00	150.00
13	250 GULDEN	28.8.1967. Olive. Mountains (Saba) at ctr.	175.00	200.00	425.00

1979–80 ISSUE

#13A–13E like #8–13. Printer: JEZ.

| 13A | 5 GULDEN | 23.12.1980; 1.6.1984. Blue. Like #8. | FV | 4.00 | 20.00 |

13B	10 GULDEN	14.7.1979; 1.6.1984. Green and blue-green. Like #9.	FV	8.00	22.50
13C	25 GULDEN	14.7.1979. Blue and blue-green. Like #10.	FV	20.00	40.00
13D	50 GULDEN	23.12.1980. Red. Like #11.	FV	40.00	100.00
13E	100 GULDEN	14.7.1979. Red-brown and violet. Like #12.	FV	75.00	120.00

MUNTBILJETTEN – Currency Notes

1955; 1964 ISSUE

Cat. #	Denomination	Date, description	VG	VF	Unc
14	2 1/2 GULDEN	1955; 1964. Blue. Ship in dock at ctr. Arms at ctr. on back. Printer: ABNC.			
		a. 1955.	4.00	17.50	65.00
		b. 1964.	4.00	20.00	80.00

1970 ISSUE

#15–16 arms at r. on back. Printer: JEZ.

			VG	VF	Unc
15	1 GULDEN	8.9.1970. Red and orange. Aerial view of harbor at l. ctr.	FV	1.00	2.00

			VG	VF	Unc
16	2 1/2 GULDEN	8.9.1970. Blue. Jetliner.	FV	2.00	5.00

Bank van de Nederlandse Antillen

1986 ISSUE

#17–22 back and wmk: Shield-like bank logo. Sign. and sign. title varieties. Printer: JEZ.

			VG	VF	Unc
17	5 GULDEN	1986; 1990; 1994. Dk. blue and m/c. Tropical bird at ctr.			
		a. 31.3.1986.	FV	FV	8.00
		b. 1.1.1990.	FV	FV	7.00
		c. 1.5.1994.	FV	FV	6.50

Cat. #	Denomination	Date, description	VG	VF	Unc
18	10 GULDEN	1986; 1990; 1994. Dk. green and m/c. Colibri (hummingbird) at ctr.			
		a. 31.3.1986.	FV	FV	15.00
		b. 1.1.1990.	FV	FV	13.50
		c. 1.5.1994.	FV	FV	12.00

			VG	VF	Unc
19	25 GULDEN	1986; 1990; 1994. Red and m/c. Flamingo at ctr.			
		a. 31.3.1986.	FV	FV	35.00
		b. 1.1.1990.	FV	FV	32.50
		c. 1.5.1994.	FV	FV	26.50

			VG	VF	Unc
20	50 GULDEN	1986; 1990; 1994. Brown-orange and m/c. Rufous (collard sparrow) at ctr.			
		a. 31.3.1986.	FV	FV	67.50
		b. 1.1.1990.	FV	FV	62.50
		c. 1.5.1994.	FV	FV	52.50

Cat. #	Denomination	Date, description	VG	VF	Unc
21	100 GULDEN	1986; 1990; 1994. Brown and m/c. Banan-aquit at ctr.			
		a. 31.3.1986.	FV	FV	100.00
		b. 1.1.1990.	FV	FV	90.00
		c. 1.5.1994.	FV	FV	85.00

Cat. #	Denomination	Date, description	VG	VF	Unc
22	250 GULDEN	1986; 1990. Purple, red-violet and m/c. Caribbean mockingbird at ctr.			
		a. 31.3.1986.	FV	FV	240.00
		b. 1.1.1990.	FV	FV	210.00

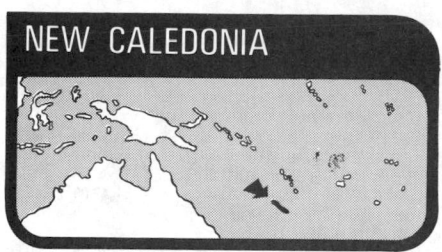

NEW CALEDONIA

The French Overseas Territory of New Caledonia, a group of about 25 islands in the South Pacific, is situated about 750 miles (1,207 km.) east of Australia. The territory, which includes the dependencies of Ile des Pins, Loyalty Islands, Ile Huon, Isles Belep, Isles Chesterfield, and Ile Walpole, has a total land area of 6,530 sq. mi. (19,058 sq. km.) and a population of 152,000. Capital: Noumea. The islands are rich in minerals; New Caledonia has the world's largest known deposit of nickel. Nickel, nickel castings, coffee and copra are exported.

British navigator Capt. James Cook discovered New Caledonia in 1774. The French took possession in 1853, and established a penal colony on the island in 1854. The European population of the colony remained disproportionately convict until 1894. New Caledonia became an overseas territory within the French Community in 1946, and in 1958 and 1972 chose to remain affiliated with France.

RULERS

French

MONETARY SYSTEM

1 Franc = 100 Centimes

Banque de l'Indochine, Nouméa

Sign. varieties.

Cat. #	Denomination	Date, description	VG	VF	Unc
26	20 FRANCS	ND. (1951–63). M/c. Youth at l., flute player at r. Fruit bowl at l., woman at r. ctr. on back.			
		a. Sign. titles: *LE PRESIDENT* and *LE DIRECTEUR GAL.* (1951).	3.00	8.00	30.00
		b. Sign. titles: *LE PRESIDENT* and *LE VICE-PRESIDENT DIRECTEUR GENERAL.* (1954; 1958).	1.50	4.50	20.00
		c. Sign. titles: *LE PRESIDENT* and *LE DIRECTEUR GENERAL.* (1963).	1.25	4.00	19.50

Cat. #	Denomination	Date, description	VG	VF	Unc
27	100 FRANCS	ND (1937–67). M/c. Woman w/wreath and sm. figure of Athena at ctr. Statue of Angkor at ctr. on back. Imprint: Seb. Laurent and Rita. 205 x 120mm.			
		a. Sign. titles: *UN ADMINISTRATEUR* and *LE DIRECTEUR GENERAL.* (1937).	5.00	15.00	65.00

Cat. #	Denomination	Date, description	VG	VF	Unc
		b. Sign. titles: *LE PRESIDENT* Borduge and *LE DIRECTEUR GENERAL* Baudouin (1937).	4.00	12.00	60.00
		c. Sign. titles: *LE PRESIDENT* and *L'ADMINISTRATEUR DIRECTEUR GENERAL* (1953).	4.00	12.00	50.00
		d. Sign. titles: *LE PRESIDENT* and *LE VICE-PRESIDENT DIRECTEUR-GENERAL* (1957).	4.00	12.00	45.00
		e. Sign. titles: *LE PRESIDENT* de Flers and *LE DIRECTEUR GENERAL* Robert (1963).	3.00	10.00	40.00

Institut d'Emission d'Outre-Mer, Nouméa.

43	100 FRANCS	ND (1969). Brown and m/c. Girl wearing wreath and playing guitar at r. W/o *REPUBLIQUE FRANÇAISE*, Intaglio printing.	3.00	12.50	45.00

44	100 FRANCS	ND (1969). Like #43 but w/ovpt: *REPUBLIQUE FRANÇAISE* at bottom ctr.			
		a. Intaglio.	1.50	3.50	22.50
		b. Lithographed. Series # beginning H2, from #51,000.	1.50	3.00	18.50

45	500 FRANCS	ND (1969–92). M/c. Fisherman at r. Man at l. on back. Sign. varieties.	6.00	8.50	13.50
46	1000 FRANCS	ND (1969). M/c. Hut under palm tree at l.; girl at r. W/o ovpt: *REPUBLIQUE FRANÇAISE*.	10.00	20.00	75.00
47	1000 FRANCS	ND (1978). M/c. Like #46 but w/ovpt: *REPUBLIQUE FRANÇAISE* ovpt. at lower l. Sign. varieties.	FV	FV	22.50

48	5000 FRANCS	ND (1969). M/c. Bougainville at l.; sailing ships at ctr. ovpt: *REPUBLIQUE FRANÇAISE*.	FV	FV	125.00

NOTE: For current 500 and 10,000 Francs see French Pacific Territories.

New Hebrides Condominium, a group of islands located in the South Pacific 500 miles (800 km.) west of Fiji, were under the joint sovereignty of Great Britain and France. The islands had an area of 5,700 sq. mi. (14,763 sq. km.) and a population of mainly Melanesians of mixed blood. Capital: Port-Vila. The volcanic and coral islands, while malarial and subject to frequent earthquakes, were extremely fertile, and produce copra, coffee, tropical fruits and timber for export.

The New Hebrides were discovered by Portuguese navigator Pedro de Quiros in 1606, visited by French explorer Bougainville in 1768, and named by British navigator Capt. James Cook in 1774. Ships of all nations converged on the islands to trade for sandalwood, prompting France and Britain to relinquish their individual claims and declare the islands a neutral zone in 1878. The New Hebrides were placed under the control of a mixed Anglo-French commission of naval officers during the native uprisings of 1887, and established as a condominium under the joint sovereignty of France and Great Britain in 1906.

RULERS

British and French to 1980

MONETARY SYSTEM

1 Franc = 100 Centimes

Institut d'Emission d'Outre-Mer, Nouvelles Hébrides

1965; 1967 (ND) ISSUE

Cat. #	Denomination	Date, description	VG	VF	Unc
16	100 FRANCS	ND (1965–71). M/c. Black on yellow and green unpt. Girl w/guitar at r. *NOUVELLE-HEBRIDES* in capital letters on back. Sign. varieties.	5.00	25.00	75.00

17 (19)	1000 FRANCS	ND (1967–71). Red. Hut w/palms at l., girl at r. *NOUVELLES HEBRIDES* in capital letters on back.	15.00	50.00	175.00

1972 (ND) ISSUE

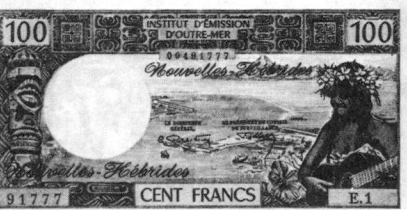

18 (17)	100 FRANCS	ND (1972). M/c. Like #16, but red and blue unpt. *Nouvelles Hebrides* in script on face and back.			
		a. Intaglio plates.	1.50	5.50	22.50
		b. Lithographed Series beginning E1, from no. 51,000.	1.35	5.00	20.00

Cat. #	Denomination	Date, description	VG	VF	Unc
19 (18)	500 FRANCS	ND (1972). Blue, green and m/c. Fisherman at r.	6.50	10.00	25.00

Cat. #	Denomination	Date, description	VG	VF	Unc
20	1000 FRANCS	ND (1972). Orange and brown. Like #17. *Nouvelles Hebrides* in script on face and back.	12.50	18.50	48.50

NOTE: For later issues see Vanuatu.

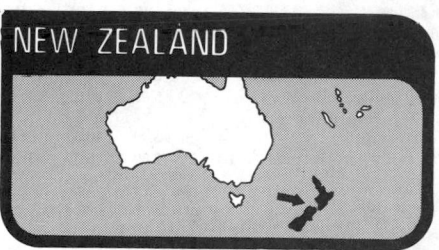

NEW ZEALAND

New Zealand, a parliamentary state located in the southwestern Pacific 1,250 miles (2,011 km.) east of Australia, has an area of 103,736 sq. mi. (269,056 sq. km.) and a population of 3.46 million. Capital: Wellington. Wool, meat, dairy products and some manufactured items are exported.

New Zealand was discovered and named by Dutch navigator Abel Tasman in 1642, and explored by British navigator Capt. James Cook who surveyed it in 1769 and annexed the land to Great Britain. The British government disavowed the annexation and for the next 70 years the only white settlers to arrive were adventurers attracted to the prospects of lumbering, sealing and whaling. Great Britain annexed the land in 1840 by treaty with the native chiefs and made it a dependency of New South Wales. The colony was granted self-government in 1852, a ministerial form of government in 1856, and full dominion status on Sept. 26, 1907. Full internal and external autonomy, which New Zealand had in effect possessed for many years, was formally extended in 1947. New Zealand is a member of the Commonwealth of Nations. The Queen of England is Chief of State.

A decimal standard currency was adopted in 1967.

RULERS
British

MONETARY SYSTEM
1 Shilling = 12 Pence
1 Pound = 20 Shillings (also 2 Dollars) to 1967
1 Dollar = 100 Cents, 1967–

REPLACEMENT NOTES
#163–167 (starting w/Wilks sign.), #169–173 Hardie sign., also #171 and 172 through Russell sign., special prefixes and asterisk at end of serial number. #177-181, ZZ prefix.

Reserve Bank of New Zealand

Pound System

1940 (ND) ISSUE

#158–162 have m/c guilloche w/arms above at ctr., portr. Capt. J . Cook at lower r. Sign. title: *CHIEF CASHIER.* Wmk: Maori chief. Printer: TDLR.

Cat. #	Denomination	Date, description	VG	VF	Unc
158	10 SHILLINGS	ND (1940–67). Brown. Kiwi at l., treaty signing at ctr. on back.			
		a. Sign. T. P. Hanna. (1940–55).	3.00	9.50	100.00
		b. Sign. G. Wilson. (1955–56).	7.50	30.00	195.00
		c. Sign. R. N. Fleming. W/o security thread. (1956–67).	1.00	5.00	37.50
		d. Sign. as c. W/security thread. (1967).	1.00	4.00	27.50

Cat. #	Denomination	Date, description	VG	VF	Unc
159	1 POUND	ND (1940–67). Purple. Sailing ship on sea at l. on back.			
		a. Sign. T. P. Hanna. (1940–55).	3.00	9.00	110.00
		b. Sign. G. Wilson. (1955–56).	5.00	20.00	185.00
		c. Sign. R. N. Fleming. W/o security thread. (1956–67).	3.00	10.00	65.00
		d. Sign. as c. W/security thread. (1967).	2.00	5.00	35.00

160	5 POUNDS	ND (1940–67). Blue. Island, water and mountains on back.			
		a. Sign. T. P. Hanna. (1940–55).	8.50	20.00	100.00
		b. Sign. G. Wilson. (1955–56).	12.50	25.00	200.00
		c. Sign. R. N. Fleming. W/o security thread. (1956–67).	8.00	17.50	90.00
		d. Sign. as c. W/security thread. (1967).	6.50	10.00	65.00

161	10 POUNDS	ND (1940–67). Green. Herd of animals on back.			
		a. Sign. T. P. Hanna. (1940–55).	30.00	55.00	275.00
		b. Sign. G. Wilson. (1955–56).	35.00	90.00	425.00
		c. Sign. R. N. Fleming. (1956–67).	12.50	30.00	100.00
		d. Sign. as c. W/security thread. (1967).	10.00	18.50	70.00

162	50 POUNDS	ND (1940–67). Red. Sailing ship at l. Dairy farm and mountain on back.			
		a. Sign. T. P. Hanna. (1940–55).	300.00	650.00	1750.
		b. Sign. G. Wilson. (1955–56).	400.00	750.00	2250.
		c. Sign. R. N. Fleming. (1956–67).	100.00	200.00	575.00

Dollar System
1967 ISSUE

#163–168 Qn. Elizabeth II on face. Birds and plants on back. Wmk: Capt. J. Cook. Printer: TDLR.

Cat. #	Denomination	Date, description	VG	VF	Unc
163	1 DOLLAR	ND (1967–81). Brown.			
		a. Sign. R. N. Fleming. (1967–68).	1.50	5.00	40.00
		b. Sign. D. L. Wilks. (1968–75).	1.50	3.00	15.00
		c. Sign. R. L. Knight. (1975–77).	1.00	1.50	6.00
		d. Sign. H. R. Hardie. (1977–81).	1.00	1.50	5.50

164	2 DOLLARS	ND (1967–81). Purple.			
		a. Sign. R. N. Fleming. (1967–68).	2.00	5.00	30.00
		b. Sign. D. L. Wilks. (1968–75).	2.00	4.00	22.50
		c. Sign. R. L. Knight. (1975–77).	1.50	2.50	11.50
		d. Sign. H. R. Hardie. (1977–81).	1.50	2.50	10.00

165	5 DOLLARS	ND (1967–81). Orange.			
		a. Sign. R. N. Fleming. (1967–68).	4.00	8.00	55.00
		b. Sign. D. L. Wilks. (1968–75).	10.00	20.00	90.00
		c. Sign. R. L. Knight. (1975–77).	3.00	5.00	25.00
		d. Sign. H. R. Hardie. (1977–81).	3.00	5.00	25.00

Cat. #	Denomination	Date, description	VG	VF	Unc
166	10 DOLLARS	ND (1967–81).Blue.			
		a. Sign. R. N. Fleming. (1967–68).	7.00	12.50	80.00
		b. Sign. D. L. Wilks. (1968–75).	8.00	15.00	135.00
		c. Sign. R. L. Knight. (1975–77).	7.00	10.00	75.00
		d. Sign. H. R. Hardie. (1977–81).	6.00	9.00	55.00

Cat. #	Denomination	Date, description	VG	VF	Unc
167	20 DOLLARS	ND (1967–81). Green.			
		a. Sign. R. N. Fleming. (1967–68).	15.00	22.50	100.00
		b. Sign. D. L. Wilks. (1968–75)	15.00	25.00	225.00
		c. Sign. R. L. Knight. (1975–77).	12.00	17.50	100.00
		d. Sign. H. R. Hardie. (1977–81).	12.00	15.00	75.00
168	100 DOLLARS	ND (1967–77). Red.			
		a. Sign. R. N. Fleming. (1967–68).	85.00	150.00	650.00
		b. Sign. R. L. Knight. (1975–77).	65.00	100.00	425.00

1981–83 ISSUE

#169–175 new portr. of Qn. Elizabeth II on face. Birds and plants on back. Wmk: Capt. J. Cook. Printer: BWC.

Cat. #	Denomination	Date, description	VG	VF	Unc
169	1 DOLLAR	ND (1981–). Dk. brown and m/c.			
		a. Sign. H. R. Hardie w/title: CHIEF CASHIER. (1981-85).	FV	1.00	3.50
		b. Sign. S. T. Russell w/title: GOVERNOR. (1985–89).	FV	1.00	3.00
		c. Sign. D. T. Brash. (1989–92).	FV	1.00	2.00

Cat. #	Denomination	Date, description	VG	VF	Unc
170	2 DOLLARS	ND (1981–). Purple and m/c.			
		a. Sign. H. R. Hardie w/title: CHIEF CASHIER. (1981–85).	FV	1.75	5.00
		b. Sign. S.T. Russell w/title: GOVERNOR. (1985–89).	FV	1.50	4.50
		c. Sign. D. T. Brash. (1989–92).	FV	1.50	4.00

Cat. #	Denomination	Date, description	VG	VF	Unc
171	5 DOLLARS	ND (1981–92). Orange and m/c.			
		a. Sign. H. R. Hardie w/title: CHIEF CASHIER. (1981–85).	FV	4.50	10.00
		b. Sign. S.T. Russell w/title: GOVERNOR. (1985–89).	FV	3.75	7.50
		c. Sign. D. T. Brash. (1989–92).	FV	3.75	7.50

Cat. #	Denomination	Date, description	VG	VF	Unc
172	10 DOLLARS	ND (1981–92). Blue and m/c.			
		a. Sign. H. R. Hardie w/title: CHIEF CASHIER. (1981–85).	FV	8.50	18.50
		b. Sign. S.T. Russell w/title: GOVERNOR. (1985–89).	FV	7.50	15.00
		c. Sign. D. T. Brash. (1989–92).	FV	7.50	13.50

Cat. #	Denomination	Date, description	VG	VF	Unc
173	20 DOLLARS	ND (1981–92). Green on m/c unpt.			
		a. Sign. H. R. Hardie w/title: CHIEF CASHIER. (1981-85).	FV	16.50	28.50
		b. Sign. S.T. Russell w/title: GOVERNOR. (1985–89).	FV	15.00	28.50
		c. Sign. D. T. Brash. (1989–92).	FV	15.00	25.00

Cat. #	Denomination	Date, description	VG	VF	Unc
174	50 DOLLARS	ND (1983–92). Yellow-orange on m/c unpt.			
		a. Sign. H. R. Hardie. (1981–85).	FV	35.00	70.00
		b. Sign. D. T. Brash. (1989–92).	FV	35.00	65.00

175	100 DOLLARS	ND (1981–). Red on m/c unpt.			
		a. Sign. H. R. Hardie w/title: CHIEF CASHIER. (1981-85).	FV	70.00	140.00
		b. Sign. S.T. Russell w/title: GOVERNOR. (1985-89).	FV	70.00	135.00

COMMEMORATIVE ISSUE

#176, 150th Anniversary of Treaty of Waitangi, 1840–1990

Cat. #	Denomination	Date, description	VG	VF	Unc
176	10 DOLLARS	1990. Blue on m/c unpt. Face design like #172, w/addition of 1990 Commission logo, the White Heron (in red and white w/date 1990) at r. of Qn. Special inscription and scene of treaty signing on back. Wmk: Capt. J. Cook. Printer: BWC.			
		a. Regular issue. Prefix letters CCC; DDD.	FV	FV	10.00
		b. Prefix letters CWB for County Wide Bank.	—	—	10.00
		c. Prefix letter FTC for Farmers Trading Co.	—	—	10.00
		d. Prefix letters MBL for Mobil Oil Co.	—	—	10.00
		e. Prefix letters RNZ for Radio New Zealand.	—	—	10.00
		f. Prefix letters RXX for Rank Xerox Co.	—	—	10.00
		g. Prefix letters TNZ for Toyota New Zealand.	—	—	10.00
		h. Special folder w/explanatory text and enclosing a single note. Prefix letters BBB.	—	—	10.00

NOTE: #176 w/prefix letters AAA was issued in 2, 4, 8, 16 and 32 subject panes. Market value is 10% over face value.

1992-93 ISSUE

#177–181 wmk: Qn. Elizabeth II. Sign. D.T. Brash. Printer: TDLR.

177	5 DOLLARS	ND (1992–). Red-brown, brown and brown-orange on m/c unpt. Mt. Everest at l., Sir Ed. Hillary at ctr. Flora w/penguin at ctr. r. on back.			
		a. Issued note.	FV	FV	5.50
		b. Uncut pair in special folder.	FV	FV	8.00
		c. Uncut block of 4 in special folder.	FV	FV	16.00

178	10 DOLLARS	ND (1993–94). Blue and purple on m/c unpt. Flowers at l., K. Sheppard at ctr. r. Pair of Whio ducks at ctr. r. on back.			
		a. Issued note.	FV	FV	11.00
		b. Uncut block of 4 in special holder.	FV	FV	30.00

Cat. #	Denomination	Date, description	VG	VF	Unc
179	20 DOLLARS	ND (1993–94). Green and m/c. Qn. Elizabeth II at r., bldg. at l. in unpt. Back pale green and blue; Karearea falcons at ctr.			
		a. Issued note.	FV	FV	20.00
		b. Uncut block of 4 in special folder.	FV	FV	60.00

180	50 DOLLARS	ND (1993–). Purple, violet and deep blue on m/c unpt. Sir A. Ngata at r., early school house at l., in unpt. Kokako crow at r. on back.			
		a. Issued note.	FV	FV	42.50
		b. Red serial #. (3000 were issued w/$50 phone card).	FV	FV	65.00
		c. Uncut block of 4 in special folder.	FV	FV	150.00

181	100 DOLLARS	ND (1993–). Violet-brown and red on m/c unpt. Lord Rutherford of Nelson at ctr., gold medallion in unpt. at l. Mohua yellowhead bird on tree trunk at ctr. r., moth at lower l. on back.			
		a. Issued note.	FV	FV	80.00
		b. Uncut block of 4 in special folder.	FV	FV	300.00

1994 ISSUE

182	10 DOLLARS	ND (1994). Like #178 but bright blue at ctr. behind Whio ducks on back.	FV	FV	10.00
183	20 DOLLARS	ND (1994). Like #179 but bright green at ctr. behind Karearea falcon on back.	FV	FV	18.00

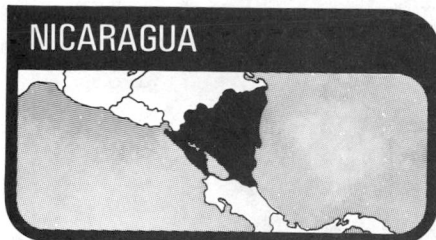

NICARAGUA

The Republic of Nicaragua, situated in Central America between Honduras and Costa Rica, has as area of 50,193 sq. mi (130,000 sq. km.) and a population of 3.87 million. Capital: Managua. Agriculture, mining (gold and silver) and hardwood logging are the principal industries. Cotton, meat, coffee and sugar and exported.

Columbus sighted the coast of Nicaragua in 1502 during the course of his last voyage of discovery. It was first visited in 1522 by conquistadors from Panama, under command of Gonzalez Davola. After the first settlements were established in 1524 at Granada and Leon, Nicaragua was incorporated, for administrative purpose, in the Captaincy General of Guatemala, which included every Central American state but Panama. The Captaincy General declared its independence from Spain on Sept. 15, 1821. The next year Nicaragua united with the Mexican Empire of Agustin de Iturbide, then in 1823 with the Central American Republic. When the federation was dissolved, Nicaragua declared itself an independent republic in 1838.

MONETARY SYSTEM
1 Cordoba = 100 Centavos, 1912–87
1 new Cordoba = 1000 old Cordobas, 1988-90
1 Cordoba Oro = 100 Centavos = 1 U.S.A. Dollar, 1991-

REPLACEMENT NOTES
1985–dated issues printed by TDLR, ZA; ZB prefix.

Banco Central de Nicaragua

SERIES A

Decreto 26.4.1962

#107–114 portr. F. Hernandez Córdoba at ctr. on back. Printer: ABNC.

Cat. #	Denomination	Date, description	VG	VF	Unc
107	1 CORDOBA	D.1962. Blue on m/c unpt. Banco Central at upper ctr.	.15	.75	4.00

| 108 | 5 CORDOBAS | D.1962. Green on m/c unpt. Portr. C. Nicarao at upper ctr. Similar to #100. | .75 | 2.50 | 10.00 |

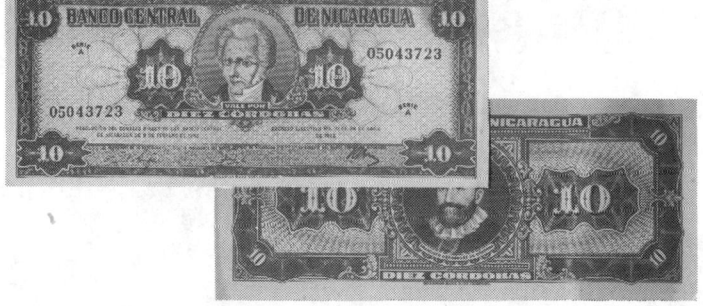

Cat. #	Denomination	Date, description	VG	VF	Unc
109	10 CORDOBAS	D.1962. Red on m/c unpt. Portr. M. de Larreynaga at upper ctr.	1.50	4.50	20.00

110	20 CORDOBAS	D.1962. Orange-brown on m/c unpt. Portr. T. Martinez at upper ctr.	3.00	10.00	40.00

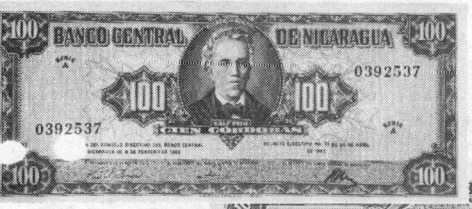

111	50 CORDOBAS	D.1962. Purple and m/c. Portr. M. Jerez at upper ctr.	6.00	25.00	75.00

112	100 CORDOBAS	D.1962. Red-brown and m/c. Portr. J. Dolores Estrada at upper ctr.	4.00	20.00	40.00
113	500 CORDOBAS	D.1962. Black and m/c. Portr. R. Dario at upper ctr.	50.00	175.00	400.00
114	1000 CORDOBAS	D.1962. Brown and m/c. Portr. A. Somoza at upper ctr.	60.00	200.00	450.00

SERIES B

Decreto 25.5.1968

#115–120 F. Hernandez Córdoba on back. Printer: TDLR.

115	1 CORDOBA	ND. Blue on m/c unpt. Like #107.			
		a. W/3 sign.	.10	.35	1.00
		b. Pres. A. Somoza hand sign. at l.	—	—	—

Cat. #	Denomination	Date, description	VG	VF	Unc
116	5 CORDOBAS	D.1968. Green on m/c unpt. Like #108.	.50	1.50	4.00
117	10 CORDOBAS	D.1968. Red on m/c unpt. Like #109.	.75	2.00	6.00
118	20 CORDOBAS	D.1968. Orange-brown on m/c unpt. Like #110.			
		a. W/3 sign.	1.00	3.00	10.00
		b. W/o r.h. sign.	—	—	—
119	50 CORDOBAS	D.1968. Purple on m/c unpt. Like #111.			
		a. W/3 sign.	4.00	7.50	27.50
		b. W/o r.h. sign.	—	—	—
120	100 CORDOBAS	D.1968. Red-brown on m/c unpt. Like #112.			
		a. W/3 sign.	3.00	6.00	17.50
		b. W/o r.h. sign.	—	—	—

NOTE: Some of #118–120 were apparently released w/o r.h. sign. after the Managua earthquake of 1972 damaged the Central Bank building.

SERIES C

Decreto 27.4.1972

#121–128 printer: TDLR.

121	2 CORDOBAS	D.1972. Olive-green on m/c unpt. Banco Central at r. Furrows at l. on back.			
		a. W/3 sign.	.10	.25	2.00
		b. W/o l.h. sign.	—	—	200.00

122	5 CORDOBAS	D.1972. Dk. green on m/c unpt. C. Nicarao standing at r. w/bow. Fruitseller at l. on back.	.25	.75	2.50

Cat. #	Denomination	Date, description	VG	VF	Unc
123	10 CORDOBAS	*D.1972.* Red on m/c unpt. A. Castro standing at r. atop rocks. Hacienda at l. on back.	.30	.85	2.50

| 124 | 20 CORDOBAS | *D.1972.* Orange-brown on m/c unpt. R. Herrera igniting cannon at r. Signing ceremony of abrogation of Chamorro–Bryan Treaty of 1912, Somoza at ctr. | .50 | 1.25 | 3.50 |

| 125 | 50 CORDOBAS | *D.1972.* Purple on m/c unpt. M. Jerez at r. Cows at l. on back. | 2.00 | 5.00 | 25.00 |

| 126 | 100 CORDOBAS | *D.1972.* Violet on m/c unpt. J. Dolores Estrada at r. Flower at l. on back. | .50 | 1.50 | 4.00 |

Cat. #	Denomination	Date, description	VG	VF	Unc
127	500 CORDOBAS	*D.1972.* Black on m/c unpt. R. Dario at r. National Theater at l. on back.	10.00	25.00	100.00

| 128 | 1000 CORDOBAS | *D.1972.* Brown on m/c unpt. A. Somoza G. at r. View of Managua at l. on back. | 12.00 | 30.00 | 120.00 |

SERIES D

Decreto of 20.2.1978

#129–130 printer: TDLR.

| 129 | 20 CORDOBAS | *D.1978.* Like #124. | .30 | 1.00 | 8.00 |

| 130 | 50 CORDOBAS | *D.1978.* Like #125. | .30 | 1.00 | 10.00 |

SERIES E
Decreto 16.8.1979
FIRST ISSUE

#131–133 w/frame. Printer: TDLR.

Cat. #	Denomination	Date, description	VG	VF	Unc
131	50 CORDOBAS	D.1979. Purple on m/c unpt. Comdt. C. Fonseca Amador at r. Liberation of 19.7.1979 on back.	.50	1.50	4.00

| 132 | 100 CORDOBAS | D.1979. Dk. brown on m/c unpt. Like #126. | .50 | 1.50 | 4.00 |

| 133 | 500 CORDOBAS | D.1979. Deep blue on m/c unpt. Like #127. | .50 | 1.25 | 5.00 |

SECOND ISSUE

#134–139 w/o frame. Wmk: Sandino. Printer: TDLR.

| 134 | 10 CORDOBAS | D.1979. Red on m/c unpt. A. Castro standing atop rocks at r. Miners on back. | .25 | .60 | 2.50 |

Cat. #	Denomination	Date, description	VG	VF	Unc
135	20 CORDOBAS	D.1979. Orange-brown on m/c unpt. Comandante G. P. Ordonez at r. Marching troops on back.	.30	.75	3.00

| 136 | 50 CORDOBAS | D.1979. Purple on m/c unpt. Comdt. C. F. Amador at r. Liberation of 19.7.1979 on back. | .35 | .85 | 3.50 |

| 137 | 100 CORDOBAS | D.1979. Brown on m/c unpt. J. D. Estrada at r. Flower on back. Sign. varieties. | .50 | 1.25 | 5.00 |

| 138 | 500 CORDOBAS | D.1979. Dk. olive-green on m/c unpt. R. Dario at r. Teatro Popular at l. on back. Sign. varieties. 3 sign. varieties. | .65 | 1.65 | 6.50 |

Cat. #	Denomination	Date, description	VG	VF	Unc
139	1000 CORDOBAS	D.1979. Blue-gray on m/c unpt. Gen. A.C. Sandino at r. Hut (Sandino's birthplace) on back. Sign. varieties.	1.50	6.00	25.00

SERIES F
Resolution of 6.8.1984

#140–143 wmk: Sandino. Printer: TDLR.

Cat. #	Denom.	Date, description	VG	VF	Unc
140	50 CORDOBAS	L.1904 (1985). Like #136.	.20	.50	2.00
141	100 CORDOBAS	L.1984 (1985). Like #137.	.20	.50	2.00
142	500 CORDOBAS	L.1984 (1985). Like #138.	.20	.50	5.00
143	1000 CORDOBAS	L.1984 (1985). Like #139.	.50	2.00	12.50

SERIES G
Resolution of 11.6.1985

#144–146 wmk: Sandino. Printer: TDLR.

144	500 CORDOBAS	L.1985 (1987). Like #142. Lithographed.	.20	.50	3.00

Cat. #	Denomination	Date, description	VG	VF	Unc
145	1000 CORDOBAS	L.1985 (1987). Like #143 but dk. gray on m/c unpt.			
		a. Engraved.	.35	1.00	4.00
		b. Lithographed.	.15	.50	2.75

146	5000 CORDOBAS	L.1985 (1987). Brown, black and m/c. Map at upper ctr., Gen. B. Zeledon at r. National Assembly bldg. on back.	.15	.50	2.50

1987 PROVISIONAL ISSUE

#147–149 black ovpt. new denomination on face and back of old Series F and G notes printed by TDLR.

147	20,000 CORDOBAS	ND (1987). Ovpt. on unissued 20 Cordobas Series F. Colors and design like #135.	.20	.50	2.25

148	50,000 CORDOBAS	ND (1987). Ovpt. on #140.	.25	.60	2.50

Cat. #	Denomination	Date, description	VG	VF	Unc
152	20 CORDOBAS	1985 (1988). Blue-black and blue on m/c unpt. Comdt. G. P. Ordonez at r. Demonstration for agrarian reform at l. on back.	.10	.35	1.25

Cat. #	Denomination	Date, description	VG	VF	Unc
149	100,000 CORDOBAS	ND (1987). Ovpt. on #144b.	.30	.75	3.00

153	50 CORDOBAS	1985 (1988). Brown and dk. red on m/c unpt. Gen. J.D. Estrada at r. Medical clinic scene at l. on back.	.10	.35	1.00

150	500,000 CORDOBAS	ND (1987). Ovpt. on #145b.	.50	1.25	5.00

Currency Reform

1 New Córdoba = 1000 Old Córdobas, 1988

1988 ISSUE (Dated 1985)

#151–156 wmk: Sandino. (W/o imprint.)

154	100 CORDOBAS	1985 (1988). Deep blue, blue and gray on m/c unpt. R. Lopez Perez at r. State council bldg. at l. on back.	.20	.50	2.00

151	10 CORDOBAS	1985 (1988). Green and olive on m/c unpt. Comdt. C. Fonseca Amador at r. Troop formation marching at l. on back.	.10	.35	1.25

155	500 CORDOBAS	1985 (1988). Purple, blue and brown on m/c unpt. R. Dario at r. Classroom w/students at l. on back.	.25	.60	2.50

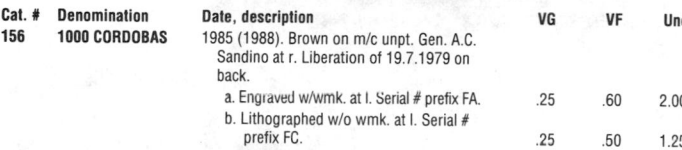

Cat. #	Denomination	Date, description	VG	VF	Unc
156	1000 CORDOBAS	1985 (1988). Brown on m/c unpt. Gen. A.C. Sandino at r. Liberation of 19.7.1979 on back.			
		a. Engraved w/wmk. at l. Serial # prefix FA.	.25	.60	2.00
		b. Lithographed w/o wmk. at l. Serial # prefix FC.	.25	.50	1.25

1988–89 PROVISIONAL ISSUE

157	5000 CORDOBAS	ND (1988). Ovpt. elements in black on face and back of #146. Face ovpt.: sign. and title: *PRIMER VICE PRESIDENTE BANCO CENTRAL DE NICARAGUA* at l., 2 lines of text at lower ctr. blocked out, guilloche added at r. Back ovpt., guilloche at l. and r., same sign. title as on face at r.	.25	.60	1.75

#158 and 159 black ovpt. of new denominations on face and back of earlier notes. ovpt. errors exist and are rather common.

158	10,000 CORDOBAS	ND (1989). Ovpt. on	.25	.75	2.25

Cat. #	Denomination	Date, description	VG	VF	Unc
159	100,000 CORDOBAS	ND (1989). Black ovpt. on face and back of #154.	.40	1.00	4.00

1989 ISSUE

#160–161 grid map of Nicaragua at ctr. on face and back. Wmk: Sandino.

160	20,000 CORDOBAS	ND (1989). Black on blue, yellow and m/c unpt. Comdt. G.P. Ordonez at r. Church of San Francisco Granada at l. on back.	.35	.85	3.50

161	50,000 CORDOBAS	ND (1989). Brown on purple, orange and m/c unpt. Gen. J.D. Estrada at r. Hacienda San Jacinto on back.	.25	.60	2.50

1990 PROVISIONAL ISSUE

#162–164, black ovpt. of new denomination on face and back of earlier notes. Ovpt. errors exist and are rather common.

162	200,000 CORDOBAS	ND (1990). Ovpt on #156b.	.15	.40	1.75

Cat. #	Denomination	Date, description	VG	VF	Unc
163	500,000 CORDOBAS	ND (1990). Ovpt. on #152.	.40	1.00	3.50

Cat. #	Denomination	Date, description	VG	VF	Unc
164	1 MILLION COR-DOBAS	ND (1990). Ovpt. on #156b.	.40	1.00	3.50

#165–166 wmk: Sandino head, repeated.

Cat. #	Denomination	Date, description	VG	VF	Unc
165	5 MILLION COR-DOBAS	ND (1990). Purple and orange on red and m/c unpt. C. Ordonez at r. Church of San francisco Granada at l., map at ctr. on back.	.20	.50	2.00

Cat. #	Denomination	Date, description	VG	VF	Unc
166	10 MILLION COR-DOBAS	ND (1990). Purple and lilac on blue and m/c unpt. Gen. J. D. Estrada at r. Hacienda San Jacinto at l., map at ctr. on back.	.25	.60	2.50

Córdoba Oro System

1 Córdoba Oro = 1 U.S.A. Dollar

1990–91 ISSUE

NOTE: Although originally issued on par with the U.S.A. Dollar, the rate of exchange has fallen to 6 Córdoba (Oro) to 1 U.S.A. Dollar.

#167–170, F. H. Córdoba at r. Arms at l., flower at r. on back. Printer: Harrison.

Cat. #	Denomination	Date, description	VG	VF	Unc
167	1 CENTAVO	ND (1991). Purple on pale green and m/c unpt.	FV	.05	.15

Cat. #	Denomination	Date, description	VG	VF	Unc
168	5 CENTAVOS	ND (1991). Red-violet on pale green and m/c unpt. 2 sign. varieties.	FV	.05	.20

Cat. #	Denomination	Date, description	VG	VF	Unc
169	10 CENTAVOS	ND (1991). Olive-green on lt. green and m/c unpt. 2 sign. varieties.	FV	.10	.25

Cat. #	Denomination	Date, description	VG	VF	Unc
170	25 CENTAVOS	ND (1991). Blue-gray on pale green and m/c unpt. 2 sign. varieties.	FV	.15	.35

#171–172 printer: CBNC.

#171–172 printer: CBNC.

Cat. #	Denomination	Date, description	VG	VF	Unc
171	1/2 CORDOBA	ND (1991). Brown and green on m/c unpt. F. H. Córdoba at l., plant at r. Arms at ctr. on green back.	FV	FV	.50

Cat. #	Denomination	Date, description	VG	VF	Unc
175	10 CORDOBAS	1990. Green on blue and m/c unpt. Sunrise over rice field at l., M. de Larreynaga at r. Back dk. green and m/c; arms at ctr. Printer: TDLR.	FV	FV	4.00

#176–177 printer: CBNC.

172	1/2 CORDOBA	ND (1992). Face like #171. Arms at l., national flower at r. on green back.	FV	FV	.50

#173-177, 2 sign. varieties.

176	20 CORDOBAS	ND (1990). Pale red-orange and dk. brown on m/c unpt. Sandino at l., coffee plant at r. E. Mongalo at l., fire in the Mesón de Rivas (1854) at ctr. on green back. 2 sign. varieties.	FV	FV	7.00

173	1 CORDOBA	1990. Blue on purple and m/c unpt. Sunrise over field of maize at l., F. H. Córdoba at r. Back green and m/c; arms at ctr. Printer: TDLR. 2 sign. varieties.	FV	FV	.85

177	50 CORDOBAS	ND (1991). Purple and violet on m/c unpt. Dr. P. J. Chamorro at l., banana plants at r. Toppling of Somoza's statue and scene at polling place on green back. 2 sign. varieties.	FV	FV	15.00

174	5 CORDOBAS	ND (1991). Red-violet and dk. olive-green on m/c unpt. Indian Chief Diriangén at l., sorghum plants at r. R. Herrera firing cannon at British warship on green back. Printer: CBNC. 2 sign. varieties.	FV	FV	3.50

178	100 CORDOBAS	1990. Blue and red on m/c unpt. Sunrise over cotton field at l., R. Darío at r. Back green and m/c; arms at ctr. Printer: TDLR.	FV	FV	27.50

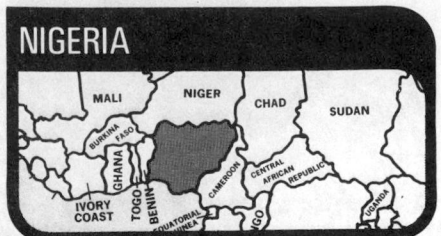

The Federal Republic of Nigeria, situated on the Atlantic coast of Africa between Benin and Cameroon, has an area of 356,667 sq. mi. (923,768 sq. km.) and a population of 88.5 million. Capital: Lagos. The economy is based on petroleum and agriculture. Crude oil, cocoa, tobacco and tin are exported.

Following the Napoleonic Wars, the British expanded their British claims to a sphere of influence in that area were recognized by the Berlin Conference of 1885, and in the following year the Royal Niger Company was chartered. Direct British control of the territory was initiated in 1900, and in 1914 the amalgamation of northern and southern Nigeria into the Colony and Protectorate of Nigeria was effected. In 1960, following a number of territorial and constitutional changes, Nigeria was granted independence within the British Commonwealth as a federation of the northern, western and eastern regions. Nigeria altered its political relationship with Great Britain on Oct. 1, 1963, by proclaiming itself a republic. It did, however, elect to remain a member of the Commonwealth of Nations. The Supreme Commander of Armed Forces is the Head of the Federal Military Government.

On May 30, 1967, the Eastern Region of the republic - an area occupied principally by the proud and resourceful Ibo tribe - seceded from Nigeria and proclaimed itself the independent Republic of Biafra. Civil war erupted and raged for 31 months. Casualties, including civilian, were about two million, the majority succumbing to malnutrition and disease. Biafra surrendered to the federal government on January 15, 1970.

After military coups in 1983 and 1985 the government was assumed by an Armed Forces Ruling Council. A transitional civilian council was formed in 1993.

RULERS
British to 1963

MONETARY SYSTEM
1 Shilling = 12 Pence
1 Pound = 20 Shillings to 1973
1 Naira (10 Shillings) = 100 Kobo, 1973–

REPLACEMENT NOTES
#14–26, DZ/# or DZ/## as the prefix.

SIGNATURE/TITLE VARIETIES

1	GOVERNOR / CHIEF OF BANKING OPERATIONS	6	
2		7	GOVERNOR / DIRECTOR OF CURRENCY OPERATIONS
3		8	
4	GOVERNOR / DIRECTOR OF DOMESTIC OPERATIONS	9	
5		10	

FEDERAL REPUBLIC OF NIGERIA

Central Bank of Nigeria

Pound System

1967 ISSUE

#6–13 bank bldg. at l. Wmk: Lion's head.

Cat#	Date, denomination	Description	VG	VF	Unc
6	5 SHILLINGS	ND (1967). Lilac and blue. Back lilac; log cutting.	3.00	15.00	85.00
7	10 SHILLINGS	ND (1967). Green and brown. Back green; stacking grain sacks.	6.50	32.50	200.00

Cat#	Date, denomination	Description	VG	VF	Unc
8	1 POUND	ND (1967). Red and dk. brown. Back red; beating plant.	.50	1.00	4.00
9	5 POUNDS	ND (1967). Blue-gray and blue-green. Back blue-gray; food preparation.	10.00	40.00	275.00

1968 ISSUE

#10–13 designs similar to previous issue. Wmk: Lion's head.

Cat#	Date, denomination	Description	VG	VF	Unc
10	5 SHILLINGS	ND (1968). Green and orange. Back green.			
		a. R. sign. title: *GENERAL MANAGER*.	4.00	20.00	125.00
		b. R. sign. title: *CHIEF OF BANKING OPERATIONS*.	5.00	25.00	150.00

Cat#	Date, denomination	Description	VG	VF	Unc
11	10 SHILLINGS	ND (1968). Blue.			
		a. R. sign. title: *GENERAL MANAGER*.	6.50	32.50	200.00
		b. R. sign. title: *CHIEF OF BANKING OPERATIONS*.	8.50	42.50	250.00
12	1 POUND	ND (1968). Olive-brown and violet. Back olive-brown.			
		a. R. sign. title: *GENERAL MANAGER*.	6.50	32.50	200.00
		b. R. sign. title: *CHIEF OF BANKING OPERATIONS*.	10.00	50.00	300.00
13	5 POUNDS	ND (1968). Red-brown and blue. Back red-brown.			
		a. R. sign. title: *GENERAL MANAGER*.	20.00	65.00	400.00
		b. R. sign. title: *CHIEF OF BANKING OPERATIONS*.	25.00	95.00	450.00

Naira System

1973; 1977 ISSUE

#14–17 bank bldg. at l. ctr. Wmk: Heraldic eagle.

Cat#	Date, denomination	Description	VG	VF	Unc
14	50 KOBO	ND (1973–78). Blue and violet on m/c unpt. Back brown; logging.			
		a. Sign. 1.	2.00	4.00	7.50
		b. Sign. 2.	1.50	5.00	30.00
		c. Sign. 3.	.50	2.00	12.50
		d. Sign. 4.	1.00	2.50	15.00
		e. Sign. 5.	.50	2.00	12.50
		f. Sign. 6.	.25	1.75	10.00
		g. Sign. 7; 8; 9.	FV	FV	.85

15	1 NAIRA	ND (1973–78). Red and brown on m/c unpt. Back red; stacking grain sacks.			
		a. Sign. 1.	2.50	5.00	10.00
		b. Sign. 2.	1.50	4.00	10.00
		c. Sign. 3.	1.50	4.00	10.00
		d. Sign. 4.	4.50	16.50	40.00

16	5 NAIRA	ND (1973–). Blue-gray and olive-green on m/c unpt. Back blue-gray; beating plant.			
		a. Sign. 1.	7.00	15.00	60.00
		b. Sign. 2.	4.00	10.00	40.00
		c. Sign. 3.	15.00	60.00	250.00
		d. Sign. 4.	20.00	75.00	300.00

17	10 NAIRA	ND (1973–78). Carmine and dk. blue on m/c unpt. Back carmine; dam at ctr.			
		a. Sign. 1.	15.00	35.00	100.00
		b. Sign. 2.	7.00	22.50	70.00
		c. Sign. 3.	35.00	125.00	375.00
		d. Sign. 4.	40.00	150.00	450.00
18	20 NAIRA	ND (1977–84). Yellow-green on m/c unpt. Gen M. Muhammed at l. Arms at ctr. r. on back.			
		a. Sign. 2.	30.00	100.00	300.00
		b. Sign. 3.	20.00	60.00	180.00
		c. Sign. 4.	8.00	20.00	60.00
		d. Sign. 5.	6.00	15.00	40.00
		e. Sign. 6.	4.00	10.00	30.00

1979 ISSUE

#19–22 sign. titles: *GOVERNOR* and *DIRECTOR OF DOMESTIC OPERATIONS*. Wmk: Heraldic eagle.

Cat#	Date, denomination	Description	VG	VF	Unc
19	1 NAIRA	ND (1979–84). Red on m/c unpt. H. Macauley at l. Mask at ctr. r. on back.			
		a. Sign. 4.	.50	1.50	4.00
		b. Sign. 5.	.30	1.00	3.00
		c. Sign. 6.	.25	.75	2.50

20	5 NAIRA	ND (1979–84). Green on m/c unpt. Alhaji Sir Abubaker Tafawa Balewa at l. Dancers at ctr. r. on back.			
		a. Sign. 4.	2.00	5.00	12.00
		b. Sign. 5.	1.50	4.00	9.00
		c. Sign. 6.	1.00	3.00	8.00

21	10 NAIRA	ND (1979–84). Brown, purple and violet on m/c unpt. A. Ikoku at l. 2 women w/bowls on heads at ctr. r. on back.			
		a. Sign. 4.	4.00	12.00	25.00
		b. Sign. 5.	3.00	8.00	20.00
		c. Sign. 6.	7.00	20.00	—
22		*Deleted*. See #18c.			

1984; 1991 ISSUE

#23–27 new colors and sign. Like #18–21 but smaller. Wmk: Heraldic eagle.

23	1 NAIRA	ND (1984–). Red, violet and green. Like #19. Back olive and lt. violet.			
		a. Sign. title at r.: *DIRECTOR OF DOMESTIC OPERATIONS*. Sign. 6.	FV	1.00	2.25
		b. Sign. title at r.: *DIRECTOR OF CURRENCY OPERATIONS*. Sign. 7.	FV	.50	1.75
		c. Titles as b. Sign. 8.	FV	FV	1.25
		d. Titles as b. Sign. 9.	FV	FV	1.25

Cat#	Date, denomination	Description	VG	VF	Unc
24	5 NAIRA	ND (1984–). Purple and brown-violet on m/c unpt. Like #20.			
		a. Sign. title at r.: *DIRECTOR OF DOMESTIC OPERATIONS*. Sign. 6.	FV	2.00	4.50
		b. Sign. title at r.: *DIRECTOR OF CURRENCY OPERATIONS*. Sign. 7.	FV	1.00	2.25
		c. Titles as b. Sign. 8.	FV	FV	1.75
		d. Titles as b. Sign. 9.	FV	FV	1.00

25	10 NAIRA	ND (1984–). Red-violet and orange on m/c unpt. Back red. Like #21.			
		a. Sign. title at r: *DIRECTOR OF DOMESTIC OPERAITONS*. Sign. 6.	FV	2.50	6.50
		b. Sign. title at r: *DIRECTOR OF CURRENCY OPERATIONS*. Sign. 7.	FV	2.50	5.00
		c. Titles as b. Sign. 8.	FV	FV	2.25
		d. Titles as b. Sign. 9.	FV	FV	2.00
		e. Titles as b. Sign. 10.	FV	FV	2.00

26	20 NAIRA	ND (1984–). Dk. blue-green, dk. green and green on m/c unpt. Like #18.			
		a. Sign. title at r.: *DIRECTOR OF DOMESTIC OPERATIONS*. Sign. 6.	FV	5.00	15.00
		b. Sign. title at r.: *DIRECTOR OF CURRENCY OPERATIONS*. Sign. 7.	FV	FV	4.50
		c. Titles as b. Sign. 8.	FV	FV	2.75
		d. Titles as b. Sign. 9.	FV	FV	1.50
		e. Titles as b. Sign. 10.	FV	FV	1.50

27	50 NAIRA	ND (1991–).Dk. blue, black and gray on m/c unpt. Four busts reflecting varied citizenry at l. ctr. Three farmers in field at ctr. r., arms at lower r. on back.			
		a. Sign. 8.	FV	3.50	10.00
		b. Sign. 9.	FV	FV	5.50
		c. Sign. 10.	FV	FV	5.00

Listing For:

Northern Ireland, see Ireland/Northern.

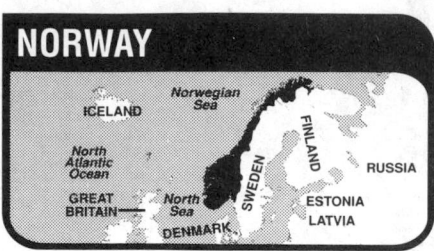

NORWAY

The Kingdom of Norway, a constitutional monarchy located in northwestern Europe, has an area of 150,000 sq. mi. (388,500 sq. km.) including the island territories of Spitzbergen (Svalbard) and Jan Mayen, and a population of 4.27 million. Capital: Oslo (Christiania until 1924). The diversified economic base of Norway includes shipping, fishing, forestry, agriculture, and manufacturing. Nonferrous metals, paper and paperboard, paper pulp, iron, steel and oil are exported.

A United Norwegian kingdom was established in the 9th century, the era of the indomitable Norse Vikings who ranged far and wide, visiting the coasts of northwestern Europe, the Mediterranean, Greenland and North America. In the 13th century, the Norse kingdom was united briefly with Sweden, then passed, through the Union of Kalmar, 1397, to the rule of Denmark which was maintained until 1814. In 1814, Norway fell again under the rule of Sweden. The union lasted until 1905 when the Norwegian Parliament arranged a peaceful separation and invited a Danish prince (King Haakon VII) to occupy the throne of an independent Kingdom of Norway.

RULERS

Olav V, 1957–1991
Harald V, 1991–

MONETARY SYSTEM

1 Krone = 100 Øre, 1873–

REPLACEMENT NOTES

30–33, 37–40 with 1945 or later dates, Z prefix. #31, 37, 38 with 1966 or later dates, X prefix. #40 with 1975 or later dates, X prefix. #34, 35 with 1971 or later dates, G prefix. #36, 41 with 1972 or later dates, either Q or H prefix.

KINGDOM

Norges Bank

1948–55 ISSUE

Cat#	Date, denomination	Description	VG	VF	Unc
30	5 KRONER	1955–63. Blue. Portr. F. Nansen at l. Fishing scene on back.			
		a. Sign. Brofoss and Thorp. 1955–57.	3.00	12.50	50.00
		b. Sign. Brofoss and Ottesen. 1959–63.	2.50	10.00	40.00

31	10 KRONER	1954–73. Yellow-brown. Portr. C. Michelsen at l. Mercury w/ships on back.			
		a. Sign. Jahn and Throp. 1954. Series A–D.	4.00	16.00	65.00
		b. Sign. Brofoss and Thorp. 1954. Series D–1958 Series N.	3.00	9.00	35.00
		c. Sign. Brofoss and Ottesen. 1959–1965. Series A.	2.50	5.00	20.00
		d. Sign. Brofoss and Petersen. 1965. Series F–1969.	2.50	4.50	18.00
		e. Sign. Brofoss and Odegaard. 1970.	2.25	3.50	11.00
		f. Sign. Wold and Odegaard. 1971–73.	2.00	2.50	8.00

Cat#	Date, denomination	Description	VG	VF	Unc
32	50 KRONER	1950–65. Dk. green. Portr. B. Bjornson at l. and as wmk., arms at ctr. Harvesting on back.			
		a. Sign. Jahn and Thorp. 1950. Series A; B.	16.50	100.00	250.00
		b. Sign. Brofoss and Thorp. 1950. Series B–1958.	13.50	30.00	125.00
		c. Sign. Brofoss and Ottesen. 1959–65.	12.50	28.50	85.00

Cat#	Date, denomination	Description	VG	VF	Unc
34	500 KRONER	1948–76. Dk. green. Portr. N. Henrik Abel at l. and as wmk. Factory workers on back.			
		a. Sign. Jahn and Thorp. 1948; 1951.	135.00	225.00	550.00
		b. Sign. Brofoss and Thorp. 1954; 1956; 1958.	125.00	200.00	500.00
		c. Sign. Brofoss and Ottesen. 1960–64.	120.00	165.00	300.00
		d. Sign. Brofoss and Petersen. 1966–69.	110.00	140.00	275.00
		e. Sign. Brofoss and Odegaard. 1970.	110.00	125.00	225.00
		f. Sign. Wold and Odegaard. 1971–76.	100.00	120.00	175.00

			VG	VF	Unc
33	100 KRONER	1949–62. Red. Portr. H. Wergeland at l. and as wmk., arms at ctr. Logging on back.			
		a. Sign. Jahn and Thorp. 1949–54. Series C.	25.00	75.00	150.00
		b. Sign. Brofoss and Thorp. 1954. Series D.	22.50	45.00	125.00
		c. Sign. Brofoss and Ottesen. 1959–62.	20.00	30.00	85.00

Cat#	Date, denomination	Description	VG	VF	Unc
35	1000 KRONER	1949–74. Red-brown. Portr. H. Ibsen at l. and as wmk. Old man and child on back.			
		a. Sign. Jahn and Thorp. 1949; 1951; 1953.	250.00	325.00	600.00
		b. Sign. Brofoss and Thorp. 1955; 1958.	240.00	300.00	525.00
		c. Sign. Brofoss and Ottesen 1961; 1962.	230.00	275.00	475.00
		d. Sign. Brofoss and Petersen. 1965–70.	220.00	265.00	400.00
		e. Sign. Brofoss and Odegaard. 1971–74.	200.00	250.00	300.00

1962–78 ISSUE

Cat#	Date, denomination	Description	VG	VF	Unc
36	10 KRONER	1972–84. Blue-black on m/c unpt. F. Nansen at l. Fisherman and cargo ship on back.			
		a. Sign. Wold and Odegaard. 1972–76.	1.50	4.50	10.00
		b. Sign. Wold and Sagård. 1977.	FV	2.00	5.00

Cat#	Date, denomination	Description	VG	VF	Unc
37	50 KRONER	1966–83. Green. B. Bjornson at l. and as wmk. Old church on back.			
		a. Sign. Brofoss and Petersen. 1966–67; 1969.	13.50	20.00	37.50
		b. Sign. Wold and Odegaard. 1971–73.	12.50	18.50	32.50
		c. As b. W/security thread. 1974–75.	11.50	16.50	27.50
		d. Sign. Wold and Sagård. 1976–83.	10.00	15.00	25.00

Cat#	Date, denomination	Description	VG	VF	Unc
38	100 KRONER	1962–77. Red-violet. H. Wergeland at l. and as wmk. Meeting at r. on back.			
		a. Sign. Brofoss and Ottesen. 1962–65. Series D.	22.50	32.50	60.00
		b. Sign. Brofoss and Petersen. 1965. Series. D–1969.	21.50	30.00	55.00
		c. Sign. Brofoss and Odegaard. 1970.	20.00	27.50	45.00
		d. Sign. Wold and Odegaard. 1971–76.	20.00	26.50	42.50
		e. Sign. Wold and Sagård. 1977.	20.00	25.00	40.00

Cat#	Date, denomination	Description	VG	VF	Unc
39	500 KRONER	1978–85. Green on brown unpt. N. Henrik Abel at l. and as wmk. Bldgs. at r. on back.			
		a. Sign. Skånland and Sagård. 1978; 1982.	FV	100.00	150.00
		b. Sign. Wold and Sagård. 1985.	FV	90.00	100.00

Cat#	Date, denomination	Description	VG	VF	Unc
40	1000 KRONER	1975–87. Brown and violet. H. Ibsen at l. and as wmk. Scenery on back.			
		a. Sign. Wold and Odegaard.1975.	FV	200.00	275.00
		b. Sign. Wold and Sagård. 1978–85. Series C.	FV	FV	250.00
		c. Sign. Skånland and Sagård. 1985. Series C–1987.	FV	FV	225.00

1977–91 ISSUE

Cat# 41	Date, denomination 100 KRONER	Description 1977–82. Purple on pink and m/c unpt. C. Collett at l. and as wmk. Date at top l. ctr. Filigree design on back. Sign. Wold and Sagård.	VG	VF	Unc
		a. Brown serial #. 1977.	FV	18.50	45.00
		b. Black serial #. 1979; 1980.	FV	18.50	40.00
		c. 1981.	FV	FV	37.50
		d. 1982.	FV	FV	35.00

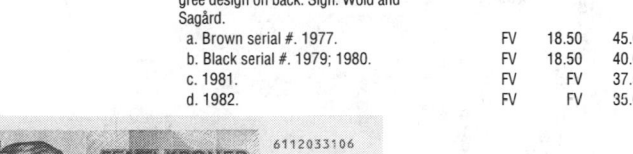

42	50 KRONER	1984–95. Green on m/c unpt. A.O. Vinje at l. Stone carving w/soldier slaying dragon on back. Wmk: 50 repeated within diagonal bars.			
		a. Sign. Wold and Sagård. 1984.	FV	10.00	25.00
		b. Sign. Skånland and Sagård. 1985–87.	FV	FV	20.00
		c. Sign. Skånland and Johnsen. 1989–90; 1993.	FV	FV	12.50
		d. Sign. Moland and Johansen. 1995.	FV	FV	11.50

43	100 KRONER	1983–. Red-violet on pink and m/c unpt. Similar to #41 but smaller printing size, and date at lower r.			
		a. Lt. brown sign. Wold and Sagård. 1983.	FV	20.00	45.00
		b. Lg. date. Dk. brown sign. 1984.	FV	FV	32.50
		c. Sign. Skånland and Sagård. Lg. date. 1985–87.	FV	FV	27.50
		d. Sign. Skånland and Johnsen. 1988–93.	FV	FV	25.00
		e. Sign. Moland and Johansen. 1994.	FV	FV	23.50

Cat# 44	Date, denomination 500 KRONER	Description 1991; 1994. Violet-blue and m/c unpt. E. Grieg at l. Floral mosaic at ctr. on back. Wmk: Multiple portr. of Grieg vertically.	VG FV	VF FV	Unc 95.00

45	1000 KRONER	1989; 1990. Purple and dk. blue on m/c unpt. C. M. Falsen at l. 1668 royal seal on back.	FV	FV	185.00

1994 ISSUE

46	50 KRONER				Expected new issue.
47	100 KRONER	1996.			Expected new issue.

48	200 KRONER	1994. Blue-black and dk. blue on m/c unpt. K. Birkeland at r. and as repeated vertical wmk. Map of the North Pole and North America and Northern Europe at l. ctr. on back.	FV	FV	45.00
49	500 KRONER				Expected new issue.
50	1000 KRONER				Expected new issue.

The Sultanate of Oman (formerly Muscat and Oman), an independent monarchy located in the southeastern part of the Arabian Peninsula, has an area of 82,030 sq. mi. (212,457 sq. km.) and a population of 2.07 million. Capital: Muscat. The economy is based on agriculture, herding and petroleum. Petroleum products, dates, fish and hides are exported.

The first European contact with Muscat and Oman was made by the Portuguese who captured Muscat, the capital and chief port, in 1508. They occupied the city, utilizing it as a naval base and factory and holding it against land and sea attacks by Arabs and Persians until finally ejected by local Arabs in 1650. It was next occupied by the Persians who maintained control until 1741, when it was taken by Ahmed ibn Sa'id of the present ruling family. Muscat and Oman was the most powerful state in Arabia during the first half of the 19th century, until weakened by the persistent attack of interior nomadic tribes. British influence, initiated by the signing of a treaty of friendship with the Sultanate in 1798, remains a dominant fact of the civil and military phases of the government, although Britain recognizes the Sultanate as a sovereign state and there is no colonial relationship between them.

Sultan Sa'id bin Taimur was overthrown by his son, Qabus bin Sa'id, on July 23, 1970. He changed the nation's name to Sultanate of Oman.

RULERS

Sa'id bin Taimur, AH1351–1390/1932–1970 AD

Qaboos bin Sa'id, AH1390–/1970 AD–

MONETARY SYSTEM

1 Rial Omani = 1000 Baiza (Baisa)

1 Rial Saidi = 1000 Baiza (Baisa)

MUSCAT AND OMAN

Sultanate of Muscat and Oman

Rial Saidi System

#1–6 arms at r. and as wmk.

Cat. #	Denomination	Date, description	VG	VF	Unc
1	100 BAIZA	ND (1970). Brown, green and m/c.	.30	.80	2.50

#2–6 different fortresses on back.

Cat. #	Denomination	Date, description	VG	VF	Unc
2	1/4 RIAL SAIDI	ND (1970). Blue, brown and m/c.	.70	1.00	3.25

Cat. #	Denomination	Date, description	VG	VF	Unc
3	1/2 RIAL SAIDI	ND (1970). Green, violet and m/c.	1.25	2.00	6.00

Cat. #	Denomination	Date, description	VG	VF	Unc
4	1 RIAL SAIDI	ND (1970). Red, olive and m/c.	2.50	4.00	10.00

Cat. #	Denomination	Date, description	VG	VF	Unc
5	5 RIALS SAIDI	ND (1970). Purple, blue and m/c.	12.50	20.00	50.00

Cat. #	Denomination	Date, description	VG	VF	Unc
6	10 RIALS SAIDI	ND (1970). Dk. brown, blue and m/c.	20.00	45.00	75.00

OMAN
Oman Currency Board
Rial Omani System

#7–12 arms at r. and as wmk.

Cat. #	Denomination	Date, description	VG	VF	Unc
7	100 BAIZA	ND (1973). Dk. brown on pale blue-green and m/c unpt.	.50	1.00	2.00

#8–12 different fortresses on back.

| 8 | 1/4 RIAL OMANI | ND (1973). Blue, brown and m/c. | .40 | 1.00 | 3.75 |

| 9 | 1/2 RIAL OMANI | ND (1973). Green, violet and m/c. | 1.75 | 2.75 | 6.00 |

| 10 | 1 RIAL OMANI | ND (1973). Red, olive and m/c. | 2.75 | 6.50 | 10.00 |

Cat. #	Denomination	Date, description	VG	VF	Unc
11	5 RIALS OMANI	ND (1973). Purple, blue and m/c.	15.00	25.00	45.00

| 12 | 10 RIALS OMANI | ND (1973). Dk. brown, blue and m/c. | 30.00 | 45.00 | 70.00 |

Central Bank of Oman
1977; 1985 ISSUE

#13–21 arms at r. and as wmk.

| 13 | 100 BAISA | ND (1977). Lt. brown on m/c unpt. Port of Qaboos on back. | FV | FV | 1.50 |

Cat. #	Denomination	Date, description	VG	VF	Unc
14	200 BAISA	ND (1985). Purple on m/c unpt. Rustaq Fortress on back.	FV	FV	2.25

| 15 | 1/4 RIAL | ND (1977). Blue and brown. Back like #8. | FV | FV | 2.50 |

| 16 | 1/2 RIAL | ND (1977). Green and violet. Back like #9. | FV | FV | 4.00 |

| 17 | 1 RIAL | ND (1977). Red and brown. Back like #10. | FV | FV | 7.00 |

| 18 | 5 RIALS | ND (1977). Lilac and blue. Back like #11. | FV | FV | 22.50 |

Cat. #	Denomination	Date, description	VG	VF	Unc
19	10 RIALS	ND (1977). Brown and m/c. Back like #12.	FV	FV	45.00

| 20 | 20 RIALS | ND (1977). Gray-blue and orange. Sultan Qaboos bin Sa'id at r. Central Bank at l. ctr. on back. Wmk: Arms. | FV | 60.00 | 90.00 |

| 21 | 50 RIALS | ND. Olive-brown, blue and dk. brown on m/c unpt. Jabreen Fort at l. ctr. on back. | FV | 145.00 | 250.00 |

1985–90 ISSUE

#22–30 Sultan Qaboos bin Sa'id at r. and as wmk.

22	100 BAISA	1987/AH1408-. Lt. brown on m/c unpt. Port of Qaboos on back.			
		a. 1987/AH1408; 1989–AH1409	FV	FV	1.25
		b. 1994/AH1414.	FV	FV	1.00

Cat. #	Denomination	Date, description	VG	VF	Unc
26	1 RIAL	1987/AH1407; 1989/AH1409. Red, black and m/c. Sohar Fort at l. on back.	FV	FV	5.00

Cat. #	Denomination	Date, description	VG	VF	Unc
23	200 BAISA	1987/AH1407-. Purple on m/c unpt. Rustaq Fort on back.			
		a. 1987/AH1407.	FV	FV	2.00
		b. 1993/AH1413; 1994/AH1414.	FV	FV	1.75

			VG	VF	Unc
27	5 RIALS	1990/AH1411. Dk. rose, brown-violet and m/c. Fort Nizwa on back.	FV	FV	22.50

			VG	VF	Unc
24	1/4 RIAL	1987/AH1407; 1989–AH1409. Blue. Dock scene on back.	FV	FV	2.00

			VG	VF	Unc
28	10 RIALS	1987–/AH1408-. Dk. brown, red-brown and blue on m/c unpt. Fort Mirani at l. ctr. on back.			
		a. 1987/AH1408.	FV	FV	45.00
		b. 1993/AH1413.	FV	FV	42.50

			VG	VF	Unc
25	1/2 RIAL	1987/AH1408. Green and m/c. City view on back.	FV	FV	3.00

			VG	VF	Unc
29	20 RIALS	1987–/AH1407-. Brown, dk. olive-brown and blue-gray on m/c unpt. Central Bank at l. ctr. on back.			
		a. 1987/AH1408.	FV	FV	85.00
		b. 1994/AH1414.	FV	FV	80.00

Cat. #	Denomination	Date, description	VG	VF	Unc
30	50 RIALS	1985–/AH1405–. Like #21 but w/*Jabreen Fort* added at lower r. on back.			
		a. 1985/AH1405.	FV	FV	210.00
		b. 1992/AH1413.	FV	FV	200.00

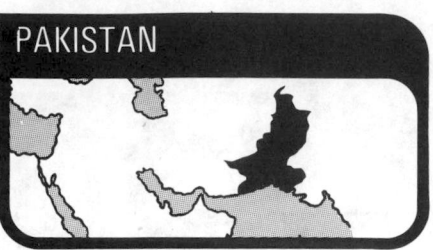

PAKISTAN

The Islamic Republic of Pakistan, located on the Indian subcontinent between India and Afghanistan, has an area of 310,404 sq. mi. (803,943 sq. m.) and a population of 114 million. Capital: Islamabad. Pakistan is mainly an agricultural land. Yarn, cotton, rice and leather are exported.

Afghan and Turkish intrusions into norhtern India between the 11th and 18th centuries resulted in large numbers of indians being converted to Islam. The idea of a separate Moslem state indepenent of Hindu India developed in the 1930's and was agreed to by Britain in 1946. The Islamic majority areas of india, consisting of the separate geographic entities known as East and West Pakistan, achieved self-government as Pakistan, with dominion status in the British Commonwealth, when the British withdrew from India on Aug. 14, 1947. Pakistan became a republic in 1956. When a basic constitutional crisis initiated by the election of Dec. 1, 1970 — the first direct general election in Pakistani history — could not be resolved by the leaders of East and West Pakistan, the East Pakistanis seceded from the Islamic Republic of Pakistan (March 26, 1971) and formed the independent People's Republic of Bangladesh.

MONETARY SYSTEM
1 Rupee = 100 Paisa (Pice), 1961–

REPLACEMENT NOTES
#24, 24A, 24B, 1/X or 2/X prefix. #25–33, X as first of double prefix letters.

> NOTE: This section has been renumbered from the old 7th Edition of General Issues

Government of Pakistan
1973 ISSUES

Cat#	Date, denomination	Description	VG	VF	Unc
10	1 RUPEE	ND (1973). Brown on m/c unpt. Arms at r. and as wmk. Archway at l. ctr. on back.	.35	1.25	3.50

State Bank of Pakistan

Dacca	Karachi	Lahore

Some notes exist w/Arabic and some w/Sanskrit ovpt. denoting city of issue, Karachi, Lahore, Dacca; these are much scarcer than the regular issues. Sign. varieties.

1957; 1964 ISSUE

#15–19A portr. of M. Ali Jinnah and as wmk.

| 15 | 5 RUPEES | ND (1957). Purple on lt. blue and maroon unpt. Jinnah at ctr. Terraces on back. 3 sign. varieties | .50 | 2.00 | 7.50 |

Cat#	Date, denomination	Description	VG	VF	Unc
20	5 RUPEES	ND (1973). Red-brown on blue and green unpt. Jinnah at ctr. Terraces on back. 3 sign. varieties	.50	2.00	3.50

Cat#	Date, denomination	Description	VG	VF	Unc
16	10 RUPEES	ND (1957). Brown and m/c. Jinnah at l. Park scene on back. 2 sign. varities w/sign. in Urdu or Latin letters.	.50	3.00	10.00
17	50 RUPEES	ND (1957). Blue-green on peach unpt. Jinnah at ctr. Back green; sailing ships. 3 sign. varities.			
		a. 1. sign.	2.50	5.00	35.00
		b. 2. sign.	2.50	6.00	40.00

			VG	VF	Unc
21	10 RUPEES	ND (1973). Green on m/c unpt. Like #16. 2 sign. varieties.	.75	3.00	7.50
22	50 RUPEES	ND (1973). Blue on m/c unpt. Like #17. 3 sign. varities	2.00	8.00	15.00

18	100 RUPEES	ND (1957). Green on violet and peach unpt. Jinnah at ctr. Mosque on back. 3 sign. varieties.			
		a. W/o city ovpt.	2.00	6.00	35.00
		b. Ovpt: *Dacca*	3.00	10.00	55.00
		c. Ovpt: *Karachi.*	3.00	8.00	50.00
		d. Ovpt: *Lahore.*	3.00	10.00	55.00

23	100 RUPEES	ND (1973). Dk. blue on m/c unpt. Jinnah at l. Mosque on back. 2 sign. varities	4.00	10.00	30.00

19	500 RUPEES	ND (1964). Red on gold and lt. green unpt. Jinnah at ctr. Bank on back. Sign. in Urdu or Latin letters. 2 sign. varieties.			
		a. Ovpt: *Dacca.*	3.50	10.00	55.00
		b. Ovpt: *Karachi.*	4.00	12.00	60.00
		c. Ovpt: *Lahore.*	4.00	12.00	60.00
19A	*Deleted.*				

1973 ISSUE

#20–23 portr. of M. Ali Jinnah and as wmk.

Government of Pakistan

SIGNATURE VARIETIES			
1	عبدالرؤف Abdur Rauf	6	رفیق اخوند Rafiq Akhind
2	آفتاب احمد خان Aftab Ahmed Khan	7	قاضی علیم اللہ السماری Qazi Alimullah Marfi
3	حبیب اللہ بیگ Habibullah Baig	8	خالد جاوید Khalid Javed
4	اظہار الحق Izhar ul-Hag	9	جاوید طلعت Javed Talat
5	سعید احمد قریشی Saeed Ahmad Qureshi	10	

1975 ISSUE

Cat. #	Denomination	Date, description	VG	VF	Unc
24	1 RUPEE	ND (1975–81). Blue on lt. green and lilac unpt. Arms at r. and as wmk. Tower on back. Sign. 1-3.	.25	1.00	2.50

1981 ISSUE

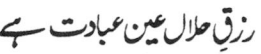

URDU TEXT LINE A	URDU TEXT LINE B

Cat. #	Denomination	Date, description	VG	VF	Unc
25 (24A)	1 RUPEE	ND (1981–82). Brown and m/c. Arms at r. and as wmk. Tomb of Allama Iqbal on back. No Urudu text line at bottom on back. Sign. 3.	FV	.40	1.00

Cat. #	Denomination	Date, description	VG	VF	Unc
26 (24B)	1 RUPEE	ND (1982). Like #24A, but w/Urdu text line A at bottom on back.			
		a. Serial # at upper ctr. Sign. 3.	FV	.15	.75
		b. Serial # at lower r. Sign. 3.	FV	.10	.40

Cat. #	Denomination	Date, description	VG	VF	Unc
27 (24C)	1 RUPEE	ND (1983–). Like #24B, but w/Urdu text line B at bottom on back.			
		a. Serial # at ctr. Sign. 3.	FV	.10	.35
		b. Serial # at lower r. Sign. 3.	FV	FV	.30
		c. As b., but sign. 4.	FV	FV	.25
		d. As b., but sign. 5.	FV	FV	.25
		e. As a., but sign. 5.	FV	FV	.25
		f. As b., but sign. 6.	FV	FV	.20
		g. Serial # at upper ctr. Sign. 7.	FV	FV	.20
		h. As b., but sign. 8.	FV	FV	.20
		i. As b., but sign. 9.	FV	FV	.15

State Bank of Pakistan

1975–78 ISSUE

#28–31 portr. of M. Ali Jinnah at r. and as wmk. Serial # and sign. varieties.

Cat. #	Denomination	Date, description	VG	VF	Unc
28 (25)	5 RUPEES	ND (1975–84). Brown on tan and pink unpt. The Khajak railroad tunnel on back. No Urdu text line beneath upper title on back.	FV	.40	1.50

Cat. #	Denomination	Date, description	VG	VF	Unc
29 (26)	10 RUPEES	ND (1975–84). Green and m/c. View of Mohanjodaro on back. No Urdu text line beneath upper title on back.	FV	.75	1.75
30 (27)	50 RUPEES	ND (1978–84). Purple and m/c. Gate of Lahore fort on back. No Urdu text line beneath upper title on back.	FV	3.00	10.00

Cat. #	Denomination	Date, description	VG	VF	Unc
31 (28)	100 RUPEES	ND (1975–84). Red, orange and m/c. Islamic College, Peshawar, on back. No Urdu text line beneath upper title on back.	FV	7.50	20.00

1985 ISSUE

Cat. #	Denomination	Date, description	VG	VF	Unc
32 (29)	*Deleted.*				

#33–36 portr. of M. Ali Jinnah at r. and as wmk.

Cat. #	Denomination	Date, description	VG	VF	Unc
33 (25A)	5 RUPEES	ND (1985). Like #28, but w/Urdu text line A beneath upper title on back.	FV	.75	2.00
34 (26A)	10 RUPEES	ND (1985). Like #29, but w/Urdu text line A beneath upper title on back.	FV	.85	2.25
35 (27A)	50 RUPEES	ND (1985). Like #30, but w/Urdu text line A beneath upper title on back.	FV	3.25	12.00
36 (28A)	100 RUPEES	ND (1985). Like #31, but w/Urdu text line A beneath upper title on back.	FV	8.50	25.00

1986–87 ISSUE

#37–43 portr. of M. Ali Jinnah at r. and as wmk.

NOTE: #37 shade varieties exist.

Cat. #	Denomination	Date, description	VG	VF	Unc
37 (29A)	2 RUPEES	ND (1986–). Pale purple on m/c unpt. Arms at r. and as wmk. Badshahi mosque on back. Urdu text line B beneath upper title on back. 5 sign. varieties.	FV	FV	.50
38 (25B)	5 RUPEES	ND (1986). Like #28, but w/Urdu text line B beneath upper title on back. 5 sign. varieties.	FV	FV	1.00
39 (26B)	10 RUPEES	ND (1986). Like #29, but w/Urdu text line B beneath upper title on back.	FV	FV	1.50

Cat. #	Denomination	Date, description	VG	VF	Unc
40 (27B)	50 RUPEES	ND (1986). Like #30, but w/Urdu text line B beneath upper title on back. 5 sign. varieties.	FV	FV	5.00

Cat. #	Denomination	Date, description	VG	VF	Unc
41 (28B)	100 RUPEES	ND (1986). Like #31, but w/Urdu text line B beneath upper title on back.	FV	FV	10.00

| 42 (30) | 500 RUPEES | ND (1986–). Deep blue-green and olive on m/c unpt. State Bank of Pakistan bldg. at ctr. on back. | FV | FV | 35.00 |

| 43 (31) | 1000 RUPEES | ND (1987–). Deep purple and blue-black on m/c unpt. Tomb of Jahangir on back. 4 sign. varieties. | FV | FV | 70.00 |

REGIONAL

Haj Pilgrim

#R1 ovpt: *FOR PILGRIMS FROM PAKISTAN/FOR USE IN SAUDI ARABIA AND IRAQ.*

| R1 | 100 RUPEES | ND. Red. | 450.00 | 1150. | — |

#R2–R7 ovpt: *FOR HAJ PILGRIMS FROM PAKISTAN/FOR USE IN SAUDI ARABIA ONLY.*

| R2 (R1) | 10 RUPEES | ND. Green. 2 sign. varieties. | 20.00 | 55.00 | 165.00 |

Cat. #	Denomination	Date, description	VG	VF	Unc
R3	10 RUPEES	ND. Green and m/c. Ovpt. on #21. 2 sign. varieties.	7.50	16.50	50.00
R4 (R2)	10 RUPEES	ND. Purple and m/c. Like #16 but w/ovpt.	1.50	3.50	5.50

| R5 (R4) | 100 RUPEES | ND. Brown and m/c. Like #23; black ovpt. 2. sign. varieties. | 25.00 | 100.00 | 225.00 |

| R6 (R5) | 100 RUPEES | ND. Gold and m/c. Like #28; dk. brown ovpt. | 10.00 | 20.00 | 55.00 |

| R7 (R6) | 10 RUPEES | ND. Blue-black on m/c unpt. Like #26; black ovpt. | .50 | 1.25 | 4.00 |

NOTE: All Haj Pilgrim notes were discontinued or destroyed in 1994.

Listing For:
 PAPEETE, see Tahiti

Papua New Guinea, an independent member of the British Commonwealth, occupies the eastern half of the island of New Guinea. It lies north of Australia near the equator and borders on West Irian. The country, which includes nearby Bismarck archipelago, Buka and Bougainville, has an area of 176,280 sq. mi. (461,691 sq. km.) and a population of 3.7 million who are divided into more than 1,000 separate tribes speaking more than 700 mutually unintelligible languages. Capital: Port Moresby. The economy is agricultural, and exports include copra, rubber, cocoa, coffee, tea, gold and copper.

New Guinea, the world's largest island after Greenland, was discovered by Spanish navigator Jorge de Menezes, who landed on the northwest shore in 1527. European interests, attracted by exaggerated estimates of the resources of the area, resulted in the island being claimed in whole or part by Spain, the Netherlands, Great Britain and Germany.

Papua (formerly British New Guinea), situated in the southeastern part of the island of New Guinea, has an area of 90,540 sq. mi. (234,499 sq. km.) and a population of 740,000. It was temporarily annexed by Queensland in 1883 and by the British Crown in 1888. Papua came under control of the Australian Commonwealth in 1901 and became the Territory of Papua in 1906. Japan invaded New Guinea and Papua early in 1942, but Australian control was restored before the end of the year in Papua and in 1945 in New Guinea.

In 1884 Germany annexed the area known as German New Guinea (also Neu-Guinea or Kaiser Wilhelmsland) comprising the northern section of eastern New Guinea, and granted its administration and development to the New-Guinea Compagnie. Administration reverted to Germany in 1889 following the failure of the company to exercise adequate administration. While a German protectorate, German New Guinea had an area of 92,159 sq. mi. (238,692 sq. km.) and a population of about 250,000. Capital: Herbertshohe, later named Rabaul. Copra was the chief crop. Australian troops occupied German New Guinea in Aug. 1914, shortly after Great Britain declared war on Germany. It was mandated to Australia by the League of Nations in 1920 and known as the Territory of New Guinea. The territory was invaded and occupied by Japan in 1942. Following the Japanese surrender, it came under U.N. trusteeship, Dec. 13, 1946, with Australia as the administering power.

The Papua and New Guinea Act, 1949, provided for the government of Papua and New Guinea as one administrative unit. On Dec. 1, 1973, Papua New Guinea became self-governing with Australia retaining responsibility for defense and foreign affairs. Full independence was achieved on Sept. 16, 1975 and Papua New Guinea is now a member of the Commonwealth of Nations. The Queen of England is Chief of State.

RULERS
British

MONETARY SYSTEM
1 Kina = 100 Toea, 1975–

Bank of Papua New Guinea

SIGNATURE VARIETIES

1	*signature*	3	*signature*
2	*signature*	4	

1975 ISSUE

#1–4 stylized bird of paradise at l. ctr. and as wmk.

Cat#	Date, denomination	Description	VG	VF	Unc
1	2 KINA	ND (1975). Green and m/c. Artifacts on back. Sign. 1.	FV	3.75	15.00

Cat#	Date, denomination	Description	VG	VF	Unc
2	5 KINA	ND (1975). Violet and m/c. Mask at ctr. r. on back. Sign. 1.	FV	7.00	30.00

| 3 | 10 KINA | ND (1975). Blue and m/c. Bowl, ring and other artifacts on back. Sign. 1. | FV | 14.00 | 55.00 |

| 4 | 20 KINA | ND (1977). Red and m/c. Boar's head at r. on back. Sign. 1. | FV | 22.00 | 85.00 |

1981–85 ISSUE

Cat#	Date, denomination	Description	VG	VF	Unc
5	2 KINA	ND (1981). Like #1. Green unpt. w/white strip 16mm wide.			
		a. Sign. 1.	FV	FV	10.00
		b. Sign. 2.	FV	FV	6.00
		c. Sign. 3.	FV	FV	5.50
6	5 KINA	ND (1981). Like #2. Pink unpt. w/white strip 22mm wide.			
		a. Sign. 1.	FV	6.50	22.50
		b. Sign. 2.	FV	7.00	25.00
7	10 KINA	ND (1985). Like #3. Blue unpt. w/white strip 18mm. wide. Sign. 1.	FV	10.00	45.00

8 Held in reserve.

Cat#	Date, denomination	Description	VG	VF	Unc
9 (10)	10 KINA	ND (1988). Similar to #7 but different design elements in unpt. representing a modern bldg. Ornate corner designs omitted on face and back.			
		a. Sign. 2.	FV	15.00	75.00
		b. Sign. 3.	FV	FV	25.00
10	20 KINA	ND. Similar to #4 but different design elements in unpt. Sign. 3.	FV	FV	45.00

| 11 | 50 KINA | ND (1989). Orange, yellow and m/c. National Parliament bldg. at ctr. Foreign Affairs Minister M. Somare at l. ctr., ceremonial masks at r. on back. Wmk: Central Bank logo. Sign. 3. | FV | FV | 75.00 |

1991 COMMEMORATIVE ISSUE

#12, 9th South Pacific Games 1991

| 12 | 2 KINA | 1991. Black on green unpt. Similar to #5 but w/design in clear circle at lower r. Plastic. | FV | FV | 6.00 |

1992 REGULAR ISSUES

| 13 | 5 KINA | ND (1992). Like #6 but most design elements much lighter. Serial # darker and heavier. Sign. 3. | FV | FV | 10.00 |
| 14 | 5 KINA | ND (1993). Like #13 but w/segmented security thread and new sign. title: *Secretary for Finance and Planning*. Sign. 4. | FV | FV | 9.00 |

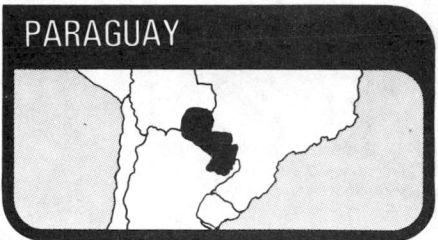

PARAGUAY

The Republic of Paraguay, a landlocked country in the heart of South America surrounded by Argentina, Bolivia and Brazil, has an area of 157,048 sq. mi. (406,752 sq. km.) and a population of 4.4 million, 95 percent of whom are of mixed Spanish and Indian descent. Capital: Asuncion. The country is predominantly agrarian, with no important mineral deposits or oil reserves. Meat, timber, oilseeds, tobacco and cotton account for 70 percent of Paraguay's export revenue.

Paraguay was first visited by Alejo Garcia, a shipwrecked Spaniard, in 1520. The interior was explored by Sebastian Cabot in 1526 and 1529, when he sailed up the Parana and Paraguay Rivers. Asuncion, which would become the center of a province embracing much of southern South America, was established by the Spanish explorer Juan de Salazar on Aug. 15, 1537. For a century and a half the history of Paraguay was largely the history of the agricultural colonies established by the Jesuits in the south and east to Christianize the Indians. In 1811, following the outbreak of the South American wars of independence, Paraguayan patriots overthrew the local Spanish authorities and proclaimed their country's independence.

MONETARY SYSTEM
1 Guarani = 100 Centimos, 1944–

Banco Central del Paraguay

Decreto Ley de No. 18 del 25 de marzo de 1952 (from Aug. 1963)

#101-110 arms at l. Sign. size and name varieties. Printer: TDLR

Cat. #	Denomination	Date, description	VG	VF	Unc
192	1 GUARANI	L.1952. Green on m/c unpt. Soldier at r. Black serial # at lower l. and lower r. Banco Central on back.	.25	1.00	4.00

193	1 GUARANI	L.1952. Green on m/c unpt. Soldier at r. Palacio Legislativo on back.			
		a. Black serial # at lower l. and lower r.	.10	.35	1.75
		b. Black serial # at upper l. and lower r.	.10	.25	1.25
194	5 GUARANIES	L.1952. Blue on m/c unpt. Girl holding jug at r., black serial # at lower l. and lower r. Hotel Guarani on back.	.25	1.50	6.00

Cat. #	Denomination	Date, description	VG	VF	Unc
195	5 GUARANIES	L.1952. Black on m/c unpt. Like #194.			
		a. Red serial # at lower l. and lower r.	.10	.30	1.50
		b. Red serial # at upper l. and lower r.	.10	.30	1.25

196	10 GUARANIES	L.1952. Deep red on m/c unpt. Gen. E. A. Garay at r. International bridge on back.			
		a. Black serial # at lower l. and lower r.	.15	.40	2.25
		b. Black serial # at upper l. and lower r.	.15	.40	2.00

197	50 GUARANIES	L.1952. Brown on m/c unpt. M. J. F. Estigarribia at r. Country road on back.			
		a. Black serial # at lower l. and lower r.	.75	1.75	7.00
		b. Black serial # at upper l. and lower r.	.20	.75	4.00

198	100 GUARANIES	L.1952. Blue-green on m/c unpt. Gen. J. E. Diaz at r. Black serial # at lower l. and lower r. Ruins of Humaita on back.	.75	3.00	15.00

NOTE: Do not confuse green #198 w/later issue #205 also in green. #198 w/value: *CIEN GUARANIES* at bottom on back.

Cat. #	Denomination	Date, description	VG	VF	Unc
199	100 GUARANIES	L.1952. Orange on m/c unpt. Like #198.			
		a. Black serial # at lower l. and lower r.	1.25	1.75	4.00
		b. Black serial # at upper l. and lower r.	.50	1.00	3.00

200	500 GUARANIES	L.1952. Blue-green on m/c unpt. Gen. B. Caballero at r. Merchant ship on back.			
		a. Black serial # at lower l. and lower r.	1.50	4.00	10.00
		b. Black serial # at upper l. and lower r.	1.00	2.00	6.00

201	1000 GUARANIES	L.1952. Purple on m/c unpt. Mariscal F. S. Lopez at r. National shrine on back.			
		a. Black serial # at lower l. and lower r.	4.00	8.00	20.00
		b. Black serial # at upper l. and lower r.	2.00	6.00	15.00
		x. As b. but w/mismatched serial #.	—	—	10.00

Cat. #	Denomination	Date, description	VG	VF	Unc
202	5000 GUARANIES	L.1952. Red-orange on m/c unpt. Arms at ctr., D. C. A. Lopez at r. Lopez Palace on back.			
		a. Black serial # at lower l. and lower r.	7.50	20.00	60.00
		b. Black serial # at upper l. and lower r.	5.00	15.00	45.00

203	10,000 GUARANIES	L.1952. Brown on m/c unpt. Arms at ctr., Dr. J. Caspar Rodriguez de Francia at r., black serial # at lower l. and lower r. Historical scene from 14.5.1811 on back.	9.00	30.00	80.00
204	10,000 GUARANIES	L.1952. Like #203 but CASPAR changed to GASPAR below Francia.			
		a. Black serial # at lower l. and lower r.	9.00	30.00	80.00
		b. Black serial # at upper l. and lower r.	FV	20.00	50.00

1982; 1990 ISSUE

#205–210 printer: TDLR.

205	100 GUARANIES	L.1952 (1982). Green on m/c unpt. Similar to #198 and 199 but value on back stated: SA GUARANI. 3 sign. varieties.	FV	FV	1.25

206	500 GUARANIES	L.1952 (1982). Similar to #200 but value on back stated: PO SA GUARANI. 3 sign. varieties.	FV	FV	1.85

207	1000 GUARANIES	L.1952 (1982). Similar to #201 but value on back stated: SU GUARANI. 3 sign. varieties.	FV	FV	2.25

Cat. #	Denomination	Date, description	VG	VF	Unc
208	5000 GUARANIES	L.1952 (1982). Similar to #202 but value on back stated: PO SU GUARANI. 3 sign. varieties.	FV	FV	6.50

209	10,000 GUARANIES	L.1952 (1982). Similar to #203 but value on back stated: PA SU GUARANI. 3 sign. varieties.	FV	FV	10.00

210	50,000 GUARANIES	L.1952 (1990). Purple and lt. blue on m/c unpt. Solider at r. Back purple and olive-green on m/c unpt. House of Independence at ctr. Wmk: Face of soldier.	FV	FV	42.50

1994 ISSUE

211	50,000 GUARANIES	L.1952 (1994). Like #210 but w/segmented foil security thread and other enhances security features.	FV	FV	40.00
212	100,000 GUARANIES	L.1952.		Expected new issue.	

1996 ISSUE

213	500 GUARANIES	L.1952 (1996). Similar to #206 but w/modified portrait. Printer: OB.	FV	FV	1.50

COLLECTOR SERIES

Cat. #	Date, denomination	Description		Issue Price	Mkt. Val.
CS1	1979 100–10,000 GUARANIES	199b–202b, 204b ovpt: SPECIMEN and w/Maltese cross prefix serial #.		14.00	25.00

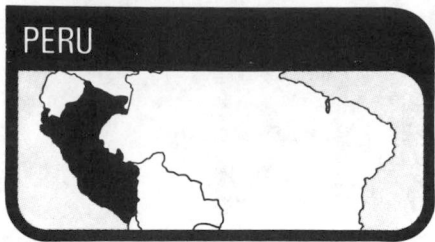

The Republic of Peru, located on the Pacific coast of South America, has an area of 496,222 sq. mi. (1,285,216 sq. km.) and a population of 21.6 million. Capital: Lima. The diversified economy includes mining, fishing and agriculture. Fish meal, copper, sugar, zinc and iron ore are exported.

Once part of a great Inca Empire that reached from northern Ecuador to Central Chile, Peru was conquered in 1531–33 by Francisco Pizarro. Desirable as the richest of the Spanish viceroyalties, it was torn by warfare between avaricious Spaniards until the arrival in 1569 of Francisco de Toledo, who initiated 2 1/2 centuries of efficient colonial rule which made Lima the most aristocratic colonial capital and the stronghold of Spain's American possessions. Jose de San Martin of Argentina proclaimed Peru's independence on July 28, 1821; Simon Bolivar of Venezuela secured it in Dec. of 1824 when he defeated the last Spanish army in South America. After several futile attempts to re-establish its South American empire, Spain recognized Peru's independence in 1879.

MONETARY SYSTEM
1 Sol = 100 Centavos (10 Dineros) to 1985
1 Libra = 10 Soles
1 Inti = 1000 Soles de Oro, 1985–91
1 Nuevo Sol = 1 Million 1 Units, 1991–

REPLACEMENT NOTES
#92–113: Z999 series number. Newer notes printed by BDDK, Y prefix. The Intis notes printed by TDLR, Z prefix and suffix. The newer notes printed by I.P.S. Roma, Y prefix.

Banco Central de Reserva del Peru

Sol System

Ley 10 535

#76–91 Liberty seated holding shield and staff at ctr. Arms at ctr. on back. Sign. and title varieties. Printer: TDLR.

Cat#	Date, denomination	Description	VG	VF	Unc
76	10 SOLES	8.7.1960; 1.2.1961. Orange on lt. green unpt. Similar to #75 but different guilloche. Serial # and series at lower l. and upper r.	.75	1.50	3.50
80	100 SOLES	1956–61. Black on lt. blue unpt. Like #79 but different guilloche. Back black.			
		a. LIMA at lower l. 22.3.1956; 24.10.1957.	2.00	7.00	22.00
		b. LIMA at lower r. w/date. 13.5.1959.	2.00	7.00	22.00
		c. Like b. Series and serial # at lower l. and upper r. 1.2.1961.	2.00	7.00	22.00
82	500 SOLES	1956–61. Brown on lt. brown and lilac unpt. Similar to #81. Back brown.			
		a. Series and serial # at upper corners. 22.3.1956; 24.10.1957.	8.00	25.00	65.00
		b. Series and serial # at lower l. and upper r. 10.12.1959; 16.6.1961.	8.00	25.00	65.00

Ley 13 958

#83–87 Liberty seated holding shield and staff at ctr. arm at ctr. on back. Printer: TDLR.

Cat#	Date, denomination	Description	VG	VF	Unc
83	5 SOLES	9.2.1962–23.2.1968. Green. Serial # at lower l. and upper r.	.30	1.00	3.00

Cat#	Date, denomination	Description	VG	VF	Unc
84	10 SOLES	8.6.1962–23.2.1968. Orange.	.30	1.00	3.00
85	50 SOLES	9.2.1962; 20.9.1963; 23.2.1968. Blue. Like #78 but serial # at lower l. and upper r.	.75	3.00	10.00
86	100 SOLES	13.3.1964; 23.2.1968. Black on lt. blue. Like #80c.	2.00	6.00	18.00

Cat#	Date, denomination	Description	VG	VF	Unc
87	500 SOLES	9.2.1962–23.3.1968. Brown on lt. brown. Like #82b.	2.75	8.00	25.00

#88–91 like #83–87 but reduced size. Printer: ABNC.

88	10 SOLES	26.2.1965. Orange. Similar to #84.	.50	1.50	4.00

Cat#	Date, denomination	Description	VG	VF	Unc
89	50 SOLES	20.8.1965. Blue. Similar to #86.	1.00	5.00	15.00
90	100 SOLES	12.9.1962; 20.8.1965. Black and blue. Similar to #88.	2.00	6.00	18.00
91	500 SOLES	26.2.1965. Brown. Similar to #90.	8.00	25.00	60.00

1968 ISSUE

#92–98 arms at ctr. 3 sign. Printer: TDLR.

Cat#	Date, denomination	Description	VG	VF	Unc
92	5 SOLES	23.2.1968. Green on m/c unpt. Artifacts at l., Inca Pachacutec at r. Back green; Fortaleza de Sacsahuaman.	.25	.50	2.50
93	10 SOLES	23.2.1968. Red-orange on m/c unpt. Bldg. at l., G. Inca de la Vega at r. Back red-orange; Lake Titicaca and boats.	.20	.65	1.75
94	50 SOLES	23.2.1968. Blue-gray on m/c unpt. Workers at l., Tupac Amaru II at r. Back blue-gray; scene of historic town of Tinta.	.25	.75	4.50

Cat#	Date, denomination	Description	VG	VF	Unc
95	100 SOLES	23.2.1968. Black on m/c unpt. Dock workers at l., H. Unanue at r. Back black; church.	.50	1.50	6.00

96	200 SOLES	23.2.1968. Purple on m/c unpt. Fishermen at l., R. Castilla at r. Frigate Amazonas on back.	1.00	3.50	10.00
97	500 SOLES	23.2.1968. Brown on m/c unpt., tan near ctr. Builders at l., N. de Pierola at r. National mint on back.	2.00	5.00	15.00
98	1000 SOLES	23.2.1968. Lilac on m/c unpt. M. Grau at l., Francisco Bolognesi (misspelled BOLOG-ÑESI) at r. Scene of Machu Picchu on back.	4.00	12.00	25.00

1969 ISSUE

#99–105 like #92–98. 2 sign. Printer: TDLR.

99	5 SOLES	1969–74. Like #92.			
		a. 20.6.1969.	.10	.30	1.50
		b. 16.10.1970; 9.9.1971; 4.5.1972.	.10	.30	1.25
		c. 24.5.1973; 16.5.1974; 15.8.1974.	.10	.25	1.00

100	10 SOLES	1969–74. Like #93.			
		a. 20.6.1969.	.10	.30	1.50
		b. 16.10.1970; 9.9.1971.	.10	.30	1.25
		c. 4.5.1972; 24.5.1973; 16.5.1974.	.10	.25	1.00
101	50 SOLES	1969–74. Like #94.			
		a. 20.6.1969.	.25	.75	4.00
		b. 16.10.1970; 9.9.1971; 4.5.1972.	.20	.60	3.00
		c. 24.5.1973; 16.5.1974; 15.8.1974.	.20	.50	2.00

Cat#	Date, denomination	Description	VG	VF	Unc
102	100 SOLES	1969–74. Like #95.			
		a. 20.6.1969.	.25	.75	4.00
		b. 16.10.1970; 9.9.1971; 4.5.1972.	.20	.60	3.00
		c. 24.5.1973; 16.5.1974; 15.8.1974.	.20	.50	2.50
103	200 SOLES	1969–74. Like #96.			
		a. 20.6.1969.	.60	2.50	8.00
		b. 24.5.1973; 16.5.1974; 15.8.1974.	.50	1.75	6.50

104	500 SOLES	1969–74. Like #97.			
		a. 20.6.1969; 16.10.1970; 9.9.1971; 4.5.1972; 24.5.1973.	1.00	3.50	12.00
		b. 16.5.1974; 15.8.1974.	.60	2.50	8.00

105	1000 SOLES	1969–73. Like #98 but BOLOGNESI correctly spelled at r.			
		a. 20.6.1969; 16.10.1970.	1.75	6.00	25.00
		b. 9.9.1971; 4.5.1972; 24.5.1973.	1.50	5.00	22.50

1975 ISSUE

#106–111 3 sign. Printer: TDLR.

106	10 SOLES	2.10.1975. Like #93.	.10	.25	1.00
107	50 SOLES	2.10.1975. Like #94.	.10	.30	1.25
108	100 SOLES	2.10.1975. Like #95.	.20	.50	2.00
109	200 SOLES	2.10.1975. Like #96.	Reported, not confirmed.		
110	500 SOLES	2.10.1975. Like #97. Pale green unpt. near ctr.	1.00	3.00	10.00
111	1000 SOLES	2.10.1975. Like #98. Name correctly spelled.	2.00	5.00	22.50

1976–77 ISSUE

#112 and 113 w/o *Pagara al Portador* at top. 3 sign. Printer: TDLR.

Cat#	Date, denomination	Description	VG	VF	Unc
112	10 SOLES	17.11.1976. Like #106.	.10	.25	.85

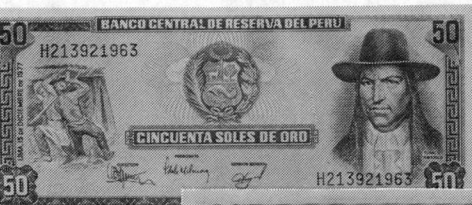

Cat#	Date, denomination	Description	VG	VF	Unc
113	50 SOLES	15.12.1977. Like #107.	.10	.30	1.00

#114 and 115 printer: IPS-Roma.

114	100 SOLES	22.7.1976. Green, brown and m/c. Arms at l., Tupac Amaru II at r. Machu Picchu on back.	.10	.30	1.25
115	500 SOLES	22.7.1976. Green, blue and yellow. Arms at ctr., J. Quinones at r. Logging scene on back.	.05	.15	.85

#116 and 117 printer: BDDK.

Cat#	Date, denomination	Description	VG	VF	Unc
116	1000 SOLES	22.7.1976. Green and m/c. Arms at ctr., M. Grau at r. Fishermen on back.	.50	2.00	6.00

117	5000 SOLES	1976–85. Brown and maroon on m/c unpt. Arms at ctr., Col. Bolognesi at r. and as wmk. 2 miners in mine on back.			
		a. 22.7.1976.	1.00	2.50	7.00
		b. 5.11.1981.	.15	.50	1.50
		c. 21.6.1985.	.05	.15	.65

1979–85 ISSUES

#118–121 portr. as wmk. Printer: TDLR.

117A	500 SOLES	18.3.1982. Like #115 but printer: DLR.	.25	.50	3.00

118	1000 SOLES	1.2.1979; 3.5.1979. Black, green and m/c. Arms at ctr., Adm. Grau at r. Fishermen and boats on back.	.50	1.00	3.00

Cat#	Date, denomination	Description	VG	VF	Unc
119	5000 SOLES	1.2.1979. Brown-violet and m/c. Similar to #117 but *CINCO MIL* added at bottom on face. Miners on back.	.50	1.50	5.00

| 120 | 10,000 SOLES | 1.2.1979, 5.11.1981. Blue, purple and m/c. Garcilaso Inca de la Vega at r. Indian digging and woman w/flowers on back. | .65 | 2.00 | 10.00 |
| 121 | 50,000 SOLES | 23.8.1985. Black, orange and m/c. N. de Pierola at r. Drilling rig at l. on back, helicopter approaching. | .75 | 2.25 | 6.50 |

#122–125 portr. as wmk. Printer: ABNC.

| 122 | 1000 SOLES | 5.11.1981. Black, green and m/c. Similar to #118 but modified guilloche in unpt. at ctr. | .05 | .15 | .65 |

| 123 | 5000 SOLES | 5.11.1981. Black and red-brown on m/c unpt. Similar to #119, but denomination is above signs. at ctr. | .35 | 1.00 | 4.00 |
| 124 | 10,000 SOLES | 5.11.1981. Similar to #120. | .50 | 1.50 | 6.00 |

| 125 | 50,000 SOLES | 5.11.1981; 2.11.1984. Like #121. | 1.00 | 3.00 | 12.50 |

1985 PROVISIONAL ISSUE

Cat#	Date, denomination	Description	VG	VF	Unc
126	100,000 SOLES	ND (ca.1985). Ovpt. bank name and new denomination in red on #122.	30.00	90.00	225.00
127	Held in reserve.				

Currency Reform

1 Inti = 1000 Soles de Oro, 1985–90

During the period from around 1984 and extending into 1990, Peru suffered from a hyperinflation that saw the Inti depreciate in value dramatically and drastically. A sudden need for banknotes caused the government to approach a number of different security printers in order to satisfy the demand for new notes of increasingly higher denominations.

1985–91 ISSUES

#128–150 involve six different printers: BDDK, CdM-B, FNMT, G&D, IPS Roma and TDLR. Listings proceed by denomination and in chronological order. All portr. appear also as wmk., and all notes have arms at ctr. on face.

| 128 | 10 INTIS | 3.4.1985; 17.1.1986. Black, dk. blue and purple on m/c unpt. R. Palma at r. Back aqua and purple; Indian farmer digging at l. and another picking cotton at ctr. Printer: TDLR. | .05 | .15 | 40 |

| 129 | 10 INTIS | 26.6.1987. Like #128. Printer: IPS-Roma. | .05 | .10 | .25 |
| 130 | 50 INTIS | 3.4.1985. Black, red-orange and green on m/c unpt. N. de Pierola at r. Drilling rig at l. on back, helicopter approaching. Printer: TDLR. | .15 | .30 | 1.00 |

Cat#	Date, denomination	Description	VG	VF	Unc
134	500 INTIS	1985; 1987. Deep brown-violet and olive-brown on m/c unpt. J. G. Condorcanqui Tupac Amaru II at r. Mountains and climber on back. Printer: BDDK.			
		a. 1.3.1985.	.15	.30	1.00
		b. 26.6.1987. Ornate red-orange vertical strip at l. end of design w/added security thread underneath.	.05	.10	.35
135	500 INTIS	6.3.1986. Similar to #134b. Printer: FNMT.	1.50	4.00	10.00

Cat#	Date, denomination	Description	VG	VF	Unc
131	50 INTIS	1986–87. Like #130. Printer: CdM-Brazil.			
		a. 6.3.1986.	.10	.20	.60
		b. 26.6.1987.	.05	.10	.35

132	100 INTIS	1985–86. Black and dk. brown on m/c unpt. R. Castilla at r. Women workers by cotton spinning frame at l. ctr. on back. Printer: CdM-Brazil.			
		a. 1.2.1985.	1.00	2.00	10.00
		b. 1.3.1985; 6.3.1986.	.15	.30	1.00

136	1000 INTIS	1986–88. Deep green, olive-brown and red on m/c unpt. Mariscal A. Avelino C. at r. Ruins of Chan Chan on back. Printer: TDLR.			
		a. 6.3.1986.	.15	.30	1.00
		b. 26.6.1987; 28.6.1988.	.05	.10	.35

133	100 INTIS	26.6.1987. Like #132. Printer: BDDK.	.05	.10	.35

137	5000 INTIS	28.6.1988. Purple, deep brown and red-orange on m/c unpt. Adm. M. Grau at r. Fishermen repairing nets on back. Printer: G&D.	.05	.15	.50
138	5000 INTIS	28.6.1988. Like #137. Printer: IPS-Roma.	.25	.80	2.50
139	5000 INTIS	9.9.1988. Like #137. W/o wmk. Printer: TDLR.	.25	.80	2.50

Cat#	Date, denomination	Description	VG	VF	Unc
140	10,000 INTIS	28.6.1988. Dk. blue, and orange on lt. green and m/c unpt. C. Vallejo at r. Black and red increasing size serial # (anti-counterfeiting device). Santiago de Chuco street scene on back. Printer: IPS-Roma.	.05	.25	.65

| 141 | 10,000 INTIS | 28.6.1988. Like #140 but w/broken silver security thread. Printer: TDLR. | .25 | .75 | 2.75 |

| 142 | 50,000 INTIS | 28.6.1988. Red, violet and dk. blue on m/c unpt. Victor Raul Haya de la Torre at r. Chamber of National Congress on back. Printer: IPS-Roma. | .15 | .50 | 1.50 |
| 143 | 50,000 INTIS | 28.6.1988. Like #142 but w/segmented foil security thread. Printer: TDLR. | .50 | 2.00 | 5.00 |

#144–150 arms at ctr. Various printers.

| 144 | 100,000 INTIS | 1988. Brown and black on m/c unpt. F. Bolognesi at r. Local boats in Lake Titicaca on back. Printer: TDLR. | | | |
| | | a. Bolognesi's printed image on wmk. area at l. 21.11.1988. | .25 | .75 | 2.25 |

Cat#	Date, denomination	Description	VG	VF	Unc
		b. Segmented silver security thread, also w/Bolognesi as regular wmk. 21.12.1988.	.50	1.65	5.00
145	100,000 INTIS	21.12.1989. Like #144b, but w/black security thread at r. of arms. Printer: BdeM.	.25	.75	2.25

146	500,000 INTIS	1988. Blue and blue-violet on m/c unpt. Face like #128. Church of *La Caridad* (charity), site of first National Congress, on back. Printer: TDLR.			
		a. R. Palma's printed image on wmk. area at l. 21.11.1988.	.30	1.50	4.50
		b. Segmented foil security thread, also w/Palma as wmk. 21.12.1988.	.35	1.65	5.00

| 147 | 500,000 INTIS | 21.12.1989. Like #146b, but w/black security thread at r. Printer: BdeM. | .20 | .60 | 1.75 |

148	1 MILLION INTIS	5.1.1990. Dk. red, green and m/c. H. Unanue at r. and as wmk. Medical college at San Fernando at l. ctr. on back. Printer: TDLR.	.25	.75	3.00
149	5 MILLION INTIS	5.1.1990. Brown, red and m/c. A. Raimondi at r. and as wmk. Indian comforting Raimundi on back. Printer: BdeM.	2.25	7.00	20.00
150	5 MILLION INTIS	16.1.1991. Similar to #149 but plants printed on wmk. area at l. on face, old bldg. at r. on back. Printer: IPS-Roma.	.65	2.00	6.00

Currency Reform
1 Nuevo (New) Sol = 1 Million Intis, 1991-

1991-92 ISSUE
#151and 152 arms at upper r.

Cat#	Date, denomination	Description	VG	VF	Unc
151	10 NUEVOS SOLES	1.2.1991. Dk. green and blue-green on m/c unpt. WW II era fighter plane as monument at upper ctr., J. Abelardo Quiñones at r. and as wmk. Biplane inverted at l. ctr. on back. Printer: TDLR.	FV	FV	8.50
152A	10 NUEVOS SOLES	10.9.1992. Like #151 but printer: IPS-Roma.	FV	FV	8.50

| 152 | 20 NUEVOS SOLES | 1.2.1991. Black and orange on m/c unpt. Archway to fountain at ctr., R. Porras B. at r. and as wmk. Palace of Torre Tagle at l. ctr. on back. Printer: TDLR. | FV | FV | 20.00 |

#153–155 arms at upper r. Printer: IPS-Roma.

| 153 | 20 NUEVOS SOLES | 25.6.1992. Like #152 but printer: IPS–Roma. | FV | FV | 16.00 |

| 154 | 50 NUEVOS SOLES | 1.2.1991; 25.6.1992; 16.6.1994. Brown, deep blue and black on m/c unpt. Bldg. at ctr., A. Valdelomar at r. and as wmk., arms at upper r. Laguna de Huacachina at l. ctr. on back. | FV | FV | 40.00 |

Cat#	Date, denomination	Description	VG	VF	Unc
155	100 NUEVOS SOLES	1.2.1991 (1992); 25.6.1992. Black, blue-black, red-violet and deep green on m/c unpt. Arch monument at ctr., J. Basadre at r. and as wmk., arms at upper r. National Library at l. on back.	FV	FV	70.00

1994 ISSUE
#156 and 157 printer: TDLR.

156	10 NUEVOS SOLES	16.6.1994. Similar to #151 but w/o wmk.	FV	FV	7.50
157	20 NUEVOS SOLES	16.6.1994. Similar to #152.	FV	FV	14.00
158	50 NUEVOS SOLES				Expected new issue.
159	100 NUEVOS SOLES				Expected new issue.

MONETARY EMERGENCY, 1985

Banco de Credito del Peru/Banco Central de Reserva del Peru

| R2 | 100,000 SOLES | 2.9.1985. Black text on lt. blue text unpt. 2 sign. varieties. | 25.00 | 65.00 | — |

Banco de la Nación/Banco Central de Reserva del Peru

CHEQUES CIRCULARES DE GERENCIA ISSUE

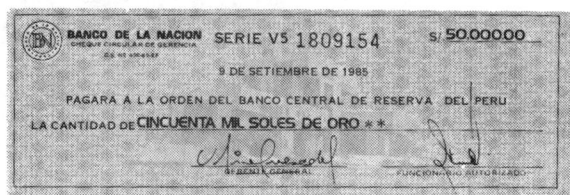

R6	50,000 SOLES	9.9.1985; 16.9.1985. Black text on tan unpt. Bank at ctr.	25.00	65.00	—
R7	100,000 SOLES	2.9.1985. Black text on lt. blue unpt. Like #R6.	25.00	65.00	—
R8	200,000 SOLES	2.9.1985. Black text on pink unpt. Like #R6.	25.00	65.00	—

PHILIPPINES

The Republic of the Philippines, an archipelago in the western Pacific 500 miles (805 km.) from the southeast coast of Asia, has an area of 115,830 sq. mi. (300,000 sq. km.) and a population of 60.9 million. Capital: Manila. The economy of the 7,000-island group is based on agriculture, forestry and fishing. Timber, coconut products, sugar and hemp are exported.

Migration to the Philippines began about 30,000 years ago when land bridges connected the islands with Borneo and Sumatra. Ferdinand Magellan claimed the islands for Spain in 1521. The first permanent settlement was established by Miguel de Legazpi at Cebu in April of 1565; Manila was established in 1572. A British expedition captured Manila and occupied the Spanish colony in Oct. of 1762, but it was returned to Spain by the treaty of Paris, 1763. Spain held the Philippines amid a growing movement of Filipino nationalism until 1898 when they were ceded to the United States of the end of the Spanish-American War. The Filipinos then fought unsuccessfully against the United States to maintain their independent Republic proclaimed by Emilio Aguinaldo. The country became a self-governing commonwealth of the United States in 1935, and attained independence as the Republic of the Philippines on July 4, 1946. During World War II the Japanese had set up a puppet republic, but this quasi-government failed to achieve worldwide recognition. The occupation lasted from late 1941 to 1945.

Ferdinand Marcos lost to Corazón Aquino in elections of 1986. Marcos then fled the country. In 1992 Fidel Ranos was elected President.

MONETARY SYSTEM
1 Peso = 100 Centavos to 1967
1 Piso = 100 Sentimos, 1967–

REPLACEMENT NOTES
#125–127, star following serial number. #132–176, sm. crosslet design instead of prefix letter.

REPUBLIC
Central Bank of the Philippines

1949–66 "ENGLISH" ISSUES

#125–131 fractional notes.

#125–127 Sign. E. Quirino and M. Cuaderno. Printer: SBNC.

Cat#	Date, denomination	Description	VG	VF	Unc
125	5 CENTAVOS	ND. Red on tan unpt. Back red.	.10	.30	1.25
126	10 CENTAVOS	ND. Brownish purple on tan unpt. Back brownish purple.			
		a. Issued note.	.25	.50	2.50
		r. Remainder w/o serial #.	—	100.00	250.00
127	20 CENTAVOS	ND. Green on lt. green unpt. Back green.			
		a. Issued note.	.30	.60	3.50
		r. Remainder w/o serial # (error).	—	100.00	250.00

#128–129 printer: W&S.

128	5 CENTAVOS	ND. LIke #125. Sign. R. Magsaysay and M. Cuaderno.	.10	.25	1.00
129	10 CENTAVOS	ND. LIke #126. Sign. R. Magsaysay and M. Cuaderno.	.10	.25	1.00

#130–131 printer: TDLR.

130	20 CENTAVOS	ND. Green on lt. green unpt. Back green.			
		a. Sign. R. Magsaysay and M. Cuaderno.	.20	.50	2.00
		b. Sign. C. Garcia and M. Cuaderno.	.10	.25	1.00
131	50 CENTAVOS	ND. Blue on lt. blue unpt. Back blue. Sign. R. Magsaysay and M. Cuaderno.	.20	.50	2.25

#132–141 larger notes. Printer: TDLR.

132	1/2 PESO	ND. Green on yellow and blue unpt. Ox-cart w/Mt. Mayon in background at ctr. Back green. Sign. C. Garcia and M. Cuaderno.	.20	.50	2.25

Cat#	Date, denomination	Description	VG	VF	Unc
133	1 PESO	ND. Black on lt. gold and blue unpt. A. Mabini at l. Back black; Barasoain Church at ctr.			
		a. Sign. E. Quirino and M. Cuaderno. *GENUINE* in very lt. tan letters just beneath top heading on face.	7.00	22.00	85.00
		b. Sign. E. Quirino and M. Cuaderno w/o *GENUINE* on face.	.50	1.50	5.00
		c. Sign. R. Magsaysay and M. Cuaderno.	.25	.75	3.00
		d. Sign. C. Garcia and M. Cuaderno.	.25	.75	2.00
		e. Sign. C. Garcia and A. Castillo w/title: *Acting Governor.*	.50	1.00	3.50
		f. Sign. D. Macapagal and A. Castillo w/title: *Governor.*	.20	.60	1.25
		g. Sign. F. Marcos and A. Castillo.	.25	.75	2.00
		h. Sign. F. Marcos and A. Calalang.	.10	.30	1.00
		s. Sign. as f. Specimen.	—	—	55.00
134	2 PESOS	ND. Black on blue and gold unpt. J. Rizal at l. Back blue; Landing of Magellan in the Philippines.			
		a. Sign. E. Quirino and M. Cuaderno.	1.00	4.00	15.00
		b. Sign. R. Magsaysay and M. Cuaderno.	.75	2.00	5.00
		c. Sign. C. Garcia and A. Castillo w/title: *Acting Governor.*	.75	1.50	4.00
		d. Sign. D. Macapagal and A. Castillo w/title: *Governor.*	.15	.50	1.50
		s1. Sign. as b. Specimen.	—	—	60.00
		s2. Sign. as d. Specimen.	—	—	60.00

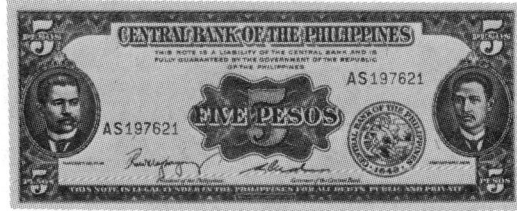

135	5 PESOS	ND. Black on yellow and gold unpt. M.H. del Pilar at l., Graciano Lopez Jaena at r. Back gold; newspaper "La Solidaridad".			
		a. Sign. E. Quirino and M. Cuaderno.	2.00	7.50	25.00
		b. Sign. R. Magsaysay and M. Cuaderno.	1.00	3.50	10.00
		c. Sign. C. Garcia and M. Cuaderno.	1.50	4.00	15.00
		d. Sign. C. Garcia and A. Castillo w/title: *Acting Governor.*	1.25	3.00	12.00
		e. Sign. D. Macapagal and A. Castillo w/title: *Governor.*	.20	.40	1.25
		f. Sign. F. Marcos and G. Licaros.	.20	.40	1.25
		s. Sign. as e. Specimen.	—	—	65.00

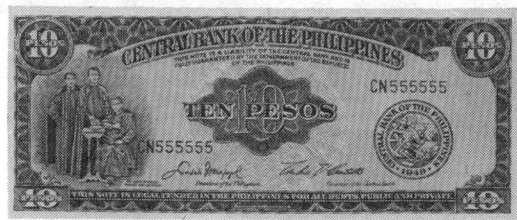

136	10 PESOS	ND. Black on tan and lt. red unpt. Fathers Burgos, Gomez and Zamora at l. Back brown; monument.			
		a. Sign. E. Quirino and M. Cuaderno.	8.00	25.00	75.00
		b. Sign. R. Magsaysay and M. Cuaderno.	2.50	7.00	20.00
		c. Sign. C. Garcia and M. Cuaderno.	3.00	7.50	22.50
		d. Sign. C. Garcia and A. Castillo w/title: *Acting Governor.*	2.50	7.00	17.50
		e. Sign. D. Macapagal and A. Castillo w/title: *Governor.*	.25	.75	2.25
		f. Sign. F. Marcos and G. Licaros.	1.00	2.50	7.50
		s1. Sign. as b. Specimen.	—	—	70.00
		s2. Sign. as d. Specimen.	—	—	70.00

137	20 PESOS	ND. Black on yellow unpt. A. Bonifacio at l., E. Jacinto at r. Back brownish orange; flag and monument.			

Cat#	Date, denomination	Description	VG	VF	Unc
		a. Sign. E. Quirino and M. Cuaderno.	10.00	30.00	85.00
		b. Sign. R. Magsaysay and M. Cuaderno.	2.75	8.00	25.00
		c. Sign. C. Garcia and A. Castillo w/title: *Acting Governor.*	2.25	7.00	20.00
		d. Sign. D. Macapagal and A. Castillo w/title: *Governor.*	.50	1.50	4.50
		e. Sign. F. Marcos and G. Licaros.	.35	1.00	3.00
		s1. Sign. as a. Specimen.	—	—	100.00
		s2. Sign. as d. Specimen.	—	—	75.00

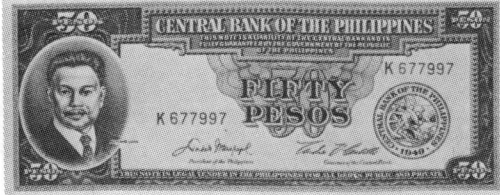

138	50 PESOS	ND. Black on pink and lt. tan unpt. A. Luna at l. Back red; scene of blood compact of Sikatuna and Legaspi.			
		a. Sign. E. Quirino and M. Cuaderno.	50.00	170.00	—
		b. Sign. R. Magsaysay and M. Cuaderno.	20.00	45.00	90.00
		c. Sign. C. Garcia and M. Cuaderno.	8.00	20.00	40.00
		d. Sign. D. Macapagal and A. Castillo.	.65	2.00	6.00
		s. Sign. as d. Specimen.	—	—	85.00

139	100 PESOS	ND. Black on gold unpt. T. Sora at l. Back yellow; regimental flags. Sign. E. Quirino and M. Cuaderno.	1.65	5.00	15.00

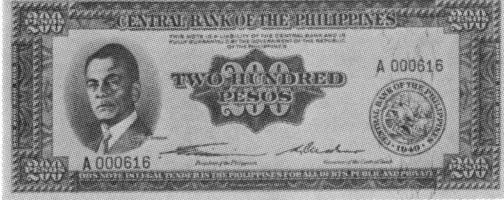

140	200 PESOS	ND. Green on pink and lt. blue unpt. Pres. Manuel Quezon at l. Back green; Legislative bldg. Sign. E. Quirino and M. Cuaderno.	2.75	8.00	25.00

141	500 PESOS	ND. Black on purple and lt. tan unpt. Pres. Manuel Roxas at l. Back purple; Central Bank. Sign. E. Quirino and M. Cuaderno.	7.00	20.00	65.00

Bangko Sentral ng Pilipinas
1969 "PILIPINO" ISSUE

#142–147 heading at top in double outline. Wmk. as portr.

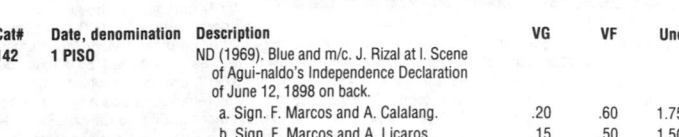

Cat#	Date, denomination	Description	VG	VF	Unc
142	1 PISO	ND (1969). Blue and m/c. J. Rizal at l. Scene of Agui-naldo's Independence Declaration of June 12, 1898 on back.			
		a. Sign. F. Marcos and A. Calalang.	.20	.60	1.75
		b. Sign. F. Marcos and A. Licaros.	.15	.50	1.50

#143–145 printer: G&D (w/o imprint).

143	5 PISO	ND (1969). Green and brown on m/c unpt. A. Bonifacio at l. in brown. Scene of the Katipunan organization on back.			
		a. Sign. F. Marcos and A. Calalang.	.50	1.50	4.50
		b. Sign. F. Marcos and G. Licaros.	.20	.60	1.75
		s. Sign. as b. Specimen.	—	—	15.00

144	10 PISO	ND (1969). Brown on m/c unpt. A. Mabini at l. Barasoain Church on back.			
		a. Sign. F. Marcos and A. Calalang.	.50	1.65	5.00
		b. Sign. F. Marcos and G. Licaros.	.50	1.65	5.00
		s. Sign. as b. Specimen.	—	—	20.00

Cat#	Date, denomination	Description	VG	VF	Unc
145	20 PISO	ND (1969). Orange and brown on m/c unpt. M.L. Quezon at l. in brown. Malakanyang Palace on back.			
		a. Sign. F. Marcos and A. Calalang.	.80	2.50	7.50
		b. Sign. F. Marcos and G. Licaros.	.80	2.50	7.50
		s. Sign. as b. Specimen.	—	—	25.00

Cat#	Date, denomination	Description	VG	VF	Unc
151	50 PISO	ND. Red on m/c unpt. Similar to #146. Seal under denomination instead of over, sign. closer, *LIMAMPUNG PISO* in one line, and other modifications.			
		a. Issued note.	3.00	8.00	25.00
		s. Specimen.	—	—	50.00

146	50 PISO	ND (1969). Red on m/c unpt. S. Osmeña at l. Legislative bldg. on back.			
		a. Sign. F. Marcos and A. Calalang.	1.35	4.00	12.00
		b. Sign. F. Marcos and G. Licaros.	1.35	4.00	12.00
		s. Sign. as b. Specimen.	—	—	30.00

#152–158 light, fully detailed bank seal w/ovpt: *ANG BAGONG LIPUNAN* **(New Society) on wmk. area, 1974–85.**

147	100 PISO	ND (1969). Purple on m/c unpt. M. Roxas at l. Old Central Bank on back.			
		a. Sign. F. Marcos and A. Calalang.	2.50	7.50	21.50
		b. Sign. F. Marcos and G. Licaros.	2.50	7.50	21.50

#148–151 heading at top in single outline. Sign. F. Marcos and G. Licaros.

148	5 PISO	ND. Green on m/c unpt. Like #143 but A. Bonifacio in green.			
		a. Issued note.	.25	.75	2.25
		s. Specimen.	—	—	20.00
149	10 PISO	ND. Brown on m/c unpt. Like #144 but w/o white paper showing at sides on face or back.			
		a. Issued note.	.25	.75	2.25
		s. Specimen.	—	—	30.00

152	2 PISO	ND. Blue on m/c unpt. J. Rizal at l., his wmk. at r. Scene of Aguinaldo's Independence Declaration of 1898 on back. Sign. F. Marcos and G. Licaros.			
		a. Issued note.	.20	.40	1.25
153	5 PISO	ND. Green on m/c unpt. Like #148. Sign. F. Marcos and G. Licaros.			
		a. Issued note.	.50	1.00	2.00
		s. Specimen.	—	—	15.00
154	10 PISO	ND. Brown on m/c unpt. Like #149. Sign. F. Marcos and G. Licaros.			
		a. Issued note.	.30	.90	1.75
		s. Specimen.	—	—	25.00
155	20 PISO	ND. Orange on m/c unpt. Like #150. Sign. F. Marcos and G. Licaros.			
		a. Issued note.	1.50	3.00	6.00
		s. Specimen.	—	—	35.00
156	50 PISO	ND. Red on m/c unpt. Like #151. Sign. F. Marcos and G. Licaros.			
		a. Issued note.	5.00	10.00	30.00
		s. Specimen.	—	—	45.00

150	20 PISO	ND. Orange and blue on m/c unpt. Like #145 but M.L. Quezon in orange.			
		a. Issued note.	.25	.75	2.25
		s. Specimen.	—	—	40.00

157	100 PISO	ND. Purple on m/c unpt. Like #147. Bank seal in purple at l.			
		a. Sign. F. Marcos and A. Calalang.	14.00	27.50	65.00
		b. Sign. F. Marcos and G. Licaros.	2.50	7.50	22.50

Cat#	Date, denomination	Description	VG	VF	Unc
158	100 PISO	ND. Purple on m/c unptc. Face resembling #157 but heading at top in single outline, green bank seal at lower r., and denomination near upper r. Back similar to #157 but denomination at bottom. Sign. F. Marcos and G. Licaros.			
		a. Issued note.	12.00	25.00	55.00
		s. Specimen.	—	—	100.00

#159–167 w/dk. silhouette bank seal.

Cat#	Date, denomination	Description	VG	VF	Unc
159	2 PISO	ND. Blue on m/c unpt. Like #152.			
		a. Sign. F. Marcos and G. Licaros.	.10	.30	1.00
		b. Sign. F. Marcos and J. Laya, w/black serial #.	.10	.30	1.00
		c. Sign. F. Marcos and J. Laya, w/red serial #.	.10	.30	1.00
		d. Sign. as b. Uncut sheet of 4.	—	—	15.00
		s. Sign. as b. Specimen.	—	—	15.00
160	5 PISO	ND. Green on m/c unpt. Like #153.			
		a. Sign. F. Marcos and G. Licaros.	.15	.40	1.50
		b. Sign. F. Marcos and J. Laya, w/black serial #.	.15	.40	1.50
		c. Sign. F. Marcos and J. Laya, w/red serial #.	.15	.40	1.50
		d. Sign. F. Marcos and J. Fernandez.	.15	.50	2.00
		e. Sign. as b. Uncut sheet of 4.	—	—	30.00
		f. Sign. as d. Uncut sheet of 4.	—	—	30.00
		s. Sign. as b. Specimen.	—	—	20.00

Cat#	Date, denomination	Description	VG	VF	Unc
161	10 PISO	ND. Brown on m/c unpt. Like #154.			
		a. Sign. F. Marcos and G. Licaros.	.30	1.00	2.50
		b. Sign. F. Marcos and J. Laya.	.25	.75	2.50
		c. Sign. F. Marcos and J. Fernandez, w/black serial #.	.20	.50	2.00
		d. Sign. F. Marcos and J. Fernandez, w/red serial #.	.20	.50	2.00
		e. Sign. as b. Uncut sheet of 4.	—	—	37.50
		f. Sign. as c. Uncut sheet of 4.	—	—	37.50
		s. Sign. as b. Specimen.	—	—	25.00
162	20 PISO	ND. Orange and blue on m/c unpt. Like #155.			
		a. Sign. F. Marcos and G. Licaros.	.30	1.00	3.00
		b. Sign. F. Marcos and J. Laya.	.30	1.00	3.00

Cat#	Date, denomination	Description	VG	VF	Unc
		c. Sign. F. Marcos and J. Fernandez.	.30	1.00	3.00
		d. Sign. as b. Uncut sheet of 4.	—	—	40.00
		e. Sign. as d. Uncut sheet of 4.	—	—	40.00
		s. Sign. as b. Specimen.	—	—	30.00
163	50 PISO	ND. Red on m/c unpt. Like #156.			
		a. Sign. F. Marcos and G. Licaros.	.50	1.50	4.50
		b. Sign. F. Marcos and J. Laya.	.50	1.50	4.50
		c. Sign. F. Marcos and J. Fernandez.	.50	1.50	4.50
		s. Sign. as b. Specimen.	—	—	35.00

Cat#	Date, denomination	Description	VG	VF	Unc
164	100 PISO	ND. Purple on m/c unpt. Face like #158. New Central Bank complex, w/ships behind on back.			
		a. Sign. F. Marcos and G. Licaros.	3.00	8.00	20.00
		b. Sign. F. Marcos and J. Laya.	2.50	7.00	18.00
		c. Sign. F. Marcos and J. Fernandez, w/black serial #.	.80	2.50	7.50
		s. Sign. as b. Specimen.	—	—	40.00

COMMEMORATIVE ISSUES

#165, Centennial Birth of Pres. Osmeña, 1978

Cat#	Date, denomination	Description	VG	VF	Unc
165	50 PISO	1978. Like #163a but w/black circular commemorative ovpt. at l.	2.25	7.00	15.00

#166, Papal Visit of John Paul II, 1981

Cat#	Date, denomination	Description	VG	VF	Unc
166	2 PISO	1981. Like #159b but w/black commemorative ovpt. at ctr. r.			
		a. Regular prefix letters before serial #.	.10	.35	1.00
		b. Special JP prefix letters and all zero numbers (presentation).	—	—	—

#167, Inauguration of Pres. Marcos, 1981

Cat#	Date, denomination	Description	VG	VF	Unc
167	10 PISO	1981. Like #161b but w/black commemorative ovpt. at ctr. r.			
		a. Regular prefix letters before serial #.	.25	.75	2.25
		b. Special FM prefix letters and all zero numbers (presentation).	—	—	20.00

1985–87 ISSUE

#168–173 portr. as wmk.

Cat#	Date, denomination	Description	VG	VF	Unc
168	5 PISO	ND (1985–). Deep green on m/c unpt. Aguinaldo at l. ctr., plaque w/cannon at r. Declaration of Independence (1898) on back.			
		a. Sign. F. Marcos and J. Fernandez.	FV	FV	2.00
		b. Sign. C. Aquino and J. Fernandez, w/black serial #.	FV	FV	1.00
		c. Sign. as b. w/red serial # (1990).	FV	FV	.75
		d. Sign. C. Aquino and J. Cuisia Jr. (1990–).	FV	FV	.75
		e. Sign. Ramos and J. Cuisia Jr.	FV	FV	.65
		f. Sign. as b. Uncut sheet of 4.	—	—	30.00
		g. Sign. as d. Uncut sheet of 4.	—	—	30.00
		h. Sign. as e. Uncut sheet of 4.	—	—	15.00
		s. Sign. as b. Specimen.	—	—	15.00
		s1. Sign. as b. Specimen.	—	—	15.00
		s2. Sign. as d. Specimen.	—	—	20.00

Cat#	Date, denomination	Description	VG	VF	Unc
169	10 PISO	ND (1985–). Dk. brown and blue-gray on m/c unpt. Mabini at l. ctr., handwritten scroll at r. Barasoain church on back.			
		a. Sign. F. Marcos and J. Fernandez.	FV	FV	2.50
		b. Sign. C. Aquino and J. Fernandez.	FV	FV	1.25
		c. Sign. C. Aquino and J. Cuisia Jr. w/black serial #.	FV	FV	1.50
		d. Sign. Ramos and J. Cuisia Jr.	FV	FV	1.25
		e. Sign. as c. w/red serial #.	FV	FV	1.25
		f. Sign. as b. Uncut sheet of 4.	—	—	38.50
		s. Sign. as b. Specimen.	—	—	25.00

Cat#	Date, denomination	Description	VG	VF	Unc
170	20 PISO	ND (1986–). Orange and blue on m/c unpt. Pres. M. Quezon at l. ctr., arms at r. Malakanyang Palace on back.			
		a. Sign. F. Marcos and J. Fernandez.	FV	FV	3.00
		b. Sign. C. Aquino and J. Fernandez.	FV	FV	2.75
		c. Sign. C. Aquino and J. Cuisia Jr. w/black serial #.	FV	FV	2.50
		d. Sign. as c. w/red serial #.	FV	FV	2.25
		e. Sign. Ramos and J. Cuisia Jr.	FV	FV	2.00
		f. Sign. as b. Uncut sheet of 4.	—	—	45.00
		s. Sign. as b. Specimen.	—	—	35.00

Cat#	Date, denomination	Description	VG	VF	Unc
171	50 PISO	ND (1987–). Red on m/c unpt. Pres. S. Osmeña at l. ctr., and gavel at r. Legislative bldg. on back.			
		a. Sign. C. Aquino and J. Fernandez.	FV	FV	3.50
		b. Sign. C. Aquino and J. Cuisia Jr.	FV	FV	2.75
		c. Sign. Ramos and J. Cuisia Jr.	FV	FV	2.50
		s1. Sign. as a. Specimen.	—	—	45.00
		s2. Sign. as b. Specimen.	—	—	9.00
		s3. Sign. as db Specimen. Uncut sheet of 4.	—	—	30.00
		s4. Sign. as a. Specimen.	—	—	45.00

Cat#	Date, denomination	Description	VG	VF	Unc
172	100 PISO	ND (1987–). Purple on m/c unpt. Pres. M. Roxas at l. ctr., US and Philippine flags at r. New Central Bank complex on back.			
		a. Sign. C. Aquino and J. Fernandez.	FV	FV	7.00
		b. Sign. C. Aquino and J. Cuisia Jr. w/ black serial #.	FV	FV	6.00
		c. Sign. as b. w/red serial #.	FV	FV	5.00
		d. Sign. Ramos and J. Cursia Jr.	FV	FV	5.00
		s1. Sign. as a. Specimen.	—	—	15.00
		s2. Sign. as b. Specimen.	—	—	13.50
		s3. Sign. as c. Specimen.	—	—	15.00
		s4. Sign. as d. Specimen.	—	—	25.00
		s5. Sign. as d. Uncut sheet of 4. Specimen.	—	—	25.00
		s6. Sign. as b. Specimen. Uncut sheet of 4.	—	—	47.50
		s7. Sign. as b. Specimen. Uncut sheet of 32.	—	—	350.00

Cat#	Date, denomination	Description	VG	VF	Unc
173	500 PISO	ND (1987–94). Black on m/c unpt. Benigno Aquino and flag at ctr., typewriter at lower r. Various scenes and gatherings of Aquino's career on back.			
		a. Sign. C. Aquino and J. Fernandez.	FV	FV	35.00
		b. Sign. C. Aquino and J. Cuisia Jr.	FV	FV	32.50
		c. Sign. Ramos and J. Cuisia Jr.	FV	FV	30.00
		s1. Sign. as a. Specimen.	—	—	55.00
		s2. Sign. as b. Specimen.	—	—	25.00
		s3. Sign. as b. Specimen. Uncut sheet of 4.	—	—	90.00
174	1000 PISO	ND (1991–94). Dk. blue on m/c unpt. J. A. Santos, Josefa L. Escoda and V. Lim at l. ctr. and as wmk. Flaming torch at r. Banawe rice terraces at l. to ctr., local carving and hut at ctr. r. on back.			
		a. Sign. C. Aquino and J. Cuisia Jr..	FV	FV	62.50
		b. Sign. Ramos and J. Cuisia Jr.	FV	FV	50.00

COMMEMORATIVE ISSUES

#175–179 uncut sheets of 4 or 8 subjects exist for certain commemorative issues.

#175, visit of Pres. Aquino to the United States

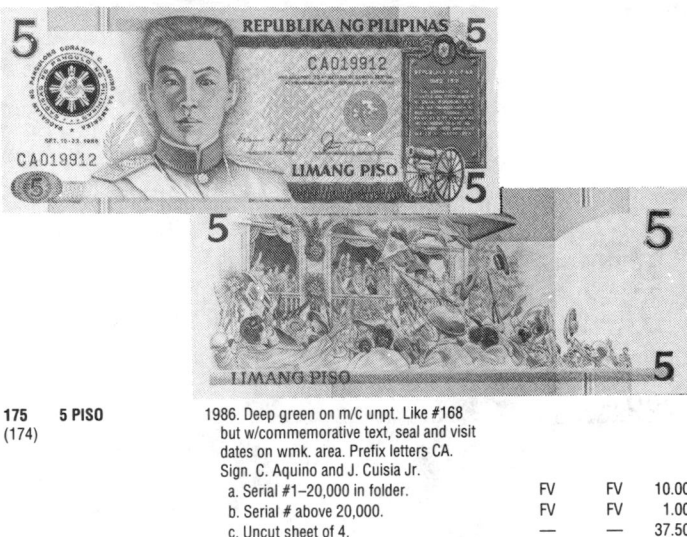

175 (174)	5 PISO	1986. Deep green on m/c unpt. Like #168 but w/commemorative text, seal and visit dates on wmk. area. Prefix letters CA. Sign. C. Aquino and J. Cuisia Jr.			
		a. Serial #1–20,000 in folder.	FV	FV	10.00
		b. Serial # above 20,000.	FV	FV	1.00
		c. Uncut sheet of 4.	—	—	37.50

#176, Canonization of San Lorenzo Ruiz

176 (175)	5 PISO	18.10.1987. Deep green on m/c unpt. Like #168 but w/commemorative design, text and date on wmk. area.			
		a. Issued note.	FV	FV	1.25
		c. Uncut sheet of 8.	FV	FV	16.00

#177, 40th Anniversary of Central Bank

Cat#	Date, denomination	Description	VG	VF	Unc
177	5 PISO	1989.Deep green on m/c unpt. Like #168 but w/red commemorative design, text and date on wmk. area.			
		a. Issued note.	FV	FV	1.00
		b. Uncut sheet of 8 in folder.	FV	FV	20.00

#178, Women's Rights 1990

178	5 PISO	1990. Like #168 but w/black commemorative design on wmk. area.	FV	FV	1.00

#179, II Plenary Council, 1991

179	5 PISO	1991. Like #168 but w/black commemorative design and date on wmk. area.	FV	FV	1.00

1995 ISSUE

#180–186 like #168 but w/redesigned Central Bank seal at r. Sign. Ramos and G. Singson.

180	5 PISO	ND (1995–). Dk. brown on m/c unpt.	FV	FV	1.00
181	10 PISO	ND (1995–). Dk. brown and blue-gray on m/c unpt.	FV	FV	1.85
182	20 PISO	ND (1995–). Orange and blue on m/c unpt.			
		a. Issued note.	FV	FV	3.50
		s. Uncut sheet of 4.	FV	FV	100.00
183	50 PISO	ND (1995–). Red on m/c unpt.	FV	FV	8.00
184	100 PISO	ND (1995–). Purple on m/c unpt.	FV	FV	15.00
185	500 PISO	ND (1995–). Black on m/c unpt.	FV	FV	28.50
186	1000 PISO	ND (1995–) Dk. blue on m/c unpt.	FV	FV	57.50

COLLECTOR SERIES

Cat. #	Date, denomination	Description	Issue Price	Mkt. Val.
CS1	1978 2–100 PISO	#159–164 ovpt: *SPECIMEN* and w/Maltese cross prefix serial #.	14.00	30.00

POLAND

The Republic of Poland, formerly the Polish Peoples Republic, located in central Europe, has an area of 120,725 sq. mi. (312,677 sq. km.) and a population of 38 million. Capital: Warsaw. The economy is essentially agricultural, but industrial activity provides the products for foreign trade. Machinery, coal, coke, iron, steel and transport equipment are exported.

Poland, which began as a Slavic duchy in the 10th century and reached its peak of power between the 14th and 16th centuries, has had a turbulent history of invasion, occupation or partition by Mongols, Turkey, Hungary, Sweden, Austria, Prussia and Russia.

The first partition took place in 1772. Prussia took Polish Pomerania. Russia took part of the eastern provinces. Austria took Galicia, in which lay the fortress city of Krakow (Cracow). The second partition occurred in 1793 when Russia took another slice of the eastern provinces and Prussia took what remained of western Poland. The third partition, 1795, literally removed Poland from the map. Russia took what was left of the eastern provinces. Prussia seized most of central Poland, including Warsaw. Austria took what was left of the south. Napoleon restored to Poland much of the territory lost to Prussia and Austria, but after his defeat another partition returned the Duchy of Warsaw to Prussia, made Kracow into a tiny republic, and declared what remained to be the Kingdom of Poland under the czar and in permanent union with Russia.

Poland re-emerged as an independent state recognized by the Treaty of Versailles on June 28, 1919, and maintained its independence until 1939 when it was invaded by, and partitioned between Germany and Russia. Poland's present boundaries were determined by the U.S.-British-Russian agreement of Aug. 16, 1945. The Polish Communist-Socialist faction won a decisive victory at the polls in 1947 and established a "People's Republic" of the Soviet type in 1952. In Dec. 1989, Poland became a republic once again.

MONETARY SYSTEM

1 Zloty = 100 Groszy

PEOPLES REPUBLIC

Narodowy Bank Polski – Polish National Bank

1948 ISSUE

#134–140 arms on face.

Cat#	Date, denomination	Description	VG	VF	Unc
134	2 ZLOTE	1.7.1948. Dk. olive green on lt. olive and lt. orange unpt. Bldg. on back. 2 serial # varieties.	.15	.65	2.50
135	5 ZLOTYCH	1.7.1948. Red-brown on brown and red-brown unpt. Farmer plowing on back. 2 serial # varieties. Wmk: Woman.	.50	1.25	5.00
136	10 ZLOTYCH	1.7.1948. Brown on lt. brown and lt. red unpt. Man at r. Stacking hay on back. 2 serial # varieties. Wmk: Woman.	.40	1.25	5.00
137	20 ZLOTYCH	1.7.1948. Dk. blue on lt. blue and lt. red unpt. Woman wearing a head scarf at r. Ornate bldg. on back. 4 serial # varieties.	.30	1.00	4.00

138	50 ZLOTYCH	1.7.1948. Green on lt. green and olive unpt. Sailor at r. Ships at dockside on back. 4 serial # varieties. Wmk: Woman.	.40	1.25	5.00

Cat#	Date, denomination	Description	VG	VF	Unc
139	100 ZLOTYCH	1.7.1948. Red on lt. red and m/c unpt. Man at r. Factory on back. 3 serial # varieties. Wmk: Woman.			

#139a   #139b

a. *100* in ctr. guilloche w/fine line around edge. Buff or white paper.	.75	2.25	6.50
b. *100* in ctr. guilloche w/o fine line around edge. Series GF.	3.00	10.00	30.00
140	500 ZLOTYCH	1.7.1948. Dk. brown on lt. brown and m/c unpt. Coal miner at r. Coal miners on back. 2 serial # varieties. Wmk: Woman.			
			.50	2.00	8.00

1965 ISSUE

141	1000 ZLOTYCH	1962; 1965. M/c. Copernicus at ctr. r. and as wmk., eagle at upper r. Zodiac signs in ornate sphere on back.			
		a. Issued note. 29.10.1965.	.85	3.00	12.50
		s1. Specimen ovpt: *WZOR.* 24.5.1962. (Not issued).	—	—	120.00
		s2. Specimen ovpt: *WZOR.* 29.10.1965.	—	—	40.00

1974–77 ISSUE

#142–147 eagle arms at lower ctr. or lower r. and as wmk. Sign. varieties.

Cat. #	Denomination	Date, description	VG	VF	Unc
142	50 ZLOTYCH	1975–88. Olive-green on m/c unpt. K. Swierczewski at ctr. Cross at l. on back.			
		a. 9.5.1975.	.10	.25	2.50
		b. 1.6.1979; 1.6.1982.	.05	.20	1.00
		c. 1.6.1986; 1.12.1988.	.05	.10	.50
		s1. Specimen ovpt: *WZOR*. 1975; 1986; 1988.	—	—	8.50
		s2. Specimen ovpt: *WZOR*. 1979.	—	—	7.00
		s3. Specimen ovpt: *WZOR*. 1982.	—	—	11.50

Cat. #	Denomination	Date, description	VG	VF	Unc
143	100 ZLOTYCH	1975–86. Brown on lilac and m/c unpt. L. Warynski at r. Old paper on back.			
		a. 15.1.1975; 17.5.1976.	.15	.50	3.00
		b. 1.6.1979; 1.6.1982.	.05	.20	1.00
		c. 1.6.1986; 1.12.1988.	.05	.10	.50
		s1. Specimen ovpt: *WZOR*. 1975; 1982.	—	—	8.50
		s2. Specimen ovpt: *WZOR*. 1976.	—	—	7.00
		s3. Specimen ovpt: *WZOR*. 1979.	—	—	11.50

Cat. #	Denomination	Date, description	VG	VF	Unc
144	200 ZLOTYCH	1976–88. Purple on orange and m/c unpt. J. Dabrowski at r. Standing woman at wall on back.			
		a. 25.5.1976.	.20	.75	3.00
		b. 1.6.1979; 1.6.1982.	FV	FV	1.00
		c. 1.6.1986; 1.12.1988.	FV	FV	.60
		s1. Specimen ovpt: *WZOR*. 1976; 1986.	—	—	8.50
		s2. Specimen ovpt: *WZOR*. 1979.	—	—	7.00
		s3. Specimen ovpt: *WZOR*. 1982.	—	—	11.50

Cat. #	Denomination	Date, description	VG	VF	Unc
145	500 ZLOTYCH	1974–82. Brown on tan and m/c unpt. T. Kosciuszko at ctr. Arms and flag on back.			
		a. 16.12.1974; 15.6.1976.	.75	2.25	8.50
		b. 1.6.1979.	.20	.65	2.00

Cat. #	Denomination	Date, description	VG	VF	Unc
		c. 1.6.1982.	.10	.25	.85
		s1. Specimen ovpt: *WZOR*. 1974; 1976.	—	—	8.50
		s2. Specimen ovpt: *WZOR*. 1979.	—	—	7.00
		s3. Specimen ovpt: *WZOR*. 1982.	—	—	11.50

Cat. #	Denomination	Date, description	VG	VF	Unc
146	1000 ZLOTYCH	1975–82. Blue on olive and m/c unpt. Copernicus at r. Atomic symbols on back.			
		a. 2.7.1975.	.75	2.25	8.50
		b. 1.6.1979.	.40	1.35	4.00
		c. 1.6.1982.	.15	.40	1.50
		s1. Specimen ovpt: *WZOR*. 1975; 1982.	—	—	11.50
		s2. Specimen ovpt: *WZOR*. 1979.	—	—	7.00

POLSKA RZECZPOSPOLITA LUDOWA
REPUBLIC OF POLAND
Narodowy Bank Polski

Cat. #	Denomination	Date, description	VG	VF	Unc
147	2000 ZLOTYCH	1977–82. Dk. green and dk. brown. Mieszko I at r. B. Chrobry on back.			
		a. 1.5.1977.	.75	2.25	8.00
		b. 1.6.1979.	.30	1.00	3.00
		c. 1.6.1982.	.20	.65	2.00
		s1. Specimen ovpt: *WZOR*. 1977.	—	—	11.50
		s2. Specimen ovpt: *WZOR*. 1979.	—	—	7.00
		s3. Specimen ovpt: *WZOR*. 1982.	—	—	15.00

1982 ISSUE

#148–149 wmk. pattern in paper.

Cat. #	Denomination	Date, description	VG	VF	Unc
148	10 ZLOTYCH	1.6.1982. Blue, green and m/c. J. Bem at l. ctr.			
		a. Issued note.	.10	.30	1.00
		s. Specimen ovpt: *WZOR.*	—	—	11.50

149	20 ZLOTYCH	1.6.1982. Brown, purple and m/c. R. Traugutt at l. ctr.			
		a. Issued note.	.05	.10	.35
		s. Specimen ovpt: *WZOR.*	—	—	11.50

150	5000 ZLOTYCH	1982–88. Black, purple and dk. green on m/c unpt. F. Chopin at r. Arms at lower ctr. and as wmk. *Polonaise* music score on back.			
		a. 1.6.1982.	.25	1.00	4.00
		b. 1.6.1986.	FV	.75	3.00
		c. 1.12.1988.	FV	FV	2.50
		s. Specimen ovpt: *WZOR.*	—	—	13.50

1987–92 ISSUE

#151–158 arms at lower ctr. or lower r. and as wmk.

151	10,000 ZLOTYCH	1.2.1987; 1.12.1988. Black and red on m/c unpt. S. Wyspianski at l. ctr. Trees and city scene on back.			
		a. Issued note.	FV	.50	3.00
		s. Specimen ovpt: *WZOR.*	—	—	8.50

Cat. #	Denomination	Date, description	VG	VF	Unc
152	20,000 ZLOTYCH	1.2.1989. Dk. brown on tan and gold unpt. M. Curie at r. Scientific instrument on back.			
		a. Issued note.	FV	1.35	4.00
		s. Specimen ovpt: *WZOR.*	—	—	7.00

153	50,000 ZLOTYCH	1.12.1989. Dk. brown and greenish-black on m/c unpt. S. Staszic at l. ctr. Staszic Palace in Warsaw on back.			
		a. Issued note.	FV	2.50	4.50
		s. Specimen ovpt: *WZOR.*	—	—	8.50

154	100,000 ZLOTYCH	1.2.1990. Black and grayish-purple on m/c unpt. S. Moniuszko at r. Warsaw Theatre at l. on back.			
		a. Issued note.	FV	5.50	7.50
		s. Specimen ovpt: *WZOR.*	—	—	11.50
155	200,000 ZLOTYCH	1.12.1989. Dk. purple and red on lt. brown and m/c unpt. Arms at r. Back purple on brown unpt.; view of Warsaw.			
		a. Issued note.	1.50	11.00	30.00
		s. Specimen ovpt: *WZOR.*	—	—	15.00

RZECZPOSPOLITA POLSKA
REPUBLIC OF POLAND

Cat. #	Denomination	Date, description	VG	VF	Unc
156	500,000 ZLOTYCH	20.4.1990. Dk. blue-green and black on m/c unpt. H. Sienkiewicz at l. ctr. Shield w/3 books, also 2 flags, on back.			
		a. Issued note.	FV	25.00	35.00
		s. Specimen ovpt: WZOR.	—	—	37.50
157	1 MILLION ZLOTYCH	15.2.1991. Brown-violet, purple and red on m/c unpt. W. Reymont at r. Tree w/rural landscape in background on back.			
		a. Issued note.	FV	45.00	65.00
		s. Specimen ovpt: WZOR.	—	—	70.00

Cat. #	Denomination	Date, description	VG	VF	Unc
158	2 MILLION ZLOTYCH	14.8.1992. Black and deep brown-violet on m/c unpt. I. Paderewski at l. ctr. Imperial eagle at l. on back.			
		a. Issued note, misspelling KONSTY-TUCYJY on back. Series A.	—	—	200.00
		b. As a., but corrected spelling KONSTY-TUCYJNY on back. Series B.	FV	90.00	110.00
		s. Specimen ovpt: WZOR.	—	—	135.00

1993 ISSUE

#159–163 similar to #153, 154, 156–158 but modified w/color in wmk. area, eagle w/crown. Wmk: Eagle's head.

Cat. #	Denomination	Date, description	VG	VF	Unc
159	50,000 ZLOTYCH	16.11.1993. Dk. blue-green and black on m/c unpt. Similar to #156.			
		a. Issued note.	FV	3.00	6.50
		s. Specimen ovpt: WZOR.	—	—	—
160	100,000 ZLOTYCH	16.11.1993. Black and grayish-purple on m/c unpt. Similar to #154.			
		a. Issued note.	FV	6.50	10.00
		s. Specimen ovpt: WZOR.	—	—	—
161	500,000 ZLOTYCH	16.11.1993. Dk. blue-green and black on m/c unpt. Similar to #156.			
		a. Issued note.	FV	27.50	40.00
		s. Specimen ovpt: WZOR.	—	—	—

Cat. #	Denomination	Date, description	VG	VF	Unc
162	1 MILLION ZLOTYCH	16.11.1993. Brown-violet, purple and red on m/c unpt. Similar to #157.			
		a. Issued note.	FV	47.50	70.00
		s. Specimen ovpt: WZOR.	—	—	—
163	2 MILLION ZLOTYCH	16.11.1993. Black and deep brown on m/c unpt. Similar to #158.			
		a. Issued note.	FV	95.00	125.00
		s. Specimen ovpt: WZOR.	—	—	—

Currency Reform, 1995

1 "new" Zlotych = 10,000 "old" Zlotych

1994 DATED ISSUE

#164–166 crowned eagle at upper r.

Cat. #	Denomination	Date, description	VG	VF	Unc
164 (159)	10 ZLOTYCH	25.3.1994. Dk. brown, brown and olive-green on m/c unpt. Prince Mieszko I at ctr. r. Medieval coin at l. ctr. on back.			
		a. Issued note.	FV	FV	7.50
		s. Specimen ovpt: WZOR.	—	—	—

Cat. #	Denomination	Date, description	VG	VF	Unc
165 (160)	20 ZLOTYCH	25.3.1994. Purple, and deep blue on m/c unpt. Kg. Boleslaw I at ctr. r. Medieval coin at l. ctr. on back.			
		a. Issued note.	FV	FV	12.50
		s. Specimen.	—	—	—

Cat. #	Denomination	Date, description	VG	VF	Unc
166 (161)	50 ZLOTYCH	25.3.1994. Blue-violet and deep blue and green on m/c unpt. Kg. Kazimierz III at ctr. r. Medallion, orb and sceptre at l. ctr. on back.			
		a. Issued note.	FV	FV	27.50
		s. Specimen.	—	—	—
167 (162)	100 ZLOTYCH	1994. Olive-green on m/c unpt. Wladyslaw II Jagie 110. Teutonic Knights' castle in Malbork on back.			
		a. Issued note.	FV	FV	52.50
		s. Specimen ovpt: *WZOR*.	—	—	—
168 (163)	200 ZLOTYCH	1994. Brown on m/c unpt. Kg. Zygmunt. Eagle in hexagon from the Zygmunt's chapel in the Wawel Cathedral and Wawel's court on back.			
		a. Issued note.	FV	FV	100.00
		s. Specimen ovpt: *WZOR*.	—	—	—

COLLECTOR SERIES

Cat.#	Date, denomination	Description	Issue Price	Mkt. Val.
CS1	1948; 1965 20-1000 ZLOTYCH	#137, 138, 139a, 140 & 141a w/deep red ovpt: *WZOR* on face; normal serial #.	—	75.00

NOTE: Issued in a special booklet by Ministry of Finance.

| CS2 | 1978 20,100 ZLOTYCH | #137, 139a w/dk. blue ovpt: *150 LAT BANKU POL-SKIEGO 1828-1978* on face. | — | 25.00 |

NOTE: Issued in a special booklet.

| CS3 | 1979-92; 20-2 MIL-LION ZLOTYCH | #142-157a, 158a w/red ovpt: *WZOR* on face; all zero serial # and additional black specimen # w/ star suffix. Red ovpt: *SPECIMEN* on back. | — | 300.00 |

NOTE: Originally #CS3 was sold in a special booklet by Pekao Trading Company at its New York City, NY, and Warsaw offices. Currently available only from the Polish Numismatic Society.

PORTUGAL

The Portuguese Republic, located in the western part of the Iberian Peninsula in southwestern Europe, has an area of 35,553 sq. mi. (92,080 sq. km.) and a population of 9.86 million. Capital: Lisbon. Portugal's economy is based on agriculture and a small but expanding industrial sector. Textiles, machinery, chemicals, wine and cork are exported.

After centuries of domination by Romans, Visigoths and Moors, Portugal emerged in the 12th century as an independent kingdom financially and philosophically prepared for the great period of exploration that would follow. Attuned to the inspiration of Prince Henry the Navigator (1394-1460), Portugal's daring explorers of the 14th and 15th centuries roamed the world's oceans from Brazil to Japan in an unprecedented burst of energy and endeavor that culminated in 1494 with Portugal laying claim to half the transoceanic world. Unfortunately for the fortunes of the tiny kingdom, the Portuguese proved to be inept colonizers. Less than a century after Portugal laid claim to half the world, English, French and Dutch trading companies had seized the lion's share of the world's colonies and commerce, and Portugal's place as an imperial power was lost forever. The monarchy was overthrown in 1910 and a republic established.

On April 25, 1974, the government of Portugal was seized by a military junta which reached agreements providing for independence for the Portuguese overseas provinces of Portuguese Guinea (Guinea-Bissau), Mozambique, Cape Verde Islands, Angola, and St. Thomas and Prince Islands (Sao Tome Principe).

MONETARY SYSTEM
1 Escudo = 100 Centavos, 1910-

NOTE: Prata = Silver, Ouro = Gold.

NOTE: This section has been renumbered since the 7th edition of Vol. II "General Issues".

Banco de Portugal

Escudo Ouro System

1960 ISSUE

Cat#	Date, denomination	Description	VG	VF	Unc
163 (69)	20 ESCUDOS	26.7.1960. Ch. 6A. Dk. green and purple. Portr. of D. Antonio Luiz de Menezes at r. and as wmk. Back purple and m/c; bank arms at l.	2.50	7.50	30.00

| 164 (79) | 50 ESCUDOS | 24.6.1960. Ch. 7A. Blue on m/c unpt. Arms at upper ctr. F. Pereira de Mello at r. and as wmk. Back dk. green and m/c; statue as "the Thinker" at l. | 3.00 | 9.00 | 35.00 |

Cat#	Date, denomination	Description	VG	VF	Unc
168 (80)	50 ESCUDOS	28.2.1964. Ch. 8. Brown-violet on pink and m/c unpt. Qn. Isabella at r. and as wmk. Old city Conimbria on back. Sign. title varieties.	.50	1.50	4.50

Cat#	Date, denomination	Description	VG	VF	Unc
165 (87)	100 ESCUDOS	19.12.1961. Ch. 6A. Black and deep violet on pink and m/c unpt. P. Nunes at r. and as wmk. Back lilac; fountain and arches at l. 3 sign. varieties.	2.00	10.00	40.00

Cat#	Date, denomination	Description	VG	VF	Unc
169 (88)	100 ESCUDOS	30.11.1965; 20.9.1978. Ch. 7. Blue and m/c. C. Castello Branco at r. and as wmk. City of Porto in 19th century at l. on back. Sign. title varieties.	1.00	1.50	6.00

Cat#	Date, denomination	Description	VG	VF	Unc
166 (108)	1000 ESCUDOS	30.5.1961. Ch. 8A. Purple on m/c unpt. Qn. at r. and as wmk. Basic design similar to #107 but many stylistic changes. Back blue. Printer: BWC (w/o imprint).	8.50	25.00	100.00

1964–66 ISSUE

Cat#	Date, denomination	Description	VG	VF	Unc
167 (70)	20 ESCUDOS	26.5.1964. Ch. 7. Olive and purple on m/c unpt. S. Antonio at r. and as wmk. Back olive; Church of Santo Antonio de Lisboa at l.			
		a. Olive brown unpt. at l. and r.	.25	.60	4.50
		b. Green unpt. at l. and r.	.25	.60	2.25

Cat#	Date, denomination	Description	VG	VF	Unc
170 (98)	500 ESCUDOS	25.1.1966; 6.9.1979. Ch. 10. Brown and m/c. Old map at ctr., João II at r. and as wmk. Ornate round design and double statue on back. Sign. title varieties. Printer: JEZ (w/o imprint).	FV	5.00	11.00

Cat#	Date, denomination	Description	VG	VF	Unc
171 (109)	1000 ESCUDOS	2.4.1965. Ch. 9. Gray-blue on red-brown and m/c unpt. Pillar at l., arms at upper ctr., D. Diniz at r. and as wmk. Scene of founding of University of Lisbon in 1290 on back. Printer: JEZ (w/o imprint).	25.00	60.00	120.00

1967 ISSUE

Cat#	Date, denomination	Description	VG	VF	Unc
172 (110)	1000 ESCUDOS	19.5.1967. Ch. 10. Blue and violet on m/c unpt. Flowers at l., Qn. Maria II at r. and as wmk. Her medallion portr. at l., Banco de Portugal in 1846 bldg. at lower r. on back. Sign. and sign. title varieties. Printer: JEZ (w/o imprint).	FV	12.00	30.00
175 (111)	1000 ESCUDOS	1968–82. Ch. 11. Blue and m/c. Don Pedro V at ctr. and as wmk. Conjoined busts at l., procession and old train at bottom ctr. and r. on back. Sign. and sign.title varieties. Printer: BWC (w/o imprint).			
		a. 28.5.1968.	FV	10.00	22.50
		b. 16.9.1980; 3.12.1981; 26.10.1982.	FV	FV	18.00

1978–79 DATED ISSUE

1968; 71 DATED ISSUE

| 173 (70A) | 20 ESCUDOS | 27.7.1971. Ch. 8. Gray, green (shades) and lt. brown. D. de Orta at r. and as wmk. Back dk. green and m/c, 18th century market in Goa. Sign. and sign. title varieties. | .25 | .60 | 2.25 |

| 176 (70B) | 20 ESCUDOS | 13.9.1978; 4.10.1978. Green and m/c. Adm. Coutinho at r. and as wmk. Airplane on back. Lg. or sm. size numerals in serial #. Sign. and title varieties. | FV | .50 | 2.25 |

| 174 (80A) | 50 ESCUDOS | 28.5.1968; 1.2.1980. Ch. 9. Brown and m/c. Arms at l., D. Maria at r. and as wmk. Sintra in 1507 on back. Sign. varieties | FV | FV | 3.75 |
| 177 (98A) | 500 ESCUDOS | 4.10.1979 (1982). Ch. 11. Brown and m/c. Old street layout of part of Braga at ctr., F. Sanches at r. and as wmk. 17th century street scene in Braga on back. Printer: JEZ (w/o imprint). | FV | 4.50 | 9.00 |

1980–87 ISSUES DATED

Cat#	Date, denomination	Description	VG	VF	Unc
178 (88A)	100 ESCUDOS	2.9.1980; 24.2.1981; 31.1.1984; 12.3.1985; 4.6.1985. Ch. 8. Dk. blue and m/c. Manuel M.B. du Bocage seated at r. and as wmk. Early 19th century scene of Rossio Square in Lisbon on back.	FV	1.25	4.50

NOTE: #178 dated 2.9.1980 has darker unpt. through ctr.

Cat#	Date, denomination	Description	VG	VF	Unc
179 (88B)	100 ESCUDOS	16.10.1986–24.11.1988. Ch. 9. Blue and pur- ple on m/c unpt. F. Pessoa at ctr. r. and as wmk. Rosebud on back. Sign. title varieties.			
		a. Regular issue.	FV	FV	3.50
		b. Prefix letters *FIL.* 12.2.1987.	—	—	4.00

NOTE: #179 was sold in a special envelope with a stamp honoring the 300th anniversary of paper money emissions of Portugal. The special prefix is taken from the Portuguese word *Filatelia* (stamp collecting).

180 (98B)	500 ESCUDOS	1987–92. Ch. 12. Brown and m/c. M. de Sil- veira at ctr. r. and as wmk. Sheaf on back. Sign. title varieties.			
		a. 20.11.1987.	FV	FV	8.00
		b. 4.8.1988.	FV	FV	7.00
		c. 4.10.1989.	FV	FV	6.50
		d. 13.2.1992.	FV	FV	6.00

181 (111A)	1000 ESCUDOS	1983–90. Ch. 12. Purple and dk. brown on m/c unpt. T. Braga at ctr. r. and as wmk. Museum artifacts on back.			
		a. 2.8.1983.	FV	FV	15.00
		b. 12.6.1986.	FV	FV	13.00
		c. 20.12.1990.	FV	FV	11.50

Cat#	Date, denomination	Description	VG	VF	Unc
183 (112)	5000 ESCUDOS	10.9.1980; 27.1.1981; 24.3.1983. Ch. 1. Brown and m/c. Antonio Sergio at l. ctr. and as wmk. A. Sergio walking at ctr. on back. Printer: TDLR (w/o imprint).	FV	FV	63.00

184 (113)	5000 ESCUDOS	12.2.1987. Ch. 2 or 2A. Olive-green, brown and m/c. A. de Quental at ctr. r. and as wmk. Six hands w/rope and chain at ctr. on back.	FV	FV	50.00
185 (115)	10,000 ESCUDOS	12.1.1989. Ch. 1. Orange, lt. brown and yel- low. Dr. E. Moniz by human brain at ctr. and as wmk. Nobel Prize medal, snakes, tree at ctr. on back.	FV	FV	95.00

1991 DATED ISSUE

186 (116)	2000 ESCUDOS	23.5.1991; 29.8.1991. Ch. 1. Dk. brown and blue on m/c unpt. B. Dias at l. and as wmk., astrolabe at ctr. Sailing ship at ctr., arms at r. on back. Sign. title varieties.	FV	FV	22.50

1993;94 DATED ISSUE

187 (117)	1000 ESCUDOS	1994. Ch. 13.			Expected new issue.
188 (118)	2000 ESCUDOS	1994. Ch. 2.			Expected new issue.
189 (119)	5000 ESCUDOS	1993. Ch. 3.			Expected new issue.
190 (120)	10,000 ESCUDOS	1993. Ch. 2.			Expected new issue.

PORTUGUESE GUINEA

Portuguese Guinea (now Guinea-Bissau), a former Portuguese province of the west coast of Africa bounded on the north by Senegal and on the east and southeast by Guinea, had an area of 13,948 sq. mi. (36,125 sq. km.). Capital: Bissau. The province exported peanuts, timber and beeswax.

Portuguese Guinea was discovered by Portuguese navigator Nuno Tristao in 1446. Trading rights in the area were granted to Cape Verde islanders but few prominent posts were established before 1851, and they were principally coastal installations. The chief export of this colony's early period was slaves for South America, a practice that adversely affected trade with the native people and retarded subjection of the interior. Territorial disputes with France delayed final demarcation of the colony's frontiers until 1905.

The African Party for the Independence of Guinea-Bissau was founded in 1956, and several years later began a guerrilla warfare that grew in effectiveness until 1974, when the rebels controlled most of the colony. Portugal's costly overseas wars in her African territories resulted in a military coup in Portugal in April 1974, that appreciably brightened the prospects for freedom for Guinea-Bissau. In August,1974, the Lisbon government signed an agreement granting independence to Portuguese Guinea effective Sept. 10, 1974. The new republic took the name of Guinea-Bissau.

RULERS
Portuguese to 1974

MONETARY SYSTEM
1 Escudo – 100 Centavos 1910–1975

PORTUGUESE INFULENCE

Banco Nacional Ultramarino, Guiné

1964 ISSUE

#40–42 ovpt: *GUINE*. Serial # prefix C.

Cat#	Date, denomination	Description	VG	VF	Unc
40	50 ESCUDOS	30.6.1964. Dk. green on lilac and m/c unpt.	4.00	15.00	45.00

Cat#	Date, denomination	Description	VG	VF	Unc
41	100 ESCUDOS	30.6.1964. Blue-green on m/c unpt.	7.50	30.00	90.00
42	500 ESCUDOS	30.6.1964. Brown on m/c unpt.	12.50	50.00	150.00

Cat#	Date, denomination	Description	VG	VF	Unc
43	1000 ESCUDOS	30.4.1964. Red-orange on m/c unpt. Portr. H. Barreto at r. Printer: BWC.	22.50	65.00	200.00

1971 ISSUE

#44–46 ovpt: *GUINE*.

Cat#	Date, denomination	Description	VG	VF	Unc
44	50 ESCUDOS	17.12.1971. Olive-green on m/c unpt. Portr. N. Tristao at r.	3.00	10.00	35.00

Cat#	Date, denomination	Description	VG	VF	Unc
45	100 ESCUDOS	17.12.1971. Blue on m/c unpt. Portr. N. Tristao at r.	3.00	12.50	55.00
46	500 ESCUDOS	27.7.1971. Purple on m/c unpt. Portr. H. Barreto at r.	10.00	40.00	135.00

NOTE: For later issues see Guinea-Bissau.

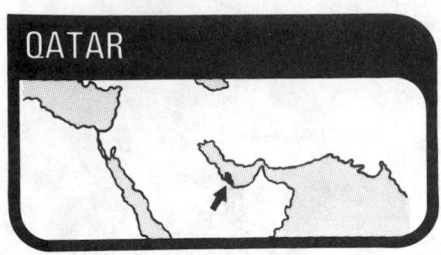

The State of Qatar, an emirate in the Persian Gulf between Bahrain and Trucial Oman, has an area of 4,247 sq. mi. (11,000 sq. km.) and a population of 382,000. Capital: Doha. Oil is the chief industry and export.

Qatar was under Turkish control from 1872 until the beginning of World War I when the Ottoman Turks evacuated the Qatar Peninsula. In 1916 Sheikh Abdullah placed Qatar under the protection of Great Britain and gave Britain responsibility for its defense and foreign relations. Qatar joined with Dubai in a Monetary Union and issued coins and paper money in 1966 and 1969. When Britain announced in 1968 that it would end treaty relationships with the Persian Gulf sheikhdoms in 1971, this union was dissolved. Qatar joined Bahrain and the seven trucial sheikhdoms (the latter now called the United Arab Emirates) in an effort to form a union of Arab emirates. However, the nine sheikhdoms were unable to agree on terms of union, and Qatar declared its independence as the State of Qatar on Sept. 3, 1971.

Also see Qatar and Dubai.

MONETARY SYSTEM

1 Riyal = 100 Dirhem

Qatar Monetary Agency

1973 (ND) ISSUE

#1–6 arms in circle at r. Wmk: Falcon's head.

Cat. #	Denomination	Date, description	VG	VF	Unc
1	1 RIYAL	ND (1973). Lilac-red on m/c unpt. Harbor at l. on back.	1.00	2.50	10.00

2	5 RIYALS	ND (1973). Lilac-brown on m/c unpt. Bldg. at l. on back.	2.00	4.50	15.00

3	10 RIYALS	ND (1973). Green on m/c. Qatar Monetary Agency bldg. at l. on back.	4.00	7.50	25.00

Cat. #	Denomination	Date, description	VG	VF	Unc
4	50 RIYALS	ND (1976). Blue. Offshore oil drilling platform at l. on back.	55.00	175.00	400.00

5	100 RIYALS	ND (1973). Olive-green and lt. brown. Modern bldg. at l. on back.	37.50	70.00	180.00

6	500 RIYALS	ND (1973). Blue-green. Mosque and minaret at l. on back.	180.00	300.00	750.00

1980's (ND) ISSUE

#7–13 arms at r. Wmk: Falcon's head.

7	1 RIYAL	ND. Brown and m/c. City street scene in Doha at l. ctr. on back.	.40	.65	3.00

Cat. #	Denomination	Date, description	VG	VF	Unc
8	5 RIYALS	ND. Red, purple and m/c. Back red-brown; sheep and plants at l. ctr.	FV	FV	3.50

Cat. #	Denomination	Date, description	VG	VF	Unc
12	500 RIYALS	ND. Blue, green and m/c. Offshore oil drilling platform on back.	FV	FV	210.00

1985 (ND) ISSUE

13	1 RIYAL	ND (1985). Face like #7. Boat beached at l. on back.	FV	FV	1.25

9	10 RIYALS	ND. Green, blue and m/c. National Museum at l. ctr. on back.	FV	FV	7.00
10	50 RIYALS	ND (1989). Blue and m/c. Face similar to #7. Industrial scene on back.	FV	FV	25.00

11	100 RIYALS	ND. Green and m/c. Qatar Monetary Agency bldg. at l. ctr. on back.	FV	FV	45.00

The State of Qatar, which occupies the Qatar Peninsula jutting into the Persian Gulf from eastern Saudi Arabia, has an area of 4,247 sq. mi. (11,000 sq. km.) and a population of 382,000. Capital: Doha. The traditional occupations of pearling, fishing and herding have been replaced in economics by petroleum-related industries. Crude oil, petroleum products, and tomatoes are exported.

Dubai is one of the seven sheikhdoms comprising the United Arab Emirates (formerly Trucial States) located along the southern shore of the Persian Gulf. It has a population of about 60,000. Capital (of the United Arab Emirates): Abu Dhabi.

Qatar, which initiated protective treaty relations with Great Britain in 1820, achieved independence on Sept. 3, 1971, upon withdrawal of the British military presence from the Persian Gulf, and replaced its special treaty arrangement with Britain with a treaty of general friendship. Dubai attended independence on Dec. 1, 1971, upon termination of Britain's protective treaty with the trucial sheikhdoms, and on Dec. 2, 1971, entered into the union of the United Arab Emirates.

Despite the fact that the sultanate of Qatar and the sheikhdom of Dubai were merged under a monetary union, the two territories were governed independently from each other. Qatar now uses its own currency while Dubai uses the United Arab Emirates currency and coins.

MONETARY SYSTEM
1 Riyal = 100 Dirhem

Qatar and Dubai Currency Board

1960's (ND) ISSUE

#1–6 dhow, derrick and palm tree at l. Wmk: Falcon's head.

Cat. #	Denomination	Date, description	VG	VF	Unc
1	1 RIYAL	ND. Dk. green on m/c unpt.	3.00	10.00	35.00

2	5 RIYALS	ND. Purple on m/c unpt.	8.00	30.00	95.00
3	10 RIYALS	ND. Gray-green on m/c unpt.	20.00	60.00	225.00
4	25 RIYALS	ND. Blue on m/c unpt.	65.00	400.00	1250.

5	50 RIYALS	ND. Red on m/c unpt.	125.00	450.00	1250.

6	100 RIYALS	ND. Olive on m/c unpt.	125.00	400.00	1000.

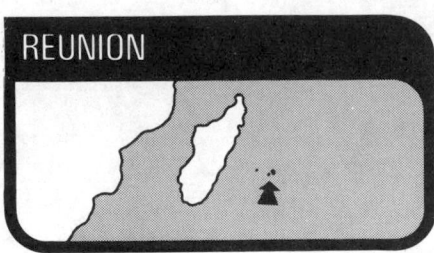

The Department of Reunion, an overseas department of France located in the Indian Ocean 400 miles (640 km.) east of Madagascar, has an area of 969 sq. mi. (2,510 sq. km.) and a population of 556,000. Capital: Saint-Denis. The island's volcanic soil is extremely fertile. Sugar, vanilla, coffee and rum are exported.

Although first visited by Portuguese navigators in the 16th century, Reunion was uninhabited when claimed for France by Capt. Goubert in 1638. It was first colonized as Isle de Burbon by the French in 1662 as a layover station for ships rounding the Cape of Good Hope to India. It was renamed Reunion in 1793. The island remained in French possession except for the period of 1810–15, when it was occupied by the British. Reunion became an overseas department of France in 1946, and in 1958 voted to continue that status within the new French Union. Baque du France notes were introduced 1.1.1973.

RULERS
French, 1638–1810, 1815
British, 1810–1815

MONETARY SYSTEM
1 Nouveaux Franc = 100 Old Francs, 1960

Département de la Réunion

Institute d'Emission des Departments d'Outre-Mer

1960 PROVISIONAL ISSUE

#54–56 ovpt. new value. 2 sign. varieties.

Cat. #	Denomination	Date, description	VG	VF	Unc
54	10 NF on 500 Francs	ND (ca. 1960). M/c. Ovpt. on #51.	5.00	27.50	85.00

55	20 NF on 1000 Francs	ND (ca. 1960). M/c Ovpt on #52.	7.50	32.50	95.00
56	100 NF on 5000 Francs	ND (ca. 1960). M/c. ovpt. on #53.	22.50	75.00	225.00

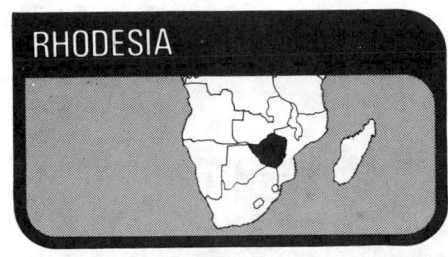

RHODESIA

The "Republic of" Rhodesia (never recognized by the British Government and was referred to as "Southern Rhodesia") (now Zimbabwe) located in the east-central part of southern Africa, has an area of 150,804 sq. mi. (390,580 sq. km.) and a population of 9.9 million. Capital: Salisbury. The economy is based on agriculture and mining. Tobacco, sugar, asbestos, copper and chrome ore and coal are exported.

The Rhodesian area, the habitat of paleolithic man, contains extensive evidence of earlier civilizations, notably the world-famous ruins of Zimbabwe, a gold-trading center that flourished about the 14th or 15th century AD. The Portuguese of the 16th century were the first Europeans to attempt to develop south-central Africa, but it remained for Cecil Rhodes and the British South Africa Co. to open the hinterlands. Rhodes obtained a concession for mineral rights from local chiefs in 1888 and administered his African empire (named Southern Rhodesia in 1895) through the British South Africa Co. until 1923, when the British government annexed the area after the white settlers voted for existence as a separate entity, rather than for incorporation into the Union of South Africa. From Sept. of 1953 through 1963 Southern Rhodesia was joined with the British protectorates of Northern Rhodesia and Nyasaland into a multiracial federation. When the federation was dissolved at the end of 1963, Northern Rhodesia and Nyasaland became the independent states of Zambia and Malawi.

Britain was prepared to grant independence to Southern Rhodesia but declined to do so when the politically dominant white Rhodesians refused to give assurances of representative government. In November 1965, the white minority government of Southern Rhodesia unilaterally declared Southern Rhodesia an independent dominion. The United Nations and the British Parliament both proclaimed this unilateral declaration of independence null and void. Following a conference In London in December 1979, the opposition government conceded and it was agreed that the British Government should resume control. In 1970, the government proclaimed a republic, but this too received no recognition. In 1979, the government purported to change the name of the Colony to Zimbabwe Rhodesia, but again this was never recognized. A British Governor soon returned to Southern Rhodesia. One of his first acts was to affirm the nullification of the purported declaration of independence. On April 18, 1980, pursuant to an act of the British Parliament, the Colony of Southern Rhodesia became independent within the commonwealth as the Republic of Zimbabwe.

RULERS
British to 1970

MONETARY SYSTEM
1 Shilling = 12 Pence
1 Pound = 20 Shillings to 1970
1 Dollar = 100 Cents, 1970–80

REPLACEMENT NOTES
#30–33 later dates, W/1, X/1, Y/1 and Z/1, respectively.

Reserve Bank of Rhodesia

Pound System

1964 ISSUE

#24–29 arms at upper ctr., Qn. Elizabeth II at r. Various date and sign. varieties. Wmk: C. Rhodes.

#24, 26 and 28 Printer: BWC. Printed in England from engraved plates.

Cat. #	Denomination	Date, description	VG	VF	Unc
24	10 SHILLINGS	30.9.1964–16.11.1964. Blue on m/c unpt. Blue portr. black serial #. Tobacco field on back.	7.50	30.00	165.00

Cat. #	Denomination	Date, description	VG	VF	Unc
26	1 POUND	3.9.1964–16.11.1964. Red on m/c unpt. Red portr. black serial #. Victoria Falls on back.	5.00	25.00	100.00

| 28 | 5 POUNDS | 10.11.1964; 12.11.1964; 16.11.1964. Blue-green on m/c unpt. Lilac portr. black serial #. Zimbabwe ruins on back. | 10.00 | 35.00 | 90.00 |

1966 ISSUE

#25, 27 and 29 printed in Rhodesia (w/o imprint). Lithographed.

| 25 | 10 SHILLINGS | 1.6.1966; 10.9.1968. Blue on m/c unpt. Similar to #24 but black portr. red serial #. | 2.50 | 10.00 | 45.00 |

| 27 | 1 POUND | 15.6.1966–14.10.1968. Pale red on m/c unpt. Similar to #26 but brown portr. red serial #. | 3.00 | 10.00 | 65.00 |

| 29 | 5 POUNDS | 1.7.1966. Blue-green on m/c unpt. Similar to #28 but purple portr. red serial #. | 15.00 | 60.00 | 235.00 |

NOTE: Before the issue of #25, 27 and 29, a series of Rhodesian banknotes was printed in Germany by Giesecke and Devrient, Munich. An injunction prevented delivery of this issue and it was never released. Subsequently it was destroyed.

REPUBLIC
Reserve Bank of Rhodesia
Dollar System
1970–72 ISSUE

#30–33 bank logo at upper ctr., arms at r. Various date and sign. varieties.

Cat. #	Denomination	Date, description	VG	VF	Unc
30	1 DOLLAR	1970–79. Blue. Back like #25.			
		a. Wmk: C. Rhodes. 17.2.1970–18.8.1971.	1.50	3.50	11.50
		b. Wmk. as a. 14.2.1973–18.4.1978.	1.00	2.50	7.50
		c. Wmk: Zimbabwe bird. 2.8.1979.	.50	1.50	6.50

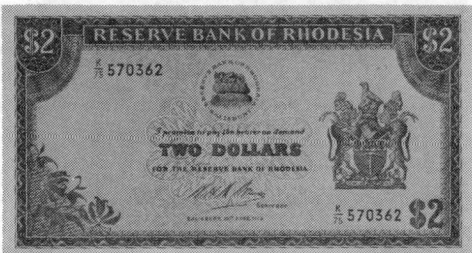

Cat. #	Denomination	Date, description	VG	VF	Unc
31	2 DOLLARS	1970–79. Red. Back like #27.			
		a. Wmk: C. Rhodes. 17.2.1970–4.1.1972.	2.00	5.00	17.50
		b. Wmk. as a. 29.6.1973–5.8.1977.	1.50	3.00	12.50
		c. Wmk. as a. 10.4.1979.	10.00	40.00	135.00
		d. Wmk: Zimbabwe bird. 10.4.1979; 24.5.1979.	1.00	2.50	10.00

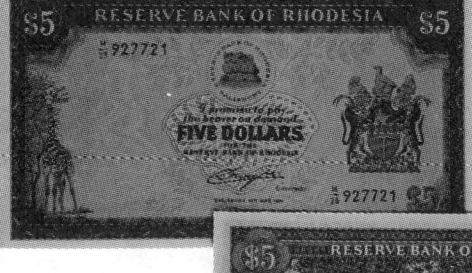

Cat. #	Denomination	Date, description	VG	VF	Unc
32	5 DOLLARS	1972–79. Brown. 2 lions on back.			
		a. Wmk: C. Rhodes. 16.10.1972.	3.00	7.00	25.00
		b. Wmk. as a. 1.3.1976; 20.10.1978.	3.00	6.00	22.50
		c. Wmk: Zimbabwe bird. 15.5.1979 (1980).	3.00	7.00	25.00

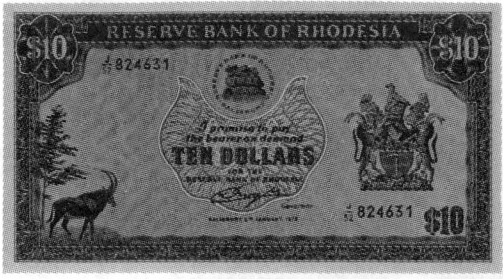

Cat. #	Denomination	Date, description	VG	VF	Unc
33	10 DOLLARS	1970–79. Blue-green. Back like #29.			
		a. Wmk: C. Rhodes. 17.2.1970–8.5.1972.	7.00	15.00	50.00
		b. Wmk. as a. 20.11.1973–1.3.1976.	5.00	10.00	27.50
		c. Wmk: Zimbabwe bird. 2.1.1979.	5.00	10.00	27.50

NOTE: For later issues see Zimbabwe.

RHODESIA & NYASALAND

The Federation of Rhodesia and Nyasaland (or the Central African Federation), comprising the British protectorates of Northern Rhodesia and Nyasaland and the self-governing colony of Southern Rhodesia, was located in the east-central part of southern Africa. The multiracial federation had an area of about 487,000 sq. mi. (1,261,330 sq. km.) and a population of 6.8 million. Capital: Salsbury, in Southern Rhodesia.

The geographical unity of the three British possessions suggested the desirability of political and economic union as early as 1924. Despite objections by the African constituency of Northern Rhodesia and Nyasaland, who by the dominant influence of prosperous and self governing Southern Rhodesia, the Central African Federation was established in Sept. of 1953. As feared, the Federation was effectively and profitably dominated by the European consituency of Southern Rhodesia despite the fact that the three component countries largely retained their prefederation political structure. It was dissolved at the end of 1963, largely because of the effective opposition of the Nyasaland African Congress. Northern Rhodesia and Nyasaland became independent states of Zambia and Malawi in 1964. Southern Rhodesia unilaterally decalred its independence as Rhodesia the following year which was not recognized by the British Government.

For earlier issues refer to Southern Rhodesia. For later issues refer to Malawi, Zambia, Rhodesia and Zimbabwe.

RULERS
British, 1953-64

MONETARY SYSTEM
1 Shilling = 12 Pence
1 Pound = 20 Shillings

Bank of Rhodesia and Nyasaland

1956 ISSUE

#20–23 Qn. Elizabeth II at r. Various date and sign. varieties. Wmk: C. Rhodes. Printer: BWC.

Cat#	Date, denomination	Description	VG	VF	Unc
20	10 SHILLINGS	3.4.1956–1.6.1961. Reddish-brown on m/c unpt. River scene on back.	10.00	50.00	200.00
21	1 POUND	3.4.1956–20.1.1961. Green on m/c unpt. Zimbabwe ruins on back.	7.50	50.00	350.00

| 22 | 5 POUNDS | 3.4.1956–1/.6.1961. Blue on m/c unpt. Victoria Falls on back. | 15.00 | 85.00 | 400.00 |
| 23 | 10 POUNDS | 3.4.1956–3.6.1960. Brown on m/c unpt. back gray-green; elephants at ctr. | 150.00 | 500.00 | 1750. |

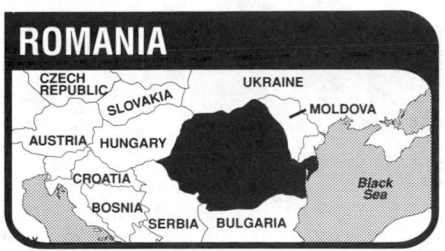

ROMANIA

The Republic of Romania (formerly the Socialist Republic of Romania), a Balkan country in southeast Europe, has an area of 91,699 sq. mi. (237,500 sq. km.) and a population of 23.2 million. Capital: Bucharest. The economy is predominantly agricultural; heavy industry and oil have become increasingly important since 1959. Machinery, foodstuffs, raw minerals and petroleum products are exported.

Romania, the ancient Roman province of Dacia, endured wave after wave of barbarian conquest and foreign domination before it declared its independence (of Turkey) in 1877. In 1881 it became a monarchy under Carol I, changing to a constitutional monarchy with a bicameral legislature in 1888. The government was reorganized along Fascist lines in 1940, and in the following year Romania joined Germany's attack on the Soviet Union. The country was subsequently occupied by the Russian Army which actively supported the program and goals of the Romanian Communists. On Nov. 19, 1946, a Communist-dominated government was installed and prompted the abdication of King Michael. Romania became a "People's Republic" on Dec. 30, 1947. With the accession of N. Ceausescu to power in 1965 a repressive and improverished domestic scene worsened. A popular protest to the eviction of a protestant pastor in 1989 escalated into a massive demonstration against the government which spread rapidly to other areas. An official rally in Bucharest turned also against the government. A state of emergency was declared but armed forces supported the uprising. Later the Ceausescus were captured and executed on Dec. 25, 1989. A provisional government was set up and after protests and riots it fell, being replaced by an interim government.

MONETARY SYSTEM
1 Leu = 100 Bani

PEOPLES REPUBLIC

Republica Populara Romana

1952 ISSUE

Cat#	Date, denomination	Description	VG	VF	Unc
83	10 LEI	1952. Brown on m/c unpt Worker at l., arms at ctr. r. Rocks loaded onto train on back.			
		a. Red serial #.	1.50	4.00	12.00
		b. Blue serial #	.50	1.50	4.00
84	25 LEI	1952. Brown on violet unpt. T. Vladimirescu at l. Wheat harvesting on back.			
		a. Red serial #.	1.50	5.00	17.00
		b. Blue serial #.	.50	1.50	4.00
85	00 LEI	1952. Blue on lt. blue unpt. N. Balcescu at l., arms at ctr. r. Lg. bldgs. on back.			
		a. Red serial #.	3.00	10.00	25.00
		b. Blue serial #.	1.50	4.00	12.50

SOCIALIST REPUBLIC

Banca Nationala a Republicii Socialiste Romania

1966 ISSUE

#86–89 arms at ctr.

| 86 | 1 LEU | 1966. Olive-brown and tan. | .05 | .10 | .25 |

| 87 | 3 LEI | 1966. Blue-gray and m/c. | .10 | .20 | .50 |

Cat#	Date, denomination	Description	VG	VF	Unc
88	5 LEI	1966. Dk. brown and blue-black on m/c unpt. Cargo ships at dockside on back.	.15	.30	.75

Cat#	Date, denomination	Description	VG	VF	Unc
92	100 LEI	1966. Dk. blue and m/c. N. Balcescu at l. Romanesque bldg. on back.	.35	.75	3.00

REPUBLIC

Banca Nationala A Romaniei

1991 ISSUE

			VG	VF	Unc
89	10 LEI	1966. Violet, grayish green and gray. Harvesting on back.	.20	.40	1.00

#90–92 arms at ctr. r.

			VG	VF	Unc
93	500 LEI	April 1991. Dk. brown on m/c unpt. C. Brancusi at r. and as wmk. Brancusi seated w/statue at l. ctr. on back. 1 sign.	FV	FV	2.50

			VG	VF	Unc
90	25 LEI	1966. Dk. green and m/c. T. Vladimirescu at l. Large refinery on back.	.30	.60	2.50

			VG	VF	Unc
91	50 LEI	1966. Dk. green and m/c. A. I. Cuza at l. Ornate bldg. on back.	.30	.60	2.50

			VG	VF	Unc
94	1000 LEI	Sept. 1991. Red-brown, blue-green and brown-orange on m/c unpt. Square topped shield at l. ctr., sails of sailing ships at lower ctr., M. Eminescu at r. and as wmk. Putna monastery on back. 2 sign.	FV	FV	5.50

1992–93 ISSUE

Cat#	Date, denomination	Description	VG	VF	Unc
95	200 LEI	Dec. 1992. Dull deep brown and brown-violet on m/c unpt. Square toped shield at l. ctr., steamboat "Tudor Vadimirescu" above heron and Sulina Lighthouse at ctr., G. Antipa at r. Herons, fish, and net on outline of Danube Delta at l. ctr. on back. Wmk: Bank monogram repeated.	FV	FV	1.50

Cat#	Date, denomination	Description	VG	VF	Unc
96	500 LEI	Dec. 1992. Dull deep green, reddish-brown and violet on m/c unpt. Square topped shield at l. ctr., sculptures at ctr., C. Brâncusi at r. Sculptures at l. and ctr. on back.			
		a. Wmk: Bust l.	FV	FV	2.25
		b. Wmk: Bust facing.	FV	FV	2.25
97	1000 LEI	May 1993. Similar to #94 but circular shield.	FV	FV	4.00

Cat#	Date, denomination	Description	VG	VF	Unc
98	5000 LEI	March 1992. Pale purple on m/c unpt. Seal at l. ctr., church ctr., A. Iancu at r. and as wmk. Church at l., "Poarta Cetatii Alba Julia" at l. ctr., seal at ctr. r. on back.	FV	4.00	20.00

Cat#	Date, denomination	Description	VG	VF	Unc
99	5000 LEI	May 1993. Similar to #98 but square topped shield.	FV	FV	6.00
100	10,000 LEI	Feb. 1994. Brown-violet and reddish brown on m/c unpt. N. Iorga at r., snake god Glycon at ctr. Historical Museum in Bucharest, statue of Fortuna and the Thinking Man of Hamangia on back.	FV	FV	11.00

RUSSIA

Russia, (formerly the central power of the Union of Soviet Socialist Republics and now of the Commonwealth of Indepedent States) which occupies the northern part of Asia and the far eastern part of Europe, in 1991 had an area of 8,649,538 sq. mi. (22,402,200 sq. km.) and a population of *288.7 million. Capital: Moscow. Exports include machinery, iron and steel, crude oil, timber and nonferrous metals.

The first Russian dynasty was founded in Novgorod by the Viking Rurik in 862 AD. Under Yaroslav the Wise (1019–54) the subsequent Kievan state became one of the great commercial and cultural centers of Europe before falling to the Mongols of the Batu Khan, 13th century, who ruled Russia until late in the 15th century when Ivan III threw off the Mongol yoke. The Russian Empire was enlarged, solidified and Westernized during the reigns of Ivan the Terrible, Peter the Great and Catherine the Great, and by 1881 extended to the Pacific and into Central Asia.

Assignats, the first government paper money of the Russian Empire, were introduced in 1769, and gave way to State Credit Notes in 1843. Russia was put on the gold standard in 1897 through the efforts of Finance Minister Count Sergei Witte, and Russia reformed her currency at that time.

All pre-1898 notes were destroyed as they were turned in to the Treasury, accounting for their uniform scarcity today.

The last Russian Czar, Nicholas II (1894–1917), was deposed by the provisional government under Prince Lvov and later Alexander Kerensky during the military defeat in World War I. This government rapidly lost ground to the Bolshevik wing of the Socialist Democratic Labor Party which attained power following the Bolshevik Revolution. During the Russian Civil War (1917–1922) many regional governments, national states and armies in the field were formed which issued their own paper money.

After the victory of the Red armies, these areas became federal republics of the Russian Socialist Federal Soviet Republic (RSFSR), or autonomous soviet republics which united on Dec. 30, 1922, to form the Union of Soviet Socialist Republics (USSR) under the premiership of Lenin.

Beginning with the downfall of the communist government in Poland, other European countries occupied since WW II began democratic elections which spread into Russia itself, leaving the remaining states united in a newly founded commonwealth developed after Mikhail Gorbachev resigned on Dec. 25, 1991. The USSR Supreme Soviet voted a formal end to the treaty of union signed in 1992 and dissolved itself.

MONETARY SYSTEM
1 Ruble = 100 Kopeks

СОЮЗ СОВЕТСКИХ СОЦИАЛИСТИЧЕСКИХ РЕСПУБЛИК

UNION OF SOVIET SOCIALIST REPUBLICS

ГОСУДАРСТВЕННЫЙ КАЗНАЧЕЙСКИЙ БИЛЕТ

State Treasury Notes

1961 ISSUE

#222–224 arms at upper l. Wmk: Stars.

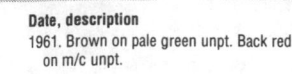

Cat. #	Denomination	Date, description	VG	VF	Unc
222	1 RUBLE	1961. Brown on pale green unpt. Back red on m/c unpt.	.05	.10	.20

Cat. #	Denomination	Date, description	VG	VF	Unc
223	3 RUBLES	1961. Greenish black on m/c unpt. View of Kremlin. Back lt. blue on green and m/c unpt.	.05	.10	.40

| 224 | 5 RUBLES | 1961. Blue on peach unpt. Kremlin Spasski tower at l. Back blue and m/c. | .05 | .15 | .50 |

БИЛЕТ ГОСУДАРСТВЕННОГО БАНКА С.С.С.Р.

State Bank Note U.S.S.R.

1961 ISSUE

Cat. #	Denomination	Date, description	VG	VF	Unc
233	10 RUBLES	1961. Red-brown on pale gold unpt. Lenin at r. Wmk: Stars.	.10	.25	.75

#234–236 Lenin at l.

| 234 | 25 RUBLES | 1961. Purple on pale lt. green unpt. Wmk: Stars. | .15 | .35 | 1.00 |

#235–236 wmk: Lenin.

Cat. #	Denomination	Date, description	VG	VF	Unc
235	50 RUBLES	1961. Dk. green and green on green and pink unpt. Kremlin at upper ctr. on back.	.35	1.00	3.50

| 236 | 100 RUBLES | 1961. Brown on lt. blue unpt. Kremlin tower at ctr. on back. | .40 | 1.25 | 4.50 |

1991 ISSUE

#237–243 similar to previous issue.

#237–239 wmk: Star in circle repeated.

| 237 | 1 RUBLE | 1991. Dk. green and red-brown on tan unpt. Similar to #222. | .05 | .10 | .20 |

Cat. #	Denomination	Date, description	VG	VF	Unc
241	50 RUBLES	1991. Dk. brown, green and red on m/c unpt. Similar to #235.	.20	.60	1.75

| 238 | 3 RUBLES | 1991. Green on blue and m/c unpt. Kremlin at ctr. Similar to #223. | .05 | .10 | .40 |

| 242 | 100 RUBLES | 1991. Deep red-brown and blue on m/c unpt. Similar to #236. | .35 | 1.00 | 3.00 |

| 239 | 5 RUBLES | 1991. Blue on lilac unpt. Tower similar to #224. | .05 | .15 | .50 |

| 243 | 100 RUBLES | 1991. Like #242 but w/added pink and green guilloche at r. in wmk. area, blue guilloche at l. on back. Wmk: Stars. | .35 | 1.00 | 3.00 |

#244–246 Lenin at l. and as wmk., arms near upper ctr. Diff. Kremlin views on back.

| 240 | 10 RUBLES | 1991. Red-brown and green on m/c unpt. Similar to #233. | .15 | .25 | .75 |

| 244 | 200 RUBLES | 1991. Green and brown on m/c unpt. | .30 | 1.00 | 3.00 |

Cat. #	Denomination	Date, description	VG	VF	Unc
245	500 RUBLES	1991. Red and green on m/c unpt.	.50	2.50	6.50

| 246 | 1000 RUBLES | 1991. Brown and blue on green and m/c unpt. | 1.00 | 3.50 | 10.00 |

1992 ISSUE

#247–250 Lenin at l. Issued after the fall of the USSR but before the formation of the CIS.

| 247 | 50 RUBLES | 1992. Brown and gray on green and m/c unpt. Similar to #241. Wmk: Star in circle repeated. | .15 | .35 | 1.25 |

| 248 | 200 RUBLES | 1992. Green and brown on m/c unpt. Similar to #244, but guilloche added in wmk. area on back. Wmk. as #247. | .30 | .90 | 2.50 |

Cat. #	Denomination	Date, description	VG	VF	Unc
249	500 RUBLES	1992. Red, violet and dk. green on m/c unpt. Similar to #245, but guilloche added in wmk. area on back. Wmk: Stars.	.25	.75	2.50

| 250 | 1000 RUBLES | 1992. Dk. brown and deep green on m/c unpt. Similar to #246, but guilloche added in wmk. area on back. Wmk: Stars. | .40 | 1.25 | 3.50 |

COMMONWEALTH OF INDEPENDENT STATES (CIS)

БАНК РОССИИ — Bank of Russia
1992 ISSUE

| 251 | 5000 RUBLES | 1992. Blue-green and maroon on m/c unpt. St. Basil's Cathedral at l. Kremlin on back. Wmk: Stars. | .45 | 1.35 | 3.50 |

Cat. #	Denomination	Date, description	VG	VF	Unc
252	10,000 RUBLES	1992. Brown, black and red on m/c unpt. Kremlin w/new tricolor flag at l. ctr. and as wmk. Kremlin towers at ctr. r. on back.	.90	2.75	5.50

РОССИЙСКАЯ ФЕДЕРАЦИЯ
(Russian Federation) Government Privatization Check
1992 ISSUE

253	10,000 RUBLES	1992. Dk. brown on m/c unpt. Scene from walkway along the Neva River is St. Petersburg at ctr. Text indicating method of redemption into shares of govt.-owned property on back. Handstamp from bank added at bottom. Valid until Dec. 31, 1993.	—	25.00	55.00

NOTE: While not a regular banknote, #253 was easily negotiable and was widely distributed by the govt. It was to provide funds to allow citizens to "buy into" a business. Worth about $35 at time of issue (early 1992), inflation since then has cut its real value dramatically.

БАНК РОССИИ — Bank of Russia
1993 ISSUE

#254–260 new tricolor flag over stylized Kremlin at l., monogram at or near upper r.

#254–256 wmk: Stars within wavy lines repeated.

254	100 RUBLES	1993. Blue-black on pink and lt. blue unpt. Kremlin, Spasski tower at ctr. r. on back.	FV	FV	.35

Cat. #	Denomination	Date, description	VG	VF	Unc
255	200 RUBLES	1993. Brown on pink and m/c unpt. Kremlin gate at ctr. on back.	FV	FV	.85

256	500 RUBLES	1993. Green, blue and violet on m/c unpt. Kremlin at l. ctr. on back.	FV	FV	2.75

257	1000 RUBLES	1993. Green, olive-green and brown on m/c unpt. Kremlin at ctr. on back. Wmk: Stars.	FV	FV	5.00

#258–260 new flag over Kremlin at l. and as wmk. Kremlin at or near ctr. on back.

Cat. #	Denomination	Date, description	VG	VF	Unc
258	5000 RUBLES	1993; 1993/94. Blue-black, brown and violet on m/c unpt.			
		a. 1993.	FV	FV	4.00
		b. 1993//94.	FV	FV	4.00

Cat. #	Denomination	Date, description	VG	VF	Unc
263	10,000 RUBLES	1995. Dk. brown and dk. gray on m/c unpt. Arch bridge at l. ctr., steeple at ctr. r. and as. wmk. Hydro-electric dam at ctr. on back.	FV	FV	4.75

Cat. #	Denomination	Date, description	VG	VF	Unc
259	10,000 RUBLES	1993; 1993//94. Violet, greenish blue, brownish purple and m/c.			
		a. 1993.	FV	FV	6.50
		b. 1993//94.	FV	FV	6.50

Cat. #	Denomination	Date, description	VG	VF	Unc
264	50,000 RUBLES	1995. Dk. brown, grayish-purple and black on m/c unpt. Monument at ctr. Fountain in St. Petersburg at upper ctr. on back. Wmk: Bldg. w/steeple.	FV	FV	22.50
265 (261)	100,000 RUBLES	1995. Purple and brown on m/c unpt. Chariot monument at ctr. Bldg. on back.	FV	FV	40.00

Cat. #	Denomination	Date, description	VG	VF	Unc
260	50,000 RUBLES	1993; 1993//94. Olive-green, black and reddish-brown on m/c unpt.			
		a. 1993.	FV	FV	27.50
		b. 1993//94.	FV	FV	13.50

1995 ISSUE

Cat. #	Denomination	Date, description		
261	1000 RUBLES	1995.		Expected new issue.

Cat. #	Denomination	Date, description	VG	VF	Unc
262	5000 RUBLES	1995. Deep blue-green and dk. olive-green on m/c unpt. Monument at l. ctr. mosque at ctr. r. and as wmk. Old towered city wall at upper l. ctr. on back.	FV	FV	2.50

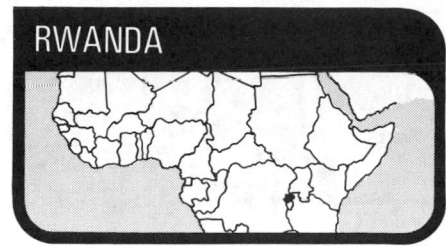

RWANDA

The Republic of Rwanda, located in central Africa between the Republic of the Congo and Tanzania, has an area of 10,169 sq. mi. (26,340 sq. km.) and a population of *7.3 million. Capital: Kigali. The economy is based on agriculture and mining. Coffee and tin are exported.

German lieutenant Count von Goetzen was the first European to visit Rwanda, 1894. Four years later the court of the Mwami (the Tutsi king of Rwanda) willingly permitted the kingdom to become a protectorate of Germany. In 1916, during the African campaigns of World War I, Belgian troops from the Congo occupied Rwanda. After the war it, together with Burundi, became a Belgian League of Nations mandate under the name of the Territory of Ruanda-Urundi. Following World War II, Ruanda-Urundi became a Belgian administered U.N. trust territory. The Tutsi monarchy was deposed by the U.N. supervised election of 1961, after which Belgium granted Rwanda internal autonomy. On July 1, 1962, the U.N. terminated the Belgian trusteeship and granted full independence to both Rwanda and Burundi.

Banknotes were used in common with the Belgian Congo, and later with Burundi.

Also see Belgian Congo, Rwanda-Burundi.

MONETARY SYSTEM
1 Franc (Amafranga, Amafaranga) = 100 Centimes

REPLACEMENT NOTES
#6e, 17:ZZ prefix, #12, VV prefix. Others probably exist.

Banque Nationale du Rwanda/Banki Nasiyonali Y'u Rwanda

1962 PROVISIONAL ISSUE

#1–5 ovpt: *BANQUE NATIONALE DU RWANDA* and sign. title: *LE GOUVERNEUR* on Banque d'Emission du Rwanda et du Burundi notes.

#1–3 stamped ovpt.

Cat. #	Denomination	Date, description	Good	Fine	VF
1	20 FRANCS	ND (1962–old date 5.10.1960). Green on tan and pink unpt. Maroon or black ovpt. on Rwanda-Burundi #3.	70.00	175.00	350.00

Cat. #	Denomination	Date, description	Good	Fine	VF
2	50 FRANCS	ND (1962–old date 15.9.1960). Red on m/c unpt. Maroon ovpt. on Rwanda-Burundi #4.	85.00	225.00	500.00

Cat. #	Denomination	Date, description	Good	Fine	VF
3	100 FRANCS	ND (1962–old dates 15.9.1960; 1.10.1960). Blue on lt. green and tan unpt. Black ovpt. on Rwanda-Burundi #5.	50.00	135.00	275.00

#4–5 embossed ovpt.

Cat. #	Denomination	Date, description	Good	Fine	VF
4	500 FRANCS	ND (1962–old date 15.9.1960). Lilac-brown on m/c unpt. Embossed ovpt. and embossed facsimile sign. on Rwanda-Burundi #6.	300.00	950.00	—
5	1000 FRANCS	ND (1962old date 1.7.1962). Green on m/c unpt. Embossed ovpt. and embossed facsimile sign. on Rwanda-Burundi #7.	250.00	850.00	—

1964 ISSUE

Various date and sign. title varieties.

Cat. #	Denomination	Date, description	VG	VF	Unc
6	20 FRANCS	1964–76. Brown and m/c. Flag of Rwanda at l. 4 young boys w/pipeline on back.			
		a. Sign. titles: *VICE GOUVERNEUR* and *GOUVERNEUR*, w/security thread. 1 7 1964; 31.3.1966; 15.3.1909, 1.9.1969.	2.50	7.50	20.00
		b. Sign. titles: *VICE GOUVERNEUR* and *ADMINISTRATEUR*, w/security thread. 1.7.1965.	3.50	8.50	25.00
		c. Sign. titles: *GOUVERNEUR* and *ADMINISTRATEUR*, w/security thread. 1.7.1971.	1.25	3.00	7.50
		d. Sign. titles: *ADMINISTRATEUR* and *ADMINISTRATEUR*, w/security thread. 30.10.1974.	.50	1.50	6.00
		e. Sign. titles: *ADMINISTRATEUR* and *GOUVERNEUR*, w/o security thread. 1.1.1976.	.50	.75	1.35
		s1. Specimen. As a. 31.3.1966; 15.3.1969	—	—	5.00
		s2. As b. Specimen. 1.7.1965.	—	—	3.50
		s3. As c. Specimen. 1.7.1971.	—	—	3.50
		s4. As d. Specimen. 30.10.1974.	—	—	6.00

Cat. #	Denomination	Date, description	VG	VF	Unc
7	50 FRANCS	1964–76. Blue and m/c. Map of Rwanda at l. Miners on back.			
		a. Sign. titles: *VICE-GOUVERNEUR* and *GOUVERNEUR*, w/security thread. 1.7.1964; 31.1.1966; 1.9.1969.	3.00	10.00	25.00
		b. Sign. titles: *ADMINISTRATEUR* and *GOUVERNEUR*, w/security thread. 1.7.1971; 30.10.1974.	.75	2.00	7.00
		c. Sign. titles: *ADMINISTRATEUR* and *GOUVERNEUR*, w/o security thread. 1.1.1976.	.50	1.00	2.00
		s1. As a. Specimen. 1.7.1964; 31.1.1966; 1.9.1969.	—	—	4.00
		s2. As b. Specimen. 1.7.1971.	—	—	4.00

Cat. #	Denomination	Date, description	VG	VF	Unc
8	100 FRANCS	1964–76. Purple and m/c. Map of Rwanda at l. Woman w/basket at l; banana trees at ctr. on back.			

Cat. #	Denomination	Date, description	VG	VF	Unc
		a. Sign. titles: *VICE GOUVERNEUR* and *GOUVERNEUR*, w/security thread. 1.7.1964; 31.3.1966; 31.10.1969.	1.00	3.00	9.00
		b. Sign. titles: *VICE GOUVERNEUR* and *ADMINISTRATEUR*, w/security thread. 1.7.1965.	5.00	12.00	30.00
		c. Sign. titles: *ADMINISTRATEUR* and *GOUVERNEUR*, w/security thread. 1.7.1971; 30.10.1974.	1.25	2.50	8.50
		d. Sign. titles: *ADMINISTRATEUR* and *GOUVERNEUR*, w/o security thread. 1.1.1976.	.75	1.50	3.00
		s1. As a. Specimen. 1.7.1964; 31.10.1969.	—	—	6.00
		s2. As c. Specimen. 1.7.1971; 30.10.1974.	—	—	6.00

Cat. #	Denomination	Date, description	VG	VF	Unc
11	500 FRANCS	19.4.1974. Green and m/c. Gen. Habyarimana at l. Back like #9.			
		a. Issued note.	7.50	12.50	22.50
		s. Specimen.	—	—	10.00

1978 ISSUE

9	500 FRANCS	1964–76. Dk. green and m/c. Arms of Rwanda at l. Man w/basket at l., rows of plants behind on back.			
		a. Sign. titles: *VICE GOUVERNEUR* and *GOUVERNEUR*. 1.7.1964; 31.3.1966; 31.10.1969.	7.00	15.00	50.00
		b. Sign. titles: *ADMINISTRATEUR* and *GOUVERNEUR*. 1.7.1971; 30.10.1974; 1.1.1976.	3.00	7.50	15.00
		s1. As a. Specimen. 1.7.1964.	—	—	12.50
		s2. As b. Specimen. 1.7.1971; 30.10.1974	—	—	12.50

12	100 FRANCS	1.1.1978. Lt. blue and m/c. Zebras. Woman and child, natural scenery on back.			
		a. Issued note.	1.00	2.50	6.00
		s. Specimen.	—	—	12.50

10	1000 FRANCS	1964–76. Red and m/c. Arms of Rwanda at l. Man and terraced hills on back.			
		a. Sign. titles: *VICE GOUVERNEUR* and *GOUVERNEUR*. 1.7.1964; 31.3.1966; 15.3.1969.	12.50	25.00	65.00
		b. Sign. titles: *ADMINISTRATEUR* and *GOUVERNEUR*. 1.7.1971; 30.10.1974.	10.00	20.00	45.00
		c. Printed sign. titles like b. 1.1.1976.	7.50	15.00	30.00
		s1. As a. Specimen. 31.3.1966; 15.3.1969.	—	—	17.50
		s2. As b. Specimen. 1.7.1971.	—	—	17.50

13	500 FRANCS	1.1.1978. Orange and m/c. Impalas. 8 drummers at l., strip mining at r. on back. Wmk: Impala's head.			
		a. Issued note.	5.00	7.50	15.00
		s. Specimen.	—	—	20.00

1974 ISSUE

Cat. #	Denomination	Date, description	VG	VF	Unc
14	1000 FRANCS	1.1.1978. Green and m/c. Boy picking tea leaves. Dancer on back. Wmk: Impala's head.			
		a. Issued note.	9.00	15.00	27.50
		s. Specimen.	—	—	25.00

1981 ISSUE

15	5000 FRANCS	1.1.1978. Green, blue and m/c. Female w/ basket on her head at l., field workers at ctr. Lake and mountains on back. Wmk: Impala's head.			
		a. Issued note.	45.00	65.00	125.00
		s. Specimen.	—	—	100.00

16	500 FRANCS	1.7.1981. Brown and m/c. Arms at l., 3 gazelle at r. Men working in field at l. on back. Wmk: Crowned crane's head.			
		a. Issued note.	FV	5.00	15.00
		s. Specimen.	—	—	20.00

17	1000 FRANCS	1.7.1981. Green, brown and m/c. 2 Watusi warriors at r. 2 gorillas at l., canoe in lake at r. on back. Wmk: Crowned crane's head.			
		a. Issued note.	FV	12.00	26.50
		s. Specimen.	—	—	32.50

1982 ISSUE

Cat. #	Denomination	Date, description	VG	VF	Unc
18	100 FRANCS	1.8.1982. Black on lilac and m/c unpt. Zebras at ctr. and r. Back purple and m/c; woman carrying baby at l., view of mountains at ctr. on back. Wmk: Impala's head.	FV	2.00	4.00

1988–89 ISSUE

#19–22 similar to #18, #17 and #15, but new spelling *AMAFARANGA* on back. Slight color differences and new sign. titles: *2E VICE-GOVERNEUR and LE GOUVERNEUR*.

19	100 FRANCS	24.4.1989. Similar to #18.	FV	1.00	3.00
20	*Deleted.*				

21	1000 FRANCS	1.1.1988; 24.4.1989. Similar to #17.	FV	12.00	22.50
22	5000 FRANCS	1.1.1988; 24.4.1989. Similar to #15.	FV	50.00	75.00

1994 ISSUE

#23–25 mountainous landscape at r. Wmk: Impala's head. Printer: G&D (w/o imprint).

Cat. #	Denomination	Date, description	VG	VF	Unc
23	500 FRANCS	1.12.1994. Blue-black, black and dk, blue-green on m/c unpt. Antelope at l. ctr. on back.	FV	FV	10.00

| 24 | 1000 FRANCS | 1.12.1994. Purple, red-brown and dk. brown on m/c unpt. Vegetation at l., water buffalo at ctr. on back. | FV | FV | 19.00 |

| 25 | 5000 FRANCS | 1.12.1994. Dk. brown, violet and purple on m/c unpt. Reclining lion at l. ctr. on back. | FV | FV | 67.50 |

RWANDA-BURUNDI

Rwanda-Burundi, a Belgian League of Nations mandate and United Nations trust territory comprising the provinces of Rwanda and Burundi of the former colony of German East Africa, was located in central Africa between the present Republic of the Congo, Uganda and mainland Tanzania. The mandate-trust territory had an area of 20,916 sq. mi. (54,272 sq. km.) and a population of 4.3 million.

For specific statistics and history of Rwanda and Burundi see individual entries.

When Rwanda and Burundi were formed into a mandate for administration by Belgium, their names were changed to Ruanda and Urundi and they were organized as an integral part of the Belgian Congo, during which time they used a common banknote issue with the Belgian Congo. After the Belgian Congo acquired independence as the Republic of the Congo, the provinces of Ruanda and Urundi reverted to their former names of Rwanda and Burundi and issued notes with both names on them. In 1962, both Rwandi and Burundi became separate independent states.

Also see Belgian Congo, Burundi and Rwanda.

MONETARY SYSTEM
1 Franc = 100 Centimes

Banque d'Emission du Rwanda et du Burundi

#1–7 various date and sign. varieties.

Cat. #	Denomination	Date, description	VG	VF	Unc
1	5 FRANCS	15.9.1960; 15.5.1961; 15.4.1963. Lt. brown on green unpt. Antelope at l.	12.50	40.00	110.00

| 2 | 10 FRANCS | 15.9.1960; 5.10.1960. Blue-gray on pink unpt. Hippopotamus at l. Printer: TDLR. | 12.50 | 50.00 | 145.00 |

Cat. #	Denomination	Date, description	Good	Fine	XF
3	20 FRANCS	15.9.1960; 5.10.1960. Green on tan and pink unpt. Crocodile at r. Printer: TDLR.	15.00	45.00	125.00

Cat. #	Denomination	Date, description	Good	Fine	XF
4	50 FRANCS	15.9.1960; 1.10.1960. Red on m/c unpt. Lioness at ctr. r.	25.00	85.00	250.00

| 5 | 100 FRANCS | 15.9.1960; 1.10.1960; 31.7.1962. Blue on lt. green and tan unpt. Zebu at l. | 17.50 | 50.00 | 140.00 |

| 6 | 500 FRANCS | 15.9.1960, 15.9.1961. Lilac-brown on m/c unpt. Rhinoceros at ctr. r. | 185.00 | 450.00 | — |

| 7 | 1000 FRANCS | 15.9.1960; 15.5.1961; 31.7.1962. Green on m/c unpt. Zebra at r. | 165.00 | 425.00 | — |

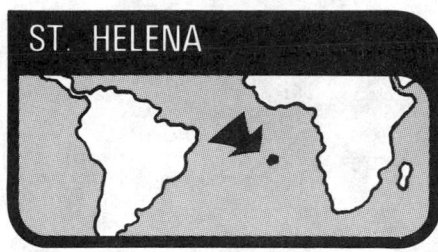

ST. HELENA

The Colony of St. Helena, a British colony located about 1,150 miles (1,850 km.) from the west coast of Africa, has an area of 47 sq. mi. (122 sq. km.) and a population of 5,700. Capital: Jamestown. Flax, lace and rope are produced for export. Ascension and Tristan da Cunha are dependencies of St. Helena.

The island was discovered and named by the Portuguese navigator Joao de Nova Castella in 1502. The Portuguese imported livestock, fruit trees and vegetables but established no permanent settlement. The Dutch occupied the island temporarily, 1645-1651. The original European settlement was founded by representatives of the British East India Company sent to annex the island after the departure of the Dutch. The Dutch returned and captured St. Helena from the British on New Year's Day, 1673, but were in turn ejected by a British force under Sir Richard Munden. Thereafter St. Helena was the undisputed possession of Great Britian. The island served as the place of exile for Napoleon, serveral Zulu chiefs, and an ex-sultan of Zanzibar.

RULERS
British

MONETARY SYSTEM
1 Pound = 20 Shillings to 1971
1 Pound = 100 New Pence, 1971

Government of St. Helena

1976; 1979 (ND) ISSUE

#5-8 views of the island at l., Qn. Elizabeth II at r.

#5-7 Royal arms w/motto at l., shield w/ship at ctr. r. on back.

Cat. #	Denomination	Date, description	VG	VF	Unc
5	50 PENCE	ND (1979). Purple on pink and pale yellow-green unpt. Correctly spelled *ANGLIAE* in motto.	1.00	1.50	3.50

NOTE: Serial #170,000–200,000 are non-redeemable.

| 6 | 1 POUND | ND (1976). Deep olive-green on pale orange and ochre unpt. Incorrect spelling *ANG-LAE* in motto. 153 x 7mm. | 2.50 | 6.00 | 2.00 |

Cat. #	Denomination	Date, description	VG	VF	Unc
7	5 POUNDS	ND (1976). Blue.			
		a. Incorrect spelling *ANGLAE* in motto.	FV	10.00	25.00
		b. Corrected spelling *ANGLIAE* in motto.	FV	FV	22.50

8	10 POUNDS	ND (1979). Lt. red. Arms on back, correctly spelled *ANGLEAE* in motto. Sign. varieties.			
		a. Issued note.	FV	FV	35.00
		b. Remainder w/o sign. or serial #.	—	—	100.00
		c. As b. Uncut sheet of 3.	—	—	275.00

1982; 1986 (ND) ISSUE

#9, 10 Qn. Elizabeth II at r. Royal arms w/motto at l., shield w/sailing ship at ctr. r. on back.

9	1 POUND	ND (1982). Deep olive-green on pale orange and ochre unpt. Like #6 but corrected spelling *ANGLIAE* in motto. Reduced size. 147 x 66mm.	FV	FV	5.00

NOTE: Serial #A/1 350,001–A/1 400,000 are non-redeemable.

10	20 POUNDS	ND (1986). Dk. brown. Harbor view at l. ctr., Back lt. brown.	FV	FV	67.50

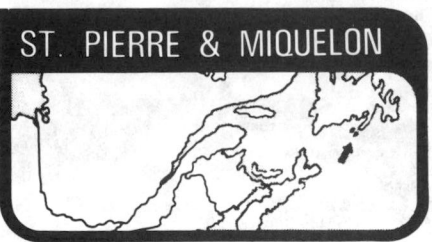

The Territorial Collectivity of St. Pierre and Miquelon, a French overseas territory located 10 miles (16 km.) off the south coast of Newfoundland, has an area of 93 sq. mi. (242 sq. km.) and a population of *6,000. Capital: St. Pierre. The economy of the barren archipelago is based on cod fishing and fur farming. Fish and fish products, and mink and silver fox pelts are exported.

The islands, occupied by the French in 1604, were captured by the British in 1702 and held until 1763 when they were returned to the possession of France and employed as a fishing station. They passed between France and England on six more occasions between 1778 and 1814 when they were awarded permanently to France by the Treaty of Paris. The rugged, soil-poor granite islands, which will support only evergreen shrubs, are all that remain to France of her extensive colonies in North America. In 1958 St. Pierre and Miquelon voted in favor of the new constitution of the Fifth Republic of France, thereby choosing to remain within the French Community.

Notes of the Banque de France circulated 1937–1942; afterwards notes of the Caisse Centrale de la France Libre and the Caisse Centrale de la France d'Outre-Mer.

RULERS
French

MONETARY SYSTEM
1 Franc = 100 Centimes
5 Francs 40 Centimes = 1 Canada Dollar

Caisse Centrale de la France d'Outre-Mer

Nouveaux Franc System

1960–64 Provisional Issue
#30–35 ovpt: *SAINT-PIERRE-ET-MIQUELON* and new denomination.

Cat#	Date, denomination	Description	VG	VF	Unc
30	1 NF on 50 Francs	ND (1960). M/c. Ovpt. on Reunion #25.	3.00	8.00	32.50

31	1 NF on 50 Francs	ND (1960). M/c. B. d'Esnambuc at l., ship at r. Woman on back.	25.00	110.00	550.00
32	2 NF on 100 Francs	ND (1963). M/c. La Bourdonnais at l., 2 women at r. Woman looking at mountains on back.	4.00	15.00	45.00
33	10 NF on 500 Francs	ND (1964). M/c. Bldgs. and sailboat at l., w women at r. Ox-carts w/wood and plants on back.	12.00	35.00	185.00

Cat#	Date, denomination	Description	VG	VF	Unc
34	20 NF on 1000 Francs	ND (1964). M/c. 2 women at r. Women at r., 2 men in small boat on back.	35.00	100.00	325.00

Cat#	Date, denomination	Description	VG	VF	Unc
35	100 NF on 5000 Francs	ND (1960). M/c. Gen. Schwelcher at ctr. r. Family on back.	85.00	275.00	700.00

The Democratic Republic of Sao Tome and Principe (formerly the Portuguese overseas province of St. Thomas and Prince Islands) is located in the Gulf of Guinea 150 miles (241 km.) off the west African coast. It has an area of 372 sq. mi. (960 sq. km.) and a population of *121,000. Capital: Sao Tome. The economy of the islands is based on cocoa, copra and coffee.

St. Thomas and St. Prince were uninhabited when discovered by Portuguese navigators Joao de Santarem and Pedro de Escobar in 1470. After the failure of their initial settlement, 1485, the Portuguese successfully colonized St. Thomas with a colony of prisoners and exiled Jews, 1493. An initial prosperity based on the sugar trade gave way to a time of misfortune, 1567–1709, that saw the colony attacked and occupied or plundered by the French and Dutch; ravaged by the slave revolt of 1595; and finally rendered destitute by the transfer of the world sugar trade to Brazil. In the late 1800s, the colony turned from the production of sugar to cocoa, the basis of its present prosperity.

The islands were designated a Portuguese overseas province in 1951. On April 25, 1974, the government of Portugal was seized by a military junta which reached agreements providing for independence for the Portuguese overseas provinces of Portuguese Guinea (Guinea-Bissau), Mozambique, Cape Verde Islands, Angola, and St. Thomas and Prince Islands. The Democratic Republic of Sao Tome and Principe was declared on July 12, 1975.

RULERS

Portuguese to 1975

MONETARY SYSTEM

1 Escudo = 100 Centavos, 1914–1976

1 Dobra = 100 Centimos, 1977–

> **NOTE:** This section has been renumbered since the 7th edition of General Issues.

PORTUGUESE INFLUENCE

Banco Nacional Ultramarino

1956–64 ISSUE

#36–39 arms at lower ctr., D. Afonso V at r. Printer: BWC.

Cat. #	Denomination	Date, description	VG	VF	Unc
36	20 ESCUDOS	20.11.1958. Brown on m/c unpt.	2.00	5.00	10.00
37	50 ESCUDOS	20.11.1958. Brown-violet on m/c unpt.	2.50	6.00	17.50
38	100 ESCUDOS	20.11.1958. Purple on m/c unpt.	3.00	8.00	32.50
39	500 ESCUDOS	18.4.1956. Blue on m/c unpt. Arms at lower r.	22.50	85.00	250.00

Cat. #	Denomination	Date, description	VG	VF	Unc
40	1000 ESCUDOS	11.5.1964. Green on m/c unpt. J. de Santarem at r.	15.00	40.00	125.00

1974 CIRCULATING BEARER CHECK ISSUE

Cat. #	Denomination	Date, description	VG	VF	Unc
41	100 ESCUDOS	31.3.1974.	—	—	—
42	500 ESCUDOS	28.4.1974.	—	—	—
43	500 ESCUDOS	31.12.1974	20.00	50.00	125.00

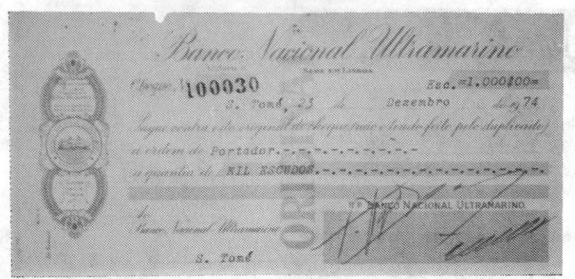

Cat. #	Denomination	Date, description	VG	VF	Unc
49	1000 ESCUDOS	23.12.1974; 31.12.1974.	20.00	50.00	125.00

DEMOCRATIC REPUBLIC

Banco Nacional de S. Tomé e Principe

1976 PROVISIONAL ISSUE

#44–48 red ovpt. new bank name ovpt. on both sides of Banco Nacional Ultramarino notes.

Cat. #	Denomination	Date, description	VG	VF	Unc
44	20 ESCUDOS	1.6.1976. Ovpt. on #36.	1.00	3.00	10.00

| 45 | 50 ESCUDOS | 1.6.1976. Ovpt. on #37. | 1.50 | 4.00 | 12.50 |

Cat. #	Denomination	Date, description	VG	VF	Unc
46	100 ESCUDOS	1.6.1976. Ovpt. on #38.	3.00	5.00	17.50

| 47 | 500 ESCUDOS | 1.6.1976. Ovpt. on #39. | 15.00 | 45.00 | 135.00 |
| 48 | 1000 ESCUDOS | 1.6.1976. Ovpt. on #40. | 1.50 | 40.00 | 120.00 |

1976 CIRCULATING BEARER CHECK ISSUE

			VG	VF	Unc
50	500 ESCUDOS	21.6.1976. 167 x 75mm.	10.00	27.50	85.00
51	1000 ESCUDOS	21.6.1976. 167 x 75mm.	13.50	33.00	100.00

1977 REGULAR ISSUE

Decreto-Lei No. 50/76

#52–53 Rei Amador at r. and as wmk. Sign. titles: *O MINISTRO DA COORDENACÃO ECONOMICA* and *O GOVERNADOR*. Printer: BWC.

| 52 | 50 DOBRAS | 12.7.1977. Red and m/c. Parrot at ctr. Scene w/2 fishermen in boats on back. | .65 | 2.00 | 5.50 |

| 53 | 100 DOBRAS | 12.7.1977. Green and m/c. Flower at ctr. Group of people preparing food on back. | 1.50 | 4.00 | 7.50 |

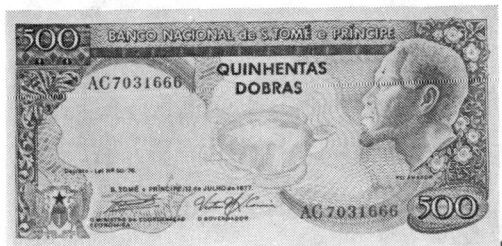

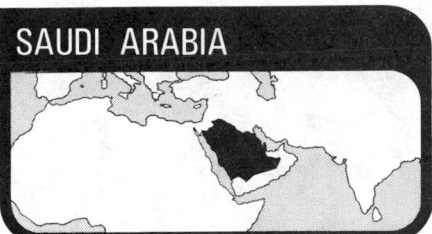

SAUDI ARABIA

The Kingdom of Saudi Arabia, an independent and absolute hereditary monarchy comprising the former sultanate of Nejd, the old kingdom of Hejaz, Asir and El Jasa, occupies four-fifths of the Arabian peninsula. The kingdom has an area of 830,000 sq. mi. (2,149,690 sq. km.) and a population of 15.4 million. Capital: Riyadh. The economy is based on oil, which provides 85 percent of Saudi Arabia's revenue.

Mohammed united the Arabs in the 7th century and his followers founded a great empire with its capital at Medina. The Turks established nominal rule over much of Arabia in the 16th and 17th centuries, and in the 18th century divided it into principalities.

The Kingdom of Saudi Arabia was created by King Ibn-Saud (1882-1953), a descendant of earlier Wahabi rulers of the Arabian peninsula. In 1901 he seized Riyadh, capital of the Sultanate of Nejd, and in 1905 established himself as Sultan. In 1913 he captured the Turkish province of Hasa; took the Hejaz in 1925 and by 1926 most of Asir. In 1932 he combined Nejd and Hejaz into the single kingdom of Saudi Arabia. Asir was incorporated into the kingdom a year later.

One of the principal cities, Mecca, is the Holy center of Islam and is the scene of an annual Pilgrimage from the entire Moslem world.

RULERS

Sa'ud Ibn Abdul Aziz, AH1373-1383/1953-1964AD

Faisal, AH1383-1395/1964-1975AD

Khaled, AH1395-1402/1975-1982AD

Fahd, AH1402-/1982AD-

MONETARY SYSTEM

1 Riyal = 20 Ghirsh

Saudi Arabian Monetary Agency

SIGNATURE VARIETIES			
1	*(signature)*	3	*(signature)*
2	*(signature)*	4	

1961 (ND) ISSUE

Law of 1.7.AH1379 (1961)

#6-10 Saudi arms (palm tree and crossed swords) on back.

Cat. #	Denomination	Date, description	VG	VF	Unc
6	1 RIYAL	L. AH1379 (1961). Brown on lt. blue and green unpt. Hill of Light at ctr. Back violet-brown and green. Sign. I.	2.00	7.50	30.00

Cat. #	Denomination	Date, description	VG	VF	Unc
7	5 RIYALS	L. AH1379 (1961). Blue and green. City wall at ctr.			
		a. Sign. #1.	15.00	60.00	225.00
		b. Sign. #2.	20.00	75.00	275.00

Cat. #	Denomination	Date, description	VG	VF	Unc
54	500 DOBRAS	12.7.1977. Purple and m/c. Turtle at ctr. Waterfall on back.	3.00	10.00	22.50

55	1000 DOBRAS	12.7.1977. Blue and m/c. Bananas at ctr. Fruit gatherer on back.	7.00	20.00	75.00

Decreto-Lei No. 6/82

#56-55 like #52-54 except sign. titles: *O MINISTRO DO PLANO* and *O GOVERNADOR*.

56	50 DOBRAS	30.9.1982. Like #52.	.40	1.25	5.00
57	100 DOBRAS	30.9.1982. Like #53.	.50	1.50	7.00
58	500 DOBRAS	30.9.1982. Like #54.	1.75	5.50	20.00

59	1000 DOBRAS	30.9.1982. Like #55.	3.00	10.00	30.00

Decreto-Lei No. 1/88

#60-62 designs like #56-59 except sign. title at l.: *O MINISTRO DA ECONOMIA E FINANCAS*. Printer: TDLR.

60	100 DOBRAS	4.1.1989. Green and m/c. Like #56.	.40	1.25	4.00
61	500 DOBRAS	4.1.1989. Red, purple and m/c. Like #58.	.90	2.00	6.00
62	1000 DOBRAS	4.1.1989. Blue, green and m/c. Like #59.	1.75	5.00	15.00

Banco Central de S.Tomé e Principe

63	1000 DOBRAS	26.8.1993. Violet and blue on m/c unpt. Similar to #62.	FV	FV	8.50
64	2000 DOBRAS				Expected new issue.
65	5000 DOBRAS				Expected new issue.

Listings For:

SALVADOR, see El Salvador

SAMOA, see Western Samoa

Cat. #	Denomination	Date, description	VG	VF	Unc
8	10 RIYALS	*L. AH1379* (1961). Green and pink. Dhows in harbor of Jedda.			
		a. Sign. #1.	15.00	65.00	250.00
		b. Sign. #2.	20.00	85.00	300.00
9	50 RIYALS	*L. AH1379* (1961). Violet and olive. Derrick.			
		a. Sign. #1.	60.00	200.00	750.00
		b. Sign. #2.	60.00	200.00	750.00

Cat. #	Denomination	Date, description	VG	VF	Unc
10	100 RIYALS	*L. AH1379* (1961). Red. Bldg. at l., archway on background at ctr., bldg. at r.			
		a. Sign. #1.	200.00	650.00	1750.
		b. Sign. #2.	175.00	550.00	1500.

1966 (ND) ISSUE

Law of 1.7.AH1379

Cat. #	Denomination	Date, description	VG	VF	Unc
11	1 RIYAL	*L. AH1379* (1966). Purple and m/c. Gov't. bldg. at r. Saudi arms on back.			
		a. Sign. #2.	.50	2.50	10.00
		b. Sign. #3.	.50	2.50	10.00

Cat. #	Denomination	Date, description	VG	VF	Unc
12	5 RIYALS	*L. AH1379* (1966). Green and m/c. Airport. Oil loading on ships at dockside on back.			
		a. Sign. #2.	2.00	7.50	30.00
		b. Sign. #3.	5.00	25.00	65.00

Cat. #	Denomination	Date, description	VG	VF	Unc
13	10 RIYALS	*L. AH1379* (1966). Gray-blue and m/c. Mosque. Al-Masa Wall w/arches on back. Sign. 2.	2.50	9.00	35.00

Cat. #	Denomination	Date, description	VG	VF	Unc
14	50 RIYALS	*L. AH1379* (1966). Brown and m/c. Court-yard of mosque at r. Saudi arms at l., row of palms at ctr. on back.			
		a. Sign. #2.	20.00	60.00	250.00
		b. Sign. #3.	18.00	55.00	225.00

Cat. #	Denomination	Date, description	VG	VF	Unc
15	100 RIYALS	*L. AH1379* (1966). Red and m/c. Gov't. bldg. at r. Derricks on back.			
		a. Sign. #2.	30.00	100.00	400.00
		b. Sign. #3.	25.00	90.00	350.00

1976–77 (ND) ISSUE
Law of 1.7.AH1379

#16-19 Kg. Faisal at r.

Cat. #	Denomination	Date, description	VG	VF	Unc
16	1 RIYAL	L. AH1379 (1977). Red-brown and m/c. Mountain at ctr. Airport on back.	.25	.50	2.00

INCORRECT

CORRECTED

17	5 RIYALS	L. AH1379 (1977). Green, brown and m/c. Irrigation canal at ctr. Dam on back.			
		a. Incorrect *Khamsa* (five) in lower ctr. panel of text.	1.50	5.00	15.00
		b. Corrected *Khamsa* (five) in lower ctr. panel of text.	1.00	2.00	6.50

18	10 RIYALS	L. AH1379 (1977). Magenta, brown and m/c. Oil drilling platform at ctr. Oil refinery on back.	FV	4.00	15.00

Cat. #	Denomination	Date, description	VG	VF	Unc
19	50 RIYALS	L. AH1379 (1976). Green, purple, brown and m/c. Arches of mosque at ctr. Courtyard of mosque on back.	FV	16.00	40.00

20	100 RIYALS	L. AH1379 (1976). Blue, turquoise and m/c. Mosque at ctr., Kg. 'Abd al-'Aziz Ibn Saud at r. Long bldg. w/arches on back.	FV	30.00	70.00

1983–84 (ND) ISSUE
Law of 1.7.AH1379

#21-24 upper l. panel also exists w/unnecessary upper accent mark in "Monetary."

INCORRECT

CORRECTED

21	1 RIYAL	L. AH1379 (1984). Dk. brown on m/c unpt. 7th century gold dinar at l., Kg. Fahd at ctr. r. Flowers and landscape on back. 2 sign. varieties.			
		a. Incorrect text.	FV	1.00	2.00
		b. Corrected "Monetary."	FV	FV	1.25

Cat. #	Denomination	Date, description	VG	VF	Unc
22	5 RIYALS	*L. AH1379* (1983). Purple, brown, and blue-green on m/c unpt. Dhows at l., Kg. Fahd at ctr. r. on back.			
		a. Incorrect text.	FV	1.50	4.50
		b. Corrected "Monetary."	FV	FV	3.25

23	10 RIYALS	*L. AH1379* (1983). Black, brown and purple on m/c unpt. Fortress at l., Kg. Fahd at ctr. r. Palm trees at ctr. r. on back.			
		a. Incorrect text.	FV	4.00	9.00
		b. Corrected "Monetary."	FV	FV	7.00

		INCORRECT		CORRECTED	
26	500 RIYALS	*L. AH1379* (1983). Purple and green on m/c unpt. Courtyard at l., Kg. 'Abd al-'Aziz Ibn Saud at ctr. r. Courtyard of Great Mosque at ctr. on back.			
		a. Incorrect "Five Hundred Riyals" in lower ctr. panel of text.	FV	FV	225.00
		b. Corrected "Five Hundred Riyals" in lower ctr. panel of text.	FV	FV	185.00

24	50 RIYALS	*L. AH1379* (1983). Dk. green and dk. brown on m/c unpt. Mosque of Omar (Dome of the Rock) in Jerusalem at l., Kg. Fahd at ctr. r. Mosque at ctr. on back.			
		a. Incorrect text.	FV	FV	30.00
		b. Corrected "Monetary."	FV	FV	25.00

#25-26 Saudi arms in latent image area at l. ctr.

25	100 RIYALS	*L. AH1379* (1984). Brown-violet and olive-green on m/c unpt. Mosque at l., Kg. Fahd at ctr. r, Mosque at ctr. on back.	FV	FV	45.00

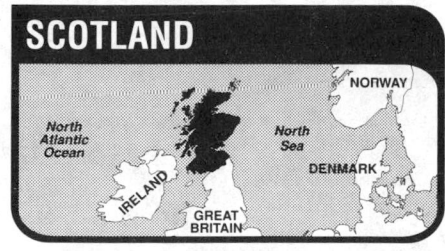

SCOTLAND

Scotland, a part of the United Kingdom of Great Britain and Northern Scotland, consists of the northern part of the island of Great Britain. It has an area of 30,414 sq. mi. (78,772 sq. km.). Capital: Edinburgh. Principal industries are agriculture, fishing, manufacturing and shipbuilding.

In the 5th century, Scotland consisted of four kingdoms; that of the Picts, the Scots, Strathclyde, and Northumbria. The Scottish kingdom was united by Malcolm II (1005–34), but its ruler was forced to do homage to the English crown in 1174. Scotland won independence under Robert Bruce at Bannockburn in 1314 and was ruled by the house of Stuart from 1371 to 1688. The personal union of the kingdoms of England and Scotland was achieved in 1603 by the accession of King James VI of Scotland as James I of England. Scotland was united with England by Parliamentary act in 1707.

RULERS
British

MONETARY SYSTEM
1 Shilling = 12 Pence
1 Pound = 20 Shillings to 1971
1 Pound = 100 New Pence, 1971–1981
1 Pound = 100 Pence, 1982 –

REPLACEMENT NOTES
#111, Z/1, Z/2 or Z/3 prefix; #112 ZA or ZB prefix; #113 ZB prefix.

Bank of Scotland

Cat. #	Denomination	Date, description	VG	VF	Unc
93	10 POUNDS	1938–63. Scottish arms in panel at l., medallion of Goddess of fortune below arms at r. ctr. Bank bldg. on back..			
		a. Sign. Lord Elphinstone and A. W. M. Beveridge.	50.00	140.00	300.00
		b. Sign. Lord Elphinstone and J. Macfarlane.	45.00	120.00	270.00
		c. Sign. Lord Elphinstone and J. B. Crawford.	40.00	100.00	240.00
		d. Sign. Lord Elphinstone and Sir Wm. Watson.	37.50	90.00	210.00
		e. Sign. Sir J. Craig and Sir Wm. Watson.	35.00	82.50	190.00
		f. Sign. Lord Bilsland and Sir Wm. Watson.	25.00	50.00	120.00

Cat. #	Denomination	Date, description	VG	VF	Unc
94	20 POUNDS	1935–65. Like #93.			
		a. Sign. Lord Elphinstone and A. W. M. Beveridge.	80.00	110.00	210.00
		b. Sign. Lord Elphinstone and J. Macfarlane.	70.00	100.00	190.00
		c. Sign. Lord Elphinstone and J. B. Crawford.	65.00	92.50	165.00
		d. Sign. Lord Elphinstone and Sir Wm. Watson.	55.00	85.00	150.00
		e. Sign. Sir J. Craig and Sir Wm. Watson.	50.00	77.50	135.00
		f. Sign. Lord Bilsland and Sir Wm. Watson.	45.00	70.00	120.00
95	100 POUNDS	1935–62. Like #93.			
		a. Sign. Lord Elphinstone and A. W. M. Beveridge.	300.00	375.00	500.00
		b. Sign. Lord Elphinstone and J. Macfarlane.	290.00	350.00	450.00
		c. Sign. Lord Elphinestone and J. B. Crawford.	280.00	330.00	425.00
		d. Sign. Lord Elphinestone and Sir Wm. Watson.	270.00	310.00	400.00
		e. Sign. Sir J. Craig and Sir Wm. Watson.	260.00	290.00	375.00
		f. Sign. Lord Bilsland and Sir Wm. Watson.	250.00	275.00	350.00

1961–66 ISSUES

Cat. #	Denomination	Date, description	VG	VF	Unc
102	1 POUND	10.5.1961–11.5.1965. Lt. brown and lt. blue. Medallion at ctr. Date below.			
		a. Imprint end: *LD*. Sign. Lord Bilsland and Sir Wm. Watson. 10.5.1961–13.2.1964.	3.00	9.00	22.50
		b. Imprint ends: *LTD*. Sign. Lord Bilsland and Sir Wm. Watson. 7.2.1964–11.5.1965.	2.50	8.00	20.00
103	5 POUNDS	14.9.1961–20.9.1961; 7.8.1962. Like #99 but reduced size.			
		a. Sign. Lord Bilsland and Sir Wm. Watson.	10.00	20.00	37.50
		b. Sign. Lord Polwarth and J. Letham.	9.00	17.50	35.00
104	*Deleted.* See #102.				
105	1 POUND	1.6.1966; 1.10.1966; 3.3.1967. Lt. brown and lt. blue. Similar to #102 but *EDINBURGH* and date at r. Sign. Lord Polwarth and J. Letham w/titles: *GOVERNOR* and *TREASURER & GENERAL MANAGER*. 2 wmk. varieties.			
		a. W/o electronic sorting marks on back. 1.6.1966.	2.50	8.00	22.50
		b. W/electronic sorting marks on back 3.3.1967.	2.50	7.50	20.00

Cat. #	Denomination	Date, description	VG	VF	Unc
106	5 POUNDS	1962–67. Blue and lt. brown. Medallion of fortune at ctr. Arms and ship on back, numeral of value filled in at base.			
		a. Sign. Lord Bilsland and Sir Wm. Watson w/titles: *GOVERNOR* and *TREASURER*. 8.8.1962; 14.8.1962; 7.10.1963; 11.1.1965; 12.1.1965.	10.00	20.00	45.00
		b. Lighter shades of printing. Sign. Lord Polwarth and J. Letham w/titles: *GOVERNOR* and *TREASURER & GENERAL MANAGER*. 7.3.1966; 1.2.1967; 2.2.1967.	10.00	20.00	45.00
		c. Sign. titles as b. W/electronic sorting marks on back. 1.11.1967.	9.00	18.50	42.50
107	*Deleted.* See #94.				
108	*Deleted.* See #95.				

1968–69 ISSUE

Cat. #	Denomination	Date, description	VG	VF	Unc
109	1 POUND	17.7.1968. 18.8.1969. Ochre and m/c. Arms at ctr. (2 women).			
		a. *EDINBURGH* 19mm in length. 17.7.1968.	2.50	6.00	22.50
		b. *EDINBURGH* 24mm in length. 18.8.1969.	2.50	6.00	20.00
110	5 POUNDS	1968–69. Green and m/c. Arms at ctr. (2 women).			
		a. *EDINBURGH* 19mm in length. 1.11.1968.	10.00	22.50	65.00
		b. *EDINBURGH* 24mm in length. 8.12.1969.	10.00	20.00	50.00
110A	20 POUNDS	5.5.1969. Like #94. Sign. Lord Polwarth and J. Letham. W/security thread. Wmk: Thistle.	40.00	80.00	—

NOTE: #110 was an emergency printing of 25,000 examples.

1970; 1974 ISSUE

#111–115 Sir W. Scott at r.

Cat. #	Denomination	Date, description	VG	VF	Unc
111	1 POUND	1970-88. Green and m/c. Sailing ship at l., arms at upper ctr., medallion of Pallas seated at r. on back.			
		a. Sign. Lord Polwarth and T. W. Walker. 10.8.1970; 31.8.1971.	4.00	8.00	30.00
		b. Sign. Lord Clydesmuir and T. W. Walker. 7.11.1972; 30.8.1973.	5.00	10.00	40.00
		c. Sign. Lord Clydesmuir and A. M. Russell. 28.10.1974–3.10.1978.	3.00	5.00	10.00
		d. Sign. Lord Clydesmuir and D. B. Pattullo. 15.10.1979; 4.11.1980.	FV	2.50	8.00
		e. Sign. T. N. Risk and D. B. Pattullo. 30.7.1981.	FV	2.50	8.00
		f. W/o sorting marks on back. Sign. like e. 7.10.1983; 9.11.1984; 12.12.1985; 18.11.1986.	FV	2.00	6.50
		g. Sign. T. N. Risk and L. P. Burt. 19.8.1988.	FV	2.00	6.50

Cat. #	Denomination	Date, description	VG	VF	Unc
112	5 POUNDS	1970–88. Blue and m/c. Back similar to #111.			
		a. Sign. Lord Polwarth and T. W. Walker. 10.8.1970.	10.00	30.00	50.00
		b. Sign. Lord Clydesmuir and T. W. Walker. 4.12.1972; 5.9.1973; 4.11.1974.	10.00	30.00	50.00
		c. Sign. Lord Clydesmuir and A. M. Russell. 1.12.1975; 21.11.1977; 19.10.1978.	8.00	10.00	22.50
		d. Sign. Lord Clydesmuir and D. B. Pattullo. 28.11.1980.	FV	10.00	22.50
		e. Sign. T. N. Risk and D. B. Pattullo. 27.7.1981; 25.6.1982.	FV	10.00	22.50
		f. W/o encoding marks. 13.10.1983; 29.2.1988.	FV	8.00	20.00

Cat. #	Denomination	Date, description	VG	VF	Unc
113	10 POUNDS	1974–90. Brown. Medallions of sailing ship at lower l., Pallas seated at upper l. ctr., arms at r. on back.			
		a. Sign. Lord Clydesmuir and A. M. Russell. 1.5.1974–10.10.1979.	16.00	22.50	50.00
		b. Sign. Lord Clydesmuir and D. B. Pattullo. 5.2.1981.	16.00	20.00	40.00
		c. Sign. T. N. Risk and D. B. Pattullo. 22.7.1981; 16.6.1982; 14.10.1983; 17.9.1984; 20.10.1986; 6.8.1987.	FV	FV	30.00
		d. Sign. T.N. Risk and P. Burt. 1.9.1989; 31.10.1990.	FV	FV	27.50

Cat. #	Denomination	Date, description	VG	VF	Unc
114	20 POUNDS	1970–87. Purple. Arms at upper l. above sailing ship w/medallion of Pallas seated below, head office bldg. at ctr. on back.			
		a. Sign. Lord Polwarth and T. W. Walker. 1.10.1970.	40.00	90.00	140.00
		b. Sign. Lord Clydesmuir and T. W. Walker. 3.1.1973.	37.50	45.00	95.00
		c. Sign. Lord Clydesmuir and A. M. Russell. 8.11.1974; 14.1.1977.	35.00	45.00	90.00
		d. Sign. Lord Clydesmuir and D. B. Pattullo. 16.7.1979; 2.2.1981.	FV	42.50	85.00
		e. Sign. T. N. Risk and D. B. Pattullo. 4.8.1981–5.12.1987.	FV	35.00	75.00
115	100 POUNDS	1971—92. Red. Arms at upper l., medallions of sailing ship at lower l., Pallas seated at lower r., head office bldg. at ctr. on back.			
		a. Sign. Lord Clydesmuir and T. W. Walker. 6.12.1971; 6.9.1973.	FV	175.00	300.00
		b. Sign. D. B. Pattullo and P. Burt. 22.1.1992.	FV	FV	225.00

1990–92 ISSUE

#116–118 similar to previous issue. Smaller size notes.

Cat. #	Denomination	Date, description	VG	VF	Unc
116	5 POUNDS	1990–. Similar to #112, but 135 x 70mm.			
		a. Sign. T. N. Risk and P. Burt. 20.6.1990.	FV	FV	16.50
		b. Sign. D. B. Pattullo and P. Burt. 18.1.1993.	FV	FV	14.00

117	10 POUNDS	7.5.1992. Deep brown on m/c unpt. Similar to #113, but 142 x 75mm. Sign. of D. B. Pattullo and P. Burt.	FV	FV	27.00
118	20 POUNDS	1.7.1991; 3.2.1992. Similar to #114 but 148 x 81mm, and *STERLING* added above sign. of D. B. Pattullo and P. Burt.	FV	FV	50.00

1995 COMMEMORATIVE ISSUE

#119–122, Bank of Scotland's Tercentenary

#119–123 Sir W. Scott at l. and as wmk., bank arms at ctr. Bank head office bldg. at lower l., medallion of Pallas seated, arms and medallion of sailing ships at r. on back. Sign. D. B. Pattullo and P. Burt. Printer: TDLR (W/o imprint).

119	5 POUNDS	4.1.1995. Dk. blue and purple on m/c unpt. Oil well riggers working w/drill at ctr. on back.	FV	FV	12.50

Cat. #	Denomination	Date, description	VG	VF	Unc
120	10 POUNDS	1.2.1995. Dk. brown and deep olive-green on m/c unpt. Workers by distilling equipment at ctr. on back.	FV	FV	22.50

121	20 POUNDS	1.5.1995. Violet and brown on m/c unpt. Woman researcher at laboratory station at ctr. on back.	FV	FV	45.00

122	50 POUNDS	1.5.1995. Dk. green and olive-brown on m/c unpt. Music director and violinists at ctr. on back.	FV	FV	110.00

Cat. #	Denomination	Date, description	VG	VF	Unc
123	100 POUNDS	17.7.1995. Red-violet and red-orange on m/c unpt. Golf outing at ctr. on back.	FV	FV	200.00

Clydesdale and North of Scotland Bank Ltd.

Formerly, and later to become the Clydesdale Bank Ltd. again.

1951 ISSUE

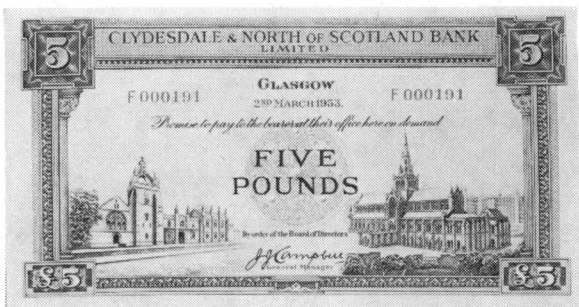

Cat. #	Denomination	Date, description	VG	VF	Unc
192	5 POUNDS	2.5.1951–1.3.1960. Purple. Bldgs. at l. and r.			
		a. Sign. J. J. Campbell.	10.00	25.00	60.00
		b. Sign. R. D. Fairbairn.	10.00	25.00	60.00
193	20 POUNDS	2.5.1951–1.8.1962. Green. 180 x 97mm.			
		a. Sign. J. J. Campbell.	35.00	70.00	125.00
		b. Sign. R. D. Fairbairn.	35.00	70.00	125.00
194	100 POUNDS	2.5.1951. Blue. 180 x 97mm. Sign. J. J. Campbell.	175.00	250.00	425.00

1961 ISSUE

Cat. #	Denomination	Date, description	VG	VF	Unc
195	1 POUND	1.3.1961; 2.5.1962; 1.2.1963. Green. Arms at r. Ship and tug on back.	5.00	10.00	40.00

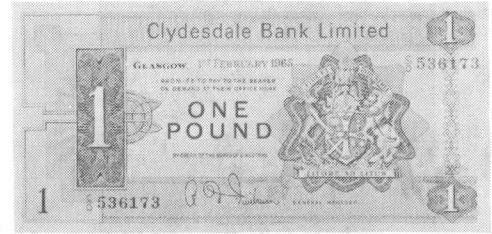

Cat. #	Denomination	Date, description	VG	VF	Unc
196	5 POUNDS	20.9.1961; 1.6.1962 (black date). Dk. blue on m/c unpt. Similar to #195.	10.00	25.00	40.00

Clydesdale Bank Limited

Formerly the Clydesdale and North of Scotland Bank Ltd. Later became Clydesdale Bank PLC.

1963-64 ISSUE

Cat. #	Denomination	Date, description	VG	VF	Unc
197	1 POUND	2.9.1963–3.4.1967. Green. Like #195.	5.00	12.00	45.00
198	5 POUNDS	1963–66. Blue and violet. Like #196.	10.00	22.50	50.00
199	10 POUNDS	1964–70. Brown. Arms at r.	20.00	45.00	90.00
200	20 POUNDS	1964–70. Carmine. Arms at r.	37.50	65.00	120.00
201	100 POUNDS	1964–70. Violet.	175.00	250.00	425.00

1967 ISSUE

| 202 | 1 POUND | 3.4.1967; 1.10.1968; 1.9.1969. Green. Like #197 but lines for electronic sorting on back. | 5.00 | 12.00 | 45.00 |

Cat. #	Denomination	Date, description	VG	VF	Unc
203	5 POUNDS	1967–69. Blue and violet. Like #198 but lines for electronic sorting on back.	10.00	20.00	50.00

1971-81 ISSUES

Cat. #	Denomination	Date, description	VG	VF	Unc
204	1 POUND	1971–81. Greenish-black on m/c unpt. Robert the Bruce at l.			
		a. Sign. R. D. Fairbairn, w/title: GENERAL MANAGER. 1.3.1971.	5.00	12.00	30.00
		b. Sign. A. R. Macmillan, w/title: GENERAL MANAGER. 1.5.1972; 1.8.1973.	8.00	15.00	40.00
		c. Sign. A. R. Macmillan, w/title: CHIEF GENERAL MANAGER. 1.3.1974–27.2.1981.	FV	2.50	8.00

Cat. #	Denomination	Date, description	VG	VF	Unc
211	1 POUND	1982–88. Like #204.			
		a. W/sorting marks. Sign. A. R. Macmillan. 29.3.1982.	FV	3.00	10.00
		b. Like a. Sign. Colg-Hamilton. 5.1.1983.	FV	2.50	8.00
		c. W/o sorting marks. Sign. Colg-Hamilton. 8.4.1985; 25.11.1985.	FV	2.50	8.00
		d. Sign. title: *CHIEF EXECUTIVE*. 18.9.1987; 9.11.1988.	FV	3.00	9.00

Cat. #	Denomination	Date, description	VG	VF	Unc
205	5 POUNDS	1.3.1971; 1.5.1972; 1.2.1980. Blue. R. Burns at l.	9.00	20.00	45.00
206	*Deleted.* See #205.				

207	10 POUNDS	1.3.1972; 1.3.1977; 31.1.1979. Brown and lt. purple. D. Livingstone at l.	FV	25.00	60.00
208	20 POUNDS	1.3.1972; 1.2.1978. Lilac. Lord Kelvin at l.	FV	50.00	100.00

212	5 POUNDS	1982–89. Like #205.			
		a. Sign. A. R. Macmillan. 29.3.1982.	8.00	14.00	35.00
		b. Sign. Colg-Hamilton. 5.1.1903.	FV	12.00	30.00
		c. W/o sorting marks. Sign. Colg-Hamilton. 8.4.1985-25.11.1986.	FV	10.00	22.50
		d. Sign. title: *CHIEF EXECUTIVE*. 18.9.1987; 2.8.1988; 28.6.1989.	FV	9.00	17.50
213	10 POUNDS	1982–87. Like #207.			
		a. Sign. A. R. Macmillan. 29.3.1982.	17.00	21.00	50.00
		b. Sign. Colg-Hamilton. 5.1.1983; 8.4.1985; 18.9.1986.	FV	17.50	32.50
		c. Sign. title: *CHIEF EXECUTIVE*. 18.9.1987.	FV	17.00	30.00

209	50 POUNDS	1.9.1981. Olive and m/c. A. Smith at l. Sailing ships, blacksmith implements and farm on back.	FV	90.00	135.00
210	100 POUNDS	1.3.1972. Red and m/c. Lord Kelvin at l. Lecture Hall at Glasgow University on back.	FV	175.00	300.00

Clydesdale Bank PLC

Formerly the Clydesdale Bank Limited.

1982–89 "Sterling" ISSUES

#211–220 wmk: Old sailing ships.

214	20 POUNDS	1982–87. Like #208.			
		a. Sign. A. R. Macmillan. 29.3.1982.	FV	45.00	100.00
		b. Sign. Colg-Hamilton. 5.1.1983; 8.4.1985.	FV	40.00	75.00
		c. Sign. title: *CHIEF EXECUTIVE*. 18.9.1987.	FV	37.50	65.00

Cat. #	Denomination	Date, description	VG	VF	Unc
215	10 POUNDS	7.5.1988; 3.9.1989. Dk. brown on m/c unpt. D. Livingstone in front of map at l. Blantyre (Livingstone's birthplace) on back. Wmk: Sailing ships.	FV	FV	40.00
216	50 POUNDS	3.9.1989. Olive-green and m/c. Similar to #209.	FV	FV	120.00
217	100 POUNDS	8.4.1985. Red and m/c. Lord Ilay at r. Balmoral Castle on back.	FV	FV	250.00

1990–92 "Sterling" ISSUE

#218–221 smaller size notes.

218	5 POUNDS	2.4.1990. Blue and m/c. Similar to #205, but 135 x 70mm.	FV	FV	13.00

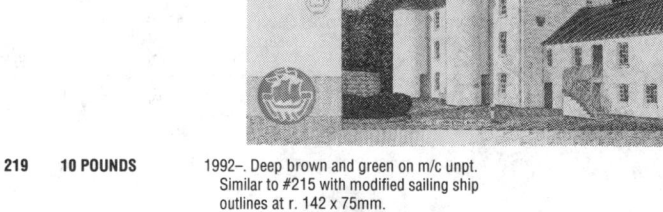

219	10 POUNDS	1992–. Deep brown and green on m/c unpt. Similar to #215 with modified sailing ship outlines at r. 142 x 75mm.			
		a. Sign. Colg-Hamilton. 3.9.1992.	FV	FV	32.50
		b. Sign. Charles-Love. 5.1.1993.	FV	FV	22.50
220	20 POUNDS	1990–93. Violet, purple, brown and brown-orange on m/c unpt. Robert the Bruce at l. His equestrian statue, Monymusk reliquary, Stirling castle and Wallace Monument on back. 148 x 80mm.			
		a. Sign. Colg-Hamilton. 30.11.1990; 2.8.1991; 3.9.1992.	FV	FV	55.00
		b. Sign. Charles-Love. 5.1.1993.	FV	FV	70.00
222	100 POUNDS	9.11.1991. Red and m/c. Similar to #217, but reduced size.	FV	FV	175.00

1994 "Sterling" ISSUE

Cat. #	Denomination	Date, description	VG	VF	Unc
223	20 POUNDS	1.9.1994. Like #220. Purple, dk. brown and deep orange on m/c unpt. Sign. F. Cicutto.	FV	FV	45.00
224	50 POUNDS			Expected new issue.	
225	100 POUNDS			Expected new issue.	

Royal Bank of Scotland

Later became the Royal Bank of Scotland Limited.

1955–66 ISSUES

324	1 POUND	1955–64. Dk. blue on yellow and brown unpt. Sign. W. R. Ballantyne. 152 x 85mm.	3.50	8.50	22.50

325	1 POUND	1.8.1964–1.7.1967. Black and brown on yellow unpt. Like #322, but 150 x 71mm.			
		a. Sign. W. R. Ballantyne. 1.8.1964–1.6.1965.	3.00	8.00	20.00
		b. Sign. G. P. Robertson. 2.8.1965–1.7.1967.	3.00	8.00	20.00
326	5 POUNDS	2.11.1964; 2.8.1965. Dk. blue, orange-brown and yellow. Uniface. Like #323, but 140 x 85mm.	12.00	25.00	50.00
327	1 POUND	1.9.1967. Green and m/c. D. Dale at l.	2.50	5.00	15.00

328	5 POUNDS	1.1.1966. Blue and m/c. D. Dale at l.	15.00	25.00	60.00

Royal Bank of Scotland Limited

Formerly the Royal Bank of Scotland. Later became the Royal Bank of Scotland plc.

1969 ISSUE

Cat. #	Denomination	Date, description	VG	VF	Unc
329	1 POUND	19.3.1969. Green. Bridge.	3.00	5.00	15.00
330	5 POUNDS	19.3.1969. Blue. Arms at l.	9.00	13.50	40.00
331	10 POUNDS	19.3.1969. Brown. Arms al ctr. Bridge on back.	20.00	37.50	85.00
332	20 POUNDS	19.3.1969. Purple. Bridge on back.	40.00	65.00	135.00

Cat. #	Denomination	Date, description	VG	VF	Unc
333	100 POUNDS	19.3.1969. Red. Bridge on back.	180.00	250.00	400.00

1970 ISSUE

Cat. #	Denomination	Date, description	VG	VF	Unc
334	1 POUND	15.7.1970. Like #329 but only 1 sign.	2.00	5.00	15.00
335	5 POUNDS	15.7.1970. Like #330 but only 1 sign.	8.50	20.00	40.00

1972 ISSUE

#336–340 arms at r. Printer: BWC.

Cat. #	Denomination	Date, description	VG	VF	Unc
336	1 POUND	5.1.1972–1.5.1981. Dk. green on m/c unpt. Edinburgh Castle on back. Wmk: A. Smith.	FV	2.50	8.00

Cat. #	Denomination	Date, description	VG	VF	Unc
337	5 POUNDS	5.1.1972–2.4.1973; 1.5.1975; 1.5.1979; 1.5.1981. Blue and m/c. Culzean Castle on back.	FV	15.00	30.00
338	10 POUNDS	5.1.1972; 2.5.1978; 10.1.1981. Brown and m/c. Glamis Castle on back.	FV	25.00	50.00

Cat. #	Denomination	Date, description	VG	VF	Unc
339	20 POUNDS	5.1.1972; 1.5.1981. Purple and m/c. Brodick Castle on back.	FV	50.00	90.00

Cat. #	Denomination	Date, description	VG	VF	Unc
340	100 POUNDS	5.1.1972; 1.5.1981. Red and m/c. Castle on back.	FV	225.00	375.00

Royal Bank of Scotland plc

Formerly the Royal Bank of Scotland Limited.

REPLACEMENT NOTE

#341–356 Z/1 prefix.

1982-86 ISSUES

#341–345 arms at r. Sign. title varieties.

Cat. #	Denomination	Date, description	VG	VF	Unc
341	1 POUND	1982–85. Like #336. Sign. C. Winter. Printer: BWC.			
		a. W/sorting marks. 3.5.1982.	2.50	5.00	25.00
		b. W/o sorting marks. 1.10.1983; 4.1.1984; 3.1.1985.	FV	2.50	8.00
341A	1 POUND	1986. Like #341. Printer: TDLR.			
		a. Sign. C. Winters. 1.5.1986.	FV	2.25	6.50
		b. Sign. R. M. Maiden. 17.12.1986.	FV	2.50	6.00

Cat. #	Denomination	Date, description	VG	VF	Unc
342	5 POUNDS	1982–85. Like #337. Printer: BWC.			
		a. W/sorting marks. 3.5.1982; 5.1.1983.	FV	15.00	45.00
		b. W/o sorting marks. 4.1.1984.	FV	13.50	40.00
		c. Sign. title larger size. 3.1.1985.	FV	12.50	45.00
342A	5 POUNDS	17.12.1986. Like #342. Printer: TDLR.	FV	11.00	22.50

Cat. #	Denomination	Date, description	VG	VF	Unc
343	10 POUNDS	3.5.1982; 4.1.1984; 17.12.1986. Like #338. Printer: BWC.	FV	25.00	40.00
343A	10 POUNDS	17.12.1986. Like #343. Printer: TDLR.	FV	22.50	35.00

Cat. #	Denomination	Date, description	VG	VF	Unc
347	5 POUNDS	25.3.1987; 22.6.1988. Black and blue-black on m/c unpt. Culzean castle on back.	FV	FV	16.50

| 348 | 10 POUNDS | 25.3.1987; 24.2.1988; 22.2.1989; 24.1.1990. Deep brown and brown on m/c unpt. Glamis castle on back. | FV | FV | 27.50 |

| 344 | 20 POUNDS | 3.5.1982; 3.1.1985. Like #339. Printer: BWC. | FV | 37.50 | 85.00 |
| 345 | 100 POUNDS | 3.5.1982. Like #340. Printer: BWC. | FV | 175.00 | 250.00 |

1987 ISSUE

#346–350 Lord Ilay at r. and as wmk. Printer: TDLR.

| 349 | 20 POUNDS | 25.3.1987; 24.1.1990. Black and purple on m/c unpt. Brodick castle on back. | FV | FV | 55.00 |
| 350 | 100 POUNDS | 25.3.1987; 24.1.1990. Red on m/c unpt. Balmoral castle on back. | FV | FV | 225.00 |

1988 ISSUE

#351–356 designs similar to #346–350, but reduced size notes.

| 346 | 1 POUND | 25.3.1987. Dk. green on m/c unpt. Edinburgh castle on back. | FV | FV | 6.50 |

351	1 POUND	1988–. Similar to #346, but 127 x 65mm. Printer: TDLR.			
		a. Sign.A. Maiden w/title: *MANAGING DIRECTOR*. 13.12.1988; 26.7.1989; 19.12.1990.	FV	FV	5.00
		b. Sign. C. Winter w/title: *CHIEF EXECUTIVE*. 24.7.1991.	FV	FV	4.50
		c. Sign. G. R. Matthewson w/title: *CHIEF EXECUTIVE*. 24.3.1992; 24.2.1993.	FV	FV	4.00
		d. W/o wmk. 23.3.1994.	FV	2.50	32.50

1992 COMMEMORATIVE ISSUE

#352, Euorpean summit at Edinburgh, Dec. 1992

Cat. #	Denomination	Date, description	VG	VF	Unc
352	1 POUND	8.12.1992. Like #351c. Additional purple ovpt. containing commemorative inscription at l.	FV	FV	4.00

REGULAR ISSUE

353	5 POUNDS	13.12.1988; 24.1.1990. Similar to #347, but 135 x 70mm. Sign. A. Maiden w/title: *MANAGING DIRECTOR.*	FV	FV	13.50
354	10 POUNDS	28.1.1992; 7.5.1992; 24.2.1993. Similar to #348, but 142 x 75mm. Sign. G. R. Matthewson, w/title: *CHIEF EXECUTIVE.*	FV	FV	22.50
355	20 POUNDS	27.3.1991. Similiar to #349 but 150 x 81mm.			
		a. Sign. C. Winter w/title: *CHIEF EXECUTIVE.* 27.3.1991.	FV	FV	50.00
		b. Sign. G. R. Mathewson. 28.1.1992.	FV	FV	42.50
356	100 POUNDS				Expected new issue.

1994 COMMEMORATIVE

#357, Robert Louis Stevenson Death Centennial

357	1 POUND	3.12.1994. Like 351c. Commemorative ovpt. in wmk area. Back Portr. Stevenson and images of his life.	FV	FV	4.00

Listings for:

SERBIA, see Bosnia & Herzegovina, Croatia or Yugoslavia

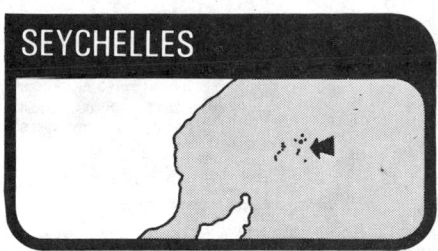

SEYCHELLES

The Republic of Seychelles, an archipelago of 85 granite and coral islands situated in the Indian Ocean 600 miles (965 km.) northeast of Madagascar, has an area of 156 sq. mi. (455 sq. km.) and a population of 70,400. Among these islands are the Aldabra Islands, the Farquhar Group, and Ile Desroches, which the United Kingdom ceded to the Seychelles upon its independence. Capital: Victoria, on Mahe. The economy is based on fishing, a plantation system of agriculture and tourism. Copra, cinnamon and vanilla are exported.

Although the Seychelles are marked on Portuguese charts of the early 16th century, the first recorded visit to the islands, by an English ship, occurred in 1609. The Seychelles were annexed to France by Captain Lazare Picault in 1743 and permanently settled in 1768, with the intention of establishing spice plantations to compete with the Dutch monopoly of the spice trade. British troops seized the islands in 1810, during the Napoleonic Wars; they were formally ceded to Britain by the Treaty of Paris, 1814. The Seychelles were a dependency of Mauritius until Aug. 31, 1903, when they became a separate British Crown Colony. The colony was granted limited internal self-government in 1970, and attained independence on June 28, 1976, becoming Britain's last African possession to do so. Seychelles is a member of the Commonwealth of Nations. The president is the Head of State and of Government.

RULERS
British to 1976

MONETARY SYSTEM
1 Rupee = 100 Cents

GOVERNMENT

1954 ISSUE

#11–13 Qn. Elizabeth II in profile at r. Denominations on back. Various date and sign. varieties. Printer: TDLR.

Cat. #	Denomination	Date, description	VG	VF	Unc
11	5 RUPEES	1954; 1960. Lilac and green.			
		a. 1.8.1954.	8.50	35.00	100.00
		b. 1.8.1960.	7.00	20.00	100.00

12	10 RUPEES	1954–67. Green and red. Like #11.			
		a. 1.8.1954.	12.50	45.00	400.00
		b. 1.8.1960.	10.00	40.00	350.00
		c. 1.5.1963.	10.00	35.00	300.00
		d. 1.1.1967.	10.00	35.00	300.00

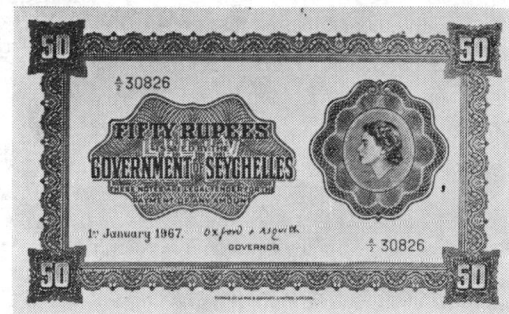

Cat. #	Denomination	Date, description	VG	VF	Unc
13	50 RUPEES	1954–67. Black. Like #11.			
		a. 1.8.1954.	30.00	100.00	650.00
		b. 1.8.1960.	25.00	90.00	650.00
		c. 1.5.1963.	25.00	85.00	650.00
		d. 1.1.1967.	25.00	85.00	650.00

1968 ISSUE

#14–18 Qn. Elizabeth II at r. Wmk: Black parrot's head. Various date and sign. varieties.

Cat. #	Denomination	Date, description	VG	VF	Unc
17	50 RUPEES	1968–73. Olive and m/c. Sailing ship at l. Word *SEX* discernible in trees at r.			
		a. 1.1.1968.	12.50	50.00	350.00
		b. 1.1.1969.	15.00	65.00	400.00
		c. 1.10.1970.	12.00	55.00	350.00
		d. 1.1.1972.	7.50	35.00	300.00
		e. 1.8.1973.	7.50	35.00	300.00

14	5 RUPEES	1.1.1968. Dk. brown and m/c. Parrot at l.	1.00	4.00	25.00

15	10 RUPEES	1968; 1974. Lt. blue and m/c. Sea tortoise at l. ctr.			
		a. 1.1.1968.	3.00	12.00	110.00
		b. 1.1.1974.	2.50	10.00	100.00

18	100 RUPEES	1968–75. Red and m/c. Land turtles at l. ctr.			
		a. 1.1.1968.	37.50	150.00	900.00
		b. 1.1.1969.	75.00	350.00	1200.
		c. 1.1.1972.	50.00	135.00	650.00
		d. 1.8.1973.	45.00	125.00	650.00
		e. 1.6.1975.	45.00	125.00	650.00

REPUBLIC

#19–22 Pres. J. R. Mancham at r. Wmk: Black parrot's head.

16	20 RUPEES	1968–74. Purple and m/c. Nesting bird at l.			
		a. 1.1.1968.	6.00	20.00	250.00
		b. 1.1.1971.	5.00	12.50	120.00
		c. 1.1.1974.	4.00	10.00	110.00

Seychelles Monetary Authority

#23–27 vertical format on back. Wmk: Black parrot's head.

Cat. #	Denomination	Date, description	VG	VF	Unc
19	10 RUPEES	ND (1976). Dk. blue and blue on m/c unpt. Seashell at lower l. Hut w/boats and cliffs on back.	1.00	2.25	8.50

Cat. #	Denomination	Date, description	VG	VF	Unc
23	10 RUPEES	ND. Blue, green and pink on m/c unpt. Nesting bird at ctr. Girl picking flowers on back.	FV	1.75	4.00

| 20 | 20 RUPEES | ND (1977). Purple on m/c unpt. Sea tortoise at lower l. Sailboat on back. | 2.00 | 4.50 | 15.00 |

| 24 | 25 RUPEES | ND. Brown, purple and gold on m/c unpt. Coconuts at ctr. Green and brown back; man and basket. | FV | 4.00 | 12.00 |

| 21 | 50 RUPEES | ND (1977). Olive on m/c unpt. Fish at lower l. Fishermen on back. | 5.00 | 10.00 | 40.00 |

| 25 | 50 RUPEES | ND. Olive, brown and lilac on m/c unpt. Turtle at ctr. Bldgs. and palm trees on back. | FV | 8.00 | 30.00 |

| 22 | 100 RUPEES | ND (1977). Red and m/c. 2 birds at lower l. Dock area and islands on back. | 10.00 | 20.00 | 70.00 |

Cat. #	Denomination	Date, description	VG	VF	Unc
26	100 RUPEES	ND. Red and lt. blue on m/c unpt. Tropical fish at ctr. Man w/tools, swordfish on back.	22.50	55.00	200.00

| 27 | 100 RUPEES | ND. Brown and lt. blue on m/c unpt. Like #26. | FV | 22.50 | 60.00 |

Central Bank of Seychelles

#28–31 like previous issue except for new bank name and sign. title. Wmk: Black parrot's head.

| 28 | 10 RUPEES | ND (1983). Like #23. | FV | FV | 5.00 |
| 29 | 25 RUPEES | ND (1983). Like #24. | FV | FV | 9.00 |

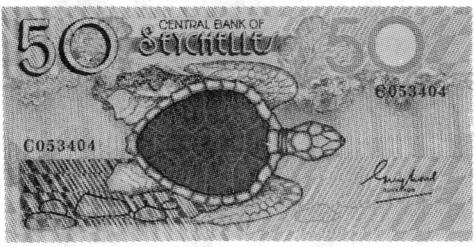

| 30 | 50 RUPEES | ND (1983). Like #25. | FV | FV | 23.50 |
| 31 | 100 RUPEES | ND (1983). Like #27. | FV | FV | 42.50 |

Central Bank of Seychelles/Labank Santral Sesel

#32–35 bank at ctr. flying fish at l. and ctr. r. Wmk: Black parrot's head.

Cat. #	Denomination	Date, description	VG	VF	Unc
32	10 RUPEES	ND (1989). Blue-black and deep blue-green on m/c unpt. Boy scouts at lower l., image of man w/flags and broken chain at r. Local people dancing to drummer at ctr. on back.	FV	FV	4.00

| 33 | 25 RUPEES | ND (1989). Purple on m/c unpt. 2 men w/coconuts at lower l., boy near palms at upper r. Primitive ox drawn farm equipment on back. | FV | FV | 10.00 |

| 34 | 50 RUPEES | ND (1989). Dk. green and brown on m/c unpt. 2 men in boat, Seychelles man at lower l., prow of boat in geometric outline at upper r. Seagulls, fishermen w/nets, modern ships on back. | FV | FV | 18.50 |

| 35 | 100 RUPEES | ND (1989). Red and brown on m/c unpt. Men in ox-cart at lower l., girl w/shell at upper r. Bldg. at ctr. on back. | FV | FV | 35.00 |

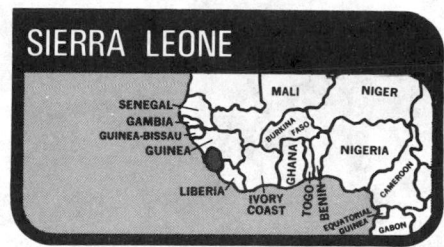

SIERRA LEONE

The Republic of Sierra Leone, a British Commonwealth nation located in western Africa between Guinea and Liberia, has an area of 27,699 sq. mi. (71,740 sq. km.) and a population of *4.1 million. Capital: Freetown. The economy is predominantly agricultural but mining contributes significantly to export revenues. Diamonds, iron ore, palm kernels, cocoa, and coffee are exported.

The coast of Sierra Leone was first visited by Portuguese and British slavers in the 15th and 16th centuries. The first settlement, at Freetown, 1787, was established as a refuge for freed slaves within the British Empire, runaway slaves from the United States and blacks discharged from the British armed forces. The first settlers were virtually wiped out by tribal attacks and disease. The colony was reestablished under the auspices of the Sierra Leone Company and transferred to the British Crown in 1907. The interior region was secured and established as a protectorate in 1896. Sierra Leone became independent within the Commonwealth on April 27, 1961, and adopted a republican constitution ten years later. It is a member of the Commonwealth of Nations. The president is Chief of State and Head of Government.

RULERS

British to 1971

MONETARY SYSTEM

1 Leone = 100 Cents

REPLACEMENT NOTES

#1d, 2d, 4–8, 15-19, Z/1 prefix (may continue on to Z/2, Z/3 etc.)

Bank of Sierra Leone

1964 (ND) ISSUE

#1–3 w/300-year-old cotton tree and court bldg. on face. Sign. varieties. Wmk: Lion's head. Printer: TDLR.

			VG	VF	Unc
1	1 LEONE	ND (1964–70). Green and m/c. Diamond mining on back.			
		a. ND (1964). Prefix A/1–A/6.	4.50	13.50	55.00
		b. ND (1969). Prefix A/7–A/8.	6.00	18.50	75.00
		c. ND (1970). Prefix A/9–A/12.	2.75	8.00	45.00

			VG	VF	Unc
2	2 LEONES	ND (1964–70). Red and m/c. Village scene on back.			
		a. ND (1964). Prefix B/1–B/21.	5.00	15.00	60.00
		b. ND (1967). Prefix B/22–B/25.	12.50	35.00	140.00
		c. ND (1969). Prefix B/26–B/30.	6.00	18.50	75.00
		d. ND (1970). Prefix B/31–B/41.	5.00	16.00	65.00

Cat. #	Denomination	Date, description	VG	VF	Unc
3	5 LEONES	ND (1964). Purple and m/c. Dockside and boats on back. Prefix C/1.	25.00	150.00	575.00

1974–80 ISSUE

#4–8 Pres. S. Stevens at l. Wmk: Lion's head. Printer: TDLR.

			VG	VF	Unc
4	50 CENTS	ND; 1979–84. Brown and m/c. Bank on back.			
		a. ND (1972). Prefix D/1–D/2.	.75	2.00	5.50
		b. ND (1974). Prefix D/3–D/5.	.75	2.00	5.50
		c. 1.7.1979.	.50	1.00	3.00
		d. 1.7.1981.	.15	.50	1.50
		e. 4.8.1984.	.10	.25	.75

			VG	VF	Unc
5	1 LEONE	1974–84. Green and m/c. Bank on back.			
		a. 19.4.1974.	.75	3.00	7.50
		b. 1.1.1978.	1.00	4.00	10.00
		c. 1.3.1980.	.25	1.00	4.00
		d. 1.7.1981.	.25	.50	2.00
		e. 4.8.1984.	.25	.50	1.00

Cat. #	Denomination	Date, description	VG	VF	Unc
6	2 LEONES	1974–85. Red-orange and m/c. Bank on back.			
		a. 19.4.1974.	1.25	3.75	11.50
		b. 1.1.1978.	6.00	15.00	45.00
		c. 1.7.1978.	1.00	4.00	12.50
		d. 1.7.1979.	.75	2.00	7.50
		e. 1.5.1980.	.75	2.00	7.00
		f. 1.7.1983.	.35	.75	3.00
		g. 4.8.1984; 4.8.1985.	.20	.45	1.25

Cat. #	Denomination	Date, description	VG	VF	Unc
7	5 LEONES	1975–85. Purple, dk. blue and m/c. Plant leaves at ctr. Parliament bldg. on back.			
		a. 4.8.1975. Prefix C/1.	3.00	10.00	32.50
		b. 1.7.1978. Prefix C/2.	2.00	7.00	25.00
		c. 1.3.1980. Prefix C/3.	1.00	4.00	12.50
		d. 1.7.1981.	.75	3.00	7.50
		e. 19.4.1984; 4.8.1984; 4.8.1985.	.50	1.00	3.50

Cat. #	Denomination	Date, description	VG	VF	Unc
8	10 LEONES	1980; 1984. Blue-gray and m/c. Dredging operation on back.			
		a. 1.7.1980.	1.00	4.00	12.00
		b. 19.4.1984; 4.8.1984.	.40	1.00	3.00

1980 COMMEMORATIVE ISSUE

#9–13 red ovpt: *COMMEMORATING THE ORGANISATION OF AFRICAN UNITY CONFERENCE / FREETOWN 1980.*

| 9 | 50 CENTS | 1.7.1980. Ovpt. in 4 lines at upper l. ctr., date twice on face. Ovpt. on #4. | — | — | 25.00 |

#10–13 ovpt. in circle around wmk. area at r., date below.

				VG	VF	Unc
10	1 LEONE	1.7.1980. Ovpt. on #5.		—	—	30.00
11	2 LEONES	1.7.1980. Ovpt. on #6.		—	—	40.00
12	5 LEONES	1.7.1980. Ovpt. on #7.		—	—	50.00
13	10 LEONES	1.7.1980. Ovpt. on #8.		—	—	60.00

NOTE: #9–13 were prepared in special booklets.

1982 ISSUE

Cat. #	Denomination	Date, description	VG	VF	Unc
14	20 LEONES	1982; 1984. Brown and m/c. Tree at ctr., Pres. S. Stevens at r. 2 youths preparing food on back. Printer: BWC. Wmk: Lion's head.			
		a. 24.8.1982.	1.00	2.50	10.00
		b. 24.8.1984.	.40	1.10	4.50

1988–93 ISSUE

#15–21 arms at upper ctr. Wmk: Lion's head.

#15–19 Pres. Dr. Joseph Saidu Momoh at r.

| 15 | 10 LEONES | 27.4.1988. Dk. green and purple on m/c unpt. Steer at l., farmer harvesting at ctr. on back. | FV | .50 | 2.00 |

| 16 | 20 LEONES | 27.4.1988. Brown, red and green on m/c unpt. Like #14, but new president at r. | FV | .65 | 2.50 |

Cat. #	Denomination	Date, description	VG	VF	Unc
17	50 LEONES	1988–89. Purple, blue and black on m/c unpt. Sports stadium at ctr. Dancers on back.			
		a. W/o imprint. 27.4.1988.	FV	1.50	3.00
		b. Printer: TDLR. 27.4.1989.	FV	.75	2.00

Cat. #	Denomination	Date, description	VG	VF	Unc
18	100 LEONES	1988–90. Blue and black on m/c unpt. Bldg. and ship at ctr. Local designs at l. and r., modern bldg. at l. ctr. on back.			
		a. W/o imprint. 27.4.1988.	FV	1.00	4.50
		b. Printer: TDLR. 27.4.1989; 26.9.1990.	FV	.65	2.50

Cat. #	Denomination	Date, description	VG	VF	Unc
19	500 LEONES	27.4.1991. Red-brown and dark green on m/c unpt. Modern bldg. below arms at l. ctr. 2 boats on back.	FV	1.00	4.00

#20-21 arms at upper ctr. Printer: TDLR.

Cat. #	Denomination	Date, description	VG	VF	Unc
20	1000 LEONES	4.8.1993. Red and yellow on m/c unpt. B. Bureh at r., carving at lower ctr. Dish antenna at l. ctr. on back.	FV	1.50	5.50

Cat. #	Denomination	Date, description	VG	VF	Unc
21	5000 LEONES	4.8.1993. Blue and violet on m/c unpt. S. Pieh at r., bldg. at lower ctr. Dam at l. ctr. on back.	FV	6.50	20.00

1995–96 ISSUE

#22–25 arms at upper ctr. Wmk: Lion's head. Printer: TDLR.

Cat. #	Denomination	Date, description	VG	VF	Unc
22	50 LEONES			Expected new issue.	
23	100 LEONES			Expected new issue.	
24	500 LEONES	27.4.1995. Blue-green, brown and green on m/c unpt. K. Londo at r., spearhead at l., bldg. at lower ctr. Fishing boats at l. ctr., artistic carp at r.	FV	FV	2.50

COLLECTOR SERIES

Cat. #	Date, denomination	Description	Issue Price	Mkt. Val.
CS1	ND 50 CENTS - 5 LEONES	#4–7 w/ovpt: *SPECIMEN* and Maltese cross prefix serial #.	14.00	20.00

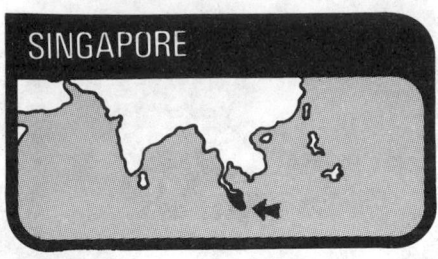

The Republic of Singapore, a British Commonwealth nation situated at the southern tip of the Malay peninsula, has an area of 224 sq. mi. (633 sq. km.) and a population of *2.7 million. Capital: Singapore. The economy is based on entrepot trade, manufacturing and oil. Rubber, petroleum products, machinery and spices are exported.

Singapore's modern history - it was an important shipping center in the 14th century before the rise of Malacca and Penang - began in 1819 when Sir Thomas Stamford Raffles, an agent for the British East India Company, founded the town of Singapore. By 1825 its trade exceeded that of Malacca and Penang combined. The opening of the Suez Canal (1869) and the demand for rubber and tin created by the automobile and packaging industries combined to make Singapore one of the major ports of the world. In 1826 Singapore, Penang and Malacca were combined to form the Straits Settlements, which was made a Crown Colony in 1867. Singapore became a separate Crown Colony in 1946 when the Straits Settlements was dissolved. It joined in the formation of Malaysia in 1963, but broke away on Aug. 9, 1956, to become an independent republic. Singapore is a member of the Commonwealth of Nations. The president is Chief of State. The prime minister is Head of Government.

MONETARY SYSTEM
1 Dollar = 100 Cents

REPLACEMENT NOTES
Z/1 (may continue on with Z/2, Z/3, etc.). #26 and higher, noted using double letters prefix have ZZ prefix.

SIGNATURE SEAL VARIETIES

Type I: Dragon, seal script, lion	Type II: Sealscript w/symbol

1967-73 ISSUE
#1-2, 6 wmk: Lion's head. Sign. varieties. Printer: BWC.

Cat. #	Denomination	Date, description	VG	VF	Unc
1	1 DOLLAR	ND (1967-72) Blue on m/c unpt. Lt. red flowers at ctr.; arms at r. Apartment bldgs. on back.			
		a. W/o red seal. Sign. Lim Kim San (1967).	.85	1.50	10.00
		b. Red sign. seal Type 1 at center. Sign. Dr. Goh Keng Swee (1970).	1.00	2.50	15.00
		c. W/o red seal. Sign. Hon Sui Sen (1971).	.75	2.00	12.00
		d. Red sign. seal Type II at ctr. Sign. Hon Sui Sen (1972).	.75	1.00	6.00

Cat. #	Denomination	Date, description	VG	VF	Unc
2	5 DOLLARS	ND (1967-73). Green on m/c unpt. Lt. orange flowers at ctr., arms at upper r. Small boats at moorings on back.			
		a. W/o red seal. Sign. Lim Kim San (1967).	3.75	10.00	50.00
		b. Red sign. seal Type I at ctr. Sign. Dr. Goh Keng Swee (1970).	20.00	100.00	300.00
		c. W/o red seal. Sign. Hon Sui Sen (1972).	6.00	12.50	80.00
		d. Red sign. seal Type II at ctr. Sign. Hon Sui Sen (1973).	3.75	5.50	40.00

#3-5, 7-8A wmk: Lion's head. Printer: TDLR.

Cat. #	Denomination	Date, description	VG	VF	Unc
3	10 DOLLARS	ND (1967-73). Red on m/c unpt. Lilac flowers at ctr., arms at lower r. 4 hands clasping wrists over map on back.			
		a. W/o red seal. Sign. Lim Kim San (1967).	7.50	10.00	50.00
		b. Red sign. seal Type I at ctr. Sign. Dr. Goh Keng Swee (1970).	9.00	18.50	110.00
		c. W/o red seal. Sign. Hon Sui Sen (1972).	8.00	11.50	60.00
		d. Red sign. seal Type II at ctr. Sign. Hon Sui Sen (1973).	7.50	10.00	40.00

Cat. #	Denomination	Date, description	VG	VF	Unc
4	25 DOLLARS	ND (1972). Dk. brown on m/c unpt. Yellow flowers at ctr., arms at upper r. Capitol on back.	18.50	30.00	75.00
5	50 DOLLARS	ND (1967-73). Blue on m/c unpt. Violet flowers at ctr., arms at lower r. Bldgs. and boats on back.			
		a. W/o red seal. Sign. Lim Kim San (1967).	37.50	60.00	140.00
		b. Red sign. seal Type I at ctr. Sign. Dr. Goh Keng Swee (1970).	40.00	65.00	160.00
		c. W/o red seal. Sign. Hon Sui Sen (1972).	37.50	60.00	150.00
		d. Red sign. seal Type II at ctr. Sign. Hon Sui Sen (1973).	35.00	50.00	100.00

Cat. #	Denomination	Date, description	VG	VF	Unc
6	100 DOLLARS	ND (1967–73). Blue and violet on m/c unpt. Red flowers at ctr., arms at r. Sailing vessels in harbor on back.			
		a. W/o red seal. Sign. Lim Kim San (1967).	75.00	90.00	225.00
		b. Red sign. seal Type I at ctr. Sign. Dr. Goh Keng Swee (1970).	85.00	300.00	725.00
		c. W/o red seal. Sign. Hon Sui Sen (1972).	77.50	100.00	240.00
		d. Red sign. seal Type II at ctr. Sign. Hon Sui Sen (1973).	72.50	90.00	200.00
7	500 DOLLARS	ND (1972). Dk. green. Lilac colored flowers at ctr. Government bldg. on back.	375.00	400.00	675.00
8	1000 DOLLARS	ND (1967–75). Purple. Lilac-brown colored flowers at ctr., arms at r. City scene on back.			
		a. W/o red seal. Sign. Lim Kim San (1967).	FV	700.00	1200.
		b. W/o red seal. Sign. Dr. Goh Keng Swee (1970).	FV	750.00	1600.
		c. Red sign. seal Type I at ctr. Sign. Dr. Goh Keng Swee (1970).	FV	750.00	1400.
		d. W/o red seal. Sign. Hon Sui Sen (1973).	FV	725.00	1325.
		e. Red sign. seal Type II at ctr. Sign. Hon Sui Sen (1975).	FV	700.00	1100.

Cat. #	Denomination	Date, description	VG	VF	Unc
8A	10,000 DOLLARS	ND (1973). Green. Orchids at ctr., arms at r. Bldg. on back. Sign. Hon Sui Sen.	FV	FV	9000.

1976-80 ISSUE

#9–17 city skyline along bottom, arms at upper r. Wmk: Lion's head.

Cat. #	Denomination	Date, description	VG	VF	Unc
9	1 DOLLAR	ND (1976). Blue-black on m/c unpt. Tern at l. Parade on back. Printer: BWC.	FV	FV	3.00

Cat. #	Denomination	Date, description	VG	VF	Unc
10	5 DOLLARS	ND (1976). Green and m/c. Bulbul at l. Skylift above river w/ships on back. Printer: BWC.	FV	FV	7.00
11	10 DOLLARS	ND (1976). Dk. brown, deep green and purple on m/c unpt. Kingfisher at l. Modern bldgs. on back. Printer: TDLR.			
		a. Straight security thread (1979).	FV	7.50	40.00
		b. Segmented security thread (1980).	FV	FV	22.50

Cat. #	Denomination	Date, description	VG	VF	Unc
12	20 DOLLARS	ND (1979). Brown, yellow and m/c. Yellow breasted sunbird at l. Back brown; Dancer at l., Concorde and airport at ctr. Printer: BWC.	FV	15.00	25.00

Cat. #	Denomination	Date, description	VG	VF	Unc
13	50 DOLLARS	ND (1976). Dk. blue and m/c. Bird of Paradise at l. High school band playing in formation on back. Printer: TDLR.			
		a. Continuous security thread.	FV	FV	60.00
		b. Interrupted security thread.	FV	FV	55.00

Cat. #	Denomination	Date, description	VG	VF	Unc
14	100 DOLLARS	ND (1977). Blue. Blue-throated bee eater. Dancers on back. Printer: BWC.	FV	FV	110.00

Cat. #	Denomination	Date, description	VG	VF	Unc
15	500 DOLLARS	ND (1977). Green and m/c. Oriole at l. Back green; view of island and refinery. Printer: TDLR.	FV	FV	500.00
16	1000 DOLLARS	ND (1978). Violet and brown. Brahminy Kite bird at l. Ship on back. Printer: TDLR.	FV	FV	950.00

Cat. #	Denomination	Date, description	VG	VF	Unc
17	10,000 DOLLARS	ND (1980). Green. White bellied Sea Eagle at l. 19th century Singapore River scene above, modern view below on back. Printer: TDLR.	FV	FV	8000.

1984-87 ISSUE

#18–25 wmk: Lion's head. Printer: TDLR.

Cat. #	Denomination	Date, description	VG	VF	Unc
18	1 DOLLAR	ND (1987). Deep blue and green. Sailing ship at l. Back deep blue; flowers and satellite tracking station at ctr.			
		a. Sign. Goh Ken Swee.	FV	FV	1.50
		b. Sign. Hu Tsu Tau.	FV	FV	1.50

Cat. #	Denomination	Date, description	VG	VF	Unc
19	5 DOLLARS	ND (1989). Green and red-violet on m/c unpt. 2 local boats at l. PSA Container Terminal at r. on back.	FV	FV	5.50

Cat. #	Denomination	Date, description	VG	VF	Unc
20	10 DOLLARS	ND (1988). Red-orange and violet on m/c unpt. Sailboat at l. Stylized map at ctr., public housing at r. on back.	FV	FV	10.00
21	Held in reserve.				
22	50 DOLLARS	ND (1987; 1994). Blue and m/c. Coaster vessel at l. 2 raised area in circles at lower r. for the blind. Bridge and city view on back.			
		a. Imbedded thin black security thread. (1987).	FV	FV	55.00
		b. Deeper blue w/silver security thread containing inscription. (1994).	FV	FV	52.00

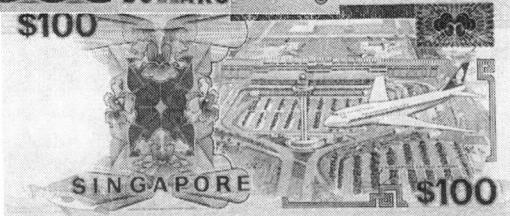

Cat. #	Denomination	Date, description	VG	VF	Unc
23	100 DOLLARS	ND (1985). Dk. brown, violet and orange-brown on m/c unpt. Ship at l. ctr. Airplane above Changi air terminal at ctr. r. on back.	FV	FV	90.00
24	500 DOLLARS	ND (1988). Green on m/c unpt. Arms at upper l. Cargo vessel at l. National defense members on back.	FV	FV	425.00

Cat. #	Denomination	Date, description	VG	VF	Unc
25	1000 DOLLARS	ND (1984). Purple and m/c. Arms at upper l. ctr., container ship at l. ctr. Repair ship on back.	FV	FV	775.00
26	10,000 DOLLARS	ND (1987). Red and m/c. Arms at upper l., bulk carrier at l., statuary at ctr. r. 1987 National Day parade on back.	FV	FV	7750.

1990-92 ISSUES

| 27 | 2 DOLLARS | ND (ca.1990). Orange and red on yellow-green unpt. Arms at upper l., 3 boats at ctr. Chingay procession on back. Wmk: Lion's head. | FV | FV | 2.50 |

| 28 | 2 DOLLARS | ND (1992). Purple and brown-violet on m/c unpt. Like #27, but w/progressively larger serial #, one of which is vertical. | FV | FV | 2.50 |

COMMEMORATIVE ISSUES

#29, 25th Anniversary of Board of Commissioners of Currency, Singapore.

Cat. #	Denomination	Date, description	VG	VF	Unc
29	2 DOLLARS	ND (1992). Logo of the Board ovpt. in red at l. beneath arms.	FV	FV	5.00

NOTE: Sheets of 25 subjects w/logo of BCCS in red only on upper r. note were offered at about $150.00.

#30-31, 25th Anniversary of Independence

| 30 | 50 DOLLARS | 9.8.1990. Red, purple and m/c. Silver hologram of Yusof bin Ishak at ctr. Old harbor scene at l., modern bldgs. at r. First parliament and group of people below flag and arms on back. Plastic. | FV | FV | 50.00 |
| 31 | 50 DOLLARS | ND (1990). Like #30 but w/o date. | FV | FV | 47.50 |

COLLECTOR SERIES

Cat. #	Date, denomination	Description	Issue Price	Mkt. Val.
CS1	ND 1 DOLLAR - 100 DOLLARS	#1a–3a, 5a and 6a ovpt. *SPECIMEN.* (77 sets)	—	1800.
CS2	ND 1 DOLLAR - 100 DOLLARS	#1c–3c, 5c and 6c ovpt. *SPECIMEN.* (89 sets).	—	1700.
CS3	ND 1 DOLLAR - 100 DOLLARS	#1d–3d, 4 and 5d and 6d ovpt. *SPECIMEN.* (82 sets)	—	2400.
CS4	ND (1989) 1-100 DOLLARS	#9–11, 13, and 14 ovpt. *SPECIMEN.* (311 sets)	—	1200.

SLOVAKIA

Slovakia as a republic has an area of 18,923 sq. mi. (49,011 sq. km.) and a population of almost 5.3 million. Capital: Bratislava. Textiles, steel, and wood products are exported.

Slovakia was settled by Slavic Slovaks in the 6th or 7th century and was incorporated into Greater Moravia in the 9th century. After the Moravian state was destroyed early in the 10th century, Slovakia was conquered by the Magyars and remained a land of the Hungarian crown until 1918, when it joined the Czechs in forming Czechoslovakia. In 1938, the Slovaks declared themselves an autonomous state within a federal Czecho-Slovak state. After the German occupation, Slovakia became nominally independent under the protection of Germany, March 16, 1939. Father Jozef Tiso was appointed President. Slovakia was liberated from German control in Oct. 1944, but in May 1945 ceased to be an independent Slovak state. In 1968 it became a constituent state of Czechoslovakia as Slovak Socialist Republic.

In January 1991 the Czech and Slovak Federal Republic was formed, and after June 1992 elections, it was decided to split the federation into the Czech Republic and Slovakia on 1 January, 1993.

MONETARY SYSTEM
1 Korun = 100 Halierov, 1993–

SLOVENSKA REPUBLIKA–REPUBLIC OF SLOVAKIA

1993 (ND) PROVISIONAL ISSUE

#15–17 Czechoslovakian issue w/adhesive stamps affixed w/*SLOVENSKA* over arms.

Cat. #	Denomination	Date, description	VG	VF	Unc
15	20 KORUN	ND (1993– old date 1988). Black and lt. blue adhesive stamp on Czechoslovakia #96.	1.00	2.50	4.00

| 16 | 50 KORUN | ND (1993– old date 1987). Black and yellow adhesive stamp on Czechoslovakia #97. | 2.25 | 3.50 | 6.50 |

17	100 KORUN	ND (1993– old date 1961). Black and orange adhesive stamp on Czechoslovakia #90b.	4.00	5.00	9.00
18	500 KORUN	ND (1993– old date 1973). Adhesive stamp on Czechoslovakia #93.	18.50	25.00	50.00
19	1000 KORUN	ND (1993– old date 1985). Adhesive stamp on Czechoslovakia #94.	35.00	45.00	90.00

Národná Banka Slovenska – Slovak National Bank

1993-95 REGULAR ISSUE

#20-26 shield at lower ctr. on back. Wmk: As portr.

#20–21 printer: BABN.

Cat. #	Denomination	Date, description	VG	VF	Unc
20	20 KORUN	1.9.1993. Black and green on m/c unpt. Prince Pribina at r. Monastery w/tall steeple at l. on back.		FV	FV	2.00

| 21 | 50 KORUN | 1.8.1993. Black, blue and aqua on m/c unpt. St. Cyril and St. Metod at r. Allegory of Cyrillic alphabet on back. | FV | FV | 4.50 |

#22, 24 and 25 printer: TDLR.

| 22 | 100 KORUN | 1.9.1993. Red and black on orange and m/c unpt. Madonna (by master woodcarver Pavel) at r. Levoca on back. | FV | FV | 8.00 |
| 23 | 200 KORUN | 1.1.1995. Dk. gray on m/c unpt. A. Bernolák. View of Trnava on back. | FV | FV | 15.00 |

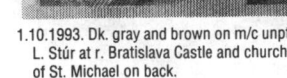

| 24 | 500 KORUN | 1.10.1993. Dk. gray and brown on m/c unpt. L. Stúr at r. Bratislava Castle and church of St. Michael on back. | FV | FV | 30.00 |

The Republic of Slovenia (formerly a part of the Kingdom of the Serbs, Croats and Slovenes which became Yugoslavia) is bounded in the north by Austria, northeast by Hungary, southeast by Croatia and to the west by Italy. It has an area of 5,246 sq. mi. (20,251 sq. km.) and a population of almost 2.0 million. Capital: Ljubljana. The economy is based on electricity, minerals, forestry, agriculture and fishing. Small industries are being developed during privatization.

The Roman Province of Pannonia (Croatia-Slavonia) was conquered by the Ostrogoths and later recovered by Justinian in 535. In 568 it was conquered by the Avars who were overthrown by the Croats around 640. After changing relations with the Franks, Byzantium, Venice, Moravia and a short-lived Bulgar State, it eventually came under Magyar conquerors led by King Koloman in 1102 who was crowned King of Croatia and Dalmatia at Belgrad. Croatia was an autonomous kingdom under the Holy Crown of St. Stephen for the next eight centuries, becoming a fortress against any further invasion by the Turks. By 1699 all Croatia-Slavonia was recovered from the Turks and was settled by many Serbian refugees from Turkey. Napoleon's rise to power created an "Illyrian" state of east Adriatic territories which Austria had acquired from Venice. All were restored by 1822. The Hungarian Revolution in 1848 developed a federalist policy dissolving any legal bond with Hungary but the Austrians remained in control. From 1868 to 1914 increased political activity developed which broke out in riots in 1883. The Croatian constitution was temporarily suspended by Hungary and a royal commissioner, Count Khuen-Héderváry, was appointed. His 20 years of rule were very humiliating for Croatia. From 1003 onwards a national feeling developed leading to quarrels with Hungary in 1907 which resulted in Cuvaj being appointed as a dictator by Hungary in 1912. The church lost its autonomy and revolutionary movements followed. The dictatorship was abolished in 1913 with somewhat of a truce with Budapest when WW I broke out. This resulted in the union of the Yugoslav Provinces on Dec. 1, 1918.

A legal opposition group, the Slovene League of Social Democrats, was formed in Jan. 1989. In Oct. 1989 the Slovene Assembly voted a constitutional amendment giving it the right to secede from Yugoslavia. On July 2, 1990 the Assembly adopted a 'declaration of sovereignty' and in Sept. proclaimed its control over the territorial defense force on its soil. A referendum on Dec. 23 resulted in a majority vote for independence, which was formally declared on Dec. 26.

In Feb. 1991 parliament ruled that henceforth Slovenian law took precedence over federal. On June 25, Slovenia declared independence, but agreed to suspend this for 3 months at peace talks sponsored by the EC. The moratorium having expired, Slovenia (and Croatia) declared their complete independence of the Yugoslav federation on Oct. 8, 1991.

MONETARY SYSTEM:

1 (Tolar) = 1 Yugoslavian Dinar

REPLACEMENT NOTES

#11–19, ZA prefix.

REPUBLIC

1990-92 ISSUE

#1–10 column pedestal at lower l., denomination numeral in guilloche over a fly in unpt. at ctr. r. Date given as first 2 numerals of serial #. Mountain ridge at l. ctr. on back. Wmk: Repeated symmetrical designs.

Cat #	Date, denomination	Description	VG	VF	Unc
1	1 (TOLAR)	(19)90. Dk. olive-green on lt. gray and lt. olive-green unpt.			
		a. Issued note.	.05	.10	.25
		s. Specimen.	—	—	7.50
2	2 (TOLARJEV)	(19)90. Dk. brown and brown on tan and ochre unpt.			
		a. Issued note.	.05	.10	.35
		s. Specimen.	—	—	8.50
3	5 (TOLARJEV)	(19)90. Maroon on lt. gray violet, lt. maroon and pink unpt.			
		a. Issued note.	.05	.15	.55
		s. Specimen.	—	—	10.00

The left column (Slovakia 1000 Korun notes):

Cat. #	Denomination	Date, description	VG	VF	Unc
25	1000 KORUN	1.10.1993. Dk. gray, purple and red violet on m/c unpt. A. Hlinka at r. Madonna of the church of Liptovké Sliace near Ruzomberok and church of St. Andrew in Ruzomberok on back.	FV	FV	55.00
26	5000 KORUN	2.4.1995. Olive-green and pale brown-orange on m/c unpt. M.R. Stefánik. Stars and tulip on back.	FV	FV	200.00

Cat #	Date, denomination	Description	VG	VF	Unc
4	10 (TOLARJEV)	(19)90. Dk. blue-green and grayish purple on lt. blue-green and lt. gray unpt.			
		a. Issued note.	FV	FV	.65
		s. Specimen.	—	—	12.50
5	50 (TOLARJEV)	(19)90. Dk. gray on tan and lt. gray unpt.			
		a. Issued note.	FV	FV	5.00
		s. Specimen.	—	—	13.50
6	100 (TOLARJEV)	(19)90. Reddish brown and violet on orange and lt. violet unpt.			
		a. Issued note.	FV	FV	4.00
		s. Specimen.	—	—	15.00
7	200 (TOLARJEV)	(19)90. Greenish black and dk. brown on lt. gray and lt. green unpt.			
		a. Issued note.	FV	FV	25.00
		s. Specimen.	—	—	17.50

Cat #	Date, denomination	Description	VG	VF	Unc
8	500 (TOLARJEV)	(19)90; (19)92. Lilac and red on pink unpt.			
		a. Issued note.	FV	FV	12.50
		s. Specimen.	—	—	20.00

Cat #	Date, denomination	Description	VG	VF	Unc
9	1000 (TOLARJEV)	(19)91; (19)92. Dk. blue-gray and gray on lt. gray and pale blue unpt.			
		a. Issued note.	FV	FV	15.00
		s. Specimen.	—	—	22.50

Cat #	Date, denomination	Description	VG	VF	Unc
10	5000 (TOLARJEV)	(19)92. Purple and lilac on pink unpt.			
		a. Issued note.	FV	FV	85.00
		s. Specimen.	—	—	25.00

Banka Slovenije

1992-93 ISSUE

#11–20 portr. as wmk.

Cat #	Date, denomination	Description	VG	VF	Unc
11	10 TOLARJEV	15.1.1992. Black, brown-violet and brown-orange on m/c unpt. Quill pen at l. ctr., P. Trubar at r. Ursuline church in Ljubljana on back.			
		a. Issued note.	FV	FV	.40
		s. Specimen.	FV	FV	8.50

Cat #	Date, denomination	Description	VG	VF	Unc
12	20 TOLARJEV	15.1.1992. Brownish black, deep brown and brown-orange on m/c unpt. Topographical outlines at l. ctr., cherub arms at r. Compass at l., J. Vajkard Valvasor at r. and topographical outlines on back.			
		a. Issued note.	FV	FV	.50
		s. Specimen.	—	—	10.00

Cat #	Date, denomination	Description	VG	VF	Unc
13	50 TOLARJEV	15.1.1992. Black, purple and brown-orange on m/c unpt. J. Vega at r., geometric design and calculations at ctr. Academy at upper l., planets and geometric design at ctr.			
		a. Issued note.	FV	FV	1.50
		s. Specimen.	—	—	12.50

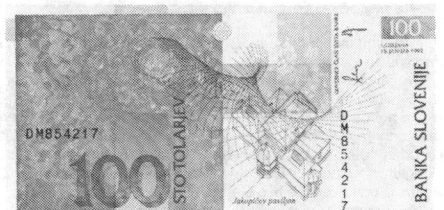

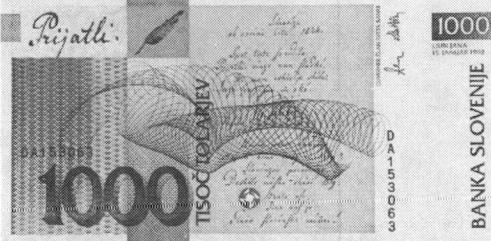

Cat #	Date, denomination	Description	VG	VF	Unc
14	100 TOLARJEV	15.1.1992. Black, blue-black and brown-orange on m/c unpt. R. Jakopic at r. Outline of the Jarkopicev Pavilion at ctr. r. on back.			
		a. Issued note.	FV	FV	2.75
		s. Specimen.	—	—	15.00

Cat #	Date, denomination	Description	VG	VF	Unc
17	1000 TOLARJEV	15.1.1992. Brownish black, deep green and brown-orange on m/c unpt. F. Preseren at r. and as wmk. The poem "Drinking Toast" at ctr. on back.			
		a. Issued note.	FV	FV	18.50
		s. Specimen.	—	—	25.00

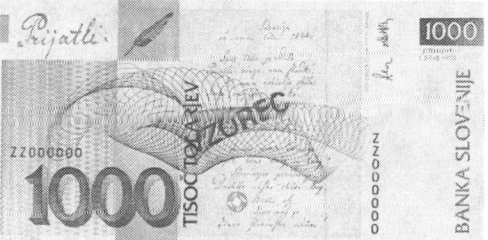

15	200 TOLARJEV	15.1.1992. Black, violet-brown and brown-orange on m/c unpt. Musical facade at l., l. Gallus at r. Drawing of Slovenia's Philharmonic bldg. at upper l., music scores at upper ctr. on back.	FV	FV	5.00
		a. Issued note.	FV	FV	5.00
		s. Specimen.	—	—	17.50

18	1000 TOLARJEV	1.6.1993. Black, deep blue-green and brown-orange on m/c unpt. Like #17 but modified portrait and other incidental changes including color.			
		a. Issued note.	FV	FV	17.50
		s. Specimen.	—	—	25.00

16	500 TOLARJEV	15.1.1992. Black, red and brown-orange on m/c unpt. J. Plecnik at r. Drawing of the National and University Library of Ljubljana at l. ctr. on back.			
		a. Issued note.	FV	FV	12.50
		s. Specimen.	—	—	20.00

19 (18)	5000 TOLARJEV	1.6.1993. Brownish-black, dk. brown and brown-orange on m/c unpt. I. Kobika at r. National Galeryin Ljubljuna at upper l.			
		a. Issued note.	FV	FV	65.00
		s. Specimen.	—	—	30.00

Cat #	Date, denomination	Description	VG	VF	Unc
20	10,000 TOLARJEV	28.6.1994. Black, purple and brown-orange on m/c unpt. I. Cankar at r. Chrysanthemum blossom at l. on back.			
		a. Issued note.	FV	FV	110.00
		s. Specimen.	—	—	35.00

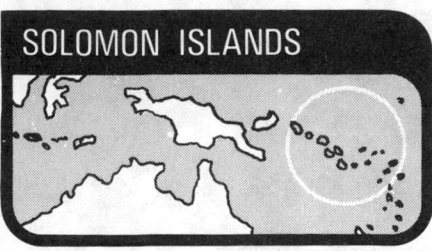

SOLOMON ISLANDS

The Solomon Islands, located in the Southwest Pacific east of Papua New Guinea, has an area of 10,983 sq. mi. (28,450 sq. km.) and a population of 325,600. Capital: Honiara. The most important islands of the Solomon chain are Guadalcanal (scene of some of the fiercest fighting of World War II), Malaitia, New Georgia, Florida, Vella Lavella, Choiseul, Rendova, San Cristobal, the Lord Howe group, the Santa Cruz islands, and the Duff group. Copra is the only important cash crop but it is hoped that timber will become an economic factor.

The Solomon Islands were discovered by Spanish navigator Alvaro de Mendana in 1567, and in 1569 he made an unsuccessful attempt to colonize them. European knowledge of the group would not be completed until the end of the 18th century. Germany declared a protectorate over the northern Solomons in 1885. The British protectorate over the southern Solomons was established in 1893. In 1899 Germany transferred its claim to all Solomon Islands except Buka and Bougainville to Great Britain in exchange for recognition of German claims in western Samoa. Australia occupied the two German islands in 1914, and administered them after 1920.

The Japanese invaded the Solomons during 1942–43, but were driven out by an American counteroffensive after a series of bloody clashes.

Following World War II, the islands returned to the status of a British protectorate. In 1976 the protectorate was abolished, and the Solomons became a self-governing dependency. Full independence was achieved on July 7, 1978. Solomon Islands is a member of the Commonwealth of Nations. The Queen of England is Chief of State.

RULERS
British

MONETARY SYSTEM
1 Shilling = 12 Pence
1 Pound = 20 Shillings to 1966
1 Dollar = 100 Cents, 1966-

REPLACEMENT NOTES

#5–12, Z/1 prefix. #13-17, Y/1 prefix.

SIGNATURE/TITLE VARIETIES					
1	*[signature]* Chairman	*[signature]* Member	4	*[signature]* Governor	*[signature]* Director
2	*[signature]*	*[signature]*	5	*[signature]*	*[signature]*
3	*[signature]*	*[signature]*	6		

Solomon Islands Monetary Authority

Dollar System

#5–8 Qn. Elizabeth II at r. Wmk: Falcon. Printer: TDLR (w/o imprint).

Cat. #	Denomination	Date, description	VG	VF	Unc
5	2 DOLLARS	ND (1977). Dk. green on pink and pale green unpt. Fishermen on back. Sign. 1.	1.00	2.00	6.00

1986 ISSUE

#13–17 arms at r. Wmk: Falcon. Sign. 5.
#13–16 backs like #5–8.

Cat. #	Denomination	Date, description	VG	VF	Unc
6	5 DOLLARS	ND (1977). Blue on m/c unpt. Long boats and hut on back.			
		a. Sign. 1.	2.25	4.00	12.00
		b. Sign. 2.	2.25	5.00	15.00

Cat. #	Denomination	Date, description	VG	VF	Unc
13	2 DOLLARS	ND (1986). Green on m/c unpt.	FV	FV	2.75

Cat. #	Denomination	Date, description	VG	VF	Unc
7	10 DOLLARS	ND (1977). Purple on gray and violet unpt. Weaver on back.			
		a. Sign. 1.	4.00	7.50	22.50
		b. Sign. 2.	4.00	8.00	25.00
14	5 DOLLARS	ND (1986). Dk. blue, deep purple and violet on m/c unpt.	FV	FV	6.50

Cat. #	Denomination	Date, description	VG	VF	Unc
15	10 DOLLARS	ND (1986). Purple and red-violet on m/c unpt.	FV	FV	10.00
16	20 DOLLARS	ND (1986). Brown on m/c unpt.	FV	FV	18.00

Cat. #	Denomination	Date, description	VG	VF	Unc
8	20 DOLLARS	ND (1981). Brown and purple on m/c unpt. Line of people on back. Sign. 3.	7.00	15.00	40.00

Central Bank of Solomon Islands

1984 ISSUE

#11 and 12 like #7 and 8 except for new bank name. Wmk: Falcon. Sign. 4.

11	10 DOLLARS	ND (1984). Purple on gray and violet unpt.	FV	FV	20.00

12	20 DOLLARS	ND (1984). Brown and purple on m/c unpt.	FV	FV	37.50

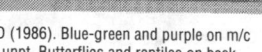

17	50 DOLLARS	ND (1986). Blue-green and purple on m/c unpt. Butterflies and reptiles on back.	FV	FV	42.50

COLLECTOR SERIES

Cat. #	Date, denomination	Description	Issue Price	Mkt. Val.
CS1	1979 2–10 DOLLARS	#5–7 w/ovpt: *SPECIMEN* and Maltese cross prefix serial #.	14.00	25.00

SOMALIA

Somalia, the Somali Democratic Repub-lic, comprising of the former Italian Somaliland, is located on the coast of the eastern projection of the African continent commonly referred to as the "Horn". It has an area of 178,201 sq. mi. (461,657 sq. km.). Capital: Mogadishu. The economy is pastoral and agricultural. Livestock, bananas and hides are exported.

The area of the British Somaliland Protectorate was known to the Egyptians at least 1,500 years B.C., and was occupied by the Arabs and Portuguese before British sea captains obtained trading and anchorage rights in 1827. The land of sandy clay and sporadic rainfall acquired a strategic importance with the opening of the Suez Canal in 1869. After negotiating treaties with the tribes, Britain declared the area a protectorate in 1888. Italy acquired Italian Somaliland in 1895 by purchase from the sultan of Zanzibar. Britain occupied Italian Somaliland in 1941 and administered it until April 1, 1950, when it was returned to Italy as a U.N. trusteeship. The British Somaliland protectorate became independent on June 26, 1960. Five days later it joined with Italian Somaliland to form the Somali Republic. The country was presently under a revolutionary military regime installed Oct. 21, 1969. After 11 years of civil war rebel forces fought their way into the capital. A. M. Muhammad became president in Aug. 1991 but interfactional fighting continued. A UN-sponsored truce was signed in March 1992 and a peace plan and pact was signed Jan. 15, 1993.

The northern Somali National Movements (SNM) declared a secession of the northwestern Somaliland Republic on May 17, 1991 which is not recognized by the Somali Democratic Republic.

MONETARY SYSTEM

1 Scellino = 1 Shilling = 100 Centesimi

REPLACEMENT NOTES

#25-28, Z001 prefix. #29-30, ZZ001 prefix. #31 and later, Z001 prefix.

REPUBLIC

Banca Nazionale Somala

1962 ISSUE

#1–16 w/dual denomination of Scellini and Shilling. Wmk: Leopard's head.
#1–4 sign. title: *PRESIDENTE* at l. Printer: OCV.

Cat. #	Denomination	Date, description	VG	VF	Unc
1	5 SCELLINI	1962. Red on green and orange unpt. Antelope at l. Back orange-brown; small sailing vessel.	15.00	35.00	125.00
2	10 SCELLINI	1962. Green on red-brown and green unpt. Flower at l. Back brown and green; river scene.	20.00	55.00	225.00

Cat. #	Denomination	Date, description	VG	VF	Unc
3	20 SCELLINI	1962. Brown on blue and gold unpt. Banana plant at l. Back brown and blue; bank bldg.	25.00	75.00	350.00

| 4 | 100 SCELLINI | 1962. Blue on green and orange unpt. Art-craft at l. Back blue and red; bldg. | 35.00 | 125.00 | 450.00 |

1966 ISSUE

#5–8 slight changes in colors and design elements; (w/o imprint).

5	5 SCELLINI	1966. Similar to #1 but different guilloche in unpt. Back w/blue unpt.	10.00	30.00	100.00
6	10 SCELLINI	1966. Similar to #2 but different guilloche in unpt. Back green w/lt. tan unpt.	15.00	50.00	225.00
7	20 SCELLINI	1966. Similar to #3 but unpt. is pink, blue and green. Brown bank bldg. on back.	25.00	65.00	350.00
8	100 SCELLINI	1966. Similar to #4 but unpt. is green, purple and tan.	35.00	120.00	485.00

1968 ISSUE

#9–12 sign. title: *Governatore* at l.

9	5 SCELLINI	1968. Red on green and orange unpt. Like #5.	12.50	35.00	150.00
10	10 SCELLINI	1968. Green on red-brown and green unpt. Like #6.	20.00	55.00	250.00
11	20 SCELLINI	1968. Brown on blue and gold unpt. Like #7.	27.50	85.00	375.00
12	100 SCELLINI	1968. Blue on green and orange unpt. Like #8.	37.50	125.00	550.00

DEMOCRATIC REPUBLIC

1971 ISSUE

#13–16 sign. titles: *GOVERNATORE* at l. and *CASSIERE* at r.

13	5 SCELLINI	1971. Purple-brown on blue, green and gold unpt. Like #9.	8.00	22.50	110.00
14	10 SCELLINI	1971. Green on red-brown and green unpt. Like #10.	10.00	27.50	185.00
15	20 SCELLINI	1971. Brown on blue and gold unpt. Like #11.	15.00	40.00	275.00
16	100 SCELLINI	1971. Blue on green and orange unpt. Like #12.	17.50	60.00	400.00

Bankiga Qaranka Soomaaliyeed/Somali National Bank

1975 ISSUE

#17–20 w/dual denominations of Scellini and Shilling. Wmk: Hassan.

Law of 11.12.1974

#17–20 arms at l.

Cat. #	Denomination	Date, description	VG	VF	Unc
17	5 SHILIN	L.1974. 1975. Violet on gold and m/c unpt. Gnus and zebras at bottom ctr. Banana harvesting on back.	1.50	5.00	17.50

18	10 SHILIN	L.1974. 1975. Dk. green on pink and m/c unpt. Lighthouse at l. ctr. Shipbuilders at work on back.	2.00	6.50	20.00
19	20 SHILIN	L.1974. 1975. Brown on m/c unpt. Bank bldg. at ctr. Cattle on back.	2.25	6.50	50.00
20	100 SHILIN	L.1974. 1975. Blue on gold and m/c unpt. Woman w/baby, rifle and farm tools at l. ctr. Dagathur monument at ctr. r. Workers in factory on back.	7.00	20.00	100.00

Bankiga Dhexe Ee Soomaaliya/Central Bank of Somalia

1978 ISSUE

Law of 6.12.1977

#20A–24 arms at l. Black series and serial #. W/dual denominations of Shilin and Shilling. Wmk: Hassan.

20A	5 SHILIN	L.1977. 1978. Violet on gold and m/c unpt. Like #17.	4.00	10.00	35.00

Cat. #	Denomination	Date, description	VG	VF	Unc
21	5 SHILIN	L.1977. 1978. Violet on gold and m/c unpt. Similar to #20A but Cape Buffalo herd at bottom ctr.	.50	2.00	8.50
22	10 SHILIN	L.1977. 1978. Dk. green on pink and m/c unpt. Similar to #18.	1.00	4.00	20.00

Cat. #	Denomination	Date, description	VG	VF	Unc
28	100 SHILIN	L.1980. 1980. Blue on gold and m/c unpt. Like #24.	2.25	9.00	35.00

Law of 9.12.1981

#29-30 wmk: Hassan.

29	20 SHILIN	L.1981. 1981. Brown on m/c unpt. Like #27.	1.00	5.50	40.00

23	20 SHILIN	L.1977. 1978. Brown on m/c unpt. Similar to #19.	1.75	7.00	35.00
24	100 SHILIN	L.1977. 1978. Blue on gold and m/c unpt. Similar to #20.	2.25	9.00	45.00

1980 ISSUE

Law of 5.4.1980

#26-28 arms at l. Red series and serial #. Different sign. title at l. Wmk: Hassan.

25	Deleted.				

30	100 SHILIN	L.1981. 1981. Blue on gold and m/c unpt. Like #28.	4.00	12.00	35.00

1983 ISSUE

Law of 30.12.1982

#31-35 arms at upper l., star at or near lower ctr. Reduced size notes.

26	10 SHILIN	L.1980. 1980. Dk. green on pink and m/c unpt. Like #22.	.60	2.50	10.00

31	5 SHILIN	L.1982. 1983-87. Brown-violet. Cape Buffalo herd at l. ctr. Harvesting bananas on back.			
		a. 1983.	.10	.50	2.00
		b. 1986-87.	.10	.40	1.50

27	20 SHILIN/	L.1980. 1980. Brown on m/c unpt. Like #23.	1.00	5.00	20.00

#32-35 wmk: Hassan.

Cat. #	Denomination	Date, description	VG	VF	Unc
32	10 SHILIN	L.1982. 1983–87. Green and m/c. Lighthouse at l. Shipbuilders on back.			
		a. 1983.	.15	.50	3.00
		b. 1986–87.	.10	.40	1.50

33	20 SHILIN	L.1982. 1983–89. Brown and m/c. Bank at l. Back similar to #19.			
		a. 1983.	.20	.80	5.00
		b. 1986–87; 1989.	.15	.70	3.50

34	50 SHILIN	1983–89. Red-brown and m/c. Walled city at l. and ctr. Watering animals at ctr. on back.			
		a. 1983.	.50	1.50	6.00
		b. 1986; 1987. 2 sign. varieties.	.15	.40	2.00
		c. 1988; 1989.	.10	.30	1.25

Cat. #	Denomination	Date, description	VG	VF	Unc
35	100 SHILIN	1983–89. Blue-black, dk. blue and dk. green on m/c unpt. Woman w/baby, rifle and farm tools at l. Dagathur monument at l. ctr. Back purple and mc/c; similar to #20.			
		a. 1983.	.60	1.85	7.50
		b. 1986; 1987. 2 sign. varieties.	.30	.85	3.50
		c. 1988; 1989.	.15	.40	2.00

1989–90 ISSUE
Law of 1.1.1989

36	500 SHILIN	L.1989. 1989; 1990. Green and blue on m/c unpt. Fishermen mending net at l. and ctr. Mosque on back. 2 sign. varieties.	.20	.65	2.50

37	1000 SHILIN	L.1989. 1990. Violet and orange on m/c unpt. Women seated weaving baskets at l. ctr; arms above. Bldgs., port. of Mogadishu on back.	.15	.50	2.00

REGIONAL

In Mogadishu-North, forces loyal to warlord Ali Mahdi Mohammed have issued currency valued in "N" Shilin. The notes may have originally been part of a plan to replace older currency.

#R1 and R2 arms at top l. ctr.

R1	20 N SHILIN	1991. Violet, red-brown, brown-orange and olive-green on m/c unpt. Trader leading camel in unpt. at l. ctr. Picking cotton at ctr. on back. Wmk: Hassan.	1.25	5.00	15.00
R2	50 N SHILIN	1991. Man working at loom on face. Young person leading a donkey w/3 children on back.	1.75	7.00	20.00

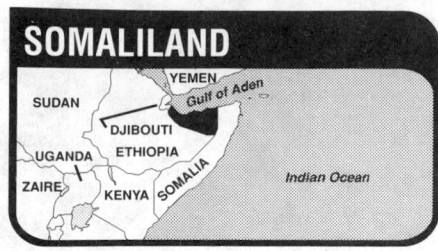

The Somaliland Republic, comprising of the former British Somaliland Protectorate is located on the coast of the northeastern projection of the African continent commonly referred to as the "Horn" on the southwestern end of the Gulf of Aden.

Bordered by Eritrea to the west, Ethiopia to west and south and Somalia to the east. It has an area of 68,000* sq. mi. (176,000* sq. km). Capital: Hargeysa. It is mostly arid and mounainous except for the gulf shoreline.

The Protectorate of British Somaliland was established in 1888 and from 1905 the territory was administered by a commissioner under the British Colonial Office. Italian Somaliland was administered as a colony from 1893 to 1941, when the territory was occupied by British forces. In 1950 the United Nations allowed Italy to resume control of Italian Somaliland under a trusteeship. In 1960 British and Italian Somaliland were united as Somalia, an independent republic outside the Commonwealth.

Civil War erupted in the late 1970's and continued until the capital of Somalia was taken in 1990. The United Nations provided aid and peacekeeptes. A UN sponsored truce was signed in March 1992 and a peace plan and pact was signed Jan. 15, 1993. The northern Somali National Movement (SMN) declared a secession of the Somaliland Republic on May 17, 1991 which is not recognized by the Somali Democratic Republic.

The currency issued by the East African Currency Board was used in British Somaliland from 1945 to 1961, Somali currency was used later until 1995.

Baanka Somaliland

#1–4 bldg. at ctr. Greater Kudu at r. Traders w/camels on back.

Cat. #	Denomination	Date, description	VG	VF	Unc
1	5 SOMALILAND SHILLINGS	1994. Bright green, olive-green and red-brown on m/c unpt.	FV	FV	1.50

| 2 | 10 SOMALILAND SHILLINGS | 1994. Violet, purple and red-brown on m/c unpt. | FV | FV | 1.50 |

| 3 | 20 SOMALILAND SHILLINGS | 1994. Brown and red-brown on m/c unpt. | FV | FV | 2.50 |

Cat. #	Denomination	Date, description	VG	VF	Unc
4	50 SOMALILAND SHILLINGS	1994. Blue-violet, blue-gray and red-brown on m/c unpt.	FV	FV	3.50

#5 and 6 bldg. at ctr. Ship dockside, herdsmen w/sheep at ctr. on back.

| 5 | 100 SOMALILAND SHILLINGS | 1994. Brownish-black and red-violet on m/c unpt. | FV | FV | 6.50 |

| 6 | 500 SOMALILAND SHILLINGS | 1994. Purple, blue-black and blue-green on m/c unpt. | FV | FV | 28.50 |

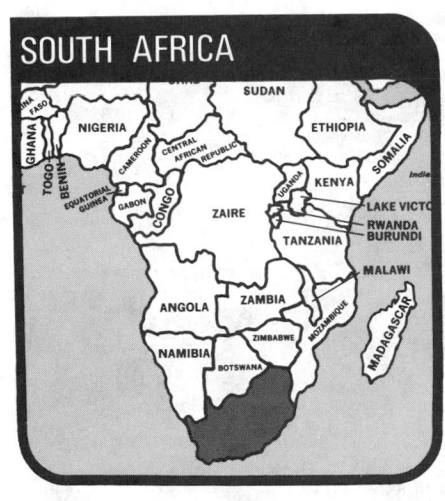

The Republic of South Africa, located at the southern tip of Africa, has an area, including the enclave of Walvis Bay, of 472,359 sq. mi. (1,221,040 sq. km.) and a population of 33.14 million. Capital: Administrative, Pretoria; Legislative, Cape Town; Judicial, Bloemfontein. Manufacturing, mining and agriculture are the principal industries. Exports include wool, diamonds, gold and metallic ores.

Portuguese navigator Bartholomeu Diaz became the first European to sight the region of South Africa when he rounded the Cape of Good Hope in 1488, but throughout the 16th century the only white men to come ashore were the survivors of ships wrecked while attempting the stormy Cape passage. The first permanent settlement was established by Jan van Riebeeck of the Dutch East India Company in 1652. In subsequent decades additional Dutch and Germans and Huguenot refugees from France settled in the Cape area to form the Afrikaner segment of today's population.

Great Britain captured the Cape colony in 1795, and again in 1806, receiving permanent title in 1814. To escape British political rule and cultural dominance, many Afrikaner farmers (Boers) migrated northward (the Great Trok) beginning in 1836, and established the independent Boer republics of the Transvaal (the South African Republic, Zuid Afrikaansche Republic) in 1852, and the Orange Free State in 1854. British political intrigues against the two republics, coupled with the discovery of diamonds and gold in the Boer-settled regions, led to the bitter Boer Wars (1880–1881, 1899–1902) and the incorporation of the Boer republics into the British Empire.

On May 31, 1910, the two former Boer republics (Transvaal and Orange Free State) were joined with the British colonies of Cape of Good Hope and Natal to form the Union of South Africa, a dominion of the British Empire. In 1934 the Union achieved status as a sovereign state within the British Empire.

Political integration of the various colonies did not still the conflict between the Afrikaners and the English-speaking groups, which continued to have a significant impact on political developments. A resurgence of Afrikaner nationalism in the 1940s and 1950s led to a referendum in the white community authorizing the relinquishment of dominion status and the establishment of a republic. The decision took effect on May 31, 1961. The Republic of South Africa withdrew from the British Commonwealth in Oct., 1961.

South African currency carries inscriptions in both Afrikaans and English.

MONETARY SYSTEM

1 Rand = 100 Cents (= 10 Shillings), 1961–

REPLACEMENT NOTES

#102–105, 109–117, 1 Rand Z/# or Z/##; 2 Rand Y/# or Y/##; 5 Rand X/# or X/##; 10 Rand W/# or W/##. #118, W/#, WW, WX prefixes; #119–122, X/#, Y/#, Z/# by de-nomination. Later notes use XX.

South African Reserve Bank

Rand System

1961 ISSUE

#102–122 portr. Jan van Riebeeck at l. and as wmk.

Cat. #	Denomination	Date, description	VG	VF	Unc
102	1 RAND	ND (1961–62). Rust brown. First line of bank name and value in English. 135 x 77mm.			
		a. Sign. Dr. M. H. de Kock (1961).	2.50	6.50	20.00
		b. Sign. Dr. G. Rissik (1962).	1.25	4.50	12.00
103	1 RAND	ND (1961–62). Rust brown. Like #102 but first line of bank name and value in Afrikaans. 137 x 78mm.			
		a. Sign. Dr. M. H. de Kock (1961).	2.50	6.50	20.00
		b. Sign. Dr. G. Rissik (1962).	1.25	4.50	12.00
104	2 RAND	ND (1961–62). Blue. Similar to #83. First line of bank name and value in English. 150 x 85mm.			
		a. Sign. Dr. M. H. de Kock (1961).	1.50	5.50	20.00
		b. Sign. Dr. G. Rissik (1962).	1.25	3.25	15.00

Cat. #	Denomination	Date, description	VG	VF	Unc
105	2 RAND	ND (1961–62). Like #104 but first line of bank name and value in Afrikaans. 150 x 85mm.			
		a. Sign. Dr. M. H. de Kock (1961).	1.50	5.50	20.00
		b. Sign. Dr. G. Rissik (1962).	1.25	3.25	15.00
106	10 RAND	ND (1961–62). Green and brown on m/c unpt. Similar to #91. First line of bank name and value in English. Sailing ship on back. 170 x 97mm.			
		a. Sign. Dr. M. H. de Kock (1961).	5.00	13.50	60.00
		b. Sign. Dr. G. Rissik (1962).	4.00	11.00	45.00
107	10 RAND	ND (1961–62). Green and brown on m/c unpt. Like #106 but first line of bank name and value in Afrikaans. 170 x 97mm.			
		a. Sign. Dr. M. H. de Kock (1961).	5.00	13.50	60.00
		b. Sign. Dr. G. Rissik (1962).	4.00	11.00	45.00
108	20 RAND	ND (1961–62). Brown-violet. First line of bank name and value in English. Machinery on back. Sign. Dr. M.H. de Kock.	10.00	27.00	135.00

Cat. #	Denomination	Date, description	VG	VF	Unc
108A	20 RAND	ND (1962). Like #108 but first line of bank name in Afrikaans. Sign. Dr. G. Rissik	9.00	25.00	110.00

1966 ISSUE

#109–114 J. van Riebeeck at l. and as wmk.

Cat. #	Denomination	Date, description	VG	VF	Unc
109	1 RAND	ND (1966–72). Dk. reddish-brown on m/c unpt. First line of bank name and value in English. Rams in field on back. 126 x 64mm.			
		a. Sign. Dr. G. Rissik (1966).	.75	2.25	11.00
		b. Sign. Dr. T. W. de Jongh (1967).	.50	1.75	9.00

Cat. #	Denomination	Date, description	VG	VF	Unc
110	1 RAND	ND (1966–72). Dk. reddish-brown on m/c unpt. Like #109 but first line on bank name and value in Afrikaans. 126 x 64mm.			
		a. Sign. Dr. G. Rissik (1966).	.75	2.25	11.00
		b. Sign. Dr. T. W. de Jongh (1967).	.50	1.75	9.00

Cat. #	Denomination	Date, description	VG	VF	Unc
111	5 RAND	ND (1966–76). Purple. Covered wagons on trail at r. corner. First line of bank name and value in English. Factory w/train on back. 133 x 70mm.			
		a. Sign. Dr. G. Rissik (1966).	3.25	9.00	30.00
		b. Sign. Dr. T. W. de Jongh. Wmk: Springbok (1967–74).	2.50	6.00	25.00
		c. Sign. Dr. T. W. de Jongh. Wmk: J. van Riebeeck (1975).	2.00	4.50	20.00

Cat. #	Denomination	Date, description	VG	VF	Unc
112	5 RAND	ND (1966–76). Purple. Like #111 but first line of bank name and value in Afrikaans.			
		a. Sign. Dr. G. Rissik (1966).	3.25	9.00	30.00
		b. Sign. Dr. T. W. de Jongh. Wmk: Springbok (1967–74).	2.50	6.00	25.00
		c. Sign. Dr. T. W. de Jongh. Wmk: J. van Riebeeck (1975).	2.00	4.50	20.00

Cat. #	Denomination	Date, description	VG	VF	Unc
113	10 RAND	ND (1966–76). Dk. green and brown. Capitol bldg. at ctr. First line on bank name and value in English. Old sailing ships on back. 140 x 76mm.			
		a. Sign. Dr. G. Rissik (1966).	7.00	12.00	35.00
		b. Sign. Dr. T. W. de Jongh. Wmk: Springbok (1967–74).	5.00	7.50	20.00
		c. Sign. Dr. T. W. de Jongh. Wmk: J. van Riebeeck (1975).	4.00	6.50	18.00
114	10 RAND	ND (1966–76). Dk. green and brown. Like #113 but first line of bank name and value in Afrikaans. 140 x 76mm.			
		a. Sign. Dr. G. Rissik (1966).	7.00	12.00	35.00
		b. Sign. Dr. T. W. de Jongh. Wmk: Springbok (1967–74).	5.00	7.50	20.00
		c. Sign. Dr. T. W. de Jongh. Wmk: J. van Riebeeck (1975).	4.00	6.50	18.00

1973–84 ISSUE

#115–122 J. van Riebeeck at l. and as wmk.

Cat. #	Denomination	Date, description	VG	VF	Unc
115	1 RAND	ND (1973–75). Brown. Like #109 but 120 x 57mm.			
		a. Sign. Dr. T. W. de Jongh. Wmk: Springbok (1973).	.65	1.00	5.00
		b. Sign. Dr. T. W. de Jongh. Wmk: J. van Riebeeck (1975).	.50	.75	4.00
116	1 RAND	ND (1973–75). Brown. Like #110 but 120 x 57mm.			
		a. Sign. Dr. T. W. de Jongh. Wmk: Springbok (1973).	.65	1.00	5.00
		b. Sign. Dr. T. W. de Jongh. Wmk: J. van Riebeeck (1975).	.50	.75	4.00

Cat. #	Denomination	Date, description	VG	VF	Unc
117	2 RAND	ND (1973–76). Blue. First line of bank name and value in Afrikaans. Hydroelectric dam on back. 127 x 62mm.			
		a. Sign. Dr. T. W. de Jongh. Wmk: Springbok (1974).	1.25	3.00	12.00
		b. Sign. Dr. T. W. de Jongh. Wmk: J. van Riebeeck (1976).	1.00	2.50	9.00

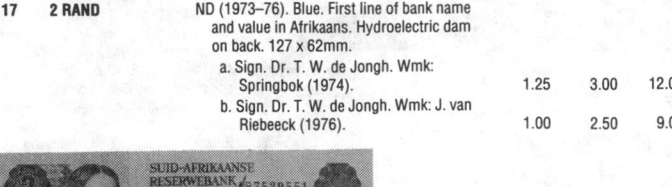

Cat. #	Denomination	Date, description	VG	VF	Unc
118	2 RAND	ND (1978–90). Blue and m/c. Electrical tower at ctr. Refinery on back. 120x57mm.			
		a. Sign. Dr. T. W. de Jongh (1978).	FV	1.00	4.00
		b. Sign. G. de Kock. (1981-90).	FV	.75	3.00
		c. Sign. Dr. C. L. Stals (1990).	FV	FV	8.00

NOTE: #118b exists w/Serial # w/sm. fractional letters and lg. numerals or larger letters w/sm. numerals.

Cat. #	Denomination	Date, description	VG	VF	Unc
119	5 RAND	ND (1978–90). Purple and m/c. First line of bank name and value in English. Diamond at ctr. Grain storage on back. 127 x 63mm.			
		a. Sign. Dr. T. W. de Jongh (1978).	FV	2.00	10.00
		b. Sign. G. de Kock (1981-90).	FV	FV	8.00
		c. Sign. Dr. C. L. Stals (1990).	FV	FV	5.00

Cat. #	Denomination	Date, description	VG	VF	Unc
120	10 RAND	ND (1978–90). Green and m/c. Flower at ctr. Bull and ram on back. 134 x 70mm.			
		a. Sign. Dr. T. W. de Jongh (1978).	FV	FV	12.50
		b. Sign. G. de Kock (1981-85).	FV	FV	9.50
		c. Sign. Dr. C. L. Stals (1990).	FV	FV	7.00

Cat. #	Denomination	Date, description	VG	VF	Unc
121	20 RAND	ND (1984–90). Brown and m/c. Bldg. at ctr. 3 sailing ships and arms on back. 144 x 77mm.			
		a. Sign. Dr. T. W. de Jongh (1978).	FV	FV	20.00
		b. Sign. G. de Kock (1984-90).	FV	FV	15.00
		c. Sign. Dr. C. L. Stals (1990).	FV	FV	13.50

Cat. #	Denomination	Date, description	VG	VF	Unc
124	20 RAND	ND (1993). Dp. brown, brown and red-brown on m/c unpt. Elephants at ctr., lg. elephant head at r. and as wmk. Open pit mining at l. ctr. on back.	FV	FV	11.50

122	50 RAND	ND (1984–90).. Red on m/c unpt. Lion at ctr. First line of bank name and value in Afrikaans. Local animals at lower l., mountains at ctr., plants at r. on back. 147 x 83mm.			
		a. Sign. G. de Kock (1904).	FV	20.00	40.00
		b. Sign. Dr. C. L. Stals (1990).	FV	17.50	32.50

1992–94 ISSUE

#123–127 sign. Dr. C. L. Stals.

125	50 RAND	ND (1992). Maroon and deep blue-green on m/c unpt. Lions w/cub drinking water at ctr., male lion head at r. and as wmk. Refinery at l. ctr. on back.	FV	FV	25.00

123	10 RAND	ND (1993). Dk. green and dk. blue on brown and m/c unpt. White rhinoceros at ctr., lg. white rhino at r. and as wmk. Ram's head over sheep at l. on back.	FV	FV	6.00

126	100 RAND	ND (1994). Blue-violet and dk. gray on m/c unpt. Water buffalo at ctr. and lg. water buffalo head at r. and as wmk. Zebras along bottom from l. to ctr. on back.	FV	FV	45.00

127	200 RAND	ND (1994). Orange on m/c unpt. Leopard at ctr., leopard's head at r. Dish antenna at upper l., modern bridge at lower l. on back.	FV	FV	82.50

SPAIN

The Spanish State, forming the greater part of the Iberian Peninsula of southwest Europe, has an area of 195,988 sq. mi. (504,714 sq. km.) and a population of *39.4 million including the Balearic and the Canary Islands. Capital: Madrid. The economy is based on agriculture, industry and tourism. Machinery, fruit, vegetables and chemicals are exported.

It isn't known when man first came to the Iberian peninsula - the Altamira caves off the Cantabrian coast approximately 50 miles west of Santander were fashioned in Palaeolithic times. Spain was a battleground for centuries before it became a united nation, fought for by Phoenicians, Carthaginians, Greeks, Celts, Romans, Vandals, Visigoths and Moors. Ferdinand and Isabella destroyed the last Moorish stronghold in 1492, freeing the national energy and resources for the era of discovery and colonization that would make Spain the most powerful country in Europe during the 16th century. After the destruction of the Spanish Armada, 1588, Spain never again played a major role in European politics. Napoleonic France ruled Spain between 1808 and 1814. The monarchy was restored in 1814 and continued, interrupted by the short-lived republic of 1873–74, until the exile of Alfonso XIII in 1931, when the Second Republic was established.

The monarchy was reconstituted in 1947 under the regency of General Francisco Franco, the king designated to be crowned after Franco's death. Franco died on Nov. 30, 1975. Two days after his passing, Juan Carlos de Borbon, the grandson of Alfonso XIII, was proclaimed King of Spain.

RULERS

Francisco Franco, 1937–75
Juan Carlos I, 1975–

MONETARY SYSTEM

1 Peseta = 100 Céntimos 1874–

REPLACEMENT NOTES

#150 and later, 9A, 9B, 9C type prefix.

Banco de España

1953–57 ISSUE

144–149 printer: FNMT.

Cat. #	Denomination	Date, description	VG	VF	Unc
144	100 PESETAS	7.4.1953 (1955). Brown on m/c unpt. J. Romero de Torres at ctr. Picture by Torres on back. Wmk: Woman's head.	FV	2.50	9.00

Cat. #	Denomination	Date, description	VG	VF	Unc
145	1 PESETA	22.7.1953. Brown and black on m/c unpt. M. de Santa Cruz at r. Old sailing ship on back.	.05	.10	.50

146	5 PESETAS	22.7.1954. Green on lt. lilac unpt. Alfonso X at r. and as wmk. Library and museum bldg. in Madrid on back.	.10	.25	1.50

147	25 PESETAS	22.7.1954. Purple on orange and m/c unpt. I. Albeniz at l. and as wmk. Patio scene of the Lion's Court of Alhambra on back.	.35	1.00	5.00
148	500 PESETAS	22.7.1954 (1958). Blue on m/c unpt. I. Zuloaga at ctr. and as wmk. Zuloaga's picture "Vista de Toledo" on back.	FV	5.00	15.00

149	1000 PESETAS	29.11.1957 (1958). Green. "Reyes Catóicos" at ctr. Arms on back.	FV	12.00	35.00

1965 ISSUE

#150–151 printer: FNMT.

Cat. #	Denomination	Date, description	VG	VF	Unc
150	100 PESETAS	19.11.1965 (1970). Brown on m/c unpt. G.A. Bécquer at r. ctr. Woman w/parasol and cathedral of Sevilla on back. Wmk: Woman's head.	FV	1.50	5.00

Cat. #	Denomination	Date, description	VG	VF	Unc
163	500 PESETAS	23.7.1971 (1973). Blue-gray, black and m/c. J. Verdaguer at r. and as wmk. View of Mt. Canigó w/village of Vignolas d'Oris on back.	FV	4.00	10.00

1974 COMMEMORATIVE ISSUE

#154, Centennial of the Banco de España's becoming the sole issuing bank, 1874–1974. Printer: FNMT.

154	1000 PESETAS	17.9.1971 (1974). Green. J. Echegaray at r. Bank of Spain in Madrid and commemorative legend on back.	FV	10.00	20.00

151	1000 PESETAS	19.11.1965 (1971). Green on m/c unpt. S. Isidoro at l. Imaginary figure w/basilica behind on back.	FV	12.00	35.00

1970–71 ISSUE

152-153 printer: FNMT.

152	100 PESETAS	17.11.1970 (1974). Brown on lt. orange unpt. M. de Falla at r. and as wmk. Patio scene of the Generalife of Granada on back.	FV	1.00	2.75

1976 REGULAR ISSUE

Cat. #	Denomination	Date, description	VG	VF	Unc
155	5000 PESETAS	6.2.1976 (1978). Purple and brown on m/c unpt. Carlos III at r. Museum of Prado on back.	FV	45.00	75.00

1982–87 ISSUE

#156–161 wmk. as portr. Printer: FNMT.

Cat. #	Denomination	Date, description	VG	VF	Unc
156	200 PESETAS	16.9.1980 (1984). Brown, orange and m/c. Cross at ctr., L. Alas (Clarin) at r. and as wmk. Tree at l. on back.	FV	1.75	3.50

| 157 | 500 PESETAS | 23.10.1979 (1983). Dk. blue and black on m/c unpt. R. de Castro at r. and as wmk. Villa on back. | FV | 4.50 | 8.50 |

Cat. #	Denomination	Date, description	VG	VF	Unc
158	1000 PESETAS	23.10.1979 (1982). Gray-blue and green on m/c unpt. Tree at ctr., B. Perez Galdos at r. and as wmk. Rock formations, mountains and map of Canary Islands on back.	FV	9.00	14.00

| 159 | 2000 PESETAS | 22.7.1980 (1983). Deep red, orange and m/c. Rose at ctr., J.R. Jimenez at r. and as wmk. Villa de la Rosa at l. on back. | FV | 17.50 | 30.00 |

| 160 | 5000 PESETAS | 23.10.1979 (1982). Brown, violet and m/c. Fleur-de-lis at ctr., Kg. Juan Carlos I at r. and as wmk. Royal Palace on back. | FV | 42.50 | 62.50 |

| 161 | 10,000 PESETAS | 24.9.1985 (1987). Gray-black on m/c unpt. Arms at ctr., Kg. Juan Carlos I at r. Back blue-gray on m/c unpt. Prince of Asturias at l. | FV | 85.00 | 130.00 |

1992 COMMEMORATIVE ISSUE

#162–165, 5th Centennial of Discovery of America. Printer: FNMT.

Cat. #	Denomination	Date, description	VG	VF	Unc
162	1000 PESETAS	18.10.1992. Green on m/c unpt. H. Cortes at r. F. Pizarro on back.	FV	FV	13.50

163	2000 PESETAS	24.4.1992. Red on m/c unpt. J.C. Mutis observing flower at r. and as wmk. Royal Botanical Garden and title page of Mutis' work on back.	FV	FV	26.50
164	5000 PESETAS	13.10.1992. Violet and m/c. Columbus at r., and as wmk. Back vertical; astrolob at lower ctr.	FV	FV	57.50
165	10,000 PESETAS	12.10.1992. Blue on m/c unpt. Kg. J. Carlos at r., Casa de America in Madrid at lower ctr. Back vertical; A. de Ulloa y de Jorge Juan above astromonical navigation diagram.	FV	FV	120.00
166	20,000 PESETAS				Expected new issue.

SHRI (SRI) LANKA

The Democratic Socialist Republic of Sri (Shri) Lanka (formerly Ceylon), situated in the Indian Ocean 18 miles (29 km.) southeast of India, has an area of 25,332 sq. mi. (65,610 sq. km.) and a population of 17.25 million. Capital: Colombo. The economy is chiefly agricultural. Tea, coconut products and rubber are exported.

The earliest known inhabitants of Ceylon, the Veddahs, were subjugated by the Sinhalese from northern India in the 6th century BC. Sinhalese rule was maintained until 1408, after which the island was controlled by China for 30 years. The Portuguese came to Ceylon in 1505 and maintained control of the coastal area for 150 years. They were supplanted by the Dutch in 1658, who were in turn supplanted by the British who seized the Dutch colonies in 1796, and made them a Crown Colony in 1802. In 1815, the British conquered the independent Kingdom of Kandy in the central part of the island. Constitutional changes in 1931 and 1946 granted the Ceylonese a measure of autonomy and a parliamentary form of government. Ceylon became a self-governing dominion of the British Commonwealth on February 4, 1948. On May 22, 1972, the Ceylonese adopted a new constitution which declared Ceylon to be the Republic of Sri Lanka - 'Resplendent Island'. Shri Lanka is a member of the Commonwealth of Nations. The president is Chief of State. The prime minister is Head of Government.

RULERS
British, 1796–1972

REPLACEMENT NOTES
#83–88, Z/1 prefix.

MONETARY SYSTEM
1 Rupee = 100 Cents

Government of Ceylon

#37–42 w/o portr.; arms of Ceylon at l. W/o English bank name. Various date and sign. varieties. Wmk: Chinze. Printer: BWC.

Cat. #	Denomination	Date, description	VG	VF	Unc
37	1 RUPEE	1956–63. Blue on orange, green and brown unpt. Ornate stairway on back.			
		a. W/o security strip. 30.7.1956–11.9.1959.	.75	2.50	8.50
		b. Security strip. 18.8.1960; 29.1.1962; 5.6.1963.	.50	1.75	5.50
38	2 RUPEES	1956–62. Brown and lilac on blue and green unpt. Pavilion on back.			
		a. W/o security strip. 30.7.1956–11.9.1959.	1.00	3.00	12.50
		b. Security strip. 18.8.1960; 29.1.1962.	1.00	2.50	10.00

39	5 RUPEES	1956–62. Orange on aqua, green and brown unpt. Standing figure on back.			
		a. W/o security strip. 30.7.1956; 31.5.1957; 10.6.1958; 1.7.1959.	2.00	5.00	17.50
		b. Security strip. 18.8.1960; 29.1.1962.	1.00	3.00	15.00

Cat. #	Denomination	Date, description	VG	VF	Unc
46	50 RUPEES	2.11.1961; 5.6.1963; 6.4.1965. Blue and m/c.	6.00	17.50	65.00
47	100 RUPEES	5.6.1963. Brown and m/c.	12.50	30.00	100.00

#48–52 statue of Kg. Parakkrama at r. W/o English bank name. Back designs like #37–42. Various date and sign. varieties. Wmk: Chinze. Printer: BWC.

Cat. #	Denomination	Date, description	VG	VF	Unc
40	10 RUPEES	1956–63. Green on violet, brown and blue unpt. Ceremonial figures on back.			
		a. W/o security strip. 30.7.1956; 7.11.1958; 11.9.1959.	3.00	8.00	25.00
		b. Security strip. 18.8.1960; 7.4.1961; 5.6.1963.	2.00	7.00	20.00
41	50 RUPEES	30.7.1956; 7.11.1958. Blue, violet and m/c. Ornate stairway on back.	17.50	50.00	150.00
42	100 RUPEES	24.10.1956. Brown and m/c. 2 women in national costumes on back.	17.50	55.00	175.00

#43–47 S. Bandaranaike at r. W/o English bank name. Back designs like #37–42. Various date and sign. varieties. Wmk: Chinze. Printer: BWC.

Cat. #	Denomination	Date, description	VG	VF	Unc
43	2 RUPEES	8.11.1962–6.4.1965. Brown on lilac, green and blue unpt.	.75	2.50	9.00

Cat. #	Denomination	Date, description	VG	VF	Unc
48	2 RUPEES	9.9.1965; 15.7.1967; 10.1.1968. Brown on lilac, lt. green and blue unpt.	.50	1.50	4.50
49	5 RUPEES	9.9.1965; 15.7.1967; 1.9.1967; 10.1.1968. Orange on brown and green unpt.	.75	2.00	7.00
50	10 RUPEES	10.1.1968. Green on purple, orange and blue unpt.	1.50	4.00	10.00
51	50 RUPEES	7.3.1967; 10.1.1968. Blue and m/c.	6.00	12.50	45.00
52	100 RUPEES	28.5.1966; 22.11.1966; 10.1.1968. Brown and m/c.	12.50	25.00	65.00

#53–57 title: CENTRAL BANK OF CEYLON added in English on face and back. Various date and sign. varieties. Wmk: Chinze. Printer: BWC.

NOTE: Earlier dates do not have the word in text lines on face.

Cat. #	Denomination	Date, description	VG	VF	Unc
44	5 RUPEES	8.11.1962; 12.6.1964. Orange on brown and green unpt.	1.00	3.00	12.00

Cat. #	Denomination	Date, description	VG	VF	Unc
53	2 RUPEES	1969–77. Like #48.			
		a. 3rd and 4th lines w/o word in text. 10.5.1969–12.5.1972.	.25	.50	1.50
		b. 3rd and 4th lines w/word in text. 21.8.1973; 27.8.1974; 26.8.1977.	.25	.50	1.25

Cat. #	Denomination	Date, description	VG	VF	Unc
45	10 RUPEES	12.6.1964; 28.8.1964; 19.9.1964. Green on purple, orange and blue unpt.	2.00	6.00	20.00

Cat. #	Denomination	Date, description	VG	VF	Unc
54	5 RUPEES	1969–77. Like #49.			
		a. 3rd and 4th lines w/o word in text. 10.5.1969; 1.6.1970; 1.2.1971.	.40	.75	3.00
		b. 3rd and 4th lines w/word in text. 21.8.1973–27.8.1974.	.40	.75	2.50

Cat. #	Denomination	Date, description	VG	VF	Unc
55	10 RUPEES	1969–77. Like #50.			
		a. 3rd and 4th lines w/o word in text. 20.10.1969; 1.6.1970; 1.2.1971; 7.6.1971.	.75	2.00	6.00
		b. 3rd and 4th lines w/word in text. 21.8.1973; 16.7.1974; 6.10.1975; 26.8.1977.	.75	2.00	5.00
56	50 RUPEES	20.10.1969. Like #51.	2.00	5.00	25.00

57	100 RUPEES	28.5.1968; 10.5.1969. Like #52.	4.00	12.50	50.00

#58–59 smiling Pres. Bandaranaike w/raised hand. Wmk: Chinze. Printer: TDLR.

Cat. #	Denomination	Date, description	VG	VF	Unc
58	50 RUPEES	26.10.1970; 9.12.1970. Blue on lilac, yellow and brown unpt. Monument on back.	3.00	12.50	45.00
59	100 RUPEES	26.10.1970. Purple and m/c. Female dancers on back.	5.50	20.00	65.00

#60–61 Pres. Bandaranaike smiling w/o hand raised. Wmk: Chinze. Printer: BWC.

60	50 RUPEES	28.12.1972; 27.8.1974. Purple and m/c. Landscape on back.	3.00	12.00	40.00

61	100 RUPEES	18.12.1971; 16.7.1974; 6.10.1975. Purple, gray and m/c. Ornate stairway on back.	5.00	18.00	60.00

SRI LANKA

Central Bank of Ceylon

1977 ISSUE

#62–63 Sri Lanka arms at r. Wmk: Chinze. Printer: BWC.

62	50 RUPEES	26.8.1977. Purple, green and m/c. Back like #60.	2.50	6.00	22.50

63	100 RUPEES	26.8.1977. Purple, black and m/c. Back like #61.	4.00	10.00	35.00

1979 ISSUE

#64–69 backs vertical format. Wmk: Chinze.

Cat. #	Denomination	Date, description	VG	VF	Unc
64	2 RUPEES	26.3.1979. Red and m/c. Fish at r. Butterfly and lizard on back.	.15	.50	1.75

Cat. #	Denomination	Date, description	VG	VF	Unc
65	5 RUPEES	26.3.1979. Gray and m/c. Butterfly and salamander at r. Flying squirrel and bird on back.	.25	1.00	3.50

Cat. #	Denomination	Date, description	VG	VF	Unc
66	10 RUPEES	26.3.1979. Green and m/c. Bird in tree at ctr. Flowers and animals on back.	.40	1.00	5.00

Cat. #	Denomination	Date, description	VG	VF	Unc
67	20 RUPEES	26.3.1979. Brown, green and m/c. Bird at ctr., monkey at r. Bird, tree and animals on back.	1.00	2.00	9.50

Cat. #	Denomination	Date, description	VG	VF	Unc
68	50 RUPEES	26.3.1979. Blue, brown and m/c. Butterfly at ctr., bird at r. Salamander and birds on back.	2.50	6.00	20.00

Cat. #	Denomination	Date, description	VG	VF	Unc
69	100 RUPEES	26.3.1979. Gold, green and m/c. Snakes and tree at ctr., birds at r. Bird in tree, butterfly below on back.	3.00	6.50	37.50

1981 ISSUE

#70–71 backs vertical format. Wmk: Chinze.

Cat. #	Denomination	Date, description	VG	VF	Unc
70	500 RUPEES	1.1.1981; 1.1.1985. Brown, purple and m/c. Elephant w/rider at r. Abhayagiri Stupa, Anuradhapura temple on hill on back.	15.00	35.00	85.00

Cat. #	Denomination	Date, description	VG	VF	Unc
74	20 RUPEES	1.1.1982; 1.1.1985. Violet on m/c unpt. Moonstone Anuradhapura at r. Shrine on back.	FV	.50	4.00

Cat. #	Denomination	Date, description	VG	VF	Unc
71	1000 RUPEES	1.1.1981. Green and m/c. Dam at r. Peacock and mountains on back.	40.00	90.00	150.00

| 75 | 50 RUPEES | 1.1.1982. Dk. blue and dk. brown on m/c unpt. Tomb at r. Back dk. blue and m/c; ruins at ctr. | FV | 1.75 | 6.00 |

1982 ISSUE

#72–76 backs vertical format. Wmk: Chinze. Printer: BWC.

| 76 | 100 RUPEES | 1.1.1982. Brown and orange on m/c unpt. Stone carving of lion at lower r. Parliament bldg. on back. | FV | 3.50 | 13.50 |

Srí Lanká Maha Bänkuva — Central Bank of Sri Lanka

1987–89 ISSUE

#77–82 wmk: Chinze.

#77–81 similar to #70, 72–76 but w/old bank name now changed in English from *CEYLON* to *Sri Lanka*. Printer: BWC.

| 72 | 5 RUPEES | 1.1.1982. Lt. red on m/c unpt. Ruins at r. Stone carving of deity and child on back. | FV | .20 | 2.00 |

| 73 | 10 RUPEES | 1.1.1982; 1.1.1985. Olive-green on m/c unpt. Temple of the Tooth at r. Shrine on back. | FV | .30 | 2.50 |

| 77 | 10 RUPEES | 1.1.1987; 21.11.1988; 21.2.1989; 5.4.1990. Green and m/c. Similar to #73 but bank name changed in English text. | FV | .35 | 1.50 |

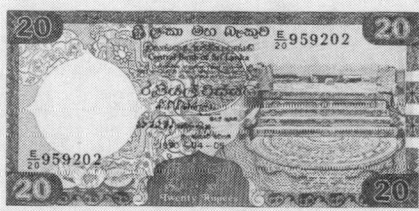

Cat. #	Denomination	Date, description	VG	VF	Unc
78	20 RUPEES	21.2.1989; 5.4.1990. Purple on m/c unpt. Similar to #74 but bank name changed in English text.	FV	.65	2.00

79	50 RUPEES	21.2.1989. Blue and brown on m/c unpt. Similar to #75 but bank name changed in English text.	FV	1.50	5.50
80	100 RUPEES	1.1.1987; 1.2.1988; 21.2.1989; 5.4.1990. Brown and orange on m/c unpt. Similar to #76 but bank name changed in English text.	FV	2.75	9.00
81	500 RUPEES	1.1.1987; 21.11.1988; 21.2.1989; 5.4.1990. M/c. Similar to #70 but w/ clearer wmk. area, vertical silver security markings, bird and borders deeper red brown. Hill and temple in violet on back.	FV	13.50	35.00

| 82 | 1000 RUPEES | 1.1.1987; 21.2.1989; 5.4.1990. Deep green on m/c unpt. Victoria dam at r. Peacock and University of Ruhuna on back. | FV | 25.00 | 65.00 |

1991 ISSUE

#83–88 backs vertical format. Wmk: Chinze. Printer: TDLR.

| 83 | 10 RUPEES | 1.1.1991; 19.8.1994. Deep brown and green on m/c unpt. Sinhalese Chinze at r. Crane above Presidential Secretariat bldg. in Colombo, flowers in lower foreground on back. | FV | FV | .65 |

Cat. #	Denomination	Date, description	VG	VF	Unc
84	20 RUPEES	1.1.1991; 19.8.1994. Purple and red on m/c unpt. Native bird mask at r. Two youths fishing, sea shells on back.	FV	FV	1.50

| 85 | 50 RUPEES | 1.1.1991; 19.8.1994. Brown-violet, deep blue and blue-green on m/c unpt. Male dancer w/local headdress at r. Butterflies above temple ruins, w/shield and ornamental sword hilt in lower foreground on back. | FV | FV | 3.50 |

86	100 RUPEES	1991–92. Dk. brown and orange on m/c unpt. Decorative urn at r. Back dk. brown on m/c unpt; tea leaf pickers, 2 parrots on back.			
		a. W/o dot on value in Tamil at l. 1.1.1991.	FV	FV	10.00
		b. W/dot on value in Tamil at l. 1.1.1991; 1.7.1992.	FV	FV	6.00

| 87 | 500 RUPEES | 1.1.1991. Dk. brown, violet and brown-orange on m/c unpt. Musicians at r., dancer at l. ctr. Kingfisher above temple and orchids on back. | FV | FV | 26.50 |

Cat. #	Denomination	Date, description	VG	VF	Unc
88	1000 RUPEES	1.1.1991; 1.7.1992. Brown, dk. green and purple on m/c unpt. Chinze at lower l., two-headed bird at bottom ctr. and elephant w/trainer at r. Peacocks on palace lawn; lotus flowers above and Octagon of the Temple of Tooth in Kandy on back.	FV	FV	50.00

1992 ISSUE

89	100 RUPEES	1.7.1992. Dk. brown and orange on m/c unpt. Like #86 but back brown-orange on m/c.	FV	FV	5.50

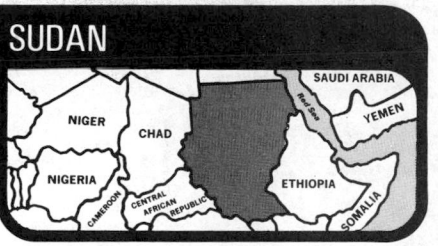

The Democratic Republic of the Sudan, located in northeast Africa on the Red Sea between Egypt and Ethiopia, has an area of 967,500 sq. mi. (2,505,810 sq. km.) and a population of 29.97 million. Capital: Khartoum. Agriculture and livestock raising are the chief occupations. Cotton, gum arabic and peanuts are exported.

The Sudan, site of the powerful Nubian kingdom of Roman times, was a collection of small independent states from the 14th century until 1820–22 when it was conquered and united by Mohammed Ali, Pasha of Egypt. Egyptain forces were driven from the area during the Mahdist revolt, 1881–98, but the Sudan was retaken by Anglo-Egyptian expeditions, 1896–98, and established as an Anglo-Egyptian condominium in 1899. Britain supplied the administrative apparatus and personnel, but the appearance of joint Anglo-Egyptian administration was continued until Jan. 9, 1954, when the first Sudanese self-government parliament was inaugurated. The Sudan achieved independence on Jan. 1, 1956 with the consent of the British and Egyptian governments. On June 30, 1989 Gen. Omar Hassan Ahmad al-Bashir overthrew the civilian government in a military coup. The rebel guerrilla PLA forces are active in the south.

Notes of Egypt were in use before 1956.

MONETARY SYSTEM

1 Ghirsh (Piastre) = 10 Millim (Milliemes)
1 Sudanese Pound = 100 Piastres to 1992
1 Dinar = 10 Old Sudanese Pounds, 1992

REPLACEMENT NOTES

Z/various numbers as Z/11, Z/49, etc. #30 and later, Z/ # prefix.

Bank of Sudan

1961-64 ISSUE

#6–10 various date and sign. varieties. Arms (desert camel rider) on back.

Cat. #	Denomination	Date, description	VG	VF	Unc
6	25 PIASTRES	1964–68. Red on m/c unpt. Soldiers in formation at l.			
		a. 6.3.1964; 25.1.1967.	6.00	15.00	85.00
		b. 7.2.1968.	5.00	12.00	70.00

7	50 PIASTRES	1964–68. Green on m/c unpt. Elephants at l.			
		a. 6.3.1964; 25.1.1967.	15.00	55.00	300.00
		b. 7.2.1968.	12.00	45.00	250.00

8	1 POUND	1961–68. Blue on yellow and m/c unpt. Dam at l.			
		a. 8.4.1961.	8.00	25.00	125.00
		b. 2.3.1965; 20.1.1966; 25.1.1967.	6.00	17.50	100.00
		c. 7.2.1968.	5.00	14.00	80.00

Cat. #	Denomination	Date, description	VG	VF	Unc
9	5 POUNDS	1962–68. Lilac-brown on m/c unpt. Dhow at l.			
		a. 1.7.1962.	20.00	50.00	400.00
		b. 2.3.1965; 20.1.1966; 25.1.1967.	10.00	40.00	300.00
		c. 7.2.1968.	8.00	37.50	250.00

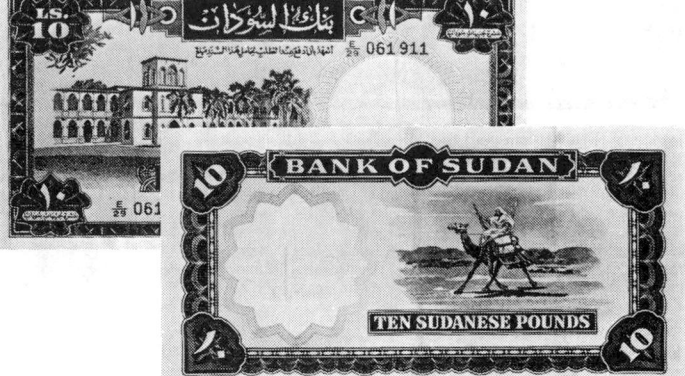

Cat. #	Denomination	Date, description	VG	VF	Unc
10	10 POUNDS	1964–68. ... Sudan bldg. at l.			
		a. 6.3.1964; 20.1.1966; 25.1.1967.	20.00	50.00	425.00
		b. 7.2.1968.	16.00	40.00	350.00

1970 ISSUE

#11–15 Bank of Sudan at l. on face. Various date and sign. varieties. Printer: TDLR.

Cat. #	Denomination	Date, description	VG	VF	Unc
11	25 PIASTRES	1970–80. Red. Textile industry on back.			
		a. Jan. 1970; Jan. 1971; Jan. 1972.	1.50	7.50	25.00
		b. 1.4.1973–28.5.1978.	.75	2.50	10.00
		c. 2.1.1980.	.50	1.00	4.50

Cat. #	Denomination	Date, description	VG	VF	Unc
12	50 PIASTRES	1970–80. Green. University of Khartoum on back.			
		a. Jan. 1970; Jan. 1971; Jan. 1972.	3.00	9.00	35.00
		b. 1.4.1973–28.5.1978.	1.00	2.50	10.00
		c. 2.1.1980.	.75	1.50	7.50

Cat. #	Denomination	Date, description	VG	VF	Unc
13	1 POUND	1970–80. Blue and m/c. Ancient temple on back.			
		a. Wmk: Rhinoceros head. Jan. 1970; Jan. 1971.	7.00	20.00	85.00
		b. Wmk: Arms (secretary bird). Jan. 1972–28.5.1978.	2.50	5.00	15.00
		c. 2.1.1980.	2.00	5.00	15.00

Cat. #	Denomination	Date, description	VG	VF	Unc
14	5 POUNDS	1970–80. Brown, lilac and m/c. Domestic and wild animals on back.			
		a. Wmk: Rhinoceros head. Jan. 1970.	17.50	50.00	185.00
		b. Wmk: Arms. Jan. 1971–28.5.1978.	7.00	15.00	75.00
		c. 2.1.1980.	7.00	15.00	60.00

Cat. #	Denomination	Date, description	VG	VF	Unc
15	10 POUNDS	1970–80. Purple, green and m/c. Transportation elements (ship, plane, etc.) on back.			
		a. Wmk: Rhinoceros head. Jan. 1970.	27.50	75.00	300.00
		b. Wmk: Arms. Jan. 1971–28.5.1978.	7.50	20.00	60.00
		c. 2.1.1980.	5.00	15.00	45.00

1981 ISSUE

#16–21 Pres. J. Nimeiri wearing national headdress at l., arms at ctr.

Cat. #	Denomination	Date, description	VG	VF	Unc
16	25 PIASTRES	1.1.1981. Brown and m/c. Kosti bridge on back.	.40	1.00	2.75

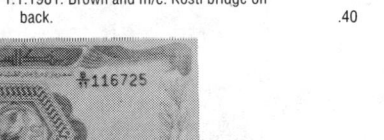

17	50 PIASTRES	1.1.1981. Purple on brown unpt. Bank of Sudan on back.	.60	1.25	3.75

#18–21 wmk: Arms.

18	1 POUND	1.1.1981. Blue and m/c. People's Assembly on back.	1.00	3.50	12.00

19	5 POUNDS	1.1.1981. Green and m/c. Back green, w/ Islamic Centre Mosque at Khartoum at r.	2.00	5.00	12.50

20	10 POUNDS	1.1.1981. Blue, brown and m/c. Kenana sugar factory on back.	7.50	15.00	75.00
21	20 POUNDS	1.1.1981. Green and m/c. Like #22 but w/o commemorative text.	10.00	20.00	85.00

COMMEMORATIVE ISSUE

#22, 25th Anniversary of Independence

Cat. #	Denomination	Date, description	VG	VF	Unc
22	20 POUNDS	1.1.1981. Green and m/c. Map at ctr., commemorative legend in circle at r. around wmk., monument at r. Unity Monument at l., People's Palace at r. on back.	15.00	35.00	90.00

1983-84 ISSUE

#23–29 like previous issue but some in different colors.

23	25 PIASTRES	1.1.1983. Red-orange on yellow unpt. Like #16.	.25	.50	1.75
24	50 PIASTRES	1.1.1983. Like #17.	.60	1.25	2.25
25	1 POUND	1.1.1983. Like #18 but bldg. on back is blue.	.50	1.25	3.00
26	5 POUNDS	1.1.1983. Like #19.	2.00	5.00	12.50
27	10 POUNDS	1.1.1983. Purple and red-brown on m/c unpt. Like #20.	4.50	10.00	22.50
28	20 POUNDS	1.1.1983. Like #21.	7.00	15.00	35.00

29	50 POUNDS	25.5.1984. Brown-orange and blue on m/c unpt. Pres. Nimeiri at l. Back blue on m/c unpt; sailing ship at ctr., modern oil tanker at r.	12.50	25.00	60.00

Law of 30.6.1985/AH1405

#30–36 outline map of Sudan at ctr. Bank of Sudan at ctr. on back. Wmk: Arms. Sign. title w/2 lines of Arabic text (Acting Governor).

Cat. #	Denomination	Date, description	VG	VF	Unc
30	25 PIASTRES	L.1985. Purple. Camels at l.	.10	.40	2.00

Cat. #	Denomination	Date, description	VG	VF	Unc
31	50 PIASTRES	L.1985. Red on lilac and peach unpt. Lyre and drum at l., peanut plant at r.	.15	.50	3.00

Cat. #	Denomination	Date, description	VG	VF	Unc
32	1 POUND	L.1985. Green on m/c unpt. Cotton boll at l. Back blue on m/c unpt.	.20	.75	4.00

Cat. #	Denomination	Date, description	VG	VF	Unc
33	5 POUNDS	L.1985. Olive and brown on m/c unpt. Cattle at l.	.50	3.00	15.00

Cat. #	Denomination	Date, description	VG	VF	Unc
34	10 POUNDS	L.1985. Brown on m/c unpt. City gateway at l.	2.00	6.00	27.50

Cat. #	Denomination	Date, description	VG	VF	Unc
35	20 POUNDS	L.1985. Green and purple on m/c unpt. Dhow at l.	10.00	25.00	100.00

Cat. #	Denomination	Date, description	VG	VF	Unc
36	50 POUNDS	L.1985. Brown, purple and red-orange on m/c unpt. Columns along pool below National Museum at l., spear at r. Back red.	7.50	22.50	90.00

1987–90 ISSUE

#37–43 sign. title in 1 line of Arabic text (Governor).

Cat. #	Denomination	Date, description	VG	VF	Unc
37	25 PIASTRES	1987. Like #30.	.05	.15	.35

Cat. #	Denomination	Date, description	VG	VF	Unc
38	50 PIASTRES	1987. Like #31.	.05	.25	.50

Cat. #	Denomination	Date, description	VG	VF	Unc
		a. 1988.	.40	1.25	4.00
		b. 1989; 1990.	2.00	5.50	22.50

1991/AH1411 ISSUE

#45–50 wmk: Arms.

Cat. #	Denomination	Date, description	VG	VF	Unc
39	1 POUND	1987. Like #32.	.10	.50	1.00

#40–43 wmk: Arms.

			VG	VF	Unc
40	5 POUNDS	1987;1989;1990. Like #33.	.25	.75	5.00

			VG	VF	Unc
45	5 POUNDS	1991/AH1411. Similar to #40 but red, orange and violet on m/c unpt. Back red-orange on m/c unpt.	.20	.60	2.75

			VG	VF	Unc
41	10 POUNDS	1987;1989;1990. Like #34.	.50	1.50	7.50

			VG	VF	Unc
46	10 POUNDS	1991/AH1411. Similar to #41 but black and deep green on m/c unpt. Back black on m/c unpt.	.30	.90	3.75

			VG	VF	Unc
42	20 POUNDS	1987;1989;1990. Like #35.	.65	2.00	12.00

			VG	VF	Unc
47	20 POUNDS	1991/AH1411. Similar to #42 but purple and violet on m/c unpt. Back violet on m/c unpt.	.25	.75	4.00

			VG	VF	Unc
43	50 POUNDS	1987;1989. Like #36.	1.00	3.00	13.50

			VG	VF	Unc
44	100 POUNDS	1988–90. Brown, purple and deep green on m/c unpt. Bldg. at l., book at r. Bank of Sudan and coin on back. Wmk: Arms.			

Cat. #	Denomination	Date, description	VG	VF	Unc
48	50 POUNDS	1991/AH1411. Similar to #43 but yellow-orange, brownish black and dk. brown on m/c unpt. Back dk. brown on m/c unpt.	.35	1.00	4.50

| 49 | 100 POUNDS | 1991/AH1411. Similar to #44 but ultramarine and blue-green on m/c unpt. Ultramarine shield at l., lt. blue green map image at ctr. Shiny lt. green coin design at r. on back. (partially engraved). | .60 | 1.75 | 7.00 |

| 50 | 100 POUNDS | 1991/AH1411; 1992/AH1412. Similar to #45 but colors rearranged. Blue-green shield at l., darker details on bldg. and ultramarine map image at ctr. Pink coin design at r. on back. (litho). | .60 | 1.75 | 7.00 |

Currency Reform, 1992
1 Dinar = 10 Pounds

1992–94 ISSUE

#51–54 People's Palace at ctr. or lower r. Wmk: Domed bldg. w/tower.

Cat. #	Denomination	Date, description	VG	VF	Unc
51	5 DINARS	1993/AH1413. Dk. brown and red-orange on m/c unpt. Plants including sunflowers on back.	FV	FV	2.75

| 52 | 10 DINARS | 1993/AH1413. Deep red and dk. brown on m/c unpt. Domed bldg. w/tower at l. ctr. on back. | FV | FV | 3.50 |

53	25 DINARS	1992/AH1412. Brownish black and green on m/c unpt. Circular design at l. on back.			
		a. W/artist's name *DOSOUGI* at lower r.	FV	FV	12.50
		b. W/o artist's name.	FV	FV	10.00
54	50 DINARS	1992/AH1412. Dk. blue-green, black and purple on m/c unpt. 2 sign varieties.			
		a. W/artist's name *DOSOUGI* at lower r. below palace.	FV	FV	20.00
		b. W/o artist's name.	FV	FV	18.00
55	100 DINARS	1994/AH1414. Black and deep brown-violet on m/c unpt. Bldg. at l. ctr. on back.	FV	FV	30.00
56	500 DINARS			Expected new issue	
57	1000 DINARS			Expected new issue	

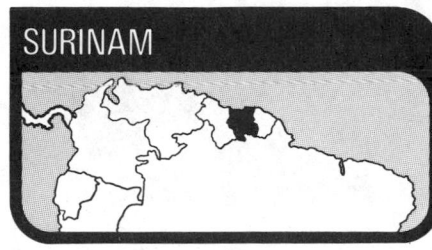

SURINAM

The Republic of Surinam, formerly known as Dutch Guiana, located on the north central coast of South America between Guyana and French Guiana, has an area of 63,037 sq. mi. (163,270 sq. km.) and a population of 404,300. Capital: Paramaribo. The country is rich in minerals and forests, and self-sufficient in rice, the staple food crop. The mining, processing and exporting of bauxite is the principal economic activity.

Lieutenants of Amerigo Vespucci sighted the Guiana coast in 1499. Spanish explorers of the 16th century, disappointed at finding no gold, departed leaving the area to be settled by the British in 1652. The colony prospered and the Netherlands acquired it in 1667 in exchange for the Dutch rights in Nieuw Nederland (state of New York). During the European wars of the 18th and 19th centuries, which were fought in part in the New World, Surinam was occupied by the British from 1799–1814. Surinam became an autonomous part of the Kingdom of the Netherlands on Dec. 15, 1954. Full independence was achieved on Nov. 25, 1975.

RULERS
Dutch to 1975

MONETARY SYSTEM
1 Gulden = 100 Cents

REPLACEMENT NOTES
#30–32, ZZ prefix. Muntbiljetten notes printed by JEZ with 6-digit serial number beginning with "1" are replacements.

DUTCH INFLUENCE
Muntbiljetten
Law 8.4.1960
#23–24 various date and sign. varieties. Printer: JEZ.

Cat. #	Denomination	Date, description	VG	VF	Unc
23	1 GULDEN	1961–86. Dk. green w/black text on pale olive-green and brown unpt. Bldg. w/ tower and flag at l. Back brown and green.			
		a. Sign. title: *De Minister van Financien* in facsimile only. 1.8.1961–1.4.1969.	.75	3.00	9.00
		b. Sign. in facsimile w/printed name below. 1.4.1971.	.50	2.00	6.00
		c. Similar to b., but name of signer at r. 1.11.1974.	.50	2.00	5.50
		d. Similar to a., but shorter text, and sign. title centered. 1.11.1974; 25.6.1979.	.40	1.50	7.00
		e. Similar to d., but sign. title: *De Minister van Financien en Planning.* 1.9.1982; 2.1.1984; 1.12.1984; 1.10.1986.	.15	.50	1.50

Cat. #	Denomination	Date, description	VG	VF	Unc
24	2 1/2 GULDEN	2.1.1961; 2.7.1967. Red-brown. Girl wearing hat at l.	.85	2.50	7.50

24A	2 1/2 GULDEN	1973; 1978. Red-brown, lt. blue and m/c. Bird on branch at l. 3 lines of text above sign. title at ctr. Lizard and Afobaka Dam on back. Printer: BWC.			
		a. Sign. title: *De Minister van Financien.* Printed name below sign. 1.9.1973.	.50	2.25	9.00
		b. W/o printed name below sign. 1.8.1978.	.20	.65	2.50

24B	2 1/2 GULDEN	1.11.1985. Like #24A but 4 lines of text above sign. W/sign. title: *De Minister Financien en Planning* at ctr.	.20	.55	2.25

Centrale Bank van Suriname
1957 ISSUE
#25-29 arms on back. Wmk: Toucan's head. Printer: JEZ.

25	5 GULDEN	2.1.1957. Blue on m/c unpt. Woman w/fruit basket at r.	3.00	7.50	35.00
26	10 GULDEN	2.1.1957. Orange on m/c unpt. Like #25.	5.00	12.50	60.00
27	25 GULDEN	2.1.1957. Green on m/c unpt. Girl and fruit at r.	10.00	25.00	100.00
28	100 GULDEN	2.1.1957. Purple on m/c unpt. Like #27.	35.00	75.00	275.00
29	1000 GULDEN	2.1.1957. Olive green on m/c unpt. Like #27.	200.00	450.00	850.00

1963 ISSUE

#30–34 different arms on back. Wmk: Toucan's head. Printer: JEZ.

Cat. #	Denomination	Date, description	VG	VF	Unc
30	5 GULDEN	1.9.1963. Blue on m/c unpt. Similar to #25. 2 serial # varieties.	.10	.25	.85

Cat. #	Denomination	Date, description	VG	VF	Unc
31	10 GULDEN	1.9.1963. Orange on m/c unpt. Similar to #26.	.10	.25	1.00

32	25 GULDEN	1.9.1963. Green on m/c unpt. Similar to #27.	2.50	7.50	20.00

33	100 GULDEN	1.9.1963. Purple on m/c unpt. Similar to #28.	8.00	20.00	65.00

Cat. #	Denomination	Date, description	VG	VF	Unc
34	1000 GULDEN	1.9.1963. Brown on m/c unpt. Similar to #29.	5.00	15.00	35.00

REPUBLIC

Central Bank van Suriname

1982 ISSUE

#35–39 soldiers and woman at r. Bldg. w/flag on back. Wmk: Toucan's head. Sign. varieties. Printer: JEZ.

35	5 GULDEN	1.4.1982. Dk. blue on m/c unpt.	.15	.35	1.00
36	10 GULDEN	1.4.1982. Red on m/c unpt.	.15	.40	1.25

37	25 GULDEN	1982; 1985. Green on m/c unpt.			
		a. 1.4.1982.	1.00	3.00	10.00
		b. 1.11.1985.	.10	.25	.85

38	100 GULDEN	1982; 1985. Purple on m/c unpt.			
		a. 1.4.1982.	5.00	15.00	45.00
		b. 1.11.1985	.30	1.25	3.50

Cat. #	Denomination	Date, description	VG	VF	Unc
39	500 GULDEN	1.4.1982. Brown on m/c unpt.	.30	1.25	4.50

NOTE: 1000 new notes of #39 were sold by the Central Bank to the numismatic community for USA $2.00 each.

1986-88 ISSUE

#40–44 Anton DeKom at l., militia at r., row of bldgs. across bottom. Toucan at l., speaker w/people at r. on back. Wmk: Toucan. Printer: TDLR.

40	5 GULDEN	1.7.1986; 9.1.1988. Blue on m/c unpt.	FV	1.00	3.25

41	10 GULDEN	1.7.1986. Orange and red on m/c unpt.	FV	1.25	4.00
42	25 GULDEN	1.7.1986. Green on m/c unpt.	FV	2.00	8.00
43	100 GULDEN	1.7.1986. Purple on m/c unpt. 2 serial # varieties.	FV	6.00	20.00
44	250 GULDEN	9.1.1988. Blue-gray on m/c unpt.	FV	7.50	35.00

Cat. #	Denomination	Date, description	VG	VF	Unc
45	500 GULDEN	1.7.1986. Brown on m/c unpt.	FV	15.00	75.00

1991–93 ISSUE

46–50 Central Bank bldg., Paramaribo at ctr. Toucan at l. ctr. and as wmk., arms at upper r. on back. Printer: TDLR.

46	5 GULDEN	9.7.1991. Deep blue and green on m/c unpt. Log trucks at upper l. Logging at ctr. r. on back.	FV	FV	1.50

47	10 GULDEN	9.7.1991. Red and green on m/c unpt. Bananas at upper l. Banana harvesting at ctr. r. on back.	FV	FV	3.00

48	25 GULDEN	9.7.1991. Green and brown-orange on m/c unpt. Track participants at upper l. Competition swimmer in breaststroke at ctr. r. on back.	FV	FV	5.00

| 49 | 100 GULDEN | 9.7.1991. Violet and purple on m/c unpt. Factory at upper l. Strip mining at ctr. r. on back. | FV | FV | 7.50 |

| 50 | 500 GULDEN | 9.7.1991. Brown and red-orange on m/c unpt. Crude oil pump at upper l. Drilling for crude oil at ctr. r. on back. | FV | FV | 15.00 |

| 51 | 1000 GULDEN | 1.7.1993. Black on m/c unpt. Combine at upper l. Combining grain at ctr. r. on back. | FV | FV | 27.50 |

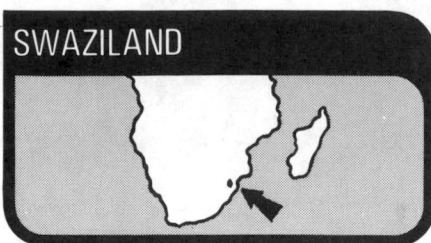

SWAZILAND

The Kingdom of Swaziland, located in southeastern Africa, has an area of 6,704 sq. mi. (17,360 sq. km.) and a population of 681,000. Capital: Mbabane (administrative); Lobamba (legislative). The diversified economy includes mining, agriculture and light industry. Asbestos, iron ore, wood pulp and sugar are exported.

The people of the present Swazi nation established themselves in an area including what is now Swaziland in the early 1800s. The first Swazi contact with the British came early in the reign of the extremely able Swazi leader Mswati when he asked the British for aid against Zulu raids into Swaziland. The British and Transvaal responded by guaranteeing the independence of Swaziland, 1881. South Africa assumed the power of protection and administration in 1894 and Swaziland continued under this administration until the conquest of the Transvaal during the Anglo-Boer War, when administration was transferred to the British government. After World War II, Britain began to prepare Swaziland for independence, which was achieved on Sept. 6, 1968. The kingdom is a member of the Commonwealth of Nations. The king of Swaziland is Chief of State. The prime minister is Head of Government.

RULERS

British to 1968

Sobhuza II, 1968–82

Queen Ntombi, as regent, 1982–86

King Mswati III, 1986–

MONETARY SYSTEM

1 Lilangeni = 100 Cents

REPLACEMENT NOTES

For all notes, Z prefix.

SIGNATURE VARIETIES					
	MINISTER FOR FINANCE	GOVERNOR		MINISTER FOR FINANCE	GOVERNOR
1	R. P. Steph	E. Hayoela	5	B. Dlamini	Sayves Nxumalo
2	Flimelane	H B O	6	Dealing	Sayves Nxumalo
3	Nxumalo	H B O	7		
4	B. Dlamini	H B O			

Monetary Authority of Swaziland

1974-78 ISSUE

#1–5 Kg. Sobhuza II at l., Parliament House at bottom ctr. r. Sign. 1. Wmk: Shield and spears. Printer: TDLR.

Cat. #	Denomination	Date, description	VG	VF	Unc
1	1 LILANGENI	ND (1974). Red-brown on m/c unpt. Sobhuza's wives dancing on back.	.60	.85	2.50

Cat. #	Denomination	Date, description	VG	VF	Unc
2	2 EMALANGENI	ND (1974). Dk. brown on pink and m/c unpt. Sugar mill on back.	1.00	2.50	5.50
3	5 EMALANGENI	ND (1974). Dk. green on yellow-green and m/c unpt. Mantenga Falls and landscape on back.	2.00	6.00	10.00

Cat. #	Denomination	Date, description	VG	VF	Unc
4	10 EMALANGENI	ND (1974). Blue-black on blue and m/c unpt. Asbestos mine on back.	7.50	17.50	45.00

Cat. #	Denomination	Date, description	VG	VF	Unc
5	20 EMALANGENI	ND (1978). Violet and dk. brown on m/c unpt. Agricultural products and cows on back.	15.00	40.00	115.00

Central Bank of Swaziland

1985 ISSUE

#6 and 7 wmk: Shield and spears.

Cat. #	Denomination	Date, description	VG	VF	Unc
6	2 EMALANGENI	ND (1985). Dk. borwn on pink and m/c unpt. Similar to #2 but new issuer's name at top.			
		a. Sign. 2.	1.75	3.75	7.50
		b. Sign. 4.	.75	1.50	3.00

Cat. #	Denomination	Date, description	VG	VF	Unc
7	5 EMALANGENI	ND (1982). Dk. green on yellow-green and m/c unpt. Similar to #3 but new issuer's name at top.			
		a. Sign. 2.	2.50	6.00	12.50
		b. Sign. 4.	1.75	3.00	6.00

1981 COMMEMORATIVE ISSUE

#8 and 9, Diamond Jubilee of Kg. Sobhuza II. Wmk: Shield and spears. Sign. 2.

Cat. #	Denomination	Date, description	VG	VF	Unc
8	10 EMALANGENI	1981. Blue-black on blue and m/c unpt. Black commemorative text on wmk. area. Back like #4.	20.00	75.00	225.00

Cat. #	Denomination	Date, description	VG	VF	Unc
9	20 EMALANGENI	1981. Violet and dk. brown on m/c unpt. Like #8. Back like #5.	15.00	65.00	200.00

1983 ISSUE

#10 and 11 wmk: Shield and spears.

Cat. #	Denomination	Date, description	VG	VF	Unc
10	10 EMALANGENI	ND (1983). Blue-black on blue and m/c unpt. Like #8 but w/o commemorative inscription on face.			
		a. Sign. 2.	7.50	12.50	40.00
		b. Sign. 3.	FV	7.50	25.00
		c. Sign. 4.	FV	4.00	9.00

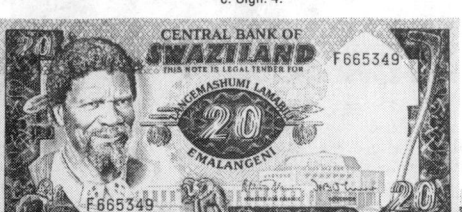

11	20 EMALANGENI	ND (1983). Violet and dk. brown on m/c unpt. Like #9 but w/o commemorative inscription on face.			
		a. Sign. 3.	FV	15.00	37.50
		b. Sign. 4.	FV	8.50	17.50

1986–88 ISSUES

12	20 EMALANGENI	ND (1986). Violet and dk. brown on m/c unpt. Kg. Mswati III at l., otherwise like #11. Printer: TDLR. Sign. 4.	FV	7.50	13.50

#13–16 Facing portr. of young Kg. Mswati III at l., arms at lower ctr. Wmk: Shield and spears. Sign. 4. Printer: TDLR

13	2 EMALANGENI	ND (1986). Dk. brown on m/c unpt. Wildlife on back.	FV	FV	2.50

Cat. #	Denomination	Date, description	VG	VF	Unc
14	5 EMALANGENI	ND (1986). Dk. green, dk. brown and bright green on m/c unpt. Warriors on back.	FV	FV	4.50

15	10 EMALANGENI	ND (1986). Dk. blue and black on m/c unpt. Hydroelectric plant at Luphohlo and bird on back.	FV	FV	12.50
16	20 EMALANGENI	ND (1988). Violet, brown and purple on m/c unpt. Cattle and truck on back.	FV	FV	22.50

1989 COMMEMORATIVE ISSUE

#17, 21st Birthday of Kg. Mswati III

17	20 EMALANGENI	19.4.1989. Like #16, w/silver commemorative text and dates ovpt. on wmk. area.	FV	8.50	18.00

1992 ISSUE

#18–22 similar to #13–16 but w/older portr. of Kg. Mswati III at l. facing half r. Backs like #13–16. Wmk: Shield and spears.

#18–21 similar to #13–16.

18	2 EMALANGENI	ND (1992–).			
		a. Sign. 4.	FV	FV	2.00
		b. Sign. 6.	FV	FV	2.00

19	5 EMALANGENI	ND (1992–95).			
		a. Sign. 4.	FV	FV	5.00
		b. Sign. 6.	FV	FV	5.00

Cat. #	Denomination	Date, description	VG	VF	Unc
20	10 EMALANGENI	ND (1992–95).			
		a. Sign. 4.	FV	FV	9.00
		b. Sign. 5.	FV	FV	11.00

21	20 EMALANGENI	ND (1992–95).			
		a. Sign. 4.	FV	FV	18.00
		b. Sign. 5.	FV	FV	21.50

22	50 EMALANGENI	ND (1992–). Sign. 4.	FV	FV	40.00

1995 ISSUE

#23–25 similar to #18–20 w/segmented foil. Sign. 7.

23	5 EMALENGENI	ND (1995). Similar to #19 but natives on back in brown. Printer: H&S.	FV	FV	5.00

#24 and 25 printer: F-CO.

24	10 EMALENGENI	ND (1995).	FV	FV	9.00
25	20 EMALENGENI	ND (1995).	FV	FV	18.00

COLLECTOR SERIES

Cat. #	Date, denomination	Description	Issue Price	Mkt. Val.
CS1	ND (1974). 1–20 EMALANGENI	#1–5 w/ovpt: SPECIMEN and Maltese cross prefix serial #.	14.00	22.50

The Kingdom of Sweden, a limited constitutional monarchy located in northern Europe between Norway and Finland, has an area of 173,732 sq. mi. (449,960 sq. km.) and a population of 8.6 million. Capital: Stockholm. Mining, lumbering and a specialized machine industry dominate the economy. Machinery, paper, iron and steel, motor vehicles and wood pulp are exported.

Sweden was founded as a Christian stronghold by Olaf Skottkonung late in the 10th century. After conquering Finland late in the 13th century, Sweden, together with Norway, came under the rule of Denmark, 1397–1523, in an association known as the Union of Kalmar. Modern Sweden had its beginning in 1523 when Gustavus Vasa drove the Danes out of Sweden and was himself chosen king. Under Gustavus Adolphus II and Charles XII, Sweden was one of the great powers of the 17th century Europe - until Charles invaded Russia, 1708, and was defeated at the Battle of Pultowa in June 1709. Early in the 18th century, a coalition of Russia, Poland and Denmark took away Sweden's Baltic empire and in 1809 Sweden was forced to cede Finland to Russia. Norway was ceded to Sweden by the Treaty of Kiel in January 1814. The Norwegians resisted for a time but later signed the Act of Union at the Convention of Moss in August 1814. The Union was dissolved in 1905 and Norway became independent. A new constitution which took effect on Jan. 1, 1975, restricts the function of the king to a ceremonial role.

RULERS
Gustaf VI, 1950–73
Carl XVI Gustaf, 1973–

MONETARY SYSTEM
1 Krona = 100 Öre

NOTE This section has been re-organized by Issue groups, but not renumbered.

REPLACEMENT NOTES

Asterisk following the serial number for note issued since 1956.

Sveriges Riksbank/Sveriges Riksba

REGULAR ISSUES

Cat. #	Denomination	Date, description	VG	VF	Unc
12	5 KRONOR	1954–61. Dk. brown on red and blue unpt. Beige paper. Kg. Gustaf VI Adolf at r. ctr. and as wmk. Svea standing w/shield on back.	1.00	3.00	10.00
13	5 KRONOR	1962–63. Dk. brown. Like #12 but wmk. E. Tegner. Paper w/security thread.	1.00	3.00	8.50

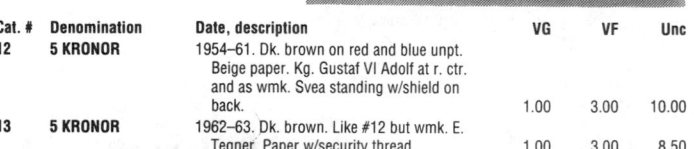

Cat. #	Denomination	Date, description	VG	VF	Unc
22	10 KRONOR	1953–62. Gray-blue. Portr. G. Vasa at l. and as wmk. Blue date and serial #.			
		a. 1953–54.	2.00	5.00	10.00
		b. 1955–56.	2.00	4.50	8.50
		c. 1957–59.	2.00	4.00	7.50
		d. 1960.	2.00	5.50	15.00
		e. 1962.	2.00	4.50	8.50

			VG	VF	Unc
33	50 KRONOR	1959–62. Like #32. Second sign. at l.	10.00	15.00	40.00
43	100 KRONOR	1959–63. Like #42. Second sign. at l.			
		a. 1959–60.	FV	35.00	65.00
		b. 1961–62.	FV	32.50	50.00
		c. 1963.	FV	30.00	45.00
53	1000 KRONOR	1952–73. Brown. Svea standing (modelled by beauty queen Greta Hoffstrom). Kg. on back and as wmk.			
		a. Blue and red safety fibers. 1952.	FV	225.00	300.00
		b. 1957.	FV	225.00	300.00
		c. 1962.	FV	220.00	300.00
		d. 1965.	FV	210.00	300.00
		e. One vertical filament. 1971.	FV	210.00	300.00
		f. 1973.	FV	210.00	300.00

			VG	VF	Unc
56	10,000 KRONOR	1958. Green and m/c. King Gustav VI Adolf at r. and as wmk. Seva standing w/shield at ctr. on back.	FV	1850.	—

1963–76 ISSUE

Cat. #	Denomination	Date, description	VG	VF	Unc
14	5 KRONOR	1965–81. Purple and m/c. G. Vasa at r. Wmk: Square w/5 repeated. Abstract design of rooster crowing on back.			
		a. W/year in dk. red letter press. 1965–69.	FV	1.25	3.50
		b. W/year in deep red offset. 1970.	FV	FV	3.00
		c. As a. 1972–74; 1976–77.	FV	FV	2.50
		d. W/year in pale red offset. 1977–79; 1981.	FV	FV	2.25

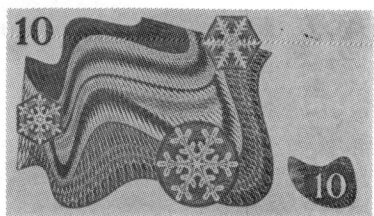

			VG	VF	Unc
23	10 KRONOR	1963–90. Dk. green and m/c. Arms at ctr., Kg. Gustaf VI Adolf at r. Abstract design of rooster crowing on back. Wmk: A. Strindberg (repeated).			
		a. W/year in dk. red letter press. 1963.	FV	FV	6.50
		b. As a. 1966; 1968.	FV	FV	5.50
		c. As a. 1971–72; 1975.	FV	FV	4.50
		d. W/year in pale red offset. Engraved sign. 1976–77; 1979; 1983; 1985.	FV	FV	4.00
		e. As d but w/offset sign. 1980–81; 1983–84; 1987–90.	FV	FV	3.50

Cat. #	Denomination	Date, description	VG	VF	Unc
34	50 KRONOR	1965–. Blue on m/c unpt. Beige paper. Kg. Gustaf III at r. C. von Linné (Linnaeus) on back. Wmk: Anna Maria Lenngren.			
		a. Sm. wmk. 1965; 1967; 1970.	FV	10.00	22.50
		b. Lg. wmk. w/year in dk. red letter press. 1974; 1976.	FV	FV	20.00
		c. Lg. wmk. as b. w/year in red-brown offset. 1978–79; 1981.	FV	FV	18.50
		d. As c. Black serial #. 1982; 1984; 1986; 1989–90.	FV	FV	17.50

44	100 KRONOR	1965–83. Red-brown and blue on lt. blue paper. Kg. Gustav II Adolf at r. Admiral Vasa and sailing ship on back. Wmk: A. Oxenstierna.			
		a. Sm. wmk. 22mm. 1965; 1968; 1970.	FV	20.00	35.00
		b. Lg. wmk. 27mm. w/year in dk. blue letter press. 1971–72; 1974; 1976.	FV	FV	32.50
		c. Lg. wmk. as b. W/year in blue-green offset. 1978; 1980–83; 1985.	FV	FV	30.00

54	1000 KRONOR	1976–83. Red-brown on green and violet unpt. Carl XIV Johan at r. Bessemer steel process on back. Wmk: J. Berzelius.			
		a. 1976–78.	FV	FV	235.00
		b. 1980; 1981; 1983–86.	FV	FV	210.00

1968 COMMEMORATIVE ISSUE

#24, 300th Anniversary of the Sveriges Riksbank

24	10 KRONOR	1968. Blue and m/c. Svea standing w/ornaments at r. Back violet-brown; old Riksbank bldg. at ctr. Wmk: Crowned monogram Kg. Charles XI.			
			2.00	3.00	6.00

1985–89 ISSUES

#57–65 the first digit of the serial number is the actual year of printing. They are usually released to circulation within the following year.

Cat. #	Denomination	Date, description	VG	VF	Unc
57	100 KRONOR	(198)6–(198)8. Blue-green and brown-violet on m/c unpt. C. von Linné (Linnaeus) at r. and as wmk., plants at l. ctr. Bee polinating flowers at ctr. on back.	FV	FV	26.50
58	500 KRONOR	(198)5; (198)6. Gray-blue and red-brown. Kg. Carl XI at r. and as wmk. C. Polhem seated on back.	FV	FV	125.00

59	500 KRONOR	(198)9; (199)1–5. Red and m/c. Similar to #58 but w/o white margin on face, also other slight changes.	FV	FV	110.00
60	1000 KRONOR	(198)9–(199)2. Brownish black on m/c unpt. Kg G. Vasa at r. and as wmk. Medievel harvest scene on back.	FV	FV	200.00

1991; 96 ISSUE

Portr. as wmk.

| 61 | 20 KRONOR | (199)1–2; (199)4–5. Deep purple on m/c unpt. Horse-drawn carriage at lower ctr., Selma Lagerlöf at r. and as wmk. Story scene w/small lad riding a goose in flight on back. | FV | FV | 5.50 |
| 62 | 50 KRONOR | (1996). Jenny Lind. | FV | FV | 13.50 |

| 63 | 100 KRONOR | ND (ca. 1992). Blue-green, brown-violet and m/c. C. von Linnéand plants on face. Bee pollinating flowers on back. | FV | FV | 27.50 |

| 64 | 500 KRONOR | ND (ca. 1993). Red and m/c. Kg. Karl XI on face. C. Polhem on back. | FV | FV | 110.00 |

| 65 | 1000 KRONOR | ND (ca. 1993). Brown, black and m/c. Kg. G. Vasa at r. Harvest and threshing on back. | FV | FV | 200.00 |

SWITZERLAND

The Swiss Confederation, located in central Europe north of Italy and south of Germany, has an area of 15,941 sq. mi. (41,290 sq. km.) and a population of 6.9 million. Capital: Bern. The economy centers about a well developed manufacturing industry. Machinery, chemicals, watches and clocks, and textiles are exported.

Switzerland, the habitat of lake dwellers in prehistoric times, was peopled by the Celtic Helvetians when Julius Caesar made it a part of the Roman Empire in 58 BC. After the decline of Rome, Switzerland was invaded by Teutonic tribes, who established small temporal holdings which, in the Middle Ages, became a federation of fiefs of the Holy Roman Empire. As a nation, Switzerland originated in 1291 when the districts of Nidwalden, Schwyz and Uri united to defeat Austria and attain independence as the Swiss Confederation. After acquiring new cantons in the 14th century, Switzerland was made independent from the Holy Roman Empire by the 1648 Treaty of Westphalia. The revolutionary armies of Napoleonic France occupied Switzerland and set up the Helvetian Republic, 1798–1803. After the fall of Napoleon, the Congress of Vienna, 1815, recognized the independence of Switzerland and guaranteed its neutrality. The Swiss Constitutions of 1848 and 1874 established a union modeled upon that of the United States.

MONETARY SYSTEM
1 Franc (Franken) = 10 Batzen = 100 Centimes (Rappen)

Schweizerische Nationalbank

1954-57 ISSUE

#174–175 printer: OFZ.

Cat. #	Denomination	Date, description	VG	VF	Unc
174	10 FRANKEN	1955–77. Red-brown and purple. Gottfr. Keller at r. Flowers across back.			
		a. 25.8.1955–2.4.1964.	FV	15.00	30.00
		b. 21.1.1965–6.1.1977.	FV	12.00	16.50

175	20 FRANKEN	1954–1976. Blue and m/c. H. Dufour at r. Sunflower at l. ctr. on back.			
		a. 1.7.1954–28.3.1963.	FV	22.50	35.00
		b. 21.1.1965–9.4.1976.	FV	18.50	27.50

Cat. #	Denomination	Date, description	VG	VF	Unc
178	500 FRANKEN	31.1.1957; 4.10.1957; 18.12.1958. Brown-orange and olive on m/c unpt. Woman looking in mirror at r. Elders w/4 girls bathing at ctr. r. on back (Fountain of Youth). Printer: W&S.	FV	500.00	700.00
178A	500 FRANKEN	21.12.1961-7.2.1974. Like #176 but printer: TDLR.	FV	450.00	525.00

Cat. #	Denomination	Date, description	VG	VF	Unc
176	50 FRANKEN	7.7.1955; 4.10.1957; 18.12.1958. Green on brown unpt. Girl at r. Family harvesting apples on back. Printer: W&S.	FV	70.00	140.00
176A	50 FRANKEN	4.5.1961-7.2.1974. Like # 176 but printer: TDLR.	FV	55.00	90.00

179	1000 FRANKEN	30.9.1954-7.2.1974. Purple. Female head at r. Allegorical scene "dance macabre" on back.		FV	900.00	1050.

1976-79 ISSUE

#180–185 series of notes printed in 4 languages - the traditional German, French and Italian plus Romansch; (Rhaeto - Romanisch), the language of the mountainous areas of Graubunden Canton. Wmk. as portr. Sign. varieties. The first 2 numerals before the serial # prefix letter are date (year) indicators. Printer: OFZ.

177	100 FRANKEN	25.10.1956-7.3.1973. Blue. Boy's head at r. St. Martin sharing his cape on back. Printer: TDLR.	FV	100.00	225.00

180	10 FRANKEN	(19)79–. Orange-brown and m/c. L. Euler at r. Planets in solor system, comet and other symbols on back.	FV	FV	14.00

Cat. #	Denomination	Date, description	VG	VF	Unc
181	20 FRANKEN	(19)78–. Blue and m/c. H-B. de Saussure at r. Fossel and early mountain expedition team hiking on back.	FV	FV	27.50

| 182 | 50 FRANKEN | (19)78–. Green and m/c. K. Gessner at r. Owl, stars and plant on back. | FV | FV | 52.50 |

| 183 | 100 FRANKEN | (19)76–. Blue and m/c. F. Borromini at r. Bldg. w/towers on back. Baroque architectural drawing and view. | FV | FV | 100.00 |

| 184 | 500 FRANKEN | (19)76–. Brown and m/c. A. von Haller at r. Anatomical mussles, heart and plant figure on back. | FV | FV | 475.00 |

Cat. #	Denomination	Date, description	VG	VF	Unc
185	1000 FRANKEN	(19)78–. Violet and m/c. A. Forel at r. Ants and ant hill on back.	FV	FV	925.00

1996–98 ISSUE

#186–191 reduced size. Excessive security features added.

186	10 FRANKEN	(1997). Orange. Le Corbusier.	Expected new issue.
187	20 FRANKEN	(1996). Red. A. Honegger.	Expected new issue.

188	50 FRANKEN	ND (1995). Deep olive-green and purple on m/c unpt. S. Taeuber-Arp at upper l. and bottom and as wmk. Examples of abstract art works on back.	FV	FV	50.00
189	100 FRANKEN	(1997). Blue. A. Giacometti.			Expected new issue.
190	200 FRANKEN	(1997). Brown. C.F. Ramuz.			Expected new issue.
191	1000 FRANKEN	(1998). Purple. J. Burckhardt.			Expected new issue.

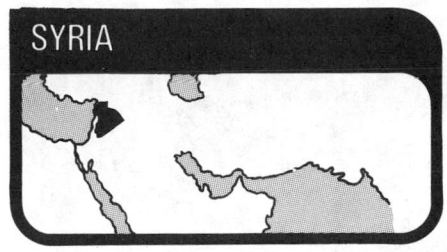

SYRIA

The Syrian Arab Republic, located in the Near East at the eastern end of the Mediterranean Sea, has an area of 71,498 sq. mi. (185,180 sq. km.) and a population of 12.6 million. Capital: Greater Damascus. Agriculture and animal breeding are the chief industries. Cotton, crude oil and livestock are exported.

Ancient Syria, a land bridge connecting Europe, Africa and Asia, has spent much of its history in thrall to the conqueror's whim. Its subjection by Egypt about 1500 BC was followed by successive conquests by the Hebrews, Phoenicians, Babylonians, Assyrians, Persians, Macedonians, Romans, Byzantines and finally, in 636 AD, by the Moslems. The Arabs made Damascus, one of the oldest continuously inhabited cities of the world, the trade center and capital of an empire stretching from India to Spain. In 1517, following the total destruction of Damascus by the Mongols of Tamerlane, Syria fell to the Ottoman Turks and remained a Turkish province until World War I. The League of Nations gave France a mandate to the Levant states of Syria and Lebanon in 1920. In 1930, following a series of uprisings, France recognized Syria as an independent republic, but still subject to the mandate. Lebanon became fully independent on Nov. 22, 1943, and Syria on Jan. 1, 1944.

On Feb. 1, 1958, Egypt and Syria formed the United Arab Republic. Yemen joined on March 8 in an association known as the United Arab States. Syria withdrew from the United Arab Republic on Sept. 29, 1961, and on Dec. 26 Egypt dissolved its ties with Yemen in the United Arab States.

MONETARY SYSTEM
1 Pound (Livre) = 100 Plastres

Central Bank of Syria

1958 ISSUE

#86–88 wmk: Arabian horse's head. Printer: The Pakistan Security Printing Corporation, Ltd., Karachi (w/o imprint).

Cat. #	Denomination	Date, description	VG	VF	Unc
86	1 POUND	1958. Brown on m/c unpt. Worker at r. Water wheel of Hama on back.			
		a. Issued note.	1.50	5.00	20.00
		s. Specimen.	—	—	25.00
87	5 POUNDS	1958. Green on m/c unpt. Like #86. Citadel of Aleppo on back.			
		a. Issued note.	3.00	15.00	50.00
		s. Specimen.	—	—	45.00

88	10 POUNDS	1958. Purple on m/c unpt. Like #86. Courtyard of Omayad Mosque on back.			
		a. Issued note.	5.00	25.00	85.00
		s. Specimen.	—	—	90.00

#89–92 wmk: Arabian horse's head. Printer: JEZ.

Cat. #	Denomination	Date, description	VG	VF	Unc
89	25 POUNDS	1958. Blue on m/c unpt. Girl w/ basket at r. Interior view of El-Azm Palace in Damascus on back.			
		a. Issued note.	12.50	65.00	225.00
		s. Specimen.	—	—	165.00
90	50 POUNDS	1958. Red, brown on m/c unpt. Like #89. Mosque of Sultan Selim on back.			
		a. Issued note.	17.50	75.00	275.00
		s. Specimen.	—	—	200.00
91	100 POUNDS	1958;1962 Olive on m/c unpt. Like #89. Old ruins of Palmyra on back.			
		a. Issued note.	25.00	125.00	350.00
		s. Specimen.	—	—	225.00
92	500 POUNDS	1958. Brown and purpleon m/c unpt. Like #105.			
		a. Issued note.	100.00	350.00	—
		s. Specimen.	—	—	500.00

1963-66 ISSUE

#93–98 wmk: Arabian horse's head. W/o imprint.

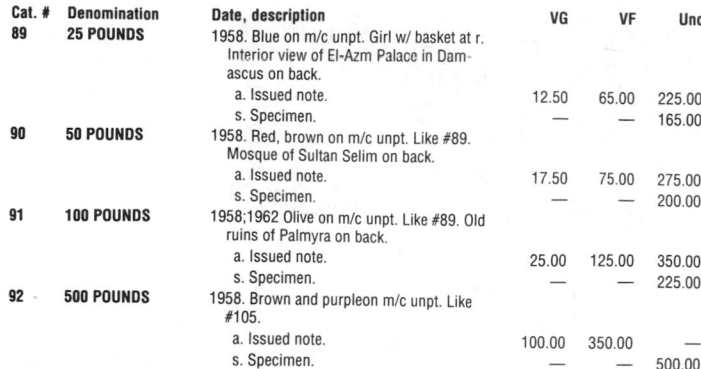

Cat. #	Denomination	Date, description	VG	VF	Unc
93	1 POUND	1963–82. Brown on m/c unpt. Like #86.			
		a. W/o security thread. 1963.	1.00	3.00	10.00
		b. 1967.	.60	2.00	6.00
		c. 1973.	.25	.75	2.00
		d. Security thread w/*Central Bank of Syria* in small letters. 1978; 1982	.15	.45	2.00
94	5 POUNDS	1963–73. Green on m/c unpt. Like #87.			
		a. 1963.	2.50	10.00	40.00
		b. 1967.	1.75	6.00	30.00
		c. 1970.	1.00	4.00	25.00
		d. 1973.	.50	2.50	12.50
95	10 POUNDS	1965–73. Purple on m/c unpt. Like #88.			
		a. 1965.	3.00	8.50	50.00
		b. 1968.	2.00	6.00	40.00
		c. 1973.	1.00	3.50	20.00

96	25 POUNDS	1966–73. Blue on m/c unpt. Worker at the loom. Ancient amphitheater on back.			
		a. 1966.	6.00	27.50	140.00
		b. 1970.	4.00	20.00	110.00
		c. 1973.	3.00	17.50	110.00

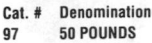

Cat. #	Denomination	Date, description	VG	VF	Unc
97	50 POUNDS	1966–73. Brown and olive on m/c unpt. Arab w/agricultural machine. Fortress on back.			
		a. 1966; 1970.	10.00	30.00	150.00
		b. 1973.	5.00	25.00	135.00

98	100 POUNDS	1966–74. Green and blue on m/c unpt. Port installation at l. Back purple; dam at ctr.			
		a. 1966; 1968.	15.00	55.00	300.00
		b. 1971.	12.50	40.00	200.00
		c. 1974.	10.00	30.00	175.00

1976–77 ISSUE

#99–105 wmk: Arabian horse's head. Shades vary between early and late printings.

99	1 POUND	1977. Orange on m/c unpt. Lg. bldg. at ctr., craftsman at r. Back red-brown; cutting wheat at ctr.			
			1.00	5.00	12.50

Cat. #	Denomination	Date, description	VG	VF	Unc
100	5 POUNDS	1977–91. Dk. green on m/c unpt. Ancient ruins and statue of female warrior at r. Cotton picking and spinning frame on back.			
		a. Security thread. 1977.	1.00	2.50	7.50
		b. Security thread. W/*Central Bank of Syria* in sm. letters. 1978; 1982.	FV	FV	3.00
		c. 1988; 1991.	FV	FV	1.00

101	10 POUNDS	1977–82. Purple and violet on m/c unpt. Palace courtyard at ctr., dancing woman at r. Water treatment plant on back.			
		a. Like #100a. 1977.	1.50	4.00	10.00
		b. Like #100b. 1978; 1982.	FV	FV	2.50
		c. 1988;1991.	FV	FV	1.65

102	25 POUNDS	1977–91. Dk. blue and dk. green on m/c unpt. Fortress at ctr., old Sultan at r. Central Bank bldg. on back.			
		a. Like #100a. 1977.	3.00	8.00	20.00
		b. Like #100b. 1978; 1982.	FV	.85	4.00
		c. 1988; 1991.	FV	FV	2.75

103   50 POUNDS
1977–82. Brown, black and green on m/c
unpt. Dam at ctr., ancient statue at r. Fortress at Aleppo on back.

a. Like #100a. 1977.	4.50	10.00	25.00
b. Like #100b. 1978; 1982.	FV	3.00	12.00
c. 1988.	FV	FV	6.00
d. 1991.	FV	FV	5.50

104   100 POUNDS
1977–82. Dk. blue and dk. green on dk.
brown on m/c unpt. Ancient ruins at ctr.,
archaic bust at r. Grain silos at Lattakia on
back.

a. Like #100a. 1977.	5.00	15.00	50.00
b. Like #100b. 1978.	FV	6.50	25.00
c. 1982.	FV	FV	12.50
d. 1990.	FV	FV	10.00

105   500 POUNDS
1976–90. Dk. violet-brown and brown on
m/c unpt. Motifs from ruins of Kingdom
of Ugarit, head at r. Ancient religious
wheel and cuneiform clay tablet on back.

a. 1976.	12.50	15.00	60.00
b. 1982.	FV	FV	50.00
c. 1986.	FV	FV	40.00
d. 1990.	FV	FV	35.00

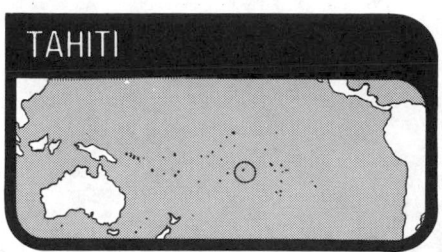

TAHITI

Tahiti, the largest island of the central South Pacific French overseas territory of French Polynesia, has an area of 402 sq. mi. (1,042 sq. km.) and a population of 79,500. Papeete on the northwest coast is the capital and administrative center of French Polynesia. Copra, sugar cane, vanilla and coffee are exported. Tourism is an important industry.

Capt. Samuel Wallis of the British Navy discovered Tahiti in 1768 and named it King George III Island. Louis-Antoine de Bougainville arrived in the following year and claimed it for France. Subsequent English visits were by James Cook in 1769 and William Bligh in the HMS "Bounty" in 1788.

Members of the Protestant London Missionary Society established the first European settlement in 1797, and with the aid of the local Pomare family gained control of the entire island and established a "missionary kingdom" with a scriptural code of law. Nevertheless, Tahiti was subsequently declared a French protectorate (1842) and a colony (1880), and is now part of the overseas territory of French Polynesia.

RULERS
French

MONETARY SYSTEM
1 (CFP) Franc = 100 Centimes

Banque de l'Indochine, Papeete

Cat. #	Denomination	Date, Description	VG	VF	Unc
15	20 FRANCS	ND (1951–63). M/c. Youth at l., flute player at r. Fruit at l., woman at r. on back. Wmk: Man w/hat.			
		a. Sign. titles: *LE PRESIDENT* and *LE DIRECTEUR GAL.* (1951).	3.50	9.00	30.00
		b. Sign. titles: *LE PRESIDENT* and *LE VICE-PRESIDENT DIRECTEUR GENERAL.* (1954–1958).	1.50	6.00	18.50
		c. Sign. titles: *LE PRESIDENT* and *LE DIRECTEUR GENERAL* (1963).	1.25	5.00	12.00

Cat. #	Denomination	Date, description	Good	Fine	XF
16	100 FRANCS	ND (1939–65). Brown and m/c. Woman wearing wreath and holding sm. figure of Athena at ctr. Angkor statue on back.			
		a. Sign. M. Borduge and P. Baudouin w/titles: *LE PRESIDENT* and *LE DIRECTEUR GAL.*	5.00	20.00	60.00
		b. Sign. titles: *LE PRESIDENT* and *LE ADMINISTRATEUR DIRECTEUR GENERAL.*	5.00	17.50	50.00
		c. Sign. titles: *LE PRESIDENT* and *LE VICE-PRESIDENT DIRECTEUR GENERAL.*	4.00	15.00	35.00
		d. Sign. titles: *LE PRESIDENT* and *LE DIRECTEUR GENERAL.*	3.00	12.50	27.0

PROVISIONAL ISSUES

16A	100 FRANCS on 20 Francs	ND. Brown, lilac and red. Woman at r. Peacock on back w/black ovpt: *CENT FRANCS* and 2 sign. vertically at l. ctr., also ovpt: *CENT* across upper ctr. and *100* at lower ctr. on old value. Punch cancelled, and handstamped: *ANNULE.*	—	Rare	—

Cat. #	Denomination	Date, description	Good	Fine	XF
17	100 FRANCS	ND(1963). Brown and m/c. Like #16, but note of Noumea w/red ovpt: *PAPEETE.*	35.00	120.00	200.00

Institut d'Emission d'Outre-Mer, Papeete

Cat. #	Denomination	Date, description	VG	VF	Unc
23	100 FRANCS	ND (1969). Brown and m/c. Girl wearing wreath holding guitar at r., w/o *REPUBLIQUE FRANCAISE* near bottom ctr. Girl at l., town scene at ctr. on back. Printed from engraved copper plates.	3.00	10.00	35.00

24	100 FRANCS	ND. M/c. Like #23, but w/*REPUBLIQUE FRANCAISE* at bottom ctr.			
		a. Printed from engraved copper plates.	1.00	4.50	17.50
		b. Offset printing.	1.00	4.00	15.00

Cat. #	Denomination	Date, description	VG	VF	Unc
25	500 FRANCS	ND (1969–92). Blue and m/c. Fisherman at r. Man at l., objects at r. on back. 4 sign. varieties.	FV	7.00	15.00
26	1000 FRANCS	ND (1969). M/c. Hut under palms at l., girl at r. W/o *REPUBLIQUE FRANCAISE* ovpt. at bottom ctr.	12.00	35.00	90.00
27	1000 FRANCS	ND (1969). M/c. Like #26 but w/*REPUBLIQUE FRANCAISE* at bottom ctr. 5 sign. varieties.	FV	12.50	20.00

Cat. #	Denomination	Date, description	Good	Fine	XF
28	5000 FRANCS	ND (1969). M/c. Bougainville at l., sailing ship at ctr. 4 sign. varieties.	FV	60.00	95.00

NOTE: For later issues refer to French Polynesia.

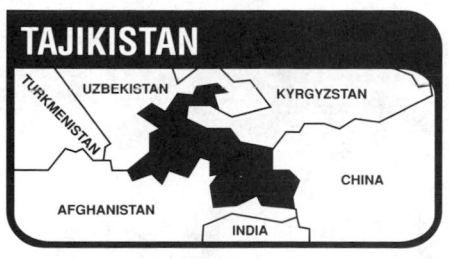

TAJIKISTAN

The Republic of Tajikistan, (Tadjiquistan, formerly the Tajik Soviet Socialist Republic) was formed from those regions of Bukhara and Turkestan where the population consisted mainly of Tajiks. It is bordered in the north and west by Uzbekistan and Kyrgyzstan; in the east by China and in the south by Afghanistan. It has an area of 55,240 sq. miles. (143,100 sq. km.) It includes 2 provinces of Khudzand and Khatlon together with the Gorno-Badakhshan Autonomous Region with a population of 5,092,603. Capital: Dush-anbe.

Tajikistan was admitted as a constituent republic of the Soviet Union on Dec. 5, 1929. In Aug. 1990 the Tajik Supreme Soviet adopted a declaration of republican sovereignty, and in Dec. 1991 the republic became a member of the CIS.

After demonstrations and fighting the Communist government was replaces by a Revolutionary Coalition Council on May 7, 1992. Following further demonstrations President Nabiev was ousted on Sept. 7, 1992. Civil war broke out, and the government resigned on Nov. 10, 1992. On Nov. 30, 1992 it was announced that a CIS peacekeeping force would be sent to Tajikistan. A state of emergency was imposed in Jan. 1993.

MONETARY SYSTEM
1 Ruble = 100 TANGA

БОНКИ МИЛЛИИ ЧУМХУРИИ ТОЧИКИСТОН

National Bank of the Republic of Tajikistan.

1994 ISSUE

#1–8 arms at upper l. or l. Bldg. w/flag at ctr. r. on back.

Cat. #	Denomination	Date, description	VG	VF	Unc
1	1 RUBLE	1994. Brown on m/c unpt.	FV	FV	.40

2	5 RUBLES	1994. Deep purple on m/c unpt.	FV	FV	.90

3	10 RUBLES	1994. Deep red on m/c unpt.	FV	FV	1.25
4	20 RUBLES	1994. Dk. green on m/c unpt.	FV	FV	2.00
5	50 RUBLES	1994. Dk. olive-green on m/c unpt.	FV	FV	3.00
6	100 RUBLES	1994. Brown on m/c unpt.	FV	FV	4.50
7	200 RUBLES	1994. Olive-green on m/c unpt.	FV	FV	8.50
8	500 RUBLES	1994. Brown-violet on m/c unpt.	FV	FV	20.00
9	1000 RUBLES				Expected new issue.

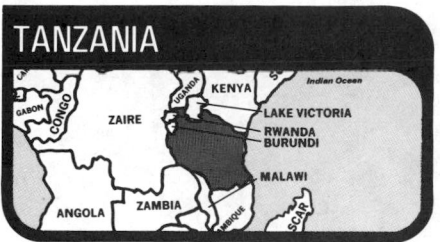

TANZANIA

The United Republic of Tanzania, located on the east coast of Africa between Kenya and Mozambique, consists of Tanganyika and the islands of Zanzibar and Pemba. It has an area of 364,900 sq. mi. (945,090 sq. km.) and a population of 25.1 million. Capital: Dar es Salaam (Haven of Peace). The chief exports are cotton, coffee, diamonds, sisal, cloves, petroleum products and cashew nuts.

German East Africa (Tanganyika), located on the coast of east-central Africa between British East Africa (now Kenya) and Portuguese East Africa (now Mozambique), had an area of 362,284 sq. mi. (938,216 sq. km.) and a population of about 6 million. Capital: Dar es Salaam. Chief products prior to German control were ivory and slaves; after German control, sisal, coffee and rubber. Germany acquired control of the area by treaties with coastal chiefs in 1884, established it as a protectorate in 1891, and proclaimed it the Colony of German East Africa in 1897. After World War I, Tanganyika was entrusted to Great Britain as a League of Nations mandate, and after World War II as a United Nations trust territory. Tanganyika became an independent nation within the British Commonwealth on Dec. 9, 1961.

The British Protectorate of Zanzibar and Pemba, and adjacent small islands, located in the Indian Ocean 22 miles (35 km.) off the coast of Tanganyika, comprised a portion of British East Africa. Zanzibar was also the name of a sultanate which included the Zanzibar and Kenya protectorates. Zanzibar has an area of 637 sq. mi. (1,651 sq. km.). Chief city: Zanzibar. Pemba has an area of 380 sq. mi. (984 sq. km.). Chief city: Chake Chake. The islands are noted for their cloves, of which Zanzibar is the world's foremost producer.

Zanzibar and Pemba share a common history. Zanzibar came under Portuguese control in 1503, was conquered by the Omani Arabs in 1698, became independent of Oman in 1860, and (with Pemba) came under British control in 1890. Britain granted the protectorate self-government in 1961, and independence within the British Commonwealth on Dec. 19, 1963. On April 26, 1964, Tanganyika and Zanzibar (with Pemba) united to form the United Republic of Tanganyika and Zanzibar. The name of the country, which remained within the British Commonwealth, was changed to Tanzania on Oct. 29, 1964.

Tanzania is a member of the Commonwealth of Nations. The president is Chief of State.

Also see East Africa and Zanzibar.

MONETARY SYSTEM
1 Shilingi (Shilling) = 100 Senti

Replacement Notes:

For all issues, ZY or ZZ prefix.

Bank of Tanzania

SIGNATURE VARIETIES					
1	*[signature]* MINISTER FOR FINANCE	*[signature]* GOVERNOR	6	*[signature]* WAZIRI WA FEDHA	*[signature]* GAVANA
2	*[signature]*	*[signature]*	7	*[signature]*	*[signature]*
3	*[signature]*	*[signature]*	8	*[signature]*	*[signature]*
4	*[signature]*	*[signature]*	9	*[signature]*	*[signature]*
5	*[signature]*	*[signature]*	10		

NOTE: Sign. 3–5 w/English titles on #2 and 3, changed to Swahili titles for later issues.

1966 ISSUE

#1–5 arms at ctr., Pres. J. Nyerere at r. Wmk: Giraffe's head.

Cat. #	Denomination	Date, description	VG	VF	Unc
1	5 SHILLINGS	ND (1966). Brown and m/c. Sign. 1. Mountain view on back.	.75	2.00	10.00

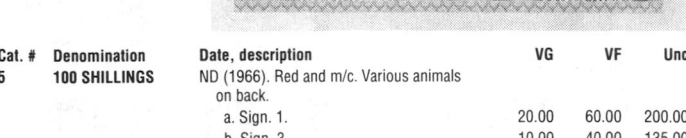

Cat. #	Denomination	Date, description	VG	VF	Unc
5	100 SHILLINGS	ND (1966). Red and m/c. Various animals on back.			
		a. Sign. 1.	20.00	60.00	200.00
		b. Sign. 3.	10.00	40.00	135.00

Cat. #	Denomination	Date, description	VG	VF	Unc
2	10 SHILLINGS	ND (1966). Green and m/c. Sisal drying on back.			
		a. Sign. 1.	1.50	3.00	7.50
		b. Sign. 2.	2.00	4.00	10.00
		c. Sign. 3.	7.50	30.00	120.00
		d. Sign. 4.	1.00	2.00	7.50
		e. Sign. 5.	1.00	2.00	6.00

Benki Kuu Ya Tanzania

1977-78 ISSUE

#6–8 arms at top ctr., Pres. J. Nyerere at r. Wmk: Giraffe's head.

			VG	VF	Unc
6	10 SHILINGI	ND (1978). Green and m/c. Monument and mountain at ctr. on back.			
		a. Sign. 5.	.25	1.50	4.00
		b. Sign. 6.	.25	1.00	2.50
		c. Sign. 3.	.25	.75	2.00

3	20 SHILLINGS	ND (1966). Blue and m/c. Work bldgs. on back.			
		a. Sign. 1.	2.00	5.00	12.50
		b. Sign. 2.	2.00	5.00	12.50
		c. Sign. 3.	3.00	7.00	17.50
		d. Sign. 4.	2.00	5.00	12.50
		e. Sign. 5.	1.50	3.00	10.00

7	20 SHILINGI	ND (1978). Blue and m/c. Cotton knitting machine on back.			
		a. Sign. 5.	1.00	2.50	6.50
		b. Sign. 6.	1.00	2.25	5.50
		c. Sign. 3.	1.00	2.25	5.50

4	100 SHILLINGS	ND (1966). Red and m/c. Sign. 1. Masai herdsman w/animals on back.	20.00	60.00	200.00

Cat. #	Denomination	Date, description	VG	VF	Unc
8	100 SHILINGI	ND (1977). Purple and m/c. Teacher and students at l., farmers at ctr. on back.			
		a. Sign. 4.	4.00	8.00	22.50
		b. Sign. 5.	4.00	7.00	20.00
		c. Sign. 6.	3.00	6.50	17.50
		d. Sign. 3.	2.50	6.00	15.00

NOTE: For #6–8, sign. are shown in chronological order of appearance. It seems sign. 3 was used again following several later combinations.

1985 ISSUE

#9–11 new portr. of Pres. J. Nyerere at r., torch at l., arms at ctr. Islands of Mafia, Pemba and Zanzibar are omitted from map on back. Sign. 3. Wmk: Giraffe's head.

| 9 | 20 SHILINGI | ND (1985). Purple, brown and m/c. Tire factory scene on back. | .15 | .50 | 2.00 |

| 10 | 50 SHILINGI | ND (1985). Red-orange, lt. brown and m/c. Brick making on back. | .30 | 1.25 | 5.00 |

| 11 | 100 SHILINGI | ND (1985). Blue, purple and m/c. Graduation procession on back. | .50 | 2.75 | 9.00 |

1986 ISSUE

#12–14 Same as #9–11 but islands of Mafia, Pemba and Zanzibar now included in map on back.

Cat. #	Denomination	Date, description	VG	VF	Unc
12	20 SHILINGI	ND (1986). Like #9 but w/islands in map.	.15	.60	2.50

| 13 | 50 SHILINGI | ND (1986). Like #10 but w/islands in map. | .25 | 1.00 | 4.50 |

14	100 SHILINGI	ND (1986). Like #11 but w/islands in map.			
		a. Sign. 3.	.50	2.00	5.00
		b. Sign. 8.	.20	.75	3.00

1986–90 ISSUE

#15–19 arms at ctr., Pres. Mwinyi at r. Wmk: Giraffe's head.

Cat. #	Denomination	Date, description	VG	VF	Unc
15	20 SHILINGI	ND (1987). Purple, red-brown and m/c. Back like #12.	.10	.40	1.50

Cat. #	Denomination	Date, description	VG	VF	Unc
16	50 SHILINGI	ND (1986). Red-orange, lt. brown and m/c. Back like #13.			
		a. Sign. 3.	.15	.60	2.50
		b. Sign. 7.	.10	.50	2.00
17	*Deleted*.				

18	200 SHILINGI	ND (1986). Black and tan on m/c unpt. 2 fishermen on back.	.50	1.50	6.00

19	500 SHILINGI	ND (1989). Dk. blue and m/c. Zebra at l. Harvesting on back.			
		a. Sign. 3.	2.50	10.00	30.00
		b. Sign. 7.	1.50	3.00	12.50
		c. Sign. 8.	1.25	1.75	7.50

Cat. #	Denomination	Date, description	VG	VF	Unc
20	1000 SHILINGI	ND (1990). Green, brown and m/c. Elephants at l. Kiwira Coal Mine at l. ctr., door to the Peoples Bank of Zanzibar at lower r. on back.	2.50	4.00	15.00

1992 ISSUE

#21–22 similar to #16 and #18 but w/modified portr. Wmk: Giraffe's head.

21	50 SHILINGI	ND (1992). Red-orange and lt. brown on m/c unpt.	.10	.50	1.75

22	200 SHILINGI	ND (1992). Black and tan on m/c unpt.	.40	1.00	4.00

1993; 1995 ISSUE

#23, 25–27 arms at ctr., Pres. Mwinyi at r. Wmk: Giraffe's head. Reduced size.

23	50 SHILINGI	ND (1993). Red-orange, brown and m/c. Animal grazing at l. Men making brick on back.	FV	FV	1.00

Cat. #	Denomination	Date, description	VG	VF	Unc
24	100 SHILINGI	ND (1993). Blue, aqua and m/c. Kudu at l., arms at ctr., J. Nyerere at r. Graduation procession on back.	FV	FV	1.75

| 25 | 200 SHILINGI | ND (1993). Black and orange on m/c unpt. Leopards at l. Back similar to #18. | FV | FV | 3.00 |

| 26 | 500 SHILINGI | ND (1993). Purple, blue-green and violet on m/c unpt. Zebra at lower l. Back similar to #19 w/arms at lower r. | FV | FV | 5.50 |

27	1000 SHILINGI	ND (1993). Dk. green, brown and orange-brown on m/c unpt. Similar to #20.	FV	FV	10.00
28	5000 SHILINGI	ND (1995).	FV	FV	18.00
29	10,000 SHILINGI	ND (1995).	FV	FV	35.00

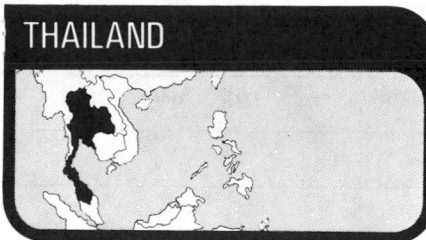

THAILAND

The Kingdom of Thailand (formerly Siam), a constitutional monarchy located in the center of mainland southeast Asia between Burma and Laos, has an area of 198,457 sq. mi. (514,000 sq. km.) and a population of 57.6 million. Capital: Bangkok. The economy is based on agriculture and mining. Rubber, rice, teakwood, tin and tungsten are exported.

The history of Thailand, the only country in south and southeast Asia that was never colonized by an European power, dates from the 6th century AD when tribes of the Thai stock migrated into the area from the Asiatic continent, a process that accelerated with the Mongol invasion of China in the 13th century. After 400 years of sporadic warfare with the neighboring Burmese, King Taksin won the last battle in 1767. He founded a new capital, Dhonburi, on the west bank of Chao Praya River. King Rama I moved the capital to Bangkok in 1782.

The Thai were introduced to the Western world by the Portuguese, who were followed by the Dutch, British and French. Rama III of the present ruling dynasty negotiated a treaty of friendship and commerce with Britain in 1826, and in 1896 the independence of the kingdom was guaranteed by an Anglo-French accord. The absolute monarchy was changed into a constitutional monarchy in 1932.

In 1909 Siam ceded to Great Britain its suzerain rights over the dependencies of Kedah, Kelantan, Trengganu and Perlis, Malay states situated in southern Siam just north of British Malaya. This eliminated any British jurisdiction in Siam proper.

On Dec. 8, 1941, after five hours of fighting, Thailand agreed to permit Japanese troops passage through the country to invade northern British Malaya. This eventually led to increased Japanese intervention and finally occupation of the country. On Jan. 25, 1942, Thailand declared war on Great Britain and the United States. A free Thai guerrilla movement was soon organized to counteract the Japanese. In July 1943, Japan transferred the four northern Malay States back to Thailand. These were returned to Great Britain after peace treaties were signed in 1946.

RULERS

Rama IX (Bhumiphol Adulyadej), 1946–

MONETARY SYSTEM

1 Baht (Tical) = 100 Satang

REPLACEMENT NOTES

#79–92, letter S-(W) in prefix number.

	SIGNATURE VARIETIES	
	MINISTER OF FINANCE รัฐมนตรีว่าการกระทรวงการคลัง	**GOVERNOR OF THE BANK OF THAILAND** ผู้ว่าการธนาคารแห่งประเทศไทย
34		
35		
36		
37		
38		
39		
40		
41		
42		
43		

**signed as Undersecretary/Deputy Finance Minister
ปลัดกระทรวงการคลังผู้ใช้อำนาจของ

44		
45		
46		
47		
48		

	MINISTER OF FINANCE รัฐมนตรีว่าการกระทรวงการคลัง	GOVERNOR OF THE BANK OF THAILAND ผู้ว่าการธนาคารแห่งประเทศไทย
49		
50		
51		
52		
53		
54		
55		
56		
57		
58		
59		
60		

SERIES 9

1953–56 ISSUE

4–78 slightly modified Kg. in Field Marshall's uniform w/collar insignia and 3 decorations. Black serial #. Printer: TDLR

Small letters in 2-line text on back.

Large letters in 2-line text on back.

Cat. # 74	Denomination 1 BAHT	Date, description ND (1955). Blue on m/c unpt. Like #69.	VG	VF	Unc
		a. Wmk: Constitution. Red and blue security threads. Sign. 34.	.25	1.00	3.50
		b. Wmk: Constitution. Metal security strip. Sign. 34; 35 (lg. size).	.25	1.00	2.50
		c. Wmk: Kg. profile. Sm. letters in 2-line text on back. Sign. 35.	.25	1.00	2.50
		d. Wmk: Kg. profile. Larger letters in 2-line text on back. Sign. 36; 37; 38; 39; 40; 41.	.20	.60	1.25

Cat. # 75	Denomination 5 BAHT	Date, description ND (1956). Purple on m/c unpt. Like #70.	VG	VF	Unc
		a. Wmk: Constitution. Red and blue security threads. Sign. 34.	.50	1.75	4.00
		b. Wmk: Constitution. Metal security strip. Sign. 34; 35 (lg. size).	.50	1.50	3.50
		c. Wmk: Kg. profile. Sm. letters in 2-line text on back. Sign. 35; 36.	.50	1.50	3.50
		d. Wmk: Kg. profile. Larger letters in 2-line text on back. Sign. 38; 39; 40; 41.	.25	.75	2.00

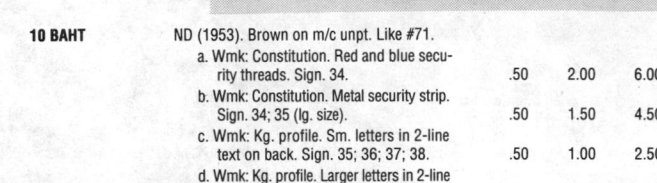

Cat. # 76	Denomination 10 BAHT	Date, description ND (1953). Brown on m/c unpt. Like #71.	VG	VF	Unc
		a. Wmk: Constitution. Red and blue security threads. Sign. 34.	.50	2.00	6.00
		b. Wmk: Constitution. Metal security strip. Sign. 34; 35 (lg. size).	.50	1.50	4.50
		c. Wmk: Kg. profile. Sm. letters in 2-line text on back. Sign. 35; 36; 37; 38.	.50	1.00	2.50
		d. Wmk: Kg. profile. Larger letters in 2-line text on back. Sign. 39; 40; 41; 42; 44.	.50	.75	2.25

Cat. # 77	Denomination 20 BAHT	Date, description ND (1953). Olive-green on m/c unpt. Like #72.	VG	VF	Unc
		a. Wmk: Constitution. Red and blue security threads. Sign. 34.	1.00	3.50	11.50
		b. Wmk: Constitution. Metal security strip. Sign. 34; 35 (lg. size).	1.00	2.50	6.00
		c. Wmk: Kg. profile. Sm. letters in 2-line text on back.	FV	1.25	3.00
		d. Wmk: Kg. profile. Larger letters in 2-line text on back.	FV	1.25	3.00

NOTE: Sign. for #77c and 77d include 35; 37; 38; 39; 40; 41; 42; 44.

Cat. # 78	Denomination 100 BAHT	Date, description ND (1955). Red on m/c unpt. Like #73.	VG	VF	Unc
		a. Wmk: Constitution. Red and blue security threads. Sign. 34.	4.50	10.00	25.00
		b. Wmk: Constitution. Metal security strip. Sign. 34; 35; 37; 38.	4.25	8.50	20.00
		c. Wmk: Kg. profile. Sm. letters in 2-line text on back.	FV	6.00	15.00
		d. Wmk: Kg. profile. Larger letters in 2-line text on back.	FV	6.00	15.00

NOTE: Sign. for #78c and 78d include 38; 39; 40; 41.

SERIES 10

1968 ISSUE

Officially described as "Series Ten".

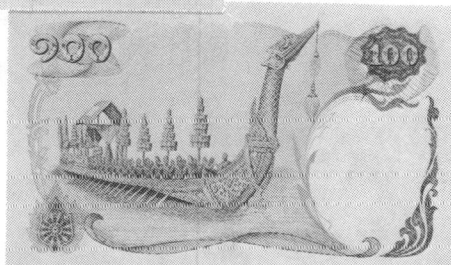

Cat. #	Denomination	Date, description	VG	VF	Unc
79	100 BAHT	ND (1968). Red, blue and m/c. Rama IX in uniform at r. and as wmk. Royal barge on back. Sign. 41; 42. Printer: TDLR.	FV	6.00	12.00

SERIES 11

Printed in Thailand by the Thai Banknote Printing Works. Officially described as "Series Eleven". Kg. Rama IX wearing traditional robes at r., sign. of Finance Minister (above) and Governor of the Bank of Thailand (below) at ctr. Wmk: Rama IX.

1969 COMMEMORATIVE ISSUE

#80–81 text at bottom: *opening of the Thai Banknote Printing Works 24 June 2512 (1969)*. Reportedly 6 or 7,000 sets issued.

| 80 | 5 BAHT | 24.6.1969. Purple and m/c. Abhorn Pimoke Throne Hall on back. Serial # prefix 00A. Sign. 41. | — | — | 150.00 |

| 81 | 10 BAHT | 24.6.1969. Brown on m/c unpt. Similar to #80. Wat Benchamabophitr temple on back. Serial # and sign. like #80. | — | — | 150.00 |

REGULAR ISSUE

Cat. #	Denomination	Date, description	VG	VF	Unc
82	5 BAHT	ND (1969). Purple on m/c unpt. Like #80 but w/o commemorative line at bottom. Sign. 41; 42.	.25	.40	1.25

| 83 | 10 BAHT | ND (1969). Brown on m/c unpt. Like #81 but w/o commemorative line at bottom. Sign. 41; 42; 43; 44; 45; 46; 47; 48; 49; 50; 51; 52; 53. | .50 | .75 | 2.25 |

| 84 | 20 BAHT | ND (1971). Dk. green, olive-green and brown-violet on m/c unpt. Royal barge on back. Sign. 11; 10; 40; 44; 45; 40; 47; 40; 49; 50; 51; 52; 53. | FV | 1.25 | 2.75 |

85	100 BAHT	ND (1972). Red-brown on m/c unpt. Emerald Buddha section of Grand Palace on back.			
		a. W/o black Thai ovpt. on face. Sign. 42; 43; 44; 45; 46; 47; 48; 49.	FV	7.00	11.50
		b. Black Thai ovpt. line just below upper sign. for change of title. Sign. 43.	6.00	10.00	25.00

Cat. #	Denomination	Date, description	VG	VF	Unc
86	500 BAHT	ND (1975). Purple on m/c unpt. Pra Prang Sam Yod Lopburi (3 towers) on back. Sign. 47; 49; 50; 51; 52; 53; 54; 55.	FV	FV	45.00

SERIES 12
1978–81 ISSUE

Kg. Rama IX wearing dk. Field Marshall's uniform at r. and as wmk. Sign. of Finance Minister (upper) and Governor of the Bank of Thailand (lower) at ctr. Official designation as "Series Twelve" not confirmed.

| 87 | 10 BAHT | ND (1980). Dk. brown on m/c unpt. Mounted statue of Kg. Chulalongkorn on back. Sign. 52; 53; 54; 56. | FV | FV | 1.50 |

| 88 | 20 BAHT | ND (1981). Dk. green and black on m/c unpt. Kg. Taksin's statue at Chantaburi w/3 armed men on back. Sign. 52; 55; 56. | FV | FV | 2.25 |

| 89 | 100 BAHT | ND (1978). Violet, red and orange on m/c unpt. Kg. Naresuan the Great on elephant's back on back. Sign. 49; 50; 52; 53; 54; 56; 57. | FV | FV | 8.50 |

1985–92 SERIES

Cat. #	Denomination	Date, description	VG	VF	Unc
90	50 BAHT	ND (1985). Dk. blue and purple on m/c unpt. Kg. Rama IX facing wearing traditional robe at r. and as wmk. Palace at l., statue of Kg. Rama VII at ctr., his arms and sign. at upper l. on back.			
		a. Kg. w/pointed eartips. Sign. 54.	FV	FV	5.50
		b. Darker blue color obscuring pointed eartips. Sign. 55; 56; 57.	FV	FV	4.50

| 91 | 500 BAHT | ND(1988). Purple and m/c. Kg. Rama IX at r. and as wmk. Statue on back. Sign. 54. | FV | FV | 32.50 |
| 92 | 1000 BAHT | ND (1992). Gray, brown, orange and m/c. Kg. at ctr. r. and as wmk. Kg. and Qn. on back. | FV | FV | 65.00 |

1987–92 COMMEMORATIVE ISSUES

#93, King's 60th Birthday

Cat. #	Denomination	Date, description	VG	VF	Unc
93	60 BAHT	BE2530 (5.12.1987). Dk. brown on m/c unpt. Kg. Rama IX seated on throne at ctr., Victory crown at l., Royal Regalia at r. Royal family seated w/ subjects on back. Sign. 55.			
		a. Issued note.	—	—	6.00
		s. Specimen in blue folder.	—	—	100.00

NOTE: A 40 Baht surcharge was added to issue price of #93, for charity work and the expense of the special envelope which came with each issued note.

#94–95, 90th Birthday of Princess Mother

#94–95 wmk: Princess Mother.

			fV	FV	
94	50 BAHT	ND (1992). Blue on m/c unpt. Similar to #90. 2 lines of text added under wmk. on face.	fV	FV	4.50
95	500 BAHT	ND (1992). Purple and m/c. Similar to #91. 2 lines of text added under wmk. on face.	FV	FV	37.50

#96, Qn. Sirikit's 60th Birthday

| 96 | 1000 BAHT | ND (1992). Gray, brown, orange and m/c. Similar to #92. Commemorative text in 3 lines under Qn.'s wmk. on back. | FV | FV | 65.00 |

1994 ISSUE

| 97 | 100 BAHT | ND (1994). Violet, red and brown-orange on m/c unpt. Kg. Rama IX at r. Statue of Kg. and prince at ctr. r. between children. | FV | FV | 8.50 |

1995 COMMEMORATIVE ISSUE

#98, 120th Anniversary of the Ministry of Finance

| 98 | 10 BAHT | ND (1995). Dk. brown on m/c unpt. Like #87 w/Commemorative text. | FV | FV | 1.25 |

MILITARY – VIETNAM WAR
Auxiliary Military Payment Certificate Coupons

Issued to Thai troops in Vietnam to facilitate their use of United States MPC. These coupons could not be used as currency by themselves.

FIRST SERIES

#M1–M8 issued probably from January to April or May, 1970. Larger shield at ctr. on face and back. Words *Coupon* below shield or at r., *Non Negotiable* at r. Small Thai symbol only at upper l. corner; denomination at 3 corners. Black print on check-type security paper.

Cat. #	Denomination	Date, description	Good	Fine	XF
M1	5 CENTS	ND. Yellow paper. Seahorse shield design.	85.00	200.00	
M2	10 CENTS	ND. Lt. gray paper. Shield w/leaping panther and *RTAVF. Not Negotiable* under shield; *Coupon* deleted.	85.00	200.00	—
M3	25 CENTS	ND. Pink paper. Shield w/*Victory Vietnam. Coupon* at r.	—	—	—
M4	50 CENTS	ND. Lt. blue paper. Circle w/shaking hands and *Royal Thai Forces Vietnam.*	—	—	—
M5	1 DOLLAR	ND. Yellow paper. Inscription *Victory Vietnam. Coupon* at r.	—	—	—
M6	5 DOLLARS	ND. Lt. gray paper. Seahorse in shield.	—	—	—
M7	10 DOLLARS	ND. Yellow paper. Shield w/leaping panther.	—	—	—
M8	20 DOLLARS	ND. Lt. green paper. Circle w/hands shaking.	—	—	—

SECOND SERIES

#M9–M16 issued April or May, 1970 to possibly Oct. 7, 1970. Shield desgns similar to previous issue, but paper colors are different. Larger shield outline around each shield at l. ctr. *Coupon* in margin at lower ctr., denomination at all 4 corners.

M9	5 CENTS	ND. Yellow paper. Shield similar to #M1.	35.00	150.00	275.00

| M10 | 10 CENTS | ND. Lt. green paper. Shield similar to #M2. | 40.00 | 175.00 | 300.00 |

M11	25 CENTS	ND. Yellow paper. Shield similar to #M3.	—	—	—
M12	50 CENTS	ND. Lt. gray paper. Shield similar to #M4.	—	—	—
M13	1 DOLLAR	ND. Pink paper. Shield similar to #M5.	—	—	—
M14	5 DOLLARS	ND. Lt. green paper. Shield similar to #M6.	—	—	—
M15	10 DOLLARS	ND. Pale yellow paper. Shield similar to #M7.	—	—	—

M16	20 DOLLARS	ND. Lt. green paper. Shield similar to #M8.	—	—	—

THIRD SERIES

#M17–M23 date of issue not known (Oct., 1970?). All notes w/hands shaking in shield at lower r. on face. Different shield designs at upper l. on back. More elaborate design across face and back.

M17	5 CENTS	ND. Lt. gray, maroon and green.	35.00	150.00	275.00

M18	10 CENTS	ND. Lt. yellow and green.	40.00	165.00	260.00

Cat. #	Denomination	Date, description	Good	Fine	XF
M19	25 CENTS	ND. Green, pink and maroon.	40.00	165.00	260.00

| M20 | 50 CENTS | ND. Yellow, green, blue and red. | 40.00 | 165.00 | 260.00 |

| M21 | 1 DOLLAR | ND. Pink, blue and green. | 110.00 | 275.00 | — |

| M22 | 5 DOLLARS | ND. Yellow, green, blue and red. | 110.00 | 275.00 | — |

| M23 | 10 DOLLARS | ND. Green, maroon and dk. red. | 70.00 | 225.00 | 475.00 |

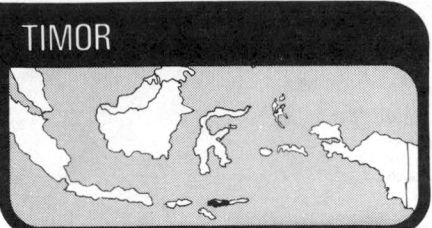

TIMOR

Timor, an island of Indonesia between the Savu and Timor Seas, has an area, including the former colony of Portuguese Timor, of 11,883 sq. mi. (30,775 sq. km.) and a population of 1.5 million. Western Timor is administered as part of Nusa Tenggara Timur (East Nusa Tenggara) province. Capital: Kupang. The eastern half of the island, the former Portuguese colony, forms a single province, Timor Timur (East Tinor). Capital: Dili. Timor exports sandalwood, coffee, tea, hides, rubber and copra.

Portuguese traders reached Timor about 1520, and moved to the north and east when the Dutch established themselves in Kupang, a sheltered bay at the southwestern tip, in 1613. Treaties effective in 1860 and 1914 established the boundaries between the two colonies. Japan occupied the entire island during World War II. The former Dutch colony in the western part of the island became part of Indonesia in 1950.

At the end of Nov., 1975, the Portuguese Province of Timor attained independence as the People's Democratic Republic of East Timur. In Des., 1975 or early in 1976 the government of the People's Democratic Republic was seized by a guerrilla faction sympathetic to the Indonesiand territorial claim to East Timur which ousted the constitutional government and replaced it with the Provisional Government of East Timur. On July 17, 1976, the Provisional Government enacted a law which dissolved the free republic and made East Timur the 24th province of Indonesia.

MONETARY SYSTEM
1 Escudo = 100 Centavos, 1958–75

PORTUGUESE INFLUENCE
Banco Nacional Ultramarino

1959 ISSUE

#22–25 J. Celestino da Silva at. r. Bank seal and crowned arms on back. Printer: BWC.

Cat. #	Denomination	Date, description	VG	VF	Unc
22	30 ESCUDOS	2.1.1959. Blue on m/c unpt.	5.00	17.50	85.00
23	60 ESCUDOS	2.1.1959. Red on m/c unpt.	5.00	20.00	110.00
24	100 ESCUDOS	2.1.1959. Brown on m/c unpt.	7.50	30.00	120.00
25	500 ESCUDOS	2.1.1959. Dk. brown and black on m/c unpt.	40.00	160.00	475.00

1963–68 ISSUE

#26–30 R. D. Aleixo at r. Bank seal and crowned arms on back. Sign. varieties. Printer: BWC.

Cat. #	Denomination	Date, description	VG	VF	Unc
26	20 ESCUDOS	24.10.1967. Olive-brown on m/c unpt.	1.50	5.00	15.00
27	50 ESCUDOS	24.10.1967. Blue on m/c unpt.	2.50	6.00	20.00
28	100 ESCUDOS	25.4.1963. Brown on m/c unpt. 2 sign. varieties.	3.00	10.00	25.00
29	500 ESCUDOS	25.4.1963. Dk. brown on m/c unpt.	10.00	25.00	100.00
30	1000 ESCUDOS	21.3.1968. Green on m/c unpt.	20.00	42.50	120.00

1969 (ND) PROVISIONAL ISSUE

Cat. #	Denomination	Date, description	VG	VF	Unc
31	500 ESCUDOS	ND (1969 – old date 22.3.1967). Brown and violet on m/c unpt. Ovpt: *PAGAVEL EM TIMOR* on Mozambique #110, face and back.	—	—	—

32	20 ESCUDOS	ND Green and m/c. Rugula Jose Nunes at l. Bank seal at ctr. local huts on pilings at r. on back. Specimen.	—	—	—

NOTE: For later issues see Indonesia listings.

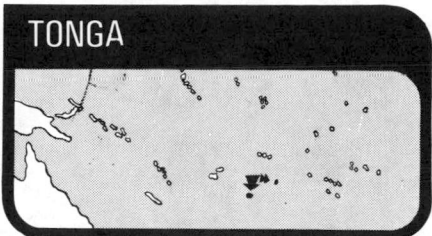

The Kingdom of Tonga (or Friendly Islands), a member of the British Commonwealth, is an archipelago situated in the southern Pacific Ocean south of Western Samoa and east of Fiji comprising 150 islands. Tonga has an area of 270 sq. mi. (748 sq. km.) and a population of 103,000. Capital: Nuku'alofa. Primarily agricultural, the kingdom exports bananas and copra.

Dutch navigators Willem Schouten and Jacob Lemaire were the first Europeans to visit Tonga in 1616. They were followed by the noted Dutch explorer Abel Tasman who visited the Tongatapu group in 1643. No further European contact was made until 1773 when British navigator Capt. James Cook arrived and, impressed by the peaceful deportment of the natives, named the islands the Friendly Islands. Within a few years of Cook's visit, Tonga was embroiled in a civil war that lasted until the great chief Taufa'ahau, who reigned as George Tubou I (1845–93), was converted to Christianity and brought unity and peace to the islands. Tonga became a self-governing protectorate of Great Britain in 1900 and a fully independent state on June 4, 1970. The monarchy is a member of the Commonwealth of Nations. The monarch is Chief of State and Head of Government.

RULERS
Queen Salote, 1918–1965
King Taufa'ahau, 1965–

MONETARY SYSTEM
1 Shilling = 12 Pence
1 Pound = 20 Shillings to 1967
1 Pa'anga = 100 Seniti, 1967–

REPLACEMENT NOTES
#18–24, Z/1 prefix.

Government of Tonga

Treasury Notes

THIRD ISSUE

#9–12 w/denomination spelled out on both sides of arms at ctr. Printer: TDLR.

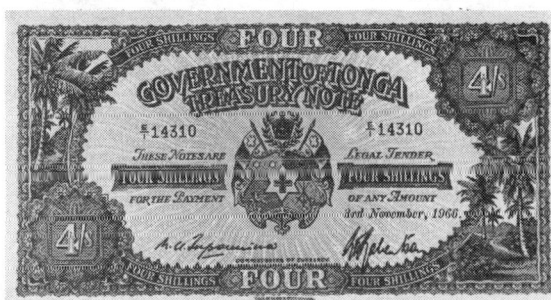

Cat. #	Denomination	Date, description	Good	Fine	XF
9	4 SHILLINGS	1941–66. Brown on m/c unpt. *FOUR SHILLINGS* at l. and r.			
		a. 1.12.1941–22.10.1946. 3 sign.	20.00	75.00	225.00
		b. 7.2.1949; 15.2.1951; 20.7.1951; 6.9.1954.	15.00	60.00	150.00
		c. 19.9.1955–30.11.1959.	5.00	25.00	65.00
		d. 24.10.1960–27.9.1966.	3.00	7.50	25.00
		e. 3.11.1966. 2 sign.	1.50	4.00	16.50
10	10 SHILLINGS	1941–66. Green on m/c unpt. *TEN SHILLINGS* at l. and r.			
		a. 19.5.1939; 17.10.1941–28.11.1944. 3 sign.	30.00	100.00	325.00
		b. 6.6.1950–1955.	25.00	70.00	150.00
		c. 2.5.1956; 22.7.1957, 10.12.1958.	6.00	15.00	70.00
		d. 24.10.1960; 28.11.1962; 29.7.1964; 22.6.1965.	3.00	8.50	30.00
		e. 3.11.1966. 2 sign.	2.00	5.00	20.00

Cat. #	Denomination	Date, description	Good	Fine	XF
11	1 POUND	1940–66. Red on m/c unpt. *ONE POUND* at l. and r.			
		a. 3.5.1940–7.11.1944. 3 sign.	35.00	110.00	325.00
		b. 15.6.1951; 11.9.1951; 19.9.1955.	30.00	85.00	175.00
		c. 2.5.1956; 10.12.1958; 30.11.1959; 12.12.1961.	10.00	22.50	50.00
		d. 28.11.1962; 30.10.1964; 2.11.1965; 3.11.1966.	5.00	12.00	35.00
		e. 2.12.1966. 2 sign.	2.00	6.00	25.00
12	5 POUNDS	1942–66. Dk. blue on m/c unpt. *FIVE POUNDS* at l. and r.			
		a. 11.3.1942–1945. 3 sign.	500.00	750.00	1000.
		b. 15.6.1951; 5.7.1955; 11.9.1956; 26.6.1958.	200.00	385.00	700.00
		c. 30.11.1959; 2.11.1965.	100.00	250.00	500.00
		d. 2.12.1966. 2 sign.	10.00	25.00	45.00

Pule' Anga 'O Tonga
(Government of Tonga)

1967 ISSUE

#13–17 arms at lower l., Qn. Salote at r. Various date and sign. varieties.

Cat. #	Denomination	Date, description	VG	VF	Unc
13	1/2 PA'ANGA	1967–73. Dk. brown on pink unpt. Back brown and blue; coconut workers.			
		a. 3.4.1967; 10.3.1970; 16.6.1970; 4.2.1971; 24.7.1972. 3 sign.	1.50	7.50	30.00
		b. 13.6.1973. 2 sign.	2.00	6.50	35.00
14	1 PA'ANGA	1967; 70–71. Olive on m/c unpt. Back olive and blue; river scene, palm trees.			
		a. 12.4.1967; 2.10.1967; 8.12.1967; 3.4.1967.	2.00	7.50	40.00
		b. 10.3.1970; 19.10.1971.	2.50	8.50	45.00

Cat. #	Denomination	Date, description	VG	VF	Unc
15	2 PA'ANGA	1967–73. Red on m/c unpt. Back red and brown; women making Tapa cloth.			
		a. 3.4.1967; 2.10.1967; 8.12.1967.	3.00	12.00	60.00
		b. 19.5.1969; 10.3.1970; 19.10.1971; 2.8.1973.	3.50	15.00	80.00

16	5 PA'ANGA	1967; 1973. Purple on m/c unpt. Back purple and olive-green; Ha'amonga stone gateway.			
		a. 3.4.1967.	7.00	25.00	95.00
		b. 13.6.1973.	8.50	30.00	110.00

17	10 PA'ANGA	3.4.1967; 2.10.1967; 8.12.1967. Dk. blue on m/c unpt. Back blue and purple; Royal Palace.	12.00	50.00	175.00

1974; 1985 ISSUE

#18–22 arms at lower l., Kg. Taufa'ahau at r. Various date and sign. varieties.

Cat. #	Denomination	Date, description	VG	VF	Unc
18	1/2 PA'ANGA	1974–83. Dk. brown on pale orange unpt. Back like #13.			
		a. 2 sign. 2.10.1974; 19.6.1975.	1.00	2.50	8.50
		b. 3 sign. 12.1.1977–29.7.1983.	.50	1.00	4.00

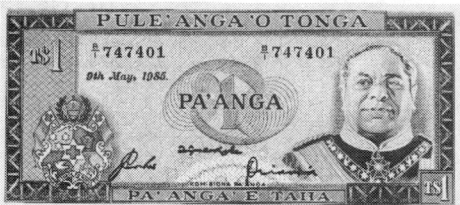

Cat. #	Denomination	Date, description	VG	VF	Unc
19	1 PA'ANGA	1974–89. Olive-green on m/c unpt. Back like #14.			
		a. 2 sign. 31.7.1974; 19.6.1975; 21.1.1981; 18.5.1983.	FV	1.50	5.50
		b. 3 sign. 17.5.1977–11.6.1980; 31.7.1981–28.10.1982; 27.7.1983–30.6.1989.	FV	FV	4.50

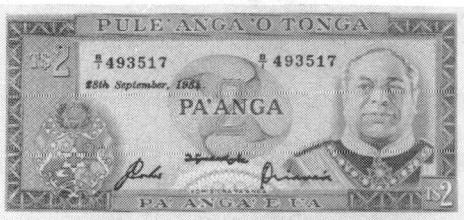

Cat. #	Denomination	Date, description	VG	VF	Unc
20	2 PA'ANGA	1974–89. Red on m/c unpt. Back like #15.			
		a. 2 sign. 2.10.1974; 19.6.1975; 21.1.1981.	FV	2.00	8.50
		b. 3 sign. 12.1.1977–27.8.1980; 31.7.1981–30.6.1989.	FV	FV	5.00

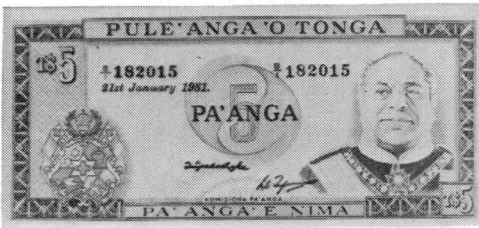

Cat. #	Denomination	Date, description	VG	VF	Unc
21	5 PA'ANGA	1974–89. Purple on m/c unpt. Back like #16.			
		a. 2 sign. 2.10.1974; 19.6.1975; 21.1.1981.	FV	4.00	17.50
		b. 3 sign. 21.12.1976–28.11.1980; 27.5.1981–30.6.1989.	FV	FV	10.00

Cat. #	Denomination	Date, description	VG	VF	Unc
22	10 PA'ANGA	1974–89. Dk. blue on m/c unpt. Back like #17.			
		a. 2 sign. 31.7.1974; 3.9.1974; 19.6.1975; 21.1.1981.	FV	7.50	27.50
		b. 3 sign. 12.12.1976–28.11.1980; 19.1.1982–30.6.1989.	FV	FV	18.50

#23–24 Kg. in new design at ctr. r. and as wmk., arms at r.

Cat. #	Denomination	Date, description	VG	VF	Unc
23	20 PA'ANGA	1985-89. Orange on green and m/c unpt. Tonga Development Bank on back.			
		a. 4.7.1985.	FV	25.00	70.00
		b. 18.7.1985; 8.1.1986; 27.2.1987; 28.9.1987.	FV	FV	45.00
		c. 20.5.1988; 14.12.1988; 23.1.1989; 30.6.1989.	FV	FV	40.00

NOTE: #23a was made in limited quanitites in celebration of the king's birthday.

Kingdom of Tonga

Cat. #	Denomination	Date, description	VG	VF	Unc
24	50 PA'ANGA	1988–89. Brown and green on m/c unpt. Vava'u Harbour on back.			
		a. 4.7.1988.	FV	50.00	110.00
		b. 14.12.1988; 30.6.1989.	FV	FV	85.00

NOTE: #24a was made in limited quantities in celebration of the king's birthday.

National Reserve Bank of Tonga

1992 ISSUE

#25–29 designs like #19–23. 2 sign. w/Tongan titles beneath.

Cat. #	Denomination	Date, description	VG	VF	Unc
25	1 PA'ANGA	ND (1992–95). Olive-green on m/c unpt.	FV	FV	2.50

Cat. #	Denomination	Date, description	VG	VF	Unc
26	2 PA'ANGA	ND (1992–95). Red on m/c unpt.	FV	FV	4.50

27	5 PA'ANGA	ND (1992–95). Purple on m/c unpt	FV	FV	10.00
28	10 PA'ANGA	ND (1992–95). Dk. blue on m/c unpt.	FV	FV	18.50
29	20 PA'ANGA	ND(1992–95). Orange and green on m/c unpt.	FV	FV	32.50

1989 COMMEMORATIVE ISSUE

#30, Inauguration of National Reserve Bank of Tonga.

30	20 PA'ANGA	1.7.1989. Orange on green and m/c unpt. w/commemorative text wmk. area on face and back	FV	25.00	50.00

1995 ISSUE

#31–34 Kg. Taufa'ahau at upper ctr. r., arms at r.

31	1 PA'ANGA	ND (1995). Olive-green on m/c unpt. River scene, palm trees on back.	FV	FV	2.25
32	2 PA'ANGA	ND (1995). Red on m/c unpt. Woman making Tapa cloth on back.	FV	FV	4.00
33	5 PA'ANGA	ND (1995). Purple on m/c unpt. Ha'amonga stone gateway on back.	FV	FV	9.00
34	10 PA'ANGA	ND (1995). Dk. blue on m/c unpt. Royal Palace on back.	FV	FV	17.00

COLLECTOR SERIES

Cat. #	Date, denomination	Description	Issue Price	Mkt. Val.
CS1	1978 1–10 PA'ANGA	#19–22 ovpt: *SPECIMEN* and Maltese cross prefix serial #.	14.00	25.00

TRANSDNIESTRA

The Transdniester Moldavian Republic was formed in 1990, even before the separation of Moldavia from Russia. It has an area of 11,544 sq. mi. (29,900 sq. km). and a population of 742,000. Capital: Tiraspol. Once the Moldavian SSR declared independence in August 1991, the natural independence route for Transdniester was pushed to a head when Russian occupation forces quelled demonstrations by force in Bendery and Doubossary.

Transdniester has a president, parliament, army and police, but as yet it is lacking international recognition.

The area was conquered from the Turks in the last 18th Century, and in 1792 the capital city of Tiraspol was founded. After 1812, the area called Bessarabia (Present Moldova and part of the Ukraine) became part of the Russian Empire. During the Russian Revolution, in 1918, the are was taken by Romanian troops, and in 1924 the Moldavian Autonomous SSR was formed. During WWII Romanian troops occupied the area, but it was soon recaptured by the Soviet troops.

See also Romania #M10–16 and #M17–M22, vol. 2.

Government

1994 PROVISIONAL ISSUE

#1–15 issued 1.24.1994, invalidated on 1.12.1994.

Cat. #	Denomination	Date, description	VG	VF	Unc
1	10 RUBLES	ND (1994– old date 1961). Green on pink tint adhesive stamp on Russia #233.	.10	.40	1.00

2	10 RUBLES	ND (1994– old date 1991). Green on pink tint adhesive stamp on Russia #240.	.30	1.25	3.00

3	25 RUBLES	ND (1994– old date 1961). Red-violet on buff tint adhesive stamp on Russia #234.	.15	.60	2.00
4	50 RUBLES	ND (1994– old date 1991). Red on pale green tint adhesive stamp on Russia #241.	.20	.80	10.00

5	50 RUBLES	ND (1994– old date 1992). Red on pale green tint adhesive stamp on Russia #237.	.20	.80	3.00
6	100 RUBLES	ND (1994– old date 1991). Black on pale blue tint adhesive stamp on Russia #242.	.25	1.00	20.00

7	100 RUBLES	ND (1994– old date 1991). Black on pale blue tint adhesive stamp on Russia #243.	.25	1.00	2.50

Cat. #	Denomination	Date, description	VG	VF	Unc
8	200 RUBLES	ND (1994– old date 1991). Green on yellow tint adhesive stamp on Russia #244.	.25	1.00	15.00
9	200 RUBLES	ND (1994– old date 1992). Green on yellow tint adhesive stamp on Russia #248.	.25	1.00	2.00
10	500 RUBLES	ND (1994– old date 1991). Blue adhesive stamp on Russia #245.	1.25	3.00	12.00

Cat. #	Denomination	Date, description	VG	VF	Unc
11	500 RUBLES	ND (1994– old date 1992). Blue adhesive stamp on Russia #249.	.20	.50	1.00
12	1000 RUBLES	ND (1994– old date 1991). Violet on yellow tint adhesive stamp on Russia #246.	1.00	2.50	10.00

Cat. #	Denomination	Date, description	VG	VF	Unc
13	1000 RUBLES	ND (1994– old date 1992). Violet on yellow tint adhesive stamp on Russia #250.	.20	.50	1.00

Cat. #	Denomination	Date, description	VG	VF	Unc
14	5000 RUBLES	ND (1994– old date 1992). Dk. brown on pale blue-gray tint adhesive stamp on Russia #251.	.00	.75	2.00
14A	5000 RUBLES	ND (1994 –old date 1961). Adhesive stamp on Russia 5 Rubles #224.	FV	FV	1.00
14B	5000 RUBLES	ND (1994 –old date 1991). Adhesive stamp on Russia 5 Rubles #239.	FV	FV	1.00

Cat. #	Denomination	Date, description	VG	VF	Unc
15	10,000 RUBLES	ND (1994– old date 1992). Purple on yellow tint adhesive stamp on Russia #252.	.50	1.00	3.50

БАНКЭ НИСТРЯНЭ – Banka Nistriana

1993–94 KUPON ISSUE

#16–18 A. V. Suvorov at r. Parliament bldg. at ctr. on back. Wmk: Block design.

Cat. #	Denomination	Date, description	VG	VF	Unc
16	1 RUBLE	1994. Dk. green on m/c unpt.	FV	FV	.30

Cat. #	Denomination	Date, description	VG	VF	Unc
17	5 RUBLEI	1994. Blue on m/c unpt.	FV	.10	.35

Cat. #	Denomination	Date, description	VG	VF	Unc
18	10 RUBLEI	1994. Red-violet on m/c unpt.	FV	.15	.50

#19–23 equestrian statue of A. V. Suvorov at r. Parliament bldg. on back. Wmk: Block design.

Cat. #	Denomination	Date, description	VG	VF	Unc
19	50 RUBLEI	1993 (1994). Olive-green on m/c unpt.	FV	.10	.35

Cat. #	Denomination	Date, description	VG	VF	Unc
20	100 RUBLEI	1993 (1994). Dk. brown on m/c unpt.	FV	.15	.50

Cat. #	Denomination	Date, description	VG	VF	Unc
21	200 RUBLEI	1993 (1994). Brown and violet on m/c unpt.	FV	.15	.50

| 22 | 500 RUBLEI | 1993 (1994). Blue-black on m/c unpt. | FV | .30 | 1.00 |

23	1000 RUBLEI	1993 (1994). Purple and red-violet on m/c unpt.	FV	.50	1.75
24	5000 RUBLEI	(1995).			Expected new issue.
25	10,000 RUBLEI	(1995).			Expected new issue.

Currency Reform, 1995–

1 "New" Rublei = 1000 "Old" Rublei

26–30	Held in reserve				
31	1000 RUBLEI	1994.	FV	FV	2.75

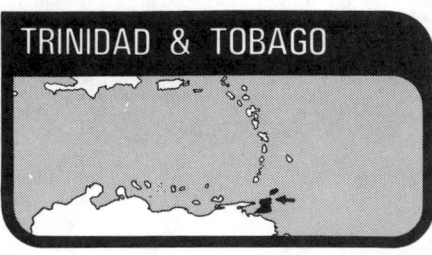

TRINIDAD & TOBAGO

The Republic of Trinidad and Tobago, a member of the British Commonwealth, situated 7 miles (11 km.) off the coast of Venezuela, has an area of 1,981 sq. mi. (5,130 sq. km.) and a population of 1.25 million. Capital: Port-of-Spain. The Island of Trinidad contains the world's largest natural asphalt bog. Birds of Paradise live on little Tobago, the only place outside of their native New Guinea where they can be found in a wild state. Petroleum and petroleum products are the mainstay of the economy. Petroleum products, crude oil and sugar are exported.

Trinidad and Tobago were discovered by Columbus in 1498. Trinidad remained under Spanish rule from the time of its settlement in 1592 until its capture by the British in 1797. It was ceded to the British in 1802. Tobago was occupied at various times by the French, Dutch and English before being ceded to Britain in 1814. Trinidad and Tobago were merged into a single colony in 1888. The colony was part of the Federation of the West Indies until Aug. 31, 1962, when it became an independent member of the Commonwealth of Nations. A new constitution establishing a republican form of government was adopted on Aug. 1, 1976. Trinidad and Tobago is a member of the Commonwealth of Nations. The president is Chief of State. The prime minister is Head of Government.

Notes of the British Caribbean Territories circulated between 1950–1964.

RULERS

British to 1976

MONETARY SYSTEM

1 Dollar = 100 Cents

REPLACEMENT NOTES

#30-41, XX prefix.

SIGNATURE VARITIES			
1	J. F. Pierce	5	W. Demas
2	A. N McLeod	6	N. Hareward
3	J. E. Bruce	7	
4	Linn OHB	8	

Central Bank of Trinidad and Tobago

Central Bank Act of Trinidad and Tobago, 1964

1964 ISSUE

#26–29 arms at l., Portr. Qn. Elizabeth II at ctr. Central Bank bldg. at ctr. on back. Wmk: Bird of paradise.

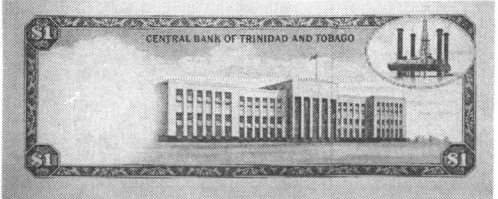

Cat. #	Denomination	Date, description	VG	VF	Unc
26	1 DOLLAR	L.1964. Red. Oil rig in water at upper r. on back.			
		a. Sign. 1.	1.50	3.50	20.00
		b. Sign. 2.	2.00	4.50	30.00
		c. Sign. 3.	1.00	2.50	12.50
		s. As a. Specimen.	—	—	250.00

Cat. #	Denomination	Date, description	VG	VF	Unc
27	5 DOLLARS	*L.1964.* Green. Crane loading sugarcane at upper r. on back.			
		a. Sign. 1.	7.50	30.00	250.00
		b. Sign. 2.	5.00	12.50	135.00
		c. Sign. 3.	2.00	7.50	60.00
		s. As a. Specimen.	—	—	350.00
28	10 DOLLARS	*L.1964.* Dk. brown. Factory at upper r. on back.			
		a. Sign. 1.	10.00	35.00	450.00
		b. Sign. 2.	9.00	30.00	400.00
		c. Sign. 3.	5.00	15.00	140.00
		s. As a. Specimen.	—	—	450.00
29	20 DOLLARS	*L.1964.* Purple. Cocoa pods at upper r. on back.			
		a. Sign. 1.	15.00	50.00	550.00
		b. Sign. 2.	12.50	35.00	450.00
		c. Sign. 3.	7.50	20.00	225.00
		s. As a. Specimen.	—	—	550.00

1977 ISSUE

#30–35 authorization date 1964. Arms at ctr. Back designs like previous issue. Wmk: Bird of paradise.

Cat. #	Denomination	Date, description	VG	VF	Unc
30	1 DOLLAR	*L.1964* (1977). Red on m/c unpt.. 2 flying birds at l.			
		a. Sign. 3.	FV	.50	2.00
		b. Sign. 4.	FV	1.00	3.00

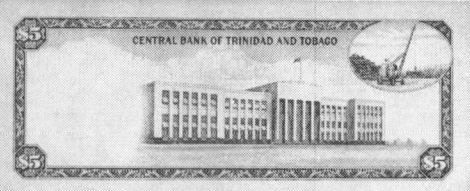

Cat. #	Denomination	Date, description	VG	VF	Unc
31	5 DOLLARS	*L.1964* (1977). Dk. green on m/c unpt. Branches and leaves at l.			
		a. Sign. 3.	FV	1.00	5.00
		b. Sign. 4.	FV	2.00	10.00

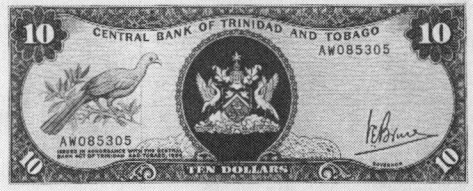

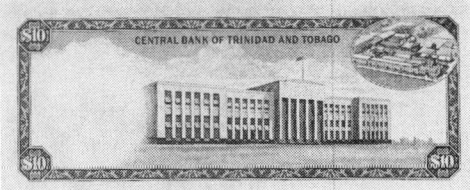

Cat. #	Denomination	Date, description	VG	VF	Unc
32	10 DOLLARS	*L.1964* (1977). Dk. brown on m/c unpt. Bird on branch at l. Sign. 3.	FV	3.00	12.00
33	20 DOLLARS	*L.1964* (1977). Purple on m/c unpt. Flowers at l. Sign. 3	FV	6.00	25.00
34	50 DOLLARS	*L.1964* (1977). Dk. brown on m/c unpt. Hummingbird at l. Net fishing at upper r. on back. Sign. 3.			
		a. 1963 (error date in authorization).	25.00	40.00	150.00
		b. 1964 (corrected authorization date).	30.00	75.00	275.00
35	100 DOLLARS	*L.1964* (1977). Deep blue on m/c unpt. Branch w/leaves and berries at l. Huts and palm trees at upper r. on back.			
		a. Sign. 3.	FV	30.00	100.00
		b. Sign. 4.	FV	35.00	125.00

1985 ISSUE

Central Bank Act Chap. 79.02

#36–41 arms at ctr. Twin towered modern bank bldg. at ctr. on back. Wmk: Bird of paradise.

Cat. #	Denomination	Date, description	VG	VF	Unc
36	1 DOLLAR	ND (1985). Red-orange and purple on m/c unpt. 2 birds at l. Oil refinery at r. on back.			
		a. Sign. 4.	FV	FV	1.00
		b. Sign. 5.	FV	FV	.85
		c. Sign. 6.	FV	FV	.75

Cat. #	Denomination	Date, description	VG	VF	Unc
37	5 DOLLARS	ND (1985). Dk. green on m/c unpt. Bird at l. Women working at r. on back.			
		a. Sign. 4.	FV	FV	3.50
		b. Sign. 5.	FV	FV	3.00
		c. Sign. 6.	FV	FV	2.75

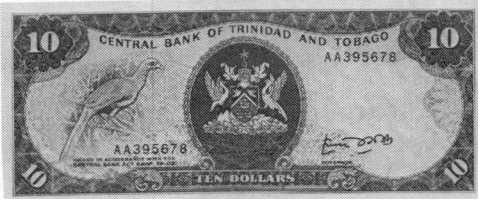

38	10 DOLLARS	ND (1985). Dk. brown on m/c unpt. Face similar to #32. Cargo ship dockside at r. on back.			
		a. Sign. 4.	FV	FV	7.00
		b. Sign. 5.	FV	FV	6.00
		c. Sign. 6.	FV	FV	5.50

39	20 DOLLARS	ND (1985). Purple on m/c unpt. Hummingbird in flowers at l. Steel drums at r. on back. Sign. 4.	FV	FV	11.50

40 (41)	100 DOLLARS	ND (1985). Deep blue on m/c unpt. Bird at l. Oil rig at r. on back. Sign. 4.	FV	FV	50.00

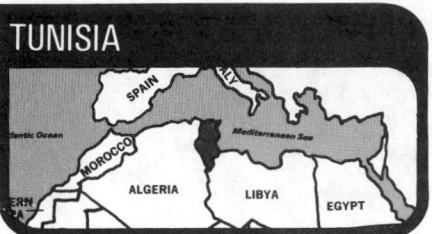

TUNISIA

The Republic of Tunisia, located on the northern coast of Africa between Algeria and Libya, has an area of 63,170 sq. mi. (163,610 sq. km.) and a population of nearly 8.4 million. Capital: Tunis. Agriculture is the backbone of the economy. Crude oil, phosphates, olive oil, and wine are exported.

Tunisia, settled by the Phoenicians in the 12th century BC, was the center of the seafaring Carthaginian empire. After the total destruction of Carthage, Tunisia became part of Rome's African province. It remained a part of the Roman Empire (except for the 439–533 interval of Vandal conquest) until taken by the Arabs, 648, who administered it until the Turkish invasion of 1570. Under Turkish control, the public revenue was heavily dependent upon the piracy of Mediterranean shipping, an endeavor that wasn't abandoned until 1819 when a coalition of powers threatened appropriate reprisal. Deprived of its major source of income, Tunisia underwent a financial regression that ended in bankruptcy, enabling France to establish a protectorate over the country in 1881. National agitation and guerrilla fighting forced France to grant Tunisia internal autonomy in 1955 and to recognize Tunisian independence on March 20, 1956. Tunisia abolished the monarchy and established a republic on July 25, 1957.

MONETARY SYSTEM
1 Dinar = 1000 Millim, 1960–

Banque Centrale de Tunisie

Dinar System

1960; 62 ISSUE

#57–58 H. Bourguiba at l.

Cat. #	Denomination	Date, description	VG	VF	Unc
57	1/2 DINAR	ND. (1962). Purple. Mosque at r. Ruins at l., arms at r. on back.	4.00	20.00	100.00
58	1 DINAR	ND. (1962). Green. Peasant and farm machine at r. Dam on back.	3.50	17.50	85.00

#59–61 H. Bourguiba at r.

59	5 DINARS	ND. (1962). Brown. Bridge at l., Arabic numerals 5 and serial #. Archways on back.	2.50	20.00	100.00

Cat. #	Denomination	Date, description	VG	VF	Unc
60	5 DINARS	1.11.1960. Brown. Similar to #59 but Western numerals *5* and serial #.	7.50	20.00	100.00
61	5 DINARS	20.3.1962. Blue. Like #60.	10.00	25.00	125.00

1965–69 ISSUE

Cat. #	Denomination	Date, description	VG	VF	Unc
62	1/2 DINAR	1.6.1965. Blue and m/c. Bourguiba at l., mosque at r. Mosaic from Monastir on back.	5.00	17.50	65.00

#63–65 H. Bourguiba at r. and as wmk.

Cat. #	Denomination	Date, description	VG	VF	Unc
63	1 DINAR	1.6.1965. Blue and m/c. Factory at l. Mosaic on back.	6.00	20.00	70.00

Cat. #	Denomination	Date, description	VG	VF	Unc
64	5 DINARS	1.6.1965. Lilac-brown and green. Sadiki College at l. Mosaic w/woman in sprays at l., arch at ctr., Sunface at lower r. on back.	10.00	25.00	125.00

Cat. #	Denomination	Date, description	VG	VF	Unc
65	10 DINARS	1.6.1969. M/c. Refinery at l. Palm trees in field on back.	15.00	50.00	225.00

1972 ISSUE

#66–68 H. Bourguiba at r. and as wmk. Printer: TDLR.

Cat. #	Denomination	Date, description	VG	VF	Unc
66	1/2 DINAR	3.8.1972. Brown and m/c. City w/river at l. View of Tunis on back.	1.00	7.50	20.50

Cat. #	Denomination	Date, description	VG	VF	Unc
67	1 DINAR	3.8.1972. Purple and m/c. Old fort at l. Minaret at l., girl at ctr. on back.	2.00	10.00	45.00

Cat. #	Denomination	Date, description	VG	VF	Unc
68	5 DINARS	3.8.1972. Green and m/c. Modern bldg. at l. Amphitheatre at El-Djem on back.	6.00	21.50	85.00

Cat. #	Denomination	Date, description	VG	VF	Unc
71	5 DINARS	15.10.1973. Dk. brown, lilac and m/c. City view at l. Montage of old and new on back.	FV	12.00	25.00

1973 ISSUE

#69–72 H. Bourguiba at l. ctr. and as wmk.

69	1/2 DINAR	15.10.1973. Green and m/c. Man w/camel and trees at l. Landscape w/sheep and	1.50	8.50	22.50

72	10 DINARS	15.10.1973. Lilac and m/c. Refinery in background at ctr. Montage w/students, column, train and drummers on back.	FV	20.00	100.00

1980 ISSUE

#74–75 and 77 Bourgaiba at r. and as wmk.

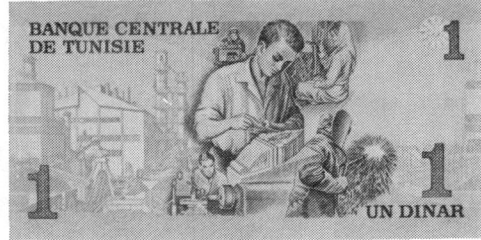

70	1 DINAR	15.10.1973. Blue, green and m/c. Bldg. at r. Industrial scenes on back.	1.50	4.50	18.50

74	1 DINAR	15.10.1980. Red-brown on dk. red and m/c unpt. Amphitheater at ctr. Town w/sea and mountain on back.	FV	2.50	16.50
75	5 DINARS	15.10.1980. Brown, green and m/c. Bldgs. at ctr. Bridge and hills at l. on back.	FV	6.50	22.50
76	10 DINARS	15.10.1980. Blue-green and bistre. Bourguiba at l., bldg. at ctr. Reservoir at ctr. on back.	FV	15.00	43.50

Cat. #	Denomination	Date, description	VG	VF	Unc
77	20 DINARS	15.10.1980. Dk. blue, brown and m/c. Amphitheater at ctr. Rowboats at dockside on back.	FV	30.00	85.00
78	Held in reserve.				

1983 ISSUE

#79–81 Bourguiba on face and as wmk.

79	5 DINARS	3.11.1983. Red-brown on lilac unpt. Bourguiba at l., desert scene at bottom ctr. Hydroelectric dam at ctr. r. on back.	FV	6.00	18.50

80	10 DINARS	3.11.1983. Blue and lilac on m/c unpt. Workers at lower l. ctr., Bourguiba at ctr., off shore oil rig at r. Modern bldg at ctr., old city gateways at r. on back.	FV	12.50	35.00

Cat. #	Denomination	Date, description	VG	VF	Unc
81	20 DINARS	3.11.1983. Lt. and dk. blue on green unpt. Bourguiba at l., bldg. at bottom ctr. Harbor on back.	FV	22.00	67.50

1986 ISSUE

84	10 DINARS	20.3.1986. Yellow-brown on green unpt. Bourguiba at l. ctr. and as wmk., agricultural scene at bottom ctr. Off-shore oil rig at l. ctr. on back.	FV	FV	27.50
85	Held in reserve.				

1992–93 ISSUE

86	5 DINARS	7.11.1993. Black, olive-brown and green. Head of Hannibal at l. ctr. and as wmk., harbor fortress at r. "Dec. 7, 1987" collage at l. ctr. on back.	FV	FV	10.00
87	10 DINARS	7.11.1994. Purple and red on m/c unpt. Ibn Khaldoun t ctr. and as wmk. Open book of *7 Novembre* at l. ctr. on back.	FV	FV	18.50

Cat. #	Denomination	Date, description	VG	VF	Unc
88	20 DINARS	7.11.1992. Deep purple, blue-black and red-brown on m/c unpt. K. Ettounsi on horse-back at l. ctr., his head as wmk., bldgs. in background. Montage of city view; a '7' over flag on stylized dove at ctr. on back.	FV	FV	35.00
89	50 DINARS				Expected new issue.

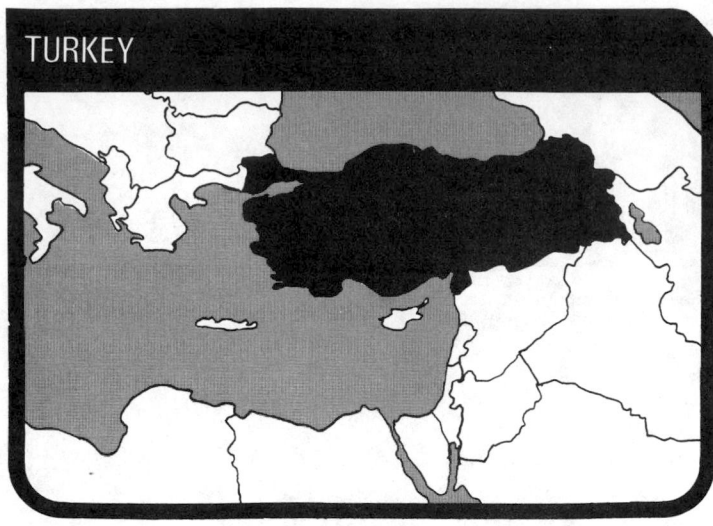

TURKEY

The Republic of Turkey, a parliamentary democracy of the Near East located partially in Europe and partially in Asia between the Black and the Mediterranean seas, has an area of 301,382 sq. mi. (780,580 sq. km.) and a population of 59.9 million. Capital: Ankara. Turkey exports cotton, hazelnuts, and tobacco, and enjoys a virtual monopoly in meerschaum.

The Ottoman Turks, a tribe from Central Asia, first appeared in the early 13th century, and by the 17th century had established the Ottoman Empire which stretched from the Persian Gulf to the southern frontier of Poland, and from the Caspian Sea to the Algerian plateau. The defeat of the Turkish navy by the Holy League in 1571, and of the Turkish forces besieging Vienna in 1683, began the steady decline of the Ottoman Empire which, accelerated by the rise of nationalism, contracted its European border, and by the end of World War I deprived it of its Arab lands. The present Turkish boundaries were largely fixed by the Treaty of Lausanne in 1923. The sultanate and caliphate, the political and spiritual ruling institutions of the old empire, were separated and the sultanate abolished in 1922 by Mustafa Kemal Atatürk. On Oct. 29, 1923, Turkey formally became a republic and Atatürk was selected as the first president.

MONETARY SYSTEM
1 Kurush (Gurush, Piastre) = 40 Para
1 Lira (Livre, Pound) = 100 Piastres

Türkiye Cümhuriyet Merkaz Bankasi
Central Bank of Turkey

1961–65 ISSUE
Central Bank Law 11 Haziran 1930

#95, 96 and 106 Pres. K. Atatürk at r. and as wmk. Sign. varieties. Printer: DBM-A (w/o imprint).

Cat. #	Denomination	Date, description	VG	VF	Unc
95	5 LIRA	L.1930 (25.10.1961). Blue w/orange, blue and m/c guilloche. Back blue; 3 peasant women w/baskets of hazelnuts at ctr.	1.75	4.00	25.00
96	5 LIRA	L.1930 (4.1.1965). Blue-green. Back blue-gray.	1.75	4.00	25.00

Cat. #	Denomination	Date, description	VG	VF	Unc
106	50 LIRA	L.1930 (1.6.1964). Brown on m/c unpt. Different sign. Soldier holding rifle at ctr. on back.	2.50	7.50	30.00

#112–114 Pres. Atatürk at r. and as wmk. Printer: DBM-A (w/o imprint).

Cat. #	Denomination	Date, description	VG	VF	Unc
112	100 LIRA	L.1930 (15.3.1962). Olive on orange and m/c guilloche. Park w/bridge in Ankara on back.	5.00	17.50	50.00

Cat. #	Denomination	Date, description	VG	VF	Unc
113	100 LIRA	L.1930 (1.10.1964). Like #112, but guilloche blue, lilac and m/c. Different sign.	5.00	17.50	50.00
114 (115)	500 LIRA	L.1930 (1.12.1962). Brown. Square w/ mosque on back.	25.00	60.00	200.00

Cat. #	Denomination	Date, description	VG	VF	Unc
120	50 LIRA	L.1970 (2.8.1971). Brown on m/c unpt. Like #106 except for different inscription at ctr., Pres. Atatürk at r., and as wmk. and 2 sign. Soldier holding rifle on back. Series O-Y.	1.00	2.50	6.00

1966–69 ISSUE

Central Bank Law 11 Haziran 1930

#115–119 Pres. Atatürk at r. and as wmk. 3 sign. Printer: DBM-A (w/o imprint).

1971–82 ISSUES

#121–128 Pres. Atatürk at r. and as wmk.

121	5 LIRA	L.1970. Like #117. 2 sign.	.10	.25	.60

115 (117)	5 LIRA	L.1930 (8.1.1968). Grayish-purple on m/c unpt. Waterfalls on back.	.10	.50	1.00
116 (118)	10 LIRA	L.1930 (4.7.1966). Green on m/c unpt. Lighthouse at l., town view at ctr. on back.	.25	.75	2.50

122	10 LIRA	L.1970. Like #118.	.10	.40	1.00

117 (119)	20 LIRA	L.1930 (15.6.1966). Red-brown on m/c unpt. Back dull brown on pale green unpt., monument at l., tomb of Atatürk at ctr. on back.	.75	1.50	5.00
118 (114)	100 LIRA	L.1930 (17.3.1969). Like #112 but modified guilloche in pinkish-red, blue and m/c. Different sign.	7.50	20.00	60.00
119 (116)	500 LIRA	L.1930 (3.6.1968). Purple, brown and m/c. Like #114.	10.00	40.00	150.00

1971 ISSUE

Law of 14 Ocak (January 26), 1970 and 11 Haziran 1930

Printer: DBM-A (w/o imprint).

123	20 LIRA	L.1970. Like #119.			
		a. Black sign. 2 varieties.	.10	.50	1.00
		b. Brown sign.	.10	.30	.75

| 124 | 50 LIRA | *L.1970.* Dk. brown on m/c unpt. New portr. at r. Fountain on back. 2 sign. varieties. | .25 | .40 | 1.00 |

| 125 | 100 LIRA | *L.1970 (15.5.1972).* Blue-green on m/c unpt. Face similar to #124. Back brown; Mt. Ararat. 2 sign. varieties. | .30 | .60 | 1.50 |

| 126 | 500 LIRA | *L.1970 (1.9.1971).* Blue-black and dk. green on m/c unpt. Gate of the University of Istanbul on back. 2 sign. varieties. | .75 | 2.00 | 4.50 |

Cat. #	Denomination	Date, description	VG	VF	Unc
127	1000 LIRA	*L.1970.* Deep purple and brown-violet on m/c unpt. River w/boat and suspension bridge on back. Sign. varieties.	1.00	2.50	6.50
128	5000 LIRA	*L.1970 (2.11.1981).* Brown and orange on m/c unpt. Atatürk at r. Mevlana Museum at ctr. and seated Mevlana at ctr. r. on back. (140 x 72 mm).	FV	7.50	20.00

| 129 | 10,000 LIRA | *L.1970 (1982).* Purpl, dk. green and dk. brown on m/c unpt. Atatürk at r. Architect M. Sinan and mosque he designed on back. Sign. varieties. Series A;B. | FV | 10.00 | 30.00 |

1984–95 ISSUES

Law 14 Ocak 1970

#130–142 Pres. Atatürk at r. and as wmk.

| 130 | 10 LIRA | *L.1970.* Dull gray-green on m/c unpt. Young boy and girl in medallion in unpt. at ctr. Children presenting flowers to Atatürk on back. | .05 | .15 | .40 |
| 130A | 10 LIRA | *L.1970.* Like #130 but black on m/c unpt. | .05 | .20 | .85 |

132	100 LIRA	*L.1970 (1984).* Violet and brown on m/c unpt. Bldg., castle on hill, document and M. A. Ersoy on back.			
		a. Wmk.: Head sm. bust facing r., dotted security thread.	.10	.25	.85
		b. Wmk.: Head lg. bust facing 3/4 r.	.05	.15	.50

Cat. #	Denomination	Date, description	VG	VF	Unc
133	500 LIRA	L.1970 (1984). Blue on m/c unpt. Tower monument at l. ctr. on back. Wmk. varieties.	.15	.35	1.25

| 134 | 1000 LIRA | L.1970 (1986). Blue-violet on m/c unpt. One dot for blind at lower l. Coastline at l., Fatin Sultan Mehmed at ctr. r. on back. | .20 | .45 | 1.50 |

| 135 | 5000 LIRA | L.1970 (1985). Dk. brown and olive-green on m/c unpt. 2 dots for blind at bottom l. Seated Mevlana at l. ctr., Mevlana Museum at ctr. on back. | FV | 1.00 | 3.50 |

Cat. #	Denomination	Date, description	VG	VF	Unc
136	5000 LIRA	L.1970 (ca.1992). Deep brown and deep green on m/c unpt. Face like #135. Afsin-Elbistan thermal power plant on back.	FV	.75	2.50

137	10,000 LIRA	L.1970. Purple and deep green on m/c unpt. 3 dots for blind at lower l. Back green; mosque at l., Mimar Sinan at ctr. on back.			
		a. Darker green back.	FV	1.50	5.00
		b. Lt. green back.	FV	.75	1.50

| 138 | 20,000 LIRA | L.1970 (1988). Red-brown and violet on m/c unpt. Central Bank bldg. in Ankara at l. ctr. on back. | FV | FV | 7.50 |
| 138A | 20,000 LIRA | L.1970 (1995). Like #138 but w/yellow unpt. Red ign. Series G–. | FV | FV | 2.25 |

| 139 | 50,000 LIRA | L.1970 (1989). Black and blue-green on m/c unpt. Atatürk at r. National Parliament House in Ankara on back. | FV | FV | 15.00 |
| 139A | 50,000 LIRA | L.1970 (1995). Like #139 but w/value in gray on back. Sereis K–. | FV | FV | 3.50 |

Cat. #	Denomination	Date, description	VG	VF	Unc
140	100,000 LIRA	L.1970 (1991). Reddish brown, dk. brown and black on m/c unpt. Equestrian statue of Atatürk at ctr. Children presenting flowers to Atatürk on back.	FV	FV	5.00

| 141 | 250,000 LIRA | L.1970 (1992). Blue-gray, dk. green and violet on m/c unpt. Triangular security device at upper r. Kizilkale Fortress at Alunya on back. | FV | FV | 12.00 |

| 142 | 500,000 LIRA | L.1970 (1993). Purple, blue-black and violet on m/c unpt. Square security device at upper r. Canakkale Martyrs Monument on back. | FV | FV | 20.00 |
| 143 | 1 MILLION LIRA | L.1970 (1995). Claret red and blue-gray on m/c unpt. Atatürk dam in Sani lurfa on back. | FV | FV | 35.00 |

TURKMENISTAN

The Turkmenistan Republic (formerly the Turkmen Soviet Socialist Republic) covers the territory of the Trans-Caspian Region of Turkestan, the Charjiui Vilayet of Bukhara and the part of Khiva located on the right bank of the Oxus. Bordered on the north by the Autonomous Kara-Kalpak Republic (a constituent of Uzbekistan), by Iran and Afghanistan on the south, by the Usbek Republic on the east and the Caspian Sea on the west. It has an area of 186,400 sq. mi. (488,100 sq. km.) and a population of 3.5 million. Capital: Ashkhabad (formerly Poltoratsk). Main occupation is agricultural products including cotton and maize. It is rich in minerals, oil, coal, sulphur and salt and is also famous for its carpets, Turkoman horses and Karakul sheep.

The Turkomans arrived in Transcaspia as nomadic Seluk Turks in the 11th century. It often became subjected to one of the neighboring states. Late in the 19th century the Czarist Russians invaded with their first victory at Kyzyl Arvat in 1877, arriving in Ashkhabad in 1882 resulting in submission of the Turkmen tribes. By Mar. 18, 1884 the Transcaspian province of Russian Turkestan was formed. During WW I the Czarist government tried to conscript the Turkmen; this led to a revolt in Oct. 1916 under the leadership of Aziz Chapykov. In 1918 the Turks captured Baku from the Red army and the British sent a contingent to Merv to prevent a German-Turkish offensive toward Afghanistan and India. In mid-1919 a Bureau of Turkistan Moslem Communist Organization was formed in Moscow hoping to develop one large republic including all surrounding Turkic areas within a Soviet federation. A Turkistan Autonomous Soviet Socialist Republic was formed and plans to partition Turkistan into five republics according to the principle of nationalities was quickly implemented by Joseph Stalin. On Oct. 27, 1924, Turkmenistan became a Soviet Socialist Republic and was accepted as a member of the U.S.S.R. on Jan. 29, 1925. The Bureau of T.M.C.O. was disbanded in 1934. In Aug. 1990 the Turkmen Supreme Soviet adopted a declaration of sovereignty followed by a declaration of independence in Oct. 1991 joining the Commonwealth of Independent States in Dec. A new constitution was adopted in 1992 providing for an executive presidency.

REPUBLIC

Türkmenistanyñ Merkezi Döwlet Banky

Central Bank of Turkmenistan

1993 (ND) ISSUE

#1–8 wmk: Rearing Arabian horse.

Cat.#	Denomination	Date, description	VG	VF	Unc
1	1 MANAT	ND (1993). Brown and tan on m/c unpt. Ylymar Academy at ctr., native craft at r. Shield at l., temple *ILARSLANYÑ YADY-GARLIGI* at ctr. Wmk: Rearing horse.	FV	FV	.40

| 2 | 5 MANAT | ND (1993). Bldg. Horse and bldg. on back. | FV | FV | 1.35 |

#3–7 Pres. S. Niazov at r.

Cat.#	Denomination	Date, description	VG	VF	Unc
3	10 MANAT	ND (1993). Bldg. at ctr. Bldg. on back.	FV	FV	2.00

| 4 | 20 MANAT | ND (1993); 1995. National library at ctr. | FV | FV | 2.50 |

| 5 | 50 MANAT | ND (1993); 1995. Monument at ctr. Anew mosque ruins on back. | FV | FV | 3.00 |

Cat.#	Denomination	Date, description	VG	VF	Unc
6	100 MANAT	ND (1993); 1995. Presidential Palace at ctr. Sultan Sanjaryn mausoleum on back.	FV	FV	5.00

| 7 | 500 MANAT | ND (1993). National theatre at ctr. Hanymym mausoleum on back. | FV | FV | 15.00 |
| 8 | 1000 MANAT | 1995. | FV | FV | 20.00 |

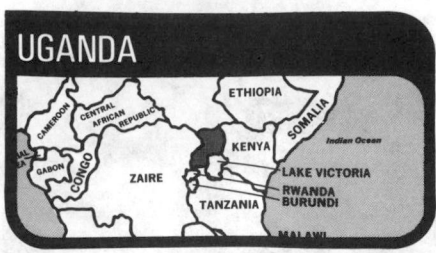

The Republic of Uganda, a former British protectorate located astride the equator in east-central Africa, has an area of 91,134 sq. mi. (236,036 sq. km.) and a population of 16.6 million. Capital: Kampala. Agriculture, including livestock, is the basis of the economy; there is some mining of copper, tin, gold and lead. Coffee, cotton, copper and tea are exported.

Uganda was first visited by Arab slavers in the 1830s. They were followed in the 1860s by British explorers searching for the headwaters of the Nile. The explorers, and the missionaries who followed them into the Lake Victoria region of south-central Africa in 1877–1879, found well developed African kingdoms dating back several centuries. In 1894 the local native Kingdom of Buganda was established as a British protectorate that was extended in 1896 to encompass an area substantially the same as the present Republic of Uganda. The protectorate was given a ministerial form of government in 1955, full internal self-government on March 1, 1962, and complete independence on Oct. 9, 1962. Uganda is a member of the Commonwealth of Nations. The president is Chief of State and Head of Government.

Notes of East African Currency Board circulated before Bank of Uganda notes were available. Also see East Africa.

MONETARY SYSTEM
1 Shilling = 100 Cents

REPLACEMENT NOTES
#5A–26, denominations use prefixes as follows: 5 and 10 Shillings, Z/1; 20 Shillings Y/1; 50 Shillings X/1; 100 Shillings W/1; 500 Shillings U/1; 1000 Shillings T/1; 5000 Shillings S/1. #27–31, ZZ prefix.

Bank of Uganda

1966 ISSUE

#1–5 sign. titles: *GOVERNOR* and *SECRETARY*. Wmk: Hand.

Cat. #	Denomination	Date, description	VG	VF	Unc
1	5 SHILLINGS	ND (1966). Dk. blue on m/c unpt. Arms at r. River and waterfall on back.	.65	2.00	4.50

Cat. #	Denomination	Date, description	VG	VF	Unc
2	10 SHILLINGS	ND (1966). Brown on m/c unpt. Arms at ctr. Workers picking cotton on back.	1.35	4.00	10.00

			VG	VF	Unc
3	20 SHILLINGS	ND (1966). Violet on m/c unpt. Arms at l. African animals on back.	1.00	3.00	7.50

			VG	VF	Unc
4	100 SHILLINGS	ND (1966). Green on m/c unpt. Crested crane at l., w/o *FOR BANK OF UGANDA* just below value at ctr. Bldg. on back.	20.00	85.00	600.00

			VG	VF	Unc
5	100 SHILLINGS	ND (1966). Green. Like #4 but w/text: *FOR BANK OF UGANDA* under value.	1.00	2.00	5.00

1973–77 ISSUE

SIGNATURE VARIETIES			
1	GOVERNOR SECRETARY	2	GOVERNOR SECRETARY

#5A–9 Pres. Idi Amin at l. Wmk: Crested crane.

Cat. #	Denomination	Date, description	VG	VF	Unc
5A	5 SHILLINGS	ND (1977). Blue and m/c. Woman picking coffee beans on back.	.50	1.00	2.75

Cat. #	Denomination	Date, description	VG	VF	Unc
8	50 SHILLINGS	ND (1973). Blue on m/c unpt. Hydroelectric dam on back.			
		a. Sign. titles: *GOVERNOR* and *DIRECTOR*.	8.50	40.00	175.00
		b. Sign. titles: *GOVERNOR* and *SECRETARY*. Sign. 1.	2.00	5.00	20.00
		c. Sign. titles as b. Sign. 2.	.50	1.35	4.00

			VG	VF	Unc
6	10 SHILLINGS	ND (1973). Brown on m/c unpt. Elephants, antelope and hippopotamus on back.			
		a. Sign. titles: *GOVERNOR* and *DIRECTOR*.	5.00	15.00	85.00
		b. Sign. titles: *GOVERNOR* and *SECRETARY*. Sign. 1.	1.00	2.50	8.00
		c. Sign. titles as b. Sign. 2.	.35	1.00	3.00

			VG	VF	Unc
9	100 SHILLINGS	ND (1973). Green on m/c unpt. Scene of lake and hills on back.			
		a. Sign. titles: *GOVERNOR* and *DIRECTOR*.	8.00	30.00	135.00
		b. Sign. titles: *GOVERNOR* and *SECRETARY*. Sign. 1.	3.00	10.00	45.00
		c. Sign. titles as b. Sign. 2.	.75	2.00	6.00

1979 ISSUE

#10–14 Bank of Uganda at l. Sign. titles: *GOVERNOR* and *DIRECTOR*. Wmk: Crested crane's head.

			VG	VF	Unc
7	20 SHILLINGS	ND (1973). Purple on m/c unpt. Lg. bldg. on back.			
		a. Sign. titles: *GOVERNOR* and *DIRECTOR*.	7.50	25.00	95.00
		b. Sign. titles: *GOVERNOR* and *SECRETARY*. Sign. 1.	1.00	3.00	10.00
		c. Sign. titles as b. Sign. 2.	.75	2.25	7.00

			VG	VF	Unc
10	5 SHILLINGS	ND (1979). Blue on m/c unpt. Back like #5A.	.10	.25	1.25

Cat. #	Denomination	Date, description	VG	VF	Unc
11	10 SHILLINGS	ND (1979). Brown and m/c. Back like #6.			
		a. Lt. printing on bank.	.25	1.50	5.00
		b. Dk. printing on bank.	.30	.90	2.75

12	20 SHILLINGS	ND (1979). Purple on m/c unpt. Back like #7.			
		a. Lt. printing on bank.	.40	2.50	6.50
		b. Dk. printing on bank.	.25	.75	3.00

13	50 SHILLINGS	ND (1979). Dk. blue, purple, and dk. blue-green on m/c unpt. Back like #8.			
		a. Lt. printing on bank.	5.00	17.50	100.00
		b. Dk. printing on bank.	.45	1.35	4.00

14	100 SHILLINGS	ND (1979). Green on m/c unpt. Back like #9.			
		a. Lt. printing on bank.	1.50	4.00	10.00
		b. Dk. printing on bank.	.85	2.50	7.50

1982 ISSUE

#15–19 arms at l. Sign. titles: *GOVERNOR* and *SECRETARY*. Wmk: Crested crane's head.

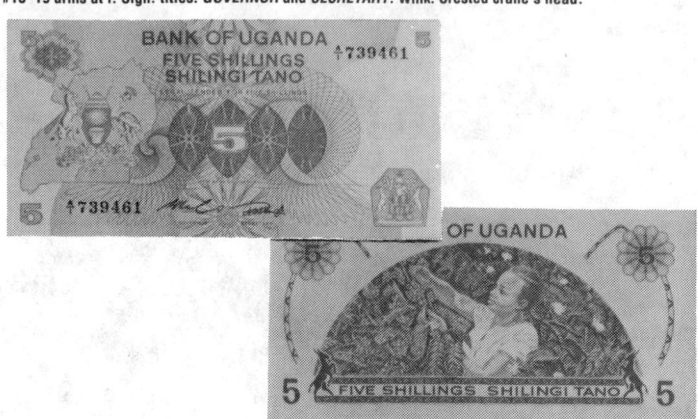

Cat. #	Denomination	Date, description	VG	VF	Unc
15	5 SHILLINGS	ND (1982). Olive-green and m/c. Back like #5A.	.10	.30	.90

16	10 SHILLINGS	ND (1982). Purple and m/c. Back like #6.	.15	.40	1.75

17	20 SHILLINGS	ND (1982). Green, red and m/c. Back like #7.	.30	1.50	4.50

18	50 SHILLINGS	ND (1982). Brown and m/c. Back like #8.			
		a. Sign. titles: *GOVERNOR* and *SECRETARY*.	.30	1.25	3.50
		b. Sign. titles: *GOVERNOR* and *DEPUTY GOVERNOR*.	.25	1.00	3.00

19	100 SHILLINGS	ND (1982). Red-violet, orange and m/c. Back like #9.			
		a. Sign. titles: *GOVERNOR* and *SECRETARY*.	.75	2.50	7.50
		b. Sign. titles: *GOVERNOR* and *DEPUTY GOVERNOR*. Sm. or lg. prefix letter and # before serial #.	.25	1.00	3.00

1983–85 ISSUE

#20–23 have Pres. Milton Obote at l. on face. Sign. titles: *GOVERNOR* and *DEPUTY GOVERNOR*. Wmk: Hand.

Cat. #	Denomination	Date, description	VG	VF	Unc
20	50 SHILLINGS	ND (1985). Brown on m/c unpt. Back like #18.	.30	.90	2.75
21	100 SHILLINGS	ND (1985). Red-violet on m/c unpt. Back like #19.	.30	1.25	5.00

Cat. #	Denomination	Date, description	VG	VF	Unc
22	500 SHILLINGS	ND (1983). Blue and m/c. Cattle and harvesting on back. Serial # prefix varieties as #19b.	.30	1.25	5.00

Cat. #	Denomination	Date, description	VG	VF	Unc
23	1000 SHILLINGS	ND (1983). Red and m/c. Bldg. on back. Serial # prefix varieties as #19b.	1.50	3.00	12.00

1985–86 ISSUE

Cat. #	Denomination	Date, description	VG	VF	Unc
24	5000 SHILLINGS	1985–86. Purple and m/c. Arms at l. Bldg. w/clock tower at ctr. r. on back.			
		a. Wmk: Hand. 1985.	2.50	8.00	24.00
		b. Wmk: Crested crane. 1986.	.75	2.25	7.00

#25 and 26 face similar to #24. Wmk: Crested crane.

Cat. #	Denomination	Date, description	VG	VF	Unc
25	500 SHILLINGS	1986. Blue and m/c. Back like #22.	.25	.75	2.50

Cat. #	Denomination	Date, description	VG	VF	Unc
26	1000 SHILLINGS	1986. Red and m/c. Back like #23.	.35	1.00	3.00

1987-95 ISSUE

#27–32 arms at upper l., map at ctr. Printer: TDLR.

27	5 SHILLINGS	1987. Brown on m/c unpt. Arms at r. also. African wildlife on back.	.10	.35	1.00

28	10 SHILLINGS	1987. Green on m/c unpt. Arms at r. also. 2 antelope grazing, 2 men fishing in canoe at ctr. on back.	.10	.35	1.25

#29–34 wmk: Crested crane's head.

29	20 SHILLINGS	1987–88. Purple, blue-black and violet on m/c unpt. Modern bldgs. at ctr. r. on back.			
		a. Imprint on back. 1987.	.20	.60	2.50
		b. W/o imprint. 1988.	.05	.25	1.00

Cat. #	Denomination	Date, description	VG	VF	Unc
30	50 SHILLINGS	1987–89. Red, orange and dk. brown on m/c unpt. Parliament bldg. at ctr. r. on back.			
		a. Imprint on back. 1987.	.20	.50	3.00
		b. W/o imprint. 1988; 1989.	.15	.40	1.50

31	100 SHILLINGS	1987–89. Deep blue-violet, black and aqua on m/c unpt. High Court bldg. w/clock tower at ctr. r. on back.			
		a. Sign. titles: *GOVERNOR* and *SECRETARY, TREASURER*. Imprint on back. 1987.	.25	.60	4.50
		b. As a. but w/o imprint on back. 1988.	.15	.25	1.50
		c. As b. but w/sign. titles: *GOVERNOR* and *SECRETARY*. 1994. W/o imprint. 1988.	FV	.20	1.00

32	200 SHILLINGS	1987; 1991. Brown, orange and olive-brown on m/c unpt. Worker in textile factory at ctr. r. on back.			
		a. 1987.	.20	.50	2.25
		b. 1991.	.20	.50	2.25

#33–35 arms at upper ctr.

Cat. #	Denomination	Date, description	VG	VF	Unc
33	500 SHILLINGS	1991–. Dk. brown and deep purple on m/c unpt. Elephant at l., arms at upper ctr. and lower r. Uganda Independence Monument at l., municipal bldg. w/clock tower at ctr. on back.			
		a. Sign. titles: *GOVERNOR* and *SECRETARY, TREASURY*.	.65	1.00	2.50
		b. Sign. titles: *GOVERNOR* and *SECRETARY*.	FV	.65	1.75

Cat. #	Denomination	Date, description	VG	VF	Unc
34	1000 SHILLINGS	1991. Black, deep brown-violet and dk. green n on m/c unpt. Farmers at l., arms at upper ctr. and lower r. Grain storage facility at ctr. on back.			
		a. Sign. titles: *GOVERNOR* and *SECRETARY, TREASURY*.	1.25	2.00	5.00
		b. Sign titles: *GOVERNOR* and *SECRETARY*.	FV	1.25	3.00

1993–94 ISSUE

35	500 SHILLINGS	1994. Like #36. Segmented foil over security thread. Ascending serial # at l.	FV	FV	2.00
36	1000 SHILLINGS	1994. Like #34. Segmented foil over security thread. Ascending serial # at l.	FV	1.25	3.00
37	5000 SHILLINGS	1993. Red-violet, deep purple and dk. green on m/c unpt. Lake Bunyoni, terraces at l. Railroad cards being loaded unto Kaawa Ferry at ctr., plant at lower r. on back.	FV	6.00	11.00
38	10,000 SHILLINGS	(1996).	FV	11.00	20.00

CAUTION: The Bank of Uganda recently had sold demonetized notes, most of which were being made available for only $1.00 a piece. Condition of notes thus sold is not reported. A listing of some pieces *NOT* available from the bank include #4, 6a, 7a, 8a and b, 9a and b, 13a, 14a, 16b, 23, and 24a and b.

The Ukraine (formerly the Ukrainian Soviet Socialist Republic) is bordered by Russia to the east, Russia and Belarus to the north, Poland, Slovakia and Hungary to the west, Romania and Moldova to the southwest and in the south by the Black Sea and the Sea of Azov. It has an area of 233,088 sq. mi. (603,700 sq. km.) and a population of 51.9 million. Capital: Kyiv (Kiev). Ukraine was the site of the Chernobyl nuclear power station disaster in 1986. Coal, grain, vegetables and heavy industrial machinery are major exports.

The territory of Ukraine has been inhabited for over 30,000 years. As the result of its location, Ukraine has served as the gateway to Europe for millennia and its early history has been recorded by Arabic, Greek, Roman, as well as Ukrainian historians.

Ukraine, which was known as *Rus'* until the sixteenth century (and from which the name Russia was derived in the 17th century), became the major political and cultural center of Eastern Europe in the 9th century. The Rus' Kingdom, under a dynasty of Varangian origin, due to its position on the intersection of the north-south Scandinavia to Byzantium and the east-west Orient ot Europe trade routes, became a focal point of world trade. At its apex Rus' stretched from the Baltic to the Black Sea and from the upper Volga River in the east, almost to the Vistula River in the west. It has family ties to many European dynasties. In 988 knyaz (king) Volodymyr adopted Christianity from Byzantium. With it came church books written in the Cyrillic alphabet, which originated in Bulgaria. The Mongol invasion in 1240 brought an end to the might of the Rus' Kingdom.

In the seventeenth century, after almost four hundred years of Mongol, Lithuanian, Polish, and Turkish domination, the Cossack State under Hetman Bohdan Khmelnytsky regained Ukrainian independence. The Hetman State lasted until the mid-eighteenth century and was followed by a period of foreign rule: Eastern Ukraine was controlled by Russia, which enforced russification through introduction of the Russian language and prohibiting the use of the Ukrainian language in schools, books and public life. Western Ukraine came under relatively benign Austro-Hungarian rule.

With the disintegration of the Russian and Austro-Hungarian Empires in 1917 and 1918, Eastern Ukraine declared its full independence on January 22, 1918 and Western Ukraine followed suit on November 1 of that year. On January 22, 1919 both parts united into one state that had to defend itself on three fronts: from the "Red" Bolsheviks and their puppet Ukrainian Soviet Republic formed in Kharkiv, from the "White" czarist Russian forces, and from Poland. Ukraine lost the war. In 1920 Eastern Ukraine was occupied by the Bolsheviks and in 1922 was incorporated into the Soviet Union. There followed a brief resurgence of Ukrainian language and culture until Stalin suppressed it in 1928. The artificial famine-genocide of 1932-33 killed 7-10 million Ukrainians, and Stalinist purges in the mid-1930s took a heavy toll. Western Ukraine was partitioned between Poland, Romania, Hungary and Czechoslovakia.

During the period of independence 1917-1920, Ukraine issued its own currency in Karbovanets denominations under the Central Rada of social-democrats (#1-11) and in Hryvnia denominations during the monarchy of Hetman Pavlo Skoropadsky (#12-19 and #25-30). During WW II German occupation forces issued Karbowanez currency.

On August 24, 1991 Ukraine once again declared its independence. On December 1, 1991 over 90% of Ukraine's electorate approved full independence from the Soviet Union. On December 5, 1991 the Ukrainian Parliament abrogated the 1922 treaty which incorporated Ukraine into the Soviet Union. Later, Leonid Kravchuk was elected president by a 65% majority.

During the changeover from the Ruble currency of the Soviet Union to the Karbovanets of Ukraine, as a transition measure and to restrict unlicensed export of scarce goods, coupon cards (202 x 82mm), similar to ration cards, were issued in various denominations (#80). They were valid for one month and were given to employees in amounts equal to their pay. Each card contained multiples of 1, 3, 5, and sometimes 10 Karbovanets valued coupons, to be cut apart. They were supposed to be used for purchases together with ruble notes. In January 1992 Ukraine began issuing individual coupons in Karbovanets denominations (printed in France and dated 1991), which are presently functioning as sole currency (#81–).

Ukraine is a charter member of the United Nations and has inherited the third largest nuclear arsenal in the world, which by recent agreement with the USA will be dismantled within the next decade. Ukrainians in the homeland and the diaspora make up 1% of the world's population.

УКРАЇНСЬКА Р.С.Р

КУПОН Ruble Control Coupons

Cat. #	Denomination	Date, description	VG	VF	Unc
82	3 KARBOVANTSI	1991. Greenish-gray and pale orange on yellow unpt. Back greenish gray.	.05	.10	.20

Cat. #	Denomination	Date, description	VG	VF	Unc
83	5 KARBOVANTSIV	1991. Dull blue-violet and pale orange on yellow unpt. Back lt. blue.			
		a. Issued note.	.05	.20	.40
		b. W/error in text on back.	.50	1.50	4.00

Cat. #	Denomination	Date, description	VG	VF	Unc
84	10 KARBOVANTSIV	1991. Pink and pale orange on yellow unpt. Back red.	.05	.20	.50

Cat. #	Denomination	Date, description	VG	VF	Unc
85	25 KARBOVANTSIV	1991. Red-violet and pale orange on yellow unpt. Back red-violet.	.15	.50	1.50

Cat. #	Denomination	Date, description	VG	VF	Unc
80	100 KARBOVANTSIV	1991. Black text on aqua unpt. Sheet of 28 coupons of various denominations w/registry at ctr. and black circular hand shamp. Uniface.			
		a. Issued full sheet.	—	3.00	5.00
		b. Coupon.	—	.15	.25

Ukranian National Bank

1991 COUPON ISSUE

Originally issued at par and temporarily to be used jointly with Russian rubles in commodity purchases as a means of currency control (similar to Ruble Control Coupons above). They soon became more popular while the ruble slowly depreciated in exchange value. This did not last very long and the karbovanets has now suffered a higher inflation rate than the Russian ruble.

#81–87 Lebbid, Viking sister of the founding brothers, at l. Cathedral of St. Sophia in Kiev at l. ctr. on back. All notes w/o serial #. Wmk: Paper. All denominations had the value, i.e. *3 KRB*, printed sideways with indelable ink at l.

Cat. #	Denomination	Date, description	VG	VF	Unc
81	1 KARBOVANETS	1991. Dull brown and pale orange on yellow unpt. Back dull brown.	.05	.10	.20

Cat. #	Denomination	Date, description	VG	VF	Unc
86	50 KARBOVANTSIV	1991. Blue-green and pale orange on yellow unpt. Back blue-green.	.10	.35	1.00

| 87 | 100 KARBOVANTSIV | 1991. Brown-violet and pale orange on yellow unpt. Back brown-violet. | .50 | 1.50 | 4.50 |

1992 ISSUE

#88–91 founding Viking brothers Kyi, Shchek and Khoryv w/sister Lebbid in bow of boat at l. Backs like #81–87. All notes w/serial #. Wmk. paper.

| 88 | 100 KARBOVANTSIV | 1992. Orange on lilac and ochre unpt. Back orange and gray. | .10 | .40 | 1.75 |

| 89 | 200 KARBOVANTSIV | 1992. Dull brown and silver on lilac and ochre unpt. Back dull brown and gray. | .25 | .85 | 2.50 |

| 90 | 500 KARBOVANTSIV | 1992. Blue-green and silver on lilac and ochre unpt. Back blue-green and gray. | .25 | .85 | 2.50 |

| 91 | 1000 KARBOVANTSIV | 1992. Red-violet and lt. green on lilac and ochre unpt. Back red-violet and gray. | .25 | 1.00 | 3.00 |

1993 ISSUE

#92–93 similar to #88–91, but trident symbol added at l. on face; at r. on back.

| 92 | 2000 KARBOVANTSIV | 1993. Blue and olive-green on aqua and gold unpt. | .35 | 1.00 | 3.00 |

Cat. #	Denomination	Date, description	VG	VF	Unc
93	5000 KARBOVANTSIV	1993; 1995. Red-orange and olive-brown on pale blue and orange-brown unpt.	.15	.50	1.50

#94–97 statue of St. Volodymyr standing w/long cross at l. Bldg. facade at l. on back. Trident at l. on face, at r. on back. Wmk: Ornamental shield repeated in a vertical row.

| 94 | 10,000 KARBOVAN-TSIV | 1993; 1995. Apple green and tan on pale blue and ochre unpt. | .10 | .35 | 1.00 |

| 95 | 20,000 KARBOVAN-TSIV | 1993–95. Lilac and lt. tan on blue and yellow unpt. | .25 | .85 | 2.50 |

| 96 | 50,000 KARBOVAN-TSIV | 1993–94. Dull orange and blue on m/c unpt. | .15 | .50 | 1.50 |

97	100,000 KARBOVAN-TSIV	1993-94. Gray-green and ochre on m/c unpt.			
		a. Prefix letters above serial #. 1993.	.25	1.00	4.00
		b. Prefix letters w/serial #. 1994.	.25	1.00	3.00

#98–99 statue of St. Volodymyr standing w/long cross at r. Opera house at l. ctr. on back.

Cat. #	Denomination	Date, description	VG	VF	Unc
98	200,000 KARBOVAN-TSIV	1993-94. Dull red-brown and lt. blue on aqua and gray unpt.			
		a. Prefix letters above serial #. Wmk: HYB. 1993.	FV	1.35	5.50
		b. Prefix letters w/serial #. Wmk: Trident shield repeated. 1994.	FV	1.25	3.75

| 99 | 500,000 KARBOVAN-TSIV | 1994. Lt. blue and lilac on yellow and gray unpt. Wmk: Trident shield repeated. | FV | 2.50 | 7.50 |

1996 ISSUE

| 100 | 1 MILLION KARBO-VANTSIV | 1995. Dk. brown, orange and blue on m/c unpt. Statue at r. Bldg. on back. | FV | 4.00 | 12.00 |
| 101 | 2 MILLION KARBO-VANTSIV | | | | Expected new issue |

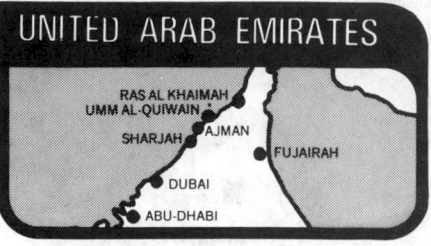

The seven United Arab Emirates (formerly known as the Trucial Sheikhdoms or States), located along the southern shore of the Persian Gulf, are comprised of the Sheikhdoms of Abu Dhabi, Dubai, Sharjah, Ajman, Umm al Qaiwain, Ras al Khaimah and Fujairah. They have a combined area of about 32,000 sq. mi. (83,600 sq. km.) and a population of 1.9 million. Capital: Abu Zaby (Abu Dhabi). Since the oil strikes of 1958–60, the economy has centered on petroleum.

The Trucial States came under direct British influence in 1892 when the maritime truce treaty, enacted after the suppression of pirate activity along the Trucial Coast, was enlarged to enjoin the states from disposing of any territory, or entering into any foreign agreements, without British consent in return for British protection from external aggression. In March of 1971 Britain reaffirmed its decision to terminate its treaty relationships with the Trucial Sheikhdoms, whereupon the seven states joined with Bahrain and Qatar in an effort to form a union of Arab emirates under British protection. When the prospective members failed to agree on terms of union, Bahrain and Qatar declared their respective independence in Aug. and Sept., 1971. Six of the Sheikhdoms united to form the United Arab Emirates on Dec. 2, 1971. Ras al Khaimah joined a few weeks later.

MONETARY SYSTEM
1 Dirham = 1000 Fils

United Arab Emirates Currency Board

#1–6 dhow, camel caravan, palm tree and oil derrick at l. Wmk: Arabian horse's head.

Cat. #	Denomination	Date, description	VG	VF	Unc
1	1 DIRHAM	ND (1973). Green on m/c unpt. Police station on back.	1.00	4.00	12.00

| 2 | 5 DIRHAMS | ND (1973). Purple on m/c unpt. Fort Fujairah on back. | 1.25 | 5.00 | 15.00 |

Cat. #	Denomination	Date, description	VG	VF	Unc
3	10 DIRHAMS	ND (1973). Gray-blue on m/c unpt. Umm Al Qaiwain (aerial photograph) on back.	2.00	8.00	25.00

| 4 | 50 DIRHAMS | ND (1973). Red on m/c unpt. Ruler's Palace of Ajman on back. | 8.00 | 32.50 | 100.00 |

| 5 | 100 DIRHAMS | ND (1973). Olive-green on m/c unpt. Ras al Khaima (village on the Gulf) on back. | 14.00 | 55.00 | 165.00 |

| 6 | 1000 DIRHAMS | ND (1976). Blue on m/c unpt. Fortress on back. | 150.00 | 300.00 | 675.00 |

United Arab Emirates Central Bank

1982 (ND) ISSUE

#7–11 arms at upper ctr., sparrowhawk at l. on back. Wmk: Sparrowhawk's head.

Cat. #	Denomination	Date, description	VG	VF	Unc
7	5 DIRHAMS	ND (1982). Brown on m/c unpt. Arms at ctr., Sharjah Market at r. Seacoast cove w/tower on back.	FV	FV	4.00

| 8 | 10 DIRHAMS | ND (1982). Green on m/c unpt. Arms at ctr., Arab dagger at r. Terraces w/trees at l. ctr. on back. | FV | FV | 7.50 |

| 9 | 50 DIRHAMS | ND (1982). Purple, dk. brown and olive on m/c unpt. Oryx at r. Al Jahilic Fort at l. ctr. on back. | FV | FV | 32.50 |

| 10 | 100 DIRHAMS | ND (1982). Red, violet and black on m/c unpt. Al Fahidie Fort at r. Dubai Trade Ctr. at l. ctr. on back. | FV | FV | 60.00 |

Cat. #	Denomination	Date, description	VG	VF	Unc
11	500 DIRHAMS	ND (1983). Dk. blue, purple and brown on m/c unpt. Sparrowhawk at r. Mosque in Dubai at l. ctr. on back.	FV	FV	250.00

1989–95 ISSUE

#12–15 and 17 similar to #7–11 w/condensed Arabic text in titles and modified designs.

Cat. #	Denomination	Date, description	VG	VF	Unc
12	5 DIRHAMS	1993/AH 1414. Dk. brown, orange and violet on m/c unpt.	FV	FV	3.50
13	10 DIRHAMS	1993/AH 1414. Green and pale olive-green on m/c unpt.	FV	FV	6.50
14	50 DIRHAMS	1995/AH 1415. Purple and violet on m/c unpt.	FV	FV	30.00
15	100 DIRHAMS	1993/AH 1414. Red, violet and black on m/c unpt.	FV	FV	50.00
16 (12)	200 DIRHAMS	1989/AH 1410. Brown, green and m/c. Sharla Court bldg. and Zayed Sprts City on face. Central bank bldg. at l. ctr. on back.	FV	FV	110.00

UNITED STATES

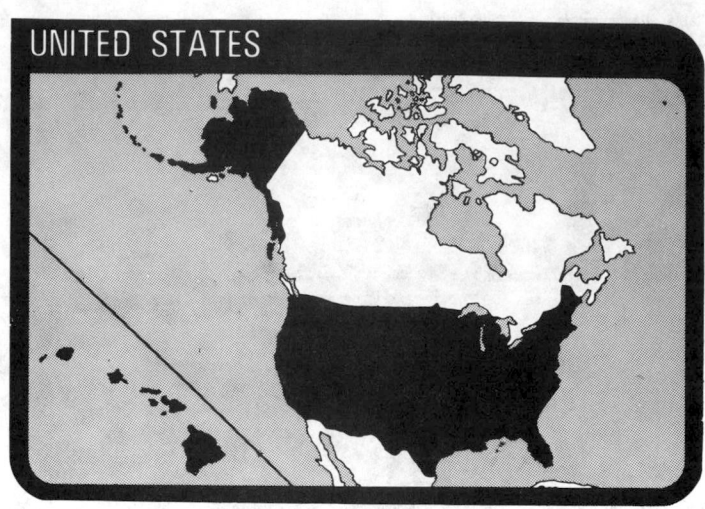

The United States of America as politically organized under the Articles of Confederation consisted of the 13 original British-American colonies — New Hampshire, Massachusetts, Rhode Island, Connecticut, New York, New Jersey, Pennsylvania, Delaware, Virginia, North Carolina, South Carolina, Georgia and Maryland — clustered along the eastern seaboard of North America between the forests of Maine and the marshes of Georgia. Under the Articles of Confederation, the United States had no national capital; Philadelphia, where the "United States in Congress Assembled" met, was the "seat of the government." The population during this formative phase of America's history (1781–1789) was about 3 million, most of whom lived on self-sufficient family farms. Fishing, lumbering and the production of grains for export were major economic endeavors. Rapid strides were also being made in industry and manufacturing, by 1775, the (then) colonies were accounting for one-seventh of the world's production of raw iron.

On the basis of the voyage of John Cabot to the North American mainland in 1497, England claimed the entire continent. The first permanent English settlement was established at Jamestown, Virginia, in 1607. France and Spain also claimed extensive territory in North America. At the end of the French and Indian Wars (1763), England acquired all of the territory east of the Mississippi River, including East and West Florida. From 1776 to 1781, the States were governed by the Continental Congress. From 1781 to 1789, they were organized under the Articles of Confederation, during which period the individual states had the right to issue money. Independence from Great Britain was attained by the American Revolution, 1775–1783. The Constitution which organized and governs the present United States was ratified on Nov. 21, 1788.

1775 Declaration of Independence: 1789 George Washington first president; 1861–1865 civil war and defeat of the Confederate States by the Union. Originally 13 states, in 1959 Alaska joined the Union as 49th and Hawaii as 50th state.

MONETARY SYSTEM
1 Dollar = 100 Cents

Bureau of Engraving and Printing Facilities

FW – Fort Worth, Texas

Note: Small prefix letters *FW* appear by the plate # at lower r. of Treasury seal.

No Destination – Washington D.C.

REPLACEMENT NOTES
All issues have a star at end of serial number.

Redemption:

All government notes of the United States, since issue of the Demand Notes in 1861, are still valid as legal tender. The different types of currency are treated in a number of specialized catalogs of such as the following:

References:

Friedberg, Robert, *Paper Money of the United States*

Hickman, John and Oakes, Dean, *Standard Catalog of National Bank Notes,* 2nd edition.

Krause, Chester L. and Lemke, Robert F., *United States Paper Money*, 14th edition.

Oakes, Dean and Schwartz, John, *Standard Guide to Small Size U.S. Paper Money*, 1st edition.

Detailed information, as given in these catalogs, is not repeated here. The following listing is limited to the individual types and their principal varieties. Sign. varieties in earlier issues are not detailed.

United States Notes

Value at l., red circular Treasury seal at r.

SERIES OF 1963

Cat. #	Denomination	Date, Description	VF	XF	Unc
382	2 DOLLARS	1963.	3.00	3.50	4.50
		a. 1963A.	3.00	3.50	4.50
383	5 DOLLARS	1963.	FV	6.50	10.00

SERIES OF 1966

384	100 DOLLARS	1966.	FV	115.00	200.00
		a. 1966A.	FV	130.00	700.00

Federal Reserve Notes

Circular black FRB indicator at l., green circular Treasury seal at r.

A-1: Boston	G-7: Chicago
B-2: New York	H-8: St. Louis
C-3: Philadelphia	I-9: Minneapolis
D-4: Cleveland	J-10: Kansas City
E-5: Richmond	K-11: Dallas
F-6: Atlanta	L-12: San Francisco

SIGNATURE VARIETIES		
Series	**Treasurer**	**Secretary**
1963	Kathryn O'Hay Granahan	C. Douglas Dillon
1963A	Kathryn O'Hay Granahan	Henry H. Fowler
1963B	Kathryn O'Hay Granahan	Joseph W. Barr
1969	Dorothy Andrews Elston	David M. Kennedy
1969A	Dorothy Andrews Kabis	David M. Kennedy
1969B	Dorothy Andrews Kabis	John B. Connally
1969C	Romana Acosta Banuelos	John B. Connally
1969D	Romana Acosta Banuelos	George P. Schultz
1974	Francine I. Neff	William E. Simon
1977	Azie Taylor Morton	W. Michael Blumenthal
1977A	Azie Taylor Morton	J. William Miller
1981	Angela M. Buchanan	Donald T. Regan
1981A	Katherine Davalos Ortega	Donald T. Regan
1985	Katherine Davalos Ortega	John A. Baker III
1988	Katherine Davalos Ortega	Nicholas F. Brady
1988A	Catalina Vasquez Villapando	Nicholas F. Brady
1993	Mary Ellen Withrow	Lloyd Bentsen

BANKNOTE DESIGNS	
1 DOLLAR	Portr. G. Washington. Great Seal flanking ONE on back.
2 DOLLAR	Portr. T. Jefferson. Monticello on back to 1963, signing of the Declaration of Independence, 1976 series.
5 DOLLAR	Portr. A. Lincoln. Lincoln Memorial on back.
10 DOLLAR	Portr. A. Hamilton. U.S. Treasury bldg. on back.
20 DOLLAR	Portr. A. Jackson. White House on back.
50 DOLLAR	Portr. U. S. Grant. U.S. Capital bldg. on back.
100 DOLLAR	Portr. B. Franklin. Independence Hall on back.

SERIES OF 1963

Market valuations are for the most common types of each denomination. Federal Reserve Branch code letters appear in parentheses.

Cat. #	Denomination	Date, Description	VF	XF	Unc
443	1 DOLLAR	1963. (A-L).	FV	FV	3.00
		a. 1963A. (A-L).	FV	FV	3.00
		b. 1963B. (B; E; G; J; L).	FV	FV	2.50

444	5 DOLLARS	1963. (A-D; F-H; J-L).	FV	FV	14.00
		a. 1963A. (A-L).	FV	FV	12.00

445	10 DOLLARS	1963. (A-H; J-L).	FV	FV	20.00
		a. 1963A. (A-L).	FV	FV	20.00

Cat. #	Denomination	Date, Description	VF	XF	Unc
446	20 DOLLARS	1963. (A-B; D-H; J-L).	FV	FV	35.00
		a. 1963A. (A-L).	FV	FV	30.00

			VF	XF	Unc
447	50 DOLLARS	1963A. (A L).	FV	FV	75.00

			VF	XF	Unc
448	100 DOLLARS	1963A. (A-L).	FV	FV	135.00

SERIES OF 1969

			VF	XF	Unc
449	1 DOLLAR	1969. (A-L).	FV	FV	2.50
		a. 1969A. (A-L).	FV	FV	2.50
		b. 1969B. (A-L).	FV	FV	2.50
		c. 1969C. (B; D-L).	FV	FV	2.50
		d. 1969D. (A-L).	FV	FV	2.50
450	5 DOLLARS	1969. (A-L).	FV	FV	10.00
		a. 1969A. (A-L).	FV	FV	12.00
		b. 1969B. (A-L).	FV	FV	14.00
		c. 1969C. (A-L).	FV	FV	10.00
451	10 DOLLARS	1969. (A-L).	FV	FV	20.00
		a. 1969A. (A-L).	FV	FV	25.00
		b. 1969B. (A-L).	FV	FV	18.00
		c. 1969C. (A-L).	FV	FV	16.00
452	20 DOLLARS	1969. (A-L).	FV	FV	30.00
		a. 1969A. (A-L).	FV	FV	30.00
		b. 1969B. (B; D-L).	FV	FV	40.00
		c. 1969C. (A-L).	FV	FV	30.00
453	50 DOLLARS	1969. (A-L).	FV	FV	75.00
		a. 1969A. (A-L).	FV	FV	70.00
		b. 1969B. (A-B; E-G; K).	FV	FV	90.00
		c. 1969C. (A-L).	FV	FV	70.00
454	100 DOLLARS	1969. (A-L).	FV	FV	130.00
		a. 1969A. (A-L).	FV	FV	130.00
		b. 1969C. (A-L).	FV	FV	125.00

SERIES OF 1974

			VF	XF	Unc
455	1 DOLLAR	1974. (A-L).	FV	FV	2.00
456	5 DOLLARS	1974. (A-L).	FV	FV	10.00
457	10 DOLLARS	1974. (A-L).	FV	FV	17.00

Cat. #	Denomination	Date, Description	VF	XF	Unc
458	20 DOLLARS	1974. (A-L).	FV	FV	30.00
459	50 DOLLARS	1974. (A-L).	FV	FV	70.00
460	100 DOLLARS	1974. (A-L).	FV	FV	120.00

1976 COMMEMORATIVE ISSUE

#461, Bicentennial of signing of the Declaration of Independence.

			VF	XF	Unc
461	2 DOLLARS	1976. (A-L).	FV	FV	4.00

NOTE: #461 is also available in uncut sheets of 4, 16 and 32 notes. A high series # range is used.

SERIES OF 1977

			VF	XF	Unc
462	1 DOLLAR	1977. (A-L).	FV	FV	2.00
		a. 1977A. (A-L).	FV	FV	2.00
463	5 DOLLARS	1977. (A-L).	FV	FV	10.00
		a. 1977A. (A-L).	FV	FV	10.00
464	10 DOLLARS	1977. (A-L).	FV	FV	17.00
		a. 1977A. (A-L).	FV	FV	16.00
465	20 DOLLARS	1977. (A-L).	FV	FV	30.00
466	50 DOLLARS	1977. (A-L).	FV	FV	65.00

			VF	XF	Unc
467	100 DOLLARS	1977. (A-L).	FV	FV	120.00

NOTE: Since Oct. 1981 the Bureau of Engraving and Printing has made available to collectors uncut sheets of 4, 16 and 32 notes of the $1.00 and $2.00 denominations. A high serial # range is used.

SERIES OF 1981

			VF	XF	Unc
468	1 DOLLAR	1981. (A-L).	FV	FV	2.00
		a. 1981A.	FV	FV	2.00
469	5 DOLLARS	1981. (A-L).	FV	FV	10.00
		a. 1981A.	FV	FV	10.00
470	10 DOLLARS	1981. (A-L).	FV	FV	15.00
		a. 1981A.	FV	FV	15.00
471	20 DOLLARS	1981. (A-L).	FV	FV	30.00
		a. 1981A.	FV	FV	30.00
472	50 DOLLARS	1981. (A-L).	FV	FV	65.00
		a. 1981A.	FV	FV	65.00
473	100 DOLLARS	1981. (A-L).	FV	FV	120.00
		a. 1981A.	FV	FV	120.00

SERIES OF 1985

			VF	XF	Unc
474	1 DOLLAR	1985. (A-L).	FV		2.00
475	5 DOLLARS	1985. (A-L).	FV	FV	10.00
476	10 DOLLARS	1985. (A-L).	FV	FV	18.00
477	20 DOLLARS	1985. (A-L).	FV	FV	30.00
478	50 DOLLARS	1985. (A-L).	FV	FV	65.00
479	100 DOLLARS	1985. (A-L).	FV	FV	120.00

SERIES OF 1988

			VF	XF	Unc
480	1 DOLLAR	1988. (A-L).	FV	FV	2.00
		a. 1988A.	FV	FV	2.00
481	5 DOLLARS	1988. (A-L).	FV	XF	10.00
		a. 1988A.	—	—	10.00

Cat. #	Denomination	Date, Description	VF	XF	Unc
482	10 DOLLARS	1988. (A-L). (Not issued).	—	—	15.00
		a. 1988A.	—	—	15.00
483	20 DOLLARS	1988. (A-L). (Not issued).	—	—	30.00
		a. 1988A.	FV	FV	30.00
484	50 DOLLARS	1988. (A-L).	FV	FV	65.00
		a. 1988A.	FV	FV	65.00
485	100 DOLLARS	1988. (A-L).	FV	FV	120.00
		a. 1988A.	FV	FV	120.00

SERIES OF 1990

#486–488 w/additional row of micro-printing: *THE UNITED STATES OF AMERICA* repeated around portr. Filament w/value and *U.S.A.* repeated inversely at l.

486	10 DOLLARS	1990. (A-L).	FV	FV	15.00
487 (486)	20 DOLLARS	1990. (A-L).	FV	FV	30.00
488 (487)	50 DOLLARS	1990. (A-L).	FV	FV	65.00
		x. Error w/filament at r.	Reported, not confirmed.		
489 (488)	100 DOLLARS	1990. (A-L).	FV	FV	115.00
		x. Error w/filament at r.	140.00	160.00	350.00

SERIES OF 1993

490 (489)	1 DOLLAR	1993. (A-L).	FV	FV	1.75
491	5 DOLLARS	1993. (A-L).	FV	FV	8.00
492	10 DOLLARS	1993. (A-L).	FV	FV	15.00
493	20 DOLLARS	1993. (A-L).	FV	FV	30.00
494	50 DOLLARS	1993. (A-L).	FV	FV	65.00

SERIES OF 1995

495	1 DOLLAR	1995.	FV	FV	2.00
496	5 DOLLARS	1995.	FV	FV	7.50
#497–502	Held in reserve.				

SERIES OF 1996

503	100 DOLLARS	1996.	Expected new issue.

MILITARY PAYMENT CERTIFICATES

REPLACEMENT NOTES

Can be identified by serial # which will have a prefix letter but no suffix letter. All replacement notes are much scarcer than regular issues which have prefix and suffix letters.

SERIES 591

26.5.1961 to 6.1.1964.

#M43–M46 Liberty at r.

Cat.#	Denomination	Date, description	Fine	VF	XF	Unc
M43	5 CENTS	ND (1961). Lilac on green and yellow unpt.	2.00	4.00	8.00	55.00
M44	10 CENTS	ND (1961). Blue on lilac unpt.	2.00	5.00	12.00	65.00
M45	25 CENTS	ND (1961). Green on purple unpt.	15.00	28.00	50.00	135.00

M46	50 CENTS	ND (1961). Brown on aqua unpt.	20.00	35.00	75.00	235.00

Cat.#	Denomination	Date, description	Fine	VF	XF	Unc
M47	1 DOLLAR	ND (1961). Red. Woman at r.	15.00	40.00	85.00	225.00
M48	5 DOLLARS	ND (1961). Blue. Woman at l.	375.00	450.00	600.00	1750.

M49	10 DOLLARS	ND (1961). Green. Woman at r.	100.00	175.00	275.00	1500.

SERIES 611

6.1.1964 to 28.4.1969.

#M50–M53 Liberty at l.

M50	5 CENTS	ND (1964). Blue.	1.00	2.00	3.00	7.00
M51	10 CENTS	ND (1964). Green.	1.50	3.00	6.00	17.00
M52	25 CENTS	ND (1964). Brown.	3.00	5.00	8.00	25.00
M53	50 CENTS	ND (1964). Lilac.	4.00	6.00	15.00	55.00

M54	1 DOLLAR	ND (1964). Green. Woman w/tiara at l.	3.50	6.00	15.00	55.00
M55	5 DOLLARS	ND (1964). Red. Woman at ctr.	70.00	100.00	175.00	450.00

M56	10 DOLLARS	ND (1964). Blue. Woman at ctr.	37.50	75.00	175.00	400.00

SERIES 641

31.8.1965 to 21.10.1968.

#M57–M60 woman at l.

Cat.#	Denomination	Date, description	Fine	VF	XF	Unc
M57	5 CENTS	ND (1965). Violet on blue.	.25	.50	1.00	4.00
M58	10 CENTS	ND (1965). Green.	.25	.75	2.00	5.00
M59	25 CENTS	ND (1965). Red.	.50	1.00	3.00	7.00
M60	50 CENTS	ND (1965). Orange.	1.00	2.00	5.00	12.00
M61	1 DOLLAR	ND (1965). Lilac. Woman at r.	2.00	3.50	8.00	20.00
M62	5 DOLLARS	ND (1965). Green. Woman w/wreath of flowers at ctr.	25.00	35.00	60.00	120.00

Cat.#	Denomination	Date, description	Fine	VF	XF	Unc
M72E	1 DOLLAR	ND (1969). Green. Woman at r.	2.00	3.00	8.00	25.00

Cat.#	Denomination	Date, description	Fine	VF	XF	Unc
M63	10 DOLLARS	ND (1965). Brown. Woman at ctr.	12.00	30.00	75.00	225.00

SERIES 661

21.10.1968 to 11.8.1969.

#M64–68 woman wearing scarf at l.

M73	5 DOLLARS	ND (1969). Brown. Woman w/wreath of flowers at ctr.	25.00	35.00	75.00	150.00
M74	10 DOLLARS	ND (1969). Violet. Woman at ctr.	25.00	35.00	80.00	200.00

SERIES 681

11.8.1969 to 7.10.1970.

#M75–M78 submarine at r.

M75	5 CENTS	ND (1969). Green and blue.	.50	1.00	1.50	5.00

Cat.#	Denomination	Date, description	Fine	VF	XF	Unc
M64	5 CENTS	ND (1968). Green and lilac.	.25	.50	1.00	4.00
M65	10 CENTS	ND (1968). Blue and violet.	.25	.75	1.00	7.00
M66	25 CENTS	ND (1968). Brown and orange.	.50	1.00	4.00	12.00
M67	50 CENTS	ND (1968). Red and green.	1.00	2.00	5.00	12.00

M76	10 CENTS	ND (1969). Violet.	.50	1.00	1.50	5.00
M77	25 CENTS	ND (1969). Claret and blue.	.50	1.00	3.00	12.00
M78	50 CENTS	ND (1969). Brown and blue.	1.00	2.00	5.00	12.00
M79	1 DOLLAR	ND (1969). Violet. Air Force pilot at r.	1.00	2.00	4.00	12.00

M68	1 DOLLAR	ND (1968). Blue. Woman at r.	2.00	3.00	6.00	15.00
M69	5 DOLLARS	ND (1968). Dk. brown. Woman holding flowers at ctr.	1.25	2.00	4.00	10.00

M80	5 DOLLARS	ND (1969). Purple and green. Sailor at ctr.	2.00	3.50	6.00	25.00

M81	10 DOLLARS	ND (1969). Blue-green. Infantryman at ctr.	10.00	20.00	35.00	150.00

M70	10 DOLLARS	ND (1968). Red. Woman holding fasces at l.	75.00	110.00	350.00	650.00
M71	20 DOLLARS	ND (1968). Black, brown and blue. Woman at ctr.	50.00	75.00	150.00	450.00

SERIES 651

28.4.1969 to 19.11.1973.

#M72A–M74 similar to Series 641 except for colors and the addition of a "Minuteman" at l.

Cat.#	Denomination	Date, description	Fine	VF	XF	Unc
M72A	5 CENTS	ND (1969).	—	—	—	3000.
M72B	10 CENTS	ND (1969).	—	—	—	3000.
M72C	25 CENTS	ND (1969).	—	—	—	3000.
M72D	50 CENTS	ND (1969).	1000.	1250.	1500.	3750.

Cat.#	Denomination	Date, description	Fine	VF	XF	Unc
M82	20 DOLLARS	ND (1969). Brown, pink and blue. Soldier wearing helmet at ctr.	10.00	20.00	45.00	110.00

SERIES 692

7.10.1970 to 15.3.1973.

#M83–M86 seated Roman warrior at l.

M83	5 CENTS	ND (1970). Brown.	.75	1.00	2.00	7.00
M84	10 CENTS	ND (1970). Green.	1.00	1.50	2.50	7.00
M85	25 CENTS	ND (1970). Blue.	2.00	3.00	4.50	15.00
M86	50 CENTS	ND (1970). Violet.	3.00	4.00	6.00	20.00

M87	1 DOLLAR	ND (1970). Blue green. Woman at l., flowers at bottom ctr.	4.00	5.00	10.00	25.00
M88	5 DOLLARS	ND (1970). Brown. Girl and flowers at ctr.	35.00	50.00	75.00	175.00

M89	10 DOLLARS	ND (1970). Blue. Indian Chief Hollow Horn Bear at ctr.	25.00	100.00	175.00	400.00

M90	20 DOLLARS	ND (1970). Violet. Indian Chief Ouray at ctr.	85.00	120.00	150.00	400.00

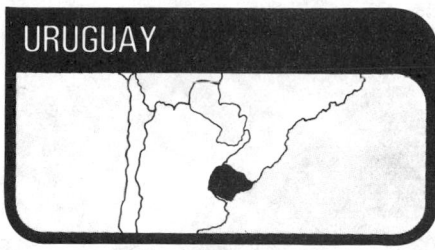

URUGUAY

The Oriental Republic of Uruguay (so called because of its location on the east bank of the Uruguay River) is situated on the Atlantic coast of South America between Argentina and Brazil. This most advanced of South American countries has an area of 68,536 sq. mi. (176,220 sq. km.) and a population of 3.12 million. Capital: Montevideo. Uruguay's chief economic asset is its rich, rolling grassy plains. Meat, wool, hides and skins are exported.

Uruguay was discovered in 1516 by Juan Diaz de Solis, a Spaniard, but settled by the Portuguese who founded Colonia in 1680. Spain contested Portuguese possession and, after a long struggle, gained control of the country in 1778. During the general South American struggle for independence, Uruguay cast off the Spanish bond, only to be reconquered by the Portuguese from Brazil in the struggle of 1816–20. Revolt flared anew in 1825 and independence was reasserted in 1828 with the help of Argentina. The Uruguayan Republic was established in 1830.

MONETARY SYSTEM
1 Peso = 100 Centesimos, 1860–1975
1 Doblon = 10 Pesos
1 Nuevo Peso = 1000 Old Pesos, 1975–93
1 Peso Uruguayo – 1000 Nuevos Pesos, 93–

REPLACEMENT NOTES
#53, 56, 57, R preceding serial number. #59 and later notes printed by TDLR, "9" starting serial #. Notes printed by CICCONE S.A. have "-R" next to series letter.

República Oriental del Uruguay
Departamento de Emisión

Ley de 2 de Enero de 1939

Cat. #	Denomination	Date, description	VG	VF	Unc
34	50 CENTESIMOS	L.1939. Green on lt. tan and brown unpt. Artigas at ctr. Series A-T. Arms at ctr. on back. Imprint: Casa de Moneda de Chile.	.20	.50	2.00

#35–41 w/a great many variations in sign. and sign. titles. Sign. titles are in overprint. All notes have 3 sign. Printer: TDLR.

35	1 PESO	L.1939. Brown on m/c unpt. Arms at upper l., Artigas at ctr. Sailing ships on back.			
		a. Paper w/fibers. Series A; B.	.30	1.25	4.00
		b. Paper w/security thread. Series C.	.25	1.00	3.50
		c. Series D.	.20	.50	2.00

Cat. #	Denomination	Date, description	VG	VF	Unc
36	5 PESOS	*L.1939.* Blue on m/c unpt. Arms at upper l., Artigas at r. Conquistadors fighting against Indians on back.			
		a. Paper w/fibers. Series A; B.	.75	2.50	7.00
		b. Paper w/security thread. Series C.	.40	1.00	3.50

Cat. #	Denomination	Date, description	VG	VF	Unc
37	10 PESOS	*L.1939.* Purple on m/c unpt. Arms at upper l., Artigas at ctr. Farmer w/3-team ox-cart on back.			
		a. Paper w/fibers. Series A.	1.00	4.00	10.00
		b. As a. Series B.	.75	3.00	7.50
		c. Paper w/security thread. Series C.	.40	1.50	5.50
		d. Series D.	.40	1.00	3.00

#38–41 wmk: Artigas.

Cat. #	Denomination	Date, description	VG	VF	Unc
38	50 PESOS	*L.1939.* Blue and brown on m/c unpt. Arms at upper l., Warrior wearing helmet at r. Group of men w/flag on back.			
		a. Paper w/fibers. Series A; B.	.75	3.00	9.00
		b. Paper w/security thread. Series C.	.40	1.50	5.00

Cat. #	Denomination	Date, description	VG	VF	Unc
39	100 PESOS	*L.1939.* Red and brown. Arms at ctr., "Constitution" at r. People in town square on back.			
		a. Paper w/fibers. Series A; B.	2.00	6.00	20.00
		b. Paper w/security thread. Series C.	.75	3.00	8.00
		c. Series D.	.50	2.00	6.00

Cat. #	Denomination	Date, description	VG	VF	Unc
40	500 PESOS	*L.1939.* Green and blue. Arms at upper l., "Industry" at r. People w/symbols of agriculture on back.			
		a. Paper w/fibers. Series A; B.	3.00	10.00	30.00
		b. Paper w/security thread. Series C.	1.00	4.00	10.00
		c. Series D.	.75	2.00	7.00

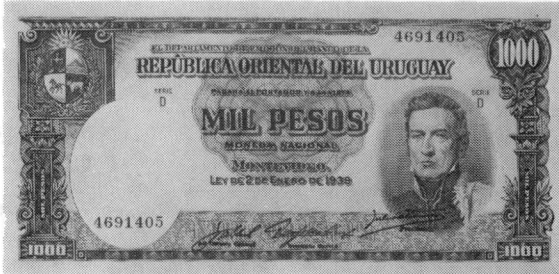

Cat. #	Denomination	Date, description	VG	VF	Unc
41	1000 PESOS	*L.1939.* Purple and black. Arms at upper l., Artigas at r. Man on horseback at ctr. on back.			
		a. Paper w/fibers. Series A; B.	10.00	25.00	75.00
		b. Paper w/security thread. Series C.	3.00	10.00	25.00
		c. Series D.	2.00	5.00	12.00

Banco Central del Uruguay

1967 PROVISIONAL ISSUE

#42–45 Banco Central was organized in 1967 and used notes of previous issuing authority w/Banco Central sign. title ovpt. All ovpt. notes are Series D.

Cat. #	Denomination	Date, description	VG	VF	Unc
42	10 PESOS	*L.1939* (1967). Purple on m/c unpt. Like #37b but all sign. titles in name of Banco Central.			
		a. Bank name below title: *Banco Central de la Republica.*	1.00	3.25	10.00
		b. Bank name below title: *Banco Central del Uruguay.*	.75	2.50	7.50
42A	50 PESOS	*L.1939* (1967). Blue and brown. Like #38b but bank name below sign. at r. Banco Central del Uruguay.			
		a. Bank name below 2 sign. at r.	.75	2.50	7.50
		b. Bank name below all 3 sign.	.75	2.00	6.00
43	100 PESOS	*L.1939* (1967). Red and brown. Like #39b.			
		a. R. sign. title: *Presidente, Banco Central de la Republica.*	—	—	—
		b. Bank name below 2 sign. at r: *Banco Central del Uruguay.*	1.00	3.00	10.00
		c. Bank name below 3 titles: *Banco Central del Uruguay.*	1.00	3.00	10.00

Cat. #	Denomination	Date, description	VG	VF	Unc
44	500 PESOS	L.1939. Green and blue. Like #40b but all sign. titles in name of Banco Central.			
		a. Sign. like #42a.	1.50	5.00	15.00
		b. Sign. like #42b.	1.50	5.00	15.00
45	1000 PESOS	L.1939. Purple and black. Like #41b. Bank name under all 3 sign: *Banco Central de la Republica.*	3.00	7.00	20.00

1967 REGULAR ISSUE

#46–51 Artigas at ctr. Sign. and sign. title varieties. #48–51 wmk: Arms. Printer: TDLR.

Cat. #	Denomination	Date, description	VG	VF	Unc
46	50 PESOS	ND (1967). Deep blue on lt. green and lilac unpt. Arms at l. Group of 33 men w/flag on back.	.10	.25	1.00

| 47 | 100 PESOS | ND (1967). Red on lilac and lt. gold unpt. Arms at l. Man presiding at independence meeting on back. | .10 | .25 | 1.00 |

| 48 | 500 PESOS | ND (1967). Green and blue on orange and lt. green unpt. Dam on back. | .50 | 1.25 | 5.00 |

Cat. #	Denomination	Date, description	VG	VF	Unc
49	1000 PESOS	ND (1967). Purple and black on blue and yellow unpt. Lg. bldg. on back.	.50	1.25	5.00

50	5000 PESOS	ND (1967). Brown and blue-green on lilac and lt. blue unpt. Bank on back.			
		a. Series A; B.	2.00	5.00	20.00
		b. Series C.	1.00	2.00	5.00
51	10,000 PESOS	ND (1967). Dk. green and black on yellow an lt. orange unpt. Bldg. on back. Series A; B.			
		a. R. sign. title: *PRESIDENTE.*	5.00	12.50	30.00
		b. R. sign. title: *VICE-PRESIDENTE.*	6.00	15.00	35.00

1974 ISSUE

#51A–53 sign. varieties. Wmk: Artigas.

51A	1000 PESOS	ND (1974). Violet and dk. green on m/c unpt. Arms at upper ctr., Artigas at r. Bldg. on back. Printer: CdeM - A.	.30	.90	2.75
52	*Deleted.* See #57.				

53	10,000 PESOS	ND (1979). Orange on m/c unpt. arms at upper ctr., Artigas at r. Palace Esteze on back. Printer: TDLR. Series A; B; C.	2.00	4.00	8.00
		a. Series A.	.90	2.75	8.00
		b. Series B.	.75	2.25	7.00
		c. Series C.	.65	2.00	6.00

Currency Reform

1 Nuevo Peso = 1000 Old Pesos, 1975

1975 PROVISIONAL ISSUE

#54–58 new value ovpt. on wmk. area.

Cat. #	Denomination	Date, description	VG	VF	Unc
54	0.50 NUEVO PESO on 500 Pesos	ND (1975). Ovpt. on #48.	.10	.35	1.00

55	1 NUEVO PESO on 1000 Pesos	ND (1975). Ovpt. on #49.	.25	.75	2.50
56	1 NUEVO PESO on 1000 Pesos	ND (1975). Ovpt. on #51A.	.25	.75	2.50
57	5 NUEVOS PESOS on 5000 Pesos	ND (1975). Brown on m/c unpt. Artigas at r., arms at ctr. w/ovpt. new value. Old Banco de Republica on back. Printer: CdM-A.	.75	2.25	7.00

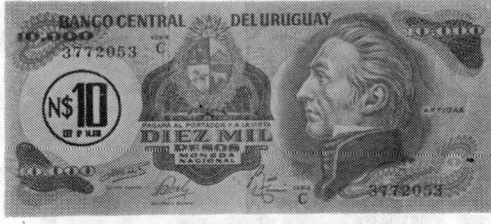

58	10 NUEVOS PESOS on 10,000 Pesos	ND (1975). Ovpt. on #53.	1.00	3.25	10.00

1975 REGULAR ISSUE

#59–60 arms near ctr., Artigas at r. and as wmk. Old govt. palace on back. Printer: TDLR.

59	50 NUEVOS PESOS	ND (1975). Deep blue on m/c unpt. Series A. 3 sign.	2.00	4.50	7.00

60	100 NUEVOS PESOS	ND (1975). Green and m/c. Series A. 3 sign.	4.00	8.00	12.00

1978-87 ISSUES

#61–64A similar to previous issue but w/o text: *PAGARA .... A LA VISTA* at ctr.

61	50 NUEVOS PESOS	ND(1978–89). Similar to #59.			
		a. 2 sign. Series B (1978).	.40	1.65	5.00
		b. 3 sign. Series C (1980).	.25	1.00	3.00
		c. 2 sign. Series D (1981).	.15	.65	2.00
		d. 3 sign. Series E (1987).	.10	.35	1.00

Cat. #	Denomination	Date, description	VG	VF	Unc
61A	50 NUEVOS PESOS	ND. Like #61 but Artigas portr. printed in wmk. Series F (1988); Series G (1989).	.05	.20	.60
62	100 NUEVOS PESOS	ND(1978–87). Similar to #60.			
		a. 2 sign. Series B (1978).	.50	2.00	5.00
		b. 3 sign. Series C (1980); Series D (1981).	.15	.65	2.00
		c. Series E (1985), Series F (1986).	.05	.15	.50
62A	100 NUEVOS PESOS	ND. Like #62 but Artigas portr. printed in wmk. Series G (1987).	.05	.25	.75
63	500 NUEVOS PESOS	ND(1978–85). Red on m/c unpt.			
		a. 2 sign. Series A (1978).	.90	3.50	10.00
		b. 3 sign. Series B (1978); Series C (1985).	.20	.80	2.50
63A	500 NUEVOS PESOS	ND. Like #63 but Artigas portr. printed in wmk. Series D (1991).	.15	.45	1.25
64	1000 NUEVOS PESOS	ND(1978–). Purple on m/c unpt.			
		a. 2 sign. Series A (1978).	2.00	4.50	10.00
		b. 3 sign. Series B (1981).	.40	1.50	4.50
64A	1000 NUEVOS PESOS	ND. Like #64 but Artigas portr. printed in wmk.			
		a. Series C (1991).	.35	1.00	3.00
		b. Series D (1992).	.10	.35	1.00

#65-67 wmk: Artigas.

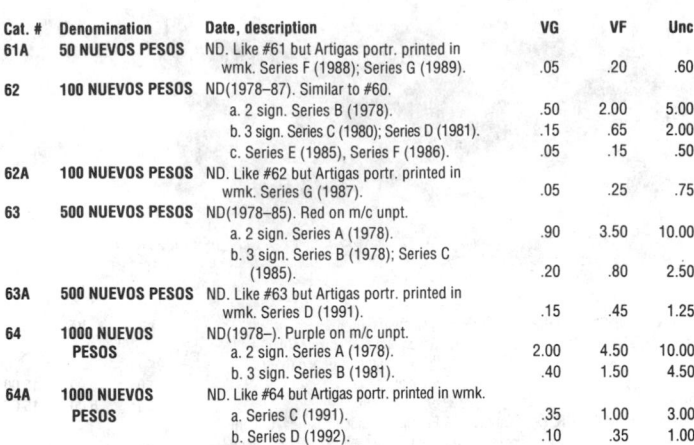

65	5000 NUEVOS PESOS	ND (1983). Brown, blue and m/c. Arms at top ctr., Brig. Gen. J.A. Lavalleja at r. Back m/c; scene of pledging allegiance ca.1830 at ctr. Series A; B. Printer: TDLR.	.35	1.10	3.50

66	200 NUEVOS PESOS	1986. Dk. and lt. green on brown and m/c unpt. Quill and scroll at l., arms at ctr., J.E. Rodo at r. Back green and brown; Rodo Monument at ctr., statuary at l. and ctr. Series A. Printer: Ciccone S.A.	.10	.35	1.00

Cat. #	Denomination	Date, description	VG	VF	Unc
67	10,000 NUEVOS PESOS	ND (1987). Blue and m/c. Plaza w/flag at ctr. 19 departmental arms on back. Printer: ABNC.			
		a. Ovpt. gold gilt bars on description and law designation. Series A.	7.50	25.00	75.00
		b. No ovpt. bars and *DECRETO-LEY NO. 14.316* at upper r. Series B; C.	FV	2.75	8.00
		s. Entire note as printed and w/o ovpt. Series A. Specimen.	—	—	—

NOTE: On #67, description *Plaza de la Nacionalidad Oriental/Monumento a la bandera* and *LEY 14.316* was ovpt. out because of a change of government from military to elected civil administration before the notes were released. The new government took the prepared notes, ovpt. the legend relating to the old government and issued them (Series A). Only Specimen notes are known w/o the ovpt.

1989–92 ISSUE

#68–73 arms at upper l. Wmk: Artigas. Printer: TDLR.

#68–73 arms at upper l., silver oval latent image at upper r. w/letters *B/CU*. Wmk: Portr. of Artigas. Printer: TDLR.

			VG	VF	Unc
68	2000 NUEVOS PESOS	1989. Black and red-orange on m/c unpt. J. M. Blanes, banker at ctr. r. Altar of the Fatherland (allegory of the Republic) on back.	FV	.50	1.50

			VG	VF	Unc
69	20,000 NUEVOS PESOS	1989; 1991. Dk. green and violet on m/c unpt. Dr. J. Zorilla de San Martin at ctr. r. Manuscript and allegorical victory w/wings on back.	FV	4.00	7.50

Cat. #	Denomination	Date, description	VG	VF	Unc
70	50,000 NUEVOS PESOS	1989; 1991. Black and violet on m/c unpt. J. P. Varela at ctr. r. Varela Monument at l. on back.	FV	10.00	17.50

			VG	VF	Unc
71	100,000 NUEVOS PESOS	1991. Purple and dk. brown on m/c unpt. E. Fabini at r. ctr. Musical allegory on back.	FV	20.00	32.50

			VG	VF	Unc
72	200,000 NUEVOS PESOS	1992. Dk. brown and violet and orange on m/c unpt. P. Figari at ctr. r. Old dance at l. on back.	FV	37.50	65.00

Cat. #	Denomination	Date, description	VG	VF	Unc
73	500,000 NUEVOS PESOS	1992. Blue-gray, violet and pale red on m/c unpt. A. Vaquez Acevedo at ctr. r. University of Monterideo at l. on back.	FV	85.00	125.00

Currency Reform

1 Peso Uruguayo = 1000 Nuevos Pesos, 1993–

1994 ISSUE

#74–77 like #69–73 but w/new denominations. Series A. Wmk: Artigas. Printer: TDLR.

74	20 PESOS URUGUAYOS	1994. Dk. green and violet on m/c unpt. Like #69.	FV	FV	7.00
75	50 PESOS URUGUAYOS	1994. Black, red and violet on m/c unpt. Like #70.	FV	FV	15.00
76	100 PESOS URUGUAYOS	1994. Purple and dk. brown on m/c unpt. Like #71.	FV	FV	27.50
77	200 PESPS URUGUAYOS	1995. Dk. brown-violet on m/c unpt. Like #72.	FV	FV	52.50
78 (77)	500 PESOS URUGUAYOS	1994. Blue-gray, violet and pale red on m/c unpt. Like #73.	FV	FV	110.00
79 (78)	1000 PESOS URUGUAYOS	(1996).			Expected new issue.
80 (79)	2000 PESOS	(1996).			Expected new issue.

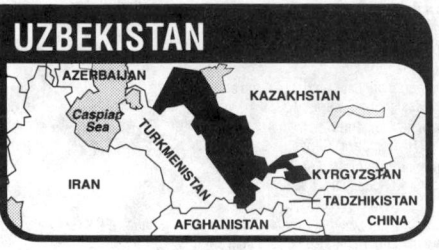

The Republic of Uzbekistan (formerly the Uzbek S.S.R.), is bordered on the north by Kazakhstan, to the east by Kirghizia and Tajikistan, on the south by Afghanistan and on the west by Turkmenistan. The republic is comprised of the regions of Andizhan, Bukhara, Dzhizak, Ferghana, Kashkadar, Khorezm (Khiva), Namangan, Navoi, Samarkand, Surkhan-Darya, Syr-Darya, Tashkent and the Karakalpak Autonomous Republic. It has an area of 172,741 sq. mi. (447,400 sq. km.) and a population of 20.3 million. Capital: Tashkent.

Crude oil, natural gas, coal, copper and gold deposits make up the chief resources, while intensive farming, based on artificial irrigation, provides an abundance of cotton.

The original population was believed to be Iranian towards the north while the southern part hosted the satrapies of Sogdiana and Bactria, members of the Persian empire and once part of the empire of Alexander of Macedon. In the 2nd century B.C. they suffered an invasion by easterners referred to by the Chinese as Yue-chi and Hiung-nu. At the end of the 7th century and into the 8th century an Arab army under Emir Kotaiba ibu Muslim conquered Khiva (Khorezm) and Bukhara (Sogdiana). Persian influence developed from the Abbasid caliphs of Baghdad. About 874 the area was conquered by the Persian Saminids of Balkh.

In 999 a Turkic Karakhanid dynasty, the first to embrace Islam, supplanted the Samanids in Samarkand and Bukhara. At the beginning of the 11th century the Seljuk Turks passed through Transoxiana and appointed a hereditary governor at Khorezm. In 1141 another dynasty appeared in Transoxiana, the Kara Kitai from north China. Under the Seljuk shahs Khorezm remained a Moslem outpost.

The Mongol invasion of Jenghiz Khan in 1219–20 brought destruction and great ethnic changes among the population. The conquerors became assimilated and adopted the Turkic language "Chagatai." At the beginning of the 16th century Turkestan was conquered by another wave of Turkic nomads, the Uzbeks (Usbegs). The term Uzbek was used in the 15th century to indicate Moslem. In the 18th century Khokand made itself independent from the emirate of Bukhara, but was soon subject to China, which had conquered eastern Turkestan (now called Sinkiang). The khanate of Khiva, in 1688, became a vassal of Persia, but recovered its independence in 1747. While the Uzbek emirs and khans ruled central Turkestan, in the north were the Kazakhs, in the west lived the nomadic Turkmens, in the east dwelled the Kirghiz, and in the southeast was the homeland of the Persian-speaking Tajiks. In 1714-17 Peter the Great sent a military expedition against Khiva which ended in a disaster. In 1853 Ak-Mechet ("White Mosque," renamed Perovsk, later Kzyl Orda), was conquered by the Russians, and the following year the fortress of Vernoye (later Alma-Ata) was established. On July 29, 1867, Gen. C. P. Kaufmann was appointed governor general of Turkestan with headquarters in Tashkent. On July 5 Mozaffar ed-Din, emir of Bukhara, signed a treaty making his country a Russian vassal state with much-reduced territory. Khiva was conquered by Gen. N. N. Golovachev, and on Aug. 24, 1873, Khan Mohammed Rakhim Kuli had to become a vassal of Russia. Furthermore, all his possessions east of the Amu Darya were annexed to the Turkestan governor-generalship. The khanate of Khokand was suppressed and on March 3, 1876, became the Fergana province. On the eve of WW I Khiva and Bukhara were enclaves within a Russian Turkestan divided into five provinces or *oblasti*. The czarist government did not attempt to Russify the indigenous Turkic or Tajik populations, preferring to keep them backward and illiterate. The revolution of March 1917 created a confused situation in the area. In Tashkent there was a Turkestan committee of the provisional government; a Communist-controlled council of workers', soldiers' and peasants' deputies; also a Moslem Turkic movement, Shuro-i-Islamiya, and a Young-Turkestan or Jaddidi (Renovation) party. The last-named party claimed full political autonomy for Turkestan and the abolition of the emirate of Bukhara and the khanate of Khiva. After the Communist *coup d'état* in Petrograd, the council of people's commissars on Nov. 24 (Dec. 7), 1917, published an appeal to "all toiling Moslems in Russia and in the east" proclaiming their right to build their national life "freely and unhindered." In response, the Moslem and Jaddidi organizations in Dec. 1917 convoked a national congress in Khokand which appointed a provisional government headed by Mustafa Chokayev (or Chokaigolu; 1890–1941) and resolved to elect a constituent assembly to decide whether Turkestan should remain within a Russian federal state or proclaim its independence. In the spring of 1919 a Red army group defeated Kolchak and in September its commander, M.V. Frunze, arrived in Tashkent with V.V. Kuibyshev as political commissar. The Communists were still much too weak in Turkestan to proclaim the country part of Soviet Russia. Faizullah Khojayev organized a Young Bukhara movement, which on Sept. 14, 1920, proclaimed the dethronement of Emir Mir Alim. Bukhara was then made a S.S.R. In 1920 the Tashkent Communist government declared war on Junaid, who took to flight, and Khiva became another S.S.R. In Oct. 1921 Enver Pasha, the former leader of the Young Turks, appeared in Bukhara and assumed command of the Basmachi movement. In Aug. 1922 he was forced to retreat into Tajikistan and died on Aug. 4, in a battle near Baljuvan. Khiva concluded a treaty of alliance with the Russian S.F.S.R. in Sept. 1920, and Bukhara followed suit in March 1921. Theoretically, a Turkestan Autonomous Soviet Socialist Republic had existed since May 1, 1918; in 1920 this "Turkrepublic," as it was called, was proclaimed part of the R.S.F.S.R. On Sept. 18, 1924, the Uzbek and Turkmen peoples were authorized to form S.S.R.'s of their own, and the Kazakhs, Kirghiz and Tajiks to form autonomous S.S.R.'s. On Oct. 27, 1924, the Uzbek and Turkmen S.S.R. were officially constituted and the former was formally accepted on Jan. 15, 1925, as a member of the U.S.S.R. Tajikistan was an autonomous soviet republic within Uzbekistan until Dec. 5, 1929, when it became a S.S.R. On Dec. 5, 1936, Uzbekistan was territorially increased by incorporating into it the Kara-Kalpak A.S.S.R., which had belonged to Kazakhstan until 1930 and afterward had come under direct control of the R.S.F.S.R.

On June 20, 1990 the Uzbek Supreme Soviet adopted a declaration of sovereignty, and in Aug. 1991, following the unsuccessful coup, it declared itself independent as the 'Republic of Uzbekistan', which was comfirmed by referendum in Dec. That same month Uzbekistan became a member of the CIS.

UZBEKISTAN REPUBLIC

Sum System

1 Sum (1 Ruble) = 100 Kopeks, 1991–

КУПОНГА КАРГОЧКА – Ruble Control Coupons

Cat. #	Denomination	Date, description	VG	VF	Unc
42A	10 COUPONS	ND (1993). Black on pale blue unpt. Sheet of 10 coupons w/registry at r. Uniface.			
		a. Issued full sheet w/circular purple hand stamp.	—	—	.50
		b. Coupon.	—	—	.05
42B	25 COUPONS	ND (1993). Black on pale blue unpt. Sheet of 12 coupons of various denominations w/registry at r. Uniface.			
		a. Issued full sheet w/circular purple hand stamp.	—	—	.75
		b. Coupon.	—	—	.10

NOTE: #42A and 42B were printed together on 1 sheet.

43	150 COUPONS	1993. Red on pale gray unpt. Sheet of 12 coupons of various denominations w/registry at r. Uniface.			
		a. Issued full sheet w/circular purple hand stamp.	—	—	1.00
		b. Coupon.	—	—	.25

NOTE: On Nov. 18, 1993, Uzbekistan converted its coupons to a legal tender currency. A fully independent currency issue not tied to the Ruble is expected.

УЗБЕКИСТОН ДАВПАТ БАНКИ

Bank of Uzbekistan

1992 DATED ISSUE

#44–53 arms at l. Mosque at ctr. on back.

44	1 SUM	1992 (1993). Blue-gray on lt. blue and gold unpt. Back gray.	.05	.10	.25

45	3 SUM	1992 (1993). Green and blue. Back green.	.05	.10	.35

Cat. #	Denomination	Date, description	VG	VF	Unc
46	5 SUM	1992 (1993). Purple on lt. blue and gold unpt. Back pale purple.	.05	.10	.40

47	10 SUM	1992 (1993). Red on lt. blue and gold unpt. Back red.	.05	.15	.60

48	25 SUM	1992 (1993). Green on lt. blue and pale orange unpt. Back green.	.05	.25	1.00

49	50 SUM	1992 (1993). Rose and blue. Back rose.	.10	.45	1.75

Cat. #	Denomination	Date, description	VG	VF	Unc
50	100 SUM	1992 (1993). Dk. brown and blue. Back blue.	.10	.35	1.50

Cat. #	Denomination	Date, description	VG	VF	Unc
54	5000 SUM	1992 (1993).	.90	3.75	15.00

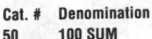

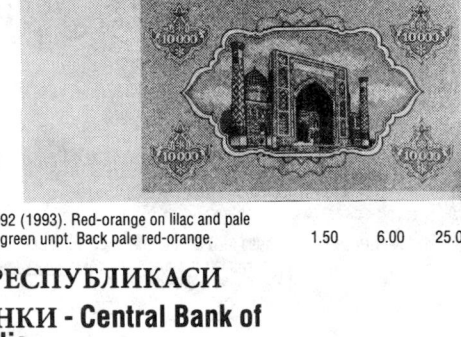

Cat. #	Denomination	Date, description	VG	VF	Unc
51	200 SUM	1992 (1993). Violet and blue. Back violet.	.10	.45	1.75

Cat. #	Denomination	Date, description	VG	VF	Unc
55	10,000 SUM	1992 (1993). Red-orange on lilac and pale green unpt. Back pale red-orange.	1.50	6.00	25.00

ЎЗБЕКИСТОН РЕСПУБЛИКАСИ
МАРКАЗИЙ БАНКИ - Central Bank of Uzbekistan Republic

Currency Reform, 1.7.1994
1 Sum (Note) = 1,000 Sum (Coupon)

1994 ISSUE

Cat. #	Denomination	Date, description	VG	VF	Unc
52	500 SUM	1992 (1993). Orange and lt. blue. Back red-brown	.10	.35	1.50

Cat. #	Denomination	Date, description	VG	VF	Unc
56	1 SUM	1994. Dk. green on m/c unpt. Arms at l. Bldg., fountain at ctr. r. on back.	FV	FV	.35
57	3 SUM	1994. Red-brown on m/c unpt. Mosque of Ça çma Ayub Mazar in Bukhara on back.	FV	FV	1.00

#58–62 arms at upper ctr. and as wmk.

Cat. #	Denomination	Date, description	VG	VF	Unc
53	1000 SUM	1992 (1993). Brown and green. Back brown.	.20	.75	3.00

Cat. #	Denomination	Date, description	VG	VF	Unc
58	5 SUM	1994. Dk. blue and red-violet on m/c unpt. Statue under kiosk at ctr. lt. on back.	FV	FV	1.75

59	10 SUM	1994. Violet and blue-gray on m/c unpt. Mosque of Mohammed Amin Khan in Khiva on back.	FV	FV	3.50

60	25 SUM	1994. Dk. blue and brown on m/c unpt. Mausoleum Kazi Zadé Rumi in the necropolis Shakhi-Zinda in Samarkand on back.	FV	FV	6.00
61	50 SUM	1994. Brown and orange on m/c u npt. Esplanade in Reghistan and the 2 medersas in Samarkand on back.	FV	FV	9.00
62	100 SUM	1994. Purple on m/c unpt. Stylized facing peacocks at ctr. "Drugja Narodov" palace in Tarshkent on back.	FV	FV	13.50
63	200 SUM				Expected new issue.

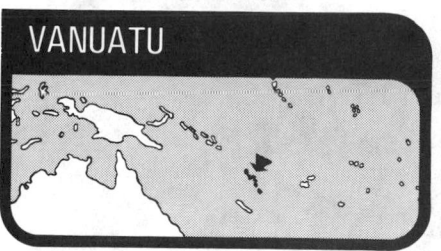

VANUATU

Vanuatu (formerly the New Hebrides Condominium), a group of islands located in the South Pacific 500 miles (800 km.) west of Fiji, were under the joint sovereignty of Great Britain and France. The islands have an area of 5,700 sq. mi. (14,763 sq. km.) and a population of *154,000, mainly Melanesians of mixed blood. Capital: Port-Vila. The volcanic and coral islands, while malarial and subject to frequent earthquakes, are extremely fertile, and produce copra, coffee, tropical fruits and timber for export.

The New Hebrides were discovered by Portuguese navigator Pedro de Quiros in 1606, visited by French explorer Bougainville in 1768, and named by British navigator Capt. James Cook in 1774. Ships of all nations converged on the islands to trade for sandalwood, prompting France and Britain to relinguish their individual claims and declare the islands a neutral zone in 1878. The New Hebrides were placed under the control of a mixed Anglo-French commission of naval officers during the native uprisings of 1887, and established as a condomiuium under the joint sovereignty of France and Great Britain in 1906. Independence for the area was attained in 1982 under the new name of Vanuatu.

RULERS
British and French to 1982

MONETARY SYSTEM
100 Vatu = 100 Francs

SIGNATURE/TITLE VARIETIES			
1	PRESIDENT GENERAL MANAGER	3	GOVERNOR MINISTER OF FINANCE
2	PRESIDENT MINISTER OF FINANCE	4	

Banque Centrale de Vanuatu/Central Bank of Vanuatu

#1–4 arms w/Melanesian chief standing w/spear at ctr. r. Wmk: Male Melanesian head. Printer: BWC.

Cat. #	Denomination	Date, description	VG	VF	Unc
1	100 VATU	ND (1982). Dk. green on m/c unpt. Cattle amongst palm trees at l. ctr. on back. Sign. 1.	1.25	2.50	8.50

2	500 VATU	ND (1982). Red on m/c unpt. 3 carved statues at l., 2 men beating upright hollow log drums at l. ctr. on back. Sign. 1.	FV	6.50	15.00

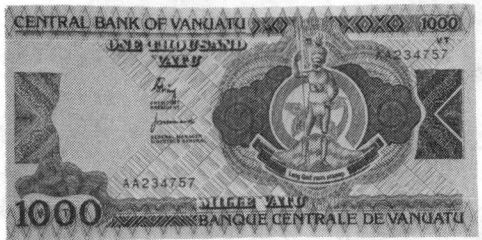

Cat. #	Denomination	Date, description	VG	VF	Unc
3	1000 VATU	ND (1982). Black on m/c unpt. 3 carvings at lower l., 3 men in outrigger sailboat at ctr. on back. Sign. 1.	FV	12.50	25.00
4	5000 VATU	ND(1989). Brown and lilac on m/c unpt. Man watching another *Gol* diving from log tower at ctr. on back. Sign. 2.	FV	50.00	80.00

Banque de Reserve de Vanuatu/Reserve Bank of Vanuatu/ Reserve Bang Blong Vanuatu

#5-7 like #2–4 but w/new bank name. Sign. 3.

5	500 VATU	ND (1993). Dk. green on m/c unpt.	FV	FV	9.00

6	1000 VATU	ND (1993). Red on m/c unpt.	FV	FV	16.00
7	5000 VATU	ND.		Expected new issue.	

VENEZUELA

The Republic of Venezuela ("Little Venice"), located on the northern coast of South America between Columbia and Guyana, has an area of 352,145 sq. mi. (912,050 sq. km.) and a population of *20.2 million. Capital: Caracas. Petroleum and mining provide 90 percent of Venezuela's exports although they employ less than 2 percent of the work force. Coffee, grown on 60,000 plantations, is the chief crop.

Columbus discovered Venezuela on his third voyage in 1498. Initial exploration did not reveal Venezuela to be a land of great wealth. An active pearl trade operated on the off-shore islands and slavers raided the interior in search of Indians to be sold into slavery, but no significant mainland settlements were made before 1567 when Caracas was founded. Venezuela, the home of Bolivar, was among the first South American colonies to revolt against Spain in 1810. Independence was attained in 1821 but not recognized by Spain until 1845. Together with Ecuador, Panama and Colombia, Venezuela was part of ""Gran Colombia" until 1830 when it became a sovereign and independence state.

MONETARY SYSTEM
 1 Bolívar = 100 Centimos, 1879–

Banco Central de Venezuela

1960–61 ISSUE

#42–44 printer: TDLR.

Cat. #	Denomination	Date, description	VG	VF	Unc
42	10 BOLÍVARES	6.6.1961. Purple on m/c unpt. S. Bolívar at l., Sucre at r. Monument and arms on back.			
		a. Issued note.	2.50	9.00	25.00
		s. Specimen.	—	—	11.00
43	20 BOLÍVARES	11.3.1960–10.5.1966. Dk. green on m/c unpt. S. Bolívar at r., bank name in 1 line. Monument at ctr. on back.			
		a. Issued note.	4.00	12.00	30.00
		s. Specimen (varieties).	—	—	12.50
44	50 BOLÍVARES	6.6.1961; 7.5.1963. Black. Modified effigy of S. Bolívar at l. Back orange; monument at ctr. on back.			
		a. Issued note.	8.00	25.00	75.00
		s. Specimen.	—	—	15.00

1963–67 ISSUE

#45–48 monument on back similar to #42–44. Printer: TDLR.

45	10 BOLÍVARES	7.5.1963–27.1.1970. Purple on m/c unpt.. Similar to #42 but much different portr. of Sucre at r.	1.00	2.50	7.50

46	20 BOLÍVARES	8.8.1967–29.1.1974. Green on orange and blue unpt. S. Bolívar at r., and as wmk., bank name in 3 lines. Arms w/o circle at l. on back.			
		a. Issued note.	1.60	4.00	12.50
		s. Specimen (varieties).	—	—	11.00

Cat. #	Denomination	Date, description	VG	VF	Unc
47	50 BOLÍVARES	2.6.1964–22.2.1972. Black. S. Bolívar at l. *CINCUENTA BOLÍVARES* above *50* at ctr. Back orange.	5.00	12.50	35.00

Cat. #	Denomination	Date, description	VG	VF	Unc
48	100 BOLÍVARES	7.5.1963–6.2.1973. Brown. S. Bolívar at r.			
		a. Issued note.	5.00	12.50	40.00
		s. Specimen (varieties).	—	—	15.00

1966 COMMEMORATIVE ISSUE

#49, 400th Anniversary of Founding of Caracas 1567–1967

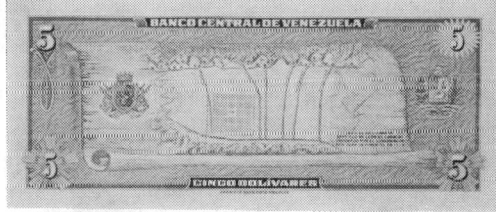

Cat. #	Denomination	Date, description	VG	VF	Unc
49	5 BOLÍVARES	10.5.1966. Blue on green and yellow unpt. Scene of the founding and commemorative text at ctr. and l., S. Bolívar at r. Back blue; city arms at l., early map (1578) of the city at ctr., national arms at r. Printer: ABNC.	2.00	5.00	15.00

1968-71 ISSUE

Cat. #	Denomination	Date, description	VG	VF	Unc
50	5 BOLÍVARES	24.9.1968–29.1.1974. Red on m/c unpt. Bolívar at l., F. de Miranda at r. Arms at l., National Pantheon at ctr. on back. Printer: TDLR.			
		a. Issued note.	.75	2.00	6.50
		b. Remainder w/o date, sign. or serial #.	—	—	7.50
		s. Specimen.	—	—	8.50

#51–52 printer: ABNC.

Cat. #	Denomination	Date, description	VG	VF	Unc
51	10 BOLÍVARES	1971–79. Purple on green and lilac unpt. Similar to #45.			
		a. Dark blue serial #. 22.6.1971–7.6.1977.	.90	2.25	7.00
		b. Black serial #. 18.9.1979.	.75	2.00	6.00
		s. Specimen (varieties).	—	—	10.00

Cat. #	Denomination	Date, description	VG	VF	Unc
52	20 BOLÍVARES	22.6.1971; 11.4.1972. Dk. green on m/c unpt. Similar to #46.			
		a. Issued note.	1.35	3.50	10.00
		s. Specimen.	—	—	10.00

1971–74 ISSUE

Cat. #	Denomination	Date, description	VG	VF	Unc
53	20 BOLÍVARES	23.4.1974; 7.6.1977; 18.9.1979. Dk. green on m/c unpt. J. Antonio Paez at r. and as wmk. Arms at l., monument of Battle of Carabobo at ctr. on back. Printer: ABNC.			
		a. Issued note.	1.00	2.50	7.50
		s. Specimen (varieties).	—	—	7.50

54	50 BOLÍVARES	21.11.1972; 29.1.1974; 27.1.1976; 7.6.1977. Purple, orange and m/c. Academic bldg. at ctr., A. Bello at r. and as wmk. Back orange; arms at l., bank at ctr. Printer: TDLR.			
		a. Issued note.	1.65	4.00	12.50
		s. Specimen.	—	—	12.50

55	100 BOLÍVARES	1972–81. Dk. brown and brown-violet on m/c unpt. S. Bolívar at r. and as wmk. National Capitol at l., arms at r. on back. Printer: BDDK.			
		a. Red serial #. 21.11.1972.	6.00	15.00	55.00
		b. Wmk. Bolívar. 6.2.1973–5.3.1974.	5.00	12.50	30.00
		c. Blue serial #. B-C added to wmk. 27.1.1976–1.9.1981.	2.75	7.00	20.00
		s. Specimen (varieties).	—	—	12.50

56	500 BOLÍVARES	9.11.1971; 11.1.1972. Brown, blue and m/c. S. Bolívar at l. and as wmk, horsemen w/rifles riding at ctr. Back brown; dam at ctr. Printer: TDLR.			
		a. Issued note.	15.00	50.00	120.00
		s. Specimen.	—	—	20.00

1980 ISSUE

Cat. #	Denomination	Date, description	VG	VF	Unc
57	10 BOLÍVARES	29.1.1980. Purple and m/c. A. J. de Sucre at r. Arms at l., officers on horseback at ctr. r. on back. Printer: ABNC.			
		a. Issued note.	.50	1.00	4.50
		s. Specimen.	—	—	8.50

1980-81 COMMEMORATIVE ISSUES

#58, Bicentennial Birth of Andres Bello 1781–1981

58	50 BOLÍVARES	27.1.1981. Dk. brown, green and m/c. A. Bello at r. and as wmk. Arms at l., scene showing Bello teaching young Bolívar on back. Printer: TDLR.	1.65	4.00	12.50

#59, 150th Anniversary Death of Simon Bolivar 1830–1980.

59	100 BOLÍVARES	29.1.1980. Red, purple and m/c. S. Bolivar at r. and as wmk., his tomb at ctr. r. Arms at l., scene of hand to hand combat on back. Printer: TDLR.			
		a. Issued note.	1.65	4.00	12.50
		s. Specimen.	—	—	12.50

1981-87 ISSUES

#60–67 w/o imprint.

Cat. #	Denomination	Date, description	VG	VF	Unc
60	10 BOLÍVARES	6.10.1981. Purple on lt. blue unpt. Similar to #57 but unpt. is different, and there are many significant plate changes.			
		a. Issued note.	FV	.75	2.50
		s. Specimen.	—	—	9.50

61	10 BOLÍVARES	1986–. Purple on lt. green and lilac unpt. Like #51, but CARACAS removed from upper ctr. beneath bank title.			
		a. 18.3.1986.	FV	FV	1.50
		b. 31.5.1990.	FV	FV	.75
		c. 8.12.1992.	FV	FV	.50

| 62 | 10 BOLÍVARES | 3.11.1900. Purple on ochre unpt. Like #45, but CARACAS removed from upper ctr. beneath bank title. | FV | FV | 1.00 |

Central design in l.h. guilloche: ➤■●◀ or ➤▸●◀

63	20 BOLÍVARES	1981–. Dk. green on m/c unpt. Similar to #53 but CARACAS deleted under bank title. Title 82mm, horizontal central design in l. ctr. guilloche.			
		a. 6.10.1981; 7.7.1987.	FV	FV	2.00
		b. 7.9.1989; 31.5.1990	FV	FV	1.25
		c. 8.12.1992.	FV	FV	1.00
		s. Specimen.	—	—	9.00

Cat. #	Denomination	Date, description	VG	VF	Unc
64	20 BOLÍVARES	25.9.1984. Like #63, but title 84mm and w/o central design in l. ctr. guilloche, also other minor plate differences. Latent image BCV in guilloches easily seen.	FV	FV	2.00

65	50 BOLÍVARES	10.12.1985–16.3.1989. Similar to #54, but CARACAS removed under bank name.	FV	FV	3.00
66	100 BOLÍVARES	1987–. Like #55 but w/o imprint.			
		a. 3.2.1987; 16.3.1989.	FV	FV	4.00
		b. 31.5.1990; 8.12.1992.	FV	FV	2.25

67	500 BOLÍVARES	1981–. Purple and black on m/c unpt. S. Bolívar at r. and as wmk. Back green and m/c; arms at l. of flowers.			
		a. 25.9.1981.	FV	10.00	35.00
		b. 3.2.1987; 16.3.1989.	FV	FV	25.00
		c. 31.5.1990.	FV	FV	9.00

1989 ISSUE

#68–70 w/o imprint.

Cat. #	Denomination	Date, description	VG	VF	Unc
68	1 BOLÍVAR	5.10.1989. Purple on blue and green unpt. Lg. *1* at l., S. Bolívar on coin at r. Arms at l., rosette at r. on back. Wmk. paper.	FV	FV	.35

Cat. #	Denomination	Date, description	VG	VF	Unc
69	2 BOLÍVARES	5.10.1989. Blue and black on lt. blue unpt. Coin head of S. Bolívar at r. Lg. *2* at l., arms at r. on back.	FV	FV	.50
70	5 BOLÍVARES	21.9.1989. Red on m/c, unpt. Like #50, but *CARACAS* removed from upper ctr. beneath bank title on face and back. Lithographed.	FV	FV	.65

1989 COMMEMORATIVE ISSUE

#68, Bicentennial Birth of Rafael Urdaneta (1789)

Cat. #	Denomination	Date, description	VG	VF	Unc
71	20 BOLÍVARES	20.10.1987 (1989). Deep green and black on m/c unpt. Gen. R. Urdaneta at r. and as wmk. Battle of Lake Maracaibo on back.	FV	FV	2.00

1990-94 ISSUE

#72–73 w/o imprint.

72	50 BOLÍVARES	31.5.1990; 8.12.1992. Similar to #65 but modified plate design, ornaments in "50's". Back, deeper orange.	FV	FV	2.00

#73–75 arms at upper r. on back.

Cat. #	Denomination	Date, description	VG	VF	Unc
73	1000 BOLÍVARES	1991; 1992. Red-violet on m/c unpt. Part of independence text at far l., S. Bolívar at l. and as wmk. Signing of the Declaration of Independence at ctr. r., arms at upper r. on back.			
		a. Dot instead of accent above *i* (error) in *Bolívares* on face and back. 8.6.1991.	FV	27.50	60.00
		b. Accent above *i* in *Bolívares* on face and back. 30.7.1992.	FV	FV	11.00
74	2000 BOLÍVARES	12.5.1994. Dk. green and black on m/c unpt. A. J. de Sucre at r. Gathering of military officers horseback at l. ctr. on back.	FV	FV	20.00
75	5000 BOLÍVARES	12.5.1994. Dk. brown and brown-violet on m/c unpt. S. Bolívar at r. and as wmk. Gathering at palace at ctr. on back.	FV	FV	45.00

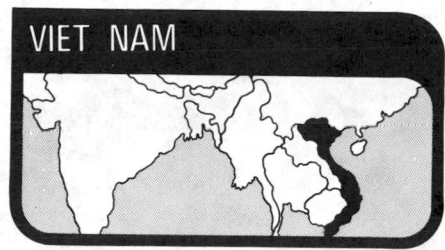

VIET NAM

The Socialist Republic of Viet Nam, located in Southeast Asia west of the South China Sea, has an area of 127,300 sq. mi. (329,560 sq. km.) and a population of *69.3 million. Capital: Hanoi. Agricultural products, coal and mineral ores are exported.

The Vietnamese originated in North China, from where they were driven southward by the Han Chinese. They settled in the Red River Delta in northern Vietnam; by 208 BC, much of present-day southern China and northern Vietnam were incorporated into the independent kingdom of Nam Viet. China annexed Nam Viet in 111 BC and ruled it until 939, when independence was reestablished. The new state then expanded until it included much of Cambodia and southern Vietnam. Vietnam was reconquered by the Chinese in 1407; they were finally driven out, but the country was divided into two, not to be reunited until 1802.

During the latter half of the 19th century, the French gradually overran Vietnam. Cochin-China, an alluvial plain of the Mekong Delta, fell to the French in 1862-67. In 1884, France established protectorates over Annam, an historic kingdom on the east coast of Indochina, and Tonkin in the north. Cambodia, Cochin-China, Annam and Tonkin were incorporated into the Indo-Chinese Union in 1887.

Vietnamese nationalists never really acquiesced to French domination, but continued to resist through a number of clandestine extra-legal organizations. At the start of World War II, many nationalists, communist and non-communist alike, fled to China where Ho Chi Minh organized the League for the Independence of Vietnam ("Viet Minh") to free Vietnam from French rule. The Japanese occupied Vietnam during World War II. As the end of the war drew near, they ousted the Vichy French administration and granted Vietnam independence under a puppet government headed by Bao Dai, emperor of Annam. The Bao Dai government collapsed at the end of the war, and on Sept. 2, 1945, Ho Chi Minh proclaimed the existence of an independent Vietnam consisting of Cochin-China, Annam and Tonkin, and set up a provisional Communist government of the Democratic Republic of Vietnam. France recognized the new government as a free state, but later reneged and in 1949 reinstalled Bao Dai as ruler of Vietnam and extended the regime independence within the French Union. Ho Chi Minh led a guerrilla war, in the first Indochina war, against the French puppet state that raged on to the disastrous defeat of the French by the Viet Minh at Dien Bien Phu on May 7, 1954.

An agreement signed at Geneva on July 21, 1954, provided for a temporary division of Vietnam at the 17th parallel of latitude, with the Communist dominated Democratic Republic of Viet Nam (North Vietnam) to the north, and the US/French-supported Republic of Viet Nam (South Vietnam) to the south. In October 1955 South Vietnam deposed Bao Dai by referendum and authorized the establishment of a new republic with Ngo Dinh Diem as president. This Republic of Vietnam was proclaimed on October 26, 1955, and was recognized immediately by the Western powers.

The Democratic Republic of Viet Nam, working through Viet Cong guerrillas, instigated subversion in South Vietnam which led to US armed intervention and the second Indochina War. This war, from the viewpoint of the North merely a continuation of the first (anti-French) war, was a bitter, protracted military conflict which came to a brief halt in 1973 (when a cease-fire was arranged and US and its other allied forces withdrew), but did not end until April 30, 1975 when South Vietnam surrendered unconditionally. The National Liberation Front for South Viet Nam, the political arm of the Viet Cong, assumed governmental power when on July 2, 1976, North and South Vietnam were united as the Socialist Republic of Viet Nam with Hanoi as the capital.

MONETARY SYSTEM
1 Hao = 10 Xu
1 Dong = 100 Xu

REPLACEMENT NOTES
#FX1–FX7 serial # prefix *EE*.

NUOC VIET NAM DAN CHU CONG HOA
DEMOCRATIC REPUBLIC OF VIET NAM
Ngan Hang Quoc Gia Viet Nam
National Bank of Viet Nam

1958 ISSUE

Cat. #	Denomination	Date, description	VG	VF	Unc
59	1 HAO	1958. Red on green unpt. Arms at ctr. Train on back.			
		a. Issued note.	.30	.75	2.50
		b. Ovpt: Cai Luu Hanj O Cua... on #59 for circulation in Haiphong.	—	—	—

Cat. #	Denomination	Date, description	VG	VF	Unc
60	2 HAO	1958. Green on tan unpt. Arms at ctr. Grazing animals near coffer dam on back.	.40	1.00	4.00

Cat. #	Denomination	Date, description	VG	VF	Unc
61	5 HAO	1958. Brown on lt. green unpt. Arms at ctr. 4 women in spinning mill on back.	2.00	7.50	30.00

Cat. #	Denomination	Date, description	VG	VF	Unc
62	1 DONG	1958. Brown on lt. green unpt. Arms at l., monument w/tower and flag at ctr. Work in rice paddies on back.			
		a. Issued note.	.75	3.00	10.00

			VG	VF	Unc
		x. US lithograph counterfeit w/propaganda message at l. 6 varities: w/o code, Code 50, Code 4540 (2 text var.), Code 4543 (2 text var.).	1.00	2.50	4.50

Cat. #	Denomination	Date, description	VG	VF	Unc
63	2 DONG	1958. Blue on green unpt. Arms at l., 4 people w/flag at ctr. r. Boats and mountains on back.			
		a. Issued note.	1.00	4.00	10.00
		x. US lithograph counterfeit w/propaganda message at r. Code 4541.	1.00	2.50	6.00

Cat. #	Denomination	Date, description	VG	VF	Unc
64	5 DONG	1958. Brown on blue unpt. Arms at l., tractor at ctr., HCM at r. Road constuction work on back.			
		a. Issued note.	1.00	4.00	12.50
		x. US lithograph counterfeit w/propaganda message at r. Code 4542.	1.00	2.50	6.00

Cat. #	Denomination	Date, description	VG	VF	Unc
65	10 DONG	1958. Red on blue and green unpt. Arms at ctr., HCM at r. factory on back.	1.00	3.00	10.00

Ngan Hang Nha Nuoc Viet Nam
State Bank of Viet Nam
1964–75 ISSUE

66	2 XU	ND (1964). Purple on green unpt. Arms at ctr.	3.50	9.00	35.00

67	5 XU	1975 (date in lt. brown above *VIET* at lower l. ctr.). Violet on brown unpt. Arms at upper r.			
		a. Wmk: 15mm stars.	.30	1.25	5.00
		b. Wmk: 30mm radiant star.	.30	1.25	5.00

68	1 HAO	1972. Violet on m/c unpt. Arms at ctr. Woman feeding pigs on back.			
		a. Wmk: 15mm. stars. Series KG-?	.30	1.25	5.00
		b. Wmk: 32mm. encircled stars. Series MK-?	.30	1.25	5.00

69	2 HAO	1975. Brownish purple on green and peach unpt. Arms at ctr. 2 men spraying rice field on back.	.30	1.25	5.00

SOCIALIST REPUBLIC

Working through Viet Cong guerrillas with material help from China and Russia, and finally with years of armed conflict, the Democratic Republic of Viet Nam (North Vietnam) toppled the U.S.A. supported Democratic government of the South. Reunion of North and South Vietnam took place on July 2, 1976, and the Socialist Republic of Viet Nam was established.

Ngan Hang Nha Nuoc Viet Nam
State Bank of Viet Nam

1976 DATED ISSUE

Issued in 1978, these notes unified the monetary systems of the South with that of the DRVN. Exchanged at par with the old DRVN notes, these replaced South Vietnam (Ngan Hang Viet Nam) transitional series (see South Vietnam #37-44) at 1 "new" = 0.8 "old South".

Cat. #	Denomination	Date, description	VG	VF	Unc
70	5 HAO	1976. Purple on m/c unpt. Arms at ctr. Coconut palms and river scene on back.	.30	.75	2.50

71	1 DÔNG	1976. Brown on m/c unpt. Arms at ctr. Factory on back.			
		a. Issued note.	.25	.65	2.00
		s. Specimen.	—	—	50.00

72	5 DÔNG	1976. Blue-gray and green on pink unpt. Arms at ctr. Back green and yellow; 2 women w/fish, boats in harbor.			
		a. Issued note.	.30	.75	2.50
		b. Block letter and serial # together. W/o wmk.	.30	.75	2.50
		s. Specimen.	—	—	55.00

73	10 DÔNG	1976. Purple and brown on m/c unpt. Arms at ctr. Elephants logging on back.			
		a. Issued note.	.15	.50	4.50
		s. Specimen.	—	—	60.00

74	20 DÔNG	1976. Blue on pink and green unpt. Arms at l., HCM at r. Tractors and dam on back.			
		a. Issued note.	.60	1.25	4.00
		s. Specimen.	—	—	60.00

Cat. #	Denomination	Date, description	VG	VF	Unc
75	50 DÔNG	1976 Reddish purple on pink and green unpt. Arms at l., HCM at r. Open pit mining scene on back (in Hongay). 2 serial # varieties.			
		a. Issued note.	85	1.65	5.00
		s. Specimen.	—	—	75.00

Cat. #	Denomination	Date, description	VG	VF	Unc
78	30 DÔNG	1981. Purple, brown and m/c. Arms at l. ctr., HCM at r. Harbor scene on back.			
		a. Issued note.	.40	1.00	4.00
		s. Specimen.	—	—	60.00

CONG HOA XA HOI CHU NGHIA VIET NAM
SOCIALIST REPUBLIC OF VIET NAM

Ngan Hang Nha Nuoc Viet Nam
State Bank of Vietnam

1981 ISSUE

76	2 DÔNG	1980. Brown on m/c unpt. Arms at ctr. River scene on back.			
		a. Issued note.	.20	.50	1.50
		s. Specimen.	—	—	50.00

79	100 DÔNG	1980. Brown, dk. blue and m/c. Arms at ctr., HCM at r. Back blue, violet and brown; boats and mountains. Lg. or sm. serial #.			
		a. Issued note.	.45	1.10	3.50
		s. Specimen.	—	—	100.00

1985 ISSUE

#A80–83 tower at l. ctr. on face.

A80	5 HAO	1985. Red-violet on lt. blue unpt.	.50	1.35	4.00

77	10 DÔNG	1980. Brown on m/c unpt. Arms at r. House at l. on back.	.25	.60	1.75

Cat. #	Denomination	Date, description	VG	VF	Unc
80	1 DÔNG	1985. Deep blue on m/c unpt. Boats along rocky coastline on back.			
		a. Issued note.	.10	.25	.75
		s. Specimen.	—	—	40.00

81	2 DÔNG	1985. Purple on m/c unpt. Boats anchored along coastline on back.			
		a. Issued note.	.15	.40	1.50
		s. Specimen.	—	—	40.00

82	5 DÔNG	1985. Green on m/c unpt. Sampans anchored in river on back.			
		a. Issued note.	.10	.30	1.00
		s. Specimen.	—	—	50.00

83	10 DÔNG	1985. Brown-violet on m/c unpt. Village along stream at ctr. on back.			
		a. Issued note.	.20	.60	2.50
		s. Specimen.	—	—	50.00

#84–87 HCM at r.

Cat. #	Denomination	Date, description	VG	VF	Unc
84	20 DÔNG	1985. Brown, dk. purple and m/c. One pillar pagoda in Hanoi on back.			
		a. Issued note.	.25	.60	1.75
		s. Specimen.	—	—	50.00

84A	30 DÔNG	1985. Blue and m/c. Lg. bldg. w/clock tower at ctr. on back.			
		a. Issued note.	.35	.85	3.50
		s. Specimen.	—	—	60.00

85	50 DÔNG	1985. Green, brown and m/c. Reservoir and electric power station on back.			
		a. Issued note.	.50	1.25	5.00
		s. Specimen.	—	—	60.00

85A	50 DÔNG	1985. Blue-gray on orange and m/c unpt. Bridge at ctr. on back.			
		a. Issued note.	.30	.75	2.50
		s. Specimen.	—	—	60.00

Cat. #	Denomination	Date, description	VG	VF	Unc
86	100 DÔNG	1985. Brown, yellow and m/c. Planting rice on back. Wmk. HCM.			
		a. Issued note.	1.00	2.50	10.00
		s. Specimen.	—	—	75.00

87	500 DÔNG	1985. Red on blue and m/c unpt. Factory at l. ctr. on back. Wmk: HCM.			
		a. Issued note.	1.25	3.25	10.00
		s. Specimen.	—	—	85.00

1987–88 ISSUE

#88–93 HCM at r.

88	200 DÔNG	1987. Red-brown and tan on m/c unpt. Peasants and tractor on back.			
		a. Issued note.	.20	.50	1.75
		s. Specimen.	—	—	85.00

Cat. #	Denomination	Date, description	VG	VF	Unc
89	500 DÔNG	1988. Red-brown and red on m/c unpt. Dockside view on back.			
		a. Issued note.	.25	.65	2.50
		s. Specimen.	—	—	50.00

#90–92 wmk: HCM.

90	1000 DÔNG	1987. Purple, dk. brown and deep olive-green on m/c unpt. Open pit mining equipment on back.			
		a. Issued note.	.40	1.00	4.00
		s. Specimen.	—	—	50.00

91	2000 DÔNG	1987. Brown, purple and olive-green on m/c unpt. Industrial plant on back.			
		a. Issued note.	.75	2.00	5.00
		s. Specimen.	—	—	60.00

Cat. #	Denomination	Date, description	VG	VF	Unc
92	5000 DÔNG	1987. Deep blue, purple and brown on m/c unpt. Offshore oil rigs on back.			
		a. Issued note.	.30	.75	3.00
		s. Specimen.	—	—	60.00
93	*Deleted.*				

1988–91 ISSUE

94	100 DÔNG	1991. Brown on m/c unpt. Arms at l. Temple and pagoda at l. ctr. on back.	FV	.25	1.00

#95–100 HCM at r.

95	1000 DÔNG	1988. Purple on m/c unpt. Arms at l. ctr. Elephant logging on back.	FV	.50	2.00

96	2000 DÔNG	1988. Brownish purple on lilac and m/c unpt. Arms at l. Women in textile factory on back.	FV	.60	2.50
97	5000 DÔNG	1991. Dk. blue on m/c unpt. Arms at l. Electric lines on back.	FV	.90	3.75

#98–100 wmk: HCM.

Cat. #	Denomination	Date, description	VG	VF	Unc
98	10,000 DÔNG	1990 (1992). Red and red-violet on m/c unpt. Arms at ctr. Back brown-violet and red; junks along coastline.	FV	1.85	6.50
99	20,000 DÔNG	1991 (1993). Blue-green on m/c unpt. Arms at ctr. Packing factory on back.	FV	4.00	16.00

100	50,000 DÔNG	1990 (1993). Dk. olive-green and black on m/c unpt. Arms at upper l. ctr. Date at lower r. Port view on back.	FV	10.00	27.50

1992 MONETARY EMERGENCY ISSUE

Negotiable Bank Cheques

101	100,000 DÔNG	(ca. Nov. 1992).	FV	12.50	—
102	500,000 DÔNG	(ca. Nov. 1992).	FV	60.00	—
103	1 MILLION DÔNG	(ca. Nov. 1992).	FV	110.00	—
104	10,000 DÔNG	1993. Like #98 but w/optical registry device at lower l., modified unpt. color around arms. Back brown-violet on m/c unpt.	FV	FV	4.00

1994 ISSUE

105 (104)	50,000 DÔNG	1994. Like #100 but w/date under portr.	FV	FV	12.50

FOREIGN EXCHANGE CERTIFICATES

Ngan Hang Ngoai Thuong
Bank For Foreign Trade

Dong B System

ND ISSUE

#FX1–FX7 bank building at ctr. on back, bank seal at upper l.

#FX1–FX5 green on lt. blue and lt. yellow unpt. Back lt. blue.

FX1	10 DÔNG B	ND. Green on pale blue and yellow unpt. Back pale blue.			
		a. Issued note. Series AA; AB.	.25	1.00	8.00
		s. Specimen. Series EE.	—	—	50.00
FX2	50 DÔNG B	ND. Green on pale blue and yellow unpt. Back pale blue.			
		a. Issued note. Series AD.	.25	1.00	8.00
		s. Specimen. Series EE.	—	—	50.00
FX3	100 DÔNG B	ND. Green on pale blue and yellow unpt. Back pale blue.			
		a. Issued note. Series AC.	.25	1.00	20.00
		s. Specimen. Series EE.	—	—	50.00
FX4	200 DÔNG B	ND. Green on pale blue and yellow unpt. Back pale blue.			
		a. Issued note. Series AD.	.25	1.00	8.00
		s. Specimen. Series EE.	—	—	50.00
FX5	500 DÔNG B	ND. Green on pale blue and yellow unpt. Back pale blue.			
		a. Issued note. Series AC.	.25	1.00	8.00
		s. Specimen. Series EE.	—	—	50.00

Cat. #	Denomination	Date, description	VG	VF	Unc
FX6	1000 DÔNG B	ND. Red-violet on pink and pale orange unpt. Back pink.			
		a. Issued note. Series AE.	.25	1.00	8.00
		s. Specimen. Series EE.	—	—	50.00
FX7	5000 DÔNG B	ND. Brown on ochre unpt. Back ochre.			
		a. Issued note. Series AA; AB.	.25	1.00	8.00
		s. Specimen. Series EE.	—	—	50.00

(U.S.A.) Dollar A System, 1981–84

#FX8–FX9 various handwritten dates.

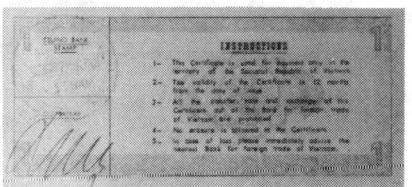

FX8	1 DOLLAR	1981-84.	—	—	—
FX9	5 DOLLARS	1981-84.	—	—	—

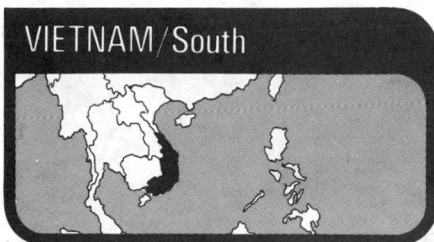

VIETNAM/South

South Vietnam (the former Republic of Viet Nam), located in Southeast Asia, bounded by North Vietnam on the north, Laos and Cambodia on the west, and the South China Sea on the east and south, had an area of 66,280 sq. mi. (171,665 sq. km.). Capital: Saigon (now Ho Chi Minh City). The economy of the area is predominantly agricultural.

South Vietnam, the direct successor to the French-dominated Bao Dai regime (also known as the Republic of Vietnam), was created after the first Indochina War (between the French and the Viet-Minh) by the Geneva agreement of 1954 which divided Vietnam at the 17th parallel of latitude. The National Bank of Vietnam, with headquarters in the old Bank of Indochina building in Saigon, came into being on October 26, 1955. Elections which would have reunified North and South Vietnam in 1956 never took place, and the North continued the war for unification of Vietnam under the communist government of the Democratic Republic of Vietnam begun at the close of World War II. South Vietnam surrendered unconditionally on April 30, 1975. With the North dominating, there followed a short period of coexistence of the two Vietnamese states, the South being governed by the National Liberation Front. On July 2, 1976, South and North Vietnam joined to form the Socialist Republic of Vietnam.

Also see Viet Nam.

MONETARY SYSTEM
1 Dong = 100 Xu = 100 Su to 1975
1 New Dong = 500 Old Dong, 1975–76

Ngân-Hâng Quôc-Gia Viêt-Nam
National Bank of Vietnam

1962–66 ISSUE

Cat. #	Denomination	Date, description	VG	VF	Unc
15	1 DONG	ND (1964). Lt. and dk. brown on orange and lt. blue unpt. Tractor on back. Wmk: Plant.	.10	.50	2.00

| 16 | 20 DONG | ND (1964). Green on m/c unpt. Stylized fish at ctr. on back. Wmk: Dragon's head. | .20 | .75 | 3.50 |

Cat. #	Denomination	Date, description	VG	VF	Unc
17	50 DONG	ND (1966). Purple on m/c unpt. Leaf tendrils at r.	1.50	5.00	20.00

| 18 | 100 DONG | ND (1966). Lt. and dk. brown on lt. blue unpt. Bldg. w/domed roof at r. Quarry and hills on back. Wmk: Plant. | .75 | 4.00 | 17.50 |

| 19 | 500 DONG | ND (1962). Green-blue on gold and pinkish unpt. Palace-like bldg. at ctr. Farmer w/2 water buffalos at r. on back. Wmk: Ngo Dinh Diem. | 30.00 | 150.00 | 375.00 |

Cat. #	Denomination	Date, description	VG	VF	Unc
20	500 DONG	ND (1964). Brown on m/c unpt. Pagoda at ctr. (Museum in Saigon). Stylized creatures at ctr. on back. Wmk: Dragon's head.	3.00	12.50	35.00

21	100 DONG	ND (1966). Red on m/c unpt. Man in national costume (Le Van Duyet) at l. Bldg. and ornate arch at ctr. r. on back.			
		a. Wmk: Le Van Duyet.	.50	2.00	7.00
		b. Wmk: Dragon's head.	.75	4.00	13.50

22	200 DONG	ND (1966). Dk. brown on m/c unpt. Famous warrior (Nguyen-Hue) at l. Warrior on horseback leading soldiers on back.			
		a. Wmk: Warrior's head.	.25	1.50	6.00
		b. Wmk: Dragon's head.	.50	3.00	10.00

| 23 | 500 DONG | ND (1966). Blue on m/c unpt. Warrior at l. (Tran-Hu'ng-Dao) and as wmk. Sailboat and rocks in water on back. | 1.50 | 5.00 | 15.00 |

1969–71 ISSUE

#24–29 bank bldg. at r. Lathework on all backs. Wmk as #23.

Cat. #	Denomination	Date, description	VG	VF	Unc
24	20 DONG	ND (1969). Red on m/c unpt.			
		a. Issued note.	.25	.60	1.50
		s. Specimen.	—	—	75.00

Cat. #	Denomination	Date, description	VG	VF	Unc
25	50 DONG	ND (1969). Blue-green on m/c unpt.			
		a. Issued note.	.25	.50	2.00
		s. Specimen	—	—	65.00

Cat. #	Denomination	Date, description	VG	VF	Unc
26	100 DONG	ND (1970). Dk. green on m/c unpt.			
		a. Issued note.	.25	.85	3.00
		s. Specimen.	—	—	75.00

Cat. #	Denomination	Date, description	VG	VF	Unc
27	200 DONG	ND (1970). Violet on m/c unpt.			
		a. Issued note.	1.00	4.00	15.00
		s. Specimen.	—	—	85.00

Cat. #	Denomination	Date, description	VG	VF	Unc
28	500 DONG	ND (1970). Orange and black on m/c unpt. Back orange and pale olive-green on m/c unpt.			
		a. Issued note.	.25	.60	3.00
		s. Specimen.	—	—	100.00
28A	500 DONG	ND (1970). Like #28 but brown and black on m/c unpt. Back brown and pale olive-green on m/c unpt.	—	—	—

Cat. #	Denomination	Date, description	VG	VF	Unc
29	1000 DONG	ND (1971). Turquoise on m/c unpt.			
		a. Issued note.	1.00	4.00	17.50
		s. Specimen.	—	—	120.00

1972–75 ISSUE

#30–36 Palace of Independence at r. Wmk: Young woman's head in profile.

Cat. #	Denomination	Date, description	VG	VF	Unc
30	50 DONG	ND (1972). Blue-gray on m/c unpt. 3 horses on back.	.20	.50	2.00

Cat. #	Denomination	Date, description	VG	VF	Unc
31	100 DONG	ND (1972). Green on m/c unpt. Farmer w/2 water buffalos on back.	.20	.50	1.50

| 32 | 200 DONG | ND (1972). Wine red on m/c unpt. 3 deer on back. | .70 | 1.75 | 6.00 |

Cat. #	Denomination	Date, description	VG	VF	Unc
33	500 DONG	ND (1972). Orange and olive-green on m/c unpt. Back orange on m/c unpt., tiger at l. ctr.	.25	.60	3.50
33A	500 DONG	ND (1972). Like #33 but brown and olive-green on m/c unpt. Back brown on m/c unpt.	.75	3.00	12.50

| 34 | 1000 DONG | ND (1972). Blue on m/c unpt. 3 elephants carrying loads on back. | .25 | .65 | 2.00 |

| 34A | 1000 DONG | ND(1975). Green and m/c. stylized fish at l.; Truong Cong Dinh at r. Dinh's mausoleum at upper l., stylized fish at r. on back. Specimen. (Not issued). | — | — | 350.00 |

#35 and #36 printer: TDLR. Wmk: Young woman's head in profile.

| 35 | 5000 DONG | ND (1975). Brown, blue and m/c. Leopard on back. (Not issued). | 20.00 | 35.00 | 65.00 |

Cat. #	Denomination	Date, description	VG	VF	Unc
36	10,000 DONG	ND (1975). Violet and m/c. Water buffalo on back. (Not issued).	27.50	45.00	85.00

NOTE: Values in italics are speculative.

Ngân-Hâng Viêt-Nam

Bank of Viet Nam

1966 DATED TRANSITIONAL ISSUE

#37–44 constitute a transitional issue of the communist National Liberation Front (Viet Cong) government which took over on April 30, 1975. Dated 1966 but issued 1975, they were used until the South's economic system was merged with that of the DRVN (North Vietnam) into a unified Socialist Republic of Vietnam.

37	10 XU	1966 (1975). Brown on m/c unpt. Drying salt at ctr. Unloading boats on back.	.35	.85	3.00
38	20 XU	1966 (1975). Blue on m/c unpt. Workers on rubber plantation at ctr. Soldiers greeting farmers w/oxen on back.	.50	2.50	7.50
39	50 XU	1966 (1975). Brownish purple on m/c unpt. Harvesting cane at ctr. Women weaving rugs on back.	.75	5.00	15.00

40	1 DONG	1966 (1975). Red-orange on m/c unpt. Boats on canal at ctr. Workers in field on back.	1.00	4.00	10.00
41	2 DONG	1966 (1975). Blue and green on m/c. Houseboats under a bridge at ctr. Soldiers and workers on back.	3.00	12.50	40.00
42	5 DONG	1966 (1975). Purple on m/c unpt. 4 women in textile factory at ctr. Armed soldiers w/ downed helicopters on back.	3.00	12.50	40.00
43	10 DONG	1966 (1975). Red on m/c unpt. 3 women and train at ctr. Soldiers and people w/flag on back.	8.00	25.00	75.00
44	50 DONG	1966 (1975). Green and blue on m/c unpt. Workers in factory at ctr. Combine harvester on back.	20.00	55.00	175.00

REGIONAL

Uy Ban Trung U'O'ng

Central Committee of the National Front for the Liberation of South Vietnam

1963 (ND) ISSUE

#R1–R8 were printed in China for use in territories under control of the National Liberation Front. They were never issued, but many were captured during a joint US/South Vietnam military operation into Cambodia. Except for #R2, relatively few survived in uncirculated condition.

Cat. #	Denomination	Date, description	VG	VF	Unc
R1	10 XU	ND (1963). Purple and m/c. Star at ctr.	.20	.60	3.00

| R2 | 20 XU | ND (1963). Red-brown on aqua and m/c unpt. Star at ctr. | .20 | .50 | 2.00 |

| R3 | 50 XU | ND (1963). Green and m/c. Star at ctr. | .30 | 1.50 | 5.00 |

| R4 | 1 DONG | ND (1963). Lt. brown on m/c unpt. Harvesting at ctr. Schoolroom on back. | 1.00 | 4.00 | 15.00 |

Cat. # Denomination	Date, description	VG	VF	Unc
R5 2 DONG	ND (1963). Blue on m/c unpt. Women in convoy at ctr. Fishermen w/boats on back.	3.00	15.00	50.00

R6 5 DONG	ND (1963). Lilac on m/c unpt. Women harvesting at ctr. Line of women fighters on back.	1.50	10.00	25.00

R7 10 DONG	ND (1963). Green on m/c unpt. Harvesting scene at ctr. War scene on back.	3.00	20.00	50.00

R8 50 DONG	ND (1963). Orange on m/c unpt. Truck convoy at ctr. Soldiers shooting down helicopters on back.	5.00	25.00	60.00

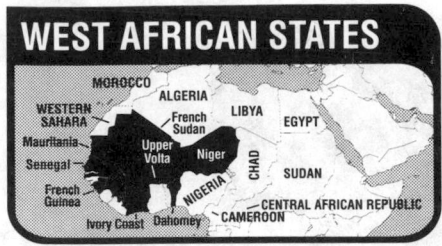

WEST AFRICAN STATES

The West African States, a former federation of eight French colonial territories on the northwest coast of Africa, had an area of 1,813,079 sq. mi. (4,742,495 sq. km.) and a population of about 17 million. Capital: Dakar. The constituent territories were Mauritania, Senegal, Dahomey, French Sudan, Ivory Coast, Upper Volta, Niger and French Guinea.

The members of the federation were overseas territories within the French Union until Sept. of 1958 when all but French Guinea approved the constitution of the Fifth French Republic, thereby electing to become autonomous members of the new French Community. French Guinea voted to become the fully independent Republic of Guinea. The other seven attained independence in 1960. The French West Africa territories were provided with a common currency, a practice which was continued as the monetary union of the West African States which provides a common currency to the autonomous republics of Dahomey (now Benin), Mali, Senegal, Upper Volta, Ivory Coast, Togo and Niger.

MONETARY SYSTEM
1 Franc = 100 Centimes

DATING
The year of issue on the current 500,1000 and 2500 Francs appears in the first 2 digits of the serial number, i.e. (19)91, (19)92, etc.

SIGNATURE VARIETIES

	LE PRÉSIDENT	LE DIRECTEUR GÉNÉRAL	Date
1		R. Julienne	Various dates – 1959 20.3.1961
2		R. Julienne	20.3.1961
3		R. Julienne	2.12.1964
4		R. Julienne	2.3.1965; ND
5		R. Julienne	ND
6		R. Julienne	ND
7		R. Julienne	ND
8		R. Julienne	ND
9		R. Julienne	ND
	LE PRÉSIDENT DU CONSEIL DES MINISTRES	LE GOUVERNEUR	Date
10		Marding	ND
11		Marding	ND (1977); 1977
12		Marding	ND (1978); 1978; 1979
13		Marding	ND (1980); 1980

14		*d/ading*	ND (1977); 1977; 1988; 1989
	LE PRÉSIDENT DU CONSEIL DES MINISTRES	**LE GOUVERNEUR**	**Date**
15		*d/ading*	ND (1981); 1981; 1982
16		*d/ading*	ND (1983); 1983
17		*d/ading*	1981; 1983; 1984
18		*d/ading*	ND (1984); 1984
19		*d/ading*	1984; 1985
20		*d/ading*	1986; 1987
21		*Alassane Ouattara*	1989
22		*Alassane Ouattara*	1991
23		*Alassane Ouattara*	1992
24		*Alassane Ouattara*	1992
25		*Alassane Ouattara*	1993
26			
27			
28			

NOTE: Begining with signatures #21 the postion has been reversed on the 500 Francs.

Banque Centrale des Etats de l'Afrique de l'Ouest

Notes of this bank were issued both w/and w/o code letters in the upper r. and lower l. corners. The code letter follows the control number and indicates which member country the note was issued for. Those w/o code letters are general issues. The code letters are as follows:

A	Ivory Coast	E	Mauritania (seceded in 1973)
B	Benin (formerly Dahomey)	H	Niger
C	Burkina Faso (formerly Upper Volta)	K	Senegal
D	Mali (seceded in 1962, rejoined 1984)	T	Togo

NOTE: Listings that follow show the specific note issues by date and sign. for each member country. As this is only the second time such a breakdown has been presented, it is fully expected that additional varieties previously unreported will be forthcoming.

Group 1 - General Issues w/o Code Letters

#1–5 have no code letters to signify member countries.

1959; (ND) ISSUE

Cat. #	Denomination	Date, Description	VG	VF	Unc
1	50 FRANCS	ND (1958). Dk. brown, blue and m/c. 3 women at ctr. Woman w/headress at ctr. on back. Sign. 1.	10.00	35.00	100.00

NOTE: #1 was not issued w/code letters.

Cat. #	Denomination	Date, Description	VG	VF	Unc
2	100 FRANCS	1959; ND. Dk. brown, orange and m/c. Mask at l., woman at r. Woman at l., carving at lower ctr. on back.			
		a. Sign. 1. 23.4.1959.	12.00	35.00	85.00
		b. Sign. 5. ND.	3.00	9.00	20.00
3	500 FRANCS	15.4.1959. Brown, green and m/c. Men doing field work at l., mask carving at r. Woman at l., farmer on tractor at r. on back. Sign. 1.	35.00	70.00	140.00
4	1000 FRANCS	17.9.1959. Brown, blue and m/c. Man and woman at ctr. Man w/rope suspension bridge in background and pineapples on back. Sign. 1.	25.00	50.00	115.00
5	5000 FRANCS	15.4.1959. Blue, brown and m/c. Bearded man at l., bldg. at ctr. Woman, corn grinders and huts on back. Sign. 1.	55.00	125.00	—

Group 2 - Issues w/letter A for Ivory Coast

1959–61 ISSUE

#101A–109A have letter A for Ivory Coast.

Cat. #	Denomination	Date, Description	VG	VF	Unc
101A	100 FRANCS	1961–65; ND. Design like #2.			
		a. Engraved. Sign. 1. 20.3.1961.	10.00	25.00	60.00
		b. Sign. 2. 20.3.1961.	10.00	25.00	60.00
		c. Litho. Sign. 2. 20.3.1961.	10.00	25.00	60.00
		d. Sign. 3. 2.12.1964.	10.00	25.00	60.00
		e. Sign. 4. 2.3.1965.	8.00	20.00	50.00
		f. Sign. 4. ND.	7.00	18.00	40.00
		g. Sign. 5. ND.	7.00	18.00	40.00
102A	500 FRANCS	1959–64; ND. Design like #3.			
		a. Engraved. Sign. 1. 15.4.1959.	15.00	40.00	75.00
		b. Sign. 1. 20.3.1961.	15.00	40.00	75.00
		c. Sign. 2. 20.3.1961.	15.00	40.00	75.00
		d. Sign. 3. 2.12.1964.	15.00	40.00	75.00
		f. Sign. 5. ND.	15.00	40.00	75.00
		g. Sign. 6. ND.	10.00	30.00	60.00
		h. Litho. Sign. 6. ND.	10.00	30.00	60.00
		i. Sign. 7. ND.	15.00	40.00	75.00
		j. Sign. 8. ND.	25.00	60.00	100.00
		k. Sign. 9. ND.	10.00	30.00	60.00
		l. Sign. 10. ND.	5.00	15.00	40.00
		m. Sign. 11. ND.	5.00	15.00	40.00
		n. Sign. 12. ND.	25.00	60.00	100.00
103A	1000 FRANCS	1959–65; ND. Design like #4.			
		a. Engraved. Sign. 1. 17.9.1959.	—	—	—
		b. Sign. 1. 20.3.1961.	15.00	45.00	90.00
		c. Sign. 2. 20.3.1961.	15.00	45.00	90.00
		d. Sign. 4. 2.3.1965.	30.00	65.00	125.00
		e. Sign. 5. ND.	8.00	20.00	50.00
		f. Sign. 6. ND.	8.00	20.00	50.00

Cat. #	Denomination	Date, Description	VG	VF	Unc
		h. Litho. Sign. 6. ND.	8.00	20.00	50.00
		i. Sign. 7. ND.	10.00	25.00	60.00
		j. Sign. 8. ND.	10.00	25.00	60.00
		k. Sign. 9. ND.	8.00	20.00	50.00
		l. Sign. 10. ND.	6.00	15.00	40.00
		m. Sign. 11. ND.	6.00	15.00	40.00
		n. Sign. 12. ND.	6.00	15.00	40.00
		o. Sign. 13. ND.	6.00	15.00	40.00

Cat. #	Denomination	Date, Description	VG	VF	Unc
104A	5000 FRANCS	1961–65, ND. Design like #5.			
		a. Sign. 1. 20.3.1961.	35.00	75.00	175.00
		b. Sign. 2. 20.3.1961.	35.00	70.00	160.00
		c. Sign. 3. 2.12.1964.	35.00	70.00	160.00
		d. Sign. 4. 2.3.1965.	40.00	80.00	200.00
		h. Sign. 6. ND.	30.00	60.00	145.00
		i. Sign. 7. ND.	30.00	60.00	145.00
		j. Sign. 8. ND.	30.00	60.00	145.00
		k. Sign. 9. ND.	25.00	50.00	125.00
		l. Sign. 10. ND.	22.00	45.00	115.00
		m. Sign. 11. ND.	22.00	45.00	115.00

1977–81 ISSUE

#105A–109A smaller size notes.

Cat. #	Denomination	Date, Description	VG	VF	Unc
105A	500 FRANCS	1979–80. Lilac, lt. olive-green and m/c. Art-work at l., longhorn animals at ctr., man wearing hat at r. Pineapple at l., aerial view at ctr., mask at r. on back.			
		a. Sign. 12. 1979.	3.00	8.00	15.00
		b. Sign. 13. 1980.	2.50	7.00	12.00

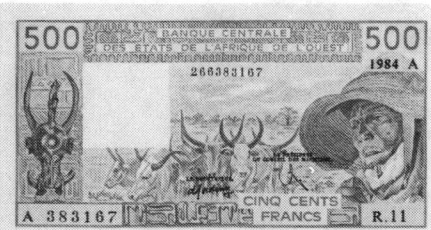

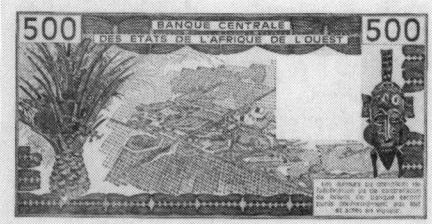

Cat. #	Denomination	Date, Description	VG	VF	Unc
106A	500 FRANCS	1981–90. Pale olive-green and m/c. Design like #105A.			
		a. Sign. 14. 1988.	FV	FV	5.00
		b. Sign. 15. 1981. (BdF).	5.00	15.00	35.00
		c. Sign. 15. 1981. (Oberthur).	FV	3.00	6.00
		d. Sign. 15. 1982. (BdF).	5.00	15.00	35.00
		e. Sign. 17. 1981. (Oberthur).	FV	3.00	6.00
		f. Sign. 17. 1983.	FV	3.00	6.00
		g. Sign. 18. 1984.	FV	3.00	6.00
		h. Sign. 19. 1984.	FV	3.00	6.00
		i. Sign. 19. 1985.	FV	3.00	6.00
		j Sign. 20. 1986.	FV	FV	6.00
		k. Sign. 20. 1987.	FV	FV	5.00
		l. Sign. 21 (reversed order). 1989.	FV	FV	5.00
		m. Sign. 22. 1990.	FV	FV	5.00

NOTE: #106A w/10-digit sm. serial # were printed by Banque de France (BdF) while those w/9-digit lg. serial # were printed by Oberthur.

Cat. #	Denomination	Date, Description	VG	VF	Unc
107A	1000 FRANCS	1981–90. Brown on m/c unpt. Artwork at l., open pit mine at ctr., woman at r. Wood carver w/finished works on back.			
		a. Sign. 14. 1988.	FV	FV	9.00
		b. Sign. 15. 1981.	FV	4.00	10.00
		c. Sign. 17. 1981.	FV	4.00	10.00
		d. Sign. 18. 1984.	FV	4.00	10.00
		e. Sign. 19. 1984.	4.00	9.00	25.00
		f. Sign. 19. 1985.	FV	4.00	10.00
		g. Sign. 20. 1986.	FV	FV	9.00
		h. Sign. 20. 1987.	FV	FV	9.00
		i. Sign. 21. 1989.	FV	FV	9.00
		j. Sign. 22. 1990.	FV	FV	9.00

Cat. #	Denomination	Date, Description	VG	VF	Unc
108A	5000 FRANCS	1977–92. Black and red on m/c unpt. Woman at l., fish and boats on shore at ctr., carving at r. Carvings, fishing boats and mask on back.			
		a. Sign. 11. 1977.	20.00	27.50	55.00
		b. Sign. 12. 1978.	20.00	27.50	55.00
		c. Sign. 12. 1979.	30.00	45.00	80.00
		d. Sign. 13. 1980.	35.00	50.00	100.00
		e. Sign. 14. 1977.	20.00	27.50	55.00
		f. Sign. 14. 1988.	FV	FV	33.00
		g. Sign. 14. 1989.	FV	FV	33.00
		h. Sign. 15. 1981.	FV	22.50	45.00
		i. Sign. 15. 1982.	FV	22.50	45.00
		j. Sign. 16. 1983.	35.00	50.00	100.00
		k. Sign. 17. 1983.	30.00	45.00	80.00
		l. Sign. 18. 1984.	30.00	45.00	80.00
		m. Sign. 19. 1984.	FV	22.50	45.00
		n. Sign. 19. 1985.	FV	22.50	45.00
		o. Sign. 20. 1986.	FV	FV	33.00
		p. Sign. 20. 1987.	FV	FV	33.00
		q. Sign. 21. 1990.	FV	FV	33.00
		r. Sign. 22. 1991.	FV	FV	33.00
109A	10,000 FRANCS	ND (1977–92). Red-brown on m/c unpt. 2 men seated operating primitive spinning apparatus, woman w/headwear at r. Figu-rine and girl at l., modern textile spinning machine at ctr. on back.			
		a. Sign. 11. ND.	40.00	50.00	90.00
		b. Sign. 12. ND.	40.00	50.00	90.00
		c. Sign. 13. ND.	40.00	50.00	90.00
		d. Sign. 14. ND.	FV	FV	90.00
		e. Sign. 15. ND.	FV	40.00	65.00
		f. Sign. 18. ND.	FV	40.00	65.00
		g. Sign. 19. ND.	40.00	50.00	90.00
		h. Sign. 20. ND.	FV	FV	60.00
		i. Sign. 21. ND.	FV	FV	60.00
		j. Sign. 22. ND.	FV	FV	60.00
		k. Sign. 23. ND.	FV	FV	50.00

1991–92 ISSUE

Cat. #	Denomination	Date, Description	VG	VF	Unc
113A	5000 FRANCS	(19)92–. Dk. brown and deep blue on m/c unpt. Woman wearing headdress adorned w/cowrie shells at r. and as wmk., smelting plant at ctr. Woman w/children and various pottery at l. ctr. on back. Sign. 23.			
		a. Sign. 23. (19)92.	FV	FV	25.00
		b. Sign. 25. (19)93.	FV	FV	25.00

Cat. #	Denomination	Date, Description	VG	VF	Unc
110A	500 FRANCS	(19)91–. Dk. brown and green on m/c unpt. Male at r. and as wmk., flood control dam at ctr. Farmer riding spray rig behind garden tractor at ctr., native art at l. on back.			
		a. Sign. 22. (19)91.	FV	FV	3.50
		b. Sign. 23. (19)92.	FV	FV	3.50
		c. Sign. 25. (19)93.	FV	FV	3.50
		d. Sign. 26. (19)94.	FV	FV	3.50
111A	1000 FRANCS	(19)91–. Dk. brown on tan, yellow and m/c unpt. Workman hauling peanuts to storage at ctr., woman's head at r. and as wmk. Twin statues and mask at l., 2 woman w/baskets, elevated riverside storage bins in background at ctr. on back.			
		a. Sign. 22. (19)91.	FV	FV	6.00
		b. Sign. 23. (19)92.	FV	FV	6.00
		c. Sign. 25. (19)93.	FV	FV	6.00
		d. Sign. 26. (19)94.	FV	FV	6.00

Cat. #	Denomination	Date, Description	VG	VF	Unc
114A	10,000 FRANCS	(19)92–. Dk. brown on m/c unpt. Headman w/scepter at r. and as wmk., skyscraper at ctr. Native art at l., woman crossing vine bridge over river at ctr. on back. Sign. 25.	FV	FV	45.00

NOTE: #113A and 114A were first issued on 19.9.1994.

Group 3 - Issues w/letter B for Benin (Dahomey).

1961 ISSUE

#201B–209B have letter B for Benin.

Cat. #	Denomination	Date, Description	VG	VF	Unc
112A	2500 FRANCS	(19)92–. Deep purple and dk. brown on lilac and m/c unpt. Dam at ctr., young woman's head at r. and as wmk. Statue at l., harvesting and spraying of fruit at l. ctr. on back. Sign. 23.			
		a. Sign. 23. (19)92.	FV	FV	16.00
		b. Sign. 25. (19)93.	FV	FV	16.00
		c. Sign. 27. (19)94.	FV	FV	16.00

Cat. #	Denomination	Date, Description	VG	VF	Unc
201B	100 FRANCS	1961–65; ND. Like #2.			
		a. Engraved. Sign. 1. 20.3.1961.	11.00	35.00	80.00
		b. Sign. 2. 20.3.1961.	11.00	35.00	80.00

Cat. #	Denomination	Date, Description	VG	VF	Unc
		c. Litho. Sign. 2. 20.3.1961.	11.00	35.00	80.00
		d. Sign. 3. 2.12.1964.	11.00	35.00	80.00
		e. Sign. 4. 2.3.1965.	10.00	30.00	70.00
		f. Sign. 4. ND.	8.00	20.00	50.00
202B	500 FRANCS	1961–64; ND. Like #3.			
		b. Engraved Sign. 2. 20.3.1961.	28.00	65.00	125.00
		d. Sign. 3. 2.12.1964.	—	—	—
		f. Sign. 5. ND.	25.00	60.00	100.00
		g. Sign. 6. ND.	10.00	32.00	65.00
		h. Litho. Sign. 7. ND.	15.00	40.00	75.00
		i. Sign. 9. ND.	10.00	30.00	65.00
		k. Sign. 10. ND.	8.00	20.00	50.00
		l. Sign. 11. ND.	8.00	20.00	50.00
203B	1000 FRANCS	1961–65; ND. Like #4.			
		a. Engraved. Sign. 1. 17.9.1959.	35.00	70.00	140.00
		b. Sign. 2. 20.3.1961.	30.00	60.00	120.00
		e. Sign. 4. 2.3.1965.	30.00	60.00	120.00
		g. Sign. 6. ND.	10.00	32.00	65.00
		h. Litho. Sign. 6. ND.	10.00	32.00	65.00
		i. Sign. 7. ND.	25.00	55.00	100.00
		j. Sign. 8. ND.	10.00	32.00	65.00
		k. Sign. 9. ND.	10.00	32.00	65.00
		l. Sign. 10. ND.	7.00	18.00	45.00
		m. Sign. 11. ND.	7.00	18.00	45.00
		n. Sign. 12. ND.	7.00	18.00	45.00
204B	5000 FRANCS	1961; ND. Like #5.			
		a. Sign. 1. 20.3.1961.	40.00	80.00	200.00
		h. Sign. 6. ND.	30.00	65.00	150.00
		j. Sign. 7. ND.	30.00	65.00	150.00
		k. Sign. 9. ND.	25.00	55.00	135.00
		l. Sign. 10. ND.	25.00	55.00	135.00

1979–81 ISSUES

#205B–209B smaller size notes.

Cat. #	Denomination	Date, Description	VG	VF	Unc
205B	500 FRANCS	1979–80. Like #105A.			
		a. Sign. 12. 1979.	5.00	15.00	35.00
		b. Sign. 13. 1980.	3.00	8.00	15.00
206B	500 FRANCS	1981–90. Like #106A.			
		a. Sign. 14. 1988.	5.00	15.00	35.00
		b. Sign. 15. 1981. (BdF).	FV	3.50	7.00
		c. Sign. 15. 1981. (Oberthur).	FV	2.50	7.00
		d. Sign. 15. 1982. (BdF).	5.00	15.00	35.00
		e. Sign. 17. 1981.	5.00	15.00	35.00
		f. Sign. 18. 1984.	FV	3.50	7.00
		g. Sign. 19. 1984.	FV	5.00	10.00
		h. Sign. 19. 1985.	FV	3.50	7.00
		i. Sign. 20. 1986.	FV	FV	6.00
		j. Sign. 20. 1987.	FV	FV	6.00
		k. Sign. 21. 1989.	FV	FV	6.00
		l. Sign. 22. 1990.	FV	FV	6.00

NOTE: #206B w/10-digit sm. serial # were printed by Banque de France (BdF) while those w/9-digit lg. serial # were printed by Oberthur.

Cat. #	Denomination	Date, Description	VG	VF	Unc
207B	1000 FRANCS	1981–90. Like #107A.			
		a. Sign. 14. 1988.	FV	FV	10.00
		b. Sign. 15. 1981.	FV	4.50	11.00
		c. Sign. 18. 1984.	FV	4.50	11.00
		d. Sign. 19. 1985.	FV	4.50	11.00
		e. Sign. 20. 1986.	FV	FV	10.00
		f. Sign. 20. 1987.	FV	FV	10.00
		g. Sign. 21. 1989.	4.00	9.00	25.00
		h. Sign. 22. 1990.	FV	FV	10.00
208B	5000 FRANCS	1977–92. Like #108A.			
		a. Sign. 12. 1979.	22.00	30.00	60.00
		b. Sign. 14. 1977.	22.00	30.00	60.00
		c. Sign. 14. 1988.	FV	FV	35.00
		d. Sign. 14. 1989.	FV	FV	35.00
		e. Sign. 15. 1981.	FV	25.00	50.00
		f. Sign. 15. 1982.	FV	25.00	50.00
		g. Sign. 17. 1983.	30.00	45.00	80.00
		h. Sign. 19. 1985.	30.00	45.00	80.00
		i. Sign. 20. 1986.	25.00	40.00	70.00
		j. Sign. 20. 1987.	FV	FV	35.00
		k. Sign. 21. 1990.	FV	FV	35.00
		l. Sign. 22. 1991.	FV	FV	35.00
		m. Sign. 22. 1992.	FV	FV	35.00
		n. Sign. 23. 1992.	FV	FV	35.00
209B	10,000 FRANCS	ND (1977–92). Like #109A.			
		a. Sign. 11. ND.	50.00	75.00	135.00
		b. Sign. 12. ND.	50.00	75.00	135.00
		c. Sign. 14. ND.	FV	FV	65.00
		d. Sign. 15. ND.	FV	50.00	85.00
		e. Sign. 16. ND.	50.00	75.00	135.00
		f. Sign. 19. ND.	FV	40.00	70.00
		g. Sign. 20. ND.	FV	FV	65.00
		h. Sign. 21. ND.	FV	FV	65.00
		i. Sign. 22. ND.	FV	FV	65.00

1991–92 ISSUE

Cat. #	Denomination	Date, Description	VG	VF	Unc
210B	500 FRANCS	(19)91–. Like #110A.			
		a. Sign. 22. (19)91.	FV	FV	4.00
		b. Sign. 22. (19)92.	FV	FV	4.00
		c. Sign. 23. (19)92.	FV	FV	4.00
		d. Sign. 25. (19)93.	FV	FV	4.00
		e. Sign. 26. (19)94.	FV	FV	4.00
211B	1000 FRANCS	(19)91–. Like #111A.			
		a. Sign. 22. (19)91.	FV	FV	7.00
		b. Sign. 22. (19)92.	FV	FV	7.00
		c. Sign. 23. (19)92.	FV	FV	7.00
		d. Sign. 25. (19)93.	FV	FV	7.00

Cat. #	Denomination	Date, Description	VG	VF	Unc
212B	2500 FRANCS	(19)92–. Like #112A.			
		a. Sign. 23. (19)92.	FV	FV	20.00
		b. Sign. 25. (19)93.	FV	FV	20.00
		c. Sign. 27. (19)94.	FV	FV	20.00
213B	5000 FRANCS	(19)92–. Like #113A.			
		a. Sign. 23. (19)92.	FV	FV	30.00
		b. Sign. 25. (19)93.	FV	FV	30.00
214B	10,000 FRANCS	(19)92–. Like #114A. Sign. 25.	FV	FV	30.00

Group 4 - Issues w/letter C for Burkina Faso (Upper Volta).

1961; ND ISSUE

#301C–309C have letter C for Burkina Faso.

Cat. #	Denomination	Date, Description	VG	VF	Unc
301C	100 FRANCS	1961–65; ND. Like #2.			
		a. Engraved. Sign. 1. 20.3.1961.	10.00	30.00	70.00
		b. Sign. 2. 20.3.1961.	10.00	30.00	70.00
		c. Litho. Sign. 2. 20.3.1961.	10.00	30.00	70.00
		d. Sign. 3. 2.12.1964.	—	—	—
		e. Sign. 4. 2.3.1965.	10.00	30.00	70.00
		f. Sign. 4. ND.	8.00	18.50	45.00
302C	500 FRANCS	1961–65; ND. Like #3.			
		c. Engraved. Sign. 2. 20.3.1961.	25.00	60.00	100.00
		e. Sign. 4. 20.3.1961.	25.00	60.00	100.00
		g. Sign. 6. ND.	15.00	40.00	75.00

Cat. #	Denomination	Date, Description	VG	VF	Unc
		h. Litho. Sign. 6. ND.	10.00	30.00	60.00
		i. Sign. 7. ND.	15.00	40.00	75.00
		j. Sign. 8. ND.	15.00	40.00	75.00
		k. Sign. 9. ND.	10.00	30.00	60.00
		m. Sign. 11. ND.	7.00	18.00	45.00
		n. Sign. 12. ND.	7.00	18.00	45.00
303C	1000 FRANCS	1961; ND. Like #4.			
		b. Sign. 1. 20.3.1961.	35.00	70.00	140.00
		d. Sign. 2. 20.3.1961.	35.00	70.00	140.00
		e. Sign. 5. ND.	—	—	—
		f. Sign. 6. ND.	25.00	60.00	100.00
		i. Sign. 7. ND.	10.00	25.00	60.00
		j. Sign. 8. ND.	30.00	65.00	120.00
		k. Sign. 9. ND.	12.00	28.00	65.00
		l. Sign. 10. ND.	6.00	15.00	40.00
		m. Sign. 11. ND	6.00	15.00	40.00
		n. Sign. 12. ND.	6.00	15.00	40.00
		o. Sign. 13. ND.	12.00	28.00	65.00
304C	5000 FRANCS	ND. Like #5.			
		a. Sign. 1. 20.3.1961.	35.00	75.00	175.00
		h. Sign. 6. ND.	30.00	60.00	145.00
		i. Sign. 7. ND.	30.00	60.00	145.00
		k. Sign. 9. ND.	30.00	60.00	145.00
		l. Sign. 11. ND.	25.00	50.00	125.00

1971–81; ND ISSUES

#305C–309C smaller size notes.

Cat. #	Denomination	Date, Description	VG	VF	Unc
305C	500 FRANCS	1979–80. Like #105A. Sign. 12.			
		a. Sign. 12. 1979.	3.00	8.00	15.00
		b. Sign. 13. 1980.	2.50	7.00	12.00

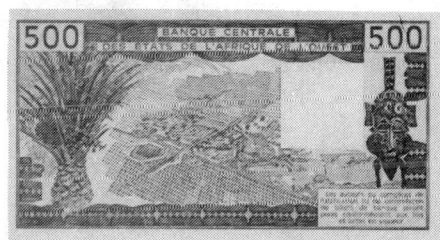

Cat. #	Denomination	Date, Description	VG	VF	Unc
306C	500 FRANCS	1981–90. Like #106A.			
		a. Sign. 14. 1988.	FV	FV	5.00
		b. Sign. 15. 1981. (BdF).	FV	3.00	6.00
		c. Sign. 15. 1981. (Oberthur).	Fv	3.00	6.00
		d. Sign. 15. 1982. (BdF).	3.00	6.00	15.00
		f. Sign. 17.1983.	3.00	6.00	15.00
		g. Sign. 18.1984.	FV	3.00	6.00
		h. Sign. 19.1984.	FV	3.00	6.00
		i. Sign. 19.1985.	Fv	3.00	6.00
		j. Sign. 20.1986.	4.00	9.00	25.00
		k. Sign. 20.1987.	FV	FV	5.00
		l. Sign. 21.1989.	FV	FV	5.00
		m. Sign. 22. 1990.	FV	FV	5.00

NOTE: #306C 10–Digit sm. serial # were printed by Banque de France (BdF) while those w/ 9–digit lg. serial # were printed by Oberthur.

Cat. #	Denomination	Date, Description	VG	VF	Unc
307C	1000 FRANCS	1981–90. Like #107A.			
		a. Sign. 14. 1988.	FV	FV	12.00
		b. Sign. 15. 1981.	FV	4.00	12.00
		c. Sign. 17. 1981.	4.00	9.00	25.00
		d. Sign. 18. 1984.	4.00	9.00	25.00
		e. Sign. 19. 1984.	4.00	9.00	25.00
		f. Sign. 19. 1985.	4.00	9.00	25.00
		g. Sign. 20. 1986.	FV	FV	12.00
		h. Sign. 20. 1987.	FV	FV	12.00
		i. Sign. 21. 1989.	FV	FV	12.00
		j. Sign. 22. 1990.	FV	FV	12.00
308C	5000 FRANCS	1977–92 Like #108A.			
		a. Sign. 12. 1978.	20.00	27.50	55.00
		b. Sign. 12. 1979.	20.00	27.50	55.00
		c. Sign. 14. 1977.	20.00	27.50	55.00
		d. Sign. 14. 1988.	FV	FV	33.00
		e. Sign. 14. 1989.	FV	FV	33.00
		f. Sign. 15. 1981.	FV	22.00	45.00
		g. Sign. 15. 1982.	FV	22.00	45.00
		h. Sign. 17. 1983.	FV	22.00	45.00
		i. Sign. 18. 1984.	FV	22.00	45.00
		j. Sign. 19. 1985.	FV	22.00	45.00
		k. Sign. 20. 1986.	25.00	35.00	75.00
		l. Sign. 20. 1987.	FV	FV	33.00
		m. Sign. 21. 1990.	FV	FV	33.00
		n. Sign. 22. 1991.	FV	FV	33.00
		o. Sign. 22. 1992.	FV	FV	33.00
		p. Sign. 23. 1992.	FV	FV	33.00
		q. Sign. 24. 1992.	FV	FV	33.00
309C	10,000 FRANCS	ND (1977–92). Like #109A.			
		a. Sign. 11.	50.00	75.00	135.00
		b. Sign. 12.	40.00	50.00	90.00
		c. Sign. 13.	40.00	50.00	90.00
		d. Sign. 14.	40.00	50.00	90.00
		e. Sign. 15.	FV	40.00	65.00
		f. Sign. 20.	FV	FV	60.00
		g. Sign. 21.	FV	FV	60.00
		h. Sign. 22.	FV	FV	60.00
		i. Sign. 23.	FV	FV	60.00

1991–92 ISSUE

Cat. #	Denomination	Date, Description	VG	VF	Unc
310C	500 FRANCS	(19)91–. Like #110A.			
		a. Sign. 22. (19)91.	FV	FV	5.00
		b. Sign. 23. (19)92.	FV	FV	5.00
		c. Sign. 25. (19)93.	FV	FV	5.00
		d. Sign. 26. (19)94.	FV	FV	3.50
311C	1000 FRANCS	(19)91–. Like #111A.			
		a. Sign. 22. (19)91.	FV	FV	9.00
		b. Sign. 22. (19)92.	FV	FV	9.00
		c. Sign. 23. (19)92.	FV	FV	9.00
		d. Sign. 25. (19)93.	FV	FV	9.00
		e. Sign. 26. (19)94.	FV	FV	6.00
312C	2500 FRANCS	(19)91–. Like #112A.			
		a. Sign. 23. (19)92.	FV	FV	20.00
		b. Sign. 25. (19)93.	FV	FV	20.00
		c. Sign. 27. (19)94.	FV	FV	18.00
313C	5000 FRANCS	(19)92–. Like #113A. Sign. 23.	FV	FV	26.00
314C	10,000 FRANCS	(19)92–. Like #114A.			
		a. Sign. 25. (19)92.	FV	FV	45.00
		b. Sign. 27. (19)94.	FV	FV	45.00

Group 5 - Issues w/letter D for Mali.

1959–61 ISSUE

#401D–408D have letter D for Mali.

Cat. #	Denomination	Date, Description	VG	VF	Unc
401D	100 FRANCS	20.3.1961. Like #2. Sign. l.	50.00	100.00	—
402D	500 FRANCS	1959; 1961. Like #3.			
		a. Sign. l. 15.4.1959.	85.00	150.00	—
		b. Sign. l. 20.3.1961.	—	—	—
403D	1000 FRANCS	1959; 1961. Like #4.			
		a. Sign. l. 17.9.1959.	60.00	125.00	—
		b. Sign. l. 20.3.1961.	50.00	100.00	—
404D	5000 FRANCS	20.3.1961. Like #5. Sign. l.	100.00	200.00	—

1981; ND ISSUE

#405D–408D smaller size notes.

Cat. #	Denomination	Date, Description	VG	VF	Unc
405D	500 FRANCS	1981–90. Like #106A.			
		a. Sign. 14. 1988.	FV	FV	5.00
		b. Sign. 15. 1981. (BdF).	FV	3.00	6.00
		c. Sign. 17. 1981. (Oberthur).	FV	3.00	6.00
		e. Sign. 19. 1985.	FV	3.00	6.00
		f. Sign. 20. 1986.	FV	FV	5.00
		g. Sign. 20. 1987.	FV	FV	5.00
		h. Sign. 21. 1989.	FV	FV	5.00
		i. Sign. 22. 1990.	FV	FV	5.00

NOTE: #405D w/10-digit sm. serial # were printed by Banque de France (BdF) while those w/9-digit lg. serial # were printed by Oberthur.

Cat. #	Denomination	Date, Description	VG	VF	Unc
406D	1000 FRANCS	1981–90. Like #107A.			
		a. Sign. 14. 1988.	FV	FV	9.00
		b. Sign. 15. 1981.	FV	4.00	10.00
		c. Sign. 17. 1981.	FV	4.00	10.00
		f. Sign. 19. 1985.	4.00	9.00	25.00
		g. Sign. 20. 1986.	4.00	9.00	25.00
		h. Sign. 20. 1987.	4.00	9.00	25.00
		i. Sign. 21. 1989.	FV	FV	9.00
		j. Sign. 22. 1990.	FV	FV	9.00
407D	5000 FRANCS	1981–92. Like #108A.			
		a. Sign. 14. 1988.	FV	FV	33.00
		b. Sign. 14. 1989.	FV	FV	33.00
		c. Sign. 15. 1981.	FV	22.00	45.00
		d. Sign. 17. 1984.	FV	22.00	45.00
		e. Sign. 18. 1984.	25.00	35.00	75.00
		f. Sign. 19. 1985.	FV	22.00	45.00
		g. Sign. 20. 1986.	FV	FV	33.00
		h. Sign. 20. 1987.	FV	FV	33.00
		i. Sign. 21. 1990.	FV	FV	33.00
		j. Sign. 22. 1991.	FV	FV	33.00
		k. Sign. 23. 1992.	FV	FV	33.00
		l. Sign. 24. 1992.	FV	FV	33.00
408D	10,000 FRANCS	ND (1981–92). Like #109A.			
		a. Sign. 14. ND.	FV	FV	60.00
		b. Sign. 15. ND.	FV	40.00	65.00
		c. Sign. 18. ND.	30.00	45.00	85.00
		d. Sign. 19. ND.	30.00	45.00	85.00
		e. Sign. 20. ND.	FV	FV	60.00
		f. Sign. 21. ND.	FV	FV	60.00
		g. Sign. 22. ND.	FV	FV	60.00

1991–92 ISSUE

Cat. #	Denomination	Date, Description	VG	VF	Unc
410D	500 FRANCS	(19)91–. Like #110A.			
		a. Sign. 22. (19)91.	FV	FV	3.50
		b. Sign. 23. (19)92.	FV	FV	3.50
		c. Sign. 25. (19)93.	FV	FV	3.50
		d. Sign. 26. (19)93.	FV	FV	3.50

Cat. #	Denomination	Date, Description	VG	VF	Unc
411D	1000 FRANCS	(19)91–. Like #111A.			
		a. Sign. 22.	FV	FV	9.00
		b. Sign. 25. (19)92.	FV	FV	6.00
		c. Sign. 25. (19)93.	FV	FV	6.00
412D	2500 FRANCS	(19)92–. Like #112A.			
		a. Sign. 23. (19)93.	FV	FV	18.00
		b. Sign. 25. (19)93.	FV	FV	18.00
413D	5000 FRANCS	(19)92–. Like #113A.			
		a. Sign. 23. (19)92.	FV	FV	26.00

Cat. #	Denomination	Date, Description	VG	VF	Unc
414D	10,000 FRANCS	(19)92–. Like #114A.			
		a. Sign. 24. (19)92.	FV	FV	45.00

Group 6 - Issues w/letter E for Mauritania.

1959–61 ISSUE

#501E–504E have letter E for Mauritania.

Cat. #	Denomination	Date, Description	VG	VF	Unc
501E	100 FRANCS	1961–65; ND. Like #2.			
		b. Sign. 1. 20.3.1961.	30.00	85.00	170.00
		c. Sign. 3. 2.12.1964.	30.00	85.00	170.00
		e. Sign. 4. 2.3.1965.	30.00	85.00	170.00
		f. Sign. 4. ND.	25.00	75.00	150.00
502E	500 FRANCS	1959–64; ND. Like #3.			
		a. Engraved. Sign. I. 15.4.1959.	50.00	110.00	300.00
		b. Sign. I. 20.3.1961.	40.00	95.00	200.00
		c. Sign. 2. 20.3.1961.	40.00	95.00	200.00
		e. Sign. 4. 2.3.1965.	40.00	95.00	200.00
		f. Sign. 5. ND.	40.00	95.00	200.00
		g. Sign. 6. ND.	40.00	95.00	200.00
		h. Litho. Sign. 6. ND.	40.00	95.00	200.00
		i. Sign. 7. ND.	40.00	95.00	200.00
503E	1000 FRANCS	1961–65; ND. Like #4.			
		b. Engraved. Sign. I. 20.3.1961.	60.00	125.00	300.00
		e. Sign. 4. 2.3.1965.	60.00	125.00	300.00
		g. Sign. 6. ND.	50.00	95.00	225.00
		h. Litho. Sign. 6. ND.	50.00	95.00	225.00
504E	5000 FRANCS	1961–65; ND. Like #5.			
		a. Sign. 1. 20.3.1961.	65.00	130.00	300.00
		b. Sign. 2. 20.3.1961.	65.00	130.00	300.00
		c. Sign. 4. 2.3.1965.	65.00	130.00	300.00
		d. Sign. 6. ND.	60.00	120.00	250.00
		e. Sign. 7. ND.	60.00	120.00	250.00

Group 7 - Issues w/letter H for Niger.

1959–61 ISSUE

#601H–608H have letter H for Niger.

Cat. #	Denomination	Date, Description	VG	VF	Unc
601H	100 FRANCS	1961–65; ND. Like #2.			
		a. Engraved. Sign. 1. 20.3.1961.	11.00	35.00	80.00
		b. Sign. 2. 20.3.1961.	11.00	35.00	80.00
		c. Litho. Sign. 2. 20.3.1961.	11.00	35.00	80.00
		d. Sign. 3. 2.12.1964.	11.00	35.00	80.00
		e. Sign. 4. 2.3.1965.	11.00	35.00	80.00
		f. Sign. 4. ND.	8.00	20.00	50.00
602H	500 FRANCS	1959–65; ND. Like #3.			
		a. Engraved. Sign. 1. 15.4.1959.	28.00	65.00	125.00
		d. Sign. 3. 2.12.1964.	25.00	60.00	115.00
		e. Sign. 4. 2.3.1965.	25.00	60.00	115.00
		g. Sign. 6. ND.	15.00	40.00	75.00
		h. Litho Sign. 6. ND.	15.00	40.00	75.00
		i. Sign. 7. ND.	—	—	—
		j. Sign. 8. ND.	20.00	55.00	100.00
		k. Sign. 9. ND.	15.00	40.00	75.00
		m. Sign. 11. ND.	10.00	32.00	65.00

Cat. #	Denomination	Date, Description	VG	VF	Unc
603H	1000 FRANCS	1959–65; ND. Like #4.			
		a. Sign. I. 17.9.1959.	—	—	—
		b. Sign. I. 20.3.1961.	35.00	65.00	145.00
		e. Sign. 4. 2.3.1965.	35.00	65.00	145.00
		f. Sign. 5. ND.	35.00	65.00	145.00
		h. Sign. 6. ND.	15.50	40.00	75.00
		i. Litho. Sign. 7. ND.	10.00	32.00	65.00
		j. Sign. 8. ND.	30.00	60.00	120.00
		k. Sign. 9. ND.	10.00	32.00	65.00
		l. Sign. 10. ND.	7.00	18.50	45.00
		m. Sign. 11. ND.	7.00	18.00	45.00
		n. Sign. 12. ND.	7.00	18.50	45.00
		o. Sign. 13. ND.	7.00	18.50	45.00
604H	5000 FRANCS	ND (1966). Like #5.			
		i. Sign. 7.	30.00	70.00	175.00
		k. Sign. 9.	30.00	70.00	175.00
		l. Sign. 10.	30.00	65.00	150.00
		m. Sign. 11.	25.00	55.00	135.00

1977–81; ND ISSUES

#605H–608H smaller size notes.

Cat. #	Denomination	Date, Description	VG	VF	Unc
605H	500 FRANCS	1979–80. Like #105A.			
		a. Sign. 12. 1979.	4.00	10.00	20.00
		b. Sign. 13. 1980.	3.00	8.00	15.00
606H	500 FRANCS	1981–90. Like #106A.			
		a. Sign. 14. 1988.	FV	FV	6.00
		b. Sign. 15. 1981. (BdF).	FV	3.50	9.00
		c. Sign. 15. 1981. (Oberthur).	FV	3.50	9.00
		d. Sign. 17. 1981. (Oberthur).	FV	3.50	9.00
		e. Sign. 18. 1984.	4.00	9.00	25.00
		f. Sign. 20. 1986.	FV	FV	7.50
		g. Sign. 20. 1987.	FV	FV	7.50
		h. Sign. 21. 1989.	FV	FV	7.50
		i. Sign. 22. 1990.	FV	FV	7.50
607H	1000 FRANCS	1981–90. Like #107A.			
		a. Sign. 14. 1988.	FV	FV	12.50
		b. Sign. 15. 1981.	FV	4.50	12.50
		c. Sign. 17. 1981.	4.00	9.00	25.00
		d. Sign. 18. 1984.	4.00	9.00	25.00
		e. Sign. 19. 1994.	4.00	9.00	25.00
		f. Sign. 19. 1985.	FV	FV	15.00
		g. Sign. 20. 1986.	FV	FV	12.50
		h. Sign. 20. 1987.	FV	FV	12.50
		i. Sign. 21, 1989.	FV	FV	12.50
		j. Sign. 22. 1990.	FV	FV	12.50

Cat. #	Denomination	Date, Description	VG	VF	Unc
608H	5000 FRANCS	1977–. Like #108A.			
		a. Sign. 12. 1978.	22.00	30.00	60.00
		b. Sign. 12. 1979.	22.00	30.00	60.00
		c. Sign. 13. 1980.	35.00	50.00	100.00
		d. Sign. 14. 1977.	22.00	30.00	60.00
		e. Sign. 14. 1989.	FV	FV	35.00
		f. Sign. 15. 1981.	FV	25.00	50.00
		g. Sign. 15. 1982.	FV	25.00	50.00
		h. Sign. 17. 1983.	FV	25.00	50.00
		i. Sign. 18. 1984.	FV	25.00	50.00
		j. Sign. 19. 1985.	FV	25.00	50.00
		k. Sign. 20. 1986.	FV	FV	35.00
		l. Sign. 20. 1987.	FV	FV	35.00
		m. Sign. 21. 1990.	FV	FV	35.00
609H	10,000 FRANCS	ND (1977). Like #109A.			
		a. Sign. 11.	40.00	55.00	95.00
		b. Sign. 12.	45.00	65.00	125.00

Cat. #	Denomination	Date, Description	VG	VF	Unc
		c. Sign. 13.	45.00	65.00	125.00
		d. Sign. 14.	FV	FV	65.00
		e. Sign. 15.	FV	40.00	70.00
		f. Sign. 18.	40.00	55.00	95.00
		g. Sign. 19.	40.00	55.00	95.00
		h. Sign. 20.	FV	FV	65.00
		i. Sign. 21.	FV	FV	65.00
		j. Sign. 22.	FV	FV	65.00

1991–92 ISSUE

Cat. #	Denomination	Date, Description	VG	VF	Unc
610H	500 FRANCS	(19)91–. Like #110A.			
		a. Sign. 22. (19)91.	FV	FV	7.00
		b. Sign. 23. (19)92.	FV	FV	7.00
		c. Sign. 25. (19)93.	FV	FV	7.00
611H	1000 FRANCS	(19)91–. Like #111A.			
		a. Sign. 23. (19)91.	FV	FV	10.00
		b. Sign. 23. (19)92.	FV	FV	10.00
		c. Sign. 25. (19)93.	FV	FV	10.00
612H	2500 FRANCS	(19)92–. Like #112A.			
		a. Sign. 23. (19)92.	FV	FV	20.00
		b. Sign. 25. (19)93.	FV	FV	20.00
613H	5000 FRANCS	(19)92–. Like #113A. Sign. 23.	FV	FV	30.00
614H	10,000 FRANCS	(19)92–. Like #114A. Sign. 25.	FV	FV	50.00

Group 8 - Issues w/letter K for Senegal.

1959–61 ISSUE

#701K - 709K have letter K for Senegal.

Cat. #	Denomination	Date, Description	VG	VF	Unc
701K	100 FRANCS	1961–65; ND. Like #2.			
		a. Engraved. Sign. 1. 20.3.1961.	10.00	30.00	70.00
		b. Sign. 2. 20.3.1961.	10.00	25.00	60.00
		c. Litho. Sign. 2. 20.3.1961.	10.00	25.00	60.00
		d. Sign. 3. 2.12.1964.	10.00	25.00	60.00
		e. Sign. 4. 2.3.1965.	10.00	25.00	60.00
		f. Sign. 4. ND.	8.00	20.00	50.00
		g. Sign. 5. ND.	8.00	20.00	50.00
702K	500 FRANCS	1959–65; ND. Like #3.			
		a. Engraved. Sign. 1. 15.4.1959.	17.00	45.00	85.00
		b. Sign. 1. 20.3.1961.	15.00	40.00	75.00
		c. Sign. 2. 20.3.1961.	15.00	40.00	75.00
		d. Sign. 3. 2.12.1964.	15.00	40.00	75.00
		e. Sign. 4. 2.3.1965.	15.00	40.00	75.00
		f. Sign. 5. ND.	17.00	45.00	85.00
		g. Sign. 6. ND.	10.00	30.00	60.00
		h. Litho. Sign. 6. ND.	10.00	30.00	60.00
		i. Sign. 7. ND.	10.00	30.00	60.00
		j. Sign. 8. ND.	15.00	42.50	75.00
		k. Sign. 9. ND.	8.00	20.00	50.00
		l. Sign. 10. ND.	5.00	15.00	40.00
		m. Sign. 11. ND.	5.00	15.00	40.00
		n. Sign. 12. ND.	5.00	15.00	40.00

Cat. #	Denomination	Date, Description	VG	VF	Unc
703K	1000 FRANCS	1959–65; ND. Like #4.			
		a. Engraved. Sign. l. 17.9.1959.	25.00	60.00	110.00
		b. Sign. l. 20.3.1961.	30.00	65.00	125.00
		c. Sign. 2. 20.3.1961.	15.00	50.00	95.00
		e. Sign. 4. 2.3.1965.	15.00	50.00	95.00
		f. Sign. 5. ND.	30.00	65.00	125.00
		g. Sign. 6. ND.	30.00	65.00	125.00
		h. Litho. Sign. 6. ND.	8.00	20.00	50.00
		i. Sign. 7. ND.	10.00	25.00	60.00
		j. Sign. 8. ND.	15.00	50.00	95.00
		k. Sign. 9. ND.	8.00	20.00	50.00
		l. Sign. 10. ND.	8.00	20.00	50.00
		m. Sign. 11. ND.	5.00	15.00	40.00
		n. Sign. 12. ND.	5.00	15.00	40.00
		o. Sign. 13. ND.	10.00	25.00	60.00
704K	5000 FRANCS	1961–65; ND. Like #5.			
		b. Sign. 1. 20.3.1961.	35.00	75.00	175.00
		c. Sign. 2. 20.3.1961.	35.00	75.00	175.00
		d. Sign. 3. 2.12.1964.	35.00	70.00	160.00
		e. Sign. 4. 2.3.1965.	35.00	70.00	160.00
		h. Sign. 6. ND.	30.00	60.00	140.00
		i. Sign. 7. ND.	35.00	70.00	160.00
		j. Sign. 9. ND.	35.00	70.00	160.00
		k. Sign. 10. ND.	25.00	50.00	125.00
		m. Sign. 11. ND.	25.00	50.00	125.00

1977–81; ND ISSUES

#705K–709K smaller size notes.

Cat. #	Denomination	Date, Description	VG	VF	Unc
705K	500 FRANCS	1979–80. Like #105A.			
		a. Sign. 12. 1979.	3.00	8.00	15.00
		b. Sign. 13. 1980.	2.50	7.00	12.00

Cat. #	Denomination	Date, Description	VG	VF	Unc
706K	500 FRANCS	1981–. Like #106A.			
		a. Sign. 14. 1988.	FV	FV	5.00
		b. Sign. 15. 1981 (BdF).	5.00	15.00	35.00
		c. Sign. 15. 1981. (Oberthur).	FV	3.00	6.00
		d. Sign. 15. 1982. (BdF).	FV	4.00	8.00
		e. Sign. 17. 1981. (Oberthur).	FV	3.00	6.00
		f. Sign. 17. 1983. (BdF).	FV	4.00	8.00
		g. Sign. 18. 1984.	FV	3.00	6.00
		h. Sign. 19. 1985.	FV	3.00	6.00
		i. Sign. 20. 1986.	FV	FV	5.00
		j. Sign. 20. 1987.	FV	FV	5.00
		k. Sign. 21. (reversed order). 1989.	FV	FV	5.00
		l. Sign. 22. 1990.	FV	FV	5.00

NOTE: #106A w/10-digit sm. serial # were printed by Banque de France (BdF) while those w/9-digit lg. sreial # were printed by Oberthur.

Cat. #	Denomination	Date, Description	VG	VF	Unc
707K	1000 FRANCS	1981–90. Like #107A.			
		a. Sign. 14. 1988.	FV	FV	9.00
		b. Sign. 15. 1981.	FV	4.00	10.00
		c. Sign. 17. 1981.	FV	4.00	10.00
		d. Sign. 18. 1984.	FV	4.00	10.00
		e. Sign. 19. 1984.	FV	6.00	15.00
		f. Sign. 19. 1985.	FV	FV	10.00
		g. Sign. 20. 1986.	FV	FV	9.00
		h. Sign. 20. 1987.	FV	FV	9.00
		h. Sign. 21. 1989.	FV	FV	9.00
		i. Sign. 22. 1990.	FV	FV	9.00
708K	5000 FRANCS	1977–. Like #107A.			
		a. Sign. 12. 1978.	20.00	27.50	55.00
		b. Sign. 12. 1979.	20.00	27.50	55.00

Cat. #	Denomination	Date, Description	VG	VF	Unc
		c. Sign. 13. 1980.	22.00	30.00	60.00
		d. Sign. 14. 1977.	20.00	27.50	55.00
		e. Sign. 14. 1989.	FV	FV	33.00
		f. Sign. 15. 1982.	20.00	27.50	55.00
		g. Sign. 16. 1983.	22.00	30.00	60.00
		h. Sign. 17. 1983.	20.00	27.50	55.00
		i. Sign. 18. 1984.	20.00	27.50	55.00
		j. Sign. 19. 1985.	22.00	30.00	60.00
		k. Sign. 20. 1986.	22.00	30.00	60.00
		l. Sign. 20. 1987.	FV	FV	33.00
		m. Sign. 21. 1990.	FV	FV	33.00
		n. Sign. 22. 1991.	FV	FV	33.00
		o. Sign. 22. 1992.	FV	FV	33.00
		p. Sign. 24. 1992.	FV	FV	33.00
709K	10,000 FRANCS	ND. (1977–). Like #109A.			
		a. Sign. 11. ND.	40.00	50.00	90.00
		b. Sign. 12. ND.	40.00	50.00	90.00
		c. Sign. 13. ND.	40.00	50.00	90.00
		d. Sign. 14. ND.	FV	FV	60.00
		e. Sign. 15. ND.	FV	40.00	65.00
		f. Sign. 16. ND.	42.00	55.00	100.00
		h. Sign. 18. ND.	FV	40.00	65.00
		i. Sign. 19. ND.	42.00	55.00	100.00
		j. Sign. 20. ND.	FV	FV	60.00
		k. Sign. 21. ND.	FV	FV	60.00
		l. Sign. 22. ND.	FV	FV	60.00
		m. Sign. 23. ND.	FV	FV	60.00

1991–92 ISSUE

Cat. #	Denomination	Date, Description	VG	VF	Unc
710K	500 FRANCS	(19)91–. Like #110A.			
		a. Sign. 22. (19)91.	FV	FV	3.50
		b. Sign. 23. (19)92.	FV	FV	3.50
		c. Sign. 25. (19)93.	FV	FV	3.50
		d. Sign. 26. (19)94.	FV	FV	3.50
711K	1000 FRANCS	(19)91–. Like #111A.			
		a. Sign. 22. (19)91.	FV	FV	6.00
		b. Sign. 23. (19)92.	FV	FV	6.00
		c. Sign. 25. (19)93.	FV	FV	6.00
712K	2500 FRANCS	(19)92–. Like #112A.			
		a. Sign. 23. (19)92.	FV	FV	18.00
		b. Sign. 25. (19)93.	FV	FV	18.00
713K	5000 FRANCS	(19)92–. Like #113A.			
		a. Sign. 23. (19)92.	FV	FV	26.00
		b. Sign. 25. (19)93.	FV	FV	26.00
714K	10,000 FRANCS	(19)92–. Like #114A.	FV	FV	45.00

Group 9 – Issues w/letter T for Togo

1959–61 ISSUE

#801T–809T have letter T for Togo.

Cat. #	Denomination	Date, Description	VG	VF	Unc
801T	100 FRANCS	1961–65. Like #2.			
		a. Engraved. Sign. 1. 20.3.1961.	10.00	30.00	70.00
		b. Sign. 2. 20.3.1961.	10.00	30.00	70.00
		c. Litho. Sign. 2. 20.3.1961.	10.00	30.00	70.00
		d. Sign. 3. 2.12.1964.	10.00	30.00	70.00
		e. Sign. 4. 2.3.1965.	8.00	20.00	50.00
		f. Sign. 4. ND.	8.00	20.00	50.00
		g. Sign. 5. ND.	8.00	20.00	50.00

Cat. #	Denomination	Date, Description	VG	VF	Unc
802T	500 FRANCS	1959-61; ND. Like #3.			
		a. Engraved. Sign. 1. 15.4.1959.	28.00	65.00	125.00
		b. Sign. 1. 20.3.1961.	28.00	65.00	125.00
		c. Sign. 2. 20.3.1961.	28.00	65.00	125.00
		g. Sign. 5. ND.	28.00	65.00	125.00
		h. Sign. 6. ND.	10.00	30.00	60.00
		i. Litho. Sign. 7. ND.	25.00	60.00	110.00
		j. Sign. 8. ND.	25.00	60.00	110.00
		k. Sign. 9. ND.	8.00	20.00	50.00
		l. Sign. 10. ND.	15.00	40.00	75.00
		m. Sign. 11. ND.	5.00	15.00	40.00
		n. Sign. 12. ND.	—	—	—
803T	1000 FRANCS	1959-65; ND. Like #4.			
		a. Engraved. Sign. 1. 17.9.1959.	35.00	70.00	140.00
		b. Sign. 1. 20.3.1961.	30.00	65.00	125.00
		c. Sign. 2. 20.3.1961.	30.00	65.00	125.00
		e. Sign. 4. 2.3.1965.	30.00	65.00	125.00
		f. Sign. 5. ND.	15.00	50.00	95.00
		g. Sign. 6. ND.	10.00	30.00	65.00
		h. Litho. Sign. 6. ND.	10.00	30.00	65.00
		i. Sign. 7. ND.	10.00	30.00	65.00
		j. Sign. 8. ND.	15.00	50.00	95.00
		k. Sign. 9. ND.	8.00	20.00	50.00
		l. Sign. 10. ND.	8.00	20.00	50.00
		m. Sign. 11. ND.	6.00	15.00	40.00
		n. Sign. 12. ND.	6.00	15.00	40.00
		o. Sign. 13. ND.	6.00	15.00	40.00
804T	5000 FRANCS	1961; ND. Like #5.			
		b. Sign. 1. 20.3.1961.	35.00	70.00	175.00
		h. Sign. 6. ND.	35.00	70.00	175.00
		i. Sign. 7. ND.	30.00	65.00	150.00
		j. Sign. 8. ND.	35.00	70.00	175.00
		k. Sign. 9. ND.	25.00	50.00	125.00
		m. Sign. 11. ND.	20.00	40.00	100.00

1977-81; ND ISSUE

#805T-809T smaller size notes.

Cat. #	Denomination	Date, Description	VG	VF	Unc
805T	500 FRANCS	1979. Like #105A. Sign. 12.	3.00	8.00	15.00

Cat. #	Denomination	Date, Description	VG	VF	Unc
806T	500 FRANCS	1981-90. Like #106A.			
		a. Sign. 14. 1988.	FV	3.00	6.00
		b. Sign. 15. 1981. (BdF).	FV	3.00	6.00
		c. Sign. 15. 1981. (Oberthur).	FV	3.00	6.00
		d. Sign. 15. 1982. (BdF).	FV	5.00	10.00
		e. Sign. 17. 1981. (Oberthur).	FV	5.00	10.00
		f. Sign. 18. 1984.	FV	5.00	10.00
		g. Sign. 19. 1994.	FV	3.00	6.00
		h. Sign. 19. 1985.	FV	3.00	6.00
		i. Sign. 20. 1986.	FV	FV	5.00

Cat. #	Denomination	Date, Description	VG	VF	Unc
		j. Sign. 20. 1987.	FV	FV	5.00
		k. Sign. 21. 1989.	FV	FV	5.00
		l. Sign. 22. 1990.	FV	FV	5.00

NOTE: #806T w/10-digit sm. serial # were printed by Banque de France (BdF) while those w/9-digit lg. serial # were printed by Oberthur.

Cat. #	Denomination	Date, Description	VG	VF	Unc
807T	1000 FRANCS	1981-90. Like #107A.			
		a. Sign. 14. 1988.	FV	FV	9.00
		b. Sign. 15. 1981.	FV	4.00	10.00
		c. Sign. 17. 1981.	FV	4.00	10.00
		d. Sign. 18. 1984.	FV	4.00	10.00
		e. Sign. 19. 1985.	FV	4.00	10.00
		f. Sign. 20. 1986.	4.00	9.00	25.00
		g. Sign. 20. 1987.	FV	FV	9.00
		h. Sign. 21. 1989.	FV	FV	9.00
		i. Sign. 22. 1990.	FV	FV	9.00
808T	5000 FRANCS	1977-92. Like #108A.			
		a. Sign. 12. 1978.	20.00	27.50	55.00
		b. Sign. 12. 1979.	20.00	27.50	55.00
		c. Sign. 14. 1977.	20.00	27.50	55.00
		d. Sign. 14. 1989.	FV	FV	33.00
		e. Sign. 15. 1981.	FV	22.50	45.00
		f. Sign. 15. 1982.	FV	22.50	45.00
		g. Sign. 17. 1983.	30.00	45.00	85.00
		h. Sign. 18. 1984.	FV	22.50	45.00
		i. Sign. 20. 1987.	FV	FV	33.00
		j. Sign. 21. 1990.	FV	FV	33.00
		k. Sign. 22. 1991.	FV	FV	33.00
		l. Sign. 22. 1992.	FV	FV	33.00
		m. Sign. 23 (19)92.	FV	FV	33.00
		n. Sign. 24. 1992.	FV	FV	33.00

Cat. #	Denomination	Date, Description	VG	VF	Unc
809T	10,000 FRANCS	ND. (1977-). Like #109A.			
		a. Sign. 11.	40.00	50.00	90.00
		b. Sign. 12.	45.00	65.00	125.00
		c. Sign. 13.	45.00	65.00	125.00
		e. Sign. 15.	FV	40.00	65.00
		f. Sign. 16.	40.00	50.00	90.00
		h. Sign. 18.	FV	40.00	65.00
		k. Sign. 22.	FV	FV	60.00
		l. Sign. 23. ND.	FV	FV	60.00

1991–92 ISSUES

Cat. #	Denomination	Date, Description	VG	VF	Unc
810T	500 FRANCS	(19)91–. Like #110A.			
		a. Sign. 22. (19)91.	FV	FV	3.50
		b. Sign. 23. (19)92.	FV	FV	3.50
		c. Sign. 25. (19)93.	FV	FV	3.50

Cat. #	Denomination	Date, Description	VG	VF	Unc
811T	1000 FRANCS	(19)91–. Like #111A.			
		a. Sign. 22. (19)91.	FV	FV	6.00
		b. Sign. 23. (19)92.	FV	FV	6.00
		c. Sign. 25. (19)93.	FV	FV	6.00
		d. Sign. 26. (19)94.	FV	FV	6.00

Cat. #	Denomination	Date, Description	VG	VF	Unc
812T	2500 FRANCS	(19)92–. Like #112A.			
		a. Sign. 23. (19)92.	FV	FV	18.00
		b. Sign. 25. (19)93.	FV	FV	18.00
813T	5000 FRANCS	(19)92. Like #113A. Sign. 23.	FV	FV	26.00
814T	10,000 FRANCS	(19)92. Like #114A. Sign. 25.	FV	FV	45.00

The Independent State of Western Samoa, located in the Pacific Ocean 1,600 miles (2,574 km.) northeast of New Zealand, has an area of 1,097 sq. mi. (2,860 sq. km.) and a population of 157,000. Capital: Apia. The economy is based on agriculture, fishing and tourism. Copra, cocoa and bananas are exported.

The Samoan group of islands was discovered by Dutch navigator Jacob Roggeveen in 1772. Great Britain, the United States and Germany established consular representation at Apia in 1847, 1853 and 1861 respectively. The conflicting interests of the three powers produced the Berlin agreement of 1889 which declared Samoa neutral and had the effect of establishing a tripartite protectorate over the islands. A further agreement, 1899, recognized the rights of the United States in those islands east of 171 deg. west longitude (American Samoa) and of Germany in the other islands (Western Samoa). New Zealand occupied Western Samoa at the start of World War I and administered it as a League of Nations mandate and U.N. trusteeship until Jan. 1, 1962, when it became an independent state.

Western Samoa is a member of the Commonwealth of Nations. The Chief Executive is Chief of State. The prime minister is the Head of Government. The present Head of State, Malietoa Tanumafili II, holds his position for life. Future Heads of State will be elected by the Legislature Assembly for five-year terms.

RULERS

British, 1914–1962

Malietoa Tanumafili II, 1962–

MONETARY SYSTEM

1 Shilling = 12 Pence

1 Pound = 20 Shillings to 1967

1 Tala = 100 Sene, 1967–

NEW ZEALAND ADMINISTRATION

Bank of Western Samoa

1960–61 PROVISIONAL ISSUE

#10–12 red ovpt. *Red Bank of Western Samoa, Legal Tender in Western Samoa by virtue of the Bank of Western Samoa Ordinance 1959* on older notes. Various date and sign. varieties.

Cat. #	Denomination	Date, description	Good	Fine	XF
10	10 SHILLINGS	1960–61. Ovpt. on #7.			
		a. Sign. title: *HIGH COMMISSIONER* blocked out at lower l., *MINISTER OF FINANCE* below. 8.12.1960; 1.5.1961.	25.00	75.00	225.00

			Good	Fine	XF
		b. Sign. title: *MINISTER OF FINANCE* in plate w/o ovpt., at lower l. 1.5.1961.	25.00	75.00	225.00

Cat. #	Denomination	Date, description	Good	Fine	XF
11	1 POUND	1960–61. Ovpt. on #8.			
		a. Sign. title: *HIGH COMMISSIONER* blocked out at lower l. *MINISTER OF FINANCE* below. 8.11.1960; 1.5.1961.	35.00	100.00	350.00
		b. Sign. title: *MINISTER OF FINANCE* in plate w/o ovpt., at lower l. 1.5.1961.	35.00	100.00	350.00
12	5 POUNDS	1.5.1961. Ovpt. on #9.	250.00	950.00	2250.

Fale Tupe o Samoa i Sisifo – Bank of Western Samoa

Pound System

1963 (ND) ISSUE

13	10 SHILLINGS	ND (1963). Dk. green on m/c unpt. Arms at l., boat at r. Hut and 2 palms on back.	2.50	8.00	35.00

Cat. #	Denomination	Date, description	Good	Fine	XF
14	1 POUND	ND (1963). Blue on m/c unpt. Palms and rising sun at l. and r., arms at ctr. Sm. bldg. and lagoon on back. 159 x 83mm.	4.00	15.00	50.00

15	5 POUNDS	ND (1963). Brown on m/c unpt. Flag over arms at r. Shoreline, sea and islands on back. 166 x 89mm.	20.00	45.00	115.00

Tala System

1967 (ND) ISSUE

#16–18 sign. varieties. Wmk: BWS repeated.

SIGNATURE VARIETIES			
1	*signature* MANAGER	3	*signature* MANAGER
2	*signature* MANAGER	4	SENIOR MANAGER

16	1 TALA	ND (1967). Dk. green on m/c unpt. Like #13.			
		a. Sign. 1.	1.50	3.50	12.00
		b. Sign. 2.	1.00	3.00	11.00
		c. Sign. 3.	1.00	3.00	11.00
		d. Sign. 4.	1.00	3.00	10.00
		s. Sign. as b. Specimen.	—	—	30.00

Cat. #	Denomination	Date, description	VG	VF	Unc
17	2 TALA	ND (1967). Blue on m/c unpt. Like #14, but 144 x 77mm.			
		a. Sign. 1.	2.50	5.00	20.00
		b. Sign. 3.	2.25	4.50	16.00
		c. Sign. 4.	2.00	3.50	15.00
		s. Sign. as b. Specimen.	—	—	40.00

Cat. #	Denomination	Date, description	VG	VF	Unc
20	2 TALA	ND (1980). Deep blue-violet on m/c unpt. Woodcarver at r. Hut w/palms on sm. island on back.	1.50	3.00	10.00

Cat. #	Denomination	Date, description	VG	VF	Unc
18	10 TALA	ND (1967). Brown on m/c unpt. Like #15, but 150 x 76mm.			
		a. Sign. 3.	12.00	20.00	65.00
		b. Sign. 4.	10.00	17.50	50.00
		s. Sign. as b. Specimen.	—	—	50.00

			VG	VF	Unc
21	5 TALA	ND (1980). Red on m/c unpt. Child writing at r. Sm. port city on back.	3.50	7.00	20.00

INDEPENDENT STATE

Komiti Faatino o Tupe a Samoa i Sisifo– Monetary Board of Western Samoa

1980–84 (ND) ISSUE

#19–23 national flag on face and back. Arms on back. Wmk: M. Tanumafili II.

			VG	VF	Unc
22	10 TALA	ND (1980). Dk. brown and purple on m/c unpt. Man picking bananas at r. Shoreline landscape on back.	7.00	12.50	40.00
23	20 TALA	ND (1984). Brown and orange-brown on m/c unpt. Fisherman w/net at r. Round bldg. at l. on back.	30.00	65.00	185.00
24	Deleted.				

Faletupe Tutotonu O Samoa – Central Bank of Samoa

1985 (ND) ISSUE

#25–30 similar to #20–23 but w/new issuer's name. Wmk: M. Tanumafili II.

			VG	VF	Unc
19	1 TALA	ND (1980). Dk. green on m/c unpt. 2 weavers at r. 2 fishermen in canoe on back.	.75	2.00	8.00

Cat. #	Denomination	Date, description	VG	VF	Unc
25	2 TALA	ND (1985). Deep blue-violet on m/c unpt. Similar to #20.	FV	FV	3.00

26	5 TALA	ND (1985). Red on m/c unpt. Similar to #21.	FV	FV	6.00

27	10 TALA	ND (1985). Dk. brown and purple on m/c unpt. Similar to #22.	FV	FV	10.00

28	20 TALA	ND (1985). Brown and orange-brown on m/c unpt. Similar to #23.	FV	FV	18.00

#29–30 M. Tanumafili II at r.

29	50 TALA	ND (ca.1990). Green and m/c. Former home of R. L. Stevenson, current residence of Head of State at ctr. Man performing traditional knife dance on back.	FV	FV	42.50
30	100 TALA	ND (ca.1990). Olive-brown, lt. brown and m/c. Flag and Parliament bldg. at ctr. Harvest scene on back.	FV	FV	85.00

1990 COMMEMORATIVE ISSUE

#31, Golden Jubilee of Service of the Head of State, Susuga Malietoa Tanumafili II, 1990

Cat. #	Denomination	Date, description	VG	VF	Unc
31	2 TALA	ND (1990). Brown, blue and purple on m/c unpt. Samoan village at ctr., M. Tanumafili II at r. Clear area at lower r. containing a Rava bowl visible from both sides. Family scene at ctr., arms at upper r. on back.			
		a. Text on face partly engraved. Serial # prefix letters AAA.	FV	FV	4.00
		b. Printing as a. Uncut sheets of 4 subjects. Serial # prefix letters AAB.	—	—	25.00
		c. Face completely lithographed, deeper blue, purple and dull brown. Serial # prefix letters AAC–.	FV	FV	3.25

NOTE: #31a was also available in a special folder.

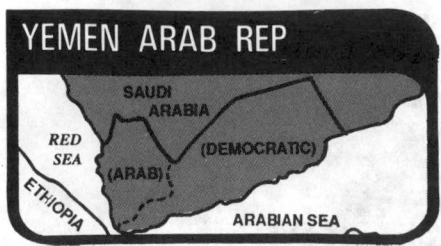

The Yemen Arab Republic, located in the southwestern corner of the Arabian Peninsula, has an area of 75,290 sq. mi. (195,000 sq. km.) and a population of 13 million. Capital: San'a. The industries of Yemen, one of the world's poorest countries, are agriculture and local handicrafts. Qat (a mildly narcotic leaf), coffee, cotton and rock salt are exported.

One of the oldest centers of civilization in the Near East, Yemen was once part of the Minaean Kingdom and of the ancient Kingdom of Sheba, after which it was captured successively by Egyptians, Ethiopians and Romans. It was converted to the Moslem religion in 628 AD and administered as a caliphate until 1538, when it came under Turkish occupation which was maintained until 1918 when autonomy was achieved through revolution.

On Feb. 1, 1958, Egypt and Syria formed the United Arab Republic. Yemen joined on March 8 in an association known as the United Arab States. Syria withdrew from the United Arab Republic on Sept. 29, 1961, and on Dec. 26 Egypt dissolved its ties with Yemen in the United Arab States.

Provoked by the harsh rule of Imam Mohammed al-Badr, last ruler of the Kingdom of Mutawwakkilite, the National Liberation Front seized control of the government on Sept. 27, 1962. Badr fled to Saudi Arabia.

An agreement for a constitution for a unified state was reached on Dec. 1989 uniting the Yemen Arab Republic with the People's Democratic Republic of Yemen into the Republic of Yemen on May 22, 1990. Both currencies are still valid but the P.D.R.Y. dinars are being phased out.

RULERS

Imam Ahmad, AH1367–1382/1948–1982AD

Imam al-Badr, AH1382–1388/1962–1968AD

MONETARY SYSTEM

1 Rial = 40 Buqshas

Arab Republic of Yemen

ND ISSUES

#1–10 sign. varieties. Wmk: Arms.

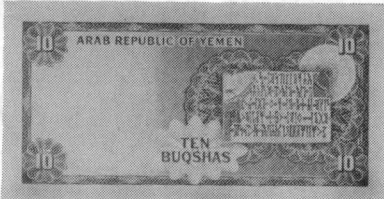

Cat. #	Denomination	Date, description	VG	VF	Unc
1	10 BUQSHAS	ND. Brown on m/c unpt. Child riding on a lion (sculpture) at l. Ancient inscription on back.	2.00	6.00	25.00

| 2 | 20 BUQSHAS | ND. Green on m/c unpt. Stylized human head (sculpture) at l. Back olive; tall ruins. | 3.50 | 13.50 | 40.00 |

Cat. #	Denomination	Date, description	VG	VF	Unc
3	1 RIAL	ND. Green on m/c unpt. Arms at l. Bldg. on back.	5.00	25.00	115.00

| 4 | 1 RIAL | ND. Green on m/c unpt. Human head (sculpture) at l. Back like #3. | 3.50 | 17.50 | 85.00 |
| 5 | 5 RIALS | ND. Red on m/c unpt. Arms at l. Sculpture like #1 face at r. on back. | 15.00 | 65.00 | 250.00 |

| 6 | 5 RIALS | ND. Red on m/c unpt. Animal sculpture (leopard head) at l. Back like #5. | 8.50 | 37.50 | 165.00 |

Cat. #	Denomination	Date, description	VG	VF	Unc
7	10 RIALS	ND. Blue-green on m/c unpt. Arms at l. Dam on back. 145 x 75mm.	25.00	100.00	375.00

| 8 | 10 RIALS | ND. Blue-green on m/c unpt. Tower at l. Back like #7. 135 x 70mm. | 10.00 | 40.00 | 150.00 |

| 9 | 20 RIALS | ND. Violet and blue-green on m/c unpt. House on rocks at l. Back violet and gold; city scene. | 25.00 | 80.00 | 250.00 |

| 10 | 50 RIALS | ND. Dk. olive on m/c unpt. Crossed daggers at l. Plants on back. | 30.00 | 85.00 | 350.00 |

Central Bank of Yemen

1973–77 (ND) ISSUES

#11–16A wmk: Arms.

Cat. #	Denomination	Date, description	VG	VF	Unc
11	1 RIAL	ND (1973). Green on m/c unpt. Mosque and minaret (Bekilia dome) at l. Plants in field w/mountains behind on back. 2 sign. varieties.	.15	.40	2.50

| 12 | 5 RIALS | ND (1973). Red on m/c unpt. Modern bldgs. at l. Back red and lt. olive; bldgs. on high rock hill. | 1.00 | 2.50 | 9.50 |

| 13 | 10 RIALS | ND (1973). Blue-green on m/c unpt. Human head (sculpture) at l. Lg. bldg. on back. 2 sign. varieties. | 1.50 | 3.00 | 10.00 |

| 14 | 20 RIALS | ND (1973). Purple on m/c unpt. Sculpture (God of Grapes) at l. Back purple and brown; terraces and rock hill. | 2.00 | 4.00 | 15.00 |

Cat. #	Denomination	Date, description	VG	VF	Unc
15	50 RIALS	ND (1973). Dk. olive and m/c. Ancient statue at l. Fortified archway on back. 2 sign. varieties.	FV	5.50	12.00

16	100 RIALS	ND (1975). Lilac on m/c unpt. Stone carving of child and mythical beast at l. City and mountain view on back.	7.50	20.00	65.00

16A	100 RIALS	ND (1977). Face like #16 but different sign. Modern bldg. on back.	FV	10.00	25.00

1979–85 (ND) ISSUES

#16B–21 wmk: Arms.

Cat. #	Denomination	Date, description	VG	VF	Unc
16B	1 RIAL	ND (1980). Like #11, but darker green and smaller serial #. Clearer unpt. design over wmk. area at r.	FV	.25	1.25

17	5 RIALS	ND (1981). Red on orange and m/c unpt. Bldg. at l. City view at foot of mountain fortress on back. 2 sign. varieties.	FV	.60	3.00

18	10 RIALS	ND (1981). Blue-green on m/c unpt. City view on rock hill at l. Mosque w/minaret on back. 2 sign. varieties.	FV	1.25	6.00

19	20 RIALS	ND (1985). Face similar to #14. View of city on back.	FV	1.25	6.50

Cat. #	Denomination	Date, description	VG	VF	Unc
21	100 RIALS	ND (1979). Lilac on m/c unpt. City view at l., mosque in foreground. City panorama w/mountains on back.	FV	5.00	25.00

1991–96 (ND) ISSUES

#22–27 wmk: Arms.

| 22 | 5 RIALS | ND (ca.1991). Red and orange on m/c unpt. Bldg. at l. City w/mountain behind on back. | FV | FV | 1.50 |

| 23 | 10 RIALS | ND (ca.1991). Blue and black on m/c unpt. Minaret, mosque at l. Dam at ctr. r., *10* at upper corners on back. | FV | FV | 3.00 |

| 24 | 10 RIALS | ND (ca.1992). Face as #23. Back design as #23, but w/*10* at upper l. and lower r. *10* w/Arabic text: *Sald Marib* near lower r. | FV | FV | 2.50 |
| 25 (25a) | 20 RIALS | ND (ca. 1992). Dk. brown on m/c unpt. Arch ended straight border across upper ctr. Sculpture of God of Grapes at l. Coastal view of Aden, dhow on back. | FV | FV | 5.00 |

Cat. #	Denomination	Date, description	VG	VF	Unc
26 (25b)	20 RIALS	ND (ca. 1994). Like #25 but w/straight border frame across upper ctr.	FV	FV	4.50

27 (26)	50 RIALS	ND (1992). Black on m/c unpt. Face like #15. City in the Hadramawt at ctr. r. on back.			
		a. City w/o Arabic title at lower l.	FV	FV	6.50
		b. W/Arabic title *Shibam Hadramawt* at lower l.	FV	FV	6.50

| 28 (27) | 100 RIALS | ND (1992). Violet, purple and black on m/c unpt. Viaduct in mountain gorge at l. City view of old San'a w/mountains behind on back. | FV | FV | 7.50 |
| 29 | 200 RIALS | ND (1996). | | Expected new issue. | |

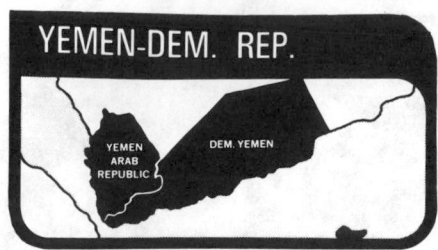

The People's Democratic Republic of Yemen, located on the southern coast of the Arabian Peninsula, had an area of 128,560 sq. mi. (332,968 sq. km.). Capital: Aden. It consists of the port city of Aden, 17 states of the former South Arabian Federation, 3 small sheikhdoms, 3 large sultanates, Quaiti, Kathiri and Mahri, which made up the Eastern Aden Protectorate, and Socotra, the largest island in the Arabian Sea. The port of Aden is the area's most valuable natural resource. Cotton, fish, coffee and hides are exported.

Between 1200 BC and the 6th century AD, what is now the People's Democratic Republic of Yemen was part of the Minaean kingdom. In subsequent years it was controlled by Persians, Egyptians and Turks. Aden, one of the cities mentioned in the Bible, had been a port for trade between the East and West for 2,000 years. British rule began in 1839 when the British East India Co. seized control to put an end to the piracy threatening trade with India. To protect their foothold in Aden, the British found it necessary to extend their control into the area known historically as the Hadramaut, and to sign protection treaties with the sheikhs of the hinterland. Eventually, 15 of the 16 Western Protectorate states, the Wahidi state of the Eastern Protectorate, and Aden Colony joined to form the Federation of South Arabia.

In 1959, Britain agreed to prepare South Arabia for full independence, which was achieved on Nov. 30, 1967, at which time South Arabia, including Aden, changed its name to the People's Republic of Southern Yemen. On Dec. 1, 1970, following the overthrowing of the new government by the National Liberation Front, Southern Yemen changed its name to the People's Democratic Republic of Yemen. On May 22, 1990 the People's Democratic Republic merged with the Yemen Arab Republic into a unified Republic of Yemen. The YDR currency is being phased out.

MONETARY SYSTEM

1 Dinar = 1000 Fils

South Arabian Currency Authority

SIGNATURE VARIETIES			
1	*signature*	3	*signature*
2	*signature*	4	*signature*

1965 (ND) ISSUE

#1–5 dhow w/coastal town in background. Each back has palm tree at ctr. but different additional plants. Wmk: Camel's head. Printer: TDLR.

Cat. #	Denomination	Date, description	VG	VF	Unc
1	250 FILS	ND (1965). Brown on m/c unpt.			
		a. Sign. 1.	2.50	6.00	25.00
		b. Sign. 2.	.50	2.00	7.50

Cat. #	Denomination	Date, description	VG	VF	Unc
2	500 FILS	ND (1965). Green on m/c unpt.			
		a. Sign. 1.	3.00	7.50	35.00
		b. Sign. 2.	2.50	6.00	25.00
3	1 DINAR	ND (1965). Blue-black on m/c unpt.			
		a. Sign. 1.	5.00	17.50	65.00
		b. Sign. 2.	4.00	15.00	45.00

Cat. #	Denomination	Date, description	VG	VF	Unc
4	5 DINARS	ND (1965). Red on m/c unpt.			
		a. Sign. 1.	17.50	40.00	125.00
		b. Sign. 2.	15.00	32.50	100.00
5	10 DINARS	ND (1965). Dk. olive on m/c unpt.			
		a. Sign. 1.	40.00	100.00	300.00
		b. Sign. 2.	35.00	85.00	250.00

Bank of Yemen

1984 (ND) ISSUE

#6–9 similar to #1–5 but w/o English on face and w/new bank name on back. Capital: *ADEN* added to bottom r. on back. Wmk: Camel's head.

Cat. #	Denomination	Date, description	VG	VF	Unc
6	500 FILS	ND (1984). Similar to #2.	.65	2.00	7.50
7	1 DINAR	ND (1984). Similar to #3.	1.00	3.00	9.00

8	5 DINARS	ND (1984). Similar to #4.			
		a. Sign. 3.	5.00	15.00	45.00
		b. Sign. 4.	3.25	10.00	37.50

9	10 DINARS	ND (1984). Similar to #5.			
		a. Sign. 3.	10.00	30.00	95.00
		b. Sign. 4.	6.50	20.00	70.00

YUGOSLAVIA

The Federal Republic of Yugoslavia, a Balkan country located on the east shore of the Adriatic Sea. It had an area of 98,766 sq. mi. (255,804 sq. km.) and a population of *10.4 million. Capital: Belgrade. The chief industries are agriculture, mining, manufacturing and tourism. Machinery, nonferrous metals, meat and fabrics are exported.

Yugoslavia was proclaimed on Dec. 1, 1918, after the union of the Kingdom of Serbia, Montenegro and the South Slav territories of Austria-Hungary; and changed its official name from the Kingdom of the Serbs, Croats, and Slovenes to the Kingdom of Yugoslavia on Oct. 3, 1929. The republic was composed of six autonomous republics: Serbia, Croatia, Slovenia, Bosnia-Herzegovina, Macedonia and Montenegro with two autonomous provinces within Serbia: Kosovo-Melohija and Vojvodina. The government of Yugoslavia attemped to remain neutral in World War II but, yielding to German pressure, aligned itself with the Axis powers in March of 1941; a few days later it was overthrown by revolutionary forces and its neutrality reasserted. The Nazis occupied the country on April 6, and throughout the remaining years were resisted by a number of guerrilla armies, notably that of Marshal Josip Broz Tito. After the defeat of the Axis powers, a leftist coalition headed by Tito abolished the monarchy and, on Jan. 31, 1046, established a "People's Republic".

The collapse of the Federal Republic during 1991–92 has resulted in the autonomous republics of Croatia, Slovenia, Bosnia-Herzegovina and Macedonia declaring their respective independence. Bosnia-Herzegovina is under military contest with the Serbian faction opposed to the Moslem populace. Besides the remainder of the older Serbian sectors, a Serbian enclave in Knin located in southern Croatia has emerged called REPUBLIKE SRPSKE KRAJINE or Serbian Republic-Krajina surrounding the city of Knin; it has also declared its independence in 1992. Croatian forces overwhelmed this enclave in August 1995. In 1992 the Federal Republic of Yugoslavia, consisting of the former Republics of Serbia and Montenegro, was proclaimed.

MONETARY SYSTEM

1 Dinar = 100 Para
1 "New" Dinar = 100 Old Dinara, 1965-89
1 "New" Dinar = 10,000 Old Dinara, 1990-92
1 "New" Dinar = 10 Old Dinara, 1992-93
1 "New" Dinar = 1 Million "Old" Dinara, 1993
1 "New" Dinara = 1 Milliard "Old" Dinara, 1.1.1994

REPLACEMENT NOTES

#73–150, 3A (ZA) prefix letters.

НАРОДНА БАНКА ЈУГОЛАВИЈЕ

Narodna Banka Jugoslavije–National Bank of Yugoslavia

1963 ISSUE

Cat. #	Denomination	Date, description	VG	VF	Unc
73	100 DINARA	1.5.1963. Red on m/c unpt. Like #69.	.10	.30	1.00

Cat. #	Denomination	Date, description	VG	VF	Unc
74	500 DINARA	1.5.1963. Dk. green on m/c unpt. Like #70.	.25	.50	2.00

Cat. #	Denomination	Date, description	VG	VF	Unc
75	1000 DINARA	1.5.1963. Dk. brown on m/c unpt. Like #71.	.35	1.00	3.00

| 76 | 5000 DINARA | 1.5.1963. Blue-black on m/c unpt. Like #72. | 1.00 | 3.00 | 22.50 |

Currency Reform

1 New Dinar = 100 Old Dinara

1965 ISSUE

Cat. #	Denomination	Date, description	VG	VF	Unc
77	5 DINARA	1.8.1965. Dk. green on m/c unpt. Like #74. 134 x 64mm.			
		a. Sm. numerals in serial #.	.20	.50	2.00
		b. Lg. numerals in serial #.	.20	.50	2.00
78	10 DINARA	1.8.1965. Dk. brown on m/c unpt. Like #75. 143 x 66mm.			
		a. Like #77a.	.20	.50	3.00
		b. Like #77b.	.20	.50	3.00
79	50 DINARA	1.8.1965. Dk blue on m/c unpt. Like #76. 151 x 72mm.			
		a. Like #77a.	.50	1.50	7.00
		b. Like #77b.	.30	1.25	6.00

80	100 DINARA	1.8.1965. Red on m/c unpt. Equestrian statue "Peace" at l.			
		a. Like #77a.	1.00	3.00	9.00
		b. Like #77b, but w/o security thread.	.75	3.25	10.00
		c. Like #77b, but w/security thread.	.25	1.00	3.00

1968–70 ISSUE

81	5 DINARA	1.5.1968. Dk. green on m/c unpt. Like #77. 123 x 59mm.			
		a. Like #77a.	.05	.20	.50
		b. Like #77b.	.05	.20	.50

82	10 DINARA	1.5.1968. Dk. brown on m/c unpt. Like #78. 131 x 63mm.			
		a. Like #77a.	.50	2.00	8.00
		b. Like #80b.	.20	.50	1.00
		c. Like #80c.	.05	.15	.25

Cat. #	Denomination	Date, description	VG	VF	Unc
83	50 DINARA	1.5.1968. Blue-black on m/c unpt. Similar to #79 but lg. *50* in circle at l. ctr. on back. 139 x 66mm.			
		a. Like #77a.	.75	3.00	10.00
		b. Like #80b.	.20	.65	2.00
		c. Like #80c.	.10	.35	1.00

84	500 DINARA	1.8.1970. Dk. olive-green on m/c unpt. N. Tesla seated w/open book at l.			
		a. W/o security thread.	.15	.50	2.00
		b. W/security thread.	1.50	6.00	15.00

1974 ISSUE

85	20 DINARA	19.12.1974. Purple on m/c unpt. Ship dock-side at l. 6 or 7-digit serial #.	.15	.40	.75
86	1000 DINARA	19.12.1974. Blue-black on m/c unpt. Woman w/fruit at l.	.50	1.65	5.00

1978–85 ISSUE

#87–92 long, 2-line sign. title at l. and different sign.

Cat. #	Denomination	Date, description	VG	VF	Unc
87	10 DINARA	12.8.1978; 4.11.1981. Like #82.	.10	.20	.75
88	20 DINARA	12.8.1978; 4.11.1981. Like #85.	.05	.15	.75
89	50 DINARA	12.8.1978; 4.11.1981. Like #83.	.05	.15	.75
90	100 DINARA	12.8.1978; 4.11.1981; 16.5.1986. Like #80.	.05	.15	.75

91	500 DINARA	1978; 1981; 1986. Like #84.			
		a. 12.8.1978.	.20	.65	2.00
		b. 4.11.1981.	.10	.40	1.25
		c. 16.5.1986.	.10	.35	1.00

92	1000 DINARA	1978; 1981. Like #86.			
		a. Sign. title: *Governor* in Cyrillic w/o letter *R* (error). Series AF.	.25	.75	7.00
		b. As a. Series AR.	3.00	12.50	50.00
		c. Corrected sign. title.	.05	.25	1.00

Cat. #	Denomination	Date, description	VG	VF	Unc
93	5000 DINARA	1.5.1985. Deep blue on m/c unpt. Tito at l. and as wmk., arms at ctr. Bldg. on hill at ctr. on back.			
		a. Error date *1930* instead of *1980* (Tito's death year)	4.00	15.00	60.00
		b. Corrected date *1980*.	.10	.25	1.00

1987–89 ISSUE

Cat. #	Denomination	Date, description	VG	VF	Unc
95	20,000 DINARA	1.5.1987. Brown on m/c unpt. Miner at l. and as wmk., arms at ctr. Mining equipment on back.	.10	.25	.75

Cat. #	Denomination	Date, description	VG	VF	Unc
96	50,000 DINARA	1.5.1988. Green and blue on m/c unpt. Girl at l., and as wmk. City of Dubrovnik on back.	.15	.3.	2.50

Cat. #	Denomination	Date, description	VG	VF	Unc
97	100,000 DINARA	1.5.1989. Violet and red on m/c unpt. Young girl at l. and as wmk. Abstract design w/letters and numbers on back.	.25	.75	3.50

Cat. #	Denomination	Date, description	VG	VF	Unc
98	500,000 DINARA	Aug. 1989. Deep purple and blue on m/c unpt. Arms at l., partisan monument "Kozara" at r. Partisan monument "Sutjeska" on back.	.35	1.50	7.50

Cat. #	Denomination	Date, description	VG	VF	Unc
99	1 MILLION DINARA	1.11.1989. Lt. olive-green on orange and gold unpt. Young woman at l. and as wmk. Sunflowers on back.	.40	1.25	7.50
100	2 MILLION DINARA	Aug. 1989. Pale olive-green and brown on lt. orange unpt. Partisan monument "Kozara" at r. Partisan "V3" monument at Kraguje-vac at ctr. on back.	3.50	13.50	55.00

Currency Reform

1 New Dinar = 10,000 Old Dinara

FIRST 1990 ISSUE

Cat. #	Denomination	Date, description	VG	VF	Unc
101	50 DINARA	1.1.1990. Purple on lilac unpt. Similar to #98.	.40	1.25	6.50
102	200 DINARA	1.1.1990. Pale olive-green and brown on lt. orange unpt. Similar to #100.	.60	1.75	7.50

SECOND 1990 ISSUE

#103–107 have lg. portr. at l. and as wmk., arms at ctr.

103	10 DINARA	1.9.1990. Violet and red on m/c unpt. Similar to #97.	.05	.20	1.50

104	50 DINARA	1.6.1990. Purple. Young boy at l. Roses on back.	.05	.25	1.50
105	100 DINARA	1.3.1990. Lt. olive-green on orange and gold unpt. Similar to #99.	.15	.45	2.00
106	500 DINARA	1.3.1990. Blue and purple. Young man at l. Mountain scene on back.	.35	1.00	5.00

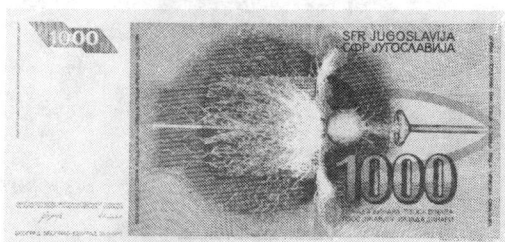

107	1000 DINARA	26.11.1990. Brown and orange. N. Tesla at l. High frequency transformer on back.	1.00	3.00	15.00

1991 ISSUE

#108–111 portr. as wmk. Year date only.

Cat. #	Denomination	Date, description	VG	VF	Unc
108	100 DINARA	1991. Black and olive-brown on yellow unpt. Similar to #105.	.10	.30	1.50

109	500 DINARA	1991. Brown, dk. brown and orange on tan unpt. Similar to #106	.25	.75	4.00

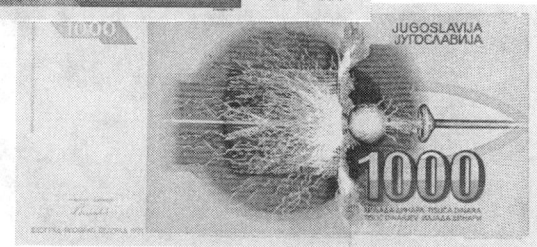

110	1000 DINARA	1991. Blue and purple. Similar to #107.	.50	1.50	7.50

Cat. #	Denomination	Date, description	VG	VF	Unc
111	5000 DINARA	1991. Purple, red-orange and violet on gray unpt. I. Andric at l. Multiple arch stone bridge on the Drina River at Visegrad on back.	.85	2.50	10.00

Currency Reform

1 New Dinar = 10 Old Dinara

1992 ISSUE

#114–120 new Republic monogram, arms at ctr. Similar to previous issues.

112	100 DINARA	1992. Pale blue and purple. Similar to #105.	.10	.25	1.00

113	500 DINARA	1992. Pale purple and lilac. Similar to #106.	.30	.50	4.50

Cat. #	Denomination	Date, description	VG	VF	Unc
114	1000 DINARA	1992. Red, orange and purple on lilac unpt. Similar to #107.	.75	2.00	5.50

115	5000 DINARA	1992. Deep blue-green, purple and deep olive-brown on gray unpt. Similar to #111.	.30	1.50	4.00

116	10,000 DINARA	1992. Varied shades of brown and salmon on tan unpt. Like #103.			
		a. W/dot after date.	.05	.25	1.25
		b. W/o dot after date.	.05	.25	1.25

Cat. #	Denomination	Date, description	VG	VF	Unc
117	50,000 DINARA	1992. Purple, olive-green and deep blue-green. Like #104.	.50	1.50	4.50

1993 ISSUE

#118–127 portr. as wmk.

118	100,000 DINARA	1993. Olive-green on orange and gold unpt. Like #112.	.50	1.50	4.50

119	500,000 DINARA	1993. Blue-violet and orange on m/c unpt. Young mam at I. Koponik Sky Center on back.	1.00	3.25	10.00

120	1 MILLION DINARA	1993. Purple on blue, orange and m/c unpt. Face like #117. Iris flowers on back.	1.25	4.00	12.50

Cat. #	Denomination	Date, description	VG	VF	Unc
121	5 MILLION DINARA	1993. Violet, lilac, turquoise and m/c. Face like #116. Vertical rendition of high frequency transformer at ctr., hydroelectric dam at r. on back.	.15	.50	2.50

122	10 MILLION DINARA	1993. Slate blue, lt. and dk. brown. Face like #115. National library on back.	.20	.60	3.00
123	50 MILLION DINARA	1993. Black and orange. Face like #116. Belgrade University on back.	.25	.75	4.00

124	100 MILLION DINARA	1993. Grayish purple and blue. Face like #113. Academy of Science on back.	.20	.60	3.00

Cat. #	Denomination	Date, description	VG	VF	Unc
125	**500 MILLION DINARA**	1993. Black and lilac. Face like #118. Faculty of Agriculture on back.	.45	1.35	4.00

Cat. #	Denomination	Date, description	VG	VF	Unc
129	**10,000 DINARA**	1993. Orange, gray and olive-green. S. Karadzic at l. Orthodox Church on back.	.50	1.50	4.50

126	**1 MILLIARD DINARA**	1993. Red and purple on orange and blue-gray unpt. Face like #123. National Assembly on back.	.50	1.50	6.00

130	**50,000 DINARA**	1993. Blue and pink. Petar II, Prince-Bishop of Montenegro at l. Monastery in Cetinje on back.	.45	1.25	3.50

127	**10 MILLIARD DINARA**	1993. Black, purple and red. Face like #121. Back like #114.	.50	1.50	7.50

Currency Reform, 1993

1 New Dinar = 1 Million "Old" Dinara

1993 REFORM ISSUE

131	**500,000 DINARA**	1993. Dk. green on blue-green and yellow-orange unpt. D. Obradovic at l. Monastery Kholovo on back.	.50	1.25	5.00

128	**5000 DINARA**	1993. Pale reddish brown, pale olive-green and orange. Face like #110. Museum on back.	FV	FV	5.00

Cat. # 132	Denomination 5 MILLION DINARA	Date, description 1993. Dk. brown on brown-orange and blue-green and pale olive-brown unpt. K. Petrovich, Prince of Serbia at l. Orthodox Church on back.	VG .55	VF 1.75	Unc 5.00

Cat. # 133	Denomination 50 MILLION DINARA	Date, description 1993. Red and purple on orange and lilac unpt. M. Pupin at l. Telephone Exchange bldg. on back.	VG .85	VF 2.50	Unc 7.50

134	500 MILLION DINARA	1993. Purple on aqua, brown-orange and dull pink unpt. J. Cvijich at l. University on back.	.85	2.50	7.50

Cat. # 135	Denomination 5 MILLIARD DINARA	Date, description 1993. Olive-brown on red-orange, lt. green, ochre and orange unpt. D. Jaksich at l. Monastery in Vrazcevsnica on back.	VG .15	VF .50	Unc 4.50

136	50 MILLIARD DINARA	1993. Dk. brown on blue-violet, orange, red-violet and gray unpt. M. Obrenovich, Prince of Serbia at l. Villa of Obrenovich on back.	.30	.90	4.50

137	500 MILLIARD DINARA	1993. Red-violet on orange, pale blue-gray and olive-brown unpt. National Library on back.	.35	1.00	5.50

Currency Reform, 1.1.1994

1 New Dinar = 1 Milliard "Old" Dinara

1994 ISSUE

138	10 DINARA	1994. Chocolate brown on brown and gray-green unpt. J. Panchih at l. Kopaonik Mountain on back. W/o serial #.	.10	.25	1.25

Cat. #	Denomination	Date, description	VG	VF	Unc
139	100 DINARA	1994. Grayish purple on purple pink and aqua unpt. N. Tesla at l. Tesla Museum on back.	.10	.30	1.50

140	1000 DINARA	1994. Dk. olive-gray on red-orange, olive-brown and lilac unpt. Like #130.	.15	.45	2.00

141	5000 DINARA	1994. Dk. blue on lilac, orange and aqua unpt. D. Obradovic at l. Monastary in Kholovo on back. Similar to #131.	.40	1.25	6.00

142	50,000 DINARA	1994. Dull red and lilac on orange unpt. K. Petrovich, Prince of Serbia at l. Orthodox Church on back. Similar to #132.	.45	1.40	7.00

Cat. #	Denomination	Date, description	VG	VF	Unc
143	500,000 DINARA	1994. Dull olive-green and orange on yellow unpt. J. Cvijich at l. Belgrade University on back. Similar to #134.	.55	1.75	6.50

1994 PROVISIONAL ISSUE

144	10 MILLION DINARA	1994 (–old date 1993). Red ovpt: *1994* on face and back w/new silver ovpt. sign. and sign. title on back on #122.	.50	1.50	7.50

Currency Reform

1 Novi (New) Dinar = 1 Deutsche Mark

1994 REFORM ISSUES

#145-147 wmk: Diamond grid.

145	1 NOVI DINAR	1.1.1994. Blue-gray and brown on pale olive green and tan unpt. J. Panchih at l. Kopa-onik Mountain on back. Similar to #138.	.10	.40	2.00

Cat. #	Denomination	Date, description	VG	VF	Unc
146	5 NOVI DINARA	1.1.1994. Red-brown and pink on ochre and pale orange unpt. N. Tesla at I. Tesla Museum on back. Similar to #139.	.35	1.75	8.50

Cat. #	Denomination	Date, description	VG	VF	Unc
149	10 NOVIKH DINARA	3.3.1995. Purple, violet and brown. Like #147.	FV	FV	15.00

150	20 NOVIKH DINARA	3.3.1995. Greenish-black, brown-orange and brown. Similar to #135.	FV	FV	28.00
151	50 NOVIKH DINARA			Expected new issue.	

147	10 NOVI DINARA	1.1.1994. Purple and pink on aqua and olive-green unpt. Petar II, Prince-Bishop of Montenegro at I. Monastery in Cetinje on back. Similar to #130 and 140.	.60	3.00	15.00

NOTE: #145–147 withdrawn from circulation on 1.1.1995.

1995 ISSUE

#148-150 arms w/double-headed eagle at upper ctr. Wmk: Symmetrical design repeated.

148	5 NOVIKH DINARA	3.3.1995. Deep purple and violet. N. Tesla at I. Back like #146.	FV	FV	8.50

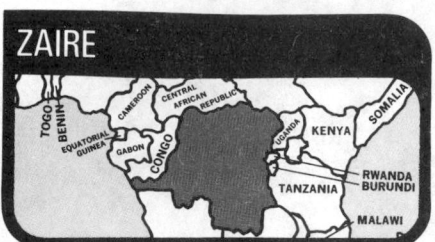

ZAIRE

The Republic of Zaïre (formerly the Belgian Congo), located in the south-central part of Africa, has an area of 905,568 sq. mi. (2,345,409 sq. km.) and a population of 38.6 million. Capital: Kinshasa. The mineral-rich country produces copper, tin, diamonds, gold, zinc, cobalt and uranium.

In ancient times the territory comprising Zaïre was occupied by Negrito peoples (Pygmies) pushed into the mountains by Bantu and Nilotic invaders. The interior was first explored by the American correspondent Henry Stanley, who was subsequently commissioned by King Leopold II of Belgium to conclude development treaties with the local chiefs. The Berlin conference of 1885 awarded the area to Leopold, who administered and exploited it as his private property until it was annexed to Belgium in 1908. Following the eruption of bloody independence riots in 1959, Belgium granted the Belgian Congo independence as the Republic of the Congo on June 30, 1960.

The Belgian Congo attained independence with the distinction of being the most ill-prepared country to ever undertake self-government. Without a single doctor, lawyer or engineer, with no organized unit capable of maintaining law and order, independence disintegrated into an orgy of anarchy. Provinces seceded. Intertribal warfare erupted. Belgian troops intervened to protect Belgian citizens from retributive massacre. By 1961, four groups were fighting for political dominance. The most serious threat to the viability of the country was posed by the secession of mineral-rich Katanga province on July 11, 1960. After two and one-half years of sporadic warfare with a U.N. military force, Katanga's leaders capitulated, Jan. 14, 1963 and the rebellious province was partioned into three provinces. The nation officially changed its name to Zaïre on Oct. 27, 1971.

See also Rwanda and Rwanda-Burundi.

MONETARY SYSTEM
1 Franc = 100 Centimes to 1967
1 Zaïre = 100 Makuta, 1967–
1 Nouveau Zaïre = 100 N Makuta = 3 million 'old' Zaïres, 1993–

REPLACEMENT NOTES
#9–12, ZZ prefix letters. #14–26, 27, 28-31, 37-38, 40-41, Z suffix letter.

CONGO (KINSHASA)
Conseil Monétaire de la République du Congo

1962–63 ISSUE
Various date and sign. varieties.

Cat. #	Denomination	Date, description	VG	VF	Unc
1	100 FRANCS	1.6.1963–8.7.1963. Green and m/c. Dam at l. Dredging at r. on back.	5.00	17.50	40.00

Cat. #	Denomination	Date, description	VG	VF	Unc
2	1000 FRANCS	15.2.1962. Purple on m/c unpt. Portr. African man at l. Text: *EMISSION DU CONSEIL MONÉTAIRE DE LA REPUBLIQUE DU CONGO* in place of wmk. Back deep violet on pink unpt; longhorn animal drinking in stream.	15.00	55.00	125.00

3	5000 FRANCS	1.12.1963. Gray-green. Portr. African woman at l. Oarsmen on back.	400.00	950.00	2000.

Banque Nationale du Congo

Franc System

1961 ISSUE

4	20 FRANCS	15.11.1961–15.9.1962. Green, blue and brown. Girl seated at r. and as wmk. Stylized tree on back. Printer: JEZ.	2.00	8.00	22.50

#5–8 have long bldg. at bottom on back.

5	50 FRANCS	1.9.1961–1.7.1962. Green. Lion at l., bridge and lake in background.	3.00	20.00	50.00

6	100 FRANCS	1.9.1961–1.8.1964. Dk. brown on m/c unpt. J. Kasavubu at l., 2 birds at r. Printer: TDLR.	3.00	17.50	40.00

Cat. #	Denomination	Date, description	VG	VF	Unc
7	500 FRANCS	15.10.1961; 1.12.1961; 1.8.1964. Lilac. Mask at l. Wmk: Bird.	10.00	35.00	100.00

Cat. #	Denomination	Date, description	VG	VF	Unc
8	1000 FRANCS	15.10 1961; 15.12.1961; 1.8.1964. Dk. blue on m/c unpt. J. Kasavubu at l., carving at r. Wmk: Antelope's head. Printer: TDLR.	8.00	25.00	75.00

Zaïre System

1967 ISSUE

#9–13 various date and sign. varieties. Printer: TDLR.

Cat. #	Denomination	Date, description	VG	VF	Unc
9	10 MAKUTA	2.1.1967–21.1.1970. Blue and olive on m/c unpt. Stadium at l., Mobutu at r. Long bldg. on back.	2.00	6.00	25.00

Cat. #	Denomination	Date, description	VG	VF	Unc
10	20 MAKUTA	24.11.1967–1.10.1970. Black on green, blue and m/c unpt. Man w/flag at ctr., P. Lumumba at r. People in long boat on back. Wmk: Antelope's head.	4.00	17.50	45.00

Cat. #	Denomination	Date, description	VG	VF	Unc
11	50 MAKUTA	2.1.1967–1.10.1970. Red and olive on m/c unpt. Stadium at l., Mobutu at r. Gathering coconuts on back.	4.50	20.00	60.00

Cat. #	Denomination	Date, description	VG	VF	Unc
12	1 ZAÏRE- 100 MAKUTA	2.1.1967–1.10.1970. Brown and green on m/c unpt. Stadium at l., Mobutu at r. Mobutu leading inoculation drive on back. Wmk: Antelope's head.	4.00	15.00	75.00

Cat. #	Denomination	Date, description	VG	VF	Unc
13	5 ZAÏRES - 500 MAKUTA	1967–70. Green and m/c. Mobutu at r. Long bldg. at l. ctr. on back. Wmk: Antelope's head.			
		a. Sign. above title: *LE GOUVERNEUR*. Green date. 2.1.1967; 24.6.1967.	12.50	55.00	200.00
		b. Sign. below title: *LE GOUVERNEUR*. Black date. 2.1.1967; 21.1.1970.	12.50	55.00	150.00

1971 ISSUE

#14–15 Mobutu at l. and as wmk., leopard at r. Printer: G&D.

Cat. #	Denomination	Date, description	VG	VF	Unc
14	5 ZAÏRES	24.11.1971. Green, black and m/c. Carving at l. ctr., hydroelectric dam at r. on back.	17.50	50.00	150.00

Cat. #	Denomination	Date, description	VG	VF	Unc
15	10 ZAÏRES	30.6.1971. Blue, brown and m/c. Arms on back w/yellow star.	20.00	60.00	100.00

ZAÏRE

Banque du Zaïre

1972–80 ISSUES

#16–25 Mobutu at l. and as wmk. Various date and sign. varieties. Printer: G&D.

Cat. #	Denomination	Date, description	VG	VF	Unc
16	50 MAKUTA	1973–78. Red, brown and m/c. Man and structure in water on back. Printed from engraved plates.			
		a. Red guilloche at l. on back. 30.6.1973–4.10.1975.	.50	1.50	6.50
		b. Red and purple guilloche at l. ctr. on back. 24.6.1976–20.5.1978.	.25	.75	4.00

Cat. #	Denomination	Date, description	VG	VF	Unc
19	1 ZAÏRE	22.10.1979; 27.10.1980; 20.5.1981. Like #18 but slight color differences and lithographed.	.15	.35	1.00

17	50 MAKUTA	24.11.1979; 14.10.1980. Like #16 but slight color differences and lithographed.	.35	1.00	3.00

20	5 ZAÏRES	24.11.1972. Green, black and m/c. Carved figure w/hydroelectric dam on back. Like #14.	15.00	35.00	100.00

18	1 ZAÏRE	1972–77. Brown and m/c. Factory, pyramid, flora and elephant tusks on back. Printed from engraved plates.			
		a. Sign. title: *LE GOUVERNEUR* placed below line. 15.3.1972–27.10.1976.	.50	1.50	5.00
		b. Sign. title: *LE GOUVERNEUR* placed above line. 27.10.1977.	.30	1.00	2.50

21	5 ZAÏRES	1974–77. Green and m/c. Similar to #20 but Mobutu w/cap.			
		a. 30.11.1974; 30.6.1975; 24.11.1975; 24.11.1976.	2.50	7.50	20.00
		b. 24.11.1977.	.50	1.50	7.00

Cat. #	Denomination	Date, description	VG	VF	Unc
22	5 ZAÏRES	20.5.1979; 27.10.1980. Blue, brown and m/c. Like #21.	.50	1.50	4.50

Cat. #	Denomination	Date, description	VG	VF	Unc
26	5 ZAÏRES	17.11.1982. Blue, black and m/c. Hydroelectric dam on back. Printer: G&D.	.25	.60	2.00
26A	5 ZAÏRES	24.11.1985. Like #26, but printer: HdMZ.	.20	.40	1.25

23	10 ZAÏRES	1972–77. Blue and m/c. Similar to #15 but arms w/hand holding torch on back.			
		a. 30.6.1972; 22.6.1974; 30.6.1975; 30.6.1976.	2.50	7.50	22.50
		b. 27.10.1977.	1.00	3.00	10.00

27	10 ZAÏRES	27.10.1982. Green, black and m/c. Hand holding torch on back. Printer: G&D.	.40	1.00	2.50
27A	10 ZAÏRES	27.10.1985. Like #27, but printer: HdMZ.	.20	.40	1.25

#28–29 printer: G&D.

24	10 ZAÏRES	24.6.1979; 4.1.1981. Green and m/c. Like #23.	1.00	3.00	10.00

28	50 ZAÏRES	24.11.1982; 24.6.1985. Purple and m/c. Back blue and m/c; natives fishing w/stick nets at ctr.	.40	1.75	2.00

25	50 ZAÏRES	4.2.1980; 24.11.1980. Red, violet, brown and m/c. Similar to #21. Arms on back.	5.00	17.50	30.00

1982–85 ISSUES

29	100 ZAÏRES	1983; 1985. Brown, orange and m/c. Bank of Zaïre on back.			
		a. 30.6.1983.	.35	1.00	3.00
		b. 30.6.1985.	.25	.75	3.00

#26–29 leopard at lower l., Mobutu in civilian dress at ctr. r. and as wmk. Sign. varieties.

#30–31 leopard at lower l., Mobutu in military dress at ctr. r. and as wmk. Printer: G & D.

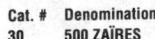

Cat. #	Denomination	Date, description	VG	VF	Unc
30	500 ZAÏRES	14.10.1984; 14.10.1985. Brown, purple and m/c. Suspension bridge over river on back.	1.25	3.50	10.00

Cat. #	Denomination	Date, description	VG	VF	Unc
34	500 ZAÏRES	24.6.1989. Brown, orange and m/c. Suspension bridge over river on back. Similar to #30.	.25	1.00	2.50

| 31 | 1000 ZAÏRES | 24.11.1985. Blue-black and green on m/c unpt. Civic bldg., water fountain at ctr. on back. | 1.00 | 3.25 | 10.00 |

| 35 | 1000 ZAÏRES | 24.11.1989. Purple, brown and m/c. Back similar to #31. | .50 | 1.65 | 5.00 |
| 36 | 2000 ZAÏRES | 1.10.1991. Violet on m/c unpt. Structure in water at l., carved figure at ctr. r. on back. (Smaller size than #35.) | .25 | .75 | 2.00 |

#37–38 printer: G&D.

1988–92 ISSUES

#32–46 Mobutu in military dress at r. and as wmk, leopard at lower l. ctr., arms at lower r. Reduced size notes.

#32–36 printer: HdMZ.

| 32 | 50 ZAÏRES | 30.6.1988. Green and m/c. Natives fishing w/stick nets on back. Similar to #28. | .10 | .25 | .85 |

| 33 | 100 ZAÏRES | 14.10.1988. Blue and m/c. Bank of Zaïre at l. on back. | .15 | .25 | .85 |

37	5000 ZAÏRES	20.5.1988. Blue, green and m/c. Factory at l., elephant tusks and plants at ctr. on back.			
		a. Brown triangle at lower r.	2.00	6.00	15.00
		b. Green triangle at lower r.	.25	.75	2.00

Cat. #	Denomination	Date, description	VG	VF	Unc
38	10,000 ZAÏRES	24.11.1989. Violet, brown-orange and red on m/c unpt. Complex of official bldgs. on back.	.35	1.00	2.50

Cat. #	Denomination	Date, description	VG	VF	Unc
43	500,000 ZAÏRES	15.3.1992. Brown and orange on m/c unpt. Hydroelectric dam at l. ctr. on back.	.50	1.50	5.00

			VG	VF	Unc
39	20,000 ZAÏRES	1.7.1991. Black on m/c unpt. Bank of Zaïre at l., other bldgs. across ctr. on back. Printer: HdMZ.	.25	.50	2.00

			VG	VF	Unc
44	1 MILLION ZAÏRES	31.7.1992. Red-violet and deep red on m/c unpt. Suspension bridge at l. ctr. on back.	.50	1.00	3.00

#40–41 printer: G&D.

			VG	VF	Unc
40	50,000 ZAÏRES	24.4.1991. Wine and blue-black on m/c unpt. Family of gorillas on back.	.75	2.00	4.50

			VG	VF	Unc
41	100,000 ZAÏRES	4.1.1992. Black and deep olive-green on m/c unpt. Domed bldg. at l. ctr. on back.	.50	1.50	4.50

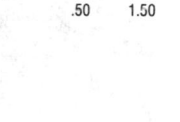

			VG	VF	Unc
45	1 MILLION ZAÏRES	17.5.1993; 30.6.1993. Like #44 but printer: HdMZ.	.50	1.00	3.00

			VG	VF	Unc
42	200,000 ZAÏRES	1.3.1992. Deep purple and deep blue on m/c unpt. Civic bldg., water fountain at l. ctr. Printer HdMZ.	.50	1.50	5.00

#43–44 printer: G&D.

Cat. #	Denomination	Date, description	VG	VF	Unc
46	5 MILLION ZAÏRES	1.10.1992. Deep brown and brown on m/c unpt. Factory, pyramids, flora and elephant tusks on back. Printer: H&S.	.40	1.00	4.50

Currency Reform

1 Nouveau Zaïre = 100 Nouveaux Makuta = 3 million old Zaïres

1993 ISSUE

#47–56 leopard at lower l., Mobutu at r., arms at lower r.

#47–48 Independence Monument at l. on back. W/o wmk. Printer: G&D.

47	1 NOUVEAU LIKUTA	24.6.1993. Tan on pink and m/c unpt.	.05	.20	.50

48	5 NOUVEAUX MAKUTA	24.6.1993. Black on pale violet and blue-green unpt.	.05	.20	.65

#49, 51 wmk: Mobutu. Printer: HdMZ (CdM-A).

49	10 NOUVEAUX MAKUTA	24.6.1993. Green on m/c unpt. Factory, pyramids, flora and elephant tusks on back.	.10	.30	1.00
50	Deleted.				

Cat. #	Denomination	Date, description	VG	VF	Unc
51	50 NOUVEAUX MAKUTA	24.6.1993. Brown-orange on lt. green and m/c unpt. Chieftan at l., natives fishing w/stick nets at ctr. on back.	.10	.30	.75

#52–54 wmk: Mobutu. Printer: G&D.

52	1 NOUVEAU ZAÏRE	24.6.1993. Violet and purple on m/c unpt. Banque du Zaïre at l. on back.	.10	.30	1.00

53	5 NOUVEAUX ZAÏRES	24.6.1993. Brown on m/c unpt. Back like #41.	.20	.50	1.50

Cat. #	Denomination	Date, description	VG	VF	Unc
54	10 NOUVEAUX ZAÏRES	24.6.1993. Dk. gray and dk. blue-green on m/c unpt. Back like #42.	.50	1.00	3.00

#55–58 wmk: Mobutu.

#55–57 printer: HdMZ (CdM-A)

Cat. #	Denomination	Date, description	VG	VF	Unc
55	10 NOUVEAUX ZAÏRES	24.6.1993. Dk. gray and dk. blue-green on m/c unpt. Back like #42.	.15	.40	1.00

Cat. #	Denomination	Date, description	VG	VF	Unc
56	20 NOUVEAUX ZAÏRES	24.6.1993. Brown and blue on pale green and lilac unpt. Back similar to #42.	.20	.60	1.75
57	50 NOUVEAUX ZAÏRES	24.6.1993. Brown and deep red on m/c unpt. Back like #43.	.20	.60	1.75
58	100 NOUVEAUX ZAÏRES	1993–94. Grayish purple and blue-violet on aqua and ochre unpt. Back like #44. Printer: G&D.			
		a. 24.6.1993.	1.00	2.00	4.00
		b. 15.2.1994.	FV	FV	3.00

1994–95 ISSUES

#59–66 leopard at lower l., Mobutu at r. and as wmk., arms at lower r.

#59–61 printer: HdMZ.

Cat. #	Denomination	Date, description	VG	VF	Unc
59	50 NOUVEAUX ZAÏRES	15.2.1994. Dull red-violet and red on m/c unpt. Like #55.	FV	FV	3.00

Cat. #	Denomination	Date, description	VG	VF	Unc
60	100 NOUVEAUX ZAÏRES	15.2.1994. Like #56.	FV	FV	4.00
61	200 NOUVEAUX ZAÏRES	15.2.1994. Deep olive-brown on m/c unpt. Natives fishing w/stick nets at l. ctr. on back.	FV	FV	1.25

Cat. #	Denomination	Date, description	VG	VF	Unc
62	200 NOUVEAUX ZAÏRES	15.2.1994. Like #59. Printer: G&D.	FV	FV	2.25

Cat. #	Denomination	Date, description	VG	VF	Unc
63	500 NOUVEAUX ZAÏRES	15.2.1994. Gray and deep olive-green on m/c unpt. Banque du Zaïre at l. ctr. on back. Printer: HdMZ.	FV	FV	1.25
64	500 NOUVEAUX ZAÏRES	15.2.1994. Like #61. Printer: G&D.	FV	FV	2.50

Cat. #	Denomination	Date, description	VG	VF	Unc
65	500 NOUVEAUX ZAÏRES	30.1.1995. Blue on m/c unpt.	FV	FV	1.25

66	1000 NOUVEAUX ZAÏRES	30.1.1995. Olive-gray and olive-green on m/c unpt. Printer: G&D.	FV	FV	3.50
67	1000 NOUVEAUX ZAÏRES	30.1.1995. Like #66. Printer: HdMZ.	FV	FV	2.50
68	5000 NOUVEAUX ZAÏRES	30.1.1995. Brown-violet and red-violet on m/c unpt. Printer: G&D.	FV	FV	6.50
69	5000 NOUVEAUX ZAÏRES	30.1.1995. Like #68. Printer: HdMZ.	FV	FV	4.50

REGIONAL

Validation Ovpt:

Type I: Circular handstamp: *REPUBLIQUE DU ZAÏRE-REGION DU BAS-ZAÏRE; GARAGE ...STA/BANANA* around arms.

NOTE: This is one example of an ovpt. applied to a note being turned in for exchange for a new issue. It appears that in some locations (i.e. Bas Fleuve, Bas Zaïre and Shaba Sons) there were not enough of the new notes to trade for the older ones. In such cases, an ovpt. was applied to the older piece indicating its validity and acceptability for future redemption into new currency. A number of diff. ovpt. are known, and more information is needed. Market values have ranged from $10-25.00

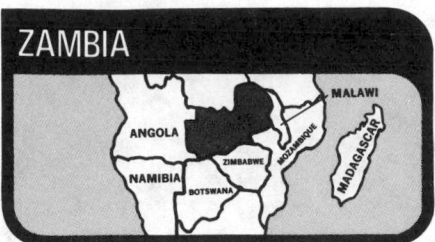

ZAMBIA

The Republic of Zambia (formerly Northern Rhodesia), a landlocked country in south-central Africa, has an area of 290,586 sq. mi. (752,614 sq. km.) and a population of nearly 8.8 million. Capital: Lusaka. The economy of Zambia is based principally on copper, of which Zambia is the world's third largest producer. Copper, zinc, lead, cobalt and tobacco are exported.

The area that is now Zambia was brought within the British sphere of influence in 1888 by empire builder Cecil Rhodes, who obtained mining concessions in south-central Africa from indigenous chiefs. The territory was ruled by the British South Africa Company, which Rhodes established, until 1924 when its administration was transferred to the British government as a protectorate. In 1953, Northern Rhodesia was joined with Nyasaland and the colony of Southern Rhodesia to form the Federation of Rhodesia and Nyasaland. Northern Rhodesia seceded from the Federation on Oct. 24, 1964, and became the independent Republic of Zambia. Zambia is a member of the Commonwealth of Nations. The president is Chief of State.

Zambia adopted a decimal currency system on Jan. 16, 1969.

Also see Rhodesia.

RULERS
British to 1964

MONETARY SYSTEM
1 Shilling = 12 Pence
1 Pound = 20 Shillings to 1969
1 Kwacha = 100 Ngwee, 1969–

REPLACEMENT NOTES
#4–22, denominations use prefixes as follows: 50 Ngwee, 1/Z; 1 Kwacha 1/Y; 2 Kwacha 1/X; 5 Kwacha 1/U; 10 Kwacha 1/W; 20 Kwacha 1/V. #23–28, 1/Z prefix.

SIGNATURE VARIETIES

#	Signature	#	Signature
1	C. Hallet, 1964–67	7	Dr. L.S. Chivuno, 1986–88
2	Dr. J.B. Zulu, 1967–70	8	F. Nkhoma, 1988–91
3	V.S. Musakanya, 1970–72	9	J.A. Bussiere, 1991–ca.1993
4	B.R. Kuwani, 1972–76, 1982–84	10	D. Mutaisho, 1993–
5	L.J. Mwananshiku, 1976–81	11	
6	D.A.R Phiri, 1984–86	12	

Bank of Zambia

Pound System

Cat. #	Denomination	Date, description	VG	VF	Unc
A1	1 Pound	1963. Blue on lilac unpt. Fisherman w/net and boat at ctr., Qn. Elizabeth II at r. Back purple; bird at l. ctr. Imprint: H&S. (Not issued).	—	—	—

1964 ISSUE

#1–3 sign. R.C. Hallet. Arms at upper ctr. Printer: TDLR. Wmk: Wildebeest head.

Cat. #	Denomination	Date, description	VG	VF	Unc
1	10 SHILLINGS	ND (1964). Brown on m/c unpt. Chaplins Barbet bird at r. Farmers plowing w/tractor and oxen on back.	15.00	50.00	200.00

| 2 | 1 POUND | ND (1964). Green on m/c unpt. Lovebird at r. Mining tower and conveyors on back. | 20.00 | 100.00 | 525.00 |

Cat. #	Denomination	Date, description	VG	VF	Unc
3	5 POUNDS	ND (1964). Blue on m/c unpt. Wildebeest at r. Waterfalls on back.	25.00	125.00	850.00

Kwacha System

1968 ISSUE

#4–8 Pres. Kaunda at r. Period between letter and value. Sign. 2. Printer: TDLR.

| 4 | 50 NGWEE | ND (1968). Red-violet on m/c unpt. Arms at l. 2 antelope on back. W/o wmk. | 3.00 | 8.00 | 50.00 |

#5–8 Arms at upper ctr. Wmk: Pres. Kaunda.

| 5 | 1 KWACHA | ND (1968). Dk. brown on m/c unpt. Farmers plowing w/tractor and oxen on back. | 3.50 | 12.50 | 60.00 |

6	2 KWACHA	ND (1968). Green on m/c unpt. Mining tower and conveyors on back.	4.00	15.00	75.00
7	10 KWACHA	ND (1968). Blue on m/c unpt. Waterfalls on back.	15.00	50.00	275.00
8	20 KWACHA	ND (1968). Purple on m/c unpt. National Assembly on back.	25.00	75.00	425.00

1969 ISSUE

#9–13 Pres. Kaunda at r., w/o period between letter and value. Backs and wmks. similar to #4–8.

Cat. #	Denomination	Date, description	VG	VF	Unc
9	50 NGWEE	ND (1969). Red-violet. Like #4.	Reported, not confirmed		
		a. Sign. 2.	2.00	6.50	27.50
		b. Sign. 3.			
		c. Sign. 4.	1.00	4.00	17.50

10	1 KWACHA	ND (1969). Dk. brown.			
		a. Sign. 2.	2.50	6.00	35.00
		b. Sign. 3.	2.00	5.00	25.00
11	2 KWACHA	ND (1969). Green.			
		a. Sign. 2.	3.00	10.00	75.00
		b. Sign. 3.	2.50	8.50	50.00

12	10 KWACHA	ND (1969). Blue.			
		a. Sign. 2.	6.00	17.50	125.00
		b. Sign. 3.	10.00	35.00	250.00
		c. Sign. 4.	8.00	25.00	175.00

13	20 KWACHA	ND (1969). Purple.			
		a. Sign. 2.	15.00	50.00	275.00
		b. Sign. 3.	20.00	70.00	350.00
		c. Sign. 4.	10.00	35.00	250.00

1973 ISSUE

#14–16, Arms at upper ctr., Pres. Kaunda at r. Printer: TDLR.

14	50 NGWEE	ND (1973). Black on purple and m/c unpt. Miners on back. W/o wmk. Sign. 4.	.50	1.50	4.00

COMMEMORATIVE ISSUE

#15, Birth of the Second Republic December 13, 1972

Cat. #	Denomination	Date, description	VG	VF	Unc
15	1 KWACHA	ND (1973). Red-orange and brown on m/c unpt. Document signing, commemorative text and crowd on back. Sign. 4. Wmk: Kaunda.	4.00	10.00	25.00

REGULAR ISSUE

16	5 KWACHA	ND (1973). Red-violet. Children by school on back. Sign. 4. Wmk: Kaunda.	15.00	75.00	300.00

1974 ISSUE

#17–18 Arms at upper ctr; Pres. Kaunda at r. and as wmk. Sign. 4. Printer: BWC.

17	10 KWACHA	ND (1974). Blue and m/c. Waterfalls on back.	17.50	75.00	200.00

18	20 KWACHA	ND (1974). Purple, red and m/c. National Assembly on back.	15.00	60.00	175.00

1974–76 ISSUE

#19–22 earlier frame design, arms at upper ctr. Older Pres. Kaunda at r. but same wmk. as previous issues. Printer: TDLR.

Cat. #	Denomination	Date, description	VG	VF	Unc
19	1 KWACHA	ND (1976). Brown. Back like #5. Sign. 5.	.50	2.00	6.00
20	2 KWACHA	ND (1974). Green. Back like #6. Sign. 4.	1.00	3.25	10.00

21	5 KWACHA	ND (1976). Brown and violet. Back like #16. Sign. 5.	3.00	12.00	38.50

22	10 KWACHA	ND (1976). Blue and m/c. Back similar to #17. Sign. 5.	5.00	20.00	75.00

1980; 86 ISSUE

#23–28 Pres. Kaunda at r. and as wmk., fish eagle at ctr. Printer: TDLR.

Cat. #	Denomination	Date, description	VG	VF	Unc
25	5 KWACHA	ND (1980–88). Brown and m/c. Hydroelectric dam on back.			
		a. Sign. 5.	.40	1.50	3.50
		b. Sign. 4.	.50	2.00	5.00
		c. Sign. 6.	.25	.75	2.50
		d. Sign. 7.	.15	.50	1.50

23	1 KWACHA	ND (1980–88). Brown and m/c. Cotton picking on back.			
		a. Sign. 5.	.20	.50	2.00
		b. Sign. 7.	.15	.40	1.50

26	10 KWACHA	ND (1980–88). Blue, green and m/c. Bank on back.			
		a. Sign. 5.	1.50	5.00	20.00
		b. Sign. 4 in black.	1.25	4.00	15.00
		c. Sign. 4 in blue.	1.25	4.00	17.50
		d. Sign. 6.	1.00	2.00	5.00
		e. Sign. 7.	.40	1.50	3.50

24	2 KWACHA	ND (1980–88). Olive and m/c. School bldg. w/teacher and student on back.			
		a. Sign. 5.	.50	1.00	4.00
		b. Sign. 6.	.25	.75	2.50
		c. Sign. 7.	.10	.25	1.50

27	20 KWACHA	ND (1980–88). Green and m/c. Woman w/basket at r. on back.			
		a. Sign. 5.	3.00	8.00	25.00
		b. Sign. 4 in black.	2.00	6.00	20.00
		c. Sign. 4 in dk. green.	2.00	6.00	25.00
		d. Sign. 6.	1.00	3.00	10.00
		e. Sign. 7.	.50	1.50	4.50

Cat. #	Denomination	Date, description	VG	VF	Unc
31	10 KWACHA	ND (1989). Dk. blue and black on m/c unpt. Back dk. blue; giraffe head at lower l., bldg. at ctr., carving of man's head at r.			
		a. Sign. 8.	.15	.40	2.00
		b. Sign. 9.	.10	.30	.85

Cat. #	Denomination	Date, description	VG	VF	Unc
28	50 KWACHA	ND (1986–88). Brown, purple, and m/c. "Chainbreaker" statue at l., modern bldg. at ctr. on back. Sign. 7.	.90	2.75	8.00

1989 ISSUE

#29–33 fish eagle at lower l., butterfly over arms at ctr., Pres. Kaunda at r. and as wmk. "Chainbreaker" statue at l. on back.

32	20 KWACHA	ND (1989). Dk. olive-green and brown on m/c unpt. Back dk. green; Dama gazelle head at lower l., bldg. at ctr., carving of man's head at r.			
		a. Sign. 8.	.15	.50	2.00
		b. Sign. 9.	.10	.30	1.00

29	2 KWACHA	ND (1989). Olive-brown on m/c unpt. Rhinoceros head at lower l., cornfield at ctr., tool at r. on back. Sign. 8.	.30	.75	2.50

33	50 KWACHA	ND (1989). Red-violet and purple on m/c unpt. Zebra head at lower l., manufacturing at ctr., carving of woman's bust at r. on back.			
		a. Sign. 8.	.50	2.00	8.00
		b. Sign. 9.	.45	1.75	7.50

30	5 KWACHA	ND (1989). Brown and red-orange on m/c unpt. Back brown; lion cub head at lower l., bldg. at ctr., jar at r. Sign. 8.	.15	.50	2.25

1991 ISSUE

#34–35 fish eagle at l., tree over arms at ctr., older Pres. Kaunda at r. and as wmk. "Chainbreaker" statue at l. on back. Sign. 9.

Cat. #	Denomination	Date, description	VG	VF	Unc
34	100 KWACHA	ND (1991). Purple and m/c. Water buffalo head at l., waterfalls w/long curved line through ctr. on back.	FV	.60	3.00
35	500 KWACHA	ND (1991). Brown on m/c unpt. Elephant at l., workers picking cotton at ctr. on back.	FV	1.50	7.50

1992 ISSUE

#36–39 seal of arms w/date at lower l., fish eagle at r. Wmk: Head of fish eagle. "Chainbreaker" statue at lower ctr. r. on back. Sign. 9. Printer: TDLR.

36	20 KWACHA	1992. Green and m/c. Kudu at l., govt. bldg. at ctr. on back.	FV	.20	.85

37	50 KWACHA	1992. Red and m/c. Zebra at l., foundry worker at ctr. on back.	FV	.30	1.25

38	100 KWACHA	1992. Dk. purple and m/c. Water buffalo head at l., waterfalls at ctr. on back.	FV	.40	1.75

39	500 KWACHA	1992. Brown and m/c. Elephant head at l., workers picking cotton at ctr. on back.	FV	1.50	3.50
40	100 KWACHA	(1996).			Expected new issue.
41	500 KWACHA	(1996).			Expected new issue.
42	10,000 KWACHA	(1996).			Expected new issue.

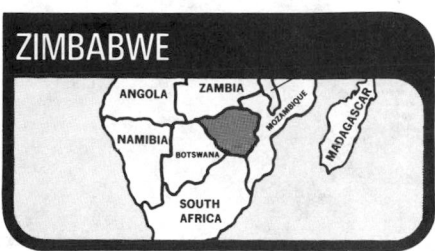

ZIMBABWE

The Republic of Zimbabwe (formerly the "Republic of" Rhodesia or Southern Rhodesia), located in the east-central part of southern Africa, has an area of 150,820 sq. mi. (390,580 sq. km.) and a population of 9.9 million. Capital: Harare (formerly Salisbury). The economy is based on agriculture and mining. Tobacco, sugar, asbestos, copper and chrome ore and coal are exported.

The Rhodesian area, the habitat of paleolithic man, contains extensive evidence of earlier civilizations, notably the world-famous ruins of Zimbabwe, a gold-trading center that flourished about the 14th or 15th century AD. The Portuguese of the 16th century were the first Europeans to attempt to develop south-central Africa, but it remained for Cecil Rhodes and the British South Africa Co. to open the hinterlands. Rhodes obtained a concession for mineral rights from local chiefs in 1888 and administered his African empire (named Southern Rhodesia in 1895) through the British South Africa Co. until 1923, when the British government annexed the area after the white settlers voted for existence as a separate entity, rather than for incorporation into the Union of South Africa. From Sept. of 1953 through 1963 Southern Rhodesia was joined with the British protectorates of Northern Rhodesia and Nyasaland into a multiracial federation. When the federation was dissolved at the end of 1963, Northern Rhodesia and Nyasaland became the independent states of Zambia and Malawi.

Britain was prepared to grant independence to Southern Rhodesia but declined to do so when the politically dominant white Rhodesianas refused to give assurances of representative government. In November 1965, the white minority government of Southern Rhodesia unilaterally declared Southern Rhodesia an independent dominon. The United Nations and the British Parliament both proclaimed this unilateral declaration of independence null and void. In 1970, the government proclaimed a republic, but this too recieved no recognition. In 1979, the government purported to change the name of the Colony to Zimbabwe Rhodesia, but again this was never recognized. Following a conference in London in December 1979, the opposition government conceded and it was agreed that the British Government should resume control. A British governor soon returned to southern Rhodesia. One of his first acts was to affirm the nullification of the purported delcaration of independence. On April 18, 1980, pursuant to an act of the British Parliament, the Colony of Southern Rhodesia became independent within the commonwealth as the Republic of Zimbabwe.

MONETARY SYSTEM
1 Dollar = 100 Cents

WATERMARKS

Type A	Type B
Rhodesia & Zimbabwe	Zimabwe
Wide Side View	Narrow 1/2-right view

REPLACEMENT NOTES

#1–4, denominations use prefixes as follows: $1, - AW; $5, - BW; $10, - CW; $20, - DW.

NOTE: For earlier issues see Rhodesia.

Reserve Bank of Zimbabwe

1980 ISSUE

#1–4 Re Matapos Rocks at ctr. r. Sign. varieties. Wmk: Zimbabwe bird.

Cat. #	Denomination	Date, description	VG	VF	Unc
1	2 DOLLARS	1980 (1981); 1983. Blue and m/c. Water buffalo at l. Tigerfish at ctr., Kariba Dam and reservoir at r. on back.			
		a. Salisbury. 1980.	FV	1.50	5.50
		b. Harare. 1983.	FV	FV	1.50
		c. 1994.	FV	FV	1.00

Cat. #	Denomination	Date, description	VG	VF	Unc
2	5 DOLLARS	1980 (1981)–1983. Green and m/c. Zebra at l. Village scene w/2 workers on back.			
		a. Salisbury. 1980.	FV	3.00	15.00
		b. Harare. 1982; 1983.	FV	FV	3.50
		c. Wmk: Type B.	FV	FV	3.00

Cat. #	Denomination	Date, description	VG	VF	Unc
6	100 DOLLARS	1995. Brownish black and purple on m/c unpt. Matapos Rocks at l. ctr. Kariba Dam and reservoir at l. ctr. on back.	FV	FV	28.50

Cat. #	Denomination	Date, description	VG	VF	Unc
3	10 DOLLARS	1980 (1981)–1983. Red and m/c. Sable antelope at l. View of Salisbury and Freedom Flame monument on back.			
		a. Salisbury. 1980.	FV	7.50	22.50
		b. Salisbury. 1982 (error).	4.00	12.50	30.00
		c. Harare. 1982; 1983.	FV	FV	6.50
		d. 1994.	FV	FV	5.00

Cat. #	Denomination	Date, description	VG	VF	Unc
4	20 DOLLARS	1980 (1982)–1983. Blue, black and dk. greenm on m/c unpt. Giraffe at l. Elephant and Victoria Falls on back.			
		a. Salisbury. 1980.	FV	1o.00	35.00
		b. Harare. 1982.	FV	20.00	65.00
		c. 1983.	FV	FV	15.00
		d. 1994.	FV	FV	10.00

1994–95 ISSUE
#5-6 Wmk: Zimbabwe bird, Type B.

			VG	VF	Unc
5	50 DOLLARS	1994. Dk. brown, olive-brown and red on m/c unpt. Matapos Rocks at l. Great Zimbabwe ruins on back.	FV	FV	15.00

STANDARD INTERNATIONAL NUMERAL SYSTEMS

PREPARED ESPECIALLY FOR THE **STANDARD CATALOG OF WORLD PAPER MONEY**

© 1995 BY KRAUSE PUBLICATIONS

	0	½	1	2	3	4	5	6	7	8	9	10	50	100	500	1000
WESTERN	0	½	1	2	3	4	5	6	7	8	9	10	50	100	500	1000
ROMAN			I	II	III	IV	V	VI	VII	VIII	IX	X	L	C	D	M
ARABIC-TURKISH	٠	١/٢	١	٢	٣	٤	٥	٦	٧	٨	٩	١٠	٥٠	١٠٠	٥٠٠	١٠٠٠
MALAY—PERSIAN	۰	۱/۲	۱	۲	۳	۴	۵	۶	۷	۸	۹	۱۰	۵۰	۱۰۰	۵۰۰	۱۰۰۰
EASTERN ARABIC	٠	½	١	٢	٣	٤	٥	٦	٧	٨	٩	١٠	٥٠	١٠٠	٥٠٠	١٠٠٠
HYDERABAD ARABIC	٠	١/٢	١	٢	٣	٤	٥	٦	٧	٨	٩	١٠	٥٠	١٠٠	٥٠٠	١٠٠٠
INDIAN (Sanskrit)	०	१/२	१	२	३	४	५	६	७	८	९	१०	५०	१००	५००	१०००
ASSAMESE	০	১/২	১	২	৩	৪	৫	৬	৭	৮	৯	১০	৫০	১০০	৫০০	১০০০
BENGALI	০	১/২	১	২	৩	৪	৫	৬	৭	৮	৯	১০	৫০	১০০	৫০০	১০০০
GUJARATI	૦	૧/૨	૧	૨	૩	૪	૫	૬	૭	૮	૯	૧૦	૫૦	૧૦૦	૫૦૦	૧૦૦૦
KUTCH	૦	૧/૨	૧	૨	૩	૪	૫	૬	૭	૮	૯	૧૦	૫૦	૧૦૦	૫૦૦	૧૦૦૦
DEVAVNAGRI	०	१/२	१	२	३	४	५	६	७	८	९	१०	५०	१००	५००	१०००
NEPALESE	०	१/२	१	२	३	४	५	६	७	८	९	१०	५०	१००	५००	१०००
TIBETAN	༠	༡/༢	༡	༢	༣	༤	༥	༦	༧	༨	༩	༡༠	༥༠	༡༠༠	༥༠༠	༡༠༠༠
MONGOLIAN	᠐	᠑/᠒	᠑	᠒	᠓	᠔	᠕	᠖	᠗	᠘	᠙	᠑᠐	᠕᠐	᠑᠐᠐	᠕᠐᠐	᠑᠐᠐᠐
BURMESE	၀	၁/၂	၁	၂	၃	၄	၅	၆	၇	၈	၉	၁၀	၅၀	၁၀၀	၅၀၀	၁၀၀၀
THAI-LAO	๐	๑/๒	๑	๒	๓	๔	๕	๖	๗	๘	๙	๑๐	๕๐	๑๐๐	๕๐๐	๑๐๐๐
JAVANESE	꧐		꧑	꧒	꧓	꧔	꧕	꧖	꧗	꧘	꧙	꧑꧐	꧕꧐	꧑꧐꧐	꧕꧐꧐	꧑꧐꧐꧐
ORDINARY CHINESE JAPANESE-KOREAN	零	半	一	二	三	四	五	六	七	八	九	十	十五	百	百五	千
OFFICIAL CHINESE			壹	貳	叄	肆	伍	陸	柒	捌	玖	拾	拾伍	佰	佰伍	仟
COMMERCIAL CHINESE			〡	〢	〣	〤	〥	〦	〧	〨	〩	十	〥十	百	〥百	〡千
KOREAN		반	일	이	삼	사	오	육	칠	팔	구	십	오십	백	오백	천

GEORGIAN

1	2	3	4	5	6	7	8	9	10	50	100	500	1000
ა	ბ	გ	დ	ე	ვ	ზ	ჱ	თ	ი	ნ	ს	ქ	ჵ

11	20	30	40	50	60	70	80	90	100	200	300	400	600	700	800
ჲ	კ	ლ	მ	ნ	ო	პ	ჟ	რ	ს	ტ	უ	ფ	ღ	ყ	შ

ETHIOPIAN

	1	2	3	4	5	6	7	8	9	10	50	100	500	1000
◆	፩	፪	፫	፬	፭	፮	፯	፰	፱	፲	፶	፻	፭፻	፲፻

20	30	40	60	70	80	90
፳	፴	፵	፷	፸	፹	፺

HEBREW

1	2	3	4	5	6	7	8	9	10	50	100	500	1000
א	ב	ג	ד	ה	ו	ז	ח	ט	י	נ	ק	תק	תתק

20	30	40	60	70	80	90	200	300	400	600	700	800
כ	ל	מ	ס	ע	פ	צ	ר	ש	ת	תר	תש	תת

GREEK

1	2	3	4	5	6	7	8	9	10	50	100	500	1000
Α	Β	Γ	Δ	Ε	ΣΤ	Ζ	Η	Θ	Ι	Ν	Ρ	Ο	Ϙ

20	30	40	60	70	80	200	300	400	600	700	800
Κ	Λ	Μ	Ξ	Ο	Π	Σ	Τ	Υ	Χ	Ψ	Ω

HEJIRA DATE
CONVERSION CHART

HEJIRA (Hijra, Hegira), the name of the Mohammedan era (A.H. = Anno Hegirae) dates back to the Christian year 622 when Mohammed "fled" from Mecca, escaping to Medina to avoid persecution from the Koreish tribesmen. Based on a lunar year the Mohammedan year is 11 days shorter.

* = Leap Year (Christian Calendar)

AH Hejira	AD Christian Date	AH Hejira	AD Christian Date	AH Hejira	AD Christian Date
1102	1690, October 5	1201	1786, October 24	1311	1893, July 15
1103	1691, September 24	1202	1787, October 13	1312	1894, July 5
1104	1692, September 12*	1203	1788, October 2*	1313	1895, June 24
1105	1693, September 2	1204	1789, September 21	1314	1896, June 12*
1106	1694, August 22	1205	1790, September 10	1315	1897, June 2
1107	1695, August 12	1206	1791, August 31	1316	1898, May 22
1108	1696, July 31*	1207	1792, August 19*	1317	1899, May 12
1109	1697, July 20	1208	1793, August 9	1318	1900, May 1
1110	1698, July 10	1209	1794, July 29	1319	1901, April 20
1111	1699, June 29	1210	1795, July 18	1320	1902, April 10
1112	1700, June 18	1211	1796, July 7*	1321	1903, March 30
1113	1701, June 8	1212	1797, June 26	1322	1904, March 18*
1114	1702, May 28	1213	1798, June 15	1323	1905, March 8
1115	1703, May 17	1214	1799, June 5	1324	1906, February 25
1116	1704, May 6*	1215	1800, May 25	1325	1907, February 14
1117	1705, April 25	1216	1801, May 14	1326	1908, February 4*
1118	1706, April 15	1217	1802, May 4	1327	1909, January 23
1119	1707, April 4	1218	1803, April 23	1328	1910, January 13
1120	1708, March 23*	1219	1804, April 12*	1329	1911, January 2
1121	1709, March 18	1220	1805, April 1	1330	1911, December 22
1122	1710, March 2	1221	1806, March 21	1331	1912, December 11*
1123	1711, February 19	1222	1807, March 11	1332	1913, November 30
1124	1712, February 9*	1223	1808, February 28*	1333	1914, November 19
1125	1713, January 28	1224	1809, February 16	1334	1915, November 9
1126	1714, January 17	1225	1810, February 6	1335	1916, October 28*
1127	1715, January 7	1226	1811, January 26	1336	1917, October 17
1128	1715, December 27	1227	1812, January 16*	1337	1918, October 7
1129	1716, December 16*	1228	1813, January 4	1338	1919, September 26
1130	1717, December 5	1229	1813, December 24	1339	1920, September 15*
1131	1718, November 24	1230	1814, December 14	1340	1921, September 4
1132	1719, November 14	1231	1815, December 3	1341	1922, August 24
1133	1720, November 2*	1232	1816, November 21*	1342	1923, August 14
1134	1721, October 22	1233	1817, November 11	1343	1924, August 2*
1135	1722, October 12	1234	1818, October 31	1344	1925, July 22
1136	1723, October 1	1235	1819, October 20	1345	1926, July 12
1137	1724, September 29*	1236	1820, October 9*	1346	1927, July 1
1138	1725, September 9	1237	1821, September 28	1347	1928, June 20*
1139	1726, August 29	1238	1822, September 18	1348	1929, June 9
1140	1727, August 19	1239	1823, September 7	1349	1930, May 29
1141	1728, August 7*	1240	1824, August 26*	1350	1931, May 19
1142	1729, July 27	1241	1825, August 16	1351	1932, May 7*
1143	1730, July 17	1242	1826, August 5	1352	1933, April 26
1144	1731, July 6	1243	1827, July 25	1353	1934, April 16
1145	1732, June 24*	1244	1828, July 14*	1354	1935, April 5
1146	1733, June 14	1245	1829, July 3	1355	1936, March 24*
1147	1734, June 3	1246	1830, June 22	1356	1937, March 14
1148	1735, May 24	1247	1831, June 12	1357	1938, March 3
1149	1736, May 12*	1248	1832, May 31*	1358	1939, February 21
1150	1737, May 1	1249	1833, May 21	1359	1940, February 10*
1151	1738, April 21	1250	1834, May 10	1360	1941, January 29
1152	1739, April 10	1251	1835, April 29	1361	1942, January 19
1153	1740, March 29*	1252	1836, April 18*	1362	1943, January 8
1154	1741, March 19	1253	1837, April 7	1363	1943, December 28
1155	1742, March 8	1254	1838, March 27	1364	1944, December 17*
1156	1743, February 25	1255	1839, March 17	1365	1945, December 6
1157	1744, February 15*	1256	1840, March 5*	1366	1946, November 25
1158	1745, February 3	1257	1841, February 23	1367	1947, November 15
1159	1746, January 24	1258	1842, February 12	1368	1948, November 3*
1160	1747, January 13	1259	1843, February 1	1369	1949, October 24
1161	1748, January 2	1260	1844, January 22*	1370	1950, October 13
1162	1748, December 22*	1261	1845, January 10	1371	1951, October 2
1163	1749, December 11	1262	1845, December 30	1372	1952, September 21*
1164	1750, November 30	1263	1846, December 20	1373	1953, September 10
1165	1751, November 20	1264	1847, December 9	1374	1954, August 30
1166	1752, November 8*	1265	1848, November 27*	1375	1955, August 20
1167	1753, October 29	1266	1849, November 17	1376	1956, August 8*
1168	1754, October 18	1267	1850, November 6	1377	1957, July 29
1169	1755, October 7	1268	1851, October 27	1378	1958, July 18
1170	1756, September 26*	1269	1852, October 15*	1379	1959, July 7
1171	1757, September 15	1270	1853, October 4	1380	1960, June 25*
1172	1758, September 4	1271	1854, September 24	1381	1961, June 14
1173	1759, August 25	1272	1855, September 13	1382	1962, June 4
1174	1760, August 13*	1273	1856, September 1*	1383	1963, May 25
1175	1761, August 2	1274	1857, August 22	1384	1964, May 13*
1176	1762, July 28	1275	1858, August 11	1385	1965, May 2
1177	1763, July 12	1276	1859, July 31	1386	1966, April 22
1178	1764, July 1*	1277	1860, July 20*	1387	1967, April 11
1179	1765, June 20	1278	1861, July 9	1388	1968, March 31*
1180	1766, June 9	1279	1862, June 29	1389	1969, March 20
1181	1767, May 30	1280	1863, June 18	1390	1970, March 9
1182	1768, May 18*	1281	1864, June 6*	1391	1971, February 27
1183	1769, May 7	1282	1865, May 27	1392	1972, February 16*
1184	1770, April 27	1283	1866, May 16	1393	1973, February 4
1185	1771, April 16	1284	1867, May 5	1394	1974, January 25
1186	1772, April 4*	1285	1868, April 24*	1395	1975, January 14
1187	1773, March 25	1286	1869, April 13	1396	1976, January 3*
1188	1774, March 14	1287	1870, April 3	1397	1976, December 23*
1189	1775, March 4	1288	1871, March 23	1398	1977, December 12
1190	1776, February 21*	1289	1872, March 11*	1399	1978, December 2
1191	1777, February 9	1290	1873, March 1	1400	1979, November 21
1192	1778, January 30	1291	1874, February 18	1401	1980, November 9*
1193	1779, January 19	1292	1875, February 7	1402	1981, October 30
1194	1780, January 8*	1293	1876, January 28*	1403	1982, October 19
1195	1780, December 28*	1294	1877, January 16	1404	1983, October 8
1196	1781, December 17	1295	1878, January 5	1405	1984, September 27*
1197	1782, December 7	1296	1878, December 26	1406	1985, September 16
1198	1783, November 26	1297	1879, December 15	1407	1986, September 6
1199	1784, November 14*	1298	1880, December 4*	1408	1987, August 26
1200	1785, November 4	1299	1881, November 23	1409	1988, August 14*
		1300	1882, November 12	1410	1989, August 3
		1301	1883, November 2	1411	1990, July 24
		1302	1884, October 21*	1412	1991, July 13
		1303	1885, October 10	1413	1992, July 2*
		1304	1886, September 30	1414	1993, June 21
		1305	1887, September 19	1415	1994, June 10
		1306	1888, September 7*	1416	1995, May 31
		1307	1889, August 28	1417	1996, May 19*
		1308	1890, August 17	1418	1997, May 9
		1309	1891, August 7	1419	1998, April 28
		1310	1892, July 26*	1420	1999, April 17
				1421	2000, April 6*